February 25–27, 2018
Monterey, CA, USA

Association for Computing Machinery

Advancing Computing as a Science & Profession

FPGA'18

Proceedings of the 2018 ACM/SIGDA International Symposium on
Field-Programmable Gate Arrays

Sponsored by:

ACM SIGDA

Supported by:

Trimberger Family Foundation, Altera, Deephi, Flexlogix, Northrop Grumman, Aldec, Algo-Logic, Atomic Rules, Lattice Semiconductor, Microsemi, Microsoft Research, Two Sigma, & Xilinx

Association for Computing Machinery

Advancing Computing as a Science & Profession

The Association for Computing Machinery
2 Penn Plaza, Suite 701
New York, New York 10121-0701

ISBN: 978-1-4503-5614-5 (Digital)

ISBN: 978-1-4503-5873-6 (Print)

Additional copies may be ordered prepaid from:

ACM Order Department
PO Box 30777
New York, NY 10087-0777, USA

Phone: 1-800-342-6626 (USA and Canada)
+1-212-626-0500 (Global)
Fax: +1-212-944-1318
E-mail: acmhelp@acm.org
Hours of Operation: 8:30 am – 4:30 pm ET

FPGA 2018 Chairs' Welcome

We are delighted to welcome you to the 2018 ACM International Symposium on Field-Programmable Gate Arrays (ACM FPGA 2018). ACM FPGA is the premiere forum for the presentation of new and exciting research on all aspects of FPGA technology, which include:

- Novel FPGA architectures and circuits.
- Advances in CAD tools for FPGAs, in areas such as technology mapping, placement, routing, and others.
- High-level design methodologies that permit FPGA design at higher levels of abstraction.
- New applications for FPGAs, particularly their use as accelerators for achieving higher computational throughput and energy efficiency.

Aside from the technical sessions, the conference provides the opportunity for FPGA researchers and practitioners from around the world to connect with long-time friends, meet new ones, and network with one another in beautiful Monterey, California, famous worldwide for its spectacular coast, Fisherman's Wharf, and Cannery Row.

This year we received 116 submissions, of which 26 were accepted as full research papers (10 pages) to appear in the main conference or the pre-conference special-session on deep learning, and 4 papers were accepted as short research papers (6 pages). All full and short papers appear in these proceedings. In addition, 31 submissions were selected to be presented as posters; abstracts of these appear in these proceedings.

At FPGA 2018, we continue to see an emphasis on the two themes causing tremendous interest in the FPGA industry: 1) the potential role for FPGAs in deep learning, and 2) the recent introduction of FPGAs in the cloud by increasing numbers of large companies, including Microsoft, Amazon, Baidu, Alibaba, Huawei, IBM and others. The panel discussion, at the Monday evening banquet, will consider whether FPGAs (as opposed to GPUs and CPUs) will ultimately succeed in becoming a widespread computing platform for deep learning. We expect a lively exchange among the panelists!

The symposium kicks off with back-to-back Sunday morning workshops on cloud-deployed FPGAs, and a parallel workshop session on using FPGAs for packet processing as specified in the P4 language. Sunday afternoon will focus on how FPGAs can be used for deep learning, with both invited presentations and research presentations. The use of low computational precision will figure prominently in the deep-learning research presented.

We would like to thank the members of the Program Committee and secondary reviewers, whose names appear on the following pages, and who devoted considerable time and effort in evaluating the submissions and providing thoughtful feedback to the authors. We would like to thank Prof. Vaughn Betz from the University of Toronto for developing and moderating the panel session. Special thanks to Lisa Tolles, Cindy Edwards, Joanne Lateulere and John Lateulere for logistical support, and our sponsors for making FPGA 2018 possible.

Welcome to ACM FPGA 2018!

Kia Bazargan
Program Chair
University of Minnesota, USA

Jason H. Anderson
General Chair
University of Toronto, Canada

Table of Contents

Special Session: Deep Learning
Session Chair: Andrew Ling *(Intel)*

Session 1: Architecture
Session Chair: Sinan Kaptanoglu *(Microsemi)*

Session 2: CAD
Session Chair: Sabya Das *(Xilinx)*

Session 3: Deep Learning
Session Chair: Peter Cheung *(Imperial College)*

Session 4: High Level Synthesis 1
Session Chair: Stephen Neuendorffer *(Xilinx)*

Session 5: Applications 1
Session Chair: John Lockwood *(Algo-Logic Systems)*

Session 6: High Level Synthesis 2
Session Chair: George Constantinides *(Imperial College)*

Session 7: Circuits and Computation Engines
Session Chair: Nachiket Kapre *(University of Waterloo)*

Session 8: Applications 2
Session Chair: Lesley Shannon *(Simon Fraser University)*

Poster Session 1

Poster Session 2

Poster Session 3

FPGA 2018 Organization

General Chair: Jason H. Anderson *(University of Toronto, Canada)*

Program Chair: Kia Bazargan *(University of Minnesota, USA)*

Finance Chair: Jonathan Greene *(Microsemi, USA)*

Publicity Chair: Nachiket Kapre *(University of Waterloo, Canada)*

Program Committee: Michael Adler, Intel, USA
Jason H. Anderson, University of Toronto, Canada
Trevor Bauer, Xilinx, USA
Kia Bazargan, University of Minnesota, USA
Vaughn Betz, University of Toronto, Canada
Michaela Blott, Xilinx, USA
Philip Brisk, UC Riverside, USA
Deming Chen, UIUC, USA
Peter Cheung, Imperial College, UK
Derek Chiou, UT Austin, USA
Paul Chow, University of Toronto, Canada
Eric Chung, Microsoft, USA
George Constantinides, Imperial College, UK
Sabya Das, Xilinx, USA
Suhaib Fahmy, University of Warwick, UK
Wenyi Feng, Microsemi, USA
Jeffrey Goeders, Brigham Young University, USA
Jonathan Greene, Microsemi, USA
Yajun Ha, National University of Singapore
James C. Hoe, CMU, USA
Brad Hutchings, Brigham Young University, USA
Mike Hutton, Intel, USA
Paolo Ienne, EPFL, Switzerland
Mahesh Iyer, Intel, USA
Nachiket Kapre, University of Waterloo, Canada
Sinan Kaptanoglu, Microsemi, USA
Alireza Kaviani, Xilinx, USA
Martin Langhammer, Intel, UK
Miriam Leeser, Northeastern University, USA
Philip Leong, University of Sydney, Australia
Jing Li, University of Wisconsin, USA
Andrew Ling, Intel, Canada
John Lockwood, Algo-Logic Systems, USA
Guojie Luo, Peking University, China
Stephen Neuendorffer, Xilinx, USA
Jonathan Rose, University of Toronto, Canada
Kyle Rupnow, Inspirit IoT, USA

Program Committee (continued):

David Rutledge, Lattice Semiconductor, USA
Graham Schelle, Xilnx, USA
Lesley Shannon, Simon Fraser University, Canada
Russ Tessier, University of Massachusetts, USA
David Thomas, Imperial College London, UK
Steve Trimberger, Consultant, USA
John Wawrzynek, UC Berkeley, USA
Scott Weber, Intel, USA
Steve Wilton, University of British Columbia, Canada
Michael Wirthlin, Brigham Young University, USA
Grace Zgheib, EPFL, Switzerland
Zhiru Zhang, Cornell University, USA

Additional Reviewers:

Abed Yassine	Greg Knox	Matei Istoan	Sitao Huang
Ana Petkovska	Guohao Dai	Mathew Hall	Skyler Windh
Andrew Boutros	He Li	Mingyi Hong	Stylianos Venieris
Aravind Dasu	Henry Wong James	Mirjana Stojilovic	Tan Nguyen
Arya Reais-Parsi	Davies	Nadesh	Thomas Preusser
Ashutosh Dhar	Jason Luu	Ramanathan	Tom Spyrou
Charles Lo	Jaydeep Kulkarni	Naif Tarafdar	Vamsi Nalluri
Chris Lavin	Jenny Huang	Nariman Eskandari	Varun Sharma
Dana How	Jialiang Zhang	Nicholas Fraser	Wei Zuo
Daniel Ly-Ma	Jiang Su	Nish Sinnadurai	Xiaofan Zhang
Daniel Rozhko	Kenneth O'Brien	Pongstorn Maidee	Yue Zha
David Munday	Kevin Murray	Ranjit Gharpurey	Zac Blair
Dmitry Denisenko	Love Singhal	Saurabh Adya	Zachary Blair
Erwei Wang	Mang Yu	Sean Nijar	Zhiqiang Liu
Giulio Gambardella			

Monday Banquet Panel:

Vaughn Betz, University of Toronto (Organizer and Moderator)
Eric Chung, Microsoft
Song Han, Stanford/MIT
Jeff Johnson, Facebook
Debbie Marr, Intel
Vivienne Sze, MIT
Kees Vissers, Xilinx

Tutorials:

Gordon Brebner, Xilinx Labs
Derek Chiou, University of Texas at Austin (Organizer and Speaker)
Paul Chow, University of Toronto (Organizer and Speaker)
Robert Green, ASIC Design Services
Robert Halstead, Xilinx Labs
Peter Hofstee, IBM
Stephen Ibanez, Stanford University
David Munday, Intel
Parimal Patel, Xilinx
Thomas Preusser, Xilinx

FPGA 2018 Sponsors and Corporate Patrons

Sponsors:

Logistics Support:

Trimberger Family Foundation

Gold Corporate Patrons:

now part of Intel

Silver Corporate Patrons:

CausaLearn: Automated Framework for Scalable Streaming-based Causal Bayesian Learning using FPGAs

Bita Darvish Rouhani
UC San Diego
bita@ucsd.edu

Mohammad Ghasemzadeh
UC San Diego
mghasemzadeh@ucsd.edu

Farinaz Koushanfar
UC San Diego
farinaz@ucsd.edu

ABSTRACT

This paper proposes CausaLearn, the first automated framework that enables real-time and scalable approximation of Probability Density Function (PDF) in the context of causal Bayesian graphical models. CausaLearn targets complex streaming scenarios in which the input data evolves over time and independence cannot be assumed between data samples (e.g., continuous time-varying data analysis). Our framework is devised using a HW/SW co-design approach. We provide the first implementation of Hamiltonian Markov Chain Monte Carlo on FPGA that can efficiently sample from the steady state probability distribution at scales while considering the correlation between the observed data. CausaLearn is customizable to the limits of the underlying resource provisioning in order to maximize the effective system throughput. It uses physical profiling to abstract high-level hardware characteristics. These characteristics are integrated into our automated customization unit in order to tile, schedule, and batch the PDF approximation workload corresponding to the pertinent platform resources and constraints. We benchmark the design performance for analyzing various massive time-series data on three FPGA platforms with different computational budgets. Our extensive evaluations demonstrate up to *two orders-of-magnitude* runtime and energy improvements compared to the best-known prior solution. We provide an accompanying API that can be leveraged by data scientists and practitioners to automate and abstract hardware design optimization.

ACM Reference Format:
Bita Darvish Rouhani, Mohammad Ghasemzadeh, and Farinaz Koushanfar. 2018. CausaLearn: Automated Framework for Scalable Streaming-based Causal Bayesian Learning using FPGAs. In *Proceedings of 2018 ACM/SIGDA International Symposium on Field-Programmable Gate Arrays (FPGA '18)*. ACM, Monterey, CA, USA, 10 pages. https://doi.org/10.1145/3174243.3174259

1 INTRODUCTION

Probabilistic learning and graphical modeling of time-series data with causal structure is a challenging task in various scientific fields, ranging from machine learning [1] and stochastic optimization [2] to economics [3] and medical imaging [4]. Bayesian networks are an important class of directed graph analytics used to model dynamic systems. Unlike undirected graphical networks such as Markov Random Field, Bayesian networks are capable of learning causal structure in time-series data. In a Bayesian network, the posterior Probability Density Function (PDF) over the model parameters should be continuously updated to accommodate for the newly added structural trends as data evolves over time. Dynamic (a.k.a., *streaming*) learning of random variables is particularly important in *time-series data analysis* to enable effective decision making before

the system encounters natural changes, rendering much of the collected data irrelevant to the current decision space.

Energy and runtime efficiency play a key role in building viable computing systems for analyzing massive and densely correlated data. Several recent theoretical works have shown the importance of data and model parallelism in analyzing Bayesian graphical networks [5–8]. These set of works, however, are designed at the algorithmic and data abstraction level and are oblivious to the hardware characteristics. Given the diminishing benefits of technology scaling, it is important to devise specialized hardware accelerators for efficient realization of different learning models [9, 10]. A number of prior research works have provided FPGA accelerators for Bayesian networks, e.g., [11, 12]. Although these works demonstrate significant improvement for deployment of specific Bayesian models, their predominant assumption is that data samples are independently and identically drawn from a certain distribution. As such, they cannot effectively capture dynamic data correlation in causal streaming applications (e.g., correlated time-series data).

We propose CausaLearn, the first *scalable FPGA* framework to compute on and update *continuous* random variables and their associated PDFs for *streaming-based* causal Bayesian analysis. Our key observation is that without simultaneous optimization of hardware resource allocation and algorithmic solution, the best performance efficiency cannot be achieved. To fulfill this objective, CausaLearn incorporates hardware characteristics into the higher-level hierarchy of the algorithmic solution and enables automated customization per application data and/or physical constraints. In particular, CausaLearn performs a one-time hardware physical profiling to find the pertinent resource constraints (e.g., memory bandwidth, computing power, and available energy). This information is automatically integrated into CausaLearn's resource-aware customization unit to tile, schedule, and batch the pertinent computational workload such that it best fits the platform. CausaLearn's automated compilation disengages users from hardware resource optimization task while providing synthesizable solutions that are co-optimized for the underlying hardware architecture and execution schedule.

CausaLearn leverages Gaussian processes (GP) to capture data dynamics in streaming settings. GP form a core methodology in probabilistic machine learning [13, 13, 14] to model the causality structure of time-series data. Markov Chain Monte Carlo (MCMC) is the mainstream method that is used in practice to explore the state space of probabilistic models such as GP. Given the wide range of MCMC applications, it is thus not surprising that a number of implementations on CPUs [15], GPUs [16–20], and FPGAs [11, 12, 21, 22] have been reported in the literature. MCMC incurs a complex data flow consisting of various sequential computing kernels to construct the pertinent Markov chain. As such, FPGAs provide a more flexible programmable substrate for MCMC acceleration compared to GPU accelerators that are particularly designed for Single Instruction Multiple Data (SIMD) operations. The existing works on FPGA, however, have mainly focused on the acceleration of MCMC for analyzing independent and identically distributed (i.i.d.) samples that are drawn from a simple multivariate Gaussian distribution, e.g., [11, 12]. Such assumption, however, does not hold for dynamic Bayesian analytics with causal structure as we illustrate in our practical design experiments. Perhaps, the only prior works on FPGA that have considered causal data dependency

Table 1: Common MCMC methodologies for analyzing Bayesian networks.

MCMC Methods	Description
Population-based	Population-based MCMC is a method designed to address the issue of multi-modality using a population of Markov chains. This method is particularly inefficient for analyzing high-dimensional data, due to the high cost of unnecessary space exploration.
State Space Model	State Space Model (SSM) MCMC targets Bayesian applications in which evaluating the closed-form PDF is not feasible. SSMs assumes the availability of unbiased estimators to compute the acceptance ratio in each MCMC step. This assumption does not often hold in practice.
Gibbs Sampling	Gibbs sampling decomposes the proposal distribution into its individual components by computing the full conditional distribution of the variable θ_i conditional on all the remaining ones. Gibbs sampling encounters serious computational inefficiency in solving high-dimensional tasks with highly correlated variables.
Slice Sampling	Slice sampling method uniformly samples from the area under the $p(\theta)$ graph as an equivalent to sampling from the probability distribution. This technique improves mixing performance in learning tasks with highly correlated variables. The complexity of Slice sampling scales exponentially with the data dimensionality.
Hamiltonian	Hamiltonian MCMC method uses the gradient of the target probability distribution to select better movements in each iteration. This method is particularly of interest as it can handle both *strong correlations* and *high-dimensionality* of the probability distribution.
Adaptive	Adaptive MCMC method adjusts the proposal distribution in the execution time to achieve a better sampling efficiency. The adaptive kernel might converge to a non-stationary distribution if not designed carefully.

in the context of Bayesian networks are [21, 22]. Authors in [21, 22] have used Dirichlet processes in *discrete space* to facilitate human T-cell analysis. We emphasize that due to the discrete nature of Dirichlet processes these works are inapplicable to the analysis of dynamic *continuous* random variables.

CausaLearn adopts Hamiltonian Markov Chain Monte Carlo (H_MCMC) to effectively explore the state space of GP parameters by moving toward the gradient of the associated PDF given the observed data samples. The prior MCMC acceleration works on FPGA, e.g., [11, 12, 21, 22] leverage random walks to sample from the target density function. Exploration of the parameters' space using random walks is particularly inefficient in analyzing *high-dimensional streaming* data due to the high cost of mitigating the impact of an unnecessary movement in constructing the Markov chain. CausaLearn overcomes this inefficiency by moving toward the gradient of the model using Hamiltonian dynamics. Computing the gradient of the target density function involves a variety of operations with complex data flows. CausaLearn provides a set of novel algorithmic and hardware optimization techniques to enable real-time execution of H_MCMC algorithm using FPGAs. In particular, our optimization includes: (i) Revising the conventional H_MCMC routine to iteratively update the corresponding gradients of the probability function using incremental data decomposition. Our algorithmic modification effectively reduces the hardware implementation complexity of computing the inverse of large matrices with no drops in the output's accuracy. (ii) Devising an automated tree-based memory management system that facilitates multiple concurrent loads/stores in order to effectively increase the system throughput by enabling data parallelism to the limits of the hardware resources. (iii) Designing an automated compilation tool to tile and schedules matrix-based computations to best fits the data dimensionality and the available resource provisioning.

We provide an accompanying API to make CausaLearn available to a broader community who rely on probabilistic data analysis and often have a limited hardware design expertise. Our API libraries can be leveraged for deployment of widely used classes of data analytics such as various regression and classification methods, belief propagation, expectation maximization, and neural networks. In summary, our explicit contributions are as follows:

- Introducing CausaLearn, the first *scalable* framework that enables *automated real-time* multi-dimensional PDF approximation for *causal* Bayesian analysis. CausaLearn provides support for streaming settings where the latent variables should be adaptively updated as data evolves over time.
- Developing a resource-aware customization tool to optimize system performance. Our automated optimization attains a balance between parallel operations and data reuse by slicing

the computation and configuring the design to best fit the intrinsic physical resources and constraints.
- Devising the first scalable floating-point realization of causal Gaussian processes on FPGA by adopting stochastic Hamiltonian Markov Chain Monte Carlo (H_MCMC).
- Designing an accompanying API to facilitate automation and adaptation of CausaLearn for rapid prototyping of an arbitrary causal Bayesian data analysis. Our API minimizes the required user interaction while providing high performance and efficiency gains for FPGA acceleration.
- Providing proof-of-concept evaluations by analyzing large time-series data on three FPGA platforms with different computational budgets. Our evaluations demonstrate up to 320-fold runtime and 770-fold energy improvement compared to a highly-optimized software deployment.

2 PRELIMINARIES

Decomposition of time-series data into estimated latent variables provides an important alternative view from the time domain perspective [1, 2]. Let us denote the input data samples $\mathbf{D}$ as the pair of $(\mathbf{x}, \mathbf{y})$ values, where $\mathbf{x} = \{x_i = [x_{i1}, ..., x_{id}]\}_{i=1}^n$ includes the input data features and $\mathbf{y} = [y_1, ..., y_n]$ are the observation values. Here, d is the feature space size and n specifies the number of data measurements that may grow over time. Each output observation y_i can be either continuous as in most regression tasks, or discrete as in classification applications. The key to performing Bayesian graph analytics is to find a *probabilistic likelihood function* that maps each input feature x_i to its corresponding observation y_i such that:

$$y_i = f(x_i) + \epsilon_i. \tag{1}$$

The variable ϵ_i is an additive observation noise that determines how different the observation vector y_i can be from the latent function value $f(x_i)$. The observation noise is usually modeled as a Gaussian distribution variable with zero mean and a variance of σ_n^2.

2.1 Gaussian Processes

In probabilistic graphical models, all parameters should be represented as random variables. *Gaussian processes* are commonly used as the prior density over the set of latent functions $\{f(x_i)\}_{i=1}^n$ for analyzing time-series data. In Gaussian processes, each data point x_i is associated with a Normally distributed random variable f_i. Every finite collection of those random variables has a multivariate Gaussian distribution. GP is represented as:

$$\mathbf{f}(\mathbf{x}) \sim \mathcal{GP}(m(\mathbf{x}), K(\mathbf{x}, \mathbf{x}')), \tag{2}$$

where $m(\mathbf{x})$ and $K(\mathbf{x}, \mathbf{x}')$ are the mean and covariance kernels that capture the correlation between data samples. With a GP prior, the observations $\mathbf{y} = [y_1, ..., y_n]$ can be assumed to be conditionally

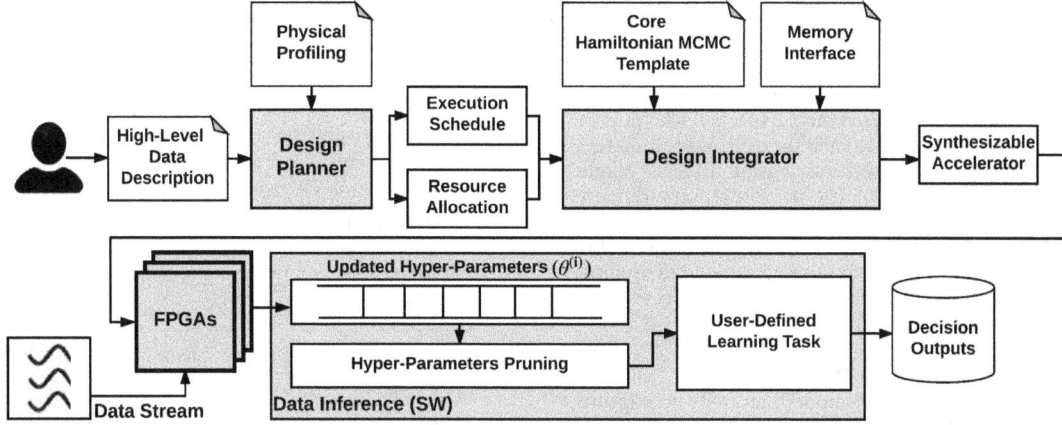

Figure 1: CausaLearn Global Flow: CausaLearn takes the stream of data samples as its input and learns the hyper-parameters of the corresponding posterior probability density function $P(\theta|\mathbf{D})$ using Hamiltonian MCMC. Our proposed Hamiltonian MCMC template is adaptively customized to the limits of the underlying platform and data structure. The updated hyper-parameters are used to perform a particular user-defined Bayesian learning task (e.g., regression or classification).

independent given the latent function $\mathbf{f}(.)$. Therefore, the likelihood $p(\mathbf{y}|\mathbf{f})$ can be factorized over data samples as $\prod_{i=1}^{N} p(y_i|f_i)$, where $\mathbf{f} = [f(x_1), ..., f(x_n)]$. Note that the observations themselves are not independent (e.g., $p(\mathbf{y}) \neq \prod_{i=1}^{N} p(y_i)$). The mean and covariance kernel of a GP are also random variables with certain hyper-parameters (γ) that should be tuned with respect to the input data. The choice of the mean and covariance kernels determines the smoothness and variability of the latent function $\mathbf{f}(.)$ to be estimated.

2.2 Bayesian Graphical Analysis

To make our notation explicit, we write the likelihood as $p(\mathbf{y}|\mathbf{f}, \sigma_n^2)$ where σ_n^2 is the parameter of the observation noise, and $p(\mathbf{f}|\gamma)$ is the GP prior. The quantities $\theta = [\gamma, \sigma_n^2]$ are the hyper-parameters of the underlying probabilistic model. The posterior distribution $p(\theta|\mathbf{D})$ must be computed to make predictions for the incoming data samples in different learning tasks including various regression and classification techniques, stochastic optimizations, and neural networks. Let us denote the function of interest to be evaluated with $g(\theta)$. Thereby, the underlying learning task can be expressed as the evaluation of the following integral:

$$E_{p(\theta|\mathbf{D})}[g(\theta)] = \int g(\theta)p(\theta|\mathbf{D})d\theta. \tag{3}$$

For instance, by setting $g(\theta) = p(y^*|\theta)$, one can predict the probability of a future observation y^* based on the previously observed data per $p(y^*|\mathbf{D}) = \int p(\mathbf{y}^*|\theta)p(\theta|\mathbf{D})d\theta$.

Given the large cardinality of the hyper-parameter set $|\theta|$, and the high dimensionality of input data in real-world applications, it is computationally impractical to analytically evaluate the integral in Eq. (3). Thus, estimation algorithms such as MCMC are often the methods of choice [23]. Table 1 summarizes different MCMC algorithms. MCMC methods work sequentially by constructing a Markov chain with each state of the chain corresponding to a new random sample from the posterior distribution $p(\theta|\mathbf{D})$. The samples are then used to approximate Eq. (3) as follows:

$$\tilde{E}_{p(\theta|\mathbf{D})}[g(\theta)] = \frac{1}{N}\Sigma_{i=1}^{N}g(\theta^{(i)}). \tag{4}$$

3 CAUSALEARN GLOBAL FLOW

Figure 1 illustrates the high-level block diagram of CausaLearn framework. CausaLearn leverages Hamiltonian MCMC to devise a

generic scalable framework that can be directly applied to different Bayesian applications. Hamiltonian technique is particularly of interest due to two main reasons: (i) It can handle both strong correlation and high-dimensionality in real-world applications by stochastically computing the gradient of the posterior distribution. (ii) It evades the requirement to compute the costly Metropolis-Hastings ratio commonly used in the alternative MCMC methods. This is because the acceptance rate tends to be high in the Hamiltonian method by moving toward the gradient of the target density function at each MCMC iteration as opposed to the use of random walks. CausaLearn involves two automated steps to schedule and customize the underlying data flow (Section 6). An API is also devised (Section 6.3) to ensure ease of use by users who do not necessarily possess a certain level of hardware-design knowledge.

(i) Design Planner. The design planner takes the high-level description of data from the user as its input. This description includes the rate of data arrival and feature space size in the target application. CausaLearn adopts platform profiling to abstract the physical characteristic of the target FPGA. The platform characteristics include the Block-RAM (BRAM) budget, available Digital Signal Processing (DSP) units, and memory bandwidth. The acquired physical characteristics along with the data description are fed into the design planner unit to find the optimal execution schedule and resource allocation (Section 6.1).

(ii) Design Integrator. The design integrator employs our core Hamiltonian MCMC (Section 5) as a template and customizes it according to the data schedule and resource allocation provided by the design planner. The integrator converters the acquired execution schedule into state machines and microcodes embedded in the target hardware design. CausaLearn tiles, batches, and pipelines the subsequent computational workload such that it best fits the target platform and application data (Section 6.2). The final synthesizable code is created after adding the memory interface to the design.

CausaLearn leverages a HW/SW co-design methodology. Bayesian analysis of streaming data involves: (i) Fine-tuning the pertinent hyper-parameters priors, and (ii) Performing a particular inference task (e.g., regression or classification) using the updated hyper-parameters. CausaLearn leverages FPGA as the primary hardware accelerator to enable real-time updating of the corresponding random variables and their associated PDFs inline with the data arrival. The FPGA is programmed with the Verilog code automatically generated as the output of the design integrator unit. The inference phase is performed on the general purpose processor that hosts the FPGA board. This is because data inference is a one-time process per input data sample and incurs a much lower computational overhead compared to that of updating the posterior distribution [6]. We use Peripheral Component Interconnect Express (PCIe) port to load the data to the FPGA and write back the updated parameters to the host. All computations are performed using IEEE 754 single precision floating-point format. Floating-point representation enables CausaLearn to be readily adopted in different learning tasks without requiring the user to modify the core implementation. It is worth noting that the fixed-point solutions are of limited applicability due to the variant nature of ultimate learning tasks and the unpredictability of data range in different applications.

4 CAUSALEARN FRAMEWORK

CausaLearn leverages a three-level model hierarchy to capture the causality structure of time-series data. It solves the following *objective function* to model the complex correlation of data samples:

$$Observation\ model : \mathbf{y}|\mathbf{f}, \sigma_n^2 \sim \prod_{i=1}^{N} p(y_i|f_i, \sigma_n^2),$$

$$GP\ prior : \mathbf{f}(\mathbf{x})|\gamma \sim \mathcal{GP}(m(\mathbf{x}), K(\mathbf{x}, \mathbf{x}'|\gamma)), \tag{5}$$

$$Hyper\ parameters\ prior : \theta = [\gamma, \sigma_n^2] \sim p(\gamma)p(\sigma_n^2),$$

where σ_n^2 is the variance of the observation noise per Eq. (1) and γ is the hyper-parameter set of the predictive function $\mathbf{f}(.)$ defined as GP. All hyper-parameters $\theta = [\sigma_n^2, \gamma]$ are iteratively updated in CausaLearn framework as data evolves over time to dynamically approximate the posterior distribution $p(\theta|\mathbf{D})$.

A GP model is fully defined by its second order statistics (i.e., mean and covariance). A common prior density choice for the GP covariance kernel is the squared-exponential function [14]:

$$K_{ij}(\mathbf{x}) = \sigma_k^2 e^{(-\frac{1}{2}(x_i - x_j)^T \Sigma^{-1}(x_i - x_j))}. \tag{6}$$

Here, σ_k^2 is the variance of the kernel function and Σ is a diagonal positive definite matrix, $\Sigma = diag[\mathcal{L}_1^2, ..., \mathcal{L}_d^2]$, in which each diagonal element is the length-scale parameter indicating the importance of a particular input dimension in deriving the ultimate output.

Algorithm 1 outlines the pseudocode of CausaLearn framework. The hyper-parameter set includes the variances of the observation noise and covariance kernel along with the length-scales variables ($\theta = [\sigma_n^2, \sigma_k^2, \mathcal{L}_1, ..., \mathcal{L}_d]$). We further assume a log-uniform prior for the variance parameter σ_k^2 and a multivariate Gaussian prior for the length-scale parameters. Algorithm 1 involves four main steps:

❶ **Platform Profiling:** CausaLearn provides a set of automated subroutine that characterize the available resource provisioning. Our subroutines measure the performance of the following four basic operations involved in the H_MCMC algorithm: matrix-matrix multiplication, dot-product, back-substitution, and random number generation. Our subroutines run the operations with varying sizes to find the target platform constraints. Note that the realization of each operation can be highly diverse depending on the target platform. For instance, based on the sizes of the matrices being multiplied, a matrix multiplication can be compute-bound, bandwidth-bound, or occupancy-bound on a specific platform.

❷ **Automated Customization:** CausaLearn design customization uses the output of physical profiling along with a set of user-defined constraints to schedule and balance the computational workload. The user-defined physical constraints can be expressed in terms of runtime (T_u), memory (M_u), and power consumption (P_u). The building blocks of the customization unit are design planner and design integrator. The details of these blocks are discussed in Section 6.

Algorithm 1 CausaLearn Pseudocode

Inputs: Stream of input data ($D = [X, Y]$), Initial parameters $\theta^{(1)}$, Desired Markov Chain length (C_{len}), discretization factor dt, number of discretization steps n_{step}, Updating frequency n_u, Mass matrix (M), Constant friction term (F), Portion of newly arrived data in each data batch η, Physical constraints $C_u = [T_u, M_u, P_u]$.

Outputs: Posterior Distribution Samples $\theta^{(i)}$, and output decision set $\mathcal{O}$.

1: $HW_{spec} \leftarrow PlatformProfiling()$ ❶
2: $[b_s, HW_{code}] \leftarrow Customization(HW_{spec}, C_u)$ ❷
3: $ProgramingFPGA(HW_{code})$
4: **for** $i = 1, 2, ..., C_{len}$ **do**
5:     **if** ($i \mod n_u$) == 0 **then**
6:       $[\tilde{X}, \tilde{Y}] \leftarrow DataPartitioning(X, Y, b_s, \eta)$
7:       *Transferring Data Batch $\tilde{D}$ to FPGA*
8:       $r^{(i)} \sim \mathcal{N}(0, M)$ ❸
9:       $(\theta_1, r_1) \leftarrow (\theta^{(i)}, r^{(i)})$
10:       $B = \frac{1}{2}\sigma_n^2 dt$
11:       $E = \sqrt{2|F - B|dt}$
12:       **for** $t = 2, ..., n_{step}$ **do**
13:         $\theta_t \leftarrow \theta_{t-1} + M^{-1}r_{t-1}dt$
14:         $\nabla \tilde{U}(\theta_t) \leftarrow gradient(\tilde{D}, \theta_t)$
15:         $r_t \leftarrow r_{t-1} - \nabla\tilde{U}(\theta_t)dt - FM^{-1}r_{t-1}dt + \mathcal{N}(0, E)$
      end for
16:       $(\theta^{(i+1)}, r^{(i+1)}) \leftarrow (\theta_{n_{step}}, r_{n_{step}})$
17:       *Sending Back $\theta^{(i+1)}$ to the Host*
18:     $\bar{\theta} = HyperParameterPrunning(\theta)$ ❹
19:     $\mathcal{O} = UserDefinedDataInference(\tilde{\theta})$
end for

---

❸ **Dynamic Parameter Updating on FPGA:** CausaLearn takes the stream of data as its input and adaptively updates the pertinent PDF model using H_MCMC. We discuss the template H_MCMC accelerator architecture and its detailed hardware implementation in Section 5. Note that our proposed accelerator architecture is the first realization of Hamiltonian MCMC on the FPGA platform.

❹ **Parameter Pruning and Data Inference:** CausaLearn leverages the hyper-parameter samples drawn form the posterior distribution $p(\theta|\mathbf{D})$ to perform a user-defined data inference task (e.g., Eq. (4)). We use autocorrelation metric $\rho(.)$ to evaluate the mixing property of the generated samples:

$$\rho_k = \frac{\Sigma_i^{N-k}(\theta_i - \bar{\theta})(\theta_{i+k} - \bar{\theta})}{\Sigma_i^{N}(\theta_i - \bar{\theta})}, \tag{7}$$

where $\bar{\theta}$ is the running average of the previous hyper-parameter samples and k is a user-defined constant that denotes the desired lag in computing the autocorrelation. CausaLearn prunes the correlated hyper-parameter samples to further reduce the computational overhead of the inference phase while providing an effective exploration of the parameters' space. We provide extensive evaluations for both regression and classification tasks in Section 8.

5 ACCELERATOR ARCHITECTURE

CausaLearn leverages batch data processing to update the hyper-parameters of the probability density function. The size of data batch to be evaluated at each MCMC iteration explicitly governs the computational workload of the underlying task. As we will discuss in Section 6, CausaLearn performs physical profiling and resource-aware customization to adjust the data batch size (b_s) and schedule the subsequent computations such that it best fits the target platform and application data requirements.

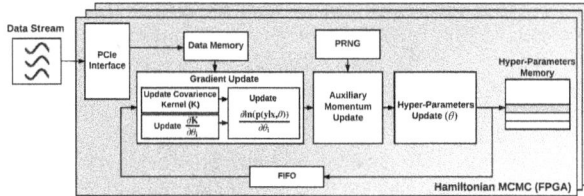

Figure 2: High-level block diagram of Hamiltonian MCMC.

Figure 2 illustrates the high-level block diagram of the H_MCMC methodology. At each H_MCMC iteration, a data batch consisting of both newly arrived data samples and a random subset of previous samples are loaded into the FPGA through PCIe to be processed using Hamiltonian dynamics (*Lines 5-7 in Algorithm 1*). We use η to denote the portion of new data in each data batch ($0 < \eta \leq 1$). Performing Hamiltonian MCMC includes three main steps:
(i) Computing the gradient of posterior distribution given the prior density function of each hyper-parameter (Line 14 of Algorithm 1). In H_MCMC, the posterior distribution of θ given a set of independent observations $\mathbf{y} \in \mathbf{D}$ is represented as $p(\theta|\mathbf{D}) \propto e^{(-U(\theta))}$, where the energy function U is:

$$U = -\Sigma_{\mathbf{y} \in \mathbf{D}} \, ln \, p(\mathbf{y}|\mathbf{x}, \theta) - ln \, p(\theta). \qquad (8)$$

(ii) Updating the auxiliary momentum variable r. CausaLearn adds a friction term to the momentum updating step as suggested in [6] to minimize the impact of injected noise as a result of bypassing the Metropolis-Hastings correction step in conventional MCMC. CausaLearn includes a scaled Pseudo Random Number Generator (PRNG) to sample from $\mathcal{N}(0, E)$ (Line 15 of Algorithm 1).

(iii) Drawing new hyper-parameter samples based on the currently computed gradients and momentum values. The Mass matrix, M, in Line 13 of Algorithm 1 is used to precondition the MCMC sampler when specific information about the target PDF is available. In many applications, the matrix M is set to the identity matrix I.

The main computational workload in Algorithm 1 is associated with computing the gradient of density function. Algorithm 2 outlines the process of computing the gradient vector $\nabla \tilde{U}(\theta_t)$ to perform H_MCMC with GP prior. Evaluating the $\frac{\partial ln(p(\mathbf{y}|\mathbf{x}, \theta))}{\partial \theta_i}$ term in Line 11 of Algorithm 2 requires computing the inverse of the covariance kernel ($K_{b_s \times b_s}$). Computing the inverse of a dense $b_s \times b_s$ matrix with $b_s \gg 2$ involves a variety of operations with complex data flow. As such, we suggest adopting QR decomposition in the MCMC routine to reduce the hardware implementation complexity and make the algorithm well-suited for FPGA acceleration.

Algorithm 3 details the incremental QR decomposition by modified Gram-Schmitt technique. QR decomposition returns an *orthogonal* matrix Q and an *upper-triangular* matrix R. Utilizing QR decomposition facilitates the gradient computing step by transforming the inversion of the dense kernel matrix into the inversion of an upper-triangular matrix ($K^{-1} = R^{-1}Q^T$), which is performed using simple back substitution (Section 5.1.3).

Algorithm 2 GP Gradient Computing

Inputs: Batch of input data ($\tilde{D} = [\tilde{X}, \tilde{Y}]$), Hyper-parameter set $\theta = [\sigma_n^2, \sigma_k^2, \mathcal{L}_1, ...\mathcal{L}_d]$
Outputs: Gradient of energy function $\nabla \tilde{U}(\theta)$.

1: $Q^{(0)} \leftarrow [\ ]$
2: $R^{(0)} \leftarrow [\ ]$
3: $H \leftarrow [0, 0, ..., 0]_{1 \times b_s}^T$
4: **for** $i = 1, 2, ..., b_s$ **do**
5:     **for** $j = 1, 2, ..., b_s$ **do**
6:         $v^2 \leftarrow \Sigma_{k=1}^d \frac{(\tilde{X}_{ik} - \tilde{X}_{jk})^2}{\mathcal{L}_k^2}$
7:         $H_j \leftarrow \sigma_k^2 exp(\frac{-v^2}{2})$
    end for
8:     $H_i \leftarrow H_i + \sigma_n^2$
9:     $[Q^{(i)}, R^{(i)}] \leftarrow QR\_Update(Q^{(i-1)}, R^{(i-1)}, H)$
end for
10: $Z_i \leftarrow R^{-1}Q^T \frac{\partial K}{\partial \theta_i}$
11: $\frac{\partial ln(p(Y|X, \theta))}{\partial \theta_i} \leftarrow -\frac{1}{2}(Tr(Z_i) + Y^T Z_i R^{-1}Q^T Y)$
12: $\nabla \tilde{U}(\theta_i) \leftarrow \frac{|D|}{|\tilde{D}|}(\frac{\partial ln(p(Y|X, \theta))}{\partial \theta_i} - ln(p(\theta_i)))$

Algorithm 3 Incremental QR decomposition

Inputs: New column H, Last iteration Q^{s-1} and R^{s-1}.
Output: Q^s and R^s.

1: $R^s \leftarrow \begin{pmatrix} R^{s-1} & 0 \\ 0 & 0 \end{pmatrix}$
2: **for** $j = 1,...,s-1$ **do**
3:     $R_{js}^s \leftarrow (Q_j^{s-1})^T H$
4:     $H \leftarrow H - R_{js}^s Q_j^{s-1}$
end for
5: $R_{ss}^s \leftarrow \|H\|_2$
6: $Q^s \leftarrow [Q^{s-1}, \frac{H}{R_{ss}^s}]$

5.1 Hardware Implementation

In this section, we explain the realization of H_MCMC module step by step. We leverage both algorithmic and hardware optimization techniques to provide an efficient implementation of H_MCMC.

5.1.1 Memory Management

To effectively pipeline the data flow in Algorithm 1 and optimize the system throughput, it is necessary to perform multiple concurrent loads and stores from a particular RAM. To cope with the concurrency, we suggest having multiple smaller-sized block memories to store particular data matrices instead of using a unified large BRAM. We devise and automate a memory management system to tile and schedule the matrix computations such that it best fits the data geometry and the physical hardware resources.

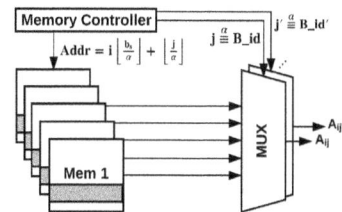

Figure 3: CausaLearn uses cyclic interleaving to facilitate concurrent load/store in performing matrix computations.

Figure 3 illustrates the schematic depiction of the memory management unit in CausaLearn framework. The block memories corresponding to a specific data matrix share the same address signal (*addr*) generated by the memory controller. The block identification index (B_id) is used in conjunction with the address signal to locate a certain element of the pertinent data matrix. To perform a matrix-based operation, one requires having access to sequential matrix indexes. CausaLearn's memory controller fills the corresponding memory blocks using *cyclic interleaving*. Employing cyclic interleaving enables accessing multiple successive elements of a matrix simultaneously which, in turn, facilitates parallelizing matrix-vector and matrix-matrix multiplications.

For a given data batch size (b_s), the number of concurrent floating-point adders/multipliers used to perform a matrix operation is directly controlled by the unrolling factor by which the data matrices are partitioned into smaller blocks. Let us denote the pertinent unroll factor with α. CausaLearn provides a set of subroutines that characterize the impact of unrolling factor α on the subsequent resource consumption. Our automated subroutines take the available resource provisioning into account and provide guidelines for an efficient hardware mapping. These guidelines are leveraged to customize the matrix-based computational workloads to the resource limits of the target platform while avoiding mapping of the data matrices into registers due to an excessive array partitioning. For instance, in Xilinx vendor libraries, every 10 floating-point numbers or less will be mapped to registers during the design synthesis. As such, α should take an integer value less than or equal to $\alpha \leq \frac{b_s}{10}$ to avoid excessive data partitioning. Note that mapping of large data matrices into the registers exhausts the LUT units on the target FPGA resulting in a complex control logic. This, in turn, translates to a larger critical path to accommodate for the underlying computations.

5.1.2 Tree-based Reduction

Performing matrix-vector and matrix-matrix multiplication results in frequent appearance of dot product operations similar to $c \mathrel{+}= A[i] \times B[i]$. Due to the sequential nature of dot products (Figure 4a), simple use of pipelining/unrolling does not significantly reduce the Initiation Interval (II) between two successive operations. As such, we suggest to transform such sequential operations ($c \mathrel{+}= A[i] \times B[i]$) into a series of operations that can be independently run in parallel (e.g., $W[i] = A[i] \times B[i]$). In particular, we implement a tree-based adder to find the final sum value c by adding up the values stored in a BRAM called W. We use cyclic interleaving for storing all the involving arrays including A, B, and W to facilitate pipelining the subsequent multiplications and additions (Figure 4b).

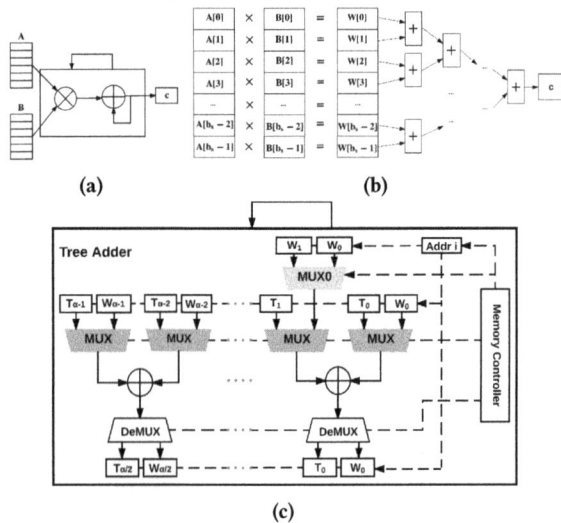

(a)   (b)

(c)

Figure 4: Facilitating matrix multiplication and dot product. (a) Conventional sequential approach. (b) Proposed tree-based model. Our approach reduces the II of dot product operations to 1. (c) The inner structure of tree-based adder.

Figure 4c illustrates the inner structure of CausaLearn tree-based adder. We utilize a temporary array T within the tree adder module to store the intermediate results. In our tree adder module, the number of additions performed at each stage is halved and the result is stored in the other array. E.g., in the even stages, the values in the array W are summed up and the results are stored in the array T. CausaLearn's memory controller generates the appropriate source/destination addresses to load/store the intermediate results at each stage of the tree. The number of floating-point adders/multipliers in the tree-based reduction module is equivalent to the unrolling factor α used to partition data matrices (assuming dual port memory blocks). Let us index the elements of arrays W and T with variable k. Each sub-block W_i and T_i in Figure 4c is filled such that $k \equiv i \mod \alpha$ where $k \in \{0, 1, ..., b_s\}$. In the tree adder structure, the multiplexer denoted by "MUX0" is necessary for performing the last b_s/α additions on the remaining values in W_{+1}. The final result (c) is stored in the address 0 of memory assigned to array W. As will be discussed in Section 5.1.4, CausaLearn attains a balance between parallel operations and data reuse by scheduling a slice of operations to be performed at each clock cycle.

5.1.3 Matrix Inverse Computation

Computing the inverse of the covariance kernel K is a key step in finding the gradient direction in the H_MCMC routine. Employing QR decomposition within the H_MCMC routine facilitates such operations given that K^{-1} can be computed as $R^{-1}Q^T$. For instance, to solve an equation similar to $V = K^{-1}B$, one needs to find the vector V such that $RV = Q^T B$. Given the upper-triangular structure of matrix R, the latter equation can be solved using back-substitution [24–26] in which (starting from the last row index) each element of the vector V can be uniquely recovered by solving a linear equation as illustrated in Figure 5. Let us denote the product of $Q^T B$ with vector C. The Processing Element (PE) in Figure 5 is a multiply-add accumulator that computes:

$$V_i = \frac{C_i - \Sigma_{j=i+1}^{b_s} R_{ij} V_j}{R_{ii}}. \tag{9}$$

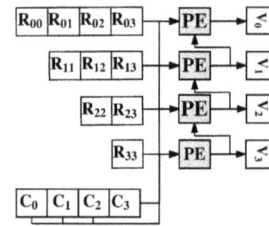

Figure 5: Schematic depiction of back-substitution.

CausaLearn performs back-substitution by parallelizing the computations as shown in Figure 6. Cyclic interleaving along the second dimension (matrix columns) is used to store the Q and R matrices. This enables us to pipeline the design and reduce the II between two successive operations into only 1 clock cycle. Indices of vectors and the second dimension of matrices in Figure 6 correspond to their actual values modulo α. We batch the operations in the back-substitution module to parallelize computations that share the same variables. E.g., in computing Line 10 of Algorithm 2, multiple columns of matrix $Z_{b_s \times b_s}$ may be batched together to facilitate computations given that the columns of matrix Z can be computed independently using the same set of Q and R values.

5.1.4 Data Parallelism

CausaLearn gains a balance between parallel operations and data reuse by partitioning matrix-based computations into smaller

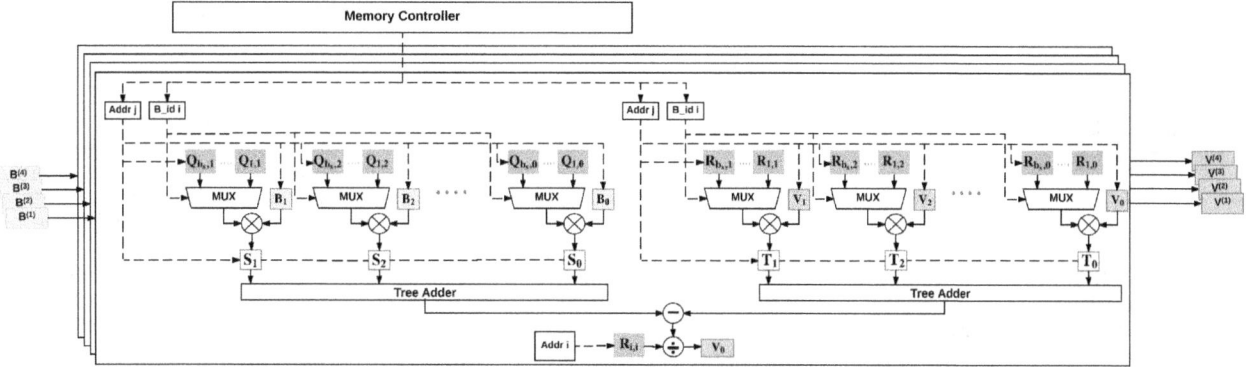

Figure 6: CausaLearn architecture for computing back-substitution. The operations in the right and left side of the equation, $R_{b_s \times b_s} V_{b_s \times b_s} = Q_{b_s \times b_s}^T B_{b_s \times b_s}$, are parallelized to optimized system throughput per iteration. We use cyclic interleaving along the second dimension to store the Q and R matrices. Each column of matrix $B^{(i)}$ is partitioned into smaller blocks to further accommodate parallelism. In this figure, we used dash lines to indicate the control signals.

slices of operations that best match the available computational resources such as DSP units. Figure 7a shows an example where multiple columns of matrix V are scheduled as a slice of operations to be evaluated in parallel in the matrix inversion unit ($R_{b_s \times b_s} V_{b_s \times b_s} = Q_{b_s \times b_s}^T B_{b_s \times b_s}$). As shown in Figure 7b, there is a trade-off between the number of samples per slice of computations and resource utilization. CausaLearn leverages this trade-off to optimize the template design such that the throughput per resource unit is maximized. The effective throughput per resource unit decreases for large values of slice factor p. This performance drop is due to the saturation of the pertinent resource provisioning which, in turn, makes it infeasible to perform more operations in parallel. We leverage batch data parallelism within different parts of the framework (e.g., tree-based reduction module, matrix inversion unit, etc.) to improve the efficiency of the system.

6 CAUSALEARN CUSTOMIZATION

The architecture discussed in Section 5 serves as a template for the accelerator's micro-architecture. Here, we outline our design customization methodology to adapt the H_MCMC routine to the resource boundaries of the target platform.

6.1 Design Planner

Table 2 details the memory footprint and runtime cost in CausaLearn framework. Memory constraint on computing platforms is one of the main limitations in big data regime. CausaLearn updates the posterior distribution samples of a dynamic data collection by breaking down the input data into data batches that best fit the memory budget. CausaLearn's memory footprint outlined in Table 2 specifies the storage requirement for the gradient matrices corresponding to each GP hyper-parameter, the covariance kernel $K = QR$, and the intermediate matrices Z_i (Line 10 in Algorithm 2).

The runtime requirement for data analysis in CausaLearn framework can be approximated as:

$$T_{CausaLearn} \propto T^{comm} + T^{Comp}. \tag{10}$$

The T^{comm} term denotes the communication overhead of sending a data batch of size $b_s \times d$ from host to the FPGA platform and reading back the updated posterior distribution parameters θ. The T^{Comp} term represents the runtime cost of updating the covariance matrix K and computing the gradients as outlined in Algorithms 1, 2, and 3. The computation and communication costs in CausaLearn framework are detailed in Table 2. As we demonstrate in Section 8,

CausaLearn's overall runtime is mainly dominated by the computational workload while the communication cost contributes to a small fraction of the overall runtime (e.g., $\leq 0.03\%$).

Table 2: CausaLearn memory and runtime characterization.

Physical Performance of CausaLearn Framework	
Memory Footprint	$M_{CausaLearn} \approx N_{bits} n_k (4 + d) b_s^2$ N_{bits}: Number of signal representation bits n_k: Number of H_MCMC units working in parallel b_s: Number of samples per data batch-size d: Feature space size of the incoming data samples
Computation Runtime	$T^{comp} \approx \beta_{flop} C_{len} n_{step} (6 b_s^2 d + b_s d)$ β_{flop}: Computational cost per floating-point operation C_{len}: Desired Markov chain's length n_{step}: Number of discretization steps in H_MCMC
Communication Runtime	$T^{comm} \approx \beta_{net} + \frac{N_{bit} C_{len} [b_s d + (d+2)]}{BW}$ β_{net}: Constant network latency BW: Operational communication bandwidth

There is a trade-off between the selected data batch size b_s and the required runtime to reach the Markov chain steady state distribution, a.k.a., *mixing time* [6, 27]. On the one hand, a high value of b_s reduces the number of iterations to reach the steady state distribution. However, it also reduces the throughput of the system as data can no longer fit in the fast BRAM of the target board. On the other hand, a low value of b_s may degrade the overall performance due to the significant increase in the number of required posterior samples to compute a steady approximation of Eq. (3). CausaLearn carefully leverages this trade-off to customize computations to the limits of the physical resources and constraints while minimally affecting the mixing time in the target application.

To deliver the most accurate approximation within the given resource provisioning, CausaLearn solves the optimization objective described in Eq. (11). CausaLearn's constraint-driven optimization can be expressed as:

$$\begin{aligned} \underset{b_s,\, n_k}{\text{minimize}} &\ (MC\ mixing\ time), \\ \text{subject to:} &\ T^{comm} + T^{Comp} \leq T_u, \\ &\ \eta n_k b_s \leq f_{data} T_u, \\ &\ M_{CausaLearn} \leq M_u, \\ &\ P_{CausaLearn} \leq P_u, \\ &\ n_k \in \mathbb{N}, \end{aligned} \tag{11}$$

where T_u, P_u, and M_u are a set of user-defined parameters that imply the application constraints in terms of runtime, power, and

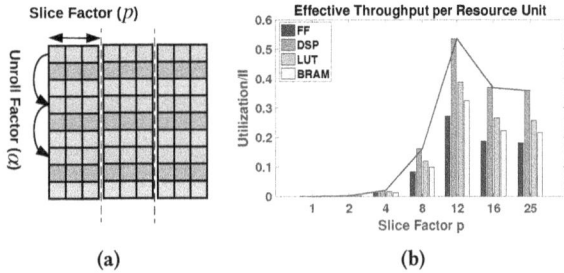

Figure 7: Example data parallelism in CausaLearn matrix inversion unit: (a) Partitioning of matrix computations into slices of operation. (b) Resource utilization divided by the pertinent initiation interval as a function of the number of samples per operation slice on Virtex-7-XC7VX485T FPGA.

memory respectively. The maximum number of newly arrived samples that should be processed in each time unit is either dictated by the arriving rate of data samples (f_{data}) or the buffer size for storing incoming samples (M_u). Here, η is the proportion of newly arrived samples versus the old ones in each data batch. For a fixed set of parameters, power consumption ($P_{CausaLearn}$) has a linear correlation with the number of MCMC modules that are run in parallel. CausaLearn tunes the number of concurrent MCMC modules accordingly to adapt to possible power limitations imposed by the target setting.

CausaLearn approximates the solution of Eq. (11) by fixing the number of parallel H_MCMC units (n_k) and solving for data batch size (b_s) using the Karush-Kuhn-Tucker (KKT) conditions. To facilitate automation, we provide a solver for our optimization approach. The solver gets the constraints from the user as inputs and uses our Mathematica-based computational software program to solve the optimization. Note that the constraint-driven optimization is a one-time process and incurs a constant, negligible overhead.

6.2 Design Integrator

The design integrator unit in CausaLearn framework takes the acquired execution schedule into consideration and generates the corresponding state machines and microcodes to manage the memory controller and data parallelisms discussed in Section 5.1. The customized synthesizable code is generated after embedding the microcodes within the template H_MCMC architecture. In our prototype designs, we leverage PCIe to transfer data back and forth between the FPGA and the general purpose processor hosting the FPGA. The PCIe interface can be replaced by any other data transfer link such as Ethernet depending on the application.

6.3 CausaLearn API

CausaLearn API consists of a set of high-level automated subroutines which perform the subsequent steps outlined in Figure 1. Programmers interact with our API only through providing the input data stream and pertinent physical constraints in terms of the available memory, runtime, and/or power inside a bash file. CausaLearn finds the optimal batch size (b_s) using our Mathematica-based optimizer as discussed in Section 6.1. The API then calls Vivado-HLS to search for optimal values of various design directives including unroll factor, slice factor, and pipeline depth that yield the maximum throughput while complying with the user-defined constraints. Eventually, the customized H_MCMC core along with the required I/O interface modules are generated to be implemented on FPGA.

In CausaLearn, API follows specific steps to find the optimal values for each HLS directive in an automated manner. For instance, the optimal value of slice factor is obtained by synthesizing the design using different values of slice factor and collecting utilization and initiation interval from the synthesis report. The optimal value

is either the local optima of the effective throughput per resource unit as depicted in Figure 7b or the maximum value that allows the design to fit user-specific constraints (when using the local optima exceeds the user constraints). After setting the slice factor, unroll factor is determined to increase data parallelism while maintaining the design metrics below the specific physical constraints. It is noteworthy that the whole customization process is automated so that data practitioners with different scientific backgrounds that do not necessarily possess any particular hardware design knowledge can benefit from CausaLearn end-to-end design.

Depending on the synthesis speed on the host machine and data dimensionality, profiling can take 5 to 30 minutes on commodity personal computers. Note that profiling is performed once per application/platform and its cost is amortized over-time as the system is used for processing data streams.

7 HARDWARE SETTING AND RESULTS

We evaluate CausaLearn using three off-the-shelf FPGA evaluation boards namely Zynq ZC702 (XC7Z020), Virtex VC707 (XC7VX485T), and Virtex UltraScale VCU108 (XCVU095) as the primary hardware accelerator. We use an Intel core-i5 CPU with 8GB memory running on the Windows OS at 2.40GHz as the general purpose processor hosting the FPGA. The software realization of CausaLearn is employed for comparison purposes. We leverage PCIe library provided by [28] to interconnect the host and FPGA platforms. Vivado HLS 2016.4 is used to synthesize and simulate our MCMC units. All FPGA platforms work at 100MHz frequency.

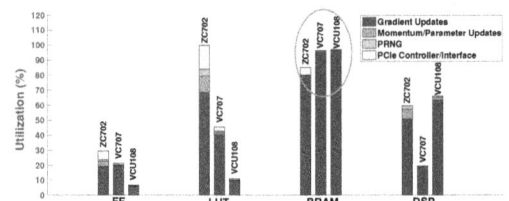

Figure 8: Resource utilization on different platforms assuming a hyper-parameter set of size $|\theta| = 10$. The output of our automated customization characterizes the hardware accelerator which, in turn, helps us to fully exploit the available on-chip memory. As shown, the resource utilization is mainly dominated by the Gradient update unit.

Figure 8 shows the breakdown resource utilization of CausaLearn deployed on three FPGAs. Each FPGA platform has a different computational budget. The total resource utilization accounts for both the H_MCMC unit (including the gradient update, momentum and parameter update, and PRNG modules) as well as the PCIe controller. Table 3 details CausaLearn performance per iteration of H_MCMC for processing different number of data samples (n). The earlier MCMC hardware accelerators are developed based on the assumption that input data samples are independent and identically distributed. These works cannot handle time-series data with causal structure as shown in Figure 9. As such, we opt to compare CausaLearn runtime (with $n_k = 1$) and energy consumption against a highly optimized C++ software solution. The software baseline is optimized using Eigen and OpenMP libraries. Eigen library exploits Intel Stream SIMD Extension (SSE) instructions to enhance the performance of intensive matrix computation. All the available cores on the Intel Core-i5 CPU (with 8GB memory running at 2.40GHz) were used to execute the H_MCMC routine.

FPGA power is simulated using Vivado power analyzer which accounts for both static and dynamic power. We use Intel Power Gadget 3.0.7. to measure CPU execution power. The power consumption for the H_MCMC unit is 0.95, 3.74, and 3.84 *Watts* for

Table 3: Relative runtime/energy improvement per H_MCMC iteration achieved by CausaLearn on different platforms compared to the optimized software implementation for $|\theta| = 10$ and $n_{step} = 100$. The conventional H_MCMC algorithm incurs $O(n^2)$ runtime complexity, whereas, our batch optimization approach scales linearly with $\left\lceil \frac{n}{b_s} \right\rceil$.

n	Communication Overhead	Runtime per Iteration SW	CausaLearn Runtime per Iteration			Runtime Improvement			Energy Improvement		
			ZC702	VC707	VCU108	ZC702	VC707	VCU108	ZC702	VC707	VCU108
256	16.92 msec	113.01 sec	96.18 sec	47.10 sec	76.71 sec	1.2×	2.4×	1.5×	8.1×	4.1×	2.4×
512	33.65 msec	902.98 sec	192.37 sec	94.23 sec	153.42 sec	4.7×	9.6×	5.9×	31.8×	16.5×	9.8×
1024	67.18 msec	8601.37 sec	384.72 sec	188.61 sec	230.13 sec	22.4×	42.7×	37.4×	136.3×	65.9×	56.3×
2048	134.19 msec	33.52 hr	769.44 sec	376.81 sec	460.26 sec	156.8×	320.2×	262.2×	769.1×	398.9×	318.2×

ZC702, VC707, and VCU108, respectively. As illustrated, the computational time in CausaLearn grows linearly with respect to the number of data samples. In this experiment, the optimal batch size for each platform is used to maximize the on-chip memory usage as shown in Figure 8. The optimal data batch sizes (output of CausaLearn customization) are 88, 256, and 360 on ZC702, VC707, and VCU108, respectively. In cases where the number of data samples is not divisible by the data batch, $\left\lceil \frac{n}{b_s} \right\rceil$ iterations are performed to analyze all data samples.

8 PRACTICAL DESIGN EXPERIENCES

We use CausaLearn to analyze three large time-series data with strong causal structure. In particular, we analyze:

(i) Dow Jones Index stock's change over time. This data [29] includes daily stock data of 30 different companies collected over 6 months. Each data sample x_i contains 8 features including different statistics of the stock price during the previous week (e.g., the highest and lowest price). The task is to predict the percentage of return for each stock in the following week.

(ii) Sensor data to classify different daily human activities. The dataset [30] comprises body motion and vital signs recordings for ten volunteers while performing different activities. Each data sample x_i includes 23 features. In this experiment, we use the data collected for two subjects to distinguish jogging and running activities. Each activity is recorded for 1 minute with a sampling rate of $50Hz$ resulting in more than $6K$ samples per subject.

(iii) Time-variant data for regression purposes [31]. The data is generated using a time-variant (unknown) function where the task is to predict the function's output given the previously observed samples. Figure 9a shows the regression's output using the posterior distribution samples learned by CausaLearn (Figure 11c). In Figure 9, we compare the regression's output using MCMC samples learned by assuming a causal GP prior versus i.i.d. data measurements with multivariate Gaussian prior (e.g., [11, 32]). The data points denoted by star signs are the training observations $\mathbf{y}$.

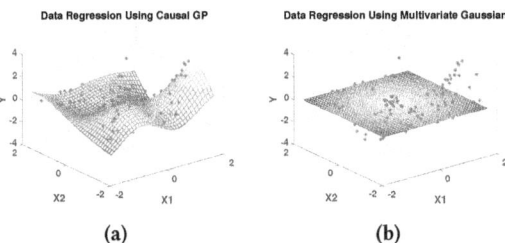

(a)   **(b)**

Figure 9: Time-variant data analysis using MCMC samples by assuming (a) causal GP prior (CausaLearn), vs. (b) i.i.d. assumption with multivariate Gaussian prior (e.g., [11, 32]).

Data batch size, b_s, is a key tunable parameter that characterizes CausaLearn's resource utilization and runtime performance as outlined in Table 2. Figure 10 demonstrates the impact of data batch size b_s on the subsequent resource utilization and system throughput per H_MCMC unit in each application. Multiple H_MCMC units can work in parallel within the confine of the resource provisioning to further boost the system throughput for smaller data batch sizes.

Figure 11 shows CausaLearn's posterior distribution samples obtained with a batch size of $b_s = 128$ in each application. The red cross sign on each graph demonstrates the maximum a posterior (MAP) estimate obtained by solving:

$$\underset{\theta}{argmax}\ ln(p(\mathbf{y}|\mathbf{x}, \theta)) + ln(p(\theta)). \tag{12}$$

Due to the space limit and high dimensionality of the target datasets, Figure 11 selectively shows the MCMC samples obtained for the observation noise variance (σ_n^2). The same trend is observed for the other hyper-parameters (e.g., σ_k^2 and $\mathcal{L}_i$).

9 RELATED WORK

Bayesian network is a key method to model dynamic systems in various statistical and machine learning tasks. Significant theoretical strides have been made to design Bayesian graphical analytics that can be used at scales by exploiting task and data level parallelism [5–8, 33]. Available Bayesian inference tools on CPUs [15], GPUs [16–18, 34], and FPGAs [21, 22], however, are either application specific or include direct mappings of algorithms to hardware. As such, the idea of customizing the Bayesian networks to make them well-suited for the underlying platform is unexplored. Recently, authors in [19, 20] have introduced a generic GPU-accelerated framework for Bayesian inference. Even these works are built based the assumption that input data samples are i.i.d; thus lack the capability to capture the inherent causal structure of time series data. To the best of our knowledge, CausaLearn is the first automated framework that enables end-to-end prototyping of complex causal Bayesian analytics with continuous random variables. CausaLearn is capable of handling both strong correlation and high-dimensionality in streaming scenarios with severe resource constraints.

FPGAs have been used to accelerate computationally expensive MCMC methods. Recent works in [11, 32, 35] have proposed reconfigurable architectures with custom precision for efficient realization of population-based MCMC routine applied to Bayesian graphical models. Authors in [11, 32, 35] targets simple multivariate Gaussian densities where observations are assumed to be independent and identically distributed. Thus, these works cannot be readily employed in more sophisticated streaming scenarios where independence cannot be assumed between data samples. To the best of our knowledge, CausaLearn is the first to provide a scalable FPGA realization of generic H_MCMC routine applied to streaming applications with large and densely correlated data samples. We emphasize that the use of data precision optimization technique proposed in [32, 36] provide an orthogonal means to our resource-aware customization for performance improvement. Therefore, CausaLearn can achieve even greater improvement by leveraging such optimizations.

10 CONCLUSION

This paper presents CausaLearn, the first automated reconfigurable framework to compute on and continuously update time-varying probability density functions for causal Bayesian analysis.

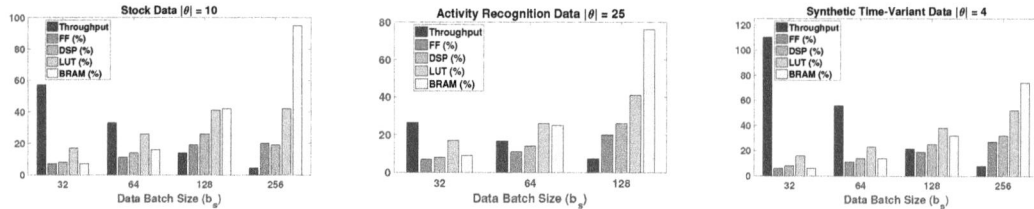

Figure 10: VC707 resource utilization and system throughput per H_MCMC unit (n_k = 1) as a function of data batch size b_s in different applications. The reported throughputs indicate batch per second processing rate corresponding to n_{step} = 100.

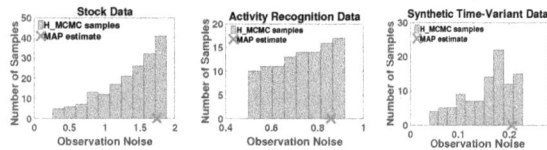

Figure 11: Example CausaLearn's posterior distribution samples. The red cross sign on each graph demonstrates the maximum a posterior estimate in each experiment.

CausaLearn targets probabilistic learning in streaming scenarios in which the number of data samples grows over time and computational resources are severely limited. To boost the computational efficiency, CausaLearn provides a scalable implementation of Hamiltonian MCMC on FPGA. We modify the conventional MCMC algorithm using QR decomposition to make it amenable for hardware-based acceleration performed by FPGA platforms. We further provide novel memory management, tree-based reduction, and data parallelism techniques to effectively pipeline and balance the underlying matrix computations on FPGA. CausaLearn is devised with an automated constraint-driven optimization unit to customize H_MCMC workload to the limits of the resource provisioning while minimally affecting the MC mixing time. An accompanying API ensures automated applicability of CausaLearn for an end-to-end realization of complex Bayesian graphical analysis on massive datasets with densely correlated samples.

REFERENCES

[1] R. Salakhutdinov, A. Mnih, and G. Hinton, "Restricted boltzmann machines for collaborative filtering," in *Proceedings of the 24th international conference on Machine learning*. ACM, 2007, pp. 791–798.

[2] L. Bottolo and S. Richardson, "Evolutionary stochastic search for bayesian model exploration," *Bayesian Analysis*, vol. 5, no. 3, pp. 583–618, 2010.

[3] T. Flury and N. Shephard, "Bayesian inference based only on simulated likelihood: particle filter analysis of dynamic economic models," *Econometric Theory*, vol. 27, no. 05, pp. 933–956, 2011.

[4] S. Brooks, A. Gelman, G. Jones, and X.-L. Meng, *Handbook of Markov Chain Monte Carlo*. CRC press, 2011.

[5] M. Welling and Y. W. Teh, "Bayesian learning via stochastic gradient langevin dynamics," in *Proceedings of the 28th International Conference on Machine Learning (ICML-11)*, 2011, pp. 681–688.

[6] T. Chen, E. B. Fox, and C. Guestrin, "Stochastic gradient hamiltonian monte carlo." in *ICML*, 2014, pp. 1683–1691.

[7] W. Neiswanger, C. Wang, and E. Xing, "Asymptotically exact, embarrassingly parallel mcmc," *arXiv preprint arXiv:1311.4780*, 2013.

[8] U. Simsekli, A. Durmus, R. Badeau, G. Richard, E. Moulines, and T. Cemgil, "Parallelized stochastic gradient markov chain monte carlo algorithms for non-negative matrix factorization," in *42nd International Conference on Acoustics, Speech and Signal Processing (ICASSP)*, 2017.

[9] D. Auras, S. Birke, T. Piwczyk, R. Leupers, and G. Ascheid, "A flexible mcmc detector asic," in *SoC Design Conference (ISOCC), 2016 International*. IEEE, 2016, pp. 285–286.

[10] M. Lin, I. Lebedev, and J. Wawrzynek, "High-throughput bayesian computing machine with reconfigurable hardware," in *Proceedings of the 18th annual ACM/SIGDA international symposium on Field programmable gate arrays*. ACM, 2010, pp. 73–82.

[11] G. Mingas and C.-S. Bouganis, "Population-based mcmc on multi-core cpus, gpus and fpgas," *IEEE Transactions on Computers*, vol. 65, no. 4, pp. 1283–1296, 2016.

[12] S. Liu, G. Mingas, and C.-S. Bouganis, "An exact mcmc accelerator under custom precision regimes," in *Field Programmable Technology (FPT), 2015 International*

Conference on. IEEE, 2015, pp. 120–127.

[13] C. E. Rasmussen, "Gaussian processes for machine learning," 2006.

[14] M. K. Titsias, N. Lawrence, and M. Rattray, "Markov chain monte carlo algorithms for gaussian processes," *Inference and Estimation in Probabilistic Time-Series Models*, vol. 9, 2008.

[15] D. Maclaurin and R. P. Adams, "Firefly monte carlo: Exact mcmc with subsets of data," *arXiv preprint arXiv:1403.5693*, 2014.

[16] M. M. Tibbits, M. Haran, and J. C. Liechty, "Parallel multivariate slice sampling," *Statistics and Computing*, vol. 21, no. 3, pp. 415–430, 2011.

[17] S. Henriksen, A. Wills, T. B. Schön, and B. Ninness, "Parallel implementation of particle mcmc methods on a gpu," *IFAC Proceedings Volumes*, vol. 45, no. 16, pp. 1143–1148, 2012.

[18] A. L. Beam, S. K. Ghosh, and J. Doyle, "Fast hamiltonian monte carlo using gpu computing," *Journal of Computational and Graphical Statistics*, vol. 25, no. 2, pp. 536–548, 2016.

[19] A. G. d. G. Matthews, M. van der Wilk, T. Nickson, K. Fujii, A. Boukouvalas, P. León-Villagrá, Z. Ghahramani, and J. Hensman, "Gpflow: A gaussian process library using tensorflow," *Journal of Machine Learning Research*, vol. 18, no. 40, pp. 1–6, 2017.

[20] D. Tran, A. Kucukelbir, A. B. Dieng, M. Rudolph, D. Liang, and D. M. Blei, "Edward: A library for probabilistic modeling, inference, and criticism," *arXiv preprint arXiv:1610.09787*, 2016.

[21] N. B. Asadi, T. H. Meng, and W. H. Wong, "Reconfigurable computing for learning bayesian networks," in *Proceedings of the 16th international ACM/SIGDA symposium on Field programmable gate arrays*. ACM, 2008, pp. 203–211.

[22] N. Bani Asadi, C. W. Fletcher, G. Gibeling, E. N. Glass, K. Sachs, D. Burke, Z. Zhou, J. Wawrzynek, W. H. Wong, and G. P. Nolan, "Paralearn: a massively parallel, scalable system for learning interaction networks on fpgas," in *Proceedings of the 24th ACM International Conference on Supercomputing*. ACM, 2010, pp. 83–94.

[23] C. Andrieu, N. De Freitas, A. Doucet, and M. I. Jordan, "An introduction to mcmc for machine learning," *Machine learning*, vol. 50, no. 1, pp. 5–43, 2003.

[24] B. D. Rouhani, A. Mirhoseini, E. M. Songhori, and F. Koushanfar, "Automated real-time analysis of streaming big and dense data on reconfigurable platforms," *ACM Transactions on Reconfigurable Technology and Systems (TRETS)*, vol. 10, no. 1, p. 8, 2016.

[25] B. D. Rouhani, E. M. Songhori, A. Mirhoseini, and F. Koushanfar, "Ssketch: An automated framework for streaming sketch-based analysis of big data on fpga," in *Field-Programmable Custom Computing Machines (FCCM), 2015 IEEE 23rd Annual International Symposium on*. IEEE, 2015, pp. 187–194.

[26] B. D. Rouhani, A. Mirhoseini, and F. Koushanfar, "Rise: An automated framework for real-time intelligent video surveillance on fpga," *ACM Transactions on Embedded Computing Systems (TECS)*, vol. 16, no. 5s, p. 158, 2017.

[27] R. Bardenet, A. Doucet, and C. Holmes, "An adaptive subsampling approach for mcmc inference in large datasets," in *Proceedings of The 31st International Conference on Machine Learning*, 2014, pp. 405–413.

[28] XILLYBUS, "http://xillybus.com/," 2017.

[29] UCI Machine Learning Repository, "https://archive.ics.uci.edu/ml/datasets/Dow+Jones+Index," 2016.

[30] ——, "https://archive.ics.uci.edu/ml/datasets/MHEALTH+Dataset," 2016.

[31] J. Vanhatalo, J. Riihimäki, J. Hartikainen, P. Jylänki, V. Tolvanen, and A. Vehtari, "Gpstuff: Bayesian modeling with gaussian processes," *Journal of Machine Learning Research*, vol. 14, no. Apr, pp. 1175–1179, 2013.

[32] G. Mingas and C.-S. Bouganis, "A custom precision based architecture for accelerating parallel tempering mcmc on fpgas without introducing sampling error," in *Field-Programmable Custom Computing Machines (FCCM), 2012 IEEE 20th Annual International Symposium on*. IEEE, 2012, pp. 153–156.

[33] Y.-A. Ma, T. Chen, and E. Fox, "A complete recipe for stochastic gradient mcmc," in *Advances in Neural Information Processing Systems*, 2015, pp. 2917–2925.

[34] C. Hall, W. Ji, and E. Blaisten-Barojas, "The metropolis monte carlo method with cuda enabled graphic processing units," *Journal of Computational Physics*, vol. 258, pp. 871–879, 2014.

[35] S. Liu, G. Mingas, and C. Bouganis, "An unbiased mcmc fpga-based accelerator in the land of custom precision arithmetic," *IEEE Transactions on Computers*, 2016.

[36] G. Mingas, F. Rahman, and C.-S. Bouganis, "On optimizing the arithmetic precision of mcmc algorithms," in *Field-Programmable Custom Computing Machines (FCCM), 21st Annual International Symposium on*. IEEE, 2013, pp. 181–188.

C-LSTM: Enabling Efficient LSTM using Structured Compression Techniques on FPGAs

Shuo Wang[1,+], Zhe Li[2,+], Caiwen Ding[2,+], Bo Yuan[3], Qinru Qiu[2], Yanzhi Wang[2] and Yun Liang[1,*]

[+]These authors contributed equally

[1]Center for Energy-Efficient Computing & Applications (CECA), School of EECS, Peking University, China

[2]Dept. of Electrical Engineering & Computer Science, Syracuse University, Syracuse, NY, USA

[3]Dept. of Electrical Engineering, City University of New York, NY, USA

[1]{shvowang,ericlyun}@pku.edu.cn, [2]{zli89,cading,qiqiu,ywang393}@syr.edu, [3]byuan@ccny.cuny.edu

ABSTRACT

Recently, significant accuracy improvement has been achieved for acoustic recognition systems by increasing the model size of Long Short-Term Memory (LSTM) networks. Unfortunately, the ever-increasing size of LSTM model leads to inefficient designs on FPGAs due to the limited on-chip resources. The previous work proposes to use a pruning based compression technique to reduce the model size and thus speedups the inference on FPGAs. However, the random nature of the pruning technique transforms the dense matrices of the model to highly unstructured sparse ones, which leads to unbalanced computation and irregular memory accesses and thus hurts the overall performance and energy efficiency.

In contrast, we propose to use a structured compression technique which could not only reduce the LSTM model size but also eliminate the irregularities of computation and memory accesses. This approach employs block-circulant instead of sparse matrices to compress weight matrices and reduces the storage requirement from $\mathcal{O}(k^2)$ to $\mathcal{O}(k)$. Fast Fourier Transform algorithm is utilized to further accelerate the inference by reducing the computational complexity from $\mathcal{O}(k^2)$ to $\mathcal{O}(k \log k)$. The datapath and activation functions are quantized as 16-bit to improve the resource utilization. More importantly, we propose a comprehensive framework called C-LSTM to automatically optimize and implement a wide range of LSTM variants on FPGAs. According to the experimental results, C-LSTM achieves up to 18.8X and 33.5X gains for performance and energy efficiency compared with the state-of-the-art LSTM implementation under the same experimental setup, and the accuracy degradation is very small.

KEYWORDS

FPGA; RNNs; LSTM; compression; block-circulant matrix; FFT

*Corresponding author.

ACM Reference Format:
Shuo Wang[1,+], Zhe Li[2,+], Caiwen Ding[2,+], Bo Yuan[3], Qinru Qiu[2], Yanzhi Wang[2] and Yun Liang[1,]. 2018. C-LSTM: Enabling Efficient LSTM using Structured Compression Techniques on FPGAs. In *FPGA'18: 2018 ACM/SIGDA International Symposium on Field-Programmable Gate Arrays, February 25–27, 2018, Monterey, CA, USA.* ACM, New York, NY, USA, 10 pages. https://doi.org/10.1145/3174243.3174253

1 INTRODUCTION

Recurrent neural networks (RNNs) represent an important class of neural networks that contain cycles to carry information across neurons while reading inputs. Long Short-Term Memory (LSTM), one of the most popular types of RNNs, achieves great success in the domains such as speech recognition, machine translation, scene analysis, etc. [25]. However, the significant recognition accuracy improvement comes at the cost of increased computational complexity of larger model size [9]. Therefore, customized hardware acceleration is increasingly important for LSTMs, as exemplified by recent works on employing GPUs [5, 17], FPGAs [13, 16] and ASICs [7] as accelerators to speedup LSTMs.

Among the numerous platforms, FPGA has emerged as a promising solution for hardware acceleration as it provides customized hardware performance with flexible reconfigurability. By creating dedicated pipelines, parallel processing units, customized bit width, and etc., application designers can accelerate many workloads by orders of magnitude using FPGAs [24]. More importantly, High-level Synthesis (HLS) has greatly lowered the programming hurdle of FPGAs and improved the productivity by raising the programming abstraction from tedious RTL to high-level languages such as C/C++ [4] and OpenCL [26].

While the benefits of FPGAs is clear, it is still challenging to design efficient designs for LSTMs on FPGAs mainly for two reasons. On one hand, the capacity of the FPGA on-chip memory (a few or tens of Mb on-chip memory) is usually not large enough to store all the weight matrices of a standard LSTM inference model (e.g. hundreds of Mb). Although the previous work ESE [13] proposes to use the parameter pruning based compression technique to compress the dense weight matrices in the LSTM model into sparse ones, the sparse matrices need extra storage and processing units to store and decode the indices of the non-zero data, respectively. The skewed distribution of the data is likely to cause unbalanced workloads among parallel compute units. Therefore, the benefits of unstructured model compression is diminished by the sparsity of weight matrices. On the other hand, the computational complexity among the operators of the LSTMs is highly skewed and the data dependencies between operator are complicated. So, it is difficult to evenly allocate computing resources under the FPGA resource constraints while guaranteeing the complex data dependencies.

In this work, we propose to compress the weight matrices in the LSTM inference model in a structured manner by using block-circulant matrix [22]. The circulant matrix is a square matrix, of which each row (column) vector is the circulant reformat of the row (column) vector. Any matrix could be transformed into a set of circulant submatrices aka block-circulant matrices. Therefore, by representing each block-circulant matrix with a vector, the storage requirement could be reduced from $\mathcal{O}(k^2)$ to $\mathcal{O}(k)$ if the block (vector) size is k. Since the compressed weight matrices are still dense, the block-circulant matrix based compression is amenable to hardware acceleration on FPGAs. In order to further speed up the computation of LSTMs, we propose to accelerate the most computation-intensive circulant convolution operator by applying Fast Fourier Transform (FFT) algorithm to reduce the computational complexity from $\mathcal{O}(k^2)$ to $\mathcal{O}(n\log n)$.

After the model is compressed, we propose an automatic optimization and synthesis framework called C-LSTM to port efficient LSTM designs onto FPGAs. The framework is composed of model training and implementation flows. The former one is in charge of iteratively training the compressed LSTM model and exploring the trade-offs between compression ratio and prediction accuracy. As for the model implementation, it mainly consists of two parts which are (1) template generation and (2) automatic LSTM synthesis framework. For the former part, after analyzing a wide range of LSTM algorithms, we generalize a suite of LSTM primitive operators which is general enough to accommodate even the most complicated LSTM variant [25]. Then, a suite of highly optimized C/C++ templates of the primitive operators are manually generated by walking through a series of optimizations such as datapath and activation quantization, DFT-IDFT decoupling and etc. As for the latter part, the well-trained LSTM inference model is first analyzed and transformed into a directed acyclic dependency graph, where each node represents an operator and each edge indicates the associated data dependency between two operators. Secondly, we propose a specialized pipeline optimization algorithm considering both coarse-grained and fine-grained pipelining schemes to schedule the operators into appropriate stages. In the third step, we use an accurate performance and resource model to enable a fast design space exploration for optimal design parameters. Lastly, the scheduling results and optimization parameters are fed to code generator and backend toolchain as to implement the optimized LSTM accelerator design on FPGAs.

Overall, the contributions of this paper are listed as:

- We employ the block-circulant matrices based structured compression technique for LSTMs which largely reduces the computation complexity and memory footprint without incurring any computation and memory access irregularities. This method results in both compression and acceleration of the LSTM models.
- We develop a general LSTM optimization and synthesis framework C-LSTM to enable automatic and efficient implementations of a wide range of LSTM variants on FPGAs.

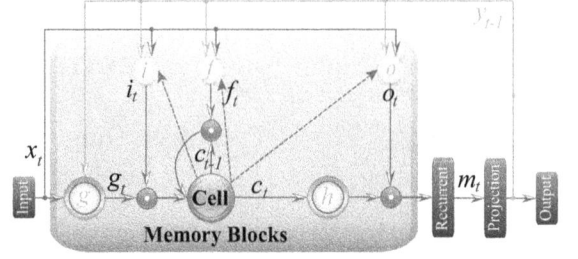

Figure 1: An LSTM based RNN architecture.

The framework mainly consists of a suite of highly optimized C/C++ based templates of primitive operators and an automatic LSTM synthesis flow.

- We present efficient implementations of LSTMs which achieve up to 18.8X and 33.5X gains in performance and energy efficiency, respectively, compared with the state-of-the-art. The proposed implementations incur very small accuracy degradation.

2 LSTM BACKGROUND

LSTM is a key component of the acoustic model in modern large-scale automatic speech recognition (ASR) systems [9, 25], and also the most computation and memory-intensive part. Due to the complicated and flexible data dependencies among gates, cells, and outputs, a lot of LSTM variants have been proposed. In this paper, we use a widely deployed variant called Google LSTM [25] as an example throughout this paper without loss of generality. The architecture details of the Google LSTM is shown in Figure 1. The LSTM accepts an input sequence $\mathbb{X} = (\mathbf{x}_1; \mathbf{x}_2; \mathbf{x}_3; ...; \mathbf{x}_T)$ (each of $\mathbf{x}_t$ is a vector corresponding to time t) with the output sequence from last step $\mathbb{Y}^{T-1} = (\mathbf{y}_0; \mathbf{y}_1; \mathbf{y}_2; ...; \mathbf{y}_{T-1})$ (each of $\mathbf{y}_t$ is a vector). The input of Google LSTM at time t depends on the output at $t-1$. The LSTM contains a special memory cell storing the temporal state of the network.It also contains three special multiplicative units which are input, output and forget gates. The output sequence $\mathbb{Y} = (\mathbf{y}_1; \mathbf{y}_2; \mathbf{y}_3; ...; \mathbf{y}_T)$ is computed by using the following equations iteratively from $t = 1$ to T:

$$\mathbf{i}_t = \sigma(\mathbf{W}_{ix}\mathbf{x}_t + \mathbf{W}_{ir}\mathbf{y}_{t-1} + \mathbf{W}_{ic}\mathbf{c}_{t-1} + \mathbf{b}_i), \tag{1a}$$

$$\mathbf{f}_t = \sigma(\mathbf{W}_{fx}\mathbf{x}_t + \mathbf{W}_{fr}\mathbf{y}_{t-1} + \mathbf{W}_{fc}\mathbf{c}_{t-1} + \mathbf{b}_f), \tag{1b}$$

$$\mathbf{g}_t = \sigma(\mathbf{W}_{cx}\mathbf{x}_t + \mathbf{W}_{cr}\mathbf{y}_{t-1} + \mathbf{b}_c), \tag{1c}$$

$$\mathbf{c}_t = \mathbf{f}_t \odot \mathbf{c}_{t-1} + \mathbf{g}_t \odot \mathbf{i}_t, \tag{1d}$$

$$\mathbf{o}_t = \sigma(\mathbf{W}_{ox}\mathbf{x}_t + \mathbf{W}_{or}\mathbf{y}_{t-1} + \mathbf{W}_{oc}\mathbf{c}_t + \mathbf{b}_o), \tag{1e}$$

$$\mathbf{m}_t = \mathbf{o}_t \odot \mathbf{h}(\mathbf{c}_t), \tag{1f}$$

$$\mathbf{y}_t = \mathbf{W}_{ym}\mathbf{m}_t, \tag{1g}$$

where symbols $\mathbf{i}$, $\mathbf{f}$, $\mathbf{o}$, $\mathbf{c}$, $\mathbf{m}$, and $\mathbf{y}$ are respectively the input gate, forget gate, output gate, cell state, cell output, and a projected output; the $\odot$ operator denotes the element-wise multiplication, and the $+$ operator denotes the element-wise addition. The $\mathbf{W}$ terms denote weight matrices (e.g. $\mathbf{W}_{ix}$ is the matrix of weights from the input vector $\mathbf{x}_t$ to the input gate), and the $\mathbf{b}$ terms denote bias vectors. Please note $\mathbf{W}_{ic}$, $\mathbf{W}_{fc}$, and $\mathbf{W}_{oc}$ are diagonal matrices for peephole connections, thus they are essentially a vector, and the matrix-vector multiplication like $\mathbf{W}_{ic}\mathbf{c}_{t-1}$ can be calculated by the $\odot$ operator. σ is the logistic activation function and h is a user-defined activation function. Here we use hyperbolic tangent (tanh) activation function as h. Overall, we have nine matrix-vector multiplications (excluding peephole connections which can be calculated by $\odot$). In one gate/cell, $\mathbf{W}_{*x}\mathbf{x}_t + \mathbf{W}_{*r}\mathbf{y}_{t-1}$ can be combined/fused in one matrix-vector multiplication by concatenating the matrix and vector as $\mathbf{W}_{*(xr)}[\mathbf{x}_t, \mathbf{y}_{t-1}]$.

3 STRUCTURED COMPRESSION

Deep neural networks (DNNs) bear a significant amount of redundancy [12] and thus model compression is a natural method to mitigate the computation and memory storage requirements for the hardware implementations on FPGAs. In this section, we propose to employ a structured compression technique to compress the weight matrices of LSTM model by using block-circulant matrices. We first introduce the block-circulant matrix and then integrate it with the inference and training algorithms of LSTMs. In the last, we explore the trade-offs between compression ratio and prediction error rate.

3.1 Block-Circulant Matrix

The circulant matrix is a square matrix whose each row (or column) vector is the circulant reformat of the row (or column) vectors [3, 22]. Any matrix could be transformed into a set of circulant submatrices (blocks) and we define the transformed matrix as a block-circulant matrix. For example, Figure 2 shows that the 8×4 weight matrix (on the left) is reformatted into a block-circulant matrix containing two 4×4 circulant matrices (on the right). Since each row vector of the circulant submatrix is a reformat of the first row vector, we could use a row vector to represent a circulant submatrix. Therefore, the first obvious benefit of the block-circulant matrix is that the number of parameters in each weight matrix is reduced by a factor of the block size $\mathcal{O}(k)$. As for the example in Figure 2, the 8×4 weight matrix (on the left) holding 32 parameters is reduced to two 4×4 circulant matrices (on the right) containing only 8 parameters, which easily leads to 4X model size reduction.

Intuitively, the model compression ratio is determined by the block size of the circulant submatrices: larger block size leads to higher compression ratio and vice versa. However, high compression ratio may degrade the prediction accuracy. Specifically, a larger block size should be selected to achieve a higher compression ratio but lower accuracy and the smaller block size provides higher accuracy but less compression ratio. The block size is 1 if no compression is utilized. It is necessary to note that block-circulant matrix based DNNs have been proved to asymptotically approach the original networks in accuracy with mathematical rigor [31]. Therefore, if the compression ratio is selected properly, the accuracy loss would be negligible. The trade-offs between compression ratio and predication accuracy are discussed in Section 3.3

3.2 Inference and Training Algorithms

The primary idea of introducing block-circulant matrix into LSTM model is to partition a $m \times n$ weight matrix $\mathbf{W}$ into $p \times q$ blocks, where $p = \frac{m}{k}$, $q = \frac{n}{k}$ and each block is a $k \times k$ circulant matrix. With bias and activation function omitted, the forward propagation

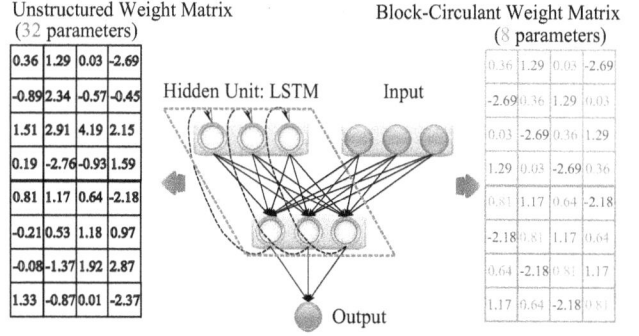

Figure 2: Block-circulant matrices for weight representation.

process of LSTM model in the inference phase is then given by:

$$\mathbf{a} = \mathbf{W}\mathbf{x} \iff \begin{bmatrix} \sum_{j=1}^{q} \mathbf{W}_{1j}\mathbf{x}_j \\ \sum_{j=1}^{q} \mathbf{W}_{2j}\mathbf{x}_j \\ \cdots \\ \sum_{j=1}^{q} \mathbf{W}_{pj}\mathbf{x}_j \end{bmatrix} = \begin{bmatrix} \mathbf{a}_1 \\ \mathbf{a}_2 \\ \cdots \\ \mathbf{a}_p \end{bmatrix}, \quad (2)$$

where $\mathbf{a}_i$ is a column vector. Since each circulant matrix $\mathbf{W}_{ij}$ could be simplified as a vector $\mathbf{w}_{ij}$, i.e., $\mathbf{w}_{ij}$ is the first row vector of $\mathbf{W}_{ij}$, the structure of block-circulant matrix enables the use of Fast Fourier Transform (FFT) algorithm to speed up the circulant convolution $\sum_{j=1}^{q} \mathbf{W}_{ij}\mathbf{x}_j$. Therefore the Equation 2 can be performed as:

$$\mathbf{a}_i = \sum_{j=1}^{q} \mathcal{F}^{-1}[\mathcal{F}(\mathbf{w}_{ij}) \odot \mathcal{F}(\mathbf{x}_j)], \quad (3)$$

where $\mathcal{F}(\cdot)$ is the Discrete Fourier Transform (DFT) operator, $\mathcal{F}^{-1}(\cdot)$ is the inverse DFT (IDFT) operator, and $\odot$ is the element-wise multiply operator. Therefore, after applying FFT algorithm to the circulant convolution, the computational complexity of the LSTM inference model is reduced from $\mathcal{O}(pqk^2)$ to $\mathcal{O}(pqk \log k)$, meaning that the computational complexity of the LSTM inference model is reduced by a factor of $\mathcal{O}(\frac{k}{\log k})$.

The backward propagation process in the training phase can also be implemented using block-circulant matrices. Here we use a_{il} to denote the l-th output element in $\mathbf{a}_i$, and L to represent the loss function. Then by using the chain rule we can derive the backward propagation process as follows:

$$\frac{\partial L}{\partial \mathbf{w}_{ij}} = \sum_{l=1}^{k} \frac{\partial L}{\partial a_{il}} \frac{\partial a_{il}}{\partial \mathbf{w}_{ij}} = \frac{\partial L}{\partial \mathbf{a}_i} \frac{\partial \mathbf{a}_i}{\partial \mathbf{w}_{ij}}, \quad (4)$$

$$\frac{\partial L}{\partial \mathbf{x}_j} = \sum_{i=1}^{p} \sum_{l=1}^{k} \frac{\partial L}{\partial a_{il}} \frac{\partial a_{il}}{\partial \mathbf{x}_j} = \sum_{i=1}^{p} \frac{\partial L}{\partial \mathbf{a}_i} \frac{\partial \mathbf{a}_i}{\partial \mathbf{x}_j}. \quad (5)$$

where $\frac{\partial \mathbf{a}_i}{\partial \mathbf{w}_{ij}}$ and $\frac{\partial \mathbf{a}_i}{\partial \mathbf{x}_j}$ are proved to be block-circulant matrices [31]. Thus, $\frac{\partial L}{\partial \mathbf{w}_{ij}}$ and $\frac{\partial L}{\partial \mathbf{a}_i} \frac{\partial \mathbf{a}_i}{\partial \mathbf{x}_j}$ can be calculated similarly as Equation (3) with the same computational complexity. The details of the training procedure for a fully-connected layer in DNNs are presented in [6, 27] and also applicable to the LSTM based RNNs.

Table 1: Comparison among different LSTM models.

Block Size	#Model Parameters	Computational Complexity	PER / PER Degradation (%)
1	8.01M	1	24.15 / 0.00
2	4.03M	0.50	24.09 / −0.06
4	2.04M	0.50	24.23 / 0.08
8	1.05M	0.39	24.57 / 0.32
16	0.55M	0.27	25.48 / 1.23

3.3 Compression and Accuracy Trade-offs

The block-circulant matrix based LSTM inference model enables a comprehensive tuning of model compression ratio by varying the block size k, thus leading to fine-grained trade-offs among the model size, computational complexity, and prediction accuracy. The proposed inference model of Google LSTM [25] is evaluated on the widely used TIMIT dataset [8]. Similar to [10], the audio data of TIMIT is preprocessed using a Fourier transform based filterbank with 50 coefficients (plus energy) distributed on a mel-scale, together with their first and second temporal derivatives. The number of features of the input speech and the architecture of Google LSTM used in this work is the same as ESE [13]. It is necessary to note that we use the widely adopted Phone Error Rate (PER) as the metric for the model prediction accuracy. The lower the PER value is, the higher the model prediction accuracy is and vice versa.

Table 1 presents the details of the trade-offs among three different metrics of Google LSTM using the block-circulant matrix based structured compression technique. We observe that the number of model parameters decreases linearly as the block size increases. Meanwhile, the PERs of different models do not have a severe degradation. For the block-circulant matrix based LSTM with block size of 2, the PER is even lower than non-compressed LSTM model whose block size is 1. For the LSTM models with block size of 8 and 16, we achieve 7.6X and 14.6X model size reduction and the computational complexity is reduced by factors of 2.6X and 3.7X while the PERs are only 0.32% and 1.23% higher than the non-compressed one, respectively. Therefore, we choose the compressed models of Google LSTM with block sizes of 8 and 16 to be further studied in this work.

4 FPGA ACCELERATION

In this section, we start by introducing a set of FPGA optimization techniques for circulant convolution operator and then apply quantizations to activation and element-wise operators. In the last, we propose an operator scheduling algorithm to generate the whole LSTM pipeline with the help of performance and resource models.

4.1 Circulant Convolution Optimization

Since the FFT based circulant convolution operator in the form of Equation 3 is the most computation-intensive operator in the LSTM inference model, we propose three techniques to further reduce the computational complexity by reducing the number of DFT and IDFT operator calls, and the redundant arithmetic operations of its complex number multiplication operators.

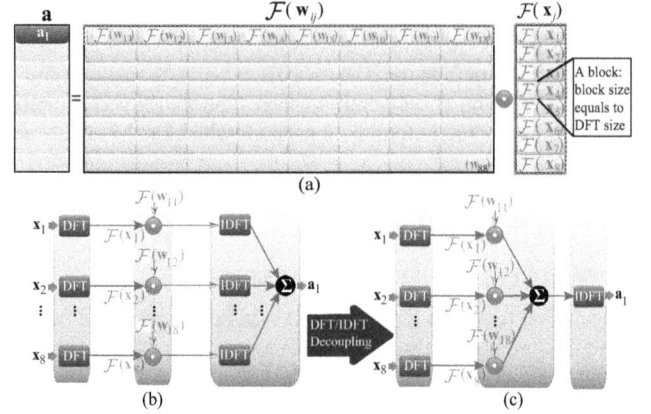

Figure 3: An illustration of the (a) circulant convolution operator; (b) its original implementation; (c) and the optimized implementation.

In order to reduce the number of IDFT calls in the circulant convolution operator, we propose the DFT-IDFT decoupling technique. Since DFT and IDFT are linear operators [21], we could decouple the DFT and IDFT operators in Equation 3 and move the IDFT operator $\mathcal{F}^{-1}(\cdot)$ outside the accumulation operator $\sum$ as following,

$$\mathbf{a}_i = \mathcal{F}^{-1}\left[\sum_{j=1}^{q} \mathcal{F}(\mathbf{w}_{ij}) \odot \mathcal{F}(\mathbf{x}_j)\right], \qquad (6)$$

where the number of IDFT operator calls for each circulant convolution operator is reduced from q to 1 and the numbers of the other operator calls are kept the same as before.

According to Equation 6, the number of DFT operator $\mathcal{F}(\cdot)$ calls in a circulant convolution operator is determined by q the number of weight vectors $\mathcal{F}(\mathbf{w}_{ij})$ and input vectors $\mathcal{F}(\mathbf{x}_j)$. Since the weight vectors $\mathbf{w}_{ij}$ are fixed when the training process is done, we could precalculate the $\mathcal{F}(\mathbf{w}_{ij})$ values and store them in the BRAM buffers of FPGAs and fetch the required values when needed instead of computing the associated DFT values at runtime. This method completely eliminates the DFT operator $\mathcal{F}(\cdot)$ calls for weight vectors and reduces the number of calls from $2qk$ to qk for each circulant convolution operator. The BRAM buffer size, however, would be doubled since the outputs of DFT values $\mathcal{F}(\mathbf{w}_{ij})$ are complex numbers whose both real and imaginary parts are needed to be stored. In order to alleviate the BRAM buffer overhead, we propose to exploit the complex conjugate symmetry property of DFT output values, where almost half of the conjugate complex numbers could be eliminated [21, 23]. Therefore, there is only negligible BRAM buffer overhead to store the DFT results of weight vectors $\mathcal{F}(\mathbf{w}_{ij})$.

The element-wise multiplication $\odot$ between two complex number vectors $\mathcal{F}(\mathbf{w}_{ij})$ and $\mathcal{F}(\mathbf{x}_j)$ requires $4k$ multiplications and $3k$ additions. Due to the complex conjugate symmetry property of DFT $\mathcal{F}(\cdot)$ results, about half of the multiplications and additions could be eliminated. Overall, Figure 3 illustrates the implementations of the original and optimized circulant convolution operators when the block size is 8.

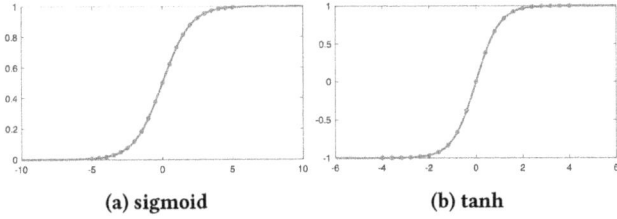

(a) sigmoid   (b) tanh

Figure 4: Piece-wise linear activation functions.

4.2 Datapath and Activation Quantization

The LSTM model size could be further compressed without accuracy degradation if the datapath of LSTM implementation on FPGA is carefully quantized into shorter bitwidth. We design a bit-accurate software simulator to study the impact of the bitwidth of datapath on the prediction accuracy. We first analyze the numerical range of the trained weights in the LSTM, and then determine the bitwidth of integer and fractional parts to avoid data overflow and accuracy degradation. We observe that 16-bit fixed point is accurate enough for implementing the LSTM inference model on FPGAs.

In order to alleviate accuracy degradation problem caused by the data truncation and overflow problems in the architecture of the proposed circulant convolution operator. It is observed that the output data of IDFT are first divided by the block size (or IDFT input size) k, which is implemented as right shifting the numbers by $\log_2^k$ bits, and then output in the last stage of IDFT pipeline. However, the more bits are right shifted, the more fractional bits are truncated and thus degrading the overall accuracy. In order to deal with the accuracy loss caused by the data truncation, we propose to evenly distribute the shift operations inside the stages of the IDFT pipeline based on the observation that right shifting one bit at a time achieves better accuracy than right shifting multiple bits at once. As for the data overflow problem, it is most likely to occur in the accumulation stage of circulant convolution operator since multiple values are summed here. We propose to move the evenly distributed right shifting operations from stages of IDFT pipeline to the ones of DFT. Since the DFT is processed before accumulation operator and right shifting makes the number to be smaller and, it is less likely to cause overflow in accumulation stage.

The activation functions in LSTMs are all transcendental functions whose implementations on FPGA are very expensive with respect to resource utilization. In order to achieve a balance between accuracy and resource cost, we propose to utilize quantized piece-wise linear functions to approximate them. Figure 4 shows that the sigmoid and tanh functions are approximated using piece-wise linear functions with 22 segments. As we can see from the figure, the approximated and the original functions are almost the same and the error rate is less than 1%. Since the linear function could be represented in the slope-intercept form like $y = ax + b$, we only need to store the associated slope a and intercept b for each piece of linear function. In the real implementation, the computation complexity of activation functions only involves a simple comparison to index the associated pair of slope and intercept and one 16-bit fixed point multiplication followed by an addition. It is necessary to note that, according to our experimental results, the piece-wise linear approximation incurs negligible accuracy degradation for LSTMs.

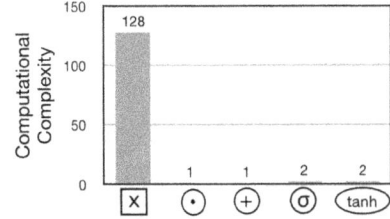

Figure 5: Computational complexity of LSTM operators.

4.3 Operator Scheduling

The recurrent nature of LSTM enforces strict data dependency among operators inside the LSTM module. In order to accommodate the complicated interactions of LSTM primitive operators, we propose a graph generator to transform the LSTM algorithm specification in the form of the equations like Equation 1 to a directed acyclic data dependency graph. Figure 6 (a) shows the generated LSTM directed operator graph from the LSTM descriptions, where each node is an LSTM primitive operator and the edge represents the data dependency between two operators. It is necessary to note that the generated graph is acyclic because we deliberately remove the feedback edges from cell output c_t to the LSTM module output y_t. Since the backward edges are taken care of by the double-buffer mechanism, this practice would never harm the correctness and efficiency of the final LSTM accelerator design.

LSTMs exhibit a highly skewed distribution of computation complexity among the primitive operators. Figure 5 shows the normalized computational complexity of the five primitive operators of the Google LSTM [25] studied in this work. The computational complexity gap between the circulant convolution operator and element-wise multiply operator ⊙ is as large as 128 times. So, if we want to pipeline these two operators we must either boost the parallelism of the former operator or make the latter operator wait (idle) for the former one. However, the reality is that the limited on-chip resources of FPGAs generally cannot sustain sufficient parallelism and the idle operators make the design inefficient. Therefore, pipelining a complex LSTM algorithm as a whole, such as the Google LSTM [25] shown in 6(a), is very inefficient on FPGAs.

In order to deal with this problem, we propose to break down the original single pipeline into several smaller coarse-grained pipelines and overlap their execution time by inserting double-buffers for each concatenated pipeline pair. For example, the original operator graph of Google LSTM [25] in 6(a) is divided into three stages in 6(b), where each stage will be implemented as a coarse-grained pipeline on FPGAs. The double-buffers added between stages are used to buffer the data produced/consumed by the previous/current stage. However, scheduling the operators to different stages in an efficient way is still a problem. We propose an operator scheduling algorithm shown in Algorithm 1 to tackle this problem. The algorithm takes the original operator graph $G = (V, E)$, operator weight set $W(V)$, and operator priority set $P(V)$ as input and outputs several operator subgraphs G_k. For original operator graph $G = (V, E)$, each vertex $v_i \in V$ represents an operator and the edge e_{ij} represents the data dependency between v_i and v_j. Each vertex v_i has a weight $W(w_i)$ which is the associated arithmetic computational complexity. The algorithm first traverses down the graph from the source vertex computing the priority of each vertex by

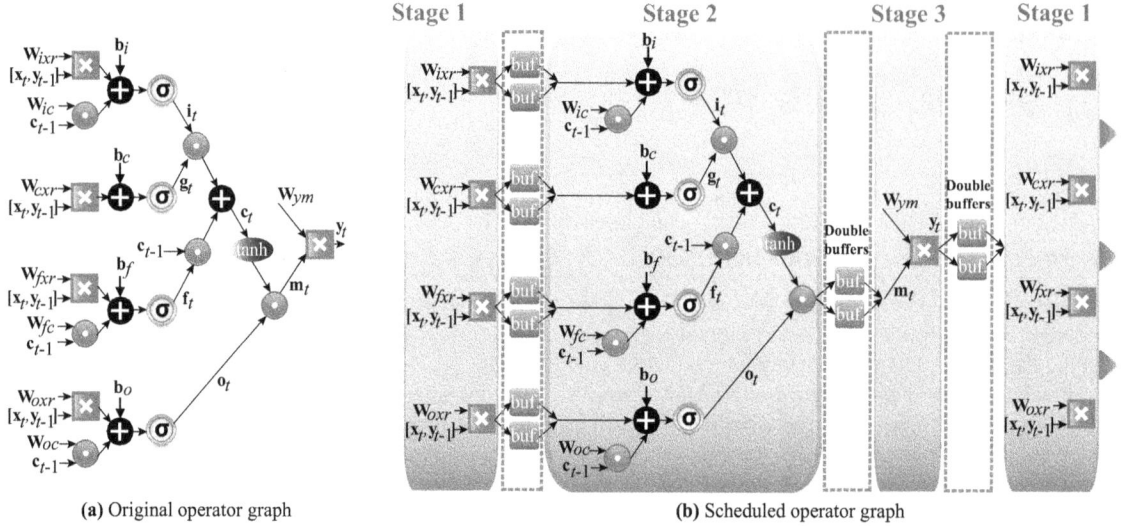

Figure 6: Illustration of operator scheduling on data dependency graph. The circle represents the element-wise operator, and the square represents the circulant convolution operator.

$$P(v_i) = \begin{cases} W(v_i) + \max\limits_{v_j \in Succ(v_i)} P(v_j), & v_i \neq v_{sink} \\ W(v_{sink}), & \text{otherwise} \end{cases} \quad (7)$$

Since $P(v_i)$ is accumulated with the maximum value of successors $P(v_j)$ as shown in Equation 7, priority set $P(V)$ is topologically ordered, which means that it is guaranteed that all predecessor operators are scheduled before scheduling a new operator [15]. After the prioritization, the algorithm selects the operator with the highest priority value and then determines the parallelism of the operator $N(v_j)$ and whether it should be added to the current or a new stage according to the resource utilization of FPGAs. Then, the operator subgraphs G_k and the operator parallelism set $N(V)$ are output by this algorithm, where each stage represents a corresponding LSTM execution stage that will be implemented as a coarse-grained pipeline on FPGAs. Since the overall throughput of this coarse-grained pipeline design is constrained by the slowest stage, we need to further determine the pipeline replication factor $R(G_k)$ for each stage. To fully utilize the resources of a certain FPGA chip, we also need to take into account of the resource utilization of each stage, and thus we propose to enumerate pipeline replication factor $R(G_k)$ to get the optimal setting with the help of our analytical performance and resource models which are presented in Section 4.4.

4.4 Performance and Resource Models

Since the throughput of the proposed coarse-grained pipeline design is constrained by the slowest stage, the analytical performance model is built as following,

$$FPS = \frac{Frequency}{\max\{T_1, T_2, ..., T_h, ...T_K\}}, \quad (8)$$

where FPS is the number of frames per second of C-LSTM accelerator, T_k represents the number of execution clock cycles of stage k,

---

Algorithm 1: Operator Scheduling Algorithm

Input: operator graph $G = (V, E)$, operator weight set $W(V)$, and priority set $P(V)$;
Output: operator subgraph of each stage $G_k = (V_k, E_k)$;
Traverse $G = (V, E)$ and compute priority set $P(V)$;
$k \leftarrow 0, N(V) \leftarrow \{1\}$;
foreach $v_i \in V$ *in decreasing order of* $P(v)$ **do**
  if $k = 0$ **then**
    $k \leftarrow k + 1$;
    $G_k \leftarrow v$; // add the operator to a new stage
  else
    foreach $N'(v_j) \in G_k$ **do**
      $N'(v_j) \leftarrow N(v_j) \cdot \lceil \frac{W(v_j)}{W(v_i)} \rceil$;
    end
    if *resource constraints are satisfied* **then**
      $G_j \leftarrow v$; // add the operator to current stage
      $N(V) \leftarrow N'(V)$; // update operator parallelisms
    else
      $k \leftarrow k + 1$;
      $G_k \leftarrow v_i$; // add the operator to a new stage
    end
  end
end
$K \leftarrow k$;
Enumerate $R(G_k)$ values to maximize throughput and fully utilize FPGA resource;
return $N(V)$, $\{G_1, G_2, ..., G_K\}$, and $\{R(G_1), R(G_2), ..., (G_K)\}$;

---

and K is the total number of stages. T_k is calculated by considering the parallelism and input data size of each stage as following,

$$T_k = \lceil \max_{v_i \in G_k} \frac{Q(v_i)}{N(v_i)} / R(G_k) \rceil + D_k \quad (9)$$

where $Q(v_i)$ is the workload of operator v_i and D_k is the pipeline depth of stage k. It is necessary to note that, the compression ratio of the block-circulant matrices based technique is large enough to store the whole LSTM model on BRAMs of FPGAs, and for each frame, we only need to load very limited size of input data which makes computation time of LSTM to be overlapped with data loading.

The resource model of the highly optimized primitive operator templates is very straightforward because the linear model with respect to the associated operator parallelism $N(v_i)$ and stage parallelism $R(G_k)$ is accurate enough to guide the design space exploration for energy-efficient designs. The models are shown in the following,

$$DSP = \sum_{k=1}^{K} R(G_k) \cdot \sum_{v_i \in V} \Delta DSP(v_i) \cdot N(v_i), \quad (10)$$

$$BRAM = \sum_{k=1}^{K} R(G_k) \cdot \sum_{v_i \in V} \Delta BRAM(v_i) \cdot N(v_i), \quad (11)$$

$$LUT = \sum_{k=1}^{K} R(G_k) \cdot \sum_{v_i \in V} \Delta LUT(v_i) \cdot N(v_i), \quad (12)$$

where $\Delta DSP(v_i)$, $\Delta BRAM(v_i)$, and $\Delta LUT(v_i)$ are obtained by profiling the resource consumption values for operator v_i on the FPGA using the manually optimized operator template.

4.5 Putting It All Together

The final hardware architecture of the Google LSTM algorithm [25] is shown in Figure 7. This design mainly consists of three coarse-grained pipeline stages corresponding to the operator scheduling result shown in Figure 6(b). At Stage 1, the input vectors $\mathbf{x}_t$ and the prestored DFT values of weight matrices $\mathbf{W}$ are convolved using the circulant convolution operator whose output is written into the double-buffer. Since all the DFT values of weight matrices are compressed small enough, they could be stored in on-chip BRAM buffers instead of off-chip DDR memory. The performance of the circulant convolution operator is thus no longer bottlenecked by off-chip memory bandwidth and the parallel compute units could be fully exploited on FPGAs. In stage 2, the input data are first read from double-buffer of the previous stage and then processed by a series of element-wise operators including addition, multiplication and activation functions in the LSTM cell module. The output of Stage 2 is also written to double-buffer for the next stage. As for Stage 3, the results of the prior stage are fetched from double-buffer and are then projected to output using the circulant convolution operator. In the last, the projected output will be forwarded to Stage 1 for the next iteration.

5   C-LSTM FRAMEWORK

In order to embrace a wide range of LSTM architectures, we propose a comprehensive framework called C-LSTM to assist the LSTM model training using the block-circulant matrix based structured compression and enable an automatic flow to generate efficient LSTM inference designs on FPGAs. As shown in Figure 8, the C-LSTM framework is mainly composed of two parts which are LSTM model training and its implementation on FPGAs. The details of the C-LSTM framework are explained in the following sections.

5.1   Model Training

The model training, which is shown on the left side of Figure 8, accepts the LSTM architecture specifications in the form of Equation 1 as input. Then, the block-circulant matrix based structured compression is applied to the weight matrices of the model. In the following, TensorFlow [1] is used as the training framework to iteratively train the LSTM model. The trade-offs between compression ratio and prediction accuracy is explored in this procedure. In the

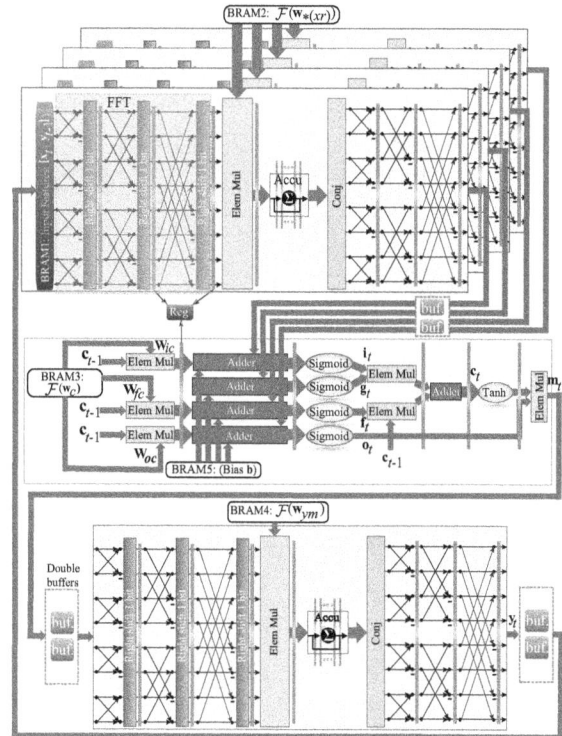

Figure 7: The proposed Google LSTM architecture.

last, the LSTM inference model is configured with the well-trained weight matrices and sent to model implementation flow for further acceleration on FPGAs.

5.2   Model Implementation

The model implementation of the C-LSTM framework is shown in the right side of Figure 8, It mainly consists of two parts which are operator templates generation (upper part) and automatic synthesis framework (lower part). Since the number of primitive operators of LSTMs is limited, we propose to manually write the template for each primitive operator. As for the LSTM algorithms studied in this work, we define hyperbolic tangent $tanh$, sigmoid σ, element-wise vector addition, element-wise vector multiplication, and circulant convolution as primitive operators. The optimization techniques presented in Section 4 are all applied to these operators. It is necessary to note that, the proposed primitive operator templates are general enough to implement almost any kind of LSTM variant to best of our knowledge.

The automatic synthesis framework is fed with the well-trained inference model provided by the model training flow. Then a directed acyclic data dependency graph is generated to represent the computation flow of LSTM. The operators in the graph are scheduled to compose a multi-stage coarse-grained pipeline as to maximize the performance under certain resource constraints with the help of analytical performance and resource models. The scheduling result is then given to the code generator. The code generator takes the operator scheduling result as input and generates the final C/C++ based code automatically by integrating the associated primitive operator templates together. Since the interface of

Model Training   **Model Implementation**

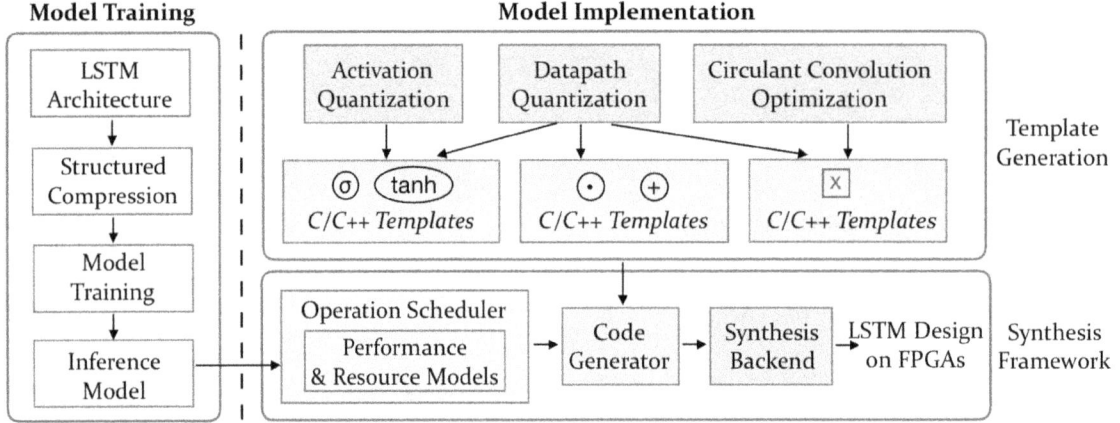

Figure 8: C-LSTM framework overview.

Table 2: Comparison of FPGA platforms

FPGA	DSP	BRAM	LUT	FF	Process
XCKU060	2,760	1,080	331,680	663,360	20nm
Virtex-7(690t)	3,600	1,470	859,200	429,600	28nm

each template is well defined and the tunable parameters are expressed using C/C++ marcos, the code generation is very efficient. The synthesis backend which is an off-the-shelf commercial HLS tool, accepts the C/C++ code as input and outputs the optimized LSTM hardware implementation on FPGAs. It is necessary to note that each commercial HLS toolchain requires specific coding style to achieve the best performance, and thus the templates of the primitive operators should be tailored accordingly [29].

6 EXPERIMENT EVALUATION

6.1 Experiment Setup

The proposed techniques for LSTMs are evaluated on two platforms: Xilinx KU060 and Alpha Data's ADM-7V3. The Xilinx KU060 platform consists of a Xilinx XCKU060 FPGA and two 4GB DDR3 memory. The ADM-7V3 board consists of a Xilinx Virtex-7 (690t) FPGA and a 16GB DDR3 memory. The comparison of the FPGA on-chip resources of the two platforms is presented in Table 2. The ADM-7V3 FPGA board is connected to the host via PCI-e 3.0 X8 interface, and the host machine is a server with Intel Core i7-4790 CPU. Xilinx SDx 2017.1 is used as the commercial synthesis backend to synthesize the C/C++ based LSTM design onto FPGAs. The proposed FPGA implementations of LSTMs are operating at 200MHz on both platforms.

We measure the latency of our C-LSTM designs on KU060 platform using the number of clock cycles times the clock period (5ns) reported by Xilinx SDx tools. To make a fair comparison with ESE [13], the latency of ESE reported in Table 3 is its theoretical time. Since we do not have the KU060 platform, we cannot give out an accurate estimation and the associated power and energy efficiency results are left blank. As for the ADM-7V3 platform, the execution time of C-LSTM designs are obtained by using Xilinx SDx runtime profiler, and the power is profiled using the TI Fusion

Power device through the associated interface on ADM-7V3 with a sampling rate of 100Hz.

Besides the LSTM based RNN architecture used in [13, 25], we also evaluated the performance on a smaller LSTM model [20], where the input feature is a 39-dimension vector (12 filterbank coefficients plus energy and its first/second temporal derivatives), and the gate/cell layers' dimension is 512. In this small model, the peephole connection and projection layer are not employed. The model contains two stacked LSTM as well. However, we used bidirectional architecture [2, 10] to get a better PER.

In order to make a convincing validation for the superiority of the proposed C-LSTM optimization framework, we compare our design with the state-of-the-art LSTM design ESE [13].The same dataset, LSTM algorithm, and FPGA platforms are used in the associated experiments as ESE to make a fair comparison.

6.2 Experimental Results of Google LSTM

With the compression technique of C-LSTM, we are able to store all the weights matrices and the projection matrix in BRAM, after performing compression on the baseline. The baseline has the same structure as the baseline in ESE.

According to the results of latency and FPS in Table 3, we achieve 3.6X and 4.3X latency reduction and 11X and 13X performance speedup for FFT8 and FFT16 based compression techniques compared with ESE on the platform of KU060. It is necessary to note that the gap between latency reduction and performance speedup stems from the coarse-grained architecture of the proposed LSTM accelerator. And thus the latency of our proposed C-LSTM accelerator for Google LSTM algorithm is the latency of one stage multiplied by 3, because each input frame needs to go through three coarse-grained pipelines. However, after three frames have been processed, the following frame could be processed at every one stage of latency.

As we can see from Table 2, the resource of the FPGA chip Virtex-7 of the ADM-7V3 platform is 30% higher than the FPGA XCKU060 of KU060 platform. Therefore, to make a fair comparison, we use the total resource of KU060 as the resource consumption bound for the ADM-7v3 platform. Compared with ESE, we achieve 10.2X and 18.8X performance speedups and 19.1X and 33.5X energy efficiency

Table 3: Detailed comparison for different LSTM designs.

	ESE [13]	C-LSTM FFT8 (Block size: 8)		C-LSTM FFT16 (Block size: 16)		C-LSTM FFT8 (Block size: 8)		C-LSTM FFT16 (Block size: 16)	
LSTM Algorithm		Google LSTM [25]				Small LSTM [20]			
Weight Matrix Size (#Parameters of LSTM)	0.73M	0.41M		0.20M		0.28M		0.14M	
Quantization	12bit fixed	16bit fixed		16bit fixed		16bit fixed		16bit fixed	
Matrix Compression Ratio	$4.5:1^1$	$7.9:1$		$15.9:1$		$7.9:1$		$15.9:1$	
Platform	KU060	KU060	7V3	KU060	7V3	KU060	7V3	KU060	7V3
DSP (%)	54.5	96.5	74.3	98.0	77.4	77.6	60.5	84.9	65.2
BRAM (%)	87.7	87.6	65.7	89.1	63.3	83.3	66.9	87.2	64.1
LUT (%)	88.6	75.2	58.7	72.8	55.3	92.5	67.6	93.6	72.3
FF (%)	68.3	58.9	46.5	63.4	48.1	61.2	49.0	70.7	54.6
Frequency (MHz)		200							
PER Degradation	0.30%	0.32%		1.23%		0.29%		1.16%	
Latency (μs)	57.0	15.4	16.7	8.1	9.1	8.9	9.8	4.8	5.4
Frames per Second (FPS)	17,544	195,313	179,687	371,095	330,275	337,838	307,432	628,379	559,257
Power (W)	41	-	22	-	23	-	21	-	22
Energy Efficiency (FPS/W)	428	-	8,168	-	14,359	-	14,640	-	25,420

[1] This estimation considers both weights and indices (there is at least one index per weight after compression in ESE).
However, this is a pessimistic estimation for ESE because indices can use fewer bits for representation than weights;

gains using FFT8 and FFT16, respectively. Since the power consumption of C-LSTM is only half of the ESE, the energy efficiency gain is higher than performance. It is necessary to note that as shown in Table 2, the manufacturing process of XCKU060 FPGA is 20nm while the process of Virtex-7 is 28nm, which means the energy efficiency gain reported here is pessimistic.

Although the promising performance and energy gains are achieved by C-LSTM, the resource utilization for LUT, FF, and BRAM are less than ESE, and more important, the relative PER degradation is very small, which are 0.32% and 1.23% using FFT8 and FFT16, respectively. After detailed analysis, we summarize the fundamental reasons for the high performance and power gains in three aspects. First, the structured compression used in this work eliminates the irregular computation and memory accesses which not only makes the design more regular but also exposes more parallelism. This could be verified in that the DSP resource consumption of the proposed method is much more than ESE. Secondly, the whole model (weights matrices and the projection matrix) could be stored on-chip without fetching data from off-chip DRAM, making the LSTM not bounded by memory. Lastly, the more efficient implementation of LSTM on FPGAs contributes to the high efficiency. For example, we use the 22-segment piece-wise linear function to approximate the activation functions while ESE employs look-up tables which break the activation down into 2048 segments and consume more resources. Moreover, we propose to employ FFT based block-circulant matrix multiplication while ESE uses sparse matrix multiplication

which needs to store extra indices for sparse matrices and thus prevents from storing the whole model on-chip.

6.3 Experimental Results of Small LSTM

In order to validate that proposed C-LSTM is not only appropriate for Google LSTM model, we also implement a Small LSTM [20] model on both FPGA platforms.

In KU060 platform, the FFT8 and FFT16 designs could achieve 19.3X and 35.9X performance speedup compared with ESE, respectively. In the ADM-7V3 platform, the performance speedups are 17.5X and 31.9X and the energy efficiency gains are 34.2X and 59.4X compared with ESE, respectively. For both platforms, the PER degradation is 0.29% and 1.16% for FFT8 and FFT16, respectively.

7 RELATED WORK

Recently, FPGA has emerged as a promising hardware acceleration platform for DNNs as it provides high performance, low power and reconfigurability. A lot of FPGA based accelerators have been proposed for convolutional neural networks (CNNs) to overcome the computing and energy efficiency challenges. [28] proposes to utilize systolic array based convolution architecture to achieve better frequency and thus performance for CNNs on FPGAs. [18] employs the Winograd algorithm to reduce the multiplication operators as to save DSP resources and accelerate matrix multiplication in CNNs. [30] proposes to take advantage of the heterogeneous algorithms to maximize the resource utilization for convolutional layers on FPGAs. Some studies also propose to transform the CNN models to frequency domains and then exploit FFT algorithms for further acceleration [14]. The FFT based acceleration scheme used in the CNN model is completely different from this work, in which we target on a totally different LSTM based RNN model and the FFT algorithm is applied to the circulant convolution operators instead of the convolution layers of CNNs.

There are also a lot of works on implementing RNN accelerators for FPGAs [11, 16, 19]. [19] designs an accelerator for the gated recurrent network (GRU) which embodies a different architecture from the LSTM based RNNs. [11] and [16] focus on LSTM based RNNs but none of these works utilize compression techniques to reduce the model size. The most relevant study to this work is ESE [13], which proposes a software and hardware co-design framework to accelerate compressed sparse LSTM model obtained by parameter pruning [12]. The performance and energy efficiency gains achieved by ESE is very promising compared with CPU and GPU based implementations. However, due to the irregular computation and memory accesses caused by the sparse weight matrices of the compressed model, the computing power of the FPGA is not fully exerted by ESE. In order to deal with this problem, this work proposes to employ a structured compression technique as to completely eliminate the irregularities of computation and memory accesses. Moreover, a suite of highly efficient optimization techniques is enabled by an automatic synthesis framework to generate LSTM accelerators with much higher performance and energy efficiency under the same conditions.

8　CONCLUSION

In this paper, we propose to employ a structured compression technique using block-circulant matrices to compress the LSTM model small enough to be fitted on BRAMs of FPGA. Besides the reduced model size, the irregular computation and memory accesses have been completely eliminated by the regular structure of the block-circulant matrices. Moreover, an efficient FFT based fast circulant convolution is applied to accelerate the LSTM computation by reducing both the computational and storage complexities. In order to accommodate a wide range of LSTM variants, we also propose an automatic optimization and synthesis framework. Overall, compared with the state-of-the-art LSTM implementation, the proposed C-LSTM designs generated by our framework achieve up to 18.8X and 33.5X gains for performance and energy efficiency with small accuracy degradation, respectively.

ACKNOWLEDGMENTS

This work is supported by Beijing Natural Science Foundation (No. L172004) and National Science Foundation under grants CNS #1704662 and CNS #1739748. We thank all the anonymous reviewers for their feedback.

REFERENCES

[1] Martín Abadi et al. 2016. Tensorflow: large-scale machine learning on heterogeneous distributed systems. *Arxiv preprint arxiv:1603.04467*.

[2] 2014. *Automatic speech recognition: A deep learning approach, author=Yu, Dong and Deng, Li*. Springer.

[3] Yu Cheng, Felix X Yu, Rogerio S Feris, Sanjiv Kumar, Alok Choudhary, and Shi-Fu Chang. 2015. An exploration of parameter redundancy in deep networks with circulant projections. In *ICCV*.

[4] J. Cong, B. Liu, S. Neuendorffer, J. Noguera, K. Vissers, and Z. Zhang. 2011. High-Level Synthesis for FPGAs: From Prototyping to Deployment. *TCAD*.

[5] Zheng Cui, Yun Liang, Kyle Rupnow, and Deming Chen. 2012. An accurate gpu performance model for effective control flow divergence optimization. In *IPDPS*.

[6] Caiwen Ding et al. 2017. Circnn: accelerating and compressing deep neural networks using block-circulant weight matrices. In *MICRO*.

[7] Steven K Esser et al. 2016. Convolutional networks for fast, energy-efficient neuromorphic computing. *Proceedings of the national academy of sciences*.

[8] John S Garofolo, Lori F Lamel, William M Fisher, Jonathon G Fiscus, and David S Pallett. 1993. DARPA TIMIT acoustic-phonetic continous speech corpus CD-ROM. NIST speech disc 1-1.1. *Nasa sti/recon technical report n*, 93.

[9] Felix A Gers and Jürgen Schmidhuber. 2000. Recurrent nets that time and count. In *Proceedings of the IEEE-INNS-ENNS International Joint Conference on Neural Networks*.

[10] Alex Graves, Navdeep Jaitly, and Abdel-rahman Mohamed. 2013. Hybrid speech recognition with deep bidirectional LSTM. In *Automatic Speech Recognition and Understanding (ASRU), 2013 IEEE Workshop on*.

[11] Yijin Guan, Zhihang Yuan, Guangyu Sun, and Jason Cong. 2017. Fpga-based accelerator for long short-term memory recurrent neural networks. In *ASP-DAC*.

[12] Song Han, Huizi Mao, and William J Dally. 2015. Deep compression: Compressing deep neural networks with pruning, trained quantization and huffman coding. *Arxiv preprint arxiv:1510.00149*.

[13] Song Han et al. 2017. ESE: Efficient Speech Recognition Engine with Sparse LSTM on FPGA. In *FPGA*.

[14] Jong Hwan Ko, Burhan Mudassar, Taesik Na, and Saibal Mukhopadhyay. 2017. Design of an Energy-Efficient Accelerator for Training of Convolutional Neural Networks Using Frequency-Domain Computation. In *DAC*.

[15] Janghaeng Lee, Mehrzad Samadi, and Scott Mahlke. 2015. Orchestrating multiple data-parallel kernels on multiple devices. In *PACT*.

[16] Sicheng Li, Chunpeng Wu, Hai Li, Boxun Li, Yu Wang, and Qinru Qiu. 2015. Fpga acceleration of recurrent neural network based language model. In *FCCM*.

[17] Yun Liang, Huynh Phung Huynh, Kyle Rupnow, Rick Siow Mong Goh, and Deming Chen. 2015. Efficient gpu spatial-temporal multitasking. *TPDS*, 26, 3.

[18] Liqiang Lu, Yun Liang, Qingcheng Xiao, and Shengen Yan. [n. d.] Evaluating fast algorithms for convolutional neural networks on fpgas. In *FCCM*.

[19] Eriko Nurvitadhi, Jaewoong Sim, David Sheffield, Asit Mishra, Srivatsan Krishnan, and Debbie Marr. 2016. Accelerating recurrent neural networks in analytics servers: comparison of fpga, cpu, gpu, and asic. In *FPL*.

[20] Christopher Olah. [n. d.] http://colah.github.io/posts/2015-08-Understanding-LSTMs. ().

[21] Alan V Oppenheim. 1999. *Discrete-time signal processing*. Pearson Education India.

[22] Victor Pan. 2012. *Structured matrices and polynomials: unified superfast algorithms*. Springer Science & Business Media.

[23] Anamitra Bardhan Roy, Debasmita Dey, Bidisha Mohanty, and Devmalya Banerjee. 2012. Comparison of FFT, DCT, DWT, WHT compression techniques on electrocardiogram and photoplethysmography signals. In *IJCA*.

[24] Kyle Rupnow, Yun Liang, Yinan Li, Dongbo Min, Minh Do, and Deming Chen. 2011. High level synthesis of stereo matching: productivity, performance, and software constraints. In *FPT*.

[25] Haşim Sak, Andrew Senior, and Françoise Beaufays. 2014. Long short-term memory recurrent neural network architectures for large scale acoustic modeling. In *Fifteenth annual conference of the international speech communication association*.

[26] Shuo Wang, Yun Liang, and Wei Zhang. 2017. FlexCL: An Analytical Performance Model for OpenCL Workloads on Flexible FPGAs. In *DAC*.

[27] Yanzhi Wang et al. 2018. Towards ultra-high performance and energy efficiency of deep learning systems: an algorithm-hardware co-optimization framework. In *AAAI*.

[28] Xuechao Wei, Cody Hao Yu, Peng Zhang, Youxiang Chen, Yuxin Wang, Han Hu, Yun Liang, and Jason Cong. 2017. Automated Systolic Array Architecture Synthesis for High Throughput CNN Inference on FPGAs. In *DAC*.

[29] Dennis Weller, Fabian Oboril, Dimitar Lukarski, Juergen Becker, and Mehdi Tahoori. 2017. Energy Efficient Scientific Computing on FPGAs Using OpenCL. In *FPGA*.

[30] Qingcheng Xiao, Yun Liang, Liqiang Lu, Shengen Yan, and Yu-Wing Tai. 2017. Exploring Heterogeneous Algorithms for Accelerating Deep Convolutional Neural Networks on FPGAs. In *DAC*.

[31] Liang Zhao, Siyu Liao, Yanzhi Wang, Jian Tang, and Bo Yuan. 2017. Theoretical Properties for Neural Networks with Weight Matrices of Low Displacement Rank. *Arxiv preprint arxiv:1703.00144*.

DeltaRNN: A Power-efficient Recurrent Neural Network Accelerator

Chang Gao
Institute of Neuroinformatics,
University of Zurich and ETH Zurich
Zurich, Switzerland
chang@ini.uzh.ch

Daniel Neil*
Institute of Neuroinformatics,
University of Zurich and ETH Zurich
Zurich, Switzerland
daniel.l.neil@gmail.com

Enea Ceolini
Institute of Neuroinformatics,
University of Zurich and ETH Zurich
Zurich, Switzerland
eceoli@ini.uzh.ch

Shih-Chii Liu
Institute of Neuroinformatics,
University of Zurich and ETH Zurich
Zurich, Switzerland
shih@ini.ethz.ch

Tobi Delbruck
Institute of Neuroinformatics,
University of Zurich and ETH Zurich
Zurich, Switzerland
tobi@ini.uzh.ch

ABSTRACT

Recurrent Neural Networks (RNNs) are widely used in speech recognition and natural language processing applications because of their capability to process temporal sequences. Because RNNs are fully connected, they require a large number of weight memory accesses, leading to high power consumption. Recent theory has shown that an RNN delta network update approach can reduce memory access and computes with negligible accuracy loss. This paper describes the implementation of this theoretical approach in a hardware accelerator called "DeltaRNN" (DRNN). The DRNN updates the output of a neuron only when the neuron's activation changes by more than a delta threshold. It was implemented on a Xilinx Zynq-7100 FPGA. FPGA measurement results from a single-layer RNN of 256 Gated Recurrent Unit (GRU) neurons show that the DRNN achieves 1.2 TOp/s effective throughput and 164 GOp/s/W power efficiency. The delta update leads to a 5.7x speedup compared to a conventional RNN update because of the sparsity created by the DN algorithm and the zero-skipping ability of DRNN.

ACM Reference Format:
Chang Gao, Daniel Neil, Enea Ceolini, Shih-Chii Liu, and Tobi Delbruck. 2018. DeltaRNN: A Power-efficient Recurrent Neural Network Accelerator. In *FPGA '18: 2018 ACM/SIGDA International Symposium on Field-Programmable Gate Arrays, February 25–27, 2018, Monterey, CA, USA*. ACM, New York, NY, USA, 10 pages. https://doi.org/10.1145/3174243.3174261

1 INTRODUCTION

Recurrent Neural Networks (**RNNs**) are fully-connected single- or multi-layered networks with complex neurons that have multiple memory states and enabled state-of-art accuracies in tasks involving temporal sequences [27] such as automatic speech recognition [2, 9] and natural language processing [23]. The prediction accuracy of

*Currently at BenevolentAI.

RNNs is further improved by adding gating units to control the data flow in and between neurons. In deep learning, Long Short-Term Memory (**LSTM**) [16] and Gated Recurrent Unit (**GRU**) [6] are two major neuron models used in gated RNNs. The gating units in the LSTM and GRU models help to mitigate the well-known vanishing gradient problem encountered during the training process.

A challenge in deploying RNN applications in mobile or always-on applications is access to hardware that achieves high power efficiency. For mobile applications, edge inference is preferable because of lower latency, reduced network bandwidth requirement, robustness to network failure, and better privacy. Recent neural network applications use GPUs ranging from high-end models such as the NVIDIA Pascal Titan X GPU to embedded system on chip (**SoC**) such as the Kepler GPU in Tegra K1 SoC or smartphone processor embedded GPU such as the Samsung Exynos Mali. The server- or desktop-targeted Titan X consumes about 200 W and achieves a power efficiency around 5 GOp/s/W in inference of an LSTM layer with 1024 neurons [12]. Embedded CPUs and GPUs consume about 1 W, but their RNN power efficiency is actually much lower (around 8 MOp/s/W during inference with an LSTM network with 2 layers of 128 LSTM neurons each, as measured in [5]). For mobile GPUs, the low efficiency is from poor matching of memory architecture to GPU, especially for small RNNs.

The energy figures from Horowitz [17] for a 45nm process show that Dynamic Random Access Memory (**DRAM**) access consumes several hundred times more energy than arithmetic operations. The power consumption of the LSTM RNN in a complete mobile speech recognition engine [22] can be estimated. The RNN is a 5-layer network with 500 units per layer, that is updated at 100 Hz. The weight matrices are too large to be stored in economical SRAM and so must be fetched from off-chip DRAM. Using the Horowitz numbers results in a power consumption of about 0.2 W with most consumed by DRAM access. Thus RNN inference energy is dominated by memory access cost; however, achieving high throughput requires high memory bandwidth for weight fetching in order to keep arithmetic units loaded as fully as possible. The key to improving power efficiency (number of arithmetic operations/W) is to reduce the total memory access therefore decreasing the energy consumption, while keeping arithmetic units fully utilized to maintain high throughput.

Sparsity in network activations or input data is a property that can be used to achieve high power efficiency. In a Matrix-Vector Multiplication (**MxV**) between a neuron activation vector and a weight matrix, zero elements in the vector result in zero partial sums that do not contribute to the final result. The multiplications between zero vector elements and their corresponding weight columns can be skipped to save memory access of weight columns. Moreover, it is also possible to skip any multiplication between a zero weight element and a non-zero vector element to further reduce operations and memory access, though this feature has not been adopted in this work yet. A common way to create sparsity in neural network parameters is weight compression, which is shown in works [14, 19]. The Delta Network algorithm [25] creates sparsity in input and activation vectors by exploiting their temporal dependency.

Although GPUs offer high peak throughput, they may suffer from irregular execution paths and memory access patterns in RNN inference, which is caused by recurrent connections and limited data reuse of RNNs [3]. In this case, it is useful to consider hardware architectures specialized for RNN inference that enhance parallelism by matching memory bandwidth to available arithmetic units. RNN inference accelerators based on FPGA have been explored because of the potentially higher power efficiency compared with GPUs. Previous works include LSTM accelerators [4, 5, 11, 21], a GRU accelerator [26] and a Deep Neural Network (**DNN**) accelerator [10] that is able to run LSTM inference. These implementations do not capitalize on the data sparsity of RNNs. The Efficient Speech Recognition Engine (ESE) proposed by Han et al. [13] employs a load-balance-aware pruning scheme, including both pruning [15] and quantization. This pruning scheme compresses the LSTM model size by 20x and a scheduler that parallelizes operations on sparse models. They achieved 6.2x speedup over the dense model by pruning the LSTM model to 10% non-zeros. However, none of these works use the temporal property of RNN data.

In this paper, a GRU-RNN accelerator architecture called the DeltaRNN (**DRNN**) is proposed. This implementation is based on the Delta Network (**DN**) algorithm that skips dispensable computations during network inference by exploiting the temporal dependency in RNN inputs and activations [25] (Sec. 2.2). The system was implemented on an Xilinx Zynq-7100 FPGA controlled by a dual ARM Cortex-A9 CPU. To provide sufficient bandwidth for arithmetic units and less external memory access, DRNN V1.0 stores the network weight matrix in BRAM blocks. It was tested on the TIDIGITS dataset using an RNN model with one GRU layer of 256 neurons.

2 BACKGROUND

2.1 Gated Recurrent Unit

A GRU RNN has similar prediction accuracy to an LSTM RNN but lower complexity of computation. We implemented the GRU which requires a smaller number of network parameters (therefore less hardware resource) than the LSTM. Fig. 1 shows the data flow within a GRU neuron.

The GRU neuron model has two gates–a reset gate r and an update gate u–and a candidate hidden state c. The reset gate determines the amount of information from the previous hidden state

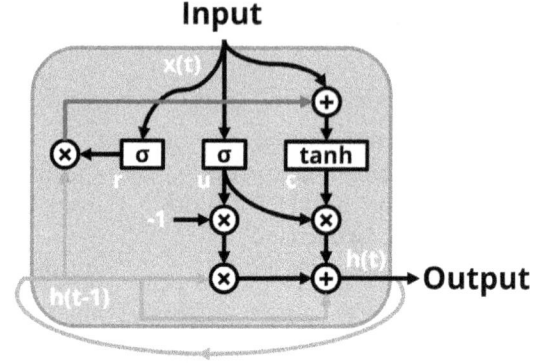

Figure 1: Data flow of GRU

that will be added to the candidate hidden state. The update gate decides to what extent the activation h should be updated by the candidate hidden state to enable a long-term memory. The GRU formulation used in this paper is shown below:

$$r(t) = \sigma[W_{xr}x(t) + W_{hr}h(t-1) + b_r] \tag{1}$$

$$u(t) = \sigma[W_{xu}x(t) + W_{hu}h(t-1) + b_u] \tag{2}$$

$$c(t) = \tanh[W_{xc}x(t) + r(t) \odot (W_{hc}h(t-1)) + b_c] \tag{3}$$

$$h(t) = (1 - u(t)) \odot h(t-1) + u(t) \odot c(t) \tag{4}$$

where x is the input vector, h the activation vector, W the weight matrix, b the bias and r, u, c correspond to the reset gate, update gate and candidate activation respectively. σ and $\odot$ signify logistic sigmoid function and element-wise multiplication respectively.

2.2 Delta Network Algorithm

This section explains the principle of the DN algorithm [25] and show how a conventional GRU-RNN model with full updates can be converted to a delta network.

The DN algorithm reduces both memory access and arithmetic operations by exploiting the temporal stability of RNN inputs and outputs. Computations associated with a neuron activation that has a small amount of change from its previous timestep can be skipped. As shown in Fig. 2, all gray circles represent neurons whose corresponding computations are skipped. The previous research on the DN algorithm [25] demonstrated for the TIDIGITS audio digit recognition benchmark that the algorithm can achieve 8x speedup with 97.5% accuracy when the network was trained as a delta network without considering sparsity in the weight matrix. Pre-trained networks can also be greatly accelerated as delta networks. The large Wall Street Journal (**WSJ**) speech recognition benchmark showed speedup of 5.7x with word error rate of 10.2%, which is the same with using a conventional RNN [25].

Fig. 3 shows how skipping a single neuron saves multiplications of an entire column in all related weight matrices as well as fetches of the corresponding weight elements. The following equations describe the conversion between an MxV with full update and one with delta updates:

$$y(t) = Wx(t) \tag{5}$$

$$y(t) = W\Delta x(t) + y(t-1) \tag{6}$$

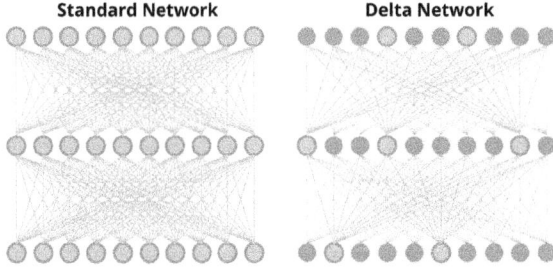

Figure 2: Comparison between a standard gated RNN network (left) and a sparse delta network (right)

where $\Delta x(t) = x(t) - x(t-1)$ and $y(t-1)$ is the MxV result from the previous timestep. The MxV in equation (6) becomes a sparse MxV if all computations with respect to small $\Delta x(t)$ elements are ignored. As shown in Fig. 3, the sparser the $\Delta x(t)$ vector, the more memory access and arithmetic operations are saved.

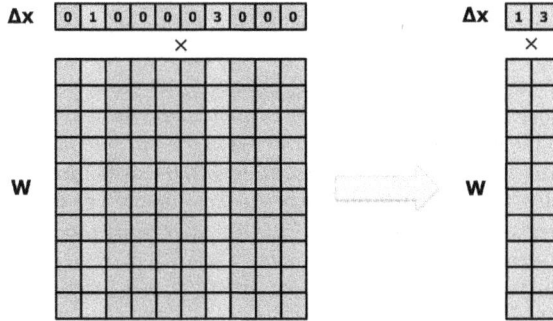

Figure 3: Skipping neuron updates save multiplications between input vectors and columns that correspond to zero $\Delta x(t)$ (also the behavior of Matrix-Vector Multiplication Channel discussed in Section 3.2.2)

Assuming the length of all vectors is n and dimension of the weight matrix W is $n \times n$, the computation cost for calculating a dense MxV is n^2 while the computation cost for calculating a DN MxV is $o_c \cdot n^2 + 2n$, where o_c is the occupancy[1] of the delta vector $\Delta x(t)$. The term $2n$ exists because calculating the delta vector $\Delta x(t)$ and adding $y(t-1)$ to $W\Delta x(t)$ respectively needs n operations. As for memory access, to calculate a dense MxV, $o_c \cdot n^2$ weight elements and n vector elements has to be fetched. The DN MxV needs to fetch $o_c \cdot n^2$ weight elements, $2n$ vector elements for $\Delta x(t)$, n vector elements for $y(t-1)$ and finally write n vector elements for $y(t)$. Thus, the theoretical computation speedup and memory access reduction approaches $1/o_c$ when $n \to \infty$. A summary of the computation cost and memory cost is shown by:

$$C_{\text{comp, dense}} = n^2 \tag{7}$$

$$C_{\text{comp, sparse}} = o_c \cdot n^2 + 2n \tag{8}$$

$$C_{\text{mem, dense}} = n^2 + n \tag{9}$$

---

[1] Occupancy is defined as the ratio of non-zero elements to all elements of a vector or a matrix

$$C_{\text{mem, sparse}} = o_c \cdot n^2 + 4n \tag{10}$$

$$\text{Speedup} = \frac{C_{\text{comp, dense}}}{C_{\text{comp, sparse}}} \approx \frac{1}{o_c} \tag{11}$$

$$\text{Memory Access Reduction} = \frac{C_{\text{mem, dense}}}{C_{\text{mem, sparse}}} \approx \frac{1}{o_c} \tag{12}$$

To skip the computations related to any small $\Delta x(t)$, the delta threshold Θ is introduced to decide when a delta vector element can be ignored. The change of a neuron's activation is only memorized when it is larger than Θ. Furthermore, to prevent the accumulation of error with time, only the last activation value that has a change larger than the delta threshold is memorized. This is defined by the following equation sets:

$$\hat{x}(t-1) = \begin{cases} x(t-1) & , |x(t) - \hat{x}(t-1)| > \Theta \\ \hat{x}(t-2) & , |x(t) - \hat{x}(t-1)| \le \Theta \end{cases} \tag{13}$$

$$\hat{h}(t-2) = \begin{cases} h(t-2) & , \left|h(t-1) - \hat{h}(t-2)\right| > \Theta \\ \hat{h}(t-3) & , \left|h(t-1) - \hat{h}(t-2)\right| \le \Theta \end{cases} \tag{14}$$

$$\Delta x(t) = \begin{cases} x(t) - \hat{x}(t-1) & , |x(t) - \hat{x}(t-1)| > \Theta \\ 0 & , |x(t) - \hat{x}(t-1)| \le \Theta \end{cases} \tag{15}$$

$$\Delta h(t-1) = \begin{cases} h(t-1) - \hat{h}(t-2) & , \left|h(t-1) - \hat{h}(t-2)\right| > \Theta \\ 0 & , \left|h(t-1) - \hat{h}(t-2)\right| \le \Theta \end{cases} \tag{16}$$

where memorized changes $\Delta x(t)$ and $\Delta h(t-1)$ are calculated by using $\hat{x}(t-1)$ and $\hat{h}(t-2)$. Next, using (13), (14), (15) and (16), the conventional GRU equation set can be transformed into its delta network version:

$$M_r(t) = W_{xr}\Delta x(t) + W_{hr}\Delta h(t-1) + M_r(t-1) \tag{17}$$

$$M_u(t) = W_{xu}\Delta x(t) + W_{hu}\Delta h(t-1) + M_u(t-1) \tag{18}$$

$$M_{cx}(t) = W_{xc}\Delta x(t) + M_{cx}(t-1) \tag{19}$$

$$M_{ch}(t) = W_{hc}\Delta h(t-1) + M_{ch}(t-1) \tag{20}$$

$$r(t) = \sigma[M_r(t)] \tag{21}$$

$$u(t) = \sigma[M_u(t)] \tag{22}$$

$$c(t) = \tanh[M_{cx}(t) + r(t) \odot M_{ch}(t)] \tag{23}$$

$$h(t) = [1 - u(t)] \odot h(t-1) + u(t) \odot c(t) \tag{24}$$

where $M_r(0) = b_r, M_u(0) = b_u, M_{cx}(0) = b_c, M_{ch}(0) = 0$.

3 IMPLEMENTATION

The DN algorithm can theoretically reduce arithmetic operations and memory access by reducing weight fetches. The main target of the DRNN accelerator is to realize efficient zero-skipping on sparse and irregular data patterns of $\Delta x(t)$ and $\Delta h(t-1)$.

Fig. 4 shows the overview of the whole system. The Programmable Logic (**PL**) part is implemented on a Xilinx Zynq-7100 FPGA chip running at 125 MHz. An AXI Direct Memory Access (**DMA**) module converts between AXI4-Stream (**AXIS**) and full AXI4 so that data can be transferred between the PL and the Processing System (**PS**). The PS is the Dual ARM-Cortex A9 CPU on the Zynq SoC. The data transfer between DRNN and AXI DMA is managed in packets. The Memory Mapped to Stream (**MM2S**) interrupt and the Stream to Memory Mapped (**S2MM**) interrupt are respectively used to indicate the end of corresponding data transfers. Read and write operations on DDR3 memory are managed by the DRAM controller of the PS [28].

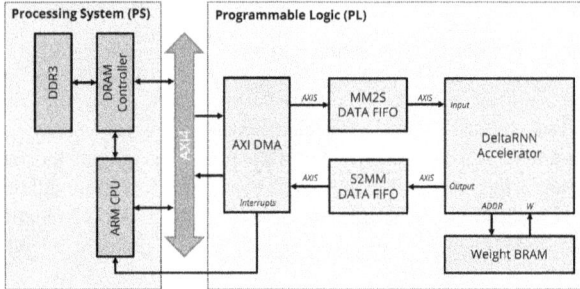

Figure 4: Acceleration system overview

The input and output interface of the DRNN accelerator uses the AXIS protocol to stream data in from the MM2S Data FIFO and out to the S2MM Data FIFO. Both the input and output interfaces are 64-bit wide in order to transfer 4 16-bit values per clock cycle. The weight BRAM block consumes 400 36-Kbit BRAM blocks (~ 1.76 MB) to store all weight matrices and biases on-chip to provide sufficient bandwidth. Input vectors are stored in DRAM to be transferred to DRNN during runtime and output vectors are written back to DRAM immediately after being produced by DRNN. Previous research shows that RNNs with quantized fixed-point parameters down to 8 and even 4 bits can still work well [18, 20]. In this work, to demonstrate the benefit of the DRNN architecture on performance gain with minimum RNN accuracy loss on practical applications, we quantize all 32-bit floating-point parameters used by the DRNN including GRU input/output vectors, weights and biases into fixed-point 16-bit Q8.8 integers by **Fixed16** = round (256 × **Float32**).

3.1 DRNN Architecture

The top-level block diagram of the DRNN Accelerator is shown in Fig. 5. It is composed of three main modules, the Input Encoding Unit (**IEU**), the **MxV** Unit which is controlled by the MxV controller, and the Activation Pipeline (**AP**).

The function of the IEU is to execute subtractions and comparisons between the input vectors from the current and previous timesteps to generate delta vectors. The MxV Unit executes Multiply-Accumulate (**MAC**) operations using the sparse IEU output. It contains 768 MAC units that performs 16-bit multiplications and 32-bit accumulations on signed integers. Accumulation results from the MxV Unit are sent to the AP module which computes the activation of the GRU layer for the current timestep. The architecture and function of each block is next presented in detail.

3.1.1 Input Encoding Unit. The IEU encodes dense input vectors $x(t)$ and $h(t-1)$ into sparse delta input vectors $\Delta x(t)$ and $\Delta h(t-1)$; however, the sparsity of these delta input vectors is not predictable and can only be known at runtime, leading to irregular data patterns. Hence another function of IEU is to format non-zero elements of delta input vectors so that they can be fetched one by one in consecutive clock cycles. This IEU is the most significant and complicated module of the DRNN.

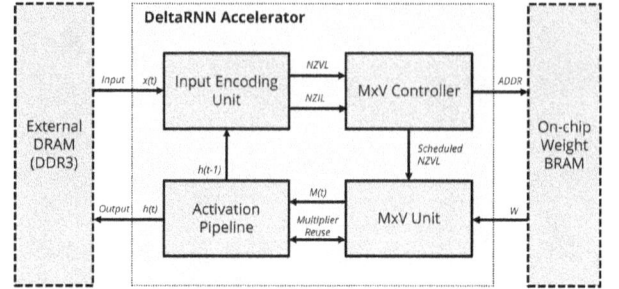

Figure 5: Top-level block diagram of the DRNN Accelerator

The structure of the IEU is shown in Fig. 6. The IEU has two identical parts that are responsible for generating $\Delta x(t)$ and $\Delta h(t-1)$ respectively. The width of the inputs of the two parts are 64 bits and 512 bits. Since both $x(t)$ and $h(t-1)$ elements are 16-bit Q8.8 integers, the two IEU parts respectively consume 4 elements of $x(t)$ and 32 elements of $h(t-1)$ per clock cycle, both of which should be set as large as possible to enhance performance but are respectively limited by the AXI-DMA bandwidth and timing requirements. The same number of delta vector elements are then calculated by the Delta Encoder by subtracting the current input from the input of last timestep stored in the Previous Time (**PT**) register file and comparing the result with the delta threshold to decide if the magnitude of change should be dropped or saved into the register file in the Delta Scheduler. After being processed by the Delta Encoder, $\hat{x}(t-1)$, $\hat{h}(t-2)$ are selected from $x(t)$, $h(t-1)$ respectively and then written into the PT Register to be used to calculate delta vectors for the next timestep. The Delta Scheduler in either of the two parts of IEU can generate 2 non-zero $\Delta x(t)$ elements or 2 non-zero $\Delta h(t-1)$ elements. Next, any non-zero values in delta vectors and their corresponding indices are respectively allocated in two groups of FIFOs to form the Non-Zero Value List (**NZVL**) and the Non-Zero Index List (**NZIL**), which is a variant of the sparsity map used in [1].

The latency of calculating a $\Delta h(t-1)$ vector with 1024 elements is at best 1024/32 = 32 cycles with all elements to be zeros (0% occupancy) and at worst 1024/2 = 512 cycles with all elements to be non-zero (100% occupancy). The DRNN is designed to calculate MxV column-wise so that the MxV computation can be started immediately after a valid delta vector element is generated. In this way, multiplications between a matrix column and a delta vector element can be easily parallelized because of the locality of the non-zero delta vector element; otherwise, if MxV is calculated row-wise, the delta encoding process might introduce a huge overhead when running a large model.

Moreover, since the IEU part for generating $\Delta x(t)$ consumes 4 elements per cycle, any input vector with an odd number of elements has to be extended to a length that is a multiple of 4 using zero-padding (this does not apply to $h(t-1)$ vectors because only even numbers of hidden layer neurons are supported by DRNN). For example, if the length of the input vectors $x(t)$ is 39, then 1 extra zero will be appended to the end of $x(t)$. Thus it takes at best 10 clock cycles and at worst 20 cycles for IEU to generate a $\Delta x(t)$ vector with 40 elements.

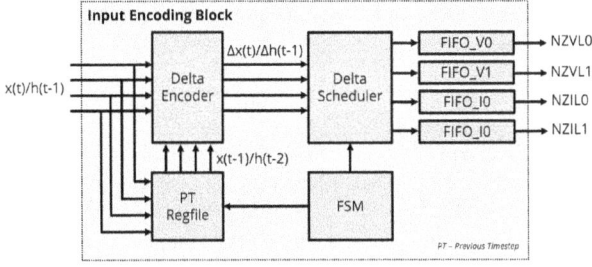

Figure 6: Block diagram of the IEU

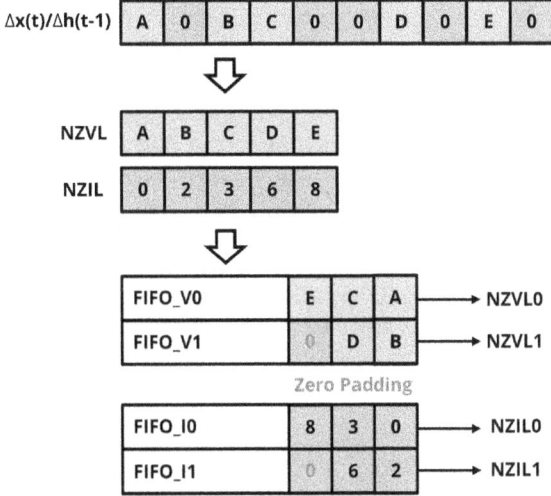

Figure 7: Principle of generating and allocating NZVL and NZIL

As shown in Fig. 7, a complete NZVL consists of all non-zero elements of $\Delta x(t)$ or $\Delta h(t-1)$ and the corresponding NZIL contains indices of elements in the NZVL and can be encoded into addresses for fetching corresponding weight columns. Either NZVL or NZIL is split and allocated in two FIFOs in ascending order of indices. Zero padding is conducted at the end of the allocation if the number of non-zero values is an odd number.

3.1.2 Matrix-Vector Multiplication (MxV) Unit. The MxV Unit performs dense matrix and sparse vector multiplications to skip columns of computations that correspond to zero vector elements in $\Delta x(t)$ and $\Delta h(t-1)$, which is different from previous works on accelerating sparse matrix-vector multiplications that mainly exploit sparsity in matrices [7, 8, 29]. The MxV Unit is composed of 3 channels, R, U and C. Channels R and U are respectively responsible for calculating memories $M_r(t)$ and $M_u(t)$ while Channel C calculates both $M_{cx}(t)$ and $M_{ch}(t)$. Each channel has 128 clusters of multipliers (**MUL**) and 128 clusters of summation adders (**ADD**) both with two instances per cluster. This is equivalent to 256 MAC units per channel. Multipliers are instantiated using DSP blocks to perform multiplications on 16-bit signed integers. Summation adders are synthesized by Look-up Tables (**LUTs**) and perform 32-bit summation. Partial sums are accumulated on the accumulation

registers (**ACC REG**). The data flow of an MxV channel is shown in Fig. 8.

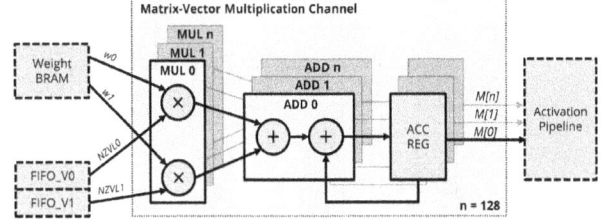

Figure 8: MxV channel

As shown in Fig. 8, in each multiplier cluster (**MUL**), the two operands of one of the multipliers are NZVL0 and the corresponding weight element in the column addressed by NZIL0. Operands of the other multipliers are driven by NZVL1 and the corresponding weight element in another column addressed by NZIL1. Operands w0 and w1 are provided by RAMB18E1 cells in the Weight BRAM block with each configured in true dual-port mode. The MxV channel is fully pipelined to fetch operands in every following clock cycle once launched. When NZVL and NZIL FIFOs are not empty, the channel starts to fetch data in all FIFOs simultaneously including any padded zeros to ensure that NZVL and NZIL are synchronized. Since $\Delta h(t-1)$ is generally longer than $\Delta x(t)$, all MxV channels calculate $W_x \Delta x(t)$ before $W_h \Delta h(t-1)$ to hide the overhead of generating $\Delta h(t-1)$ under the computation time. Accumulation results, $M_r(t)$, $M_u(t)$, $M_{cx}(t)$ and $M_{ch}(t)$, are held in ACC REGs. Channel C has two clusters of ACC REGs to store $M_{cx}(t)$ and $M_{ch}(t)$ respectively while Channels R and U each have one cluster of ACC REGs to store $M_r(t)$ and $M_u(t)$ respectively.

Fig. 9 illustrates the computation pattern of MxV channels. One MxV channel can simultaneously calculate multiplications between two non-zero delta vector elements and weight elements in two corresponding columns, reducing the total number of fetching/writing accumulation registers by approximately 2x. The MxV channel calculates the MxV in a column-wise style. The Channel Width equals to the number of multiplier clusters in each MxV channel, so that it denotes the amount of column elements that can be processed by the channel in each clock cycle. The Channel Worksize indicates how many clock cycles the MxV channel needs to finish processing a column. In this design, the Channel Width is 128 and the Channel Worksize is 2. It takes 2 clock cycles for each MxV channel to process 2 columns.

3.1.3 Activation Pipeline (AP). The AP produces the final hidden layer activation from the accumulation results held in ACC REGs. Fig. 10 shows the data flow of the AP, which has 6 pipeline stages, S0-S5. The GRU formulation is divided into 6 steps correspond to each pipeline stage.

The latency of the AP affects the utilization rate of the MxV Unit. Although the part of IEU that processes input $x(t)$ keeps working whenever there are new input vectors coming from the M2SS Data FIFO, the other part that works on $h(t-1)$ must be stalled until a new activation vector is generated by the AP. The condition to launch the MxV Unit is when both NZVL FIFOs for $\Delta x(t)$ and $\Delta h(t-1)$ are not empty. Thus, during this period, the MxV Unit

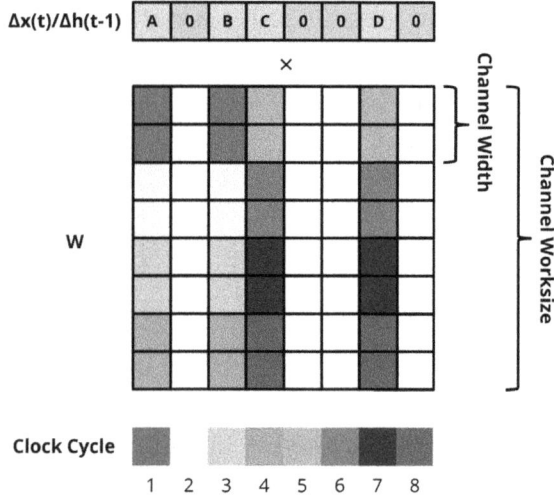

Figure 9: MxV Channel computation pattern

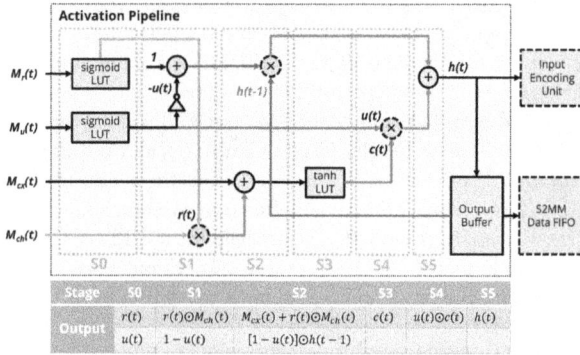

Figure 10: Data flow of the Activation Pipeline module; blue arrows denote data paths from AP to MxV multipliers and red arrows denote those from MxV multipliers to AP

is in idle state due to no new non-zero $\Delta h(t-1)$ elements coming from the IEU. When running larger models, the MxV Unit will run for more clock cycles per timestep compared to the AP and thus the MxV Unit utilization rate is improved. In this case, to enhance the utilization rate of the MxV Unit, multiplications in AP are conducted by reusing the MxV Unit. Multiplexers and demultiplexers are used to control the data paths between AP and multipliers in MxV Unit. Adders in the AP are synthesized by LUT. Adders in S1 and S5 perform 16-bit integer summation and those in S2 perform 32-bit integer summation to calculate $M_c(t) = M_{cx}(t) + M_{ch}(t)$. 32-bit Q16.16 outputs of 'virtual' multipliers in S2 and S4 are transformed into 16-bit Q8.8 before reaching adders in S5. Sigmoid and tanh functions in the AP are realized by using the Range Addressable Lookup Table (RALUT) [24]. A RALUT can save hardware resources by quantizing the non-linear functions within a given input range and any input that exceeds the range will give an output which is saturated to the maximum or minimum of the corresponding non-linear function. The precision and range of the inputs and outputs of sigmoid and tanh RALUTs are shown in Table 1.

Table 1: Precision and range of inputs and outputs of RA-LUTs in AP

	sigmoid	tanh
Input Precision	signed 16-bit Q8.8	signed 16-bit Q8.8
Sampling Range	[-0x0008,0x0008)	[-0x0008,0x0008)
Sampling Points	4096	4096
Output Precision	unsigned 9-bit Q1.8	signed 10-bit Q2.8
Output Range	[0x0000,0x0100]	[-0xFF00, 0x0100]

The activation vector is stored into the Output Buffer, which can independently write outputs into the S2MM Data FIFO so that computations for the next timestep can be immediately started after the activation vector of current timestep is generated.

4 RESULTS

4.1 Experimental Setup

Vivado 2017.2 was used for synthesis and implementation of the design. After place and route, the system is able to operate at 125 MHz. As shown in Fig. 11, the system is implemented on an Xilinx Zynq-7000 All Programmable SoC Mini-Module Plus (MMP) system-on-a-module (SOM) mounted on a customized baseboard with a power module. It has a dual ARM Cortex-A9 CPU, a Kintex-7 XC7Z100 FPGA, and 1 GB DDR3 SDRAM.

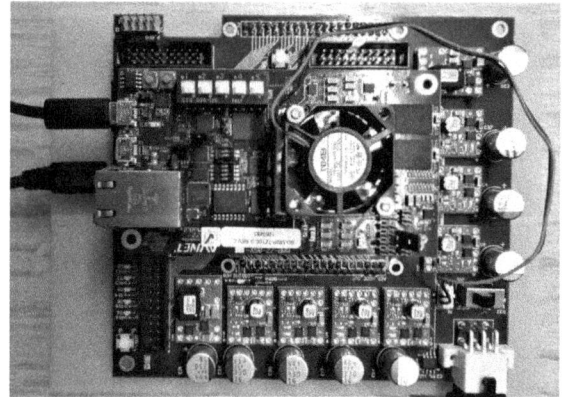

Figure 11: Our customized baseboard supporting Xilinx Zynq-7100 All Programmable SoC Mini-Module Plus from AVNET

DRNN is used to accelerate a single-layer GRU-RNN with 256 neurons that forms part of a classifier to enable real-time spoken digit recognition. The network structure is shown in Fig. 12. The GRU RNN is trained by applying the DN algorithm with different delta thresholds Θ from 0x00 to 0x80 [2] on the TIDIGITS dataset using 32-bit single precision floating-point parameters. The test set has 128 samples, each of which has different numbers of timesteps due to the different audio sequence lengths. Outputs of the GRU RNN layer are processed by two Fully-Connected (**FC**) layers to

---

[2]The delta threshold is in 16-bit Q8.8 format. For example, 0x80 in Q8.8 corresponds to 0.5 in 32-bit floating-point numbers.

Input

39

| GRU |

256

| FC1 |

200

| Leaky ReLU |

200

| FC2 |

10

| Softmax |

10

Output

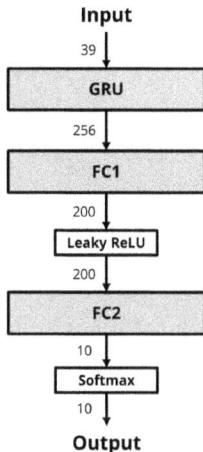

Figure 12: Network structure of the test RNN model

generate the final classification results. Computations of FC layers are handled by the ARM CPU. For training, all samples were zero-padded to have the same length of 249 timesteps. The final classification is done for all the samples on their last timestep. The input dimension is 39 and the input vectors are quantized into 16-bit Q8.8 fixed-point numbers. They are stored in the off-chip DRAM and are transferred to the DRNN one sample at a time during runtime using the AXI-DMA. Hidden layer outputs are written back to the off-chip DRAM to be used by the CPU to produce classification results.

The dimensions of the weight matrices corresponding to inputs and activations are 256×39 and 256×256 respectively. All matrices are quantized into the same format as the input vectors, which gives the total size of 0.43 MB, which are initialized in BRAM blocks together with biases. The test bench is a bare metal C program compiled in the Xilinx SDK environment and is passed to Zynq MMP by USB-JTAG on the baseboard. The range of parameter values before and after quantization is summarized in Table 2.

Table 2: Quantization of the input vector and weight matrices (trained at $\Theta = 0.5$)

	Range (Float-32)	Range (Fixed-16 Q8.8)
$x(t)$	[-8.3845, 12.1637]	[0xF79E, 0x0C2A]
W_{xr}	[-0.4260, 0.3914]	[0xFF93, 0x0064]
W_{xu}	[-0.4505, 0.4107]	[0xFF8D, 0x0069]
W_{xc}	[-0.3862, 0.3649]	[0xFF9D, 0x005D]
W_{hr}	[-0.4249, 0.4426]	[0xFF93, 0x0071]
W_{hu}	[-0.5975, 0.4878]	[0xFF67, 0x007D]
W_{hc}	[-0.4617, 0.4566]	[0xFF8A, 0x0075]

4.2 Hardware Resource Utilization

The hardware resource utilization percentage is shown in Table 3. The maximum number of DSPs used in this design is limited by the maximum bandwidth that RAMB18E1 cells in the weight BRAM block can provide to enable a weight fetch in 1 clock cycle for each

DSP cell and also the available LUTs to synthesize adders in the MxV Unit.

Table 3: Hardware utilization of DRNN

	FF	LUT	DSP	BRAM
Available	554800	277400	2020	755
Used	119260	261357	768	457.5
Percentage	21.50%	94.22%	38.02%	60.60%

4.3 Performance

4.3.1 Numerical Accuracy. RNN models trained at different delta thresholds are first computed by an Intel i7-8700k CPU in 32-bit floating-point precision on the 128 test samples. Then the numerical accuracy is calculated as the percentage of same classification results generated by DRNN in 16-bit fixed-point precision compared to those by the CPU. Results shown in Fig. 13 indicate that the same delta threshold Θ should be used in both training and inference to achieve better numerical accuracy. For example, the model with the best numerical accuracy 98.43% (126 out of 128 correct classifications vs. CPU) achieved during inference at $\Theta = 0x80$ is trained also at $\Theta = 0x80$. There is no numerical accuracy loss when $\Theta <= 0x40$ if using the same Θ in both training and inference.

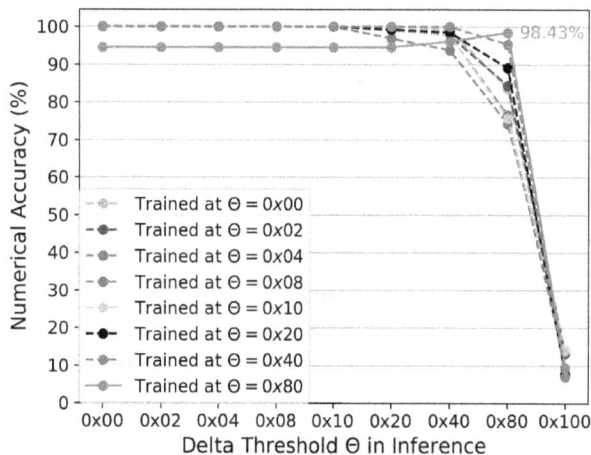

Figure 13: Numerical accuracy of classification results obtained by DRNN running test RNN models trained at different delta thresholds

4.3.2 Throughput. According to the standard GRU formulation, the total Operations per Timestep (OPsT) is:

$$\text{OPsT} = 6 \times \text{LX} \times \text{LH} + 6 \times \text{LH} \times \text{LH} = 453120 \quad (25)$$

where LX is the length of the input vectors and LH is the length of the activations. Since MxV operations dominate the total number of operations, all element-wise multiplications, additions and nonlinear functions are ignored. For this test model, LX = 39 and LH = 256. Then the effective throughput is defined as:

$$\text{Eff. Throughput} = \frac{\text{OPsT} \times \text{Timesteps}}{\text{Time}} \quad (26)$$

The effective throughput of the DRNN is evaluated by streaming 128 input samples to DRNN and measuring the time to process all samples. Padded zeros in each sample are removed. The total number of timesteps of the 128 samples is 12263 leading to a total number of operations equaling $12263 \times 453120 = 5.56$ GOp. Time used by DRNN to finish computing all GRU layer outputs and corresponding effective throughputs at each delta threshold are shown in Table 4. Increasing Θ increases throughput. The highest throughput of 1.2 TOp/s is obtained at $\Theta = 0x80$, which is the delta threshold where optimal throughput with negligible numerical accuracy loss can be achieved. According to Fig. 13 and our previous research [25], delta thresholds larger than 0.5 may cause dramatic accuracy loss.

Table 4: DRNN effective throughput with respect to delta threshold

Delta Threshold	Time [ms]	Eff. Throughput [GOp/s]
0x00	26.43	210.37
0x02	22.77	244.18
0x04	18.89	294.34
0x08	14.61	380.56
0x10	11.12	500.00
0x20	8.14	683.05
0x40	6.04	920.53
0x80	4.64	1198.28

Fig. 14 shows the occupancy of delta input vectors Δx and delta activation vectors Δh averaged across all timesteps, as well as the speedup of GRU layer computation with respect to the delta threshold Θ. When $\Theta = 0x00$ the occupancy of either Δx or Δh is not 100%, indicating that both inputs and activations already have some sparsity without the delta threshold. When $\Theta = 0x80$, the occupancy of Δx and Δh are respectively reduced to 57% and 2%, which means that the total arithmetic operations and memory access are reduced by 43% and 98% for Δx and Δh, respectively. Thanks to the zero-skipping capability, DRNN achieved 5.7x speedup when $\Theta = 0x80$ compared to that when $\Theta = 0x00$. Together with Fig. 13, Fig. 14 also indicates that DRNN can achieve 4.4x speedup without any numerical accuracy loss on the test samples.

The occupancy of Δx is much higher than that of Δh at $\Theta = 0x80$, which indicates that the possibility of IEU to give an invalid output is much higher for Δh than for Δx. For example, if the occupancy of Δh is zero at any timestep, it will take 8 clocks for IEU to consume a Δh vector with 256 elements without generating any valid operand that is useful for the MxV Unit. To reduce the possibility of the MxV Unit idling at the beginning of IEU encoding delta vectors, DRNN calculates $W_h \Delta h(t-1)$ after $W_x \Delta x(t)$ because Δx might provide valid operands more frequently.

4.3.3 MAC Computation Efficiency. The MAC computation efficiency measures how efficiently the hardware makes use of MAC units and is defined as:

$$\text{MAC Comp. Efficiency} = \frac{\text{Eff. Throughput}}{\text{Peak Throughput}} \qquad (27)$$

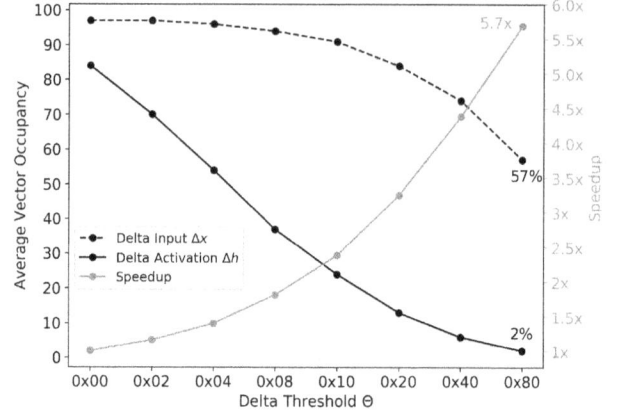

Figure 14: Average vector sparsity and speedup with respect to delta threshold

where peak throughput is defined as $2 \times \#MAC \times f$ and #MAC is the total number of MAC units, each of which contains a multiplier and an accumulator. Thus the peak throughput of DRNN is calculated as $2 \times 768 \times 125 \times 10^6 = 192$ GOp/s and the MAC computation efficiency of DRNN is $1198/192 = 623.96\%$ for this example workload and delta threshold.

4.3.4 DSP Utilization Efficiency. Here we propose a method to estimate the efficiency of utilizing DSP blocks for MAC computations without considering the bandwidth limitation of memory access. For example, a DSP block in Xilinx FPGAs consists of a 25-bit x 18-bit multiplier followed by an accumulator; thus potentially every DSP can be instantiated as a MAC unit to perform 16-bit fixed-point multiplications or 32-bit floating-point multiplications [3] and accumulation. In this case, assuming each DSP can be used as a MAC unit, we calculate the potential peak throughput in terms of the number of DSPs instantiated in the design:

$$\text{Potential Peak Throughput} = 2 \times \#DSP \times f \qquad (28)$$

where *#DSP* is the number of DSPs after synthesis and implementation. Thus the DSP utilization efficiency is defined as:

$$\text{DSP Util. Efficiency} = \frac{\text{Eff. Throughput}}{\text{Potential Peak Throughput}} \qquad (29)$$

Note that any techniques that synthesize multipliers by LUT or use low precision operands, such as 8-bit or 4-bit numbers, to produce multiple products out of a single DSP should result in higher DSP utilization efficiency.

4.3.5 Power. We measured the wall-plug power using a Voltcraft 4500ADVANCED Energy Monitor (Fig. 15).

As shown in Fig. 15, the power of the baseboard plus the fan when the Zynq MMP is not mounted is 7.9 W. It also includes the power of the power supply. It increases to 9.4 W when the Zynq MMP is mounted without programming the FPGA so that the Zynq MMP is in idle state. After programming the FPGA, the power rises to 10.0 W and further to 15.2 W when the system is iteratively

---

[3]A single-precision (32-bit) floating-point multiplier can be synthesized using multiple DSPs to achieve high performance or single DSP at the expense of potentially longer latency and higher LUT usage.

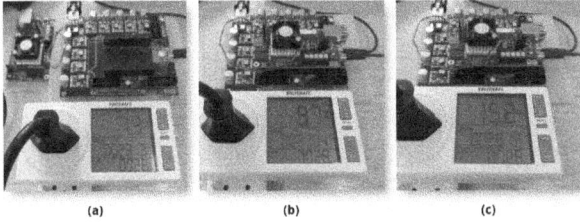

Figure 15: (a): Measured power of the baseboard plus the fan; (b) measured power of the whole system with the Zynq MMP in idle; (c) measured power of the whole system when DRNN is fully loaded by iteratively calculating GRU layer outputs

calculating the hidden layer outputs. Thus the power consumption of the Zynq MMP is $15.2 - 7.9 = 7.3$ W and the on-chip power, i.e, the power of the FPGA PL, is $15.2 - 9.7 = 5.5$ W. This number is nearly identical to 5.503 estimated from the Xilinx Power Analyzer using a switching rate of 50%. The power analyzer shows that the power of DRNN and weight BRAM are respectively 2.727 W and 2.284 W. The measured power consumption is summarized in Table 5.

Table 5: Power consumption hierarchy of the system

	Power (W)
Total (Running DRNN)	15.2
Baseboard + Fan	7.9
Baseboard + Fan + Zynq MMP	9.7
Zynq MMP	7.3
FPGA	5.5

4.3.6 Power Efficiency. When the delta threshold is 0x80, the effective power efficiency of the DRNN is $1198/5.5 = 218$ GOp/s/W with respect to the FPGA on-chip power or $1198/7.3 = 164$ GOp/s/W with respect to the power of the Zynq MMP board. A summary of the DRNN performance is shown in Table 6.

Table 6: Summary of DRNN Performance

Parameter	Value
Delta Threshold	0.5 (0x80)
Frequency	125 MHz
Effective Throughput	1198 GOp/s
Potential Peak Throughput	192 GOp/s
MAC Computation Efficiency	623.96%
Power Efficiency (FPGA)	217.82 GOp/s/W
Power Efficiency (Board)	164.11 GOp/s/W

4.4 Comparison to Prior Work, CPU & GPU

Table 7 shows performance of DRNN compared to prior work, an Intel i7-8700K CPU, and an NVIDIA GTX 1080 Ti GPU. The total power of the Zynq MMP development board measured by the wall plug power meter is used in this comparison. Ref. [10] supports either 32-bit floating-point or 16-bit fixed-point precision and we use results obtained in fixed-point precision. Ref. [4] has three different implementations, and we used the one called "DeepStore" that stores weights on BRAM in Table 7, which is the closest one to our work. To measure the performance of CPU/GPU on the same task discussed in Section 4.3, we try to follow a method similar to the one used in Ref. [13]. For the CPU benchmark, we run the test model in Theano with Intel Software Optimization (Intel MKL 2018), and the CPU power is measured by using the Stress Terminal UI monitoring tool[4] since our CPU does not support the Intel pcm-power utility. For GPU, the model is run in Theano with CUDA 9 and cuDNN 7 while the GPU power is measured using the nvidia-smi utility. With batch size = 128, the CPU/GPU finished the task in 295.87/45.05 ms with 35.6/95.9 W average power. On this task, DRNN is 63.8x/9.7x faster and 312.7x/128.5x more power efficient than CPU/GPU.

5 CONCLUSION

In this paper, we illustrate how high power efficiency can be achieved for RNN inference by combining the DN algorithm, of which the training process is already integrated in Lasagne powered by Theano, with our proposed DRNN hardware architecture. The DRNN features the ability to reduce MxV operations and corresponding weight fetches by skipping dispensable neuron activation changes below a threshold. The DRNN allows trade-off between accuracy and runtime cost. Our previous research on the DN algorithm [25] showed that pre-trained RNNs can also be accelerated by simply running them as delta networks, but the accuracy will be higher if the RNN is trained as a delta network.

The DRNN is implemented on an Xilinx Zynq-7100 FPGA embedded on a Zynq MMP development board running at 125 MHz. Without weight compression and using 16-bit parameters, the DRNN achieved an effective throughput of 1.2 TOp/s and MAC computation efficiency of 623.96% with negligible numerical accuracy loss in a simple speech RNN. The power consumption of the Zynq MMP board with a programmed DRNN is 7.3 W, leading to a power efficiency of 164 GOp/s/W. The use of pruning and other optimizations allowed Han et. al [13] to achieve 2520 GOp/s, which is impressive considering they used external DRAM for weights. Chang et. al [4] proposed an implementation using BRAM for weights, but achieved 0.45 GOp/s/W. The power efficiency achieved by DRNN shows the utility of the delta network approach even without any other optimizations.

The main limitation of our work is the low scalability limited by the available number of BRAM blocks. Moreover, to provide sufficient bandwidth, space in BRAM is not fully utilized. In the future, we will address these limitations to target a lower power design with better scalability to process large multi-layered RNNs.

ACKNOWLEDGMENTS

This work was supported by Samsung Advanced Institute of Technology (SAIT), University of Zurich and ETH Zurich. We thank A. Rios-Navarro, R. Morales and A. Linares-Barranco from the University of Seville for creating the baseboard. We also thank A. Aimar,

---

[4]https://github.com/amanusk/s-tui

Table 7: Comparison to prior works and CPU, GPU

	This work	[13]	[10]	[4]	CPU	GPU
Hardware Model	XC7Z100	XCKU060	GSMD5	XC7Z045	i7-8700K	GTX 1080 Ti
Frequency [MHz]	125	200	150	142	-	-
Input Precision	Fixed16	Fixed16	Fixed16	Fixed16	Float32	Float32
Weight Precision	Fixed16	Fixed12	Fixed16	Fixed16	Float32	Float32
#DSP	768	1504	1036	-	-	-
#Multiplier	768	1536	-	-	-	-
#MAC	768	1024	-	-	-	-
Peak Throughput [G(FL)Op/s]	192	409.6	-	-	-	-
Effective Throughput [G(FL)Op/s]	1198	2520	315.85	1.04	18.78	123.34
MAC Comp. Efficiency	623.96%	615.23%	-	-	-	-
DSP Util. Efficiency	623.96%	418.88%	101.62%	-	-	-
Power [W]	7.3	41	25	2.3	35.6	95.9
Power Efficiency [G(FL)Ops/s/W]	164.11	61.46	12.63	0.45	0.53	1.29

E. Calabrese and other Sensors Group members for support on the FPGA implementation.

REFERENCES

[1] A. Aimar, H. Mostafa, E. Calabrese, A. R. Navarro, R. T. Morales, I-A. Lungu, M. B. Milde, F. Corradi, A. Linares-Barranco, S-C. Liu, and T. Delbrück. 2017. NullHop: A Flexible Convolutional Neural Network Accelerator Based on Sparse Representations of Feature Maps. *CoRR* abs/1706.01406 (2017). arXiv:1706.01406
[2] D. Amodei, R. Anubhai, E. Battenberg, C. Case, J. Casper, B. Catanzaro, J. Chen, M. Chrzanowski, A. Coates, G. Diamos, E. Elsen, J. Engel, L. Fan, C. Fougner, T. Han, A. Y. Hannun, B. Jun, P. LeGresley, L. Lin, S. Narang, A. Y. Ng, S. Ozair, R. Prenger, J. Raiman, S. Satheesh, D. Seetapun, S. Sengupta, Y. Wang, Z. Wang, C. Wang, B. Xiao, D. Yogatama, J. Zhan, and Z. Zhu. 2015. Deep Speech 2: End-to-End Speech Recognition in English and Mandarin. *CoRR* abs/1512.02595 (2015).
[3] N. Bell and M. Garland. 2008. *Efficient Sparse Matrix-Vector Multiplication on CUDA*. NVIDIA Technical Report NVR-2008-004. NVIDIA Corporation.
[4] A. X. M. Chang and E. Culurciello. 2017. Hardware accelerators for Recurrent Neural Networks on FPGA. In *2017 IEEE International Symposium on Circuits and Systems (ISCAS) (ISCAS '17)*.
[5] A. X. M. Chang, B. Martini, and E. Culurciello. 2015. Recurrent Neural Networks Hardware Implementation on FPGA. *CoRR* abs/1511.05552 (2015).
[6] K. Cho, B. v. Merrienboer, Ç. Gülçehre, F. Bougares, H. Schwenk, and Y. Bengio. 2014. Learning Phrase Representations using RNN Encoder-Decoder for Statistical Machine Translation. *CoRR* abs/1406.1078 (2014).
[7] R. Dorrance, F. Ren, and D. Marković. 2014. A Scalable Sparse Matrix-vector Multiplication Kernel for Energy-efficient Sparse-blas on FPGAs. In *Proceedings of the 2014 ACM/SIGDA International Symposium on Field-programmable Gate Arrays (FPGA '14)*. ACM, New York, NY, USA, 161–170.
[8] J. Fowers, K. Ovtcharov, K. Strauss, E. S. Chung, and G. Stitt. 2014. A High Memory Bandwidth FPGA Accelerator for Sparse Matrix-Vector Multiplication. In *Proceedings of the 2014 IEEE 22Nd International Symposium on Field-Programmable Custom Computing Machines (FCCM '14)*. IEEE Computer Society, Washington, DC, USA, 36–43.
[9] A. Graves, A. Mohamed, and G. E. Hinton. 2013. Speech Recognition with Deep Recurrent Neural Networks. *CoRR* abs/1303.5778 (2013).
[10] Y. Guan, H. Liang, N. Xu, W. Wang, S. Shi, X. Chen, G. Sun, W. Zhang, and J. Cong. 2017. FP-DNN: An Automated Framework for Mapping Deep Neural Networks onto FPGAs with RTL-HLS Hybrid Templates. In *2017 IEEE 25th Annual International Symposium on Field-Programmable Custom Computing Machines (FCCM)*. 152–159.
[11] Y. Guan, Z. Yuan, G. Sun, and J. Cong. 2017. FPGA-based accelerator for long short-term memory recurrent neural networks. In *2017 22nd Asia and South Pacific Design Automation Conference (ASP-DAC)*. 629–634.
[12] K. Guo, S. Han, S. Yao, Y. Wang, Y. Xie, and H. Yang. 2017. Software-Hardware Codesign for Efficient Neural Network Acceleration. *IEEE Micro* 37, 2 (Mar 2017), 18–25.
[13] S. Han, J. Kang, H. Mao, Y. Hu, X. Li, Y. Li, D. Xie, H. Luo, S. Yao, Y. Wang, H. Yang, and W. J. Dally. 2017. ESE: Efficient Speech Recognition Engine with Sparse LSTM on FPGA. In *Proceedings of the 2017 ACM/SIGDA International Symposium on Field-Programmable Gate Arrays (FPGA '17)*. ACM, New York, NY, USA, 75–84.

[14] S. Han, H. Mao, and W. J. Dally. 2015. Deep Compression: Compressing Deep Neural Network with Pruning, Trained Quantization and Huffman Coding. *CoRR* abs/1510.00149 (2015).
[15] S. Han, J. Pool, J. Tran, and W. J. Dally. 2015. Learning Both Weights and Connections for Efficient Neural Networks. In *Proceedings of the 28th International Conference on Neural Information Processing Systems (NIPS'15)*. MIT Press, Cambridge, MA, USA, 1135–1143.
[16] S. Hochreiter and J. Schmidhuber. 1997. Long Short-Term Memory. *Neural Comput.* 9, 8 (Nov. 1997), 1735–1780.
[17] M. Horowitz. 2014. 1.1 Computing's energy problem (and what we can do about it). In *2014 IEEE International Solid-State Circuits Conference Digest of Technical Papers (ISSCC)*. 10–14.
[18] I. Hubara, M. Courbariaux, D. Soudry, R. El-Yaniv, and Y. Bengio. 2016. Quantized Neural Networks: Training Neural Networks with Low Precision Weights and Activations. *CoRR* abs/1609.07061 (2016). arXiv:1609.07061
[19] D. Kadetotad, S. Arunachalam, C. Chakrabarti, and Jae sun Seo. 2016. Efficient memory compression in deep neural networks using coarse-grain sparsification for speech applications. In *2016 IEEE/ACM International Conference on Computer-Aided Design (ICCAD)*. 1–8.
[20] S. Kapur, A. K. Mishra, and D. Marr. 2017. Low Precision RNNs: Quantizing RNNs Without Losing Accuracy. *CoRR* abs/1710.07706 (2017). arXiv:1710.07706
[21] M. Lee, K. Hwang, J. Park, S. Choi, S. Shin, and W. Sung. 2016. FPGA-Based Low-Power Speech Recognition with Recurrent Neural Networks. *CoRR* abs/1610.00552 (2016).
[22] I. McGraw, R. Prabhavalkar, R. Alvarez, M. G. Arenas, K. Rao, D. Rybach, O. Alsharif, H. Sak, A. Gruenstein, F. Beaufays, and C. Parada. 2016. Personalized speech recognition on mobile devices. In *2016 IEEE International Conference on Acoustics, Speech and Signal Processing (ICASSP)*. 5955–5959.
[23] T. Mikolov, M. Karafiát, L. Burget, J. Cernocký, and S. Khudanpur. 2010. Recurrent neural network based language model.. In *Interspeech*, Vol. 2. 3.
[24] A. H. Namin, K. Leboeuf, R. Muscedere, H. Wu, and M. Ahmadi. 2009. Efficient hardware implementation of the hyperbolic tangent sigmoid function. In *2009 IEEE International Symposium on Circuits and Systems*. 2117–2120.
[25] D. Neil, J. H. Lee, T. Delbruck, and S-C. Liu. 2017. Delta Networks for Optimized Recurrent Network Computation. In *Proceedings of the 34th International Conference on Machine Learning (Proceedings of Machine Learning Research)*, Doina Precup and Yee Whye Teh (Eds.), Vol. 70. PMLR, International Convention Centre, Sydney, Australia, 2584–2593.
[26] E. Nurvitadhi, J. Sim, D. Sheffield, A. Mishra, S. Krishnan, and D. Marr. 2016. Accelerating recurrent neural networks in analytics servers: Comparison of FPGA, CPU, GPU, and ASIC. In *2016 26th International Conference on Field Programmable Logic and Applications (FPL)*. 1–4.
[27] J. Schmidhuber. 2014. Deep Learning in Neural Networks: An Overview. *CoRR* abs/1404.7828 (2014).
[28] Xilinx. 2017. *Zynq-7000 All Programmable SoC Data Sheet: Overview*. https://www.xilinx.com/support/documentation/data_sheets/ds190-Zynq-7000-Overview.pdf
[29] L. Zhuo and V. K. Prasanna. 2005. Sparse Matrix-Vector Multiplication on FPGAs. In *Proceedings of the 2005 ACM/SIGDA 13th International Symposium on Field-programmable Gate Arrays (FPGA '05)*. ACM, New York, NY, USA, 63–74.

A Lightweight YOLOv2: A Binarized
CNN with A Parallel Support Vector Regression for an FPGA

Hiroki Nakahara
Tokyo Institute of Technology
nakahara@ict.e.titech.ac.jp

Haruyoshi Yonekawa
Tokyo Institute of Technology
yonekawa@ict.e.titech.ac.jp

Tomoya Fujii
Tokyo Institute of Technology
t-fujii@ict.e.titech.ac.jp

Shimpei Sato
Tokyo Institute of Technology
satos@ict.e.titech.ac.jp

ABSTRACT

A frame object detection problem consists of two problems: one is a regression problem to spatially separated bounding boxes, the second is the associated classification of the objects within realtime frame rate. It is widely used in the embedded systems, such as robotics, autonomous driving, security, and drones - all of which require high-performance and low-power consumption. This paper implements the YOLO (You only look once) object detector on an FPGA, which is faster and has higher accuracy. It is based on the convolutional deep neural network (CNN), and it is a dominant part both the performance and the area. However, the object detector based on the CNN consists of a bounding box prediction (regression) and a class estimation (classification). Thus, the conventional all binarized CNN fails to recognize in most cases. In the paper, we propose a lightweight YOLOv2, which consists of the binarized CNN for feature extraction and the parallel support vector regression (SVR) for both classification and localization. To our knowledge, this is the first time binarized CNN's have been successfully used in object detection. We implement a pipelined based architecture for the lightweight YOLOv2 on the Xilinx Inc. zcu102 board, which has the Xilinx Inc. Zynq Ultrascale+ MPSoC. The implemented object detector archived 40.81 frames per second (FPS). Compared with the ARM Cortex-A57, it was 177.4 times faster, it dissipated 1.1 times more power, and its performance per power efficiency was 158.9 times better. Also, compared with the nVidia Pascall embedded GPU, it was 27.5 times faster, it dissipated 1.5 times lower power, and its performance per power efficiency was 42.9 times better. Thus, our method is suitable for the frame object detector for an embedded vision system.

CCS CONCEPTS

• **Hardware → Hardware accelerators**; **Reconfigurable logic applications**;

KEYWORDS

Convolutional Deep Neural Network; Object Detection; Binarized Deep Neural Network

ACM Reference Format:
Hiroki Nakahara, Haruyoshi Yonekawa, Tomoya Fujii, and Shimpei Sato. 2018. A Lightweight YOLOv2: A Binarized CNN with A Parallel Support Vector Regression for an FPGA. In *FPGA '18: 2018 ACM/SIGDA International Symposium on Field-Programmable Gate Arrays, February 25–27, 2018, Monterey, CA, USA*. ACM, New York, NY, USA, 10 pages. https://doi.org/10.1145/3174243.3174266

1 INTRODUCTION

1.1 Frame Object Detection

An object detection problem consists of two problems: one is a regression problem to spatially separated bounding boxes and associated class probabilities as shown in Fig. 1. A frame object detection is used in an embedded vision systems, such as a robot, an automobile, a security camera, and a drone. These applications require high-performance computation and low-power consumption by an inexpensive device. Current frame object detection systems re-purpose classifiers to perform detection. To detect an object, these systems take a classifier for that object and evaluate it at various locations and scales in a test image.

1.2 Related Work

Before the advent of convolutional neural networks (CNNs), state of the art for those two approaches was Deformable Part Model (DPM) [9] and Selective Search[1]. Recently, the dramatic improvement of the R-CNN [11] has been proposed. It combines selective search region proposals and a CNN, however, it requires the classification of thousands of image crops, which is expensive and time-consuming. The SPPnet [13] speeds up the original R-CNN approach significantly by introducing a spatial pyramid pooling layer that is more robust to region size and scale, and it allows the classification layers. The Fast R-CNN [10] extends the SPPnet so that it can fine-tune all layers end-to-end by minimizing a loss for both confidence and bounding box regression, which

Figure 1: Object detection problem.

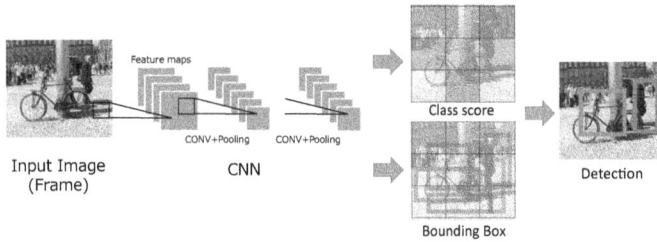

Figure 2: You Only Look Once (YOLO) algorithm.

Table 1: Comparison of frame object detectors using PASCAL VOC2007 dataset [20].

Detection Algorithms	Accuracy (mAP)	Speed (FPS)
Fast R-CNN	70.0	0.5
Faster R-CNN w/ VGG-16 [26]	73.2	7
Faster R-CNN w/ ResNet [12]	76.4	5
YOLOv1	63.4	45
SSD300	74.3	46
YOLOv2 288 × 288	69.0	**91**
YOLOv2 416 × 416	**76.8**	67

was first introduced in Multi-Box [8] for learning objectness. The second set of approaches improve the quality of proposal generation using CNNs. In the most recent works [8, 27], the Selective Search region proposals, which are based on low-level image features, are replaced by proposals generated directly from a separate CNN. The Faster R-CNN [23] replaces selective search proposals by ones learned from a region proposal network (RPN), and introduces a method to integrate the RPN with Fast R-CNN. The SSD [15] is very similar to the RPN in the Faster R-CNN, which uses a fixed set of boxes for prediction. Then, it simultaneously produces a score for each object category in each box.

1.3 YOLO version 2

As shown in Fig. 2, the YOLO (You Only Look Once) [14] uses a single CNN, that simultaneously predicts multiple bounding boxes and class probabilities for those boxes. It trains on full images and directly optimizes detection performance. This unified model has several benefits compared

with the conventional object detectors. Most detection frameworks rely on the VGG-16 CNN as the base feature extractor, which requires 30.69 billion floating point operations for a single pass over a single image at 224 × 224 size. The YOLO version 2 (YOLOv2) uses a new classification model (darknet-19) to be used as the base feature extractor. Similar to the VGG models, it uses mostly a 3 × 3 convolutional operation and applies a pooling operation. Following the previous work on Network-in-network, it uses global average pooling to make predictions as well as 1 × 1 convolutional operation. Also, they used a batch normalization to stabilize training, speed up convergence, and regularize the model. Table 1 compares the YOLOv2 with the other object detection systems. Although the YOLOv2 achieved the real time frame per second (FPS), it was realized by the NVidia Corp. GTX Titan X GPU, which consumes much power. Thus, it cannot be realized on the embedded vision system requiring a limited power source. Since these algorithms are based on the CNN, we focus on the efficient realization one on the FPGA.

2 LIGHTWEIGHT YOLOV2 FOR AN FPGA

2.1 Binarized CNN

Recent work by Microsoft showed that the FPGA based deep learning leads us the performance per power efficiency. Furthermore, the low-precision CNN has been shown [5, 22, 30] which uses only one- or two- bit quantization strategy to reduce the hardware size with considerable accuracy. It is suitable for the FPGA implementation, since it can realize such a low-precision circuit, while the GPU cannot. Recently, a flexible heterogeneous streaming binarized architecture [28], and a variable-width line buffer implementation [29] have been reported. The evaluation results [19] by Intel reported that the binarized CNN could deliver orders of magnitude improvements in performance and performance/watt over well-optimized software on the CPU and the GPU. Although the FPGA is less efficient than the ASIC, the FPGA-ASIC gap may be reduced for designs that heavily utilize hard blocks. Additionally, more attractive results including a ternarized CNN [3], a high-performance parallel realization [16], and a low-latency implementation [25] have been proposed. Hence, FPGA offers an attractive solution, which delivers superior efficiency improvements over software, without having to lock into a fixed ASIC solution.

2.2 Known Problem of Object Detection

From previous works, a binarization of both weights and inputs is suitable for a hardware realization. Also, it has been found that classification does not degrade recognition accuracy with batch normalization. Fig. 3 shows a typical convolutional deep neural network (CNN) for an image classification. Note that, bottom scatter diagrams are illustrated by principal component analysis (PCA) and it denotes the distribution of the output of each layer. It shows that a typical

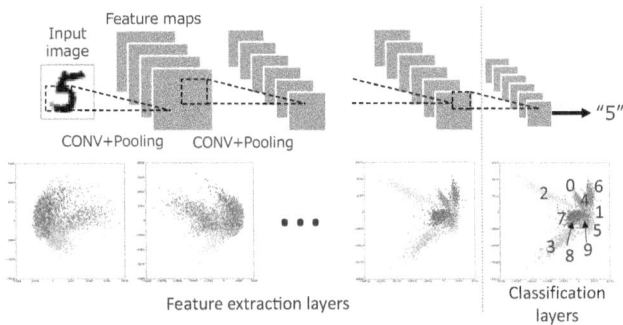

Figure 3: Typical convolutional deep neural network (CNN) for image classification. Note that, bottom scatter diagrams are illustrated by principal component analysis (PCA) and it denotes the distribution of the output of each layer. It shows that a typical CNN consists of a feature extraction layer and a classification layer.

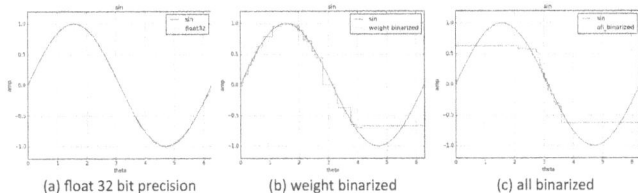

(a) float 32 bit precision   (b) weight binarized   (c) all binarized

Figure 4: Comparison of regressions for different precision.

CNN consists of a feature extraction layer and a classification layer. Even if we use a binarized convolutional layer, it can classifies a given image with sufficient layers.

However, the object detection task requires accurate inference (in other words, regression) of localization. We did a simple experiment on whether binarized neural network can regress accurately with an elementary function $sin\ (x)$. The result of regression using a fully connected three-layer neural network is shown in Fig. 4. In the experiment, we used *LeakyReLU* activation function used in YOLOv2, optimizer was the SGD, and trained 1,000 epochs. From Fig. 4, a float32 bit precision neural network (NN) can regress almost exactly, however, as for the binarized NNs (weight binarized (b) and all binarized (c)), the regression errors were large. Therefore, the existing low precision NN cannot be applied to the current regression task including the localization one.

To realize localization, it is a realistic method to use a mixed-precision CNN which has the former feature extraction layers using all binarized precision and the latter all float32 bit precision ones. However, even if a part of it is realized with binarized precision, we only meet again the wall [21], that is, the sum of products computation and the weight memory size.

2.3 Proposed Lightweight YOLOv2

We propose to use other machine learning regression into the localization layer where highly accurate regression is required. In this paper, the support vector regression (SVR), which has excellent regression performance, is used in parallel for both the localization and the classification. Another reason for choosing SVR is that it corresponds to on-line (sequential) training corresponding to a large amount of training data. In the paper, we used around 10,000 images (Pascal VOC 2007 data set) for the experiment, which can be trained by batch learning, however, we can keep up with even if it needs to train many images in the future.

The existing YOLOv2 adopts the FCN (fully convolutional network) structure, and the convolution operation is executed in all layers. From the profile analysis [21], since the product of sum operation is a bottleneck in the convolutional layer, and the weight requires a large size of memory. Compared with the convolutional operation, the SVR has a small amount of computation and a small size of a weight, thus it can be stored into the FPGA. In the paper, we compare the FCN based existing YOLOv2 with proposed Lightweight one and show that the proposed method is practical. In addition, the paper clarifies training method and its recognition accuracy.

2.4 Contributions of the Paper

1. We showed that the object detector based on the CNN, which consists of a bounding box prediction (regression) and a class estimation (classification). Thus, the conventional all binarized CNN fails to recognize in most cases. We opened the new problem to this research area, and proposed a lightweight YOLOv2 which consists of the conventional binarized CNN with parallel SVRs. We showed the architecture for such a mixed low precision CNN and SVRs on the FPGA.

2. We demonstrate a performance-per-power efficient object detector on an FPGA. We implemented a proposed lightweight YOLOv2 on the Xilinx Inc. zcu102 Zynq Ultra Scale+ MPSOC evaluation board. We compared with the embedded CPU and the embedded GPU with respect to the YOLOv2 (batch size was 1). Compared with the ARM Cortex-A57, it was 177.4 times faster, it dissipated 1.1 times lower power, and its performance per power efficiency was 158.9 times better. Also, compared with the Pascal embedded GPU, it was 27.5 times faster, it dissipated 1.5 times lower power, and its performance per power efficiency was 42.9 times better.

3 YOLOV2

In this section, first, we introduce the You Only Look Once version 2 (YOLOv2) algorithm, which is a based on one-shot object detector using the CNN. In the paper, we estimated that the pre-trained binarized CNN for the YOLOv2 has already given, then, considering the inference on the FPGA.

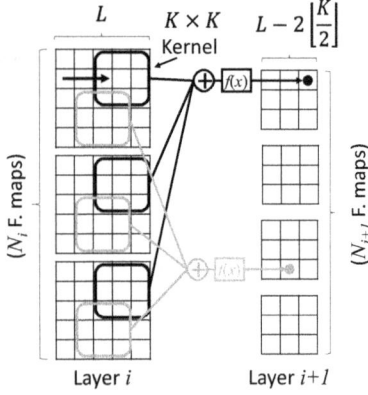

Figure 5: 2D convolutional operation.

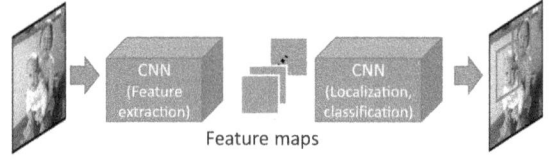

Figure 6: Conventional YOLOv2 based on an FCN structure.

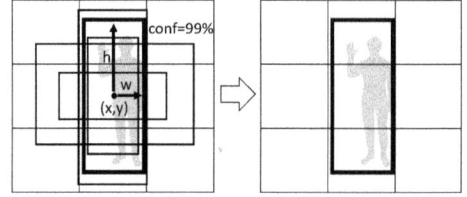

Figure 7: Bounding box.

We unify the separate components of object detection into a single neural network. It uses features from the entire image to predict each bounding box. It also predicts all bounding boxes for an image simultaneously. The YOLO design enables end-to-end training and real-time speeds while maintaining high average precision.

3.1 Convolutional Deep Neural Network (CNN)

Let n be a bit precision, $X = (x_0, x_1, \ldots, x_n)$ be the input, $Y = (y_0, y_1, \ldots, y_n)$ be the internal variable, $W = (w_0, w_1, \ldots, w_n)$ be the weight, f_{act} be the activation function, and $Z = (z_0, z_1, \ldots, z_n)$ be the output. Note that, in this paper, a capital letter denotes an integer, while a small letter denotes a binary value. The following expression shows an operation for **an artificial neuron (AN)**:

$$Y = \sum_{i=0}^{n} W_i X_i, \qquad (1)$$
$$Z = f_{act}(Y),$$

where X_0 is a constant one and W_0 denotes **a bias** which corrects the deviation of the given data. Typically, the activation function is realized by a sigmoid, a tanh, a ReLU [18], and so on. **A deep neural network (DNN)** consists of multiple of ANs. **A convolutional deep neural network (CNN)** has multiple **layers**. The typical layer consists of **a 2D convolutional layer, a pooling layer**, and **a classification layer**. Each layer consists of multiple **feature maps**. To recognize the input image, first, the feature map reacts corresponding subdivided training data by 2D convolutional layers with pooling layers. Then, the classifier selects the appropriate reactions from feature maps. Usually, the classifier is realized by the fully connected neural network. In this paper, for layer i, K_i denotes the kernel size, N_i denotes the number of feature maps, and L_i denotes the feature map size. Fig. 5 shows the 2D convolution operation. It computes the output by shifting a $K \times K$ size **kernel**, and applies the MAC operation similarly to the AN. For (x, y) at the output

feature map value $i + 1$, the MAC (multiply-accumulation) operation is performed as follows:

$$Y_{i+1,x,y} = \sum_{k=0}^{N_i-1}(\sum_{m=0}^{K-1}\sum_{n=0}^{K-1} X_{k,x+m,y+n}W_{k,m,n}) \quad (2)$$
$$Z_{i+1,x,y} = f_{act}(Y_{i+1,x,y}).$$

In the 2D convolutional operation, Z is mapped to (x, y) at the output feature map $i + 1$. In the fully connected layer, $L_i = 1$ and $K_i = 1$. By inserting the non-linear and low-imaging operations into the convolution layers, we can reduce the number of computations in the convolution layers, while we can obtain the movement invariance. We call this **a pooling operation**, which can be realized by a simple circuit. In this paper, we implement the max-pooling operation. Its operation can be realized by a comparator for selecting the maximum value in the kernel. It is much smaller than the 2D convolution operation circuit.

3.2 YOLOv2 Overview

Fig 6 shows an overview of the YOLOv2 algorithm. It consists of the feature extraction layers and the localization and classification layers, and based on a fully convolution network (FCN) structure. It divides the input image into a $S \times S$ grid. If the center of an object falls into a grid cell, that grid cell is responsible for the object detection. Each grid cell predicts bounding boxes and confidence scores for those boxes. These confidence scores reflect how confident the model is that the box contains an object and also how accurate it thinks the box is that it predicts. Formally, it defines confidence as $Pr(Object) * IOU_{pred}^{truth}$. If no object exists in that cell, the confidence scores should be zero. Otherwise, its confidence score to equal the intersection over union (IOU) between the predicted box and the ground truth.

Each bounding box consists of 5 predictions: x, y, w, h, and confidence as shown in Fig. 7. The (x, y) coordinates

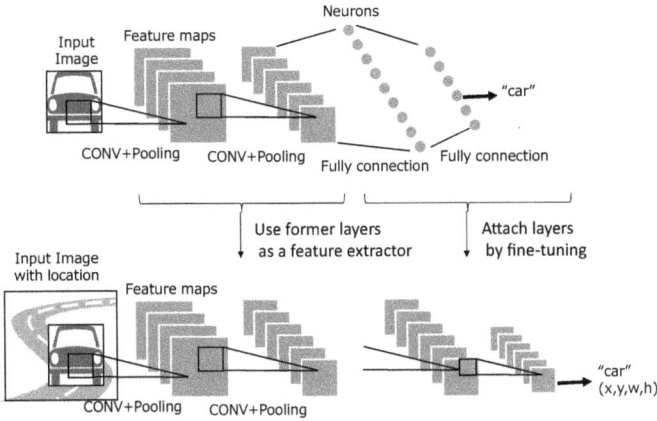

Figure 8: Two steps training for the YOLOv2.

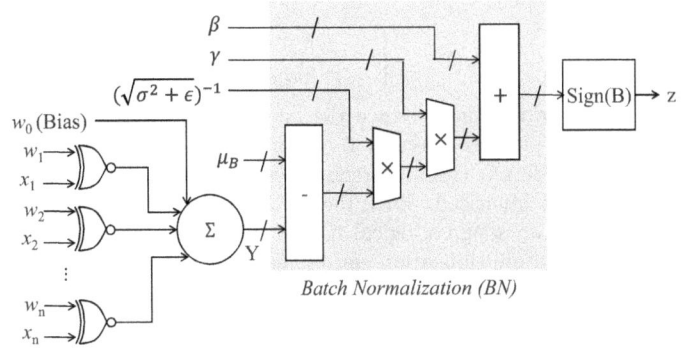

Figure 9: Binarized AN with batch normalization (BN).

represent the center of the box relative to the bounds of the grid cell. The width and height are predicted relative to the whole image. Finally, the confidence prediction represents the IOU between the predicted box and any ground truth box. Each grid cell also predicts C conditional class probabilities, $Pr(Class_i \mid Object)$. These probabilities are conditioned on the grid cell containing an object. It only predicts one set of class probabilities per a grid cell, regardless of the number of boxes B. At inference time we multiply the conditional class probabilities and the individual box confidence predictions shown in the followings:

$$Pr(Class \mid Object) * Pr(Object) * IOU_{pred}^{truth}$$
$$= Pr(Class_i) * IOU_{pred}^{truth}, \qquad (3)$$

which gives us class-specific confidence scores for each box. These scores encode both the probability of that class appearing in the box and how well the predicted box fits the object. For evaluating YOLO on PASCAL VOC2007 [20], we use $S = 7$, $B = 2$. PASCAL VOC2007 has 20 labelled classes so $C = 20$. Our final prediction is a $7 \times 7 \times 30$ tensor.

Most object detection algorithms rely on VGG16 as the base feature extractor. In the YOLOv2, it is based on the darknet-19, which is a combination of the VGG-16 CNN and the Network-in-network one. It uses 3×3 convolution layer to extract the feature, while uses 1×1 convolution to compress the feature map. Also, to stabilize training, speed up convergence, and regularize model, it uses the batch normalization for each output of the convolution layer. Table 2 compares the parameter size for the original (8bit fixed-point precision) YOLOv2 with that for the binarized one. The YOLOv2 has 22 convolutional layers and 6 max pooling layers.

As shown in Fig. 8, for the training of the YOLOv2, it takes two steps to finish the training from the given images. First, it performs the training for classification using the base feature extractor. In our design, we used the original darknet-19. Then, it performs the fine-tuning for the detection by using pre-trained feature extractor. In this step, we

modify the darknet-19 by removing the last convolutional layer, then attached on four convolutional layers. In the training, we used a similar data augmentation including a random crop, color shifting, etc.

4 LIGHTWEIGHT YOLOV2

In the object detection task including YOLOv2, the class and localization of the object are simultaneously detected. In Introduction, the localization task is a regression problem, and it cannot be realized by the binarized CNN since the error increases in binarization. In the paper, a binarized CNN is used for object feature detection, and parallel support vector regression (SVR) is used for localization and classification. First, we introduce a binary CNN and an SVR, and the proposed Lightweight YOLOv2 which combines these methods. We also show the training method of the Lightweight YOLOv2.

4.1 Binarized CNN

As shown in Fig. 5, the 2D convolutional operation consisting of the AN operation and the memory access for the feature maps. In the 2D convolutional operation, the MAC operation is a dominant of computation time. To focus on the efficient realization of the MAC operation, in this part, we discuss the binarization of the AN operation.

As shown in Exprs (1) and (2), the 2D convolutional operation is an extension of the AN operation. In this section, to briefly explain, we introduce the binarization of the AN. Recently, Courbariaux et al. proposed **the binarized CNN** [5], which restricts the weights and inputs to only -1 and 1. The binarized AN operation performs the following expression:

$$Y = \sum_{i=0}^{n} w_i x_i, \qquad (4)$$
$$z = f_{sgn}(Y),$$

where $f_{sgn}(Y)$ denotes the signed activation function as follows:

$$f_{sgn}(Y) = \begin{cases} 1 & (if \ Y \geq 0) \\ -1 & (otherwise) \end{cases}$$

In the first layer, since the input is the RGB color images, the bit precision for the input is 8 bits. Note that, the binarized AN, the bit precision of internal variable would not be a binarized. Since the FPGA cannot directly represent -1, we assign a logical zero to -1. In this case, since the binarized multiplication can be realized by an XNOR gate, the hardware area for the integer multiplier is drastically reduced. Also, the other advantage is that the binarized weight can reduce the memory bandwidth than the integer one. For two reasons, although the binarized CNN is area and performance efficient one, it requires the additional hardware for batch normalization, which is a mathematical trick to retain the classification accuracy.

4.2 Batch Normalization

Typically, to accelerate training time and convergence, a set of training data (mini-batch) is back-propagated and it updates weights at a time. It is called by a mini-batch training. In this case, since the impact on the difference in the distribution of data for each batch (internal covariate shift), the convergence of the training tends to be slow, and the trainer must carefully determine the initial value of the parameters. These problems are solved by **batch normalization (BN)** [24] which corrects the difference in the distribution by a shift and a scaling operation. At the training, the BN finds parameters γ and β to regularize the variance to 1 and the average to 0 for each mini-batch. The normalized output B_i by the BN algorithm is calculated as follows:

$$\begin{aligned} \hat{Y}_i &= \frac{Y_i - \mu}{\sqrt{\sigma_B^2 + \epsilon}} \\ B_i &= \gamma \hat{Y}_i + \beta, \end{aligned} \tag{5}$$

where Y_i is an i-th input of the mini-batch, μ is a mean value of the mini-batch, σ_B^2 is a variance of the mini-batch, and ϵ is a hyperparameter. Expr. (5) performs the normalization for each mini-batch. Since both γ and β have been already trained during classification, the AN with BN just reads them from the off-chip memory. It means that the AN with BN requires additional cost for the multiplier and the adder, while the memory access for parameters. Fig. 9 shows the binarized AN with BN.

Although the BN is an essential technique for the binarized CNN, it requires additional area for the multiplier and the adder, and the memory access for parameters. The previous work showed that the BN is converted into the equivalent integer value. In the paper, we merge the bias and the equivalent value into a single value [28].

4.3 Support Vector Regression

A support vector machine (SVM) [4] is a supervised learning model that analyzes data used for classification and regression analysis. For a given training data having each

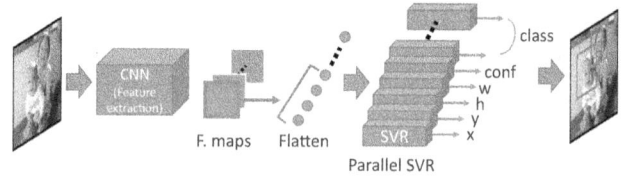

Figure 10: Proposed lightweight YOLOv2.

marked as belonging to one or the other of two categories, an SVM training algorithm builds a model that assigns new examples to one category or the other. It makes a non-probabilistic binary linear classifier. An SVM model is a representation of the examples as points in space, hence the examples of the separate categories are divided by a clear gap that is as wide as possible. New examples are then mapped into that same space and predicted to belong to a category based on which side of the gap they fall. In addition to performing linear classification, SVMs can efficiently perform a non-linear classification using what is called the kernel trick, implicitly mapping their inputs into high-dimensional feature spaces.

A regression version of SVM was proposed in 1996 [7], which is called support vector regression (SVR). The model produced by support vector classification depends only on a subset of the training data, since the cost function for building the model does not care about training points that lie beyond the margin. Analogously, the model produced by SVR depends only on a subset of the training data, since the cost function for building the model ignores any training data close to the model prediction. The regression for n-tuple input is performed by the following expression:

$$y = \sum_{i=1}^{n} \langle w, x_i \rangle + b, \tag{6}$$

where w is a weight, x_i is an i-th input, and b is a bias. The regression of the SVR is similarly to the perception computation. On the other hand, training the original SVR minimizes a cost function $C(w)$ as follows:

$$C(w) = \frac{1}{2} \|w\|^2,$$

with considering following conditions:

$$\begin{cases} y_i - \langle w, x_i \rangle - b \leq \varepsilon \\ \langle w, x_i \rangle + b - y_i \leq \varepsilon \end{cases}$$

where x_i is a training sample with target value y_i. The inner product plus intercept $\langle w, x_i \rangle + b$ is the prediction for that sample, and ε is a hyperparameter that serves as a threshold. All predictions have to be within an ε range of the true predictions. Slack variables are usually added into the above to allow for errors and to allow approximation in the case the above problem is infeasible.

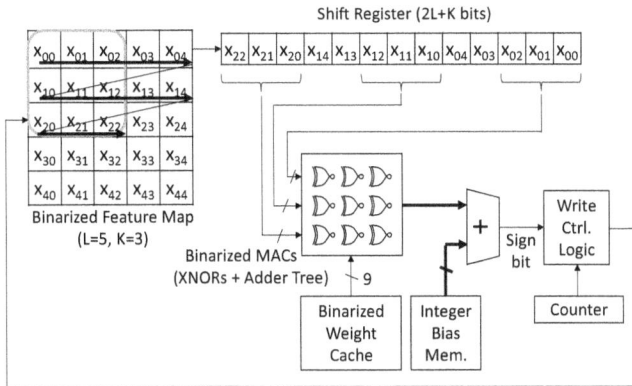

Figure 11: Streaming binarized 2D convolutional circuit.

4.4 Lightweight YOLOv2

Fig. 10 shows a proposed lightweight YOLOv2. The proposed one uses a binarized CNN for a feature extraction and a parallel SVR for both a localization and a classification. Compared with the original YOLOv2, since the binarized CNN is used, its memory size and amount of computation can be reduced and features can be extracted at high speed by a binary multiply-add operation. The original YOLOv2 adopts the FCN structure, and localization and classification are also performed in the convolution layer. From the profile analysis [21], in the FPGA realization, it meets the problem of the memory size and the computation intensive. Since the operation used in the parallel SVR is an equivalent to a single layer perception, it is possible to suppress the amount of computation. Also, the weight is also relatively lightweight and can be stored in an on-chip memory on the FPGA. Therefore, it has advantages for power and speed than an off-chip memory implementation.

Next, we introduce the training method. Similarly to the original YOLOv2 training, first, it is performed only on the classification of the object to be recognized on the feature extraction CNN. To do this, we attached the fully connection layer to the feature extraction CNN. After finished the feature extraction training, we remove the latter fully connection layer, then attach the parallel SVR to the binarized CNN for feature extraction. The output of the feature extraction CNN is set as new training data of the parallel SVR, then the parallel SVR is trained. When we use a large amount of training data, we can use an on-line (sequential) training SVR [17], which supports to use kernel tricks to increase the recognition accuracy. Also, to reduce the SVR model size, we used a discard technique [6]. Since we assume that the localization of the object can be estimated by a relatively simple linear regression, we decided to use the linear kernel in the paper.

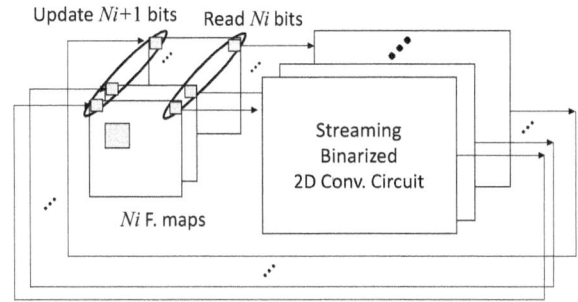

Figure 12: Shared streaming binary 2D convolutional circuit.

5 FPGA IMPLEMENTATION

5.1 Shared XNOR-MAC Circuit with Streaming Operation

Although we used the binarized MAC operation instead of the floating-point one, it consumes much hardware to realize the fully parallel XNOR-MAC operation. Since the typical CNN has the different number of feature maps in the layer, a heterogeneous streaming architecture requires many LUTs for a large size of XNOR operations.

In the paper, to realize the high-performance with less hardware, we proposed a shared XNOR-MAC circuit supporting a streaming operation as shown in Fig. 11. The architecture is a binarized version of the pipelined 2D convolvers [2]. To reduce the memory access, we use the shift register to make a streaming data flow from the memory for the feature map. Also, it shares the different size of XNOR-MAC circuit into a single bitwise XNOR circuit followed by adder-trees, bias adder, and a write controller. The circuit reads the corresponding inputs from the shift register, then it applies to the bitwise binarized MAC operation. Next, it adds the pre-computed bias, which is obtained by both the pre-trained bias and the batch normalization value. Since the kernel crosses the boundary of the feature map, we attach the write control logic to the output of the circuit.

To further increase the performance, we propose the shared streaming binary 2D convolutional circuit shown in Fig. 12. To flexibility access to all feature maps, multiple on-chip BRAMs are used to realize multi-port with wide band memory access speed. In contrast, to read the weight, we use the off-chip memories, since the convolutional operation reads it at intervals for each feature map. Since we use the binarized CNN, the memory size is drastically reduced compared with non-binarized one. Since our CNN eliminates internal FC layers, the weight memories also eliminated.

5.2 Parallel SVRs

Fig. 13 shows the parallel SVR. The feature map of the binarized CNN for the feature extraction is stored into the binarized feature map memory. The parallel SVR sequentially finds the regressed parameters in each grid. It generates the localization parameters (x, y, h, w), its confidence ($conf$),

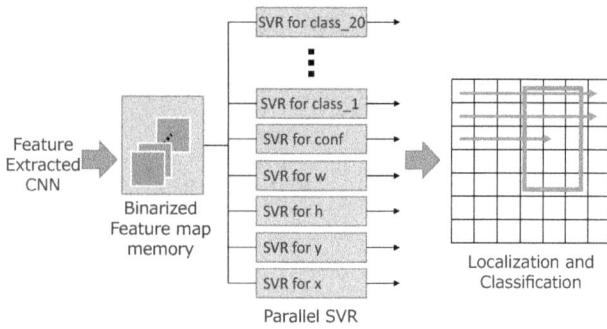

Figure 13: Parallel SVR for a localization and a classification.

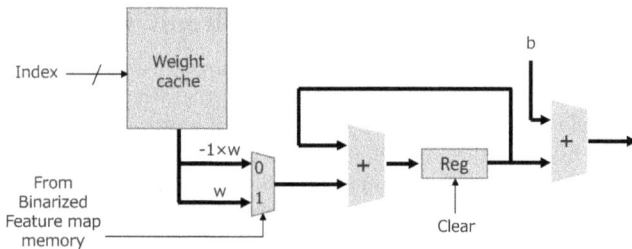

Figure 15: Overall architecture.

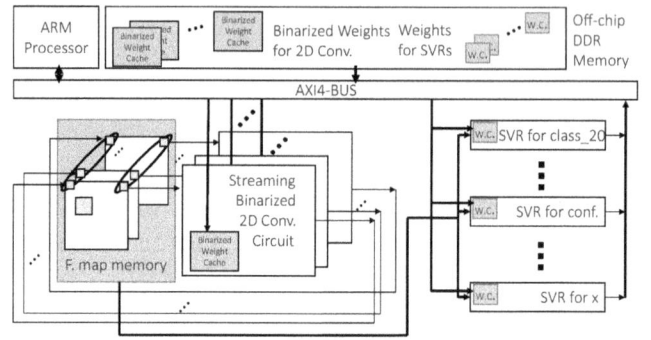

Figure 14: Circuit for an SVR.

This architecture sequential evaluates each layer. As shown in Fig. 12, it uses the shift registers and buffers to access indices for the corresponding kernel. In our implementation, the XNOR gates are used in the binarized convolution, while as shown in Fig. 14, it uses DSP48 blocks to compute a parallel SVRs. Thus, our architecture efficiently uses of the BRAMs and DSP blocks while it saves additional memory and keeps the performance. The result is sent to the host ARM processor, then a post-processing is done since it is a light processing. Also, our implementation achieves higher computation speed than conventional one, since it performs a convolutional operation for feature maps at a time.

6   EXPERIMENTAL RESULTS

6.1   Implementation Results

We implemented the proposed lightweight YOLOv2 on the Xilinx Inc. Zynq UltraScale+ MPSoC zcu102 evaluation board, which has the Xilinx Zynq UltraScale+ MPSoC FPGA (ZU9EG, 274,080 LUTs, 548,160 FFs, 1,824 18Kb BRAMs, 2,520 DSP48Es). We used the Xilinx Inc. SDSoC 2017.4 with timing constraint 299.97 MHz. Our implementation used 135,381 LUTs, 370,299 FFs, 1,706 18Kb BRAMs, and 377 DSP48Es. Table 3 shows a detail of the resource consumption. Also, it satisfied the timing constraint for real-time applications. Since our architecture computed an image with 24.5 msec, the number of frames per second (FPS) was 40.81. We measured the dynamic board power consumption: It was 4.5 Watt. Thus, the performance per power efficiency was 9.06 (FPS/W).

6.2   Comparison of Model Size

We considered that the input image size is 224× 224, and we trained our designed YOLOv2 by using the Pascal VOC dataset [1]. Table 2 compares the proposed lightweight YOLOv2 with the conventional fixed-point precision one. In the paper, we propose the CNN using the binarized weight for feature extraction, while using the parallel SVR for the regression. Compared with the fixed-point precision CNN, the proposed one requires less memory size. To concern the scenario, we

and each class probability ($class_i$) of the detected object. Since we replicate the YOLOv2, we set the number of classes to 20. Since two bounding boxes have been trained for a grid, 50 SVRs are operated in parallel. For an input image, since it is divided into 7×7 grids, the parallel SVR is sequentially executed by 49 times. It uses weights and intermediate values in 32-bit floating point precision, which are stored in the weight cache. Fig. 14 shows the configuration of each SVR. It sequentially reads the trained weights and sequentially computes the SVR. Since the input value is the binarized value of the feature maps of the binarized CNN, it can be realized by adding of weights, thus a multiplication circuit is unnecessary. Therefore, it can be realized with small size hardware. After finished the completion of all inputs, it reads the bias (b) value and adds it.

5.3   Overall Architecture

Fig. 15 shows the overall architecture for the proposed YOLOv2. Our architecture has weight caches. The binarized one is used for the 2D convolutional binarized neural network, while the weight cache is used for the SVRs. The off-chip DDR memory stores all weights. Since the load operations for the weight is not a dominant for the CNN and the SVR computations, the proposed architecture achieves a high performance object detector. Note that, the temporary data (F. map memory) is frequently loaded, we realize it by using the on-chip memory on the FPGA.

---

[1]Original paper evaluates the input image from 288× 288 to 544× 544.

Table 2: Parameters for the original (Floating precision) CNN and the binarized CNN of the YOLOv2.

Layer	# In. Fmaps	Kernel Size	# Out. F Size	Conventional Fixed Point FCN Type	Mem	Proposed BinCNN+SVRs Type	Mem
(Feature Extraction)							
Conv1	3	3×3	224×224	Int	13.8K	Int	13.8K
Max Pool	64	1×1	112×112				
Conv2	64	3×3	112×112	Int	294K	Bin	36.8K
Max Pool	128	1×1	56×56				
Conv3	128	3×3	56×56	Int	589K	Bin	73.7K
Conv4	64	3×3	56×56	Int	65.6K	Bin	8K
Conv5	128	3×3	56×56	Int	589K	Bin	73.7K
Max Pool	256	1×1	28×28				
Conv6	256	3×3	28×28	Int	2.3M	Bin	294K
Conv7	128	3×3	28×28	Int	262K	Bin	32.7K
Conv8	256	3×3	28×28	Int	2.3M	Bin	294K
Max Pool	512	1×1	14×14				
Conv9	512	3×3	14×14	Int	9.4M	Bin	1.1M
Conv10	256	3×3	14×14	Int	1.0M	Bin	131K
Conv11	512	3×3	14×14	Int	9.4M	Bin	1.1M
Conv12	256	3×3	14×14	Int	1.0M	Bin	131K
Conv13	512	3×3	14×14	Int	9.4M	Bin	1.1M
Max Pool	1024	1×1	7×7				
Conv14	1024	3×3	7×7	Int	37.7M	Bin	4.7M
Conv15	512	3×3	7×7	Int	4.1M	Bin	524K
Conv16	1024	3×3	7×7	Int	37.7M	Bin	4.7M
Conv17	512	3×3	7×7	Int	4.1M	Bin	524K
Conv18	1024	3×3	7×7	Int	37.7M	Bin	4.7M
Max Pool	1024	1×1	7×7	Int			
(Localization+Classification)							
Conv19	1024	3×3	512	Int	37.7M	float	20.0M
Conv20	512	3×3	512	Int	18.8M		
Conv21	512	3×3	512	Int	18.8M		
Conv22	512	3×3	1470	Int	45.1M		
(Total)					279M		39.5M
Accuracy (mAP)					69.1		67.6

Table 3: Details of resource consumptions for a binary 2D-convolution, a binary CNN, and a parallel SVRs.

Module	# LUTs	# FFs	# 18Kb BRAMs	# DSPs
Binary CNN	108,138	358,868	1680	135
(2D bin. conv)	(103,924)	(313,839)	(0)	(0)
Parallel SVR	27,243	11,431	26	242
Total	135,381	370,299	1,706	377

trained two types of CNNs for the YOLOv2. Also, Table 2 compares recognition accuracy for the Pascal VOC2007 data set. A complication caused by the mixed precision CNN, since there is a tradeoff between the hardware size and the recognition accuracy. The binarization reduces the recognition accuracy by 1-2In the implementation, as shown in Table 2, the accuracy was reduced by 1.5However, for the practical application, it slightly decreases.

6.3 Comparison with other Embedded Platforms

We compared our binarized CNN with other embedded platforms. We used the NVidia Jetson TX2 board which has both the embedded CPU (ARM Cortex-A57) and the embedded GPU (Pascal GPU). For both the embedded platform, we used the original YOLO version 2 from the Darknet deep learning framework [14]. Also, we measured the dynamic power consumption. Note that, in the experiment, to measure the latency, we set the number of batch size to one. Table 4 compares our FPGA implementation with other platforms. Compared with the ARM Cortex-A57, it was 177.4

Table 4: Comparison with embedded platforms with respect to the YOLOv2 detection (Batch size is 1).

Platform	Embedded CPU	Embedded GPU	FPGA
Device	Quad-core ARM Cortex-A57	256-core Pascal GPU	Zynq Ultra. MPSoC
Clock Freq.	1.9 GHz	1.3 GHz	0.3 GHz
Memory	32 GB eMMC Flash	8 GB LPDDR4	32.1 Mb BRAM
Time [msec] (FPS) [sec^{-1}]	4210.0 (0.23)	715.9 (1.48)	**24.5** **(40.81)**
Power [W]	4.0	7.0	4.5
Efficiency [FPS/W]	0.057	0.211	**9.06**

times faster, it dissipated 1.1 times more power, and its performance per power efficiency was 158.9 times better. Also, compared with the Pascal GPU, it was 27.5 times faster, it dissipated 1.5 times lower power, and its performance per power efficiency was 42.9 times better. Thus, our method is suitable for the frame object detector for an embedded system.

7 CONCLUSION

This paper implemented the lightweight YOLOv2 on an FPGA, which was a combination of the binarized CNN and the parallel SVR. It performs a bounding box prediction (regression) and a class estimation (classification) at a time. We used the binarized CNN for the classification, while used the parallel SVR for both the classification and the localization. In the paper, we showed the efficient implementation of the lightweight YOLOv2 on the FPGA. We implemented the proposed one on the Xilinx Inc. Zynq UltraScale+ MPSoC zcu102 evaluation board. Compared with the ARM Cortex-A57, it was 177.4 times faster, it dissipated 1.1 times more power, and its performance per power efficiency was 158.9 times better. Also, compared with the Pascal GPU, it was 27.5 times faster, it dissipated 1.5 times lower power, and its performance per power efficiency was 42.9 times better. Thus, our method is suitable for the frame object detector for an embedded system.

8 ACKNOWLEDGEMENTS

This research is supported in part by the Grants in Aid for Scientist Research of JSPS, and the New Energy and Industrial Technology Development Organization (NEDO). Also, thanks to the Xilinx University Program (XUP), Intel University Program, and the NVidia Corp.'s support.

REFERENCES

[1] M. B. Blaschko and C. H. Lampert, "Learning to localize objects with structured output regression," *In Computer Vision ECCV 2008*, pp. 2-15, Springer, 2008.

[2] B. Bosi, G. Bois and Y. Savaria, "Reconfigurable pipelined 2-D convolvers for fast digital signal processing," *IEEE Trans. on Very Large Scale Integration (VLSI) Systems*, Vol. 7, No. 3, pp. 299-308, 1999.

[3] A. P. Boucle, A. Bourge, F. Petrot, H. Alemdar, N. Caldwell and V. Leroy, "Scalable High-Performance Architecture for Convolutional Ternary Neural Networks on FPGA," *FPL*, 2017.

[4] C. Cortes, and V. Vapnik, "Support-vector networks", *Machine Learning*, No. 20, Vol 3, pp. 273-297, 1995.

[5] M. Courbariaux, I. Hubara, D. Soudry, R.E.Yaniv, Y. Bengio, "Binarized neural networks: Training deep neural networks with weights and activations constrained to +1 or -1," *Computer Research Repository (CoRR)*, Mar., 2016, http://arxiv.org/pdf/1602.02830v3.pdf

[6] T. Downs, K. E. Gates and A. Masters, "Exact simplification of support vector solutions," *Journal of Machine Learning Research*, Vol. 2, 2001, pp. 293-297.

[7] H. Drucker, C. J. C. Burges, L. Kaufman, A. J. Smola and V. N. Vapnik, "Support Vector Regression Machines," *Neural Information Processing Systems*, No. 9, *NIPS* 1996, pp. 155-161, 1997.

[8] D. Erhan, C. Szegedy, A. Toshev, D. Anguelov, "Scalable object detection using deep neural networks," *In: CVPR*, 2014.

[9] P. F. Felzenszwalb, R. B. Girshick, D. McAllester, and D. Ramanan, "Object detection with discriminatively trained part based models," *IEEE Trans. on Pattern Analysis and Machine Intelligence*, No. 32, Vol. 9, 2010, pp. 1627-1645.

[10] R. Girshick, "Fast R-CNN," *In: ICCV*, 2015.

[11] R. Girshick, J. Donahue, T. Darrell and J. Malik, "Rich feature hierarchies for accurate object detection and semantic segmentation," *In: CVPR*, 2014.

[12] K. He, X. Zhang, S. Ren, and J. Sun, "Deep residual learning for image recognition," *arXiv preprint arXiv:1512.03385*, 2015.

[13] K. He, X. Zhang, S. Ren and J. Sun, "Spatial pyramid pooling in deep convolutional networks for visual recognition," *In: ECCV*, 2014.

[14] J. Redmon and A. Farhadi, "YOLO9000: Better, Faster, Stronger," *arXiv preprint arXiv:1612.08242*, 2016.

[15] W. Liu, D. Anguelov, D. Erhan, C. Szegedy, S. Reed, C.. Y. Fu and A. C. Berg, "SSD: Single Shot MultiBox Detector," *In: ECCV*, 2016.

[16] Y. Ma, Y. Cao, S. Vrudhula and J. Seo, "An Automatic RTL Compiler for High-Throughput FPGA Implementation of Diverse Deep Convolutional Neural Networks," *FPL*, 2017.

[17] M. Martin, "On-Line Support Vector Machine Regression," *ECML*, pp.282-294, 2002.

[18] V. Nair and G.E. Hinton, "Rectified linear units improve restricted Boltzmann machines," *Int'l Conf. on Machine Learning (ICML)*, 2010, pp. 807-814.

[19] E. Nurvitadhi, D. Sheffield, J. Sim, A. Mishra, G. Venkatesh and D. Marr, "Accelerating Binarized Neural Networks: Comparison of FPGA, CPU, GPU, and ASIC," *FPT*, pp.1-8, 2016.

[20] The PASCAL Visual Object Classes 2007: http://host.robots.ox.ac.uk/pascal/VOC/

[21] J. Qiu, J. Wang, S. Yao, K. Guo, B. Li, E. Zhou, J. Yu, T. Tang, N. Xu, S. Song, Y. Wang and H. Yang, "Going deeper with embedded FPGA platform for convolutional neural network," *FPGA*, 2016, pp. 26-35

[22] M. Rastegari, V. Ordonez, J. Redmon, and A. Farhadi, "XNOR-Net: ImageNet Classification Using Binary Convolutional Neural Networks," https://arxiv.org/pdf/1603.05279.pdf

[23] S. Ren, K. He, R. Girshick, and J. Sun, "Faster R-CNN: Towards real-time object detection with region proposal networks," *arXiv preprint arXiv:1506.01497*, 2015.

[24] I. Sergey and S. Christian, "Batch normalization: Accelerating deep network training by reducing internal covariate shift," 2015.

[25] S. Venieris and C. Bouganis, "Latency-Driven Design for FPGA-based Convolutional Neural Networks," *FPL*, 2017.

[26] K. Simonyan and A. Zisserman, "Very deep convolutional networks for large-scale image recognition," *ICLR*, 2015.

[27] C. Szegedy, S. Reed, D. Erhan and D. Anguelov, "Scalable, high-quality object detection," *arXiv preprint arXiv:1412.1441*, 2015.

[28] Y. Umuroglu, N. J. Fraser, G. Gambardella, M. Blott, P. Leong, M. Jahre, and K. Vissers, "FINN: A Framework for Fast, Scalable Binarized Neural Network Inference," *ISFPGA*, 2017.

[29] R. Zhao, W. Song, W. Zhang, T. Xing, J.-H. Lin, M. Srivastava, R. Gupta and Z. Zhang, "Accelerating Binarized Convolutional Neural Networks with Software-Programmable FPGAs," *ISFPGA*, 2017, pp.15-24.

[30] S. Zhou, Y. Wu, Z. Ni, X. Zhou, H. Wen and Y. Zou, "DoReFa-Net: Training Low Bitwidth Convolutional Neural Networks with Low Bitwidth Gradients," http://arxiv.org/pdf/1606.06160v2.pdf

Architecture and Circuit Design of an All-Spintronic FPGA

Stephen M. Williams
University of Central Florida
Department of Electrical and Computer Engineering
Orlando, FL, U.S.A.
Stephen.Williams@knights.ucf.edu

Mingjie Lin
University of Central Florida
Department of Electrical and Computer Engineering
Orlando, FL, U.S.A.
Member, IEEE

ABSTRACT

Reconfigurable logic device, such as FPGA, has been well-known to be the driver of cutting-edge device technology. In the last five years, there have been extensive studies on constructing novel FPGA devices using CMOS technology combined with emerging spintronic devices. Unfortunately, although spintronic device technology promises desirable features such as non-volatility and high area density, its relatively slow switching speed makes it quite challenging to use them as drop-in replacements for CMOS transistors. As such, to fully unlock the performance benefits of spintronic devices, it is imperative to develop innovative design techniques of circuit and architecture that are custom-made for building high-performance FPGA devices. In this paper, we aim at fully extracting the benefits of new spin-based device technology through innovative circuit and architecture design techniques for FPGAs. Specifically, we exploit the unique characteristics of a domain-wall logic device called the mCell to achieve a direct mapping to NAND-NOR logic and in doing so create a high-throughput non-volatile alternative to LUT-based CMOS reconfigurable logic.

To empirically validate our approach, we have performed extensive HSpice circuit simulations. Our simulation results have shown that, for a similar logic capacity, the NAND-NOR FPGA design with mCell devices excels across all metrics when compared to the CMOS NAND-NOR FPGA design. Not only do we reduce average delay by about 17%, but we also improve path delay variance between different logic block configurations by about 59%, which can ease the burden on the FPGA timing analysis CAD tools by having more consistent delay between configurations. To judge the performance of our mCell FPGA in practical applications, we measured it against the Stratix IV LUT-based FPGA for the MCNC and VTR benchmark suites. Our mCell-based FPGA devices prove to be quite competitive against the CMOS LUT-based FPGA design, on average reducing delay and area by approximately 26% and 64% for the MCNC benchmark, and 13% and 55% for the VTR benchmark respectively.

CCS CONCEPTS

• **Hardware → Programmable logic elements**; **Emerging architectures**;

KEYWORDS

Spintronic; FPGA; mCell

ACM Reference Format:
Stephen M. Williams and Mingjie Lin. 2018. Architecture and Circuit Design of an All-Spintronic FPGA. In *FPGA '18: 2018 ACM/SIGDA International Symposium on Field-Programmable Gate Arrays, February 25–27, 2018, Monterey, CA, USA.* ACM, New York, NY, USA, 10 pages.
https://doi.org/10.1145/3174243.3174256

1 INTRODUCTION

With Moore's law dwindling quickly, the physical limits of CMOS technology make it almost intractable to achieve high energy efficiency if the traditional logic design methodology still dominates. In fact, a modern FPGA device built with CMOS transistors operating at 0.6V, about 50% of its total energy consumption will be "wasted" as the leakage from idle transistors [17]. Therefore, we need to explore new area-energy efficient device technology and architectures in order to effectively tackle the upcoming "zettabytes" data explosion in computing. However, between new device technology and the corresponding microarchitecture, which is the best path forward in terms of optimal pairing remains to be unclear. Among many emerging device technologies, spin-based devices, commonly referred to as spintronics, have been shown to be quite promising because they have good scalability, non-volatility, and ultra-low energy [11], all of which may enable fundamental shifts in our computation paradigm that were not possible with CMOS technology. Specifically, the non-volatility of spintronic devices has the potential to bring massive energy savings in special applications such as normally-off computation [3, 16]. Unfortunately, despite many compelling advantages of adopting spintronic devices, studies on all-spin logic designs are relatively sparse. In fact, most existing approaches to using spintronic devices often involve a mixed-mode usage of CMOS devices, which may face challenges in the fabrication stage. Another benefit of an all-spintronic design is that they are naturally hardened against bit flips due to radiation [9]. As such, it is of great interest to further pursue competitive logic circuit design methodologies using only spintronic devices, thus exploiting a more optimized fabrication process and increasing its viability as an alternative to the standard CMOS technology.

Among all computing devices, contemporary FPGA design, based on the Look-Up Table (LUT) for logic realization and switch point interconnections for routing, can be a natural candidate for exploring all-spintronic circuit design. Spintronic devices, such as domain walls and magnetic tunnel junctions, have been used in FPGA architecture research, however it is often used to replace only the configuration SRAM bits as spin-technology has a proven track record for memory [4, 18]. Little work has been targeted at the logic block design or the routing interconnections. To our knowledge, no existing work has presented an FPGA architecture made purely of domain-wall devices. This is not without good reasons. First, spintronic devices, when comparing with the most cutting-edge CMOS technology, have relatively low switching ratio. Therefore, CMOS-based sense amplifiers are used to compensate for the low switching ratios of spin-based devices and to aid in fanout. Second, relative to CMOS devices, spintronic devices are also relatively slow in terms of switching speed. In modern spintronic digital circuit design, nanosecond range switching delay is considered adequate, though newer spintronic materials have the potential to improve that [12]. On the device engineering side, faster switching can also be obtained through larger terminal voltages/injection current; however, this can cause excessive heating and device degradation. Ultimately, directly using spintronic devices in the same CMOS circuit design style typically yields poor results. The best path forward in terms of optimal pairing between new device technology and the corresponding microarchitecture remains unclear.

Despite the above technical challenges, there are several promising opportunities to fully exploit the potential of spintronic devices in constructing a modern FPGA device. For example, in a modern FPGA device such as a Stratix IV, a complex logic block is composed of an 8-input LUT and a multiplexor to choose between registered and sequential output. As a result, as many as 256 6T SRAM bits are required to store the configuration of a single logic block. These memory bits incur not only a large area overhead, but an energy and time overhead due to the SRAM needing to be reprogrammed upon each boot cycle, all of which could be better purposed as dedicated computation blocks, communication links, or more reconfigurable cells. Second, the programming time for an SRAM based Zynq FPGA-SOC can be upwards of 10ms [8], which greatly limits the prospects of dynamic reconfigurability for real-time applications such as autonomous vehicle navigation. Third, intermittent power supply also poses an issue as it can interrupt device operation and cause the configuration to be dropped or lost from the SRAM bits, requiring a lengthy reconfiguration period. We believe that all these issues can be mitigated by adopting non-volatile spintronic devices.

Of course, in order to truly unlock the full potential of spintronic devices in building FPGA devices, simple drop-in device replacements is far from enough. To put our work into perspective, in Fig. 1, we present a simple categorization of relevant prior work and our study. Specifically, our work explores a new frontier of the FPGA microarchitecture design process. We approach the problem from the architectural, logical, and device technology points of view. This provides interesting opportunities to fully extract the benefits of new spin-based technology. We utilize the unique characteristics of domain-wall logic devices to achieve a direct mapping to NAND-NOR logic and in doing so create a high-throughput non-volatile alternative to LUT-based CMOS reconfigurable logic. Overall, our contributions can be summarized as

(1) We have developed various innovative mCell-based circuit design techniques and redesigned all crucial circuit components in a modern FPGA device including logic block, MUX-based interconnects, and configuration bits. All of this helps in reducing the fabrication complexity when compared with the hybrid Spin-CMOS FPGA implementations, simply due to the lower number of process stages.

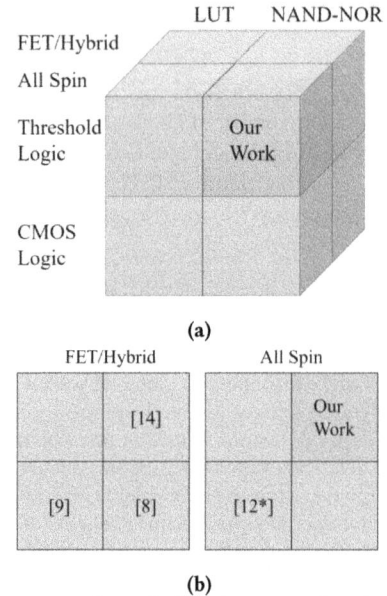

Figure 1: Context of Work. [*] denotes related work in non-reconfigurable logic.

(2) Instead of forcing new spintronic devices into the LUT-based FPGA architecture, we precisely matched the logic block design with the unique device characteristics of spintronic devices. As such, we replace the LUT structure with an area-efficient NAND-NOR cone network, interconnect structures based on hardware-efficient MUX-based switching trees, and 6T-SRAM configuration memory bits with 2-mCell non-volatile memory. NAND-NOR is ideal as spintronics can easily implement the majority function from which both NAND and NOR can be obtained. All of these new circuit design techniques are both scalable and flexible, and potentially usable for other conic logic structures (AIC, MIG).

(3) We have demonstrated through simulations that not only can spintronic devices be used for compact FPGA circuit designs, but also can realize delay competitive designs against standard CMOS solutions with the added benefit of non-volatility.

The rest of the paper is structured as follows: Section 2 briefly describes the physical mechanism of mCell devices and the pros and cons of using mCell devices to construct logic circuits. We then proceed with exploring various circuit architectures to implement FPGA logic blocks in Section 3. In Section 4, we investigate the best circuit design techniques to implement various core logic components within a modern FPGA device, e.g., interconnect structures, configuration bits, and logic block. In particular, we discuss how mCell-based circuit design achieves logic registrations cheaply and naturally, which paves way to ultra-fine micro-pipelining. Finally, in Section 6 and 7, we provide a representative circuit layout and various HSpice simulation results.

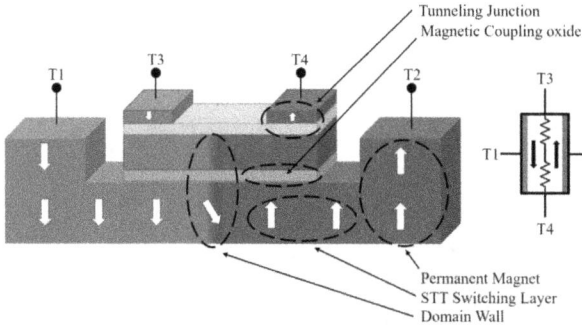

Figure 2: 3D view of an mCell domain wall device with STT (Spin Transfer Torque) write path.

Device Parameter	Value
hold Current Density [MA/cm^2]	4
MTJ Resistance*Area [$\omega \cdot \mu m^2$]	2
Tunnel Magnetoresistance Ratio	200%
Domain Wall Depinning Time [ps]	100
Spin Polarization	120%
Read Path Low Resistance [ω]	1.25K
Read Path High Resistance [ω]	2.5K
Write Path Resistance [ω]	100
Device Width [nm]	20
Device Length [nm]	40

Table 1: mCell Device parameter values used in this paper.

2 THE MCELL, A SPIN-COUPLED DOMAIN-WALL DEVICE

Among many physical realizations of a spintronic device, we focus on those which are based upon domain-wall motion in a ferromagnetic nanowire. Typically, such a domain-wall device has electrically connected read and write pathways to provides a signal output and to set the domain wall position, respectively. However, this leads to the problem of needing separate read and write phases, along with a few access transistors, further exacerbating the longer delay inherent to spin-devices. In [14], the authors designed a domain wall device, called the mCell shown in Fig. 2, in which the read and write pathways are electrically isolated. This is achieved by placing a magnetic coupling oxide between two magnetic free layers. Applying a voltage across terminals T1 and T2 causes a spin-polarized current to flow which moves the lower domain wall via spin-transfer torque. This in turn moves the upper domain wall between terminals T3 and T4 via dipolar coupling. Magnetic tunneling junctions are formed by the magnetic materials and oxide at terminals T3 and T4. As the domain wall sweeps from one far end to the other, the resistance between T3 and T4 varies between R_{low} and R_{high}. In our work, we replace the MTJ at terminal T4 with a lower resistance ohmic contact, this further allows for larger current flow leading to faster switching times. Thanks to the isolated read and write paths, the mCell, as well as similar magnetically coupled spin-devices, can be used to design improved spintronic logic circuits. The magnetization state is non-volatile which can aid in achieving lower energy designs. Until now, the mCell has been only been used in ASIC like designs and not for a full FPGA architecture. Table 1 lists all essential parameters values used to simulate the mCell circuits used in this paper. The model can be

made to use a Giant Spin Hall Effect (GSHE) write path through a basic change of parameters given above. Domain-wall devices which utilize GSHE switching have been shown to achieve ultra-low energy consumption as low as 100aJ/bit, 100mV terminal voltage, and switching delay as low as 10ps [12].

2.1 Circuit Design using the mCell

Despite many advantageous properties spintronic devices have, such as non-volatility and high area density, performing logic circuit design with them turns out to be challenging. In fact, we believe that new circuit design techniques and styles have to be invented in order to fully unleash their performance potential. For example, most work assumes reliable domain wall movement and settling points; however, precise domain-wall movement is unreliable [13]. This can lead to errors when temperature, dopant, and geometric variations are inevitably introduced during fabrication. In [6], the authors propose a spintronic logic block. They use the domain-wall device as a tunable resistance to achieve reconfigurability, which is hard to achieve given today's spintronic device technology. Their approach relies on auxiliary transistors for core functionality, which adds additional fabrication stages and will likely create roadblocks to a competitive computation alternative to CMOS transistors. In our work, we use domain-wall devices to create a simple two-state device with reliable transitions between the states as all that is required is full domain-wall movement vs partial movements.

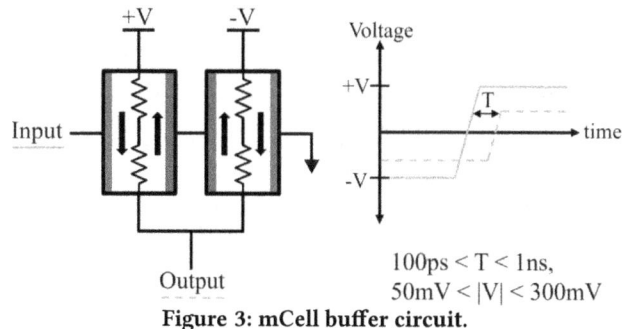

Figure 3: mCell buffer circuit.

Shown in Fig. 3 is the core building block of all circuits presented in this work. Using two mCells, we create a voltage divider which swings between V+ and V- based on the direction of current applied at the Input terminal. If the current from Input to ground is positive then the output is set to V+, likewise if the current is negative then the output is set to V-. When connected as shown the device acts like a buffer, however if the voltage supply polarity is reversed, then it becomes an inverter. We use this simple buffer-/inverter circuit to create a programmable inverter which has an intrinsically balanced delay. This helps in solving a large part of the delay variance inherent in CMOS NAND-NOR logic. Fanout is achieved by connecting a load in series so that each load is driven by the same current. Fanout with mCell devices is energy efficient and uses as little as 1.4fJ in comparison to the 23fJ required by a typical tapered CMOS buffer chain.

The output current is given in Equation 1(a) where RPU and RPD are the switchable MTJ resistances which range from Rlow and Rhigh, and V/2 is the magnitude of the positive or negative voltage supplies. Gain is provided by increasing the voltage supply at a given buffering stage. In our design we use a +/- 65mV terminal voltage for the core logic supplies and +/- 100mV for stages with large fanout.

$$I = \frac{V\left(\frac{1}{R_{\text{PU}}} + \frac{1}{R_{\text{PD}}}\right)}{2k}, \text{ where } k = 1 + R_{\text{output}}\left(\frac{1}{R_{\text{PU}}} + \frac{1}{R_{\text{PD}}}\right). \quad (1)$$

3 LOOKUP-TABLE VS NAND-NOR AS BASIS FOR RECONFIGURABLE LOGIC

We rethink the entire FPGA design from the ground up by first examining the the most fundamental circuit component of an FPGA device—the logic blocks. It is well-known that, with the CMOS device technology, the LUT-based logic block architecture has long been dominant. However, this traditional LUT circuit design requires many multiplexors, in which the area and delay scale almost exponentially and logarithmically as the number of inputs increases. Unfortunately, directly duplicating such an LUT-based circuit design with delay-constrained spin-devices incurs technical issues such as excessive delay and path design imbalance. Furthermore, when the input number of LUTs increases, building a high-input multiplexor becomes quite challenging if using only spin-devices, at least when using the spin-mux design shown in this paper. As such, in consideration of the area, energy, and delay overheads from cascading many multiplexors to create the LUT, we attempt to explore more efficient implementations for reconfigurable logic. Reconfigurable logic cones such as the AND-Inverter-Cone (AIC) [15, 19] have been presented as an alternative to LUT-based FPGAs. The AIC cone consists of a binary tree of AND-INVERTER basic logic elements (BLE). More recently Huang et al. [7] improved upon the AIC with the similarly constructed NAND-NOR-Cone. In fact, the authors of [7] have shown that CMOS-based NAND-NOR logic can lead to a compact high-speed FPGA, reducing the delay-area product by 44% and 21% for the MCNC and VTR benchmarks, compared to a CMOS LUT-based solution. In this study, we attempt to show that, although the CMOS NAND-NOR-Cone introduces more logical flexibility while improving the cone delay variance issues compared to the AIC, there is still much room for improvement as the NAND-NOR cone requires 63 6T SRAM bits to hold the configuration, and overhead of 378 transistors per cone. Despite improvements compared to the AIC, the NAND-NOR cone input-to-output delay varies based on chosen configuration by as much as 20%. This poses challenges in timing analysis performed by the CAD tools and as a result, dynamic reconfigurability becomes a daunting task due to the large delay variation between different configurations; furthermore, the circuit must be clocked at a slow enough frequency to accommodate the blocks which are using a slower configuration.

NAND-NOR logic is based around a binary tree of gates which can be programmed to perform NAND or NOR operations. The first level is unique with the inputs having programmable inverters, this allows for a greater number of functions to be realized by the NAND-NOR cluster. The NAND-NOR element can implement eight basic functions: AB, $A\text{fi}B\text{fi}$, $A\text{fi}B$, $AB\text{fi}$, $A + B$, $A\text{fi} + B\text{fi}$, $A\text{fi} + B$, and $A + B\text{fi}$. Unfortunately input delay variance is introduced by the input CMOS inverter and an additional gate delay is introduced vs the non-inverted case. This is treated as a delay error which can accumulate across long chains of logic. The schematic for a three level NAND-NOR is shown in Fig. 4(a). The two critical elements are the Enhanced NAND-NOR element and the basic

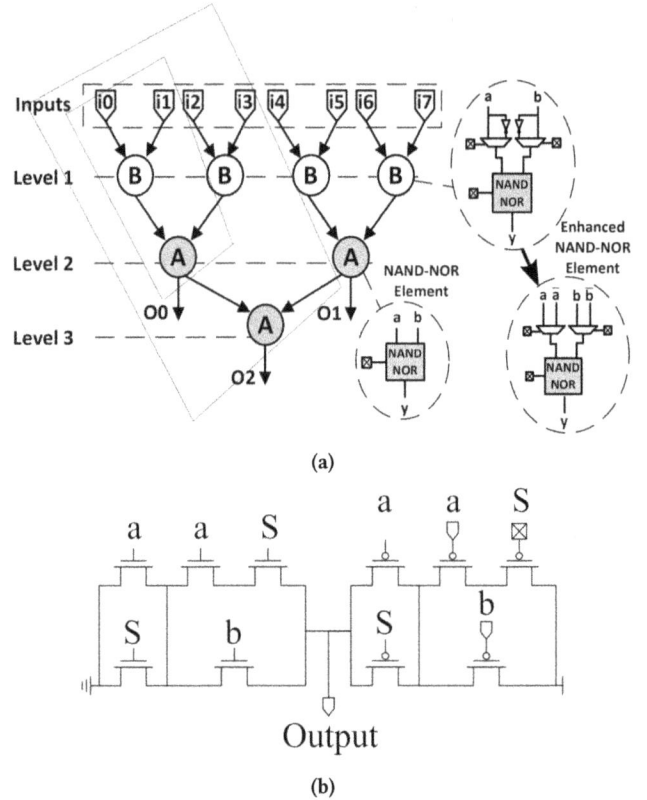

(a)

Output

(b)

Figure 4: (a) NAND-NOR logic cone. (b) NAND-NOR basic logic element CMOS schematic [7].

NAND-NOR element. The input inverters can be moved to the input crossbar, allowing the whole NAND-NOR cone to be composed of basic NAND-NOR elements. NAND-NOR can reduce logic replication which is a problem with LUT-based FPGAs, causing large area overheads. In the NAND-NOR scheme, the inner level outputs can be routed out of the cluster to save resources by reusing the inner parts of the cluster. It is this sharing of resources that allows for NAND-NOR to provide compact logic realizations.

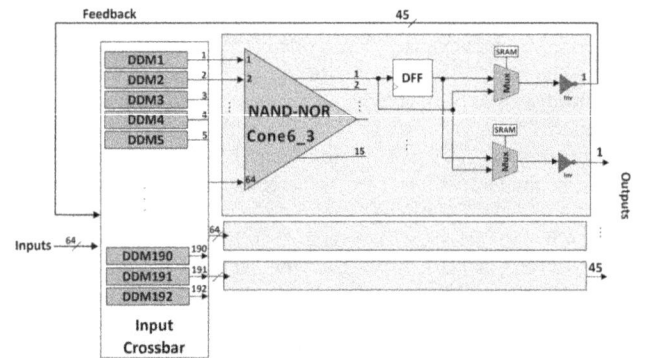

Figure 5: NAND-NOR cluster. Composed of three logic cones and routing [7].

The overall NAND-NOR cluster layout from [14] is shown in 5. It can be viewed as the equivalent of a complex logic block and associated interconnect for LUT-based FPGA designs. The cluster consists of a 192 multiplexer input crossbar, three six-level reconfigurable logic cones in parallel providing 192 inputs, and an output registration stage. Here, the final level output is provided both registered and directly, as well as 15 inner layer outputs from each of the three cones, for a total of 45 outputs per cluster. The outputs are sent through a feedback path in addition to being routed to the next cluster, this allows for sequential logic to be realized by the cluster. Due to area and energy constraints, logic registration is are provided only at the last level before the interconnect.

3.1 Challenges Facing CMOS NAND-NOR Logic

A CMOS inverter is composed of a single pair of transistors and as result has delay greater than that of a direct connection or through a buffer. NAND-NOR logic requires a programmable-inverter on each gate input, this leads to delay-variation between the inputs. This delay-variation accumulates and with sufficiently long chains of combinatorial logic, it can cause errors and increases the complexity of timing analysis. In [7], the authors utilized a delay-balancing crossbar matrix to achieve nearly equal delay for the various cone configurations, but overall cone delay-discrepancy is still significant at 20%.

We design our spintronic NAND-NOR block in such a way that the input inverters have a delay equal to that of a buffered connection. We do so by inverting the power supply to a spintronic buffer using a few extra mCells. Additionally, non-volatile spintronic devices can provide low cost logic registration [14] allowing for registers to be embedded within the cone providing much finer pipeline granularity. However, for the sake of a more direct comparison to the CMOS design we use register the same number of outputs at the same points in the cone.

4 MCELL NAND-NOR RECONFIGURABLE LOGIC

Using the mCell and the basic Spin Logic Element design from Section 2, we can construct our logic cluster, interconnect, configuration bits, and logic registration. Our Spin NAND-NOR logic element consists of two mCells for the gate and two mCells for the configuration bit, in comparison to the 16 transistors required by the CMOS design. This allows for an extremely compact logic cluster design with an area savings of up to 50% compared to CMOS. The input crossbar is functionally equivalent to the CMOS crossbar and provides the programmable input inversion capabilities. This reduces mCells in the cluster and removes one level of mCell delay from the critical path of the crossbar and cluster. Due to the non-volatile nature of the mCell, we can implement logic registration using the mCell gate itself by replacing its power rail by a clock signal. This allows us to have cheap logic registration and the ability to increase pipeline granularity than what is feasible with CMOS. This also helps reduce static power consumption in the logic cone as it only consumes energy during switching when the clock line is strobed. This is similar to power gating in CMOS designs, admittedly this may be challenging to implement in practice due and we leave the power gating circuit design to future work. Finally, maybe most importantly, with the area savings from our design, we can implement much deeper NAND-NOR cones than with CMOS in the same amount of area. However, for this work we compare an equivalent 6-level NAND-NOR cone structure with a single register stage as in [7] for both the mCell and CMOS designs. This provides an initial reference point; future work could

examine the benefits of finer granularity pipelines and the effects of having deeper cones.

4.1 Basic and Enhanced Spin NAND-NOR Logic Elements

When using domain-wall devices as direct drop-in replacements in a CMOS-style design, the overall circuit performance may actually suffer. This is due to the relatively low switching ratio inherent in domain-wall devices [14]. It is crucial to use design methods which can tolerate the low switching ratios, threshold logic has been shown [5] to be a good candidate for domain-wall logic due to the simple mapping from function to device leading to area-energy efficient implementations. The NAND-NOR programmable gate requires only four mCells when using a threshold logic approach; using a CMOS-style design requires four mCells for a fixed function NAND-only gate. In this simple example, by using threshold logic we are able to extract twice the functionality for the same device count.

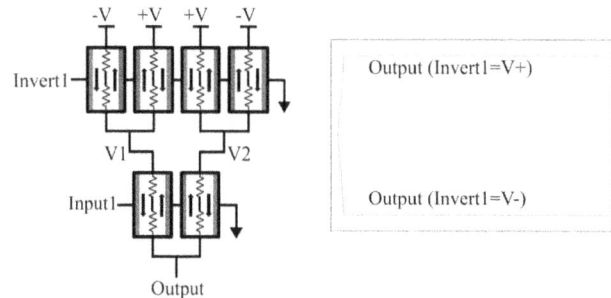

Figure 6: Programmable inverter. Input to output delay is identical for inverting and non-inverting modes.

Programmable input inversion is achieved by inverting the power supply applied to a signal buffer. As shown in Fig. 6, this functionality is provided by four mCells, two per supply rail which form the Voltage Supply Inverter (VSI). A programming signal is applied to the VSI which sets the positions of the non-volatile domain walls. Unlike in CMOS, inverting a signal with this method does not add any additional delay compared to the non-inverted case. This helps to reduce the delay discrepancy between the best and worst-case configurations of the overall NAND-NOR cone by 59% compared to the CMOS design.

The mCell NAND-NOR basic logic element (NNBLE) is shown in Fig. 7. It consists of an output buffer mCell which performs thresholding based on the number of active inputs. Each input is passed through a programmable inverter. A current summation is performed at the output register input node, if the current is positive then the output is asserted positive whenever the power supply is active. If the current is negative then the output is asserted negative. The configuration bit, composed of two mCells, provides a bias current to the input of the threshold gate. This is what determines whether the gate acts as a NAND or NOR. It can be viewed as a three-input majority gate in which the configuration bit biases the third input low or high. When the program signal is asserted to V-, the domain walls in the configuration bit are set and the logic element acts as a NAND gate. Likewise, when the program signal is asserted to V+, the logic element acts as a NOR gate.

(a)

(b)

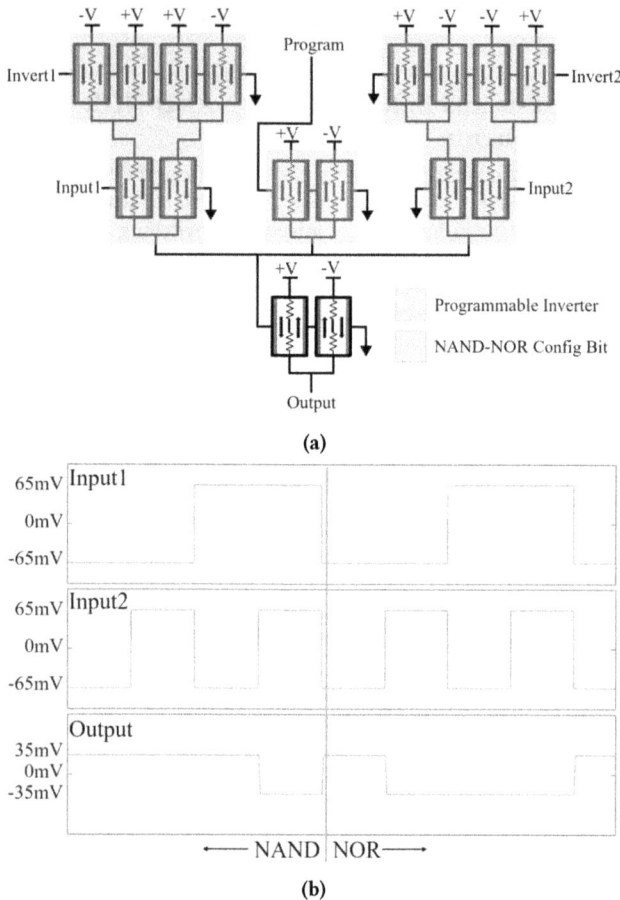

Figure 7: (a) mCell NAND-NOR enhanced logic element, (b) sample HSpice simulation showing NAND-NOR functionality, plots created in Matlab.

4.2 MUX-Based Input Interconnect

To create the routing network between logic blocks, we use a multiplexor-based interconnection composed of cascaded 4-to-1 multiplexors. Each signal input to the multiplexor passes through a parallel pair of programmable inverters before reaching the multiplexor output buffer. To select an input, each of its programmable inverters must be set to the same mode. If the input signal needs to be inverted, both are set to inversion mode, otherwise they are left in the buffer mode. The non-selected inputs have their programmable inverter pairs set to opposite modes, this provides a zero sum of current at the input to the multiplexor output buffer. Fig. 8 depicts the ba-sic circuit design of a 4-input MUX and its HSpice simulation re-sults. Note that the buffer-like structure after the MUX achieves low signal degradation at the output, which is critical in designing and implementing mCell-based logic circuits. If additional inputs are needed then another pair of programmable inverters need to be connected to the input node of the multiplexor output buffer. This works well until around 10 inputs for a single stage multiplexor, after which the input-to-output delay increases past that of an equivalent input number cascaded design.

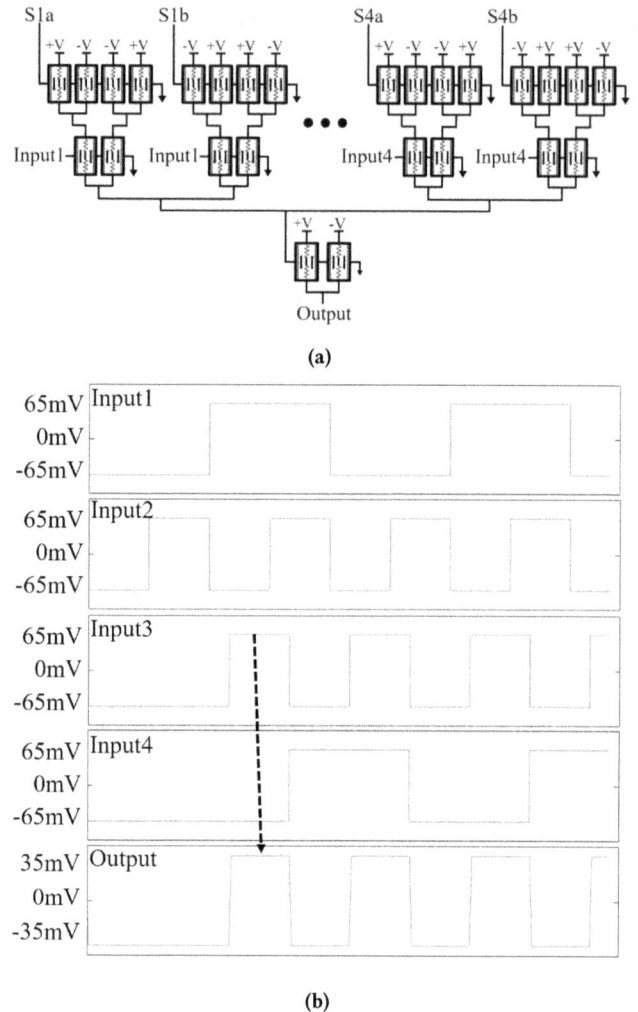

(a)

(b)

Figure 8: (a) 4-Input MUX implemented with only mCells. (b) HSpice simulation demonstrates that the mCell MUX can select Input3 with little degradation due to other inputs.

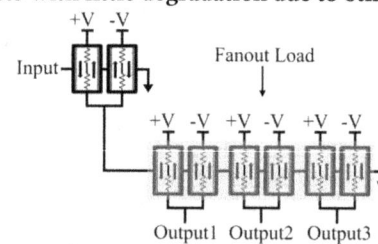

Figure 9: Series fanout ensures each downstream load receives the same current.

4.3 Fanout

When using the mCell, fanout is handled in a much different manner than with CMOS. Since the output signal is current-based, a serial fanout scheme is required for each downstream gate input to receive the same amount of current, which can be modeled simply as a series combination of resistors. Fanout with mCells is much more efficient in terms of energy than CMOS. CMOS fanout requires a tapered buffer chain to drive large loads which can consume 23fJ to drive 100um of metal, much of which is dominated by the large load capacitance. In comparison, only 1.4fJ is required for an equivalent STT based mCell fanout to a 700ω load, a savings of nearly 20% [14]. The savings are even greater when using a GSHE based mCell. Given that the interconnect and fanout can account for up to 90% of total FPGA power use [10], this savings can have a good impact on overall circuit energy consumption. In contrast, for CMOS NAND-NOR, the overhead due to interconnections can be detrimental to performance and with certain connectivity schemes. The fanout delay can potentially exceed that of the entire logic cluster, negating much of the delay benefit CMOS has in comparison to spin devices. Fig. 9 presents an example of mCell-based 3-fanout.

4.4　Low-Area Configuration Bits

Due to the non-volatility of the mCell, it is possible to use the position of the configuration bit mCells' domain walls to store the FPGA configuration. As shown in Fig. 7, we dedicate two mCells for each configuration bit, providing a more area efficient alternative to the traditional 6T SRAM bit used in CMOS FPGAs. The direction of the current applied between the Program and ground terminals sets the domain wall position fully to the left or right. Which provides either positive or negative output current to bias the NAND-NOR element output buffer to act as either a NAND or NOR gate. After the spin FPGA has been initially programmed, device boot-up is instantaneous upon receiving power as the configuration doesn't have to be loaded over a slow SPI interface from external flash to the internal SRAM. This opens the doors to new instant-sleep/wake FPGA designs. Design of the programming circuitry is left to future work, here we manually configure the FPGA in Hspice.

4.5　Logic Registration

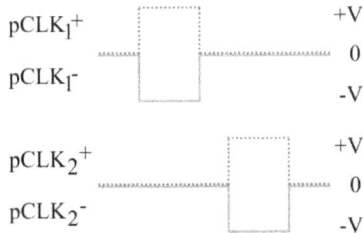

Figure 10: From [14], power supply strobing signals. When inactive the circuit is in a zero-energy consumption state.

Logic registration represents an area, energy, and delay overhead; due to this, pipelining is often only provided every 12 logic stages in CMOS logic designs [14]. CMOS NAND-NOR provides pipeline registers roughly every 6 logic stages for the same reasons. Due to the isolated domain walls in the mCell, it is possible to efficiently implement registered logic at a low area cost. This is done by using a pulsed power supply which can propagate data through adjacent mCells like a flip-flop. The voltage supply to the mCell is replaced by a clock source as shown in Fig. 10. Clock buffering and distribution would be managed in a similar fashion to CMOS designs. The area cost of an mCell clock tree would be lower than with CMOS designs as it completely replaces the supply rail routing for registered logic. In a simple pipeline, the first

logic stage would receive pCLK1, while the second stage would receive pCLK2. Stage one has its input domain-wall positions set by upstream logic, during this pCLK1 is idle and as a result stage one consumes no energy. Stage one then receives a pulse on pCLK1 which allows it to pass the processed data to stage two by setting the input domain-walls in stage two. pCLK2 is pulsed allowing stage two to pass its data to downstream logic. The mCell registers and their preceding logic only receives power when data is ready to be processed, otherwise they sit idle with zero leakage energy during this time. To achieve minimal energy consumption with the mCell FPGA, it is crucial to use heavy pipelining and registered logic whenever possible. This is due to the leakage through a powered idle mCell being a concern in large circuits. Although the mCell operates at a 65mV supply voltage, its low switching ratio and off resistance of 2.5K ohms leads to a small current leakage that adds up quickly in large designs. As device engineering improves and better spintronic devices are produced, this will be less of an issue.

5　MCELL NAND-NOR LOGIC CLUSTER

6 Level NAND-NOR Performance Metrics	CMOS	mCell
Best Case Delay	372.8	316.1
Worst Case Delay	466.4	358.1
Average Delay	424.2	337.1
ΔT	51.2	20.99

Table 2: Comparison of mCell vs CMOS delay and delay variance for logic cone and input crossbar.

By combining the previously discussed elements, we can form a NAND-NOR cone of any depth. Fig. 11 depicts a 3-level mCell NAND-NOR cone which has 8 inputs. Highlighted in pink are the non-volatile configuration bits, each equivalent to a 6T SRAM bit cell in a CMOS design. Highlighted in green is the logic registration for each NAND-NOR element output, though in our final design we selectively chose our registered outputs to maintain equivalence to the CMOS NAND-NOR cone we are comparing against. Logic registration is essentially free, incurring minimal delay and area penalties. This results in an extremely compact overall NAND-NOR cone implementation that reduces area and delay by over 45% and 15% respectively, compared to CMOS NAND-NOR. Table 2 lists various delay value comparisons between CMOS and mCell-based circuit of a 6-level NAND-NOR network.

As in [7], we move the programmable inverters from the logic cluster to the input interconnect. This is because both the input interconnect and the programmable inverters need higher voltage levels for fanout. By integrating the programmable inversion into the input interconnect, we reduce the number of mCells connected to the higher voltage supply used and save energy. This also further reduces the logic cluster device count and area. Each NAND-NOR element requires just four mCells, two for the configuration bit and two for the gate itself. This is in comparison to the CMOS NAND-NOR element which requires 16 transistors, six for the configuration bit and ten for the NAND-NOR gate itself. This leads to our entire circuit, both the input crossbar and the logic cluster, to require only 9,972 mCells in comparison to nearly 20,000 transistors in the CMOS NAND-NOR design.

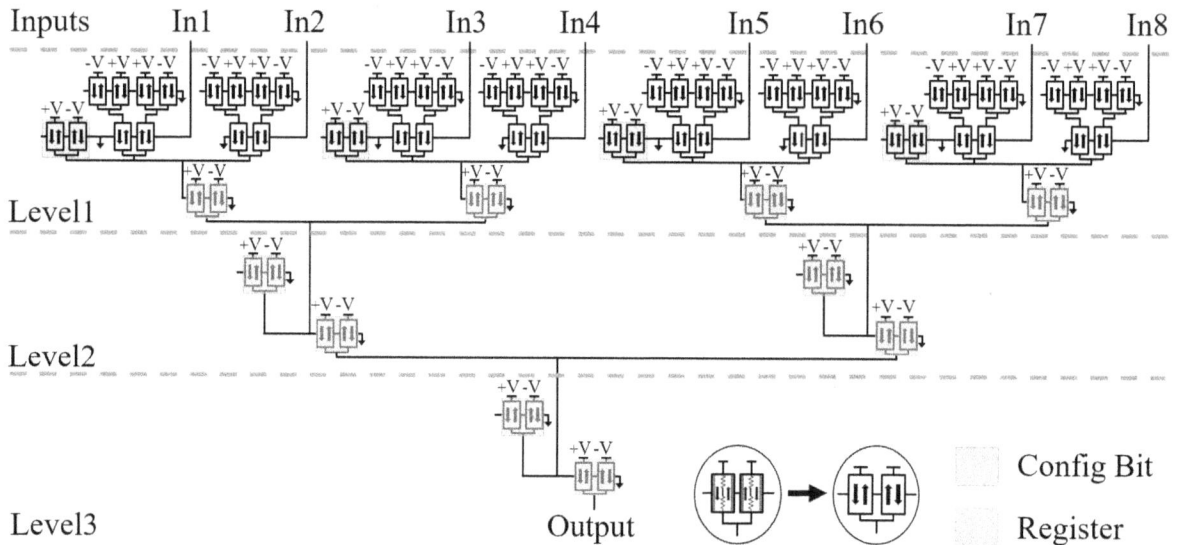

Figure 11: Full NAND-NOR logic cone.

6 DEVICE LAYOUT

Schematically we represent the mCell circuit as pair of mCell between a positive and negative voltage. However, during layout each pair is combined on a single STT/GSHE write path. Sharing the write path between the two mCells allows for dense device integration. We use a layout style similar to [4], which used an mCell scaled in size to 5.5 metal tracks by 2 metal tracks, giving it a net area comparable to a 10nm FinFET device. In our work, we relax device scaling, this was done to maintain a fair comparison to the previous CMOS NAND-NOR design as it doesn't use highly scaled CMOS device technology. As such, area calculations in the results section are based on these larger mCells. It is important to note that our spintronic FPGA provides flexibility, and can be tuned in terms of delay, area, and energy based on design requirements; this is done by simply increasing or decreasing the device voltage or device size, as the mCell can tolerate large supply voltage variations with little to no issues [14].

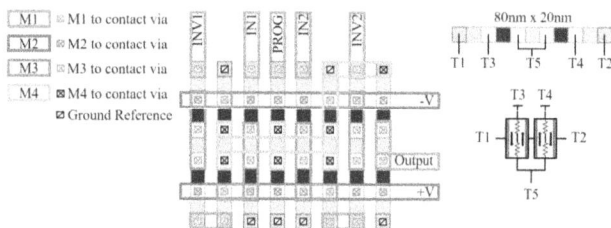

Figure 12: Layout for NAND-NOR logic cone, including programmable inverters and three configuration bits. 32 CMOS transistors compared to 14 mCell are required to implement an equivalent logic element. Layout style inspired by [4].

7 EXPERIMENTS AND RESULTS

7.1 Experimental Setup

We use a VerilogA device model from [14] to design the circuits presented here. It has been tuned to match real device behavior,

and mCell circuits have been successfully fabricated which gives us confidence in the VerilogA model accuracy. The model can be edited to adjust device geometry as well the Tunneling Magneto-Resistance Ratio (TMR), write path resistance, domain-wall depinning time, write path material, and a choice between an MTJ or an ohmic contact at T3. This allows us to simulate our mCell circuit and take advantage of the more efficient GSHE switching mechanism. The VerilogA mCell model is used in conjunction with Hspice to simulate the circuit from which we calculate energy, delay, and area. The only device component used in our simulation is the mCell itself and the voltage sources for the circuit's power supply. We estimate total dynamic circuit energy by calculating the energy for a single gate transition and assume maximum switching activity. We found agreement within 9% in our estimated energy consumption with [14]. Device count for the CMOS NAND-NOR cone is calculated based on the schematics and information provided in [7]. CMOS NAND-NOR delay performance is taken from [7] and their results are based on 40 nm technology. Energy calculations were not provided in the reference CMOS NAND-NOR design so we used a 45nm PTM high performance CMOS model to obtain an approximate figure. All calculations are based only on the logic clusters, LUTs, and interconnect hardware that is used in the benchmark. As the Stratix IV is a fully-featured FPGA device, the extra hardware it contains (IO blocks, clock management tiles, dedicated multipliers, etc.) was not included in the results section. This was done to provide a clear comparison between NAND-NOR and LUT based logic architectures.

7.2 Results

Given in Table III are the results from our Hspice simulation for a single NAND-NOR cluster. Our mCell NAND-NOR FPGA design shows improvements across all metrics compared to the CMOS design. Not only do we reduce average delay by 17%, but we also improve path delay variance between different logic block configurations by 59%. This eases the burden on the FPGA timing analysis CAD tools by having more consistent delay between configurations.

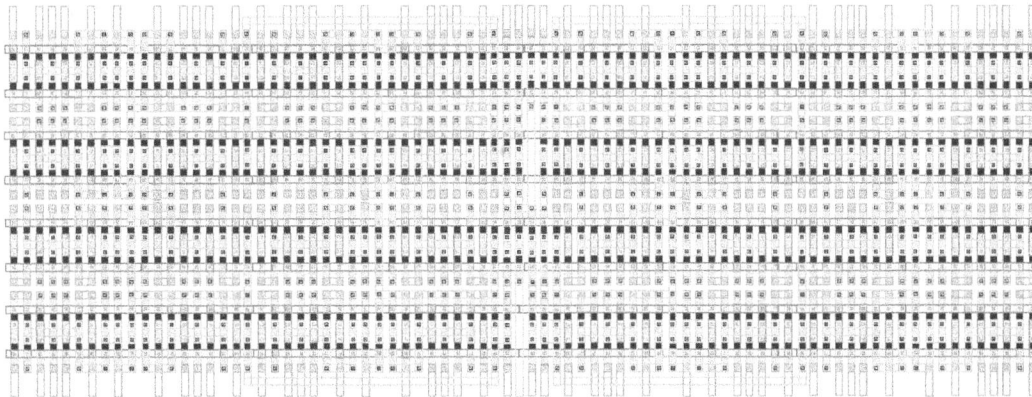

Figure 13: mCell layout for 6-level cone including the 64-input programmable inverter layer. Composed of 636 mCells compared to 1,575 CMOS transistors for equivalent functionality.

Performance Metric	Improvement
Average Delay	17.3%
Path Delay variance	59.1%
Total Device Count	47.4%
Energy Consumption	56.7%

Table 3: Summary of improvements in mCell NAND-NOR cluster compared to CMOS.

To judge the performance of our mCell FPGA in practical applications, we compare it to the Stratix IV LUT-based FPGA [1] for the MCNC and VTR benchmark suites based on data from [7]. 1 The results from the benchmarks are provided in Table IV. Our mCell FPGA competes well with the CMOS LUT-based FPGA design, reducing delay and area by 26% and 64% for the MCNC benchmark, and 13% and 55% for the VTR benchmark respectively. While the number of clusters used in the mCell FPGA can be greater than that of the CMOS LUT-based FPGA, the mCell logic clusters themselves are smaller which leads to an overall area reduction.

In certain benchmarks, the NAND-NOR FPGA has worse performance than its LUT-based counterpart. For the stereovision3 this is due to delay being compromised for area by the packing and routing algorithms for and stereovision3 benchmarks, this is due to a known issues in the technology mapper [7].

8 CONCLUSION

Overall, we have shown that spintronic devices can be used to completely realize an area-delay efficient FPGA microarchitecture. Compared to recent CMOS designs we reduce the device count by 47%, with and delay variance by 59%, improving many of the flaws found in the original CMOS NAND-NOR design. This work is unique in that we use only spintronic devices in our circuit design, in comparison to the many hybrid approaches which use both CMOS transistors and spin-devices for the core logic block to achieve the same goal. We demonstrated via simulation that by taking advantage of the latest developments in spin materials, an all Spin NAND-NOR cone can surpass the top CMOS NAND-NOR design in terms of delay, energy, and area. We used device parameters which are in line with current research [12]. This paints a promising picture for the future of spin-based reconfigurable logic.

Our future work will focus on further improvement in the performance of the Spin NAND-NOR cone while increasing its logical

	Delay Reduction (%)	Area Reduction (%)	Number of Clusters	
MCNC benchmark	w.r.t. LUT	w.r.t. LUT	LUT	mCell NAND-NOR
s298	36.46	74.15	52	49
pdc	42.06	63.27	193	153
diffeq	41.07	57.09	58	48
alu4	44.22	60.37	62	51
misex3	43.51	65.66	56	47
apex2	35.52	75.54	80	74
seq	44.23	69.69	76	61
s38417	-2.41	67.96	222	315
bigkey	25.63	70.95	80	75
s385841	27.73	61.37	198	200
apex4	32.36	67.10	57	55
tseng	19.86	51.69	50	55
ex1010	19.54	70.62	212	235
Elliptic	38.95	62.11	140	112
dsip	32.51	72.99	83	76
clma	15.82	63.27	285	345
spla	10.02	61.92	141	175
des	5.65	60.20	69	111
frisc	39.53	60.17	155	130
ex5p	-10.30	65.19	47	73
Geomean	26.01	64.96	98	98

	Delay Reduction (%)	Area Reduction (%)	Number of Clusters	
VTR benchmark	w.r.t. LUT	w.r.t. LUT	LUT	mCell NAND-NOR
stereovision0	-16.54	56.86	1041	1554
ch_intrinsics	40.94	68.96	16	13
diffeq1	17.01	52.90	37	67
mkSMAdapter4B	35.66	60.32	114	111
boundtop	26.04	64.39	172	182
or1200	17.75	38.91	205	243
stereovision1	-23.23	36.97	986	1693
mkDelayWorker32B	54.22	70.28	55	39
Raygentop	16.70	58.54	158	215
stereovision3	11.87	68.33	15	18
diffeq2	15.04	48.12	25	64
mkPktMerge	51.35	48.76	11	11
Sha	-14.29	58.50	157	261
blob_merge	-7.83	49.65	387	586
Geomean	13.51	55.48	96	123

Table 4: Comparison to LUT-based FPGA for MCNC and VTR benchmarks, based on data from [7].

flexibility. Logical flexibility can be increased by using the NAND-NOR element configuration bit optionally as a third gate input,

(a)

(b)

(c)

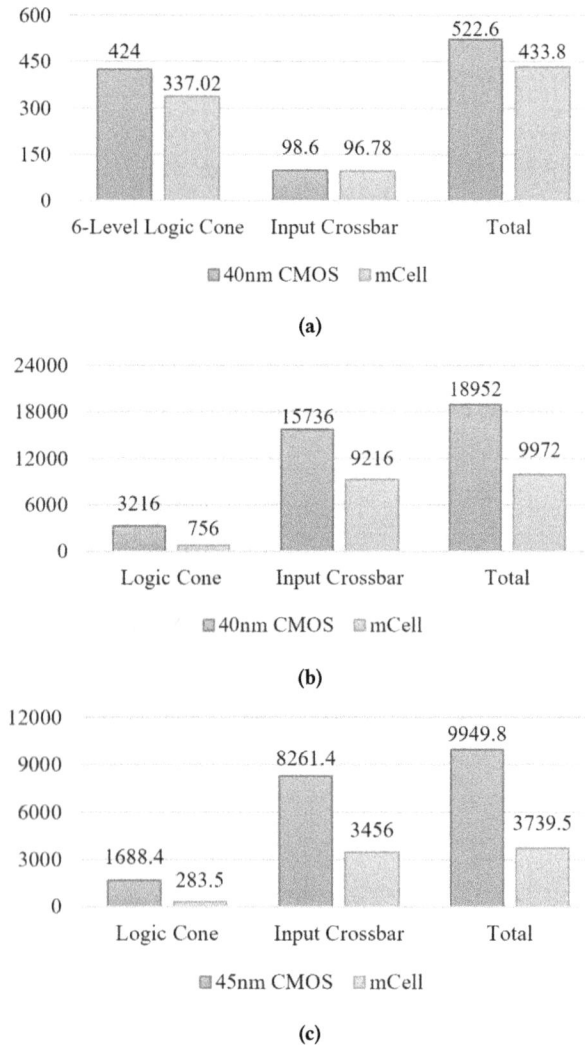

Figure 14: Simulation results for both the CMOS and the mCell NAND-NOR cluster design shown in Figure 5. (a) delay in pico-seconds, (b) overall device count, and (c) energy in femto-Joules. (0.525fJ/switch CMOS, 0.375fJ/switch mCell).

transforming the NAND-NOR cone into logic cone which can realize a both NAND-NOR and Majority Inverter Graphs (MIGs). Benefits of MIG representation have been discussed here [2], but until now the area overhead in CMOS MIGs has limited their use to purely logic optimization in CAD tools. Our design can implement compact logic registration, embedding registers in logic with a finer granularity than the CMOS NAND-NOR cone. This has the potential to further reduce logic replication and waste by allowing for simple micro-pipelines which when using CMOS would quickly consume the NAND-NOR clusters.

ACKNOWLEDGEMENT

This material is based upon work supported by the National Science Foundation under Grant No. 1319884 and 1553056.

REFERENCES

[1] 2016. *Altera Stratix IV Device Handbook*. Technical Report. Altera Corporation.
[2] L. AmarĂž, P. E. Gaillardon, and G. De Micheli. 2016. Majority-Inverter Graph: A New Paradigm for Logic Optimization. *IEEE Transactions on Computer-Aided Design of Integrated Circuits and Systems* 35, 5 (May 2016), 806–819. https://doi.org/10.1109/TCAD.2015.2488484
[3] K. Ando, S. Fujita, J. Ito, S. Yuasa, Y. Suzuki, Y. Nakatani, T. Miyazaki, and H. Yoda. 2014. Spin-transfer torque magnetoresistive random-access memory technologies for normally off computing (invited). *Journal of Applied Physics* 115, 17 (2014), 172607. https://doi.org/10.1063/1.4869828 arXiv:http://dx.doi.org/10.1063/1.4869828
[4] D. M. Bromberg, H. E. Sumbul, J.-G. Zhu, and L. Pileggi. 2015. All-magnetic magnetoresistive random access memory based on four terminal mCell device. *Journal of Applied Physics* 117, 17 (2015), 17B510. https://doi.org/10.1063/1.4913279 arXiv:http://dx.doi.org/10.1063/1.4913279
[5] D. Fan, M. Sharad, and K. Roy. 2014. Design and Synthesis of Ultralow Energy Spin-Memristor Threshold Logic. *IEEE Transactions on Nanotechnology* 13, 3 (May 2014), 574–583. https://doi.org/10.1109/TNANO.2014.2312177
[6] Z. He and D. Fan. 2017. Energy Efficient Reconfigurable Threshold Logic Circuit with Spintronic Devices. *IEEE Transactions on Emerging Topics in Computing* 5, 2 (April 2017), 223–237. https://doi.org/10.1109/TETC.2016.2633966
[7] Zhihong Huang, Xing Wei, Grace Zgheib, Wei Li, Yu Lin, Zhenghong Jiang, Kaihui Tu, Paolo Ienne, and Haigang Yang. 2017. NAND-NOR: A Compact, Fast, and Delay Balanced FPGA Logic Element. In *Proceedings of the 2017 ACM/SIGDA International Symposium on Field-Programmable Gate Arrays (FPGA '17)*. ACM, New York, NY, USA, 135–140. https://doi.org/10.1145/3020078.3021750
[8] Heewon Joung Iljung Yoon and Jooheung Lee. 2016. Zynq-Based Reconfigurable System for Real-Time Edge Detection of Noisy Video Sequences. 2016 (12 2016).
[9] Wang kang, Weisheng Zhao, Erya Deng, Jacques-Olivier Klein, Yuanqing Cheng, DafinĂŤ Ravelosona, Youguang Zhang, and Claude Chappert. 2014. A radiation hardened hybrid spintronic/CMOS nonvolatile unit using magnetic tunnel junctions. *Journal of Physics D: Applied Physics* 47, 40 (2014), 405003. http://stacks.iop.org/0022-3727/47/i=40/a=405003
[10] Yan Lin, Fei Li, and Lei He. 2005. Routing track duplication with fine-grained power-gating for FPGA interconnect power reduction. In *Proceedings of the ASP-DAC 2005. Asia and South Pacific Design Automation Conference, 2005.*, Vol. 1. 645–650 Vol. 1. https://doi.org/10.1109/ASPDAC.2005.1466243
[11] Sasikanth Manipatruni, Dmitri Nikonov, and Ian A. Young. 2012. Material Targets for Scaling All Spin Logic. 5 (12 2012).
[12] Sasikanth Manipatruni, Dmitri Nikonov, and Ian A. Young. 2013. Voltage and Energy-Delay Performance of Giant Spin Hall Effect Switching for Magnetic Memory and Logic. 7 (01 2013).
[13] Guido Meier, Markus Bolte, René Eiselt, Benjamin Krüger, Dong-Hyun Kim, and Peter Fischer. 2007. Direct Imaging of Stochastic Domain-Wall Motion Driven by Nanosecond Current Pulses. *Phys. Rev. Lett.* 98 (May 2007), 187202. Issue 18. https://doi.org/10.1103/PhysRevLett.98.187202
[14] D. Morris, D. Bromberg, J. G. Zhu, and L. Pileggi. 2012. mLogic: Ultra-low voltage non-volatile logic circuits using STT-MTJ devices. In *DAC Design Automation Conference 2012*. 486–491. https://doi.org/10.1145/2228360.2228446
[15] Hadi Parandeh-Afshar, Hind Benbihi, David Novo, and Paolo Ienne. 2012. Rethinking FPGAs: Elude the Flexibility Excess of LUTs with And-inverter Cones. In *Proceedings of the ACM/SIGDA International Symposium on Field Programmable Gate Arrays (FPGA '12)*. ACM, New York, NY, USA, 119–128. https://doi.org/10.1145/2145694.2145715
[16] G. Prenat, K. Jabeur, P. Vanhauwaert, G. D. Pendina, F. Oboril, R. Bishnoi, M. Ebrahimi, N. Lamard, O. Boulle, K. Garello, J. Langer, B. Ocker, M. C. Cyrille, P. Gambardella, M. Tahoori, and G. Gaudin. 2016. Ultra-Fast and High-Reliability SOT-MRAM: From Cache Replacement to Normally-Off Computing. *IEEE Transactions on Multi-Scale Computing Systems* 2, 1 (Jan 2016), 49–60. https://doi.org/10.1109/TMSCS.2015.2509963
[17] H. Qi, O. Ayorinde, and B. H. Calhoun. 2016. An energy-efficient near/sub-threshold FPGA interconnect architecture using dynamic voltage scaling and power-gating. In *2016 International Conference on Field-Programmable Technology (FPT)*. 20–27. https://doi.org/10.1109/FPT.2016.7929183
[18] Ramtin Zand, Arman Roohi, Deliang Fan, and Ronald F. DeMara. 2017. Energy-Efficient Nonvolatile Reconfigurable Logic Using Spin Hall Effect-Based Lookup Tables. *IEEE Trans. Nanotechnol.* 16, 1 (Jan. 2017), 32–43. https://doi.org/10.1109/TNANO.2016.2625749
[19] Grace Zgheib, Liqun Yang, Zhihong Huang, David Novo, Hadi Parandeh-Afshar, Haigang Yang, and Paolo Ienne. 2014. Revisiting And-inverter Cones. In *Proceedings of the 2014 ACM/SIGDA International Symposium on Field-programmable Gate Arrays (FPGA '14)*. ACM, New York, NY, USA, 45–54. https://doi.org/10.1145/2554688.2554791

Liquid Silicon: A Data-Centric Reconfigurable Architecture Enabled by RRAM Technology

Yue Zha
Department of Electrical and Computer Engineering
University of Wisconsin Madison
yzha3@wisc.edu

Jing Li
Department of Electrical and Computer Engineering
University of Wisconsin Madison
jli587@wisc.edu

ABSTRACT

This paper presents a data-centric reconfigurable architecture, namely *Liquid Silicon*, enabled by emerging non-volatile memory, i.e., RRAM. Compared to the *heterogeneous* architecture of commercial FPGAs, *Liquid Silicon* is inherently a *homogeneous* architecture comprising a two-dimensional (2D) array of identical "tiles". Each tile can be configured into one or a combination of four modes: TCAM, logic, interconnect, and memory. Such flexibility allows users to partition resources based on applications' needs, in contrast to the fixed hardware design using dedicated hard IP blocks in FPGAs. In addition to better resource usage, its "memory friendly" architecture effectively addresses the limitations of commercial FPGAs i.e., scarce on-chip memory resources, making it an effective complement to FPGAs. Moreover, its coarse-grained logic implementation results in shallower logic depth, less inter-tile routing overhead, and thus smaller area and better performance, compared with its FPGA counterpart. Our study shows that, on average, for both traditional and emerging applications, we achieve 62% area reduction, 27% speedup and 31% improvement in energy efficiency when mapping applications onto *Liquid Silicon* instead of FPGAs.

ACM Reference format:
Yue Zha and Jing Li. 2018. Liquid Silicon: A Data-Centric Reconfigurable Architecture Enabled by RRAM Technology. In *Proceedings of 2018 ACM/SIGDA International Symposium on Field-Programmable Gate Arrays, Monterey, CA, USA, February 25–27, 2018 (FPGA '18)*, 10 pages.
https://doi.org/10.1145/3174243.3174244

1　INTRODUCTION

Field-Programmable Gate Arrays (FPGAs) exhibit superior performance as hardware accelerators to assist general purpose processors in performing compute-intensive tasks [32][35]. While FPGAs provide the lucrative benefit of fine-grained parallelism and highly reconfigurable capability, they also face several challenges that impede the performance improvement. First, the total capacity of on-chip embedded memory blocks (EMBs) is limited (∼ 200's Mb [14]), which makes it inefficient in performing large-scale data processing. Second, chip area devoted to unused EMBs cannot be efficiently utilized even with "large-LUT-mapping" technique [37], leading to a waste of on-chip resources. Moreover, the fixed locations of EMBs also prevent users from flexibly exploiting data locality to minimize energy consumption [7].

In addition, FPGA architecture cannot efficiently implement ternary content addressable memory (TCAM) or TCAM-equivalent search engines. Most existing FPGA-based TCAM implementations are based on brute-force methods to emulate the search function using EMBs. Although a recent work proposed a scalable TCAM design with improved capacity and throughput [17], this approach is fundamentally limited by its exponential dependence on the memory size.

Another widely known architectural limitation of FPGAs is the *routing overhead*, as commercial FPGAs are designed to have extensive bitwise routing structure. Numerous studies indicate that more than 60% of dynamic and static power is dissipated in the interconnect network [30][33][38]. Additionally, for a typical FPGA device, the elaborate interconnect network also accounts for about 70% area in the deep submicron processes.

In this paper, we propose a new paradigm, namely *Liquid Silicon* (also referred to as *L-Si*) - a collaborative software/hardware technique to address the challenges of state-of-art FPGAs. *L-Si* is enabled by the emerging resistive random-access memory (RRAM) [40]. However, rather than being a direct drop-in replacement of SRAMs in existing FPGAs, it is designed to fully exploit the great potentials of RRAM, i.e., the unprecedented capacity, CMOS-compatible monolithic 3D integration, non-volatility and bit-alterability, by re-thinking reconfigurable architecture from the ground up.

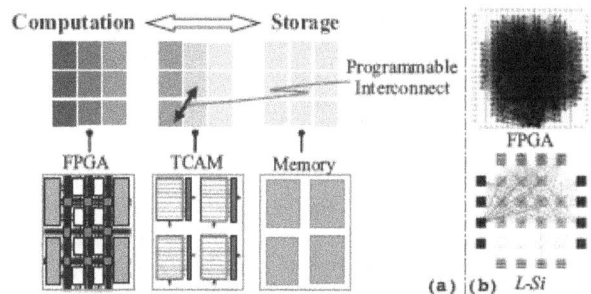

Figure 1: (a) *L-Si* **can be configured to implement computation (FPGA), search (TCAM), storage (Memory) and interconnect. (b) One example illustrates the reduced routing pressure due to the coarse-grained logic implementation in** *L-Si*.

As shown in Fig. 3, *L-Si* is a *homogeneous* architecture that comprises *identical* tiles organized in a two-dimensional array, similar to memory. Thus, it inherits the cost advantage of semiconductor memory due to its highly dense and regular structures. In *L-Si*, computation is performed in the crossbar arrays for energy efficiency, while communication is performed by CMOS circuits for resilience. It is also worth noting that, *L-Si* employs on-chip *non-volatile* configuration memory (Section 4.2.1) to internally store the bitstreams and user data. This reduces the energy consumption for configuration as it does not need to load bistreams from external memory when it is powered on. This also improves the security as it effectively eliminates the security vulnerability caused by the loading process.

L-Si supports both *coarse-grained* and *fine-grained* configurations. At the coarse-grained level, each tile can be configured into one of four operation modes, 1) light-weight compute mode (native TCAM function), 2) heavy-weight compute mode (arbitrary logic function), 3) interconnect mode (routing) and 4) memory mode (embedded block RAM) (Fig. 1a). At the fine-grained level, each tile can be further partitioned between heavy-weight compute mode (logic) and interconnect mode (routing) based on the actual usage to improve the resource utilization. These abundant configuration options are utilized by our CAD tool set (Section 5) to flexibly partition resources to better match applications' characteristics, leading to better mapping quality. It also provides flexibility to exploit memory locality to minimize energy consumption as suggested in [7]. In addition, in contrast to the fine-grained logic implementation in FPGAs (6-input lookup-table), *L-Si* provides a coarse-grained logic implementation (~ 30-input Sum-Of-Products, Section 5) that results in shallower logic depth and lower routing pressure (less nets to route, Fig. 1b).

In particular, compared to prior work, we make the following contributions in this paper:

1. We develop a data-centric reconfigurable architecture named *Liquid Silicon*. It effectively addresses the limitations in state-of-the-art FPGAs by providing both *fine-grained* and *coarse-grained* configurations, and four operation modes supporting search (TCAM), computation, routing and storage functions, and thus become an effective complement to FPGAs.

2. We develop detailed circuits for a full-fledged implementation of *L-Si*. This circuit implementation is validated through HSPICE simulation, which also gives the performance of the circuits that is used in the architecture evaluation. In addition, by leveraging the monolithic 3D integration of RRAM, we develop a new physical design and wiring strategy to optimally hide the CMOS circuits beneath the RRAM array for higher density.

3. We conduct comprehensive experiments to characterize the various performance/area trade-offs in *L-Si* and provide a thorough comparison with: 1) SRAM-based FPGAs (baseline); 2) RRAM-based FPGAs; 3) SRAM-based *L-Si*. We show our design outperforms the other three in delay, area, and energy efficiency, thereby concluding that *L-Si* is the best companion for RRAM to maximize the benefits.

The rest of the paper is organized as follows. Section 2 discusses RRAM device, access device and several related architecture works. Section 3 describes the architecture of *L-Si* and its operating principle in various configuration modes. Section 4 presents a detailed circuit implementation. Section 5 describes CAD design flow for application mapping. Section 6 presents evaluation results, followed by Section 7 to highlight the open issues and conclude the paper.

2 BACKGROUND

This section introduces the basis of RRAM device and access device. A discussion of the related works is also presented.

2.1 RRAM Device

Resistive random access memory (RRAM) has emerged as one of the most promising non-volatile memories due to its small cell size ($4F^2$), fast switching time (<10ns) [36], excellent scalability (<10nm) [41], and good endurance (up to 10^{12} cycles) [21]. Benefiting from its CMOS-compatible monolithic 3D fabrication process, RRAM cells can be organized into an ultra-dense crossbar array (Fig. 3), which does not consume die area since the array can be stacked atop CMOS circuits in the back end of line (BEOL).

In this work, we use the TaO_x RRAM device from Panasonic [40], which has already been in mass production since 2013 [29], to build

the crossbar arrays in *L-Si*. The structure and the resistive switching I-V curve of the TaO_x RRAM cell are shown in Fig. 2.

2.2 Access Device

In the crossbar array, an access device is needed to pair with one RRAM device to suppress the leakage current on the sneak path, thereby reducing the power consumption when programming (writing) the RRAM array [3]. It also eliminates the sneak path leakage during computation, as discussed in Section 4.1. Among various access devices [34][39], we choose the FAST selector [19] to build *L-Si*. It is a two-terminal bi-directional diode, which has a high selectivity ($\sim 10^{10}$), a steep turn on slop ($< 5mV/dec$), a BEOL-compatible fabrication process, and an adjustable turn on voltage.

2.3 Related Work

Several works have proposed to use the nanowire-based crossbar array to build nanoscale reconfigurable computing architectures [6][8][10][31]. In these architectures, a group of logic gates can be implemented by the nanowire-based crossbar arrays. Due to the small feature size of the nanowire, they consume less area and achieve higher performance than the CMOS-based implementations. *L-Si* is different from them in two aspects. At first, besides implementing logic functions, crossbar arrays in *L-Si* can also implement other functions, e.g., memory and TCAM, thereby improving hardware utilization for supporting diverse workloads. In addition, these nanowire-based architectures require the logic functions mapped onto one crossbar have the same data-flow direction, i.e., all inputs need to be applied on the word-lines and all outputs are on the bit-lines, and vice versa. On the contrary, *L-Si* allows more fine-grained control, i.e. inputs and outputs can have different data-flow directions in one crossbar (Section 3.3). This flexibility is utilized by our CAD tool set (Section 5) to improve the mapping quality.

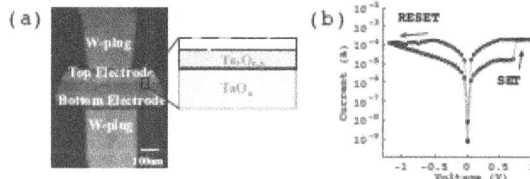

Figure 2: (a) The $Ir/Ta_2O_{5-\delta}/TaO_x/TaN$ structure [40] of one RRAM cell. (b) The resistive switching I-V curve.

Numerous research efforts have been devoted to investigate novel FPGA architectures based on non-volatile memory (NVM) technologies [4][5][9][13][24]. In these architectures, NVM cells (e.g. RRAMs) are used to either 1) replace the SRAM cells in LUTs, 2) replace the pass gates in routing fabric (connection blocks and switch blocks) as programmable switches, or 3) build dense on-chip memory blocks. Benefiting from the BEOL-compatible fabrication process and non-volatility, these implementations reduce the chip area and power consumption, without changing the basic architecture of FPGAs. Nevertheless, these implementations use NVM cells as a direct drop-in replacement of the SRAM cell. *L-Si*, on the contrary, provides a radically different reconfigurable architecture that is tailored to the RRAM technology, which allows flexible resource partitioning among computation, storage and routing.

In another interesting work, a configurable memory array is built upon a crossbar array using conventional SRAM [16], which can also be configured to perform TCAM/CAM function and bit-wise logic operations. It stores words *column-wise* in TCAM/CAM mode, but *row-wise* in logic mode. Consequently, it requires data reshuffling when performing different operations, thereby reducing the flexibility and efficiency. On the contrary, *L-Si* does not have any of these restrictions, and words (data entries) can be stored in either direction. Additionally, this work only implements a single SRAM block to realize simple bit-wise logic function (e.g. AND and NOR), while *L-Si* can implement *arbitrary* complex logic with a full-fledged CAD tool to support the application mapping.

3 HARDWARE ARCHITECTURE

L-Si is a homogeneous architecture, which comprises a 2D array of *identical* building blocks (also referred to as "tile"), as shown in Fig. 3. Thus, it is inherently different from the classic island-style FPGA architecture. In *L-Si*, each tile can be configured into four distinct modes: 1) light-weight compute mode, 2) heavy-weight compute mode, 3) interconnect mode, and 4) memory mode. This coarse-grained (tile-wise) configuration allows *L-Si* to provide an adjustable *compute-to-memory access ratio* (defined in [46]) to support diverse workloads. In addition, *L-Si* provides a fine-grained configuration since one tile can be partitioned between heavy-weight compute mode (logic) and the interconnect mode (routing) (Fig. 5c) based on the actual usage, resulting in more efficient resource utilization than the dedicated routing structure in FPGAs. In the following subsections, we will start with an overview of the *L-Si* architecture and then present the operations of these four modes.

3.1 Architecture Overview

Despite the rich configuration modes it supports, the tile structure is relatively simple. As shown in Fig. 3, each tile comprises two core components: a crossbar array and a set of connection nodes.

The crossbar array has a native array structure, where one cell containing 1 diode and 1 RRAM (1D1R) is placed at the intersection of a word-line (WL) and a bit-line (BL), as shown in Fig. 3. An 8Mb multi-layered crossbar array using the TaO_x-based 1D1R cell has been demonstrated by Panasonic [20]. As the focus of this paper is not on technology, more details for building RRAM crossbar array can be found in [20].

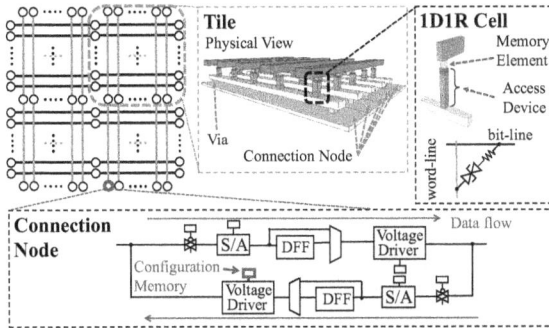

Figure 3: Conceptual diagram of *L-Si* architecture comprising a 2×2 array of tiles. In one tile, the 1D1R-based crossbar array is stacked atop connection nodes (CMOS circuits) and does not consume die area. The key building blocks of one connection node is also highlighted.

The connection node is used for connecting WLs (or BLs) of two adjacent crossbar arrays, the key building blocks are sense amplifiers (S/As), skippable flip-flop, voltage driver and configuration memories. The S/A detects signal changes on a WL (or a BL) in one array, then generates a full-swing output to drive the corresponding WL (or BL) in the adjacent array and vice versa. The skippable flip-flop is used to implement sequential circuit. The voltage driver can be configured to generate different drive voltages for four modes, controlled by the configuration memories. The configuration memories also control the direction of the connection node, which is designed with two copies of circuits to operate *bidirectionally*. We note that

connection nodes can also be disabled if not in use to save power. More details of the circuit design is presented in Section 4.2.

3.2 Light-weight Compute Mode

In this mode, each tile can be configured as an embedded TCAM block. The first 1Mb hardware prototype [23] proved the feasibility of applying NVMs to build cost-effective TCAM. Inspired by the fact that an NVM-based TCAM shares the same physical design as a memory array, we extend the RRAM crossbar array to directly implement TCAM function as a dedicated configuration mode.

Fig. 4 illustrates the search operation in this mode. More specifically, the search key from top/bottom (or left/right) tile is applied on WLs (or BLs), and compared with data entries that are horizontally (or vertically) stored in the crossbar array. After the parallel search, the connection nodes output the match vector to adjacent tiles for post-match processing.

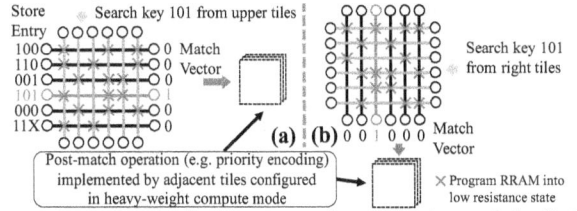

Figure 4: An example illustrates the operations of the light-weight compute mode. All data entries are stored in the same direction in one tile, either (a) horizontally or (b) vertically. The data set stored in example (a) and (b) are same, and the matched data entry is highlighted in yellow.

We note that this configuration mode provides three unique flexibilities that are not available in other TCAM designs [23][25]. At first, users can flexibly define their own post-match operations, which are implemented by the adjacent tiles configured in heavy-weight compute mode (Section 3.3). In addition, this mode can implement TCAMs with different capacities and aspect ratios by coalescing multiple adjacent tiles. Finally, the data-flow direction is adjustable, i.e., data entries are stored horizontally or vertically.

3.3 Heavy-weight Compute/Interconnect Mode

Due to the similarities between heavy-weight compute mode and interconnect mode, we will discuss them together in this section. In the Berkeley Logic Interchange Format (BLIF) [2], an AND logic function can be represented by a combination of '0', '1' and '-'. For example, function $F = ABC$ is represented as '111', while $F = \bar{A}\bar{B}\bar{C}$ (or $F = \overline{A+B+C}$) is represented as '000'. In case of unused inputs, '-' will be used to mask them. For example, when the inputs are A, B, C and D, the function $F = \bar{A}B\bar{C}$ is represented as '010-'. We observe that this representation is *fully compatible* with the TCAM function, i.e., we can apply the three states in TCAM ('0', '1' and 'X'[1]) to represent the three states ('0', '1' and '-') in BLIF to implement AND logic functions, and use search keys to represent its logic inputs.

Based on this observation, we further extend our tile design from light-weight compute mode to heavy-weight compute mode, in which each tile can be configured to implement multiple combinational logic functions, i.e., one data entry for one multi-input-single-output function. Sequential circuits can be implemented by configuring a skippable flip-flop in the connection node. In contrast to light-weight compute mode, data-flow direction in this mode can be controlled at highly fine-grained granularity (entry level instead of tile level) as shown in Fig. 5a. This feature is utilized by our CAD tool (Section 5) to optimize the mapping.

---

[1] 'X' is don't care state.

The interconnect mode can be treated as a special case of heavy-weight compute mode, in which one data entry implements a buffer function ($F = A$). As shown in Fig. 5b, one input can be routed to any of the other three directions in a tile by programming the crossbar array and the connection nodes accordingly. Additionally, this mode is able to co-exist with the heavy-weight compute mode in the same tile (Fig. 5c). Such a feature is exploited by our CAD tool set (Section 5) to improve the mapping quality.

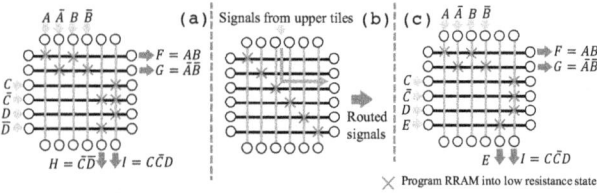

Figure 5: (a) Four logic functions with different data-flow directions are mapped in one tile configured in heavy-weight compute mode. (b) The operation of the interconnect mode is illustrated. (c) The heavy-weight compute mode (implement functions F, G and I) and interconnect mode (route signal E) can co-exist in the same tile.

3.4 Memory Mode

In contrast to FPGAs, *L-Si* is designed to be "memory friendly", as each tile can also be configured as an EMB. For simplicity, we have restricted our design to be a single-port RAM. In this mode, four tiles are used to implement a memory block (Fig. 6). One of them is configured as a memory array, a small fraction ($\sim 4.7\%$ in this design) of which is used to implement the column address decoding logic, while the other three tiles are configured to implement row address decoder and read/write column select logic, respectively.

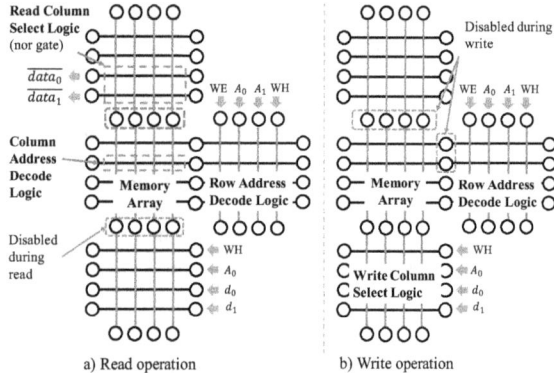

Figure 6: An example illustrates (a) the read operation and (b) the write operation in the memory mode. This memory block stores 4 2-bit words.

The read operation is performed in several steps (Fig. 6a). First, the row address is decoded by the row address decoding logic (right tile), and the outputs are sent to the memory array (central tile). Meanwhile, the column address is also sent to the column address decoding logic in the memory array in the same direction as the decoded row address. After performing sensing by the connection nodes (highlighted in blue), the read column select logic (NOR gates in the top tile) is applied on the outputs of the memory array to generate the final read results. Note that, the write column select logic (bottom tile) is disabled during read operation.

The write operation is performed in two consecutive steps to write logic 1's and logic 0's, controlled by the write high (WH) signal. In write operation, row address decoding logic and write column select

logic generates the appropriate drive voltages, based on the address, WH, and the write data. Note that during write, the read column select logic and column address decode logic are disabled (Fig. 6b).

It appears that using four tiles to implement one memory block is likely to be inefficient. However, due to the ultra-dense array organization and much simplified pitch match between the array and the periphery, the overhead is negligible in our experimental evaluation (Section 6.2). Moreover, since all peripheral circuits are implemented in a soft-logic style (instead of ASIC), users can flexibly adjust the logical aspect ratio of the memory array. Our custom CAD tools support varying logical aspect ratios from $4b \times 15616$ to $32b \times 1952$ ($61kb$ in total) by default, and more logical aspect ratios can be realized by configuring the peripheral circuits.

4 CIRCUIT IMPLEMENTATION

This section presents detailed circuit implementations for *L-Si*, including digital circuits, physical design and optimization.

4.1 Crossbar Array

In *L-Si*, each tile contains one crossbar array, which is built upon 1D1R cells comprising a RRAM device and an access device placed at the intersection of a bit-line (BL) and a word-line(WL), as discussed in Section 3.1. When one tile is configured to implement one of the four modes (Section 3), the RRAM cells in the crossbar are programmed into appropriate resistance states (LRS or HRS), and the BLs (or WLs) in the crossbar are either driven or sensed by the connection nodes.

Proper voltages are applied on BLs (or WLs) to eliminate the sneak path leakage during computation. More specifically, when one BL (or WL) is driven by the connection node, it can have two voltage levels, i.e., V_{input0} and V_{input1} to represent logic '0' and '1', respectively. When it is sensed by the connection node, the voltage on this line is between $V_{precharge}$ and $V_{discharge}$ based on the sensing scheme (Section 4.2.1). To eliminate the sneak path leakage, these voltages need to satisfy the following requirements[2].

(1) $V_{input1} - V_{input0} < V_T$ (2) $V_{precharge} - V_{discharge} < V_T$
(3) $V_{precharge} - V_{input0} > V_T$ (4) $V_{precharge} - V_{input1} < V_T$

Satisfying the requirement (1) means that when one BL and one WL are both driven by the connection nodes, the access device (diode) at the intersection is turned off, therefore no direct path is formed between two voltage sources (no static current). Satisfying the requirement (2) indicates that when one BL and one WL are both sensed by the connection nodes, the access device at the intersection is turned off, thereby disconnecting these two lines. Requirements (3)-(4) are given by the sensing scheme, which will be discussed in Section 4.2.1.

Based on these requirements, the voltages used in *L-Si* are $V_{input0} = -0.3V$, $V_{input1} = 0V$, $V_{precharge} = 0.5V$, $V_{disharge} = 0.3V$ and $V_T = 0.6V$.

4.2 Connection Node

The circuit implementation of one connection node is depicted in Fig. 7. The key building blocks are 1) sense amplifier (S/A) for sensing the voltage changes on the connected BL (or WL), 2) configurable dynamic inverter to assist implementing the OR gates in the Sum-Of-Product (SOP) terms, 3) flipflops for implementing sequential circuits, 4) voltage driver to generate the required voltages for different modes, and 5) RRAM-based configuration memories to control the various operations of the connection node.

Particularly, it is worth noting that configurable dynamic inverters are included to improve the mapping quality. As discussed in Section 5, applications are synthesized into SOP terms in the technology mapping stage, where each SOP term comprises a group of

---

[2]V_T is the turn on voltage for the access device, and $V_{dd} = 1V$ under 45nm technology.

AND gates and one OR gate. While it is efficient to map the group of AND gates onto tiles, it leads to a low utilization when mapping the OR gates onto tiles. More specifically, these OR gates do not share their inputs with other logic gates, and when mapping them onto tiles, the WLs (or BLs) they occupy cannot be utilized by other gates mapped in the same tile. This reduces the amount of logic gates that can be mapped onto one tile and results in a degraded performance (e.g. area). Using configurable dynamic inverters to implement these OR gates can improve the mapping quality.

In the following subsections, we will present the detailed implementation of the building blocks and discuss several techniques applied to reduce the power consumption.

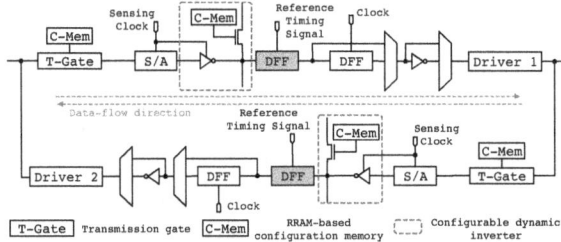

Figure 7: Detailed implementation of one connection node.

4.2.1 Implementation of Building Blocks.

Sense Amplifier. The circuit implementation of the S/A is presented in Fig. 8, which contains three parts: 1) precharging circuit (P1 and the transmission gate), 2) discharging circuit (N1 and N2), and 3) inverters to generate a full swing output. To illustrate the sensing scheme used in this S/A design, we assume that the data entry is stored on BLs, and inputs are applied on WLs by driving them to V_{input0} or V_{input1}. Note that, the same sensing circuit and scheme can still be applied when the data entry is stored on WLs.

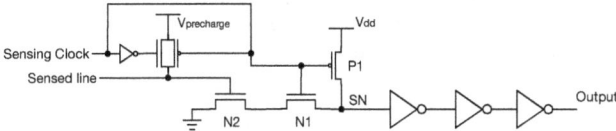

Figure 8: The implementation of the S/A design.

The sensing operation is controlled by the sensing clock and is performed in two stages: precharge and evaluation. In the precharge stage, the BL is charged to $V_{precharge}$ through the transmission gate, and the node SN is precharged to V_{dd} through P1. Then, in the evaluation stage, BL is floating and starts to discharge (Fig. 9b) at a rate depending on the number of WLs that are pulled down to V_{input0} (requirement 3) and the resistance states of RRAMs on the BL (Fig. 9a). Note that, no discharging current flows through the WLs that connected to V_{input1} (requirement 4) due to the isolation of the access device, regardless of the resistance states of RRAMs. At the same time, node SN is also discharging to ground since N1 and N2 are opened (Fig. 9c), and the discharging rate is controlled by the gate voltage of N2, i.e., the voltage of the BL. In a match case (BL_1 in Fig. 9), SN has a higher discharging rate and the output switches to logic '1' in a shorter time, compared to the mismatch case (BL_0, Fig. 9d).

Configurable Dynamic Inverter. The circuit implementation of a configurable dynamic inverter is shown in Fig. 10, which contains one dynamic inverter and one NMOS. The dynamic inverter is controlled by the same sensing clock that is applied to the S/A, and its operation is illustrated in Fig. 9e. The NMOS can be configured to connect the adjacent connection nodes, therefore, a multi-input dynamic NOR gate can be formed among adjacent nodes.

Flip-flops. As shown in Fig. 7, one connection node contains two flip-flops for one data-flow direction. One flip-flop is conditionally included to implement the sequential circuit. The other one (marked in grey in Fig. 7) is included to latch the output (Fig. 9f) of the configurable dynamic inverter, which is controlled by the reference timing signal. This reference timing signal is locally generated by one reserved entry (WL or BL) in every tile. This allows each tile to have its own reference timing control, therefore, it works for all configuration modes without any modification.

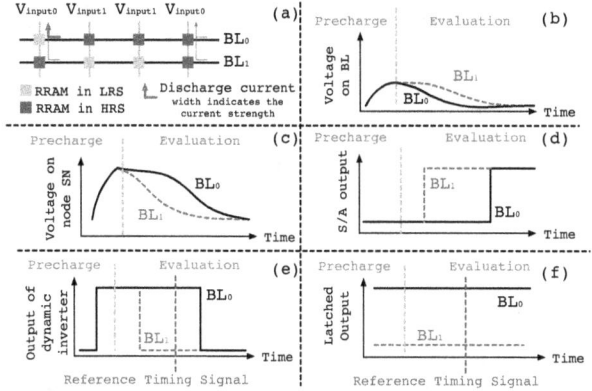

Figure 9: (a) The voltages on WLs and the RRAM states are presented. The corresponding discharge current for these two BLs are also drawn. (b) The voltages on these two BLs. (c) The voltage on the node SN in the S/A. (d) The output of S/A. (e) The output of the configurable dynamic inverter, and (f) this output is latched by the reference timing signal.

Driver Circuits. Driver circuits are included to generate the correct drive voltages based on the input signal and the sensing clock. Controlled by one configuration memory, they also can be disabled to save power. Two types of driver circuits are used in the connection node. Driver 1 contains a negative voltage level shifter to generate the V_{input0}, and the driver 2 extends the driver 1 by adding a positive voltage level shifter to provide the write voltages for the memory mode. Since the row address decode logic and write column select logic (Fig. 6) can only be placed on the right and bottom side of the memory array, only one data-flow direction needs to use the large driver circuits (Driver 2), as shown in Fig. 7.

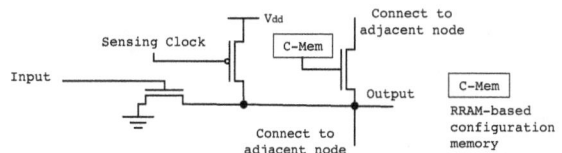

Figure 10: Circuit design of the configurable dynamic inverter.

Configuration Memory. In *L-Si*, we also use RRAM devices to build *non-volatile* configuration memory in the connection node. Each configuration memory is structured with a 3D2R cell, two inverters, and two MOSFETs (Fig. 11a) and can be organized as a crossbar array (Fig. 11b), by connecting the WLs (WL_T and WL_B), BLs and LOAD lines. Information is stored in each configuration memory cell using two RRAM devices, which are programmed to have complementary states (one in HRS and the other in LRS). For example, the RRAM device in blue (Fig. 11a) is programmed into LRS to store logic 1, otherwise it stores logic 0.

To program the RRAM device in configuration memory, the "V/3" write scheme [3] is used, and one example (Fig. 11b) is given to illustrate the applied voltages for writing one RRAM device (blue).

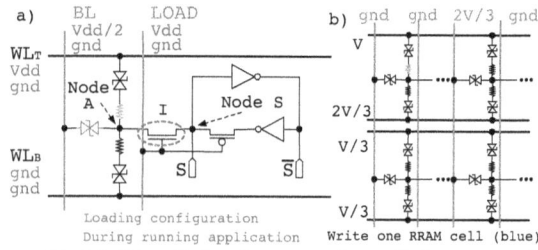

Figure 11: (a) Circuit implementation of the non-volatile configuration memory, and voltage setups for three operations are highlighted. (b) 3D2R cells can be organized in a crossbar structure and the voltage setup to program one RRAM cell (in blue) is illustrated.

In the read operation, WL_T is connected to V_{dd}, and WL_B is connected to gnd. A voltage divider is formed between two WLs, and the voltage on Node A (Fig. 11a) is determined by the resistance states of the two RRAM devices. The degraded voltage level on Node A due to the limited resistance ratio is restored to a full voltage swing by the inverters to generate final digital outputs. In addition, $V_{dd}/2$ is applied on BL to turn off the access device in red (Fig. 11a), thereby disconnecting 3D2R cells from BL and isolating them from each other. Finally, the LOAD line is connected to V_{dd}, and the stored configuration bit is loaded into the storage node (Node S).

During normal operations, WLs, BL and LOAD line are all connected to gnd (Fig. 11a). Therefore, 3D2R cells have zero standby power consumption, and configuration bits are retained without the need of an external power supply.

4.2.2 Power-Saving Techniques.

S/A is the most power consuming part in the connection node because it needs to frequently precharge the BL or WL (large capacitance). To reduce the power, we apply two techniques when designing the S/A. The first technique is that we reduce the precharging voltage, i.e., using $V_{precharge}$ instead of V_{dd}. In addition, instead of a rail-to-rail voltage swing, the voltage on the BL or WL is a small voltage difference between $V_{discharge}$ and $V_{precharge}$, which is 0.2V in this design. This technique reduces the power consumption for one precharging operation.

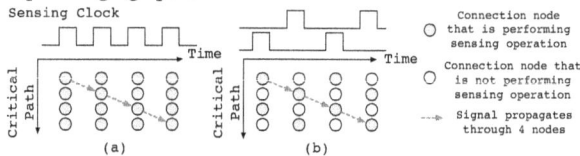

Figure 12: One example illustrates sensing operations when providing (a) one sensing clock or (b) two sensing clocks.

The other technique is that, instead of only having one sensing clock, multiple sensing clocks that have same the frequency but different phases are provided, and S/As choose one of them to perform the sensing operation. This can reduce the operation frequency of the S/A, thereby reducing the power consumption, as illustrated in Fig. 12. More specifically, one critical path of the mapped application can have n connection nodes. If only one sensing clock is provided, then in order to run the application under frequency f, the sensing clock frequency needs to be nf. On the contrary, if two sensing clocks are provided, then the sensing clock frequency can be reduced to $nf/2$. More sensing clocks lead to lower power consumption,

but they require more multiplexers and configuration memories for selecting clocks (large area). In this design, we choose to include two sensing clocks which reduces the power consumption of *L-Si* without noticeably increasing the design complexity.

4.3 Physical Design

As described in Section 2, the fabrication process of the RRAM and access device is BEOL compatible. Therefore, the crossbar arrays are implemented on upper level metals i.e., M3 and M4 layers while the connection nodes use lower level metals, i.e., M1 and M2 layers for local routing and are buried underneath the arrays. We perform layout optimization by judiciously increasing the pitch size of the crossbar array, which will ease the placement of connection nodes *fully* below the array to achieve the minimal Si area. Additionally, we share common circuits (e.g. S/A and voltage driver) as much as possible between tiles to further reduce the area. As shown in Fig. 13, we complete the physical design using 40nm CMOS technology. The area of one tile is measured to be $87.87\mu m \times 87.24\mu m$. The physical design information will be used for the evaluation in Section 6.

4.4 Configuration and Other Issues

In Section 4.2.1, we discussed the methods to program configuration memory in the connection nodes. In this Section, we present the method to program crossbar array.

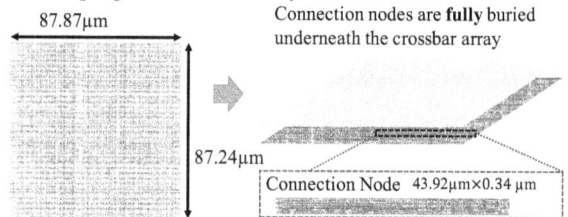

Figure 13: Physical design of a tile under 40nm technology.

In *L-Si*, buffers are inserted between crossbar arrays, which can be configured to connect or disconnect multiple WLs (or BLs) in the adjacent tiles when programming *L-Si*. Logically, *L-Si* only contains one crossbar array during configuration, and it can be programmed by the widely used write scheme (e.g. "V/3" or "V/2" write scheme)[3]. Additionally, write-and-verify schemes can be applied to program RRAM cells into the required resistance level. Physically, WLs and BLs are separated by the buffers, therefore the configuration process does not have severe IR-drop issue. The configuration bitstream is generated by the CAD tool (Section 5) in an offline process.

With the manufacturing process getting mature, there has been steady improvement in RRAM technologies based on engineering approaches. Rather than taking over the dominant markets of incumbent technologies such as DRAM or FLASH, a relative low-hanging fruit is to apply RRAM to *L-Si*, as it has less stringent requirements on endurance, write speed and power, etc., from the technology point of view. For RRAMs of interest, 10^8 cycles of endurance is likely sufficient to sustain the life time of *L-Si*, which is quite achievable in commercial products. For the memory mode, since any tile can be configured as memory blocks, wear leveling can be performed by optimally placing the memory blocks, thereby reducing the pressure on endurance. Evaluation of this technique will be our future work. High write power and low write speed per bit compared to SRAMs is less of a concern, as configuration is not done as frequently as updates on main memory and not all applications utilize the memory mode.

5 CAD TOOL SET

In order to efficiently map applications onto *L-Si*, we develop a complete CAD tool set based on the VTR framework [26]. As shown in

Fig. 14, this tool set takes applications written in Verilog as input, and generates bitstreams to configure *L-Si*. It comprises three core tools: ODIN II [15] for parsing Verilog codes, ABC [27] for technology mapping, and a custom tool for placement and routing. Finally, the mapping results are validated by checking the utilization, and if one tile is overutilized or all tiles are underutilized, the place and route process will be repeated with an adjusted amount of tiles.

Due to the architectural difference between FPGA and *L-Si*, the ODIN II and ABC tools (originally developed for FPGA) in VTR have been modified. More specifically, the ODIN II is modified to synthesize memory modules into logic primitives (e.g. memory array and address decoders), instead of hard IP blocks (e.g. on-chip block RAM). It is also modified to synthesize the new TCAM modules. Additionally, the modified ODIN II also exploits the flexibility (capacity and aspect ratio) provided by the memory and light-weight compute modes (Section 3.4, 3.2) to efficiently synthesize large memory and TCAM modules. For the ABC tool, we applied the cut enumeration with priority cut algorithm [28] to map logics into K-input Sum-Of-Product terms. In the experiments, we observe that a large K value leads to better performance but a longer run time. In order to complete the mapping of applications in a reasonable run time, we choose the value of K to be ~30.

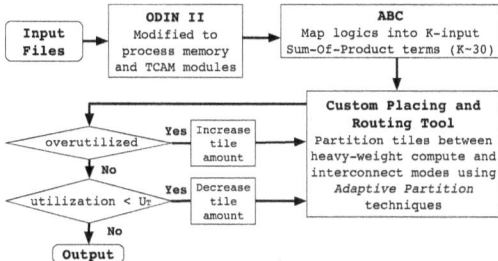

Figure 14: Workflow of the provided CAD tool set.

In order to utilize the unique routing structure in *L-Si*, the custom tool developed by Zha et al. [45] is adapted to perform placement and routing. This custom tool improves the mapping quality through three key techniques. At first, it applies the Adaptive Partition techniques [45] to efficiently utilize the resources in tiles. More specifically, tiles (not configured in memory and light-weight compute modes) are partitioned between heavy-weight compute mode (logic) and interconnect mode (routing) based on the actual usage, i.e., tiles in routing congested area allocate more resources for routing and other tiles allocates more resources for logic. Secondly, this tool places logic primitives that have shared inputs in the same tile to reduce the amount of interconnections among tiles. Finally, it optimizes the data-flow direction of each logic primitive to reduce the length of routing paths. Consequently, the resources used for routing is minimized (19.4% of used resources) and the routing delay is reduced (42.2% of total delay).

More details on the modified ODIN II, the modified ABC and the custom placing and routing tool are discussed in [45].

6 ARCHITECTURE EVALUATION

In this section, we evaluate the performance (area, delay and energy efficiency) of *L-Si* by running applications under three representative usage cases: 1) logic only, 2) logic + memory and 3) TCAM. For that purpose, our benchmark circuits comprise of traditional MCNC benchmark circuits [43], circuits provided by VTR project, and two new TCAM benchmark circuits that we created to accelerate packet classification in networking and join operation in database. We note that the future applications of *L-Si* will not be limited to applications

developed for commercial FPGAs. Nonetheless, it can effectively complement FPGA in developing new applications particularly data-intensive applications that are traditionally considered not suitable for FPGAs.

In this evaluation, the SRAM-based FPGA is chosen as the baseline. Moreover, the goal of this work is to provide insights in comparing two architectures (*L-Si*, FPGA) paired with two different technologies (RRAM, SRAM). To ensure the benefits (area and delay) that we gained in *L-Si* are not simply due to the advance in technology, i.e., a direct drop-in replacement for SRAMs with dense RRAMs, we also included two more cases (RRAM-based FPGAs and SRAM-based *L-Si*). The RRAM-based FPGAs is a drop-in replacement for the commercial SRAM-based FPGA, and maintain the same architecture as most prior works did. Similarly, in the SRAM-based *L-Si*, the RRAMs are replaced with SRAMs.

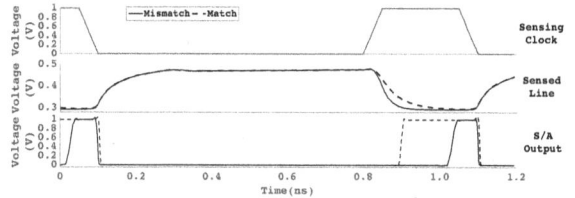

Figure 15: The simulated waveform of a sensing operation.

We use the VTR[3] to estimate the area, delay and power when mapping applications onto FPGAs. For *L-Si*, our custom CAD tool set is applied to map applications and outputs the amount of used tiles (N_T) and the amount of tiles on the critical path (L). It also outputs the average tile utilization (U), i.e., the ratio between used entry (e.g WL) and total entry, for calculating the power consumption. The area of one tile (A_T) is measured at 40nm technology node based on the physical design (Section 4.3), and the area for one application is $N_T \times A_T$. The performance of one tile is obtained from the HSPICE simulation (Fig. 15) under 45nm technology [1] and scaled to 40nm. The behaviors of RRAM cells and access device are simulated using Verilog-A modules [18]. The ON/OFF ratio of RRAM cells are $R_{on} = 1k\Omega$ and $R_{off} = 150k\Omega$. The capacitance of one WL (or BL) is estimated based on its length obtained from physical design. Multiple input patterns and stored patterns are simulated to accurately estimate the power and delay, and the peak power and maximum operation frequency of one tile are $P_{max} = 7.2\mu W$ per entry and $f_{max} = 1.13GHz$, respectively. For one mapped application, the power consumption is estimated as $N_T \times U \times P_{max}$. The operation frequency of it is calculated $F = f_{max}/L$, as one signal needs to propagate through the L tiles on the critical path.

6.1 Logic Only Evaluation

In this experiment, we applied MCNC benchmark set and several benchmarks from VTR to evaluate the aforementioned four architectures, when *L-Si* is configured to operate in heavy-weight compute and interconnect modes.

As shown in Fig. 16, for all the benchmark circuits, *L-Si*, on average, outperforms the other three architectures in area, delay and energy efficiency. In particular, it achieves 62% area saving comparing to SRAM-based FPGAs. We also observe that it consumes 13% less area than RRAM-based FPGAs, which implies that such an area saving is not simply due to a drop-in replacement for SRAMs with dense RRAMs. It is also worth noting that among the four architectures, SRAM-based *L-Si* has the largest area cost, indicating that *L-Si* architecture is most beneficial to pair with RRAM technology.

---

[3]"k6_frac_N10_frac_chain_mem32K_40nm.xml" architecture file is applied

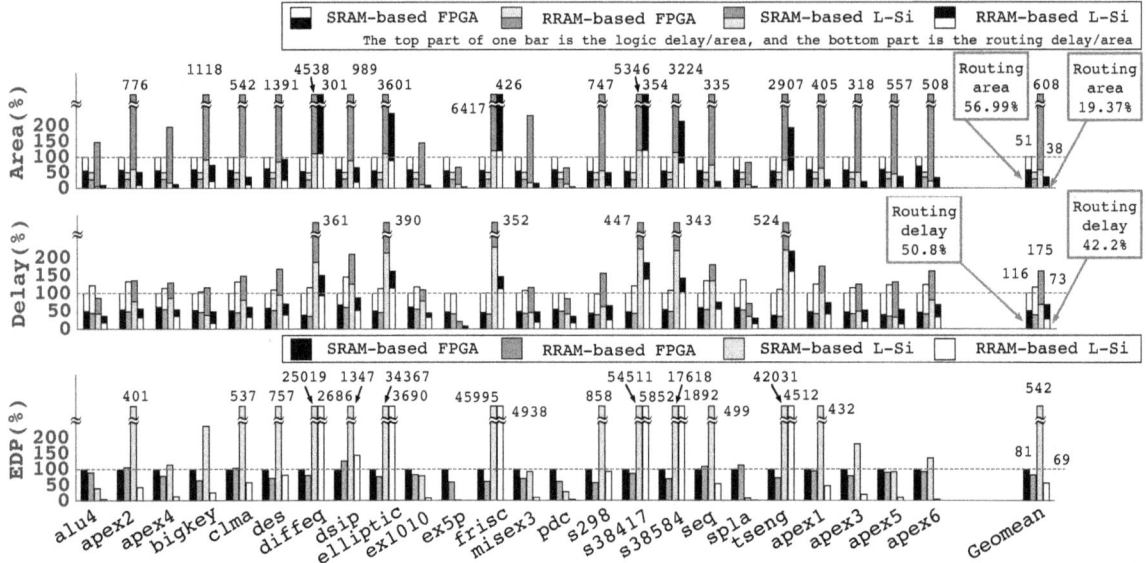

Figure 16: Area (top), delay (middle) and energy efficiency (energy-delay-product, EDP, bottom) results are presented. Results of the SRAM-based FPGA are used as the baseline, and other results are normalized to them. The ratio between routing area and total used area (top), and the ratio between routing delay and total delay (middle) are also presented.

On the other hand, benefiting from the coarse-grained configurable architecture of *L-Si*, technology mapping stage generates net lists with much shallower depth. Therefore, the delay of *L-Si* is 27% less than that of baseline FPGAs, on average, whereas the delays of SRAM-based *L-Si* and RRAM-based FPGA increase by 75% and 16% respectively, compared to the baseline. The delay become worse in SRAM-based *L-Si* is because the increase in unit delay per tile due to longer wires (larger RC constant) is much more significant than the decrease in logic depth. The minor increase in delay for RRAM-based FPGA is because of the longer sensing time of RRAM devices, due to its higher R_{on} compared to that of a MOSFET.

Another advantage of *L-Si* is that it makes better use of routing resources as compared with FPGAs, due to its coarse-grained architecture and flexibility of partitioning resources between logic and routing. Overall, the area consumed by routing in RRAM-based *L-Si* is only 19% of the total used area, compared to 57% in the SRAM-based FPGA, as shown in Figure 16. Moreover, the delay contributed by routing in RRAM-based *L-Si* is only 42% of the total delay, as compared with 51% in the baseline architecture.

Moreover, RRAM-based *L-Si* also achieves 31% improvement in energy efficiency (energy-delay-product) over the SRAM-based FPGA. We also note that the energy efficiency of RRAM-based *L-Si* is 12% higher than that of the RRAM-based FPGA. This indicates that this improvement does not only come from the advance RRAM technology, but also because of the *L-Si* architecture.

From the fact that *L-Si* on average outperforms the other three evaluated architectures in area, delay and energy efficiency, we conclude that it is beneficial to implement programmable logic device using RRAMs and vice-versa. However, we also observe that several benchmarks show slightly different trends. The problem is caused by the high resource usage for routing. In these benchmark circuits, more than 30% hardware resources are used for routing connection nets. Since less resources in tiles is left for logic functions, the amount of tiles for these applications increases. Logic functions are scattered in more tiles, thereby increasing the average length of routing paths (long routing delay as shown in Fig. 16), and further increasing the

routing pressure. The contention of the hardware resources between routing and logic leads to a slightly degraded performance. One possible solution is using a hybrid routing structure. More specifically, several tiles are grouped and the interconnection mode is used for the local routing inside this group, while an FPGA-like routing structure (i.e. connection block and switch block) can be applied for the global routing among these groups. More investigation on this problem and the hybrid routing structure will be our future work.

6.2 Memory Evaluation

In this section, *L-Si* is evaluated by applying a set of benchmark circuits that contains memory blocks. When mapping these benchmark circuits onto *L-Si*, the hardware resources is partitioned between memory and logic among tiles, i.e., some tiles are configured into the memory mode while others are configured into the heavy-weight compute mode. We note that, *L-Si* architecture only supports single port RAM. Therefore, in our evaluation, we restricted out analysis to benchmarks with single port memory only.

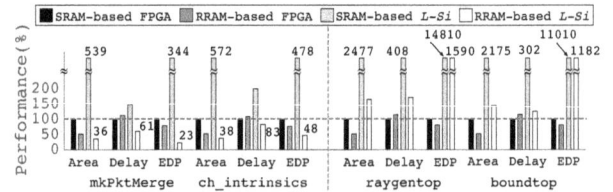

Figure 17: Area, delay and energy efficiency (energy-delay-product, EDP) results of benchmarks using single-port memory block. The benchmarks are divided into large-memory (left) and small-memory benchmarks (right), based on the amount of resource consumed by memory blocks. The results of the SRAM-based FPGA are used as the baseline.

According to the resource usage of memory and logic, these benchmark circuits can be divided into two groups. The benchmark ch_intrinsics and mkPktMerge have simple logic functions, and more than 30% hardware resources are consumed by memory blocks (large-memory benchmarks). On the contrary, the benchmark raygentop and boundtop have complex logic function, and less than 3% hardware resources are used to implement memory blocks (small-memory benchmarks).

As shown in Figure 17, *L-Si* achieves the best results in area, delay and energy efficiency when implementing the large-memory benchmarks. On average, 64%, 29% and 65% improvement is achieved in area, delay and energy efficiency, respectively, compared to that of the SRAM-based FPGA. On the other hand, for the small-memory benchmarks, the benefits of the flexible and dense memory block (memory mode) is overshadowed by the routing pressure (discussed in Section 6.1). Therefore, it is not efficient to implement these circuits on *L-Si*. Additionally, we further decrease the size of memory block in the benchmark ch_intrinsics, and change it from a large-memory benchmark to a small-memory benchmark. Much less performance improvement (less than 10% decrease in area compared to SRAM-based FPGA) is observed when mapping it onto *L-Si*. These results indicate that *L-Si* is advantageous in running large-memory applications, which have large memory footprint and high memory bandwidth requirement. The larger the memory size and the higher the bandwidth, the better efficiency.

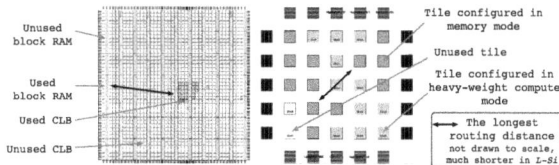

Figure 18: Implementing benchmark *mkPktMerge* on FPGAs and *L-Si*. Memory blocks are at fixed locations in FPGAs (left), while their locations can be configured in *L-Si*(right)

We note that the efficiency gain in *L-Si* is mainly due to three reasons. The first one is the high storage density. For instance, in this evaluation, the storage density of the memory block in *L-Si* is $1.93 bit/um^2$, compared to $0.62 bit/um^2$ for the SRAM-based FPGA. Advanced technologies such as multi-bit cell [44] or multi-level cell [22] will further improve the density. Additionally, since every tile in *L-Si* can be configured to implement memory block, it supports a large dynamic range of memory capacity/bandwidth, which can be configured by users. For the same chip area (iso-area), *L-Si* can be configured to have $61Kb \sim 1.43Gb$ storage capacity, while commercial FPGAs only have a fixed and limited on-chip storage capacity ($\sim 150Mb$ [42]). The last reason is the flexible placement of memory blocks in *L-Si* (Figure 18), which is a highly desirable feature for programmable logic devices to have. As discussed in [7], spatial computation through data partition within a computation substrate is more energy efficient than to dump all data into a large monolithic memory block. In other words, the size and location of memory blocks have to be optimized towards different applications from an energy stand point. However, current FPGA does not support such feature. Although we did not evaluate energy in this work, the advantages we gained in both area and delay indicate that, better application mapping and thus better energy efficiency is achieved on *L-Si* due to the highly flexible hardware architecture.

We believe the "memory friendly" architecture of *L-Si* effectively addresses the limitation of state-of-art FPGA in large scale data processing. It becomes increasingly more important as emerging applications are more data-intensive at the era of "Big Data".

6.3 TCAM Evaluation
From an application perspective, a TCAM is an attractive hardware solution for a wide range of data-intensive applications such as IP address lookup, intrusion detection, etc. Due to these advantages, TCAM design using FPGA has been gaining popularity in recent

years. However, most ideas are based on brute-force implementations to mimic the TCAM function using EMBs, resulting in severe efficiency loss. To improve the efficiency, a recent work from Xilinx proposed a methodology to make better use of on-chip memory resources for implementing a TCAM [17]. In particular, one TCAM is logically partitioned into smaller blocks, each of which is implemented by a set of small-size EMBs. This approach greatly improves the scalability and efficiency, leading to an improved resource utilization. However, it still has a substantially higher implementation cost compared to a dedicated TCAM ASIC design in *L-Si*. The fundamental reason for that is the exponential dependence on RAM size (2^w) when implementing an equivalent TCAM function with a size of W. To fully address the issue, *L-Si* provides a dedicated mode (light-weight compute mode) to directly implement a TCAM, which effectively closes the efficiency gap with its ASIC counterpart.

To quantitatively evaluate the benefits of implementing a TCAM on *L-Si*, we will need to run benchmark circuits which are specifically developed to exercise a TCAM design. However, we could not find such applications from existing benchmark suites due to the high implementation cost on FPGAs. Therefore, we made our best efforts to create two benchmark circuits for our study by implementing 1) a *search* function to perform longest prefix match for packet classification [17]. 2) a *join* function in database application. These benchmarks are coded in Verilog, and are run through the design flow described in Section 5.

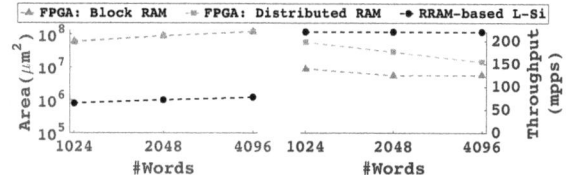

Figure 19: Area(left) and throughput(right) of implementing TCAM on FPGA and *L-Si*. The number of words (x-axis) and area (y-axis) are plotted in logarithmic scale. The results of FPGAs are from [17].

The first *L-Si*-based benchmark circuit comprises two parts: 1) a TCAM array to generate the match vector and 2) a priority encoder to compress the match vector to generate the index of match words with the highest priority. To ensure a fair comparison, we chose Xilinx's FPGA-based TCAM design [17] as the baseline. The *L-Si* implementation of TCAM array is quite straightforward and can be mapped directly on soft blocks configured in light-weight compute mode. The implementation of priority encoder is equivalent to designing digital logic, which can be synthesized on soft blocks configured in heavy-weight compute mode. We note that by nature, it is costly to implement a priority encoder in FPGA because its Boolean functions have a large number of shared inputs, which, nevertheless, are highly efficient to be mapped on *L-Si*. Our evaluation results show that on average, the area of *L-Si*-based design is only 1% of Xilinx's design for implementing the same TCAM capacity (Figure 19[4]). Additionally, *L-Si* also reduces the power consumption by 94% and achieves 30% higher throughput compared to the FPGA-based design.

Moreover, when TCAM size grows to be deeper or wider, the logic and the routing complexities become more pronounced in FPGA, as it will need to bitwise-AND wide bit vectors and compress a deep match vector, decreasing the achievable clock rate, which determines the peek throughput of the RAM-based TCAM [17]. In contrast, our *L-Si*-based implementation is much more scalable, meaning thereby

---
[4] mpps: million packet per second. The width of search key is 150 bit in both experiments.

we can maintain nearly constant clock rate and thus peak throughput, independent of the size of TCAM.

In the second benchmark, we define a data array (one tile) placed adjacent to a TCAM block. The output of the TCAM block (match vector) is used as an index to access the data array, thereby realizing an efficient search operation on key-value pairs. One restriction of this design is that any two keys in one TCAM block cannot be same. However, this problem can be addressed by carefully partitioning the data entries before dumping them into TCAM blocks. Note that, this partition operation is a one-time operation, thereby resulting in negligible overhead.

On the contrary, most FPGA-based designs are based on the hash join algorithm [11][12]. Complex logic circuits are implemented to hash the search key, and a dedicated storage structure (e.g. a linked list) is applied to resolve the collision caused by an imperfect hashing function. Compared to our design, previous FPGA implementation [11] requires 24% more storage capacity, and much more complex logic circuits (thus lower throughput) to realize the search operation. Additionally, the compact TCAM blocks in our design result in much lower routing pressure, and thus, the frequency of our implementation can easily achieve above 300MHz, compared to 200MHz in the FPGA-based design.

In summary, the area-efficient, high-performance and flexible TCAM mode in *L-Si* provides an attractive hardware solution for accelerating numerous search-based data-intensive applications.

7 DISCUSSION AND CONCLUSION

Our evaluation results show great promise, and we believe it opens up rich research opportunities in driving new reconfigurable architectures to better complement FPGAs, developing new design tools and new data-intensive applications which were not generally considered to be suitable for FPGA-based accelerations. However, there are several open issues we list below for future research.

1) Heterogeneous architecture. *L-Si* is likely to experience similar limitations to the state-of-art FPGAs in performing a specific set of computations such as floating-point operations. The current homogeneous architecture can be enhanced by adding embedded hard IP blocks, at the cost of reduced flexibility. Additionally, hybrid routing structure (as discussed in Section 6.1) may be applied to increase the routing efficiency.

2) Benchmark development. We believe a full spectrum of applications and algorithms is still under-developed that can fully exploit the flexible resources of *L-Si*, especially the TCAM feature. *L-Si* is likely to be an enabler for such opportunities.

ACKNOWLEDGEMENT

We appreciate the insightful comments and feedback from Prof. Katherine Morrow (UW-Madison), Prof. Zhiru Zhang (Cornell), Prof. Jonathan Rose (U. Toronto), Dr. Jonathan Greene (Microsemi), Dr. Steve Trimberger (Xilinx) and the anonymous reviewers. This work was supported by DARPA Young Faculty Award D16AP00122.

REFERENCES

[1] 2008. Predictive Technology Model (PTM). http://ptm.asu.edu/. (2008).
[2] UC Berkeley. 1992. Berkeley logic interchange format (BLIF). (1992), 197–247.
[3] An Chen. 2013. A comprehensive crossbar array model with solutions for line resistance and nonlinear device characteristics. *IEEE Transactions on Electron Devices* 60, 4 (2013), 1318–1326.
[4] Yi-Chung Chen et al. 2012. Non-volatile 3D stacking RRAM-based FPGA. In *FPL*.
[5] Jason Cong et al. 2014. FPGA-RPI: A novel FPGA architecture with RRAM-based programmable interconnects. *IEEE Transactions on VLSI* 22, 4 (2014), 864–877.
[6] André Dehon. 2005. Nanowire-based programmable architectures. *ACM Journal on Emerging Technologies in Computing Systems (JETC)* 1, 2 (2005), 109–162.
[7] André M. DeHon. 2013. Location, Location, Location: The Role of Spatial Locality in Asymptotic Energy Minimization. In *FPGA*. ACM, 137–146.
[8] Chen Dong et al. 2007. 3-D nFPGA: A reconfigurable architecture for 3-D CMOS/nanomaterial hybrid digital circuits. *IEEE Transactions on Circuits and Systems I: Regular Papers* 54, 11 (2007), 2489–2501.
[9] Pierre-Emmanuel Gaillardon et al. 2012. GMS: Generic memristive structure for non-volatile FPGAs. In *VLSI-SoC*. IEEE, 94–98.
[10] Seth Copen Goldstein and Mihai Budiu. 2001. NanoFabrics: Spatial Computing Using Molecular Electronics. In *ISCA 01*. Citeseer.
[11] Robert J Halstead et al. 2013. Accelerating join operation for relational databases with FPGAs. In *FCCM*. IEEE, 17–20.
[12] Robert J Halstead et al. 2015. FPGA-based Multithreading for In-Memory Hash Joins.. In *CIDR*.
[13] Kejie Huang et al. 2014. A low active leakage and high reliability phase change memory (PCM) based non-volatile FPGA storage element. *IEEE Transactions on Circuits and Systems I: Regular Papers* 61, 9 (2014), 2605–2613.
[14] Intel. 2016. Stratix GX FGPA Family Data Sheet. www.altera.com/content/dam/altera-www/global/en_US/pdfs/literature/ds/ds_sgx.pdf. (2016).
[15] Peter Jamieson et al. 2010. Odin II-an open-source verilog HDL synthesis tool for CAD research. In *FCCM*. IEEE, 149–156.
[16] Supreet Jeloka et al. 2016. A 28 nm Configurable Memory (TCAM/BCAM/SRAM) Using Push-Rule 6T Bit Cell Enabling Logic-in-Memory. *JSC* 51, 4 (2016).
[17] W. Jiang. 2013. Scalable Ternary Content Addressable Memory implementation using FPGAs. In *ANCS*. 71–82. https://doi.org/10.1109/ANCS.2013.6665177
[18] Zizhen Jiang et al. 2014. Verilog-A compact model for oxide-based resistive random access memory (RRAM). In *SISPAD*. IEEE, 41–44.
[19] Sung Hyun Jo et al. 2014. 3D-stackable crossbar resistive memory based on Field Assisted Superlinear Threshold (FAST) selector. In *IEDM*. IEEE.
[20] A. Kawahara et al. 2013. An 8 Mb Multi-Layered Cross-Point ReRAM Macro With 443 MB/s Write Throughput. *JSSC* 48, 1 (Jan 2013), 178–185.
[21] Myoung-Jae Lee et al. 2011. A fast, high-endurance and scalable non-volatile memory device made from asymmetric Ta_2O_{5-x}/TaO_{2-x} bilayer structures. *Nature materials* 10, 8 (2011), 625–630.
[22] Seung Ryul Lee et al. 2012. Multi-level switching of triple-layered TaOx RRAM with excellent reliability for storage class memory. In *VLSIT*. IEEE, 71–72.
[23] Jing Li et al. 2014. 1 Mb 0.41 μm^2 2T-2R Cell Nonvolatile TCAM With Two-Bit Encoding and Clocked Self-Referenced Sensing. *JSSC* 49, 4 (April 2014), 896–907.
[24] Young Yang Liauw et al. 2012. Nonvolatile 3D-FPGA with monolithically stacked RRAM-based configuration memory. In *ISSCC*. IEEE, 406–408.
[25] Chien-Chen Lin et al. 2016. 7.4 A 256b-wordlength ReRAM-based TCAM with 1ns search-time and 14× improvement in wordlength-energyefficiency-density product using 2.5 T1R cell. In *ISSCC*. IEEE, 136–137.
[26] Jason Luu et al. 2014. VTR 7.0: Next generation architecture and CAD system for FPGAs. *TRETS* 7, 2 (2014), 6.
[27] Alan Mishchenko et al. 2007. ABC: A system for sequential synthesis and verification. *URL http://www.eecs.berkeley.edu/~alanmi/abc* (2007).
[28] A. Mishchenko et al. 2007. Combinational and sequential mapping with priority cuts. In *ICCAD*. 354–361. https://doi.org/10.1109/ICCAD.2007.4397290
[29] Panasonic. 2013. Panasonic Starts World's First Mass Production of ReRAM Mounted Microcomputers. (2013).
[30] Arifur Rahman et al. 2004. Evaluation of Low-leakage Design Techniques for Field Programmable Gate Arrays. In *FPGA*. ACM, New York, NY, USA, 23–30.
[31] Wenjing Rao et al. 2009. Logic mapping in crossbar-based nanoarchitectures. *IEEE Design & Test of Computers* 26, 1 (2009), 68–77.
[32] Yi Shan et al. 2010. FPMR: MapReduce Framework on FPGA. In *FPGA*. ACM, New York, NY, USA, 93–102. https://doi.org/10.1145/1723112.1723129
[33] Li Shang et al. 2002. Dynamic Power Consumption in Virtex™-II FPGA Family. In *FPGA*. ACM, New York, NY, USA, 157–164.
[34] Rohit S Shenoy et al. 2014. MIEC (mixed-ionic-electronic-conduction)-based access devices for non-volatile crossbar memory arrays. *Semiconductor Science and Technology* 29, 10 (2014), 104005.
[35] Bharat Sukhwani et al. 2012. Database Analytics Acceleration Using FPGAs. In *PACT*. ACM, New York, NY, USA, 411–420.
[36] Antonio C Torrezan et al. 2011. Sub-nanosecond switching of a tantalum oxide memristor. *Nanotechnology* 22, 48 (2011), 485203.
[37] S. M. Trimberger. 2015. Three Ages of FPGAs: A Retrospective on the First Thirty Years of FPGA Technology. *Proc. IEEE* 103, 3 (March 2015), 318–331.
[38] Tim Tuan et al. 2003. Leakage power analysis of a 90nm FPGA. In *CICC*. 57–60.
[39] Ching-Hua Wang et al. 2010. Three-dimensional 4F 2 ReRAM cell with CMOS logic compatible process. In *IEDM*. IEEE, 29–6.
[40] Zhiqiang Wei et al. 2014. Switching and reliability mechanisms for ReRAM. In *IEEE International Interconnect Technology Conference*. 349–352.
[41] H-S Philip Wong et al. 2012. Metal-oxide RRAM. *Proc. IEEE* 100, 6 (2012).
[42] Xilinx. 2017. UltraScale Architecture and Product Data Sheet: Overview. (2017).
[43] Saeyang Yang. 1991. *Logic synthesis and optimization benchmarks user guide: version 3.0*. MCNC.
[44] Xiang Yang et al. 2013. Demonstration and modeling of multi-bit resistance random access memory. *Applied Physics Letters* 102, 4 (2013), 043502.
[45] Yue Zha et al. 2016. Reconfigurable in-memory computing with resistive memory crossbar. In *ICCAD*. IEEE, 1–8.
[46] Jialiang Zhang and Jing Li. 2017. Improving the Performance of OpenCL-based FPGA Accelerator for Convolutional Neural Network. In *FPGA*. ACM, 25–34.

Improving FPGA Performance with a S44 LUT Structure

Wenyi Feng, Jonathan Greene
Microsemi Corporation SOC Products Group, San Jose
{wenyi.feng, jonathan.greene}@microsemi.com

Alan Mishchenko
Department of EECS, University of California, Berkeley
alanmi@berkeley.edu

ABSTRACT

FPGA performance depends in part on the choice of basic logic cell. Previous work dating back to 1999-2005 found that the best look-up table (LUT) sizes for area-delay product are 4-6, with 4 better for area and 6 for performance. Since that time several things have changed. A new "LUT structure" mapping technique can target cells with a larger number of inputs (cut size) without assuming that the cell implements all possible functions of those inputs. We consider in particular a 7-input function composed of two tightly-coupled 4-input LUTs. Changes in process technology have increased the relative importance of wiring delay and configuration memory area. Finally, modern benchmark applications include carry chains, math and memory blocks. Due to these changes, we show that mapping to a 7-input LUT structure can approach the performance of 6-input LUTs while retaining the area and static power advantage of 4-input LUTs.

ACM Reference format:
Wenyi Feng, Jonathan Greene, and Alan Mishchenko. 2018. Improving FPGA Performance with a S44 LUT Structure. In *FPGA'18: 2018 ACM/SIGDA International Symposium on Field-Programmable Gate Arrays, Feb. 25–27, 2018, Monterey, CA, USA. ACM, New York, NY, USA,* 6 pages. DOI: https://doi.org/10.1145/3174243.3174272

1. INTRODUCTION

Modern FPGA architectures [1-4] use clusters of look-up tables (LUTs). Previous studies [6,7] sought combinations of LUT size (the number of inputs) and cluster size (the number of LUTs in the cluster) providing the best area-delay tradeoffs. LUT sizes of 4-6 were found to offer the best area-delay product with LUT4 slightly better for area and LUT6 for performance. Since static power tends to correlate with area, LUT4 is also better for static power.

LUT4s are used widely in commercial FPGAs, including Altera's Stratix [2], Lattice's ECP series [3], Microsemi's IGLOO2 and PolarFire families [1], and Xilinx's early Virtex series [4]. Starting about 2005, LUT6-based architectures were developed for improved performance, including by Altera since StratixII [9] and by Xilinx since Virtex5 [4]. Since the relevant netlists still contain a significant fraction of smaller LUTs which would under-utilize a simple LUT6, these architectures used different techniques to enhance area efficiency. Altera developed an adaptive logic module (ALM) [9], while Xilinx employed a dual-output LUT6 [4]. More sophisticated software is required to leverage these cells (e.g., [10]), and there is some performance

cost due to the additional constraints on clustering and placement. Since in this paper we are concerned with performance, we sidestep these issues and focus on a simple LUT6. (But we comment on this matter further in the Discussion section below.)

Since the advent of LUT6 architectures, several things have changed. First, process technology has scaled considerably since the 180nm node considered in [7], with current design activity at 14 and 7nm. Wire delay has come to dominate logic delay. Has this caused the 15% performance benefit of LUT6 vs LUT4 reported in [7] to grow or shrink?

Another impact of advancing technology is that configuration bit cell area has not been keeping up with scaling. From 150nm to 16nm a shrink of 88x would be expected but SRAM FPGA configuration bit cell area has shrunk by only about 36x. Other things being equal, slower scaling of the bit cell will tend to make larger LUTs more costly since the number of bits in a LUT grows exponentially with the number of inputs. This is another motivation to check if the performance benefit of LUT6 is still significant.

Second, new logic synthesis and mapping algorithms have been developed. The main advantage of larger LUTs is the reduction in the number of levels of logic in the critical path. The authors of [7] suggested that if there is "a way to achieve the depth properties of a LUT7 without paying the heavy area price, then such a seven-input function may well be a good choice." A recent algorithm for mapping to "LUT structures" provides a way to do just that [12]. Consider the "S44" structure shown in Fig. 1(a). This is a 7-input structure composed of two tightly-coupled 4-input LUTs. While it cannot implement all 7-input functions, it can implement almost all 5-input functions, 98% of 6-input functions, and 75% of 7-input functions observed in the designs studied here (re-evaluated by the methods of [12]). The addition of a two-input mux and an additional output, as shown in Fig. 1(b), allow this structure to also implement two ordinary LUT4s.

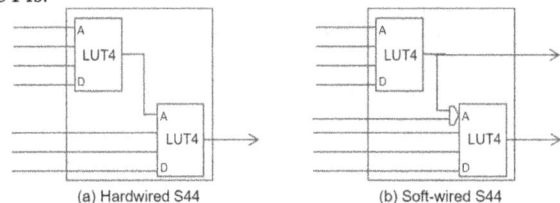

Figure 1. Hardwired and soft-wired S44s

Third, modern designs contain more than just the simple LUTs considered in [6,7]. They now include carry chains, which have a significant impact on the critical path [20], as well as embedded math and memory blocks.

These three changes motivate us to do a practical evaluation of S44 mapping, and to reexamine the performance benefits of LUT6 architectures in the context of 14nm technology, S44 mapping, and industrial benchmark designs. Our contributions are as follows:

- We show how scaling has affected the relative delays of logic, intra-cluster wiring, and inter-cluster wiring, and explain why this would tend to reduce the benefit of LUT6.
- It was shown in [12] that the reduction in logic levels with the S44 structure incurred an increase in area for public benchmark designs (e.g., MCNC20 designs). We show that for more realistic industrial designs, S44 mapping provides both a delay and area benefit, and explain why.
- The prior study [12] considered only mapping. We show that the delay benefits of mapping to a soft-wired S44 are sustained through a complete clustering, placement and routing flow in a commercial architecture setting.
- We show that the post-routing performance benefit of LUT6 (or S44) over LUT4 is often much less for industrial designs that include carry chains and embedded blocks than for public designs that do not.
- We show that the combined effect of 14nm technology, S44 mapping and industrial benchmarks is to significantly narrow the performance benefit of LUT6 vs LUT4.

2. TECHNOLOGY SCALING AND ITS IMPACT ON FPGA ARCHITECTURES

2.1 Scaling of Various Delay Components

As is well-known, wire resistance is not scaling well, and as a result interconnect delay is increasing relative to logic delay [21]. Table 1 shows the ratio of various delays in similar architectures [17] optimized for 65nm and 14nm. Values are given for the average delay through a LUT4, a representative intra-cluster connection, and a representative longer connection of length 5 clusters.

Table 1: Delay Scaling from 65nm to 14nm

Delay	Ratio (65nm/14nm)
LUT4	4.1
intra-cluster routing	3.3
inter-cluster routing	2.4

It is apparent that the same architecture at a more advanced technology would exhibit critical paths with an increased contribution from inter-cluster routing and decreased contribution from logic.

How does this trend affect the relative speed of architectures using different LUT sizes? The simple explanation for the performance benefit of a larger LUT is that fewer levels of logic are required. The implicit assumption is that delay is proportional to the number of logic levels, as is commonly assumed in mapping algorithms [14]. However, this assumption may not be valid, especially in clustered architectures. The eliminated levels will more likely be intra-cluster connections (which are relatively fast) than inter-cluster connections (which are relatively slow). To gain intuition into how many intra- vs inter-cluster connections appear in critical paths of LUT4 vs LUT6 architectures, we propose the following thought experiment.

2.2 A Thought Experiment

Consider three architectures:

- ArchA: cluster of 8 LUT6s

- ArchB: cluster of 8 hard-wired S44 cells. Within each S44, one input from the first LUT4 is merged with one of the three free inputs from the second LUT4 to form a 6-input cell.
- ArchC: cluster of 6 soft-wired S44 cells

Each LUT6 in ArchA corresponds to an S44 in ArchB. Since ArchA and ArchB have the same number of logic cell inputs and outputs per cluster, they can use identical routing networks.

Given a LUT6 netlist placed in ArchA, we attempt to convert it to a functionally identical netlist placed in ArchB as follows. Consider each instance of a LUT6:

- If the LUT6 has no more than 4 used inputs, we can map it to one of the two corresponding LUT4s in ArchB trivially.
- If the LUT6 has 5 or 6 used inputs, we check whether the same function can be implemented in an S44. If so, we can use the S44 with no problem. As mentioned above, this will happen >98% of the time. We ignore the remaining cases for now since they will not change the big picture.

It is apparent that the resulting LUT4 netlist in ArchB has the same number of inter-cluster connections as in ArchA, up to 8 connections per cluster between LUT4s in the same S44, and the same number of other intra-cluster connections as in ArchA. The routing delays of the two implementations are similar, with the difference only in logic delays and the (very fast) direct connections internal to an S44.

One limitation of the conversion is pin swappability. As we map a 5- or 6-input function to a S44 structure, the S44 mapping might require some inputs to be assigned to the first LUT, some to the second LUT and some to both LUTs. So there is some potential reduction in routing flexibility. However, at worst we could solve this by adding additional muxes at the S44 inputs to guarantee the routing can stay the same during conversion, and lump the delay of these muxes into the cell delay.

Now consider converting the implementation from ArchB to ArchC. A typical LUT6 netlist has less than 50% LUTs using 5 or 6 inputs [15]. So a cluster from ArchA or ArchB can typically be reimplemented by a cluster from ArchC, packing two independent LUT4s into an S44 when necessary.

This conversion may occasionally fail (for example, when all S44 instances in an ArchB cluster use 5 or 6 inputs). However, it gives us some intuition why most additional logic levels in a LUT4 netlist can be routed using short connections. As technology scales, the longer routing delays will increasingly dominate over the short connection and logic delays, and the performance disadvantage of LUT4 will tend to shrink.

2.3 Prior Results Using VPR/VTR

While intuition is nice, it is desirable to confirm it by actual experiments using architectures tuned for two different process nodes, benchmarks, and a CAD flow such as VTR. Fortunately, such data is available. We compiled the detailed LUT4 vs. LUT6 performance results from the original 180nm study ([7], Figure 14; detail in [8], appendix E), and a recent 65nm study ([18], Figure 6.6(b); numerical values provided by private communication). Table 2 compares them. The 180nm study provides results for cluster size 1-10; while the 65nm study provides data for cluster size 4-15. Both use a similar methodology and MCNC benchmarks. We compute the ratio of critical path delays for LUT4 vs LUT6 for each cluster size, and summarize three ways: "AvgAll" is the average of all available cluster sizes (1-10 for 180nm, 4-15 for 65nm); "AvgCommon" is the average of cluster size 4-10 (common to both); and "Best Delay" is for the best achieved LUT4 or LUT6 performance of any cluster size. All three averages show the difference shrinking from 180nm to 65nm, corroborating our hypothesis. Following this trend, further reductions of the difference are expected at smaller nodes.

Table 2: Critical Path Delays

	Ahmed, 2001 [8]			Zgheib, 2017 [18]		
Node	180nm			65nm		
Cluster Size	LUT4 (ns)	LUT6 (ns)	Ratio	LUT4 (ns)	LUT6 (ns)	Ratio
1	25.9	21.0	124%			
2	22.3	18.2	123%			
3	19.6	17.0	116%			
4	19.4	17.3	112%	4.9	4.3	114%
5	19.8	16.5	120%	4.9	4.1	121%
6	19.2	15.6	123%	4.8	4.2	115%
7	18.5	15.6	119%	4.6	4.1	112%
8	17.9	15.9	113%	4.5	4.1	109%
9	18.3	15.8	116%	4.5	4.1	110%
10	17.5	15.3	114%	4.9	4.4	110%
11				4.5	4.3	106%
12				4.7	4.4	107%
13				4.6	4.2	110%
14				4.6	4.3	107%
15				5.0	4.4	114%
AvgAll			117.8%			111.2%
AvgCommon			116.6%			113.0%
Best Delay	17.5	15.3	114.4%	4.5	4.1	111.2%

3. REVIEW OF LUT STRUCTURE MAPPING

3.1 LUT Structures

Approximating a large LUT with a combination of smaller LUTs and fast internal connections is a natural idea that has existed for some time. An XC4000 CLB has 2 LUT4s plus a LUT3 with two inputs driven directly by the two LUT4s [4]. A hard-wired S44 was studied in [8], but area-delay results were found to be consistently worse than for simple LUT4s. In its CAD flow, LUT structures were formed during the packing stage. The author stated that direct mapping into LUT structures held the promise of better results, but such a capability was not then available.

Various other LUT structures are proposed in [12] and [13].

3.2 Mapping into LUT Structures

ABC is a system for synthesis and verification [16]. It initially supported mapping into simple LUTs [14,15]. More recently, ABC has been extended to support direct mapping into LUT structures by these two modifications [12]:

- A checker determines whether a cut can be implemented using the structure. If the cut is no larger than the base LUT size, the check may be skipped.
- A "library file" is required to specify an area and delay cost for each number of used inputs up to the total number of inputs of the targeted structure. Mapping into a simple LUT has the same area and delay cost for any number of inputs up to the LUT size.

S44 mapping has two flavors depending on the library used, one for area optimization and one for delay optimization. Since our goal is performance we use the latter, which is reflected in Table 3. For 1-4 inputs, area and delay costs are set to 1. For 5-7 inputs, the area cost is set to 2 (since both constituent LUTs in the S44 are used), and delay cost is set to 1.2. The incremental delay cost of 0.2 approximates the delay of the additional LUT plus the direct connection between LUTs internal to the S44 relative to the delay of a LUT plus a normal routing connection. Further details can be found in [12].

Table 3: Mapping Costs for LUT4, S44, and LUT6

	LUT4		S44		LUT6	
Inputs	Area	Delay	Area	Delay	Area	Delay
1-4	1	1	1	1	1	1
5-6	N/A	N/A	2	1.2	1	1
7	N/A	N/A	2	1.2	N/A	N/A

3.3 Prior Results for LUT Structure Mapping

Mapping into an S44 structure reduces the logic depth by 28% at the expense of 5% area for a set of public benchmarks compared to simple LUT4 mapping [12].

Two factors affect the area of an S44 mapping. The ability to examine cuts of size up to 7 allows greater scope for optimization than cuts of size up to 4 for simple LUT4 mapping; this is good for area. On the other hand, achieving optimal delay in S44 mapping may require that some logic be duplicated. For example, suppose a node in the And-Inverter-Graph used by the mapper has two fanouts and both are critical. S44 mapping might have to cover the node twice in two S44 structures for optimal delay; this is bad for area.

S44 mapping requires about 3 times the runtime of simple LUT4 mapping, but is still quite practical even for industrial-sized designs.

4. EXPERIMENTAL METHODS

4.1 Architectures

The experimental architecture is roughly the same as that of [17] but with technology scaled to 14nm. A cluster has 12 LUT4s and 12 flip-flops. The inter-cluster routing consists of various length segments. The input interconnect block has three levels, providing excellent routing flexibility. A direct connection is available from each LUT's output (Y) to the fast input (A) of the next LUT in the cluster. Thus any adjacent pairs of LUTs (up to 6 pairs per cluster) can implement a soft-wired S44, and remaining LUTs can implement independent LUT4s. The architecture also supports carry chains and embedded blocks. The carry cell is a LUT4 with an additional carry input CI, carry output CO and sum output S (Figure 3 in [5]).

For comparison, an architecture with clusters of 8 LUT6s and 8 flip-flops is also created. The inter-cluster routing and input interconnect block remain unchanged. The quantity and fan-in of the output muxes are also unchanged, but to continue to use them fully the fanout of the LUTs and flip-flops is increased in a balanced way. Such an architecture is reasonable due to the similar logic capacity of the two clusters (12xLUT4 vs 8xLUT6). The floor plan of the cluster and resulting area and delay models are updated to reflect the changes.

The cluster layouts assume non-volatile configuration memory. But since performance depends mainly on the routing architecture and logic cell rather than configuration bits, we would expect to see similar results for equivalent SRAM architectures as well.

Due to CAD limitations, we use the same 4-input carry cell even in the LUT6 architecture. (This has negligible impact on our results; see below.)

4.2 CAD Flow

The CAD flow used in our experiments takes as input a netlist produced by a commercial synthesis tool that infers carry, math and memory blocks. The flow consists of the following: re-synthesis and mapping (using ABC), packing, placement and routing. The latter three steps are done using a modified version of the Libero® SoC Design Suite [1]. Because ABC does a re-synthesis from an And-Inverter-Graph, any possible bias in the incoming netlist should be neutralized.

ABC is enhanced to handle "boxes" representing carry chains or embedded blocks. Carry chains are treated as white boxes, which are kept intact during optimization but whose function and delay are considered by ABC. (See [19] for a description of white boxes.) Delay costs of the carry cell are normalized relative to the average LUT delay as follows: 1.5 from LUT inputs to CO, 0.1 from CI to CO, and 0.2 from CI to S. Embedded blocks are registered at their inputs and outputs. Critical paths may start at a block output, or end at a block input, but do not go through any block.

For the LUT4 (baseline) case, mapping is done with command (dch; if)^4 using the LUT4 library [12]. The placer and router are aware of the Y-to-A direct connects inside the clusters and attempt to use them effectively.

For the S44 case, mapping is done with commands (dch; if -S 44)^4 using the S44 library. The mapped netlist represents a mixture of S44 and ordinary LUT4 instances. During packing, each individual LUT4 has weight 1 and each true S44 cell (consisting of 2 LUT4s) has weight 2. The placer ensures the two LUTs comprising an S44 cell are adjacent so the direct Y-to-A connection can be used during routing.

For the LUT6 case, mapping is done with command (dch; if)^4 using the LUT6 library. Packing, placement, and routing work with clusters of size 8 instead of 12.

To reduce the impact of random fluctuations in the CAD flow, we run placement five times per design with different random seeds and report average values.

4.3 Benchmark Designs

We use two suites of designs in our experiments. The "public" suite consists of the MCNC20 set excluding a few designs (clma, eliptic, and s298) with fewer than 120 LUTs. These designs lack carry and embedded blocks, but are useful for comparison with prior work. The "industrial" suite consists of proprietary designs including serial protocols, error correction, MACs, soft processors and complete customer applications. They include carry and embedded blocks. The suite includes designs using up to 54% of the LUT4s for muxes.

5. EXPERIMENTAL RESULTS

Results for the public suite are shown in Table 4, and for the industrial suite in Table 5. "S44 area" is determined as per the S44 mapping area cost in Table 3, and may be compared to the number of cells in the LUT4 mapping. "S44 cells" counts any S44 as one, and may be compared to the number of cells in the LUT6 mapping. The number of "Carry Cells" is not affected by the type of mapping. "Logic levels" are determined as per the appropriate delay cost in Table 3, and for the carry cell as described above.

Table 4: Results for Public Suite

| Design | Non-carry Cells | | | | Carry Cells | Logic Levels | | | Crit Path Delay | |
	LUT4	S44 area	S44 cells	LUT6		LUT4	S44 / LUT4	LUT6 / LUT4	S44 / LUT4	LUT6 / LUT4
alu4	432	471	308	311	0	8.0	0.73	0.63	0.93	0.88
apex2	419	448	300	289	0	8.0	0.85	0.75	0.92	0.90
apex4	852	931	623	617	0	6.0	0.77	0.67	0.92	0.90
bigkey	1263	1305	974	788	0	4.0	0.85	0.75	0.97	0.94
des	1538	1577	1212	1172	0	6.0	0.77	0.83	0.91	0.96
diffeq	658	740	507	499	0	9.0	0.78	0.67	0.91	0.92
dsip	1121	1284	1046	891	0	4.0	0.80	0.75	1.01	1.02
ex1010	1005	1052	716	731	0	7.0	0.80	0.71	0.97	0.92
ex5p	182	194	167	145	0	3.0	0.80	1.00	0.96	0.92
frisc	2277	2463	1805	1806	0	15.0	0.72	0.73	0.91	0.97
misex3	320	332	223	235	0	5.0	0.92	0.80	0.94	0.93
pdc	318	355	248	247	0	5.0	0.72	0.80	0.92	0.94
s38417	2648	2804	1956	1866	0	8.0	0.73	0.75	0.92	0.97
s38584_1	3367	3249	2355	2302	0	8.0	0.73	0.75	0.94	0.95
seq	796	855	613	646	0	6.0	0.77	0.67	0.91	0.89
spla	328	323	246	247	0	5.0	0.88	0.80	0.95	0.93
tseng	653	659	550	549	0	10.0	0.84	0.80	0.89	0.90
Total	18177	19042	13849	13341	0					
Ratio	1.00	1.05		0.73	0.00					
Ratio	1.36		1.04	1.00	0.00					
Geomean							0.79	0.75	0.93	0.93

Table 5: Results for Industrial Suite

Design	Non-carry Cells				Carry Cells	Logic Levels			Crit Path Delay	
	LUT4	S44 area	S44 cells	LUT6		LUT4	S44 / LUT4	LUT6 / LUT4	S44 / LUT4	LUT6 / LUT4
D1	12915	12395	8493	8913	108	9.1	0.88	0.86	0.96	0.97
D2	19386	18522	12572	13014	117	10.2	0.78	0.80	0.95	0.94
D3	4581	4396	3342	3141	340	7.0	0.90	0.91	0.99	1.07
D4	10327	9843	7536	7396	460	7.3	0.92	0.86	1.02	1.02
D5	9461	9090	7147	6992	400	8.0	0.74	0.71	0.93	1.02
D6	4117	3886	2711	2728	390	13.1	1.00	1.00	0.96	1.01
D7	97770	93937	74782	73636	11233	13.0	0.80	0.74	0.97	1.02
D8	195785	187973	149695	147320	22484	14.0	0.76	0.76	0.94	1.02
D9	389862	373636	297763	293324	44967	14.0	0.81	0.79	0.97	0.94
D10	2824	2748	2157	2014	122	5.8	0.83	0.86	0.99	0.93
D11	4439	4287	3417	3180	143	5.9	0.83	0.83	0.99	0.94
D12	9820	9297	6843	6475	134	6.7	0.78	0.75	0.96	0.90
D13	2065	2026	1473	1470	61	13.0	0.72	0.77	0.91	0.96
D14	4723	4639	3441	3343	16	8.0	0.75	0.75	0.90	0.90
D15	4300	3570	2476	2468	0	5.0	0.92	0.80	0.99	0.93
D16	171937	165451	119162	107562	4822	10.0	0.89	0.84	1.08	1.07
D17	5555	5387	3567	3852	26	6.1	1.00	1.00	0.98	0.93
D18	11153	10490	7956	6569	52	5.1	1.00	1.00	1.03	1.00
D19	5177	5037	3848	3791	635	8.1	0.85	0.81	0.92	0.93
D20	6005	5683	4386	4149	574	11.4	0.93	0.91	0.98	1.01
Total	972202	932293	722767	701337	87084					
Ratio	1.00	0.96		0.72	0.09					
Ratio	1.39		1.03	1.00	0.12					
Geomean							0.85	0.83	0.97	0.97

"Crit Path Delay" is determined using post-route timing models (based on transistor-level circuits) for the applicable architecture.

For the public suite, comparing S44 vs LUT4, we see results similar to [12] with a reduction in logic levels (0.79) but some increase in area (1.05). Comparing LUT6 vs LUT4, we see a somewhat better reduction in logic levels (0.75).

Results for the industrial suite show two important differences. First, the area is lower for S44 than LUT4 (0.96) rather than higher. This appears to be due to less logic at critical or near critical paths that might trigger duplication. Indeed, the proportion of such logic (with a slack of 0 or 1 logic level) is found to be <10% for the industrial suite while >40% for the public designs. This makes mapping to S44 a win for area as well as logic levels. Second, the logic level reduction is smaller for both S44 and LUT6 mapping. This is due to the expected ([20]) significant contribution to critical paths from carry logic.

Recall that CAD limitations precluded the possibility of merging additional logic into the carry cell in our LUT6 mappings. To bound the impact of this potential issue, we separately mapped the industrial suite using another synthesis tool that did handle LUT6 carry cells, and checked for any occasions where a critical path contained at least one carry and had fewer logic levels than in our regular flow. This occurred only once and could have only minimal impact on the overall results.

For the public suite, LUT6 reduces critical path delay by a factor of 0.93 compared to LUT4, or 7%. This is smaller than the 11% reported for 65nm in [18], but is reasonable in light of the further scaling to 14nm here.

For the industrial suite, LUT6 reduces critical path delay by a factor of 0.97 compared to LUT4, or only 3%, less than the 7%

seen for the public suite. Some of this is again due to the introduction of carry logic. Carry accounts for about 40% of the combinational logic delay in the critical paths of the industrial suite (in line with the findings of [20]). Another reason is that the industrial suite contains embedded blocks. When a critical path starts or ends at flip-flops, the flip-flops can be placed in the same cluster as the connected LUTs. This is not the case for embedded blocks, which have their own special routing clusters. This forces the relevant connections to be inter-cluster, incurring bigger delays that cannot be reduced by S44 or LUT6 mapping.

Comparing S44 and LUT6 mappings, we find that S44 ranges from 7% slower (D15) to 9% faster (D8) than LUT6 based on the design. To better understand why S44 can approximate the speed of LUT6, we show a breakdown of the critical path delays for the public suite in Table 6.

Table 6: Delay Breakdown for Public Suite

	LUT4	S44- way1	S44- way2	LUT6
Total Delay (ns)	144.8	134.7	134.7	134.9
Logic Delay (ns)	34.0	31.7	36.6	31.9
Intra-cluster delay (ns)	18.3	12.5	7.6	11.3
Inter-cluster delay (ns)	92.5	90.6	90.6	91.7
Total connections	638	616	461	493
Intra-cluster connections	301	305	150	182
Inter-cluster connections	337	311	311	311

"Total Delay" is the sum of the critical path delay over all runs of all designs. S44 is accounted for in two ways: "way1" is to treat the S44 netlist as a LUT4 netlist, considering the soft-wired net delay within the S44 as part of intra-cluster routing delay; "way2" is to treat S44 as single cell and the soft-wired net delay as part of the cell delay. The number of true S44 used is 155 (=305-150, the difference of intra-cluster connections between way1 and way2). Comparing S44-way1 with LUT4, we see the benefits of S44 mapping: reduced logic delay (due to fewer logic levels and more use of the fastest A-to-Y LUT delay), reduced intra-cluster routing delay (due to the extensive use of fast Y-to-A connections internal to the S44), and reduced inter-cluster routing delay (due to the reduction in inter-cluster connections, offset by higher average inter-cluster connection delays).

Alternatively, we can compare S44-way2 with LUT6. Total delay for LUT6 is similar. As suggested by our thought experiment, we see that the number and total delay of inter-cluster connections are very similar between S44 and LUT6. The only significant disadvantage for S44 is in logic delay, the relative importance of which is expected to decrease with further scaling.

One other explanation for the improved performance of S44 is its ability to implement a 4-input mux. The fast connection from Y to A within the S44 reduces the delay by about 10% for typical bus muxes compared with conventional LUT4 mappings.

6. DISCUSSION

As mentioned above, some commercial LUT6 architectures employ a dual-output LUT6 to improve area efficiency. Algorithms to pack two smaller LUTs into a dual-output LUT6 are discussed in [10]. These can achieve a 9.5% area saving at the expense of 1.6% performance loss, or 15.6% area saving at 12% performance loss in a more aggressive version. We have two observations on these results.

First, these more complex architectures can save area but are unlikely to improve performance compared to a simple LUT6. So the performance comparisons reported above should still be valid.

Second, does the dual-output technique eliminate the area cost of LUT6 vs LUT4? Using values from Table 5, see that on average it takes (701337/8)/(932293/12) = 1.13 times as many clusters of 8xLUT6 versus 12xLUT4 to accommodate a given design. Furthermore, from trial layouts at 14nm we estimate the LUT6 cluster would occupy at least 10% more silicon area. The combined 23% area cost for LUT6 is clearly not outweighed by the 10-15% area savings from dual-output LUTs, which anyway would cost performance.

An obvious question is whether the LUT structure idea can be applied to a LUT6 architecture as well, using an S66 cell. We believe some improvement is possible but it will be much less than the improvement seen with S44 over LUT4. The simple reason is that there is a large logic level reduction from LUT4 mapping to LUT7 mapping, and S44 can capture most of the reduction. The reduction will be much less from LUT6 mapping to LUT11 mapping, making S66 much less interesting.

7. CONCLUSIONS

We conclude that:

- Contrary to earlier results with public benchmarks, we find that with industrial benchmarks S44 mapping saves area as well as logic levels. This is due to the fact that the industrial benchmarks have fewer near critical paths and require less logic duplication for optimal delay mapping.

- S44 mapping can effectively optimize use of fast direct connections between LUTs, and its benefits are sustained after placement and routing.

- The combined effect of technology scaling, S44 mapping, and use of industrial benchmarks allows 4-input LUTs to approach the performance of 6-input LUTs while retaining their area and static power advantage.

8. ACKNOWLEDGEMENTS

The authors would like to thank Sinan Kaptanoglu, Joel Landry, and Fei Li for their support and extensive discussions throughout this work.

9. REFERENCES

[1] Microsemi SoC products group (formerly Actel). http://www.microsemi.com/products/fpga-soc.

[2] Intel FPGA and SoC (formerly Altera). http://www.altera.com.

[3] Lattice Semiconductor Corp. http://www.latticesemi.com.

[4] Xilinx Corp. http://www.xilinx.com.

[5] PolarFire FPGA Fabric User Guide, downloadable from https://www.microsemi.com/products/fpga-soc/fpga/polarfire-fpga#documentation

[6] V. Betz, J. Rose and A. Marquardt. Architecture and CAD for Deep-submicron FPGAs. Kluwer Academic Publishers, February, 1999.

[7] E. Ahmed and J. Rose, The effect of LUT and cluster size on deep-submicron FPGA performance and density, IEEE Trans. on VLSI, vol. 12, pp. 288-298, 2004.

[8] E. Ahmed, The effect of logic granularity on deep-submicron FPGA performance and density, Master Thesis, Univ. of Toronto, 2001.

[9] D. Lewis, et al., The Stratix II logic and routing architecture, FPGA 2005, pp. 14-20.

[10] T. Ahmed, P. Kundarewich, J. Anderson, Packing techniques for Virtex-5 FPGAs, ACM TRETS, vol.2, No. 3, Article 18, 2009.

[11] J. Luu, et al., VTR 7.0: Next Generation Architecture and CAD System for FPGAs, ACM TRETS, vol. 7, No. 2, Article 6, 2014.

[12] S. Ray, et al., Mapping into LUT structures, DATE 2012, pp. 1579-1584.

[13] A. Mishchenko, LUT structure for delay: cluster or cascade, IWLS 2012, pp. 84-88.

[14] A. Mishchenko, et al., Combinational and sequential mapping with priority cuts, ICCAD 2007, pp. 354-361.

[15] S. Jang, et al., WireMap: FPGA technology mapping for improved routability and enhanced LUT merging, ACM TRETS, vol. 2, No. 2, Article 14, 2009.

[16] Berkeley Logic Synthesis and Verification Group, ABC: A System for Sequential Synthesis and Verification. http://www.eecs.berkeley.edu/~alanmi/abc/

[17] J. Greene, et al., A 65nm flash based FPGA fabric optimized for low cost and power, FPGA 2011, pp. 87-96.

[18] G. Zgheib, Leading the blind: automated transisttor-level modeling for FPGA architects, Ph.D Thesis, EPFL, 2017.

[19] S. Jang, et al., SmartOpt: An industrial strength framework for logic synthesis, FPGA 2009, pp. 237-240.

[20] K. Murray, et al., Timing-driven Titan: enabling large benchmarks and exploring the gap between academic and commercial CAD, ACM TRETS, vol. 8, No. 2, Article 10, 2015.

[21] G. Yeric, Moore's Law at 50: Are we planning for retirement?, IEEE Int'l Electron Devices Meeting, 2015.

ParaDRo: A Parallel Deterministic Router Based on Spatial Partitioning and Scheduling

Chin Hau Hoo
Department of Electrical & Computer Engineering
National University of Singapore
chinhau.hoo@u.nus.edu

Akash Kumar
Center for Advancing Electronics
Technische Universität Dresden
akash.kumar@tu-dresden.de

ABSTRACT

Routing of nets is one of the most time-consuming steps in the FPGA design flow. Existing works have described ways of accelerating the process through parallelization. However, only some of them are deterministic, and determinism is often achieved at the cost of speedup. In this paper, we propose ParaDRo, a parallel FPGA router based on spatial partitioning that achieves deterministic results while maintaining reasonable speedup. Existing spatial partitioning based routers do not scale well because the number of nets that can fully utilize all processors reduces as the number of processors increases. In addition, they route nets that are within a spatial partition sequentially. ParaDRo mitigates this problem by scheduling nets within a spatial partition to be routed in parallel if they do not have overlapping bounding boxes. Further parallelism is extracted by decomposing multi-sink nets into single-sink nets to minimize the amount of bounding box overlaps and increase the number of nets that can be routed in parallel. These improvements enable ParaDRo to achieve an average speedup of 5.4X with 8 threads with minimal impact on the quality of results.

KEYWORDS

FPGA; EDA; Parallel Routing

ACM Reference Format:
Chin Hau Hoo and Akash Kumar. 2018. ParaDRo: A Parallel Deterministic Router Based on Spatial Partitioning and Scheduling. In *FPGA '18: 2018 ACM/SIGDA International Symposium on Field-Programmable Gate Arrays, February 25–27, 2018, Monterey, CA, USA.* ACM, New York, NY, USA, 10 pages. https://doi.org/10.1145/3174243.3174246

1 INTRODUCTION

Moore's law has enabled the fabrication of FPGAs of increasing capacity, and modern FPGAs can accommodate state-of-the-art designs that are larger and more complex. To fully utilize the capacity of modern FPGAs, high-quality EDA tools are required. However, the long execution time of the tools causes a productivity gap where the capacity of FPGAs is growing faster than the ability of engineers to effectively utilize it. It is also one of the major factors that are preventing the wide adoption of FPGAs as a general computing platform.

Among the tools for packing, placement and routing for FPGAs, routing contributes almost 45% to the total execution time for Titan [7] benchmarks. One possible way of reducing the FPGA route time is by using a faster processor. Unfortunately, the failure of Dennard's scaling limits the maximum speed of a single processor. Therefore, recent works focus on the development of parallel FPGA routers to reduce the time spent in routing. Existing parallel routers are based on Pathfinder [6], which is one of the most widely used algorithms for sequential FPGA routing. The Pathfinder algorithm works by iteratively increasing the costs of using overused routing resources (RRs) until congestion is eliminated.

The sequential nature of Pathfinder poses a huge challenge to the design of a scalable **and** deterministic parallel FPGA router. In fact, existing works generally sacrifice scalability for determinism and vice versa. To guarantee determinism, the congestion costs seen by a net must be the same across different runs of the Pathfinder algorithm. In other words, race conditions on the congestion costs must be prevented by ensuring that nets routed by different threads/processes do not modify the congestion cost associated with the same RRs. Some existing works [3, 10] achieve this by spatially partitioning the FPGA and routing nets that are located within different partitions in parallel. Since nets in different partitions access disjoint subgraphs of the RR, there is no possibility of race conditions. However, the maximum speedup is limited by the fact that nets within the same partition must be routed sequentially. In this paper, we improve upon the idea of spatial partitioning and attempt to extract further parallelism by scheduling nets within a partition to be routed in parallel while guaranteeing determinism. **In summary, our contributions are as follows:**

- A parallel FPGA router based on spatial partitioning with enhancements to improve speedup.
- Multi-sink net decomposition and bounding box minimization heuristic to increase the number of nets within a partition that can be routed in parallel.
- Mapping of the net scheduling problem to a graph coloring problem and a fast heuristic to solve it.

The rest of this paper is organized as follows. Section 2 describes background of the FPGA routing problem. Section 3 surveys the existing works on parallel FPGA routing. Section 4 explains the design of ParaDRo and its various enhancements. Section 5 presents the experimental setup while Section 6 discusses the performance of ParaDRo in terms of speedup and quality of results. The paper is concluded in Section 7.

2 BACKGROUND

Given a set of nets to be routed, routing connects the source to the sinks of each net using the RRs in the FPGA such that each RR is utilized by at most one net. The RRs are modeled as a graph where the nodes represent the wires in the FPGA and input/output pins of the computation elements while the edges of the graph represent the programmable switches between the wires and input/output pins.

One of the most effective algorithms for solving the FPGA routing problem is Pathfinder [6]. In Pathfinder, Dijkstra's shortest path algorithm is used to find a path from the RR node of the source to the RR nodes of the sinks of a net. The cost of a RR node during the neighbor expansion of Dijkstra's algorithm is a weighted sum of the delay of the node and two additional cost components, the present and history congestion costs. The present congestion costs are updated after routing every net while the history congestion costs are updated after routing all the nets. The rationale behind the congestion costs is to penalize the overuse of RRs so that the overuse is eliminated eventually.

Since the present congestion costs are updated after routing each net, the costs seen by a net depends on the routes taken by previous nets. As a result, the present congestion costs introduce dependencies among nets and pose challenges to effective parallelization of the Pathfinder algorithm.

3 RELATED WORKS

In this section, we review existing works on parallel deterministic FPGA routers.

TDR [1] is a parallel router where each processor is allocated a disjoint subgraph of the RR graph and a subset of nets to be routed. To generate the disjoint subgraphs, TDR requires the FPGA to have the disjoint switch box topology. Since processors do not share RR, there is no need to synchronize congestion costs among them during routing. As a result, TDR achieved close to linear speedup.

Gort and Anderson [3] proposed a parallel router where congestion costs are synchronized among processors using the message passing interface (MPI). The costs are sent in a non-blocking manner to other processors once a processor finishes routing a net. Determinism is guaranteed by receiving the congestion costs in a blocking manner. Unfortunately, the blocking receive reduces the speedup because of increased stall time when there is load imbalance among the processors. Gort and Anderson tried to solve the problem by spatially partitioning the FPGA. A processor can route nets whose bounding boxes are within a partition without communicating with other processors that are routing nets in other partitions.

Another parallel router based on spatial partitioning is by Shen and Luo [10]. While [3] routes nets within a partition with multiple processors, Shen and Luo route nets within a partition sequentially. Therefore, the communication overhead of Shen and Luo is lower because there is no need to synchronize congestion costs among processors.

Gort and Anderson [2] found that 68% of the total route time is spent on the maze expansion step of Pathfinder and attempted to parallelize the step. In sequential maze expansion, a minimum cost node is popped from the priority queue, and neighbors of the node are sequentially pushed into the queue after the cost of using them are calculated by a single thread. On the other hand, Gort exploited fine-grained parallelism by calculating the costs of a node's neighbors in parallel with multiple worker threads and pushing the neighbors into the priority queue of the thread that calculated their costs. The worker threads wait at a barrier to ensure that all neighbors are expanded before moving on to the next minimum cost node.

Another fine-grained parallel router is Corolla [11], a GPU-accelerated router based on Bellman Ford's algorithm. Since running Bellman Ford's algorithm on the entire RR graph increases the problem size unnecessarily, Corolla executes the algorithm only on the subgraph within the bounding box of the net being routed. The subgraph is dynamically expanded until a legal routing solution is found. To extract sufficient parallelism, Corolla applies the operator formulation [9] where each RR node is mapped to a GPU thread to be processed in parallel. In addition to the fine-grained parallelism, Corolla also exploits coarse-grained parallelism where multiple nets are routed in parallel as long as they do not have overlapping bounding boxes.

4 PARADRO

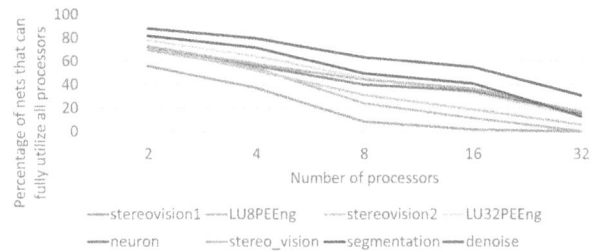

Figure 1: Percentage of nets that fully utilize all processors versus number of processors

Designing a scalable **and** deterministic parallel FPGA router is a non-trivial task. The deterministic parallel routers presented in Section 3 are based on either partitioning or fine-grained parallelism. Partitioning based routers [1, 3, 10] route multiple nets in parallel only if the nets access disjoint subgraphs of the RR graph to prevent race conditions. Instead of routing multiple nets in parallel, fine-grained routers parallelize either the classic maze expansion algorithm [2] or the Bellman Ford algorithm [11] to route a single net.

Unfortunately, routers based on partitioning [3, 10] do not scale well. As shown in Figure 1, the percentage of nets that can fully utilize all the processors reduces as the number of processors increases, resulting in diminishing speedup. While the figure assumes that the FPGA is partitioned into equally sized segments, the trend shown in the figures applies to the partitioning described in [3, 10]. Therefore, we propose ParaDRo, a Parallel Deterministic Router, based on spatial partitioning and scheduling to address the limitations of existing partitioning-based routers.

ParaDRo is based on recursive spatial bi-partitioning of the FPGA. The bi-partitioning forms a perfect binary tree where each node represents a region on the FPGA and contains nets whose bounding boxes fit entirely within the region. An example of a bi-partitioning tree is shown in Figure 2. Since the regions represented the nodes at each level of the tree are spatially independent, nets in one node can be routed in parallel with nets in other nodes while still guaranteeing determinism. For example, in Figure 2, nets A and B can be routed in parallel with nets D and E. Unfortunately, this simple bi-partitioning approach does not produce a good speedup because the number of interior (non-leaf) nodes at any level of the tree is less than the number of threads, which results in underutilization of the threads. In Figure 2, the number of nodes at level zero is one, which

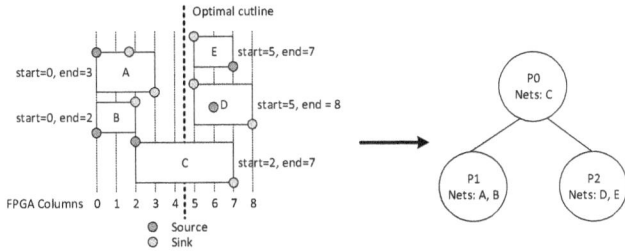

Figure 2: An example of a 2-level bi-partitioning tree. Partition P0 contains nets that cross the partition cutline whereas partitions P1 and P2 contain nets whose bounding boxes entirely fit into the left and right partition respectively.

is less than two, the number of threads that the tree is generated for. ParaDRo addresses this problem with three enhancements.

Firstly, interior nodes are further bi-partitioned to extract additional parallelism. The direction of this extra bi-partitioning is orthogonal to the direction that created the initial children of each interior node.

Secondly, ParaDRo schedules nets in interior nodes to be routed in parallel as long as they have non-overlapping bounding boxes. In order to minimize the overlap between nets, ParaDRo reduces the bounding box size of nets by decomposing multi-sink nets into single-sink nets called virtual nets. The bounding box size of virtual nets is further reduced by restricting the routes of a virtual net to be along the perimeter of its bounding box. Since there are two ways of routing virtual nets along the perimeter (bottom half or top half), a heuristic is introduced to choose the optimal bounding box shape for virtual nets. This heuristic is similar to global routing where coarse-grained routing channels are assigned to nets to minimize the overall congestion. After determining the bounding box shapes of the virtual nets, a schedule is generated for each node in the bi-partitioning tree to route the nets in the node in parallel whenever possible. The scheduling problem is reduced to a graph coloring problem where the graph models the nets to be routed and the overlap among them. The overlap graph is built such that virtual nets of the same net are scheduled to be routed sequentially. Therefore, subsequent sinks can reuse the existing route tree in a similar manner as VTR.

Thirdly, due to the smaller bounding boxes of the virtual nets, it was observed that ParaDRo fails to converge to a congestion-free state for some benchmarks circuits. Therefore, ParaDRo reroutes only congested nets when the number of congested nets is less than a predefined threshold. In this stage, ParaDRo expands the bounding box of the virtual nets to an axis-aligned bounding box covering the source and sink of the net to increase the routing flexibilty when eliminating congestion.

4.1 Recursive Bi-partitioning

ParaDRo starts by recursively splitting the FPGA into two disjoint regions while minimizing the difference in the workload of routing the nets in the two regions as shown in Algorithm 1. When determining where to cut the FPGA into two regions, ParaDRo leverages on the discrete nature of the FPGA architecture so that only a finite number of cutlines needs to be considered. For example, if the number of rows and columns in an FPGA are n_{rows} and $n_{columns}$, there are only $n_{rows} + 1$ horizontal and $n_{columns} + 1$

Algorithm 1 The recursive bi-partitioning algorithm

1: **procedure** RECURSIVE_BIPART(bb, $nets$, n_levels, cur_level, $node$)
2:     **if** $cur\_level < n\_levels - 1$ **then**
3:         $nets\_before$, $nets\_after$, opt_cut ← get_opt_cut(bb, $nets$)   ▷ Algorithm 2
4:         $nets\_crossing ← nets - nets\_before - nets\_after$
5:         $node.nets ← nets\_crossing$
6:         bb_before, bb_right ← split_bounding_box(bb, opt_cut)
7:         recursive_bipart(bb_before, $nets\_before$, n_levels, $cur\_level + 1$, $node.right$)
8:         recursive_bipart(bb_after, $nets\_after$, n_levels, $cur\_level + 1$, $node.left$)
9:     **else**
10:         $node.nets ← nets$
11:     **end if**
12: **end procedure**

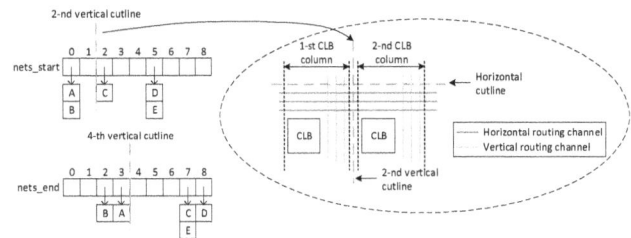

Figure 3: *nets_start* **and** *nets_end* **generated based on the nets in Figure 2**

vertical cutlines respectively. While the discrete nature of FPGAs significantly reduces the search space for an optimal cut, a naive way of performing bi-partitioning might lead to an inefficient algorithm. For example, finding the most load balanced cutline by calculating the total workload of nets that are located before and after every possible cutline leads to an inefficient $O(kN)$ algorithm where k is the number of cutlines and N is the number of nets. The bottleneck in this example lies in repeatedly determining the side of every net relative to every possible cutline, which requires the list of nets to be iterated k times.

In ParaDRo, the list of nets is only iterated once as shown in Algorithm 2. During the iteration, the contents of four arrays *nets_start*, *nets_end*, *total_workload_before* and *total_workload_after* are computed. These arrays allow the optimal cutline to be determined in $O(N + k)$ instead of $O(kN)$.

nets_start and *nets_end* are 2D arrays with the i-th element being an array of nets whose bounding boxes start and end at the i-th FPGA row/column respectively. The bounding box of a net can be represented as a 4-tuple $\langle xmin, xmax, ymin, ymax \rangle$, and the meaning of the start and end of a net bounding box depend on the orientation of the cutline. For a vertical cutline, the start and end of a bounding box are $xmin$ and $xmax$. Similarly, for a horizontal cutline, the start and end of a bounding box are $ymin$ and $ymax$. As shown in Algorithm 2, the start and end of a net are used to index into *nets_start* and *nets_end* respectively when adding the net to the arrays. Figure 3 shows an example of *nets_start* and *nets_end* that are generated based on the five nets shown in Figure 2. It also shows how a cutline is positioned relative to the CLBs and routing channels.

Algorithm 2 Fast heuristic to determine the optimal cutline

1: **procedure** GET_OPT_CUT(bb, $nets$)
2:     $nets\_start \leftarrow \{\{\}\}$
3:     $nets\_end \leftarrow \{\{\}\}$
4:     $total\_workload\_before \leftarrow \{0\}$
5:     $total\_workload\_after \leftarrow \{0\}$
6:
7:     **for** $net \in nets$ **do**
8:         $nets\_start[net.start] \leftarrow nets\_start[net.start] \cup net$
9:         $nets\_end[net.end] \leftarrow nets\_end[net.end] \cup net$
10:         $total\_workload\_before[net.end]$ $\leftarrow$
    $total\_workload\_before[net.end] + net.workload$
11:         $total\_workload\_after[net.start]$ $\leftarrow$
    $total\_workload\_after[net.start] + net.workload$
12:     **end for**
13:     $total\_workload\_before$ $\leftarrow$ prefix   sum   of
    $total\_workload\_before$ starting from **first** element
14:     $total\_workload\_after$ $\leftarrow$ prefix   sum   of
    $total\_workload\_after$ starting from **last** element
15:
16:     $opt\_cut \leftarrow -1$
17:     $min\_diff \leftarrow \infty$
18:     **for** $cut \in$ cut indices **do**
19:         $diff$ $\leftarrow$ $|total\_workload\_before[cut]$ $-$
    $total\_workload\_after[cut + 1]|$
20:         **if** $diff < min\_diff$ **then**
21:             $min\_diff \leftarrow diff$
22:             $opt\_cut \leftarrow cut$
23:         **end if**
24:     **end for**
25:     **return** $\bigcup_{i=0}^{opt\_cut} nets\_end[i]$,
    $\bigcup_{i=opt\_cut+1}^{last} nets\_start[i]$, opt_cut
26: **end procedure**

$nets\_start$ and $nets\_end$ allow the nets that are located after and before a specific cutline respectively to be determined easily. The list of nets located after the n-th cutline is simply $\bigcup_{i=n}^{last} nets\_start[i]$. Similarly, the list of nets located before the n-th cutline is $\bigcup_{i=0}^{n-1} nets\_end[i]$. For example, from Figure 3, the list of nets located after the 2-nd cutline is $\{C, D, E\}$ while the list of nets located before the 4-th cutline is $\{A, B\}$.

$total\_workload\_before$ and $total\_workload\_after$ are 1D arrays whose i-th element represents the total workload of all nets before the $(i + 1)$-th cutline and after the i-th cutline respectively. They are generated in 2 steps. The first step is done while iterating through the list of nets. For each net, its workload, which is approximated by the number of sinks, is added to the element of $total\_workload\_after$ and $total\_workload\_before$ at indices equal to the start and end of the net's bounding box respectively. The second step performs in-place prefix sums on both the arrays to generate the final values. The prefix sums are calculated starting from the first and last element for $total\_workload\_before$ and $total\_workload\_after$ respectively. The steps are illustrated in Figure 4 and 5.

After generating the arrays, the optimal cutline can be determined by finding an index opt_cut such that the absolute difference between $total\_workload\_before[opt\_cut]$ and $total\_workload\_after[opt\_cut + 1]$ is minimum. Based on opt_cut, the nets that are before and after the cutline can be obtained directly as $nets\_before = \bigcup_{i=0}^{opt\_cut} nets\_end[i]$ and $nets\_after = \bigcup_{i=opt\_cut+1}^{last} nets\_start[i]$

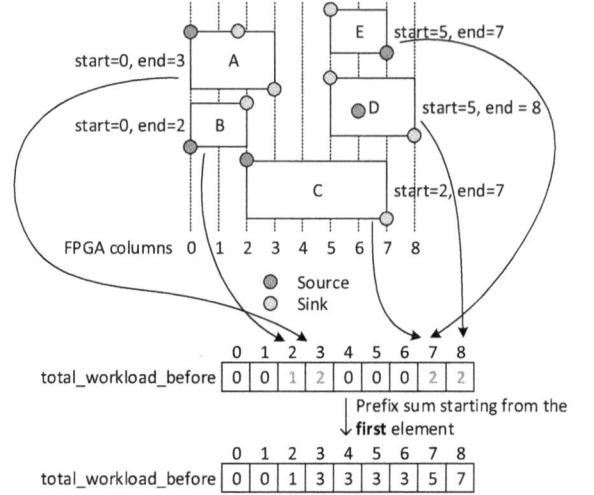

Figure 4: The process of generating $total\_workload\_before$

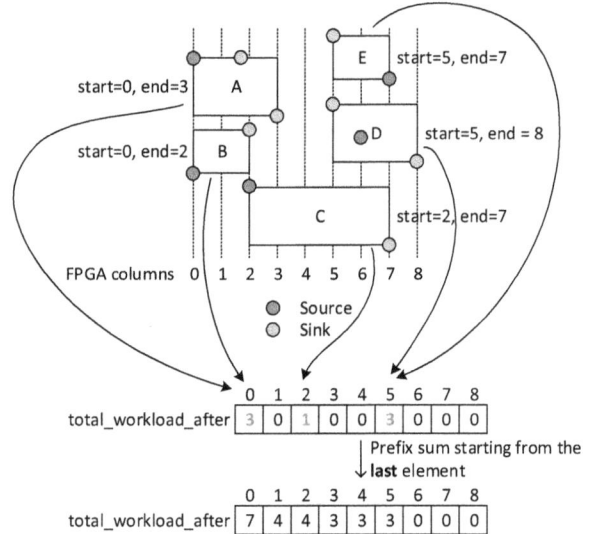

Figure 5: The process of generating $total\_workload\_after$

respectively. Nets that are not in $nets\_before$ and $nets\_after$, $nets\_crossing$, are contained in the parent node of the two child nodes that contain nets in $nets\_before$ and $nets\_after$. The biparitioning process is repeated for nodes that contain $nets\_before$ and $nets\_after$. ParaDRo also repeats the bi-partitioning process for the nets in $nets\_crossing$ to extract further parallelism. For simplicity purposes, the bi-partitioning process of $nets\_crossing$ is not shown in Algorithm 1.

Figure 2 shows the optimal cut and the associated bi-partitioning tree when ParaDRo is run with two threads. The FPGA is bi-partitioned once for two threads, and $|total\_workload\_before[opt\_cut] - total\_workload\_after[opt\_cut + 1]| = 0$.

4.2 Scheduling

After building the bi-partitioning tree, a directed task graph is generated for each node of the tree to identify nets that can be routed in parallel. The motivation behind this is the decreasing potential parallelism as the depth of a node, which is the number of edges between the node and the root of the tree, decreases. The worst case happens at a depth of zero where the potential parallelism is one because there is only one node, which is the root of the tree.

However, maximizing the number of nets that can be routed in parallel within a node is nontrivial due to a large number of overlapping nets. In order to guarantee determinism, these overlapping nets cannot be routed in parallel. By modeling the overlap between nets as a graph where the nodes represent the nets while the edges represent the bounding box overlap between the nets, it is easy to see that maximizing the number of nets that can be routed in parallel is equivalent to finding the chromatic number in graph coloring. The chromatic number is the minimum number of distinct colors that is required to color every node of a graph such that no adjacent nodes have the same color. A smaller chromatic number results in a higher number of nets that can be routed in parallel.

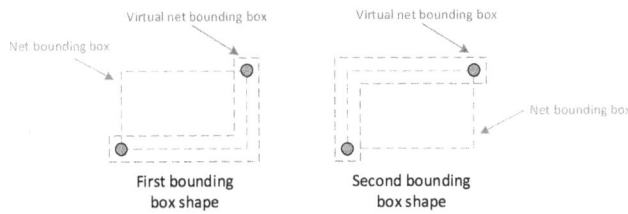

Figure 6: Two possible bounding box shapes for virtual nets

In order to maximize the number of nets that can be routed in parallel, it is important to reduce the bounding box overlap between the nets before performing graph coloring. Therefore, ParaDRo decomposes multi-sink nets into single-sink nets called virtual nets, which have smaller bounding boxes. Since a virtual net has only one sink, its bounding box size can be further reduced by restricting its route to be on the perimeter of its bounding box. Figure 6 shows the two possible routes that are on the perimeter and their associated bounding boxes. Figure 7 shows the process of decomposing two nets, A and B, into virtual nets A1, A2 and B1. It can be seen that virtual net B1 is no longer overlapping with virtual net A1 and A2 after the decomposition and a proper choice of bounding box shapes. The algorithm to make such a choice is described in Section 4.3.

After generating the virtual nets, an overlap graph is built based on their bounding boxes. The vertices of the graph represent the virtual nets while the edges represent a bounding box overlap between two virtual nets. An example of the overlap graph is shown in Figure 8. Since virtual nets of the same net always overlap at the source, the subgraph induced by their corresponding nodes forms a complete graph in the overlap graph. In Figure 8, the complete graph is between nodes A1 and A2. The complete graph ensures that sinks of the same net are routed sequentially so that each sink can reuse the route tree of sinks routed before it. While this is similar to the route tree reuse in VTR, the caveat is that the amount

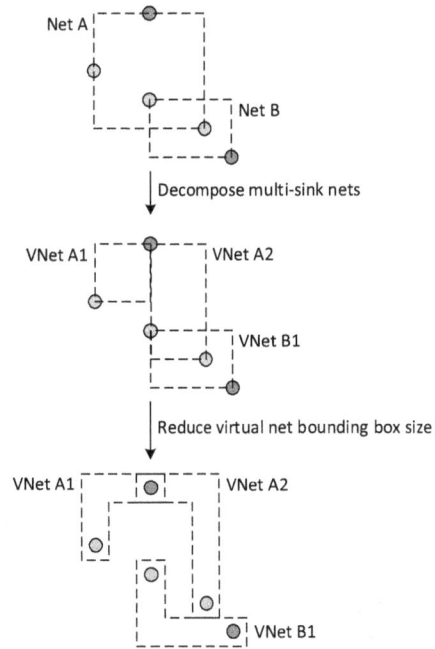

Figure 7: The process of decomposing multi-sink nets and reducing their bounding box sizes

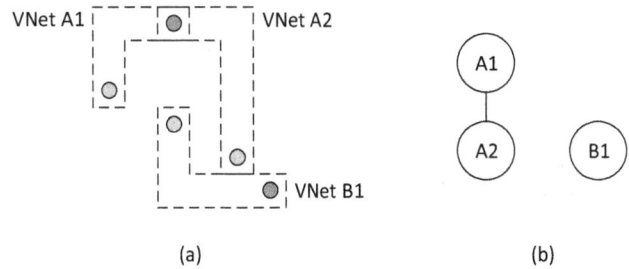

Figure 8: (a) Virtual nets (b) Their corresponding overlap graph

of reuse is lower because the bounding box of each sink is smaller than that of VTR's.

Although graph coloring is an NP-complete problem, there is a greedy algorithm to solve it. The greedy algorithm works by iterating through the nodes of the overlap graph in a certain order and greedily assigns each node a color that is not used by its neighbor. The quality of the coloring depends heavily on the order in which the nodes are colored. In ParaDRo, the nodes are visited in a smallest last ordering. The ordering is generated by repeatedly finding a node with the smallest degree and removing it from the graph until the graph is empty. Then, the nodes are returned in an order reverse to that in which they were found.

A simple way of routing the colored virtual nets would be in a bulk synchronous manner where nets of the same color have to finish routing in parallel before nets of the next color can be routed. However, this could lead to unnecessary waiting as shown in Figure 9(a). The bottleneck can be solved by converting the undirected overlap graph into a directed acyclic task graph shown in Figure

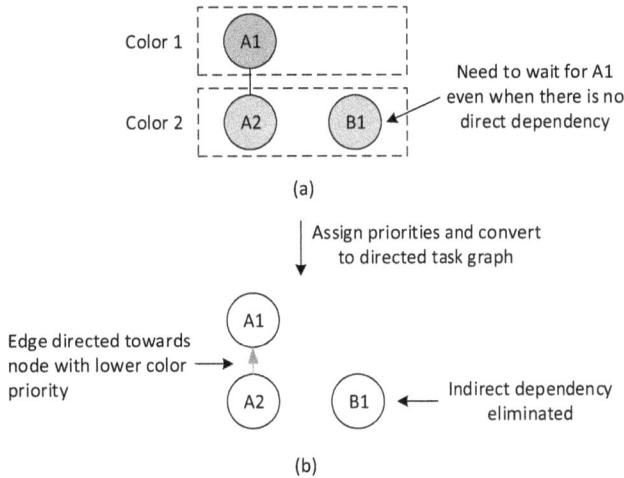

Figure 9: (a) An example of routing the overlap graph in Figure 8(b) where a net (B1) has to wait for another net (A1) to complete routing even when there is no direct dependency between them (b) Solving the waiting problem by converting the undirected overlap graph to a directed task graph

9(b). The task graph is similar to the overlap graph in that the nodes represent the nets but the edges impose an order in which the nodes are routed. Based on the task graph, a net can be routed as soon as all its parents have been routed.

The conversion works by assigning a priority to every color and setting the direction of overlap edges based on the color priority of the nodes that are connected by the edge. The color priority is determined by summing the number of sinks of all nets of the color. Then, edges are set to point from the node with a higher sum to the node with a lower sum. The rationale is that higher fanout nets should be routed first to ensure better convergence. The conversion imposes a partial order on the overlap graph nodes to ensure determinism.

4.3 Global Routing of Virtual Nets

As described in the previous section, there are two possible bounding box shapes of virtual nets. In this section, a heuristic is proposed to determine the shapes that minimize the total overlap between virtual nets. The heuristic is motivated by the following observations. Firstly, reducing the amount of overlap increases the number of nets that can be routed in parallel, which is the main goal of ParaDRo. Secondly, the amount of overlap has a direct impact on the congestion during routing.

Determining the bounding box shapes is similar to assigning routing channels to nets in global routing, and this similarity forms the basic idea of the proposed heuristic. One of the most important factors in the heuristic is the order in which nets are routed. Unfortunately, the actual order can only be determined after the scheduling described in Section 4.2, which requires the bounding box shapes in the first place to generate the overlap graph. In order to break the dependency loop, the net order is approximated by traversing the bi-partitioning tree in a breadth-first manner and adding the virtual nets in the node, after sorting them in decreasing number of sinks of their original net, to the list of virtual nets to be routed, *global_netlist*. The original net of a virtual net refers to the

multi-sink net before decomposition. This approximation makes sense because, during scheduling, virtual nets whose original nets have higher number of sinks are scheduled to be routed earlier.

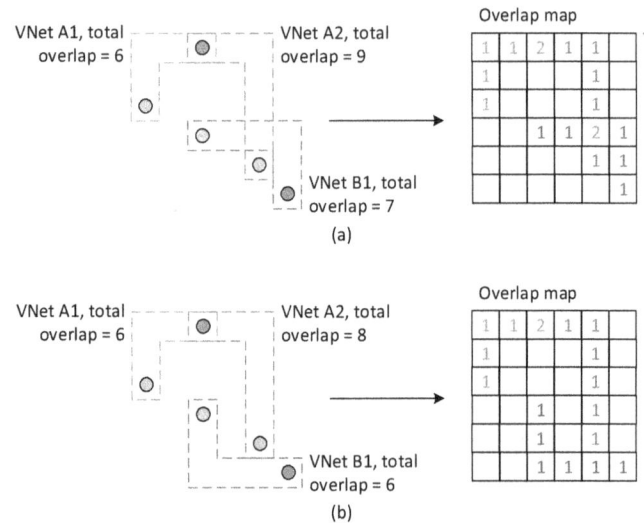

Figure 10: Different virtual net bounding boxes and their corresponding overlap maps

For each virtual net, *vnet*, in *global_netlist*, the optimal bounding box is determined by finding the box with the least overlap with virtual nets ordered before *vnet* in *global_netlist*. The decision to find the locally optimum bounding box is intentional to reduce the algorithmic complexity of the global routing so that its execution time does not outweigh the increased parallelism generated by it. The amount of overlap can be determined quickly by maintaining an overlap map, which is a 2D array of the same size as the FPGA grid. Each element of the array represents a discrete point in the FPGA grid and stores the number of globally routed virtual nets with bounding boxes that contain the point. With the overlap map, the total overlap of the two possible bounding boxes, *Box1* and *Box2*, of *vnet* can be calculated by summing the elements of the map that corresponds to the points contained in *Box1* and *Box2*. The box with the least total overlap is set as the bounding box for *vnet*. Figure 10 shows two different bounding box shapes for virtual net B1 and their corresponding overlap maps. It also illustrates how choosing the shape in Figure 10(b) for virtual net B1 leads to a lower total overlap of 6, assuming virtual net A1 and A2 are globally routed before B1. The choice of bounding boxes in Figure 10(b) not only enables virtual nets A2 and B1 to be routed in parallel, but also completely eliminates congestion between the them.

4.4 Actual Routing

After building the bi-partitioning tree and directed task graphs, the actual routing process starts from the root of the bi-partitioning tree. All nets with no parents in the directed task graph associated with the root of the bi-partitioning tree are routed in parallel. During routing, ParaDRo keeps track of the indegree of the nodes in the task graph. After routing a task graph node, the indegree of the children of the node is decremented by one. As soon as the indegree of a task graph node reaches zero, it can be scheduled to be routed

Table 1: Summary of benchmarks used in the experiments

Benchmark	Total nets	Total blocks	Minimum channel width
stereovision1	10,797	1,217	104
LU8PEEng	15,990	2,373	114
stereovision2	34,501	2,926	154
LU32PEEng	53,199	7,536	174
neuron	54,056	3,512	206
stereo_vision	61,883	3,434	228
segmentation	125,592	9,047	292
denoise	257,425	18,600	310

Table 2: Notations

Notation	Meaning
seq	Nets in nodes of the bi-partitioning tree are routed **sequentially**
par	Nets in nodes of the bi-partitioning tree are routed in **parallel**
normal	The bi-partitioning tree of *nets_crossing* is routed **sequentially**
extra	The bi-partitioning tree of *nets_crossing* is routed in **parallel**

in parallel. After routing all the nets in the task graph associated with the root of the bi-partitioning tree, the process is repeated recursively for the two children of the root.

Except for the root of the bi-partitioning tree, multiple task graphs are processed in parallel. In addition, the number of task graphs doubles each time the level of the tree increases by one. Coupled with routing nets in the task graphs in parallel whenever possible, ParaDRo can keep all the threads busy during routing. Another property that minimizes idling time during routing is that a node in the bi-partitioning tree can be routed as soon as its parent is done routing without waiting for other nodes in the same level to complete. This is because the FPGA region associated with a node only overlaps with the region associated with its parent, and nodes at the same level of the bi-partitioning tree are spatially independent.

4.5 Serial Equivalence

The number of levels of the bi-partitioning tree affects the route order of virtual nets and in turn the route solution. ParaDRo is implemented in such a way that the number of levels can be set independently of the number of threads because nets from the bi-partitioning tree are simply dispatched to a pool of worker threads to be routed. By keeping the number of levels constant, ParaDRo produces the same result even when the size of worker thread pool is changed. Therefore, ParaDRo is serially equivalent [4]. The number of levels in the bi-partitioning tree can be chosen carefully to strike a good balance between the amount of exposed parallelism and the overhead of task switching.

5 EXPERIMENTAL SETUP

ParaDRo was evaluated on a server equipped with two Intel Xeon E5-2680 V3 without hyper-threading and 128 GB of RAM. The operating system is Red Hat Enterprise 6.8 with Linux kernel version 2.6.32. gcc 7 with optimization flag -O3 was used to compile both ParaDRo and VTR [5].

The benchmarks used for evaluation were obtained from the VTR [5] and Titan [8] packages, and they are summarized in Table 1. The Titan benchmarks were chosen to cover a wide range of circuit sizes with *neuron* being the smallest and *denoise* being the largest out of the 23 Titan benchmarks. The benchmarks were packed and placed with default parameters using VTR of the same version as the Titan paper [8] (7.0 r4292) because the release version of VTR (7.0) crashes when loading Titan benchmarks due to a netlist loading bug. The architecture files used are k6_frac_N10_mem32K_40nm.xml and

stratixiv_arch.timing.xml for VTR and Titan benchmarks respectively. The minimum channel widths in Table 1 are obtained by running VTR's routing in binary search mode.

The notations used to refer to different variants of ParaDRo are shown in Table 2.

6 EXPERIMENTAL RESULTS

In this section, two important performance metrics of ParaDRo, speedup and critical path delay, are presented.

6.1 Speedup Across Different Benchmarks

Figure 11 shows the speedups of different ParaDRo variants relative to their single-threaded variant. The time required to build the bi-partitioning tree is not included in the speedup calculation. Bi-partitioning tree generation for 2, 4, and 8 partitions currently requires on average 67.7%, 27.2%, and 15.6% of the routing time of single-threaded ParaDRo respectively. The tree generation takes longer for a smaller number of partitions because of the larger number of nets within a partition. Fortunately, generation of the bounding box overlap graph, which is the most time-consuming part of the tree building, is embarrassingly parallel because the bounding box overlaps of each net can be determined independently of other nets. The parallelization of the overlap graph generation is left as a future work.

It can be seen that LU32PEEng has significantly higher speedup than other benchmarks. On the other hand, stereovision1, neuron and stereo_vision are among the worst performing benchmarks in terms of speedup. The reason for this observation can be found in Figure 13, which shows the total time spent routing nets in all threads normalized to single-threaded ParaDRo. Only the **par extra** variant of ParaDRo is shown in Figure 13 because the total time measures only the raw time spent routing nets, which is the same for all variants of ParaDRo. The total time gives an approximation of the amount of work that is done by the router. In order to achieve good speedup, the amount of work must remain relatively constant as the number of threads increases. Unfortunately, this is not the case for most benchmarks as shown in Figure 13. The workload of ParaDRo depends on the order in which the virtual nets are routed. Therefore, the workload changes depending on the number of threads because a different number of threads generates a different bi-partitioning tree, which results in a different order in which the nets are routed. For LU32PEEng, the workload reduces significantly as the number of threads increases, which explains the super-linear speedup in Figure 11. On the other hand, the workload of stereovision1, neuron, and stereo_vision for more than one thread is actually more than

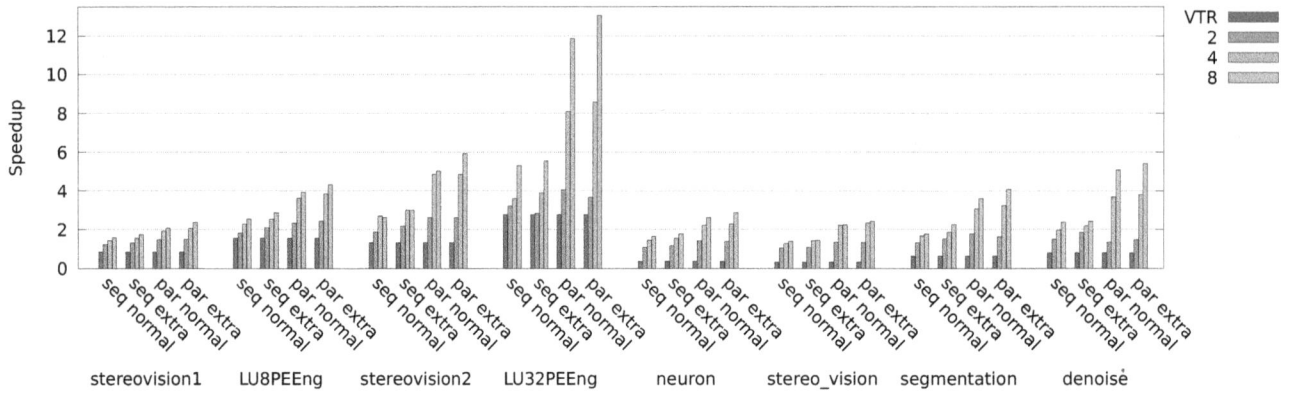

Figure 11: Speedups of different ParaDRo variants and VTR with 140% channel width normalized to single-threaded ParaDRo

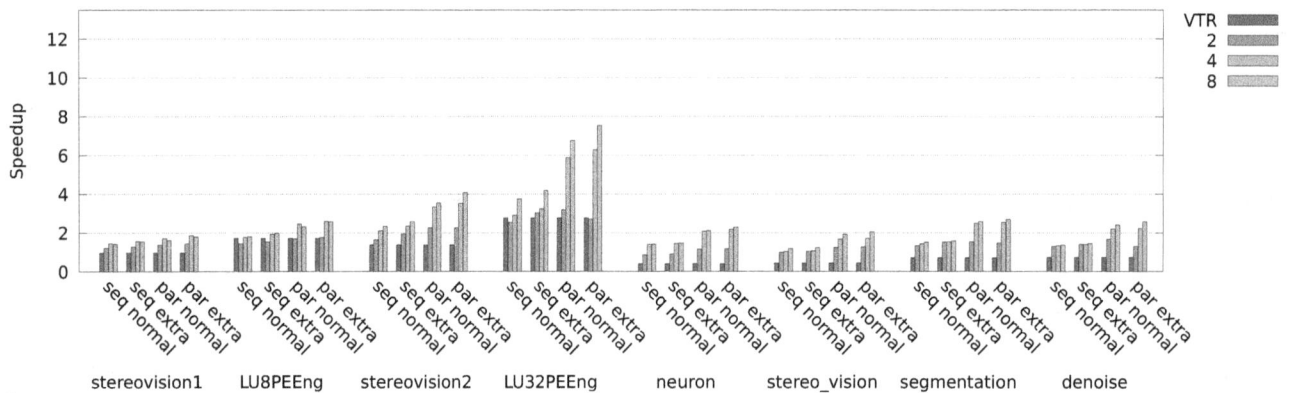

Figure 12: Speedups of different ParaDRo variants and VTR with 120% channel width normalized to single-threaded ParaDRo

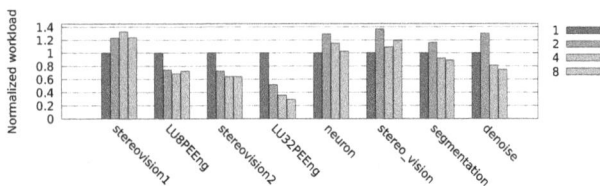

Figure 13: Total net route time of par extra ParaDRo with 140% channel width normalized to single-threaded par extra ParaDRo

that of single thread ParaDRo. Therefore, their speedups are among the worst in Figure 13.

Unfortunately, due to the difference in the route order, the workload when routing LU32PEEng with one thread is higher than that of VTR, causing ParaDRo to be slower than VTR for LU32PEEng. On the other hand, ParaDRo is significantly faster than VTR when routing Titan benchmarks. This is because an enhancement proposed by Gort [3] is added to ParaDRo. The enhancement is motivated by the fact that the Logic Array Block (LAB) in stratixiv_arch.timing.xml has equivalent output pins. The equivalence causes convergence issues because the packer assumes that each net will use only one

LAB output pin but nets with multiple sinks tend to use more than one of those pins during routing. In order to solve the problem, the enhancement forces the router to use the same output pin to route the rest of the sinks once the first sink of the net has been routed.

Another observation that can be made from Figure 11 is that enabling the enhancements proposed in Section 4.1 and 4.2 improve speedup by different amounts for different benchmarks. This is because different benchmarks have different amounts of overlap between nets. Benchmarks with less number of overlaps allow more parallelism to be exploited when nets in nodes of the bi-partitioning tree are scheduled to be routed in parallel. For example, routing LU32PEEng with the **par** variant of ParaDRo improves speedup significantly as compared to routing with the **seq** variant of ParaDRo. stereovision1, on the other hand, does not exhibit such a huge improvement.

The speedup of ParaDRo when routing resources are more scarce is shown in Figure 12. It can be seen that the speedup of ParaDRo with only 20% higher than the minimum channel width is worse than that of ParaDRo with 40% higher than the minimum channel width. This is due to the restrictive virtual net bounding boxes when ParaDRo is run with more than one thread. Since virtual nets can only use RR on the perimeter of their bounding box, the flexibility of avoiding congestion is lower than when all the RRs in

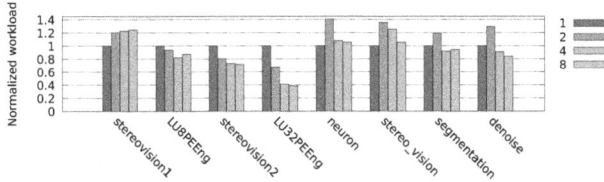

Figure 14: Total net route time of par extra ParaDRo with 120% channel width normalized to single-threaded par extra ParaDRo

the bounding box are available. The reduction in flexibility causes ParaDRo to work harder to resolve congestion as shown in Figure 14.

6.2 Effects of Proposed Enhancements

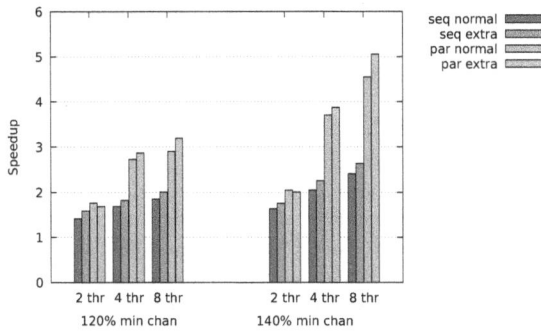

Figure 15: Average self-relative speedups of different ParaDRo variants

In this section, the effects of the enhancements discussed in Section 4.1 and 4.2 on ParaDRo's speedup are shown in Figure 15. The speedups in the figures are averaged across the benchmarks in Table 1.

Figure 15 shows that routing nets in nodes of the bi-partitioning tree in parallel results in higher speedup than routing them sequentially. In addition, the increase in speedup is more significant for 4 and 8 threads where the increase is almost two-fold. This improvement validates the hypothesis in Section 4.2 that spatial partitioning alone does not expose sufficient parallelism to keep the threads busy especially for higher number of threads. On the other hand, the improvement in speedup by routing the bi-partitioning tree of *nets_crossing* in parallel is not as significant as routing the main bi-partitioning tree in parallel.

6.3 Critical Path Delay

Figure 16 and 17 show the critical path delay of ParaDRo normalized to that of VTR with 40% and 20% higher than minimum channel width respectively. It is important to note that the different variants of ParaDRo shown in Section 6.2 are equivalent to one another in terms of the route solution produced. Therefore, their critical path delays are the same and not shown separately in the figures.

As shown in Figure 16 and 17, the worst degradation in critical path delay is only 5%. In addition, single thread ParaDRo is able

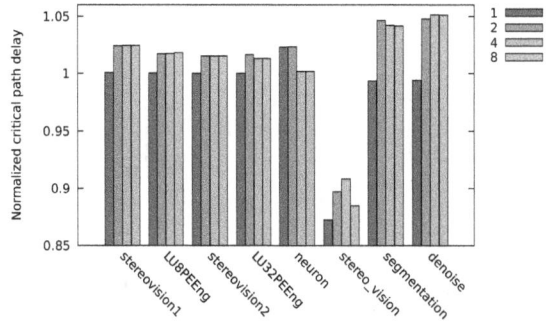

Figure 16: Critical path delay of ParaDRo with 140% channel width normalized to that of VTR

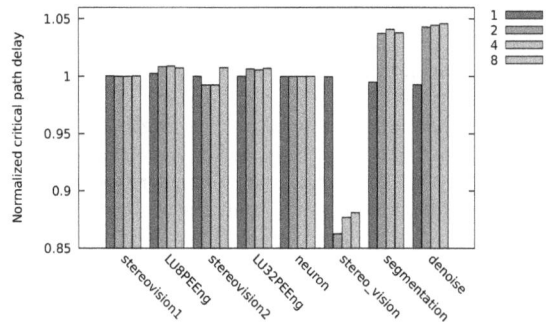

Figure 17: Critical path delay of ParaDRo with 120% channel width normallized to that of VTR

to produce critical path delay that is very close to VTR's for most benchmarks.

6.4 Total wirelength

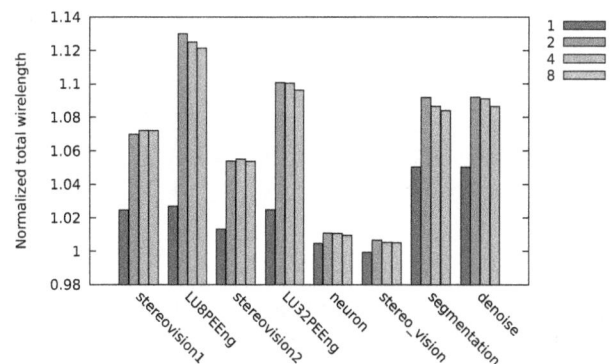

Figure 18: VTR normalized total wirelength of ParaDRo with 140% channel width

Due to the more restrictive bounding boxes of the virtual nets, nets might take longer routes to avoid congestion. In addition, the restriction also reduces the opportunity for route tree reuse in

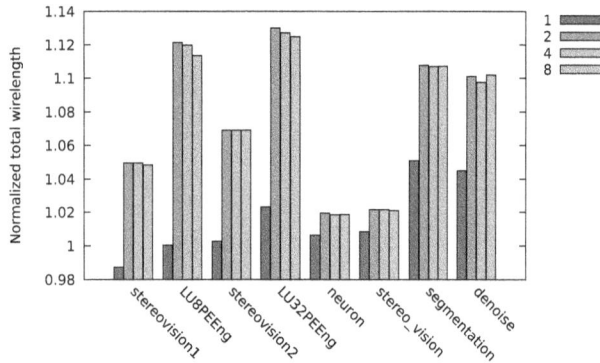

Figure 19: VTR normalized total wirelength of ParaDRo with 120% channel width

ParaDRo as compared to VTR. The effect of these factors on the total wirelength is shown in Figure 18 and 19.

Virtual nets are not generated for single-threaded ParaDRo because nets cannot be routed in parallel. However, the total wirelength of single-threaded ParaDRo is still higher than that of VTR for most benchmarks because the bounding box expansion factor (bb_factor) is lower than that of VTR. This is to be consistent with multi-threaded ParaDRo where the lower bb_factor increases the amount of parallelism by reducing the overlap between nets.

The absence of virtual nets in single-threaded ParaDRo is also the reason why single-threaded ParaDRo has significantly lower total wirelength than multi-threaded ParaDRo in Figure 18 and 19.

6.5 Impact of Serial Equivalence on Speedup

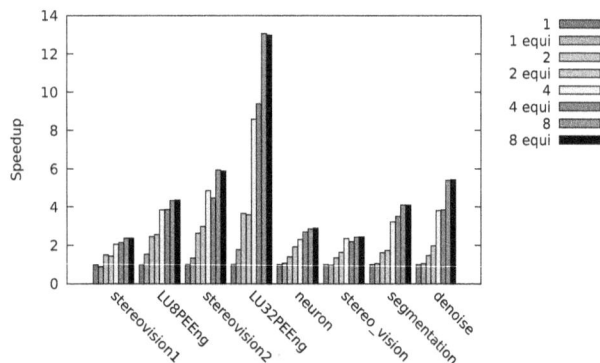

Figure 20: Speedup of serially equivalent versus non serially equivalent ParaDRo relative to single-threaded non serially equivalent ParaDRo

Figure 20 shows the effect of enforcing serial equivalence [4] on the speedup of ParaDRo. The channel width is set to 40% higher than the minimum, and the number of levels in the bi-partitioning tree is fixed to 4. As can be seen in the figure, the performance of serially equivalent ParaDRo is comparable to that of non serially equivalent ParaDRo.

6.6 Comparison with Existing Works

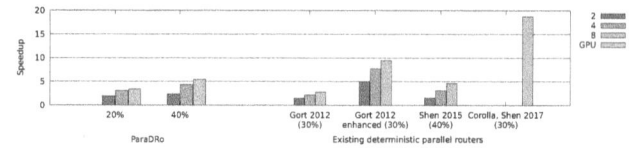

Figure 21: VTR normalized average speedup of ParaDRo and other existing works

Figure 21 compares the speedup of **par extra** ParaDRo to existing works. ParaDRo is faster than Shen's [10] and Gort's [3] router because ParaDRo routes nets within a partition in parallel while Shen and Gort do not.

On the other hand, Gort's enhanced router [3] is faster than ParaDRo because even though both routers are capable of rerouting only congested nets, the former does so for every routing iteration while the latter only does it when the number of congested nets drops below a threshold. Corolla [11] is also significantly faster than ParaDRo but its scalability is unclear because the authors did not evaluate Corolla with varying number of CUDA cores.

7 CONCLUSIONS

In this paper, we propose ParaDRo, a parallel deterministic router based on spatial partitioning. To improve speedup, nets within a partition are scheduled to be routed in parallel. Multi-sink nets are decomposed into single-sink nets, and their bounding boxes are shrunk to increase the number of nets that can be routed in parallel. With these enhancements, ParaDRo achieves a maximum speedup of 5.4X with 8 threads.

ACKNOWLEDGMENTS

This work is supported in part by the German Research Foundation (DFG) within the Cluster of Excellence "Center for Advancing Electronics Dresden" (cfaed) at the Technische Universität Dresden.

REFERENCES

[1] Lucídio AF Cabral, Júlio S Aude, and Nelson Maculan. 2002. TDR: A distributed-memory parallel routing algorithm for FPGAs. In *Field-Programmable Logic and Applications: Reconfigurable Computing Is Going Mainstream.* Springer, 263–270.
[2] Marcel Gort and Jason H Anderson. 2010. Deterministic multi-core parallel routing for FPGAs. In *FPT.* IEEE, 78–86.
[3] Marcel Gort and Jason H Anderson. 2012. Accelerating FPGA routing through parallelization and engineering enhancements, special section on PAR-CAD 2010. *IEEE TCAD* 31, 1 (2012), 61–74.
[4] Adrian Ludwin and Vaughn Betz. 2011. Efficient and deterministic parallel placement for FPGAs. *TODAES* 16, 3 (2011), 22.
[5] Jason Luu, Jeffrey Goeders, Michael Wainberg, Andrew Somerville, Thien Yu, Konstantin Nasartschuk, Miad Nasr, Sen Wang, Tim Liu, Nooruddin Ahmed, et al. 2014. VTR 7.0: Next generation architecture and CAD system for FPGAs. *TRETS* 7, 2 (2014), 6.
[6] L. McMurchie and C. Ebeling. 1995. PathFinder: a negotiation-based performance-driven router for FPGAs. In *FPGA.*
[7] Kevin E Murray, Scott Whitty, Suya Liu, Jason Luu, and Vaughn Betz. 2013. Titan: Enabling large and complex benchmarks in academic CAD. In *FPL.* IEEE, 1–8.
[8] Kevin E Murray, Scott Whitty, Suya Liu, Jason Luu, and Vaughn Betz. 2015. Timing-driven Titan: Enabling large benchmarks and exploring the gap between academic and commercial CAD. *TRETS* 8, 2 (2015), 10.
[9] Keshav Pingali, Donald Nguyen, Milind Kulkarni, Martin Burtscher, M Amber Hassaan, Rashid Kaleem, Tsung-Hsien Lee, Andrew Lenharth, Roman Manevich, Mario Méndez-Lojo, et al. 2011. The tao of parallelism in algorithms. *ACM Sigplan Notices* 46, 6 (2011), 12–25.
[10] Minghua Shen and Guojie Luo. 2015. Accelerate FPGA routing with parallel recursive partitioning. In *ICCAD.* IEEE, 118–125.
[11] Minghua Shen and Guojie Luo. 2017. Corolla: GPU-Accelerated FPGA routing based on subgraph dynamic expansion. In *FPGA.* 105–114.

Routing Magic: Performing Computations Using Routing Networks and Voting Logic on Unary Encoded Data

Soheil Mohajer
Department of Electrical and
Computer Engineering
University of Minnesota
Minneapolis, MN 55455
soheil@umn.edu

Zhiheng Wang
Department of Electrical and
Computer Engineering
University of Minnesota
Minneapolis, MN 55455
wang3868@umn.edu

Kia Bazargan
Department of Electrical and
Computer Engineering
University of Minnesota
Minneapolis, MN 55455
kia@umn.edu

ABSTRACT

The binary number representation has dominated digital logic for decades due to its compact storage requirements. However, since the number system is positional, it needs to "unpack" bits, perform computations, and repack the bits back to binary (*e.g.*, partial products in multiplication). An alternative representation is the unary number system: we use N bits, out of which the first M are 1 and the rest are 0 to represent the value M/N. We present a novel method which first converts binary numbers to unary using thermometer encoders, then uses a "scaling network" followed by voting gates that we call "alternator logic", followed by an adder tree to convert the numbers back to the binary format. For monotonically increasing functions, the scaling network is all we need, which essentially uses only the routing resources and flip-flops on the FPGA architecture. Our method is especially well-suited to FPGAs due to the abundant availability of routing and FF resources, and for the ability of FPGAs to realize high fanout gates for highly oscillating functions. We compare our method to stochastic computing and to conventional binary implementations on a number of functions, as well as on two common image processing applications. Our method is clearly superior to the conventional binary implementation: our area×delay cost is on average only 3%, 8% and 32% of the binary method for 8-, 10-, and 12-bit resolutions respectively. Compared to stochastic computing, our cost is 6%, 5%, and 8% for those resolutions. The area cost includes conversions from and to the binary format. Our method out performs the conventional binary method on an edge detection algorithm. However, it is not competitive with the binary method on the median filtering application due to the high cost of generating and saving unary representations of the input pixels.

CCS CONCEPTS

•**Hardware → Hardware accelerators;** *Reconfigurable logic applications;* Programmable logic elements;

KEYWORDS

Unary Computing, Scaling Network, Alternator Logic, Stochastic Computing, Thermometer Code

ACM Reference format:
Soheil Mohajer, Zhiheng Wang, and Kia Bazargan. 2018. Routing Magic: Performing Computations Using Routing Networks and Voting Logic on Unary Encoded Data. In *Proceedings of 2018 ACM/SIGDA International Symposium on Field-Programmable Gate Arrays, Monterey, CA, USA, February 25–27, 2018 (FPGA 2018),* 10 pages.
DOI: http://dx.doi.org/10.1145/3174243.3174267

1 INTRODUCTION

Digital logic has relied on Binary representation of data for decades. The advantage of the *positional* binary representation is obvious: its logarithmic space requirements, *i.e.*, to represent N discrete values, we need only $\log(N)$ bits to represent data. However, the binary representation comes with a cost: computations such as multiplication and addition need to "unpack" the number by either generating partial products in the case of multiplication, or working with a carry chain in the case of addition.

Given the increasingly larger available pool of flip-flops and deeply buffered routing resources on modern FPGAs, we can consider simpler data formats that are not as compact as binary in storage, but allow drastically simpler logic to perform the same calculations, hence reducing the area × delay product. This is true especially when the resolution of the data is not high, *e.g.*, when the data is 8-12 bits wide.

In this paper we present a novel way of evaluating functions by first converting their binary representation to the "flushed unary" data representation. Without loss of generality, we only focus on real numbers $x \in [0, 1]$, represented with a resolution of $1/N$. All finite range set of discrete numbers can be scaled to the $[0, 1]$ range with the desired resolution. The real number i/N, where $N = 2^W$ and $i \in \{0, 1, \cdots, N\}$ can be represented using W bits in binary to show the value of i in base 2. The same number can be represented in the "unary" format by using a total of N bits, in which i bits are 1's and $N - i$ bits are zeros, and the order of the appearance of 1's and 0's does not matter. Unlike the binary representation in which each bit has half the weight of the bit immediately to its left, all bits in the unary format have the same weight. As an example, 0.101_2 represents the number 5/8, whereas the same number can be represented as either 11111000_1, 00011111_1, 11010110_1 or any other sequence of 1's and 0's that has five 1's and three 0's.

We are interested in a canonical unary representation for consistency and for being able to make circuits that have multiple levels of logic, *e.g.*, feeding the input pixel values in the canonical unary format to a Gamma correction unit, and taking the canonical unary output of the Gamma correction unit and feeding it to an edge detection unit. We have chosen the "left-flushed unary" representation in which all the 1's appear first in the string of bits (similar to [10]). Our method uses N wires (flip-flops) to represent a unary number in the $[0, 1]$ range with a resolution of $1/N$.

Our method can be summarized as follows. More details are presented in Sec. 3 and figures 2 and 3.

- We use an efficient binary-to-thermometer encoder to convert the input data from binary to the left-flushed unary representation [16].
- Once the unary representation is generated on the input wires, monotonically increasing functions can be implemented by a simple rewiring network that stretches or contracts the bits and routes them to the output wires, hence requiring only flip-flops and routing. We call this the "scaling network", and its architecture is designed using the discrete derivative of the function.
- The output wires can be fed to an adder tree to convert the value to the binary format.
- For non-monotonic functions, we divide the function into piece-wise monotonically increasing or decreasing regions. For each region we design the scaling network, and combine the outputs of these regions using a voting (or as well call them "alternator") logic.
- For univariate functions and for monotonically increasing multivariate functions, the output of our scaling network + alternator logic is also in the canonical format of left-flushed unary representation, so we can synthesize logic with a cascade of modules and amortize on the cost of the binary-to-thermometer encoder and thermometer-to-binary decoder. We cannot guarantee the output would be in the canonical format for non-monotonic multivariate functions, but in practice, deviations from the canonical format result in about 1% error (*e.g.*, see Fig. 14 and the 1.1% error mentioned in the caption).

The advantages of our method are:

(1) The unary representation requires less logic compared to binary computations in most cases. For monotonically increasing functions, once data is converted to the flushed-unary format, we can do computations with no logic at all.

(2) Our method makes good use of the abundant buffered routing resources in FPGAs. Additionally, FPGA architectures are particularly suitable for our method because they can easily handle large fanouts (10's - 100's), which are required when implementing oscillating functions.

(3) On average, our method has an area×delay cost that is only 3% of that of conventional binary implementations with a resolution of 8 bits. Although our method is still competitive for higher resolutions, the gap between the

conventional binary and our method shrinks as the resolution goes higher (our cost is 8% and 32% of the conventional at 10- and 12-bit resolutions).

(4) Our method also has a clear advantage over stochastic computing methods, as will be discussed later.

The rest of the paper is organized as follows. Section 2 discusses relevant prior work and the context in which our work should be evaluated. The overall architecture of our method is discussed in Section 3), followed by the details of the scaling network and the alternator logic (sections 4 and 5). Experimental results are presented in Section 6. Section 7 concludes the paper and discusses future directions of the research.

2 RELEVANT PREVIOUS WORK

The closest line of work that is similar to our proposed approach is "Stochastic Computing", which essentially uses a non-canonical unary number representation with random streams of bits. Traditionally, Stochastic Computing (SC) has been defined as an alternative digital approach to real arithmetic in which a real value $x \in [0, 1]$ is encoded as a Bernoulli sequence of length N, where the probability of a bit in the stream to be at logic 1 equals x. The expected value of the stream is $\frac{M}{N} = x$, M being the number of 1's in the stream. The resolution of this representation is $1/N$, and if $N = 2^W$, an equivalent binary representation with the same resolution would need only W bits to represent numbers.

The idea of performing arithmetic using stochastic bit-streams dates back to 1956 and resurfaced sporadically up until 2001[1–3]. In the past few years (2008-present), there has been renewed interest in stochastic computing [4], showing significant benefits including remarkable hardware cost reductions and high degrees of fault tolerance [5, 9].

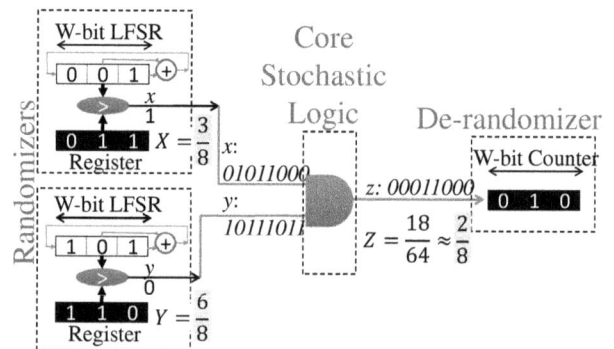

Figure 1: Previous work: stochastic multiplication.

Figure 1 shows how multiplication is performed in the first generation of stochastic computing using only a single AND gate (the middle box in the figure). The randomizer (also called binary-to-stochastic converter) and the de-randomizer (also called stochastic-to-binary converter) blocks are shown to the left and to the right of the core stochastic logic respectively. It can be seen that the randomizer and de-randomizer logic offset the potentially large area savings offered by the core stochastic logic. This architecture is serial: it waits for a long latency of L bits to get the desired resolution on the output. Due to its use of random number generators, the architecture also has an inherent random fluctuation in the output, resulting in inaccuracies when evaluating functions.

New generations of stochastic computing circuits are emerging: the authors in [10] favored abandoning randomness in generating bit streams and essentially using the convolution of two deterministic bit streams to evaluate a two-input function such as an AND gate. The method amounts to using input streams of length $N = 2^W$, and generating an output that has N^2 bits. The growth would be exponential as the circuit depth increases. We will not compare our work against [10] in this paper since their delay is N^2, which will not make it competitive to our work.

Another recent effort used a more compact stochastic function logic that minimized the use of constant coefficients, and proposed a parallel implementation of the circuit [15]. The work in [15] is similar to our work in two respects: it uses thermometer encoding of data, and it has a network of connections called a "shuffling network", followed by the "core logic" to implement functions. However, the core logic in their method is based on stochastic logic that belongs to the class of Bernstein Polynomials [6, 7]. Our method is fundamentally different from that work because:

- We rely mostly on the routing network to *compute* functions. Our method is not bound by Bernstein polynomials or stochastic logic at all.
- The Bernstein Polynomials can only approximate a limited class of real polynomial functions. The value of a Bernstein function $f(x)$ can be 0 or 1 only at $x = 0$ or $x = 1$. For example, a Bernstein Polynomial cannot approximate the functions shown in Fig. 12.

In summary, our method is superior to stochastic computing in terms of the set of functions it can implement (*e.g.*, Fig. 12), its accuracy (see Fig. 11), and its area × delay product (by 26x at a resolution of 12 bits. See Table 4).

3 OVERALL ARCHITECTURE

As discussed in the introduction, we convert binary numbers to a left-flushed unary number format to make the computation logic simple. Figure 2 shows the overall architecture of our method. A W–bit binary input value M is converted to thermometer code (2^W parallel bits, the first M of which are 1's, and the rest are zeros). A "scaling network" designed using the slope of the function takes the parallel bits, stretching or contracting the bits corresponding to monotonically increasing or decreasing regions of the function, feeding the result to the "alternator logic" that decides on the value of each bit based on the region of the function. Sections 4 and 5 discuss how these components are synthesized. Finally, the 2^W output bits are fed to an adder tree that converts the output to binary.

If a value is to be evaluated using multiple levels of computations (*e.g.*, first using a Gamma correction filter on an image, and then performing edge detection), they can be cascaded without extra conversions between the unary and binary number formats as shown in Fig. 3. To minimize errors, the output of the first level of the alternator should also be in the canonical unary format. As mentioned before, we can guarantee that for all univariate functions and all monotonically increasing multivariate functions. Based on our experiments, when bits are not necessarily in the left-flushed

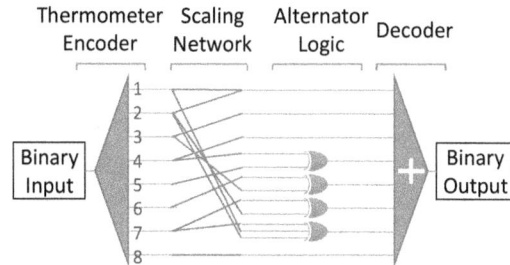

Figure 2: The overall architecture of our method.

format, there will be a small error of about 1% in the calculations of Level 2.

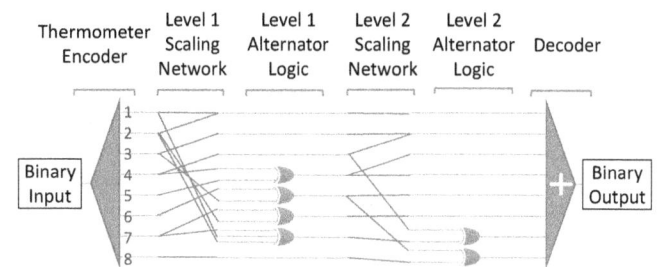

Figure 3: The overall architecture of our method: two-level logic.

4 UNIVARIATE FUNCTIONS

In this section we introduce our synthesis method which results in an optimum approximation for computing an arbitrary function $f : [0, 1] \to [0, 1]$.

The main idea in our method is to utilize the structure of the unary representation, in which each bit of the output contributes $1/N$ in the value of the function calculated as the sum of all bits.

We first define the *discrete derivative* of function $f(x)$ as

$$\dot{f}(x) = \frac{f(x) - f(x - 1/N)}{1/N} = N(f(x) - f(x - 1/N)).$$

Similar to integration, we can recover the original function from its discrete derivative and an initial value of $f(0)$ using

$$f(x) = \frac{1}{N}\left(Nf(0) + \sum_{y=1}^{x} \dot{f}(y)\right).$$

Assume that we have a scaling network and alternator logic which is capable of computing $y = f(x)$ for some

$$x = \frac{i}{N} = \underbrace{11\ldots1}_{i}\underbrace{00\ldots0}_{N-i},$$

and outputs

$$y = \frac{\lfloor Ny \rfloor}{N} = \underbrace{11\ldots1}_{\lfloor Ny \rfloor}\underbrace{00\ldots0}_{N-\lfloor Ny \rfloor}.$$

Now for $x' = x + 1/N$ the network should modify the output to

$$y' = f(x') = f(x + 1/N)$$

$$= f(x) + (f(x + 1/N) - f(x)) = y + \frac{1}{N}\dot{f}\left(x + \frac{1}{N}\right)$$

Note that the difference between the unary representation of x and x' is only the $(i + 1)$-th bit which is 0 in x, and 1 in x'. This implies that this single bit flip should change the output by $\dot{f}(x + 1/N)/N$. To mimic this analysis in our network, we should set $\dot{f}(x+1/N)/N$ of the output bits to 1 when the $(i + 1)$-th bit of the input is 1.

In the following we further elaborate this technique through a sequence of examples. To this end we start from the simplest configuration, i.e., the identity function $f(x) = x$ (Sec. 4.1), and address more sophisticated properties of functions step by step in the subsequent sections.

4.1 The Unit Slope Function

For the simple function of $f(x) = x$ we have $\dot{f}(x) = 1$. Hence each zero-to-one flip in the input (i.e., going from a value of $x = p/N$ to a value of $x = (p + 1)/N$) results in a zero-to-one flip in the output (going from $f(p)$ to $f(p+1)$). To implement this the network directly outputs the input bits. This is illustrated in Fig. 4 for $N = 100$, where on the left we show the scaling network between the bits of input and output in the unary representation. No alternator logic gates are needed in this case. In the scaling network, the input value is represented using the canonical unary representation (the 1's are grouped together on the left). The output is also in the canonical representations with all the 1's stacked at the bottom of the column. The top-right figure shows the function itself, and the bottom-right figure shows the derivative of the function.

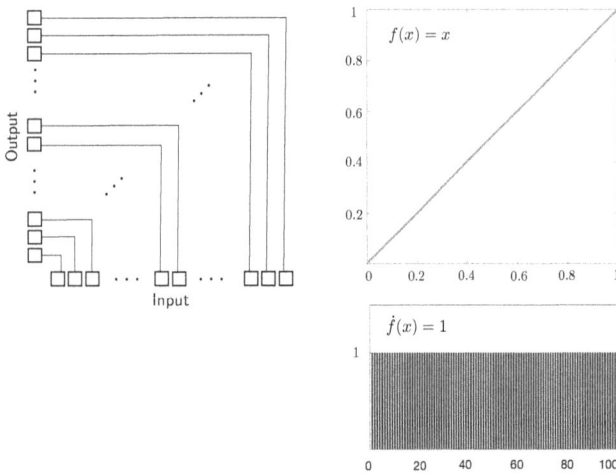

Figure 4: $f(x) = x$

4.2 Piece-Wise Linear Monotonically Increasing Functions

Next we consider a piece-wise linear function, namely,

$$f(x) = \begin{cases} x/2 & \text{if } x \leq 2/3, \\ 2x - 1 & \text{if } x \geq 2/3. \end{cases}$$

Note that this is still a monotonically increasing function with positive but varying derivatives:

$$\dot{f}(x) = \begin{cases} 1/2 & \text{if } x < 2/3, \\ 2 & \text{if } x > 2/3. \end{cases}$$

This implies that for $x \leq 2/3$ we have to implement a zero-to-one flip in the output for every two flips in the input. On the other hand, when $x \geq 2/3$, every flip in the input results in two flips in the output string. This can be done by changing the connections in the scaling network as shown in Fig. 5.

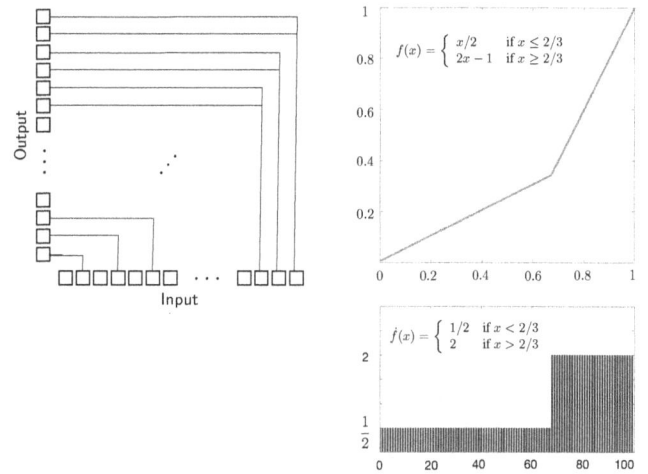

Figure 5: A piece-wise linear function.

4.3 General Monotonically Increasing Functions

The re-wring technique discussed above can be applied to any function, as long as the discrete derivative is non-negative. To this end, the zero-to-one flip structure need to be individually revised for each single bit of the output. This can be easily determined by the discrete derivative of the function.

The network to compute function

$$f(x) = \frac{1 + \tanh(4(2x - 1))}{2}$$

is shown in Fig. 6. As devised by the discrete derivative values, zero-to-one flip in the output bits occur very sparsely, after few input flips when $x \approx 0$ or $x \approx 1$ (the bundle of neighboring bits are contracted when connecting to the output). However, for $x \approx 0.5$, the discrete derivative can be as large as 4, and hence the network consists of four zero-to-one output flips per each input flip (stretching the bundle of neighboring wires when connecting them to output, hence the name "scaling network" in Fig. 2). Note that we still do not need any "alternator" gates.

4.4 Monotonically Increasing Functions with an Initial Offset

All the functions discussed above have a common property that $f(0) = 0$. When $f(0) > 0$, the initial $i = \lfloor Nf(0) \rfloor$ bits of the

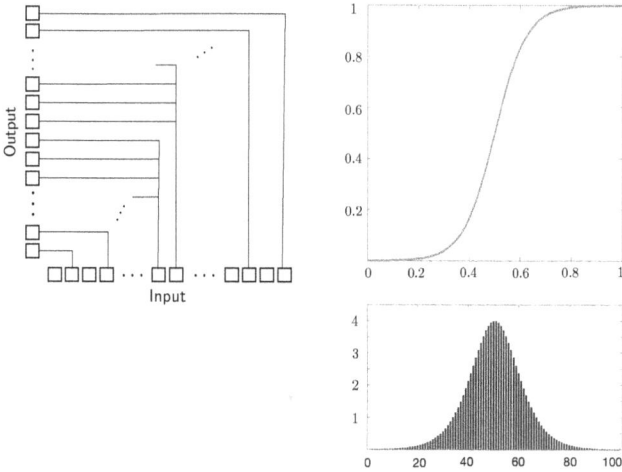

Figure 6: A general monotonically increasing function.

output should be set to 1 regardless of the input value. These bits are essentially dummy outputs hardwired to '1', that is, the first $i = \lfloor N f(0) \rfloor$ output bits are set to 1. A simple example is shown in Fig.7 for

$$f(x) = \frac{x + 1}{2}.$$

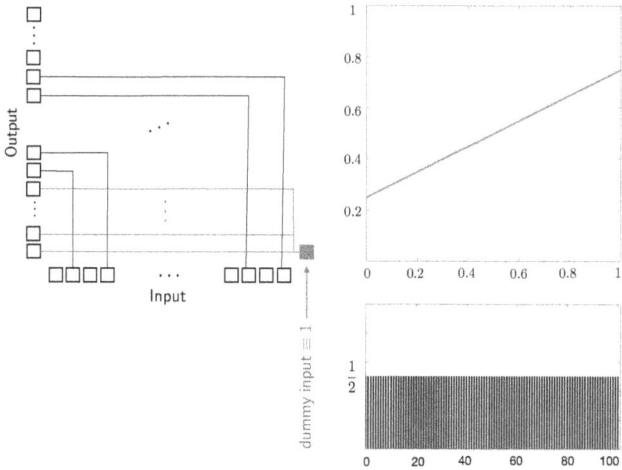

Figure 7: A monotonically increasing function with an off-set.

It is also worth noting that the maximum value the function takes is $f(1) = 3/4$. Hence, the last $N/4$ bits of the outputs are always zero, regardless of the input x.

4.5 Oscillating Piece-wise Linear Functions

When a function is decreasing its discrete derivative will be negative at that point. Consider some $x = i/N$ for which we have

$$y' - y = \frac{1}{N} \dot{f} \left(x + \frac{1}{n} \right)$$

$$= f \left(x + \frac{1}{N} \right) - f(x) < 0$$

This means once the $(i + 1)$-th bit of the input is set to 1, the output value should decrease by $|\frac{1}{N} \dot{f} \left(x + \frac{1}{n} \right)|$, which is equivalent to flipping $|\dot{f} \left(x + \frac{1}{n} \right)|$ already set-to-1 bits of the output string back to 0. Recall that a 1 in the output string is set to 1 when it is triggered by another input zero-to-one flip, say X_j. Thus, we can flip the output bit back to 0 by assigning the XOR of the original trigger X_j and the newly observed bit X_{i+1}. This only holds due to the left-flushed structure of the inputs which guarantees that $X_j = 1$ only when $X_{i+1} = 1$. More precisely, an output bit $Y = X_j \oplus X_{i+1}$ takes the values

$$\begin{cases} 0 \leq x < \frac{j}{N} & \Rightarrow X_j = 0, X_{i+1} = 0 \Rightarrow Y = 0, \\ \frac{j}{N} \leq x \leq \frac{i}{N} & \Rightarrow X_j = 1, X_{i+1} = 0 \Rightarrow Y = 1, \\ \frac{i+1}{N} \leq x \leq 1 & \Rightarrow X_j = 1, X_{i+1} = 1 \Rightarrow Y = 0. \end{cases}$$

In Fig. 8 we show an explicit example of functions with negative discrete derivatives for

$$f(x) = \frac{1}{2} - \left| x - \frac{1}{2} \right| \tag{1}$$

$$= \begin{cases} x & \text{if } 0 \leq x \leq 0.5 \\ 1 - x & \text{if } 0.5 \leq x \leq 1 \end{cases} \tag{2}$$

with

$$\dot{f}(x) = \begin{cases} 1 & \text{if } 0 \leq x \leq 0.5 \\ -1 & \text{if } 0.5 \leq x \leq 1 \end{cases}$$

In Fig. 8a we first design the scaling network for $x \in [0, 0.5]$, with $\dot{f} = 1$, similar to the increasing functions discussed above. The last two input bits of this stage are colored in yellow and blue for illustration purposes. As we continue building the network for values $x > 1/2$, we have to start adding "alternator" XOR gates to make sure the function value is correct in all regions of the function. Let us focus on the blue and the green inputs in Fig. 8b. When the thermometer code sets the blue bit to 1 and the green bit to 0 ($x = 0.5$), the output of the XOR is 1, which is correct. However, for an input value $x = 0.5 + 1/N$, $f(x)$ should be $1/N$ less than $f(0.5)$, which means the last 1 bit that we added because of the blue bit, has to be canceled, hence XORing the blue and the green bits. The same process is used on the yellow and the purple bits: the yellow bit sets the output, the purple bit resets it. Continuing this modification on the remaining gates, we obtain the network in Fig 8c which can compute the function for all $x \in [0, 1]$.

Note that there is no *sequential* process here: the thermometer code does not progressively change the values of the yellow, blue, green and purple bits. They all take their values in one cycle and the XOR gates do the voting in parallel. Also note that the final output will still be in the canonical unary format.

4.6 General Oscillating Functions

In the previous section we discussed functions that are increasing and then decreasing. In general, a function can go up and down multiple times. The XOR gate discussed above allows the output bit to switch between 0 and 1 for an arbitrary number of times, only changing the fan-in of the gate. The gate output should be set to 1 whenever function increases, and to 0 whenever it decreases. It should be set back to 1 if the function started going up again.

(a) The increasing part of the function of Eq. 1.

(b) The first deductions in the function value.

(c) The complete function evaluation.

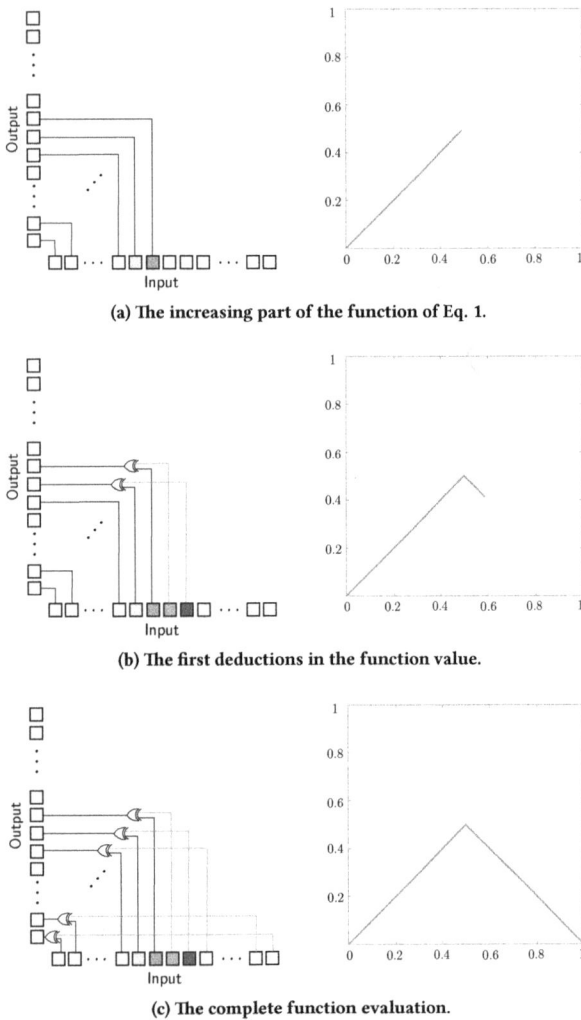

Figure 8: Modification of the gates to address negative discrete derivatives in the function of Eq. 1.

In Fig. 9 we demonstrate the implementation of an arbitrary function. As shown in the figure, function $f(\cdot)$ is increasing in regions (a) and (b), decreasing in region (c), and again increasing in regions (d) and (e). However, there is a fundamental difference between regions (d) and (e): In (d) the function value is still below the maximum value that function has taken up to that point. Hence, in order to construct $f(x)$ one needs to make sure that the already defined gates are set to 1. In (e), however, the function value is greater that the maximum value the function has taken up to that point. Hence, even if all the predetermined gates are set to 1, the circuit still cannot keep up with the growth of the function, and thus new direct line connections should be added to set the corresponding output bits to 1 when the thermometer code sets the right-most group of bits of the input to 1.

5 MULTIVARIATE FUNCTIONS

A techniques similar to what was described above can be utilized to design a network to evaluate/approximate a multivariate function.

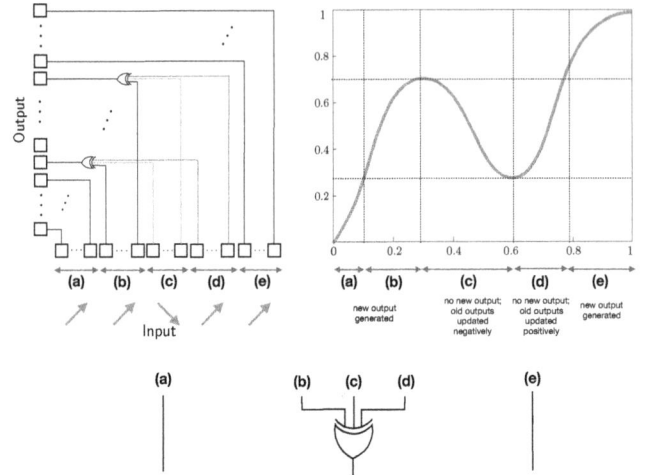

Figure 9: A general oscillating function.

Recall the basic ingredients of circuit development for a univariate function: (1) an output bit Y_i is triggered by an X_j when $x = j/N$ is the first time the function value exceeds $y = i/N$, and (2) after being triggered, output bits are alternated by multiple input bits through XOR operations to mimic the increasing and the decreasing behavior of the function of interest.

5.1 Monotonically Increasing Functions

A similar recipe can be used to design a circuit for multivariate functions, in which triggering and alternating will be performed by a tuple from the function inputs. Such tuple is implemented by ANDing a subset of the input bits, one from each of the function inputs. For a relatively simple class of monotonically increasing functions, no alternating is needed, and we only have to properly determine triggering points for each output bit. However, the main difference is that the notion of "the first time the function exceeds a certain value" is not meaningful. To further elaborate we consider a simple example of designing a circuit for $z = f(x,y) = 10x \cdot y$ with unary bit length of $N = 10$. This function reaches $z = 0.4$ at $(x,y) \in \{(0.1, 0.4), (0.2, 0.2), (0.4, 0.1)\}$, where one cannot establish an ordering of these tuples. Hence, Z_4 should be triggered by *either* of such combinations. This can be implemented by

$$Z_3 = (X_1 \wedge Y_4) \vee (X_2 \wedge Y_2) \vee (X_4 \wedge Y_1).$$

5.2 Oscillating Functions

Once an output bit is triggered, it can alternate between zero and one frequently by XORing the original triggering sequence by all alternators. It is worth noting that each alternator input is again a tuple of input bits, one from each function input.

In the following we present a toy example, and we assume $N = 4$ for the sake of simplicity. An output gate defined as

$$Z = [(X_1 \wedge Y_3) \vee (X_2 \wedge Y_1)] \oplus (X_2 \wedge Y_2) \oplus (X_3 \wedge Y_4)$$

gets triggered by either of $(X_1, Y_3) = (1, 1)$, *i.e.*, $(x,y) = (1/4, 3/4)$ or $(X_2, Y_1) = (1, 1)$, *i.e.*, $(x,y) = (2/4, 1/4)$. After being triggered by (X_2, Y_1), it will be switched back to zero by $(X_2, Y_2) = (1, 1)$, *i.e.*,

$(x, y) = (2/4, 2/4)$. Later at $(X_3, Y_4) = (1, 1)$, i.e., $(x, y) = (3/4, 4/4)$, it will again take the value one. The behavior of this output gate is shown in Fig. 10.

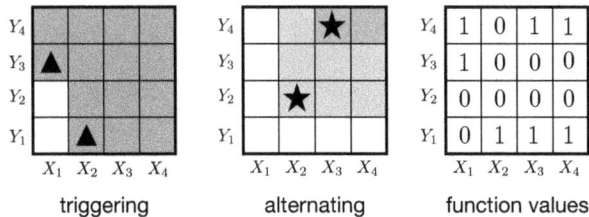

Y_4				
Y_3	▲			
Y_2				
Y_1		▲		
	X_1	X_2	X_3	X_4

triggering

Y_4			★	
Y_3				
Y_2		★		
Y_1				
	X_1	X_2	X_3	X_4

alternating

Y_4	1	0	1	1
Y_3	1	0	0	0
Y_2	0	0	0	0
Y_1	0	1	1	1
	X_1	X_2	X_3	X_4

function values

Figure 10: The first table shows the triggering of the gate, while the second shows alternations. The gate value determined by these two is reported in the third table.

5.3 The Median Function

As a practical example, we describe the design of a function that computes the median of nine inputs, A, B, C, $\cdots$, H, and I. We can show that $z = \text{median}(a, b, c, \cdots, h, i)$ can be computed and represented in N-bit unary format, given by

$$Z_k = \begin{cases} 0 & \text{if } 0 \leq \text{sum}(A_k, B_k, \cdots, I_k) \leq 4 \\ 1 & \text{if } 5 \leq \text{sum}(A_k, B_k, \cdots, I_k) \end{cases}$$

In other words, if at least 5 out of the nine bits at position k are 1, the output at that bit position is 1. Interestingly, Z_k only depends on the k-th bit of the inputs, and hence, the corresponding adder tree has only nine inputs.

Calculation of the median filter in the unary format is almost trivial due to the fact that the unary representation has already "unpacked" the bits from binary, hence making the sorting problem needed in a conventional binary approach redundant. Intuitively, if we visualize the nine canonical unary values as a set of vertical bar graphs, and start sweeping them from bottom-up using a horizontal cut line, the first time we get to a point that only four of the bars are still cutting the horizontal cut line is the point that we have past exactly five smallest values behind, and the horizontal cut line shows the value of the fifth bar graph.

Table 1: The functions that we use to evaluate our work. The last column shows previous stochastic work that has implemented that function.

Function Name	Equation	Stochastic Reference
$\gamma(x)$	$x^{0.45}$	[5]
tanh	$(1 + \tanh(4(2x - 1)))/2$	[13]
cosh	$\cosh(x) - 1$	[12]
exp	$e^{(x-1)}$	[12]
$f_{x6}(x)$	$\mu x(1 - x)$	[8]
sin	$\frac{1}{2}(1 + \sin(15x))$	–
M-shaped	$30x(1 - x)(x - 0.4)^2$	–
Robert's Cross edge detection	$\sqrt{(x_{TL} - x_{BR})^2 + (x_{TR} - x_{BL})^2}$	–
Median	$\text{median}(x_1, x_2, \cdots, x_9)$	–

6 EXPERIMENTAL RESULTS

We compared our method to previous stochastic works that include Bernstein Polynomial implementation [5], state-machine-based methods [13], combinational logic implementing Maclaurin series [12], dynamical systems with feedback [8], and the recent parallel implementation of stochastic logic [15]. We did not compare against [10] as their latency numbers were much higher than other previous work.

Table 1 shows the functions we used to compare our work against previous work. The name we use to refer to functions are listed in the first column. The second column shows the real-valued function that it represents. The third column shows the stochastic computing reference that implemented that function. In addition to previous stochastic implementations, we also compared our work against conventional binary implementations. The Robert's Cross edge detection algorithm takes four pixels $x_{TL}, x_{BR}, x_{TR}, x_{BL}$ as input. The subscripts T, B, L, R correspond to top, bottom, left and right. The median filter finds the median pixel value in a 3x3 window.

We compared our work to the previous work in terms of accuracy of computation (Sec. 6.1), hardware resource usage and computation latency (Sec. 6.2). The accuracy comparisons were done using 10-bit binary resolutions (Fig. 11 and Table 2). Image processing applications such as Gamma correction, Robert's cross and median were done using an 8-bit resolution. Hardware comparisons were done using 8-, 10-, and 12-bit resolutions.

6.1 Approximation Error

Table 2 shows the mean absolute error (MAE) numbers of our method and previous work. The "This work" column shows the results of our architecture of Fig. 2 with $N = 1024$ parallel input bits. It can be seen that our method is about 1-2 orders of magnitude more accurate compared to previous work. All experiments in this subsection were done in MATLAB. Except for [15] which does not use randomness, for all previous stochastic computing work we generated random bit streams using MATLAB's rand function (in practice, low-cost LFSRs are used in stochastic computing, which have lower quality).

Fig. 11 shows graphs of the functions using our method (top row) and previous work (bottom two rows). It can be seen that our method shows significantly smaller approximation errors.

Table 2: The mean absolute error (MAE) between the real-valued functions and various approximations

Function	This work	Parallel [15]	Prev. Stoch. Work
$\gamma(x)$	2.39×10^{-4}	2.45×10^{-2}	2.10×10^{-2} [5]
tanh	2.49×10^{-4}	1.74×10^{-2}	4.59×10^{-2} [13]
cosh	2.40×10^{-4}	4.50×10^{-3}	7.45×10^{-3} [12]
exp	2.42×10^{-4}	7.69×10^{-2}	1.24×10^{-2} [12]
$f_{x6}(x)$	2.42×10^{-4}	5.29×10^{-3}	9.84×10^{-3} [8]
sin	2.41×10^{-4}	–	–
M-shaped	2.47×10^{-4}		

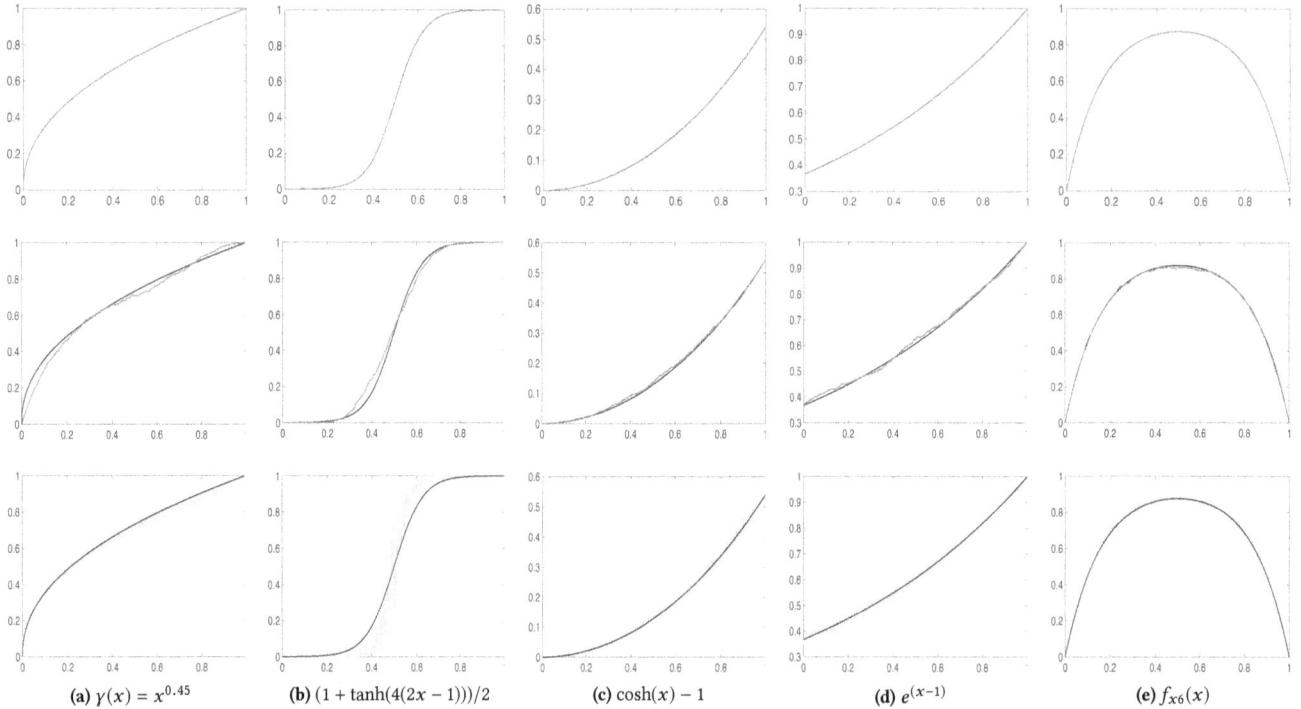

(a) $\gamma(x) = x^{0.45}$　　**(b)** $(1 + \tanh(4(2x - 1)))/2$　　**(c)** $\cosh(x) - 1$　　**(d)** $e^{(x-1)}$　　**(e)** $f_{x6}(x)$

Figure 11: Comparison of our method (top row), parallel stochastic method (middle row) [15] and previous stochastic work (bottom row) [5, 8, 12, 13].

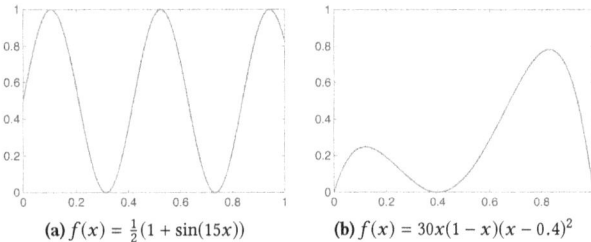

(a) $f(x) = \frac{1}{2}(1 + \sin(15x))$　　**(b)** $f(x) = 30x(1 - x)(x - 0.4)^2$

Figure 12: Approximation of oscillating function using the proposed method.

6.2 Hardware Comparisons

We implemented all designs in Verilog and compiled them on Kintex 7 XC7K325T-1FFG900C FPGAs using the Xilinx Vivado default design flow. For each function, we used three methods to implement it: W-bit wide conventional binary, 2^W-bit serial stochastic (previous work) and our method: 2^W-bit unary encoding, and set $W = 8, 10, 12$. Table 4 shows the area and delay results, and is divided into three groups for each resolution. Columns 2-4 show the number of LUTs and FFs used to implement the function, and the critical path delay. Column 5 labeled "Cy" shows the number of clock cycles needed to calculate the function (more details below). The $A \times D$ column shows the area×delay product, which is the multiplication of the LUT, Delay, and Cy columns. Finally, the "Ratio" column shows the ratio of the previous stochastic and our method to the conventional binary.

For the conventional implementation of tanh, cosh and exp, we tried both polynomial approximation[1] and CORDIC [14], and in all three cases CORDIC resulted in better area×delay, so we used CORDIC for those functions. It takes W iterations of CORDIC to evaluate cosh and exp, hence the number W under the "Cy" column for these designs. For tanh, we need an additional W cycles to perform division using CORDIC. For the previous stochastic methods, we implemented the circuit and used LFSRs for the random number generators. For our implementation of the functions, we used the architecture of Fig. 2, including the thermometer encoder and the decoder. It can be seen that our method takes only 3% of the A×D of the conventional binary method, and 6% of previous stochastic approaches on average for an 8-bit resolution. When the resolution gets higher, stochastic methods start to perform increasingly worse compared to their binary counterparts, as the number of cycles in stochastic logic increases exponentially. Our method also suffers from an exponential increase in the size of the scaling network and the alternating logic. As can be seen, our method still outperforms the conventional binary implementation (8% and 32% of the cost in terms of A×D at resolutions of 10 and 12 bits), but we expect our method not to be competitive with conventional binary implementations for higher resolutions such as $W = 16$. Due to space limitations, we did not include comparisons of our method against the parallel stochastic paper [15]. That work had 14% the A×D of the conventional binary at $W = 10$, compared to our 8% ratio. Furthermore, the method of [15] cannot implement functions similar to those in Fig. 12 because it uses core stochastic logic based on Bernstein Polynomials.

---
[1] 5-order Taylor Series were used to get the 2^{-10} accuracy.

(a) Original figure

(b) Gamma Correction 0.45 with average error of 0.15%

(c) Gamma Correction 0.25 with average error of 0.23%

(d) Gamma Correction 0.75 with average error of 0.17%

Figure 13: Gamma Correction with different gamma coefficients.

6.3 Image Processing Applications

In this section we show the results of our image processing implementations, in which pixels are represented using 8-bit binary grayscale values. We used MATLAB simulations to generate the images using our architectures of figures 2 and 3. Gamma correction only needed one level of logic.

We first attempted to implement the Robert's Cross algorithm using a one-level network with four unary inputs. However, that resulted in a complex circuit that would take our synthesis method a long time to generate, and we quit the program after about 15 minutes. Then we tried a two-level network (Fig. 3): in the first level we calculate the square of differences, and in the second level we calculate the square root of the sum. We designed the network in such a way that the output of the first level was in the canonical unary format. That architecture created a maximum fanout of 2000 for the XOR gate of the Level 1 network. Relaxing the canonical format resulted in much better maximum fanout[2] of 250. The penalty for not using the canonical unary format is the introduction of errors in the calculation.

Figure 13 shows the original image, and the output of four different scaling networks designed for different gamma values. The average error of all cases are below 0.25%. Figure 14 shows the output of the Robert's Cross algorithm using our two-level network. It can be seen that the error rose to 1.1%, which is due to

---

[2]The exact fanouts were: Level 1, fanout of OR:4, fanout of XOR:2. Level 2, fanout OR fanout: 250 max, XOR fanout: 0

the use of a non-canonical two-level network as discussed above. Table 3 shows the hardware comparison of our method against the

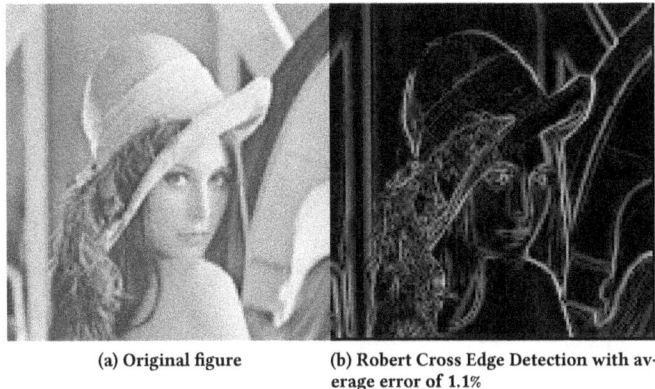

(a) Original figure

(b) Robert Cross Edge Detection with average error of 1.1%

Figure 14: Robert's Cross Edge detection.

conventional binary method. In our median filter implementation, we used three thermal encoder units for the three new pixels that are introduced as the 3×3 pixel window moves across the image. We also allocate six 256-bit registers to hold the values of the old pixels from the previous location of the window. The high cost of generating / storing the unary representations puts our method at a disadvantage: our method has 80% higher cost compared to the binary method.

In the case of the conventional binary Robert's Cross method, we used a CORDIC unit to calculate the square root, hence the 16 cycles that do not allow us to use pipelining and increase throughput. Our method has 26% the cost of the conventional method.

Table 3: Image Processing Hardware Comparisons

Function	LUT	FF	Delay	Cycle	A x D	Ratio
Conventional Robert Cross	1218	276	9.10	16	177340.80	1.00
Proposed Robert Cross	8240	791	5.73	1	47215.20	0.26
Conventional Median Filter	421	8	15.45	1	6504.45	1.00
Proposed Median Filter	1723	2058	5.76	1	11854.08	1.8

7 CONCLUSIONS

We showed a novel approach that converts binary input to the canonical unary format, and synthesizes a scaling network and alternator logic to implement complex functions using much smaller area compared to conventional binary, especially for 8-bit and 10-bit resolutions. Our method achieves much smaller area×delay products compared to the binary methods. Our approach takes advantage of two main features of FPGAs: the abundance of routing resources that can handle large fanouts (especially needed in multivariate functions), and large fanin LUTs.

ACKNOWLEDGEMENTS

This work was supported in part by the National Science Foundation, under grant number 1408123 (CCF-SHF).

Table 4: FPGA area and delay results. Our method is compared against the conventional binary, and previous stochastic computing methods. All are implemented on the same FPGA chip.

Func	LUT	FF	Delay	Cy	A×D	Ratio	LUT	FF	Delay	Cy	A×D	Ratio	LUT	FF	Delay	Cy	A×D	Ratio
Conventional Binary Architecture with W = 8							Conventional Architecture with W = 10							Conventional Architecture with W = 12					
γ	5944	8	24.00	1	143k	1	11335	10	29.99	1	340k	1	14504	12	30.42	1	441k	1
tanh	1193	260	9.10	16	174k	1	1193	260	9.10	20	217k	1	1193	260	9.10	24	261k	1
cosh	1193	260	9.10	8	87k	1	1193	260	9.10	10	109k	1	1193	260	9.10	12	130k	1
exp	1203	270	9.10	8	88k	1	1203	270	9.10	10	109k	1	1203	270	9.10	12	131k	1
M_Sh	880	8	17.35	1	15k	1	1380	10	22.52	1	31k	1	1907	12	23.37	1	45k	1
Avg					101k	1					134k	1					202k	1
Previous Stochastic Work with W = 8							Previous Work with W = 10							Previous Work with W = 12					
γ	92	81	4.32	256	102k	0.71	92	81	4.32	1024	407k	1.19	92	81	4.32	4096	1628k	3.69
tanh	111	10	1.10	256	31k	0.18	111	10	1.10	1024	125k	0.57	111	10	1.10	4096	500k	1.91
cosh	154	99	0.99	256	39k	0.45	154	99	0.99	1024	156k	1.44	154	99	0.99	4096	624k	4.79
exp	100	70	0.98	256	25k	0.28	100	70	0.98	1024	100k	0.92	100	70	0.98	4096	101k	3.06
M_Sh	Can't implement this kind of function						Can't implement this kind of function							Can't implement this kind of function					
Avg					49k	0.49					197k	1.47					788k	3.91
Our Architecture with W = 8							Our Architecture with W = 10							Our Architecture with W = 12					
γ	290	195	5.75	1	1.6k	0.01	918	72	8.01	1	7.4k	0.02	2243	1738	8.12	1	18k	0.04
tanh	208	150	5.32	1	1.1k	0.01	813	652	7.67	1	6.2k	0.03	1534	130	8.25	1	13k	0.05
cosh	218	194	5.19	1	1.1k	0.01	840	710	7.43	1	6.2k	0.06	4520	3960	8.76	1	39k	0.30
exp	253	216	5.48	1	1.3k	0.02	858	70	7.73	1	6.6k	0.06	4652	4008	8.80	1	41k	0.31
M_Sh	301	203	5.56	1	1.6k	0.11	884	404	7.67	1	7.4k	0.24	4700	3746	8.54	1	40k	0.90
Avg					1.4k	0.03					6.8k	0.08					30k	0.32
Our method/prev stochastic						0.06						0.05						0.08

REFERENCES

[1] J. von Neumann, "Probabilistic logics and the synthesis of reliable organisms from unreliable components", *Automata Studies*, pp. 43-98, Princeton University Press, 1956.

[2] B.R. Gaines, "Stochastic Computing Systems," *Advances in Information Systems Science J.F.Tou, ed.*, vol.2, chapter 2, pp.37-172, New York: Plenum, 1969.

[3] B. Brown and H. Card, "Stochastic neural computation I: Computational elements", *IEEE Trans. Comput.*, vol. 50, no. 9, pp. 891-905, 2001.

[4] Armin Alaghi and John P. Hayes, "Survey of Stochastic Computing," *ACM Transactions on Embedded Computing Systems (TECS)*, 2013.

[5] Weikang Qian, Xin Li, Marc D. Riedel, Kia Bazargan, and David J. Lilja, "An Architecture for Fault-Tolerant Computation with Stochastic Logic," *IEEE Transactions on Computers*, Vol. 60, No. 1, pp. 93–105, 2011.

[6] Weikang Qian and Marc Riedel, "The Synthesis of Robust Polynomial Arithmetic with Stochastic Logic" *ACM/IEEE Design Automation Conference*, pp. 648–653, 2008.

[7] Weikang Qian, Marc Riedel, and Ivo Rosenberg, "Uniform Approximation and Bernstein Polynomials with Coefficients in the Unit Interval," *European Journal of Combinatorics*, Vol. 32, No. 3, pp. 448–463, 2011.

[8] Zhiheng Wang; Naman Saraf; Kia Bazargan; Arnd Scheel, "Randomness meets feedback: Stochastic implementation of logistic map dynamical system" *Design Automation Conference (DAC)*, June 2015.

[9] A. Alaghi; Cheng Li; and J.P. Hayes, "Stochastic circuits for real-time image-processing applications" *Design Automation Conference (DAC)*, June 2013.

[10] Devon Jenson; and Marc Riedel, "A deterministic approach to stochastic computation" *ICCAD*, 2016.

[11] Z. Jaworski, "Verilog HDL model based thermometer-to-binary encoder with bubble error correction" *MIXDES - 23rd International Conference Mixed Design of Integrated Circuits and Systems*, Lodz, 2016, pp. 249-254.

[12] S. A. Salehi, Y. Liu, M. D. Riedel, and K. K. Parhi, "Computing Polynomials with Positive Coefficients using Stochastic Logic by Double-NAND Expansion", *Proc. of the on Great Lakes Symposium on VLSI*, pp. 471–474, 2017.

[13] P. Li, D. Lilja, W. Qian, M. D. Riedel, and K. Bazargan, "Logical Computation on Stochastic Bit Streams with Linear Finite State Machines", *IEEE Transactions on Computers*, Vol. 63, No. 6, pp. 1473–1485, June 2014.

[14] F. L. Yuan et al., "A throughput-agnostic 11.9fi?!13.6GOPS/mW multi-signal classification SoC for cognitive radios in 40nm CMOS,", *Symposium on VLSI Circuits (VLSI Circuits)*, Kyoto, 2015, pp. C150-C151.

[15] blind review, "blind review," *blind review*, 2018.

[16] Yongsang Yoo and Minkyu Song, "Design of a 1.8V 10bit 300MSPS CMOS digital-to-analog converter with a novel deglitching circuit and inverse thermometer decoder," *Asia-Pacific Conference on Circuits and Systems*, 2002, pp. 311-314 vol.2.

A Full-System VM-HDL Co-Simulation Framework for Servers with PCIe-Connected FPGAs

Shenghsun Cho, Mrunal Patel, Han Chen, Michael Ferdman, Peter Milder

Stony Brook University

ABSTRACT

The need for high-performance and low-power acceleration technologies in servers is driving the adoption of PCIe-connected FPGAs in datacenter environments. However, the co-development of the application software, driver, and hardware HDL for server FPGA platforms remains one of the fundamental challenges standing in the way of wide-scale adoption. The FPGA accelerator development process is plagued by a lack of comprehensive full-system simulation tools, unacceptably slow debug iteration times, and limited visibility into the software and hardware at the time of failure.

In this work, we develop a framework that pairs a virtual machine and an HDL simulator to enable full-system co-simulation of a server system with a PCIe-connected FPGA. Our framework enables rapid development and debugging of unmodified application software, operating system, device drivers, and hardware design.

Once debugged, neither the software nor the hardware requires any changes before being deployed in a production environment. In our case studies, we find that the co-simulation framework greatly improves debug iteration time while providing invaluable visibility into both the software and hardware components.

CCS CONCEPTS

• **Hardware** → **Reconfigurable logic and FPGAs**; **Functional verification**; *Hardware-software codesign*; • **Computer systems organization** → *Heterogeneous (hybrid) systems*;

ACM Reference Format:
Shenghsun Cho, Mrunal Patel, Han Chen, Michael Ferdman, Peter Milder. 2018. A Full-System VM-HDL Co-Simulation Framework for Servers with PCIe-Connected FPGAs. In *FPGA'18: The 2018 ACM / SIGDA International Symposium on Field-Programmable Gate Arrays, February 25–27, 2018, Monterey, CA, USA.* ACM, New York, NY, USA, Article 4, 10 pages. https://doi.org/10.1145/3174243.3174269

1 INTRODUCTION

FPGAs are gaining popularity as an accelerator technology to offload complex computation and data flows. The combination of programmability, a high degree of parallelism, and low power consumption make FPGAs suitable for environments with rapidly changing workloads and strict power consumption limits, such as data centers. To put FPGAs into existing systems, PCIe has become the most common connection choice, due to its wide availability in server systems. Today, the majority of FPGAs in data centers are communicating with the host system through PCIe [2, 12].

Unfortunately, developing applications for PCIe-connected FPGAs is an extremely slow and painful process. It is challenging to develop and debug the host software and the FPGA hardware designs at the same time. Moreover, the hardware designs running on the FPGAs provide little to no visibility, and even small changes to the hardware require hours to go through FPGA synthesis and place-and-route. The development process becomes even more difficult when operating system and device driver changes are required. Changes to any part of the system (the OS kernel, the loadable kernel modules, the application software or hardware) can frequently hang the system without providing enough information for debugging, forcing a tedious reboot. The combination of these problems results in long debug iterations and a slow development process, especially in comparison to the quick iteration of the software development process familiar to application developers.

The traditional way to test and debug hardware designs without running on a hardware FPGA platform is by writing simulation testbenches, either using Hardware Description Languages (HDLs) or Hardware Verification Languages (HVLs), sometimes combined with Bus Functional Models (BFMs) provided by the FPGA vendors. However, this approach prevents the hardware from being tested together with the software and operating system. Moreover, writing testbenches with high coverage is an extremely time-consuming and error-prone process. While some vendors provide hardware-software co-simulation environments [3, 5, 7, 18], these environments skip the operating system and driver code and provide a limited environment for development, typically restricting the use of the co-simulation to simple designs while still requiring considerable development and debugging effort for porting the designs from the co-simulation framework to the hardware FPGA platform. There have been several efforts to provide frameworks to connect instruction-set simulators to HDL simulators to perform full-system simulation. However, full-system simulation of datacenter servers is itself an open research challenge and the speed of full-system simulation of the servers alone limits their use for software development [17]. As such, existing full-system simulation-based frameworks target system-on-chips—typically, ASICs with ARM cores—as tools for early stage design exploration, software development, and functional verification, rather than the cycle-accurate simulations required to verify or debug FPGA-accelerated servers.

We observe that, although there are no available full-system simulation environments of servers with PCIe-connected FPGAs, we can extend existing mature and robust tools to build a co-simulation framework for rapid development and debugging of such systems. In particular, modern datacenters employ virtual machines (VMs) in production environments to provide security and isolation. Because of this, virtual machines are effective for high-performance emulation of full server systems, including CPUs, disks, memory, and network interfaces. This makes VMs a natural fit to emulate the server system in an FPGA development environment. Moreover, FPGA vendors provide sophisticated HDL simulation software, allowing cycle-accurate simulation of the designs as they would run on the target hardware FPGA platform. Although virtual machines and HDL simulators separately provide effective software and hardware development environments, the key missing enabler is a link between a VM's virtual PCIe and NIC devices and the PCIe and network blocks in an HDL simulation platform. This link should be transparent both to the operating system and software running inside the VM, and to the hardware design in the HDL simulator.

In this work, we developed a co-simulation framework by providing PCIe and NIC communication channels between a VM and an HDL simulator. On the VM side, we created a software pseudo device to represent the FPGA and proxy all device interactions to the HDL simulator. The operating system and software running inside the VM see the same PCIe-attached device as if they were running in a hardware system with an FPGA plugged in.

On the HDL side, we developed a PCIe simulation bridge to communicate with the VM and proxy all hardware events to the software pseudo device in the VM. The PCIe simulation bridge is pin-compatible with the PCIe block of the hardware FPGA platform. Similarly, we developed a pin-compatible NIC simulation bridge to allow the FPGA simulation to exchange Ethernet frames with a host network. The FPGA design observes the same interfaces toward PCIe and network; thus it requires no modification or porting to work with the co-simulation framework. To the FPGA development tools, the PCIe and NIC simulation bridges appear as regular hardware blocks and have no impact on the simulation flow.

To demonstrate our VM-HDL co-simulation framework, we prototyped two server systems: a sorting accelerator and a network card, both using a PCIe-connected FPGA. Our experience indicates that the co-simulation framework significantly reduces the debug iteration time and enables rapid design exploration and debugging that was not previously possible with the available vendor tools. Moreover, our framework provides invaluable visibility into both the hardware design and the operating system, making it easier and faster to identify problems while developing and debugging. The framework allows single-stepping the host kernel software instruction by instruction, and examining variable contents and interactions with the hardware, while simultaneously recording and visualizing all signal waveforms in the hardware design.

The rest of this paper is organized as follows: Section 2 provides an in-depth discussion of co-simulation requirements and the motivation behind our approach. Section 3 describes our co-simulation framework. Section 4 describes the framework implementation. Section 5 presents our case studies and evaluation. Lastly, Section 6 discusses related work and Section 7 gives concluding thoughts.

2 MOTIVATION AND APPROACH

The continually rising demand for data processing in datacenters fuels the need for efficient accelerators. However, to achieve widespread adoption, accelerator technologies must not only achieve high performance and efficiency, but they must also be convenient for application developers. Engineers and their managers have

specific expectations of what constitutes a practical development environment and reasonable debug iteration time, stemming from their experience in software development for CPUs and GPUs. Unfortunately, even ignoring the fact that FPGA development requires a unique and expert set of skills beyond those of a typical software engineer, the development of the hardware and software needed for FPGA acceleration in datacenters presents fundamental challenges in terms of full-system test, debug iteration time, and visibility into the design internals during development.

2.1 Challenges of Development and Debugging

Full-System Test. A major challenge with existing FPGA development environments is the inability to simulate full systems including the OS, device drivers, application software, network, and the accelerator logic. As a result, accelerators are developed in isolation from the software. In traditional FPGA design, developers rely on simulation and carefully-crafted hardware testbenches. However, the complexity of server systems and the expected fluidity of rapid prototyping during the early stages of system development make testbench-driven design impractical for datacenter applications.

Existing SoC co-simulation environments address this problem by simulating embedded CPUs with the entire software stack. However, performing per-instruction CPU emulation in hardware simulation cannot be used for production server software, as simulation is many orders of magnitude less than "interactive" performance expected by developers [17]; even if a simulation platform could be configured to emulate a typical multi-core x86-64 server system, it would take days to just boot the server in such an environment.

Seeing these problems, vendors targeting datacenter accelerators have adopted development platforms that connect HDL simulators with user-level libraries that wrap accelerator functionality. However, the interfaces used for these libraries are non-standard and brittle, developed by small teams for very specific use cases and a very limited user base. Once an initial prototype is developed in such an environment, a significant porting and debugging effort must still take place to move the design to the hardware FPGA platform and integrate it with the production software stack.

Moreover, FPGA accelerators in datacenters may have network connectivity beyond the host server. To support network connectivity, FPGA vendors provide IP blocks that interconnect on-chip data streams with off-chip high-speed interfaces, including all functionality (e.g., MAC, PCS, etc.). Developing and testing network functionality with hand-written testbenches is impractical, because the testbench would need to supply many carefully-crafted network packets whose contents depend on the responses received from the hardware design. As a result, these systems are currently developed and debugged directly on hardware FPGA platforms.

Debug Iteration Time. After a design is implemented on the hardware FPGA platform and integrated with the software stack, the next challenges are debugging and rapidly iterating over design changes. A fundamental challenge is caused by the difficulty of synthesizing, placing, and routing a design for large modern FPGAs. For example, despite large-scale investments in FPGA infrastructure from Microsoft [4], Intel [6], and Amazon [2], the environments used to develop accelerators in these frameworks are not amenable to rapid iteration. Each change to the FPGA design requires hours of waiting before the new design can be tested. While such times are acceptable in an ASIC or embedded appliance development environment, wide-scale adoption of FPGAs for datacenter applications is severely stunted by such slow development practices.

Considering these challenges alongside the difficulties associated with full-system test, FPGA designers face a difficult dilemma: either attempt to debug in simulation (using testbenches and isolating the hardware from the software stack), or work with the production hardware and software, sacrificing the ability to iterate quickly.

Visibility. In addition to the needs of fast iteration and running full-system tests throughout the development process, rapid accelerator development requires visibility into both the server software and the accelerator hardware as expected for traditional software development. However, existing platforms offer limited introspection for system software and hardware. For example, running tests on hardware FPGA platforms limits visibility if the system freezes, which leads to debugging with printf() and frequent rebooting.[1] On the hardware side, tools such as SignalTap [1] and Integrated Logic Analyzer [20] permit the insertion of probes on a select subset of signals in the hardware design. However, the number of signals that can be probed is limited, the amount of time for which signals can be recorded is limited, and changing the set of signals monitored (or in some cases, the trigger events) requires place and route of the design. Developers must wait for hours before re-running an experiment whenever an additional signal needs to be collected.

2.2 Our Approach

In this work, we set out to create a co-simulation framework that allows for full-system test, rapid debug iteration, and complete visibility into the system under development. Moreover, our goal was to construct a flexible platform based on robust, mature, and production-ready components, so that it can be quickly adopted by a wide range of projects without discouraging accelerator developers due to platform limitations, brittleness, and poor performance. To this end, we developed a co-simulation framework that connects a virtual machine (running production server software) with an HDL simulation (running unmodified accelerator hardware designs). The resulting system addresses the challenges described above.

Enabling Full-System Test. Our co-simulation framework enables development and debugging to take place in a full-system environment without any software modifications to the operating system, device drivers, and application software and without any modifications to the accelerator hardware design. Precisely the same software and HDL code are used in the development environment as the production environment. All software components and any part of the accelerator hardware can be modified and debugged in co-simulation. This allows all components of the design to be seamlessly moved between the production environment and the co-simulation environment without modification.

Our system employs a virtual machine (VM) that mimics the production server environment. The VM can use CPU virtualization features, which allow it to execute nearly as fast as bare-metal hardware. In fact, in some cases, such as during the system reboot process, the VM runs faster than bare metal due to the host's disk

cache, which can service requests faster than a physical disk. This setup provides a functionally-correct fast and convenient development environment. Additionally, to help developers debug more obscure timing-sensitive problems, our system supports transitioning in and out of "lock-step" mode, where the VM's execution speed is paired with the HDL simulation's clock.

In addition to the PCIe connection to the host, FPGA platforms often include connections to Ethernet networks. For example, the latest Microsoft Catapult FPGAs use a bump-in-the-wire arrangement [4] where network traffic intended for the host passes through the FPGA fabric on its way to the host's built-in NIC. Other prominent FPGA platforms, such as the NetFPGA SUME [23] and the Xilinx VCU118 [19], feature multiple network ports that can be used to configure these platforms as a "Smart NIC" for the host.

To support debugging systems with external network connections, our co-simulation framework includes a network interface simulation bridge, providing network connectivity to the FPGA. Virtual machines have extensive support for network connectivity through software-defined networking (SDN) components. We leverage this infrastructure to link the HDL simulator into the VM network, enabling the developer to use standard SDN tools to bridge the accelerator hardware running in simulation into test networks (including real LANs or virtual LANs), and even provide direct connectivity between the simulated hardware and the public Internet. This feature is invaluable for debugging network-connected FPGAs, as it allows the developer to make the FPGA participate in real bi-directional network traffic during development and debugging.

Reducing Debug Iteration Time. The use of standard HDL simulation tools for the accelerator design allows hardware designers to use a familiar simulation workflow. Importantly, modifications to the accelerator HDL sources can be done quickly, avoiding the synthesis and place-and-route process which would be necessary when targeting a hardware FPGA platform. Changes to the hardware design require only a quick rebuild or restart of the HDL simulation infrastructure, which ranges between seconds to at most several minutes, depending on the design complexity.

The software and hardware simulation components can be restarted independently. During the debugging process, developers frequently face the need to restart application software and unload and reload kernel device drivers, which can be done freely in our co-simulation framework. In addition to these, sometimes it is necessary to reboot the system or reset the hardware (for example, when the operating system source code or the hardware design are modified). By connecting the virtual machine and HDL simulator using a fault-tolerant high-level message queue implementation, either side of the co-simulation can be independently restarted and the sides will automatically reconnect and continue communicating as though they were never disconnected or modified.

Providing Full Visibility. The co-simulation framework offers complete visibility into both software and hardware. In software, the VM environment supports a remote gdb debugger interface that permits temporarily freezing the VM and stepping through the source code of the software running inside, line by line or instruction by instruction, and observing variable contents in memory. In hardware, HDL simulators offer the capability of tracing all signal waveforms from the beginning of simulation without requiring simulation restarts or prior selection of specific signals to monitor.

---

[1]The situation is exacerbated further for bump-in-the-wire systems [4], where an error in the FPGA logic can lead to complete loss of connectivity to the server.

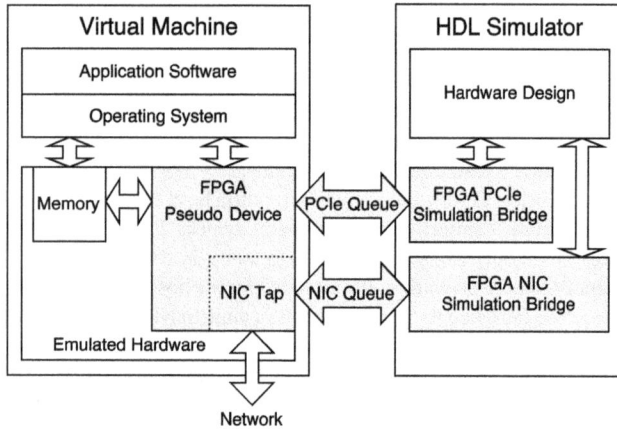

Figure 1: Our VM-HDL co-simulation framework (new components we developed are shaded gray)

3 VM-HDL CO-SIMULATION FRAMEWORK

We built our VM-HDL co-simulation framework by coupling several mature technologies. A high-level architecture of the framework in shown Figure 1. On the host side (left), a virtual machine is used in place of the server. On the FPGA side (right), the hardware design runs in a commercial HDL simulator. The key framework components are the links between the hypervisor[2] and the HDL simulator, comprising the *PCIe link* between the server and the FPGA and the *NIC link* between the FPGA and the Ethernet network. Critically, these links provide exactly the same interfaces and functionality as their hardware FPGA platform counterparts, allowing seamless back-and-forth transitions between the co-simulation framework and deployment on production hardware. All other parts of the system, including the FPGA accelerator design, operating system, device drivers, and application software run in co-simulation and on the production hardware without any modifications.

3.1 FPGA Pseudo Device

On the VM side, we created an FPGA pseudo device module for the hypervisor. From the perspective of the hypervisor, this module emulates a hardware platform's FPGA and its interfaces (PCIe and NIC). To the guest operating system running inside the virtual machine, the pseudo device appears exactly like a PCIe-connected FPGA in the target platform. The device exposes the same number and size of the Base Address Register (BAR) regions and Message Signaled Interrupt (MSI) capabilities. The hypervisor interacts with the pseudo device using high-level abstractions such as Memory-Mapped I/O (MMIO), Direct Memory Access (DMA), and interrupts. We maintain this high level of abstraction when sending these operations over the communication links, thereby avoiding low-level protocol details.

A typical NIC module for a hypervisor has two interfaces. One exposes the NIC to the guest VM as a PCIe device, and the second exposes the NIC to the host system as a *tap* network interface. To support debugging FPGA designs with network interfaces, our

---

[2]We use the term *hypervisor* to refer to the software application used to emulate the virtual hardware and launch a virtual machine.

pseudo device creates a host tap network interface and relays Ethernet frames between this interface and the NIC link connected to the HDL simulator. This enables the developer to use standard software defined networking tools such as bridges and virtual switches to connect the exposed tap interface to virtual or physical networks.

3.2 FPGA PCIe Simulation Bridge

On the HDL side, we developed an FPGA PCIe simulation bridge to replace the PCIe bridge IP in the FPGA platform. The PCIe simulation bridge is pin-compatible with the PCIe bridge IP provided by the FPGA vendor, exposing exactly the same interface and functionality to the FPGA hardware design. Because of this, all interactions between the FPGA hardware and the host are identical in the co-simulation and production environments. Because the interface is unchanged, the FPGA hardware design is entirely unaware of the fact that it is operating in simulation. No modifications are required to run hardware designs in co-simulation, and the design can glide freely between the production environment and co-simulation.

The PCIe bridge offers three functions: forwarding the host's MMIO requests to the FPGA interconnect, forwarding the FPGA interconnect's DMA requests to the host, and raising interrupts on the host in response to the bridge interrupt pins. Notably, the PCIe bridge operates at two different levels of abstraction on its two sides. When communicating to the hypervisor, the bridge maintains the same high level of abstraction as the FPGA pseudo device. The data transfers use high-level operations rather than low-level PCIe transactions. However, on the side of the hardware design, the bridge faithfully emulates the hardware FPGA platform and uses the same low-level cycle-accurate protocol models to receive messages from (and deliver messages to) the FPGA interconnect.

3.3 FPGA NIC Simulation Bridge

Support for the bump-in-the-wire and NIC scenarios in a full-system setup is facilitated by an FPGA NIC Simulation Bridge. Just as the PCIe bridge shuttles PCIe operations between the hypervisor and HDL simulation, the NIC bridge is responsible for shuttling Ethernet frames between the network components of the hardware design in simulation and the hypervisor.

The NIC bridge is pin-compatible with the vendor provided IP, which handles all protocol details and expects for the off-chip interfaces to connect to an Ethernet network. Our co-simulation NIC bridge interacts with the rx and tx streams in the same way as the vendor-provided IP. However, rather than interacting with a physical network, the received and transmitted frames are communicated as high-level operations to the hypervisor NIC tap functions.

Although our current prototype assumes Ethernet networks, we note that this approach is not limited to a specific protocol and is not restricted to communication only with other VMs and servers. For example, a NIC bridge can be used to connect multi-FPGA systems in the co-simulation framework. Multiple concurrently-running HDL simulators, each with its own NIC bridge, can be used for co-simulation of a system like the Amazon F1.16xlarge [2] instance, where each FPGA connects to the server host via PCIe and to the other FPGAs via a 400Gbps bi-directional ring.

3.4 VM-HDL Link Queues

The PCIe link and NIC link provide communication between the hypervisor and HDL simulator. These links can be implemented using domain or network socket APIs. However, rather than directly relying on a low-level stream protocol, we construct the links using a high-level message queuing library. Messages are guaranteed to be reliably delivered to the destination process in their entirety and communication is non-blocking, allowing the sending process to continue running after enqueuing a message.

Beyond simplifying the implementation, the queue-based approach offers functional benefits. The queue abstraction allows independently restarting the VM or the HDL simulator (e.g., after making changes to the hardware design). The system automatically re-establishes the connections and continues exchanging high-level messages after restart. The queue interface also allows to independently pause and resume execution of the VM or HDL simulator (for example, to examine their internal state), without incurring timeouts and aborts from the side that is not paused.

3.5 Untimed and Lock-Step Modes

Our co-simulation framework enables an optional *lock-step* mode, which forces the VM and the HDL simulation to have a consistent view of time. This option can be invaluable in resolving timing bugs or verifying complex time-sensitive interactions between the server software and hardware design. This mode contrasts with the standard *untimed* mode, where the VM operates on real-world time and the HDL simulator advances time as fast as it can.

Lock-step mode was easily added to the co-simulator framework because both the hypervisor and the HDL simulator have mechanisms to control the advance of time. On the software side, we can place a hypervisor into a mode where it acts similar to an instruction-set simulator, with a mechanism to advance time one instruction at a time. On the hardware side, we can easily control when the clock signal advances in the HDL simulation environment. By adding an extra link between them, we can synchronize the passage of time, allowing them to proceed in lock-step according to a user-provided clock ratio (e.g., eight server cycles to one FPGA cycle to simulate a 2GHz server with a 250MHz FPGA).

The downside to this approach is that using a hypervisor in this mode imposes a very high performance overhead. Our system aims to minimize the effect of this by allowing the developer to switch between untimed and lock-step mode dynamically, as needed.

3.6 Debugging and Development Interfaces

Our co-simulation framework enables extensive debugging and development capabilities that take the process of working with PCIe-connected FPGAs a step closer to the simplicity and ease-of-use of traditional software-development environments.

For software debugging, the hypervisor can act as a remote target for command-line and graphical debuggers. Developers can use familiar tools such as *gdb* to connect to the hypervisor to examine the contents of memory and registers inside the virtual machine and for single-step execution. Remote target support allows debugging not only the application software running within the VM, but also to debug the device drivers and operating system, including interrupt handlers, providing complete access to memory and registers and supporting single-stepping at both the C statement and the assembly instruction granularity. Moreover, the interface allows the developer to modify memory and register contents on the live system to experiment with various scenarios and on-the-fly fixes.

For hardware debugging, developers can use the HDL simulator to record all hardware signals during the entire simulation. As a result, the co-simulation framework provides greater visibility than using an in-hardware virtual logic analyzer, which limits the number of probed signals and requires place-and-route to add probes. Our approach not only provides full visibility into all signals in the system at the current time, but also allows examining the HDL state at any point in the past, enabling the developer to quickly trace back and identify the origin of a bug, regardless of how far in the past it occurred. Similar to the software debug interface, the HDL simulator also supports single-step operation, examining all register contents, and forcing signal and memory values.

In addition to enabling the classic approaches above, our co-simulation infrastructure offers a new hybrid mode of development and debugging, combining the practices and expectations of developing on a hardware FPGA platform with the debugging capabilities of simulation. Specifically, software and hardware developers find it natural to edit, compile, run, and debug code directly on the target platform. Because of the high (near bare metal) performance of the VM in co-simulation, including an additional network interface in the VM allows it to be used by the developers just like a hardware FPGA platform. The VM can fulfill all expectations of a traditional development environment by including all editors and build tools needed to work with code, mounting remote NFS or SMB filesystems, and allowing interaction with remote code repositories. When the co-simulation framework is deployed in a datacenter, developers can use ssh or remote desktop to log into the co-simulation VM and use it exactly as if logging into a hardware FPGA platform in a production cloud environment. However, while the platform behaves like a server system with a PCIe-connected FPGA, it comes with the added benefits of full visibility into the hardware waveforms and the ability to make changes to the hardware design and see them immediately reflected on the live system.

4 FRAMEWORK IMPLEMENTATION

In this section, we describe our design decisions and provide the key implementation details of our co-simulation framework.

4.1 Hypervisor

To emulate the server system, we use QEMU, an open-source hypervisor that is widely deployed in production environments. QEMU includes many features that make it particularly well-suited for this work: it has robust emulation models of server system components, it provides a rich API for developing new device models such as the FPGA Pseudo Device, it offers bare-metal speeds using hardware-accelerated virtualization via KVM [8], it includes an instruction-set simulator-like mode to enable single-step execution, and it supports a standard remote target debugger interface.

FPGA Pseudo Device. To allow the VM to interact with the simulated FPGA device, we developed a QEMU virtual device to serve as a proxy for the FPGA, supporting PCIe transactions and

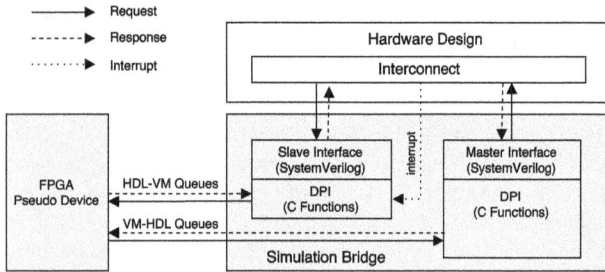

Figure 2: FPGA PCIe simulation bridge

network communication. We based our implementation on a QEMU reference design of a NIC. The QEMU API supports customization of all PCIe device parameters, enabling our implementation to exactly mimic the target PCIe-connected FPGA system. The pseudo device identifies itself using the vendor and device ID of the hardware FPGA platform, and matches the Base Address Register (BAR) address widths, sizes, pre-fetch capabilities, and the number of Message Signaled Interrupt (MSI) interrupts. For NIC devices, the API also includes functions to declare network interfaces, read and configure their MAC addresses, and send out Ethernet frames.

To enable the device to respond to events, QEMU provides an interface for the device model to register callback routines. Our implementation registers callbacks for handling the VM's MMIO reads and writes on the FPGA BAR regions and a callback for receiving Ethernet frames from the network interfaces. Additionally, QEMU supports registering file descriptors with its event loop and triggering custom callbacks when there is activity on those file descriptors. We leverage this functionality to enable efficient receipt of messages from the HDL simulator by registering callbacks on the network sockets underlying our PCIe and NIC message queues.

Network Interfaces. QEMU network devices create a *tap* virtual network interface on the host. Frames sent by the device model are transmitted by QEMU on the tap interface. Frames received by the tap interface trigger a QEMU callback, which forwards frames to the HDL simulator. The tap interface is the standard mechanism for virtual machine network connectivity. It can be bridged into the physical network of the simulation host via software-defined networking components (e.g., a Linux bridge), in a manner identical to a production setup in a cloud environment. From the perspective of all other devices connected to the same network, the simulated hardware is indistinguishable from a plugged-in physical device. Alternatively, the tap interface can be bridged into a private virtual network, together with other VMs running on the same host. These VMs can use a full-system software stack to act as a traffic generator and to expose the hardware design to a variety of test loads.

When the tap interface is bridged into a physical Ethernet network, the hardware design in the co-simulation framework is exposed to all traffic from this network segment. Such networks routinely observe a significant amount of background chatter, such as ARP requests and other broadcast protocols, which serves as an excellent way to expose the hardware design to a diversity of real packet contents and timing scenarios in addition to the test traffic.

4.2 Hypervisor-Simulator Message Queues

Rather than directly relying on a stateful connection-oriented bi-directional stream protocol, we link the QEMU and the HDL simulator using pairs of unidirectional high-level message queues constructed with the ZeroMQ (ZMQ) messaging library [22]. ZMQ is a high-level message library that wraps the low-level details of inter-process communication. The library provides reliable message delivery, which is particularly helpful when one side of the co-simulation framework slows down, crashes, or simply needs to be restarted, allowing the other side to continue without interruption. The loose coupling of the processes enables high performance operation and makes the system very robust, freeing our implementations of the pseudo device and simulation bridges from the responsibility of handling incomplete messages and flow control.

Each communication link comprises a pair of unidirectional channels. There are two communication links for performing PCIe operations between QEMU and HDL simulation: one for QEMU to HDL simulator messages and another for HDL simulator to QEMU messages. The NIC bridge uses two unidirectional channels, one for transmitting outgoing frames and one for receiving incoming frames. Each message sent over a channel contains a structure comprising the operation type and attributes, such as the address offset, data, data length, BAR number, etc. The structure and content of the messages can be easily modified or extended, as the details of reliably delivering the messages is handled by ZMQ.

4.3 Co-Simulation Bridge IPs

The co-simulation bridge IPs serve as interfaces between the hardware design and the hypervisor, linking the HDL simulation with QEMU (via ZMQ channels). The bridges are built using SystemVerilog's direct programming interface (DPI), which allows interactivity between the HDL simulation and external software. The bridges are pin-compatible with Xilinx-provided IPs for PCIe and Ethernet controllers. The bridges are parameterized to allow them to be easily configured to match different hardware FPGA platforms (e.g., PCIe interfaces with differing numbers of lanes).

FPGA PCIe Simulation Bridge. Figure 2 shows a block diagram of the FPGA PCIe simulation bridge. Like the Xilinx PCIe bridge IP, the simulation bridge has AXI slave and master interfaces and an MSI interrupt input. The master interface facilitates MMIO requests from the host to the hardware design and the slave interface supports memory requests from the hardware to the host.

In the simulation bridge, each interface's functionality is split between SystemVerilog code (which drives the hardware-facing AXI interfaces), and C functions (which interact with the ZMQ channels to communicate with QEMU); SystemVerilog DPI is used to link the two. The slave interface code is activated by the (simulated) clock. On each positive clock edge, the interface module checks for a new request from the hardware design via its AXI port. When an AXI read or write is detected, the interface calls a C function, which translates the request to a high-level message for the FPGA pseudo device and places the message into the HDL-VM ZMQ channel.

To handle responses coming back from QEMU, the interface calls a C function to poll the ZMQ response channel. The polling function is invoked on the positive clock edge of each simulated cycle. When it detects a response on the channel, the C function triggers a state machine within the interface module, which feeds the response data into the corresponding AXI port. Lastly, the slave interface has an MSI interrupt input port. Whenever the SystemVerilog code detects that the interrupt is raised, it calls a C function to write the interrupt request message into the HDL-VM channel.

The master interface works similarly. The interface uses a clock-edge activated SystemVerilog block to call a C function which polls the VM-HDL channel for MMIO requests from QEMU; when one is detected, the C function triggers a state machine that feeds the request data into the AXI port. Responses (which arrive from the hardware via the AXI port) are detected on positive clock edges and are sent (using a C function) to the VM-HDL response channel.

FPGA NIC Simulation Bridge. The NIC bridge has a similar structure to the PCIe bridge, with two notable differences. First, the NIC bridge only needs one ZMQ channel pair to handle incoming and outgoing frames. Second, the NIC bridge uses unidirectional AXI Stream interfaces to interact with the hardware design (rather than connecting to an AXI interconnect). The NIC bridge indicates frame boundaries by setting the Start of Frame (SOF) and End of Frame (EOF) symbols on the rx stream and uses the EOF symbol on the tx stream as an indication that a complete frame has been received from the hardware and should now be sent to QEMU.

4.4 Lock-Step Mode

We created a *lock-step* mode, which builds on QEMU's *icount* mode to synchronize the execution of the VM and simulated hardware. The icount mode disables hardware virtualization support, falling back to an instruction-set simulator with IPC 1 (one instruction per cycle), and modifying the VM's notion of time to be relative to the number of instructions executed (e.g., two billion instructions corresponds to one second of execution). Our variant of this mode further restricts QEMU such that it runs in sync with the HDL simulator, allowing the two to perceive the same notion of time.

The lock-step mode allows co-simulating timing-sensitive interactions between the server software and hardware design. In this mode, the HDL simulator includes an additional unidirectional ZMQ channel to transmit a *clock* message to QEMU on every positive clock edge. We modified the QEMU interpreter loop to perform a blocking read on this channel after QEMU executes the number of instructions corresponding to a single cycle of the hardware design. For example, when targeting a 2GHz server CPU and 250MHz FPGA hardware design, each clock message allows QEMU to advance by eight instructions. To maintain high performance, QEMU internals sometimes cause simulation to advance by more than one instruction before re-entering the interpreter loop. To account for this, our implementation keeps track of the actual number of instructions executed by QEMU and adjusts the number of instructions that are permitted to execute on the subsequent clock message. As a result, any deviation between the server's and the HDL simulator's notion of time is eliminated as soon as it is detected.

The lock-step mode is orders of magnitude slower than the untimed co-simulation running with hardware virtualization. Booting the server in lock-step mode would take multiple days. To make this mode practical for debugging, we support dynamically toggling lock-step execution on a running QEMU instance. Lock-step mode can be disabled to allow QEMU to run without waiting for

Table 1: Co-Simulation and Hardware FPGA Platform

Target FPGA Board	NetFPGA SUME (xc7vx690tffg1761-3)
Co-Sim Host	Xeon E5-2620v3, 64GB DDR4
FPGA Compilation Host	Xeon E5-2620v3, 64GB DDR4
Operating System	Ubuntu 16.04, Linux 4.4.0 with KVM
Hypervisor	QEMU 2.7.50
FPGA Tool	Xilinx Vivado 2017.1
HDL Simulator	Synopsys VCS J-2014.12-SP3-8 (with GCC 4.4)
Message Passing Library	ZeroMQ 4.2.1

the HDL simulator while booting the guest operating system and while the developer works on setting up the debugging experiment, and enabled immediately before the start of the experiment.

5 EVALUATION

This section presents an evaluation of our VM-HDL co-simulation framework. For this evaluation, we developed two test cases: an FPGA accelerator for sorting of data, and an FPGA network card device. Using these test cases, we demonstrate how the co-simulation framework allows full-system simulation including hardware, application software, device driver, and operating system, and we evaluate how the co-simulator improves the developer's design and debug experience, in terms of the debug iteration time and the visibility into the internal state of the hardware and software.

5.1 Methodology

We list the details of the hardware and software platform we use for our evaluation of both test designs in Table 1. We intentionally use the same hardware for the co-simulation framework measurements as for the hardware FPGA platform, and use the same versions of the operating system and all software in both.

Sorting Accelerator Design. The sorting accelerator design represents a common style of coarse-grained accelerators. Such hardware designs typically comprise one or several compute units for processing data and a DMA engine to perform data transfers. The software running on the server prepares the input data and triggers the accelerator's DMA and compute unit. The DMA engine fetches input data from the server memory and sends it to the compute unit. After the compute unit finishes processing the input data and generates the result, the DMA engine stores the result back to the server memory and notifies the application software.

We automatically generate the sorting unit using the Spiral Sorting Network IP Generator [24]. The sorting unit takes a stream of input data and produces a stream of output data after a fixed number of cycles. Xilinx DMA IP is used in *basic* mode to fetch input data from the server memory through PCIe, stream data through the sorting unit, and write the results back to the server memory.

Network Card Design. The network card device is an example system that connects the FPGA hardware to a network interface. Compared to the sorting accelerator, the NIC has a more complex dataflow, including finer-granularity interaction with the server operating system. The NIC design uses the Xilinx DMA IP to transfer packets to/from the VM memory, but the controller is configured in *scatter/gather* mode. When sending data to the network, the device driver prepares the packets in server memory and triggers the DMA to fetch them through PCIe and stream them to the FPGA MAC's

Table 2: Run time comparison for operations (µs)

	Hardware Platform	Untimed Co-Sim
MMIO Read	0.74	42,400
DMA and Sorting	23.33	2,830,000

transmit interface. In the hardware FPGA platform, the MAC interface then sends data to the wire; in the co-simulation environment, the NIC FPGA simulation bridge will instead transfer this data to the pseudo device in QEMU. When receiving data, the FPGA MAC's receive interface streams the packets into the DMA unit, where they are transferred to the server memory. After a transfer finishes, the DMA sends an interrupt to the operating system to notify it.

5.2 Full-System Performance

PCIe Bridge Performance. To evaluate the performance of our PCIe simulation bridge, we timed the same operations running on a hardware FPGA platform and in co-simulation. For MMIO, we performed dependent serialized MMIO reads from a block RAM in the hardware design. For DMA, we measured the execution time of the sorting accelerator task, including DMA transfers.

Table 2 shows the performance of our framework compared to the hardware FPGA platform. As expected, the co-simulation runs slower than the hardware FPGA platform, because the co-simulation performs cycle-accurate HDL simulation. By comparing the simulation run time with and without the VM-HDL communication channels, we found that communication with the VM does not noticeably impact performance. The VM runs on a separate host CPU core from the HDL simulation, and polling of the ZMQ channels takes negligible CPU time. Although the poor HDL simulator performance requires developers to still be cautious regarding long test cases while debugging using the co-simulation platform, the performance impact of doing HDL simulation as part of the co-simulation framework is small and is well worth the benefits.

Untimed Mode Time Dilation. When using our co-simulation framework in untimed mode, the QEMU VM runs at bare-metal speed, and time in the VM equals wall-clock time. However, the HDL simulator is running cycle-accurate simulation and is slower than a hardware FPGA platform. Because QEMU and the HDL simulator run independently, the user observes a time dilation between the VM and the hardware design. The performance measurements in Table 2 show this effect to be approximately five orders of magnitude; a hardware design at 250MHz appears as though it is running at approximately 2.5KHz to the software in the VM. However, despite the time dilation, the system remains completely functional and can be used for interactive development and debugging.

Lock-step Mode Performance. To overcome time dilation for timing-sensitive simulations, we utilize the lock-step mode of our framework to force a realistic clock ratio between the VM and the hardware design running inside the HDL simulator.

To measure the accuracy of the co-simulation in lock-step mode, we target a CPU frequency of 2GHz at an IPC of 1 (QEMU *shift=1* setting, which instructs QEMU to treat two billion instructions as equivalent to one second). We target a 250MHz hardware design to set the lock-step multiplier, which means that every HDL simulator clock cycle permits the QEMU VM to advance by eight instructions.

We used a simple *sleep* application to measure time in the virtual machine. We observed that, although the wall clock elapsed time is approximately three orders of magnitude longer than the requested sleep time, the elapsed time observed by both the VM and HDL simulator match the requested sleep time. This indicates that, although the simulation runs much slower than real time, the VM's notion of time remains self-consistent. We also tested our network card design in lock-step mode. We used ping to test the network latency between the VM and its host. Unlike the untimed mode, which resulted in higher latency than on a real system due to the VM observing time faster than HDL simulation, the reported latency in lock-step mode is very similar to a real system. This happens because the time taken by ping outside the co-simulation environment appears instantaneous to the co-simulation (just like when a real host pings itself), resulting in the latency reported by the VM corresponding to the actual number of cycles that elapsed in the lock-step co-simulation framework. This further demonstrates that the notion of time is self-consistent between the VM and the HDL simulator in lock-step mode.

NIC Bridge Performance. Our framework presents new opportunities for debugging FPGA hardware designs with network connectivity by exposing them to the LAN and Internet traffic. However, network packets between real hosts have a higher packet rate than expected by the co-simulation setup, and can overwhelm the co-simulation when processing the test traffic. We therefore use firewall rules on the co-simulation host to filter out background ARP chatter and packets not sent to the co-simulated host. We then use *HTTP file transfer* to evaluate the bandwidth and *ping* to evaluate the latency of network traffic from the co-simulation environment when running network card hardware in HDL simulation.

In the untimed mode, our experiments show that the platform can sustain 15KB/sec connections. The platform introduces an extra 80ms round-trip latency on each ping, indicating that the network card hardware in simulation takes approximately 40ms to process a packet. These results demonstrate that the platform is fast enough to sustain network connectivity to to the real world, without the remote end timing out or retransmitting packets, despite the packets passing through a cycle-accurate HDL simulation of the network card. We also performed these tests in lock-step mode. Due to significant slowdown of the virtual machine, the round-trip ping times observe an additional 400ms of latency. Network transfers from real-world hosts become impractical, as the co-simulation environment falls too far behind to send TCP acknowledgments in a timely fashion and the remote end closes the connection.

5.3 Debug Iteration Time

Hardware Design Changes. While developing and debugging applications, developers frequently need to modify the hardware design due to bugs, design changes, or simply to observe the effects of different design decisions. If working with the hardware FPGA platform, this would require the developer to run the FPGA synthesis and place-and-route process. However, in our co-simulation framework the developer only needs to launch the simulation. We quantify this difference using our sorting accelerator. As shown in Table 3, when compared to a hardware FPGA platform, which takes

Table 3: Run-time comparison (minutes:seconds)

	Hardware Platform	Co-Simulation
Launch Simulator	-	1:10
Synthesis	18:03	-
Place and Route	35:40	-
Reboot	2:33	0:25
Execution	≈0	0:02.8
Total	56:16	1:38

Table 4: System boot time comparison (minutes:seconds)

	Local disk	iSCSI	VM
BIOS	0:55	1:10	0:05
OS	0:33	1:23	0:14
Total	1:26	2:33	0:19

Table 5: Visibility overhead (minutes:seconds)

	1st Change	2nd Change	3rd Change
Hardware FPGA Platform:			
Synthesis	17:48	-	-
Place and Route	39:16	42:22	58.52
Reboot	1:26	1:26	1:26
Execution	≈0	≈0	≈0
Total	58:30	43:48	60:18
Co-Simulation:			
Launch Simulator	1:10	-	-
Reboot	0:19	-	-
Execution	0:04.2	-	-
Total	1:33	0	0
Speedup	over 30x	∞	∞

about an hour to go through the FPGA synthesis and place-and-route process, the co-simulation framework can achieve an over 30x reduction in iteration time. Changes in the FPGA platform can run in the co-simulation framework in just a few minutes.

Software Reboot. When debugging accelerators on a hardware FPGA platform, instability in the hardware, software, and device driver can all frequently hang the entire system, requiring slow and tedious reboots. An advantage of our co-simulation framework is that VMs are typically faster to reboot. To illustrate this, Table 4 compares: the boot time from a local disk, the same server booting from an iSCSI disk, and the VM in our co-simulation framework, all running the same version of Linux. The results indicate that the VM reboot time is consistently faster than server reboot.

Additionally, the developer can use VM snapshots to achieve nearly-instant reboot. Although server reboot time seems negligible compared to the FPGA synthesis and place-and-route, frequent and slow system reboots greatly contribute to the slow debug process.

5.4 Full Hardware Visibility

Adding Logic Analyzer Probes. When debugging on a hardware FPGA platform, developers frequently use embedded logic analyzers such as Xilinx ILA [20] or Altera SignalTap II [1] to observe the values of internal signals over time. This approach places practical limitations on the number of signals observed and the number of cycles of data that can be recorded. Naturally, these limitations mean that developers gradually adjust the set of signals they monitor during the debug process. Each time the set of monitored signals changes, the developer must re-run at least place-and-route.

We use our sorting accelerator as a case study to quantify the cost of re-configuring the embedded logic analyzer (Xilinx ILA). For the hardware FPGA platform, we follow a typical debug workflow, where the developer iterates several times, changing the locations of the limited embedded logic analyzer probes each time. We first configured the logic analyzer to observe the ports of the sorting unit (408 pins) for 8192 cycles. We then synthesized and implemented the design, as the developer would need to do to program the FPGA. In the next step, we added one AXI port (659 pins) to the monitored signals and repeated the process. In the third step, we swapped monitoring one AXI port for another one (806 pins). To compare

with the time required to observe the same signals using our co-simulation framework, we simply configured the HDL simulator to store all signals from the start to the end of the entire simulation.

Table 5 compares the time required for these changes in the two scenarios. On the hardware FPGA platform, the first insertion of the debug core requires both synthesis and place-and-route, which requires nearly an hour even for this relatively small design. Further changes to the monitoring signal set do not require re-synthesis, but the place-and-route time increases along with the number of the signals being observed. In contrast, our co-simulation framework has full visibility into the hardware design after only one simulation run because all signal values in the design are stored. The co-simulator's first iteration is already over 30x faster than the hardware FPGA platform; further iterations are unnecessary.

Cost of Full Visibility. By storing the entire waveform history for every signal in the hardware design, it is possible for our co-simulation framework to enable full visibility of all internal values in the FPGA from a single simulation run. There are two costs associated with storing this large number of signals: the time overhead of writing the data to disk, and the amount of storage required.

To quantify the runtime differences, we compare the co-simulation execution times in Table 3 (which do not record internal signals) and Table 5 (which saves all signals for the entire execution). We observe a 50% increase in execution time when saving signals. As shown in Table 5, this performance overhead is still much lower than the cost of having to re-run place-and-route to reconfigure the hardware FPGA platform's embedded logic analyzer probes. The other cost is the disk space. Experiments shows that a two-hour (wall clock time) simulation of our network card design creates an 8GB waveform file in the FSDB format, suggesting that it is affordable with today's storage capacity even for long simulations.

6 RELATED WORK

HW-SW Co-Sim. Several frameworks introduced by academia, EDA companies, FPGA vendors, and cloud service providers with FPGA offerings aim to co-simulate FPGA hardware and application software. These systems, such as the Message-passing Simulation Framework (MSF) [13], Intel OpenCL for FPGA [5], Intel AFU Simulation Environment (ASE), Xilinx SDAccel [18], and Amazon F1 [3] allow software testbenches to drive HDL simulation environments. However, these systems are limited to executing application software, rather than allowing full-system co-simulation. In contrast, our framework supports co-simulating and debugging the operating system, device drivers, application software, and hardware designs. Like our approach, the open-source VPCIe co-simulation project [15] uses QEMU to support full-system device driver development in the co-simulation environment. However, while similar in spirit, VPCIe is a proof-of-concept system that significantly restricts the hardware designs that can be simulated and uses interfaces that require extensive modification to QEMU and to the hardware design to allow them to work in co-simulation.

Full-System Simulation for SoC ASICs. Another class of related work targets simulation and design exploration for system-on-chip (SoC) ASICs. In this situation, designers' needs and motivations are quite different than those of developers targeting FPGA-accelerated datacenters. In this context, designers typically aim to study design trade-offs or perform early software development alongside high-level models of hardware systems. For example, [9, 11, 14, 16, 21] use QEMU as an instruction-set simulator, connecting it to high-level models of virtual platforms written in SystemC, and there are commercial tools like [10] that can do full-system simulation with hardware designs in HDL. However, all these platforms generally focus on ARM-based SoC ASICs using early-stage hardware models. This contrasts starkly with the approach and goals of our system, where we require full cycle-accurate simulation of the exact hardware design because we aim to analyze and debug the exact hardware and software that will run in the production environment on the target hardware FPGA platform.

7 CONCLUSIONS

FPGAs hold great promise as accelerators in datacenters; in recent years, we have seen several large-scale deployments of FPGA-accelerated servers. Although the performance and energy advantages of FPGAs are well known, a major challenge to wide-spread use is the difficulty of designing, debugging, and integrating FPGA accelerators. Better methodologies and tools, which can reduce the impact of these obstacles, are crucially needed to improve developer productivity and increase adoption of FPGA accelerators.

In this work we aim to improve a challenging drawback in the typical FPGA accelerator workflow: namely, that testbenches are insufficient for testing and debugging full server systems, but debugging on hardware FPGA platforms is slow and cumbersome, due to the long synthesis and place-and-route process, frequent and tedious system reboots, and insufficient visibility. The combination of these problems results in a time-consuming development process, hindering the effective use of FPGA-equipped servers.

Our VM-HDL co-simulation framework leverages existing and widely used mature technologies: virtual machines (which allow fast execution of the operating system, device driver, and application software), and commercial HDL simulators (which provide cycle-accurate simulation of the FPGA design). We join these together by designing new pin-compatible bridge IP for the FPGA's PCIe and NIC interfaces, allowing developers to move seamlessly between the co-simulation framework and hardware FPGA platform, with identical hardware designs, software, and operating

system code. By avoiding the FPGA synthesis and place-and-route process, our framework can drastically reduce the debug iteration time, while providing full visibility of the entire system by enabling the use of standard software debuggers and by comprehensively recording waveforms for all hardware signals. The end result is a co-simulation framework that enables rapid development of FPGA accelerators in datacenter systems.

REFERENCES

[1] Altera. 2017. *Quartus Prime Standard Edition Handbook*.
[2] Amazon 2017. Amazon EC2 F1 FPGA Instances. (2017). https://aws.amazon.com/ec2/instance-types/f1
[3] Amazon 2017. Amazon EC2 F1 FPGA Simulation Environment. (2017). https://github.com/aws/aws-fpga/blob/master/hdk/docs/RTL_Simulating_CL_Designs.md
[4] A. M. Caulfield, E. S. Chung, A. Putnam, H. Angepat, J. Fowers, M. Haselman, S. Heil, M. Humphrey, P. Kaur, J. Y. Kim, D. Lo, T. Massengill, K. Ovtcharov, M. Papamichael, L. Woods, S. Lanka, D. Chiou, and D. Burger. 2016. A cloud-scale acceleration architecture. In *2016 49th Annual IEEE/ACM International Symposium on Microarchitecture (MICRO)*. 1–13.
[5] Intel 2015. Intel OpenCL for FPGA. (2015). https://www.altera.com/products/design-software/embedded-software-developers/opencl/overview.html
[6] Intel 2016. Intel-Altera Heterogeneous Architecture Research Platform Program. (2016). https://cpufpga.files.wordpress.com/2016/04/harp_isca_2016_final.pdf
[7] Intel 2017. Intel AFU Simulation Environment. (2017). https://opae.github.io/docs/ase_userguide/ase_userguide.html
[8] KVM 2016. Kernel Virtual Machine (KVM). (2016). https://www.linux-kvm.org/
[9] J. W. Lin, C. C. Wang, C. Y. Chang, C. H. Chen, K. J. Lee, Y. H. Chu, J. C. Yeh, and Y. C. Hsiao. 2009. Full System Simulation and Verification Framework. In *2009 Fifth International Conference on Information Assurance and Security*, Vol. 1. 165–168.
[10] Mentor Seamless 2016. Mentor Seamless. (2016). https://www.mentor.com/products/fv/seamless/
[11] M. Monton, A. Portero, M. Moreno, B. Martinez, and J. Carrabina. 2007. Mixed SW/SystemC SoC Emulation Framework. In *2007 IEEE International Symposium on Industrial Electronics*. 2338–2341.
[12] A Putnam, A M Caulfield, E S Chung, D Chiou, K Constantinides, J Demme, H Esmaeilzadeh, J Fowers, G P Gopal, J Gray, M Haselman, S Hauck, S Heil, A Hormati, J Y Kim, S Lanka, J Larus, E Peterson, S Pope, A Smith, J Thong, P Y Xiao, and D Burger. 2014. A reconfigurable fabric for accelerating large-scale datacenter services. In *2014 ACM/IEEE 41st International Symposium on Computer Architecture (ISCA)*. 13–24.
[13] M Saldana, E Ramalho, and P Chow. 2008. A Message-Passing Hardware/Software Co-simulation Environment to Aid in Reconfigurable Computing Design Using TMD-MPI. In *2008 International Conference on Reconfigurable Computing and FPGAs*. 265–270.
[14] S. T. Shen, S. Y. Lee, and C. H. Chen. 2010. Full system simulation with QEMU: An approach to multi-view 3D GPU design. In *Proceedings of 2010 IEEE International Symposium on Circuits and Systems*. 3877–3880.
[15] VPCIe 2013. vpcie: virtual PCIE devices. (2013). https://github.com/texane/vpcie
[16] Chen-Chieh Wang, Ro-Pun Wong, Jing-Wun Lin, and Chung-Ho Chen. 2009. System-level development and verification framework for high-performance system accelerator. In *VLSI Design, Automation and Test, 2009. VLSI-DAT'09. International Symposium on*. IEEE, 359–362.
[17] Thomas F. Wenisch, Roland E. Wunderlich, Michael Ferdman, Anastasia Ailamaki, Babak Falsafi, and James C. Hoe. 2006. SimFlex: Statistical Sampling of Computer System Simulation. *IEEE Micro* 26, 4 (2006), 18–31.
[18] Xilinx 2015. Xilinx SDAccel Development Environment. (2015). https://www.xilinx.com/products/design-tools/software-zone/sdaccel.html
[19] Xilinx 2016. Xilinx Virtex UltraScale+ FPGA VCU118 Evaluation Kit. (2016). https://www.xilinx.com/products/boards-and-kits/vcu118.html
[20] Xilinx 2017. Integrated Logic Analyzer (ILA). (2017). https://www.xilinx.com/products/intellectual-property/ila.html
[21] Tse-Chen Yeh and Ming-Chao Chiang. 2012. On the interfacing between QEMU and SystemC for virtual platform construction: Using DMA as a case. *Journal of Systems Architecture* 58, 3 (2012), 99 – 111. http://www.sciencedirect.com/science/article/pii/S1383762112000045
[22] ZeroMQ 2017. ZeroMQ. (2017). http://zeromq.org
[23] Noa Zilberman, Yury Audzevich, G Adam Covington, and Andrew W Moore. 2014. NetFPGA SUME: Toward 100 Gbps as research commodity. *IEEE Micro* 34, 5 (2014), 32–41.
[24] Marcela Zuluaga, Peter A. Milder, and Markus Püschel. 2016. Streaming Sorting Networks. *ACM Transactions on Design Automation of Electronic Systems* 21, 4 (2016), 55.

Towards a Uniform Template-based Architecture for Accelerating 2D and 3D CNNs on FPGA

Junzhong Shen, You Huang, Zelong Wang, Yuran Qiao, Mei Wen, Chunyuan Zhang
National University of Defense Technology
College of Computer, National Key Laboratory for Parallel and Distributed Processing
Changsha, Hunan, China
{shenjunzhong,youhuang,wangzelong15,qiaoyuran,meiwen,cyzhang}@nudt.edu.cn

ABSTRACT

Three-dimensional convolutional neural networks (3D CNNs) are used efficiently in many computer vision applications. Most previous work in this area has concentrated only on designing and optimizing accelerators for 2D CNN, with few attempts made to accelerate 3D CNN on FPGA. We find accelerating 3D CNNs on FPGA to be challenge due to their high computational complexity and storage demands. More importantly, although the computation patterns of 2D and 3D CNNs are analogous, the conventional approaches adopted for accelerating 2D CNNs may be unfit for 3D CNN acceleration. In this paper, in order to accelerate 2D and 3D CNNs using a uniform framework, we propose a uniform template-based architecture that uses templates based on the Winograd algorithm to ensure fast development of 2D and 3D CNN accelerators. Furthermore, we also develop a uniform analytical model to facilitate efficient design space explorations of 2D and 3D CNN accelerators based on our architecture. Finally, we demonstrate the effectiveness of the template-based architecture by implementing accelerators for real-life 2D and 3D CNNs (VGG16 and C3D) on multiple FPGA platforms. On S2C VUS440, we achieve up to 1.13 TOPS and 1.11 TOPS under low resource utilization for VGG16 and C3D, respectively. End-to-end comparisons with CPU and GPU solutions demonstrate that our implementation of C3D achieves gains of up to 13x and 60x in performance and energy relative to a CPU solution, and a 6.4x energy efficiency gain over a GPU solution.

CCS CONCEPTS

• **Computer systems organization** → *Special purpose systems*;

KEYWORDS

3D CNN; Winograd Algorithm; Uniform Templates

ACM Reference Format:
Junzhong Shen, You Huang, Zelong Wang, Yuran Qiao, Mei Wen, Chunyuan Zhang. 2018. Towards a Uniform Template-based Architecture for Accelerating 2D and 3D CNNs on FPGA. In *Proceedings of 2018 ACM/SIGDA International Symposium on Field-Programmable Gate Arrays (FPGA 2018).*

ACM, New York, NY, USA, 10 pages. https://doi.org/http://dx.doi.org/10.1145/3174243.3174257

1 INTRODUCTION

Convolutional Neural Networks (CNNs) have been implemented with great success in the field of computer vision. However, the improvements in accuracy provided by CNNs have exacerbated the computational complexity of the computational layers. Since general-purpose CPUs have failed to provide the massive computational parallelism required by modern CNNs, many hardware accelerators (such as GPUs [8], ASICs [6] and FPGAs [2, 14, 21]) have been developed to boost CNN performance. Of these platforms, FPGAs have become a particularly attractive option due to their reconfigurability and abundant logic resources. Moreover, the availability of commercial high-level synthesis (HLS) tools greatly reduces both the programming difficulty and development time required for FPGA accelerators, meaning that FPGA-based solutions have become more popular.

Abundant studies [2, 12, 14, 20–23] have focused on accelerating 2D CNNs on FPGAs, while the accelerations of three-dimensional convolutional neural networks (3D CNNs) on FPGA are not as well-researched. However, 3D CNNs have proven to be very effective in many complicated computer vision tasks including video classification [17], human action recognition [5] and medical image analysis [7].

Our studies reveal that while the computation patterns of 2D and 3D CNNs are very similar, 3D CNNs have higher computational complexity and greater memory bandwidth demands. In addition, the design space for 3D CNN acceleration has been further expanded, making it more difficult to determine the optimal solution. More importantly, widely studied approaches in the 2D CNN field may not be a good fit for 3D CNNs. For instance, the ordinary convolutional approach adopted in [14, 20] will cause higher computation complexity when adopted in a 3D CNN acceleration application; moreover, our studies suggest that the approach of unrolling the convolution to matrix multiplication [16] could introduce high degree of data replication. Therefore, designing an efficient 3D CNN accelerator on FPGA demands more intensive design efforts than have been applied in previous works.

Motivated by the insight that the computation patterns of 2D and 3D CNNs are very similar, we here attempt to unify the 2D and 3D CNNs into a single acceleration framework rather than designing an accelerator for a given 2D or 3D CNN. In other words, we aim to use uniform templates as building-blocks to support the accelerations of both 2D and 3D CNNs. This template-based methodology, which was also adopted in [13], has a number of appealing advantages: 1.

it can make good use of the reconfigurability of FPGAs by building accelerators for complex 2D and 3D CNNs in a short period of time; 2. the scalability of the template-based design enables the generation of accelerators that match the CNN's specific need, as well as the resource constraints of the FPGA platform; 3. use of the templates makes it easy to exploit the fine-grained parallelism of CNN algorithms, which in turn contributes to high-throughput solutions.

Based on this idea, we propose a template-based design methodology for accelerating 2D and 3D CNNs on FPGA in this work. Due to its ability to reduce the complexity of convolutions, as well as its good extensibility, we first select the Winograd algorithm as the common approach to the computation of the convolutional layers in 2D and 3D CNNs. We then design uniform templates based on the common operations extracted from the 2D and 3D Winograd algorithms; these templates constitute a hierarchical architecture capable of exploiting all sources of parallelism in CNNs. Finally, we present detailed optimization strategies for improving both on-chip and off-chip memory bandwidth.

Previous design space exploration schemes [16, 20, 21] have been applicable only to 2D CNN accelerators, making them unsuitable for our architecture. Since the sizes of the design space of 2D and 3D CNN accelerators are different, determining the optimal design options for both by using two different design space exploration schemes will inevitably be costly. To resolve this issue, we propose a uniform analytical model to efficiently explore the design space of both 2D and 3D CNN accelerators. We conduct an in-depth analysis of the performance of the proposed architecture by taking the computation capacity of the computation engine and memory bandwidth into consideration. The main contributions of this work are summarized as follows:

(1) We propose a uniform template-based architecture for accelerating 2D and 3D CNNs on FPGA. With the help of uniform templates, which are based on the Winograd algorithm, we are able to build accelerators for 2D and 3D CNNs in only a short time.

(2) We develop a uniform analytical model for efficient design space explorations of both 2D and 3D CNN accelerators.

(3) As a case study, we implement two accelerators for state-of-the-art 2D and 3D CNNs: VGG16 and C3D, respectively. Experimental results show that our implementation of VGG achieves comparable performance with recent 2D CNN accelerators under conditions of low resource utilization. Furthermore, the C3D implementation achieves up to 13x and 60x gains in performance and energy over the CPU solution, as well as a 6.4x energy efficiency gain over the GPU solution.

The rest of this paper is organized as follows: Section 2 provides a background for 3D CNN and the Winograd algorithm. Section 3 presents the details of the proposed template-based architecture. Section 4 discusses the design space exploration. Section 5 shows our experimental results. Section 6 discusses related work and Section 7 concludes this paper.

2 BACKGROUND

The computation pattern of the CONV layers in 3D CNN is more complicated than that of the CONV layers in 2D CNN, which can

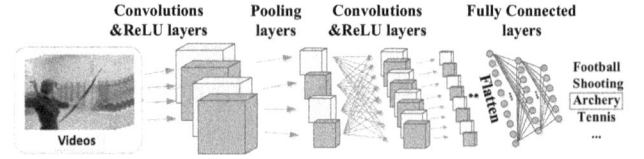

Figure 1: A real-life 3D CNN model for video classification.

Table 1: Analysis of C3D

Layers	Ops (GFLOPS)	Data Transfer(MB) In+Out	Data Transfer(MB) Weights	Time (ms)
CONV	38.4(99.9%)	99.0(27.7%)	17.7(26.7%)	31.9(97.3%)
ReLU	0.0(0%)	96.7(27.1%)	0.0(0.0%)	0.0(2.3%)
Pool	0.0(0%)	161.0(45.1%)	0.0(0.0%)	0.0(0.2%)
FC	0.0(0.1%)	0.1(0.0%)	48.8(73.3%)	0.7(0.2%)

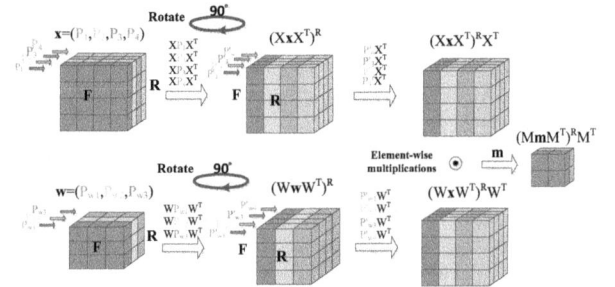

Figure 2: The process of the 3D Winograd algorithm.

be described as follows:

$$Out[m][z][r][c] = \sum_{n=0}^{N} \sum_{k=0}^{K_d} \sum_{i=0}^{K_r} \sum_{j=0}^{K_c} \tag{1}$$
$$W[m][n][k][i][j] * In[n][S*z+k][S*r+i][S*c+j],$$

where In/Out and W define the three-dimensional input/output feature maps and filters, respectively. In each layer, a set of N input feature maps of size $D \times H \times W$ are convolved by M sets of $N \times Ksize$ filters ($Ksize = K_d * K_r * K_c$), yielding M output feature maps of size $Z \times R \times C$. In each of M sets, N filters slide across the corresponding input feature maps with a stride of S. It can be seen that the computational complexity of the CONV layers in 3D CNN is much higher than that of the CONV layers in 2D CNN (i.e. $2*M*N*R*C*K_r*K_c$ for 2D CNN and $2*M*N*Z*R*C*K_d*K_r*K_c$ for 3D CNN).

In addition, the computation pattern of the FC layers in 3D CNN is a dense matrix-vector multiplication, which is identical to that of the FC layers in 2D CNN. In this paper, our template-based design is targeted at the CONV and FC layers. Although the Activation and POOL layers are also supported by our proposed architecture, we omit the discussions of these layers due to their relative simplicity.

2.1 In-depth Analysis of 3D CNN

Previous studies [4, 8, 15] have demonstrated that the convolutional operations take up over 90% of computation time. Our study draws a similar conclusion with regards to 3D CNN. To better illustrate this, the profiling results of C3D are presented in Table 1 (here, the execution time is measured on a NVIDIA Tesla K40 GPU). Three observations can be drawn from Table 1: firstly, similar to 2D CNN, the CONV layers in 3D CNN are computationally-intensive and occupy the majority of the computation time (over 97%). Secondly, the FC layers are memory-intensive, since they require 73.3% of the weights but only occupy 0.1% of the computation cost. Thirdly, the amount of intermediate data that needs to be transferred between the layers is far larger than the weights (356.7 MB vs. 66.5 MB).

It can be seen that although C3D is relatively small (66.5 MB weights), it contains a larger number of computations (38.5 GOPs) than recent large-scale 2D CNN networks such as AlexNet [8] (~240 MB weights, 1.46 GOP/image) and VGG-16 [15] (~500 MB weights, 30.9 GOPs/image). This is mainly due to the fact that the sizes of both input and output data are extended in 3D CNN. More importantly, the performance of the computation-centric CONV layers may become more sensitive to the memory bandwidth due to the huge intermediate data transfer between layers.

2.2 Winograd Algorithm Extension

The Winograd algorithm, which was proposed in [19] to reduce the arithmetic complexity of the convolutional operation, can be applied to 1D, 2D and even higher-dimensional convolutions. To simplify the discussion, we begin with an illustration of the 1D Winograd algorithm. We denote a 1D convolution as $F(m, r)$, which has an ordinary computation pattern that is given by:

$$\mathbf{y}_i = \sum_{j=0}^{r-1} \mathbf{x}_{i+j} \mathbf{w}_j, i = 0, 1, \cdots m - 1. \tag{2}$$

Here, $\mathbf{x}$ is an 1D image data of size n $(n = m + r - 1)$, and $\mathbf{w}$ is a filter of size r. To be more specific, we can consider the Winograd algorithm for $F(2, 3)$, which can be represented as follows:

$$\mathbf{y} = M[(X\mathbf{x}) \odot (W\mathbf{w})], \tag{3}$$

where $\odot$ is denoted as element-wise multiplication, and M, X, W are transformation matrices with constant values:

$$X = \begin{pmatrix} 1 & 0 & -1 & 0 \\ 0 & 1 & 1 & 0 \\ 0 & -1 & 1 & 0 \\ 0 & 1 & 0 & -1 \end{pmatrix}, W = \begin{pmatrix} 1 & 0 & 0 \\ \frac{1}{2} & \frac{1}{2} & \frac{1}{2} \\ \frac{1}{2} & -\frac{1}{2} & \frac{1}{2} \\ 0 & 0 & 1 \end{pmatrix},$$

$$M = \begin{pmatrix} 1 & 1 & 1 & 0 \\ 0 & 1 & -1 & -1 \end{pmatrix} \tag{4}$$

The transformation matrices are determined for a given m and r. Note that the proof of equivalence of Equation 2 and Equation 3 is provided in [19]. The simplicity of the transformation matrices contributes to reducing the overall arithmetic complexity.

We now further consider the 2D Winograd algorithm for $F(m \times m, r \times r)$, which is given by the following equation:

$$Y = M[(X\mathbf{x}X^T) \odot (W\mathbf{w}W^T)]M^T \tag{5}$$

Here, $\mathbf{x}$ is redefined as an $n \times n$ image tile, while $\mathbf{w}$ is an $r \times r$ filter. If we regard $\mathbf{x}$ as having n column vectors of size n, then $X\mathbf{x}$ can be calculated by left multiplying all column vectors of $\mathbf{x}$ by the transformation matrix X. Similarly, $X\mathbf{x}X^T$ can be obtained by right multiplying all row vectors of $X\mathbf{x}$ by X^T, where $X\mathbf{x}$ is regarded as n row vectors of size n. When we take a similar approach to the rest of the transformation procedures in Equation 5, it emerges that the 2D Winograd algorithm can be nested by the 1D Winograd algorithm [10].

In [9], Lan et al. propose a nested technique for the 3D convolution $F(m \times m \times m, r \times r \times r)$, i.e. the 3D Winograd algorithm. In this work, we signify this algorithm using the following equation:

$$Z = (M((X\mathbf{x}X^T)^R X^T \odot (W\mathbf{w}W^T)^R W^T)M^T)^R M^T, \tag{6}$$

where $\mathbf{x}$ and $\mathbf{w}$ are extended to an $m \times m \times m$ image and $r \times r \times r$ filter, respectively. R represents the operation of rotating the transformed image or filter tiles 90 degrees clockwise. We illustrate the process of the 3D Winograd algorithm in Figure 2. Here, it can be seen that the transformations on the 3D input data can be performed by transformations on multiple 2D data plains (e.g. P_1, P_2, P_3, P_4). However, unlike the 2D Winograd algorithm, the transformation procedures employed in the 3D Winograd algorithm are asymmetric; for instance, the algorithm only applies row transformations (right multiply X^T) on the rotated image. Therefore, the 3D Winograd algorithm is the combination of the 1D and 2D Winograd algorithms. More importantly, since the 2D Winograd transformation procedure can be further broken up into 1D transformation procedures, the 3D Winograd algorithm can also be nested by the 1D Winograd algorithm. This demonstrates that the Winograd algorithm has good extensibility.

3 TEMPLATE-BASED ACCELERATOR DESIGN

We first define the key features of the uniform templates for 2D and 3D CNNs, as follows: 1. the templates can be regarded as common computational building blocks for 2D and 3D CNNs, allowing us to generate CNN accelerators with different configurations; 2. the templates can exploit the fine-grained parallelism inherent in the computation components of CNN algorithms; 3. the templates are resource-saving, in that they can be developed quickly.

3.1 Algorithms

Since CONV layers have the highest computational cost in both 2D and 3D CNNs, we primarily aim to design templates for computation of the CONV layers in this work. Our first concern is to determine the best algorithm for the uniform template-based design. We require this algorithm to be extensible, meaning that the algorithm for 2D CNN can be easily extended to accelerate 3D CNNs with minimal new operations; in this way, the computation procedures for both 2D and 3D CNNs can share a large number of common operations. In addition, the computational complexity and storage requirements of the selected algorithm must not be too high when it is adopted in 2D and 3D CNNs.

The most commonly adopted approach for computation of the CONV layers in 2D CNNs is the convolutional Matrix-Multiplication (MM), which is illustrated in Equation 1. Owing to the high computational complexity of this approach, many studies parallelize the kernel computation by combining different UNROLL strategies [12]. While the algorithm is extensible, such that the 3D convolution can be transformed into multiple 2D convolutions, the computational complexity of this approach grows cubically when it is adopted in 3D CNN; as a result, the optimization strategies employed need to become more complex if the optimal design is to be achieved.

An alternative approach is to map the convolution to matrix multiplication [16], which is also widely used in many deep-learning software frameworks [20]. However, it should be noted that the

Table 2: Comparisons of the ordinary convolution and Winograd algorithms

	$F(2,3)$		$F(2^2,3^2)$		$F(2^3,3^3)$	
Algorithms	muls	adds	muls	adds	muls	adds
Ordinary	6	4	36	32	216	208
Winograd	4	11	16	77	64	419

mapping procedure will introduce data replication for the input feature maps. Zhang et al. [20] reveal that the input feature maps in AlexNet require 25x more data when adopting this approach for a CONV layer computation. According to our study, the data replication worsens in 3D CNN applications. Theoretically, the data replication ratio of the input feature maps is $\frac{Size_{filter} * Size_{Out}}{Size_{In}}$, where $Size_{In}$, $Size_{out}$ and $Size_{filter}$ are the sizes of the input/output feature maps and filters of a given CONV layer, respectively. Therefore, using this approach for 3D CNN acceleration may stress the memory system, potentially leading to a bottleneck. More importantly, it is difficult to implement the mapping procedures in 2D and 3D CNN by means of uniform templates.

Owing to its advantageous ability to reduce the complexity of convolutions, the Winograd algorithm has attracted increasing attention in the field of CNN acceleration in recent research [2, 9, 10]. Table 2 presents the comparisons of the ordinary convolution (i.e. convolutional MM) and the Winograd algorithm with respect to the the number of arithmetic operations, demonstrating that the Winograd algorithm can efficiently reduce the number of multiplications in convolutions. While the Winograd algorithm does also increase the number of additions, the computational complexity is reduced overall. Additionally, the discussions in Section 2.2 demonstrate the good extensibility of the Winograd algorithm, which is beneficial for developing uniform templates to implement both 2D and 3D algorithms. Furthermore, use of the Winograd algorithm will not introduce any data replication. In light of the above, we here select the Winograd algorithm as the common approach for computing the CONV layers in 2D and 3D CNNs. Note that we use $F(m,r)$,$F(m^2,r^2)$ and $F(m^3,r^3)$ to represent the 1D, 2D and 3D Winograd algorithms for the rest of this paper.

3.2 Extracting Common Operations

Since uniform templates are to be used for performing the common operations of the 2D and 3D CNNs, a key step is extraction of the common operations from the procedures of these CNNs. We first apply the Winograd algorithms to the computation of the CONV layers. As shown in Figures 3(a) and 3(b), the major common operations of the algorithms can be found in the transformations, element-wise multiplications and accumulations, which are marked using dashed boxes. As discussed in Section 2.2, both the 2D and 3D Winograd algorithms can be nested by the 1D Winograd algorithm. Therefore, the 1D Winograd transformations can be used as the common operations of the 2D and 3D transformation procedures. Additionally, due to the operator-level parallelism of the element-wise multiplications, these element-wise multiplications on the 3D tiles can be performed repeatedly by multiplications on the 2D tiles. Therefore, the element-wise multiplication of a 2D input tile and a 2D filter tile can also be considered a common operation of the two algorithms. Similarly, since the accumulations of the elements

```
L1: for(row=0;row<R; row+=2){
L2:  for(col=0;col<C; col+=2){
L3:   for(m=0; m<M; m++){
L4:    for(n=0; n<N; n++){
         Load(In, n); //4*4 input tile
         Load(W, m ,n); //3*3 filter tile
         2D_Trans_X(In, Tin);
         2D_Trans_W(W, Tw);
         2D_Mul(Tin,Tw, P);
         2D_Trans_M(P, Tp);
         2D_Accumulate(Sum,Tp);
     }
     Send(Out,Sum,m); //2*2 output tile
}}}
```

(a) CONV layers of 2D CNN

```
L1:for(dep=0;dep<Z;dep+=2){
L2: for(row=0;row<R; row+=2){
L3:  for(col=0;col<C; col+=2){
L4:   for(m=0; m<M; m++){
L5:    for(n=0; n<N; n++){
         Load(In, n); //4*4*4 input tile
         Load(W, m ,n); //3*3*3 filter tile
         2D_Trans_X(In, Tin);
         2D_Trans_W(W, Tw);
         Rotate(Tin, Tin^R);
         Rotate(Tw, Tw^R);
         1D_Trans_X(Tin^R, Tin^1);
         1D_Trans_W(Tw^R, Tw^1);
         3D_Mul(Tin^1,Tw^1, P);
         2D_Trans_M(P, Tp);
         Rotate(Tp, Tp^R);
         1D_Trans_M(Tp^R, Tp^1);
         3D_Accumulate(Tp^1,Sum);
     }
     Send(Out, Sum,m); //2*2*2 output tile
}}}}
```

(b) CONV layers of 3D CNN

Figure 3: Simplified pseudocode of CONV layers in 2D and 3D CNNs with Winograd algorithms.

in one intermediate result tile are independent of each other, the accumulations of a 3D tile can be performed by the accumulations of the 2D tiles that have split from the 3D tile. Therefore, the accumulation of the transformed 2D result tile across the input channels is the common operation of the algorithms.

3.3 Template Design

Figure 4 shows the proposed templates based on the extracted common operations, including three kinds of transformation templates (TX, TW and TM), the element-wise multiplication template and the accumulation template.

Transformation templates. The 1D Winograd transformation procedure is essentially the matrix-vector multiplications. We observe that the transformation matrices in Equation 4 contain many 1s and -1s, meaning that we can replace the multiplications here with additions or subtractions. In addition, we can utilize the sparsity of the transformation matrices to reduce the number of operations. Moreover, special multiplications/divisions (e.g. $*2$, $*\frac{1}{4}$) can be replaced by shifting operations, thus further reducing the computational complexity. Figures 4(a), (b) and (c) show the transformation templates for $F(2,3)$. It can be seen that no multipliers or dividers are required in the templates.

Element-wise multiplication template. This template is responsible for multiplying a transformed input tile with its corresponding filter tile. As shown in Figure 4(d), the template consists of a group of dot-product units that can perform multiplications independently. The maximum degrees of parallelization of the element-wise multiplications in $F(m^2,r^2)$ and $F(m^3,r^3)$ are n^2 and n^3, respectively. Therefore, n^2 dot-product units are integrated in the element-wise multiplication template to maximize throughput and minimize latency.

Accumulation template. As shown in Figure 4(e), the accumulation template offers a certain number of accumulators to iteratively sum up the intermediate transformed products. Much like the element-wise multiplication template, we integrate m^2 (i.e. the maximum degrees of parallelization of accumulations in $F(m^2,r^2)$) accumulators to achieve the highest throughput and lowest latency.

It should be noted here that, due to their simplicity, all proposed templates can be implemented easily by means of the HLS tool, which contributes to the rapid development of the accelerators.

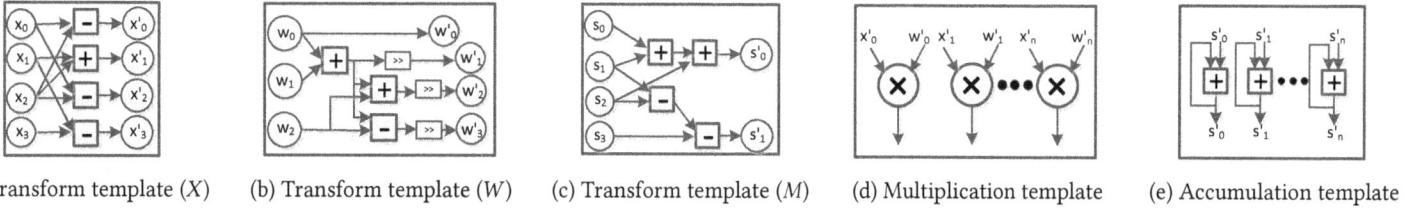

(a) Transform template (X)   (b) Transform template (W)   (c) Transform template (M)   (d) Multiplication template   (e) Accumulation template

Figure 4: Proposed templates for 2D and 3D CNNs ($F(2,3)$).

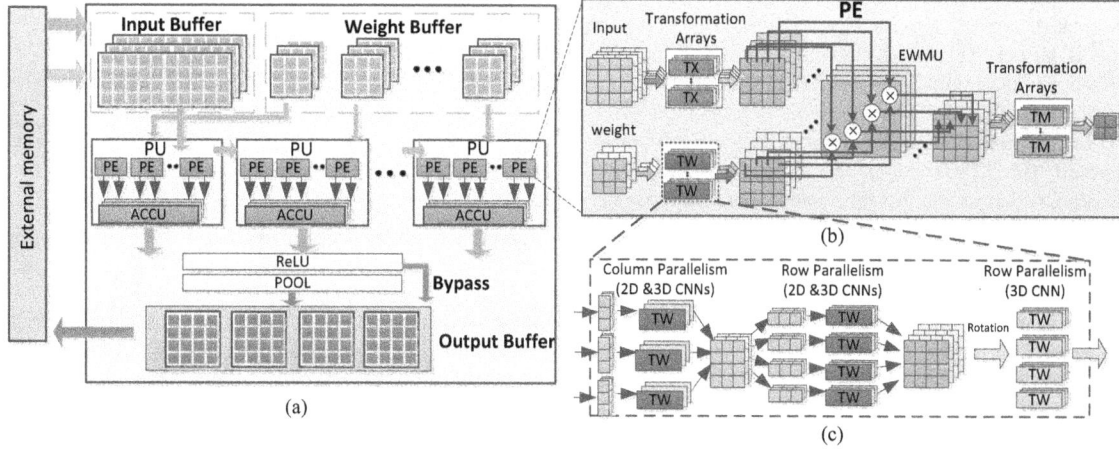

Figure 5: (a) Overview of the template-based architecture; (b) Processing element; (c) Architecture of the transformation arrays.

3.4 Template-based Architecture

```
Computation_Engine<To,Ti>(Tz,Tr,Tc):
L1:for(tz=0;tz < Tz;tz+=2){//loop flattened (only for 3D CNN)
 L2: for(           r+=2){//loop flattened
  L3:  for(tc=0;tc < Tc;tc+=2){
#Pragma HLS PIPELINE
  Load(In,Bin); //load input tiles Bin from In[Ti][Td*Th*Tw]
  Load(W,Bw); //load filter tiles from W[To][Ti][Ksize]
  L4:  for(to=0;to < To; to++){
#Pragma HLS UNROLL
   PU(Bin,Bw,Bout,to,tz,tr,tc){  //parallelism in PUs
    L5:    for(ti=0;ti < Ti; ti++){
#Pragma HLS UNROLL
     PE(Bin,Bw,to,ti); //parallelism in PEs
}
Accumulations(Bout,to,ti); }}
store(Bout,Out);//store output tiles Bout to Out[To][Tz*Tr*Tc]
}}}
```

Listing 1: Simplified pseudocode of the computation engine.

Figure 5(a) presents an overview of the proposed template-based architecture. Due to the limited on-chip memory capacity of the FPGA platform, holding all input feature maps and weights in on-chip Block RAM (BRAM) would be unrealistic; consequently, we store both the initial data and the final results in the external memory. In addition, we identify data reuse opportunities in the feature maps, as each feature map is convolved many times by M different filters; therefore, caching more filters on-chip will be beneficial for input feature data reuse. However, it is infeasible to cache all filters on-chip, since the number of filters increases significantly as the network goes deeper. Therefore, we opt to apply the tiling method on both the input/output feature maps and the filters. As shown in Figure 5(a), we manage three kinds of buffers to store the tiled data. Note that the sizes of the tiled input/output

feature maps and filters are $T_i * T_d * T_h * T_w$, $T_o * T_z * T_r * T_c$ and $T_o * T_i * Ksize$ (T_d and T_z equal to 1 for 2D CNN), where T_o and T_i are tiling factors of M and N, respectively; T_d, T_h and T_w are tiling factors for the input feature maps (i.e. T_d for D, T_h for H and T_w for W), and T_z, T_r and T_c are tiling factors of output feature maps (similarly, T_z for Z, T_r for R and T_c for C).

Computation Engine. The computation engine is the kernel component of the architecture. The scalable architecture implemented has two levels of hierarchy, namely the Processing Units (PUs) and a set of Processing Engines (PEs) in each PU. The proposed templates are integrated inside the PEs. Similar to [2, 14, 20], the computation engine can be used to accelerate both the CONV and FC layers (more details in Section 3.6). As can be seen, we also map the Activation (ReLU) and pooling layers (POOL) into the architecture. In particular, the network configuration allows the pooling layer to be optionally bypassed. Consequently, the entire CNN can be perfectly mapped to our proposed architecture.

Listing1 shows the pseudocode of the computation engine. As shown in the figure above, we unroll Loops $L4$ and $L5$ in Listing1 to explore two parallelisms: 1. the inter-output parallelism, by using T_o PUs to compute multiple output feature maps in parallel; 2. the inter-input parallelism, by integrating T_i PEs in each PU to process multiple input feature maps in parallel. In addition, we also pipeline loop $L3$ in Listing1 so that the processing of different tiles can be overlapped, which leads to the computation engine having high throughput. Moreover, we also flatten $L1$ and $L2$ in Listing1, thus minimizing the latency of the computation engine.

Processing Engine (PE). PEs are the fundamental computing units that perform the major procedure of the Winograd algorithm.

The function of a PE unit is to fetch an input tile and its corresponding filter tile, then yield an intermediate result tile to be accumulated in PU. As shown in Figure 5(b), the templates presented in Figure 4 are used to build the major components of the PEs, namely the transformation arrays (*TX*, *TW* and *TM*) and the *EWMU* (Element-Wise Multiplication Unit). It can be seen that the 2D and 3D Winograd algorithms are perfectly mapped to the structure of the PE. Note that the dataflow of the 2D algorithm is depicted in lighter colors, while the dataflow of 3D algorithm is depicted in darker colors. It can be seen that both of the dataflows can be organized by the proposed templates.

Figure 5(c) illustrates the micro-architecture of the transformation arrays. In order to minimize the computational latency of the transformation procedure, multiple transformation templates are integrated to support both column (transformation) and row (transformation) parallelism. Consequently, the transformation arrays are perfectly pipelined, meaning that they can process a new tile in every cycle. For 3D CNN, extra templates (as identified by dashed blocks) are required to support transformations on multiple data plains as well as the rotated transformed tiles.

Processing Unit (PU). We manage multiple identical PUs to enable re-use of the input feature maps. This means that every time the process is run, all PUs share the same input feature tiles but fetch T_o different sets of filter tiles, yielding T_o result tiles that belong to T_o output feature maps. If all PUs are connected directly to the input feature buffer, our design may experience some difficulties in making the timing closure when the clock rate is high [18]. To solve this problem, we organize the PUs according to a systolic array architecture, as in [2, 18, 20]. As shown in Figure 5, only the leftmost PU is directly connected to the input buffers, while the other PUs are connected to the adjacent PUs. Every time a PU receives T_i input tiles from the preceding PU for processing, it also delivers the data to the adjacent PU intermediately. Local buffers are required in each PU so that the the input tiles may be cached. In order to overlap computation and data delivery, we manage double buffers in each PU. The result tiles generated by the local PEs are accumulated in the *ACCU* module of each PU, which consists of multiple accumulation templates. The temporary sum generated by the *ACCU* will then be read to add the newly generated results until all the input feature maps have been traversed.

3.5 Memory Access Optimization

As discussed in Section 2.1, the bandwidth sensitivity of the CONV layers in 3D CNNs is exacerbated due to the cubical growth of input/output data. In addition, the improvement in computation engine throughput demands higher on-chip memory bandwidth. Optimization strategies for both off-chip DRAM and on-chip memory access are provided in this subsection so that the memory bandwidth can be matched with the computational capacity of the computation engine.

3.5.1 Optimization for the external memory bandwidth. There are two main aspects to our strategies for optimizing external memory access: reducing the number of memory transfers and increasing the efficient memory bandwidth. As shown in Table 3, we observe that the selection of tiling factors affects the effective external memory bandwidth. It can be seen that using Strategy 1 will result

Table 3: Tiling strategies

	Tiling Strategies	# of Transfers[*]	Burst Length
1	$T_z <= Z, T_c < C, T_r <= R$	$T_d * T_h * \frac{W}{T_w}$	$\frac{T_w * Bw_{on}}{Bw_{off}}$
2	$T_z <= Z, T_c = C, T_r < R$	T_d	$\frac{T_h * W * Bw_{on}}{Bw_{off}}$
3	$T_z <= Z, T_c = C, T_r = R$	1	$\frac{T_d * H * W * Bw_{on}}{Bw_{off}}$

[*] $T_w = T_c * S - S + K, T_h = T_r * S - S + K, T_d = T_z * S - S + K.$

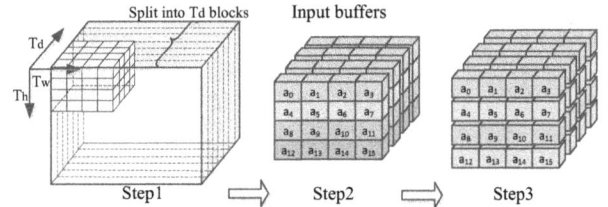

Figure 6: Step-by-step optimization for on-chip memory access.

in poor memory bandwidth efficiency, since this may result in a large number of memory transfers with short burst lengths; this is not favored by the external memory. Using Strategy 2 can result in higher effective bandwidth than Strategy 1, as it significantly increases the burst length and thereby reduces the number of memory transfers. Although Strategy 3 seems to be the best option, it requires a large amount of on-chip memory to store the data to be processed. Accordingly, we propose a flexible optimization strategy to tackle this issue. For convolutional layers where the size of the input feature maps is large, we select Strategy 2 to facilitate a good tradeoff between on-chip memory consumption and external memory bandwidth. In addition, we apply Strategy 3 only for those convolutional layers with small input feature maps.

From Table 3, it can be further concluded that the bit-widths of the external memory Bw_{off} and on-chip buffer Bw_{on} also affect the burst length. The work in [20] demonstrates that higher Bw_{off} can result in better peak bandwidth. In addition, according to [3], enlarging the data width of the on-chip buffer can lead to a larger data transfer width and thus a higher DRAM bandwidth. In this work, we increase both Bw_{on} and Bw_{off} to facilitate fast DRAM-BRAM transfer. More importantly, we also use multiple memory ports to load and store multiple input/output feature maps simultaneously.

3.5.2 Optimization for on-chip buffer access. In order to parallelize the executions of PEs in each PU, we first split the input feature buffers into T_i blocks. In this way, it is possible to read T_i input feature tiles for the corresponding T_i PEs independently. Similarly, the weight buffer is partitioned into T_o blocks to support parallelism among PUs. In a departure from prior works, we adopt the Winograd algorithm that each time a PE needs to read an input feature tile and a filter tile simultaneously. If all pixels of the input feature tile are stored in the same memory bank, the on-chip memory access conflicts can be very severe, thereby limiting the throughput of the computation pipeline. Moreover, fully splitting the memory blocks into register files is infeasible, as this may result in a great number of multiplexers which in turn cost a large number

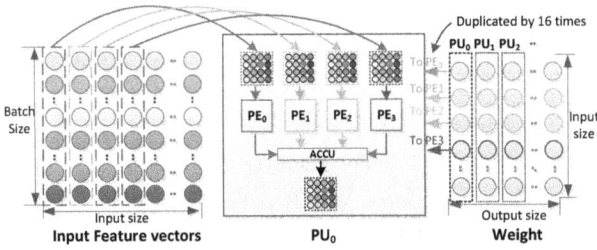

Figure 7: An illustration of FC layer mapping.

of LUTs (Loop-Up Tables). To resolve this issue, we propose a step-by-step optimization strategy that can significantly improve the on-chip memory bandwidth with moderate memory consumption. To promote better understanding, an example of this is shown in Figure 6 (For simplicity's sake, we assume $T_i = 1$ in this example).

Step 1: Each of the T_i input buffer blocks is further split into T_d partitions, as shown in Figure 6. In this way, data located at different depths of the input feature tile can be fetched simultaneously, which significantly reduces memory access conflicts by a factor of 4 (i.e. $m + r - 1$) for each PU. Note that this step can only be applied for 3D CNN.

Step 2: Further optimization is achieved by enlarging the width of the on-chip buffers. As the example shows, after this optimization method is applied, four consecutive data $a_i \sim a_{i+3}$ ($i = 0, 1, 2, 3$) (marked as the same color) can be read simultaneously. However, it should be noted that data marked in different colors still cannot be fetched in parallel, suggesting substantial room for improvement.

Step 3: We utilize the "ARRAY_PARTITION" directive provided by the HLS tool to achieve higher bandwidth. The "cyclic" partition strategy is used in this work to split the original on-chip buffers into blocks of equal size, interleaving the elements. As the example shows, $a_0 \sim a_3$ and $a_4 \sim a_7$ are stored in different blocks that can be fetched simultaneously. Finally, we can simply use the dual-port BRAMs to implement the buffers for further improvement. Use of this method means that each buffer can handle two concurrent memory accesses. As in [21], we use double buffering in the input/output feature maps and weights to overlap data transfer time with computation, thereby further reducing the overall latency.

3.6 Fully Connected Layers

The proposed architecture can be reused to accelerate the FC layers. Since the computation pattern of the FC layers is inner-product, which mainly includes multiplications and additions, we can reuse the computation engine for FC layers by bypassing the transformation modules in PEs, such that only the *EWMU* and *ACCU* modules are used. Figure 7 depicts the mapping from an FC layer to the template-based architecture. In order to reuse the weights in FC layers thereby reducing data access, a batch of input feature vectors are organized as the input of the FC layers. The input feature tile fetched by each PE is made up of the pixels from the same location of different input feature vectors (i.e, data in the same dashed box in Figure 7 (left)). Therefore, the batch size is equal to the tile size. In addition, according to the computation pattern of the FC layers, the pixels belong to the same tile are multiplied by the same weight. As it turns out, each PE requires only a weight each time the process is run. In order to perform element-wise multiplications in each PE,

each weight needs to be duplicated by 16 (i.e. the size of input tile, 16 for 2D CNN and 64 for 3D CNN) times before being sent to each PU. Subsequently, the *ACCU* in each PU accumulates the intermediate results from all local PEs. Once all the pixels of the input feature vectors are traversed, the PUs deliver the accumulated results to the output buffer. Since the size of the output feature vectors is small, these vectors are stored in on-chip buffers in order to reduce amount of the off-chip communication. Moreover, as the weights to be transferred are very large, double buffering is also adopted to overlap the computation with the memory access, similar to the process applied to the CONV layers.

4 ANALYTICAL MODEL FOR DESIGN SPACE EXPLORATION

In this section, we propose a uniform analytical model for the design space explorations of our proposed template-based architecture.

4.1 Computational Roof

To ensure uniform mathematical representation of the analytical model for both 2D and 3D CNN accelerators, we regard 2D CNN as a special form of 3D CNN with $Z = T_z = 1$. We first estimate the peak computation performance of our accelerator by calculating its computational roof (CR), which is given by:

$$Computational\ Roof\ = \frac{total\ computational\ operations}{execution\ cycles}. \quad (7)$$

Considering that the Winograd algorithm is essentially the fast algorithm for the convolution, the number of operations can be defined by Equation 8, which is identical to the ordinary convolutional algorithm.

$$OPs = 2 \times Z \times R \times C \times M \times N \times Ksize. \quad (8)$$

Here, $Ksize$ denotes the size of the filters. With reference to Listing1, the execution cycles can be calculated as follow:

$$EC_w = \lceil \frac{M}{T_o} \rceil \times \lceil \frac{N}{T_i} \rceil \times \frac{Z}{T_z} \times \frac{R}{T_r} \times \frac{C}{T_c} \times (\frac{T_z \times T_r \times T_c \times I}{m^{dim}} + L), \quad (9)$$

where I and L denote the iteration interval and latency of the computation pipeline, and dim is the number of dimensions of the input data (i.e., $dim = 2$ for 2D CNN and $dim = 3$ for 3D CNN). Note that for the sake of simplicity, we assume T_z, T_r and T_c are divisors of Z,R and C, respectively. Consequently, the computational roof can be calculated by:

$$CR = \frac{OPs}{EC_w} = \frac{2 \times M \times N \times Ksize \times m^{dim}}{\lceil \frac{M}{T_o} \rceil \times \lceil \frac{N}{T_i} \rceil \times I}. \quad (10)$$

Note that we omit L in Equation 10 due to its negligible impact on the execution cycles. When a comparison is drawn with the computational roof discussed in [21], it can be found that using the Winograd algorithm can allow for a higher computational roof to be reached than when the ordinary convolutional algorithm is used (given that $\frac{m^{dim}}{I} > 1$ in this work). In addition, we can observe that the computational roof is mainly determined by T_o and T_i, especially when M and N are integer multiples of T_o and T_i respectively. Increasing T_o or T_i can thus lead to a higher computational roof.

4.2 Performance Modeling

We mainly focus on modeling the execution time of a given convolutional layer. Since external memory transfer significantly affects the total execution time, we first model the transfer time of the input and output data required each time by the computation engine illustrated in Listing1:

$$V_{in} = T_i \times (S \times T_z + K - S)^{dim-2} \times (S \times T_r + K - S) \times (S \times T_c + K - S) \quad (11)$$

$$V_w = T_o \times T_i \times Ksize \quad (12)$$

$$V_{out} = T_o \times T_z \times T_r \times T_c \quad (13)$$

$$T_{trans}^i = \frac{(V_{in} + V_w) \times Data\_Width}{BW_{eff}} \quad (14)$$

$$T_{trans}^o = \frac{V_{out} \times Data\_Width}{BW_{eff}}, \quad (15)$$

where V_{in}, V_w and V_{out} denote the amount of required input/output feature maps and filters respectively. BW_{eff} is defined as the effective bandwidth of the off-chip memory, while $Data\_Width$ denotes the data widths of the input/output and weights. We define T_{com} as the computation time of $L3$ in Listing1, which can be modeled as follows:

$$T_{com} = \frac{T_z \times T_r \times T_c \times I}{m^{dim} \times Freq}. \quad (16)$$

Considering the bandwidth limitation of the FPGA platform, it is not possible for the computation time to be directly calculated calculated by $\frac{EC_w}{Freq}$. Instead, given that we have adopted double buffering in the input and output to hide the transfer latency, the total execution time for a given convolutional layer can be calculated as follows:

$$T_{total} = \frac{Z}{T_z} \times \frac{R}{T_r} \times \frac{C}{T_c} \times (\lceil \frac{M}{T_o} \rceil \times \lceil \frac{N}{T_i} \rceil \times \max\{T_{com}, T_{trans}^i\} + T_{trans}^o), \quad (17)$$

where $Freq$ is the frequency of the accelerator. Note that we remove the transfer time of the output from Equation 17 due to its negligible impact on total execution time.

5 EXPERIMENTAL RESULTS

In this section, we evaluate the template-based architecture by implementing two accelerators for state-of-the-art 2D and 3D CNNs, respectively. In addition, multiple FPGAs are used to test the portability of our designs.

5.1 Experimental Setup

Benchmarks. As a case study, we evaluate our design using two representative CNN models: VGG16 and C3D. All convolutional layers of the selected CNNs have uniform $3 * 3$ and $3 * 3 * 3$ filters, which fit well with the Winograd algorithm.

CPU and GPU setup. We evaluated our FPGA implementation of C3D through comparison with other platforms , namely (1) the high-performance ten-core Intel E5 2680 v2 CPU, which operates at 2.8 GHz, (2) the NVIDIA Tesla K40m GPU with 2880 SIMD cores and (3) the NVIDIA GeForce GTX 1080 GPU with 2560 SIMD cores.

FPGA platform setup. We use two evaluation boards to evaluate our accelerators for 2D and 3D CNNs: Xilinx VC709 and S2C VUS440. The VC709 platform contains a Virtex-7 690t FPGA and two 4GB DDR3 DRAMs. Our implementations are clocked at 150MHz on

Table 4: Uniform cross-layer parameters

Networks	Winograd	T_i	T_o	Bw_{off}	Bw_{on}	# of Ports
VGG16	$F(2^2, 3^2)$	4	64	256bit	64bit	4
C3D	$F(2^3, 3^3)$	4	32	256bit	64bit	4

Table 5: FPGA resource utilization

Device		Resource	DSP	BRAM	LUT	FF
VC709		Available	3600	2940	433K	866K
	2D	Used	1376	1232	175K	202K
		Utilization	38%	42%	40%	23%
	3D	Used	1536	1508	242K	286K
		Utilization	42%	52%	56%	33%
VUS440		Available	2880	5040	2532K	5065K
	2D	Used	1376	1232	170K	189K
		Utilization	48%	24%	6.7%	3.7%
	3D	Used	1536	1476	209K	285K
		Utilization	53%	30%	8.3%	5.6%

this platform. To test the portability of our architecture, we implement our designs on S2C VUS440; this integrates a Xilinx VCU440 FPGA and an 8GB DDR4, which can provide a higher bandwidth. Our designs run at 200MHz on this platform.

Design tools. We use Xilinx Vivado HLS 2016.4 to implement the proposed templates, as well as to generate the template-based accelerators. All synthesized results are obtained from Xilinx Vivado 2016.4.

5.2 Performance Analysis

In our experiment, we design an accelerator with unified unroll factors for all convolutional layers in each CNN model rather than creating an optimal design for each layer. In this way the overhead of reprogramming the FPGA for different layers is removed. Note that we primarily evaluate the $F(2^2, 3^2)$ and $F(2^3, 3^3)$ due to the associated benefits in saving DSPs as well as the simplicity of template designs. Table 4 presents the uniform cross-layer parameters for all layers of the benchmarks, including the tiling factors and memory system configurations. Although the selected uniform parameters are sub-optimal for some layers (e.g. the optimal $< T_o, T_i >$ for the Conv1 in C3D is $< 3, 32 >$ instead of $< 4, 32 >$), our results suggest that the overall performance degradation is minimal compared to the condition in which each layer uses the optimal $< T_o, T_i >$. In addition, the configurations in Table 4 also contribute to the optimal on-chip and off-chip bandwidth, according to our on-board memory test.

Table 5 presents the FPGA resource utilization of the implementations for 2D and 3D CNNs. Here, it is evident that the DSPs are no longer the limiting resource on VC709, which demonstrates the benefit of using the Winograd algorithm. Instead, LUTs, which are mainly utilized for the transformation and accumulation templates, dominated the resource consumption. Since VUS440 contains an FPGA with a larger amount of LUTs (5.8x) but fewer DSPs than VC709, it can be seen that our implementations consume over 48% of DSPs but few LUTs ($< 10\%$) on this platform. In summary, the overall resource consumption on VUS440 is lower which contributes to the frequency improvement on this platform.

Figure 8 and Figure 9 present the evaluation results on multiples FPGA platforms for VGG and C3D, respectively. For both

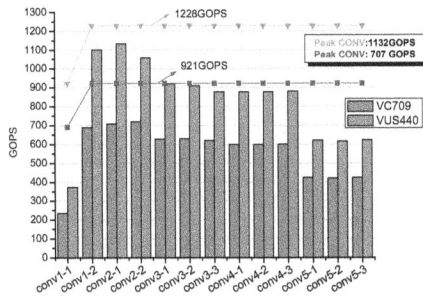

Figure 8: Evaluation results of VGG16.

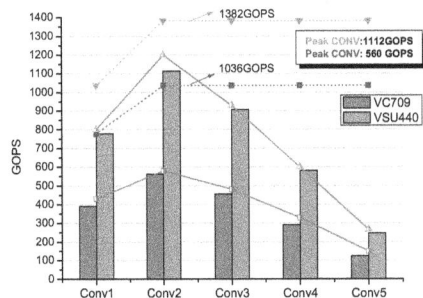

Figure 9: Evaluation results of C3D.

Table 6: Bandwidth comparison on multiple FPGA platforms for C3D

Platform	Freq. (MHz)	BW (GB/s)	C1	C2	C3	C4	C5
VC709	150	Req.	4.15	4.23	4.89	7.24	17.02
		Act.	2.47	2.27	2.14	2.02	2.01
VUS440	200	Req.	5.53	5.65	6.52	9.65	22.7
		Act.	4.98	4.55	4.29	4.05	4.04

benchmarks, implementations on VUS440 can achieve higher peak performance (1132 GOPS for VGG and 1112 GOPS for C3D) and higher overall performance of all CONV layers (902 GOPS for VGG and 940 GOPS for C3D). To explain this result, we compare the required bandwidth with the actual bandwidth of each CONV layer of C3D, with the results presented in Table 6: as it can be seen, VUS440 provides higher bandwidth than VC709 (an average of 2.0x improvement). In addition, both implementations are bounded by the memory bandwidth on the platforms. Moreover, the gap between required and actual bandwidths increases from Conv1 to Conv5 on both platforms. This is because the size of the input feature maps decreases in the latter CONV layers, resulting in inefficient memory access (short burst length).

As a result, the performance of the latter layers (especially Conv5) is poorer compared to that of the former layers. One interesting phenomenon that emerges from Figure 8 and Figure 9 is that the first layers of the benchmarks show relatively lower performance, despite having higher bandwidth; this occurs because these layers only have three input feature maps, which fail to utilize the double buffering in the input buffers ($N < T_i$). In addition, the dashed lines in Figure 8 and Figure 9 indicate the computational roofs of the CONV layers in both networks. This demonstrates that our implementations of VGG and C3D can reach up to 92% and 80%, respectively, of the computational roof on VUS440.

The solid lines in Figure 9 represent the estimated performance of each CONV layer in C3D (green line for VC709 and red line for VUS440). This shows that our analytical model perfectly matches the on-board results, in that the average error is < 5%, which is evidence of the accuracy of our model. Overall, our designs achieve high performance for both 2D and 3D CNNs, thus demonstrating the effectiveness of our proposed template-based architecture.

5.2.1 Comparison with previous work. A performance comparison between our accelerator and the previous FPGA implementations of 2D CNN is presented in Table 7. Throughput and DSP efficiency were used as performance metrics. It can be seen that our work achieves state-of-the-art performance with the second-lowest DSP utilization (38% on VC709) of the implementations listed in Table 7, after [16]), which demonstrates the advantages of utilizing the Winograd algorithms for CNN acceleration. In addition, our work outperforms most of previous work in terms of DSP efficiency except for [2] and [23]. [2] also utilizes the Winograd algorithm in its design. However, the DSPs used in [2] can perform two 16-bit floating-point multiplies and adds, while the DSPs used in this work only supports one 16-bit fixed-point multiply and add. Moreover, our experience suggests that it is difficult to reach high frequency with over 90% of DSP utilization using the Xilinx HLS tool, while [2] and [23] use Intel SDK for OpenCL, which makes this easier. Therefore, it can be concluded that differences in FPGA types and HLS tools between [2, 23] and the present work indicate that it is unfair to draw a direct comparison.

5.2.2 Comparison with SW implementation. Since there is no FPGA implementation for 3D CNN (to the best of our knowledge), we compare our implementation of C3D with the CPU and GPU solutions only. The results of this comparison are presented in Table 8. Note that OpenBLAS and CuDNN libraries are used for optimizing the CPU and GPU solutions. The results demonstrate that on VC709, our implementation achieves an end-to-end performance 7.3x greater than that of CPU and with 3.6x the energy efficiency of K40m GPU. Better results are attained on VUS440; here, our implementation achieves a speedup of 13.4x relative to the CPU solution and a 6.4x increase in energy efficiency relative to K40m GPU. In addition, it can also be seen that when compared with the state-of-the-art GTX 1080 GPU, our design on VUS440 still achieves better energy efficiency.

6 RELATED WORK

An abundance of research exists into designing FPGA-based accelerators for 2D CNN. However, the majority of these studies have only implemented the convolutional layers of CNNs. A representative work by Zhang et al. [21] proposes a roofline model to maximize computational resources on FPGA under the memory bandwidth limitations. As the convolutional layers are accelerated, the other unaccelerated layers become a performance bottleneck. To resolve this issue, several studies [14, 16, 20] attempt to accelerate the entire CNN on an FPGA. Suda et al. [16] transform the 3D convolution to 2D general purpose matrix multiplication and design a matrix multiplication accelerator for both convolutional and fully connected layers. The work by Qiu [14] presents a dynamic-precision data quantization method and uses a convolver design

Table 7: Comparison with previous implementations for 2D CNN

	[14]	[16]	[20]	[12]	[2]	[23]	Ours	
FPGA	Xilinx Zynq XC7Z045	Altera Stratix-V	Xilinx Virtex 690t	Arria10 GX1150	Arria10 GX1150	Arria10 GX1150	Xilinx Virtex 690t	Xilinx VCU440
Frequency (MHz)	150	120	150	150	303	385	150	200
CNN	VGG	VGG	VGG	VGG	AlexNet	VGG	VGG	VGG
Precision	16-bit fixed	8-16 bits fixed	16-bit fixed	8-16 bits fixed	16-bit float	16-bit fixed	16-bit fixed	16-bit fixed
DSP Utilization	780(87%)	727(37%)	2833(78%)	1518(100%)	1476(97%)	2756(91%)	1376(38%)	1376(48%)
Throughput (Gops)	137	118	354	645	1382	1790	570	821
DSP Efficiency (Gops/DSPs)	0.18	0.16	0.12	0.43	0.98	0.65	0.41	0.60

Table 8: End-to-end comparison with CPU/GPU for C3D

Platforms	CPU	GPU		FPGA	
Device	E5-2680	K40	GTX1080	VC709	VUS440
Technology	22nm	28nm	16nm	28nm	20nm
Power (W)	115	250	180	25	26
CONV (Gops)	60.3	1206.5	4375.7	474.3	940.6
CNN (Gops)	58.7	1174.0	4101.9	430.7	784.7
Latency(ms)	656.2	32.8	8.8	89.4	49.1
Speedup	1x	20.0x	69.9x	7.3x	13.4x
(Gops/W)	0.5 (1x)	4.7 (9.2x)	22.8 (44.6x)	17.1 (33.8x)	30.2 (60.3x)

for all layers in the CNN, while Zhang et al. [20] propose a uniform convolutional matrix multiplication representation to accelerate both the convolutional and fully connected layers on FPGAs. All these works mentioned above process the networks layer by layer. The works in [1, 11] take opposite approaches by making all layers working concurrently in a pipelined structure. In [1], the authors use a pyramid-shaped multi-layer sliding window to fuse the processing of adjacent CNN layers, thereby minimizing the off-chip transfer. Li et al. [11] map all the layers of the CNN on one chip and make different layers work concurrently in a pipelined structure. However, in order to store the intermediate results between layers, these works require massive memory usage for large scale CNNs in order to store the intermediate results between layers.

Currently, a few studies utilize the fast algorithms to reduce the computation complexity of CNNs. Zhang et al. [22] propose a 2D convolver in frequency domain to accelerate convolutional layers on FPGA, leaving other layers computed by CPU. However, the FFT-based approach shows less efficiency for convolutions with small filters [10]. Aydonat et al. [2] utilize the 1D Winograd algorithm for arithmetic optimization that greatly improves the DSP utilization. However, it stores all input feature maps in on-chip memory, which can only support small CNN models. To the best of our knowledge, we are the first to explore 3D CNN acceleration using the Winograd algorithm on FPGA. More importantly, we unify the 2D and 3D CNNs into a single acceleration framework.

7 CONCLUSIONS

In this work, we propose a template-based methodology for 2D and 3D CNN acceleration on FPGA. We use uniform templates to build accelerators for 2D and 3D CNNs based on the Winograd algorithm. We also develop uniform analytical model for our template-based

architecture, along with performance modeling that efficiently explores the design space. We evaluate our architecture by realizing the implementations for VGG16 and C3D across multiple FPGA platforms. Experimental results show that our template-based architecture is capable of accelerating both 2D and 3D CNNs efficiently.

ACKNOWLEDGMENTS

This work was supported by National Program on Key Basic Research Project 2016YFB1000401 and 2016YFB1000403.

REFERENCES

[1] M. Alwani et al., "Fused-layer cnn accelerators," In *MICRO*, pages 1–12. IEEE, 2016.
[2] U. Aydonat et al., "An opencl deep learning accelerator on arria 10," *arXiv preprint arXiv:1701.03534*, 2017.
[3] J. Cong et al., "Bandwidth optimization through on-chip memory restructuring for hls," *Design Automation Conference (DAC)*, pages 1–6. IEEE, 2017.
[4] K. He et al., "Deep residual learning for image recognition," In *CVPR*, pages 770–778, 2016.
[5] S. Ji et al., "3d convolutional neural networks for human action recognition," *IEEE transactions on pattern analysis and machine intelligence*, 35(1):221–231, 2013.
[6] N. P. Jouppi et al., "In-datacenter performance analysis of a tensor processing unit," *arXiv preprint arXiv:1704.04760*, 2017.
[7] K. Kamnitsas et al., "Efficient multi-scale 3d cnn with fully connected crf for accurate brain lesion segmentation," *Medical image analysis*, 36:61–78, 2017.
[8] A. Krizhevsky et al., "Imagenet classification with deep convolutional neural networks," In *NIPS*, pages 1097–1105, 2012.
[9] Q. Lan et al., "High performance implementation of 3d convolutional neural networks on a gpu," In https://www.hindawi.com/journals/cin/aip/8348671/.
[10] A. Lavin and S. Gray, "Fast algorithms for convolutional neural networks," In *CVPR*, pages 4013–4021, 2016.
[11] H. Li et al., "A high performance fpga-based accelerator for large-scale convolutional neural networks," In *FPL*, pages 1–9. IEEE, 2016.
[12] Y. Ma et al., "Optimizing loop operation and dataflow in fpga acceleration of deep convolutional neural networks," In *FPGA*, pages 45–54. ACM, 2017.
[13] D. Mahajan et al., "Tabla: A unified template-based framework for accelerating statistical machine learning," In *HPCA*, pages 14–26. IEEE, 2016.
[14] J. Qiu et al., "Going deeper with embedded fpga platform for convolutional neural network," In *FPGA*, pages 26–35. ACM, 2016.
[15] K. Simonyan et al., "Very deep convolutional networks for large-scale image recognition," *arXiv preprint arXiv:1409.1556*, 2014.
[16] N. Suda et al., "Throughput-optimized opencl-based fpga accelerator for large-scale convolutional neural networks," In *FPGA*, pages 16–25. ACM, 2016.
[17] D. Tran et al., "Learning spatiotemporal features with 3d convolutional networks," In *ICCV*, pages 4489–4497, 2015.
[18] X. Wei et al., "Automated systolic array architecture synthesis for high throughput cnn inference on fpgas," In *DAC*, page 29. ACM, 2017.
[19] S. Winograd. "On multiplication of polynomials modulo a polynomial," *SIAM Journal on Computing*, 9(2):225–229, 1980.
[20] C. Zhang et al., "Caffeine: Towards uniformed representation and acceleration for deep convolutional neural networks," In *ICCAD*, pages 1–8. IEEE, 2016.
[21] C. Zhang et al., "Optimizing fpga-based accelerator design for deep convolutional neural networks," In *FPGA*, pages 161–170. ACM, 2015.
[22] C. Zhang et al., "Frequency domain acceleration of convolutional neural networks on cpu-fpga shared memory system," In *FPGA*, pages 35–44. ACM, 2017.
[23] J. Zhang and J. Li, "Improving the performance of opencl-based fpga accelerator for convolutional neural network," In *FPGA*, pages 25–34. ACM, 2017.

A Customizable Matrix Multiplication Framework for the Intel HARPv2 Xeon+FPGA Platform

A Deep Learning Case Study

Duncan J.M. Moss*, Srivatsan Krishnan[†], Eriko Nurvitadhi[†], Piotr Ratuszniak[†‡], Chris Johnson[†],
Jaewoong Sim[†], Asit Mishra[†], Debbie Marr[†], Suchit Subhaschandra[†] and Philip H.W. Leong*

[†]Intel Corporation, [‡]Koszalin University of Technology,*The University of Sydney
duncan.moss@sydney.edu.au,{srivatsan.krishnan,suchit.subhaschandra}@intel.com

ABSTRACT

General Matrix to Matrix multiplication (GEMM) is the cornerstone for a wide gamut of applications in high performance computing (HPC), scientific computing (SC) and more recently, deep learning. In this work, we present a customizable matrix multiplication framework for the Intel HARPv2 CPU+FPGA platform that includes support for both traditional single precision floating point and reduced precision workloads. Our framework supports arbitrary size GEMMs and consists of two parts: (1) a simple application programming interface (API) for easy configuration and integration into existing software and (2) a highly customizable hardware template. The API provides both compile and runtime options for controlling key aspects of the hardware template including dynamic precision switching; interleaving and block size control; and fused deep learning specific operations. The framework currently supports single precision floating point (FP32), 16, 8, 4 and 2 bit Integer and Fixed Point (INT16, INT8, INT4, INT2) and more exotic data types for deep learning workloads: INT16xTernary, INT8xTernary, BinaryxBinary.

We compare our implementation to the latest NVIDIA Pascal GPU and evaluate the performance benefits provided by optimizations built into the hardware template. Using three neural networks (AlexNet, VGGNet and ResNet) we illustrate that reduced precision representations such as binary achieve the best performance, and that the HARPv2 enables fine-grained partitioning of computations over both the Xeon and FPGA. We observe up to 50x improvement in execution time compared to single precision floating point, and that runtime configuration options can improve the efficiency of certain layers in AlexNet up to 4x, achieving an overall 1.3x improvement over the entire network.

ACM Reference Format:
Duncan J.M. Moss*, Srivatsan Krishnan[†], Eriko Nurvitadhi[†], Piotr Ratuszniak[†‡], Chris Johnson[†], Jaewoong Sim[†], Asit Mishra[†], Debbie Marr[†], Suchit Subhaschandra[†] and Philip H.W. Leong* and [†]Intel Corporation, [‡]Koszalin University of Technology,*The University of Sydney. 2018. A Customizable Matrix Multiplication Framework for the Intel HARPv2 Xeon+FPGA Platform: A Deep Learning Case Study. In *FPGA '18: 2018 ACM/SIGDA International Symposium on Field-Programmable Gate Arrays, February 25–27, 2018, Monterey, CA, USA.* ACM, New York, NY, USA, 10 pages. https://doi.org/10.1145/3174243.3174258

1 INTRODUCTION

High performance and scientific computing (HPC & SC) workloads rely on the basic linear algebra (BLAS) [1] subroutines to perform many of their most time intensive functions. BLAS libraries are optimized for high performance and consist of three separate levels with level 3 routines focused on matrix operations. The general matrix to matrix multiplication (GEMM) level 3 routine is arguably the most time intensive and widely used function in HPC and SC. Hence when designing an accelerator for these applications, targeting the GEMM routine often leads to the highest improvement in performance.

In the past, architectures for accelerating these HPC and SC algorithms have been developed for discrete FPGA or FPGAs with embedded soft/hard processors, with all functions handled by the FPGA fabric. Often resources which would be better allocated to accelerating specific bottlenecks, such as GEMM, need to be traded off to implement the other less compute intensive portions of the algorithm. Recently, heterogeneous CPU+FPGA platforms have been proposed as an alternative to discrete FPGAs. By close integration with a CPU, the FPGA's resources can be better utilized to optimize the most compute intensive parts of the application, while less FPGA friendly functions are handled by the CPU. The Intel HARPv2 [12] combines a 14 core Broadwell Xeon CPU and an Arria 10 GX1150 FPGA. It provides access to the standard x86 ecosystem, coherent access to the CPU's memory and high bandwidth to the FPGA. In contrast to embedded heterogeneous platforms, the Xeon is designed for high performance, giving the users flexibility to partition the heavy compute in a way which best suits the FPGA and CPU. By using a heterogeneous CPU+FPGA platform like HARPV2, the designer has freedom to explore architectures that advantageously exploit collaboration between the FPGA and CPU. Hence, better performance can be achieved via specialized high speed accelerators that focus on the computational bottleneck, and rely on a high performance CPU to handle the rest.

Deep learning is quickly becoming a disruptive technology with state-of-the-art accuracy shown in applications such as computer

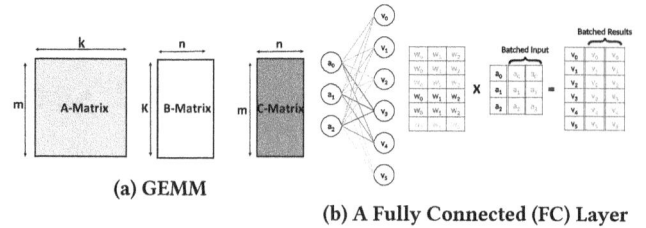

(a) GEMM

(b) A Fully Connected (FC) Layer

Figure 2: (a) Matrix layout for a GEMM. m and n are the leading dimension and k is the common dimension. (b) Each neuron takes in activations (a_i) from the previous set of neurons and performs the dot product with its weights (w_i) to produce its output (v_i).

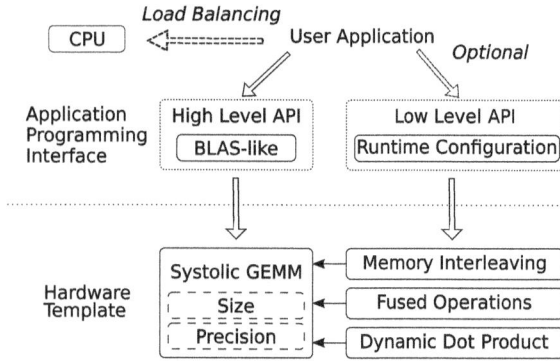

Figure 1: The framework consists of an application programming interface and hardware template. The high level API provides a function call similar to those used in BLAS libraries. The low level API is optional and allows the developer to configure certain aspects of the hardware template at runtime.

vision, autonomous driving, speech-to-text and artificial intelligence. It is still a very active area of research with work focusing on new topologies and reduced precision methods [3, 10, 17, 20, 21, 26, 26, 30]. While single precision floating point representation is still used in training, it has been shown that reduced precision representations all the way down to a single bit can be sufficient for inference. Due to lack of native low precision support in CPUs and GPUs, FPGAs are well positioned to take full advantage of exotic data types supported by their fine grained reconfigurable architecture. It has been shown [2, 4] that GEMM plays a significant role in deep learning.

This paper presents a customizable matrix multiplication framework on Intel's HARPv2, and an overview is shown in Fig. 1. It consists of a highly configurable hardware template with a streamlined software stack and runtime application programming interface (API), which allows for a wide range of different precisions, various core sizes and tunable runtime configurable parameters. We take deep learning as a case study to evaluate performance and flexibility of our framework. Various HW/SW co-design and heterogeneous load balancing techniques are applied to achieve synergistic collaboration between the Xeon CPUs and FPGA. Specifically, the contributions of this work are as follows:

- The first runtime configurable heterogeneous GEMM implementation which supports arbitrary matrix sizes and offers a wide range of precision, blocking, fusing of operations, buffering schemes and load balancing.
- A systolic GEMM template that allows runtime customization of memory interleaving, offering performance improvements of up to 2.7x on small matrices and 4x for certain neural networks. In addition, it incorporates a scheme for fusing operations so inline computation such as ReLU, Batch Norm and Clipping can be done in FPGA hardware, minimizing CPU overhead.
- A dynamic dot product, enabling mixed precision training and binary inference which leverages the HARPv2 architecture, providing up to a 1.67x improvement over a 14 core CPU.
- An evaluation of performance using popular deep neural networks (AlexNet, VGGNet and ResNet) on the HARPv2

platform used for ILSVRC15[23], and a study on the efficiency of the hardware template and its impact on deep learning performance. The resulting binary implementation is, to our knowledge, the fastest and most flexible reported to date.

The rest of this paper is organized as follows. Sec. 2 focuses on GEMM and neural networks. The API, hardware template and HARPv2 specific details are presented in Sec. 3 and Sec. 4. The fused operations and the dynamic dot product are presented in Sec. 5. The results are presented in Sec. 6 and related work is discussed in Sec. 7. Finally, conclusions are drawn in Sec. 8.

2 BACKGROUND

GEMM is a key function in many HPC and SC workloads and can be expressed as Equ. 1.

$$C = alpha * op(A) * op(B) + beta * C \qquad (1)$$

Where A, B and C are the input and result matrices, alpha and beta are scaling factors and op is a separate function that performs a matrix transpose if needed. The most computational intensive part of the operation is the $A * B$ matrix multiplication. As illustrated in Fig. 2a, matrices A and B share a dimension, k, named the common dimension and another unrestricted dimensions m and n named the leading dimensions. The output of the matrix multiplication is accumulated with the C matrix and has dimension, m and n. For each element in the result matrix a k-length dot product needs to be performed. Hence the number of multiply accumulates can be generalized to $m * n * k$, expressed as $O(n^3)$ in big-O notation.

2.1 Neural Networks

Neural networks (NNs) are a class of machine learning algorithms that are described as a connected graph of basic compute nodes named neurons. The fundamental compute in each neuron is a dot product of the inputs, named activations, and a set of weights that are unique to that particular neuron. In addition to the dot product, an activation function (tanh, ReLU, sigmoid, etc.) is applied to the output. Equ. 2 shows the operation performed by each neuron.

$$v_j = f(\sum_{i=0}^{n} w_i^j * a_i + b^j) \qquad (2)$$

As illustrated in Fig. 2b, a NN is layered such that the output from one layer is passed to each neuron in a subsequent layer, these are named fully connected (FC) layers. The operations for each neuron in a layer can be combined such that the problem is described as a matrix-vector multiplication. For large workloads, multiple inputs are often batched together and the problem is expressed as a matrix-matrix multiplication. Stacking multiple FC layers together creates a multilayer perceptron (MLP).

Convolutional Neural Networks (CNNs) are a sub-class of NNs designed for image recognition, classification, segmentation and object detection. The main layer in a CNN is the convolution (CONV) layer and is represented as a 3 dimensional block of neurons, often named a filter. Similar to an FC layer, each filter performs a dot product followed by an activation function. The input into a convolution layer is a collection of 2 dimensional input images (or channels) named input feature maps (IFMs). These IFMs are fed into a four dimensional filter array to produce another collection of 2 dimensional output images (or channels) named output feature maps (OFMs). This process is repeated across the image for all filters within the array.

When considering architectures for accelerating deep learning, it is standard practice [2, 4, 19] to use GEMM for recurrent and MLP neural networks given that batching is used across all topologies. However, as presented in a previous study [16], three different methods are commonly used to perform a convolution: (1) GEMM, (2) Winograd and (3) FFT. DeepBench [19] suggests that although convoluation specific functions such as Winograd and FTT exist, GEMM still accounts for over 50% of the highest performing benchmark configurations. Finally, when considering typical data center workloads, previous work [14] has shown that CNNs only account for 5% of the deep learning workloads performed in their data center. Hence by targeting a GEMM for accelerating deep learning we are pursuing an architecture that provides the most benefit for a wide gamut of workloads.

2.2 Reduced Precision Networks

With significant research [8, 9, 20–22, 26, 30] indicating that 8 bit or lower precision is sufficient for inference, dedicated hardware such as the Google TPU [14] and the NVIDIA V100 GPU [7], which are optimized for lower precisions have been reported. The benefit of moving to a reduced precision format for neural network computation lies in the efficiency of the multiply and accumulate operations. By moving from single precision floating point to a 32 bit fixed point, normalization is removed and scaling is simplified resulting in smaller hardware. Hence, the area and time complexity is reduced for both the addition and multiplication, improving performance but sacrificing dynamic range. Additionally, by lowering the number of bits, B, in the representation, the area requirements of the multiplication and addition generally reduce by factors of B^2 and B respectively.

3 API

The hardware template presented in Sec. 4 is implemented on the Intel HARPv2 platform with an accompanying software stack and API. As illustrated in Fig. 1, the API contains a high-level function interface for easy integration and a low-level templated interface for fine-grained control. To maintain consistency with other GEMM implementations, the high level API is modeled off other linear algebra libraries. Given Equ. 1 and previous BLAS libraries, the simplified GEMM signature for the FP32 version is:

Table 1: Tunable Options

Parameters	Type	Options
Systolic Array Size (Sec. 4)	C	*Logic & Memory Limited
Precision (Sec. 4.1)	C	FP32, INT16, INT8, INT4, Ternary, Binary
Accumulator Width (Sec. 4.1)	C	*Logic & Memory Limited
Interleaving (Sec. 4.2)	C&R	*Memory Limited
Fused Ops (Sec. 5.1)	C&R	Scaling, Batch Norm, Clip, Rounding, ReLU

***Limited by the size of the systolic array and available hardware resources.
Features are controllable at compile (C) time, runtime(R) or both (C&R)**

```
void gemm( trans a, trans b, int m, int n, int k, float
    alpha, float* a, int lda, float* b, int ldb, float
    beta, float* c, int ldc);
```

This signature is provided in a set of libraries that is easily compiled into the developers code base. For most projects this should provide sufficient performance as optimizations are performed within the function without interaction from the developer.

Tab. 1 presents a list of the current parameters tunable in the GEMM implementation. Both the precision and accumulator width are configurable at compile time when the systolic GEMM bitstream is generated. If multiple precisions are required for a workload, the API provides a single function for partial reconfiguration that allows for fast precision switching. Post processing fused operations such as value scaling, clipping, rounding and a few deep learning specific operations such as ReLU and Batch Norm can be performed while the results are transfered back to the system memory. These post processing operations are enabled at compile time to be added into the design and can be configured to be bypassed at runtime. For precisions other than FP32, the developer can set the desired accumulator width at compile time, however this does affect memory and logic resource utilization. Similarly, the developer has access to the systolic array interleaving factors. These allow the developer to make fine-grained adjustments to trade off bandwidth with compute efficiency. Sec. 4.2 covers this in more detail. The maximum interleaving level is set at compile time and is bound by the number of memory resources available on the device. However the exact level of interleaving (up to the set maximum) can be controlled at runtime via the lower level APIs.

3.1 Runtime Support

The API exposes various configurable parameters to the user-level software. Applications running using our framework leverage the Intel HARPv2 user mode runtime and kernel driver to set these parameters. Intel HARPv2 comes with its own driver stack called Intel Accelerator Abstraction Layer (Intel AAL). The integration of runtime software with the hardware accelerator template is shown

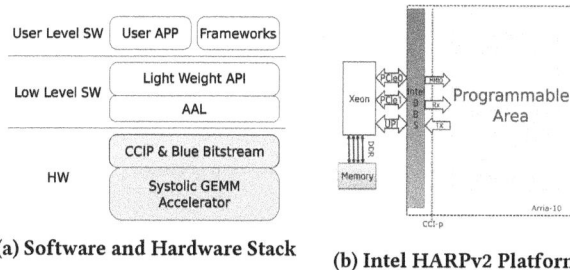

(a) Software and Hardware Stack

(b) Intel HARPv2 Platform

Figure 3: (a) The CCIP, blue bitstream and AAL are provided by the HARPv2 platform. (b) The blue bitstream communicates directly with the Xeon and makes memory requests to system memory.

in Fig. 3a. The hardware template and API chooses between the different memory links, the default setting performs bandwidth balancing between all three. There are three key components in the integration.

```
template <typename T1, typename T2>
void fpga_gemm<T1,T2>::fpga_gemm( trans a, trans b,
int m, int n, int k, float alpha, T1* a, int lda,
T2* b, int ldb, float beta, T1* c, int ldc
int i_a_lead_interleave, int i_b_lead_interleave, int
    i_feeder_interleave, GEMM_MODE i_mode);
```

Application API: The low-level functions are templated to support different precisions and modes in Tab. 1. Depending upon the precision, the number of elements packed into cacheline also changes. The low level API is shown above. "a_rows" and "b_cols" refers to the number of rows and columns in A and B matrices respectively. The "common" parameter refers to the common dimension in both the matrices. "i_alpha" and "i_beta" refer to the scaling parameters and "i_mode" refers to the mode in which the hardware accelerator template is set. "i_a_lead_interleave", "i_b_lead_interleave" and "i_feeder_interleave" are the interleaving parameters. These parameters can be used by the runtime to control the memory interleaving and improve the compute efficiency. Internally, the application API uses the AAL user mode runtime to access and initialize the FPGA device. Switching the precision during runtime is supported by the dynamic configuration API.

Intel AAL: The AAL layer provides the necessary runtime services and API to access the FPGA device. The framework's API is built on top of the AAL user-mode API's and services. At a very high level, AAL services can be briefly classified into two categories. The AAL user-mode runtime are interfaces that abstract the FPGA hardware via a service oriented model. The AAL kernel-mode driver includes interfaces for allocation of Direct Memory Access (DMA) buffers with shared addressing between the hardware accelerator template and the users application. It provides interfaces to access Memory Mapped IO (MMIO) registers in the hardware template. It also provides interfaces to perform partial reconfiguration on the FPGA device. The AAL kernel mode driver utilizes Intel Blue Bitstream to enumerate the device and perform partial reconfiguration.

Intel Blue Bitstream (BBS): Intel BBS is the infrastructure shell component in the FPGA. It abstracts the UPI (Cache Coherent Xeon Link) and the PCIe links to provide a simple load-store like interface called the Cache Coherent Interface (CCI) to the user's accelerator. Intel BBS also handles partial reconfiguration and contains the AAL kernel visible MMIO registers. The AAL kernel driver uses the configuration registers for FPGA device enumeration and initialization.

3.1.1 *Heterogeneous Load Balancing*. The hardware template also supports heterogeneous load balancing. At runtime the workload is partitioned across both the FPGA and CPU. In the case of a GEMM, the A and B matrices are divided into sub blocks and the computation is balanced across the two compute engines. This is useful for particularly large workloads in which the majority of the work is taken by the GEMM function.

4 HARDWARE TEMPLATE

The hardware template illustrated in Fig. 1 contains the systolic GEMM, described below, and several modules handling: memory interleaving, explored in Sec. 4.2, a fused operation scheme and dynamic dot product presented in Sec. 5. As illustrated in Fig. 4a, the hardware template is a systolic array of processing elements (PEs), each containing a dot product module and two memory buffers, named the cache buffer and drain buffer. The systolic array operates by iteratively processing chunks of the input matrices stored in the feeders. There are two orthogonal feeders that connect to their respective edges of the array. The design is fully pipelined, hence each cycle data is fed into the array through the feeders and propagated along the appropriate rows and columns. The feeders are by default double buffered to ensure that multiple read requests are in-flight to saturate the system bandwidth and that compute stalls due to insufficient memory are minimized. The data management unit (DMU) is responsible for requesting the input data, filling the feeders, draining out completed sections of the compute and generating write requests to the system memory. Within the systolic array, input vectors are interleaved into each PE to take advantage of data reuse and help meet the bandwidth requirements of the system. Since the input is interleaved, a small cache within each PE is necessary to store the partial results for accumulation later in the computation.

The feeders are memory modules that manage the flow of data into the array. Each feeder is by default double buffered such that one buffer can be operated while the other is being filled. The number of buffers is configurable at compile time and can be used to alleviate issues related to periods of inconsistent bandwidth.

The drain is a large interconnect that controls the flow of data down the columns of the systolic array. When the signal to drain is given, the 'drain' memories at the bottom of the array start to empty. Each column acts as a large FIFO that produces a result every cycle.

4.1 Processing Element

The PE contains a dot product module with two memories, a partial results 'cache' and completed results 'drain'. Input vectors are passed into each PE every cycle where the dot product is performed and any partial results are accumulated. In cases where the dot

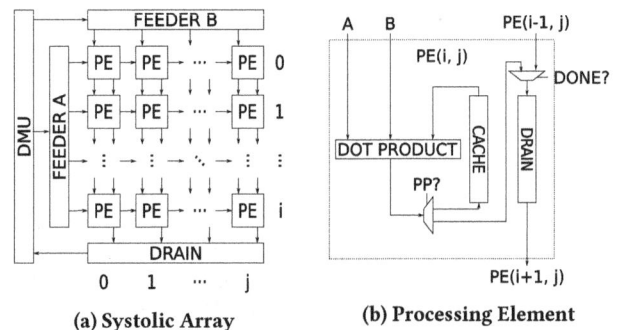

(a) Systolic Array   **(b) Processing Element**

Figure 4: The hardware template: (a) The array size is configurable with one limitation, the drain bus width must be ≤ 64 bytes. For FP32 this limits the number of columns to $j = 16$. (b) This is a PE for a given row (i) and column (j).

product is larger than the input vector length, the partial result is stored in the cache which will be used later in the computation. If the dot product length is smaller than the input vector length, or more commonly the final partial input vectors have been passed in to the PE, the completed result is stored in the drain and is ready to be taken out of the array. To ensure high throughput, reading out the array, i.e. 'draining', can be performed while partial results of the next chunk are produced and stored in the cache, as both memories operate independently. The one exception is when a set of complete results would be written into a non-empty drain. In this case the computation is stalled until the drain is empty. The array control signals for the computation stage are passed across rows whereas the control for the draining is passed across columns. Each PE is responsible for passing data in a linear fashion along its row and column. Additionally, each PE is fully pipelined such that the result of a single dot product is produced every cycle.

Depending on the desired bit width, the dot product is either performed in DSPs, constructed using logic resources or a combination of both. The PE currently supports single precision floating point (FP32), 16, 8, 4 and 2 bit Integer and Fixed Point (INT16, INT8, INT4, INT2) and more exotic data types for deep learning workloads: INT16xTernary, INT8xTernary, BinaryxBinary (BINxBIN).

For the integer and fixed point data types, the bit width of the each stage of the adder tree in the dot product is increased by one. Apart from FP32, the accumulator bit width is configurable at compile time for all data types. After accumulation and before storing into the 'cache' or 'drain', the results are truncated and rounded. Currently stochastic rounding and round to nearest are supported by the framework and are configurable at compile time.

4.2 Blocking and Interleaving

During GEMM each element in matrix A is used n times and each element in matrix B is used m times. The bandwidth can be minimized by storing both A and B on-chip and reusing each element. However, the number of on chip memories quickly becomes the limiting factor when dealing with larger matrices. To handle larger matrix sizes both A and B are partitioned into chunks and sent down in batches. This is usually referred to as blocking and is a standard practice in GEMM implementations to achieve high performance.

Interleaving on the other hand, is an architecture specific optimization designed to enable data reuse on a fine-grained level. It takes advantage of the data reuse in a GEMM and operates by feeding the same vectors into the PEs in a specific order. Both the leading dimension of matrices A and B, m and n respectively, have independent interleaving factors that are controlled at both compile and run time. Fig. 5 shows a simplified example, 1x1 array, of how interleaving operates within our hardware template. The interleaving factors for feeder A and B are 3 and 2 respectively. Each row in Feeder A and column in Feeder B are partitioned into two separate blocks, a_x and b_x respectively, the result of these partitions are accumulated to create the final 3x2 matrix.

At $t = 0$, a_0 and b_0 are passed into the PE and the partial result is stored in the first location in the cache. At $t = 1$, the pointer to memory location a is incremented, b_0 is reused and a_1 is passed into the PE; with the partial result stored in the second location in the cache. This continues on to $t = 3$ where the a memory pointer

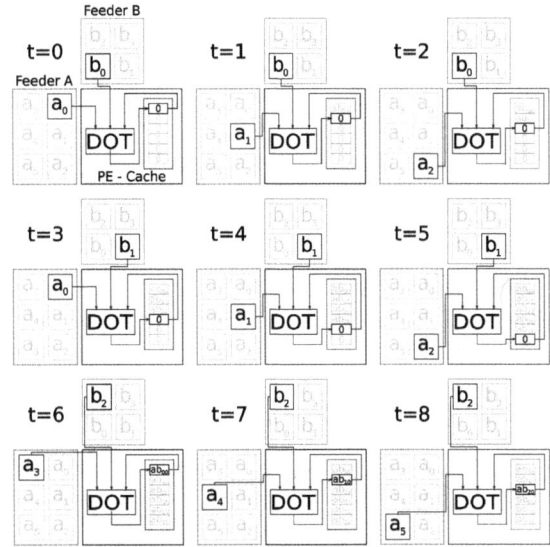

Figure 5: Interleaving Example: This shows a simplified example of how the PE operates and the concept of interleaving.

is reset back to zero and the b memory pointer is updated. Now a_0 is reused and b_1 is passed into the PE; the partial result is stored in the fourth location in the cache. At $t = 6$, the first column and row of A and B respectively, have been processed and the pointers move on to the second row and column. Instead of accumulating zeros, the previous value from $t = 0$, $a_0 b_0$, is added to the result of a_3 and b_2 and is stored back into the first location. This process continues in a similar fashion for $t = 7, ..., 11$ until all rows and columns have been processed.

Both blocking and interleaving are used together to improve performance. The blocking size is determined by the interleaving factor as well as the number of row and columns in the systolic array. Initially the interleaving size was fixed at compile time. While the systolic array would perform at near peak theoretical performance for large matrices, for smaller matrix sizes there was a significant decrease in performance. Since both matrix A and B would need to be padded with zeros until they were a multiple of the block size. We observed that by adding configurable memory interleaving support at runtime, the performance significantly improved as discussed later in Sec. 6.1.2. In most cases the optimal interleaving size can be directly calculated using $I = \min_{x_L, ..., x_H} modulo(DIM, x)$. x is the range of different interleaving values supported by the hardware template, and DIM is the leading dimension of either the A or B input matrices. Hence the size of the block's leading dimension for A and B can be calculated using $S_A = I_A * HW_{ROWS}$ and $S_B = I_B * HW_{COLS}$ respectively.

Now, given the dot product size (S_D) and the length of the block's common dimension (S_C), the number of cycles per block can be calculated using the A and B interleaving sizes (I_A and I_B) as illustrated in $Cycles = I_A * I_B * \frac{S_C}{S_D}$. Given the block sizes of A (S_AxS_C), B (S_BxS_C) and C (S_AxS_B) and $Cycles = I_A * I_B * \frac{S_C}{S_D}$, the read and write bandwidth requirements can be calculated directly using Equ. 3

$$Bandwidth = f \frac{Bytes(S_A S_C + S_B S_C + S_A S_B)}{Cycles} \quad (3)$$

where f is the operating frequency of the design and *Bytes* is the number of bytes used to represent each element of A, B and C.

5 DEEP LEARNING

This section discusses the deep learning specific optimization and hardware template features available in our framework. We describe the fused operations and dynamic dot product modules from Fig. 1.

5.1 Fused Operations

In the context of deep learning, often additional operations such as the activation function or batch normalization are performed after the FC or CONV layers.

As presented in Fig. 6a, as the results are drained out of the systolic array a post processing module can apply some basic operations. The post processing module contains a common interface such that extra functions such as sigmoid, tanh or custom scaling schemes can be added without modification to the systolic array.

5.2 Dynamic Dot Product

Training neural networks on FPGA hardware has been challenging since the gradient update step requires a higher precision. Recent work [17] has shown that through the use of a novel quantization scheme, hardware friendly backprogation is possible if a mixed precision FP32x(Binary/Ternary/Integer) dot product can be performed. To support this we added the ability to dynamically switch between dot product types during runtime. Fig. 6b presents the necessary change to the PE. To illustrate the advantages of this change, we implemented a BINxBIN dot product and a FP32xFP32 dot product. With the addition of dynamic dot product switching, both training and inference is supported on the FPGA.

For a typical layer in a state-of-the-art BNN [17] the FPGA performs the BIN X BIN operations very efficiently, hence the CPU can be freed during that time to perform other tasks in its pipeline. Tab. 2 illustrates the required operations of the middle and end portions for a binarized AlexNet. It shows that different layers can be partitioned, for both forward and backward passes, across the FPGA, CPU or using heterogeneous load balancing (FPGA+CPU). The RELU operation during the forward and backward pass can be performed on the FPGA or CPU depending on which device the result was calculated on. For the batch norm operation the forward pass can be performed on the FPGA as it is a scale and shift operation. At this time the hardware template does not support the backward computation of batch norm or pool operations and adding support is future work. To further support mixed precision,

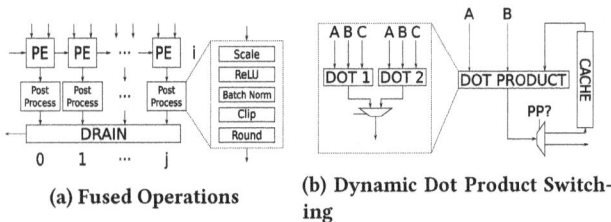

(a) Fused Operations

(b) Dynamic Dot Product Switching

Figure 6: (a) The post processing module is configurable at compile time and runtime. (b) Dynamic dot product switching allows for greater micro-architecture exploration and flexibility when designing for reduced precision networks.

Table 2: Mixed Precision Inference and Training

Layer	Location		Type	
	Forward	Backward	Forward	Backward
...	...	...	...	...
conv	FPGA	FPGA+CPU	BINxBIN	FPxBIN
c&r	FPGA	N/A	INT	STE
relu	FPGA	FPGA+CPU	INT	FP
norm	FPGA	CPU	FP	FP
pool	CPU	CPU	FP	FP
...	...	...	...	...
fc	CPU	CPU	FPxFP	FPxFP
prob	CPU	CPU	FP	FP

For the standard configuration of a BNN, a mixed precision implementation on the Xeon+FPGA utilizing the dynamic dot product could operate in this manner. The straight through estimator (STE) is used for the clipping and rounding (c&r) layer, hence no operation is required on the backwards pass.

in the future we plan to include a hybrid 2-D systolic array with mixed precision PEs between different rows or columns to alleviate routing congestion due to multiplexing between DOT types.

6 RESULTS

The results are presented in two section, first we show the performance of the GEMM for the various precisions and compare to a NVIDIA Titan X Pascal GP102 GPU on 16nm process. We illustrate the benefit of memory interleaving on various matrix sizes for three precisions, FP32, INT16 and INT8. We present our results of heterogeneous load balancing and the effect of the different partitioning sizes across the FPGA and CPU. The second section focuses on the deep learning workload. Results for three different binary network topologies, (AlexNet [15], VGGnet [25] and ResNet [13]) are presented and are evaluated against the GPU. We illustrate the impact of memory interleaving on AlexNet at various batch sizes for FP32 and discuss further possible optimizations. Finally, we investigate several possible mixed precision implementations and evaluate their performance for both training and inference. All FPGA results were gathered by measuring the wall time of the function call for each configuration on the HARPv2 system.

Since the systolic array size is configurable at compile time, it can be tailored to the resources available on the FPGA. In the case of the HARPv2, all of the available area was used to implement the hardware template minus the area taken by the Intel BBS. However, other modules could be implemented along side the hardware template at the cost of array size. For FP32, this results in 160 PEs, with an array size of 10 rows and 16 columns, operating at 312.5Mhz. With the dot product size configured to 8, this uses 1280 of the 1285 DSP available. Even though our measurements are performed on the HARPv2, the hardware template, written in SystemVerilog, is only dependent on the CCI interface and can be implemented on larger or smaller FPGAs.

6.1 GEMM

Fig. 7a presents the performance of the GEMM architecture presented in Sec. 4 on the Arria 10. Since a floating point addition and multiplication is needed for all FP32 modes, all operations are

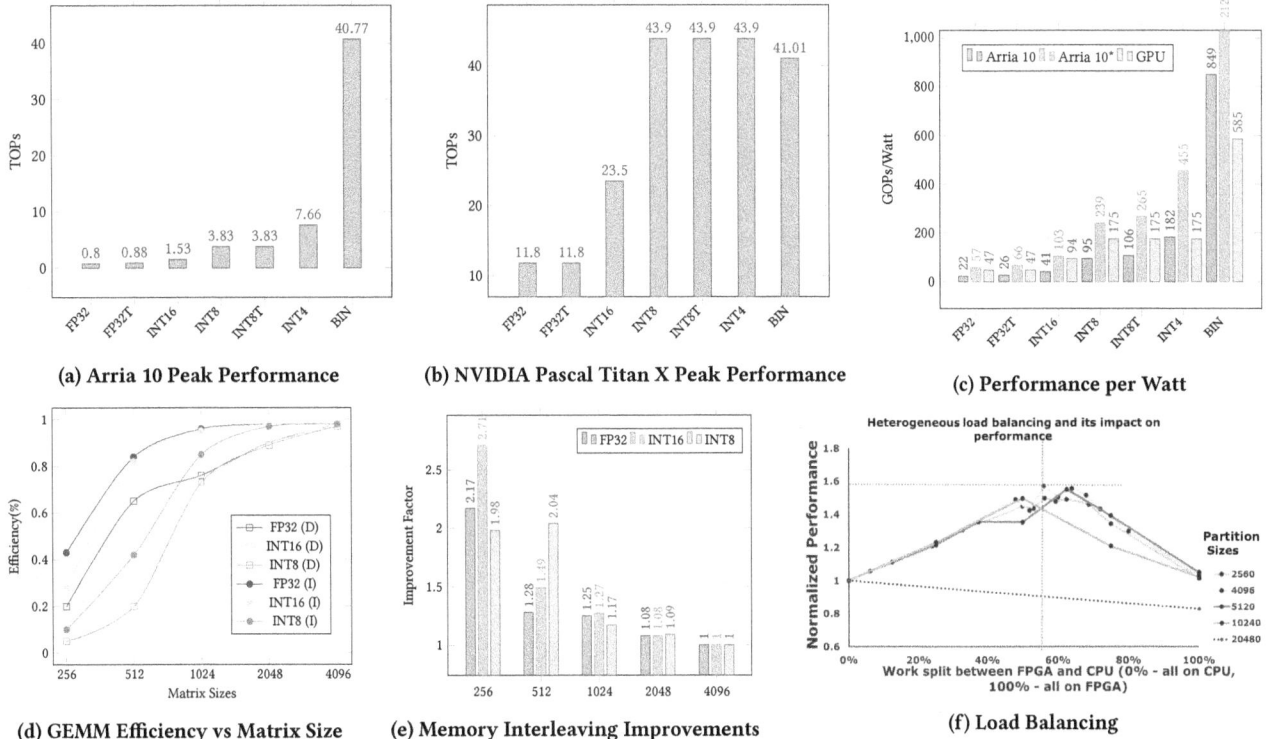

(a) Arria 10 Peak Performance

(b) NVIDIA Pascal Titan X Peak Performance

(c) Performance per Watt

(d) GEMM Efficiency vs Matrix Size

(e) Memory Interleaving Improvements

(f) Load Balancing

Figure 7: GEMM MCP Performance. (a) shows the current peak performance of the framework for a few selected precisions. (b) gives the GPU results for same precision selected in (a). (c) shows the current performance per watt for both the GPU and Arria 10 as well as *modified Arria 10 results which normalize for process node. (d) & (e) illustrates the difference between the framework with (I) and without (D) memory interleaving. (f) illustrates the load balancing results.

performed in the DSP. While it is possible to implement these operations in logic it quickly becomes very expensive and the design is constrained by routing resource when increasing the array size. Hence the performance is limited by the number of DSPs available on the chip. For FP32T (FP32xTernary) further optimizations can be made by removing the multiplication and implementing a simplified multiplexer unit.

For integer precisions we observe a better than linear scaling of performance. As the bit width becomes smaller, the dot product is a good fit for the FPGA architecture. INT16 doubles the FP32 performance since each DSP can perform two multiplications and two additions. The hardware template supports the use of logic resources when implementing a larger array. However specifically for INT16, the multiplication utilization and routing resources become a significant issue and only result in a small improvement in the peak tera-operations per second (TOPs). Since the DSP architecture does not natively support 8 bit operations, doubling the performance is achieved by using a dot product built out of both DSP and logic elements. For INT8 and INT4, extra rows are added to the array since there is sufficient logic resources available to implement additional math operations. Moving to INT8T (INT8xTernary) provides a performance per watt improvement over INT8 since: (1) each multiplication is replaced by a multiplexer (2) with the removal of the multiplication, the accumulator bit width can be reduced. The BIN GEMM is implemented completely in logic and uses an XOR and lookup-table based dot product.

6.1.1 GPU Comparison. GPUs are known for their linear algebra performance as shown in Fig. 7b, reported performance from previous studies [17, 21]. Compared to the Arria 10, the GPU has higher raw performance for all cases apart from the binary GEMM. Considering power, the FPGA shows superior performance for binary and 4 bit integer which are not a good fit for the GPU architecture. However considering that the GPU is at a newer processes node than the FPGA, TSMC 16nm and 20nm respectively, we have plotted a normalized Arria 10 result of the same design and frequency while cutting power by 60% [6]. In the normalized case, the FPGA out performs the GPU especially for the binary GEMM.

6.1.2 Memory Interleaving. Efficiency is calculated by comparing the measured TOPs to the theoretical maximum value for a given design. The theoretical TOPs are calculated by simply taking the number of compute units and multiplying by the frequency, disregarding any time for data transfer. Fig. 7d and Fig. 7e illustrate the efficiency of the array at different matrix sizes as well as the improvement of the memory interleaving optimization. The sizes tested were square matrices of the x axis labels, i.e., for 256 the A, B and C matrices are all 256x256.

For the smallest matrix size 256, we can see that for the unoptimized designs (D) the efficiency for FP32, INT16 and INT8 are all below 20%. In these cases the low efficiency is caused by an inefficient use of blocking. Memory interleaving alleviates these issues as per Equ. 3. With runtime configurable memory interleaving (I), presented in Sec. 4.2, we see a 2.7x improvement in efficiency for the smaller matrix sizes. In some cases even with memory interleaving, the efficiency of the design is quite low. Usually the data transfer of the next chunk in the input matrix is hidden during the computation of previous chunks. For smaller matrix sizes, the number of chunks are small and hence the transfer cost cannot be amortized by the compute. Additionally, the initial transfer time for the first chunks of A and B as well as the transfer of C account for the majority of the measured execution time. This issue can be resolved by staging multiple GEMMs such that transfer of the A, B and C chunks overlap with the compute from the previous GEMM. This is similar to how larger single GEMMs are performed. For matrix sizes past 512, the efficiency for all precision is above 80% and becomes 90% past 1024 where it quickly reaches peak performance. For square matrix size 4096 the effectiveness of memory interleaving has been diminished, however as discussed later in Sec. 6.2.2, non-square matrix sizes still see significant improvements.

6.1.3 Heterogeneous Load Balancing. Fig. 7f presents the performance of the FP32 GEMM when load balancing is performed over the FPGA and a 14 core Xeon CPU. Peak performance is achieved as the work split approaches 60% on the FPGA and 40% on the CPU. In this configuration the FPGA and CPU contribute similar peak performance. This is consistent for most partitioning sizes apart from 20480. In this case, the whole compute is performed on either the CPU or the FPGA. For small partitioning size either the CPU or FPGA becomes memory bound and peak performance drops. Interestingly, for this particular workload the optimal partitioning size is 4096, showing that a finer-grained partitioning of the problem performs better than coarse-grained sizes such as 10240. This illustrates that the CPU and FPGA working in tandem can achieve a 1.6x improvement in performance over a 14 core implementation.

6.2 Neural Network Evaluation

In this section we extend on previous work [18] and apply our customizable GEMM framework to three deep learning workloads: AlexNet [15], VGGnet [25] and ResNet [13]. While the GEMM targets many different precisions, we specifically target binary neural networks since: (1) from Fig. 7a, this clearly offers the best performance over a GPU and (2) recent work [17] has shown that implementations can achieve high accuracy even for binary weight and activation networks. Additionally, we provide a study on the effectiveness of memory interleaving on layer efficiency for the AlexNet topology running in FP32. Finally, we present a mixed precision training and inference scheme targeted at leverage heterogeneity and the dynamic dot product module

The evaluation was performed on both the CONV and FC layers for inference with the standard mini-batch size used for each topology. The total network performance and Images per Second (IPS) is calculated based on the weighted average of the layers operation contribution to the overall network. A runtime breakdown

Table 3: Network Performance

Device	FPGA				GPU			
	TOPs	GOPS/W	IPS	IPS/W	TOPS	GOPs/W	IPS	IPS/W
AlexNet	31.54	657.27	1610	33.54	37.60	568.09	1626	25.02
VGGNet	31.18	649.67	114	2.39	35.85	522.59	121	1.78

of each topology was collected using the 14 core Xeon Broadwell CPU running Caffe with Intel MKL2017.

6.2.1 Binary Network Performance. As shown in Fig. 7a, Fig. 7b and Fig. 7c the FPGA and GPU achieve 40.77 TOPs and 41.01 TOPs for the binary GEMM respectively, which is within 99% of their theoretical peak performance. Compared to the GPU, the FPGA achieved 849.38 GOPs per Watt which results in a 1.44x improvement in energy efficiency over the GPU at 585.86 GOPs per Watt.

As illustrated in Tab. 3, the FPGA, without load balancing, achieves 83% and 86% of the GPU raw performance for AlexNet and VGGNet. However in terms of energy efficiency (GOPs/Watt) the FPGA surpasses the GPU by 1.15x and 1.23x for AlexNet and VGGnet respectively. When extrapolating to Images per Second (IPS) the difference in network performance is less stark with the FPGA achieving 99% and 94% of the GPUs IPS for AlexNet and VGGNet respectively. Hence, the FPGA shows better Images per Second per Watt compared to the GPU for both AlexNet and VGGNet resulting in a 1.34x improvement for both topologies.

For ResNet-34 the FPGA achieves 70% of the GPU performance at 23.47 and 33.34 TOPs respectively. However it is on par for energy efficiency at 489.05 GOPs/Watt for the FPGA and 485.68 GOPs/Watt for the GPU, showing a 1.03x improvement. This drop in FPGA performance compared to AlexNet can be understood by examining the layer breakdown presented in Fig. 8a. The GPU out performs the FPGA for the first three layer sets which contribute 50% of the total operations. While increasing the batch size can alleviate some of this discrepancy, this is undesirable since it can affect training rate and total execution time.

If we examine specifically the first layer, the FPGA achieves 7.88 TOPs, which is 19% of the measured peak performance presented in Fig. 7a. The main cause of this inefficiency is introduced by the padded zeros in the common dimension of the input matrices. As future work we are planning to enable runtime configurable memory interleaving for the common dimensions of the matrices. This should result in significant performance improvements since the majority of the padded zero computations will be avoided.

6.2.2 Effect of Memory Interleaving on AlexNet. Fig. 8b and Fig. 8c show the performance of the first five convolutional layers in AlexNet for FP32. Different batch sizes ranging from 1 to 64 illustrate the performance improvement that is provided by memory interleaving. For a batch size of 1, A and B are long-skinny/short-fat matrices. Hence with fine control of the interleaving we can see 1.8x and 1.6x improvement for the first two layers, while for layer 3,4 and 5 the improvement is over 3x and up to 4x. For batch sizes of 4, 16 and 64, the A and B matrices are becoming increasingly square. Hence we don't see the same level of improvement, however it achieves near peak performance. The improvement for the first layer is more significant than the other since the first layer exhibits the worst long-skinny/short-fat matrix sizes. However it is clear that memory interleaving significantly improves the efficiency, achieving a 1.3x up to 4x improvement.

6.2.3 Dynamic Dot Product. As discussed in Sec. 5.2, mixed precision GEMMs are needed to handle both the forward and backwards pass. Typically, the first convolution and last fully connected layers are performed at full precision while the inner layers are

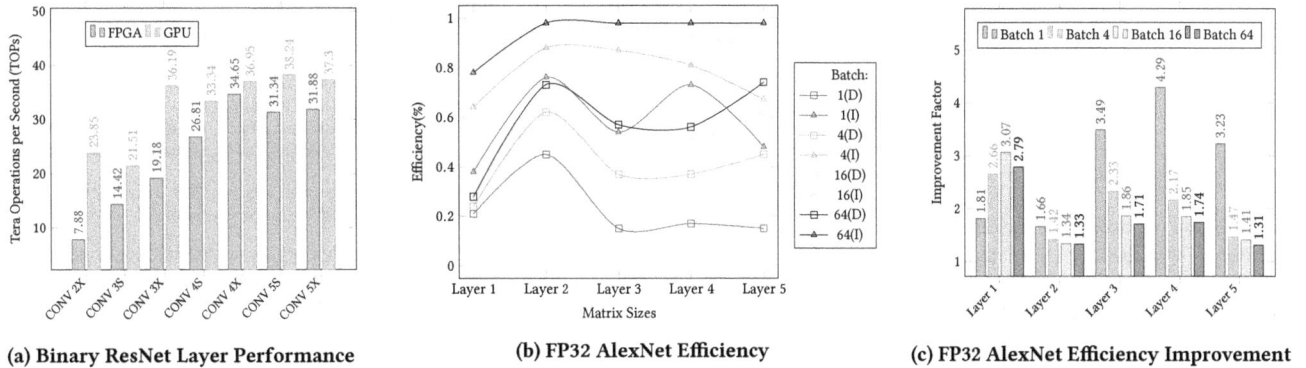

(a) Binary ResNet Layer Performance   (b) FP32 AlexNet Efficiency   (c) FP32 AlexNet Efficiency Improvement

Figure 8: (a) Binarized ResNet layer performance. (b) & (c) Breakdown of static design (D) vs configurable interleaving (I) for different batch sizes on AlexNet at FP32 precision.

performed at lower precision [17]. As shown in Tab. 2, during the backward pass, the gradients are computed using single precision floating point hence the operation is a FP32xBIN GEMM. While our framework contains an API for switching between different precisions (Sec. 3.1) the latency is determined by the partial reconfiguration (PR) time. In the cases where the PR latency is too high, a dynamic dot product may be more appropriate.

By examining the breakdown for binarized AlexNet, similar to Tab. 2, we designed three FPGA implementations, two with dynamic dot product modules, targeting different portions of the topology: (1) a single BINxBIN, (2) a BINxBIN and FPxFP, (2H) a version of (2) that performs the FPxFP GEMM utilizing heterogeneous load balancing (FPGA+CPU) and finally (3) a BINxBIN and FPxBIN. All other layer operations not supported are assumed to be implemented in software on all cores of the Xeon. Implementation (1) and (2) were synthesized for the HARPv2 whereas (3) was extrapolated using the results of (2) and the analysis from Sec. 6.1 (2) is able to perform the FPxBIN operations by representing the BIN values as floating point. Inference and training take 421ms and 892ms respectively, implementation (1) accelerates the BINxBIN operations which account for 272ms of the execution time (all in the forward pass). This corresponds to 65% and 30% of the total interference and training time respectively. (2) accelerates the most layers with the BINxBIN and FPxFP operations accounting for 327ms (77%) and 735ms (82%) of the total execution time. Finally, (3) accelerates the BINxBIN and FPxBIN operations accounting for 272ms (65%) and 593ms (66%) of inference and training time respectively.

As illustrated in Tab. 4, for pure inference, implementation (1) achieves the best results, reporting the fastest forward execution time. However for training (Forward+Backward), implementation

Table 4: Implementation Peak Performance

Impl.	BINxBIN (TOPs)	FPxFP (TFLOPs)	FPxBIN (TFLOPs)	Forward (ms)	Backward (ms)	Total (ms)
SW	-	-	-	421	471	892 (1x)
(1)	40.77	0	0	158 (F)	471 (C)	630 (1.41x)
(2)	25.4	0.8	0.8	164 (F)	537 (F)	702 (1.23x)
(3)	25.4	0	0.88	165 (F)	502 (F)	668 (1.33x)
(2H)	25.4	1.4	1.4	163 (F+C)	369 (F+C)	533 (1.67x)

Where possible, the operation was performed on the FPGA (F), the 14 core CPU (C) or using heterogeneous load balancing (F+C).

(2H) and (3) show a greater speedup, achieving 1.67x and 1.41x improvement over a software only implementation. Implementations (2), (3) and (2H) use the dynamic dot product, hence the BINxBIN performance suffers since a smaller systolic array size is used to accommodate the extra routing resources. Although implementation (2) implements all operations on the FPGA, this reduces the amount of hardware that can be dedicated to the bottlenecks, resulting in the lowest speed up, 1.23x. The CPU+FPGA implementations (1), (3) and (2H) show that the best overall performance is achieved by leveraging the CPU and specializing the implementations for only the most profitable parts of the algorithm, or by utilizing heterogeneous load balancing. Compared to other CPU+FPGA platforms, the same network performance would not be achieved since SoC type CPUs have relatively low FLOPS compared to Xeon CPU.

7 RELATED WORK

Compared to other work, our hardware template in the BINxBIN configuration achieves the highest peak TOPs, MOPs / LE and the second highest GOPs / Watt. We appreciate that comparing across different devices and manufacturers is difficult and try to ensure that accurate comparisons are made. While the results reported in [26] are for an older process node and lower frequency, [10] shows their framework performance on a device of similar size and process node as our own. It is expected that [26] should achieve better energy efficiency since the device is targeted at low power SOC applications, while ours is a data center target device. One key advantage of our hardware template is that it provides several other data types and customizations that benefit applications outside of deep learning. Additionally, with the Xeon CPU able to provide high floating point compute power, any changes to the underlying neural network algorithms, such as those presented in [17] can be supported without changes to the hardware architecture.

7.1 Existing accelerators on Xeon+FPGA

As the Xeon+FPGA platform continues to gain popularity there has been prior work that studied acceleration on this platform, such as [28, 29]. [29] studied CNN with math optimization (e.g., FFT transformation). [28] studied irregular pointer chasing applications. Heterogeneous CPU-Accelerator platforms are quickly becoming pervasive throughout computational systems and clusters. With the fast adoption of machine learning and deep learning in business, the

Table 5: Previous Work

	[26]	[10]	[30]	Our Work
Platform	Zynq z7045	Kintex US KU115	Zynq 7Z020	Arria 10 GX1150
Logic Elements (LEs)	350K	1,451K	85K	1,150K
Power (W)	11.3	41	4.7	48
TOPs (Peak)	11.612	14.8	0.32	40.77
MOPs / LE	33.17	10.19	4.43	35.45
GOPs / Watt	1027.68	360.97	44.2	849.38

computation requirements of cloud and local distributed systems is increasing at an exponential rate.

Several studies [5, 24, 27] have focused on key workloads to better understand the requirements of these algorithms and their performance on CPU+FPGA systems. [5] provides a quantitative analysis of a QPI based CPU+FGPA system compared to a PCI-E based CPU+FPGA system. Key differences between the two platforms such as different memory models and peak bandwidth were highlighted and a decision tree based flowchart was provided as a guide to assist developers when choosing a platform.

7.2 Existing NN FPGA accelerators

Previous work has been done on NN accelerators [3, 11, 20, 21, 26, 30] and our work differs in these key areas. We studied a flexible hardware template where the CPU and FPGA work in tandem to accelerate only the functions well suited to each device. Previous work has mainly focused on inference while we examined potential mixed precision implementations that accelerate both inference and training. Training is more complex than inference, as it requires more variety of operations. We showed that an "All-FPGA approach" may yield sub-optimal performance when compared to a tailored or heterogeneous approach. We handled training of NNs by relying on the Xeon CPU to leverage the existing x86 software ecosystems.

8 CONCLUSION

We presented a customizable matrix multiplication framework that includes a simple software API and a hardware template for designing custom GEMM accelerators on the HARPv2. We demonstrated that for deep learning workloads, the FPGA was either on par or exceeded what the GPU could perform in the case of binary neural networks and offered insight into some of the issues faced when designing for this system. We evaluated several heterogeneous implementations and illustrated that by dedicating FPGA resources to accelerating specific bottlenecks and utilizing the CPU for other operations, results in higher performance implementations. While the HARPv2 is still an emerging technology, it is able to stay competitive with a high performance discrete GPU by taking advantage of close collaboration between the FPGA and CPU.

ACKNOWLEDGMENT

This research was supported under the Australian Research Councils Linkage Projects funding scheme (project number LP130101034) and Zomojo Pty Ltd.

REFERENCES

[1] 2002. An Updated Set of Basic Linear Algebra Subprograms (BLAS). *ACM Trans. Math. Softw.* 28, 2 (June 2002), 135–151. https://doi.org/10.1145/567806.567807
[2] Firas Abuzaid, Stefan Hadjis, Ce Zhang, and Christopher Ré. 2015. Caffe con Troll: Shallow Ideas to Speed Up Deep Learning. *CoRR* abs/1504.04343 (2015). http://arxiv.org/abs/1504.04343
[3] Utku Aydonat, Shane O'Connell, Davor Capalija, Andrew C Ling, and Gordon R Chiu. 2017. An OpenCL (TM) Deep Learning Accelerator on Arria 10. In *ISFPGA*.
[4] Sharan Chetlur, Cliff Woolley, Philippe Vandermersch, Jonathan Cohen, John Tran, Bryan Catanzaro, and Evan Shelhamer. 2014. cuDNN: Efficient Primitives for Deep Learning. *CoRR* abs/1410.0759 (2014). http://arxiv.org/abs/1410.0759
[5] Young-kyu Choi, Jason Cong, Zhenman Fang, Yuchen Hao, Glenn Reinman, and Peng Wei. 2016. A quantitative analysis on microarchitectures of modern CPU-FPGA platforms. In *DAC*.
[6] Taiwan Semiconductor Manufacturing Company. 2013. TSMC 16/12nm Technology. (2013). http://www.tsmc.com/english/dedicatedFoundry/technology/16nm. htm
[7] NVIDIA Corporation. 2017. *NVIDIA TESLA V100 GPU ARCHITECTURE*. Technical Report WP-08608-001. NVIDIA Corporation. https://images.nvidia.com/content/volta-architecture/pdf/Volta-Architecture-Whitepaper-v1.0.pdf
[8] Matthieu Courbariaux, Yoshua Bengio, and Jean-Pierre David. 2015. BinaryConnect: Training Deep Neural Networks with Binary Weights During Propagations. In *NIPS*.
[9] Matthieu Courbariaux, Itay Hubara, Daniel Soudry, Ran El-Yaniv, and Yoshua Bengio. 2016. Binarized Neural Networks: Training Deep Neural Networks with Weights and Activations Constrained to +1 or -1. *arXiv:1602.02830* (2016).
[10] Nicholas J. Fraser, Yaman Umuroglu, Giulio Gambardella, Michaela Blott, Philip Leong, Magnus Jahre, and Kees Vissers. 2017. Scaling Binarized Neural Networks on Reconfigurable Logic. In *PARMA-DITAM*.
[11] Yijin Guan, Hao Liang, Ningyi Xu, Wenqiang Wang, Shaoshuai Shi, Xi Chen, Guangyu Sun, Wei Zhang, and Jason Cong. 2017. FP-DNN: An Automated Framework for Mapping Deep Neural Networks onto FPGAs with RTL-HLS Hybrid Templates. In *FCCM*.
[12] PK Gupta. 2016. Accelerating Datacenter Workloads. In *FPL*.
[13] Kaiming He, Xiangyu Zhang, Shaoqing Ren, and Jian Sun. 2016. Deep Residual Learning for Image Recognition. In *CVPR*.
[14] Norman P. Jouppi, Cliff Young, Nishant Patil, David Patterson, and et. al. 2017. In-Datacenter Performance Analysis of a Tensor Processing Unit. *CoRR* abs/1704.04760 (2017). http://arxiv.org/abs/1704.04760
[15] Alex Krizhevsky, Ilya Sutskever, and Geoffrey E. Hinton. 2012. ImageNet Classification with Deep Convolutional Neural Networks. In *NIPS*.
[16] Andrew Lavin. 2015. Fast Algorithms for Convolutional Neural Networks. *CoRR* abs/1509.09308 (2015). http://arxiv.org/abs/1509.09308
[17] Asit K. Mishra, Eriko Nurvitadhi, Jeffrey J. Cook, and Debbie Marr. 2017. WRPN: Training and Inference using Wide Reduced-Precision Networks. *CoRR* abs/1709.01134 (2017). http://arxiv.org/abs/1709.01134
[18] Duncan Moss, Eriko Nurvitadhi, Jaewoong Sim, Asit Mishra, Suchit Subhaschandra, and Debbie Marr. 2017. High Performance Binary Neural Networks on the Xeon+FPGA Platform. In *FPL*.
[19] Sharan Narang. 2016. DeepBench. (2016). https://svail.github.io/DeepBench/
[20] Eriko Nurvitadhi, David Sheffield, Jaewoong Sim, Asit Mishra, Ganesh Venkatesh, and Debbie Marr. 2016. Accelerating Binarized Neural Networks: Comparison of FPGA, CPU, GPU, and ASIC. In *FPT*.
[21] Eriko Nurvitadhi, Ganesh Venkatesh, Jaewoong Sim, Debbie Marr, Randy Huang, Jason Ong Gee Hock, Yeong Tat Liew, Krishnan Srivatsan, Duncan Moss, Suchit Subhaschandra, and Guy Boudoukh. 2017. Can FPGAs Beat GPUs in Accelerating Next-Generation Deep Neural Networks?. In *ISFPGA*.
[22] Mohammad Rastegari, Vicente Ordonez, Joseph Redmon, and Ali Farhadi. 2016. XNOR-Net: Imagenet Classification Using Binary Convolutional Neural Networks. In *ECCV*.
[23] Olga Russakovsky, Jia Deng, Hao Su, Jonathan Krause, Sanjeev Satheesh, Sean Ma, Zhiheng Huang, Andrej Karpathy, Aditya Khosla, Michael Bernstein, Alexander C. Berg, and Li Fei-Fei. 2015. ImageNet Large Scale Visual Recognition Challenge. *International Journal of Computer Vision (IJCV)* 115, 3 (2015), 211–252. https://doi.org/10.1007/s11263-015-0816-y
[24] David Sidler, Zsolt István, Muhsen Owaida, and Gustavo Alonso. 2017. Accelerating pattern matching queries in hybrid CPU-FPGA architectures. In *Proceedings of the 2017 ACM International Conference on Management of Data*.
[25] Karen Simonyan and Andrew Zisserman. 2014. Very Deep Convolutional Networks for Large-scale Image Recognition. *arXiv:1409.1556* (2014).
[26] Yaman Umuroglu, Nicholas J Fraser, Giulio Gambardella, Michaela Blott, Philip Leong, Magnus Jahre, and Kees Vissers. 2017. FINN: A Framework for Fast, Scalable Binarized Neural Network Inference. In *ISFPGA*.
[27] Xuechao Wei, Yun Liang, Tao Wang, Songwu Lu, and Jason Cong. 2017. Throughput optimization for streaming applications on CPU-FPGA heterogeneous systems. In *ASP-DAC*. IEEE.
[28] Gabriel Weisz, Joseph Melber, Yu Wang, Kermin Fleming, Eriko Nurvitadhi, and James C Hoe. 2016. A study of pointer-chasing performance on shared-memory processor-FPGA systems. In *ISFPGA*.
[29] Chi Zhang and Viktor Prasanna. 2017. Frequency Domain Acceleration of Convolutional Neural Networks on CPU-FPGA Shared Memory System. In *FPGA*.
[30] Ritchie Zhao, Weinan Song, Wentao Zhang, Tianwei Xing, Jeng-Hau Lin, Mani Srivastava, Rajesh Gupta, and Zhiru Zhang. 2017. Accelerating Binarized Convolutional Neural Networks with Software-Programmable FPGAs. In *ISFPGA*.

A Framework for Generating High Throughput CNN Implementations on FPGAs

Hanqing Zeng
University of Southern California
Ming Hsieh Department of Electrical Engineering
zengh@usc.edu

Ren Chen
University of Southern California
Ming Hsieh Department of Electrical Engineering
renchen@usc.edu

Chi Zhang
University of Southern California
Department of Computer Science
zhan527@usc.edu

Viktor Prasanna
University of Southern California
Ming Hsieh Department of Electrical Engineering
prasanna@usc.edu

ABSTRACT

We propose a framework to generate highly efficient accelerators for inferencing on FPGAs. Our framework consists of multiple algorithmic optimizations for computation complexity and communication volume reduction, a mapping methodology for efficient resource utilization, and a tool for automatic `Verilog` generation. The algorithmic optimizations improve throughput of frequency domain convolution so as to satisfy a given set of hardware constraints. While the Overlap-and-Add (OaA) technique has been known, it performs "wasted" computation at the edges. We propose a novel Concatenate-and-Pad (CaP) technique, which improves OaA significantly by reducing the "wasted" computation on the padded pixels. The proposed CaP used in conjunction with OaA enables us to choose a fixed FFT size at design time, and achieve low computation complexity for layers with various image sizes and kernel window sizes. We also develop a novel frequency domain loop tiling technique to further boost the throughput by improving data reuse. Our mapping methodology optimizes the architecture for the target device by fast design space exploration. We quantitatively categorize FPGAs by capturing their DSP resources, on-chip memory size and external memory bandwidth into a device coefficient. We identify the optimal architectural parameters based on the tradeoff between computation and communication cost. Our framework includes a tool to automatically generate fully synthesizable `Verilog`. We demonstrate the framework by generating high throughput accelerators for state-of-the-art CNN models on Intel HARP heterogeneous platform. Using our framework, we achieve throughput of 780.6 *GOPS*, 669.1 *GOPS* and 552.1 *GOPS* for AlexNet, VGG16 and FCN-16s respectively. These correspond to 6.8× (AlexNet) and 4.9× (VGG16) improvement compared with the state-of-the-art implementations.

FPGA'2018, February 25–27, 2018, Monterey, CA, USA
© 2018 Association for Computing Machinery.
ACM ISBN 978-1-4503-5614-5/18/02...$15.00
https://doi.org/10.1145/3174243.3174265

KEYWORDS

Convolutional Neural Networks; Algorithmic Optimization; Hardware Mapping; Software-Hardware Co-design; FPGA;

ACM Reference Format:
Hanqing Zeng, Ren Chen, Chi Zhang, and Viktor Prasanna. 2018. A Framework for Generating High Throughput CNN Implementations on FPGAs. In *FPGA'18: 2018 ACM/SIGDA International Symposium on Field-Programmable Gate Arrays, February 25–27, 2018, Monterey, CA, USA.* ACM, New York, NY, USA, 10 pages. https://doi.org/10.1145/3174243.3174265

1 INTRODUCTION

Convolutional Neural Networks (CNNs) are one of the most influential innovations in machine learning and computer vision [9, 15, 16]. With proliferation of deep learning models, the complexity and diversity of state-of-the-art CNNs has increased significantly.

Several challenges exist in accelerating CNNs on FPGAs:

- *Computation complexity*: Convolution layers of CNNs perform computationally expensive operations.
- *Hardware efficiency*: Efficiently accelerating various convolution layers is hard, due to the large variation of CNN model parameters across layers. The problems to be addressed are:
  - *Reconfiguration*: Hardware runtime reconfiguration can potentially meet the diverse computational requirements of various layers. However, time and resource overhead are incurred to support the flexibility in hardware.
  - *Wasted computation*: Using fixed hardware for acceleration avoids reconfiguration overhead. However, significant amount of computation can be wasted due to padding.
  - *Data reuse*: Given an on-chip memory of limited size, the accelerator needs to efficiently reuse on-chip data so as to reduce the communication volume to external memory.

Motivated by the above challenges, we propose a framework to generate high throughput accelerators for diverse CNN models. The inputs of the framework are the CNN model parameters (image size, kernel filter window size, number of input and output feature maps) and the FPGA device meta data (DSP resources, on-chip memory size and external bandwidth). The output is the automatically generated architecture on the target device specified in `Verilog`. To address the *computation complexity challenge*, our framework alleviates the computation burden of spatial convolution by frequency domain convolution. To address the *hardware utilization challenge*, we solve the problems in *reconfiguration*, *wasted computation* and *data reuse* by multiple algorithmic optimizations. The Overlap-and-Add (OaA) operation has been used in [21] to implement frequency domain convolution with a fixed-size FFT module. We significantly improve the OaA approach by a novel Concatenate-and-Pad (CaP) operation. Compared with OaA, CaP achieves much lower computation complexity by filling the paddings with pixels from other images within the same batch. By applying CaP in conjunction with OaA, we identify a fixed FFT size in design time. Thus, without runtime reconfiguration, the accelerator achieves high throughput for layers with diverse image sizes and kernel filter window sizes. We further propose the frequency domain loop tiling technique which partitions the data blocks returned from the CaP-OaA step. Total communication volume to external memory is reduced as a result of increased reuse of on-chip data. In summary, our algorithmic optimizations perform light weight data layout rearrangement so that data from various layers are efficiently blocked into identical shapes before loaded onto FPGA. To optimize the architecture based on the FPGA resources, we then propose a hardware mapping methodology. A simplified performance model leads to fast design space exploration, which identifies the optimal architectural parameters by saturating the computation or communication capacity of the target device. Finally, a tool is developed to automatically generate implementations in `Verilog`. Our main contributions are:

- We propose algorithmic optimizations to improve throughput:
  - Concatenate-and-Pad (CaP) operation, a dual of Overlap-and-Add (OaA), which significantly improves the OaA based approach by reducing computation on paddings.
  - A data blocking methodology, which enables a fixed size FFT module to achieve low computation complexity for layers with various image and kernel window sizes.
  - Frequency domain loop tiling, which increases reuse of on-chip data by partitioning the feature map dimensions.
- We propose hardware mapping that incorporates the above algorithmic optimizations:
  - A generic architecture, which accelerates diverse CNNs on the target device without runtime reconfiguration.
  - A device coefficient, which measures the computation and communication capacity of the target FPGA by on-chip DSP resources, memory size and external bandwidth.
  - Fast design space exploration methodology, which identifies optimal architectural parameters on the target device.
- We develop a code generation tool that outputs fully synthesizable `Verilog` based on the resulting hardware mapping.
- We show that on Intel HARP platform, our techniques lead to throughput of 780.6 *GOPS*, 669.1 *GOPS* and 552.1 *GOPS* for AlexNet, VGG16 and FCN-16s respectively. The throughput corresponds to 6.8× (AlexNet) and 4.9× (VGG16) improvements compared with the state-of-the-art designs.

2 BACKGROUND

2.1 Frequency Domain Convolution and Overlap-and-Add (OaA)

We start from reviewing the convolution algorithm for 2D matrices.

Let I (shape: $l_{img} \times l_{img}$) and K (shape: $l_{kern} \times l_{kern}$) be the input and kernel matrices. Let M (shape: $l'_{img} \times l'_{img}$) be the output

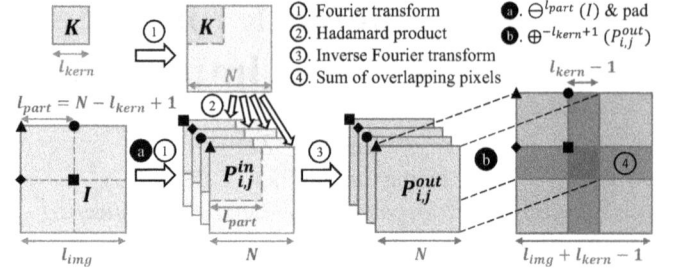

Figure 1: Frequency domain convolution using OaA

matrix. After transforming I and K into frequency domain representation, the sliding window operation of space convolution turns into the Hadamard product operation ($\circ$). *Equation 1* summarizes the algorithm for frequency domain convolution, where $\mathcal{F}$ and $\mathcal{F}^{-1}$ denote Fourier transform and its inverse operation.

$$M = I * K = \mathcal{F}^{-1}\big(\mathcal{F}(I) \circ \mathcal{F}(K)\big) \qquad (1)$$

To perform the Hadamard product operation, dimensions l_{img}, l_{kern} of I, K need to be zero-padded to the same size before Fourier transform. When l_{img} is large (as is often the case for the first few convolution layers of a CNN), computing FFT on the complete I is not efficient. The Overlap-and-Add (OaA) technique [5] addresses the problem by partitioning I before the Fourier transform step.

The following describes the procedures of computing $I * K$ using OaA. Suppose we convolve I with K using N-point 2D FFT units (where $N > l_{kern} - 1$). First, we partition I into $P^{in}_{i,j}$ of shape $l_{part} \times l_{part}$ (where $l_{part} + l_{kern} - 1 = N$). Then, after zero padding $P^{in}_{i,j}$ to shape $N \times N$, we compute the intermediate output matrices $P^{out}_{i,j}$ using *Equation 2*. The final output matrix M is obtained by placing $P^{out}_{i,j}$ so that their up-left corners (pixel $(0, 0)$) are located at pixels $(i \cdot l_{part}, j \cdot l_{part})$ of M. Value of each pixel in M is the sum of the overlapping pixels in $P^{out}_{i,j}$, as shown in *Equation 3* and *Figure 1*.

$$P^{out}_{i,j} = \mathcal{F}^{-1}\big(\mathcal{F}(P^{in}_{i,j}) \circ \mathcal{F}(K)\big) \qquad (2)$$

$$M[p][q] = \sum_{i,j} \big(P^{out}_{i,j}[p - i \cdot l_{part}][q - j \cdot l_{part}]\big)$$

$$\text{where} \quad \begin{cases} 0 \leqslant p - i \cdot l_{part} < l_{part} \\ 0 \leqslant q - j \cdot l_{part} < l_{part} \end{cases} \qquad (3)$$

Value enclosed by square brackets ([*][*]) indicates the pixel index within the matrix. All indices i, j, p, q start from 0.

We define operators $\ominus$ and $\oplus$. Operation $\ominus^y(I)$ partitions I into matrices of shape $y \times y$; $\oplus^{-x}(P)$ generates a large matrix from a set of matrices $\{P\}$ with x pixels overlapped, based on *Equation 3*.

2.2 Convolution Layers Using OaA

A convolution layer operates on a set of I and K, and outputs a set of M. Define I^{layer}, K^{layer} and M^{layer} as the high dimensional arrays of input, kernel filters and output feature maps of a layer. For batch processing, I^{layer}, K^{layer} and M^{layer} are of dimension $Batch \times f_{in} \times l_{img}^2$, $f_{out} \times f_{in} \times l_{kern}^2$ and $Batch \times f_{out} \times l_{img}'^2$ respectively, where f_{in}, f_{out} are number of input, output feature maps. Let b, n and m index into the *Batch*, f_{in} and f_{out} dimensions. *Equation 4* specifies the operations of a convolution layer.

$$M_{b,m}^{layer} = \sum_{n < f_{in}} (I_{b,n}^{layer} * K_{m,n}^{layer}) \tag{4}$$

Algorithm 1 shows the operations of a convolution layer using OaA. Since K^{layer} is fixed for a trained CNN, we calculate $K^{freq} = \mathcal{F}(K^{layer})$ prior to the CNN inferencing computation.

Algorithm 1: Batch processing of a convolution layer using the OaA technique

---

Input : I^{layer} of shape $Batch \times f_{in} \times l_{img}^2$
$\quad\quad\quad$ K^{freq} of shape $f_{out} \times f_{in} \times N^2$
Output: M^{layer} of shape $Batch \times f_{out} \times l_{img}'^2$

1 **for** $b = 0$ to $(Batch - 1)$ **do**
2 $\quad$ **for** i, j iterating matrices of $\ominus^{l_{part}}(I_b^{layer})$ **do**
3 $\quad\quad$ **for** $n = 0$ to $(f_{in} - 1)$ **do**
4 $\quad\quad\quad$ $P_{n,i,j}^{in,freq} \leftarrow \mathcal{F}(P_{n,i,j}^{in,padded})$
5 $\quad\quad$ **for** $m = 0$ to $(f_{out} - 1)$ **do**
6 $\quad\quad\quad$ **for** $n = 0$ to $(f_{in} - 1)$ **do**
   $\quad\quad\quad\quad$ // Element-wise MAC operation
7 $\quad\quad\quad\quad$ $P' \leftarrow P_{n,i,j}^{in,freq} \circ K_{m,n}^{freq}$
8 $\quad\quad\quad\quad$ $P_{m,i,j}^{out,freq} \leftarrow P_{m,i,j}^{out,freq} + P'$
9 $\quad\quad\quad$ $P_{m,i,j}^{out} \leftarrow \mathcal{F}^{-1}(P_{m,i,j}^{out,freq})$
10 $\quad$ **for** $m = 0$ to $(f_{out} - 1)$ **do**
11 $\quad\quad$ $M_{b,m}^{layer} \leftarrow \oplus^{-l_{kern}+1}(P_{m,*,*}^{out})$
12 **return** M^{layer}

2.3 CNN Applications and Models

Feature extraction is fundamental to many applications. With little preprocessing on input images, CNNs extract high dimensional features associated with receptive fields of various sizes. Thus, variations of CNNs can be developed for specific applications.

We select three large scale state-of-the-art CNNs: AlexNet [9], VGG16 [15] and FCN-16s [11]. AlexNet and VGG16 can perform the tasks of feature extraction as well as image classification. FCN-16s is designed specifically for image segmentation. For feature extraction of AlexNet and VGG16, we execute all the convolution, ReLU and pooling layers, and skip the final fully connected layers. The input images can be of any l_{img} value. For image classification of AlexNet and VGG16, we execute all the layers including the fully-connected layers. The input images are scaled to be 224×224 pixels before feeding into the networks. For semantic segmentation of FCN-16s, we deploy deconvolution layers to replace fully connected layers. FCN-16s takes images of any l_{img} value as its input.

The above three CNNs are representatives of a wide range of recently developed deep CNNs. In general, the model parameters $l_{img}, l_{kern}, f_{in}$ and f_{out} change dramatically from the first convolution layer to the last. As an example, *Table 1* summarizes the variation of these parameters for AlexNet, VGG16 and FCN-16s.

Table 1: Variation of model parameters

CNN	Conv. Layers	l_{kern}	$\frac{\max l_{img}}{\min l_{img}}$	$\frac{\max f_{in}}{\min f_{in}}$	$\frac{\max f_{out}}{\min f_{out}}$
AlexNet	5	11,5,3	17	128	4
VGG16	13	3	16	170	8
FCN-16s	18	7,3,1	50	1365	64

3 ALGORITHMIC OPTIMIZATIONS

Due to the large variation of $l_{kern}, l_{img}, f_{in}$ and f_{out}, using a fixed architecture to accelerate various CNN models, or even for various layers of the same CNN model is very challenging. We show in this section three algorithmic optimizations to block input data into identical shapes after data layout rearrangement. As a result, computation complexity and communication cost are reduced, and a fixed hardware architecture (*Section 4*) on a target FPGA efficiently accelerates various CNNs. We show the procedure of hardware mapping and performance analysis in *Section 5*.

3.1 OaA Using Fixed FFT Size

For *native* frequency domain convolution, the FFT size is equal to $(l_{img} + l_{kern} - 1)$ and FFT is applied to the complete I at once without partitioning. The native approach is hard to be realized by accelerators, as hardware does not efficiently support FFT of arbitrary sizes. Previous work [21] addressed the hardware limitation by using the OaA technique. Their complexity analysis was based on 2D convolution without considering the f_{in} and f_{out} dimensions. We show in this section a more accurate complexity analysis on high dimensional convolution performed by a CNN layer. We also discuss how to select an appropriate FFT size for various l_{kern}.

According to *Algorithm 1*, for an FFT size N, number of operations performed by a convolution layer is calculated as:

$$O_{total} = \left(O_{part,FFT} + O_{part,MAC} + O_{part,IFFT} + O_{part,OaA} \right) \cdot \left\lceil \frac{l_{img}}{N - l_{kern} + 1} \right\rceil^2 \tag{5}$$

where:

$$O_{part,FFT} = C_1 \cdot N^2 \cdot \log N \cdot f_{in}$$
$$O_{part,IFFT} = C_1 \cdot N^2 \cdot \log N \cdot f_{out}$$
$$O_{part,MAC} = C_2 \cdot N^2 \cdot f_{in} \cdot f_{out}$$
$$O_{part,OaA} = C_3 \cdot N \cdot (l_{kern} - 1) \cdot f_{out}$$

C_* are constants reflecting the cost of addition or multiplication.

We perform the following approximation to *Equation 5*: (1) Ignoring $O_{part,FFT}$ and $O_{part,IFFT}$: OaA performs partitioning of matrix I (l_{img}: order of 10^1 or 10^2), so it is reasonable to assume N to be in the order of 10^1. Observing that f_{in} and f_{out} are typically in the order of 10^2, the coefficient $\log N$ of $O_{part,FFT}$ ($O_{part,IFFT}$) is negligible compared with the coefficient f_{out} (f_{in}) of $O_{part,MAC}$. (2) Ignoring $O_{part,OaA}$: As required by OaA, ($l_{kern} - 1$) should be less than N. So $O_{part,OaA} < C_3 \cdot N^2 \cdot f_{out} \ll O_{part,MAC}$. (3) Ignoring the ceiling function: We will discuss the effect of $\lceil * \rceil$ in detail in *Section 3.2*. We approximate *Equation 5* by:

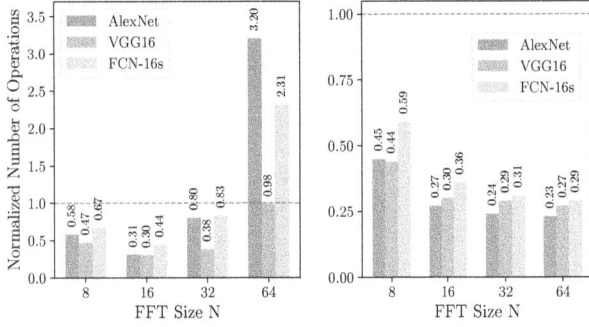

(a) OaA Approach   **(b) CaP-OaA Approach**

Figure 2: Number of operations for three CNNs. For AlexNet we exclude the first convolution layer, as 8-point FFT cannot be applied to l_{kern} of 11 using OaA. The images input to the CNNs are of size 224×224, 224×224 and 500×500 for AlexNet VGG16 and FCN-16s respectively.

$$O_{total}^{approx} \approx C_2 \cdot f_{in} \cdot f_{out} \cdot \left(\frac{l_{img}}{1 - (l_{kern} - 1)/N} \right)^2 \quad (6)$$

We conclude that:

(1) Number of operations decreases as N increases;

(2) Benefit of increasing N diminishes when N is sufficiently larger than $(l_{kern} - 1)$.

From *Table 1*, we observe that for the three CNNs, all l_{kern} are less than 10 (except the first convolution layer of AlexNet). Taking the radix-$2n$ FFT architecture [6] as an example, this means that setting N to be as small as 16 likely results in low enough computation complexity. *Figure 2a* shows the number of operations for AlexNet, VGG16 and FCN-16s according to *Equation 5*. Number of operations for OaA using various N (bars) are normalized by number of operations for spatial convolution (dashed line).

We observe that the best configuration is $N = 16$. If N keeps increases, computation complexity increases as opposed to the conclusion on *Equation 6*. This is because when N is 32 or 64, value of N is much larger than l_{img} of deep layers. Ceiling function in *Equation 5* then comes into picture. We show in *Section 3.2* the CaP operation to address this issue and justify our approximation to the ceiling function. We also observe that by applying OaA with a 16-point FFT module, we achieve significant reduction compared with spatial convolution. OaA using an uniform FFT size thus potentially processes convolution layers of various l_{kern} very efficiently. Note that our computation complexity is even much lower than the results in [21]. This is due to an additional optimization to utilize the imaginary channel for complex number operations (*Section 3.4*).

3.2 CaP for Reducing Wasted Computations

OaA requires the shape of each partition to be $N \times N$. The analysis on *Equation 6* ignores the useless computation on the zero paddings of $P_{i,j}^{in}$. Such approximation is not always valid, as can be seen in *Figure 2a* when $N = 32$ or 64. Two examples are shown in *Figure 3*. Scenario 1 is for deep layers when l_{img} is small and scenario 2 happens when l_{img} is larger.

One possible solution is to select an appropriate N which fits well l_{img} of most layers. The first problem is, this technique significantly

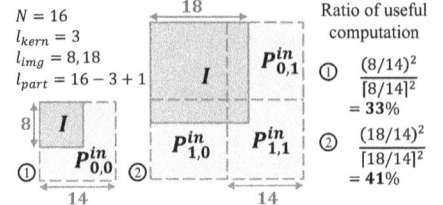

Figure 3: Examples showing that the majority of computa-

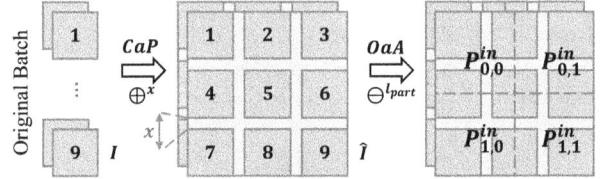

Figure 4: An example showing the CaP technique

limits the choices of N, leaving little freedom for architectural tuning on a target FPGA (*Section 5*). More importantly, identifying such an N value is often impossible. l_{img} can be of arbitrary value. This is especially the case for feature extraction applications, where images are not scaled to a fixed size before fed into the CNNs. An alternative solution is to mask the padded pixels. This saves number of operations, but still leads to low resource efficiency in hardware.

Instead of avoiding computation on paddings, we solve the problem from another perspective by filling the padded pixels with useful information. Based on *Equation 4*, out of the two dimensions involved in I^{layer} (Batch and f_{in}), f_{in} is shared between I^{layer} and K^{layer}. Batch is independent of K^{layer}. Thus, we fold the Batch dimension and expand I to solve the padding issue of OaA.

We call our operation Concatenate-and-Pad (CaP) [19]. Given a batch of d^2 images I of equal size $l_{img} \times l_{img}$, we arrange the images I in a $d \times d$ mesh, with x pixels of zero paddings between the vertically or horizontally adjacent images. CaP outputs a large image $\widehat{I}$ by concatenating multiple input images I. Parameter x is defined as the padding size of CaP. Parameter d is defined as the Batch folding factor. *Figure 4* illustrates how CaP reduces the wasted computation of OaA.

We observe the following with respect to the CaP operation. (1) *Aliasing* among adjacent images: The OaA operation that follows CaP may apply kernel windows covering pixels of multiple images (Step 2 in *Figure 1* and step OaA in *Figure 4*). It can be shown that aliasing among adjacent I in $\widehat{I}$ can be avoided iff $x \geq l_{kern} - 1$. (2) *Duality* of the OaA and CaP operations: OaA *partitions* images, and CaP *combines* images. OaA processes a set of matrices by *overlapping* pixels (Step 4 in *Figure 1*), and CaP processes a set of matrices by *padding* pixels (Step CaP in *Figure 4*). Since CaP is a dual of OaA, we can extend the $\oplus^x$ operator (*Section 2.1*). If the superscript x is negative, then we use $\oplus^x$ to compute step b in *Figure 1*. If x is positive, we use $\oplus^x$ to compute $\widehat{I} = \oplus^x(I)$ in CaP.

In summary, we CaP the I_{layer} array so that input of $Batch \times f_{in} \times l_{img}^2$ is reshaped to $\frac{Batch}{d^2} \times f_{in} \times \widehat{l_{img}}^2$, where $\widehat{l_{img}} = d \cdot l_{img} + (d - 1) \cdot (l_{kern} - 1)$. We then apply OaA to $\widehat{I}$. Abbreviate such operations

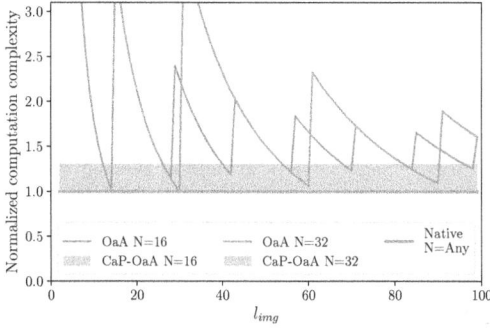

Figure 5: Comparison of computation complexity

as CaP-OaA. It is worth noticing that the various frequency domain convolution algorithms discussed so far are closely related to each other. CaP-OaA reduces to OaA when $d = 1$. OaA further reduces to native frequency domain convolution when $N \geqslant l_{img} + l_{kern} - 1$. Therefore, CaP-OaA is the most general version among these frequency domain convolution algorithms. CaP-OaA also achieves the highest hardware efficiency.

We further quantitatively analyze the computation complexity of CaP-OaA. CaP introduces a new variable d whose value can be set to approximate the ceiling function in *Equation 5*. It can be shown that by setting $d = \frac{N-(l_{kern}-1)}{\gcd(l_{img}+l_{kern}-1,\,N-(l_{kern}-1))}$ (where gcd means Greatest Common Divisor), the complexity of CaP-OaA is:

$$O_{CaP-OaA} < C_2 \cdot f_{in} \cdot f_{out} \cdot \left(\frac{l_{img} + l_{kern} - 1}{1 - (l_{kern} - 1)/N} \right)^2 \quad (7)$$

We compare OaA and CaP-OaA with the native approach as follow, where $O_{native} = C_2 \cdot f_{in} \cdot f_{out} \cdot (l_{img} + l_{kern} - 1)^2$.

$$\frac{O_{OaA}}{O_{native}} = \left(\frac{\lceil \frac{l_{img}}{N - l_{kern} + 1} \rceil \cdot N}{l_{img} + l_{kern} - 1} \right)^2$$

$$\frac{O_{CaP-OaA}}{O_{native}} < \left(\frac{1}{1 - (l_{kern} - 1)/N} \right)^2 \quad (8)$$

The native approach achieves the lowest computation complexity compared with OaA and CaP-OaA. However, it requires the hardware to support FFT of arbitrary size. In the best case, OaA requires the same amount of computation as the native approach. Yet performance of OaA is highly dependent on N. As for CaP-OaA, as long as N is sufficiently larger than $(l_{kern} - 1)$, it ensures its computation complexity to be close to the native approach.

Figure 5 verifies our computation complexity analysis on the three algorithms. We vary l_{img} from 3 to 100, and fix l_{kern} to be 3. Complexity of CaP-OaA and OaA are normalized by complexity of the native approach. Colored areas for CaP-OaA show the possible ranges of its computation complexity according to *Equation 8*.

Figure 2b shows the number of operations for three CNNs using CaP-OaA. Compared with *Figure 2a*, we conclude that given any fixed N, CaP-OaA achieves low computation complexity consistently for convolution layers of various l_{kern} and arbitrary l_{img}.

3.3 Frequency Domain Loop Tiling

The CaP-OaA technique manipulates the data dimensions l_{img} and l_{kern}. To block data of convolution layers into identical shapes, we still need optimization on the f_{in} and f_{out} dimensions.

We revisit *Algorithm 1*. Tiling of the loop dimensions in lines 5 and 6 performs partitioning of f_{in} and f_{out}. In runtime, the kernel filters and image data are partitioned into fixed shapes, and the tiles are loaded onto FPGA. Tiling on top of CaP-OaA makes the data flow of diverse CNNs on a target device identical to each other. The tiling factor f is the same for various convolution layers. After CaP-OaA transforms the kernel filters and images to an uniform $N \times N$ shape, value of f becomes independent of the CNN model parameters, and is solely bound by the on-chip memory size. The motivation for loop tiling is to reduce the communication volume to external memory by increased reuse of on-chip data [4]. For frequency domain convolution, tradeoff exists between N and f to balance computation complexity and data reuse. Analysis on the algorithm-architecture co-design is made in *Section 5*.

Although loop optimization for CNNs on FPGAs has been extensively studied, previous work [4, 8, 12] focused on convolution in space domain. Existing techniques cannot be directly applied to frequency domain CNNs, since data flow of sliding window operations is different from Hadamard product operations. On the other hand, our three techniques proposed in *Section 3.1*, 3.2 and 3.3 can all be understood as loop optimizations in frequency domain. OaA is analogous to loop tiling of l_{img}, and CaP is analogous to loop tiling and unrolling of the *Batch* dimension.

With the optimizations in *Section 3.1*, 3.2 and 3.3, we derive *Algorithm 2* from *Algorithm 1*. Lines 6 to 13 shows the workload on FPGA. The rest of the algorithm specifies the operations by CPU. Loop unrolling of lines 9 and 10 is discussed in *Section 4*.

3.4 Composing a Complex Image

Fourier transform converts a real number image into complex number representation. A straightforward implementation feeds input image data to the real channel and zeros to the imaginary channel. To better utilize the hardware resources, a better implementation feeds two images within a batch to the real and imaginary channels simultaneously. Thus, given two images I_1, I_2 and kernel filter K, we perform $(I_1 + j \cdot I_2) * K = \mathcal{F}^{-1}\left(\mathcal{F}(I_1 + j \cdot I_2) \circ \mathcal{F}(K) \right) = (I_1 * K) + j \cdot (I_2 * K)$, where I_1, I_2 and K are all of real values.

Composing a complex image reduces the computation complexity *by half*, and *doubles* the efficiency of hardware DSPs. The technique in this section can be easily combined with OaA-CaP.

4 SYSTEM ARCHITECTURE

We define throughput (bandwidth) as the number of complex words transferred per unit time. Also, the number of DSPs used in implementing a complex multiplier-accumulator as the unit of DSP resources; bytes per complex word as the unit of on-chip memory. Hardware parallelism is measured in terms of number of parallel operations on complex data.

4.1 Data Reuse Scheme

Image or kernel oriented data reuse schemes have both been explored in previous work [3] for spatial convolution. In our design,

---

Algorithm 2: Batch processing of a convolution layer using CaP-OaA and f_{in}, f_{out} loop tiling

---

Input: I^{layer} of shape $Batch \times f_{in} \times l_{img}^2$
K^{freq} of shape $f_{out} \times f_{in} \times N^2$; $K^{freq} = \mathcal{F}(K^{layer})$

Output: M^{layer} of shape $Batch \times f_{out} \times l_{img}'^2$

1 **for** $b = 0$ to $(Batch - 1)$, **stride by** D **do**   // $D = d^2$
2   **for** $m = 0$ to $(f_{out} - 1)$, **stride by** f **do**
3   **for** $n = 0$ to $(f_{in} - 1)$, **stride by** f **do**
4           $\widehat{I^{tile}} \leftarrow \oplus^{lkern-1}(I^{layer}_{b:b+D, n:n+f})$
5           $K^{tile,freq} \leftarrow K^{freq}_{m:m+f, n:n+f}$
          /* FPGA starts to process tiled data. */
6   **for** i, j iterating matrices of $\ominus^{lpart}(\widehat{I^{tile}})$ **do**
7   **for** $n' = 0$ to $(f - 1)$ **do**
8                 $P^{in,freq}_{n',i,j} \leftarrow \mathcal{F}(P^{in,padded}_{n',i,j})$
9   **for** $m' = 0$ to $(f - 1)$ **do**
10   **for** $n' = 0$ to $(f - 1)$ **do**
11                     $P' \leftarrow P^{in,freq}_{n',i,j} \circ K^{tile,freq}_{m',n'}$
12                     $P^{out,freq}_{m',i,j} \leftarrow P^{out,freq}_{m',i,j} + P'$
13                 $P^{out}_{m',i,j} \leftarrow \mathcal{F}^{-1}(P^{out,freq}_{m',i,j})$

          /* FPGA ends processing. */
14   **for** $m' = 0$ to $(f - 1)$ **do**
15              $M' \leftarrow \oplus^{-lkern+1}(P^{out}_{m',*,*})$
16              $M'' \leftarrow$ Reshape M' to $D \times 1 \times (l_{img})^2$
17              $M^{layer}_{b:b+D, m+m'} \leftarrow M^{layer}_{b:b+D, m+m'} + M''$

18 **return** M^{layer}

---

the element-wise Hadamard product results in a clean data movement pattern, so we simply calculate the amount of data reuse to make our design choice. Reuse of image pixels are proportional to f, and reuse of kernel pixels are proportional to the batch size. We use the kernel-oriented data reuse scheme. Before execution, a tile of kernel filters is pre-loaded onto FPGA. The kernel loading time is amortized for a large enough batch. Our reuse scheme is equivalent to loop interchanging of line 1 with 2, 3 in *Algorithm 2*.

4.2 Overall System Design

Based on *Algorithm 2*, we design the hardware modules on FPGA to execute the workload from line 6 to 13. Prior to FPGA execution, a kernel filter tile $K^{tile,freq}$ is pre-loaded to on-chip memory BUF$_K$. When data streams in from external memory, a 2D FFT module transforms partitions of I^{layer} into frequency domain (lines 7, 8). Outputs of the FFT module are stored in the on-chip memory BUF$_I$. After reading matrices from BUF$_I$ and BUF$_K$, the Hadamard-Accumulation (HAC) module performs element-wise multiplication-accumulation (lines 9 to 11). HAC feeds its accumulated outputs to a 2D IFFT module, which transforms the partitions back to space domain (line 13). The IFFT module sends its outputs directly to external memory. *Figure 6* shows the overall system design. Note

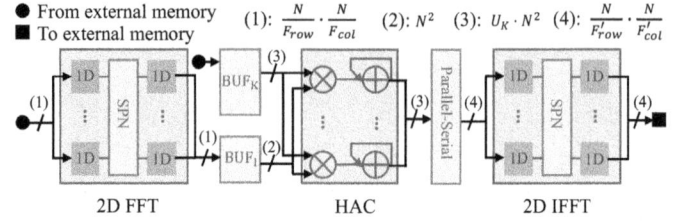

Figure 6: Overall FPGA architecture

that a small buffer is placed between the HAC and IFFT module. It serves as a parallel-serial converter. We will see later on that data parallelism of HAC should be larger than the IFFT module.

HAC module. The key benefit of frequency domain convolution is that sliding window operation in spatial convolution turns into Hadamard product operation. Thus, all loop carried dependencies are automatically eliminated. Massive parallelism can then be exploited by the HAC module. Based on the FPGA resources, we unroll the loop of line 9, *Algorithm 2*. Each cycle, HAC takes as input U_K slices of $N \times N$ matrices from BUF$_K$, and 1 slice from BUF$_I$. Each slice is also fully unrolled to a 1D array of length N^2. Thus, data parallelism of HAC is $U_K \cdot N^2$. Every f^2/U_K cycles, HAC traverses the f^2 slices of $K^{tile,freq}$. During the period, f slices of inputs are read from BUF$_I$, and each slice is reused for f times. On the output side, f slices are generated and fed in the IFFT module. Throughput of HAC is thus $U_K \cdot \frac{N^2}{f}$.

2D FFT (IFFT) module. FFT on a $N \times N$ complex number matrix involves two computation phases. In both phases, N-point 1D FFT is performed on each of the N rows of the 2D matrix. Input to phase 1 is the original matrix. Input to phase 2 is the transposed output matrix of phase 1. For each phase, a straightforward implementation deploys N 1D FFT pipelines where each 1D FFT pipeline supports data parallelism of N. Since the throughput of 2D FFT is bounded by the external memory bandwidth and the throughput of the HAC module, we may either increase the data parallelism of 2D FFT by unrolling the loop in line 7 in *Algorithm 2*, or decrease the parallelism by folding the FFT pipelines. Under the current memory technology, it is very unlikely that the external bandwidth is large enough to transfer more than N^2 complex words per cycle (N: order of 10^1 or 10^2). Thus, we set the FFT unrolling factor to be 1. Folding can be performed along each of the two dimensions. Let F_{col} and F_{row} be the column and row folding factors. Column folding reduces the number of 1D FFT pipelines from N to $\frac{N}{F_{col}}$. Row folding reduces data parallelism of each 1D FFT pipeline from N to $\frac{N}{F_{row}}$ [2]. Data parallelism of the 2D FFT module is thus $\frac{N}{F_{col}} \cdot \frac{N}{F_{row}}$.

Matrix transpose between phase 1 and phase 2 for the 2D FFT architecture is implemented by a Streaming Permutation Network (SPN) [2]. The resource efficient in-place permutation in time algorithm of SPN requires a single port memory of size N^2 to support data parallelism of $\frac{N}{F_{col}} \cdot \frac{N}{F_{row}}$.

For the 2D IFFT module, we use the same architectural parameters as 2D FFT (F_{col} and F_{row}).

On-chip memory. Data in BUF$_I$ are reused f times (f/U_K times temporal reuse, U_K times spatial reuse) before they are replaced by the next tile. Thus, we use the double buffering technique for BUF$_I$.

Data communication latency is completely hidden if throughput of HAC is no less than the streaming FFT module (*Section 5.1*). BUF_K and BUF_I store one kernel tile and one image tile respectively. So the BUF_K size is $M_K = f^2 \cdot N^2$ and the BUF_I size is $M_I = f \cdot N^2$.

5 ARCHITECTURE MAPPING

Define **M**, **L** as the total memory size and DSP resources on chip, **B** as the total external memory bandwidth.

5.1 Performance Model

By our data reuse scheme, we ignore the kernel communication cost and utilize the full bandwidth **B** to read and write image tiles.

By calculating the throughput of each individual hardware module, we derive the overall system throughput R_{sys}:

$$R_{sys} = \min \left\{ \frac{N}{F_{col}} \cdot \frac{N}{F_{row}}, \quad U_K \cdot \frac{N^2}{f}, \quad \frac{1}{2} \cdot \mathbf{B} \right\} \quad (9)$$

To execute one layer for a batch of complex images, we first keep one kernel tile in BUF_K, and load the image tiles belonging to $\widehat{I}$ one by one into BUF_I. Then we replace the data in BUF_K with the next kernel tile belonging to the same layer, and repeat the loading of image tiles. The execution time averaged for one input I is:

$$t_{img} = \left\lceil \frac{f_{in}}{f} \right\rceil \cdot \left\lceil \frac{f_{out}}{f} \right\rceil \cdot \left\lceil \frac{\widehat{l_{img}}}{N - l_{kern} + 1} \right\rceil^2 \times \frac{f \cdot N^2}{R_{sys}} \times \frac{1}{d^2} \quad (10)$$

We may further simplify R_{sys}. First of all, we observe that the architectural parameters should be set such that throughput of FFT, IFFT and HAC are matched. Secondly, for **L** and **M**, we observe that: (1) Most of the DSP resources are consumed by the HAC module to perform Hadamard product. This observation is consistent with the conclusion in *Section 3.1*. (2) Most of the on-chip memory is consumed by the kernel tile. The size of the kernel tile is in the order of $f^2 \cdot N^2$, and the size of the image tile is in the order of $f \cdot N^2$. Thus, we approximate R_{sys} as follows.

$$R_{sys} = \min \left\{ N \cdot \frac{\mathbf{L}}{\sqrt{\mathbf{M}}}, \quad \frac{1}{2} \cdot \mathbf{B} \right\} \quad (11)$$

We then get throughput of a convolution layer by t_{img} and R_{sys}.

5.2 Device Coefficient

The two terms in *Equation 11* show the potential computation and communication bounds of the target device. As N increases, the system shifts from being computation bound to communication bound. We analyze the system performance for various N. Based on this, we quantitatively categorize FPGA devices by **L**, **M** and **B**.

Case 1: small N. The system throughput R_{sys} is determined by **L** and **M**. So $R_{sys} = N \cdot \frac{\mathbf{L}}{\sqrt{\mathbf{M}}}$. By approximating $\left\lceil \frac{f_{in}}{f} \right\rceil \cdot \left\lceil \frac{f_{out}}{f} \right\rceil \approx \frac{f_{in}}{f} \cdot \frac{f_{out}}{f}$ and $\left\lceil \frac{\widehat{l_{img}}}{N - l_{kern} + 1} \right\rceil \approx \frac{d \cdot (l_{img} + l_{kern} - 1)}{N - l_{kern} + 1}$. We update *Equation 10*:

$$t'_{img} \approx f_{in} \cdot f_{out} \cdot (l_{img} + l_{kern} - 1)^2 \cdot \left(\frac{N}{N - l_{kern} + 1} \right)^2 \cdot \frac{1}{\mathbf{L}} \quad (12)$$

Case 2: large N. The system throughput R_{sys} is determined by **B**. Therefore, $R_{sys} = \frac{1}{2} \cdot \mathbf{B}$. By approximating $\left\lceil \frac{f_{in}}{f} \right\rceil \cdot \left\lceil \frac{f_{out}}{f} \right\rceil \approx \frac{f_{in}}{f} \cdot \frac{f_{out}}{f}$ and $\frac{N}{N - l_{kern} + 1} \approx 1$. We derive *Equation 10* as:

$$t''_{img} \approx f_{in} \cdot f_{out} \cdot (l_{img} + l_{kern} - 1)^2 \cdot (2 \cdot N) \cdot \frac{1}{\sqrt{\mathbf{M}} \cdot \mathbf{B}} \quad (13)$$

As N grows from a small value, latency t'_{img} decreases due to lower computation complexity (*Section 3.1*). However, with limited on-chip memory size, larger N means smaller f and lesser data reuse. At some point, external bandwidth saturates. As N increases, latency t''_{img} becomes larger, since communication cost then becomes the dominant factor. When sweeping N, expressions on the right side of *Equation 12* and *13* forms two curves, which are the performance asymptotic bounds. We define the common term $f_{in} \cdot f_{out} \cdot (l_{img} + l_{kern} - 1)^2$ as the *model coefficient* $\mathbf{K_{CNN}}$, which scales performance of the architecture by the complexity of CNN.

Imagine a device with infinite bandwidth **B**. It is never bound by communication. Thus, its maximal achievable throughput according to *Equation 12* is $R^{max}_{comp} = \max \frac{1}{t'_{img}} = \frac{1}{\mathbf{K_{CNN}}} \cdot \mathbf{L}$, which is the theoretical computational upper bound.

Dividing the reciprocal of t'_{img} and t''_{img} by R^{max}_{comp}, we get the asymptotic bounds for normalized throughput:

$$\begin{aligned} C_{comp}(N) &= \left(\frac{N - l_{kern} + 1}{N} \right)^2 \\ C_{comm}(N) &= \left(\mathbf{B} \cdot \mathbf{M}^{\frac{1}{2}} \cdot \mathbf{L}^{-1} \right) \cdot \left(\frac{1}{2 \cdot N} \right) \end{aligned} \quad (14)$$

We define $\mathbf{K_{FPGA}} = \mathbf{B} \cdot \mathbf{M}^{\frac{1}{2}} \cdot \mathbf{L}^{-1}$ as the *device coefficient*. For a target device, it measures the ratio of communication capacity over computation capacity. Based on $\mathbf{K_{FPGA}}$, we map the architecture onto the target device by balancing the computation complexity and data reuse. Details of the mapping are shown in the next section.

5.3 Design Space Exploration

We note some important properties of C_{comp} and C_{comm}. The model coefficient $\mathbf{K_{CNN}}$ disappears in the process of normalization. Furthermore, $\mathbf{K_{FPGA}}$ captures the device characteristics in C_{comm}. For diverse CNNs, we can use a constant $l_{kern} (= 3)$ to approximate C_{comp}, so the computation bound is a single curve. On the other hand, for a given target device, the communication bound is also a single curve since $\mathbf{K_{FPGA}}$ keeps as a constant regardless of the CNNs. In this sense, $\mathbf{K_{FPGA}}$ intrinsically determines the device performance, and the normalized throughput is independent of the CNN model parameters.

With $\mathbf{K_{FPGA}}$, design space exploration is as simple as identifying the intersection point of two curves. We propose a *design chart* (*Figure 7*). The red and blue solid lines are the computation and communication rooflines bounding the actual performance. Intersection of the rooflines shows the optimal N for the target device. Parameters f, U_K, F_{row} and F_{col} are calculated based on N. *Algorithm 3* shows the procedure for a radix-$2n$ FFT architecture.

In the design chart, we use the device coefficient ($\mathbf{K_{Stratix-V}}$) of our experimental platform as reference. For this device, $N = 16$ is the best configuration. For devices with their coefficients

Algorithm 3: Design space exploration using the design chart

Input: L, M, B of the target device
Output: N chosen for the architecture

1 $K_{FPGA} \leftarrow B \cdot M^{\frac{1}{2}} \cdot L^{-1}$
2 Get the curve of communication bound $C_{comm}(N)$
3 $N_0 \leftarrow$ Intersection of $C_{comm}(N)$ and $C_{comp}(N)$
4 $N' \leftarrow 2^{\lfloor \log_2 N_0 \rfloor}$; $\quad N'' \leftarrow 2^{\lceil \log_2 N_0 \rceil}$
5 **return** $\quad C_{comp}(N') > C_{comm}(N'') \quad ? \quad N' : N''$

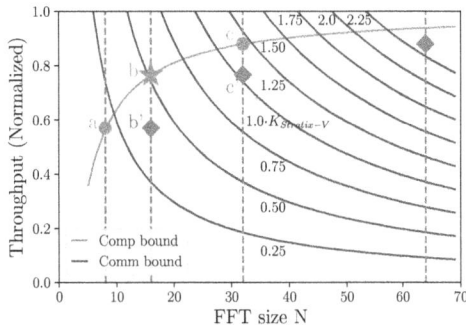

Figure 7: Design chart for hardware mapping

falling between 0.2 to 0.35, 0.52 to 1.05, 1.45 to 2.37, the designs are computation bound. Optimal N is 8, 16 and 32 respectively (these are shown by three red marks a, b, c). Similarly, for other devices, the designs are communication bound (design points falling between b and b', c and c'). Using the design chart, we can identify target devices that are best suited for our architecture. Devices with their roofline intersections falling at the blue vertical lines ($N = 8, 16, 32, 64$) have perfectly balanced resources in terms of L, M and B (e.g., devices with $K_{FPGA} = 0.2, 0.5$ or 1.18).

6 AUTOMATIC CODE GENERATION

We have developed a tool [20] to automatically generate the architecture on the target device. *Figure 8* shows the workflow of the tool. The inputs are the CNN model parameters for each convolution layer (l_{img}, l_{kern}, f_{in} and f_{out}), and the meta data of the target device (B, L and M). The outputs includes C++ code for book-keeping the data blocks (lines 1-5 and 14-18, *Algorithm 2*), and synthesizable Verilog performing the computational expensive convolution (lines 6-13, *Algorithm 2*). The Mapping Engine feeds the CaP-OaA parameters (N, d) and tiling factor (f) into Software Generation Engine, and feeds architectural parameters into Hardware Generation Engine. Optionally, users can specify additional constraints to the tool such as available FFT sizes and maximum d.

Software Generation. Although the optimal batch folding factor d varies across convolution layers, we use a uniform d for all layers of a CNN in implementation. This ensures that the output of the previous layer can be directly fed into the following layer without further layout rearrangement.

Hardware Generation. The 2D FFT module consists of 1D FFT pipelines and Streaming Permutation Networks (SPN) for matrix

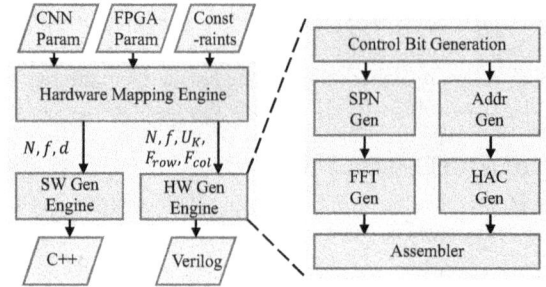

Figure 8: Tool workflow

transpose. We take the 1D FFT template from [13]. SPN is a folded CLOS network including two spatial permutation stages and one temporal permutation stage. We implement the in-place permutation in time algorithm [2] to generate the control bits. HAC includes a memory controller to fetch data from BUF_I and BUF_K. Since our architecture does not involve any runtime reconfiguration, Hardware Generation Engine statically computes all the SPN control bits and HAC input addresses in design time. The Assembler connects the 2D FFT, 2D IFFT, HAC, BUF_I and BUF_K based on *Figure 6*.

7 EXPERIMENTAL RESULTS

7.1 Experimental Setup

We use Intel Heterogeneous Research Platform (HARP) [1] for evaluation. HARP has shared memory accessible to the CPU and FPGA. The FPGA is an Intel Stratix V GXA7 device, with 5 GB/s bandwidth to external memory, 6.25 MB on-chip memory, 256 $DSPs$ and 234720 $ALMs$. The CPU of HARP is a 10-core Intel Xeon E5-2600 v2 processor. We use 16-bit fixed-point data representation to compute CNNs. The designs were synthesized by Quartus II (version 13.1.0).

In the following, throughput is calculated as the total number of operations for *spatial* convolution divided by the average execution time per image for our *frequency domain* approach. Numerator for spatial convolution let us make fair comparison with other works. The execution time is the actual execution time on HARP.

The architecture for *all* CNNs under evaluation is configured as: $N = 16$, $f = 64$, $U_K = \frac{1}{2}$, $F_{row} = 4$, $F_{col} = 16$. We set an upper limit for d ($\leqslant 15$) to bound the batch size.

For workload distribution between FPGA and CPU, FPGA executes all convolution layers of AlexNet, VGG16 and FCN-16s except the first convolution layer of AlexNet, while the CPU executes all the remaining layers (pooling, ReLU, fully connected and first convolution of AlexNet). In summary, the CPU executes 15%, 1% and 1% of the total computation for AlexNet, VGG16 and FCN-16s respectively. We implement the first convolution layer of AlexNet using the BLAS [17] library. By a simple batch processing pipeline, execution time of CPU is completely hidden by FPGA.

7.2 Impact of Algorithmic Optimizations

To vary the input image size, we use AlexNet and VGG16 to execute feature extraction by skipping their fully-connected layers. We execute all layers of FCN-16s.

Effect of CaP. We use the architecture configuration as specified in *Section 7.1*. We vary l_{img} of the first convolution layer from 160 to 304 for AlexNet and VGG16, and from 320 to 608 for FCN-16s (In other words, l'_{img} of the last convolution layer for the three CNNs vary from 10 to 19). *Figure 9* shows the comparison of computation complexity for frequency domain convolution using CaP-OaA, OaA and spatial convolution. Each bar is vertically stacked by the number of operations for each convolution layer of the CNNs. *Figure 10* shows the comparison of the measured throughput on HARP.

When l_{img} is divisible by $(N - l_{kern} + 1)$ (e.g., $l_{img} = 224$ for AlexNet and VGG16), performance of OaA is identical to CaP-OaA. However, in other cases, CaP-OaA delivers much better performance than OaA. For example, when $l_{img} = 240$ for AlexNet, VGG16 and $l_{img} = 352$ for FCN-16s, CaP-OaA leads to 2.3×, 1.5× and 1.7× complexity reduction, and 2.3×, 1.5× and 1.7× throughput improvement. Furthermore, we observe that the performance of OaA is highly sensitive to image sizes. For AlexNet and VGG16, performance drops significantly when the image size increases from 224 to 240. This reflects the padding effect of OaA.

Effect of N. Next, we experiment how selecting various N affects the throughput of the system. Since parameters N and f are together dependent on the on-chip memory size, by varying N, we are exploring the effect of loop tiling as well. *Figure 11* shows the normalized throughput of the three CNNs on the design chart when using $N = 8, 16, 32$. The corresponding f values are $128, 64, 32$.

As predicted by the design chart, $N = 16$ is the best configuration on the Stratix-V GXA7 device. When $N = 8$, the increased computation complexity degrades the performance. When $N = 32$, the low data reuse makes external bandwidth the bottleneck. Furthermore, despite the dramatically different network structure, the normalized throughput of the three CNNs are very close to each other. This demonstrates the effect of our algorithmic optimization.

7.3 Comparison with State-of-the-Art

For AlexNet and VGG16, we use the ImageNet dataset ($l_{img} = 224$).

Table 2 summarizes the comparison with state-of-the-art designs. All the designs except [21] use similar or lower precision data representation than our designs. In [21], frequency domain convolution using the OaA technique was employed. However, their analysis was based on a metric called "delay-multiplier product" evaluating convolution of a single image rather than a complete layer. Using the same FPGA, we show 9.4× (AlexNet) and 5.4× (VGG16) speed up in throughput as a result of a deeper analysis on frequency domain convolution. All other works are based on spatial convolution. Compared with [18] which uses the same target FPGA and data representation as this project, we achieve 5.8× speedup. Compared with [7], [8] and [12], when we use the same data representation (16-bit fixed point), our designs achieve 1.4×, 4.9× and 1.0× speedup, even though our target device has 14.0×, 3.4× and 5.9× less DSP resources. Using a device with 5.9× more DSPs, [22] achieves 2.7× higher throughput than us. One main reason is the difference in the clock rate. We can not achieve higher clock rate, since HARP requires the FPGA to operate at exactly 200 *MHz*.

To understand such significant improvement in throughput, we use [18] as an example to show the improvement breakdown. Out of the 5.8× improvement, approximately 3× comes from the reduction in computation complexity (*Figure 2b*). The remaining 2× comes from the clock rate improvement. The Hadamard product operation

leads to much less number of operations and much simpler data flow compared with the sliding window operation.

To the best of our knowledge, this is the first work that accelerates FCN-16s on FPGAs. As shown in *Figure 10*, approximately, throughput of 550 *GOPS* is achieved for images of various sizes.

8 RELATED WORK

Accelerating spatial convolution has been extensively studied from the perspective of loop operation optimization [4, 12] and data flow optimization [3]. Work in [4] proposed a roofline model to capture various techniques including loop tiling, unrolling and interchanging. [12] further optimized performance by a thorough design space exploration. [22] boosted throughput under the OpenCL framework. Spatial convolution based approaches will eventually be bound by the computation complexity of the convolution algorithm. On the other hand, alternatives such as convolution by Winograd transform and frequency domain convolution have been proposed and implemented [10, 14, 21]. Winograd based approaches do not easily generalize to CNNs with various kernel window sizes. While the approaches based on frequency domain convolution are more flexible, further optimizations to [21] can be performed when processing high dimensional data of convolution layers (this work).

9 CONCLUSION

We presented a framework for generating high throughput CNN accelerators. Combining the CaP, OaA and frequency domain loop tiling techniques together, our framework generates architectures accelerating diverse CNNs without runtime reconfiguration.

In the future, we will explore the hybrid algorithm combining convolution in space and frequency domain. Spatial convolution is as efficient as frequency domain convolution for 1×1 kernels. In such cases, we may switch to spatial convolution which leads to better hardware utilization. In addition, as techniques have been developed to make use of the sparsity in spatial convolution, we will explore if similar techniques can be applied in frequency domain.

10 ACKNOWLEDGEMENTS

This work was supported by the US NSF under grants CNS-1643351, ACI-1339756 and CCF-1320211. This work is also supported in part by Intel Strategic Research Alliance funding. Equipment grant from the Intel Hardware Accelerator Research Program is gratefully acknowledged.

REFERENCES

[1] 2015. Intel Inc. Xeon+FPGA Platform for the Data Center. (2015). https://www.ece.cmu.edu/calcm/carl/lib/exe/fetch.php?media=carl15-gupta.pdf
[2] R. Chen, H. Le, and V. K. Prasanna. 2013. Energy efficient parameterized FFT architecture. In *2013 23rd Intl. Conf. on Field programmable Logic and Applications.*
[3] Y. H. Chen, J. Emer, and V. Sze. 2017. Using Dataflow to Optimize Energy Efficiency of Deep Neural Network Accelerators. *IEEE Micro* 37, 3 (2017).
[4] Chen Zhang, et al. 2015. Optimizing FPGA-based Accelerator Design for Deep Convolutional Neural Networks. In *Proceedings of the 2015 ACM/SIGDA International Symposium on Field-Programmable Gate Arrays (FPGA '15)*. ACM.
[5] Ali Daher, et al. 2010. Overlap-save and overlap-add filters: Optimal design and comparison. *IEEE Transactions on Signal Processing* 58, 6 (2010).
[6] P. Duhamel and H. Hollmann. 1984. 'Split radix' FFT algorithm. *Electronics Letters* 20, 1 (January 1984).
[7] Huimin Li, et al. 2016. A high performance FPGA-based accelerator for large-scale convolutional neural networks. In *2016 26th International Conference on Field Programmable Logic and Applications (FPL)*.

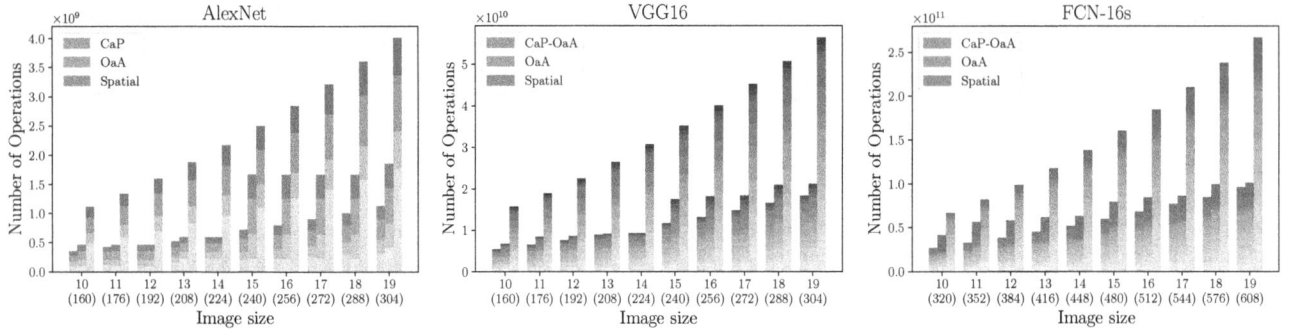

Figure 9: Number of operations performed by various convolution algorithms

Table 2: Comparison with state-of-the-art AlexNet and VGG16 implementations (FX: fixed point, FT: floating point)

	[7] AlexNet	[18] AlexNet	[21] AlexNet	[8] VGG16	[12] VGG16	[22] VGG16	[21] VGG16	Proposed: AlexNet	Proposed: VGG16
FPGA	Virtex-7 VC709	Stratix-V GXA7	Startix-V GXA7	Zync XC7Z045	Arria-10 GX1150	Arria-10 GX1150	Stratix-V GXA7	Stratix-V GXA7	Stratix-V GXA7
Frequency (MHz)	156	100	200	150	150	385	200	200	200
Precision	16 bit FX	8-16 bit FX	32 bit FT	16 bit FX	8-16 bit FX	16 bit FX	32 bit FT	16 bit FX	16 bit FX
DSP Usage	2144 (60%)	256 (100%)	224 (88%)	780 (89%)	1518 (100%)	1378 (91%)	224 (88%)	256 (100%)	256 (100%)
Logic Usage	274K (63%)	121K (52%)	200K (85%)	183K (84%)	161K (38%)	–	200K (85%)	107K (46%)	107K (46%)
On-chip RAM	956 (65%)	1152 (61%)	1208 (64%)	486 (87%)	1900 (70%)	1450 (53%)	1208 (64%)	1377 (73%)	1377 (73%)
Throughput (GOPS)	565.9	134.1	83.0	137.0	645.3	1790	123.5	780.6	669.1

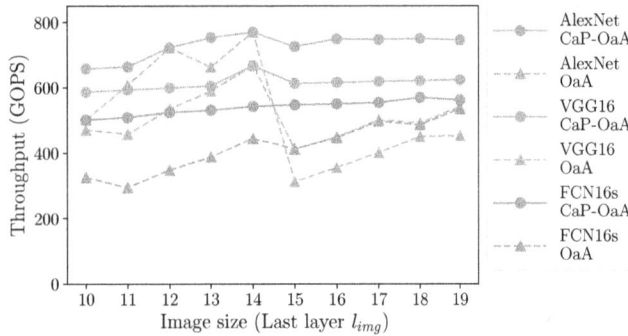

Figure 10: Throughput of AlexNet, VGG16 and FCN-16s

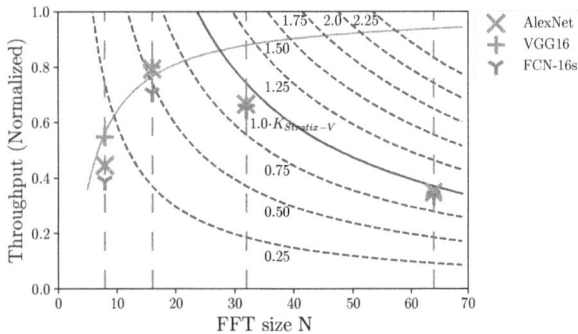

Figure 11: Actual throughput (normalized) for various N

[8] Jiantao Qiu, et al. 2016. Going Deeper with Embedded FPGA Platform for Convolutional Neural Network. In *Proceedings of the 2016 ACM/SIGDA International Symposium on Field-Programmable Gate Arrays (FPGA '16)*. ACM.

[9] Alex Krizhevsky, Ilya Sutskever, and Geoffrey E. Hinton. 2012. Imagenet classification with deep convolutional neural networks. In *NIPS'12*.

[10] Andrew Lavin. 2015. Fast Algorithms for Convolutional Neural Networks. *CoRR* abs/1509.09308 (2015).

[11] Jonathan Long, Evan Shelhamer, and Trevor Darrell. 2014. Fully Convolutional Networks for Semantic Segmentation. *CoRR* abs/1411.4038 (2014).

[12] Yufei Ma, et al. 2017. Optimizing Loop Operation and Dataflow in FPGA Acceleration of Deep Convolutional Neural Networks. In *Proceedings of the 2017 ACM/SIGDA Intl. Symposium on Field-Programmable Gate Arrays (FPGA '17)*.

[13] Markus Püschel, et al. 2005. SPIRAL: Code Generation for DSP Transforms. *Proceedings of the IEEE, special issue on "Program Generation, Optimization, and Adaptation"* 93 (2005).

[14] A. Podili, C. Zhang, and V. Prasanna. 2017. Fast and efficient implementation of Convolutional Neural Networks on FPGA. In *2017 IEEE 28th International Conference on Application-specific Systems, Architectures and Processors (ASAP)*.

[15] Karen Simonyan and Andrew Zisserman. 2014. Very Deep Convolutional Networks for Large-Scale Image Recognition. *CoRR* abs/1409.1556 (2014).

[16] Christian Szegedy, Wei Liu, Yangqing Jia, Pierre Sermanet, Scott E. Reed, Dragomir Anguelov, Dumitru Erhan, Vincent Vanhoucke, and Andrew Rabinovich. 2014. Going Deeper with Convolutions. *CoRR* abs/1409.4842 (2014).

[17] Xianyi Zhang, et al. 2017. OpenBLAS. (2017). "www.openblas.net"

[18] Yufei Ma, et al. 2016. Scalable and modularized RTL compilation of Convolutional Neural Networks onto FPGA. In *2016 26th International Conference on Field Programmable Logic and Applications (FPL)*.

[19] Hanqing Zeng, Ren Chen, and Viktor K. Prasanna. 2017. *Optimizing Frequency Domain Implementation of CNNs on FPGAs*. Technical Report. University of Southern California. http://ceng.usc.edu/techreports/2017/Prasanna%20CENG-2017-3.pdf

[20] Hanqing Zeng, Chi Zhang, and Viktor Prasanna. 2017. Fast Generation of High Throughput Customized Deep Learning Accelerators on FPGAs. In *2017 International Conference on ReConFigurable Computing and FPGAs (ReConFig)*.

[21] C. Zhang and V. Prasanna. 2017. Frequency Domain Acceleration of Convolutional Neural Networks on CPU-FPGA Shared Memory System. In *Proceedings of the 2017 ACM/SIGDA Intl. Symp. on Field-Programmable Gate Arrays (FPGA '17)*.

[22] Jialiang Zhang and Jing Li. 2017. Improving the Performance of OpenCL-based FPGA Accelerator for Convolutional Neural Network. In *Proceedings of the 2017 ACM/SIGDA Intl. Symposium on Field-Programmable Gate Arrays (FPGA '17)*.

Dynamically Scheduled High-level Synthesis

Lana Josipović, Radhika Ghosal, and Paolo Ienne
Ecole Polytechnique Fédérale de Lausanne (EPFL)
School of Computer and Communication Sciences
CH–1015 Lausanne, Switzerland

ABSTRACT

High-level synthesis (HLS) tools almost universally generate statically scheduled datapaths. Static scheduling implies that circuits out of HLS tools have a hard time exploiting parallelism in code with potential memory dependencies, with control-dependent dependencies in inner loops, or where performance is limited by long latency control decisions. The situation is essentially the same as in computer architecture between *Very-Long Instruction Word* (VLIW) processors and dynamically scheduled superscalar processors; the former display the best performance per cost in highly regular embedded applications, but general purpose, irregular, and control-dominated computing tasks require the runtime flexibility of dynamic scheduling. In this work, we show that high-level synthesis of dynamically scheduled circuits is perfectly feasible by describing the implementation of a prototype synthesizer which generates a particular form of latency-insensitive synchronous circuits. Compared to a commercial HLS tool, the result is a different trade-off between performance and circuit complexity, much as superscalar processors represent a different trade-off compared to VLIW processors: in demanding applications, the performance is very significantly improved at an affordable cost. We here demonstrate only the first steps towards more performant high-level synthesis tools adapted to emerging FPGA applications and the demands of computing in broader application domains.

ACM Reference Format:
Lana Josipović, Radhika Ghosal, and Paolo Ienne. 2018. Dynamically Scheduled High-level Synthesis. In *Proceedings of 2018 ACM/SIGDA International Symposium on Field-Programmable Gate Arrays (FPGA 2018)*. ACM, New York, NY, USA, 10 pages. https://doi.org/10.1145/3174243.3174264

1 INTRODUCTION

The use of FPGAs in datacenters by Microsoft [7, 35] and Amazon [2] as well as the acquisition of Altera by Intel [10] signal one of the greatest opportunities for FPGAs since they were first introduced. One of the many challenges ahead is whether software programmers will ever manage to extract enough performance through modern programming paradigms. While there is conspicuous research activity on this front, practically all attempts ultimately rely on classic forms of *High-Level Synthesis* (HLS) to generate the actual circuits. In turn, HLS tools almost universally rely on building datapaths that are controlled following *static schedules*—that is, the cycle

when every operation is executed is fixed at synthesis-time [20]. The similarity to code generation for *Very-Long Instruction Word* (VLIW) processors is all but accidental: much of the key transformations to exploit fine-grain parallelism between operators derives from VLIW compilation techniques [28, 37]. This analogy with computer architecture is enlightening: Around two decades ago, Intel started working on the now defunct Itanium architecture [17], the first and only VLIW processor aimed to general-purpose markets. Unfortunately, it turned out significantly more difficult than expected for a compiler to extract the parallelism that dynamically scheduled processors routinely exploit. Today, VLIW processors are successful only in markets with extremely regular and predictable applications, and where it is acceptable to tune code manually.

Perhaps HLS and FPGAs are following the same trajectory: Statically scheduled HLS serves well applications that are fairly regular and when development time is measured against coding in RTL languages. But, with FPGAs moving to datacenters and facing broader classes of applications, the ability of dynamic scheduling to automatically extract parallelism may prove essential. With dynamic scheduling, not only complex loop transformations (and related hints from the programmers) are often unnecessary, but more parallelism can be extracted in the presence of control and memory dependencies undecidable at compile time. Although beyond the scope of this paper, dynamically scheduled circuits open the door to speculative execution, one of the most powerful ideas ever in computer architecture. If FPGAs should compete with CPUs running on one order of magnitude faster clocks, they will need every ounce of exploitable operation parallelism with minimal programmer effort.

This paper presents a methodology to automatically generate dynamically scheduled circuits from C code. Our approach borrows several ideas from the asynchronous domain, but produces perfectly synchronous designs which are directly comparable to standard HLS techniques. The paper is organized as follows: Section 2 explores an example of one of the situations where dynamic extraction of operation-level parallelism proves essential to performance. Section 3 details our circuit generation methodology as implemented in our prototype tool. Section 4 gives the results of the comparison of our technique with static HLS and contrasts our methodology with previous efforts to create dynamically scheduled circuits. In Section 5, we discuss some of the future perspectives opened by our circuit generation strategy. In Section 6, we outline what others have done to circumvent some of the problems of statically scheduled HLS, before concluding the paper in Section 7.

2 WHY DYNAMIC SCHEDULING?

To illustrate the limitations of standard HLS approaches, consider the code in Figure 1a. In this loop there is a control flow decision (if) which depends on the actual data being read from arrays A[] and B[]. The operation which might take place in a specific iteration (s = s + d) introduces a dependency between iterations and delays

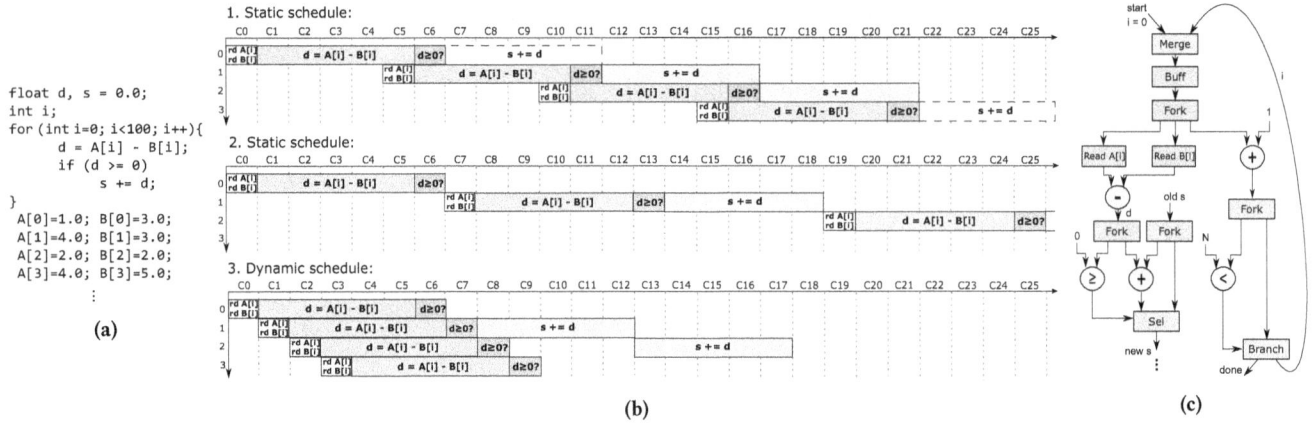

Figure 1: Limitations of static scheduling. Figure 1a gives a code segment where dependencies cannot be determined at compile time. Figure 1b contrasts two possible schedules (top and middle) created by an HLS tool with a dynamic schedule (bottom). Figure 1c shows a portion of a dynamically scheduled circuit achieving the optimal execution schedule of Figure 1b.

the next iteration whenever the condition is true. When pipelining this loop, a typical HLS tool needs to create a static schedule—that is, a conservative execution plan for the various operations in the loop which is valid in every possible case. Such a schedule is shown on the top of Figure 1b: in the example the condition is true only for the second and third iteration but "space" is reserved in the schedule as if the condition were true everywhere. An alternative could be to avoid pipelining the loop and creating a sequential finite-state machine. The result could be the middle schedule in Figure 1b, where indeed cycles are spent for the addition only when needed; however, the decision of not pipelining the loop has removed one of the foremost potentials for parallelism (in this case, the memory reads, the subtraction, and the comparison are perfectly independent across iterations and could be pipelined). Obviously, a good schedule is the bottom one in Figure 1b: the operations of different iterations are overlapped as much as possible and the parallelism is reduced only when the dependency is actually there (that is, when the addition is executed). Such behavior is beyond what a statically scheduled HLS tool can achieve.

This example is representative of one case where generating a schedule at synthesis time has a negative impact on performance. Another well-known situation is the presence of dependencies through memory: a write in a previous iteration may address the same memory location as the read in a successive one and thus creates a dependency imposing serialization; yet, if these two accesses address different locations, they can be executed out of order. When an HLS tool is not able to guarantee independence between two memory accesses, it must assume the worst case scenario and thus limit the exploitable parallelism—exactly as above but for a different reason. In recent years, many authors have been exploring workarounds to some cases of potential dependencies through memory—we will discuss them in Section 6—but dynamically scheduled circuits represent the most general solution to the problem.

2.1 Elastic Circuits

The key to avoid the limitations of static scheduling is to refrain from triggering the operators through a centralized pre-planned controller but to take scheduling decisions locally in the circuit as

it runs: as soon as all conditions for execution are satisfied (e.g., the operands are available or critical control decisions are resolved), an operation starts. In line with the computer architecture analogy of the introduction, this is exactly what dynamically scheduled processors do through their reservation stations [23]. The rest of this section looks informally at one dynamically scheduled circuit paradigm to give the reader a flavor of what we want to achieve.

Figure 1c shows a simplified version of an *elastic* circuit [11] implementing the loop of Figure 1a. Besides normal datapath components, this circuit uses a few control components labelled Buff, Merge, Sel, Fork, and Branch. All data signals are accompanied by handshake control signals. The handshake signals are two, in opposite direction, indicating respectively the availability of a new piece of data from the source component and the readiness of the target component to accept it. The loop to the right of the figure shows the part of the circuit which updates the iterator i: At the beginning, the constant 0 is sent from the start node. The Merge node takes this value and passes it further. The elastic buffer node Buff is the register which holds i and distributes it on the next clock cycle to three consumers through the Fork node; all successors must consume the value before Fork accepts a new input value. The right branch compares the incremented i with the loop bound; if the bound is not reached, the new value of i is sent back to the register by the Branch node through Merge. Meanwhile, the other outputs of the first Fork use i to access A[] and B[] and to compute the subtraction, which is propagated to the rest of the circuit.

The key to a good execution of this loop is that, ideally, a new value of i should be used to start computing A[i] - B[i] on every cycle. This is the case in this circuit, contrary to a conservative statically scheduled one: The cycle on the right of Figure 1c is completely combinational excluding the register Buff and thus a new value for i can be computed on every cycle. It is the left part of the circuit which can delay this: when the if is not taken, the result of the addition is dumped by the Sel node as soon as it arrives and the old value of s becomes immediately the new value that is sent back to the adder on the following cycle (loop and Buff omitted for simplicity); if, on the other hand, the result is needed, Sel will wait for the sum to complete, the adder will be stalled next cycle waiting for its right operand, a new subtraction will not be computed and the memory accesses will not be performed due to backpressure from the adder. Ultimately, the top Fork will not allow a new i to proceed on the right branch. This slows down the initiation of the loop and is exactly what the dynamic schedule in Figure 1b shows.

2.2 Dynamic vs. Static Scheduling

As the example above shows, loop pipelining happens naturally in an elastic circuit such as the one in Figure 1c. Again, this is in line with the experience in computer architecture: whereas complex compilation techniques have been developed for VLIWs with the purpose of transforming loops to exploit instruction-level parallelism (often requiring either complex heuristics to drive the optimization or pragmas from the programmers), dynamically scheduled out-of-order processors are capable of achieving good levels of parallelism on-the-fly and without extensive code preparation. Apart from the advantage of exploiting parallelism when static scheduling cannot, this ability to find the "good" solution without help may be critical in a future where HLS will not be driven by hardware designers (available to study the generated circuits and to restructure the input code) but by higher-level code generation tools (e.g., Delite [22]) and ultimately by software programmers.

It is clear that, as in the case of processors, taking scheduling decisions dynamically costs resources and time (such as the area and delay of the control elements in Figure 1c). Our purpose in this paper is (1) to show how one can generate automatically dynamically scheduled circuits from C-programs and (2) to compare their circuit complexity and critical path with those of circuits obtained through state-of-the-art HLS tools. Although the potentials of gain in terms of cycles saved are at least qualitatively clear, to the best of our knowledge, the problems at bullet (1) have never been thoroughly studied in the domain of modern, synchronous HLS and the comparison at bullet (2) has never been attempted.

3 SYNTHESIZING ELASTIC CIRCUITS

In this section, we describe the process we use to convert an arbitrary piece of code into a dynamically scheduled circuit. As evoked in Section 2.1, we have chosen the elastic circuits [11] as the paradigm for the circuits we produce. This section is organized as follows: In Section 3.1, we describe the elastic components and Section 3.2 shows how to use them to build datapaths corresponding to basic blocks of code. Section 3.3 discusses a few problems which appear when datapaths from different basic blocks are interconnected following the control flow of the program. Section 3.4 illustrates how we add registers to our circuits to produce correct functionality. The next problem is connecting the design to memory, which we describe in Section 3.5. There is an essential optimization to extract reasonable performance; we outline it in Section 3.6.

3.1 Elastic Components

This section provides an overview of the elastic primitives we use. Inspired by asynchronous circuits, elastic circuits are strictly synchronous and perfectly adapted to traditional VLSI and FPGA flows.

Most elastic components are immediately equivalent to ordinary datapath components but they implement latency-insensitivity by communicating with their predecessors and successors through point-to-point pairs of handshake control signals: a *valid* signal

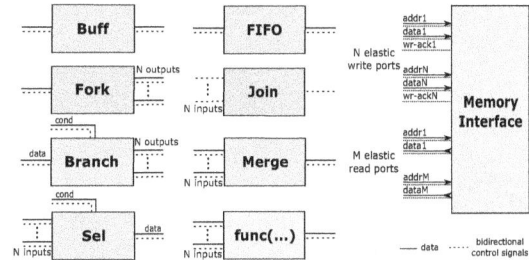

Figure 2: Elastic components.

indicates that a component is sending a valid piece of data to its successor(s), whereas the *ready* signal informs the predecessor(s) that a component can accept a new piece of data. The availability of a piece of data is colloquially indicated as the presence of *token*, for analogy with Petri nets; tokens indicate valid data and a transition (event) occurs as a component absorbs the token [32].

Figure 2 outlines the elastic components we use. Their gate-level descriptions can be found in literature [11, 25] and none is original of this piece of work. All have the above-mentioned *ready* and *valid* control signals and most are associated to a data component.

- *Elastic Buffers* (Buffs) are the elementary storage structure of elastic circuits and the immediate equivalent of D flip-flops or registers in regular circuits.
- *Elastic FIFOs* (FIFOs) are ordinary first-in first-out queues with the appropriate handshaking signals.
- An *Eager Fork* (Fork) replicates every token received at the input to multiple outputs; it outputs tokens to each successor as soon as possible (i.e., as soon as each individual successor is ready to accept the data) but does not accept any new token until all successors have accepted the previous one.
- A *Lazy Fork* (LFork) performs essentially the same function as an eager fork, but it outputs tokens only when all successors are ready. It is, in general, a less optimized version of an eager fork, as the more conservative triggering rule reduces the opportunities for out-of-order execution. Yet, it will be useful in Section 3.5 in a very specific part of the circuit where we will need to emit tokens in a particular order.
- A *Join* (Join) is the reciprocal of an Fork—it acts like a synchronizer by waiting to receive a token on each and every one of its inputs before emitting a token at its output. We seldom employ Joins explicitly but they are used in components requiring multiple operands to trigger advancement.
- A *Branch* (Branch) implements program control-flow statements (i.e., *if* or *switch*) by dispatching a token (and, sometimes, the corresponding piece of data) received at its single input to one of its multiple outputs based on a condition.
- A *Merge* (Merge) is a reciprocal of a Branch—it propagates a token and data received on any input to its output. Merges are analogous to Φ functions in the static single assignment form, inserted in points where control-flow paths meet [40].
- A *Select* (Sel) acts as a multiplexer—it waits for the required input to produce the output and discards the tokens at the nonselected inputs as soon as they arrive.

In addition, we use any functional unit the code requires, such as integer and floating point units. Components that require multiple operands contain a Join to trigger the operation only when all inputs

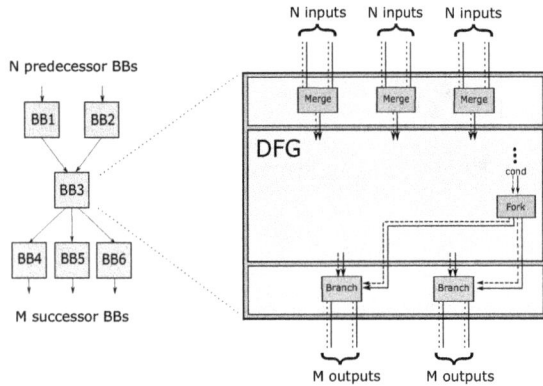

Figure 3: The basic block template.

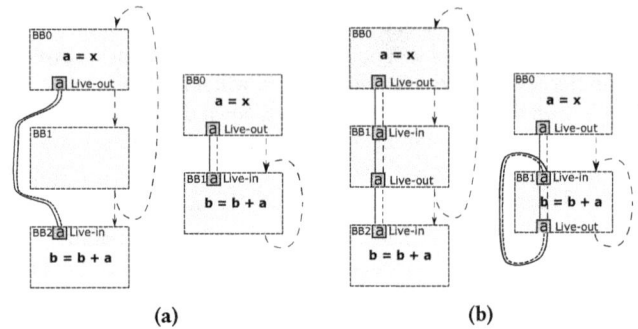

(a)   (b)

Figure 4: Implementing control flow. Figure 4a shows two cases where a direct conversion of a data and control flow graph into an elastic circuit would fail. Coupling data and control to ensure correct token transfers between BBs is given in Figure 4b.

are available. Finally, we interface with memory through *elastic memory ports*. The write port has two inputs (*data* and *address*) and a control-only signal from the memory interface indicates successful completion. The read port sends an address to memory and receives data with its corresponding elastic control. Yet, to achieve correct execution in an intrinsically out-of-order system, interfacing to memory is more challenging than just connecting to the appropriate memory ports; this will be addressed in Section 3.5.

3.2 From Basic Blocks to Datapaths

We use the standard data and control flow graphs obtained by a compiler as the starting point of our circuit generation. First, we create a datapath for each *basic block* (BB)—i.e., for each straight piece of code not containing conditionals. The basic conversion is a literal translation of the data flow graph into an elastic circuit: every operator corresponds to a functional unit, edges are connections between the components, and a Fork is added when a node has more than one direct successor and at least one is in the same basic block. At this point, our circuit does not contain any register (Buff).

BBs are connected by directed edges representing data and control transfers. Once the datapath of each BB has been built, we need to connect them to other datapaths (or BBs). We have chosen the conversion template of Figure 3. We allocate a Merge node for every variable entering the BB (*live-in*). Every Merge receives a piece of data with the corresponding token from one of the predecessor BBs and forwards it to the main datapath. In the example in Figure 3, BB3 accepts three live-in variables from one of its two predecessor BBs—note that, as the circuit follows the control flow, only one of the predecessor blocks is active at any point in time (i.e., *BB1* and *BB2* will never send tokens to *BB3* simultaneously) and this is key to deadlock avoidance (see Section 3.4).

To implement control flow decisions, for every value used by any successor BB (*live-out*), we place a Branch at the BB output. If the successor block does not require a particular data, the output of the corresponding Branch is discarded into a sink.

3.3 Implementing Control Flow

Connecting the datapath elements corresponding to BBs (Figure 3) is relatively straightforward, except for a couple of problems which arise from the fundamental difference of software programs implemented on a processor compared to elastic circuits.

Figure 4a shows two examples: (1) In the example on the left, the variable a is defined in BB0 and used in BB2. A typical representation in a compiler propagates the desired information directly from the source to the destination block (i.e., a live-in of a basic block comes from a basic block which is not its immediate predecessor). This flow does not pose problems in software, as successive values of a would be stored in a register of a processor or in memory and the last value used when BB2 is reached. (2) In the example on the right, BB1 is the only BB in the body of a loop and uses a value a produced in BB0. The value of a does not change during the execution of BB1 and is used at every execution of BB1. Again, there would be no problem in a processor—the value would be stored in a register or memory and read as many times as needed.

Directly implementing such connections in an elastic circuit would result in incorrect behavior because every value is associated with a control token: the number of generated tokens must exactly match the number of distinct uses. Both cases in Figure 4a violate this principle: (1) In the first case, if the control flow were {BB0-BB1-BB0-BB1-BB2}, two new values (with the respective tokens) for a would have been generated and sent to BB2; yet, BB2 can take only a single token and wants only the most recent value. Execution would be incorrect or the circuit would not terminate because the tokens not absorbed by BB2 would create backpressure to BB0 and stop it indefinitely. (2) In the second case, BB1 would not be able to execute repeatedly due to a starving input. Assuming the control flow is {BB0-BB1-BB1}, the first execution of BB1 will consume the single data token for a and any further execution of BB1 would stall indefinitely waiting for a token.

The solution to both problems corresponds to strictly coupling data propagation with control flow, as Figure 4b shows. We modify the data and control flow graphs to ensure that (1) every BB provides a live-out for every live-in of all of its immediate successor BBs and exclusively to them, and that (2) every BB receives all of its live-ins from its immediate predecessor BBs and exclusively from them. We implement this by identifying the origin block for every live-in variable of every BB. We then find all the paths of the control flow graph connecting the origin BB and the BB that the live-in belongs to, and we reconnect the variable through these paths. This approach guarantees that every piece of data for a BB receives a fresh token each and every time the BB actually executes.

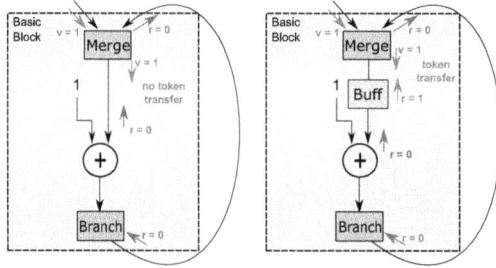

Figure 5: Adding registers. A combinational cycle causes deadlock, as the token with the updated data cannot propagate back into the Merge node. Breaking the combinational loop with an Buff enables the token to loop back.

3.4 Adding Registers

So far, our circuits do not contain any registers. Before illustrating our strategy for Buff placement, we discuss their impact on the circuit functionality and their role in avoiding deadlock.

Elastic buffers and circuit functionality. Elastic systems use distributed handshake signals to control the flow of data in the datapath. These signals implicitly take care of stalling early data items when they need to synchronize with late items [21]. Although Buffs shift the values in time with respect to the pure synchronous behavior, their presence or absence does not affect the functional correctness of the system, as any consumer of multiple values synchronizes the corresponding valid tokens. Contrary to registers in traditional synchronous designs, this characteristic allows the insertion of Buffs on any wire without any effect on functionality but only on performance. In other words, insertion or removal of Buffs is correct by construction, as it preserves flow equivalence and guarantees an unchanged order of valid data [11, 21].

Elastic buffers and avoiding deadlock. The necessary and sufficient condition for deadlock-free execution requires any cycle in the circuit to contain at least one Buff [12, 19]. Figure 5 contrasts a design of a simple cycle with and without a Buff on the cyclic path—in the first case, a token inserted into the Merge node cannot propagate through the loop due to the combinational relationship of the valid and ready tokens on the cycle (labeled as v and r in the figure). As in traditional synchronous circuits, the combinational loop needs to be broken through a register. Adding a Buff ensures that a token can propagate through the cycle [11]. Once the cyclic combinational relations have been resolved, all tokens will flow through the circuit in the absolute execution order specified by the original program; if the program terminates, the token inserted in the start BB will eventually reach the end BB, following the control flow of the program; this guarantees the absence of deadlock.

Once the requirement above is satisfied, adding more Buffs has no influence on functionality but only on performance by (1) delaying the corresponding piece of data by a clock cycle and (2) by breaking a combinational path in the circuit into two paths, possibly reducing the critical path of the circuit. A Buff can be placed on any edge of the graph of elastic nodes (i.e., between any two elastic components). Each edge is associated with its weight, equivalent to the number of bits of the corresponding data. We define an optimal Buff placement as one which ensures that (1) every graph cycle is cut by at least one Buff or sequential element within a functional

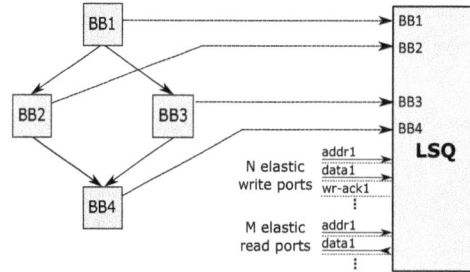

Figure 6: The load-store queue required for correct out-of-order memory accesses.

unit and (2) the sum of the weights of all cut edges is minimized. In our experiments we implement a simple heuristic to approximate this optimal placement (and, in practice, we think that in all our experiments the placement is optimal in the above sense).

3.5 Connecting to Memory

Figure 2 shows a memory component with elastic read and write ports (i.e., an elastic interface to a traditional memory hierarchy). Connecting every load or store operation to a read and write port respectively seems a natural decision, but the result may be incorrect. Access requests will arrive to the memory interface in arbitrary order (this is the dynamic out-of-order feature that, in general, we desire) and this may lead to the violation of memory dependencies. For instance, if a write happens at the same address as some successive read, and if the read token arrives in the elastic circuit before the write token, the result of the read will be incorrect.

The solution is to use a *load-store queue* (LSQ) similar to those present in dynamically scheduled processors. Yet, we have shown that building a LSQ for elastic circuits has one fundamental difference [26]: the LSQ must be given explicit information on the original program order of the memory accesses, so that it can allocate them into the queue in the right order and thus resolve them in a semantically correct way. The details are beyond the scope of this paper; it suffices to say that the key condition for the LSQ to execute correctly is to receive tokens which follow the actual order of execution of the basic blocks of the circuit. This ordering enables the LSQ to determine and resolve dependencies as memory access arguments from different basic blocks arrive out-of-order.

Consider a program containing four basic blocks as given in Figure 6. The difference from the simple memory interface of Figure 2 is only in the additional elastic control signals (e.g., BB1, BB2). These signals indicate to the LSQ the start of the particular BB. When the program starts, BB1 sends a token to the LSQ. Assuming that the control flow determines the execution of BB2 afterwards, BB2 will send a token to the LSQ next. The order of these tokens enables the LSQ to appropriately handle out-of-order memory accesses; accesses from BB1 need to be completed before those from BB2. If, for instance, a read request arrives from BB2 before all writes from BB1 have been completed (or determined independent of the read), the LSQ will appropriately stall the execution of the read.

Our challenge here is to guarantee that the BBi signals needed for the LSQ are produced *in order* by a circuit which we have otherwise designed to be as aggressively out-of-order as we could. To this end, we generate a control path that follows the control flow of

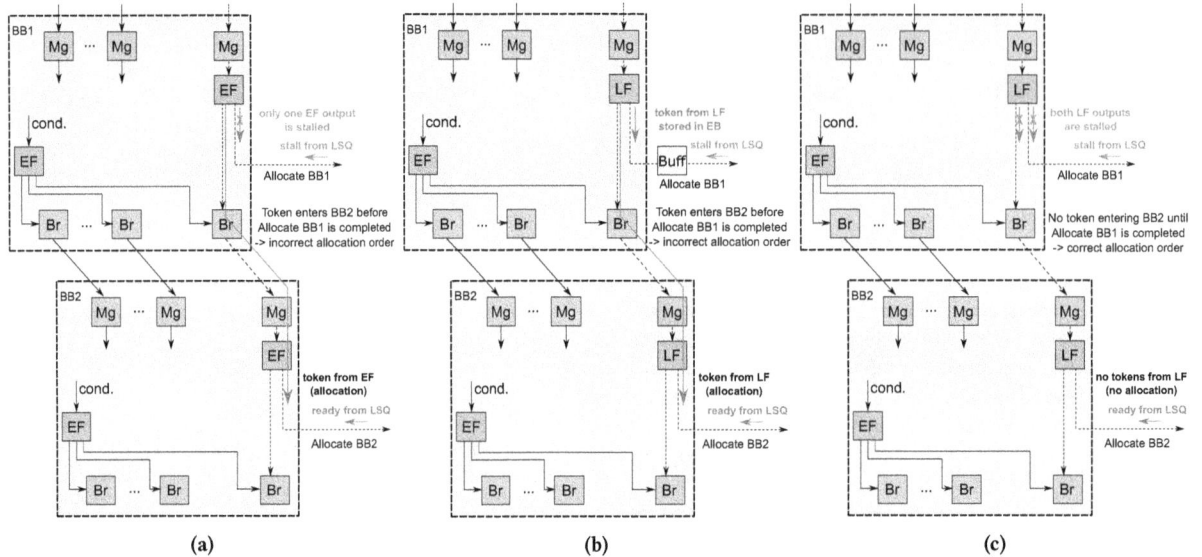

Figure 7: Connecting the elastic circuit to the memory interface. Figures 7a and 7b give examples of incorrect connections. In Figure 7a, the Eager Fork may send an allocation to BB2 before the allocation of BB1 completes. In Figure 7b, the allocation order may be reversed due to the storage element on the control line between the circuit and the LSQ. Figure 7c shows the correct way to connect the LSQ—an allocation cannot occur unless all predecessor allocations have been completed.

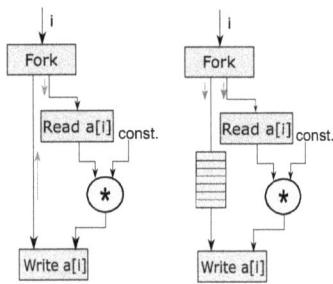

Figure 8: Increasing parallelism by adding FIFOs.

the program through the BBs—essentially, as a data-less variable which is a live-in and live-out of each and every BB. The tokens in this path trigger the allocation of BBs as soon as the control flows there (i.e., as soon as a decision has been made to enter a particular BB). However, applying the standard elastic circuit design strategy described in the previous sections might result in the incorrect order of token arrival to the LSQ. Here are two example situations leading to a potentially wrong execution: (1) If the token is forked to the LSQ using the typical Eager Fork (Fork), one of the fork outputs might send a token to the next BB before the LSQ has accepted a token from its predecessor (Figure 7a). (2) Although placing Buffs in elastic circuits has no impact on correctness (as discussed in Section 3.4), an Buff on the fork output connected to the LSQ might compromise the order of token arrival to the queue—if the token remains stored in the Buff, the successor BB could send a new token before the prior allocation has been completed (Figure 7b).

The correct way to connect the LSQ to the elastic circuit is given in Figure 7c: (1) The forks used to send the tokens to the LSQ are Lazy Forks (LFork)—if one of the fork outputs is stalled, the other one will stall as well. (2) No sequential elements (Buffs) are

allowed on the fork outputs connected to the LSQ. This ensures that a token can be passed to the successor BB only when the allocation of its predecessor BB has been completed—if an allocation is deferred (e.g., due to limited space in the LSQ), the token stalls and no further allocation requests reach the LSQ. To connect our datapaths to memory, we leverage compiler analysis to simplify our memory interface. Whenever the compiler can disambiguate memory accesses, groups of accesses that cannot mutually conflict use separate LSQs, while accesses which cannot have dependencies with any other accesses are connected to simple memory interfaces.

3.6 Decoupling Paths for More Parallelism

The methodology described so far results in semantically correct circuits; however, they may not yet be competitive with statically scheduled circuits: A Fork, used to distribute some value to potentially independent pipelines, does pass the token to any successor as soon as it is ready to take it, but, as mentioned in Section 3.1, does not accept a new token until all successors have consumed the previous one. Since some paths through a basic block take longer to process a token, a Fork may prevent a shorter path to execute faster. A critical example is the Fork distributing the condition to all Branches, shown in Figure 3: Even if the control decision is resolved quickly, the Fork accepts a new condition only when all Branch nodes receive their values. This prevents hardware pipelining; even if the need for another iteration can be decided very fast, the new iteration will not start until the current iteration finishes.

To increase the effective parallelism, we decouple the fast and slow paths of the basic block by inserting FIFOs into the paths with longer latency. This allows token accumulation without blocking the Fork and thus allows to trigger the faster paths at a higher rate. Figure 8 contrasts the naive slow design with the FIFO-optimized version. This modification is sufficient to overlap iterations of a loop at a rate which corresponds to the speed at which the control decision can be made. Algorithmically determining the optimal size of the FIFOs seems akin to buffer sizing in networking and has been discussed in the context of dataflow machines [13]. We have not yet properly studied the problem, given the fact that it affects only performance and not correctness. In this work, we place a FIFO on every Fork output and experimentally determine its optimal size.

3.7 A Complete Flow

This section has shown how an arbitrary program described in a high-level language can be transformed into a dynamically scheduled circuit. The resulting circuit executes operations out-of-order, naturally implements hardware pipelining, and handles efficiently potential memory dependencies. Although our transformation flow is susceptible to improvements, we think it is interesting to compare it with a mature HLS tool producing statically-scheduled circuits, as well as with approaches similar to ours.

4 EVALUATION

We describe here our prototype synthesizer, then give an overview of our methodology to compare with a commercial HLS tool, and finally discuss our benchmarks before presenting our results.

4.1 Prototype Synthesizer

Our hardware generation flow uses the LLVM compiler framework [30]: (1) The clang frontend parses the C/C++ program and produces a *static single assignment* (SSA) intermediate representation (LLVM IR) [40]. (2) The LLVM optimizer applies standard transformation and analysis passes on the IR. (3) Our custom-made pass transforms the optimized LLVM IR into an elastic circuit. The main steps of this transformation are described in Section 3. (4) The IR of the elastic circuit is converted into a VHDL netlist of the elastic primitives described in Section 3.1. Our flow still includes a few semimanual steps (including some for the comparisons of the next section), but nothing more than what is described in Section 3.

4.2 Methodology

To demonstrate the benefits of using an elastic hardware generation strategy in HLS, we compare our circuits with designs generated by Vivado HLS [43], a state-of-the-art commercial HLS tool. In all Vivado designs, we apply the pipelining optimization directive.

To provide a fair comparison of our designs against those generated by Vivado, we employ the same arithmetic units used by Vivado into our designs. We extract the components manually from Vivado's results and create custom wrappers with handshake signals. We use the same RAMs for our design as Vivado employs. We rely on the same memory analysis as Vivado: when a compiler cannot disambiguate memory accesses, we manually employ the LSQ in our designs and connect it to the RAM interface; otherwise, we connect the elastic read/write ports directly to the RAM.

We simulated the designs in ModelSim [31] and used a set of test vectors for functional verification. We obtain the loop initiation interval (II) from the simulation and the clock period (CP) from the post-routing timing analysis to calculate the total execution time. Placing and routing the designs using Vivado gives us the resource usage (i.e., the number of CLB slices, with the corresponding LUT and FF count, as well as the number of DSP units).

4.3 Benchmarks

The designs that we discuss in this section are simple kernels which represent typical cases where static scheduling is known to run into its fundamental limits while dynamic scheduling should make a significant difference. We also consider a simple kernel where static scheduling is fully successful, to show that dynamically scheduling achieves virtually the same result with small overheads.

- *Histogram* reads an array of features and increases the value of the corresponding histogram bins. The memory access pattern cannot be determined at compile time—the loop may contain read-after-write dependencies if the same bin is updated in neighbouring iterations.
- *Matrix Power* performs a series of matrix-vector multiplications. Each iteration of a nested loop reads a row and a column coordinate and updates the corresponding matrix element. At compile time, it is not possible to determine if successive iterations perform conflicting writes and reads.
- *Loop with condition 1* is the kernel discussed in Section 2, with a potential dependency across iterations dependent on the data from arrays A and B.
- *Loop with condition 2* is a variation of the previous kernel where we replace the conditional addition with a multiplication of the same variables and which we will contrast with the previous kernel in terms of resource utilization.
- *FIR filter* is an ordinary FIR filter calculating the output based on the inputs and the coefficients. The memory reads and writes are independent and disambiguated at compile time.

4.4 Results: Comparison with Static HLS

Table 1 summarizes the timing and resource results for all kernels and Figure 9 shows our results relative to those from Vivado HLS (results to the left or below the red circle are better).

Timing. Avoiding conservative assumptions on memory and control dependencies results in a significant improvement of the execution time in all of the corresponding benchmarks (note that the dynamic results are data dependent: the average II can, in all these examples, be as low as 1 and never larger than the statically computed II). This increases the throughput with usually an acceptable impact on the CP due to the additional handshake signals between elastic components. The strongest impact on the CP is when we use the LSQ, whose critical path is extremely sensitive to the number of queue entries [26]. Although this timing overhead is quite tangible, it is still conspicuously small when compared to the potential improvement in II and, consequently, the net performance. On the *FIR* benchmark, static HLS techniques produce a highly optimized pipeline because memory accesses can be disambiguated at compile time. The static HLS tool depends on techniques akin to modulo scheduling [37] to restructure and pipeline the loop, whereas we effortlessly compile the LLVM IR into an elastic circuit as-is: this is the only example of design where our result is Pareto dominated by the static one, but the impact of the elastic circuitry on the CP appears not to be a cause of major concern—especially since nothing was yet attempted to optimize the elastic circuits.

Resource utilization. The right of Table 1 contrasts the resource utilization of statically and dynamically scheduled circuits. The overhead in slices of the dynamic designs, notable across all benchmarks, is partially due to the control logic that the elastic

Benchmark	II$_{avg}$		CP (ns)		Execution time (us)		Slices		LUTs		FFs		DSPs	
	STAT	DYN	STAT	DYN	STAT	DYN	STAT	DYN	STAT	DYN	STAT	DYN	STAT	DYN
Histogram	11	2.3	3.3	5.7	36.3	13.3	130	200 + 901	296	3,632	447	1,734	2	2
Matrix power	16	4.2	3.4	6.0	20.7	9.6	219	352 + 1113	500	4,237	790	2,050	5	5
Loop with condition 1	9	1.3	2.8	4.8	25.3	6.2	161	289	391	767	525	984	2	4
Loop with condition 2	5	1.2	3.4	4.8	17.1	5.7	187	240	409	659	623	811	5	5
FIR	1	1	3.3	4.4	3.3	4.4	62	127	89	341	224	382	3	3

Table 1: Dynamically scheduled results (our elastic circuits) contrasted to statically scheduled results (Vivado HLS). The slice count for *Histogram* and *Matrix Power* is given as slices of kernel + slices of LSQ.

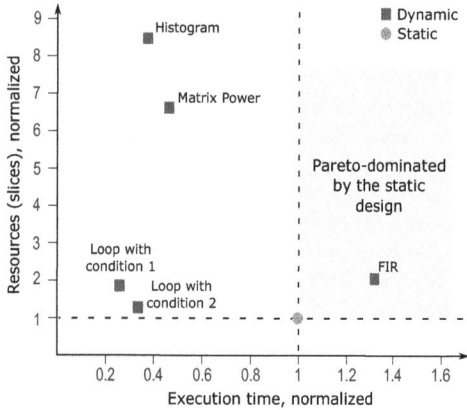

Figure 9: Resource utilization and execution time of the dynamically scheduled designs, normalized to the corresponding static designs produced by Vivado HLS.

circuits contain and which allows them to achieve the latency-insensitivity which we desire. The overhead of the FIFOs that we introduced to increase throughput, as discussed in Section 3.6, is probably overblown by the simplicity of the examples with only a few functional units. Additionally, we have not yet looked into time-multiplexing of functional units—we trivially allocate a new unit per operator, whereas the allocation and binding algorithms that Vivado employs allow a single unit to be shared: see for instance *Loop with condition 1* where our design requires two functional units to perform the addition and the subtraction whereas Vivado HLS time-multiplexes the same one. To show this, we replaced one of the operations with a multiplication (*Loop with condition 2*) and verified that the resource difference is now significantly smaller.

It is immediately visible from Figure 9 that the circuits requiring an out-of-order memory interface demand significant additional resources. Although others have accelerated similar kernels to a qualitatively comparable extent and with only insignificant overhead [15], their solution is highly specific and solves only a subset of problems discussed in this work. It should be emphasized that the resource and timing overhead could be minimized by implementing the LSQs as hard-macros, in the same way as other memory hierarchy components might be in the future (e.g., caches and TLBs).

4.5 Results: Comparison of Dynamically Scheduled Techniques

In this section, we compare our work to two approaches that are perhaps the closest ones to ours, and discuss some issues preventing them to attain the performance we strive for.

Huang et al. generated elastic circuits from C code, to be mapped to a coarse-grain reconfigurable array [25]. Their circuit generation approach differs from ours in two aspects: (1) They use a single Branch node at the output of each basic block, which forces them to synchronize all the basic block outputs and, consequently, prevents loop iterations from overlapping (i.e., loops are not pipelined). (2) Their approach does not employ a LSQ at the memory interface and, thus, all memory accesses which cannot be disambiguated at compile time need to be conservatively sequentialized.

Budiu et al. described a compiler for generating *asynchronous circuits* from C code [3, 4]. Although their final circuits are fundamentally different from ours (our circuits are *perfectly synchronous* and avoid the traditional difficulties associated with asynchronous designs), the generation strategy is similar to ours. Unfortunately, the exact methodology is never described in full detail and examples across different papers by the same authors do not seem perfectly consistent. Nevertheless, their best results appear to match qualitatively ours, except when memory accesses are involved: they present two strategies for handling memory dependencies and both are more conservative than ours.

We implemented our two benchmarks with memory dependencies following the design strategies above and compared their timing and resource requirements to our designs. In the case of Budiu et al., we have replaced their asynchronous components with the corresponding synchronous elastic components. Table 2 shows the results. The designs of Huang et al. cannot achieve any pipelining, which results in performances lower than even those of the static HLS designs. For the designs by Budiu et al., we provide two sets of results, corresponding to the two approaches for handling memory dependencies that the authors present: The first version (labeled *CASH 1* in the table) contains no LSQ at the memory interface; as in the work by Huang et al., the authors conservatively sequentialize memory accesses which are potentially dependent; however, they manage to create a pipeline across iterations and achieve some performance improvement compared to Huang et al. In the second version, the authors add an LSQ but use a conservative allocation policy which inserts an entry into the LSQ only when an address or a data item for the corresponding access is known; despite increasing the pipeline throughput, this strategy still cannot match the performance that we achieve using our group allocation policy.

5 PERSPECTIVES

Although many results of Section 4 appear attractive to us, it is also clear that our synthesizer is still primitive in many respects. We think it is fair to emphasize that statically scheduled HLS benefits from decades of research that the automatic design of latency insensitive circuits cannot sport. We spend this section to evoke

Benchmark	II_{avg}				CP (ns)				Execution time (us)				Slices			
	Huang	CASH 1	CASH 2	DYN	Huang	CASH 1	CASH 2	DYN	Huang	CASH 1	CASH 2	DYN	Huang	CASH 1	CASH 2	DYN
Histogram	12	11	3.7	2.3	4.9	4.8	5.9	5.7	58.9	52.9	21.2	13.3	134	149	182+901	200+901
Matrix power	17	16	5.0	4.2	4.1	3.9	6.3	6.0	26.6	23.8	11.9	9.6	204	233	332+1113	352+1113

Table 2: Dynamically scheduled results (our elastic circuits, DYN) contrasted to other dynamic approaches.

some of the most important areas where dynamically scheduled HLS could improve in the future.

5.1 Pipelining and Area Optimizations

Pipelining ordinary synchronous circuits is a thoroughly studied problem [16]. Our heuristic in Section 3.4 is nothing more than first working shot, certainly susceptible of significant improvements—for instance, we did not even try to break critical paths with sequential elements. Other typical concerns of HLS which we did not address here are allocation and binding: deciding how many units of a specific type to implement and how to time-multiplex them to perform needed operations. Elastic circuits can time-multiplex functional units [6] and we will try to exploit this.

5.2 Partial Schedule Rigidification

One optimization aspect which is immediately manifest when looking at the circuits we generate is that we allow latency insensitivity through any component and on any path. Although in some cases this is exactly the strength of our methodology, in many cases it is an expensive overkill: many computational paths may be constructed with fixed-latency components (ALUs, floating-point operators, etc.) and never really profit from the control flexibility. There may be optimizations that "rip-off", under some conditions, complex control paths from the corresponding datapaths and replace them with simpler, customized control structures. One could see this as a selective rigidification of the schedule where dynamism is not really needed. This is a completely unexplored avenue which might reduce significantly the area and timing overhead of elasticity.

5.3 Speculative Execution

Finally, as in computer architecture, dynamic scheduling paves the way to one of the most powerful ideas in computing: executing some operations before one has the certitude that they are actually needed or that it is correct to execute them. Speculation can significantly improve the execution of loops where the iteration interval is very large due to a condition on the loop continuation that takes very long to compute: control speculation can predict very early (possibly with an iteration interval of one) whether it makes sense to execute *tentatively* another iteration. Similarly, speculation can further improve the problem of memory dependencies, not only by reordering accesses once the lack of dependency is known but even by assuming independence early on and reverting back if the prediction was wrong. The ability to implement speculation depends on reliable mechanisms to revert state changes due to wrongly executed operations—what in processors is entrusted to reorder buffers and store queues. In the scope of elastic circuits, first steps of speculative execution (much more limited compared to the above goals) have been shown already [21] and suggest that latency insensitive protocols can be modified to accommodate tentative and reversible execution.

6 RELATED WORK

Recent advances in HLS have explored methods to overcome the conservatism in static scheduling. Several techniques [1, 29] generate multiple schedules which are dynamically selected during runtime, once the values of all parameters are known. Tan et al. [39] describe an approach called ElasticFlow to apply loop pipelining on a particular class of irregular loops. Dai et al. [14] propose methods for pipeline flushing by performing scheduling for multiple initiation intervals of the pipeline; they later developed application-specific dynamic hazard detection circuitry [15] and have shown the ability of speculation but with stringent constraints (e.g., stateless inner-loop datapath). Nurvitadhi et al. [34] perform automatic pipelining, assuming that the datapath is already partitioned into pipeline stages. The underlying methodology in all these techniques is still based on static scheduling opportunistically adapted to enable some level of dynamic behavior, which limits the achievable performance improvements only to some particular cases.

Different authors exploited latency-insensitive protocols [5, 11, 19] to construct dynamic circuits. Elastic circuits [11] are probably the best-studied form of latency insensitivity, but the original paradigm used in most of the papers by Cortadella et al. is too restrictive for HLS. Several approaches [8, 24] extended the SELF protocol [11] with constructs similar to the Branch and Merge which we use in this work. Kam et al. [27] testified of the ability of elastic circuits to create dynamic pipelines, but do not provide generic transformations to create elastic circuits out of high-level descriptions. Efforts in the asynchronous circuit domain, such as Balsa [18] and Haste/TiDE [33], applied syntax-driven approaches for mapping a program into a structure of handshake components [38], and a synchronous backend for Haste/TiDE has later been developed. Putnam et al. [36] have also explored synthesizing dataflow-like circuits from high-level specifications. However, all these approaches provide little information on some critical aspects of the conversion which are at the heart of this paper; to our best knowledge, these approaches have never been contrasted to modern HLS tools. The efforts closest to ours (i.e., the work by Huang et al. [25] and Budiu et al. [3, 4]) have been discussed in Section 4.5.

Cheng et al. [9] describe circuits as networks of processes in which hardware accelerators exchange data via dynamic communication channels. We are here interested in exploring dynamicity on a finer grain and thus we do not face some of the deadlock issues that are critical in their work. Standard HLS tools [43] also often interconnect with handshakes various datapaths from nested loops and functions but, again, we care here for the fine-grain schedule of individual datapaths. Townsend et al. [41] used a functional programming intermediate representation as a starting point for synthesizing dataflow networks. Elastic circuits, with their handshake signals, immediately bring to mind Bluespec and its firing rules [42]. However, nothing in these two approaches is directly related to our goal: transforming a program written in an imperative, high-level language into a dynamically scheduled circuit.

7 CONCLUSIONS

With FPGAs finding their way into datacenters, HLS tools are set to play a key role in the future of reconfigurable computing. Yet, they are relying on a paradigm which is conceptually identical to the problem of compilation for VLIW processors: generating good static circuits from high-level languages requires peculiar code restructuring algorithms (e.g., modulo scheduling), demands expert user interaction (e.g., pragmas), forces worst-case assumptions on important issues (e.g., memory and control dependencies), and precludes key performance optimizations (e.g., general forms of speculative execution). In this paper, we have described a dynamically scheduled form of HLS and run a simple synthesizer on a few relevant kernels to compare results to a commercial, statically scheduled HLS tool. When static HLS exploits the maximum parallelism available, our technique achieves similar results with minimal degradation in cycle time; when static HLS misses some key performance optimization opportunities, our circuits seize them, achieving large performance improvements with the investment of more resources. Although much remains to be done to refine the optimizations and to add key features we have only evoked so far, we believe our work points to a very promising avenue to make HLS truly valuable on irregular and control-dominated applications.

REFERENCES

[1] M. Alle, A. Morvan, and S. Derrien. Runtime dependency analysis for loop pipelining in high-level synthesis. In *Proceedings of the 50th Design Automation Conference*, pages 51:1–51:10, Austin, Tex., June 2013.

[2] Amazon.com, Inc. *Amazon EC2 F1 Instances*.

[3] M. Budiu, P. V. Artigas, and S. C. Goldstein. Dataflow: A complement to superscalar. In *Proceedings of the IEEE International Symposium on Performance Analysis of Systems and Software*, pages 177–86, Austin, Tex., Mar. 2005.

[4] M. Budiu and S. C. Goldstein. Pegasus: An efficient intermediate representation. Technical Report CMU-CS-02-107, Carnegie Mellon University, May 2002.

[5] L. P. Carloni, K. L. McMillan, and A. L. Sangiovanni-Vincentelli. Theory of latency-insensitive design. *IEEE Transactions on Computer-Aided Design of Integrated Circuits and Systems*, CAD-20(9):1059–76, Sept. 2001.

[6] J. Carmona, J. Júlvez, J. Cortadella, and M. Kishinevsky. A scheduling strategy for synchronous elastic designs. *Journal Fundamenta Informaticae*, 108(1–2):1–21, Jan. 2011.

[7] A. M. Caulfield, E. S. Chung, A. Putnam, H. Angepat, J. Fowers, M. Haselman, S. Heil, M. Humphrey, P. Kaur, J. Kim, D. Lo, T. Massengill, K. Ovtcharov, M. Papamichael, L. Woods, S. Lanka, D. Chiou, and D. Burger. A cloud-scale acceleration architecture. In *Proceedings of the 49th International Symposium on Microarchitecture*, pages 1–13, Taipei, Taiwan, Oct. 2016.

[8] S. Chatterjee, M. Kishinevsky, and U. Y. Ogras. xMAS: Quick formal modeling of communication fabrics to enable verification. *IEEE Design & Test of Computers*, 29(3):80–88, June 2012.

[9] S. Cheng and J. Wawrzynek. Synthesis of statically analyzable accelerator networks from sequential programs. In *Proceedings of the International Conference on Computer-Aided Design*, pages 126–33, Austin, Tex., Nov. 2016.

[10] D. Chiou. Intel acquires Altera: How will the world of FPGAs be affected? In *Proceedings of the 2016 ACM/SIGDA International Symposium on Field-Programmable Gate Arrays*, page 148, Monterey, Calif., Feb. 2016.

[11] J. Cortadella, M. Kishinevsky, and B. Grundmann. Synthesis of synchronous elastic architectures. In *Proceedings of the 43rd Design Automation Conference*, pages 657–62, San Francisco, Calif., July 2006.

[12] J. Cortadella, M. G. Oms, M. Kishinevsky, and S. S. Sapatnekar. RTL synthesis: From logic synthesis to automatic pipelining. *Proceedings of the IEEE*, 103(11):2061–75, Nov. 2015.

[13] D. E. Culler and Arvind. Resource requirements of dataflow programs. In *Proceedings of the 15th Annual International Symposium on Computer Architecture*, pages 141–150, Honolulu, Hawaii, May 1988.

[14] S. Dai, M. Tan, K. Hao, and Z. Zhang. Flushing-enabled loop pipelining for high-level synthesis. In *Proceedings of the 51st Design Automation Conference*, pages 1–6, San Francisco, Calif., June 2014.

[15] S. Dai, R. Zhao, G. Liu, S. Srinath, U. Gupta, C. Batten, and Z. Zhang. Dynamic hazard resolution for pipelining irregular loops in high-level synthesis. In *Proceedings of the 25th ACM/SIGDA International Symposium on Field Programmable Gate Arrays*, pages 189–194, Monterey, Calif., Feb. 2017.

[16] G. De Micheli. *Synthesis and Optimization of Digital Circuits*. McGraw-Hill, New York, 1994.

[17] J. C. Dvorak. *How the Itanium Killed the Computer Industry*, Jan. 2009.

[18] D. Edwards and A. Bardsley. Balsa: An asynchronous hardware synthesis language. *The Computer Journal*, 45(1):12–18, Jan. 2002.

[19] S. A. Edwards, R. Townsend, and M. A. Kim. Compositional dataflow circuits. In *Proceedings of the 15th ACM-IEEE International Conference on Formal Methods and Models for System Design*, pages 175–184, Vienna, Austria, Sept. 2017.

[20] M. Fingeroff. *High-Level Synthesis Blue Book*. Xlibris Corporation, first edition, 2010.

[21] M. Galceran-Oms, J. Cortadella, and M. Kishinevsky. Speculation in elastic systems. In *Proceedings of the 46th Design Automation Conference*, pages 292–95, San Francisco, Calif., July 2009.

[22] N. George, H. Lee, D. Novo, T. Rompf, K. Brown, A. Sujeeth, M. Odersky, K. Olukotun, and P. Ienne. Hardware system synthesis from domain-specific languages. In *Proceedings of the 23rd International Conference on Field-Programmable Logic and Applications*, pages 1–8, Munich, Sept. 2014.

[23] J. L. Hennessy and D. A. Patterson. *Computer Architecture: A Quantitative Approach*. Morgan Kaufmann, fifth edition, 2011.

[24] G. Hoover and F. Brewer. Synthesizing synchronous elastic flow networks. In *Proceedings of the Design, Automation and Test in Europe Conference and Exhibition*, pages 306–11, Munich, Mar. 2008.

[25] Y. Huang, P. Ienne, O. Temam, Y. Chen, and C. Wu. Elastic CGRAs. In *Proceedings of the 21st ACM/SIGDA International Symposium on Field Programmable Gate Arrays*, pages 171–80, Monterey, Calif., Feb. 2013.

[26] L. Josipović, P. Brisk, and P. Ienne. An out-of-order load-store queue for spatial computing. *ACM Transactions on Embedded Computing Systems (TECS)*, 16(5s):125:1–125:19, Sept. 2017.

[27] T. Kam, M. Kishinevsky, J. Cortadella, and M. Galceran-Oms. Correct-by-construction microarchitectural pipelining. *Proceedings of the 27th International Conference on Computer-Aided Design*, pages 434–41, Nov. 2008.

[28] M. S. Lam. Software pipelining: An effective scheduling technique for VLIW machines. In *Proceedings of the 1988 ACM Conference on Programming Language Design and Implementation*, pages 318–28, Atlanta, Ga., June 1988.

[29] J. Liu, S. Bayliss, and G. A. Constantinides. Offline synthesis of online dependence testing: Parametric loop pipelining for HLS. In *Proceedings of the 23rd IEEE Symposium on Field-Programmable Custom Computing Machines*, pages 159–62, Vancouver, May 2015.

[30] The LLVM Compiler Infrastructure. *http://www.llvm.org*.

[31] Mentor Graphics. ModelSim, 2016.

[32] T. Murata. Petri nets: Properties, analysis and applications. *Proceedings of the IEEE*, 77(4):541–80, Apr. 1989.

[33] S. F. Nielsen, J. Sparsø, J. B. Jensen, and J. S. R. Nielsen. A behavioral synthesis frontend to the Haste/TiDE design flow. In *Proceedings of the 15th International Symposium on Asynchronous Circuits and Systems*, pages 185–94, Chapel Hill, N.C., May 2009.

[34] E. Nurvitadhi, J. C. Hoe, T. Kam, and S.-L. L. Lu. Automatic pipelining from transactional datapath specifications. *IEEE Transactions on Computer-Aided Design of Integrated Circuits and Systems*, 30(3):441–54, Mar. 2011.

[35] A. Putnam, A. M. Caulfield, E. S. Chung, D. Chiou, K. Constantinides, J. Demme, H. Esmaeilzadeh, J. Fowers, G. P. Gopal, J. Gray, M. Haselman, S. Hauck, S. Heil, A. Hormati, J.-Y. Kim, S. Lanka, J. Larus, E. Peterson, S. Pope, A. Smith, J. Thong, P. Y. Xiao, and D. Burger. A reconfigurable fabric for accelerating large-scale datacenter services. In *Proceedings of the 41st International Symposium on Computer Architecture*, pages 13–24, Minneapolis, Minn., June 2014.

[36] A. R. Putnam, D. Bennett, E. Dellinger, J. Mason, and P. Sundararajan. CHiMPS: A high-level compilation flow for hybrid CPU-FPGA architectures. In *Proceedings of the 16th ACM/SIGDA International Symposium on Field Programmable Gate Arrays*, pages 173–178, Monterey, Calif., Feb. 2017.

[37] B. R. Rau. Iterative modulo scheduling. *International Journal of Parallel Programming*, 24(1):3–64, Feb. 1996.

[38] J. Sparsø. Current trends in high-level synthesis of asynchronous circuits. In *Proceedings of the 16th IEEE International Conference on Electronics, Circuits, and Systems*, pages 347–50, Yasmine Hammamet, Tunisia, Dec. 2009.

[39] M. Tan, G. Liu, R. Zhao, S. Dai, and Z. Zhang. ElasticFlow: A complexity-effective approach for pipelining irregular loop nests. In *Proceedings of the 34th International Conference on Computer-Aided Design*, pages 78–85, Austin, Tex., Nov. 2015.

[40] L. Torczon and K. Cooper. *Engineering a Compiler*. Morgan Kaufmann, second edition, 2011.

[41] R. Townsend, M. A. Kim, and S. A. Edwards. From functional programs to pipelined dataflow circuits. In *Proceedings of the 26th International Conference on Compiler Construction*, pages 76–86, Austin, TX, USA, Feb. 2017.

[42] M. Vijayaraghavan and Arvind. Bounded dataflow networks and latency-insensitive circuits. In *Proceedings of the 9th International Conference on Formal Methods and Models for Codesign*, pages 171–80, Cambridge, MA, July 2009.

[43] Xilinx Inc. *Vivado High-Level Synthesis*.

A Scalable Approach to Exact Resource-Constrained Scheduling Based on a Joint SDC and SAT Formulation

Steve Dai, Gai Liu, Zhiru Zhang

School of Electrical and Computer Engineering, Cornell University, Ithaca, NY

{hd273,gl387,zhiruz}@cornell.edu

ABSTRACT

Despite increasing adoption of high-level synthesis (HLS) for its design productivity advantage, success in achieving high quality-of-results out-of-the-box is often hindered by the inexactness of the common HLS optimizations. In particular, while scheduling forms the algorithmic core to HLS technology, current scheduling algorithms rely heavily on fundamentally inexact heuristics that make ad hoc local decisions and cannot accurately and globally optimize over a rich set of constraints. To tackle this challenge, we propose a scheduling formulation based on system of integer difference constraints (SDC) and Boolean satisfiability (SAT) to exactly handle a variety of scheduling constraints. We develop a specialized scheduler based on conflict-driven learning and problem-specific knowledge to optimally and efficiently solve the resource-constrained scheduling problem. By leveraging the efficiency of SDC algorithms and scalability of modern SAT solvers, our scheduling technique is able to achieve on average over 100x improvement in runtime over the integer linear programming (ILP) approach while attaining optimal latency. By integrating our scheduling formulation into a state-of-the-art open-source HLS tool, we further demonstrate the applicability of our scheduling technique with a suite of representative benchmarks targeting FPGAs.

ACM Reference format:

Steve Dai, Gai Liu, Zhiru Zhang. 2018. A Scalable Approach to Exact Resource-Constrained Scheduling Based on a Joint SDC and SAT Formulation. In *Proceedings of 2018 ACM/SIGDA International Symposium on Field-Programmable Gate Arrays, Monterey, CA, USA, February 25–27, 2018 (FPGA '18)*, 10 pages.

https://doi.org/10.1145/3174243.3174268

1 INTRODUCTION

The breakdown of Dennard scaling has led to the rapid growth of specialized hardware accelerators to meet the ever more stringent performance and energy requirements. However, great performance-per-watt comes at the cost of enormous development effort. With the traditional register-transfer-level (RTL) design flow, designers must constantly wrestle with low-level hardware description languages (HDLs) and manually explore a large multidimensional solution space. With the RTL design methodology, it is difficult to re-target multiple design points because the timing and micro-architecture are essentially fixed by design.

As the process of RTL optimization becomes unequivocally difficult, if not already unsustainable, high-level synthesis (HLS) has emerged as a promising alternative to the RTL design methodology

for tackling the design productivity gap [19]. HLS raises the abstraction of input from HDL to software programming language by providing the capability to automatically synthesize untimed high-level software programs into cycle-accurate RTL implementations. Lower design complexity and faster simulation speed enable shorter time-to-market, which is especially relevant in today's rapidly-evolving technology landscape. Most recently, HLS has successfully accelerated the design of complex and realistic applications [22, 30, 37] as well as system-on-chip [1]. The productivity advantage has led to growing adoption of commercial and open-source HLS tools, including Vivado HLS [7] and LegUp [4].

Because HLS transforms an untimed, possibly sequential, description with no concept of clock into a timed parallel implementation with registers, scheduling has been recognized as one of the most important problems in HLS. Scheduling extracts parallelism from the input high-level program and determines the clock cycle at which different computation and communication operations should be executed. With exclusive control on timing at the front-end of the hardware flow, scheduling is in a unique position to influence the micro-architecture and quality of the generated hardware. Nevertheless, finding an optimal schedule is intractable in general, and thus necessitates a tradeoff between optimality and efficiency.

For example, HLS traditionally solves the classic resource-constrained scheduling problem, which minimizes latency given a limited number of functional units of each type. It is an NP-hard problem which can be optimized exactly with integer linear programming (ILP). However, it is typically approximated using heuristics for better scalability. One heuristic is list scheduling, a constructive algorithm that sorts ready operations based on an established priority and schedules them one clock cycle at a time considering resource availability [27]. It is a fast local optimization algorithm for minimizing latency under resource constraints, albeit sub-optimally. State-of-the-art HLS tools typically employ the more versatile scheduling heuristic based on system of integer difference constraints (SDC) [8]. SDC-based scheduling is rooted in a linear programming formulation and can globally optimize over design constraints that can be represented in the integer difference form (e.g., cycle time constraints, latency constraints). Notably however, resource constraints must be heuristically transformed into integer difference form to be considered. As a result, SDC-based scheduling is unable to optimally handle resource constraints.

While scheduling heuristics are fast and scalable, they are fundamentally inexact with no guarantee on optimality. First, scheduling heuristics are designed to consider only a restrictive set of constraints and are unable to handle more complex scheduling problems. Second, they lack the ability to perform global optimization and may miss valuable optimization opportunities that can otherwise be discovered by exact techniques. In some cases, these challenges introduce a quality-of-results (QoR) gap whose severity remains unknown to both the designer as well as the tool itself. This gap may be exacerbated as the quantity and variety of constraints increase for HLS to accommodate emerging application domains.

To address these challenges, we propose a scheduling formulation based on SDC coupled with Boolean satisfiability (SAT) to exactly model a rich set of scheduling constraints. Inspired by satisfiability modulo theory (SMT) [13], our proposed approach exploits the efficiency of SDC while leveraging the scalability of modern SAT solvers to quickly prune away infeasible schedule space and derive optimal schedule. Our scheduling technique aims to push the limit on what is practically scalable with exact scheduling as well as the variety of constraints that can be efficiently encoded and solved. Our specific contributions are as follows:

(1) We propose a novel resource-constrained scheduling formulation, which combines SDC and SAT problems, to exactly and efficiently encode both resource and timing constraints in HLS.

(2) We devise an exact yet fast resource-constrained scheduling algorithm for HLS based on conflict-driven learning by leveraging the efficiency of SDC and scalability of modern SAT solvers.

(3) We employ problem-specific knowledge to specialize our scheduling algorithm to enable optimization and incremental scheduling techniques that further improve scalability.

(4) We apply our specialized scheduler within the open-source HLS tool LegUp to efficiently synthesize high-quality RTL for a range of representative benchmarks targeting FPGAs.

The rest of this paper is organized as follows: Section 2 provides background on scheduling and relevant theories, as well as motivation for our approach; Section 3 details our scheduling formulation; Section 4 describes our specialized conflict-driven scheduler; Section 5 presents experimental results; Section 6 provides related work and additional discussions, followed by conclusions in Section 7.

2 PRELIMINARIES

A typical HLS flow employs a software compiler (e.g., LLVM, GCC) to compile the input high-level program into a control data flow graph (CDFG) on which scheduling is then performed. In this paper, we focus on the resource-constrained scheduling problem, which is also a classic optimization problem in operation research. In the context of HLS, the problem is described as follows:

Given: (1) A CDFG $G(V_G, E_G)$ where V_G represents the set of operations in the CDFG and E_G represents the set of edges; (2) A set of scheduling constraints, which may include dependence constraints, resource constraints, cycle time constraints, and relative timing constraints.

Objective: Construct a minimum-latency schedule so that every operation is assigned to at least one clock cycle while satisfying all scheduling constraints.

We illustrate the three types of scheduling formulation using the data flow graph (DFG) in Figure 1(a). As our running example, we would like to schedule the DFG targeting a clock period T_{clk} of 5ns. We assume that each add or store operation incurs a delay of 1ns, and each load operation incurs a delay of 3ns. We further assume that only two memory read ports are available, so at most two load operations can be scheduled within the same cycle. add and store operations are unconstrained.

2.1 SDC-Based Formulation

SDC is a system of inequality constraints in the integer difference form $x_i - x_j \leq b_{ij}$, where b_{ij} is an integer, and x_i and x_j are variables. The system is feasible if there exists a solution that satisfies all inequalities in the system. Because of the restrictive form of the constraints, SDC can be solved efficiently. For SDC-based scheduling [8], a schedule variable s_i is declared for each operation i in the CDFG to denote the clock cycle at which operation i is scheduled. All SDC scheduling constraints are then expressed in the integer difference form so that the system consists of a totally unimodular constraint matrix over which an optimal integer solution can be guaranteed in polynomial time. For resource-constrained scheduling, we minimize

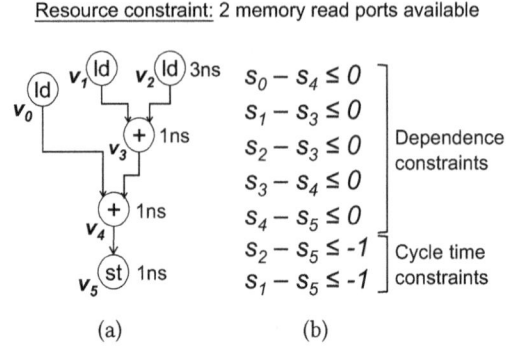

Resource constraint: 2 memory read ports available

(a)   (b)

Figure 1: Motivational and running example for this paper — (a) DFG for our example. Delay of each operation type is indicated next to the corresponding node. Resource constraint denotes that only two memory read ports are available. No resource constraints are imposed on add or store operations. (b) Dependence constraints and cycle time constraints corresponding to the DFG for a target clock period of 5ns.

the objective l such that $l > s_i \; \forall i$, where l represents the latency of the design.

To handle data dependence, SDC creates the following difference constraint for each data edge from operation i to operation j in G.

$$s_i - s_j \leq 0 \qquad (1)$$

In our example, because there is an edge from node v_0 to node v_4, SDC will impose the difference constraint $s_0 - s_4 \leq 0$ to ensure that v_4 is scheduled no earlier than v_0. Similar constraints are constructed for other data dependence edges. To honor the target clock period T_{clk}, SDC identifies the maximum critical combination delay $D(ccp(v_i, v_j))$ between pairs of operations i and j and constructs the following different constraint to ensure that the combinational path with total delay exceeding the target cycle time T_{clk} must be partitioned into $\lceil D(ccp(v_i, v_j))/T_{clk} \rceil$ number of clock cycles.

$$s_i - s_j \leq -(\lceil D(ccp(v_i, v_j))/T_{clk} \rceil - 1) \qquad (2)$$

In our example, because the maximum critical delay from v_2 to v_5 $(D(ccp(v_2, v_5)) = 6ns)$ exceeds the target clock period of 5ns, SDC will impose the constraint $s_2 - s_5 \leq -1$ to ensure that v_5 is scheduled at least one cycle after v_2. Similar constraints are imposed for combinational paths from v_1 to v_5 and v_0 to v_5. The aforementioned dependence and cycle time constraints are indicated in Figure 1(b).

While SDC is able to model timing constraints exactly, it must heuristically transform resource constraints into the integer difference form by imposing a particular heuristic linear ordering on the resource-constrained operations. This process separates resource-constrained operations appropriately into different cycles to ensure that sufficient resources are available to execute operations scheduled within the same cycle. The linear ordering consists of a set of precedence relationships between pairs of resource-constrained operations i and j represented in the form of

$$s_i - s_j \leq -L_i \qquad (3)$$

where L_i denotes the latency (in cycles) of operation i. Although the linear ordering results in a legal schedule that satisfies all resource constraints, the schedule is likely sub-optimal because the linear ordering is devised heuristically. There are many possible such legal linear orderings, some resulting in better schedules than others. However, SDC can simply pick one particular linear ordering heuristically and without knowledge of whether it is optimal.

Resource constraint: 2 memory read ports available

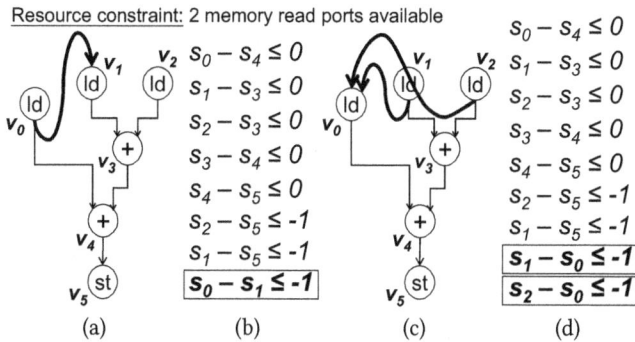

$$s_0 - s_4 \leq 0$$
$$s_1 - s_3 \leq 0$$
$$s_2 - s_3 \leq 0$$
$$s_3 - s_4 \leq 0$$
$$s_4 - s_5 \leq 0$$
$$s_2 - s_5 \leq -1$$
$$s_1 - s_5 \leq -1$$
$$\boxed{s_0 - s_1 \leq -1}$$

$$s_0 - s_4 \leq 0$$
$$s_1 - s_3 \leq 0$$
$$s_2 - s_3 \leq 0$$
$$s_3 - s_4 \leq 0$$
$$s_4 - s_5 \leq 0$$
$$s_2 - s_5 \leq -1$$
$$s_1 - s_5 \leq -1$$
$$\boxed{s_1 - s_0 \leq -1}$$
$$\boxed{s_2 - s_0 \leq -1}$$

(a)   (b)   (c)   (d)

Figure 2: Partial ordering edges are heuristically imposed on the DFG, and subsequently in the SDC, to satisfy the resource constraints — Partial ordering edges are shown in bold, and corresponding difference constraints are boxed. (a)-(b) represent a different combination of partial ordering edges than (c)-(d). Minimum latency differs depending on the particular combination.

For our example, SDC must impose partial orderings among the resource-constrained load operations because only two memory read ports are available for the three load operations (v_0, v_1, and v_2). On one hand, SDC can impose an edge from v_0 to v_1 as shown in bold in Figure 2(a) to separate v_0 and v_1 into different cycles so that each cycle has at most two load operations. With this heuristic partial ordering, the DFG requires at least three cycles to execute due to the critical path delay from v_0 to v_5. Given the target clock period of 5ns, v_0 and v_1, each of which incurs a delay of 3ns, must be scheduled in separate cycles given the partial ordering edge between them. v_5 cannot be scheduled in the same cycle as v_1 because there is no slack remaining in the clock cycle after scheduling v_3 and v_4. On the other hand, if SDC instead imposes an edge from v_1 to v_0 and another edge from v_2 to v_0 as shown in bold in Figure 2(c), the DFG can achieve a better latency of only two cycles while ensuring that each cycle has at most two load operations. In Figure 2, corresponding SDC constraints are shown in (b) and (d), respectively, with appended partial ordering ("resource") constraints boxed.

From this example, we see that it is necessary to enumerate all possible combinations of partial orderings and solve an SDC for each combination of imposed "resource" edges to find the optimal (minimum-latency) schedule. However, attempting all combinations is not scalable in the general case for an arbitrary number of resource-constrained operations. For this reason, SDC heuristically imposes one particular partial ordering without guarantee of optimality and proceed with solving the scheduling problem without regards to the effect of any sub-optimality on the solution.

2.2 ILP-Based Formulation

Applying ILP in the context of resource-constrained scheduling problem has been a well-studied topic [24]. ILP is a linear program with linear objective and constraints in which all variables are restricted to be integers. For the ILP-based formulation, we focus on the special case of 0-1 ILP in which all variables are binary. The formulation declares a binary variable x_{it} to denote whether operation i starts at clock cycle t, where i and t are integers bounded by the total number of operations and maximum allowable latency, respectively. With these binary variables, the start time s_i of operation i can be expressed as

$$s_i = \sum_{t=0}^{L-1} t \cdot x_{it} \qquad (4)$$

where L denotes the maximum latency. Because s_i is analogous to the corresponding schedule variable in SDC, dependence constraints in ILP can be equivalently represented as the difference between pairs of schedule variables as in Eq. 1. For our example, we can safely assume a maximum start time equal to the number of operations $N = 6$. It follows that we declare variables $\{x_{00}, x_{01}, x_{02}, x_{03}, x_{04}, x_{05}\}$ for operation v_0 and denote that $s_0 = \sum_{t=0}^{6-1} t \cdot x_{0t}$. Variables are similarly declared and derived for operations v_1 to v_5. The objective is same as that defined in Section 2.1 for the SDC formulation.

Unlike in SDC, resource constraints can be encoded exactly as linear constraints in ILP. To ensure that the number of active operations of type r in clock cycle t does not exceed the number of available type-r resources a_r, the ILP formulation imposes the resource constraint

$$\sum_{i:RT_i=r} \sum_{t'=t-L_i}^{t} x_{it'} \leq a_r \qquad (5)$$

where RT_i and L_i denote the resource type and latency of operation i, respectively. For our example, the ILP formulation needs to impose the constraints $\sum_{i=0}^{2} x_{it} \leq 2$ for each clock cycle t because only two memory ports are available. These constraints apply to the resource-constrained load operations v_0, v_1, and v_2 (i.e., $i = 0, 1, 2$). The second summation is omitted because the latency of load operation is zero-cycle in our example. The ILP formulation also requires the following unique start time constraint for each operation i to ensure that operation i starts at only one particular clock cycle.

$$\sum_{t} x_{it} = 1 \qquad (6)$$

While modern ILP solvers can handle problems of non-trivial size, ILP is in general NP-hard and difficult to scale. In comparison to SDC for scheduling, ILP requires significantly more variables for encoding the same problem and cannot take advantage of special matrix structure to efficiently solve the problem.

2.3 SAT-Based Formulation

SAT stands for the Boolean satisfiability problem, which determines if there exists an assignment of the Boolean variables that satisfies a Boolean formula. A SAT problem consists of a set of Boolean clauses, all of which must be satisfied by some assignment of the Boolean variables for the problem to be satisfiable. The problem is unsatisfiable otherwise. In general, a SAT-based scheduling formulation [16] uses Boolean variable x_{it} to denote whether operation i starts at clock cycle t, and employs Boolean variable u_{it} to denote whether operation i is active at clock cycle t. Dependence and resource constraints can be expressed as clauses of these variables.

Modern SAT solvers perform systematic search based on variations of the Davis-Putnam-Logemann-Loveland (DPLL) algorithm [12] of *decide*, *propagate*, and *backtrack*. These solvers recursively *decide* the value (true or false) of an unassigned variable, *propagate* the effects of this decision using deduction rules, and *backtrack* if conflicts dictate that a different value should be attempted for the variable. In particular, conflict-driven SAT solvers complements DPLL with extra features to achieve significant improvement in efficiency. Extra features may include clause learning, non-chronological backtracking, adaptive branching, unit propagation, and random restart [36]. Although SAT remains a well-known NP-complete problem, SAT procedures based on the DPLL algorithm have demonstrated scalability with hundreds of thousands of variables and clauses [23]. In the domain of design automation, SAT has been successfully applied to solve problems in hardware/software model checking, test pattern generation, equivalence checking, etc.

However, it is interesting to note that although the scheduling problem can be encoded completely in SAT, the encoding is often too large and too inefficient even considering the capability of modern SAT solvers [26]. Moreover, SAT is only concerned with whether the problem is satisfiable and does not inherently support optimization of an objective, such as minimizing latency.

3 JOINT SDC AND SAT SCHEDULING

In resource-constrained scheduling, there has always been an inherent tension between scalability and quality. On one hand, heuristic scheduling is fast and scalable, but generates sub-optimal QoR. On the other hand, exact scheduling creates optimal QoR, but is slow and difficult to scale. As described in Section 2, the SDC heuristic achieves fast runtime but generates sub-optimal schedule because resource constraints cannot be represented exactly with integer difference constraints. The ILP-based formulation can model both timing and resource constraints exactly but is not scalable in general. As a result, resolving the tension between scalability and quality is key to achieving both global optimization and fast runtime.

To this end, we propose a scheduling algorithm that integrates SDC and SAT to exactly handle different types of constraints and optimally solve the resource-constrained scheduling problem defined in Section 2. To achieve global optimization, our algorithm leverages SDC to represent constraints that can be readily expressed in the integer difference form and employs SAT to encode constraints that do not naturally fall under the SDC framework. A joint SDC and SAT formulation allows us to leverage the advantages of SDC and SAT while exactly encoding both timing and resource constraints.

Figure 3 shows the high-level structure of our scheduler, mainly composed of a conflict-based SAT solver integrated with a graph-based SDC solver. On the left, the SAT solver takes advantage of conflict-based search (detailed in Section 3.1) to quickly propose partial orderings that satisfy the resource constraints. These partial orderings are converted to SDC constraints and appended to the SDC problem. On the right, the SDC solver leverages a graph-based algorithm (detailed in Section 3.2) to efficiently check the feasibility of the proposed partial orderings. Any infeasibility will be encoded as a conflict clause in SAT and appended back into the SAT problem. The solver iterates between SAT and SDC until it finds a feasible solution or proves that such solution does not exist.

Because a particular binding (set of partial orderings) proposed by SAT may not be consistent with the given SDC timing constraints, it is necessary to communicate any SAT binding decision to the SDC so that constraints in SDC and SAT are jointly considered. At the same time, any infeasibility must be communicated back from SDC to SAT so that SAT can learn from the mistakes of its previous proposals and make better proposals in the future. This process of conflict-driven learning is key to enabling accelerated convergence of our proposed scheduler. It is important to note that despite the benefits of conflict-driven learning, the problem remains NP-hard. Nevertheless, our approach demonstrates better efficiency and scalability than ILP. While our approach is inspired by and bears resemblance to SMT, we will discuss the key differences in Section 6.

3.1 SAT for Resource Constraints

As shown in Figure 3, our algorithm leverages SAT to model the resource constraints based on which partial orderings are proposed. In our formulation, let binding variable B_{ik} denote whether operation i is bound to resource instance k. We employ one binding variable to denote the binding of each resource-constrained operation to each resource instance. For our example, operations v_0, v_1, and v_2 are resource-constrained load operations, each of which can be bound to one of two memory read ports (i.e., $k = 0, 1$). Therefore,

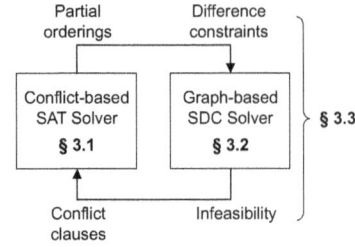

Figure 3: Overall structure of our scheduler — Composed of a SAT solver integrated with an SDC solver to enable conflict-driven learning. This solver checks the feasibility of a particular latency. Latency optimization (Section 3.4) is built on top of this solver.

we declare $\{B_{00}, B_{01}, B_{10}, B_{11}, B_{20}, B_{21}\}$ for the different operation-resource pairs. By adding the appropriate clause $\sum_k B_{ik} = 1 \; \forall i$ to enforce that each operation is bound to exactly one resource, the binding variables are responsible for assigning each operation to a resource instance without exceeding the resource availability.

Based on the definition of binding variable, a sharing variable R_{ij} can be derived to denote whether operation i is sharing the same resource with operation j. For each pair of operations (i, j) mapped to the same type of resource,

$$R_{ij} = \bigvee_{k \in T} (B_{ik} \wedge B_{jk}) \tag{7}$$

where T denotes the set of resources of the particular type. R_{ij} is true if both operations i and j are bound to the same resource instance by the binding variable. With R_{ij}, we can then define the partial ordering variable $O_{i \to j}$ to denote whether operation i is scheduled in an earlier cycle than operation j. $O_{i \to j}$ maps to integer difference constraint in SDC between i and j as follows:

$$O_{i \to j} = True \; \mapsto \; s_i - s_j \leq -1 \tag{8}$$

$$O_{i \to j} = False \; \mapsto \; \emptyset \tag{9}$$

As shown in Eq. (8), assigning $O_{i \to j}$ to true dictates that operation i must be scheduled in an earlier cycle than operation j and therefore maps to the difference constraint $s_i - s_j \leq -1$. As shown in Eq. (9), assigning $O_{i \to j}$ to false maps to an empty set of constraints, indicating that it is not necessary to impose any partial ordering between operations i and j because no particular partial ordering is required by the proposed resource binding. Given the mapping between SAT and SDC, we include the following partial ordering clauses in SAT for each pair of operations (i, j) mapped to the same type of resource.

$$R_{ij} \to (O_{i \to j} \vee O_{j \to i}) \tag{10}$$

$$\neg(O_{i \to j} \wedge O_{j \to i}) \tag{11}$$

Eq. (10) indicates that if operation i and j shares the same resource instance, it implies that operation i must be scheduled either in an earlier cycle or in a later cycle than operation j. Eq. (11) ensures that operation i cannot be simultaneously scheduled both in an earlier cycle and later cycle than operation j.

Figure 4(a) shows the partial ordering clauses for our problem where a pair of clauses is specified for every combination of resource-constrained load operations (v_0, v_1, and v_2). Among other types of clauses described, only the partial ordering clauses are shown because they contain the partial ordering variables to be mapped to SDC. In this figure, for example, the first clause indicates that if v_0 and v_1 share the same resource instance, v_0 must be scheduled either in an earlier cycle or in a later cycle than v_1, and not both. A similar line of logic follows with the other clauses in the figure. SAT clauses like these (e.g., Eq. (7), (10), (11)) can be translated into conjunctive normal form commonly accepted by SAT solvers. Subsequently, the resulting assignments of $O_{i \to j}$ and $O_{j \to i}$ satisfying these clauses will be mapped to integer difference constraints or lack thereof in SDC based on Eq. (8) and (9). For instance, $O_{0\to1}$ assigned to true will be mapped to $s_0 - s_1 \leq -1$.

3.2 SDC for Timing Constraints

As shown in Figure 3, our algorithm uses SDC to solve the difference constraints, which consist of incoming partial ordering constraints from SAT and the original set of timing constraints (e.g., dependence and cycle time constraints) of the problem previously shown in Figure 1(b) and reproduced for convenience in Figure 4(b). From Figure 4(b), we see the difference constraints can be conveniently represented using a constraint graph where each variable maps to a node and each constraint maps to an edge. The constraint graph contains edges to represent dependence constraints and cycle time constraints. Inequalities whose right-hand side is 0 represent dependence constraints, while those whose right-hand side is −1 represent cycle time constraints, both described in Section 2.1. For each of these constraints in integer difference form $s_u - s_v \leq d_{u,v}$, the constraint graph includes an edge of weight $d_{u,v}$ from node v to u. For clarity, weights are omitted for zero-weight edges.

By representing SDC as a constraint graph, we can detect infeasibility of the difference constraints by the presence of negative cycle in the graph. This property will be useful for checking whether the proposed partial orderings from SAT are consistent with the given SDC timing constraints. In addition, the negative cycle serves as a certificate of any inconsistency between the proposed resource binding and given timing constraints. In Section 3.3, we will describe how we leverage the negative cycle to provide feedback from SDC to SAT for enabling conflict-driven learning. Furthermore, we can obtain a feasible schedule, either as late as possible (ALAP) or as soon as possible (ASAP) schedule, by solving a single source shortest path problem on the graph. ASAP schedules all operations to the earliest possible clock cycle, and ALAP schedules all operations to the latest possible clock cycle given a latency constraint.

In our solver, it is necessary to detect whether the addition of each partial ordering edge induces a negative cycle in the constraint graph. However, it is wasteful to solve the entire SDC with all nodes and edges for each edge added when only a small part of graph is affected by the addition. Doing so cuts directly into the bottom line of our scheduler because SDC is a crucial component of conflict-driven learning. Quick propagation and convergence of the scheduler rely on having a highly efficient SDC solver and a method to quickly identify any negative cycle in the constraint graph. To accelerate the process of conflict identification in SDC, we propose to leverage an efficient incremental algorithm for maintaining a feasible solution and detecting negative cycle for a dynamically changing SDC constraint graph [28].

To enable incremental SDC solving, our scheduler initializes with a feasible solution (shortest path solution) of the original graph (without partial ordering edges). For each edge added to the constraint graph or each tightened edge weight, the algorithm traverses only the affected subgraph and update the distances of only affected nodes. This incremental update guarantees that the updated node values continue to maintain a feasible solution. Because the algorithm is essentially applying Dijkstra's algorithm to modify only affected edges and nodes, the addition (or tightening) of a constraint incurs a marginal time complexity $O(\Delta e + \Delta v \log \Delta v)$, where Δe and Δv denote the number of affected edges and nodes, respectively. The algorithm is able to delete or relax an edge in constant time. Because deletion or relaxation results in a less constrained system, the current feasible solution remains feasible.

Using the incremental SDC algorithm, our scheduler inserts one edge at a time until the constraint graph becomes infeasible. The

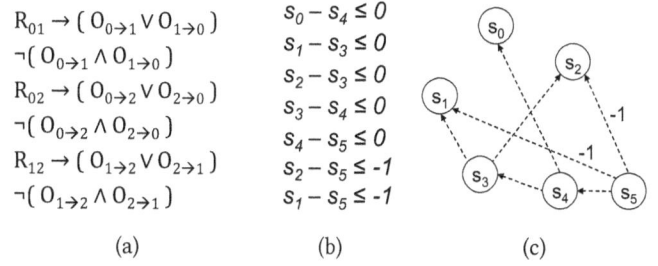

$$R_{01} \to (\, O_{0\to1} \lor O_{1\to0}\,)$$
$$\neg(\, O_{0\to1} \land O_{1\to0}\,)$$
$$R_{02} \to (\, O_{0\to2} \lor O_{2\to0}\,)$$
$$\neg(\, O_{0\to2} \land O_{2\to0}\,)$$
$$R_{12} \to (\, O_{1\to2} \lor O_{2\to1}\,)$$
$$\neg(\, O_{1\to2} \land O_{2\to1}\,)$$

$$s_0 - s_4 \leq 0$$
$$s_1 - s_3 \leq 0$$
$$s_2 - s_3 \leq 0$$
$$s_3 - s_4 \leq 0$$
$$s_4 - s_5 \leq 0$$
$$s_2 - s_5 \leq -1$$
$$s_1 - s_5 \leq -1$$

(a)   (b)   (c)

Figure 4: Constraints for our running example — *(a)* Resource constraints in SAT. *(b)* Timing constraints in SDC. *(c)* Corresponding SDC constraint graph.

algorithm detects such infeasibility when the distance of the source node of the inserted edge is updated during the traversal of the affected subgraph. This indicates a negative cycle in the affected subgraph because the distances of the nodes will continue decrease as long as we continue to traverse the subgraph. At this point, our algorithm traces backward on the predecessors along the shortest path computed by Dijkstra's algorithm to extract the edges involved in the negative cycle. Our algorithm then reports partial ordering edges in the negative cycle back to SAT because SAT is concerned with resource-related partial orderings. Other edges represent hard constraints and are not influenced by SAT.

3.3 Conflict-Driven Learning

As shown in Figure 3, SAT and SDC interact closely within a feedback loop to enable conflict-driven learning. For each iteration of the loop, SAT proposes partial orderings that satisfy the SAT clauses described by Eq. (10) and (11). These partial orderings are converted to SDC constraints based on Eq. (8) and (9) and appended to the SDC problem. SDC then checks the feasibility of the proposed partial orderings and report any infeasibility as a conflict clause back to the SAT.

We illustrate the power of conflict-driven learning in Figure 5 using our running example. Here we would like to determine if the DFG in Figure 1(a) can be scheduled within two cycles. The corresponding SAT formulation for resource constraints is reproduced on the top of Figure 5(a), while the initial SDC constraint graph for timing constraints is shown on the bottom. As the solver progresses, resource-related edges mapped from the partial ordering variables will be added to the constraint graph in a manner similar to that of timing constraints described in Section 3.2. It is important to note that the constraint graph contains a latency edge of weight 1 from s_0 to s_5 to indicate a maximum allowable clock cycle index of 1 for our target two-cycle schedule starting with cycle 0.

To solve the feasibility problem of determining whether the graph can be scheduled within two cycles, SAT starts with an initial proposal of the assignment of the partial ordering variables as shown on the top of Figure 5(b). For clarity, we show only partial ordering variables that are assigned to True because they are the ones that will influence the constraint graph. On the bottom of the figure, SDC adds the corresponding edges (shown with solid lines) proposed by SAT into the constraint graph. With these additional edges, SDC detects a negative cycle (shown in bold) among the initial edges and the partial ordering edge from $O_{0\to1}$. SDC then reports the conflict back to SAT using the conflict clause $\neg O_{0\to1}$ to ensure that any partial ordering involving v_0 before v_1 should no longer be proposed by SAT. As shown in Figure 5(c), after the conflict clause is added to the SAT problem, SAT makes a different proposal based on the updated set of clauses. In this case, SDC detects a different negative cycle involving the edge proposed by $O_{0\to2}$ and adds the

$R_{01} \leftrightarrow (O_{0\rightarrow1} \vee O_{1\rightarrow0})$

$\neg (O_{0\rightarrow1} \wedge O_{1\rightarrow0})$

$R_{02} \leftrightarrow (O_{0\rightarrow2} \vee O_{2\rightarrow0})$

$\neg (O_{0\rightarrow2} \wedge O_{2\rightarrow0})$

$R_{12} \leftrightarrow (O_{1\rightarrow2} \vee O_{2\rightarrow1})$

$\neg (O_{1\rightarrow2} \wedge O_{2\rightarrow1})$

Proposal

$O_{0\rightarrow1}$ = True

$O_{0\rightarrow2}$ = True

$O_{1\rightarrow2}$ = True

Conflict clauses

$\neg O_{0\rightarrow1}$

Proposal

$O_{1\rightarrow0}$ = True

$O_{0\rightarrow2}$ = True

$O_{1\rightarrow2}$ = True

Conflict clauses

$\neg O_{0\rightarrow1}$, $\neg O_{0\rightarrow2}$

Proposal

$O_{1\rightarrow0}$ = True

$O_{2\rightarrow0}$ = True

Conflict clauses

$\neg O_{0\rightarrow1}$, $\neg O_{0\rightarrow2}$

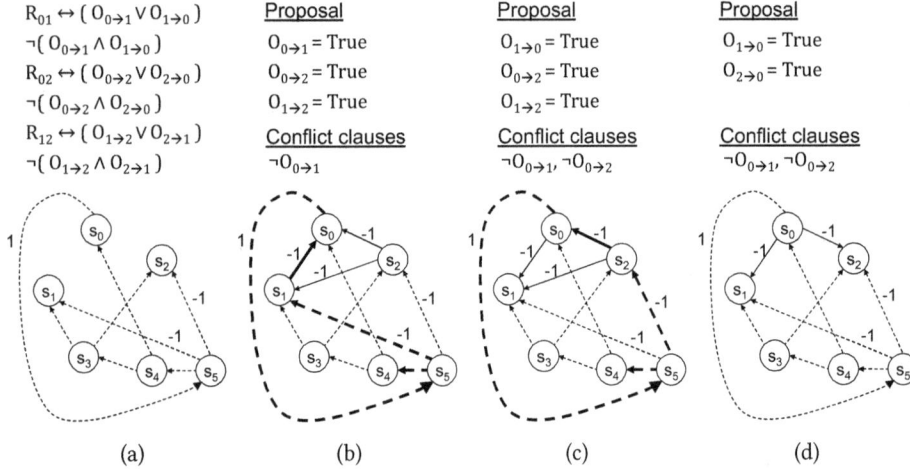

(a)　　　　　　　(b)　　　　　　　(c)　　　　　　　(d)

Figure 5: Illustration of conflict-driven learning with SDC and SAT using our running example from Figure 1 — (a) Resource constraints in SAT on the top and initial SDC constraint graph on the bottom. (b)-(d) The progression of joint SAT and SDC scheduling. Corresponding partial ordering proposals by SAT are shown on the top. For conflict clauses, ¬ denotes negation of the SAT variable. For constraint graphs, dashed lines represent hard constraints. Solid lines represent partial ordering constraints proposed by SAT. Bold lines trace negative cycles.

conflict clause $\neg O_{0\rightarrow2}$ to the SAT. During conflict-driven scheduling, a negative cycle indicates that the resource binding proposed by SAT is inconsistent with the (hard) timing constraints of the problem. No schedule is able to achieve the desired latency while satisfying both the timing constraints and the proposed resource binding. As a result, a different resource binding needs to be attempted.

Based on the feedback up until this point from SDC, conflict clauses dictate that any schedule with v_0 before v_1 or v_0 before v_2 will be infeasible and need not be attempted. Notice that these conflict clauses are short, allowing SAT to prune out a large search space because it no longer needs to propose any combination involving these infeasible orderings. Shorter conflict clauses lead to a larger search space that can be pruned and therefore faster propagation and convergence for our scheduler. As such, it is crucial to derive conflict clauses that are as short as possible. Negative cycle satisfies this property because it is guaranteed to be an irreducibly inconsistent set of constraints [34]. It is a minimal set of inconsistent constraints in which the removal of any edge in the negative cycle will also remove the negative cycle in its entirety.

With two short conflict clauses, SAT has a much better understanding of the search space. As shown in Figure 5(d), SAT now makes a proposal whose corresponding edges no longer generate any negative cycle in the constraint graph. Because the constraint graph is now feasible, SDC returns a feasible solution that satisfies all timing and resource constraints. For efficiency, our scheduler uses the shortest path distances of the constraint graph as the feasible solution because the shortest path has already been computed in the process of detecting negative cycle.

3.4 Minimizing Latency

Because SAT has its root in decision problems, we have so far limited our discussion to checking the feasibility of a particular latency value. To minimize latency as in the case of resource-constrained scheduling, we propose to perform binary search over the range of possible latency values based on an initial upper and lower bound. During the binary search, we solve a series of feasibility problems as described in Section 3.3, each of which returns either a feasible solution or a proof that the problem is infeasible. A feasible answer allows our scheduler to decrease the upper bound, while an infeasible answer requires increasing the lower bound. The binary search terminates when the upper and lower bounds coincide.

Because the convergence of the scheduler depends on the number of latency values the binary search needs to process, we propose

to leverage specialized knowledge we can obtain for the scheduling problem to establish upper and lower latency bounds to reduce the range of latency values that need to be searched. Specifically, we propose to leverage the original SDC heuristic scheduling algorithm [8] for upper bounding to establish a good initial solution that has already globally optimized over a subset of constraints. Furthermore, we propose to apply the resource-aware lower bounding algorithm [29] (described later in Section 4.1) to establish a lower bound so that the scheduler does not waste time exploring too many unmeaningful latency values. While the upper and lower bounds are not necessarily tight, they provide a good starting point from which exact scheduling can initialize.

4 SCHEDULER SPECIALIZATION

As mentioned in Section 3.4, it is possible to extract knowledge we have specific to the resource-constrained scheduling problem to further reduce the search space and improve runtime. In this section, we describe how we leverage various heuristics to specialize our scheduler for the scheduling problem. These techniques maintain the exactness of the algorithm and the optimality of the solution.

4.1 Resource-Aware Lower Bounding

Resource-aware lower bounding applies a greedy algorithm to solve a relaxed version of the resource-constrained scheduling problem [29]. While the algorithm eliminates dependence constraints for the relaxation, it uses the ASAP schedule to determine the earliest clock cycle each operation can be scheduled and minimizes the tardiness of each operation in respect to the ALAP schedule. The greedy algorithm selects the operation with minimum ALAP value and assigns it to the earliest clock cycle based on the ASAP schedule and resource constraints. This process continues until all operations have been scheduled. The resulting lower bound is determined by adding the maximum tardiness (in cycles) among all operations to the critical path latency for the entire design, which considers only dependence.

While we have discussed in Section 3.4 the application of resource-aware lower bounding to establish tighter lower bound in optimization, the same exact algorithm can be helpful for accelerating the propagation for conflict-driven learning described in Section 3.3. Recall that partial ordering edges are inserted one-by-one into the SDC constraint graph until the graph becomes infeasible. The fewer the number of inserted partial ordering edges, the shorter the conflict clause and larger the search space that can be pruned by SAT based on the conflict clauses. In addition to detecting negative cycle, our scheduler can also incrementally determine the lower bound

Resource constraint: 1 memory read port available

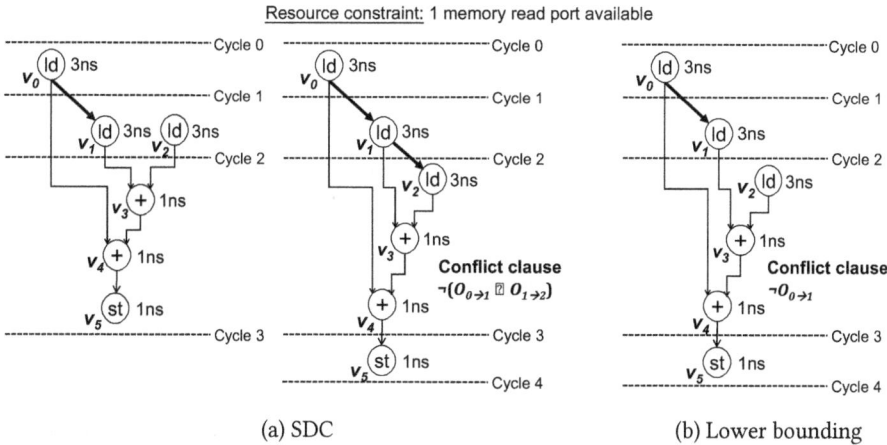

(a) SDC

(b) Lower bounding

Figure 6: Illustration of the advantage of lower bounding over SDC in conflict-driven learning — Assume one memory read port and $T_{clk} = 5ns$. Actual DFGs, instead of constraint graphs, are shown in these figures. *(a)* SDC requires two "resource" edges (in bold) to determine that the DFG requires at least 4 cycles. *(b)* The lower bounding algorithm requires only one edge to determine the same 4-cycle latency because it pushes v_2 to the next cycle due to resource constraint.

upon the insertion of each new edge. After identifying the first edge that results in an infeasible system, our scheduler uses the deletion filtering algorithm [6] to remove previously added edges that do not contribute to the infeasibility. An edge does not contribute to the infeasibility if the graph remains infeasible even after the edge has been removed. The remaining set of edges then compose an irreducibly inconsistent set of constraints. Because the lower bounding algorithm is aware of the limited resource availability, it is actually able to prove infeasibility, in certain cases, with fewer partial ordering edges than SDC which has no sense of resource constraints other than those imposed by partial ordering. As such, lower bounding improves solution space pruning during conflict-driven learning.

We illustrate one such case in Figure 6 with the same DFG as in Figure 1(a). Here we would instead like to determine if the DFG can be executed within three cycles, assuming one memory read port and a target clock period of 5ns. To separate the resource-constrained load operations (v_0, v_1, and v_2) into different cycles due to the availability of only one read port, let's further assume that partial ordering edges are added in the order corresponding to partial ordering variables $\{O_{0 \to 1}, O_{1 \to 2}\}$. In Figure 6, note that edges are shown within the DFG instead of the constraint graph. With the first partial ordering edge from v_0 to v_1 in Figure 6(a), SDC is unable to rule out the feasibility of executing the DFG in three cycles. Because SDC is unaware of the number of available read ports, it schedules v_2 in the same cycle as v_1. Only with the second edge from v_1 to v_2, as shown in Figure 6(a), does SDC pushes v_2 to the next cycle and realize that the DFG requires at least four cycles. Because the DFG cannot complete in three cycles with the two edges, SDC will return the conflict clause $\neg(O_{0 \to 1} \wedge O_{1 \to 2})$ to reflect the irreducibly

inconsistent set of two edges. SDC requires both partial ordering edges (the complete resource binding) to decide infeasibility.

With resource-aware lower bounding, however, it is possible to determine that the DFG requires at least four cycles after adding only the first partial ordering edge from v_0 to v_1. As demonstrated in Figure 6(b), the algorithm does not attempt to schedule v_2 in the same cycle as v_1 even without the second edge, because the algorithm is aware that only one read port can be used in each cycle. As a result, v_2 is pushed to the next cycle, increasing the latency to at least four cycles. With lower bounding, the scheduler generates a more concise conflict clause $\neg O_{0 \to 1}$ for this example, which enables more effective pruning of the search space in SAT. Lower bounding is able to determine infeasibility with only a partial resource binding, thus resulting in speedup.

4.2 Incremental Learning

Because the proposed SAT formulation in Section 2.3 includes variables for all resource-constrained operations, conflict-driven learning described in Section 3.3 considers all resource-constrained operations equally. In reality, however, some operations tend to be located in congested region of the schedule and must compete for a very limited number of resources within a limited number of time steps. Other operations do not fall in the congested region and can be freely scheduled. The congested region constitutes the problematic part of the schedule because there are more operations that need to be scheduled than the number of available resources for these operations. As a result, it would be more effective to emphasize our SAT's resource constraints over operations that are likely to encounter resource contention and allow non-contending operations to be scheduled by SDC's (hard) timing constraints only. This approach attempts to reduce the size of the NP-hard part of the problem and leverages SDC as much as possible in finding a feasible schedule.

To implement this idea, we propose an incremental learning mode for our scheduler. Incremental learning leverages problem-specific knowledge to specifically target operations that are likely to cause resource contention. The flow of incremental learning mode is shown in Figure 7. Based on this flow, the scheduler starts with an empty SAT formulation, with no resource constraints initially. The scheduler then performs conflict-driven learning by propagating SDC and/or lower bounding (denoted as LB in the figure) with SAT. If the SDC graph reports a negative cycle, the problem is not satisfiable even with only timing constraints. In this case, the solver returns unsatisfiable and terminates. If the SDC graph does not detect any negative cycle, which is the more likely scenario, the scheduler checks the legality of the schedule against resource constraints. If the schedule is legal, the scheduler returns with the feasible schedule. If the

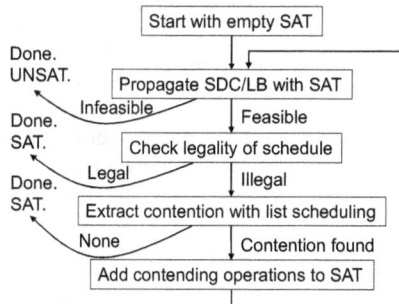

Figure 7: Incremental learning flow — Starts with no resource constraints and incrementally imposes resource constraints on operations that have encountered resource contention in previous iterations of the loop in this flow.

Table 1: Runtimes are reported in seconds for our proposed joint SDC and SAT scheduling (SDS for short) compared to default ILP scheduling using CPLEX and CBC — `%variables`: percentage of variables in non-incremental mode activated in incremental mode; speedup of `Non-incremental` and `Incremental` shown respectively in parentheses against CPLEX and CBC. TO: timeout after 300 seconds. n/a: not applicable. `Optimal Latency`: optimal latency in clock cycles for each benchmark and represents the latency achieved by both SDS scheduler and default ILP scheduling. `LegUp Latency`: latency achieved by LegUp using SDC-based scheduling heuristic.

Benchmark	# Operations	Runtime for SDS Scheduling (sec)		Runtime for Default ILP Scheduling (sec)		Optimal Latency	LegUp Latency
		Non-incremental	Incremental (% Variables)	CPLEX	CBC		
ARAI	44	0.01	0.01 (39.5%)	0.12 (12x, 12x)	1.18 (118x, 118x)	8	9
PR	52	0.02	0.01 (31.3%)	0.86 (43x, 86x)	3.70 (185x, 370x)	12	14
WANG	54	0.01	0.01 (8.29%)	0.86 (86x, 86x)	12.2 (1220x, 1220x)	12	14
LEE	58	0.01	0.01 (3.02%)	0.26 (26x, 26x)	2.88 (288x, 288x)	12	14
MCM	74	0.54	0.34 (10.4%)	6.19 (11x, 18x)	24.6 (46x, 72x)	15	16
DIR	76	0.14	0.01 (6.18%)	1.51 (11x, 151x)	11.5 (82x, 1550x)	14	15
HONDA	105	0.02	0.02 (0.95%)	9.06 (453x, 453x)	104 (5200x, 5200x)	27	33
CHEM	349	TO	1.42 (0.12%)	TO (n/a, n/a)	TO (n/a, n/a)	85	89
U5ML	857	0.01	0.01 (0.00%)	20.8 (2080x, 2080x)	TO (n/a, n/a)	261	264

schedule is illegal, likely in the initial iterations of this flow because no resource constraints have been considered, the scheduler will extract the contending operations with a list scheduling like heuristic. During the extraction process, the heuristic attempts to reorder operations to remove resource contention. If the heuristic succeeds in removing all resource contention, the scheduler also returns a feasible schedule. If contention remains, however, the scheduler adds the clauses of those contending operations to the SAT and repeats the flow starting with another iteration of conflict-driven learning.

The ultimate goal of incremental learning is to dramatically reduce the search space and improve runtime by using well-known heuristics (e.g., list scheduling, SDC-based scheduling) to direct the search toward the more difficult region of the schedule. Nevertheless, it is important to emphasize that these heuristics are used simply to guide the solver in a more promising path toward the solution and should in no way jeopardize the exactness of the scheduler. When incremental learning returns satisfiable, it always provides a legal schedule in regards to both timing and resource constraints and satisfies the given latency bound. Incremental learning is performed for different latency bounds in the binary search manner described in Section 3.4 to determine the schedule with the optimal latency.

5 EXPERIMENTS

We implement our proposed scheduler (detailed in Section 4) in C++ interfaced with LLVM compiler and Lingeling SAT solver [2]. We execute our scheduler on an Intel Xeon CPU running at 2.50GHz, and evaluate it on a set of compute-intensive benchmarks listed in Table 1. These benchmarks include a chemical plant controller and a number of DSP algorithms such as discrete cosine transforms. We constrain the scheduling process such that these benchmarks contain a large portion of resource-constrained operations useful for stress-testing our scheduler.

Our first set of experiments aim to compare the runtimes of our scheduler against those of state-of-the-art commercial and open-source ILP solvers. A comparison of runtime results between our joint SDC and SAT scheduling (SDS for short) and default ILP scheduling is shown in Table 1. For our SDS scheduler, we provide results for the scheduler running in non-incremental mode and in incremental mode. `Non-incremental` column provides results from applying conflict-driven learning from Section 3.3 with the full set of SAT variables. `Incremental` column provides results from applying incremental learning from Section 4.2 by selectively targeting a subset of SAT variables. For default ILP scheduling, the formulation presented in Section 2.2 is solved in CPLEX [9], a state-of-the-art commercial ILP solver, as well as in CBC [14], a best-in-class open-source ILP solver. Speedup values achieved by non-incremental and incremental modes against each ILP solver are shown respectively in parentheses in the corresponding columns.

Table 2: Runtimes in seconds for different combinations of resource constraints on multiplier and memory port — Results are shown for SDS scheduling in incremental mode.

Benchmark	# Operations	Runtime for Incremental Scheduling (sec)				
		1 mult 1 port	2 mult 2 port	3 mult 3 port	4 mult 4 port	6 mult 6 port
ARAI	44	0.01	0.01	0.01	0.01	0.01
PR	52	0.01	0.01	0.01	0.01	0.02
WANG	54	0.01	0.01	0.01	0.01	0.02
LEE	58	0.01	0.01	0.01	0.01	0.02
MCM	74	0.05	0.34	0.01	0.13	0.07
DIR	76	0.02	0.01	0.01	0.01	0.01
HONDA	105	0.01	0.03	0.04	0.09	0.24
CHEM	349	1.49	1.42	1.10	2.92	4.33
U5ML	857	0.01	0.01	0.01	0.01	0.01

Based on the results in Table 1, SDS scheduler running in non-incremental mode is faster than the open-source ILP solver by around two orders of magnitude and sometimes three orders of magnitude in all cases except CHEM for which both solvers time out. In non-incremental mode, SDS scheduler can also beat the commercial ILP solver by at least one order of magnitude, and up to two or three orders of magnitude for the same set of benchmarks. These results demonstrate the effectiveness of setting upper and lower latency bounds and exploiting negative cycle and lower bounding in propagation to quickly prune out the entire search space. It is interesting to note that benchmark U5ML achieves a low runtime because it is much more constrained by timing than by resource. Timing constraints dictate that its latency cannot be further reduced regardless of resource assignment.

With incremental mode enabled, Table 1 shows that SDS scheduler is able to complete the previously difficult benchmark CHEM and locate the optimal solution while both the commercial and open-source solvers struggle and time out. At the same time, incremental mode also improves the runtime of other benchmarks by various degrees. The improvement from incremental mode stems from the fact that only a small fraction of operations are actually involved in resource contention. Based on Table 1, mostly less than 10% of the SAT variables are needed to resolve resource constraints and converge to an optimal solution. The percentage becomes small for large benchmarks. With problem-specific knowledge, we specifically target contending operations to achieve significant speedup.

Table 2 shows the runtime in seconds for different combinations of constraints on the number of multipliers and memory ports. In general, an increase in the number of resources leads to additional SAT binding variables while the number of SAT partial ordering variables remains unchanged. The overall increase in the number of SAT variables may lead to longer runtime for the SAT solver. However, increasing the number of resources also loosens the resource constraints and decreases the number of partial ordering edges that

Table 3: Experiments on synthesizing CHStone benchmarks targeting the Intel Cyclone V FPGA at a clock period of 10ns — #Ops: number of operations in the program. #States: number of states in the generated schedule for each function; benchmarks achieving state reduction with SDS are highlighted in bold. CP: achieved clock period in ns. ALM, LUT, FF, DSP, and RAM: number of corresponding resources used on the target device. Runtime: time in seconds taken to solve the SDS scheduling problem.

Benchmark	#Ops	SDC-Based Scheduling							SDS Scheduling						
		#States	CP	ALM	LUT	FF	DSP	RAM	Runtime	#States	CP	ALM	LUT	FF	DSP	RAM
ADPCM	850	25, 58	11.2	5316	8948	9851	122	7	0.03	25, **54**	12.5	5549	9166	9894	146	7
AES	812	37, 25, 17, 46	10.6	5313	7817	9568	0	10	0.05	37, 25, 17, **42**	11.5	5506	8147	9755	0	10
BLOWFISH	687	74, 36	7.5	2209	3330	4035	0	29	0.02	**70**, 36	7.8	2402	3709	4582	0	29
DFADD	361	4, 4	7.3	1439	1770	2124	0	1	0.01	4, 4	7.4	1442	1778	2105	0	1
DFDIV	361	65	9.7	3179	4383	6776	48	2	0.01	65	9.6	3170	4385	6769	48	2
DFMUL	279	5	9.6	1125	1601	1494	32	1	0.01	5	9.7	1126	1630	1492	32	1
DFSIN	1067	4, 9, 65	10.2	8584	10677	14568	82	5	0.05	4, 9, 65	9.6	8541	10594	14557	82	5
GSM	966	7	10.2	3256	4747	5204	54	7	0.03	7	10.6	3233	4697	5154	62	7
JPEG	2255	36, 9, 6, 7, 9, 7, 53	13.4	17066	28087	21211	87	83	0.11	36, 9, 6, 7, 9, 7, 53	13.7	17020	28112	21016	87	83
MIPS	346	5	11.7	1036	1468	928	6	4	0.01	5	11.8	1029	1468	947	6	4
MOTION	284	4, 7	8.4	5577	8257	8495	0	6	0.01	4, 7	9.0	5729	8339	8985	0	6
SHA	314	11, 11	6.1	1350	1596	2650	0	20	0.01	11, 11	6.3	1375	1603	2687	0	20

needs to be inserted into the SDC (when the solver is running in incremental mode). The resulting set of SDC constraints are more likely to be consistent, making it easier for SDC to return a feasible solution after fewer iterations in propagation. Table 2 shows that SDS scheduler running in incremental mode remains scalable as the number of resources in the constraints increases.

To demonstrate the applicability of SDS, we further integrate SDS scheduler into LegUp [4], a state-of-the-art open-source HLS tool. We leverage LegUp's front-end to compile the input program into a CDFG and extract the relevant scheduling (e.g., timing, resource) constraints. SDS scheduler schedules the CDFG based on the constraints extracted from LegUp and returns the generated schedule to LegUp for post-scheduling processing and RTL generation. For experiments, we synthesize a set of applications from the CHStone benchmark suite [15] targeting the Intel Cyclone V FPGA at a clock period of 10ns.

Using LegUp, we compare the QoR of the synthesized hardware produced by SDC-based scheduling against the QoR of hardware produced by our SDS scheduler. For each benchmark, Table 3 reports the total number of operations of the program, runtime of SDS scheduling, as well as the key quality metrics post place-and-route generated by SDC-based scheduling and our SDS scheduler. Table 3 shows that our SDS scheduling approach achieves QoR comparable to that of SDC-based scheduling. On average, we observe small increase in clock period with small reduction in resource usage. Because most of the CHStone benchmarks are not dominated by resource constraints, they do not benefit from reduction in the number of states with the exception of ADPCM, AES, and BLOWFISH. Nevertheless, these experiments demonstrate that the SDS scheduling approach is practical for real-life applications of non-trivial size. We note that the achieved clock period exceeds the target clock period for several benchmarks regardless of the scheduling approach applied. We believe this is a result of inaccurate delay estimation in HLS tools instead of an artifact of our proposed scheduling approach. Table 4 demonstrates that ADPCM, AES, BLOWFISH, and DFMUL can achieve further state reduction after we tighten the resource constraints in LegUp to one memory port and one multiplier.

6 RELATED WORK AND DISCUSSIONS

Resource-constrained scheduling has been the subject of extensive study, resulting in a line of heuristics, including Hu's Algorithm, List Scheduling, and Force-Directed Scheduling, to solve the problem efficiently. Iterative metaheuristics, such as simulated annealing and ant colony optimization, have also been demonstrated as viable options [24]. Because resource-constrained scheduling maps naturally to a constraint satisfaction problem consisting of logical connectives of linear constraints, it can also be solved with modern SMT solvers,

Table 4: Benchmarks achieving further state reduction after tightening resource constraints — Results are shown for one memory port and one multiplier. Same notations are followed as in Table 3.

Benchmark	SDC-Based Scheduling		SDS Scheduling		
	#States	CP	Runtime	#States	CP
ADPCM	31, 64	12.0	0.04	**26, 60**	11.3
AES	37, 49, 33, 55	10.4	0.05	37, 49, 33, **47**	10.5
BLOWFISH	118, 57	8.2	0.02	**108**, 57	8.5
DFMUL	7	9.4	0.02	**6**	9.6

which integrate specialized (linear) solvers with propositional satisfiability search techniques to achieve conflict-driven learning [13]. In particular, a subset of SMT solvers focus on determining the satisfiability of a Boolean combination of difference constraints [35]. These solvers take advantage of an graph-based algorithm to efficiently explore the search space.

Our scheduler is inspired by the concept of SMT and employs a graph-based algorithm to perform conflict-based learning to quickly prune out the infeasible search space. However, unlike generic SMT solvers in which SAT assumes a principal role in driving the underlying theory solver, our solver treats SAT and the underlying theory as equal partners. Notably, our underlying theory is able to influence the subset of SAT clauses that need to be included at each iteration of the feedback loop and determine the appropriate problem that needs to be solved by SAT. In addition, our solver makes heavy use of well-established heuristics specific to the resource-constrained scheduling problem to significantly improve the efficiency of propagation. These problem-specific knowledge provides supports for the key features of our solver, including optimization, resource-aware lower bounding, and incremental learning described in Section 4.

Branch-and-bound style pruning is another popular approach for solving the resource-constrained scheduling problem [5, 25]. This type of approach divides the problem into sub-problems and computes the lower and upper bounds of each sub-problem. A subproblem is solved optimally when the lower and upper bounds coincide. While these branch-and-bound style schedulers employ problem-specific knowledge from lower and upper bounding to reduce overall scheduling time, our scheduler applies conflict-driven learning tightly coupled with various scheduling heuristics (including upper and lower bounding) to achieve additional runtime improvement. Our approach combines the power of conflict-driven learning and problem-specific knowledge to realize significant speedup. While previous schedulers are designed to work with only resource-constrained scheduling problems, our proposed joint SDC and SAT formulation allows more expressive encoding of a rich set of constraints. With a combination of SAT and SDC, our approach provides the flexibility to make tradeoffs among different constraints and select the encoding most suitable for each type of constraints.

While this work focuses on HLS, the proposed scheduling approach can equally apply to resource-constrained scheduling problems in many other fields of study. Moreover, our scheduling framework is designed to generalize to a wide range of constrained scheduling problems with a variety of constraints. For example, the framework can be extended to consider constraints arising from various forms of pipeline scheduling [3, 10, 32, 39], which are also typically handled by heuristics for efficiency. In addition, recent interest in dynamically scheduled HLS [11, 18, 20, 21, 33] necessitates a tradeoff between runtime hardware overhead and performance that may not be easily optimized. A scheduling formulation with SAT will enable modeling of the hardware resource overhead so it can be co-optimized during scheduling. Our scheduling approach can also be extended to handle cross-layer HLS optimizations, such as mapping-aware scheduling [31, 40] and place-and-route aware HLS [41], as well as low-power optimizations in HLS [17, 38]. Because many constraints cannot be anticipated by heuristics, the gap to optimality is expected to only widen. Efforts in exact scheduling is therefore crucial for handling a rich set of current and future constraints.

7 CONCLUSIONS

Current HLS scheduling algorithms rely on inexact heuristics that make ad hoc local decisions and cannot accurately and globally optimize over a rich set of constraints. To provide guarantee on QoR out-of-the-box, we propose an exact scheduling approach based on a joint SDC and SAT formulation to precisely handle a variety of scheduling constraints. We develop a specialized scheduler based on conflict-driven learning and problem-specific knowledge to efficiently solve the resource-constrained scheduling problem. By pushing the boundary of what is practically scalable, our scheduler demonstrates orders-of-magnitude improvement in runtime over current exact scheduling approach. Given the flexibility of SAT, we envision that our approach can be effectively applied to a wide range of constrained scheduling problems. As ongoing research, we are further enhancing the proposed scheduler to handle pipeline scheduling and enable more intelligent static optimization techniques for dynamically scheduled HLS.

ACKNOWLEDGEMENTS

We would like to thank the anonymous reviewers for their insightful comments. This research was supported in part by DARPA Award HR0011-16-C-0037, a DARPA Young Faculty Award, NSF Awards #1337240, #1453378, #1618275, Semiconductor Research Corporation, and a research gift from Xilinx, Inc.

REFERENCES

[1] T. Ajayi et al. Celerity: An Open-Source RISC-V Tiered Accelerator Fabric. *Hot Chips: A Symp. on High Performance Chips*, 2017.
[2] Armin Biere. Lingeling, Plingeling and Treengeling Entering the SAT Competition 2013. *SAT Competition*, 2013.
[3] Andrew Canis, Stephen D. Brown, and Jason H. Anderson. Modulo SDC Scheduling with Recurrence Minimization in High-Level Synthesis. *Int'l Conf. on Field Programmable Logic and Applications (FPL)*, 2014.
[4] A. Canis et al. LegUp: High-Level Synthesis for FPGA-Based Processor/Accelerator Systems. *Int'l Symp. on Field-Programmable Gate Arrays (FPGA)*, 2011.
[5] Mingsong Chen, Saijie Huang, Geguang Pu, and Prabhat Mishra. Branch-and-Bound Style Resource Constrained Scheduling using Efficient Structure-Aware Pruning. *IEEE Computer Society Annual Symposium on VLSI (ISVLSI)*, 2013.
[6] John W. Chinneck and Erik W. Dravnieks. Locating Minimal Infeasible Constraint Sets in Linear Programs. *ORSA Journal on Computing*, 1991.
[7] J. Cong, B. Liu, S. Neuendorffer, J. Noguera, K. Vissers, and Z. Zhang. High-Level Synthesis for FPGAs: From Prototyping to Deployment. *IEEE Trans. on Computer-Aided Design of Integrated Circuits and Systems (TCAD)*, 2011.
[8] Jason Cong and Zhiru Zhang. An Efficient and Versatile Scheduling Algorithm Based on SDC Formulation. *Design Automation Conf. (DAC)*, 2006.
[9] IBM ILOG CPLEX. V12.6: User's Manual for CPLEX. *International Business Machines Corporation*, 2015.
[10] Steve Dai, Mingxing Tan, Kecheng Hao, and Zhiru Zhang. Flushing-Enabled Loop Pipelining for High-Level Synthesis. *Design Automation Conf. (DAC)*, 2014.
[11] Steve Dai, Ritchie Zhao, Gai Liu, Shreesha Srinath, Udit Gupta, Christopher Batten, and Zhiru Zhang. Dynamic Hazard Resolution for Pipelining Irregular Loops in High-Level Synthesis. *Int'l Symp. on Field-Programmable Gate Arrays (FPGA)*, 2017.
[12] Martin Davis, George Logemann, and Donald Loveland. A Machine Program for Theorem-Proving. *Communications of the ACM*, 1962.
[13] Leonardo De Moura and Nikolaj Bjørner. Satisfiability Modulo Theories: Introduction and Applications. *Communications of the ACM*, 2011.
[14] John Forrest. CBC User Guide. *IBM Research*, 2005.
[15] Yuko Hara, Hiroyuki Tomiyama, Shinya Honda, Hiroaki Takada, and Katsuya Ishii. CHStone: A Benchmark Program Suite for Practical C-Based High-Level Synthesis. *Int'l Symp. on Circuits and Systems (ISCAS)*, 2008.
[16] Andrei Horbach. A Boolean Satisfiability Approach to the Resource-Constrained Project Scheduling Problem. *Annals of Operations Research*, 2010.
[17] Wei Jiang, Zhiru Zhang, Miodrag Potkonjak, and Jason Cong. Scheduling with Integer Time Budgeting for Low-Power Optimization. *Asia and South Pacific Design Automation Conf. (ASP-DAC)*, 2008.
[18] Lana Josipovic, Philip Brisk, and Paolo Ienne. From C to Elastic Circuits. *Asilomar Conf. on Signals, Systems, and Computers*, 2017.
[19] Yun Liang, Kyle Rupnow, Yinan Li, Dongbo Min, Minh N. Do, and Deming Chen. High-Level Synthesis: Productivity, Performance, and Software Constraints. *Journal of Electrical and Computer Engineering*, 2012.
[20] Gai Liu, Mingxing Tan, Steve Dai, Ritchie Zhao, and Zhiru Zhang. Architecture and Synthesis for Area-Efficient Pipelining of Irregular Loop Nests. *IEEE Trans. on Computer-Aided Design of Integrated Circuits and Systems (TCAD)*, 2017.
[21] Junyi Liu, Samuel Bayliss, and George A. Constantinides. Offline Synthesis of Online Dependence Testing: Parametric Loop Pipelining for HLS. *IEEE Symp. on Field Programmable Custom Computing Machines (FCCM)*, 2015.
[22] Xinheng Liu, Yao Chen, Tan Nguyen, Swathi Gurumani, Kyle Rupnow, and Deming Chen. High Level Synthesis of Complex Applications: An H.264 Video Decoder. *Int'l Symp. on Field-Programmable Gate Arrays (FPGA)*, 2016.
[23] Sharad Malik and Lintao Zhang. Boolean Satisfiability from Theoretical Hardness to Practical Success. *Communications of the ACM*, 2009.
[24] Giovanni De Micheli. *Synthesis and Optimization of Digital Circuits*. McGraw-Hill Higher Education, 1994.
[25] M. Narasimhan and J. Ramanujam. A Fast Approach to Computing Exact Solutions to the Resource-Constrained Scheduling Problem. *ACM Trans. on Design Automation of Electronic Systems (TODAES)*, 2001.
[26] Robert Nieuwenhuis. SAT and SMT are Still Resolution: Questions and Challenges. *Automated Reasoning*, 2012.
[27] Alice C. Parker, Jorge T. Pizarro, and Mitch Mlinar. MAHA: A Program for Datapath Synthesis. *Design Automation Conf. (DAC)*, 1986.
[28] Ganesan Ramalingam, Junehwa Song, Leo Joskowicz, and Raymond E. Miller. Solving Systems of Difference Constraints Incrementally. *Algorithmica*, 1999.
[29] Minjoong Rim and Rajiv Jain. Lower-bound Performance Estimation for the High-Level Synthesis Scheduling Problem. *IEEE Trans. on Computer-Aided Design of Integrated Circuits and Systems (TCAD)*, 1994.
[30] Nitish Kumar Srivastava, Steve Dai, Rajit Manohar, and Zhiru Zhang. Accelerating Face Detection on Programmable SoC Using C-Based Synthesis. *Int'l Symp. on Field-Programmable Gate Arrays (FPGA)*, 2017.
[31] Mingxing Tan, Steve Dai, Udit Gupta, and Zhiru Zhang. Mapping-Aware Constrained Scheduling for LUT-Based FPGAs. *Int'l Symp. on Field-Programmable Gate Arrays (FPGA)*, 2015.
[32] Mingxing Tan, Bin Liu, Steve Dai, and Zhiru Zhang. Multithreaded Pipeline Synthesis for Data-Parallel Kernels. *Int'l Conf. on Computer-Aided Design (ICCAD)*, 2014.
[33] Mingxing Tan, Gai Liu, Ritchie Zhao, Steve Dai, and Zhiru Zhang. ElasticFlow: A Complexity-Effective Approach for Pipelining Irregular Loop Nests. *Int'l Conf. on Computer-Aided Design (ICCAD)*, 2015.
[34] J.N.M. Van Loon. Irreducibly Inconsistent Systems of Linear Inequalities. *European Journal of Operational Research*, 1981.
[35] Chao Wang, Franjo Ivančić, Malay Ganai, and Aarti Gupta. Deciding Separation Logic Formulae by SAT and Incremental Negative Cycle Elimination. *Logic for Programming, Artificial Intelligence, and Reasoning*, 2005.
[36] Lintao Zhang, Conor F. Madigan, Matthew H. Moskewicz, and Sharad Malik. Efficient Conflict Driven Learning in a Boolean Satisfiability Solver. *Int'l Conf. on Computer-Aided Design (ICCAD)*, 2001.
[37] X. Zhang, X. Liu, A. Ramachandran, C. Zhuge, S. Tang, P. Ouyang, Z. Cheng, K. Rupnow, and D. Chen. High-Performance Video Content Recognition with Long-Term Recurrent Convolutional Network for FPGA. *Int'l Conf. on Field Programmable Logic and Applications (FPL)*, 2017.
[38] Zhiru Zhang, Deming Chen, Steve Dai, and Keith Campbell. High-Level Synthesis for Low-Power Design. *IPSJ Transactions on System LSI Design Methodology (T-SLDM)*, 2015.
[39] Zhiru Zhang and Bin Liu. SDC-Based Modulo Scheduling for Pipeline Synthesis. *Int'l Conf. on Computer-Aided Design (ICCAD)*, 2013.
[40] Ritchie Zhao, Mingxing Tan, Steve Dai, and Zhiru Zhang. Area-Efficient Pipelining for FPGA-Targeted High-Level Synthesis. *Design Automation Conf. (DAC)*, 2015.
[41] Hongbin Zheng, Swathi T. Gurumani, Kyle Rupnow, and Deming Chen. Fast and Effective Placement and Routing Directed High-Level Synthesis for FPGAs. *Int'l Symp. on Field-Programmable Gate Arrays (FPGA)*, 2014.

P4-Compatible High-Level Synthesis of Low Latency 100 Gb/s Streaming Packet Parsers in FPGAs

Jeferson Santiago da Silva, François-Raymond Boyer and J.M. Pierre Langlois
Polytechnique Montréal, Canada
{jeferson.silva,francois-r.boyer,pierre.langlois}@polymtl.ca

ABSTRACT

Packet parsing is a key step in SDN-aware devices. Packet parsers in SDN networks need to be both reconfigurable and fast, to support the evolving network protocols and the increasing multi-gigabit data rates. The combination of packet processing languages with FPGAs seems to be the perfect match for these requirements.

In this work, we develop an open-source FPGA-based configurable architecture for arbitrary packet parsing to be used in SDN networks. We generate low latency and high-speed streaming packet parsers directly from a packet processing program. Our architecture is pipelined and entirely modeled using templated C++ classes. The pipeline layout is derived from a parser graph that corresponds to a P4 code after a series of graph transformation rounds. The RTL code is generated from the C++ description using Xilinx Vivado HLS and synthesized with Xilinx Vivado. Our architecture achieves a 100 Gb/s data rate in a Xilinx Virtex-7 FPGA while reducing the latency by 45% and the LUT usage by 40% compared to the state-of-the-art.

CCS CONCEPTS

• **Hardware** → **Reconfigurable logic applications**; • **Networks** → *Programming interfaces*;

KEYWORDS

FPGA; packet parsers; HLS; programmable networks; P4

ACM Reference Format:
Jeferson Santiago da Silva, François-Raymond Boyer and J.M. Pierre Langlois. 2018. P4-Compatible High-Level Synthesis of Low Latency 100 Gb/s Streaming Packet Parsers in FPGAs. In *FPGA '18: 2018 ACM/SIGDA International Symposium on Field-Programmable Gate Arrays, February 25–27, 2018, Monterey, CA, USA.* ACM, New York, NY, USA, 6 pages. https://doi.org/10.1145/3174243.3174270

1 INTRODUCTION

The emergence of recent network applications have opened new doors to FPGA devices. Dataplane realization in Software-defined Networking (SDN) [10] is an example [13, 15] of such applications. In SDN networks, the data and control planes are decoupled, and they can evolve independently of each other. When new protocols

are deployed in a centralized intelligent controller, new forwarding rules are compiled to the data plane element without changing the underlying hardware. FPGAs, therefore, offer the right degree of programmability expected by these networks, by offering fine grain programmability with sufficient and power-efficient performance.

A standard SDN forwarding element (FE) is normally implemented in a pipelined-fashion [3]. Incoming packets are parsed in order to extract header fields to be matched in the processing pipelines. These pipelines are organized as a sequence of match-action tables. In SDN FEs, a packet parser is expected to be programmable, and it can be reconfigured at run time whenever new protocols are deployed.

Recent packet processing programming languages, such as POF [9] and P4 [4], allow describing agnostic data plane forwarding behavior. Using such languages, a network programmer can specify a packet parser to indicate which header fields are to be extracted. He can as well define which tables are to be applied, and the correct order in which they will be applied.

The main focus of this work is to propose a high-level and configurable approach for packet parser generation from P4 programs. Our design follows a configurable pipelined architecture described in C++. The pipeline layout and the header layout templates are generated by a script after the P4 compilation.

The contributions of this paper are classified into two classes: architectural and microarchitectural. The summary of the architectural contributions of this work is listed as follows:

- an open-source framework for generation of programmable packet parsers[1] described in a packet processing language;
- a modular and configurable hardware architecture for streaming packet parsing in FPGAs; and
- a graph transformation algorithm to improve the parser pipeline efficiency.

The contributions related to the microarchitectural improvements are as follows:

- a data-bus aligned pipelined architecture for reducing the complexity in the header analysis; and
- a lookup table approach for fast parallel barrel-shifter implementation.

The rest of this paper is organized as follows. Section 2 presents a review of the literature, Section 3 draws the methodology adopted in this work, Section 4 shows the experimental results, and Section 5 draws the conclusions.

2 RELATED WORK

Packet processing languages. The SDN [10] paradigm has brought programmability to the network environment. OpenFlow [11] is

---

[1]Available at https://github.com/engjefersonsantiago/P4HLS

the standard protocol to implement the SDN networks. However, the OpenFlow realization [7] is protocol-dependent, which limits the genericity expected in SDN.

Song [9] presents the POF language. POF is a protocol-agnostic packet processing language, where the user can define the behavior of the network applications. A POF program is composed of a programmable parser and match-action tables.

P4 [4] is an emergent protocol-independent packet processing language. P4 provides a simple network dialect to describe the packet processing. The main components of a P4 program are the header declarations, packet parser state machine, match-action tables, actions, and the control program. Recently, P4 has gained adoption in both academia and industry, and this is why we have chosen P4 as the packet processing language in this work.

Packet parsers design. Gibb *et al.* present in [6] a methodology to design fixed and programmable high-speed packet parsers. However, this work did not show results for FPGA implementation.

Attig and Brebner [1] propose a 400 Gb/s programmable parser targeting a Xilinx Virtex-7 FPGA. Their methodology includes a domain specific language to describe packet parsers, a modular and pipelined hardware architecture, and a parser compiler. The deep pipeline of this architecture allows very high throughput at the expense of longer latencies.

Benácek *et al.* [2] present an automatic high-speed P4-to-VHDL packet parser generator targeting FPGA devices. The packet parser hardware architecture is composed of a set of configurable parser engines [8] in a pipelined-fashion. The generated parsers achieve 100 Gb/s for a fairly complex set of headers, however the results showed 100% overhead in terms of latency and resources consumption when compared to a hand-written VHDL implementation.

P4-to-FPGA mappers have been recently proposed [13, 14]. P4-SDNet translator is partially compatible with the $P4_{16}$ specification and it maps a P4 code to custom Xilinx FPGA logic. One limitation of P4-SDNet is the lack of support for variable-sized headers.

In this work, we deal with some of the pitfalls of previous works [1, 2], trading-off design effort, latency, performance, and resources usage. Our pipeline layout leads to lower latencies compared to the literature [1, 2]. Moreover, the FPGA resource consumption in terms of lookup tables (LUTs) is reduced compared to [2], since instead of generating each parser code we parametrize generic hand-written templated C++ classes targeted to FPGA implementation.

3 DESIGN METHODOLOGY

This section presents the methodology followed in this work. Section 3.1 draws the high-level architectural view. Section 3.2 deals with details on microarchitectural aspects. Section 3.3 presents our method to generate the parser pipeline.

3.1 High-Level Architecture

A packet parser can be seen at a high-level as a directed acyclic graph (DAG), where nodes represent protocols and edges are protocol transitions. A parser is implemented as an abstract state machine (ASM), performing state transition evaluations at each parser state. States belonging to the path connecting the first state to the last state in the ASM compose the set of supported protocols of an FE.

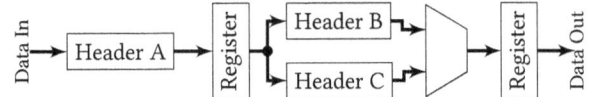

(a) High-level packet parser pipeline layout

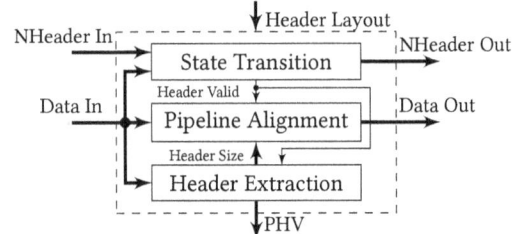

(b) Internal header block architecture

Figure 1: High-level architecture

Figure 1a depicts the high-level view of the packet parser realization proposed in this work. The proposed architecture is a streaming packet parser, requiring no packet storage. Header instances are organized in a pipelined-fashion. Headers that share the same previous states are processed in parallel. Throughout this work, we say that those headers belong to the same parser (graph) level. The depth of the parser pipeline is the length of the longest path in the parser graph. For sake of standardization, thick arrows in the figures throughout this work indicate buses, while thin arrows represent single signals.

The internal header block architecture is shown in Figure 1b. This block was carefully described using templated C++ classes to offer the right degree of configurability required by the most varied set of protocol headers this architecture is intended to support. This design choice was also taken to improve bit accuracy by accordingly setting arbitrary integer variables, reducing FPGA resources usage.

In Figure 1b, the *Header Layout* is a configuration parameter. It is a set of data structures required to initialize the processing objects. It includes key match offsets and sizes for protocol matching, lookup tables to determine data shift values, expressions to determine the header size, last header indication, and so forth. *Data In* is a data structure that contains the incoming data to be processed in a header instance. It is composed of the data bus to be analyzed and some metadata. These metadata include data start and finish information for a given packet and packet identifier. The packet identifier is used to keep track of the packet throughout the processing pipeline and to identify which headers belong to the same packet. *NHeader In* is assigned by the previous header instance indicating which is the next header to be processed. *PHV* is a data structure containing the extracted fields. It includes the extracted data, number of bits extracted, a data valid information, and header and packet identifier. Signals labelled with *In* and *Out* are mirrored, which means that *In* signals undergo modifications before being forwarded to *Out*.

Internal sub-blocks execute in parallel with minimum data dependency. In fact, only the *Header Valid* information must propagate among the blocks within the same clock cycle and it is generated from a basic combinational logic. *Header Size* also transits from the *Header Extraction* to the *Pipeline Alignment* module. However, this information is only required in the next cycle, which does not constitute a true data hazard.

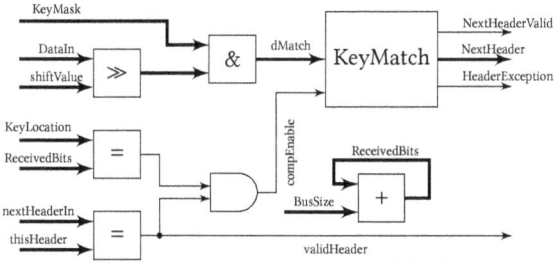

Figure 2: Station transition block

3.2 Microarchitectural Aspects

This subsection presents microarchitectural aspects of this work. We start by presenting the state transition block. Details of the header extraction module are drawn followed by the pipeline alignment block. Then, we present the case of variable-sized headers.

3.2.1 State Transition Block.
Figure 2 shows the state transition block which implements part of the ASM that represents the whole parser. Each *state* (header) of this ASM performs state transition evaluations by observing a specific field in the header and matching against a table storing the supported next headers for a given state. In this work, this table is filled at compilation time and it is part of what we call *Header Layout*.

The state transition block uses only barrel-shifters, counters, and comparators to perform state evaluations. Such operations can be easily done in an FPGA within a single clock cycle.

In Figure 2, *validHeader* is the result of a comparison between the *nextHeaderIn* and *thisHeader*. *thisHeader* is hardwired and it is part of the header layout. *validHeader* is used as an enable signal for all stateful components in the header instance. *ReceivedBits* is a counter that keeps track of the number of bits received in the same header. This information is used to check if the current data window belongs to the same window in which the *KeyValue* is placed in (*KeyLocation*). A barrel-shifter is used to shift the *DataIn* and to align it with the *KeyMask*. The bitwise AND (&) operation after the barrel-shifter guarantees this alignment. Finally, the *KeyMatch* compares the key aligned input data and the key table. If a match is found, the *NextHeader* is assigned to the value corresponding to the match and the *NextHeaderValid* is set. *HeaderException* is asserted otherwise.

3.2.2 Header Extraction Block.
Figure 3 shows the header extraction block which retrieves the header information from a raw input data stream. Similarly to the state transition block, this module is implemented using barrel-shifters, comparators, and counters. Additionally, this module calculates header sizes derived from the raw input data in case of variable-sized headers. For fixed-sized headers, the header size information is hardwired at compile time.

In the header extraction module architecture, the counter *ReceivedWords* is used to delimit the header boundaries for comparison with the *HeaderSize*. It is also used to index a table that stores the shift amounts for the barrel-shifter. This table is fixed and it is filled at compile time. The bitwise OR (|) acts as an accumulator, receiving the current shifted and value accumulating it with the results from previous cycles. *HeaderDone* indicates that a header has been completely extracted.

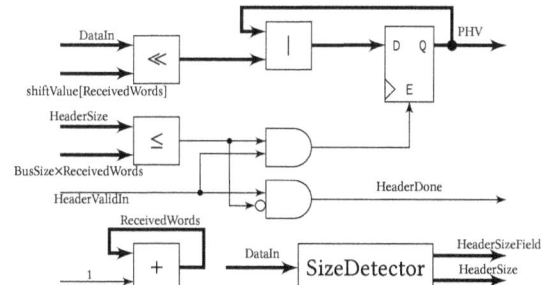

Figure 3: Header extraction block

The *SizeDetector* sub-block is hardwired for fixed-sized headers. For variable-sized headers, this sub-block has a behavior similar to the state transition module, returning the header size and the value of the field corresponding to the header size. More details regarding variable-sized headers are given in Section 3.2.4.

3.2.3 Pipeline Alignment Block.
Unlike previous works, we opt for a bus-aligned pipeline architecture. That means that each stage in the parser pipeline aligns the incoming data stream before sending it to the next stage. This design choice reduces the complexity of the data offset calculation at the beginning of a stage. The bus alignment is done in parallel with other tasks within a stage and therefore has a low overall performance impact. The pipeline alignment block microarchitecture is depicted in Figure 4.

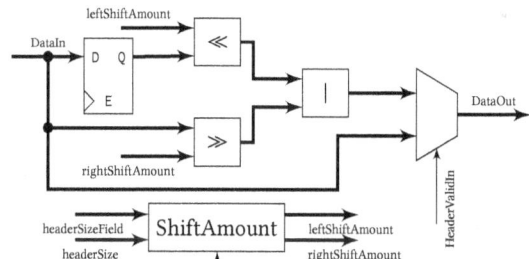

Figure 4: Pipeline alignment block

This block delays the input data and performs bit-shifts to remove the already extracted data at the same parser stage. Shift amounts are functions of the header size and the bus size. In the case of fixed-size headers, these shift amounts are hardwired. For variable-sized headers, they are calculated by the *ShiftAmount*, which is explained in more details in Section 3.2.4.

The output bus is then composed of data belonging to the current input data stream and from the previous cycle. When the current header instance is not to be processed, in the case where *HeaderValidIn* is not set, this block just passes the input data to the output bus, playing the role of a bypass unit.

3.2.4 Handling Variable-sized Headers.
It is not unusual to have a network protocol in which the header size is unknown until the packet arrives at a network equipment. The header size is inferred from a header field. IPv4 is such an example.

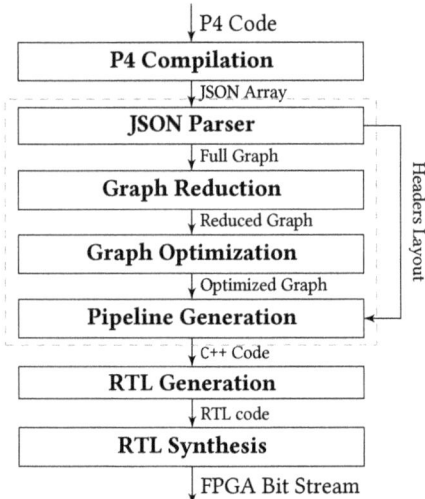

Figure 5: Parser pipeline generation

Algorithm 1: Graph balancing algorithm

> **input** : List of nodes representing a transitive reduced graph
> **input** : Ordered list of nodes belonging to the longest path
> **output**: Optimized balanced graph
> **Data:** A node is a data structure that has pointers to
> $successors/predecessors$ and methods to add/remove them. A node
> $level$ represents the graph level and it is unassigned at the beginning.

1 **Function** graphBalance(*tReducedGraph, longestPath*)
   /* Compute the distance of all nodes to the root   */
2   computeNodesLevel(*tReducedGraph*)
   /* Remove edges to successors from nodes not in the longest
      path   */
3   **for** *node* in *tReducedGraph* **do**
4   **if** *node* ∉ *longestPath* **then**
5   **for** *sucNode* in *node*.successors() **do**
6   removeEdge(*node, sucNode*)
   /* Adding spare edges to balance the graph   */
7   **for** *node* in *tReducedGraph* **do**
8   **if** *node* ∉ *longestPath* **then**
9   addEdge(*node, longestPath*[*node.level* + 1])
10   **return** *tReducedGraph*

One approach to handle variable-sized headers would be to directly generate the required arithmetic circuit from the high-level packet processing program. However, this is an inefficient option based on our bus-aligned pipeline layout. In our architecture, supporting variable-sized headers would require dynamic barrel-shifters. Recall that a brute-force approach to design barrel-shifters uses a chain of multiplexers, resulting in $O(N \log(N))$ and $O(\log(N))$ space and time complexity respectively, which compromises both FPGA resources and performance.

To avoid dynamic barrel-shifters, we are inspired by a technique available in modern high-level programming languages known as template metaprogramming. Template metaprogramming uses the compiler capabilities to compute expressions at compilation time, improving the application performance. Based on this technique, during the P4 compilation in our framework, we calculate all valid results of arithmetic expressions and store them into ROM memories. These expressions include header size calculation and shift amount taps for static barrel-shifters. The results for a variable-sized IPv4 header instance show 13% LUT and 15% FF usage reduction when implementing these ROM memories rather than dynamic barrel-shifters.

3.3 Pipeline Layout Generation

The procedure to generate the parser pipeline is depicted in Figure 5. The input P4 code is compiled using the P4C compiler [12] producing a JSON array. We have chosen to use the result of the P4 back-end compilation (p4c-bm2-ss driver) for sake of simplicity.

Our work is limited to what is enclosed by the dashed rectangle in Figure 5 and it is written in Python. It starts with the parsing of the JSON array file. While parsing, the script extracts the data structures necessary to initialize the multiple C++ *Header* instances that compose the parser pipeline. The JSON parser also extracts the full parser graph. Figure 6a presents a full parser graph generated from a header stack comprising the following protocols: Ethernet, IPv4, IPv6, IPv6 extension header, UDP, and TCP.

For an efficient pipelined design, the graph illustrated in Figure 6a is not suitable. In that representation, almost all pipeline stages need

bypass schemes to skip undesired state transitions, introducing combinational delays and increasing the resource usage due to the bypass multiplexers. We propose to simplify the original graph in order to have a more regular pipeline layout.

The graph simplification starts with the graph reduction phase that receives the full graph as input. This step performs a transitive reduction of the original graph in order to eliminate redundant graph edges. This phase also extracts the longest possible path of the parser graph. The result of this phase is shown in Figure 6b.

The graph presented in Figure 6c is an alternative representation for the reduced graph from Figure 6b. In this graph, a dummy node is introduced to offer the same reachability while balancing the graph. This dummy node only acts as a bypass element and therefore has no implementation cost, thus, it can be merged with existent nodes at the same graph level.

We propose a graph balancing algorithm in Algorithm 1 to optimize the reduced graph. It receives as parameters the transitive reduced parser graph and the longest path in the graph. As output, the algorithm returns a balanced graph tailored to our pipelined architecture. The first function call (line 2) in the algorithm executes the node level computation in relation to the root for all nodes. The first loop (lines 3 - 6) iterates over the nodes that are not in the longest path. It deletes the edges from these nodes to their children. The last loop (lines 7 - 9) iterates again over the nodes that are not part of the longest path and assigns a child to them. The chosen child is the first one belonging to the next graph level. Finally, the algorithm returns an optimized graph on line 10. An example of balanced graph is shown in Figure 6d.

The last step of the proposed approach illustrated in Figure 5 is the code generation. This phase receives as input a set of data structures representing the supported header layouts and the balanced graph. The header layouts are used to initialize both template and construction parameters for the C++ objects. The pipeline layout is drawn based on the balanced graph, with multiplexer insertion when required. The result of this phase is a synthesizable C++ code.

The generated C++ code is tailored for FPGA implementation. The next step in the processing chain is to generate RTL code for FPGA synthesis and place-and-route. Vivado HLS 2015.4 is used in

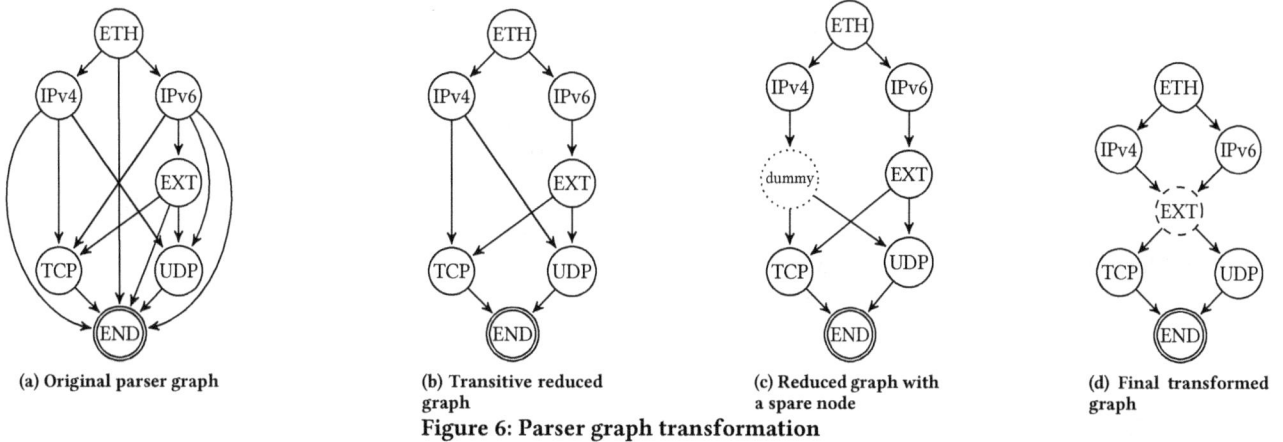

(a) Original parser graph

(b) Transitive reduced graph

(c) Reduced graph with a spare node

(d) Final transformed graph

Figure 6: Parser graph transformation

this phase. Then, the generated RTL is synthesized under Vivado, which produces a bit stream file compatible with Xilinx FPGAs.

4 EXPERIMENTAL RESULTS

To demonstrate and evaluate our proposed method, we conducted two classes of experiments, the same ones performed in [2], to simplify comparisons. These two classes are defined as follows:

- **Simple parser**: Ethernet, IPv4/IPv6 (with 2 extensions), UDP, TCP, and ICMP/ICMPv6; and
- **Full parser**: same as simple parser plus MPLS (with two nested headers) and VLAN (inner and outer).

We used Vivado HLS 2015.4 to generate synthesizable RTL code. The RTL code was afterwards synthesized under Vivado 2015.4. The target FPGA device of this work was a Xilinx Virtex-7 FPGA, part number XC7VX690TFFG1761-2.

Table 1 shows a comparison against other works present in the literature [2, 6] that support fixed- and variable-sized headers. In the case of [6], because they do not provide FPGA results, we reproduced their results based on a framework provided by the authors [5]. For that, we developed a script that converts the P4 code to the data structures needed in the framework.

Analysing the data from Table 1, both this work and [2] outperform [6], which is expected since the framework proposed in that work for automatic parser generation was designed for ASIC implementation and not for FPGA.

We assume as a golden model, labelled as Golden [2] in Table 1, a hand-written VHDL implementation presented in [2], which the authors used to evaluate their method.

For the full parser, our work achieves the same throughput as [2], while not only reducing latency by 45% but also the LUT consumption by 40%. However, our architecture consumes more FFs, which is partially explained by the additional pipeline registers inferred by the Vivado HLS. Nonetheless, we can even have a lower overall slice utilization compared to [2], since in a Virtex-7 each slice has four LUTs and eight FFs, and our architecture does not double the number of used FFs.

Also, a notable resource consumption reduction is noticed when the number of extracted fields are reduced from all fields to 5-tuple,

since a large amount of resources is destined to store the extracted fields, which matches with the findings reported in [6].

To compare the impact of our proposed pipelined layout, we implemented the pipeline organization proposed in [2] using the proposed header block architecture illustrated in Figure 1b since their source code was unavailable. This experiment is marked as "Hybrid [2] and this work" in Table 1. For the simple parser, our proposed architecture improves latency by more than 33%, while reducing by 16% and 10% the number of used FFs and LUTs, respectively. In the case of the full parser, the latency was reduced by 39%, while the resource consumption follows the results of the simple parser.

Moreover, this hybrid solution also outperforms the original work [2] in both latency and LUT consumption. It shows that our microarchitectural choices are more efficient in these aspects. In addition, these better results can also be related to the language chosen to describe each architecture. In [2], they generated VHDL code from a P4 description. Our design uses templated C++ classes, which can fill the abstraction gap between the high-level packet processing program and the low-level RTL code.

When comparing to the golden model, the results obtained with our architecture are comparable in terms of latency. However, our design utilizes nearly twice the overall amount of logic resources, following what has been reported in [2]. Such area overhead is explained by the hand-crafted low-level VHDL optimizations manually performed by the authors in [2].

As shown in Table 1, the present work achieves the best maximum frequency comparing to the state-of-the-art, which allows scaling to data rates higher than 100 Gb/s. Figure 7 presents the design scalability results for data rates ranging from 10 Gb/s up to 160 Gb/s. It is worth noting that the data rate scaling causes a non-expressive impact in terms of LUTs, corresponding to an increase of 35 $^{LUTs}/_{Gbps}$ in the case of the full 160 Gb/s parser. To achieve higher throughputs (> 160 Gb/s) in a single parser, a larger data bus (> 512 bits) is required. As a consequence, more than one minimum-sized Ethernet frame (64 bytes) could span over a single input data stream, requiring more complex hardware to detect frame boundaries. Therefore, multiple parser instances are required to support higher throughputs.

Table 1: Parser results comparison

Work	Performance				Resources			Extracted Fields
	Data Bus [bits]	Frequency [MHz]	Throughput [Gb/s]	Latency [ns]	LUTs	FFs	Slice Logic (LUTs+FFs)	
Simple Parser								
[6]	256	184.1	47	N/A	14 906	2963	17 869	All fields
[6]	256	178.6	46	N/A	6865	1851	8716	TCP/IP 5-tuple
Golden [2]	512	195.3	100	15	N/A	N/A	5000	TCP/IP 5-tuple
[2]	512	195.3	100	29	N/A	N/A	12 000	TCP/IP 5-tuple
Hybrid [2] and this work	320	312.5	100	28.8	4699	7254	11 953	TCP/IP 5-tuple
This work	320	312.5	100	19.2	4270	6163	10 433	TCP/IP 5-tuple
This work	320	312.5	100	19.2	5888	10 448	16 336	All fields
Full Parser								
[6]	64	172.2	11	N/A	6946	2600	9546	All fields
[6]	64	172.2	11	N/A	3789	1425	5214	TCP/IP 5-tuple
Golden [2]	512	195.3	100	27	N/A	N/A	8000	TCP/IP 5-tuple
[2]	512	195.3	100	46.1	10 103	5537	15 640	TCP/IP 5-tuple
Hybrid [2] and this work	320	312.5	100	41.6	6450	10 308	16 758	TCP/IP 5-tuple
This work	320	312.5	100	25.6	6046	8900	14 946	TCP/IP 5-tuple
This work	320	312.5	100	25.6	7831	13 671	21 502	All fields

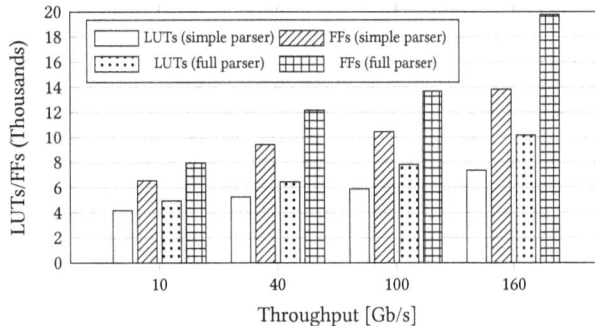

Figure 7: Synthesis results for multiple data rate parsers

5 CONCLUSION

FPGAs have increasingly gained importance in today's network equipment. FPGAs provide flexibility and programmability required in SDN-based networks. SDN-aware FEs need to be reconfigured to be able to parse new protocols that are constantly being deployed.

In this work, we proposed an FPGA-based architecture for high-speed packet parsing described in P4. Our architecture is completely described in C++ to raise the development abstraction. Our methodology includes a framework for code generation, including a graph reducing algorithm for pipeline simplification. From modern high-level languages, we borrowed the idea of metaprogramming to perform offline expressions calculation, reducing the burden of calculating them at run-time.

Our architecture performs as well as the state-of-the-art while reducing latency and LUT usage. The latency is reduced by 45% and the LUT consumption is reduced by 40%. Our proposed methodology allows a throughput scalability ranging from 10 Gb/s up to 160 Gb/s, with a moderate increase in logic resources usage.

ACKNOWLEDGMENTS

The authors thank A. Abdelsalam, I. Benacer, M. D. Souza Dutra, T. Stimpfling, T. Luinaud, and the anonymous reviewers for their thoughtful comments. This work is supported by the CNPQ/Brazil.

REFERENCES

[1] Michael Attig and Gordon Brebner. 2011. 400 Gb/s Programmable Packet Parsing on a Single FPGA. In *Proceedings of the 2011 ACM/IEEE Seventh Symposium on Architectures for Networking and Communications Systems (ANCS '11)*. IEEE Computer Society, Washington, DC, USA, 12–23. https://doi.org/10.1109/ANCS.2011.12

[2] P. Benácek, V. Pu, and H. Kubátová. 2016. P4-to-VHDL: Automatic Generation of 100 Gbps Packet Parsers. In *2016 IEEE 24th Annual International Symposium on Field-Programmable Custom Computing Machines (FCCM)*. 148–155. https://doi.org/10.1109/FCCM.2016.46

[3] Pat Bosshart et al. 2013. Forwarding Metamorphosis: Fast Programmable Match-action Processing in Hardware for SDN. *SIGCOMM Comput. Commun. Rev.* 43, 4 (Aug. 2013), 99–110. https://doi.org/10.1145/2534169.2486011

[4] Pat Bosshart et al. 2014. P4: Programming Protocol-independent Packet Processors. *SIGCOMM Comput. Commun. Rev.* 44, 3 (July 2014), 87–95. https://doi.org/10.1145/2656877.2656890

[5] G. Gibb. 2013. Network Packet Parser Generator . https://github.com/grg/parser-gen. (2013).

[6] G. Gibb et al. 2013. Design principles for packet parsers. In *Architectures for Networking and Communications Systems*. 13–24. https://doi.org/10.1109/ANCS.2013.6665172

[7] N. Gude et al. 2008. NOX: towards an operating system for networks. *SIGCOMM Comput. Commun. Rev.* 38 (2008), 105–110.

[8] Viktor Pus, Lukas Kekely, and Jan Korenek. 2012. Low-latency Modular Packet Header Parser for FPGA. In *Proceedings of the Eighth ACM/IEEE Symposium on Architectures for Networking and Communications Systems (ANCS '12)*. ACM, New York, NY, USA, 77–78. https://doi.org/10.1145/2396556.2396571

[9] Haoyu Song. 2013. Protocol-oblivious Forwarding: Unleash the Power of SDN Through a Future-proof Forwarding Plane. In *Proceedings of the Second ACM SIGCOMM Workshop on Hot Topics in Software Defined Networking (HotSDN '13)*. ACM, New York, NY, USA, 127–132. https://doi.org/10.1145/2491185.2491190

[10] The Open Networking Foundation. 2012. Software-Defined Networking: The New Norm for Networks. (April. 2012).

[11] The Open Networking Foundation. 2014. OpenFlow Switch Specification. (Dec. 2014).

[12] The P4 Language Consortium. 2017. P4 Compiler. https://github.com/p4lang/p4c. (2017).

[13] Han Wang et al. 2017. P4FPGA: A Rapid Prototyping Framework for P4. In *Proceedings of the Symposium on SDN Research (SOSR '17)*. ACM, New York, NY, USA, 122–135. https://doi.org/10.1145/3050220.3050234

[14] Xilinx Inc. 2017. P4-SDNet Translator User Guide. https://www.xilinx.com/support/documentation/sw_manuals/xilinx2017_1/ug1252-p4-sdnet-translator.pdf. (2017).

[15] S. Zhou, W. Jiang, and V. K. Prasanna. 2014. A flexible and scalable high-performance OpenFlow switch on heterogeneous SoC platforms. In *2014 IEEE 33rd International Performance Computing and Communications Conference (IPCCC)*. 1–8. https://doi.org/10.1109/PCCC.2014.7017053

Combined Spatial and Temporal Blocking for High-Performance Stencil Computation on FPGAs Using OpenCL

Hamid Reza Zohouri, Artur Podobas, Satoshi Matsuoka
Tokyo Institute of Technology, Tokyo, Japan
{zohouri.h.aa@m,podobas.a.aa@m,matsu@is}.titech.ac.jp

ABSTRACT

Recent developments in High Level Synthesis tools have attracted software programmers to accelerate their high-performance computing applications on FPGAs. Even though it has been shown that FPGAs can compete with GPUs in terms of performance for stencil computation, most previous work achieve this by avoiding spatial blocking and restricting input dimensions relative to FPGA on-chip memory. In this work we create a stencil accelerator using Intel FPGA SDK for OpenCL that achieves high performance without having such restrictions. We combine spatial and temporal blocking to avoid input size restrictions, and employ multiple FPGA-specific optimizations to tackle issues arisen from the added design complexity. Accelerator parameter tuning is guided by our performance model, which we also use to project performance for the upcoming Intel Stratix 10 devices. On an Arria 10 GX 1150 device, our accelerator can reach up to 760 and 375 GFLOP/s of compute performance, for 2D and 3D stencils, respectively, which rivals the performance of a highly-optimized GPU implementation. Furthermore, we estimate that the upcoming Stratix 10 devices can achieve a performance of up to 3.5 TFLOP/s and 1.6 TFLOP/s for 2D and 3D stencil computation, respectively.

CCS CONCEPTS

• **Hardware → Reconfigurable logic and FPGAs**; *High-level and register-transfer level synthesis*;

KEYWORDS

FPGA, Stencil, OpenCL, Spatial Blocking, Temporal Blocking

ACM Reference Format:
Hamid Reza Zohouri, Artur Podobas, Satoshi Matsuoka. 2018. Combined Spatial and Temporal Blocking for High-Performance Stencil Computation on FPGAs Using OpenCL. In *FPGA '18: 2018 ACM/SIGDA International Symposium on Field-Programmable Gate Arrays, February 25–27, 2018, Monterey, CA, USA.* ACM, New York, NY, USA, 10 pages. https://doi.org/10.1145/3174243.3174248

1 INTRODUCTION

FPGA designs have traditionally been described using Hardware Description Languages (HDLs) such as VHDL and Verilog. These low-level languages require deep understanding of hardware design,

which has prevented large-scale adoption of FPGAs in the High Performance Computing (HPC) community. However, with the recent improvements in High Level Synthesis (HLS), especially the OpenCL programming model, new opportunities have opened up for using FPGAs in HPC.

Stencils are an important computation pattern in HPC, used for solving differential equations, weather, seismic and fluid simulations, and convolution neural networks. Many real-world simulations involve very large 3D stencils with dimensions in the order of tens of thousands of cells that are accelerated using world-class supercomputers [3, 21, 24]. Such stencils are generally so large that even when the problem space is spatially distributed over thousands of nodes, the per-node problem size is still hundreds of cells wide in each dimension. Furthermore, the problem size for such simulations is increasing due to the need for higher resolution and accuracy [6, 12].

Previous work [1, 9, 20, 22] have shown that FPGAs can achieve GPU-level performance in stencil computation. Most of such work achieve this level of performance by relying on temporal blocking *without* spatial blocking. By avoiding spatial blocking, design complexity is significantly reduced and performance can scale near-linearly with the degree of temporal parallelism. However, depending on on-chip memory size, lack of spatial blocking comes at the cost of limiting width for 2D stencils to a few thousands cells [9, 20, 22], and plane size for 3D stencils to 128×128 cells or even less [20, 22]. Furthermore, lack of spatial blocking prevents supporting larger input sizes by spatial distribution over multiple FPGAs. Hence, even though such implementations could show the potential of FPGAs for stencil computation, they have limited use cases in accelerating real-world HPC applications. The main motivation of our work is to avoid restricting input size by combing spatial and temporal blocking in a deep-pipelined FPGA design, and show that it is still possible to achieve comparable performance to high-end GPUs. This paves the way for using FPGAs to accelerate real-world stencil-based computations.

We propose a parametrized accelerator based on Intel FPGA SDK for OpenCL that, to the best of our knowledge, achieves the highest performance for stencil computation on a single FPGA without restricting input size. We show that despite limited external memory bandwidth on current FPGA boards, shift register-based spatial blocking coupled with deep-pipelined temporal blocking allows us to achieve comparable performance to high-end GPUs. Our contributions can be summarized as follows:

- We propose a parameterized OpenCL-based FPGA accelerator which combines spatial and temporal blocking. We tackle issues arisen from the added design complexity by utilizing multiple FPGA-specific optimizations, and achieve high throughput without restricting input size.

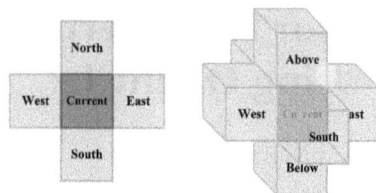

Figure 1: Example of 2D and 3D stencils

- We devise a performance model for predicting performance and pruning parameter search space.
- We evaluate our accelerator with two 2D, and two 3D stencils, each having different memory and compute characteristics. We show that the trade-off between vectorization and degree of temporal parallelism should be exploited in different ways for 2D and 3D stencils, to achieve the best performance.
- We demonstrate that our FPGA-based accelerator can compete with high-end GPUs in terms of performance, and based on a conservative performance projection, estimate that the upcoming Stratix 10 FPGAs can offer similar or even better performance compared to their same-generation GPUs.

2 BACKGROUND

2.1 Stencil Computation

In stencil computation, a grid (typically 2D or 3D) is iteratively traversed from a starting cell, and each grid cell is updated based on a set of coefficients and the values of its neighboring cells. The stencil radius and shape determine how many cells, and in which directions, are used in the computation. Fig. 1 shows typical first-order (radius of one) 2D 5-point and 3D 7-point stencils. In each iteration (time-step), input cells are read from one buffer, and updated cells are written to another. These two buffers are then swapped before the next iteration is started.

Stencil computation exhibits good spatial locality. To reduce the number of high-latency accesses to external memory and improve performance, the input grid is generally divided into blocks that are read into internal memory. Then, the computation uses this internal buffer instead. This widely-used technique is called *spatial blocking*. Stencil computation also exhibits good temporal locality. When one spatial block is computed and its output is stored in internal memory, it is possible to start computing the next iteration for this block, without fully computing the first iteration for the whole grid. This technique, called *temporal blocking*, allows further reduction of accesses to external memory.

2.2 OpenCL

OpenCL is an open, portable standard defined by Khronos Group [10] for writing software targeting heterogeneous platforms in a host/device-based fashion. Using OpenCL involves creating a *host code*, usually written in C/C++, that runs on the host processor, and a *kernel code* written in C, that runs on the device/accelerator. Usually, the host code is compiled using a C/C++ compiler, and the kernel code is compiled at runtime using a compiler that supports the target device. OpenCL provides APIs to manage the device and abstract away the communications between the host and the device. The unit of computation in

OpenCL is a *work-item*. Work-items are grouped into *work-groups* in a multidimensional descriptor called an *NDRange*. The work-items in each work-group can share data using *local memory*, which is generally implemented on-chip.

2.3 Intel FPGA SDK for OpenCL

Altera SDK for OpenCL (now called Intel FPGA SDK for OpenCL) was released in 2013 [4]. With this SDK, Altera (now Intel PSG) FPGAs became more widely available to software programmers since it allowed them to program FPGAs using a software programming language and a standard API. *Compiling* the kernel code for FPGAs involves compiling OpenCL to LLVM Intermediate Representation (IR) and then to Verilog, followed by the standard EDA flow. Because of this, the kernel code has to be compiled offline, and loaded at run time to reconfigure the FPGA.

Apart from the standard NDRange kernel programming model, Intel FPGA SDK for OpenCL also provides a *single work-item* kernel programming model. In this model, no thread-level parallelism exists, and the compiler will instead extract pipeline-parallelism from the loops in the kernel code. This model more closely matches the traditional deep-pipeline approach of programming FPGAs.

3 IMPLEMENTATION

Our design goals are to enable unrestricted input sizes for stencil computation, without sacrificing performance. The first goal requires using spatial blocking, while the low external memory bandwidth of current FPGA boards mandates utilizing temporal blocking to achieve the second one. Combing spatial and temporal blocking creates new challenges, including area overhead and lowered operating frequency due to multiply-nested loops, and memory access alignment issues. Furthermore, our design needs to be parameterized so that we can efficiently use the FPGA area by tuning these parameters. To realize all of these goals, apart from spatial and temporal blocking, we employ multiple FPGA-specific optimizations in a parameterized deep-pipelined OpenCL design.

The outline of our implementation is similar to [16] which targets CPUs and GPUs. We use the single work-item kernel programming model for two reasons. First, shift registers which are the most efficient on-chip storage type for stencil computation can only be inferred in this model. Second, an NDRange implementation will require barrier-based synchronization between threads which will result in pipeline flushes on the FPGA and reduce pipeline efficiency. Hence, we believe that a thread-based implementation using the NDRange model would likely not be able to fully exploit the advantages of FPGAs for stencil computation.

We use a multi-kernel design, with a *read*, a *compute* and a *write* kernel. As shown in Fig. 2, the compute kernel consists of multiple replicated Processing Elements (PEs). Data is streamed from external memory through the PEs using on-chip channels, and is written back to external memory in the end.

3.1 Spatial Blocking on FPGAs

We employ spatial blocking to avoid input size restrictions. We use shift registers as on-chip buffers to take advantage of the regular memory access pattern in stencil computation. This is a well-known optimization that is employed in many deep-pipeline

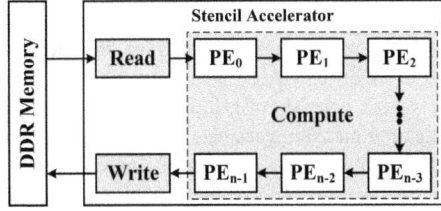

Figure 2: Overview of our multi-kernel design

implementations of stencil computation on FPGAs [9, 20, 22]. This optimization is not applicable to CPUs and GPUs due to lack of hardware support for this storage type. Furthermore, shift registers cannot be used in a thread-based implementation since they require sequential static addressing known at compile-time.

Fig. 3 shows how all neighbors for a 2-D 5-point stencil are buffered in a shift register. Incrementing the starting address of the buffer shifts the stencil forward, while all the neighbors stay at the same distance relative to the starting point (static addressing). New cells are written to the head of the shift register every clock, and old ones are evicted from the tail. This type of storage can be efficiently mapped to FPGA on-chip Block RAMs.

Using shift registers allows us to minimize the size of on-chip memory buffers by only storing cells of the spatial block that are needed. This is in contrast with spatial blocking on GPUs (or similar highly-threaded hardware) where all of the spatial block is stored on-chip until it has been computed. Supporting shift registers is one of the architectural advantages of FPGAs for stencil computation, which enables us to use larger spatial blocks or more temporal parallelism on FPGAs, compared to GPUs.

We use 1D and 2D spatial blocking for 2D and 3D stencils, respectively. Computation starts from the left or top left block, and each block is computed in all dimensions before going to the next one. Computation of spatial blocks is streamed (no blocking) in the y dimension for 2D, and z dimension for 3D stencils. We also vectorize the computation and coalesce memory accesses simultaneously by loop unrolling. In theory, if the dimensions of the spatial block are $bsize_{\{x|y\}}$, for a stencil of radius rad and a vector size of par_{vec}, the size of the shift register will be equal to:

$$size = \begin{cases} 2 \times rad \times bsize_x + par_{vec}, & 2D \\ 2 \times rad \times bsize_x \times bsize_y + par_{vec}, & 3D \end{cases} \quad (1)$$

In practice, due to multiple accesses to the shift register per loop iteration, and limited number of ports per FPGA Block RAM, all or parts of the shift register need to be replicated to support all the parallel accesses. This further increases Block RAM utilization. Altera (Intel) OpenCL Compiler (AOC) automatically performs this

operation, while minimizing Block RAM utilization. As we manually cache data, we disable the private cache that is created by AOC for every external memory access to save Block RAMs.

As shown in Fig. 4, we use *overlapped blocking (tiling)* to avoid synchronization between adjacent spatial blocks. Overlapping blocks adds redundant memory accesses and computations, but removes the read-after-write (RAW) dependency between time-steps, allowing us to compute multiple iterations for the same spatial block in parallel. The overlapped parts of the blocks are called *halos* or *ghost zones*. In absence of temporal blocking, the width and height of this region is directly proportional to rad, and $bsize_{\{x|y\}}$, respectively, with 2 and 4 such regions existing per spatial block for 2D and 3D stencils, respectively. It is worth noting that we do not require the input dimensions to be divisible by $bsize_{\{x|y\}}$ and hence, there can be a significant amount of out-of-bound computation in the last row and last column of blocks, as also shown in Fig. 4. For inputs that are very large compared to the spatial block size, this overhead will be negligible.

3.2 Temporal Blocking on FPGAs

To realize temporal blocking, we use a compute kernel that consists of multiple replicated PEs. Each PE will compute a different time-step of the same spatial block, with a distance of rad rows (for 2D) or planes (for 3D) from the previous PE. Data is transfered between PEs using shallow on-chip channels.

In a standard OpenCL design, having multiple PEs will require creating one kernel for each, and creating multiple queues in the host code to invoke each of the kernels separately. To avoid this issue, we use the *autorun* kernel type provided by Intel FPGA SDK for OpenCL. This kernel type allows any kernel that does not have an interface to host or device memory to be replicated without needing to modify the host code. Each replica in this case can be customized using a static compiler-supplied ID, and will run automatically without needing to be invoked from the host. Another important advantage of this kernel type is that the compiler can better optimize the pipeline and hence, operating frequency scales very well even with tens of PEs in the design.

To use temporal blocking with overlapped spatial blocking, we need to further increase the width of halo regions. In this case, the width of each halo region in the last PE will be:

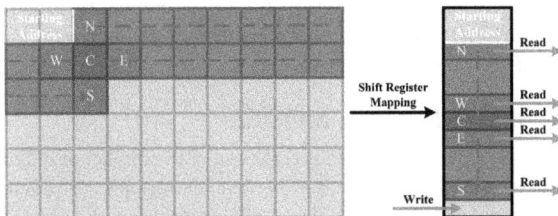

Figure 3: Shift register-based spatial blocking

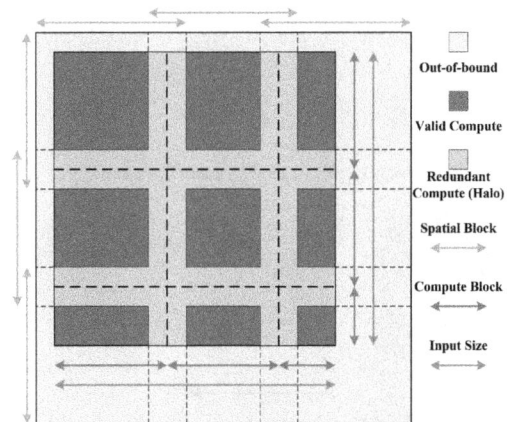

Figure 4: Overlapped blocking (tiling)

$$size_{halo} = rad \times par_{time} \qquad (2)$$

par_{time} is the number of parallel time-steps, which also equals the number of PEs. Fig. 5 shows how the halo size increases as we go further towards the last parallel time-step. Here, block size stays the same regardless of the time-step, and only the region with valid computation will become smaller. Large halos cause *thread divergence* on architectures like GPUs, since the threads that process the halos go through a different path compared to the ones that perform valid computation. Avoiding this issue on GPUs requires complex optimizations like Warp Specialization [14]. In a deep-pipelined FPGA design, however, both paths of a control flow statement are created, where the result of the control flow is multiplexed out based on the evaluated condition. This technique removes flow divergence at the cost of an area penalty. In our design, we reduce this area penalty by redundantly computing halo regions, and only controlling the flow of writes to external memory. Lack of thread divergence and the need for Warp Specialization is another advantage of using FPGAs for stencil computation, which allows better scaling with temporal blocking, compared to GPUs.

When the number of iterations is not a multiple of par_{time}, the unused PEs will just forward the data to the next PE in the chain. Even though forwarding adds overhead, as the number of iterations increases, this overhead will diminish.

3.3 FPGA-Specific Optimizations

3.3.1 Loop Collapsing. Stencil computation with spatial blocking requires multiple nested loops to iterate over dimensions and blocks. Using nested loops in an FPGA design has two disadvantages. First, to achieve an iteration interval (II) of one for all of the loops, the exit conditions of all of them need to be determined in one clock cycle. This creates a long critical path and reduces operating frequency. Second, preserving the state of variables in such loops incurs additional area and memory overhead. Because of these reasons, we collapse all of our loops into one as shown in the conversion from Listing 1 to Listing 2.

Listing 1: Original

```
1  for(y = 0; y < m; y++)
2  {
3    for(x = 0; x < n; x++)
4    {
5      compute(x,y);
6    }
7  }
```

Listing 2: Loop Collapsed

```
1  int x = 0, y = 0;
2  while(y != m) {
3    compute(x,y);
4    x++;
5    if (x == n) {
6      x = 0;
7      y++; }}
```

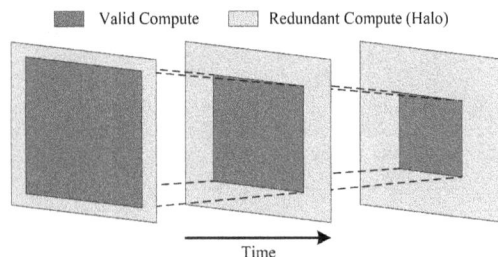

Figure 5: Halo size variance in temporal blocking

3.3.2 Exit Condition Optimization. While loop collapsing reduces area usage, the critical path of the design remains unchanged. This critical path is on the loop's exit condition calculation, which consists of a long chain of comparisons and state updates on dimension variables. We shorten this critical path by manually calculating the number of times the collapsed loop will iterate, on the host, and converting the exit condition to a single accumulation followed by an integer comparison. Listing 3 shows how this optimization is applied to Listing 2. This optimization allowed us to increase operating frequency from 200 MHz to over 300 MHz. Our results indicate that after this optimization, the critical path still consists of the remaining comparison and state updates for the dimension variables.

Listing 3: Exit Condition Optimization

```
1  int x = 0, y = 0, index = 0;
2  while (index != m * n) {
3    index++;
4    compute(x,y);
5    x++;
6    if (x == n) {
7      x = 0;
8      y++; }}
```

3.3.3 Padding. We observed that external memory accesses which are not 512-bit aligned are split by the memory controller at runtime, resulting in significant memory bandwidth waste. In our implementation, valid memory accesses start from the beginning of the top left compute block (brown area in Fig. 4), which is $size_{halo}$ floats apart from the beginning of the spatial block; hence, unless $size_{halo}$ is a multiple of 512 bits, the starting access and every access after that will not be 512-bit aligned. Furthermore, since our spatial blocks overlap, even if the starting point of the first compute block is aligned and $bsize_{\{x|y\}}$ are multiples of 512 bits, the starting point of other blocks might not be 512-bit aligned. Here, the distance between the starting point of two adjacent spatial blocks is equal to $bsize_{\{x|y\}} - 2 \times size_{halo}$. For single-precision floating-point grid cells, assuming that par_{time} is a multiple of eight, and $bsize_{\{x|y\}}$ and input dimensions are divisible by 512 bits, this distance and $size_{halo}$ will be multiples of 512 bits. Because of this, all accesses can be aligned for such values of par_{time}. For other cases, however, either $size_{halo}$ or the distance between two adjacent spatial blocks will not be a multiple of 512 bits and hence, some memory accesses could be unaligned.

To alleviate this issue, we pad the device buffers by par_{time} % 8 words. This forces the starting point of the first compute block to be always 512-bit aligned and hence, we can achieve fully-aligned accesses also for values of par_{time} that are multiples of four, and improve performance by over 30%. For other values of par_{time}, the distance between two adjacent spatial blocks will not be a multiple of 512 bits and even though alignment will be improved, many accesses will still be unaligned.

4 PERFORMANCE MODEL

We created a performance model to predict the impact of different parameters on performance, and perform design space exploration for our accelerator. Table 1 shows the description of parameters we use in our model. Iterative stencil computation generally has

Table 1: Parameters Description

Parameter	Description	Unit
rad	Stencil radius	Cells
par_{vec}	Compute vector size (width)	N/A
par_{time}	Number of parallel time-steps	N/A
f_{max}	Kernel operating frequency	Hz
$size_{cell}$	Size of each grid cell	Bytes
$size_{input}$	Number of cells in input grid	Cells
$size_{halo}$	Width of each halo region	Cells
num_{read}	External memory reads per cell update	N/A
num_{write}	External memory writes per cell update	N/A
num_{acc}	External memory accesses per cell update	N/A
$bsize_{\{x|y\}}$	Size of spatial block in x or y dimension	Cells
$csize_{\{x|y\}}$	Size of compute block in x or y dimension	Cells
th_{mem}	Memory throughput	GB/s
th_{max}	Maximum memory throughput	GB/s
$dim_{\{x|y|z\}}$	Input size per dimension	Cells
$bnum_{\{x|y\}}$	Number of spatial blocks per dimension	Cells
$trav_{\{x|y\}}$	Number of traversed cells per dimension	Cells
$iter$	Number of iterations	N/A

higher bytes-to-FLOP ratio compared to what is available on most hardware and hence, is generally memory-bound [16]. For our model we assume the computation is memory-bound, and external memory latency is hidden by the deep pipeline. To predict run time and throughput, we need to estimate external memory throughput and correctly count the number of accesses to external memory.

We observe that external memory performance on FPGAs scales with both kernel operating frequency, f_{max}, and compute vector size, par_{vec}, until the maximum throughput of the external memory is reached. This maximum throughput is determined by the memory bus width and the frequency of external memory DIMMs. We estimate memory performance in GB/s[1] as follows:

$$num_{acc} = num_{read} + num_{write}$$

$$th_{mem} = min\left(\frac{f_{max} \times par_{vec} \times size_{cell} \times num_{acc}}{10^9}, th_{max}\right) \quad (3)$$

To calculate the number of memory accesses we first calculate the number of total accesses to external memory, including the redundant and out-of-bound ones. We define *compute block* as the region in each spatial block with only valid computation (dark blue arrows in Fig. 4). The dimensions of the compute block are:

$$csize_{\{x|y\}} = bsize_{\{x|y\}} - 2 \times size_{halo} \quad (4)$$

Since the spatial blocks are overlapped in a way that in the last PE, the compute blocks are consecutive (as seen in Fig. 4), each dimension of the input is traversed up to a point that the index in that dimension is a multiple of $csize_{\{x|y\}}$. Hence, number of spatial/compute blocks in each dimension is:

$$bnum_{\{x|y\}} = \left\lceil \frac{dim_{\{x|y\}}}{csize_{\{x|y\}}} \right\rceil \quad (5)$$

[1]All throughput numbers in this paper are in GB/s = 10^9 B/s, and not GiB/s = 2^{30} B/s

Consequently, the number of cells that are read from external memory for each input buffer is calculated as follows:

$$t_{cell} = \begin{cases} bnum_x \times bsize_x \times dim_y, & 2D \\ bnum_x \times bsize_x \times bnum_y \times bsize_y \times dim_z, & 3D \end{cases} \quad (6)$$

Since we avoid out-of-bound memory reads and writes, and also memory writes to halo regions, the number of reads from external memory will be equal to t_{cell} minus out-of-bound cells, multiplied by the number of reads per cell update. The number of writes will also be equal to input size multiplied by the number of writes per cell update. For example, the total number of reads from external memory for a 2D stencil will be:

$$trav_x = bnum_x \times csize_x + 2 \times size_{halo}$$

$$t_{read} = \left(t_{cell} - (trav_x - dim_x) \times dim_y\right) \times num_{read} \quad (7)$$

Now we can calculate run time (seconds) and throughput (GB/s):

$$run\_time = \frac{\left\lceil \frac{iter}{par_{time}} \right\rceil \times (t_{read} + t_{write}) \times size_{cell}}{10^9 \times th_{mem}} \quad (8)$$

$$throughput = \frac{num_{acc} \times size_{input} \times size_{cell} \times iter}{10^9 \times run\_time} \quad (9)$$

Throughput can be converted to compute performance (GFLOP/s) by using the bytes-to-FLOP ratio of the stencil.

5 METHODOLOGY

5.1 Benchmarks

For evaluating our accelerator, we use four stencils, two 2D and two 3D. We use the 2D and 3D version of the Hotspot benchmark from Rodinia Benchmark Suite [2], and also Diffusion 2D and 3D [14]. Table 2 shows the computation and characteristics of these stencils. The bytes per cell update (Bytes PCU) numbers reported in this table assume full spatial locality optimization.

All of these benchmarks use single-precision floating-point numbers. All the variables except $TEMP_{AMB}$ (compile-time constant) are passed to the kernel as arguments in form of values

Table 2: Benchmarks

Benchmark	Computation	FLOP PCU	Bytes PCU	Bytes / FLOP
Diffusion 2D	$c_c \times val_c + c_w \times val_w + c_e \times val_e + c_s \times val_s + c_n \times val_n$	9	8	0.889
Diffusion 3D	$c_c \times val_c + c_w \times val_w + c_e \times val_e + c_s \times val_s + c_n \times val_n + c_b \times val_b + c_a \times val_a$	13	8	0.615
Hotspot 2D	$val_c + sdc \times (power_c + (val_n + val_s - 2.0 \times val_c) \times Ry\_1 + (val_e + val_w - 2.0 \times val_c) \times Rx\_1 + (TEMP_{AMB} - val_c) \times Rz\_1)$	15	12	0.800
Hotspot 3D	$val_c \times c_c + val_n \times c_n + val_s \times c_s + val_e \times c_e + val_w \times c_w + val_a \times c_a + val_b \times c_b + sdc \times power_c + c_a \times TEMP_{AMB}$	17	12	0.706

or arrays, and can be changed without kernel recompilation. The subscripts show direction (current, north, south, west, east, above, and below). Apart from arithmetic intensity, Hotspot also differs from Diffusion in memory characteristics since it needs two reads from external memory per cell update. In our implementation, both reads are cached using shift registers, though the shift register for the *power* input will be smaller than the one used for the main input since only the *current* value needs to be cached. In all of the stencils, all out-of-bound neighbors of grid cells on the grid boundaries will fall back on the boundary cell itself.

5.2 Hardware and Software Setup

We evaluate our implementation on the Terasic DE5-net board with a Stratix V GX A7 FPGA, and the Nallatech 385A board with an Arria 10 GX 1150 FPGA. We compare our results with four generations of high-end NVIDIA GPUs. Table 3 contains a comprehensive comparison of these devices. To keep comparison fair, we disable ECC on the GPUs. We compile our OpenCL host code using GCC 5.3.1, and kernel code using Quartus and AOC v16.1.2, and use CUDA v8.0/9.0 for compiling GPU kernels.

For power measurement, we use the NVIDIA NVML [18] library for GPUs, and Nallatech's API on the Arria 10 board, to access the on-board power sensors. In both cases the sensor is queried every 10 ms during kernel execution, and average power is calculated. For the Stratix V board, no power sensor exists on the board. As a conservative estimate, we run Quartus PowerPlay on the place-and-routed OpenCL design with a 25% toggle rate (default is 12.5%) and add 2.34 Watts (obtained from the datasheet of a similar memory model [11]) to the obtained value as the maximum power consumption of the external memory.

We choose $dim_{\{x|y\}}$ to be a multiple of $csize_{\{x|y\}}$ to minimize the number of out-of-bound cells, and clearly show the potential of our accelerator. We use square and cubic inputs, for 2D and 3D stencils, respectively, with at least 1 GB of external memory usage. We observe that as long as $dim_{\{x|y\}}$ are multiples of $csize_{\{x|y\}}$, performance variation with input size is negligible. We only measure kernel run time, and ignore initialization and data transfer time between host and device. Each benchmark is run with 1000 iterations, and average of five runs is reported. In our case, benchmark run times were at least 3 seconds for 2D, and 7 seconds for the 3D stencils, with a variation of less than 5 ms.

5.3 Parameter Tuning

To achieve maximum performance with the available FPGA area, we need to tune three parameters: $bsize_{\{x|y\}}$, par_{vec} and par_{time}. Increasing $bsize_{\{x|y\}}$ reduces redundancy and improves performance scaling with higher par_{time}. However, both of these values affect Block RAM utilization which creates an area/performance trade-off. Another such trade-off exists between par_{vec} and par_{time}, both of which increase performance (with different scaling factors) at the cost of higher DSP utilization. We use the area report generated by AOC to determine how many DSPs are necessary for one cell update, and then use our model and the device DSP count to optimize the trade-off between par_{time} and par_{vec}. Predicting Block RAM utilization is not straightforward due to Block RAM packing during mapping, and

also mapping of some buffers to distributed memory instead of Block RAMs. Hence, we experimentally optimize the trade-off between par_{time} and $bsize_{\{x|y\}}$. Furthermore, we put the following restrictions on our parameters:

- We use square spatial blocks for 3D stencils. Even though our implementation allows non-square blocks, doing so reduces our parameter search space with little effect on performance.
- We assume $bsize_{\{x|y\}}$ are powers of two so that the block indexes can be updated using an efficient *mod* operation. Other block sizes can be supported using conditional branching, at the cost of 5-20 MHz lower operating frequency.
- $bsize_x$ must be divisible by par_{vec}
- Since the compiler only creates coalesced access ports to external memory with a width that is a power of two, we limit par_{vec} to powers of two to avoid bandwidth waste.
- We prefer multiples of four for par_{time} to avoid unaligned accesses.

Performance predictions from our model combined with the compiler's area report allow us to limit the number of candidate configurations per stencil per board to less than six, which significantly reduces the time and compute resources that are needed for placement and routing.

5.4 Compiler Optimizations

5.4.1 Flat Compilation. Using Intel FPGA SDK for OpenCL, FPGA reconfiguration is automatically performed at runtime by the OpenCL runtime. On Stratix V devices, this reconfiguration is performed using Configuration via Protocol (CvP). However, CvP update is not supported on Arria 10 [8] and runtime reconfiguration instead happens using Partial Reconfiguration (PR) through PCI-E. Due to the additional placement and timing constraints imposed on placement and routing to support PR, fitting and routing quality for OpenCL kernels is reduced on Arria 10, especially when area utilization is high. Because of this, we used flat compilation for this device which disables PR and place and routes the OpenCL kernel and the Board Support Package (BSP) as a flat design. In our experience, most of our best-performing kernels either failed to fit or route with the default PR-based flow, or exhibited noticeably lower operating frequency compared to the flat flow (up to 100 MHz lower). However, flat runtime reconfiguration happens through JTAG with takes longer (15-20 seconds vs. less than 5 seconds for PR through PCI-E).

5.4.2 Seed and F_{max} Sweep. By default, AOC balances the pipeline stages for a target f_{max} of 240 MHz. It is possible to increase this value to achieve higher operating frequency, at the cost of extra logic and memory utilization. For each stencil on each device, we compile all candidate configurations using the default f_{max} target and measure their performance on the device. Then, to eliminate the effect of f_{max} variability, we normalize the measured values for a fixed f_{max} to find the best-performing candidate. After that we recompile the best version with multiple f_{max} targets higher than default, as long as II remains one, to maximize its f_{max}. If logic utilization is high (>80%), increasing f_{max} target will instead reduce f_{max} due to more routing congestion. In such cases we instead change the random seed for placement and routing to maximize f_{max}.

Table 3: Hardware Comparison

Device	Peak Memory Bandwidth (GB/s)	Peak Compute Performance (GFLOP/s)	Production Node (nm)	Transistors (Billion)	On-chip Memory (MiB) [a]	On-board Memory (GiB)	TDP (Watt)	Release Year
Stratix V GX A7	25.6	200	28	3.8	6.25 + 0.895	4	40	2011
Arria 10 GX 1150	34.1	1450	20	5.3	6.62 + 1.585	8	70	2014
Tesla K40c	288.4	4300	28	7.08	3.75 + 1.5	12	235	2013
GTX 980Ti	336.6	6900	28	8	5.5 + 3	6	275	2015
Tesla P100 PCI-E	720.9	9300	16	15.3	14 + 4	16	250	2016
Tesla V100 SXM2	900.1	14900	12	21.1	20 + 6	16	300	2017

[a]FPGAs: M20K + MLAB, GPUs: Register + L2

6 RESULTS

6.1 FPGA Performance

Table 4 shows the results for all of our evaluated stencils on both FPGA boards. The highest estimated performance (adjusted to post-place-and-route f_{max} for correct accuracy calculation) for each kernel on each board is marked in yellow, the highest measured performance is marked in green, and the resource bottleneck for the best configuration on each board is marked in red.

We achieve over twice higher throughput in 2D stencils, versus 3D. This is expected since the much higher Block RAM requirement of 3D stencils significantly reduces $bsize_{\{x|y\}}$, and limits scaling with temporal parallelism. For 2D stencils, however, since $bsize_x$ is sufficiently-high, redundancy is minimized and we can achieve close-to-linear scaling with temporal parallelism. This difference brings us to a very important conclusion: **For 3D stencils, it is better to spend FPGA resources to support a larger vector size, rather than more temporal parallelism**, since the former allows better performance scaling. **For 2D stencils, however, it is more efficient to spend FPGA resources on increasing temporal parallelism, rather than vector size**; the latter achieves close-to-linear performance scaling, while performance scaling with the former depends on the behavior of the memory controller which in our experience, is sub-linear except for very small vector sizes (up to four). Still, higher degree of temporal parallelism will result in higher logic utilization and consequently, more routing complications and lower f_{max}. Because of this, using the highest par_{time} and lowest par_{vec} will not necessarily result in the highest performance.

For the 2D stencils on Stratix V, Hotspot achieves higher throughput than Diffusion despite lower par_{time}. This is due to the fact that the higher num_{acc} in Hotspot allows better utilization of the memory bandwidth with the narrow vector size. It is not possible to fully utilize the DSPs on Stratix V for Hotspot since this stencil has a high number of floating-point addition and subtractions which are not natively supported by the DSPs on this device and hence, performance scaling is constrained by logic utilization. On Arria 10, however, throughput is 40% higher in Diffusion compared to Hotspot since both are constrained by DSP utilization, while the much lower compute intensity of Diffusion allows a twice wider vector at the same par_{time}. This is enough to offset the better memory bandwidth utilization of Hotspot due to higher num_{acc}. This 40% difference is exactly equal to the ratio of $num_{acc} \times par_{vec} \times f_{max}$ between these two stencils.

For the 3D stencils on Stratix V, total degree of parallelism ($par_{vec} \times par_{time}$) is the same and computation throughput is very close. Hotspot 3D achieves lower f_{max} due to 100% Block RAM and DSP utilization, but this is offset by the higher num_{acc} in this stencil. Also on Arria 10, the computation throughput of the 3D stencils is close. On this device, Diffusion 3D benefits from the higher total degree of parallelism and bigger $bsize_{\{x|y\}}$, while Hotspot 3D benefits from higher num_{acc} and f_{max}.

As shown in Table 4, we achieve an f_{max} of over 300 MHz in cases that routing is not constrained by area utilization. This shows that our implementation maps well to the underlying FPGA architecture, and that we have been successful in optimizing the critical path. Since 2D stencils have less dimension variables, their critical path is shorter compared to 3D stencils, and f_{max} is higher.

As a final note on power consumption, in many cases we are using over 70 Watts on the Arria 10 board, which is over its TDP. This further asserts that we are pushing the boundaries of performance on this device.

6.2 Model Accuracy

We define model accuracy as ratio of the measured performance on the board, to estimated performance by our model for a fixed f_{max}. As show in Table 4, even though our model can correctly predict the trend of performance for different configurations, for 2D stencils we achieve 65-90% of the estimated performance and for 3D we achieve 55-70%. One reason for this discrepancy is that even though we assume memory performance scales linearly with f_{max} and par_{vec}, in practice, scaling with par_{vec} is sub-linear except for very small values. Scaling with f_{max} also depends on the effectiveness of the memory controller in runtime coalescing. Linear scaling can be achieved if the kernel f_{max} is lower than the operating frequency of the memory controller (200 and 266 MHz for Stratix V and Arria 10, respectively), but this linearity is lost for higher values which is the general case in our implementation. Apart from this, since more data is read from external memory, than written to it, writes are more likely to be stalled and such stalls can potentially propagate all the way to the top of the pipeline. Since halo regions are not written to external memory, some writes need to be masked and potentially split into two or more accesses by the memory controller. This further increases bandwidth waste and lowers performance and model accuracy. Profiling the kernels using Intel's OpenCL profiler shows that the average burst size is always lower than par_{vec}, and does not go beyond eight words, which implies some accesses are being split into smaller ones at runtime.

Table 4: FPGA Results

Kernel	Device	bsize	par_{vec}	par_{time}	dim	Estimated Performance (GB/s)	Measured Performance (GB/s|GFLOP/s|GCell/s)	f_{max} (MHz)	Logic	Memory (Bits|Blocks)		DSP	Power (Watt)	Model Accuracy
Diffusion 2D	S-V	4096	8	6	16336	107.861	93.321|104.986|11.665	281.76	62%	10%	32%	95%	26.575	86.5%
		4096	4	12	16288	111.829	97.440|109.620|12.180	294.20	63%	14%	40%	95%	27.509	87.1%
		4096	2	24	16192	114.720	99.582|112.030|12.448	302.48	69%	22%	52%	95%	29.845	86.8%
	A-10	4096	16	16	16256	540.119	359.664|404.622|44.958	311.62	46%	20%	45%	85%	53.447	66.6%
		4096	8	36	16096	780.500	673.959|758.204|84.245	343.76	55%	38%	83%	95%	72.530	86.3%
		4096	4	72	15808	635.003	542.196|609.971|67.775	281.61	67%	65%	100%	95%	65.310	85.4%
Hotspot 2D	S-V	4096	8	6	16336	153.068	110.452|138.065|9.204	272.47	91%	13%	43%	77%	33.654	72.2%
		4096	4	12	16288	128.667	112.206|140.258|9.351	225.83	95%	21%	53%	77%	24.271	87.2%
		4096	2	20	16224	128.950	112.218|140.273|9.352	269.97	84%	27%	61%	64%	33.361	87.0%
	A-10	4096	8	16	16256	468.024	355.043|443.804|29.587	308.35	39%	27%	42%	85%	41.623	75.9%
		4096	4	36	16096	547.904	474.292|592.865|39.524	322.47	47%	53%	94%	95%	50.129	86.6%
		4096	2	72	15808	483.921	415.012|518.765|34.584	287.43	72%	88%	100%	95%	52.179	85.8%
Diffusion 3D	S-V	256	8	4	744	75.422	62.435|101.457|7.804	301.02	62%	36%	67%	91%	21.135	82.8%
		256	8	5	738	59.019	39.918|64.867|4.990	189.50	72%	44%	81%	100%	22.825	67.6%
	A-10	256	16	8	720	261.159	178.784|290.524|22.348	294.81	38%	65%	76%	60%	57.083	68.5%
		256	16	12	696	379.230	230.568|374.673|28.821	286.61	60%	94%	100%	89%	71.628	60.8%
		128	8	24	640	282.839	160.222|260.361|20.028	308.64	52%	52%	96%	89%	73.208	56.6%
Hotspot 3D	S-V	256	8	4	496	92.527	63.603|90.104|5.300	246.18	76%	68%	100%	100%	36.126	68.7%
		128	4	8	560	78.818	61.157|86.639|5.096	238.32	74%	37%	76%	100%	34.085	77.6%
	A-10	128	16	8	560	235.145	165.876|234.991|13.823	256.47	45%	37%	73%	77%	53.933	70.5%
		128	8	16	576	321.361	194.406|275.409|16.201	299.85	47%	67%	100%	77%	66.210	60.5%
		128	8	20	528	355.284	228.149|323.211|19.012	296.20	62%	81%	100%	96%	73.398	64.2%

Table 5: Stratix 10 Device Specifications

Device	DSP	Memory Blocks	External Memory Spec.	External Memory Bandwidth (GB/s)
GX 2800	5,760 (3.8x)	11,721 (4.3x)	4-bank DDR4-2400 [15]	76.8 (2.25x)
MX 2100	3,744 (2.5x)	6,501 (2.4x)	4-tile HBM [13]	512 (15x)

For 2D stencils, since par_{vec} is small, this issue has a smaller effect on performance, but for the 3D stencils, the effect is larger since we use higher values of par_{vec}. This is the reason why 2D stencils achieve better model accuracy compared to 3D ones.

In Table 4, our model correctly predicts the best configuration in every case, except for Hotspot 2D on Stratix V. The reason is that, as discussed in Section 3.3.3, fully-aligned accesses can only be achieved if par_{time} is a multiple of four and hence, a configuration with $par_{time} = 6$ cannot achieve the predicted performance.

6.3 Performance Projection for Stratix 10

To evaluate the potential of future FPGAs for stencil computation, we use our model to predict the performance of two of the upcoming Stratix 10 devices. Table 5 shows the specifications of these devices, and improvement ratio compared to Arria 10 GX 1150.

Designs on the Stratix 10 family are expected to reach an f_{max} of up to 1 GHz, enabled by the latest 14 nm manufacturing node and HyperFlex technology [7]. The extended register insertion and re-timing capabilities offered by HyperFlex are expected to improve f_{max} in case of routing congestion. However, when f_{max} is instead limited by the critical path in the design, HyperFlex will have limited effect. For the specific case of stencil computation, as discussed in Section 3.3.2, the critical path of the design will be the chain of operations that update the state of dimension variables and hence, we expect limited f_{max} improvement with HyperFlex on Stratix 10 devices. Due to this reason, we only assume a conservative 100-MHz increase in f_{max} compared to Arria 10 for stencil computation.

To predict the performance of our stencils for Stratix 10, we estimate the DSP and memory utilization on these devices by extrapolating usage on Arria 10. We assume the devices will have enough logic available to support every configuration. For memory utilization we assume overutilization only if the bits count goes above 100%. Then we use our model alongside with the area utilization estimations to predict the best configuration and performance on Stratix 10. Table 6 shows our estimation results for 5000 iterations and an input size that is a multiple of $csize_{\{x|y\}}$. Based on measured model accuracy from real executions (Table 4), we use a calibration factor of 80% and 60%, for 2D and 3D stencils, respectively, to calibrate our predictions on Stratix 10.

Even with a conservative estimation, we expect the high DSP and Block RAM count of the Stratix 10 GX 2800 device to allow over 3.5 TFLOP/s of compute performance for 2D stencil computation, which will likely outperform its same-generation GPUs. Furthermore, we expect the high memory bandwidth of the MX 2100 device to enable up to 1.6 TFLOP/s for 3D stencils, which will be competitive against its same-generation GPUs. Even though the MX 2100 device has much higher external memory bandwidth, we predict that it will achieve only slightly higher

Table 6: Stratix 10 Performance Estimation

FPGA	Stencil	$bsize$	par_{vec}	par_{time}	f_{max} (MHz)	Calibration Factor	Performance (GB/s|GFLOP/s)	Used Memory Bandwidth (GB/s|%)	Memory Utilization (Bits|Blocks)	DSP Utilization
GX 2800	Diffusion 2D	8192	8	140	450	80%	3162.7|3558.0	28.8| 38%	59%| 88%	97%
	Hotspot 2D	8192	4	140	450	80%	2362.8|2953.5	21.6| 28%	80%| 91%	97%
	Diffusion 3D	256	32	24	400	60%	917.4|1490.8	76.8|100%	44%| 47%	93%
	Hotspot 3D	256	16	24	400	60%	868.8|1230.8	76.8|100%	91%|100%	61%
MX 2100	Diffusion 2D	8192	8	92	450	80%	2078.6|2338.5	28.8| 6%	69%|100%	98%
	Hotspot 2D	8192	4	92	450	80%	1555.0|1943.8	21.6| 4%	94%|100%	98%
	Diffusion 3D	512	128	4	400	60%	975.3|1584.8	409.6| 80%	53%| 56%	96%
	Hotspot 3D	256	32	12	400	60%	991.1|1404.1	153.6| 30%	81%|100%	93%

performance compared to GX 2800 for 3D stencils. This is due to the fact that the MX 2100 device has much less resources, and the computation becomes area-bound before the external bandwidth can be fully utilized. **We conclude that a too-high or too-low "external memory bandwidth to compute performance" ratio on FPGAs will result in either area or memory bandwidth bottleneck for stencil computation.**

6.4 Comparison with GPUs

To avoid biased comparisons, we only compare our Diffusion 3D results with the highly-optimized implementation from [14]. We tune the parameters from this implementation for every GPU, and use an input size of 512^3 which achieves the best performance on these devices. This GPU implementation restricts $dim_{\{x|y\}}$ to values that are a multiple of $bsize_{\{x|y\}}$. Even though Rodinia includes CUDA implementations of both Hotspot 2D and 3D, these implementations are not optimized well, to the point that our implementations on Arria 10 achieve over twice the performance of Tesla P100; hence, we avoid using them for comparison.

Fig. 6 shows the performance and power efficiency of our implementation of Diffusion 3D on FPGAs, compared to GPUs. The roofline performance is the achievable GFLOP/s by full utilization of external memory bandwidth on each device, without temporal blocking. We also add our estimated performance and power efficiency for the Stratix 10 MX 2100 device. Based on [17], we estimate the power consumption of the Stratix 10 GX 2800 FPGA between 140 to 150 Watts for an f_{max} of 400 to 450 MHz. For the smaller MX 2100 device, we will assume a typical power consumption of 125 watts for estimating its power efficiency.

As seen in the graph, we achieve higher performance on Arria 10 compared to Tesla K40c, despite more than eight times lower memory bandwidth. **The performance advantage of Arria 10 is due to better scaling of temporal blocking on FPGAs, compared to GPUs, which allows achieving multiple times higher performance than the roofline.** Despite the fact that Arria 10 cannot reach the performance of the more modern GPUs, our results clearly show the advantage of FPGAs for stencil computation over GPUs. It noteworthy that Arria 10 also achieves better power efficiency compared to GTX 980 Ti, which further asserts the superior power efficiency of FPGAs compared to GPUs of their age. Based on our estimation, the upcoming Stratix 10 MX 2100 FPGA will achieve better performance and power efficiency compared to the Tesla P100 GPU, and better power efficiency compared to the state-of-the-art Tesla V100.

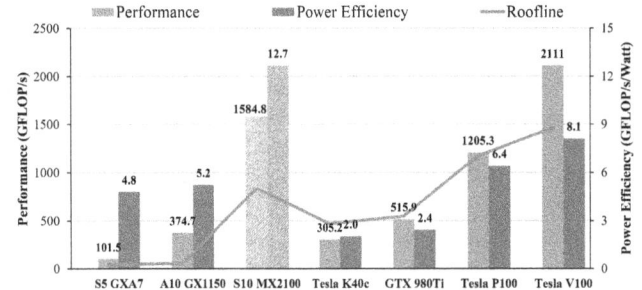

Figure 6: Performance comparison with GPUs

As a final note, we compare the code complexity of our FPGA implementation against the GPU code from [14]. Our FPGA kernel is ~250 lines and can be ported to same-shape stencils in a matter of minutes, and to same-order but differently-shaped stencils in a few hours. Furthermore, block size, vector width and degree of temporal parallelism have been parameterized in our implementation. In contrast, the GPU kernel is ~400 lines, only parameterizes block size, and requires more effort for porting to other stencils.

7 RELATED WORK

In [25] we reported an early optimization analysis of Hotspot 2D which only achieved comparable *power efficiency* to GPUs due to lack of temporal blocking and the FPGA-specific optimizations discussed here. In [23], the authors implement multiple stencils using Xilinx SDAccel with both spatial and temporal blocking. Their work uses a thread-based implementation which, as discussed in Section 3, cannot use shift register-based spatial blocking. They also do not employ 3.5D blocking [16]. Since they do not report run time or FLOP/s, we cannot compare our results with theirs. [5, 19] are examples of similar automated frameworks for stencil computation on FPGAs that use dependency analysis and the polyhedral model. These frameworks focus on automation rather than achieving high performance, and use thread-based implementations which suffer from the same shortcoming as [23]. [5] reports 8 GFLOP/s for Jacobi 2D, while we achieve over 110 GFLOP/s on Stratix V (and much more on Arria 10) for Diffusion 2D which has the exact same stencil characteristics. We achieve this large performance advantage despite the fact that the Kintex-7 XC7Z045 FPGA they use has more DSPs and roughly half of the logic and Block RAM count of our Stratix V A7 FPGA.

[1, 9, 20, 22] present the recent high-performing deep-pipelined implementations of stencil computation on FPGAs, all of which avoid spatial blocking and hence, put hard limits on input dimensions relative to on-chip memory size. In contrast, we do employ spatial blocking to avoid such restrictions which limit usability in real-world HPC applications, and show that it is still possible to achieve high performance. Compared to [22], we achieve only 9% lower performance on the same Stratix V device, but with an input size that is not supported by their implementation unless it is modified to use bigger shift registers at the cost of multiple times lower degree of temporal parallelism. In that case, our implementation will have a clear performance advantage. Compared to [9], we achieve 4x higher performance in Hotspot 2D which has similar characteristics to their FDTD 2D (same num_{acc} and one higher FLOP PCU). Compared to [1], we achieve 5x and 40x higher performance for Diffusion 2D and 3D on Stratix V A7, respectively, compared to their results for Jacobi 2D and 3D on a Virtex-7 XC7VX485T FPGA. [20] uses a 2nd order stencil and hence, their results are not comparable with ours.

8 CONCLUSION

We studied the potential of FPGAs for accelerating 2D and 3D stencil computation in real-world HPC applications. Using combined spatial and temporal blocking allowed us to, unlike many previous work on FPGAs, achieve high performance without restricting input size. With a parameterized OpenCL-based design and a performance model to guide parameter tuning, we achieved a compute performance of up to 760 and 375 GFLOP/s on an Arria 10 device, for 2D and 3D stencil computation, respectively, which rivals the performance of a highly-optimized implementation on high-end GPUs. Furthermore, we used our performance model for estimating the performance of two of the upcoming Stratix 10 devices in stencil computation, and showed that these devices will be even more competitive against their same-generation GPUs.

Since many real-world HPC applications use high-order stencils, investigating the effectiveness of temporal blocking on FPGAs for such stencils is the subject of our future work. Furthermore, we plan to evaluate spatial distribution of large stencils on multiple FPGAs for accelerating real-world HPC applications in future.

ACKNOWLEDGMENTS

This work was supported by MEXT, JST-CREST under Grant Number JPMJCR1303, JSPS KAKENHI under Grant Number JP16F16764, the JSPS Postdoctoral fellowship under grant P16764, and performed under the auspices of the Real-world Big-Data Computation Open Innovation Laboratory, Japan. We would like to thank Intel for donating licenses for their FPGA toolchain through their university program, and also thank Mohamed Wahib Attia for helping us with extracting the GPU results.

REFERENCES

[1] R. Cattaneo, G. Natale, C. Sicignano, D. Sciuto, and M. D. Santambrogio. 2015. On How to Accelerate Iterative Stencil Loops: A Scalable Streaming-Based Approach. ACM Trans. Archit. Code Optim. 12, 4, Article 53 (Dec 2015), 26 pages.

[2] S. Che, M. Boyer, J. Meng, D. Tarjan, J. W. Sheaffer, S. Lee, and K. Skadron. 2009. Rodinia: A Benchmark Suite for Heterogeneous Computing. In IEEE International Symposium on Workload Characterization (IISWC). 44–54.

[3] Y. Cui, E. Poyraz, K. B. Olsen, J. Zhou, K. Withers, S. Callaghan, J. Larkin, C. Guest, D. Choi, A. Chourasia, Z. Shi, S. M. Day, P. J. Maechling, and T. H. Jordan. 2013. Physics-based Seismic Hazard Analysis on Petascale Heterogeneous Supercomputers. In Proceedings of the International Conference

[4] on High Performance Computing, Networking, Storage and Analysis (SC '13). ACM, New York, NY, USA, Article 70, 12 pages.

[4] T. S. Czajkowski, U. Aydonat, D. Denisenko, J. Freeman, M. Kinsner, D. Neto, J. Wong, P. Yiannacouras, and D. P. Singh. 2012. From OpenCL to high-performance hardware on FPGAs. In 22nd International Conference on Field Programmable Logic and Applications (FPL). 531–534.

[5] G. Deest, T. Yuki, S. Rajopadhye, and S. Derrien. 2017. One Size Does Not Fit All: Implementation Trade-Offs for Iterative Stencil Computations on FPGAs. In 27th International Conference on Field Programmable Logic and Applications (FPL). 1–8.

[6] Peter R. Gent, Stephen G. Yeager, Richard B. Neale, Samuel Levis, and David A. Bailey. 2010. Improvements in a half degree atmosphere/land version of the CCSM. Climate Dynamics 34, 6 (01 May 2010), 819–833.

[7] M. Hutton. 2015. Stratix 10: 14nm FPGA delivering 1GHz. In IEEE Hot Chips 27 Symposium (HCS). 1–24.

[8] Intel Corporation. 2016. Arria 10 CvP Initialization and Partial Reconfiguration over PCI Express User Guide. (October 2016). https://www.altera.com/en_US/pdfs/literature/ug/ug_a10_cvp_prop.pdf

[9] T. Kenter, J. Förstner, and C. Plessl. 2017. Flexible FPGA design for FDTD using OpenCL. In 27th International Conference on Field Programmable Logic and Applications (FPL). 1–7.

[10] Khronos OpenCL Working Group. 2011. The OpenCL Specification: Version 1.0. (October 2011). https://www.khronos.org/registry/cl/specs/opencl-1.0.pdf

[11] Kingston Technology. 2013. Kingstone KVR16S11S6/2 Memory Module Specification. (December 2013). http://www.kingston.com/dataSheets/KVR16S11S6_2.pdf

[12] B. P. Kirtman, C. Bitz, F. Bryan, W. Collins, J. Dennis, N. Hearn, J. L. Kinter, R. Loft, C. Rousset, L. Siqueira, C. Stan, R. Tomas, and M. Vertenstein. 2012. Impact of ocean model resolution on CCSM climate simulations. Climate Dynamics 39, 6 (01 Sep 2012), 1303–1328.

[13] Manish Deo, Jeffrey Schulz, Lance Brown. 2017. Intel Stratix 10 MX Devices Solve the Memory Bandwidth Challenge. (2017). https://www.altera.com/content/dam/altera-www/global/en_US/pdfs/literature/wp/wp-01264-stratix10mx-devices-solve-memory-bandwidth-challenge.pdf

[14] Naoya Maruyama and Takayuki Aoki. 2014. Optimizing Stencil Computations for NVIDIA Kepler GPUs. In Proceedings of the 1st International Workshop on High-Performance Stencil Computations, Armin Größlinger and Harald Köstler (Eds.). Vienna, Austria, 89–95.

[15] Nallatech. 2017. Nallatech 520 Product Brief. (2017). http://www.nallatech.com/wp-content/uploads/Nallatech-520-Product-Brief-v2-4.pdf

[16] A. Nguyen, N. Satish, J. Chhugani, C. Kim, and P. Dubey. 2010. 3.5D Blocking Optimization for Stencil Computations on Modern CPUs and GPUs. In 2010 ACM/IEEE International Conference for High Performance Computing, Networking, Storage and Analysis (SC '10). 1–13.

[17] E. Nurvitadhi, G. Venkatesh, J. Sim, D. Marr, R. Huang, J. Ong Gee Hock, Y. T. Liew, K. Srivatsan, D. Moss, S. Subhaschandra, and G. Boudoukh. 2017. Can FPGAs Beat GPUs in Accelerating Next-Generation Deep Neural Networks?. In Proceedings of the 2017 ACM/SIGDA International Symposium on Field-Programmable Gate Arrays (FPGA '17). ACM, New York, NY, USA, 5–14.

[18] Nvidia Corp. 2015. NVML API Reference Guide. (May 2015). http://docs.nvidia.com/deploy/pdf/NVML_API_Reference_Guide.pdf

[19] Prashant Rawat, Martin Kong, Tom Henretty, Justin Holewinski, Kevin Stock, Louis-Noël Pouchet, J. Ramanujam, Atanas Rountev, and P. Sadayappan. 2015. SDSLc: A Multi-target Domain-specific Compiler for Stencil Computations. In Proceedings of the 5th International Workshop on Domain-Specific Languages and High-Level Frameworks for High Performance Computing (WOLFHPC '15). ACM, New York, NY, USA, Article 6, 10 pages.

[20] K. Sano and S. Yamamoto. 2017. FPGA-Based Scalable and Power-Efficient Fluid Simulation using Floating-Point DSP Blocks. IEEE Transactions on Parallel and Distributed Systems 28, 10 (Oct 2017), 2823–2837.

[21] Takashi Shimokawabe, Takayuki Aoki, and Naoyuki Onodera. 2014. High-productivity Framework on GPU-rich Supercomputers for Operational Weather Prediction Code ASUCA. In Proceedings of the International Conference for High Performance Computing, Networking, Storage and Analysis (SC '14). IEEE Press, Piscataway, NJ, USA, 251–261.

[22] H. M. Waidyasooriya, Y. Takei, S. Tatsumi, and M. Hariyama. 2017. OpenCL-Based FPGA-Platform for Stencil Computation and Its Optimization Methodology. IEEE Transactions on Parallel and Distributed Systems 28, 5 (May 2017), 1390–1402.

[23] S. Wang and Y. Liang. 2017. A comprehensive framework for synthesizing stencil algorithms on FPGAs using OpenCL model. In 54th ACM/EDAC/IEEE Design Automation Conference (DAC '17). 1–6.

[24] W. Xue, C. Yang, H. Fu, X. Wang, Y. Xu, J. Liao, L. Gan, Y. Lu, R. Ranjan, and L. Wang. 2015. Ultra-Scalable CPU-MIC Acceleration of Mesoscale Atmospheric Modeling on Tianhe-2. IEEE Trans. Comput. 64, 8 (Aug 2015), 2382–2393.

[25] H. R. Zohouri, N. Maruyama, A. Smith, M. Matsuda, and S. Matsuoka. 2016. Evaluating and Optimizing OpenCL Kernels for High Performance Computing with FPGAs. In SC16: International Conference for High Performance Computing, Networking, Storage and Analysis. 409–420.

A HOG-based Real-time and Multi-scale Pedestrian Detector Demonstration System on FPGA

Jan Dürre, Dario Paradzik, and Holger Blume
Institute of Microelectronic Systems
Leibniz Universität Hannover
Hanover, Germany
{jan.duerre, dario.paradzik, holger.blume}@ims.uni-hannover.de

ABSTRACT

Pedestrian detection will play a major role in future driver assistance and autonomous driving. One powerful algorithm in this field uses HOG features to describe the specific properties of pedestrians in images. To determine their locations, features are extracted and classified window-wise from different scales of an input image. The results of the classification are finally merged to remove overlapping detections. The real-time execution of this method requires specific FPGA- or ASIC-architectures. Recent work focused on accelerating the feature extraction and classification. Although merging is an important step in the algorithm, it is only rarely considered in hardware implementations. A reason for that could be its complexity and irregularity that is not trivial to implement in hardware. In this paper, we present a new bottom-up FPGA architecture that maps the full HOG-based algorithm for pedestrian detection including feature extraction, SVM classification, and multi-scale processing in combination with merging. For that purpose, we also propose a new hardware-optimized merging method. The resulting architecture is highly efficient. Additionally, we present an FPGA-based full real-time and multi-scale pedestrian detection demonstration system.

ACM Reference format:
Jan Dürre, Dario Paradzik, and Holger Blume. 2018. A HOG-based Real-time and Multi-scale Pedestrian Detector Demonstration System on FPGA In FPGA '18: 2018 ACM/SIGDA International Symposium on Field-Programmable Gate Arrays, February 25–27, 2018, Monterey, CA, USA. ACM, New York, NY, USA, 10 pages. https://doi.org/10.1145/3174243.3174249

1 INTRODUCTION

Fully automatic pedestrian detection is a desirable service in a wide field of applications, e.g. driver assistance and autonomous driving. Object detection is one of the most challenging fields in computer vision. Much effort is put into improving the detection performance of such algorithms. Additionally, algorithms in this area are very computational intensive. Thus, optimized implementations are often necessary for real-time execution, especially if run under certain boundary conditions. In many applications, e.g. autonomous driving, mere FPGA or ASIC architectures are required to achieve efficient real-time processing under the strict requirement of very low power consumption.

An algorithm presented by Dalal and Triggs [1] is one of the current state-of-the-art methods for people detection. The algorithm is based on the description of characteristic features of pedestrians with histograms of oriented gradients (HOG) and subsequent classification with a support vector machine (SVM). Although newer methods based on convolutional neural networks (CNN) are able to achieve better detection performance [2], real-time execution of CNN-based algorithms currently requires desktop or server systems with power-consuming GPUs to even process low resolution images [2] [3]. To our knowledge, no efficient FPGA implementation of pedestrian detection with neural networks exists in literature. This makes HOG-based methods still highly relevant for certain low-power applications. Ongoing research focusses on accelerating the HOG feature extraction on all kinds of homogenous and heterogeneous platforms, due to the high computational nature of the algorithm. Although the classification of pedestrians in different sizes and the fusion of overlapping detections is an important part of the algorithm, most publications of dedicated ASIC or FPGA architectures do not include this step genuinely.

In this paper, we present a new highly efficient FPGA architecture for pedestrian detection with HOG and SVM. The implementation includes the important merging process, making the setup of an efficient stand-alone, real-time and multi-scale pedestrian detector system possible.

The paper is organized as follows. In section 2 the HOG-based algorithm for pedestrian detection by Dalal and Triggs is described in detail. This preamble is necessary for better understanding of related work to this paper, presented in Section 3. Part 4 gives an overview on the main contributions of our work. In section 5 a detailed description and evaluation of the proposed FPGA architecture for feature extraction, classification and merging is given. The setup of a real-time demonstration system for pedestrian detection with camera processing is described in section 6. The paper is summarized in the final section 7.

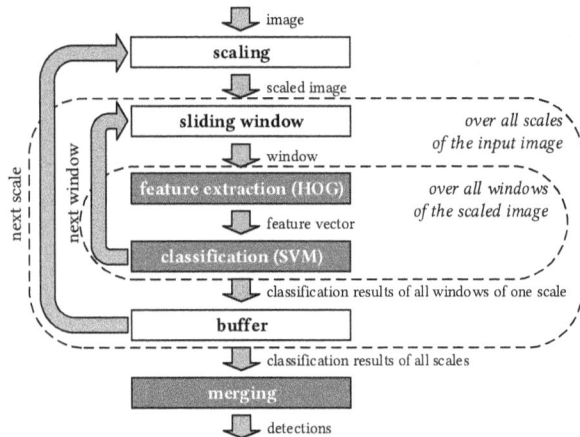

Fig. 1: Overview of the HOG- and SVM-based algorithm for pedestrian detection as proposed in [1] and [5].

2 HOG-BASED PEDESTRIAN DETECTION

Dalal and Triggs presented their algorithm for pedestrian detection in 2005 [1], Dalal continued enhancing and improving the method in his PhD-thesis in 2006 [5].

2.1 Algorithm Overview

The algorithm as described by the authors is shown in Fig. 1. The detection method is based on an overlapping sliding window approach. The required number of pixels for satisfying detection results defines the size of the sliding window. In [1] a window size of 64×128 pixel is described as sufficient. This window size predetermines the size of detectable objects. To detect larger objects the input image can be scaled down. In order to scan an image of size $w \times h$ for detections in all sizes the input frame has to be processed in multiple scales, starting from the original resolution down to the smallest resolution determined by the window size. For 4:3 or 16:9 aspect ratios, this is typically limited by the window height of 128 pixels. The number of scale stages and the step-size between the scales depends on the resolution of the input and the desired detection density. Dalal suggests in [5] that a scaling ratio from 1.01 to 1.30 in-between two stages leads to reasonable results.

Thus, the first step of the algorithm is the scaling of a single input frame. After that, the sliding window is applied. For each of the resulting windows the HOG features are calculated and classified with an SVM. The step-size and overlap of the sliding window influences the accomplishable detection density. This overlap also fundamentally affects the required computational effort for the feature extraction of subsequent windows. Some specific step-sizes are much more efficient to implement. A stride of 8 pixels in each direction is a reasonable compromise between the detection density and the computational cost [1]. The classification results for each window of an image-scale are subsequently collected in a buffer, and the next scaling size is processed. After the classification results of each window of each scaling stage have been calculated and collected, the last step to determine the final detections is the merging process. Since objects typically lead to

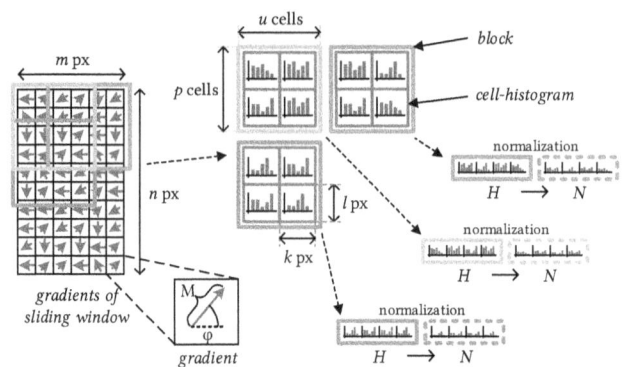

Fig. 2: Hierarchical breakdown of sliding detection window into overlapping blocks and cells. The figure shows only three exemplary blocks.

multiple overlapping positive window classifications, also throughout different scaling stages, this final step is necessary to merge multiple detections belonging to a single object. Furthermore, the merging can be utilized to remove single positive detections since they are most likely not caused by an object.

The HOG feature extraction, SVM classification and merging are explained in detail in the following paragraphs.

2.2 HOG Feature Extraction

The HOG features describe the distribution of geometric edges within local areas in a detection window, and thus are able to describe shapes of objects. For that purpose, a window of $m \times n$ pixels is handled on three different hierarchical levels. The lowest level is the pixel region. Each $k \times l$ pixels form a local cell. Last, the highest level, $u \times p$ cells form overlapping blocks. Fig. 2 illustrates the hierarchy. As mentioned before, a window contains 64×128 pixels and overlaps 8 pixels to neighboring windows. In [1] it is furthermore suggested to use 8×8 pixels in each cell and 2×2 cells in a block with a single cell overlap in both directions. Since the cell size and the block-overlap equals the window stride, a large number of the cells and blocks in a window are identical to those in its neighbor windows.

First, for each pixel P the magnitude M and direction φ of its RGB-gradients are calculated according to (1) – (4). Subsequent, the largest magnitude of the three color channels is selected for each pixel. A simplified version of the algorithm uses only the luminance of each pixel for computing the gradient. This results in a minor decreased detection rate, but is typically used in hardware implementations due to benefits regarding computational effort. For the application of pedestrian detection, it is recommended to consider φ solely as unsigned, from 0° to 180° (0 to π) [1].

$$G_x(x, y) = P(x + 1, y) - P(x - 1, y) \qquad (1)$$

$$G_y(x, y) = P(x, y + 1) - P(x, y - 1) \qquad (2)$$

$$M(x, y) = \sqrt{G_x^{\,2}(x, y) + G_y^{\,2}(x, y)} \qquad (3)$$

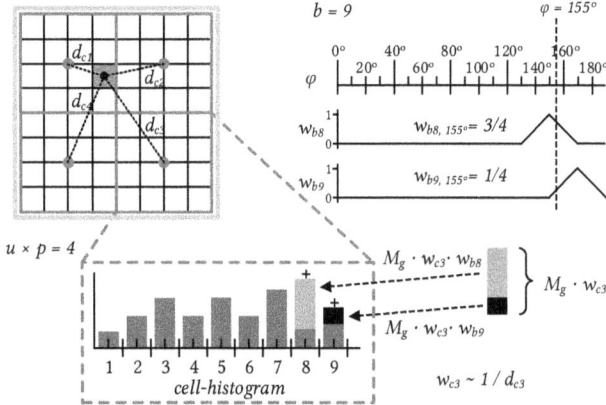

Fig. 3: Trilinear interpolation to determine cell-histograms from gradients, carried out in two steps. First, linear interpolation in-between histogram-bins, depending on the gradient angle φ. Second, inter-cell interpolation subject to the current pixel position within a block.

$$\varphi(x, y) = \tan^{-1} \frac{G_y(x,y)}{G_x(x,y)} \tag{4}$$

A Gaussian filter, as in (5), is applied to the magnitudes M on the block hierarchy in the second step. This step lowers the influence of pixel gradients near block borders, and makes the features more robust against image noise. According to [1] $\sigma = 8$ leads to good results in pedestrian detection.

$$M_g(\mathrm{x}, \mathrm{y}) = M(x, y) \cdot \frac{1}{2\pi\sigma^2} \cdot e^{-\frac{x^2+y^2}{2\sigma^2}} \tag{5}$$

Next, the gradients are processed to create cell-histograms over their orientations. For that purpose, the possible range of angles (0° to 180°) is divided into b bins. Dalal and Triggs standard detector uses 9 bins in total [1]. The filtered magnitudes M_g are sorted into all cell-histograms within a block according to their corresponding angle φ. To prevent aliasing effects the compilation of histograms is interpolated in two ways. First, all magnitudes are portioned linearly in-between neighboring bins. This step is illustrated in Fig. 3 exemplarily for an angle of 155°. Second, an additional interpolation is carried out between cell-histograms in both spatial dimensions within each block. This step is applied for each magnitude in a block with regard to the centers of the four neighboring cells, as can be seen in Fig. 3. Depending on the distance of a magnitude's location to the cell- centers, it is weighted linearly into all cell-histograms within a block. The distribution in two bins within a cell and the two dimensional distribution in-between cells is called trilinear interpolation.

After creating the cell-histograms, each $u \times p = 4$ histograms are concatenated to form a block-histogram H:

$$\vec{H} = [h_1 \ldots h_{u \cdot p \cdot b}] \tag{6}$$

Each resulting block contains $u \cdot p \cdot b = 36$ values, and is then normalized to balance different illumination conditions within an image. Different norms are suggested in [1] to receive the normalized block vector N. These are L1-norm, L1-sqrt, L2-norm and L2-hys. Norms differ in detection performance and

computational effort. Equation (7) exemplarily shows the L1-sqrt norm.

$$\vec{N} = \sqrt{\vec{H} \cdot \frac{1}{\sum_{i=1}^{u \cdot p \cdot b}|h_i| + \varepsilon}} \tag{7}$$

Finally, a feature vector W is formed by concatenating all blocks in a window according to (8). Each window contains $K=105$ different blocks with each 36 bin values, leading to a final window feature vector dimension of 3,780.

$$\vec{W} = [\vec{N_1} \ldots \vec{N_K}] \tag{8}$$

2.3 SVM Classification

A trained support vector machine describes the position of a hyperplane, able to split a multi-dimensional feature space into separate classes. For a two-class problem, as it is the case in pedestrian detection, the class of a feature vector W can be calculated by determining the distance between the vector and the hyperplane [6]. The hyperplane within an SVM is described through a normal vector v and an offset o. The distance between W and hyperplane can be determined with a multiplication of W and v and a subsequent addition of o. The sign of the result specifies the class f of vector W, as described by (9).

$$f(\vec{W}) = \mathrm{sgn}(\vec{v} \cdot \vec{W} + o) \tag{9}$$

Furthermore, it is possible to determine the probability of a classification result being correct. This so called confidence score P is calculated with (10).

$$P(\vec{W}) = \frac{1}{1 + e^{A \cdot (\vec{v} \cdot \vec{W} + o) + B}} \tag{10}$$

Vector v and offset o are determined with a training process, described in [1]. Parameters A and B are fit using maximum likelihood estimation, presented in [7]. The offset o can be utilized to virtually move the hyperplane after training, to influence the ratio of false positive and false negative classifications.

2.4 Merging

Dalal suggests in [5] a method called non-maximum suppression for fusion of overlapping detections. After mapping all positive detections of every scale into a 3-dimensional space of position and scale, a mean shift algorithm is applied to locally smooth the detections. For that purpose, the detections are iteratively moved towards local centers of mass within regions of interest. (11) describes the computational formula for a single iteration step for a detection y_i of n total detections. y_m is calculated until it does not change anymore. Additionally, each step requires the calculation of two covariance matrices H and a transformation function $t(P_i)$, based on the confidence score.

$$y_m = H_h(y_m) \cdot \left[\sum_{i=1}^{n} \left(\frac{|H_i|^{-\frac{1}{2}} \cdot t(P_i) \cdot e^{-\frac{1}{2}(y_m - y_i)^T \cdot H_i^{-1} \cdot (y_m - y_i)}}{\sum_{i=1}^{n} |H_i|^{-\frac{1}{2}} \cdot t(P_i) \cdot e^{-\frac{1}{2}(y_m - y_i)^T \cdot H_i^{-1} \cdot (y_m - y_i)}} \right) \cdot H_i^{-1} \cdot y_i \right] \tag{11}$$

As (11) implies, the computational effort for the merging is comparable to the feature extraction and classification with a runtime complexity of $O(n^2)$. The number of iteration steps depends on the location of detections and the total number of detections within a region of interest.

3 RELATED WORK

Since Dalal and Triggs published their work in 2005, many FPGA- or ASIC-architectures for HOG-based pedestrian detection have been published.

In 2009, an architecture for accelerating the HOG-feature extraction was published [8]. The architecture follows the sliding-window approach of the algorithm and achieves 3 FPS on processing VGA images with a single instance. [9] presented a more advanced architecture in 2011. This implementation introduces a more efficient block-based feature extraction. Furthermore, the architecture includes a window-based classification, including a less complex AdaBoost- classification. With this architecture, the authors are able to process VGA images at 112 FPS. Although the miss rate is increased by factor 2, due to the more simple classification algorithm. In [10] and [11] the block-based approach is further advanced, including an SVM-classification. The architecture in [10] is able to process SVGA images with 72 FPS through SRAM-based buffering. [11] introduced a very efficient pipeline with fewer buffers, thus being able to accelerate the processing of HD images to 64 FPS with much lower hardware costs.

Additionally, many approaches for heterogeneous FPGA-SoC implementations are made. In [13] for example a HOG/AdaBoost-based architecture is implemented on a Virtex Zynq system. The presented approach uses a DDR-memory for buffering and is able to process HD images at 40 FPS. Furthermore, only four DSPs are required due to many simplifications of the algorithm. This also leads to a lower detection rate, compared to the original algorithm [1].

The mentioned architectures are only a selection of the ones available in literature. In general, the feature extraction and the classification have undergone a significant amount of optimization, sometimes with the cost of reduced detection rates due to simplifications of the algorithm. Although Dalal emphasizes in [5] that the merging of multiple overlapping window detections throughout different scales is a crucial part of the pedestrian detection process, only very few publications include this step in their architecture. Even the processing of multiple image scales that is necessary for merging, is often not included in presented systems, but only estimated based on a single unscaled processing chain. Thus, published information about processing speed in FPS usually refers to a single unscaled image.

Some exceptions can be found in literature. The authors in [11] were able to build a system that can process 6 scales in parallel and 3 in time with the proposed pipeline. However, no merging is considered and the given FPS refers only to the processing in parallel. In [14] a very large heterogeneous system with 3 scales in parallel and 11 in time is presented. The architecture is able to process 68 VGA frames per second with all scales. The scaling and

Tab. 1: Comparison of implemented processing steps. The neutral marker is used for significantly simplified implementations, e.g. AdaBoost instead of SVM.

Processing step	Publication							
	[8] 2009	[9] 2011	[10] 2012	[11] 2013	[12] 2015	[13] 2015	[14] 2015	this 2017
Scaling	×	×	×	✓	×	×	×	✓
HOG feat. extr.	✓	✓	✓	✓	✓	✓	✓	✓
SVM classification	×	∘	✓	✓	✓	∘	✓	✓
Multi-scale processing	×	×	×	✓	×	×	✓	✓
Merging	×	×	×	×	∘	×	×	✓

gradient calculation is done prior in software, and no merging is included. A rare example for an approach including some sort of merging-step can be found in [12]. In this work, a block-based FPGA-implementation with real-time processing of SVGA camera-images is presented. The introduced system processes only a single scaling stage, but considers the classification results of neighboring window-detections to determine if a current detection is valid. The authors define a detection as invalid if any of the 12 sequentially preceding windows has been a valid detection. This means that all final detections have to be 12 sequential windows apart. This simple method prevents some overlapping detections, but is not able to determine the most probable location of a person or remove single false positive detections.

A reason for the lack of merging in implementations could be the complex, irregular and data-depended merging process that is not trivial to implement in hardware. Furthermore, a fully synchronized processing chain of the feature extraction and classification on multiple scales is required to implement the final step of merging in a meaningful way. This can be challenging especially when processing camera frames with constant cyclic data transfers in a real-time stand-alone system.

4 CONTRIBUTIONS

In this work, we present a full pedestrian detector architecture with genuine multi-scale processing of the HOG feature extraction and SVM classification, and a new powerful merging algorithm implemented on an FPGA. The setup is capable of processing a non-stop pixel stream e.g. from a camera in real-time. Tab. 1 shows a comparison of implemented processing steps of this work and recent work from literature.

The pipeline for feature calculation and classification of this work is one of the most efficient architectures compared to the ones found in literature. Furthermore, only few simplifications regarding extracting the feature vector are considered to achieve best detection results for a reasonable amount of hardware costs.

Based on the fusion processes proposed in [2] and [15] we present a new merging algorithm that is suitable for a cost-efficient hardware implementation. The new algorithm shows very good results in practice and is capable of performing a validity check for classification results to determine the real position of a person and even remove many false positive detections.

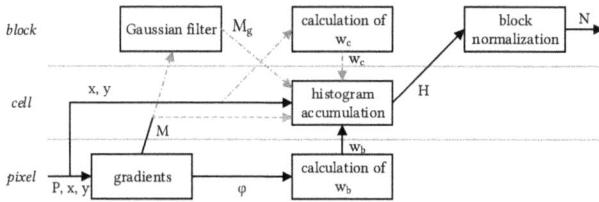

Fig. 4: Data flow visualization of processing steps for HOG feature extraction on different hierarchy levels. The flow of the reference algorithm is shown in red (dash-dot), our proposed bottom-up approach is highlighted in green (dash).

Finally, based on the proposed architecture, a stand-alone demonstration system with camera processing, multi-scale feature extraction and classification, merging and live display of detections is presented in this work. For that purpose, we were able to map the highly efficient architecture even on a small low-cost FPGA. The multi-scale processing and merging significantly improves the usability over other systems. Solely the inclusion of the merging process in the hardware architecture, makes the real-time and multi-scale implementation of an efficient stand-alone system possible.

5 HARDWARE IMPLEMENTATION

The goal to process images in a real-time system comes with certain restrictions, due to the typical way a CCD-sensor camera provides pixel information. Usually, an image is transferred one pixel per clock, line after line. In addition, in-between lines there are often certain pauses. This leads to specific requirements for a pedestrian detection system being able to process each pixel in real-time. In worst case, each clock cycle a pixel has to be processed. The FPGA pipeline designed and implemented in this work is capable of fulfilling this requirement. To achieve an efficient architecture, a fixed point data representation was selected.

5.1 HOG- / SVM-Pipeline

As mentioned before, cell-histogram information is valid for neighboring windows due to their high overlap. The same is true for the normalized blocks. Therefore, a window-based processing is highly inefficient. Much more efficient is a cell- and block-based approach, where overlapping data is processed for multiple windows. Similar approaches can be found in previous works, e.g. [10] and [11]. This approach generally requires storing less redundant data.

As described in section 2 the feature extraction processes data on different hierarchy levels: pixels, cells and blocks. Some processing steps jump back and forth between the pixel, cell- and block-hierarchy, as shown in Fig. 4 in red. First, pixel-magnitudes are weighted with a Gaussian filter on block-level. Then, magnitudes are accumulated into cell-histograms while individually interpolating on pixel- and block-level. After all magnitudes within a block are processed, a block-wise normalization is applied. Considering a clock-wise line-by-line

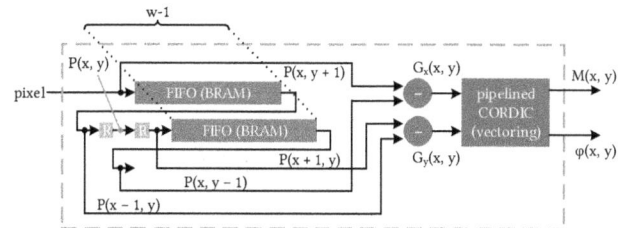

Fig. 5: Pipelined architecture to calculate gradients. For a better overview, no pipeline registers and logic for image border handling are shown.

pixel input, processing becomes much less complex and fewer information has to be stored, when following a strict bottom-up hierarchy processing. However, this would require omitting or simplifying some of the processing steps. Namely the Gaussian filter and the block-wise interpolation interfere with a strict bottom-up hierarchy.

The authors of the algorithm evaluated in [1], that the skipping of the Gaussian filter has only a minor influence of a 1%-increased miss rate at the reference point of 10^{-4} false positives per window (FPPW) in pedestrian detection. Furthermore, the authors did not evaluate the disadvantage of skipping the block-wise inter-cell interpolation. Hence, we analyzed the algorithm by using a software reference to evaluate whether it is reasonable to leave it out. For that purpose, we compared the detection rates with trilinear interpolation and with solely linear bin-interpolation in Matlab by means of the INRIA data set [1]. Here we found another 1.5%-increase of the detection miss rate at 10^{-4} FPPW. A summarized increase of ~3% miss rate is reasonable for a much more efficient architecture. Hence, we omit the Gaussian filter and only use linear bin-interpolation to be able to maintain strict bottom-up processing, as highlighted in green in Fig. 4. Furthermore, this approach leads to identical cell-histograms in overlapped block-areas since all block-specific weighting of magnitudes is skipped. Hence, fewer histograms have to be computed and stored in memory.

The following section describes the design of our bottom-up FPGA architecture for feature extraction and SVM-classification, based on the clock-wise line-by-line pixel input.

5.1.1 Gradient Calculation
As the first step of gradient calculation in (1) and (2) implies, two prior lines of pixels are required to be stored. This can be achieved with a BRAM-based line-buffer. Fig. 5 shows the buffer concept to automatically access the required pixels. The transfer from Cartesian to polar coordinates with (3) and (4) can be achieved with a pipelined CORDIC-module. In vectoring mode, the CORDIC algorithm is capable of calculating both (3) and (4) in a single iteration run.

5.1.2 Cell-Histograms
Without the Gaussian filter, the next processing step is the creation of cell-histograms. In order to process the cell-histograms further, all histograms of a block are required at the same time. Due to the order in which gradients are available for histogram processing and the strict bottom-up approach, cells-per-block-height times cells-per-image-width ($p \cdot w / k$) are required to be

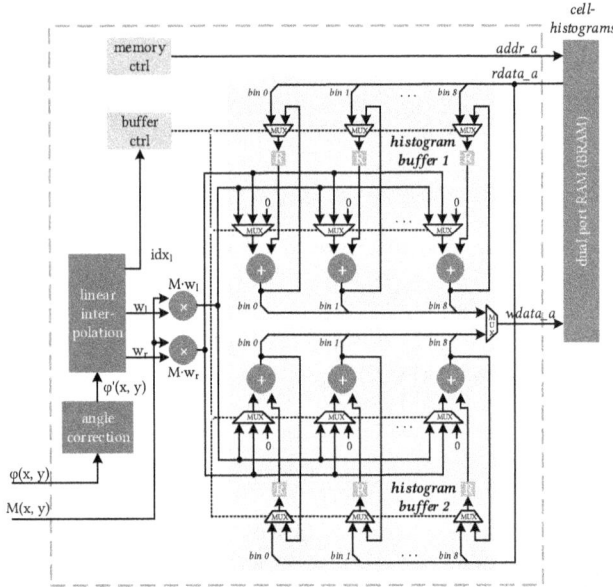

Fig. 6: Block diagram of the histogram creation including linear bin-interpolation. For a better overview, no pipeline registers are shown.

stored in memory until block normalization is possible. Since new gradients have to be processed in each clock cycle, the histograms in memory have to be continuously updated, while finished sets of histograms have to be read from memory and normalized. On an FPGA an efficient BRAM should be used for storage, to prevent the utilization of more expensive registers.

However, BRAMs are somewhat limited in simultaneous access. On most FPGAs BRAMs are available with at most two access ports, each being capable of reading and writing. Since one dedicated port is required for the reading of histograms for normalization, only one port is available for updating the histograms. The bins of the cell-histograms are stored concatenated at a single address of a BRAM, leading to a most efficient memory organization.

Fig. 6 shows the architecture of the histogram creation including the linear interpolation. First, an angle correction is applied to ensure that the value is between 0 to π. If not, the angle is mirrored into the first quadrant. After that, the index of the left bin (*idxl*) is determined through threshold comparison and the weights for the right (*wr*) and left (*wl*) bins are calculated.

The magnitude is multiplied with both weights and added to the buffered histogram. The module uses two histogram-buffer for accumulation to be able to process a new pixel each cycle, since only a single port of the BRAM is available. Due to pixel order, each eight pixels are accumulated alternating into the buffers. While one histogram buffer is used, the other buffer is written back to BRAM and the next histogram is loaded.

5.1.3 Block-Normalization
Subsequent to the creation of cell-histograms follows the block-wise normalization. As mentioned before, the authors evaluated the influence of the different norms on the detection rate. In [1] L1-Sqrt, L2-Norm and L2-Hys produce approximately the same

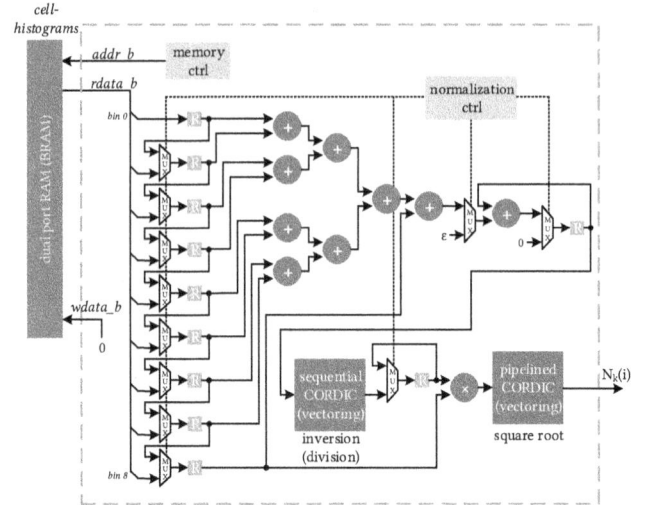

Fig. 7: L1-Sqrt Block normalization. For a better overview, no pipeline registers are shown.

detection results. The L1-Norm causes a 5% higher miss rate at reference point, skipping the normalization entirely leads to a 27% higher miss rate. Because the computational effort for the L1-Sqrt given in (8) is the lowest of the three equally best norms, we chose it for our architecture. The required computation of the division and square root can be done iteratively with additional CORDIC-modules.

All previous processing steps are fully pipelined, because in worst case incoming pixels are transferred in each clock cycle. In contrast, the block normalization does not have to be conducted in every cycle, due to the order of incoming pixels and the necessity for all cells of a block being available. Due to the overlap of blocks, only one new cell-histogram, processed from *l·k* pixels, is required between two blocks being ready. Hence, independent of the pixel order, on average *l·k=64* clock cycles are available for one block normalization. This leaves enough time to sequentially read and accumulate each four cell-histograms of a block, conduct the calculation of the division resource-efficient with a not-pipelined CORDIC, read the four cell-histograms again for multiplying, and finally calculating the square root. Fig. 7 illustrates the details of the architecture.

5.1.4 SVM Classification
To the block-normalization follows the classification of the concatenated blocks of a window. From (9) it is evident that the vector multiplication can be done partially, as described in (12) and (13).

$$d(\overrightarrow{W}) = \sum_{k=1}^{K} \overrightarrow{v_k} \cdot \overrightarrow{N_k} \qquad (12)$$

$$f(\overrightarrow{W}) = \text{sgn}(d(\overrightarrow{W}) + o) \qquad (13)$$

Hence, it is not necessary to store the normalized blocks until all are available for classification. Instead, a partial classification value can be stored in BRAM, and accumulated with each partial block vector multiplication. This results in a significantly smaller memory. To keep control more simple, the partial classifications of all windows in a frame are stored. Furthermore, each block can belong to 105 different windows with the given overlap of a single

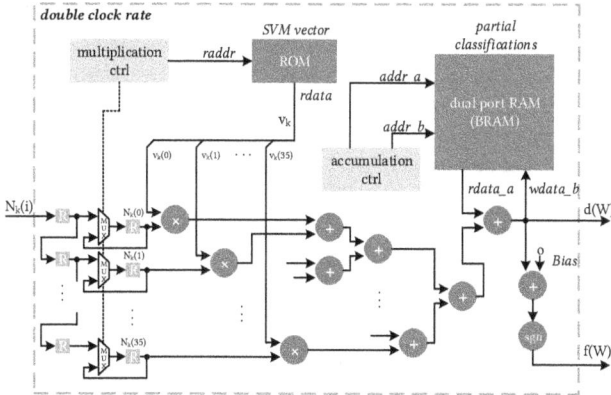

Fig. 8: Block diagram of the architecture for SVM classification. For a better overview, pipeline registers and dual-clock FIFOs at in-/output are not shown.

cell in both directions. Thus, each block of four cells, nine bins each, have to be multiplied and accumulated with 105 different v_k. In total a large amount of 3,780 multiply-accumulate operations (MAC) are required to process a single normalized block. Due to the same reasons described in conjunction with the normalization, on average 64 clock cycles are available for the operations. To achieve enough computational power the proposed architecture (see Fig. 8) conducts one partial block classification of 36 MAC-operations each clock cycle with a doubled clock rate. Synchronization is accomplished with minimum sized dual-clock FIFOs at in- and output. Incoming block-normalized bins are collected in a shift register. The 36-dimensional vector N_k is then consecutively vector-multiplied with 105 different partial SVM vectors v_k. Each vector product is accumulated to its corresponding partial window classification in the BRAM. The required partial SVM-vectors v_k are stored as constants in a ROM. After all blocks of a window are processed, the bias o is added to receive the window class. Each class $f(W)$ and vector multiplication result $d(W)$ are put out for merging.

5.2 Multi-Scale Merging

The merging procedure proposed by Dalal in [5] is not well suited for hardware implementation, due to the high computational requirements, the irregular structure and the high runtime. In literature, a less complex algorithm can be found. In [15] detection results are at first sorted by confidence score. Then beginning with the highest score, each overlapping window is removed. The runtime complexity of this algorithm is small. But cluster sizes are not considered, thus the merging results are not as good as with the original method from [5]. Based on [5] and [15], we propose a new algorithm that is fast and considers cluster sizes, as described in Alg. 1. The method performs a plausibility check, considering the following aspects:

- A high confidence score implies high likelihood of a true positive detection.

- Highly overlapping detections are most likely multiple detections of the same object.

```
Input[N]: array containing all positive classifications of all
scales

function Merge_Detections
  detections = Sort(Input) // sort descending by confidence score

  for i=0 to N-3 loop
    if detections[i].flag = false then
      count = 0
      for j=i+1 to N-1 loop
        if area of windows i and j overlap at least 50% then
          detections[j].flag = true // mark entry as handled
          count = count + 1
        end if
      end for

      if count >= 2 then
        detections[i].valid = true // mark entry as valid
      end if
    end if
  end for

  return all detections that are valid
end function
```

Alg. 1: Proposed merging algorithm for fusion of overlapping pedestrian detections.

- Objects always cause multiple overlapping detections, single non-overlapping detections are most likely false.

Initially, positive detection results are sorted by confidence score. For each detection, lower scoring detections are searched for overlaps of 50% or more. If at least two overlapping detections are found, the current entry is a true positive detection. Overlapped detections are removed from the list.

The new method is very suitable for hardware implementation, containing only a few loop runs. Calculating the overlap requires only simple arithmetic operations. For highest efficiency, instead of calculating the arithmetically complex confidence score with (10), we use (12) that is already computed for classification and is proportional to $P(W)$, and thus also suitable for ranking detections regarding the probability of a true positive detection. The architecture, mapping the proposed algorithm, is shown in Fig. 9. For initial sorting after collecting the positive detection results in a BRAM, we use the well-known heap-sort algorithm. The area overlap is calculated from the window position and size. x and y describe the window top-left coordinate. Window sizes are

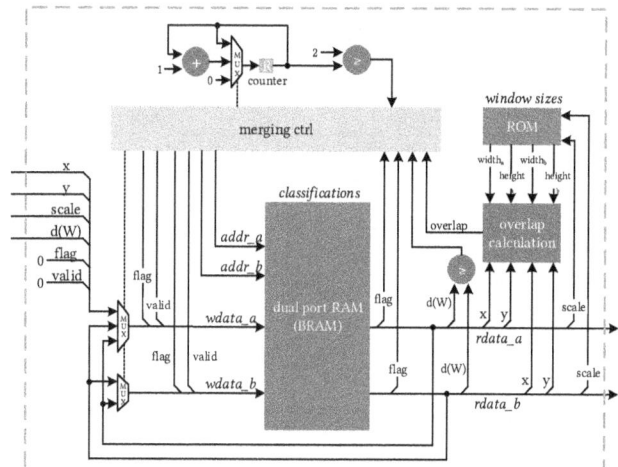

Fig. 9: Block diagram of the merging unit. For a better overview, pipeline registers are not shown.

Tab. 2: Synthesis results of HOG-feature extraction and SVM classification for different image resolutions.

Altera Cyclone IV EP4CE115	800×600 70+140 MHz, 145 FPS				1920×1080 70+140 MHz, 33 FPS			
	LUTs	Reg.	DSPs	BRAM [kBit]	LUTs	Reg.	DSPs	BRAM [kBit]
HOG feature ex.	3,676	1,479	11	59	3,686	1,492	11	143
Pixel-line buffer	0	0	0	19	0	0	0	46
Gradients	239	87	0	0	250	93	0	0
Histograms	2,005	679	5	0	1,998	683	5	0
Cell-line buffer	0	0	0	40	0	0	0	97
Block norm.	1,432	713	6	0	1,438	716	6	0
SVM class.	1,167	1,214	36	169	1,251	1,259	36	706
Block class.	1,167	1,214	36	0	1,251	1,259	36	0
SVM-vector	0	0	0	34	0	0	0	34
Part. class. buffer	0	0	0	135	0	0	0	672
Total (% of available)	4,843 (4%)	2,693 (2%)	47 (9%)	228 (5%)	4,937 (4%)	2,751 (2%)	47 (9%)	849 (21%)

constant, and read from a ROM. Thus, only a scale-index has to be stored in memory.

5.3 Evaluation of HOG- / SVM-Pipeline

In this section, we evaluate our architecture towards other implementations. As mentioned, a fair comparison is somewhat difficult since a wide variety of algorithm simplifications are used, and multi-scale processing and merging is often not considered. Therefore, we only compare the feature extraction and window classification of a single scale instance to evaluate the efficiency. The merging unit is examined in the next section, in which a multi-scale demonstration system is presented.

The proposed architecture is able to continuously process one pixel each clock cycle. Multiple frames can be processed uninterrupted. Thus, the throughput of our implementation depends only on the clock rate. For a low-end Altera Cyclone IV FPGA we were able to synthesize the architecture with 70 MHz, respectively 140 MHz for the SVM module. The architecture is configurable regarding image resolution. The bit widths of data paths were carefully selected, to achieve a minimized impact on

detection results. Still, DSPs are a limited resource on FPGAs. Since the SVM architecture requires a large multiplier network, we optimized the bit widths to fit available DSP sizes to prevent cascading. Synthesis results for two exemplary resolutions are shown in Tab. 2. Buffer sizes increase with image size. Pixel-line and cell-line buffer only increase with image width. The buffer for partial classifications increase with both image dimensions. All other resources are almost constant for different input image sizes. The achievable clock rate is also independent of resolution, since only very few logic, namely counter comparisons, becomes more complex with larger images, and the critical path lies within the SVM vector multiplication.

To further evaluate the proposed architecture, Tab. 3 shows a comparison to other exemplary work. In general, implementations are very difficult to compare. First, target FPGAs or SoCs differ considerably regarding available resources, LUT- and DSP-sizes, performance, and costs. In some SoC solutions, even external DDR-memory is used. Second, almost every work uses different algorithm simplifications, which sometimes significantly influence the detection performance. Furthermore, presented detection rates often relate to different operating points of FPPW. Typically, classification training and parametrization allows a tradeoff between both rates. This tradeoff also depends on the data set used for training and testing.

To nearly enable architecture comparison to different FPGA classes despite algorithm differences, we synthesized the proposed architecture for a low-performance FPGA (Cyclone IV) and a more modern high-performance FPGA (Stratix V). Main differences are sizes of LUTs (4 and 6 inputs), DSPs (9×9 and 27×27 inputs), and the general performance. As is evident in Tab. 3, our architecture significantly benefits from larger LUTs, DSPs and higher performance. In general, most architectures in Tab. 3 use high-performance FPGAs, and should be compared to our synthesis results for Stratix V. [10] also uses a low-performance Cyclone IV.

Tab. 3: Comparison of resource costs, performance, LUT efficiency and detection rates between recent publications and this work. All results refer to the feature extraction and classification of a single scale stage. The table shows synthesis results of the proposed architecture for low-cost FPGA (Cyclone IV) and a high-performance FPGA (Stratix V) for better comparison with the FPGAs in other works.

Publication	Year	FPGA	LUTs	Reg.	DSPs	BRAM [kBit]	Clock rate [MHz]	Resolution	Data rate [FPS]	LUT eff. η	Detection rate / FPPW	Comment
[8]	2009	Altera Stratix II EP2S180	3,794 [LUT6]	6,699	12 [18×18]	?	127.49	640×480	3	1.27	- / -	no Gaussian filter, interpolation + classification
[9]	2011	Xilinx Virtex-5 XC5VLX50	17,383 [LUT6]	2,181	36 [25×18]	?	44.85	640×480	112	29.42	96% / 0.2 (2×10⁻¹)	no Gaussian filter + interpolation, AdaBoost
[10]	2012	Altera Cyclone IV EP4CE115	34,403 [LUT4]	23,247	68 [18×18]	340	40	800×600	72	25.11	87% / 0.0001 (10⁻⁴)	no Gaussian filter
[11]	2013	Xilinx Virtex-5 XC5VFX200T	5,188 [LUT6]	5,178	49 [25×18]	1,188	135 + 270	1920×1080	64	63.16	84% / 0.001 (10⁻³)	no interpolation
[12]	2015	Xilinx Spartan-6 XC6SLX150T	9,955 [LUT6]	13,350	66 [18×18]	208	100	800×600	47	15.11	? / ?	
[13]	2015	Xilinx Zynq XC7Z020	21,297 [LUT6]	5,942	4 [25×18]	-	82.2	1920×1080	40	31.59	90% / 0.04 (4×10⁻²)	no Gausian filter + interp., AdaBoost, external DDR
[14]	2015	Xilinx Virxtex-6 XC6VLX760	98,642 [LUT6]	8,694	63 [25×18]	4,579	150	640×480	250 (est.)	3.45	90% / 0.0001 (10⁻⁴)	
this work	2017	Altera Cyclone IV EP4CE115	4,937 [LUT4]	2,751	47 [9×9]	849	70 + 140	1920×1080	33	101.28	87% / 0.0001 (10⁻⁴)	no Gaussian filter, linear bin-interpolation
this work	2017	Altera Stratix V 55GXMA4	3,529 [LUT6]	2,657	26 [27×27]	815	142 + 284	1920×1080	68	94.46	87% / 0.0001 (10⁻⁴)	no Gaussian filter, linear bin-interpolation

For a quantitative comparison, we compute a LUT efficiency η by normalizing the data rate in pixels per second to the number of required LUTs, weighted with LUT size factor α, and the clock rate in MHz, as shown in (14).

$$\eta = \frac{\text{Pixels/s}}{(\alpha \cdot \#\text{LUTs}) \cdot f_{\text{clk}}} \qquad (14)$$

In order to enable an approximate comparison between different LUT sizes, we used a correction factor of 1.0 for 4-input, and a value of 1.5 for 6-input LUTs. As is evident from Tab. 3, the LUT efficiency of our architecture is higher for the Cyclone IV FPGA with 4-input LUTs, than for the Stratix V FPGA with 6-input LUTs. This shows, that on the Stratix device a larger number of 6-input LUTs are not fully utilized, when compared to the smaller LUTs of the Cyclone device. From other works, only [11] achieves comparable LUT efficiency to our architecture. Both architectures are somewhat similar regarding a dual-clock approach to handle computational requirements. In [11] a much larger portion of the architecture runs with doubled clock rate, which might explain the almost double number of required registers. Still, the overall hardware costs of the proposed architecture are significantly smaller, with slightly better performance. The reason for that could be our strict bottom-up approach, in contrast to the mixed hierarchy architecture in [11] (see Fig. 4).

With regard to the detection rate, only performance results with the same FPPW operating point should be compared directly. Since [14] does not use any algorithm simplifications, the architecture achieves the same detection performance as the reference algorithm. Still, our approach only results in a minor decrease in detection performance, at a significantly higher hardware efficiency. [10] achieves similar detection results to our approach, at a four times lower LUT efficiency.

6 DEMONSTRATOR SETUP

Based on the proposed architecture, a real-time and multi-scale pedestrian detector demonstrator system on a COTS Altera DE2-115 development board was implemented. The system is shown in Fig. 10, and detects pedestrians in input image of 800×600 pixels in 9 different scales.

For image-recording a CCD-sensor with Bayer-array is used. Captured image and detection results are displayed via VGA. For

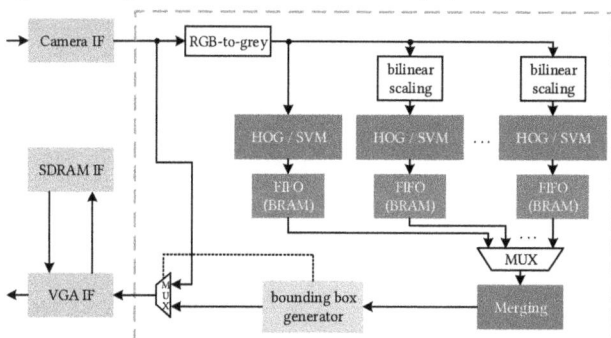

Fig. 10: Block diagram of final demonstrator setup. For communication with camera and VGA interface a framework for rapid prototyping is used [16].

Tab. 4: Synthesis results of the full pedestrian detector demonstration system for 9 scales from 800×600 to 170×128.

Altera Cyclone IV EP4CE115	800×600, 50+100 MHz, 9 scales in parallel			
	LUTs	Reg.	DSPs	BRAM [kBit]
Pedestrian Detector	47,175	25,158	491	1,222
HOG/SVM (9 instances)	41,906	23,138	423	1,137
Bilinear scaling (8 instances)	1,611	664	64	6
Merging	1,249	109	4	28
Infrastructure (Framework [16])	3,343	2,137	0	543
Camera Interface	889	552	0	432
VGA Interface	903	488	0	51
SDRAM Interface	1081	870	0	59
Total	50,518	27,295	491	1,765
(% of available)	(44%)	(24%)	(92%)	(45%)

that purpose, we use interfaces that are part of a rapid prototyping framework that runs at a clock rate of 50 MHz [16]. The camera interface handles data transfers, Bayer-to-RGB conversion and provides a serial pixel stream. The VGA interface utilizes external SDRAM for synchronized double buffering of output frames, and allows direct write access to individual pixel. The framework is able to capture and display SVGA images with 20 FPS. The framerate is limited by the relatively slow SDRAM on the development board.

An incoming frame is written to the VGA frame buffer. In parallel, the RGB-pixels are converted to luminance values, and then processed in 9 parallel scale stages from 800×600 to 170×128. For that, scaled images are created for 8 out of the 9 stages through bilinear scaling. The resulting images are processed with the proposed HOG-/SVM-architecture, detection results are collected and buffered in small FIFOs. The FIFOs are sequentially scanned for positive detections, which are transferred to the merging unit. The merging results are converted to bounding boxes and written to the frame buffer. Fig. 11 shows two photos of the physical setup.

Tab. 4 shows the synthesis results for the full setup. The merging unit is configured to merge a maximum of 576 positive detections. Still, the costs for merging are marginal compared to the rest of the system. Available DSP resources limit the number of scale stages. Nonetheless, 9 different scales at SVGA-resolution result in a scaling factor of approximately 1.1, leading to very good detection results of different pedestrian sizes.

7 SUMMARY

In this paper, we presented an efficient bottom-up FPGA implementation of multi-scale HOG-based pedestrian detection.

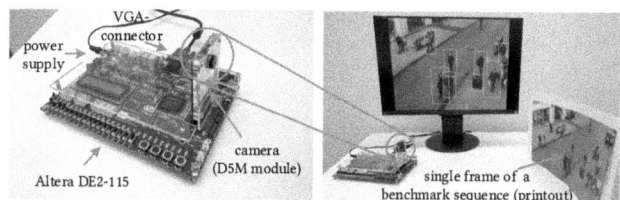

Fig. 11: Physical setup of the stand-alone demonstrator. The left image shows the COTS prototyping board DE2-115 with D5M camera module and VGA connector. To the right an exemplary detection of pedestrians in a frame-printout of a benchmark sequence is shown.

The proposed architecture includes HOG-feature extraction, SVM classification and merging of multi-scale detections. The HOG/SVM pipeline is able to process an incoming pixel stream in every clock cycle. Proposed algorithm simplifications only decrease the detection performance by approximately 3% at 10^{-4} FPPW. Due to the complexity of current merging approaches, we proposed a new algorithm, suitable for hardware implementation. In a comparison of our implementation to other publications, we were able to show its very high efficiency with a data rate of 68 HD-frames per second on a Stratix V FPGA. Furthermore, no comparable multi-scale merging is currently available as hardware implementation in literature.

Finally, due to the new architecture's very high efficiency, we were able to implement a live demonstrator system even on a low-cost DE2-115 FPGA development board. The system uses a framework for rapid prototyping and is capable of processing 20 SVGA frames per second from a camera with 9 image scales in parallel at a clock rate of 50 MHz. Solely the inclusion of the merging process in the architecture, makes the real-time and multi-scale implementation of this efficient stand-alone system possible.

REFERENCES

[1]   Dalal, N. and Triggs, B. "Histograms of oriented gradients for human detection" Computer Vision and Pattern Recognition, 2005. CVPR 2005. IEEE Computer Society Conference on. IEEE, 2005

[2]   Zhang, S. et al. "Towards Reaching Human Performance in Pedestrian Detection" *IEEE transactions on pattern analysis and machine intelligence.* IEEE, 2017

[3]   Angelova, A. et al. "Real-Time Pedestrian Detection with Deep Network Cascades" *Proceedings of the Britsh Mashine Vision Conference.* BMVC, 2015

[4]   Wu, B. et al. "SqueezeDet: Unified, Small, Low-Power Fully Convolutional Neural Networks for Real-Time Object Detection for Autonomous Driving" *Computer Vision and Pattern Recognition Workshops, IEEE Conference on.* IEEE, 2017

[5]   Dalal, N. "Finding People in Images and Videos". *PhD-Thesis.* Institut National Polytechnique de Grenoble / INRIA Grenoble, 2006

[6]   Schuldt, C., Laptev, I. and Caputo, B. "Recognizing human actions: A local SVM approach" In *Pattern Recognition, 2004. ICPR 2004. Proceedings of the 17th International Conference on.* IEEE, 2004

[7]   Platt, J. C. "Probabilistic Outputs for Support Vector Machines and Comparisons to Regularized Likelihood Methods" In *Advances in large Margin Classifiers.* MIT Press, 1999

[8]   Kadota, R. et al. "Hardware architecture for HOG feature extraction" Intelligent Information Hiding and Multimedia Signal Processing, 2009. IIH-MSP'09. Fifth International Conference on. IEEE, 2009

[9]   Negi, K. et al. "Deep pipelined one-chip FPGA implementation of a real-time image-based human detection algorithm" *Field-Programmable Technology (FPT), 2011 International Conference on.* IEEE, 2011

[10]   Mizuno, K. et al. "Architectural study of HOG feature extraction processor for real-time object detection" *Signal Processing Systems (SiPS), 2012 IEEE Workshop on.* IEEE, 2012

[11]   Hahnle, M. et al. "FPGA-based real-time pedestrian detection on high-resolution images" *Proceedings of the IEEE Conference on Computer Vision and Pattern Recognition Workshops.* 2013

[12]   Yuan, X. et al. "A two-stage hog feature extraction processor embedded with SVM for pedestrian detection" *Image Processing (ICIP), 2015 IEEE International Conference on.* IEEE, 2015

[13]   Rettkowski, J., Boutros, A., and Göhringer, D. "Real-time pedestrian detection on a xilinx zynq using the HOG algorithm" *ReConFigurable Computing and FPGAs, 2015 International Conference on.* IEEE, 2015

[14]   Ma, X. Najjar, W. A., and Roy-Chowdhury, A. K. "Evaluation and acceleration of high-throughput fixed-point object detection on FPGAs" *IEEE Transactions on Circuits and Systems for Video Technology 25.6.* IEEE, 2015

[15]   Felzenszwalb, P. F. et al. "Object detection with discriminatively trained part-based models" *IEEE transactions on pattern analysis and machine intelligence 32.9.* IEEE, 2010

[16]   Dürre, J. and Blume, H. "SF3: A scalable and flexible FPGA-framework for education and rapid prototyping" *2017 IEEE International Conference on Microelectronic Systems Education (MSE).* IEEE, 2017

Scalable Window Generation for the Intel Broadwell+Arria 10 and High-Bandwidth FPGA Systems

Greg Stitt, Abhay Gupta, Madison N. Emas, David Wilson, Austin Baylis

University of Florida, Department of Electrical and Computer Engineering

gstitt@ece.ufl.edu,abhayg271@gmail.com,madisel@ufl.edu,d.wilson@ufl.edu,abaylis@ufl.edu

ABSTRACT

Emerging FPGA systems are providing higher external memory bandwidth to compete with GPU performance. However, because FPGAs often achieve parallelism through deep pipelines, traditional FPGA design strategies do not necessarily scale well to large amounts of replicated pipelines that can take advantage of higher bandwidth. We show that sliding-window applications—an important subset of digital signal processing—demonstrate this scalability problem. We introduce a window generator architecture that enables replication to over 330 GB/s, which is an 8.7× improvement over previous work. We evaluate the window generator on the Intel Broadwell+Arria10 system for 2D convolution and show that for traditional convolution (one filter per image), our approach outperforms a 12-core Xeon Broadwell E5 by 81× and a high-end Nvidia P6000 GPU by an order of magnitude for most input sizes, while improving energy by 15.7×. For convolutional neural nets (CNNs), we show that although the GPU and Xeon typically outperform existing FPGA systems, projected performances of the window generator running on FPGAs with sufficient bandwidth can outperform high-end GPUs for many common CNN parameters.

CCS CONCEPTS

• **Hardware** → **Hardware accelerators**;

KEYWORDS

FPGA, convolution, neural networks

ACM Reference format:
Greg Stitt, Abhay Gupta, Madison N. Emas, David Wilson, Austin Baylis. 2018. Scalable Window Generation for the Intel Broadwell+Arria 10 and High-Bandwidth FPGA Systems. In *Proceedings of 2018 ACM/SIGDA International Symposium on Field-Programmable Gate Arrays, Monterey, CA, USA, February 25–27, 2018 (FPGA '18),* 10 pages.
https://doi.org/10.1145/3174243.3174262

1 INTRODUCTION

Digital signal processing applications commonly use field-programmable gate arrays (FPGAs) or graphics-processing units (GPUs), but GPUs are generally the more popular alternative for most high-performance

use cases. Although FPGAs often provide more performance per unit of memory bandwidth (e.g., [7]), GPUs tend to provide external memory bandwidth that is at least an order-of-magnitude higher than FPGA systems. For example, the Nvidia P100 provides 732 GB/s [19], whereas most FPGA boards provide on the order of tens of GB/s (e.g., [8, 15, 21]).

Traditionally, high-performance FPGA designs have dealt with limited memory bandwidth using deep pipelines (e.g., [6, 13, 27]). Pipeline replication and loop unrolling are also common FPGA optimizations, but with limited bandwidth such replication provides limited improvements. For FPGAs to compete with GPU performance, emerging and future FPGAs will need to significantly increase memory bandwidth [16].

Although higher-bandwidth FPGA systems enable increased replication, not all FPGA design patterns scale well to large amounts of pipeline replication. We show that sliding-window generation has limited replication scaling, which is a significant problem for FPGAs given the prevalence of sliding windows in convolutional neural nets (CNNs) and other image-processing applications [6, 26].

Previous approaches provide window generators that are either limited to one window per cycle [4, 9], lack scalability to numerous windows [23], or support a specific window and/or image size [20]. For data-center usage, an FPGA circuit must support a wide range of window and image sizes due to prohibitively long reconfiguration times. Although previous approaches can support different window and image sizes by padding the input, such padding is often an expensive overhead, which in our tests exceeded the FPGA execution times of the presented case studies.

In this paper, we introduce a window generator architecture that greatly improves scalability, enabling generation of numerous windows in parallel to support anticipated bandwidth increases, while addressing flexibility problems by supporting runtime-configurable window and image sizes with no padding overhead. Our results demonstrate pipeline replication to more than 330 GB/s of memory bandwidth, which to our knowledge is more than any existing FPGA system and an 8.7× improvement over previous work [23].

Although the window generator can be used with any sliding-window application, we evaluate 2D convolution running on an Intel Broadwell+Arria 10 (BDW+A10) [10]. For traditional convolution (one filter per image), our approach outperforms optimized implementations from DeepBench [22] and the Intel Math Kernel Library (MKL) [24] running on a 12-core Xeon Broadwell E5 and a high-end Nvidia P6000 GPU with 3,840 CUDA cores. Despite the FPGA having a theoretical peak performance that is comparable to the Xeon and significantly less than the P6000, our approach achieves an average speedup of 81× over the Xeon and 12.6× over the P6000. We obtain these improvements by exploiting different types of parallelism that provide near-peak FPGA performance in situations where existing Xeon and GPU implementations leave many resources underutilized. Energy improvements are even more significant, with improvements of 96× and 15.7× for the Xeon and GPU, respectively. Even for the ideal situation where a GPU can completely avoid or amortize PCIe transfers, our approach achieves an average speedup of 1.2× and energy improvement of 1.5×.

We also evaluate our approach using convolution parameters common to CNNs for theoretical bandwidth improvements. Although the P6000 outperforms existing FPGA systems for CNNs, we show that our approach running on a shared-memory Stratix 10 system with sufficient bandwidth is projected to outperform the P6000 for common CNN use cases.

2 RELATED WORK

The most closely related study is the window generator from [23], which had similar goals of generating multiple windows per cycle, while also supporting runtime-configurable window and image sizes. We show that the previous approach does not scale past 256 parallel windows on the BDW+A10, and has clock speeds that are more than 2× slower than the presented approach for 64 or more parallel windows. Overall, the presented approach is able to support memory bandwidth that is 8.7× higher than this previous work.

Although there are many previous window-generation studies [4, 9, 20, 23], none of those studies address scalability, high clock frequencies, and runtime-configurable inputs with no padding overhead. A recent approach [20] investigated minimizing register usage during loop coarsening with high-level synthesis. Our approach has an alternative goal of maximizing scalability, which sacrifices register usage for improved clock speeds and scalability up to 1024 replicated pipelines, whereas the previous study reports up to 64. Although a direct comparison is not feasible due to the previous approach only providing high-level synthesis estimates, that approach complements our work with new border-handling techniques.

Tradeoff analyses between FPGAs, GPUs, and microprocessors for sliding-window applications are a well-studied topic [1, 3, 6, 26], and have established Pareto-optimal implementations for different use cases. This paper complements those studies with a window generator that improves FPGA performance, especially for emerging high-bandwidth systems.

FPGA performance evaluations for CNNs have received significant attention recently. Zhang [27] evaluated an FFT-based FPGA implementation for CNNs on a shared-memory system. Our work is complementary, focusing on sliding windows needed by time-domain implementations. The two approaches could be combined to efficiently support CNNs over many use cases, with time-domain implementations for smaller windows and frequency-domain implementations for larger windows [2]. Nurvitadhi et al. [18] compared Arria 10 performance with a CPU, GPU, and ASIC for binarized neural networks. In more recent work, Nurvitadhi et al. [17] presented Stratix 10 performance and energy projections compared to a Titan X GPU for CNNs, which showed projections similar to our presented work. Our work is complementary by presenting a window generator capable of realizing such projections for high-bandwidth FPGA systems. In general, the focus of our paper is on efficient

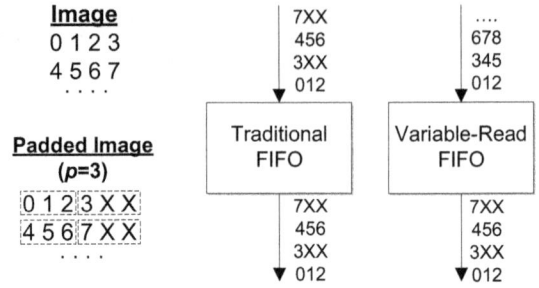

Figure 1: Unlike traditional FIFOs, the variable-read FIFO obviates padding for parallel windows (e.g., $p = 3$), which reduces pre-processing and PCIe overhead.

sliding-window generation, which we evaluate using different convolution use cases, whereas earlier studies focus primarily on an architectural tradeoff analysis for CNNs.

3 WINDOW GENERATOR

Sliding-window applications are a domain of digital signal processing that perform application-specific computation on "windows" (sub-images) of an image. Applications generally slide these windows across an image from left to right at the top of the image, then move down one row and repeat until all windows have been processed. Although there are a variety of different sliding behaviors, we focus on single strides where each window slides by one column, and fully immersed windows where the window does not slide past the image borders. Our approach can be easily adapted to other variations, albeit with potentially less reuse for larger strides.

In this section, we present an architecture for generating all necessary windows independently from the application-specific computation. For consistency, we adopt the same terminology as the previous approach in [23], where the inputs are an image i with i_r rows and i_c columns, and a window w with w_r rows and w_c columns. We define the top-left pixel of an image to be $i[0, 0]$. We use p to represent the number of pixels provided each cycle, the number of windows generated each cycle, and the amount of pipeline replication, which are all equivalent in our architecture.

The window generator consists of a variable-read FIFO, a window buffer, and a window coalescer. Initially, the user passes a stream of pixels (p each cycle) to the variable-read FIFO (Section 3.1), which provides a variable number of pixels from that stream to the window buffer to obviate input padding. The window buffer assembles the pixels into columns of window data that the coalescer combines into approximately p complete windows each cycle (Section 3.2).

3.1 Variable-Read FIFO

The variable-read FIFO (VRF) streams pixels into the window buffer in a way that enables the window buffer to generate p windows in parallel, while eliminating the need for input padding. Although padding the image to have columns that are a multiple of p can eliminate the need for the VRF, such padding has a software pre-processing and PCIe overhead. In our experiments, software padding times often exceeded the FPGA execution time, which significantly reduced or eliminated speedup. Although such padding is conceptually easy to implement on the FPGA, creating a circuit that adds

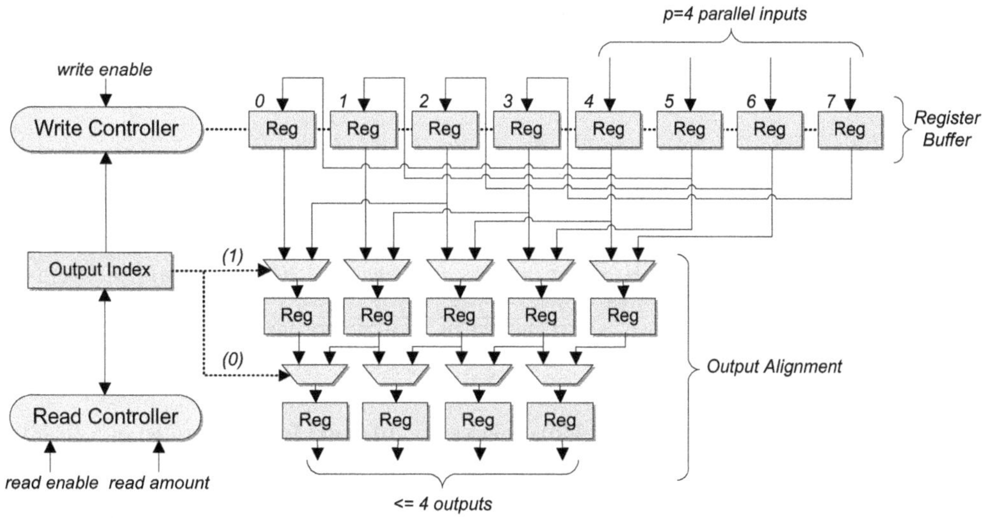

Figure 2: Variable-read FIFO architecture for four parallel inputs and outputs ($p = 4$).

variable padding based on runtime parameters with no performance overhead is not trivial. The VRF provides this functionality.

Figure 1 compares the difference between input streams when using a traditional FIFO with padding and the VRF. For an image with four columns and a system that can provide three pixels ($p = 3$) each cycle, the first read from the FIFO provides elements 0-2. To complete the processing of the first row, the application only needs element 3. However, if the FIFO provides three elements instead of one, the application will either be corrupted with invalid data for the first row, or must buffer the extra data somewhere internally. Since the FIFO already provides buffering, it makes more sense to read a variable amount of data from the FIFO instead of adding additional buffering elsewhere, which would also need to support variable amounts. With the VRF, the application reads three pixels to get pixels 0-2, then one pixel (3) to complete the first row, then pixels 4-6, then pixel 7, etc. This approach eliminates up to $p - 1$ padded pixels from the right edge of each image row, which is critically important for large p values where the padding overhead could be prohibitive.

Figure 2 illustrates the VRF architecture. The structure is conceptually similar to the FIFO in [23], but has been modified to improve timing scalability for larger p. Both approaches write p pixels into a fixed set of registers within a buffer of $2p$ registers. In this buffer, the output index varies depending on previous reads. Initially, the output index starts at 0 and then increases after each read by the number of elements read from the FIFO. When the output index exceeds $p - 1$, the write controller shifts the register buffer left by p positions to ensure the index is always between 0 and $p - 1$.

Because the output index changes, the read controller must align the outputs with the appropriate p registers. The previous approach implemented output alignment using p separate p:1 muxes to select the appropriate register for each output, which is a significant timing-closure bottleneck. Although those muxes could potentially be pipelined, muxes in general are an expensive FPGA resource. To avoid this problem, and to ensure better scalability, our new

approach ensures that the critical-path propagation delay (ignoring routing delays) is independent of p.

In our approach, the VRF aligns outputs using a pipelined barrel shifter that shifts by the amount in the output index. Although this approach creates a several-cycle output delay, the user can still read every cycle. With this strategy, there is never more than a 2:1 mux in between registers for any value of p, which potentially enables the architecture to scale indefinitely up to any resource constraint without experiencing a timing-closure bottleneck.

In addition to the logic in the figure, the VRF outputs a count of the words in the FIFO, in addition to bits that specify the validity of each output. For example, when the user requests one output, the VRF will provide p outputs, but will mark $p - 1$ outputs as invalid. Although the propagation delay of the count logic increases with larger p, that increase is logarithmic. For any realistic value of p, the count logic is is not a timing-closure bottleneck. Even for $p = 1024$, the count logic only requires a 10-bit adder and subtractor.

3.2 Window Buffer and Coalescer

The window buffer is responsible for buffering the input stream of pixels into separate rows, and then passing p columns from each row into the window coalescer each cycle.

Figure 3(a) provides an overview of the window-buffer architecture. The basic structure is a chained sequence of w_r FIFOs, which each buffer an entire row of the image. The window buffer reads p pixels at a time from the VRF into the bottom row FIFO, where each word consists of p pixels. When there are fewer than p pixels left in a row of the image, the window buffer requests the remaining number of pixels from the VRF (e.g, pixel 3 in Figure 1). In this case, the window buffer marks any extra pixels as invalid to avoid including them in windows.

A previous approach [23] similarly used w_r FIFOs, but after outputting an entire row of windows, that approach would erase the top FIFO. The previous approach would then reuse the top FIFO for the next row of the image. As a result, the first row of each window gradually moves into different FIFOs. Similar to the VRF,

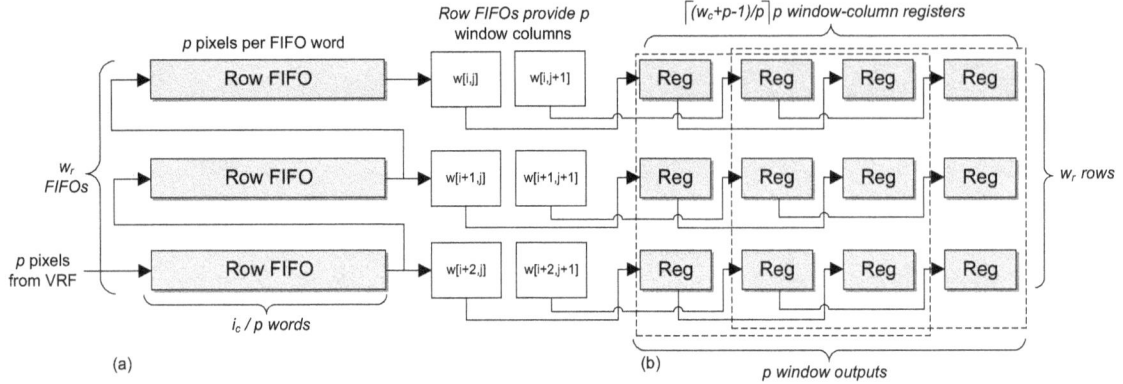

Figure 3: Overview of the (a) window buffer and (b) coalescer architecture for two parallel ($p = 2$) 3×3 windows.

the previous approach maintained an index that specified which FIFO stored the top window row. To align the outputs, that approach used w_r separate w_r:1 muxes, which created another significant scalability bottleneck that has similar problems to the previous VRF.

Our approach uses an alternative strategy that completely eliminates the need for alignment by always using the top FIFO as the top row of a window, the bottom FIFO as the bottom row, etc. To enable this functionality, the window buffer initially writes all incoming pixels into the bottom FIFO, storing p pixels per word. When the bottom FIFO contains $\lceil i_c/p \rceil$ words (an entire image row), every new write into the bottom FIFO also triggers a read from that FIFO. For each FIFO read, the buffer writes the read data into the next higher FIFO, which enables the pixels to gradually shift to the top FIFO. This process repeats until all w_r FIFOs contain $\lceil i_c/p \rceil$ words.

At this point, a controller (not shown) starts reading from all FIFOs, which passes p columns each cycle into the coalescer (Figure 3(b)). The coalescer assembles p windows by dividing each window into w_c register columns that get shifted by p positions for every new set of columns from the window buffer. After $\lceil (w_c + p - 1)/p \rceil$ shifts, the coalescer contains p complete windows, where the index of the first window starts at the first column, the second window at the second column, etc. Overall, the coalescer consists of $\lceil (w_c + p - 1)/p \rceil \cdot p$ columns, where each column has w_r registers.

The controller continues streaming columns from the buffer for $\lceil i_c/p \rceil$ cycles, and then returns to buffering incoming data. The controller continues to buffer new pixels while outputting columns. If pixels arrive every cycle, the controller will immediately begin outputting columns again after completing the current row. If the window buffer outputs all the current columns before another i_c pixels arrive, the controller delays the next set of columns until all the FIFOs have sufficient pixels.

In addition to removing all muxes, one critically important timing optimization was the removal of register enable logic. The previous approach stalled the coalescer by clearing an enable until all FIFOs were not empty. Because that enable had to control every register in the coalescer, the previous approach had a timing-closure bottleneck resulting from a prohibitive enable fanout of $\lceil (w_c + p - 1)/p \rceil \cdot p w_r d$, where d is the bit width of each pixel.

We address this problem by removing all enable logic from the coalescer. To remove the logic, the controller delays reads from the window buffer until the row FIFOs contain all required pixels for the next row of windows. When the controller starts reading, the p column inputs to the coalescer will always be valid until the end of the row, which eliminates the need for an enable. Although this approach delays the first columns, the throughput is identical. Most importantly, this optimization eliminates the fanout, which results in propagation delays that are independent of p.

To support any window size, the controller determines how far to slide the maximum-sized window across the image. For example, if the FPGA provides a 10×10 window, but the user requests a 3×3 window, the controller would slide the 10×10 window seven pixels past the right edge and bottom edge of the image. The controller pads all unused window elements with 0, which is done automatically on reset. With this strategy, although many window elements are unused, generation times for 3×3 windows are similar regardless of the maximum window size, with the only overhead being the initial time to fill up the extra row FIFOs. To support arbitrary image sizes, the architecture sets the FIFO depth to the maximum image width divided by p, and then simply starts reading from the FIFOs when the requested image columns i_c are buffered in each FIFO ($\lceil i_c/p \rceil$ words).

4 2D CONVOLUTION ON BDW+A10

In this section, we describe our custom RTL implementation of 2D convolution on the Broadwell+Arria 10 (BDW+A10). Because convolution implementations have been widely studied [6], we focus on BDW+A10 specific issues due to space constraints.

The BDW+A10 shares the Xeon's main memory with the FPGA, which the FPGA accesses over both PCIe and/or QPI. To access memory, the BDW+A10 provides a cache coherent interface (CCI) that provides basic memory-access mechanisms. In VHDL, we extended the provided mechanisms with our own DMA memory interface that provided memory access reordering, virtual-to-physical address translation, in addition to width conversion to enable the application to request any data width from memory. We also went to great effort with timing optimizations to ensure the DMA interface can run at 400 MHz to maximize memory bandwidth. Intel provides a Memory Properties Factory core that enables much of this functionality, which we have not yet evaluated, but could potentially improve reported memory bandwidth.

In our BDW+A10 implementation, software initially loads the bitfile and initializes page tables inside the FPGA using memory-mapped I/O (MMIO) to enable sharing of memory between software and the FPGA. For data-center usage, such functionality would normally be done while booting. Next, the software transfers the convolution kernel into FPGA registers, specifies the convolution parameters, and starts the FPGA execution, all using MMIO. The FPGA circuit then starts a DMA access to read the image from memory, which the circuit streams into the window generator from Section 3. After receiving enough pixels, the window generator generates a stream of parallel windows that are pushed into replicated 2D convolution pipelines. The FPGA also initiates another DMA access to simultaneously write results to memory.

Each 2D convolution pipeline uses a row of $w_r w_c$ multipliers, one for each element of the convolution kernel, followed by a balanced adder tree consisting of $w_r w_c - 1$ adders. The pipelines include registers between each operation, which eventually provides an output from each pipeline every cycle.

For the floating-point implementation, we use a different strategy to maximize DSP utilization and clock frequency. Arria 10 DSPs can perform both a single-precision multiply and addition. The DSPs also contain chained routing that connects each DSP to an adjacent DSP. Our implementation utilizes this chaining, which has the side-effect of converting the balanced adder tree with a depth that grows logarithmically with the kernel size into a sequence of adds whose length grows linearly. This chaining improves clock frequencies at the cost of each adder input requiring a longer alignment delay than in the balanced tree. To handle these delays, we use registers when the delay is below a certain threshold and switch to block RAM for larger delays. Such an approach will not scale to large kernel sizes due to limited block RAM, in which case a combination of the balanced approach and chaining approach can be used.

To improve clock frequency, we performed a number of timing optimizations. Chaining the DSPs made a significant impact on timing by avoiding routing delays from numerous 32-bit signals. We also performed an optimization similar to Section 3.2 where we eliminated stall functionality for each individual pipeline stage to eliminate the enable signal's fanout. We replaced the fine-grained stall strategy with a strategy that uses a large FIFO to absorb the entire state of the pipeline when writes to output memory have to stall. When this FIFO is almost full, it triggers the window generator to stop producing windows. An additional advantage of this strategy is the enabling of Stratix 10 HyperFlex interconnect registers, which should further improve clock frequencies in future work.

One critical timing optimization for the 2D convolution pipelines was register duplication. Because the window coalescer (Section 3.2) shares registers for window elements that overlap in consecutive windows, many of these registers will fanout to numerous pipelines, which can significantly restrict maximum clock frequency for large values of p. Although we could not find an exact description of register-duplication restrictions in Quartus, we removed the fine-grained stalling of each individual register, removed combinational logic before the first pipeline register, and added registers before the multipliers, at which point Quartus started replicating the registers with high fanout. We plan to manually evaluate area/clock tradeoffs for manually specified replication thresholds, but lengthy compilation times prohibited such analysis for this study.

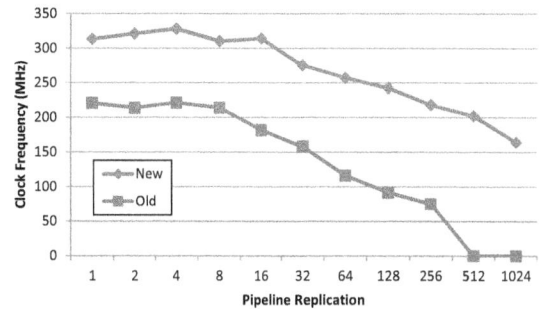

Figure 4: A comparison of Arria 10 clock frequencies for the presented (*new*) window generator and previous work (*old*) for different amounts of pipeline replication.

5 EXPERIMENTS

In this section, we first evaluate the scalability of the window generator (Section 5.1). We then provide performance and energy comparisons between the BDW+A10, Broadwell Xeon E5, and Nvidia P6000 for traditional 2D convolution (Section 5.2), in addition to performance projections for convolutional neural nets (Section 5.3).

5.1 Scalability

Figure 4 compares the maximum clock frequency of the presented approach with previous work [23], which we evaluated using the open-source release at https://github.com/ARC-Lab-UF/window_gen. We use Quartus 16 Prime Pro to determine the maximum clock frequency after synthesis, placement, and routing on an Arria 10 GX1150 FPGA. Results use 3×3 windows and image sizes of 2048×2048. Frequencies for other window and image sizes were similar.

The figure demonstrates the potential scalability problem in window generation with the previous approach decreasing to under 100 MHz for 128 pipelines, whereas the new approach runs at 242 MHz. More importantly, the old approach does not scale past 256 pipelines, whereas we were able to evaluate the new approach for 1024 pipelines. Although the frequency of both approaches decreases with more replication, the new approach decreases at a slower rate, and provides frequencies over 200 MHz even for 512 pipelines. Overall, the maximum bandwidth that the new approach can leverage is 336 GB/s, compared to 38.4 GB/s in the old approach—an improvement of 8.7×. These results suggest that the presented approach will enable FPGAs to fully utilize increased memory bandwidth for the foreseeable future.

Table 1(a) compares lookup table (LUT), flip flop (FF), and block RAM (RAM) utilizations between the presented approach and previous work for different window sizes and replication amounts. For almost all examples, the new approach used fewer LUTs, with an average reduction of 40% from eliminating muxes as described in Section 3.2. Register usage (FFs) increased by an average of 20%, which is likely an attractive trade off considering the 8.7× bandwidth improvement. RAM usage increased on average by 40%. Note that the previous approach does not synthesize past 256 pipelines.

Table 1(b) shows resource counts for the new approach. The Arria 10 GX1150 has over one million LUTs and FFs, which likely

Table 1: (a) Resource utilization relative to previous work for window sizes from 3×3 to 9×9. (b) Absolute resource numbers for the presented approach.

Replication	3x3			5x5			7x7			9x9		
	LUTs	FFs	RAM	LUTs	FFs	RAM	LUTs	FFs	RAM	LUTs	FFs	RAM
1	0.7x	1.1x	1.3x	0.6x	1.0x	1.2x	0.6x	1.0x	1.1x	0.6x	1.0x	1.1x
2	0.7x	1.1x	1.7x	0.6x	1.0x	1.4x	0.6x	1.0x	1.3x	0.6x	1.0x	1.2x
4	0.7x	1.2x	1.7x	0.6x	1.1x	1.4x	0.6x	1.1x	1.3x	0.5x	1.0x	1.2x
8	0.9x	1.3x	1.7x	0.7x	1.2x	1.4x	0.7x	1.1x	1.3x	0.5x	1.1x	1.2x
16	0.9x	1.4x	1.7x	0.7x	1.3x	1.4x	0.7x	1.2x	1.3x	0.6x	1.1x	1.2x
32	0.9x	1.5x	1.7x	0.7x	1.3x	1.4x	0.6x	1.2x	1.3x	0.5x	1.2x	1.2x
64	1.0x	1.6x	1.7x	0.4x	1.4x	1.4x	0.4x	1.3x	1.3x	0.5x	1.2x	1.2x
128	0.3x	1.6x	1.7x	0.3x	1.4x	1.4x	0.4x	1.3x	1.3x	0.5x	1.2x	1.2x
256	0.2x	1.7x	1.7x	0.3x	1.5x	1.4x	0.4x	1.3x	1.3x	0.5x	1.3x	1.2x
512	n/a	n/a	n/a	n/a	n/a	n/a	n/a	n/a	n/a	n/a	n/a	n/a
Avg	0.7x	1.4x	1.6x	0.6x	1.2x	1.4x	0.6x	1.2x	1.3x	0.5x	1.1x	1.2x

(a)

Replication	3x3			5x5			7x7			9x9		
	LUTs	FFs	RAM	LUTs	FFs	RAM	LUTs	FFs	RAM	LUTs	FFs	RAM
1	425	631	4	602	917	6	805	1278	8	1040	1695	10
2	461	704	5	638	1032	7	859	1428	9	1107	1891	11
4	560	990	5	763	1366	7	996	1952	9	1264	2377	11
8	823	1632	10	1158	2252	14	1528	2856	18	1911	3484	22
16	1379	3017	20	1925	4121	28	2489	5231	36	3059	6354	44
32	2444	5919	35	3216	8070	49	3997	10176	63	4742	12284	77
64	4826	11967	65	6265	16119	91	7711	20290	117	9218	24465	143
128	10001	24661	130	12747	32879	182	15494	41194	234	18306	49486	286
256	20704	51117	260	26262	67636	364	31603	83955	468	37062	100310	572
512	43360	106385	515	54097	1E+05	721	64928	2E+05	927	75862	204114	1133

(b)

makes these amounts acceptable for most use cases. All results use a maximum image size of 2048×2048, which makes the RAM usage pessimistic for common use cases with smaller images.

5.2 2D Convolution on BDW+A10

This section evaluates the window generator using 2D convolution on the Intel BDW+A10, while comparing performance and energy to a GPU and parallelized software.

5.2.1 Experimental Setup. All experiments compare the BDW+A10 with a 12-core Broadwell Xeon E5 and an Nvidia Quadro P6000 GPU. The P6000 is a high-end GPU using the latest Pascal architecture, which has 3840 CUDA cores, 24 GB of GDDR5X RAM, and costs approximately $5000. The BDW+A10 does not have a publicly announced price, but uses an Arria 10 GX1150 FPGA, which costs several thousand dollars [5].

To evaluate software, we used the optimized convolution from DeepBench [22], which provides two algorithms that leverage the Intel Math Kernel Library (MKL) 2017 Update 3 [24]. We also created our own MKL-based implementation to optimize for large images. All software implementations used AVX2 instructions on 12 cores. For the GPU, we used DeepBench GPU code, which selects from eight different algorithms for a given input. We also used Nvidia *convolutionFFT2D* code from the CUDA-8.0 SDK to include an optimized frequency-domain implementation. FPGA details are given in Section 4. For synthesis, we used Quartus 16 Prime Pro, which is required for the BDW+A10. All examples run the convolution pipelines at 271 MHz and the DMA interface at 400 MHz.

To measure performance, we used *gettimeofday()* around relevant regions of code. For all devices, measurements exclude initialization that is common to all devices. We also exclude times for device initialization on all devices, which would be amortized over many executions when used in a data center. On the FPGA, we excluded

time for bitstream configuration and memory allocation, which requires several seconds. For the GPU, we exclude the time of the first execution, which adds 0.3 seconds. For all devices, we exclude the time to initialize the convolution kernel, which generally changes infrequently. All FPGA results include PCIe and QPI transfer times for accessing memory.

We measured Xeon and memory power using the RAPL (Running Average Power Limit) component of Performance API (PAPI) 5.5.1.0 [25]. RAPL uses the Model Specific Registers (MSR) kernel module to read registers that capture the energy and time between two points in the code. To measure power, we performed convolution in a loop, capturing the PAPI readings before and after the loop to give an average value.

For Arria 10 power measurements, we used *tempPowMon* from system release 5.0.3, which reads power and temperature measurements from the FPGA. To get total system power for the FPGA, we added FPGA power to the measured Xeon and memory power during FPGA execution.

To measure GPU power, we used *nvmlDeviceGetPowerUsage* from the Nvidia Management Library, which provided power of the entire GPU board. For the GPU, we measured power and time in separate executions because the power measurements significantly increased time measurements. For total system power with the GPU, we added the GPU power to the idle Xeon power and idle memory power. Ideally, we would measure Xeon power during GPU execution, but since we could not put the GPU in the server with the Broadwell processor, such power would not be a fair comparison. Therefore, total system power for the GPU is likely optimistic.

For all devices, we measured time and power by putting the relevant code in a loop and averaging numerous measurements, with the exact amount depending on the variation for each device.

Because 2D convolution can be used for a variety of purposes, a complete analysis is outside the scope of this paper. This section focuses on traditional use cases of one filter per image, using kernel sizes of 3×3, 5×5, 7×7, and 9×9, along with images ranging from 256×256 to 2048×2048. All examples use inseparable kernels to get worst-case performances. Color channels are 8 bits.

5.2.2 Performance Evaluation. To ensure good FPGA performance, we replicated the 2D convolution pipelines using the presented window generator. Figure 5 demonstrates the improvements in FPGA execution time for different amounts of pipeline replication for a 3×3 kernel on a 2048×2048 image using 8-bit color channels. Trends were similar for other window and image sizes.

The results show near-perfect performance improvements initially, with each replication achieving a 1.99× speedup over the previous amount of replication. However, for 32 replications, that improvement fell to 1.18× due to memory bandwidth being exhausted. For 64 replications, there was no improvement. For nearly all the presented results, this trend was the main performance bottleneck. Average DSP utilization was only 52% of the available 1280 DSPs, with additional DSP usage being prevented primarily by insufficient bandwidth. This utilization suggests improved memory bandwidth can provide significantly improved performance.

Table 2 presents BDW+A10 speedup over the Xeon for both a 16-bit fixed-point kernel and a 32-bit floating-point kernel. The software baseline only uses floating point due to MKL not including

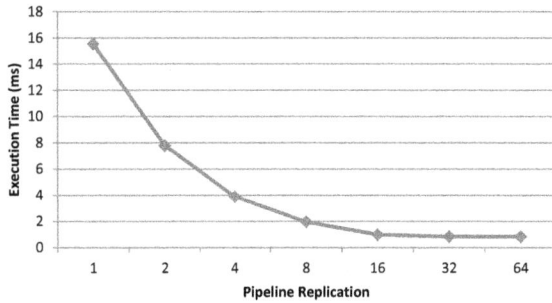

Figure 5: FPGA 2D convolution execution times with varying amounts pipeline replication (unrolling) for a 3x3 kernel, 2048x2048 image, and 8-bit color channels.

Table 2: BDW+Arria10 2D convolution speedup compared to a 12-core Xeon Broadwell E5.

| Precision | Kernel Size | Image Size | | | | |
		256x256	512x512	1024x1024	2048x2048	Avg
16-bit Fixed	3x3	29×	38×	52×	55×	44×
	5x5	57×	96×	135×	146×	108×
	7x7	50×	115×	126×	145×	109×
	9x9	38×	80×	110×	123×	88×
	Avg	44×	82×	106×	117×	
32-bit Float	3x3	27×	38×	52×	55×	43×
	5x5	57×	96×	136×	146×	109×
	7x7	48×	97×	109×	123×	94×
	9x9	27×	48×	58×	62×	49×
	Avg	40×	70×	89×	97×	

fixed-point implementations. The BDW+A10 shows clear improvements over the Xeon, with speedups ranging from 27× to 146×, and an average of 81× across all examples. Speedup from fixed-point implementations tended to be larger than floating point, primarily due to a larger amount of pipeline replication at larger kernel sizes.

The FPGA speedup is achieved from several contributing factors. Most significantly, the FPGA exploited a massive amount of parallelism every cycle. For example, the fixed-point 5×5 kernel is capable of 1,600 multiplies and 1,536 adds every cycle at 271 MHz, which is approximately 850 GOPS. Floating-point results are similar, with the 5×5 kernel performing 800 single-precision multiplies and 768 adds each cycle. Although memory bandwidth prevented those resources from being fully realized, the parallelism still far exceeded that achieved by the Xeon. For fixed-point kernels, the pipeline replication was 64 for 3×3 windows, 64 for 5×5, 32 for 7×7, and 16 for 9×9. These pipelines used 576, 1600, 1568, and 1296 multipliers, respectively, and a similar number of adders. For floating-point kernels, the replication was 64 for 3×3 windows, 32 for 5×5, 16 for 7×7, and 8 for 9×9, which used 576, 800, 784, and 648 DSP resources, respectively, with each performing a multiply and add.

For traditional convolution, the Xeon efficiency was surprisingly low considering its peak potential throughput of 700 GFLOPS when using AVX2 across 12 cores. We have observed that DeepBench and MKL appear to exploit parallelism across larger kernel sizes and larger numbers of kernels, as opposed to computing multiple outputs from the same kernel in parallel. As as a result, much of the potential parallelism of the Xeon is left underutilized. It may be

possible to optimize the Xeon code to exploit such parallelism, but for current convolution software implementations, our presented approach is able to exploit parallelism that is not leveraged by the Xeon.

Another significant contributor to FPGA performance compared to previous studies is that the BDW+A10 has negligible overhead for initiating FPGA execution. For systems using FPGAs on PCIe boards, the application generally has to copy all relevant inputs to the FPGA board, and then read back all results. On the BDW+A10, even though the FPGA accesses memory over PCIe and/or QPI, the FPGA shares the Xeon's memory, which provides a significant performance improvement by eliminating such copying. For the BDW+A10, execution time is roughly equivalent to the time to read inputs and write outputs to memory.

Figure 6 compares BDW+A10 execution times with the GPU for different kernel and image sizes. GPUs can be used in a variety of usage scenarios, where in some cases inputs and outputs must be transferred over PCIe every execution, and in others results are reused from GPU memory for a large number of execution. In these results, we evaluate the maximum possible GPU performance by excluding all PCIe transfers from the GPU execution times. Note that all FPGA results still include all PCIe and QPI transfer times.

For 256×256 images, the fixed-point FPGA implementation always provided the best performance, with the floating-point FPGA version achieving nearly identical results, except for the 9×9 kernel size. The GPU DeepBench implementation was slightly slower, with FPGA speedup ranging from 1.0× to 1.4×. The GPU CUDA-SDK implementation was significantly slower at this image size due to the added initial overhead of performing the FFT. For 512×512 images, trends are similar, with the FPGA speedup range increasing from 1.4× to 2.3×.

At 1024×1024, performances of the GPU CUDA-SDK and FPGA fixed-point version were comparable, with the GPU slightly overtaking the FPGA at the 9×9 kernel size. The FPGA floating-point version experienced a 2× slowdown for the 9×9 kernel due to lower parallelism than the fixed-point version. Trends were similar for 2048×2048 images, with the GPU CUDA-SDK slightly increasing its advantage.

Table 3 shows BDW+A10 speedup across all inputs compared to the fastest GPU implementation. The left side of the table summarizes the results from Figure 6, which excluded PCIe transfers. The right side shows the BDW+A10 speedup with GPU PCIe transfers. The results show that GPU transfers are an expensive overhead, resulting in FPGA speedup of more than an order of magnitude in most cases. Overall, the average FPGA speedup increased from 1.2× with no GPU PCIe transfers to 12.6× with PCIe transfers.

Like the Xeon, the P6000 performed far below its peak performance of 12 TFLOPS. The decreasing speedup for larger window sizes suggests that current GPU implementations parallelize across large windows, and as shown later, across multiple filters per image. Because traditional convolution uses a single kernel per image, the P6000 was significantly underutilized, whereas the FPGA was able to exploit parallelism across multiple outputs of the same kernel.

5.2.3 Energy Comparison. In this section, we repeat the experiments from the previous section for energy consumption using power measurements described in Section 5.2.1.

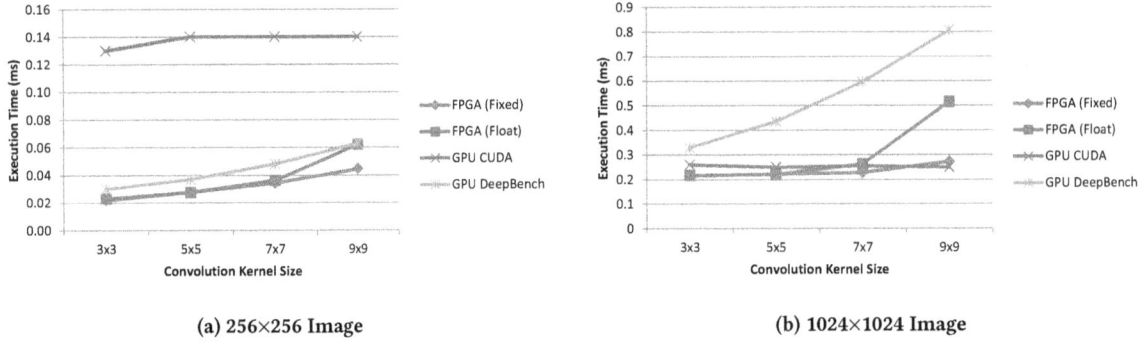

(a) 256×256 Image

(b) 1024×1024 Image

Figure 6: 2D convolution execution times for different kernel and image sizes. FPGA results include 16-bit fixed point and 32-bit floating point. GPU results include CUDA SDK and DeepBench implementations and *exclude* all PCIe transfer times.

Table 3: BDW+Arria10 speedup over the P6000 GPU when excluding (left) and including (right) GPU PCIe transfer times.

GPU PCIe	Precision	Kernel Size	Image Size				Avg
			256x256	512x512	1024x1024	2048x2048	
Excluded	16-bit Fixed	3x3	1.4×	1.4×	1.2×	0.9×	1.2×
		5x5	1.3×	1.7×	1.1×	0.9×	1.3×
		7x7	1.4×	2.2×	1.1×	0.9×	1.4×
		9x9	1.4×	2.3×	0.9×	0.8×	1.3×
		Avg	1.4×	1.9×	1.1×	0.9×	
	32-bit Float	3x3	1.3×	1.4×	1.2×	0.9×	1.2×
		5x5	1.3×	1.7×	1.1×	0.9×	1.3×
		7x7	1.3×	1.9×	1.0×	0.8×	1.2×
		9x9	1.0×	1.3×	0.5×	0.4×	0.8×
		Avg	1.2×	1.6×	0.9×	0.8×	

GPU PCIe	Precision	Kernel Size	Image Size				Avg
			256x256	512x512	1024x1024	2048x2048	
Included	16-bit Fixed	3x3	13.1×	16.4×	14.5×	14.1×	14.5×
		5x5	11.1×	15.5×	14.6×	14.5×	13.9×
		7x7	9.3×	15.7×	14.9×	15.1×	13.7×
		9x9	7.0×	12.6×	13.2×	13.4×	11.5×
		Avg	10.1×	15.0×	14.3×	14.3×	
	32-bit Float	3x3	12.5×	16.4×	14.5×	14.0×	14.3×
		5x5	11.1×	15.7×	14.7×	14.5×	14.0×
		7x7	8.8×	13.3×	12.9×	12.8×	12.0×
		9x9	5.0×	7.5×	7.0×	6.8×	6.6×
		Avg	9.4×	13.2×	12.3×	12.0×	

Table 4: BDW+Arria10 2D convolution energy improvements over a Xeon Broadwell E5.

Precision	Kernel Size	Image Size				Avg
		256x256	512x512	1024x1024	2048x2048	
16-bit Fixed	3x3	35×	47×	67×	68×	54×
	5x5	68×	116×	171×	179×	133×
	7x7	58×	135×	153×	164×	128×
	9x9	44×	98×	135×	148×	106×
	Avg	51×	99×	131×	140×	
32-bit Float	3x3	33×	46×	65×	66×	53×
	5x5	64×	111×	162×	169×	127×
	7x7	55×	113×	131×	139×	109×
	9x9	32×	58×	71×	75×	59×
	Avg	46×	82×	108×	112×	

Table 4 compares BDW+A10 energy with the Xeon. BDW+A10 energy improvements were more significant than performance improvements, with the FPGA providing an average 96× improvement in energy. FPGA device power ranged from 8.9 W to 15.4 W. Memory power during FPGA execution added another 33 W, and the Xeon power added 42 W. For software execution on the Xeon, Xeon power ranged from 53 W to 77 W, with memory power ranging from 25 W to 49 W. Overall, the average system power across all FPGA tests was 87 W, compared to 105 W when running software.

Table 5 compares BDW+A10 energy to the most energy-efficient GPU implementation for each input. When excluding GPU PCIe transfers, the BDW+A10 achieved an average energy improvement of 1.5×, and was more efficient than the GPU for all but two examples. When including CPU PCIe transfers, the BDW+A10 shows significant improvements, achieving an average energy improvement of 15.7×. GPU device power ranged from 61 W to 190 W. The

FPGA device power ranged from 8.9 W to 15.4 W. Total system power with the GPU ranged from 98 W to 227 W, whereas the total system power for the FPGA was from 84 W to 90 W.

One potential power optimization for the FPGA is to use interrupts instead of polling to check for completion. Although FPGA-generated interrupts are not documented yet for the BDW+A10, we imitated this optimization by putting the processor to sleep during FPGA execution. For these tests, the Xeon power and memory during FPGA execution decreased to 27 W and 24 W, respectively, reducing the average total system power to 62 W.

5.3 CNN Performance Projections

In this section, we evaluate the window generator for convolution parameters common to CNNs. Specifically, we use an image size of 256×256, filter sizes of 3×3 and 5×5, filters per image ranging from 32 to 512, which are common to DeepBench and AlexNet [14].

Unlike traditional convolution, the Xeon and P6000 outperform existing FPGA systems for most CNN use cases due to efficient parallelization across multiple filters for an image. Because this paper focuses on the benefits of scalable window generation, in these experiments we evaluate projected performance of shared-memory FPGA systems with theoretical amounts of memory bandwidth that would achieve full utilization of the presented 2D convolution pipelines up to the resource limits of an Arria 10 GX1150 and a Stratix 10 GX2800. For the FPGA projections, we manually determined a parallelization strategy for each example that both replicated pipelines and performed multiple filters per pipeline without exceeding resource constraints. We then simulated the

Table 5: BDW+Arria10 2D convolution energy improvements over the P6000 GPU when excluding (left) and including (right) GPU PCIe transfer times.

GPU PCIe	Precision	Kernel Size	Image Size				Avg
			256x256	512x512	1024x1024	2048x2048	
Excluded	16-bit Fixed	3x3	1.6×	1.7×	1.5×	1.4×	1.5×
		5x5	1.5×	2.1×	1.4×	1.3×	1.6×
		7x7	1.6×	2.8×	1.3×	1.3×	1.7×
		9x9	1.7×	3.3×	1.1×	1.1×	1.8×
		Avg	1.6×	2.5×	1.3×	1.3×	
	32-bit Float	3x3	1.5×	1.7×	1.5×	1.3×	1.5×
		5x5	1.5×	2.0×	1.3×	1.3×	1.5×
		7x7	1.5×	2.3×	1.1×	1.1×	1.5×
		9x9	1.2×	2.0×	0.6×	0.5×	1.1×
		Avg	1.4×	2.0×	1.1×	1.0×	

GPU PCIe	Precision	Kernel Size	Image Size				Avg
			256x256	512x512	1024x1024	2048x2048	
Included	16-bit Fixed	3x3	15.5×	19.8×	19.4×	19.0×	18.4×
		5x5	12.9×	18.6×	19.5×	19.8×	17.7×
		7x7	10.5×	18.2×	19.7×	20.5×	17.2×
		9x9	8.1×	15.3×	16.9×	18.6×	14.7×
		Avg	11.8×	18.0×	18.9×	19.5×	
	32-bit Float	3x3	14.6×	19.4×	19.0×	18.6×	17.9×
		5x5	12.2×	17.8×	18.6×	18.7×	16.8×
		7x7	9.9×	15.2×	16.9×	17.3×	14.8×
		9x9	5.8×	9.0×	8.9×	9.4×	8.3×
		Avg	10.6×	15.4×	15.8×	16.0×	

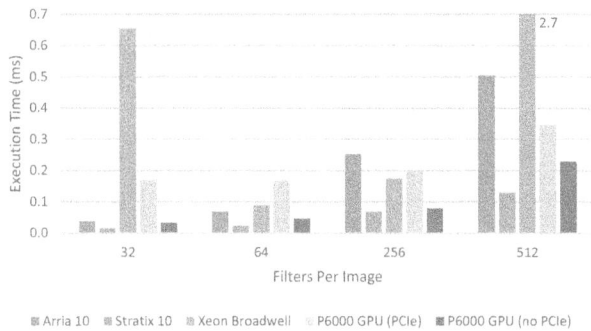

(a) 3×3 Filter

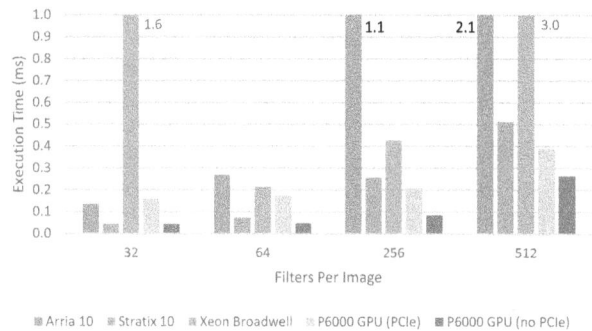

(b) 5×5 Filter

Figure 7: A CNN performance comparison of the Xeon Broadwell and P6000 GPU with projections of the Arria 10 and Stratix 10 using the presented window generation with hypothetical increases in memory bandwidth.

existing pipelines for this strategy, using memory and communication latencies obtained from the BDW+A10 experiments. Due to space constraints, these experiments only use 16-bit fixed-point kernels, which are common for CNNs [11]. GPU examples use single-precision floating point due to DeepBench not providing fixed-point implementations. We also evaluated half precision, but the results are omitted due to worse performance than single precision, which is a known issue on GPUs [12]. DeepBench can potentially be optimized for half precision, but is outside the scope of this paper. We omit power and energy in this section due to the use of projections for envisioned optimizations and the lack of a Stratix 10 to physically measure.

Figure 7 compares CNN performance, again including GPU results both with and without PCIe transfers. For 3×3 filters and 32 filters per image, the Stratix 10 outperforms all other devices. The Arria 10 outperforms the GPU when including PCIe transfers, and is comparable to the GPU excluding PCIe transfers. For 64 filters per image, the Arria 10 performance falls behind the GPU excluding PCIe transfers, but the Stratix 10 is still 2× faster without GPU PCIe transfers, and 7× faster than the GPU when including PCIe transfers. Trends are similar at 256 and 512 filters per image, but with reduced FPGA speedup.

For 5×5 filter sizes, the GPU has significantly better performance due to extra parallelism from the larger filter. However, when including PCIe transfers, the Stratix 10 projections are better or comparable up to 256 filters per image. At 512 filters per image, the

GPU begins to outperform the Stratix 10 both with and without PCIe transfers, achieving speedups of 1.9× and 1.3×, respectively.

Table 6 shows the parallelism strategy used by each FPGA example, where p is the number of replicated pipelines, and k is the filters per pipeline. BW is the required bandwidth in GB/s to achieve this parallelism without stalls. $Perf$ is the resulting performance in tera-operations per second (TOPS). In general, most examples used both replicated pipelines and performed multiple filters in each pipeline. For the larger number of filters per image, some examples did not use pipeline replication and instead used all available resources to maximize the number of parallel filters. On average, the Arria 10 and Stratix 10 achieved a sustained performance of 1.1 TOPS and 4.2 TOPS, respectively, which required bandwidth ranging from 18 GB/s to 286 GB/s. Required bandwidth was calculated by multiplying the number of inputs and outputs by the clock frequency (271 MHz). For example, the 3×3 Stratix 10 example for 32 filters/image had 32 inputs each cycle and $32 \cdot 32$ outputs each cycle for a total of $(32 + 32 \cdot 32)271 = 286$ GB/s. Performance was calculated as the number of multiplies each cycle ($pkw_r w_c$) added with the number of adds each cycle ($pkw_r w_c - p$), multiplied by the clock frequency.

The reason for the large differences in required bandwidth is due to lower resource utilization for a particular parallelization strategy. For example, for the 5×5 Stratix 10 examples, all of the circuits used 6400 multipliers, which is only 54% of the 11,721 available multipliers. The reason for this underutilization is that the existing version of the convolution code only supports replication in powers of two, where the next highest power would exceed 11,721

Table 6: FPGA parameters from Figure 7, where p is pipeline replication, k is filters per pipeline, BW is required memory bandwidth in GB/s, and $Perf$ is performance in tera-ops/s.

		Filters Per Image															
		32				64				256				512			
Device	Filter	p	k	BW	Perf	p	k	BW	Perf	p	k	BW	Perf	p	k	BW	Perf
Arria 10	3x3	8	32	72	1.2	4	64	70	1.2	1	256	70	1.2	1	256	70	1.2
	5x5	2	32	18	0.9	2	32	18	0.9	2	32	18	0.9	2	32	18	0.9
Stratix 10	3x3	32	32	286	5.0	16	64	282	5.0	4	256	279	5.0	2	512	278	5.0
	5x5	8	32	72	3.5	4	64	70	3.5	1	256	70	3.5	1	256	70	3.5

multipliers. Ideally, we would replicate by non-powers of two to ensure that all examples achieve closer to 100% utilization of DSP resources. We will investigate such optimization in future work, but even without this optimization, these projections show that the presented window generator enables emerging FPGA systems to achieve performance that is better or comparable to the P6000 GPU for many CNN use cases.

6 CONCLUSIONS

In this paper, we introduced a sliding-window generator architecture that enables scalable pipeline replication to over 330 GB/s of memory bandwidth, while also eliminating software pre-processing and PCIe overheads from input padding. We evaluated the window generator for 2D convolution on the Intel Broadwell+Arria 10 and demonstrated order-of-magnitude speedup over software running on the Xeon and a high-end P6000 GPU. Although the GPU outperforms any existing FPGA for CNN usage, we demonstrate that the presented window generator running on a Stratix 10 system with sufficient memory bandwidth can outperform the GPU for many common CNN use cases.

ACKNOWLEDGMENTS

This work was supported by the I/UCRC Program of the National Science Foundation under Grant No. EEC-0642422 and IIP-1161022. We would like to thank and acknowledge the donations and support from Intel, and the help provided by Ken Hill and Pawel Cieslewski.

REFERENCES

[1] S. Asano, T. Maruyama, and Y. Yamaguchi. 2009. Performance comparison of FPGA, GPU and CPU in image processing. In *Field Programmable Logic and Applications, 2009. FPL 2009. International Conference on*. 126–131. https://doi.org/10.1109/FPL.2009.5272532

[2] Patrick Cooke, Jeremy Fowers, Greg Brown, and Greg Stitt. 2015. A Tradeoff Analysis of FPGAs, GPUs, and Multicores for Sliding-Window Applications. *ACM Trans. Reconfigurable Technol. Syst.* 8, 1, Article 2 (March 2015), 24 pages. https://doi.org/10.1145/2659000

[3] B. Cope, P.Y.K. Cheung, W. Luk, and S. Witt. 2005. Have GPUs made FPGAs redundant in the field of video processing?. In *Field-Programmable Technology, 2005. Proceedings. 2005 IEEE International Conference on*. 111 –118. https://doi.org/10.1109/FPT.2005.1568533

[4] Yazhuo Dong, Yong Dou, and Jie Zhou. 2007. Optimized Generation of Memory Structure in Compiling Window Operations onto Reconfigurable Hardware. In *Proc. of the Int. Symp. on Applied Reconfigurable Computing*. 110–121.

[5] Mouser Electronics. 2017. Intel Arria 10 GX 1150 Series FPGA - Field Programmable Gate Array. (September 2017). http://www.mouser.com/Intel/Semiconductors/Programmable-Logic-ICs/FPGA-Field-Programmable-Gate-Array/Arria-10-GX-1150-Series/_/N-3oh9p?P=1ypc7usZ1yy6lwu

[6] Jeremy Fowers, Greg Brown, John Wernsing, and Greg Stitt. 2013. A Performance and Energy Comparison of Convolution on GPUs, FPGAs, and Multicore Processors. *ACM Trans. Archit. Code Optim.* 9, 4, Article 25 (Jan. 2013), 21 pages. https://doi.org/10.1145/2400682.2400684

[7] Jeremy Fowers, Kalin Ovtcharov, Karin Strauss, Eric S. Chung, and Greg Stitt. 2014. A High Memory Bandwidth FPGA Accelerator for Sparse Matrix-Vector

Multiplication. In *Field-Programmable Custom Computing Machines (FCCM), 2014 IEEE 22nd Annual International Symposium on*. 36–43. https://doi.org/10.1109/FCCM.2014.23

[8] Gidel. 2017. Proc10A PCIe Arria 10 Accelerator Boards. (2017). http://www.gidel.com/HPC-RC/Proc10A_HPC.asp

[9] Zhi Guo, Betul Buyukkurt, and Walid Najjar. 2004. Input data reuse in compiling window operations onto reconfigurable hardware. In *Proceedings of the 2004 ACM SIGPLAN/SIGBED Conference on Languages, Compilers, and Tools for Embedded Systems (LCTES '04)*. ACM, New York, NY, USA, 249–256. https://doi.org/10.1145/997163.997199

[10] PK Gupta. 2016. Accelerating Datacenter Workloads. (2016). http://www.fpl2016.org/slides/Gupta%20--%20Accelerating%20Datacenter%20Workloads.pdf FPL 2016 Keynote.

[11] Suyog Gupta, Ankur Agrawal, Kailash Gopalakrishnan, and Pritish Narayanan. 2015. Deep Learning with Limited Numerical Precision. In *Proceedings of the 32Nd International Conference on International Conference on Machine Learning - Volume 37 (ICML'15)*. JMLR.org, 1737–1746. http://dl.acm.org/citation.cfm?id=3045118.3045303

[12] Nhut-Minh Ho and Weng-Fai Wong. 2017. Exploiting half precision arithmetic in Nvidia GPUs. In *IEEE High Performance Extreme Computing Conference*.

[13] S. Kestur, J.D. Davis, and O. Williams. 2010. BLAS Comparison on FPGA, CPU and GPU. In *VLSI (ISVLSI), 2010 IEEE Computer Society Annual Symposium on*. 288–293. https://doi.org/10.1109/ISVLSI.2010.84

[14] Alex Krizhevsky, Ilya Sutskever, and Geoffrey E Hinton. 2012. ImageNet Classification with Deep Convolutional Neural Networks. In *Advances in Neural Information Processing Systems 25*, F. Pereira, C. J. C. Burges, L. Bottou, and K. Q. Weinberger (Eds.). Curran Associates, Inc., 1097–1105. http://papers.nips.cc/paper/4824-imagenet-classification-with-deep-convolutional-neural-networks.pdf

[15] Nallatech. 2017. Nallatech 385A FPGA Accelerator Card. (2017). http://www.nallatech.com/store/fpga-accelerated-computing/pcie-accelerator-cards/nallatech-385a-arria10-1150-fpga/

[16] Nallatech. 2017. Nallatech 510T Compute Acceleration Card. (2017). http://www.nallatech.com/store/fpga-accelerated-computing/pcie-accelerator-cards/nallatech-510t-fpga-computing-acceleration-card/

[17] E. Nurvitadhi et al. 2017. Can FPGAs Beat GPUs in Accelerating Next-Generation Deep Neural Networks?. In *Proceedings of the 2017 ACM/SIGDA International Symposium on Field-Programmable Gate Arrays (FPGA '17)*. ACM, New York, NY, USA, 5–14. https://doi.org/10.1145/3020078.3021740

[18] E. Nurvitadhi, D. Sheffield, Jaewoong Sim, A. Mishra, G. Venkatesh, and D. Marr. 2016. Accelerating Binarized Neural Networks: Comparison of FPGA, CPU, GPU, and ASIC. In *2016 International Conference on Field-Programmable Technology (FPT)*. 77–84. https://doi.org/10.1109/FPT.2016.7929192

[19] Nvidia. 2017. Tesla P100: The Most Advanced Data Center GPU Ever Built. (2017). http://www.nvidia.com/object/tesla-p100.html

[20] M. A. Ozkan, O. Reiche, F. Hannig, and J. Teich. 2017. Hardware design and analysis of efficient loop coarsening and border handling for image processing. In *2017 IEEE 28th International Conference on Application-specific Systems, Architectures and Processors (ASAP)*. 155–163. https://doi.org/10.1109/ASAP.2017.7995273

[21] A. Putnam et al. 2014. A Reconfigurable Fabric for Accelerating Large-scale Datacenter Services. In *Proceeding of the 41st Annual International Symposium on Computer Architecture (ISCA '14)*. IEEE Press, Piscataway, NJ, USA, 13–24. http://dl.acm.org/citation.cfm?id=2665671.2665678

[22] Baidu Research. 2017. DeepBench. (2017). https://svail.github.io/DeepBench/

[23] Greg Stitt, Eric Schwartz, and Patrick Cooke. 2016. A Parallel Sliding-Window Generator for High-Performance Digital-Signal Processing on FPGAs. *ACM Trans. Reconfigurable Technol. Syst.* 9, 3, Article 23 (May 2016), 22 pages. https://doi.org/10.1145/2800789

[24] Endong Wang, Qing Zhang, Bo Shen, Guangyong Zhang, Xiaowei Lu, Qing Wu, and Yajuan Wang. 2014. *Intel Math Kernel Library*. Springer International Publishing, Cham, 167–188. https://doi.org/10.1007/978-3-319-06486-4_7

[25] V. M. Weaver, M. Johnson, K. Kasichayanula, J. Ralph, P. Luszczek, D. Terpstra, and S. Moore. 2012. Measuring Energy and Power with PAPI. In *2012 41st International Conference on Parallel Processing Workshops*. 262–268. https://doi.org/10.1109/ICPPW.2012.39

[26] Haiqian Yu and M. Leeser. 2006. Automatic Sliding Window Operation Optimization for FPGA-Based Computing Boards. In *Field-Programmable Custom Computing Machines, 2006. FCCM '06. 14th Annual IEEE Symposium on*. 76 –88. https://doi.org/10.1109/FCCM.2006.29

[27] Chi Zhang and Viktor Prasanna. 2017. Frequency Domain Acceleration of Convolutional Neural Networks on CPU-FPGA Shared Memory System. In *Proceedings of the 2017 ACM/SIGDA International Symposium on Field-Programmable Gate Arrays (FPGA '17)*. ACM, New York, NY, USA, 35–44. https://doi.org/10.1145/3020078.3021727

High-Performance QR Decomposition for FPGAs

Martin Langhammer
Intel, Programmable Solutions Group
UK

Bogdan Pasca
Intel, Programmable Solutions Group
France

ABSTRACT

QR decomposition (QRD) is of increasing importance for many current applications, such as wireless and radar. Data dependencies in known algorithms and approaches, combined with the data access patterns used in many of these methods, restrict the achievable performance in software programmable targets. Some FPGA architectures now incorporate hard floating-point (HFP) resources, and in combination with distributed memories, as well as the flexibility of internal connectivity, can support high-performance matrix arithmetic. In this work, we present the mapping to parallel structures with inter-vector connectivity of a new QRD algorithm. Based on a Modified Gram-Schmidt (MGS) algorithm, this new algorithm has a different loop organization, but the dependent functional sequences are unchanged, so error analysis and numerical stability are unaffected. This work has a theoretical sustained-to-peak performance close to 100% for large matrices, which is roughly three times the functional density of the previously best known implementations. Mapped to an Intel Arria 10 device, we achieve 80us for a 256x256 single precision real matrix, for a 417 GFLOP equivalent. This corresponds to a 95% sustained to peak ratio, for the portion of the device used for this work.

CCS CONCEPTS

• **Computing methodologies** → **Linear algebra algorithms**;
• **Hardware** → **Reconfigurable logic applications**; *Arithmetic and datapath circuits*; *Hardware accelerators*;

KEYWORDS

QRD; MGS; FPGA; Arria10; throughput

ACM Reference Format:
Martin Langhammer and Bogdan Pasca. 2018. High-Performance QR Decomposition for FPGAs. In *Proceedings of 2018 ACM/SIGDA International Symposium on Field-Programmable Gate Arrays (FPGA 2018)*. ACM, New York, NY, USA, 6 pages. https://doi.org/10.1145/3174243.3174273

1 INTRODUCTION

The nature of FPGA architecture is changing. Originally, devices contained soft logic and programmable interconnect, with the majority of the die area devoted to programmability. Embedded functions started being added, first memory blocks, followed by hard multipliers, and more recently, floating-point (FP) support. The

embedded features have also changed the power envelope of the FPGA; on one hand the hardened features allow for much greater functionality, measured either per mm^2, or by functional density. On the other hand, the greater power density in the ever increasing embedded features has left less thermal capacity for the traditional functionality within the typical FPGA package and for environmental constraints.

Contemporary applications therefore need to rely less on the traditional soft logic for datapath construction and instead utilize the embedded features. Soft logic will only be used for assembling datapaths, as well as supplying a resource for bit-level operations such as state machines and control logic. Software programmable solutions, such as CPUs and GPUs, are limited by the data transfer paths of a load-store architecture. In contrast, FPGAs are hardware programmable solutions, with flexible and configurable data movements. In this paper, we will show that we can take advantage of multiple degrees of freedom in data movement: parallelism as well as independence in data sources and destinations. For instance, data can be written back to memory and simultaneously to another datapath, all without instruction overhead.

We select MGS for the QRD implementation, as it lends itself readily to be parallelized, as all data accesses are column-wise. In contrast, Householder QRD requires alternating row and column accesses. Although Householder QRD exhibits better stability than MGS, the MGS implementations described in this paper reduce cumulative rounding errors.

In this paper, we will use sustained to peak performance as our quantitative measure, which can clearly show computational and algorithm efficiency. This can also scale well for comparisons with future FPGA and other architectures, where the resource mix and/or speed changes. As a qualitative measure, we will also examine resource use - our goal is to improve efficiency by using the smallest possible amount of soft logic, and map as much of the design to memories and DSP Blocks.

2 PREVIOUS WORK

Typically, FPGA implementations of QRD have focused on small matrices, with relatively low throughputs. Often, logic intensive approaches such as CORDIC have been employed, even in recent works. In [12], a 4x4 16-bit fixed-point QRD is implemented using an unrolled CORDIC approach, requiring 2671 4LUTs and 12 DSP48E of a Xilinx Virtex5 device, with a clock frequency of 254MHz. The first FP (IEEE-754 single-precision) FPGA QRD was in [15], where a 7x7 systolic array was implemented. This design required 126K 4LUTs, 102 DSP48E Blocks, and 56 BRAMs of a Xilinx Virtex5 device, achieving a clock rate of 132MHz. Neither publication explicitly specifies whether the number format is real or complex, although [6] describes a 4x4 complex QRD using the SGR (Squared Givens Rotation) method on a custom FP format (6-bit exponent, 14-bit fraction) in an earlier work.

In [10], a vectorized algorithm was introduced, which was able to calculate a much larger complex QRD on an FPGA efficiently. In [13] this QRD was mapped onto an Arria 10 device to take advantage of the FP DSP Blocks; a 200x100 QRD required 423 DSP Blocks and 12K ALMs, or about 25% of the device. A 78 GFLOP performance was calculated, which corresponds to 30% sustained to peak of the consumed resources, at a 300MHz clock rate. From [10], the QRD requires about 45% of the FLOPs of a simple STAP radar processing core. As the QRD is a n^3 process, and the other key signal processing components (such as generating the covariance matrices, finding the interference covariance matrix, and calculating the steering vectors using back-substitution) are n^2, the QRD will increase as a fraction of the computational load with increasing system complexity.

A number of ASIC implementations with some aspects of [10, 13] have also been published. A 4x4 fixed point, real numbered QRD systolic array is described in [4] and improved in [9], but both appear to rely on a combination of low precision numbers and the performance of ASIC technology to achieve the single cycle arithmetic operations required to unroll the calculation. An FPGA version of this is implemented in [3], but again with a low precision 4x4 matrix, and a modest performance of 133MHz.

Another recent MGS FP FPGA implementation is described in [11]. Although poorly documented, we calculate that the presented 128x64 matrix requires 1.4GFLOPs at the stated throughput. From [1], the number of DSP48E blocks can support 37.6 GFLOPs at the stated frequency, which corresponds to a 3.7% sustained to peak ratio. Interestingly, we will see that this is close to the expected hardware implementation of the unoptimized canonic MGS.

In [14], the GPU is evaluated for radar signal processing applications, with particular emphasis on QRD, and higher level algorithms (STAP) containing QRD. The work explains that matrix sizes of 200x100 are representative of the complexity for this type of application. The QRD on individual matrices has a very low performance of a fraction of 1% sustained to peak, although a STAP system using multiple parallel iterations of QRD approached 23% sustained to peak; however, it must be noted that only the R portion of the result was calculated in this case. In [5], GPU results for QRD showed 15% sustained to peak performance for matrices of size 8192x8192, and 25% for larger matrices. Smaller matrices were not reported, but the steep slope in GFLOPs from the 8K to 9K sizes suggests that smaller matrices performed poorly. Kerr [7] also reports a 8K matrix QRD throughput of about 15%, but smaller matrices appear to have a much lower throughput. These three sources correlate closely; a QRD algorithm implemented on a GPU may achieve a sustained to peak of 15% for larger matrices, or carefully organized smaller matrices, but will show dramatically lower performance for typical matrix sizes used in embedded applications.

3 ALGORITHM

We will first review the canonic MGS algorithm in order to highlight the importance of the sequence of operations on expected throughput. We will then show the best known algorithm for parallel datapaths, which approaches 50% sustained to peak throughput, and confirm that although the grouping of operations is different

---

Algorithm 1: Gram-Schmidt–based QR factorization

1 function QRD (A);
    Input : Matrix A (square)
    Output: Matrix Q (orthogonal) and R (upper-triangular)
2 **for** $i=1{:}n$ **do**
3      $r_{i,i} = |a_i|$
4      $q_i = a_i/r_{i,i}$
5   **for** $j=i+1{:}n$ **do**
6          $r_{i,j} = \langle q_i, a_j \rangle$
7          $a_j = a_j - r_{i,j}q_i$

---

than the canonic MGS, the order of dependent operations is essentially the same. Finally, the new MGS algorithm, which trends towards 100% sustained to peak, will be introduced. The grouping of operations is again changed, but the order of dependent operations is the same.

The input matrix is A, a $n \times n$-element square matrix formed out of the column vectors $a_k, k \in \{1..n\}$:

$$A = [a_1|a_2|...|a_n].$$

We denote by $\langle x, y \rangle$ the dot-product $x^T y$, and by $|x|$ the norm of the column vector x. The L2-norm used in this article is:

$$|x| = |(x_1, ..., x_n)^T| = \sqrt{x_1^2 + ... + x_n^2}$$

For the purposes of illustration, we will use a 256×256 matrix as the basis for our discussion. This will allow us to show the effects of realistic datapath and operator latencies for current FPGAs in the context of the QRD. In this paper, we will use the following terminology: a *vector operation* denotes a dot-product and a *scalar operation* denotes a multiply-add or multiply-subtract.

3.1 Canonic MGS Algorithm

The canonic MGS algorithm is shown in Algorithm 1. There are n outer loop iterations $i \in \{1..n\}$ - in this case, 256. At the beginning of each iteration ($k \in \{1..n\}$), the norm of the column vector a_k, is calculated. This can be computed as the dot-product $\langle a_k, a_k \rangle$, followed by a square root. Both the dot-product and the square root are long latency operations.

In an FPGA with HFP cores, a 256-length dot-product may require 25 or more cycles (depending on the target frequency), with an additional 10 to 20 cycles for the square root, which in practice is often replaced by the lower latency inverse square root and a multiply. This creates a data dependency for the following divide function, which creates a 45-cycle stall before the following column can be processed.

The following columns $j \in \{i + 1..n\}$ are processed by the inner loop. The first operation is a dot-product, followed by a multiply-subtract. The dot-product again has a relatively long latency, and creates a data dependency for the multiply-subtract. In contrast, the multiply-subtract has a relatively short latency, of typically 5 clock cycles.

Looking at the number of clock cycles required for a single iteration for mid-algorithm ($i = 128$), the normalization calculation requires around 45 cycles, and the following 127 inner loop iterations require 30 cycles each. Clearly, this is very inefficient, with

Algorithm 2: QRD improved algorithm (from [10])

1   function QRD (A);
  Input : Matrix A (square)
  Output: Matrix Q (orthogonal) and R (upper-triangular)
2   **for** i=1:n **do**
3     $r2_{i,i} = \langle a_i, a_i \rangle$
4   **for** j=i+1:n **do**
5       $rn_{i,j} = \langle a_i, a_j \rangle$
6     $r_{i,i} = \sqrt{r2_{i,i}}$
7     $q_i = a_i / r_{i,i}$
8   **for** j=i+1:n **do**
9       $a_j = a_j - \frac{rn_{i,j}}{r2_{i,i}} a_i$
10   **for** j=i+1:n **do**
11       $r_{i,j} = \frac{rn_{i,j}}{r_{i,i}}$

Algorithm 3: Proposed QRD algorithm

1   function QRD (A);
  Input : Matrix A (square)
  Output: Matrix Q (orthogonal) and R (upper-triangular)
2   $p_{1,1} = \langle a_1, a_1 \rangle$
3   $ir_{1,1} = \frac{1}{\sqrt{p_{1,1}}}$ /* via the reciprocal square-root   */
4   **for** j=2:n **do**
5     $p_{1,j} = \langle a_1, a_j \rangle$
6     $s_{1,j} = \frac{p_{1,j}}{p_{1,1}}$ /* via the divider   */
7     $r_{1,j} = p_{1,j} \times ir_{1,1}$ /* via the multiplier   */
8   **for** i=1:n-1 **do**
9     $q_i = a_i \times ir_{i,i}$
10   **for** j=i+1:n **do**
11       $a_j = a_j - s_{i,j} a_i$
12   **if** j=i+1 **then**
13         $p_{i+1,i+1} = \langle a_{i+1}, a_{i+1} \rangle$
14         $ir_{i+1,i+1} = \frac{1}{\sqrt{p_{i+1,i+1}}}$
15         $r_{i+1,i+1} = \sqrt{p_{i+1,i+1}}$
16   **else**
17         $p_{i+1,j} = \langle a_{i+1}, a_j \rangle$
18         $s_{i+1,j} = \frac{p_{i+1,j}}{p_{i+1,i+1}}$
19         $r_{i+1,j} = p_{i+1,j} \times ir_{i+1,i+1}$
20   $q_n = a_n \times ir_{n,n}$

the sustained to peak ratio in the region of 3%, based on the amount of time stalled, however, the true cost can be much higher, if the scalar and vector structures are on independent datapaths.

3.2 Improved MGS Algorithm

An improved form of the MGS algorithm is presented in [10] and rewritten as Algorithm 2. The algorithm loops and operations are restructured in order to reduce and hide loop-carried dependencies.

Examining the multiply-add operation $a_j = a_j - r_{i,j}q_i$ (line 7 in Algorithm 1) we can substitute the definitions of $r_{i,j}$ and q_i to make an equivalent calculation:

$$a_j = a_j - \frac{\langle a_i, a_j \rangle}{|a_i|} \frac{a_i}{|a_i|} = a_j - \frac{\langle a_i, a_j \rangle}{\langle a_i, a_i \rangle} a_i$$

The new update equation for a_j removes the $r_{i,j}$ and $q_{i,j}$ computations from the critical path and requires computing the scalar division $rn_{i,j}/r2_{i,i}$. The $rn_{i,j}$ elements are processed in a separate loop (line 5 in Algorithm 2) to that containing the a_j updates. As these elements become available at the output of the dot-product unit, they feed directly into a second parallel compute core. This core computes the quotients $rn_{i,j}/r2_{i,i}$ and square-roots $\sqrt{r2_{i,i}}$. When all the a_i, a_j inputs are fed into the dot-product unit, and as the first quotient becomes available, the main compute cores will start processing the a_j updates. After all a_j are updated we can proceed to the next outer loop iteration.

The vector calculation (dot-product and the normalization) requires different hardware than the multiply-subtract calculation. As all of the vectors for the r calculation must have been read before the multiply-add begins, typically one structure will be mostly idle while the other is being utilized. This results in a maximum sustained-to-peak performance of roughly 50%.

The architecture proposed in [10] requires parallel transfers between memories and the datapath cores – the dot-product and mult-subtract units. The potentially distant geographical fanout from the memory blocks may limit timing closure and requires more elaborate pipelining.

3.3 Proposed MGS Algorithm

In [8] we presented a new loop structure of the MGS algorithm where the scalar datapath feeds the vector datapath. This makes near 100% sustained to peak performance possible, as both datapaths are active at the same time. Additionally, the memory fanout is reduced to 1 as memories connect directly to the scalar datapath, and the scalar datapath feeds the vector datapath in turn.

Algorithm 3 updates [8] with operation mapping considerations. The first part (lines 2-6) still requires the vector datapath, which is used to calculate the normalization ($ir_{1,1}$) and $s_{1,j}$ values for the first pass, using the optimizations of the improved MGS algorithm described previously. The main loop (lines 9-19) calculates q_i and all of the a_j updates (the multiply-subtract values), and writes these back to memory. At the same time, the $ir_{i+1,i+1}$ and the $s_{i+1,j}$ values for the next loop iteration are calculated from the a_j just computed; the multiply-subtract datapath feeds both the memory write port, as well as the vector datapath, so that the scalar and vector datapaths are utilized simultaneously. The first ir in each loop iteration (line 14) is the normalization value, and is calculated by the inverse square root of the dot-product of the first vector written back. For subsequent js the $s_{i+1,j}$ values (line 18) are the quotients resulting from dividing the dot-products $p_{i+1,j}$ by the pre-computed $p_{i+1,i+1}$ used for the first ir. The q vector, which is the first output of each loop, is also calculated using the scalar datapath; for this case the input to the subtracter is zeroed.

The pre-loop values (lines 2-6) are also calculated with the chained scalar and vector datapaths. The scalar datapath is bypassed, by latching one of the multiplier inputs to zero. Therefore only one datapath structure is needed, thereby reducing routing

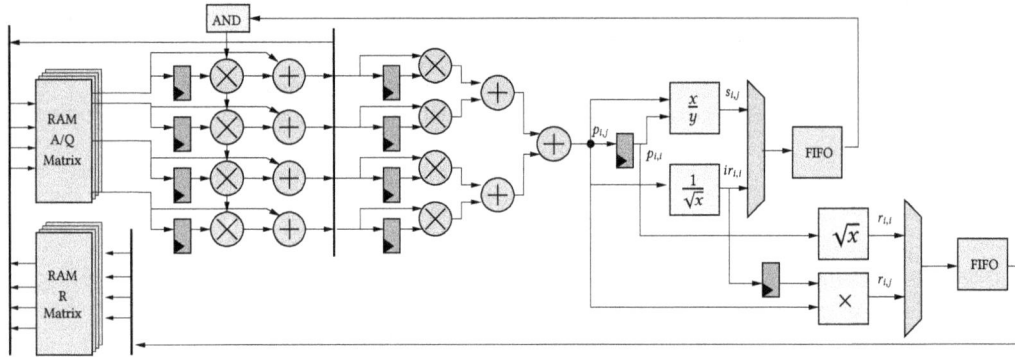

Figure 1: Proposed MGS Algorithm Architecture

stress, removing the need for a multiplexer, and simplifying the control logic.

The final pass consists of a single vector division implemented as a multiplication by the inverse. This is again handled by the scalar structure, similar as for the q calculations of the previous columns, by zeroing one input of the subtracter.

3.4 Architecture

Figure 1 shows the architecture of a QRD core implementing the new MGS algorithm. The RAM block is made up of one memory per column element, so that the entire column can be accessed in parallel. The first column in an iteration, a_i, is always latched at the input of the multipliers. The other input of the multipliers is a common input from the math functions, either the inverse square root for the normalization of the vector ($ir_{i,i}$, the subtracter is zeroed in this case), or the divider ($s_{i,j}$), to apply the projection of the first vector onto the rest. A FIFO, or other delay mechanism, is provided to align the output of the math functions (which are generated for the previous iteration) with the vectors a_j for the current iteration. The new a_j is written back to the RAM block, and at the same time is input to the vector datapath.

The vector datapath latches the first vector it receives for an iteration, which is the normalized a_i, or normalized vector, and calculates the inner product of $p_{i,i} = \langle a_i, a_i \rangle$. This is latched at the denominator input of the divider, and is also used at the input of the inverse square root function, to generate the normalization value for the next iteration $ir_{i,i}$. The first dot-product $p_{i,j}$ is passed through the square root block in order to compute $r_{i,i}$. The output of the inverse square root ($ir_{i,i}$) is latched at the input of the multiplier. The following vector outputs, the inner products of $p_{i,j} = \langle a_i, a_j \rangle$, are divided by the latched value to produce $s_{i+1,j}$, used to calculate the angle between the first and following vectors for the next pass. At the same time $p_{i,j}$ values are multiplied by the latched $ir_{i,i}$ for obtaining $r_{i,j}$.

From Figure 1, it can be seen that for single-precision and when targeting HFP-enabled FPGAs, most of the functionality can be mapped to the HFP blocks. All the FP multiplies and the adders are mapped to the HFP blocks in gray. The math functions ($\div$, $\sqrt{x}$, $1/\sqrt{x}$) together with the muxing and latching logic require small amounts

of soft logic resources. The counting and decoding logic in the controller uses a relatively negligible amount of logic.

Although the implementation and analysis presented here is a fully parallel implementation, a multi-cycle version is also possible. Resource savings would primarily be in the FP scalar and vector datapaths, with the elementary functions unchanged. The number of memory bits is also constant, with any change in the number of RAM blocks dependant on the ratio of matrix size to memory size.

4 PERFORMANCE ANALYSIS

In this section we will estimate the expected sustained to peak performance of the new MGS algorithm, assuming real-world implementations. Although the theoretical sustained to peak performance is close to 100%, pipelining will reduce this by introducing stalls, as well as a smaller component of initial pipeline fill. The larger the matrix, the lower the incidence of stalling.

Although QRD is an n^3 process, our implementation will require n^2 steps as we will read an entire column vector per clock. For a $n \times n$ matrix, there will be n iterations, with the number of columns processed per iteration decreasing by 1 every pass. Ignoring pipelining, QRD therefore takes $n^2/2$ cycles.

The roundtrip through the multiply-subtract core is relatively short, comprising of the registered memory interfaces, the four or five pipeline stages of the multiply-subtract core, and a small number of additional registers, such as the multiplier input latch, and the registered multiplexer (to provide external read and write access to the RAM) on the input of the memory. Additional pipelining may be used for fitting purposes; breaking up long paths for the many FP datapaths can improve the timing closure of complex designs. Typically, the total delay in the multiply-subtract path will be less than 10. The scalar roundtrip path will have minimal impact on system performance, which will be dominated by the vector and elementary function depth instead, and will include the scalar outbound (to the output of the subtracter). Before the next iteration can be started, the angle between the previously calculated vector and the current vectors must be available. This will be the sum of the scalar outbound depth, the vector depth, and the division operator, along with the various hold latches and pipelines added for fitting. The scalar outbound depth is close to the scalar roundtrip path, perhaps 8. The vector depth is dependent on the vector size,

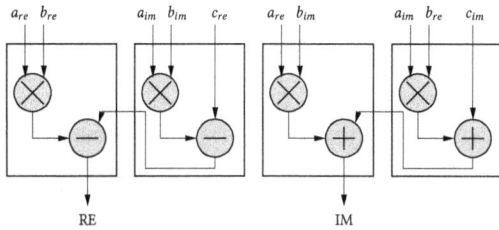

Figure 2: Complex Mult-Add Mapping to HFP DSP Blocks

and in current devices is several times the scalar path:

$$\text{vectorDepth} = 8 + (4 + 3\lceil log_2(n)\rceil) + 15 + x.$$

The divider has a latency of about 15, n is the column height of the matrix, and x represents the additional pipeline depth - this is usually small. For our 256×256 example, the vector depth would be in the order of 55 cycles. If the number of columns in the iteration is greater than the vector depth, then this latency would be hidden in the processing time of the iteration, as the result of the vector pipeline is not required until the iteration is complete.

The QRD implementation would therefore require approximately the following number of cycles:

$$t_{\text{QRD}} = \sum_{i=1}^{n} \max(i, \text{vectorDepth})$$

For our 256×256 example, this is in the order of 34,025 cycles, compared to the untimed maximum of 32,768, for a sustained to peak ratio of 96%. The amount of time for the pre-main loop calculation, which only uses the vector datapath, is included here as the nth sum; although the scalar datapath is not used for this first pass through the core, the data still flows through it.

For smaller matrices, such as 64x64, the latency of the pipeline is exposed, leading to a lower efficiency, here 64%. A multi-cycle version (m cycles per column, which will reduce datapath resources by $1/m$) will require the following cycles:

$$t_{\text{QRD}} = \sum_{i=1}^{n} \max(m \cdot i, \text{vectorDepth}) \tag{1}$$

Our 64x64 case increases to 8570 from 3570 cycles (2.4x) but improves system efficiency by about 50%, as the datapath structures are about 25% the size.

5   RESULTS

Our proposed algorithm is implemented in a core generator written in C++which takes as input the matrix dimension n, the target FPGA and the objective frequency. The datapath structures of our design (the scalar and vector cores), and the math functions (division and inverse square root), are generated for the Arria 10 device using the Intel DSPBA [2].

Table 1 presents the latencies of these compute cores when targeting the Arria 10 device (-I1), with an objective frequency set to 400MHz, for IEEE754 single-precision. With increasing n the vector latency increases roughly with $2 + 4 log_2(n)$. As it can be observed, as n increases from 128 to 512 the latency increases by only 8 cycles for a fully pipelined implementation.

Table 1: Latency of the QRD components for various configurations

n, v	Type	Latency			
		div	rsqrt	scalar	vector
64, 64	real	17	11	4	26
128, 128	real	17	11	4	30
256, 256	real	17	11	4	34
384, 384	real	17	11	4	34
512, 512	real	17	11	4	38

Table 2: Synthesis results for various size QRD designs

	n, v	Results			
		Freq.	ALMs	DSPs	M20K
Real					
	64, 64	461 MHz	4808	135	72
	128, 128	445 MHz	11207	265	136
ours	256, 256	430 MHz	22013	526	264
	384, 384	388 MHz	32726	787	392
	512, 512	371 MHz	43404	1047	520
Complex					
ours	32,32	455 MHz	7814	270	76
[13]	32,8	368 MHz	11K	68	31
[13]	32,16	368 MHz	16.9K	118	44
ours	64,64	407 MHz	14826	530	139
[13]	64,8	368 MHz	13.6K	68	75
[13]	64,16	368 MHz	19.5K	118	83
ours	128,128	366 MHz	28865	1050	267
[11] (Figure 7)	128x64,-	150 MHz	7114 LUT	24 DSP48	72 BRAM_18K
[11] (Figure 8)	128x64,-	147 MHz	75900 LUT	392 DSP48	128 BRAM_18K

The synthesis results for this architecture, for both real and complex versions, are presented in Table 2.

The complex multiply-add can be optimized to use the HFP DSP Blocks more effectively, and is depicted in Figure 2.

$$\begin{aligned} AB + C &= (a_{re} + i \cdot a_{im})(b_{re}) + i \cdot b_{im}) + (c_{re} + i \cdot c_{im}) \qquad (2) \\ &= (a_{re}b_{re} - a_{im}b_{im} + c_{re}) + i \cdot (a_{re}b_{im} + a_{re}b_{im} + c_{im}) \\ &= (a_{re}b_{re} - (a_{im}b_{im} - c_{re})) + i \cdot (a_{re}b_{im} + (a_{re}b_{im} + c_{im})) \end{aligned}$$

The complex dot-product is split element-wise into 4 real dot-products of size n. The final real and imaginary components are assembled using an adder and a subtracter. The only subtlety is the dot-product $\langle x, y \rangle$ which requires a conjugate transpose of x.

The architectures presented in Table 2 have extra stages of pipeline on the control and other high-fanout signals. With increasing n, the physical distance between the placement of the control FSM and the controlled structures increases. A variable number of pipeline stages are added (depending on n) on these control signals. The output of the FIFO also feeds n mult-add blocks and therefore requires appropriate pipelining. The extra delays are accounted for at FSM generation time. Synthesis results confirm that the pipelining strategy is effective for obtaining high-frequency, chip-filling designs.

Table 3 shows how the sustained to peak performance ratio improves with increasing matrix size. Our proposed architecture achieves over 95% sustained-to-peak performance for $n = 256$, and increases to over 98% for $n = 512$. The performance in GFlops is

Table 3: Sustained-to-peak and absolute performance

	n,v	Datapath latency	Peak Latency	Real Latency	Ratio	Perf. (GFlops)	μs
			Real				
ours	64,64	51	2080	3355	61%	71.7	7.27
	128,128	55	8256	9741	84%	190.9	21.8
	256,256	59	32896	34607	95%	417.8	80.4
	384,385	60	73920	75690	97%	577.6	195
	512,512	65	131328	133408	98%	744.2	359.5
			Complex				
ours	32,32	51	528	1888	27%	62.6	4.1
[13]	32,8	-	-			13.9	19.4
[13]	32,16	-	-			17.6	15.3
ours	64,64	56	2080	3620	57%	237	8.8
[13]	64,8	-	-			20.2	105
[13]	64,16	-	-			33.8	62.9
ours	128,128	61	8256	10086	81%	606.5	27.5
[11] Fig.7	128x64,-	-	-	13466627	1%	0.046	89553
[11] Fig.8	128x64,-	-	-	420163	3.7%	3.6	2852.9

reported using the frequency numbers from Table 2. We can observe that we can achieve over 744 GFlops while utilizing only 1047 DSPs out of the 1687 DSPs available in the largest Arria 10 device, or about 62% of the DSPs. The logic utilization is of 43404 ALMs out of 251680 ALMs, which is only 17%. Having a comfortable margin on logic utilization, we expect that frequency can be further improved by 10-20% for a 10% logic increase.

We have also compared our work against [13] which to our knowledge is currently the fastest complex QRD FPGA implementation. The results in [13] have the vector width always smaller than the matrix size, and are therefore expected to consume fewer resources, and have a longer latency than our proposed solution. This holds true for DSPs and memory blocks, but our solution consumes fewer ALMs.

The algorithmic improvements are also observed when analyzing latency. For $n = 64$ our implementation takes $8.8\mu s$ ($v = 64$) and is expected to take $21.55\mu s$ ($v = 16$) according to Equation 1. In comparison, the latency reported in [13] for $n = 64$, $v = 16$ is $62\mu s$. This shows that for similar hardware cost, our implementation is three times faster.

We have added the work in [11] for completeness. The sustained to peak ratio is about 3.7%, which agrees with the expectation for an unoptimized MGS mapping. This also illustrates the validity of the sustained to peak metric in comparing matrix decomposition results, as we are able to compare the quality of an algorithm and implementation independently of device resources. The Xilinx devices do not have FP support, so we expect the soft logic utilization to be much higher, and we expect that a careful redesign would also improve frequency, as the individual operators are capable of about 3x the reported speed in a recent device [1].

6 CONCLUSION

We have successfully demonstrated a number of contributions. First, our sustained to peak ratios approach 100% for even medium sized matrices, as commonly used for embedded applications such as radar. We have shown that even relatively large matrices, such as 256x256, can close timing near the maximum possible speed of the device, which is limited to around 460MHz in FP mode. Secondly, as current FPGA devices contain as many embedded FP functions as

their GPU counterparts – in the order of 1TFLOPs on the lower-end to 10 TFLOPs on the higher-end – the higher efficiency of the FPGA solution (near 100% compared with a typical GPU ratio of 15% or less) means that FPGAs offers higher performance matrix decomposition processing. We have shown an ever increasing improvement in QRD performance, by careful tuning of the algorithm and implementation. Our results, in both efficiency (sustained to peak) and cost (resource utilization) are superior to previous hardware implementations. Finally, our new designs show low soft-logic usage (ALMs). The traditional soft logic and routing resources are used to support the embedded functions, rather than the typical reverse of this. The soft routing is used for zero overhead movement of data, for example when the output of the scalar cores are written back to memory and forward to the vector core simultaneously. Soft logic, when used, often only holds a vector constant in time, which both reduces power (as there is no toggling of the registers) and memory bandwidth, which further reduces power, as the constant vector is not continuously read from memory or a register file.

REFERENCES

[1] 2012. *LogiCORE IP CORDIC v6.0.* https://www.xilinx.com/support/documentation/ip_documentation/floating_point/v6_0/ds816_floating_point.pdf.

[2] 2017. DSP Builder Advanced Blockset. (2017). https://www.altera.com/products/design-software/model---simulation/dsp-builder/overview.html.

[3] A. Alhamed and S. Alshebeili. 2016. FPGA implementation of complex-valued QR decomposition. In *2016 5th International Conference on Electronic Devices, Systems and Applications (ICEDSA)*. 1–4. https://doi.org/10.1109/ICEDSA.2016.7818557

[4] R. C. H. Chang, C. H. Lin, K. H. Lin, C. L. Huang, and F. C. Chen. 2010. Iterative QR Decomposition Architecture Using the Modified Gram-Schmidt Algorithm for MIMO Systems. *IEEE Transactions on Circuits and Systems I: Regular Papers* 57, 5 (May 2010), 1095–1102. https://doi.org/10.1109/TCSI.2010.2047744

[5] Peng Du, Piotr Luszczek, Stan Tomov, and Jack Dongarra. 2013. Soft error resilient QR factorization for hybrid system with GPGPU. *Journal of Computational Science* 4, 6 (2013), 457 – 464. https://doi.org/10.1016/j.jocs.2013.01.004 Scalable Algorithms for Large-Scale Systems Workshop (ScalA2011), Supercomputing 2011.

[6] M. Karkooti, J. R. Cavallaro, and C. Dick. 2005. FPGA Implementation of Matrix Inversion Using QRD-RLS Algorithm. In *Conference Record of the Thirty-Ninth Asilomar Conference onSignals, Systems and Computers, 2005.* 1625–1629. https://doi.org/10.1109/ACSSC.2005.1600043

[7] Andrew Kerr, Dan Campbell, and Mark Richards. 2009. QR Decomposition on GPUs. In *Proceedings of 2Nd Workshop on General Purpose Processing on Graphics Processing Units (GPGPU-2)*. ACM, New York, NY, USA, 71–78. https://doi.org/10.1145/1513895.1513904

[8] M. Langhammer. 2017. QRD for Parallel Arithmetic Structures. In *2017 IEEE 24th Symposium on Computer Arithmetic (ARITH)*. 146–147. https://doi.org/10.1109/ARITH.2017.26

[9] C. Liu, C. Tang, L. Yuan, Z. Xing, and Y. Zhang. 2016. QR decomposition architecture using the iteration look-ahead Modified Gram-Schmidt algorithm. *IET Circuits, Devices Systems* 10, 5 (2016), 402–409. https://doi.org/10.1049/iet-cds.2015.0349

[10] V. Mauer and M. Parker. 2011. Floating point STAP implementation on FPGAs. In *2011 IEEE RadarCon (RADAR)*. 901–904. https://doi.org/10.1109/RADAR.2011.5960667

[11] Luke Miller. 2014. Adaptive Beamforming for Radar: Floating-Point QRD+WBS in an FPGA. *Xilinx Whitepaper* (June 2014). https://www.xilinx.com/support/documentation/white_papers/wp452-adaptive-beamforming.pdf.

[12] S. D. Muñoz and J. Hormigo. 2015. High-Throughput FPGA Implementation of QR Decomposition. *IEEE Transactions on Circuits and Systems II: Express Briefs* 62, 9 (Sept 2015), 861–865. https://doi.org/10.1109/TCSII.2015.2435753

[13] M. Parker, V. Mauer, and D. Pritsker. 2016. QR decomposition using FPGAs. In *2016 IEEE National Aerospace and Electronics Conference (NAECON) and Ohio Innovation Summit (OIS)*. 416–421. https://doi.org/10.1109/NAECON.2016.7856841

[14] Jimmy Pettersson and Ian Wainwright. 2010. Radar Signal Processing with Graphics Processors (GPUs). In *SAAB*.

[15] Xiaojun Wang and Miriam Leeser. 2009. A Truly Two-dimensional Systolic Array FPGA Implementation of QR Decomposition. *ACM Trans. Embed. Comput. Syst.* 9, 1, Article 3 (Oct. 2009), 17 pages. https://doi.org/10.1145/1596532.1596535

ADAM: Automated Design Analysis and Merging for Speeding up FPGA Development

Ho-Cheung Ng, Shuanglong Liu and Wayne Luk
Department of Computing, Imperial College London, UK
{h.ng16,s.liu13,w.luk}@imperial.ac.uk

ABSTRACT

This paper introduces ADAM, an approach for merging multiple FPGA designs into a single hardware design, so that multiple place-and-route tasks can be replaced by a single task to speed up functional evaluation of designs, especially during the development process. ADAM has three key elements. First, a novel approximate maximum common subgraph detection algorithm with linear time complexity to maximize sharing of resources in the merged design. Second, a prototype tool implementing this common subgraph detection algorithm for dataflow graphs derived from Verilog designs; this tool would also generate the appropriate control circuits to enable selection of the original designs at runtime. Third, a comprehensive analysis of compilation time versus degree of similarity to identify the optimized user parameters for the proposed approach. Experimental results show that ADAM can reduce compilation time by around 5 times when each design is 95% similar to the others, and the compilation time is reduced from 1 hour to 10 minutes in the case of binomial filters.

KEYWORDS

Design productivity; FPGA; Maximum common subgraph; Design merging

ACM Reference Format:
Ho-Cheung Ng, Shuanglong Liu and Wayne Luk. 2018. ADAM: Automated Design Analysis and Merging for Speeding up FPGA Development. In *Proceedings of 2018 ACM/SIGDA International Symposium on Field-Programmable Gate Arrays (FPGA '18)*. ACM, New York, NY, USA, 10 pages. https://doi.org/10.1145/3174243.3174247

1 INTRODUCTION

FPGA accelerators have shown to be promising candidates to improve system performance and power efficiency for more than two decades [20, 33, 39]. However, the low productivity in developing FPGA-based applications compared to software development remains a huge obstacle that hinders widespread utilization of FPGA devices in main-stream systems [26].

One of the major challenges when designing applications on FPGA devices is the lack of efficient implementation, optimization and debugging facilities [27]. In particular, compiling a hardware

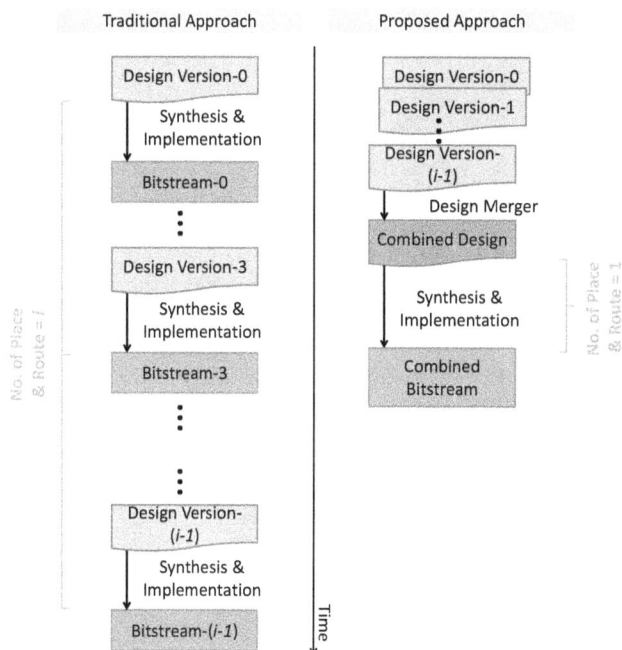

Figure 1: Comparison between the traditional approach and the proposed approach during the optimization phase of an FPGA design. Traditional optimization flow (left) requires placing and routing the design i times, while the proposed approach (right) reduces the number of compilations but requires the use of a design merger.

design using standard design tools could involve a tremendous amount of time. This long compilation time limits the amount of implement/optimize-debug-edit cycles [23] per day and, as a consequence, hinders the productivity of the designers.

During the optimization process, it is usual to have multiple versions [34] of an FPGA design project being experimented on actual hardware to test the functional correctness or to evaluate their accuracy. In particular, **there exist many real-life applications that perform optimization by fine-tuning each version of the design**, where the derivation of each version can be independent of each other and the results from one version are not required for deriving the other versions. For instance, Aubury and Luk [2] propose the use of binomial filters to implement and approximate Gaussian filtering on FPGA. The depth of the binomial filter structure can be adjusted in each version to determine the accuracy and the frequency response. Also, Targett et al. [42] carry out a precision and resolution exploration for shallow water equations for climate modeling. Such study includes reducing the bitwidth of mantissa length of variables in each version of design to balance the tradeoff between precision and accuracy. Other work such as [1] includes changing the specialized filters in each version of short read aligner to cater for different sequencing errors and genetic diversity. Such fine-tuning activities can improve the resulting design significantly, but can be time-consuming due to the repeated and prolonged process of placing and routing for each of the design version.

To address the above design optimization challenge, we propose the use of an automatic merger that combines multiple versions of a design project into a single hardware implementation. The proposed merger can identify common computational kernels between versions, perform the necessary merging and generate a final hardware design in linear time. Instead of placing and routing each individual version every time separately as shown in Figure 1, the developer can implement the generated hardware once and hence improve optimization productivity. We note that this approach is still useful for the scenario where the derivation of each version is dependent on a former one because developers can sometimes predict the possible parameters for the succeeding versions.

Furthermore, based on the statistics from ICFPT 2015 and 2016, 75% of the full papers in the application sections utilize less than half of the resources on FPGA. In other words, **there remains adequate area on chip for insertion of extra logic with the proposed merger, especially when there are only minor discrepancies between each version of the design.** We collect the statistic from ICFPT instead of other conferences because there are more application-based contributions in this conference. Finally, **by relaxing the timing constraints, the proposed merger enables designers to focus on checking functional correctness in hardware which is faster and more accurate than software simulation.**

This paper presents ADAM, an **A**utomated **D**esign **A**nalysis and **M**erging approach to improve the design optimization process. Given i versions of a design, this approach first parses each of them and generates the respective dataflow graphs. Then a maximum subgraph algorithm is applied to determine the common computational kernels among them with linear time complexity. Common signals with different bitwidths across the versions are also analyzed and merged if possible in order to further minimize resource consumption. Finally, the user can select a particular version of design by providing appropriate control signals to the generated hardware implementation. The proposed approach can also be applied to merge unrelated designs targeting a large FPGA.

Since the users do not need to follow the low-level details of the generated hardware implementation, the proposed approach can be considered as an *overlay* [23] where a virtual programmable intermediate architecture is overlaid on top of the physical fabric as a way to address the productivity challenge.

The main contributions of this work are the following:

- A novel approximate maximum common subgraph detection algorithm with linear time complexity that maximizes the sharing of resources for merging of different design versions (Section 2).

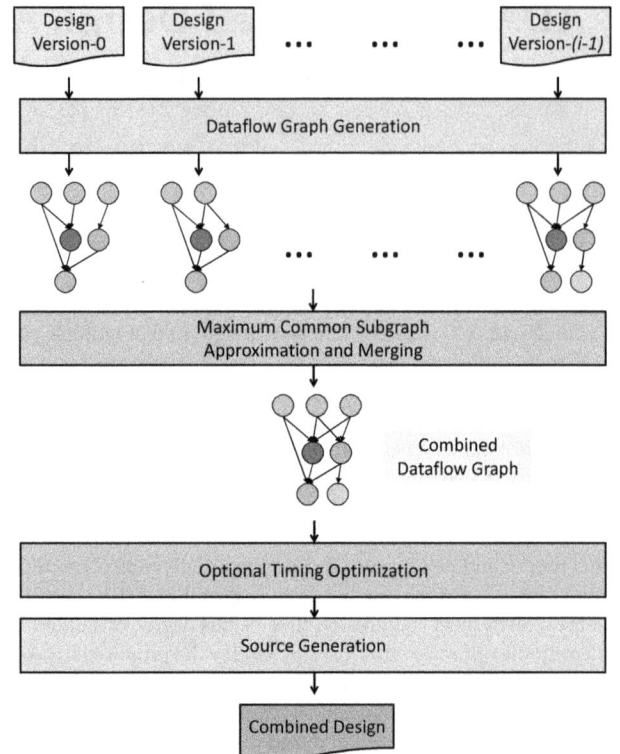

Figure 2: The workflow of the proposed approach.

- A prototype tool implementing a common subgraph detection algorithm for dataflow graphs derived from Verilog designs, which in addition generates the appropriate control circuits to enable selection of each design version at runtime (Section 3).
- A comprehensive analysis of compilation time versus degree of similarity to identify the optimized user parameters for the proposed approach. (Section 4).

The next section presents the details of the proposed framework. We then describe the prototype tool and evaluate the performance of ADAM in Section 3. A comprehensive analysis of compilation time versus degree of similarity is given in Section 4, and related work is discussed in Section 5. We make conclusions in Section 6.

2 THE ADAM FRAMEWORK

This section provides a comprehensive overview of ADAM. Figure 2 illustrates the complete workflow of the design merger. To begin with, we consider the dataflow graphs for multiple versions of a design. As there are only minor discrepancies between each version, every dataflow graph will look remarkably similar. To identify the common subgraph between versions, a maximum common subgraph algorithm is launched and the corresponding nodes are merged, including the nodes of the common signal that can be different in bitwidth across different versions of design. Then the combined dataflow graph is directed to the compiler to generate a final hardware design.

The proposed approach has two novel aspects. First, ADAM supports merging of multiple design versions in linear time based on an approximate maximum common subgraph algorithm. Second, it covers merging of common variables that have different bitwidths across versions. In the following subsections, we describe each of the modules within the merger and their interactions in detail.

2.1 Dataflow Graph

A dataflow graph is a directed graph where the nodes represent the basic operations and variables of a design while the edges between them represent specific paths that data elements follow [44]. Every hardware circuit can be translated into a dataflow graph and vice versa, since every node in the graph corresponds to a hardware unit that can be allocated on the chip surface and every edge represents a wire between two units.

In the proposed approach, a dataflow graph is first extracted from each version v, where $v = 0, 1, ..., i - 1$ of the hardware design with a source-to-source compiler. Then, in order to recognize the common computational kernels, a maximum subgraph algorithm is subsequently applied between every version of dataflow graphs $G_0, G_1, ..., G_{i-1}$ to identify the maximum amount of connected hardware elements that can be merged and shared.

2.2 Maximum Common Subgraph Algorithm

Essentially, precise detection of maximum common subgraph (MCS) in random graphs is an NP-complete problem. Existing algorithms such as McGregor or Durand-Pasari suffer from prolonged execution latency because of their exponential time complexity [6]. Therefore, such algorithms are inappropriate for adoption in the proposed design merger.

Approximate Algorithm for MCS Detection — It is noticed that the dataflow graph extracted from hardware circuits carries certain properties that can aid in the quick search for MCS. In general, nodes are connected by a few edges since most operators consist of only one or two parents and one output, and the majority of the nodes are normally labels such as signal or port names. As a result, the dataflow graph extracted is so sparse that an approximate algorithm such as [37] (time complexity: $O(n)$, where n is the number of nodes) can be used to obtain a set of MCS with decent quality.

To approximate the MCS between two graphs G_a and G_b, a mapping M_{ab} is constructed from the vertices $v_a \in V_a$ of graph G_a onto the equivalent vertices $v_b \in V_b$ of graph G_b. In [37], Rutgers et al. present a greedy algorithm which uses best-first search to traverse the graph G_a and G_b. In each round of search, a vertex v_a is heuristically chosen from G_a so as to find a mapping to a vertex v_b of G_b. For every possible v_b, the best candidate to choose from is determined by the following heuristic. To begin with, vertices in V_a with fewer possible mapping candidates in V_b are handled first, as the probability of selecting an incorrect vertex decreases with a lower number of candidates. After a vertex v_a is chosen from V_a, the selection of the corresponding v_b depends on the similarities of v_a and v_b neighbors. Lastly, when a round of search completes, the vertex v_a is finished and will not be selected again regardless of the search result.

To initiate the above MCS algorithm, the set of inputs I_a and outputs O_a of G_a are matched against the set of inputs I_b and outputs I_b of G_b respectively, and this constructs the initial common vertices in M_{ab}. Since every version of the same design is highly similar during the design optimization process, the io interface of each version must share some common signals such as the clock or reset input. After initialization, the above heuristic, denoted by $Rutgers(G_a, G_b, M_{ab})$, is subsequently launched until all the vertices in V_a are exhausted so as to return the MCS M_{ab}. For further information about the approximation algorithm, please refer to [37] .

Obviously, there are several conditions to check before two nodes can be identified as common. First, both nodes need to implement the same operation, and they also have to operate on the same data type. Furthermore, associative operations such as $(a + b) + c$ and $a + (b + c)$ must be extracted before performing MCS detection, and commutative operations such as $a + b$ and $b + a$ must also be recognized as the same to minimize the area cost of the final implementation.

MCS Algorithm for Multiple Graphs — Since [37] can only determine the set of MCS between two dataflow graphs, the algorithm has to be launched iteratively until a final set of MCS for every version is obtained. The set of notations adopted in this section are given by:

- i is the total number of versions for a given design;
- G_p is the dataflow graph for each version, where $p = \{0, 1, ..., i - 1\}$;
- C_q is the set of MCS between every G_p, where $q = \{0, 1, ..., i - 2\}$;
- $C = C_{i-2}$ is the set of MCS between every version of dataflow graphs;
- $\overline{C}$ is the negation of C which contains all the uncommon subgraphs;
- $find\_MCS((G_0, G_1, ..., C_{j-3}), G_{j-1})$ refers to the algorithm that identifies the set C_q, where $2 < j \leq i$.

To identify the set of MCS between every version of dataflow graphs, an initial set of MCS C_0 is obtained by comparing G_0 and G_1. This newly calculated C_0, together with G_0 and G_1, are matched against G_2 to compute C_1. This process repeats $i - 2$ times until the final C_{i-2} is obtained. Note that the set C_{i-2}, which is equivalent to C, contains every set of MCS across all i versions of design. Other nodes that are not in any of the MCS fall into the set $\overline{C}$.

Data: $G_0, G_1, ..., C_{j-3}, G_{j-1}$, where $2 < j \leq i$
Result: C_{j-2}

1 $G_a = \{G_0, G_1, ..., G_{j-2}\}$
2 $G_b = \{G_{j-1}\}$
3 $M_{ab} = \{\}$
4 **for** g in G_A **do**
5 | $M_{ab} = M_{ab} \cup$ MATCH_IO(g, G_b)
6 **end**
7 $M_{ab} = Rutgers(G_a, G_b, M_{ab})$
8 $C_{j-2} = C_{j-3} \cup M_{ab}$

Algorithm 1: Pseudocode of a single iteration of MCS approximation for multiple dataflow graphs. Assume that C_0 is already computed for consistent input data format.

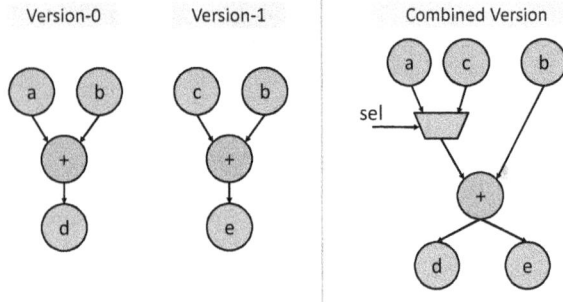

Figure 3: Example of multiplexing when dataflow graphs of two separate versions are combined and merged.

A simple illustration of each iteration of the merging process, i.e. $find\_MCS((G_0, G_1, ..., C_{j-3}), G_{j-1}))$, is displayed in Algorithm 1. In each iteration, G_b is initialized with the graph to be matched against, while G_a is composed of multiple dataflow graphs across versions, which can be conceptually considered as a single dataflow graph with numerous unconnected subgraphs. After that, the common input and output ports are mapped and inserted into M_{ab}, and $Rutgers(G_a, G_b, M_{ab})$ is then executed to compute a partial MCS. Finally, the information about the current MCS and the MCS from the previous iteration are joined to obtain a complete MCS. This final step is crucial because only one vertex in G_a can be mapped to a candidate in G_b based on Rutgers et al. Yet in reality multiple vertices can be matched because G_a is composed of dataflow graphs from every version. The MCS formulated in the previous version provides the information about rest of the mapped vertices, and hence the union of C_{j-3} and M_{ab} contributes to a complete search result.

Since the number of versions i is relatively small, the overall time complexity is given by:

$$O(find\_MCS(G_0, G_1)) + O(find\_MCS((G_0, G_1, C_0), G_2)) +$$
$$... + O(find\_MCS((G_0, ..., G_{i-2}, C_{i-3}), G_{i-1}))$$
$$= O(n) + O(2n + n) + ... + O(i \times n + n)$$
$$= O(i^2 n)$$
$$= O(n),$$

which means such algorithm is acceptable for the proposed design merger because of its linear time complexity.

Final Dataflow Graph Generation — In order to generate the final hardware which is logically identical to the originals, every MCS in C are first combined to generate a merged dataflow graph. The inputs and outputs of the merged graph are reconnected to the nodes in $\overline{C}$ as well.

Essentially, the inputs to the MCS in C are multiplexed and the sel signal is fed to the output interface. To activate a particular version of the original design, an associated value is asserted at sel so that a correct signal from $\overline{C}$ can be directed to the merged hardware. The outputs of the merged node, on the other hand, have to be connected back to the nodes of the versions that originally use the results. Figure 3 displays an example that explains the process of multiplexing.

2.3 Analysis and Merging of Common Signals/Variables with Different Bitwidths

As our goal is to minimize the resource consumption for the combined implementation, we are also interested in merging the common signals based on their literal name even though they are different in bitwidth across various versions of design.

In the above MCS search, the common signals mentioned are considered to be non-identical because of their discrepancies in bitwidth. In order to merge these signals, the maximum bitwidth of every common signal is first obtained and the value is used to update every node that carries the same variable. After that, the same set of MCS algorithms is applied on $\overline{C}$, which identifies a new group of MCS C' composed only of the newly-formed common signals. To provide a clear explanation, another set of notations is adopted in this subsection and they are defined as:

- C' is the set of newly obtained MCS which is composed of the common signals with different bitwidths;
- $\overline{C'} = \overline{C} - C'$ contains all the graphs in various versions that cannot be combined or merged with any of the methods proposed.

Assignment Nodes — Of course, since every common signal in C' is unique, extra hardware node is inserted in the dataflow graph during the merging phase of C' to ensure correctness. This includes appending multiplexers, partially-selecting and sign/zero-extending the low-level bit when the signal is appeared as an assignment node. A signal or a variable is assigned when it is either attached to the output of an operator, or directly connected to another signal in the dataflow graph.

Figure 4 shows an example of the above process when the output signals are attached to an addition operator in two separate versions. Initially, the common signal Y is of width 8-bit and 16-bit in version-0 and version-1 respectively. Then, the operator is merged and its output is partially-selected and sign-extended. This enables the 16-bit signal to imitate an 8-bit signal and contributes to the same computational result.

As illustrated in the above example, different number of bits should be selected and different values should be appended in regards to the signal type and the operators attached. Normally, sign extension is applied when the signal adopts signed number representation while for unsigned number representation zero extension would suffice.

Comparison Operator — Furthermore, for every common signal that is connected to a comparison operator (e.g. == < ≤ > ≥), partially-selecting the low-level bit is required. This is due to the fact that comparison is based on the left-to-right evaluation, and the sign/zero-extension process performed above will incur an incorrect comparison result if left unattended.

Connection to the MCS in C — Depending on the original structure of the dataflow graph, the inputs or outputs of each MCS in C' can be connected to the previously formed MCS in C, or simply connected to the nodes in $\overline{C'}$. The following description summarizes all possible combinations and provides a detailed explanation for each scenario.

(1) *C′ and C Unconnected* — In this scenario, every input and output of an MCS in *C′* are connected to the uncommon subgraphs in set $\overline{C'}$. Similar to the multiplexing mechanism as shown in Figure 3, the inputs are multiplexed and the sel signal is fed to the control interface. Also, the outputs of the merged graph must be connected back to the nodes in the uncommon graphs that use the calculated results.

(2) *Outputs of C′ connected to Inputs of C* — This is the case where the outputs of a MCS in *C′* are connected to any input nodes of a MCS in *C*. To link both MCS together, the outputs are first partially-selected and sign/zero-extended, which is similar to the example in Figure 4. The multiplexers inserted in Section 2.2 are also slightly modified. The inputs of the original multiplexer in *C* are disconnected so that the sign/zero-extended outputs and the unmodified outputs can connect to them.

(3) *Inputs of C′ connected to Outputs of C* — In this case, the outputs of an MCS in *C* can be connected to the inputs of an MCS in *C′* directly, without the need to introduce extra hardware. This is because the partial-selection and bit-extension process during assignment can always guarantee that a common signal will carry a correct value.

Currently, merging of common signals with multi-bitwidth always takes place regardless of hardware cost, which may be less desirable for low-cost operations such as addition. In the future, we plan to extend the merging heuristic by considering multiplexing versus operator savings to further minimize the final resource consumption.

2.4 Optional Timing Optimization

Based on [44], the throughput of a hardware mainly depends on the number of data items that the design can process in one cycle, and also the maximum clock frequency that the design can support. Therefore, the proposed design merger provides an optional mechanism for users to perform certain re-pipelining if the dataflow graph is direct acyclic.

It is often hard to fulfill timing constraints when an output signal is connected to many hardware nodes. Since it is difficult for the synthesis and implementation tool to place the hardware nodes in close proximity, the resulting wire length will consequently increase. To address this challenge, the proposed approach can insert registers in a tree-like fashion such that each register only consists of a limited amount of outputs if the timing optimization mechanism is activated by the users.

2.5 Final Implementation Generation

After detecting and approximating the MCS and merging the common nodes with the methods proposed, the final dataflow graph, which is formed by C, C' and $\overline{C'}$, can be supplied to the source-to-source compiler to generate the final implementation.

Usually, the compiler can produce the final hardware that is in the same language as the original design. However, depending on the needs of the designers, the compiler can be extended to produce the corresponding source code in another programming language such as Chisel [3] or Verilog to promote productivity.

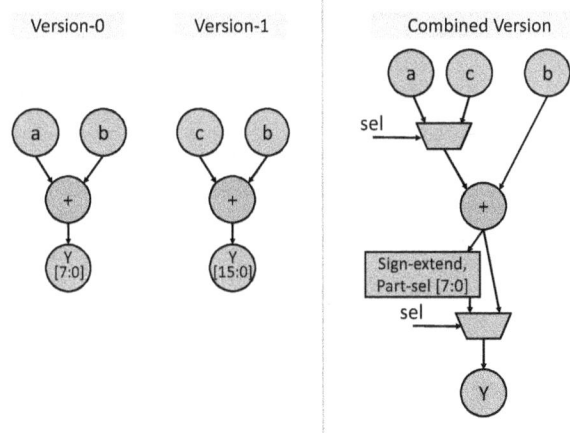

Figure 4: **Example of appending multiplexers, partially-selecting and sign-extending the low-level bit when the common signal with multi-bitwidth is merged.**

3 PROTOTYPE TOOL & BENCHMARKS

3.1 Prototype tool for Pyverilog

With the objective to improve designers productivity during the optimization process of FPGA implementations, the key goal of ADAM is to merge every version of a design automatically while minimizing resource consumption. To demonstrate the feasibility and viability of ADAM, we prototype the proposed approach with Pyverilog [41] to support the functionality mentioned in Section 1 and Section 2 as a proof of concept.

Pyverilog is an open-source toolkit that provides register transfer level design analysis and code generation of Verilog HDL. Written in the Python programming language, Pyverilog incorporates multiple libraries such as parser, dataflow analyzer and Verilog code generator that are useful to realize the proposed design merger. In our prototype, we use the given parser and dataflow analyzer to generate the dataflow graph for each version of a Verilog-based design. Then, we approximate and combine the MCS iteratively in linear time using the algorithm presented by Rutgers et al. [37]. To further optimize the tool efficiency, we also perform the search and the necessary merging of the common signals that are different in bitwidth during the above iterative MCS detection. Optional timing optimization is performed by analyzing the number of fan-out of any outputs. The final dataflow graph is processed by the Verilog code generator to produce a final, Verilog-based hardware description.

Moreover, the decision to implement the proposed approach based on Verilog is mainly a consideration for design productivity and tool portability. Verilog is one of the most-used design languages to describe a hardware structure at the register transfer level for FPGA-based implementations. In addition, Verilog and VHDL are usually used as an intermediate representation for open-source or vendor EDA tools in modern high-level synthesis and next-generation HDL research [41].

With Pyverilog extended to support the proposed approach, we run the design merger on HP EliteDesk 800 G2 Tower PC with Intel

Table 1: Resource consumption and maximum frequency of the generated hardware versus the originals for different applications.

Application	Version	Difference	LUTs		Registers		BRAMs	DSPs	Max. Freq.
diffeq1 Array (Array Size=64)	0	for all signals: bitwidth = 8	5928	4 %	5540	2 %	0	0	125 MHz
	1	for all signals: bitwidth = 16	5638	4 %	8256	3 %	0	256	78.74 MHz
	2	for all signals: bitwidth = 24	17 497	13 %	15 827	6 %	0	384	60.24 MHz
	3	for all signals: bitwidth = 32	20 790	15 %	20 608	8 %	0	576	58.82 MHz
	Merged	–	**22 399**	**17 %**	**20 544**	**8 %**	**0**	**576**	**53.19 MHz**
bgm	0	Macro: BITS = 8	7318	5 %	2665	1 %	0	22	78.13 MHz
	1	Macro: BITS = 16	7356	5 %	3401	2 %	0	22	78.13 MHz
	2	Macro: BITS = 32	11 518	9 %	6030	3 %	0	22	78.13 MHz
	Merged	–	**12 728**	**10 %**	**8276**	**4 %**	**0**	**22**	**70.42 MHz**
LU8PEEng	0	Macro: PRECISION = 8	8369	6 %	3903	1 %	28	16	19.46 MHz
	1	Macro: PRECISION = 16	9946	7 %	4136	2 %	28	16	19.42 MHz
	2	Macro: PRECISION = 32	15 366	11 %	4637	2 %	28	16	19.30 MHz
	Merged	–	**15 910**	**12 %**	**6048**	**2 %**	**28**	**16**	**83.33 MHz**

i7-6700 3.40GHz CPU and 32GB RAM, and the merged hardware is synthesized and implemented onto Xilinx Artix-7 AC701 Evaluation Platform using Vivado 2016.3 edition to recognize the overall performance and limitations.

3.2 Benchmarks from VTR

Experimental Setup — We select several parameterizable Verilog designs from the VTR Benchmarks [28, 36] and automatically combine them with the prototype merger in order to understand its implications in terms of real-life applications. These applications include bgm, LU8PEEng and array of diffeq1 which provide macros or parameters for users to explore different hardware structures and to offer multiple versions of a single design.

Table 1 illustrates the configuration details for these applications. In diffeq1, each version is obtained by adjusting the bitwidth of all signals, while for bgm and LU8PEEng the macros BITS and PRECISION are altered respectively so that different precision can be used to calculate the final results. As lowering the precision and changing the corresponding macros eliminate certain parts of the original circuit, the resulting dataflow graphs vary across different versions. Additionally, the adjustment of the macros changes the width of several signals, and hence creating common signals with different bitwidths for merging.

Finally, the generated hardware and original hardware are synthesized and implemented individually using Vivado with the default settings, and data about the area cost and compilation time are collected subsequently. Also, the maximum frequency for each implemented hardware is obtained by specifying different timing values in the constraint file and compiling separately until the tool fails to meet the timing constraint. Optional timing optimization is not activated for these benchmarks.

Experimental Results — For each application, the area cost and the maximum frequency for every version, including the combined

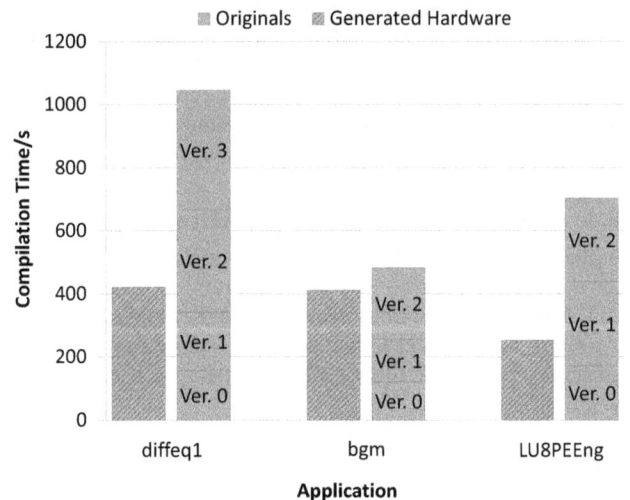

Figure 5: Compilation time of the generated hardware versus the combined compilation time of each hardware application.

ones, are displayed in Table 1. The percentage values are relative to available resources of the targeted FPGA device.

As expected, the reduction in bitwidth of certain signals between versions contributes to a decrease in total resource consumption, and sometimes improves the maximum frequency of the implemented hardware. The generated hardware, on the other hand, shares similar properties in terms of area cost and timing when compared to the original implementations. The resources consumed are increased only by around 2 % with reference to the Artix-7 AC701 FPGA, which is one of the smallest FPGAs in the Xilinx 7-series.

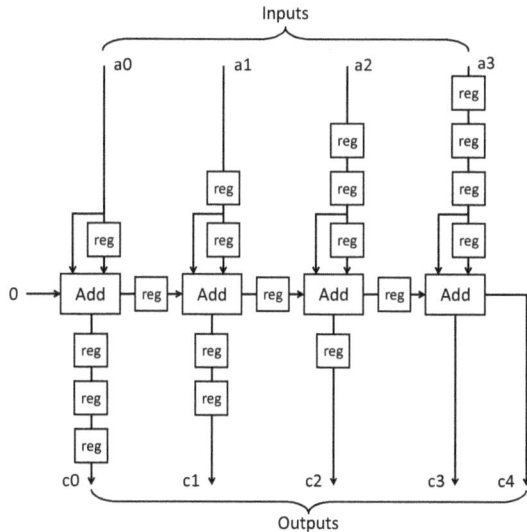

Figure 6: A fully-pipelined binomial filter where $n = 4$.

Table 2: Resource consumption of the generated hardware versus the original hardware for binomial filter. The usage of BRAMs and DSPs are not displayed because they are not used.

Version	Difference	LUTs		Registers	
0	$n = 14$	40 763	30 %	67 632	25 %
1	$n = 15$	43 549	33 %	72 464	27 %
2	$n = 16$	46 335	35 %	77 312	29 %
3	$n = 17$	49 887	37 %	82 176	31 %
4	$n = 18$	52 929	40 %	87 056	33 %
5	$n = 19$	55 715	42 %	91 952	35 %
6	$n = 20$	58 501	44 %	96 864	36 %
Merged	-	**58 501**	**46 %**	**101 420**	**38 %**

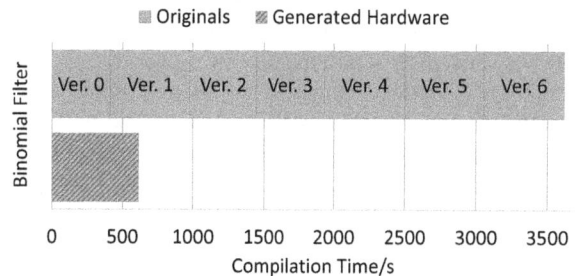

Figure 7: Compilation time of the generated hardware versus the combined compilation time of the originals for the binomial filter.

Moreover, the maximum frequencies in diffeq1 and bgm are reduced by 10 to 12 %, which are moderate given the functionality that ADAM provides.

The maximum frequency supported by the merged hardware in LU8PEEng, on the contrary, is improved by around 4 times when compared to the original implementation. This unexpected result arises from a similar timing and fan-out issue mentioned in Section 2.4. Originally, the register recResult in LU8PEEng is assigned by a wide multiplexer where the inputs are connected to repeating subsets of the same signal. Such assignment incurs a large fan-out and subsequently limits the maximum frequency of every version of implementation. Nevertheless, the bitwidth of recResult is defined with macro PRECISION and as a result, it is resolved as a common signal with different bitwdiths during the merging process. The insertion of registers for zero-extension increases the number of driving gates for recResult and hence the number of fan-out is reduced, which in turn improves the overall timing. We note that such an improvement in the maximum frequency can be obtained by fan-out optimization [18], which can be applied in addition to dataflow graph merging.

Finally, Figure 5 shows the total compilation time of the generated hardware versus the sum of compilation time of each hardware application. The time recorded includes the duration of synthesis as well as implementation.

3.3 Case Study: Binomial Filters

This subsection presents a case study on one of the applications mentioned in Section 1: Binomial Filters. Such filters are efficient structures based on binomial coefficients to realize Gaussian filtering on FPGA. There are numerous possible variations of the basic binomial filter structure and therefore an analysis of the accuracy and frequency response is required when implemented on FPGA [2]. In particular, an analysis with actual hardware is important for such filters because it usually provides more accurate results such as

frequency response with respect to signal inputs when compared to software simulation.

An example of a binomial filter used in this experiment is shown in Figure 6. The structure of the binomial filter is derived from the polynomial $(1 - z^{-1})^n$, and it can be implemented with a cascade of adders with one of the inputs delayed by a register. Such a cascade is arranged in a pipeline structure where the depth is given by the parameter n. The quality of the approximation to Gaussian filter depends on n where the error is reduced to a small value for large filters. For further information about binomial filters, please refer to [2].

Experimental Setup — We populate multiple binomial filters on the FPGA to allow parallel processing where each of them supports 64-bit calculation. The FPGA is populated with 32 filters so that the total resource consumption is around 40%. As mentioned above, the depths of the filters need to be fine-tuned to determine the accuracy of the binomial filters. Therefore, in this experiment, the depth of the filters is varied in each version while the target frequency is fixed at 100 MHz. Similar to the previous benchmarks, optional timing optimization is not activated in this case study, and the generated hardware and the original design versions are synthesized and implemented individually using Vivado with the default settings.

Table 2 illustrates the configuration details for every version and also the corresponding implementation results.

Evaluation Results — The area cost of every version and of the combined hardware are shown in Table 2. Obviously, the reduction of depth contributes to a decrease in total area cost in each version, while the resource consumption of the combined hardware remains competitive compared to the originals. The LUTs and registers consumed are only increased by around 2% with reference to the target Artix-7 AC701 FPGA. This clearly showcases the efficiency of the MCS approximation algorithm since the bitwidth is set to be identical across versions, and the merging of common signals with different bitwidths is not executed in this case study.

The total compilation time, on the other hand, is presented in Figure 7. Similar to the VTR benchmark, the time recorded includes the duration of synthesis as well as implementation. From the figure, it can be seen that the speedup in compilation time is around 5.9 times when compared to the combined compilation time of all the originals. In particular, the overall compilation time is reduced from 1 hour to around 10 minutes. Such a significant result is due to the increase in version counts and also the relatively high similarity between versions. It shows that the MCS algorithm proposed in Section 2 is able to identify most of the common vertices among all the dataflow graphs, and this contributes to a promising speedup in compilation time with only a minor increase in resource consumption. Also, it is expected that the overall compilation speedup will be more significant if more versions are supplied to the proposed design merger. Finally, the execution time for MCS detection and dataflow graph merging is only 1.43 seconds and is insignificant compared to the synthesis and compilation time.

4 EVALUATION

As the above experiment is based on the architecture of the applications provided by VTR Benchmarks and binomial filters, the variations or the degree of similarity between versions cannot be adjusted randomly. In this evaluation, we explore the relationship between compilation time and degree of similarity by varying the number of design versions i and its resource consumption on FPGA.

Evaluation Setup — We populate the FPGA with multiple diffeq1 modules so that 30 %, 40 % and 50 % of the FPGA slices are initially occupied by each unmerged design version. After that, we introduce discrepancies between versions by changing the signal names literally. This enables a fine-grained adjustment of the degree of similarity between versions. Then all the design versions are applied to the prototype merger to generate a merged design, which is passed to Vivado subsequently to record the compilation time. The original versions are also synthesized and implemented separately in order to make a comparison.

Essentially, the compilation time of the unmerged designs is the summation of the synthesis and implementation time of all the versions. For the merged designs, the compilation time simply refers to its own synthesis and implementation time. The degree of similarity is defined as the proportion of computational hardware that is common between versions. We note that we do not use the context of dataflow graph for this definition because each node can represent different hardware types which contribute to different area costs.

Evaluation Results — Figure 8 displays a summary of the experimental results which demonstrates the scalability of the proposed approach. Note that 100% similarity refers to the scenario that every design version is logically equivalent, and it indicates the scope of the maximum compilation speedup. The soaring compilation time in the figure illustrates the failure of placement and routing in which the merged hardware is larger than the area of the given FPGA.

Originally, the total compilation time is linearly proportional to the number of versions as indicated by the flat lines in the figure, whereas the compilation time of the generated hardware is independent of the version counts. Since the synthesis and implementation time of the merged designs purely depends on the degree of similarity, extra logic is only introduced when there exist variations between versions. Thus, the compilation time increases with the decrease of similarity until the FPGA runs out of resources for the generated hardware.

It is also noticed that the compilation time of the generated hardware is largely similar regardless of the numbers of versions when every version is 85 % to 100 % in common. The compilation time is around 400 s to 1000 s which is at least 3 times faster when there are seven versions of the same design. The compilation speedup can be further improved to around 5 times if the versions are 95 % similar. It is expected that, based on the assumption that there is adequate space on chip, the improvement will be larger when more designs are merged. Finally, we note that although the performance numbers are based on diffeq1, parameters such as relative compilation speedup are important specifications for other applications when ADAM is employed by designers to perform FPGA design optimization.

5 RELATED WORK

The concept of supporting multiple versions is described in [43] where conservation cores, i.e. specialized processors that focus on reducing energy, are designed to run both past and future versions of code. However, the notation of versions in [43] is different from our work since each version in the proposed approach is independent of each other. In other words, all the variants between versions are already known at the time when designers need to synthesize and implement the hardware.

Automated dataflow graph merging has been extensively studied in the context of runtime reconfiguration, high-level synthesis and instruction set extension. Fazlali et al. [9, 10] propose a datapath merging algorithm based on approximating the maximum weighted clique to shorten the bitstream and to reduce reconfiguration time. Voss et al. [44] present a cost-driven heuristic to minimize the area cost within an HLS application. Other work such as [5, 30, 35, 40, 45] focuses on resource sharing of multiple instruction set extensions (ISEs) for extensible base processors. For example, a path-based heuristic approach is presented in [5] in which a set of ISEs is transformed to a hardware datapath. Maximal subsequences problem is then applied to maximize area reduction. Zuluaga and Topham later extend the work by introducing latency constraints in the merging process [45]. Similarly, a heuristic that uses the construction of compatibility graph is proposed in [30] and a nonexact method is suggested to perform datapath merging. Such heuristic is also

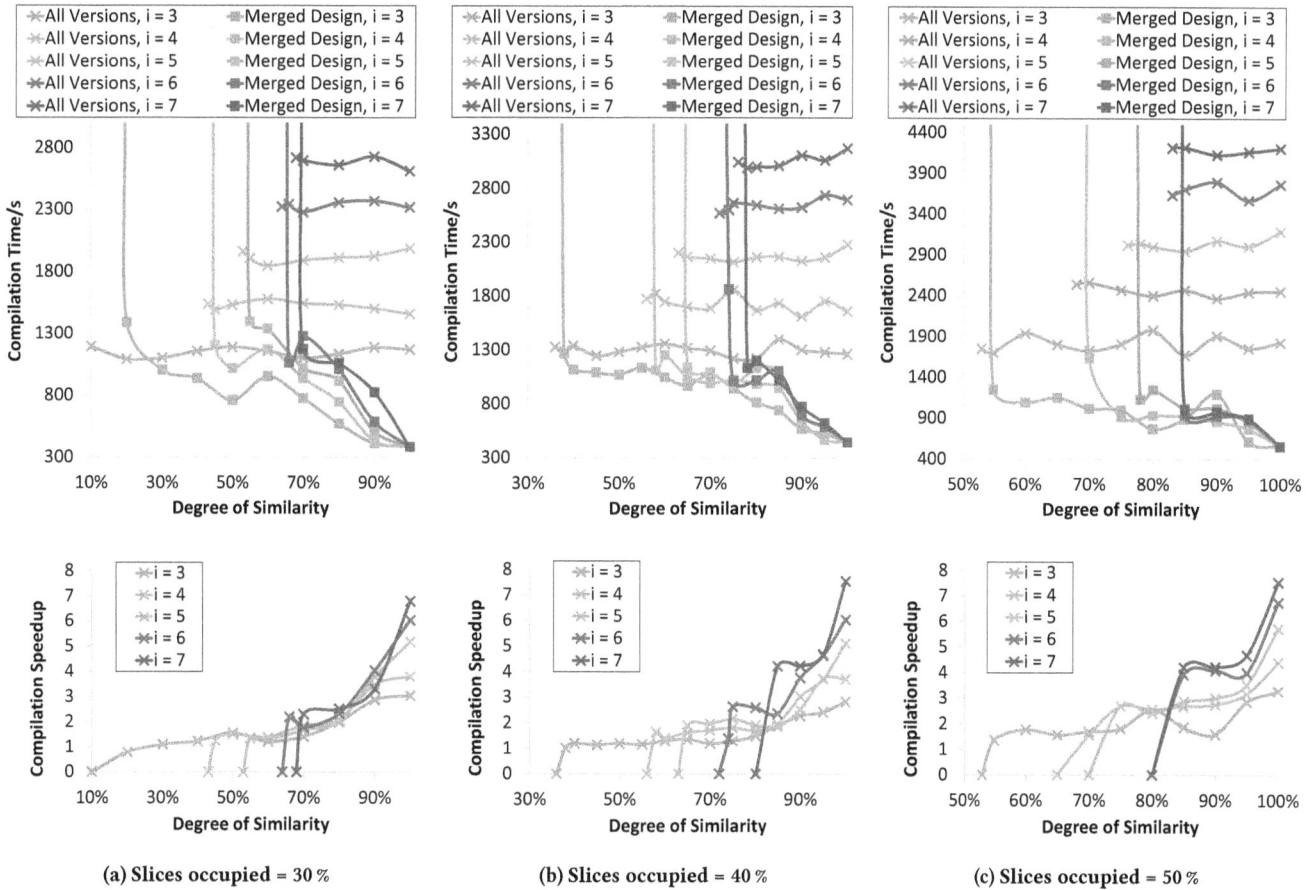

(a) Slices occupied = 30 %　　　　　(b) Slices occupied = 40 %　　　　　(c) Slices occupied = 50 %

Figure 8: The relationship between compilation time and degree of similarity.

employed in [35] to increase area reduction by accounting for the cost of multiplexers.

Since the merging latency is not a prior concern in most of the work mentioned (from exponential to polynomial time complexity), the corresponding algorithms are less appropriate for ADAM. A linear time heuristic is proposed in this paper to minimize the merging time because reducing compilation time is an important objective of the proposed approach.

On the other hand, researchers have tackled the challenge of prolonged hardware implementation, optimization and debugging runtime in many different ways. For example, overlay architectures have been leveraged to offer faster compilation as well as improved programmability and runtime management. Recently, overlays with different granularity ranging from virtual FPGAs [4, 8, 15, 22], soft processors [16, 17, 32] to CGRA overlays [7, 11, 19, 26, 27] and GPU-like overlays [21] have been proposed.

In addition, some have addressed the challenge from a design methodology's perspective. In [24, 25], the authors propose the use of pre-built hard macros and modular design flow to minimize the placement and routing process. A similar approach is also presented in [14] where a library of precompiled macros is constructed for

HLS. Finally, some researchers have devoted their efforts to low-level FPGA EDA tools to improve implementation speed.　31], the authors accelerate the placement and routing process by making quality-runtime tradeoffs. The implementation runtime can also be improved by parallelizing the placement algorithm [13, 29]. Dynamic partial reconfiguration is leveraged in [38] and [12] to shorten runtime by effectively reducing the user design size.

Compared to these contributions, the proposed approach represents an orthogonal solution to improve designers productivity by eliminating the need to perform placement and routing for different design versions repeatedly. It is possible to use ADAM together with the above optimization techniques to reduce compilation time, and such opportunities will be explored in the next section.

6　CONCLUSION AND FUTURE WORK

A new approach, ADAM, is proposed for merging multiple FPGA designs into a single design to support rapid functional evaluation. ADAM is based on a novel approximate maximum common subgraph detection algorithm with linear time complexity, which is developed to maximize the sharing of resources after merging designs. Preliminary results show that ADAM can reduce compilation time by 3 to 5 times. Further research includes studying additional optimization such as adopting pre-placed macros for ADAM, extending ADAM to support multi-chip implementations, signal merging for floating-point numbers, inclusion of additional applications and incremental compilation to evaluate the proposed approach. Finally, we note that the concept of multiple graphs analysis and merging can be applied to multiple designs at the dataflow graph level for many purposes, we just focus on one of the possibilities which is to improve design productivity in this work.

ACKNOWLEDGMENT

The support of the Lee Family Scholarship, the EU Horizon 2020 Research and Innovation Programme under grant agreement number 671653 and the UK EPSRC (EP/L00058X/1, EP/L016796/1, EP/N031768/1 and EP/P010040/1) is gratefully acknowledged.

REFERENCES

[1] J. Arram et al. 2013. Reconfigurable Filtered Acceleration of Short Read Alignment. In *2013 International Conference on Field-Programmable Technology (FPT)*. 438–441.

[2] M. Aubury and W. Luk. 1996. Binomial Filters. *Journal of VLSI Signal Processing Systems for Signal, Image and Video Technology* 12, 1 (Jan. 1996), 35–50.

[3] J. Bachrach et al. 2012. Chisel: Constructing Hardware in a Scala Embedded Language. In *2012 Design Automation Conference (DAC)*. 1212–1221.

[4] A. Brant and G. G. F. Lemieux. 2012. ZUMA: An Open FPGA Overlay Architecture. In *IEEE 20th International Symposium on Field-Programmable Custom Computing Machines (FCCM)*. 93–96.

[5] P. Brisk et al. 2004. Area-efficient Instruction Set Synthesis for Reconfigurable System-on-chip Designs. In *Proceedings of the 41st Annual Design Automation Conference (DAC)*. 395–400.

[6] H. Bunke et al. 2002. A Comparison of Algorithms for Maximum Common Subgraph on Randomly Connected Graphs. In *Joint IAPR International Workshops on Statistical Techniques in Pattern Recognition (SPR) and Structural and Syntactic Pattern Recognition (SSPR)*. 123–132.

[7] D. Capalija and T. S. Abdelrahman. 2013. A High-performance Overlay Architecture for Pipelined Execution of Data Flow Graphs. In *23rd International Conference on Field Programmable Logic and Applications (FPL)*. 1–8.

[8] J. Coole and G. Stitt. 2010. Intermediate Fabrics: Virtual Architectures for Circuit Portability and Fast Placement and Routing. In *IEEE/ACM/IFIP International Conference on Hardware/Software Codesign and System Synthesis (CODES+ISSS)*. 13–22.

[9] M. Fazlali et al. 2009. High Speed Merged-datapath Design for Run-time Reconfigurable Systems. In *2009 International Conference on Field-Programmable Technology (FPT)*. 339–343.

[10] M. Fazlali et al. 2012. Efficient Datapath Merging for the Overhead Reduction of Run-time Reconfigurable Systems. *J. Supercomput.* 59, 2 (Feb. 2012), 636–657.

[11] R. Ferreira et al. 2011. An FPGA-based Heterogeneous Coarse-grained Dynamically Reconfigurable Architecture. In *Proceedings of the 14th International Conference on Compilers, Architectures and Synthesis for Embedded Systems (CASES)*. 195–204.

[12] T. Frangieh et al. 2010. PATIS: Using Partial Configuration to Improve Static FPGA Design Productivity. In *2010 IEEE International Symposium on Parallel Distributed Processing, Workshops and PhD Forum (IPDPSW)*. 1–8.

[13] J. B. Goeders et al. 2011. Deterministic Timing-Driven Parallel Placement by Simulated Annealing Using Half-Box Window Decomposition. In *2011 International Conference on Reconfigurable Computing and FPGAs (ReConFig)*. 41–48.

[14] M. Gort and J. Anderson. 2014. Design Re-use for Compile Time Reduction in FPGA High-level Synthesis Flows. In *2014 International Conference on Field-Programmable Technology (FPT)*. 4–11.

[15] D. Grant et al. 2011. A CAD Framework for Malibu: An FPGA with Time-multiplexed Coarse-grained Elements. In *Proceedings of the 19th ACM/SIGDA International Symposium on Field Programmable Gate Arrays (FPGA)*. 123–132.

[16] J. Gray. 2016. GRVI Phalanx: A Massively Parallel RISC-V FPGA Accelerator Accelerator. In *IEEE 24th Annual International Symposium on Field-Programmable Custom Computing Machines (FCCM)*. 17–20.

[17] F. Hannig et al. 2014. Invasive Tightly-Coupled Processor Arrays: A Domain-Specific Architecture/Compiler Co-Design Approach. *ACM Trans. Embed. Comput. Syst.* 13, 4s, Article 133 (April 2014), 29 pages.

[18] H. J. Hoover et al. 1984. Bounding Fan-out in Logical Networks. *J. ACM* 31, 1 (Jan 1984), 13–18.

[19] A. K. Jain et al. 2015. Efficient Overlay Architecture Based on DSP Blocks. In *IEEE 23rd Annual International Symposium on Field-Programmable Custom Computing Machines (FCCM)*. 25–28.

[20] C. Kachris and D. Soudris. 2016. A Survey on Reconfigurable Accelerators for Cloud Computing. In *26th International Conference on Field Programmable Logic and Applications (FPL)*. 1–10.

[21] J. Kingyens and J. G. Steffan. 2011. The Potential for a GPU-Like Overlay Architecture for FPGAs. *International Journal of Reconfigurable Computing* 2011, Article 514581 (2011), 15 pages.

[22] D. Koch et al. 2013. An Efficient FPGA Overlay for Portable Custom Instruction Set Extensions. In *23rd International Conference on Field Programmable Logic and Applications (FPL)*. 1–8.

[23] D. Koch et al. 2016. *FPGAs for Software Programmers*. Springer International Publishing.

[24] S. Korf et al. 2011. Automatic HDL-Based Generation of Homogeneous Hard Macros for FPGAs. In *IEEE 19th Annual International Symposium on Field-Programmable Custom Computing Machines (FCCM)*. 125–132.

[25] C. Lavin et al. 2013. Improving Clock-rate of Hard-macro Designs. In *2013 International Conference on Field-Programmable Technology (FPT)*. 246–253.

[26] C. Liu et al. 2015. Automatic Nested Loop Acceleration on FPGAs Using Soft CGRA Overlay. In *2nd International Workshop on FPGAs for Software Programmer (FSP)*. 13–18.

[27] C. Liu et al. 2015. QuickDough: A Rapid FPGA Loop Accelerator Design Framework Using Soft CGRA Overlay. In *2015 International Conference on Field Programmable Technology (FPT)*. 56–63.

[28] J. Luu et al. 2014. VTR 7.0: Next Generation Architecture and CAD System for FPGAs. *ACM Trans. Reconfigurable Technol. Syst.* 7, 2, Article 6 (July 2014), 30 pages.

[29] Y. O. M. Moctar and P. Brisk. 2014. Parallel FPGA routing based on the Operator Formulation. In *51st ACM/EDAC/IEEE Design Automation Conference (DAC)*. 1–6.

[30] N. Moreano et al. 2005. Efficient Datapath Merging for Partially Reconfigurable Architectures. *IEEE Transactions on Computer-Aided Design of Integrated Circuits and Systems* 24, 7 (July 2005), 969–980.

[31] C. Mulpuri and S. Hauck. 2001. Runtime and Quality Tradeoffs in FPGA Placement and Routing. In *Proceedings of the ACM/SIGDA Ninth International Symposium on Field Programmable Gate Arrays (FPGA)*. 29–36.

[32] H. C. Ng et al. 2016. A Soft Processor Overlay with Tightly-coupled FPGA Accelerator. In *2nd International Workshop on Overlay Architectures for FPGAs (OLAF)*. 31–36.

[33] H. C. Ng et al. 2017. Reconfigurable Acceleration of Genetic Sequence Alignment: A Survey of Two Decades of Efforts. In *27th International Conference on Field Programmable Logic and Applications (FPL)*. 1–8.

[34] B. O'Sullivan. 2009. *Mercurial: The Definitive Guide*. O'Reilly Media.

[35] N. Pothineni et al. 2010. A High-level Synthesis Flow for Custom Instruction Set Extensions for Application-specific Processors. In *15th Asia and South Pacific Design Automation Conference (ASP-DAC)*. 707–712.

[36] J. Rose et al. 2012. The VTR Project: Architecture and CAD for FPGAs from Verilog to Routing. In *Proceedings of the ACM/SIGDA International Symposium on Field Programmable Gate Arrays (FPGA)*. 77–86.

[37] J. H. Rutgers et al. 2010. An Approximate Maximum Common Subgraph Algorithm for Large Digital Circuits. In *13th Euromicro Conference on Digital System Design: Architectures, Methods and Tools*. 699–705.

[38] N. Shirazi et al. 1998. Automating Production of Run-time Reconfigurable Designs. In *Proceedings. IEEE Symposium on FPGAs for Custom Computing Machines (FCCM)*. 147–156.

[39] I. Skliarova and A. de Brito Ferrari. 2004. Reconfigurable Hardware SAT Solvers: A Survey of Systems. *IEEE Trans. Comput.* 53, 11 (Nov 2004), 1449–1461.

[40] C. C. de Souza et al. 2005. The Datapath Merging Problem in Reconfigurable Systems: Complexity, Dual Bounds and Heuristic Evaluation. *J. Exp. Algorithmics* 10 (Dec 2005).

[41] S. Takamaeda-Yamazaki. 2015. Pyverilog: A Python-Based Hardware Design Processing Toolkit for Verilog HDL. In *Applied Reconfigurable Computing: 11th International Symposium (ARC)*. 451–460.

[42] J. S. Targett et al. 2015. Lower Precision for Higher Accuracy: Precision and Resolution Exploration for Shallow Water Equations. In *2015 International Conference on Field Programmable Logic and Applications (FPT)*. 208–211.

[43] G. Venkatesh et al. 2010. Conservation Cores: Reducing the Energy of Mature Computations. In *International Conference on Architectural Support for Programming Languages and Operating Systems (ASPLOS)*. 205–218.

[44] N. Voss et al. 2016. Automated Dataflow Graph Merging. In *2016 International Conference on Embedded Computer Systems: Architectures, Modeling and Simulation (SAMOS)*. 219–226.

[45] M. Zuluaga and N. Topham. 2008. Resource Sharing in Custom Instruction Set Extensions. In *2008 Symposium on Application Specific Processors (ASAP)*. 7–13.

Graph-Theoretically Optimal Memory Banking for Stencil-Based Computing Kernels

Juan Escobedo
University of Central Florida
Department of Electrical and Computer Engineering
Orlando, FL, U.S.A.
johne1312@knights.ucf.edu

Mingjie Lin
University of Central Florida
Department of Electrical and Computer Engineering
Orlando, FL, U.S.A.
Member, IEEE

ABSTRACT

High-Level Synthesis (HLS) has advanced significantly in compiling high-level "soft" programs into efficient register-transfer level (RTL) "hard" specifications. However, manually rewriting C-like code is still often required in order to effectively optimize the access performance of synthesized memory subsystems. As such, extensive research has been performed on developing and implementing automated memory optimization techniques, among which memory banking has been a key technique for access performance improvement. However, several key questions remain to be answered: given a stencil-based computing kernel, what constitutes an optimal memory banking scheme that minimizes the number of memory banks required for conflict-free accesses? Furthermore, if such an optimal memory banking scheme exists, how can an FPGA designer automatically determine it? Finally, does any stencil-based kernel have the optimal banking scheme? In this paper we attempt to optimally solve memory banking problem for synthesizing stencil-based computing kernels with well-known theorems in graph theory. Our graph-based methodology not only computes the minimum memory partition factor for any given stencil, but also exploits the repeatability of coloring entire memory access conflict graph, which significantly improves hardware efficiency.

CCS CONCEPTS

• Hardware → Hardware accelerators; High-level and register-transfer level synthesis; Logic synthesis;

KEYWORDS

Graph coloring; Chromatic Number; Memory Banking

ACM Reference Format:
Juan Escobedo and Mingjie Lin. 2018. Graph-Theoretically Optimal Memory Banking for Stencil-Based Computing Kernels. In *FPGA '18: 2018 ACM/SIGDA International Symposium on Field-Programmable Gate Arrays, February 25–27, 2018, Monterey, CA, USA.* ACM, New York, NY, USA, 10 pages. https://doi.org/10.1145/3174243.3174251

1 INTRODUCTION

Even with the help of sophisticated High-Level Synthesis (HLS) tools, compiling high-level "soft" C-like programs into efficient

register-transfer level (RTL) "hard" specifications requires significant amount of "tweaking" if the access performance of synthesized memory subsystems needs to be effectively optimized. As such, one central research topic in the high-level synthesis (HLS) of FPGA is how to automatically construct parallel memory access architectures and schemes that allow for simultaneous, conflict-free, accesses to all the data required for continuous executions. Among all developed methodologies so far, memory banking has been a key technique for effectively improving memory access performance. In the past, innovative memory banking schemes such as [9] proved to be quite successful. However, all existing memory banking techniques, to the best of our knowledge, can not guarantee solution optimality, or a lower bound for partition factor, for all stencils. Therefore, several key questions remain to be answered: 1) Given a stencil-based computing kernel, what constitutes an optimal memory banking scheme that minimizes the number of memory banks required for conflict-free accesses? 2) Furthermore, if such an optimal memory banking scheme exists, how can an FPGA designer automatically determine it? 3) Finally, does any stencil-based kernel have the optimal banking scheme? We believe that all these questions possess especial interests as High Level Synthesis (HLS) gradually gains popularity among FPGA designers.

In this paper, we present an innovative graph-based approach to optimally solve memory banking for any given shape of stencil. Our key idea is to construct and optimally color a so-called extended stencil graph. Our specific contributions include:

- To the best of our knowledge, none of existing memory banking techniques can mathematically compute the minimally required memory banks for any given stencil in order to achieve conflict-free memory access. For the first time, our graph-based approach can formally compute such number through optimal graph coloring a small-sized conflict graph.
- Furthermore, using latest discoveries in graph theory, we formally prove that, for a perfect extended stencil, the optimal coloring of an entire memory access conflict graph is periodic. This is significant because: 1) The problem of optimal memory banking can be reduced to solving a much smaller induced subgraph problem, therefore bypassing the NP-hardness of the traditional graph coloring algorithm. 2) Because the overall coloring can be formed by "stitching" a large number of identical small graph coloring, the hardware usage for computing memory mapping can be greatly reduced.
- Solving memory banking through graph coloring offers a powerful new framework, and may offer new insights to solving other memory-related optimization problems. For example, we found that optimal memory banking for multi-port memory banks can be readily solved by defective coloring.

The rest of the paper is divided as follows: Section 2 presents a motivational example of our graph-based optimal memory banking algorithm. We then review some related works and summarize their limitations. When possible, we compare the conceptual difference between our method and these existing approaches. After offering the algorithm overview and the detailed methodology of our graph-based optimal memory banking scheme in Section 4, we formally prove all necessary aspects of solution optimality in Section 5. Subsequently in Section 6, we present the results obtained after performing graph coloring to stencil, and affine non-stencil code using several graph coloring techniques. Finally, Section 7 concludes by summarizing the main results and discussing possible extension to this study.

2 MOTIVATIONAL EXAMPLE

Figure 1: (a) Code snippet for a motivational example. (b) 12-point example stencil.

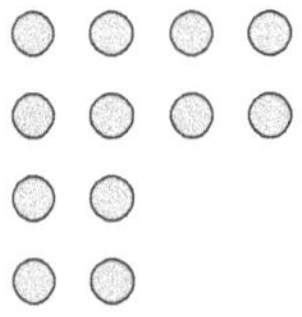

The code snippet listed in Fig. 1(a) contains a computing kernel that produces the stencil depicted in Fig. 1(b). The same stencil form has also been considered in [7]. Through directly following the hyper-plane-based memory banking method from [9], we can obtain a partition factor of 14 with a block size of 1, i.e., totally 14 independent memory banks are required to ensure conflict-free memory accessing. The question we ask is: What is the minimally required number of memory banks that full parallelizes all memory accesses while still having a practical memory address mapping scheme? With our graph-coloring-based methodology, we now believe that, 12 memory banks are not only sufficient to guarantee conflict-free memory accesses but also can be formally proven to be optimal.

Our key idea is to use optimal graph coloring to determine the optimal partition factor. Since the problem can be arbitrarily large, doing an optimal coloring of the entire conflict graph is infeasible, even for relatively small problem sizes given the NP-complete nature of the algorithm. To solve this, we attempt to instead optimally only a small induced subgraph of the original entire memory access conflict graph, and subsequently "stitching" this obtained much smaller obtained solution to form the complete coloring solution of the entire conflict graph. In this paper, we generate what we call *the Extended Stencil Graph*. This graph is the smallest graph we need to color to obtain both the optimal partition factor and an usable coloring. The details of our algorithm and the definitions of various graph-related concepts that are essential to our method can found in Section 4. Specifically in Section 5, using the recently discovered theorems in graph theory, we formally prove that the solutions obtained by our algorithm will be optimal.

To illustrate, our final obtained solution is depicted in Fig. 2, where each cell denotes a memory location and its alphabetical label represents its allocated memory bank index. For clarity, we omitted the edges in the figure. The geometry of this graph is the

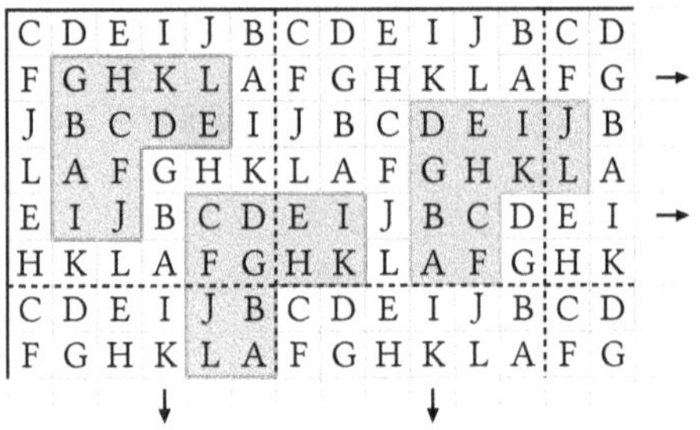

Figure 2: Coloring of the data space. Black lines indicate where the pattern repeats. Light gray areas are instances of the stencil

equivalent of considering each memory location in the memory space a node and taking a single node (any node) in it as a reference along all nodes that also belong to any stencils of which the pivot node is part of, keeping their relative positions. As we can see in figure 2, this coloring forms a pattern that can be repeated in any direction, and can be used to cover a memory space of any size using only a fixed, and more importantly: finite, coloring scheme. As we can see from Fig. 2, after memory banking is finished, if we move stencil instances around (denoted with color blue, purple, and red), in each instance, there is no memory conflict,

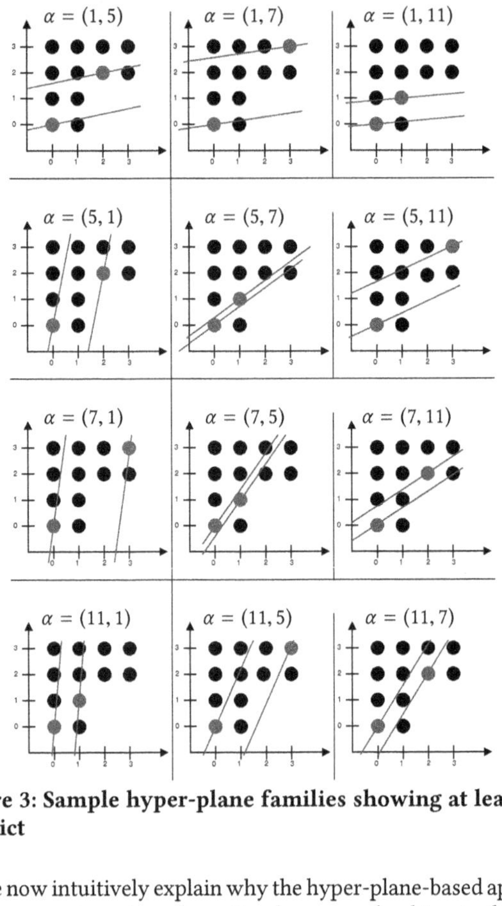

Figure 3: Sample hyper-plane families showing at least one conflict

We now intuitively explain why the hyper-plane-based approach alone may not produce the optimal memory banking in this case. In Fig. 3, we have enumerated multiple possible hyper-plane families. We found that, no matter what hyper-plane family we use, we always have at least one conflict. This is also supported by the claim made in [7], where the authors studied this particular stencil and found no linear skewing scheme in mod 12 that ensures conflict free partition of the memory space. Also in [1], Cilardo *et. al.* re-stated that having a single hyper-plane family might lead to missing certain solutions with a better partition factor. If we consider the memory banking problem abstractly, all memory locations can be treated as multi-dimensional data points scattered over a multi-dimensional space. All previous methods, including hyper-plane-based and lattice-based [1], attempt to find the most suitable multi-dimensional planes to separate these data points in order to avoid conflicts (or minimize them for a given bank number in the case of [1]). But, these multi-dimensional planes are confined to be affine in mod n, therefore these approaches may miss better solutions which are somewhat non-linear in nature.

3 RELATED WORK

Study of memory partition schemes dates back to the first days of computer science and memory organization. Work in [7]studied how to partition the memory space in the fewest number of banks for kernels that had stencil memory access in SIMD machines following a technique to generate the bank and address on the fly called skewing schemes that relied on hyperplanes and on the fact that if the stencil tessellates the plane, then there should exist a linear skewing scheme to do the partition. The limitation of this technique and all others using the same partition scheme with just one family of hyperplanes is that it does not ensure the solution will indeed be optimal for all stencils and does not provide an upper bound to the maximum partition factor it might need. Later work by [12] proved a conjecture by [7] that claimed there exist a valid linear skew, if there exists a valid periodic skewing scheme. The advantage of this skewing scheme being periodic is that it allows for an efficient and simple way to locate the data. This work also proved there is a polynomial time algorithm to prove if a stencil tessellates the memory space. In [13], they refined the theory behind the skewing schemes on the basis that previous mathematical definitions where imprecise. The most significant contribution of this paper is the fact that an upper bound to the maximum number of banks needed to generate a linear skewing scheme is stated, being the first prime $> N$ for an N-point stencil. Similar results were compiled and polished in [11]. In more recent years, study [2] translated the concept of using hyperplanes to do the memory partitioning to the HLS world with their AMP method. This method maintained the same single family of hyperplanes for bank calculation method but added a memory padding technique that allowed for a much more simple way to calculate the address of a memory location in a particular bank at cost of some memory overhead. This method still lack an optimality proof, namely the minimum number of banks and the actual values of the hyperplane are unknown and a heuristic search needs to be performed plus the addition that it does not always give the true optimal. Further work on the area by [9] introduced the concept of block, where two or more contiguous memory locations where assigned the same bank, each with a different address inside the bank, which allowed to reduce the number of the partition factor needed for some cases. They also refined the padding technique to reduce memory waste. Some of the main limitations is that the blocs only extend in one of the dimensions of the memory space and still there is no formal proof of what is the minimum partition factor needed to do the mapping. In [5], the authors introduces a method that uses the geometric information

from the stencil itself and can find a valid solution (partition factor and orientation of the hyperplane family) to do the mapping much faster than previous methods with much less arithmetic operations needed. This solution does not always guarantee the same partition factor, but it ensures all banks are balanced (contain the same number of elements) and reduces memory overhead.

In addition to the hyperplane mapping strategy, there has also been a line of research based in lattices that tries to overcome the limitations of the aforementioned method. In [3] the authors propose the use of lattices to solve the problem of memory reuse. Although they are trying to solve a different problem, they set a solid mathematical background to do the analysis of memory access under the lattice framework. This work, based on the liveliness of a variable and tries to reduce the memory needed for the execution of algorithm. They make the connection between an integer lattices and a modular mapping of the indexes of the array, a mapping strategy of the same dimension of the data space. One of the main limitation of the this method is that, since their goal is not to solve the memory partition problem, the partition factor considered optimal is the determinant of the used lattice, which does not guarantee will be the optimal in terms of the smallest factor. The definition of conflict also differs from the one considered in the partition problem. Instead of it being simultaneous accesses to the same bank in a loop execution, they consider a conflict when there are some indexes considered alive simultaneously under a given schedule. Work in [1] improves and expands on the idea and focuses explicitly in memory partition problem. They use Z-polyhedra model to do the analysis and follow the same concept of integer lattices and a modular mapping of the indexes of the array to do the mapping. The main idea is that they explore all lattices of the same rank as the memory space such that the determinant corresponds to the number of memory banks to use, and the optimization problem is formulated around the minimization of an objective function that minimizes the number of conflicts. In this case, we have a solution that is analogous to using as many families of hyperplanes as the dimensionality of the data space, this guarantees that the optimal partition factor can indeed be found. Note that this also means that any solution obtained in the hyperplane partitioning method using a single family can also be represented here, making it only a subset of the possible solutions. They also tackle the problem of memory minimization, solving a minimization problem that ensures either asymptotically zero or a small, fixed, and arbitrary amount of memory waste. The main limitation is that this paper starts from the concept that one has the number of banks to be used (although an heuristic search to find the best determinant is considered) and not find the smallest factor from the start. Another main limitation of this work is that it relies on and the assumes that the code is already parallelized and the loops properly rearranged.

In [4], the concept of tessellation to the HLS framework, specifically to be sued in FPGAs, was introduced. In it, the authors further developed and expanded on the concept of block introduced in [9], relating it with the concept of multi-dimensional loop unrolling, thus making the block a hyper-rectangle of the same dimension as the problem. they also made the connection between the concept of lattice (and the associated families of hyperplanes) and tessellation, using this as their basis to claim that they can indeed find the optimal partition factor. The main idea of this work is the introduction of the Supertile, the smallest hyper-rectangle such that the mapping contained in it can be used to cover the entire data domain just by repeating it, and allows for conflict free access. This solution, as well as the intra bank offset calculation methods, offers not only a simplified bank and address calculating logic, eliminating the need for DSP slices entirely, reducing overall resource utilization, and achieving higher clock speeds, but in many cases, a reduction in memory waste in comparison with state-of-the-art methods. The main disadvantage is the fact that still no upper bound to the partition factor is given.

More recently, a new approach by [14] uses the trace of the memory addresses accessed and the associated bits to generate a mask for a solution with N banks using $log_2(N)$ bits. Then, each of the masked address is considered a node and addresses that need to be accessed in the same iteration are joined by an edge. If the maximum clique is larger than N, then N needs to be increased and the whole process repeats until this condition is met. The bank assignment is then done using optimal graph coloring. The solution is then stored in a multi-level lookup table. The main advantage from this method, contrary to [1] and [4], is that it can in theory be used for any kind of kernel, stencil or not, with better results than [9] for non-stencils and no worse for stencils. The disadvantage is the time it takes to test all possible masks to find the best and there is still no guarantees on the upper limit needed to achieve an optimal solution.

4 PROBLEM FORMULATION AND OVERALL SOLVING STRATEGY

The central task of high-level synthesis is to transform a C-like software code segment into efficient and high-performance hardware circuit description. Typically, within a given code segment, the largest percentage of computation will be concentrated on iteratively executing a small-size computing kernel, which often access multiple data items stored in one or several data arrays as shown in Fig. 1. Mathematically, during each iteration, all the memory accesses within such a kernel K can be defined as a set of m data points $P = \{\vec{A_0}, \vec{A_1}, \ldots, \vec{A_{m-1}}\}$, where each data point $\vec{A}$. is stored in a d-dimensional array structure. The main objective of memory banking is to distribute all array elements into multiple independent memory banks such that fully parallel memory accesses can be enabled. In other words, during any iteration i, all accessed memory points in P will be read from totally independent memory banks with zero memory reading conflicts. Mathematically, the memory banking problem of an n-dimensional array can be defined as finding a pair of mapping functions $f(\vec{x})$ and $g(\vec{x})$, where $f(\vec{x})$ assigns a distinct memory bank and $g(\vec{x})$ generates its corresponding intra-bank offset for a given data element, respectively. Clearly, an access conflict between two memory references $\vec{x_j}$ and $\vec{x_k}$ occurs if $f(\vec{x_j}) = f(\vec{x_k})$, which means accessing the same memory bank during the same iteration. Again, we assume single-port memory banks here. As such, the memory banking problem under our consideration consists of two mapping problems: memory bank mapping and intra-bank offset mapping. Formally:

PROBLEM 1 (BANK MINIMIZATION). *Given an l-level loop on the iteration domain $\mathcal{D}$ with m affine memory references $\vec{x_0}, \vec{x_1}, \ldots, \vec{x_{m-1}}$ on the same array, find a partition factor N such that:*

$$Minimize: N = max_{0 \le n < m}\{f(\vec{x_i})\} \tag{1}$$

$$s.t. \ \forall \vec{x_j}, \vec{x_k} \in \mathcal{D}, f(\vec{x_j}) \ne f(\vec{x_k}), 0 \le j < k < m$$

Eqn. 1 defines the objective function of memory partitioning, ensuring no access conflict between any two references. After bank mapping, a data element in the original array should be allocated a new intra-bank location. For correctness, two different array elements will be either mapped onto different banks or the same bank with different intra-bank offsets. An intra-bank offset function is valid if and only if:

$$\forall \vec{x_j}, \vec{x_k} \in \mathcal{D}, \vec{x_j} \ne \vec{x_k} \to (f(\vec{x_j}), g(\vec{x_j})) \ne (f(\vec{x_k}), g(\vec{x_k}))$$

which means either

$$f(\vec{x_j}) \ne f(\vec{x_k}) \ or \ f(\vec{x_j}) = f(\vec{x_k}), g(\vec{x_j}) \ne g(\vec{x_k})$$

PROBLEM 2 (STORAGE MINIMIZATION). *Given an l-level loop on the iteration domain $\mathcal{D}$ with m affine memory references $\vec{x_0}, \vec{x_1}, \ldots, \vec{x_{m-1}}$ on the same array, find a partition factor N, find an intra-bank offset mapping function g with minimum storage requirement S such that:*

$$Minimize: \sum_{j=0}^{N-1} max_{\forall i \, s.t. \, f(\vec{x_i})=j}(g(\vec{x_i})) \tag{2}$$

$$s.t. \ \forall \vec{x_j}, \vec{x_k} \in \mathcal{D}, \vec{x_j} \ne \vec{x_k} \to (f(\vec{x_j}), g(\vec{x_j})) \ne (f(\vec{x_k}), g(\vec{x_k}))$$

Eqn. 2 defines the objective function of partitioning with minimum storage overhead, ensuring a valid partition.

Theoretically, one can optimally solve the memory banking problem by optimally coloring the complete memory access conflict graph. Here, a memory access conflict graph is generated by considering all accessed memory locations as nodes and adding edges between nodes that need to be accessed together, forming a clique, during a particular iteration for all iterations in the iteration domain. In other words, whenever two array elements M_i and M_j are accessed during the same iteration, we consider them are conflicting and need to allocated into two different memory banks. Here, we assume all memory banks to be single-ported for simplicity. After solving the optimal single-port memory banking problem, it can be readily shown that multiple-port memory banking can be solved by defective coloring scheme with the same strategy.

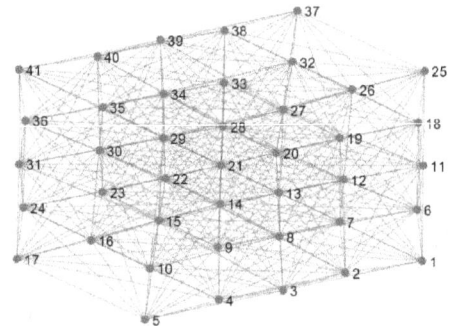

Figure 4: A small portion of the entire memory access conflict graph generated by the stencil in Fig. 1.

The biggest advantage of such graph-coloring-based approach is its generality, i.e., this method imposes no limitation on the regularity of loop structure or the affiness of memory accesses. Unfortunately, in practice, this graph-based methodology is infeasible due to two critical issues. First, for any realistic code segment of loop, the size the memory access graph quickly increases with its associated array size, therefore simple too big for any existing graph coloring algorithm to handle optimally. For example, for the 12-point stencil S shown in Fig. 1(b), even a tiny portion of its complete memory access conflict graph becomes quite complex as shown in Fig. 4, thus infeasible to optimally color. Second, even if we can optimally solve this graph coloring problem, the resulted memory address mapping will simply be too large, therefore completely impractical to implement with hardware.

In this paper, we first limit our research scope to only the stencil-based kernel code. As such, all memory accesses we consider will be affine, which means that the array index of each d-dimensional memory access $\vec{x} = (x_0, x_1, \cdots, x_{d-1})^T$ we consider is a linear transformation of a l-dimensional iteration vector $\vec{i}$ in the form of:

$$\vec{x} = A_{d \times l} \cdot \vec{i} + \vec{C}$$

$$A_{d \times l} = \begin{bmatrix} a_{0,0} & \cdots & a_{0,l-1} \\ \vdots & \ddots & \vdots \\ a_{d-1,0} & \cdots & a_{d-1,l-1} \end{bmatrix}, \vec{C} = \begin{bmatrix} a_{0,l} \\ \vdots \\ a_{d-1,l} \end{bmatrix}$$

where $A_{d \times l}$ is a coefficient matrix, $a_{k,j} \in \mathbb{Z}$ is the coefficient of the j-th iteration vector on the k-th dimension, and $\vec{C}$ is a a column vector with constants. Moreover, within each kernel K, the relative displacements between all memory locations will be invariant throughout all iterations.

By focusing on only stencil-based computing kernel, we show in the following that the repeatability of a complete memory access conflict graph can be exploited to produce a much smaller-sized kernel expansion graph. As such, the optimally coloring the complete conflict graph can be greatly reduced to optimally coloring a much smaller graph, which typically is only within two times of the kernel size. Furthermore, the reduced graph coloring method also will only require a much smaller memory address mapping, thus completely practical for hardware implementation. Maybe most importantly, to the best of our knowledge, our graph-theoretic approach is the first work that offers the provable optimality of its memory banking solutions.

Before describing our algorithm in detail, we mathematically define several important concepts in our methodology. Let $G = (V, E)$ denote the memory access conflict graph, coloring G is the process of assigning each vertice $v \in V$ with a distinct color, such that no two adjacent vertices connected by an edge $e \in E$, have the same color. In mathematics, if a graph G can be colored with k colors, the graph is termed as k-colorable, and the smallest k for which the graph G is k-colorable is defined as the chromatic number of G, denoted as $\chi(G)$. For example, in Fig. 5, we present a tiny example of stencil-based kernel. Given the code snippet in Fig. 5(a), a 3-point stencil depicted in Fig. 5(b) can be readily extracted. During each loop iteration, three memory locations will be accessed in parallel. As such, we construct a clique with three conflict edges. If we iterate through all iterations, we will obtain the total memory access conflict graph G_0 in Fig. 5(c). If we proceed with optimally coloring this conflict graph, it can easily computed that only three colors needed to color this conflict graph, therefore G_0 is 3-colorable and its chromatic number is 3. Despite of the elegance of solving the small problem in Fig. 5, unfortunately, it is well-known that even determining if a graph G is k-colorable for $k \geq 3$ proves to be NP-complete [10]. This makes solving a realistic large-scale memory banking problem infeasible.

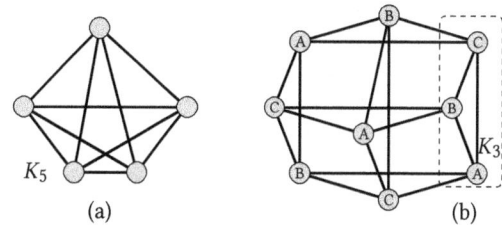

Figure 6: (a) A 5-node clique K_5. (b) A perfect graph of 9 nodes.

In addition, two graph theory concepts are essential to the development of our memory banking algorithm. First, in graph theory, a clique is a subset of vertices of an undirected graph such that every two distinct vertices in the clique are adjacent; that is, its induced subgraph is complete. Cliques are one of the basic concepts of graph theory and are used in many other mathematical problems and constructions on graphs. One example of 5-node clique K_5 is shown in Fig. 6(a). It can be noted that, within our memory conflict graph, any instance of one stencil will clearly form a clique because all nodes inside this particular stencil instance will conflict with each other, i.e., they can not be allocated into the same memory bank in order to avoid any access conflict. Second, a perfect graph is a graph in which the chromatic number of every induced subgraph equals the size of the largest clique of that subgraph. One example of 9-node perfect graph is depicted in Fig. 6(b) and shows a lot similarity with a typical extended stencil graph in topology. One important consequence of a perfect graph is that its optimal coloring can be solved in polynomial time. As shown in Fig. 6(b), all 9 nodes in the perfect graph G are colored optimally with exactly three colors A, B, and C, hence $\chi G = 3$. More importantly, when a graph proves to be perfect, we can be sure its chromatic number will be equal to its largest clique number. Note that in Fig. 6(b), G has six equal-sized cliques, each of which consists of 3 nodes.

One crucial observation in this paper is that, the stencil-induced memory access conflict graph is formed by combining many cliques

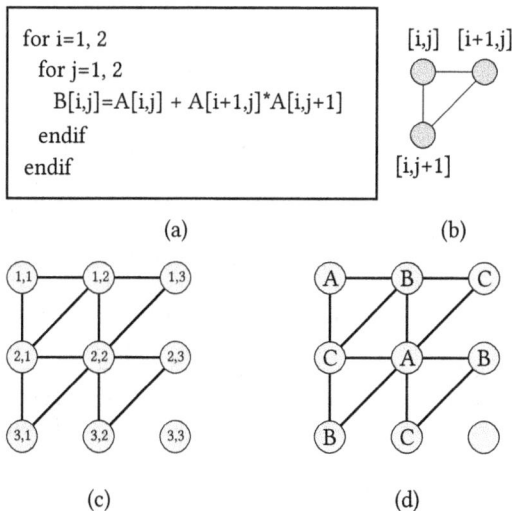

Figure 5: (a) Kernel code snippet. (b) Stencil S. (c) Extended stencil graph ($ESG(S)$). (d) Optimal coloring $ESG(S)$. A, B, and C denote different colors.

corresponding to all loop iterations. The key to the success of our memory banking algorithm is to exploit the special graph-theoretical property of our target memory access conflict graph while avoiding the NP-hardness of optimally coloring a large-sized complete memory access conflict graph.

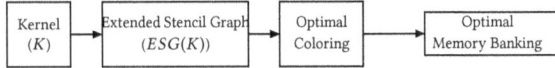

Figure 7: Flow diagram of our algorithm.

Fig. 7 presents the overall flow diagram of our graph-based algorithm. Given a stencil-based computing kernel S, we first construct its Extended Stencil Graph or $ESG(S)$. We then optimally color this $ESG(S)$ using the Matlab toolbox from [6] and obtain its chromatic number $\chi(ESG(S))$. If $\chi(ESG(S))$ equals to the number of nodes in the given stencil S, i.e., the extended stencil graph $ESG(S)$ is perfect, we complete our memory banking scheme by allocating each array element to a distinct memory bank denoted by a distinct color. In Section 5, we will prove that not only this coloring scheme is optimal but also the resulted coloring results can be repeated to cover the whole memory array space. Otherwise, if $\chi(ESG(S))$ is larger than the stencil size, i.e. $ESG(S)$ is not perfect, we will show the the entire conflict graph can be colored with that many colors, but we make no claims on the existence of an usable mapping function we will start to modify the given stencil by adding more nodes. During each iteration, we treat the modified stencil shape as a new one and repeat the above steps. This iterative process will stop if the resulting kernel graph becomes perfect. More details about how we iteratively modify the stencil, why this algorithm is guaranteed to terminate, and why the resulting solution will be optimal will be further discussed in Section 5.

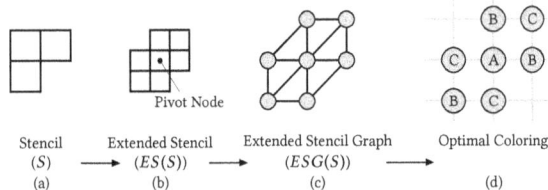

Figure 8: (a) An 3-point stencil example S. (b) Its extended stencil $ES(S)$. (c) Its extended stencil graph $ESG(S)$. (d) Optimal coloring of $ESG(S)$.

Clearly, the key component in our algorithm is to construct the expanded stencil graph ESG of a given kernel-induced stencil. This construction consists of two steps. First, we construct an expanded stencil by overlapping multiple stencil instances that intersects or touches a fixed point. For example, exactly three instances of the given stencil depicted in Fig. 8(a) forms an expanded version of stencil in Fig. 8(b). Subsequently, by selecting all nodes in this expanded stencil, we can readily induce a subgraph from the overall memory access conflict graph. In graph theory, an induced subgraph of a graph is another graph, formed from a subset of the vertices of the graph and all of the edges connecting pairs of vertices in that subset. By including all necessary conflict edges, we then construct a graph, which we termed as the extended stencil graph $(ESG(S))$ in Fig. 8(c). Finally, we perform the optimal coloring on $ESG(S)$ in order to obtain the coloring of each node. In the

next section, we will formally prove that (1) the chromatic number of an extended stencil graph equals the the chromatic number of a total memory access conflict graph and (2) the obtained coloring can be repeatedly utilized to optimally color all memory space. Note that both results are significant because the algorithm listed in Fig. 7 not only can be proven to be optimal but also, because typically the size of expanded stencil graph is much small than the complete memory conflict graph, the optimally memory banking problem can be efficiently solved.

5 PROOF OF ALGORITHMATIC OPTIMALITY AND HARDWARE IMPLEMENTATION EFFICIENCY

Our optimal memory banking methodology largely depends on effectively manipulating memory conflict graph through exploiting its special properties. In this section, we formally prove two key theorems that ensure the optimality of our memory banking solutions and the practical guarantee of hardware efficiency. Specifically, we will prove that, for any given kernel stencil, our methodology will always find the optimal memory banking scheme with the smallest possible number of memory banks. Furthermore, we will prove that, for any given kernel stencil, we only need to optimally color an extended stencil graph, only a small portion of the overall memory access conflict graph, and the complete graph coloring problem can be solved by repeatedly "stamping" this small coloring throughout the overall conflict graph. This ensures that the required memory banking indexes and offsets can be computed efficiently.

5.1 Minimum Memory Bank Number

When constructed as in Section 2, a given extended stencil graph ESG has three important properties. First, any given ESG has a pivot node in the center, which a number of stencil instances surround. Moreover, by definition, the number of stencil instances equals the number of nodes in a given stencil. Second, an expanded stencil includes all possible scenarios how two stencil instances intersect. This is important because this loosely but intuitively explains why optimally coloring an expanded stencil graph, an induced subgraph, infers optimal coloring the entire memory access conflict graph. Third, graphically, an expanded stencil graph combines multiple subgraphs, each of which is formed by an individual stencil. In fact, the induced conflict subgraph generated by each stencil is a graph clique. Moreover, because each stencil contains the same number of nodes, all cliques found in an extended stencil graph are equal in size. This property turns out to be critical to our optimality proof.

Following the steps in Fig. 7, it is clear that a complete memory access conflict graph can be readily partitioned as a number of extended stencil graphs. This is expanded and proved in section 5.2. Furthermore, these extended stencil graphs are connected with each other through stencil-induced conflict graph cliques. Without loss of generality, let us consider two individual extended stencil graphs ESG_a and ESG_b that joined at a stencil-induced clique K_n, where n is the clique size. According to the theorem in [8], in general, for graphs G_1 and G_2, $\chi(\frac{G_1+G_2}{K_n}) = \max\{\chi(G_1), \chi(G_2)\}$, where operation $\chi(\cdot)$ denotes finds chromatic number and $\frac{G_1+G_2}{K_n}$

denotes a joined graph of G_1 and G_2 at a complete graph K_n. Fortunately, in our case, a clique generated by a n-node stencil is trivially a complete graph K_n. Additionally, two individual extended stencil graphs ESG_a and ESG_b under our consideration is isomorphic, thus $\chi(ESG_a = \chi(ESG_b) = c$. As such, we conclude that $\chi(\frac{ESG_a + ESG_b}{K_n}) = \max\{\chi(ESG_a), \chi(ESG_a)\} = c$. In other words, expanding one extended stencil graph through joining at a stencil-induced clique will preserve the chromatic number of the original extended stencil graph. Therefore, by continuously expanding a starting extended stencil graph, we can cover the whole memory space and reconstruct the entire memory access conflict graph. Because we know that the starting chromatic number is optimally obtained by coloring a extended stencil graph, the inferred chromatic for the entire conflict graph must also be optimal.

5.2 Graph Repeatability

Previous section proves that, given a stencil S, the chromatic number of its extended stencil graph $\chi(ESG(S))$ equals to the optimal partition factor of the entire memory access conflict graph, i.e., the minimum number of independent memory banks are needed to ensure conflict-free memory accesses throughout all loop iterations. However, this result doesn't by itself provide a valid and hardware-efficient memory address mapping. In the following, we prove by construction that the optimal coloring of an extended stencil graph repeats itself across the entire memory domain, thus providing a very efficient memory address mapping scheme if the considered extend stencil graph is perfect. Otherwise, we need to augment the original stencil by adding more nodes until the induced extended stencil graph becomes perfect. We will prove that such augmentation will terminate and always have an optimal solution.

As mentioned in Section 4, an extended stencil graph is formed by overlapping multiple stencil instances. By definition, each extended stencil graph ESG has a center point p. In addition, the conflict graph of each stencil constitutes a clique and the coloring of each node contained in this clique is unique. We now show that, a valid optimal coloring of a given ESG can be readily expanded in all directions with repeated patterns. Clearly, if this is true, we only need to store a small-size coloring in order to infer every node's color assignment.

In Fig. 9, we consider one extended stencil graph ESG. Pick one of its cliques and call its particular coloring B. By definition, B assigns a distinct color to all the nodes in this clique. In particular, its previously defined "pivot" node is colored in orange, which will be shared by the other cliques, generating a partial coloring. Note that, even after fixing its "pivot" node with a specific color, any given n-size clique will still has $(n-1)!$ possible valid colorings. Without loss of generality, let us select exactly one of the other $n-1$ nodes from this fully colored clique with B and define this to be a "link" node colored in green. Now consider another extended stencil graph ESG' and again choose two cliques in it. Note that these two cliques may not be the same ones considered previously. One of these cliques can be chosen such that it has the same coloring B, but its "link" node is now the "pivot" node of this particular ESG as seen in Fig.9(b). If the ESG is perfect, then all the cliques must have all the colors, so there must exist another clique in ESG' such that it contains the "pivot" node, keeping the corresponding green color in that particular location, and can keep the partial coloring from the clique in ESG plus (color that particular node in orange). Let's call this coloring of a clique

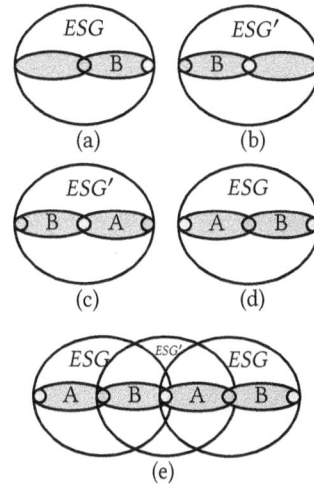

Figure 9: (a) Instance of the ESG with two cliques colored.(b) Instance of the gluing ESG (ESG') with the coloring reversed.(c) continuous sequence ESG-$ESG'$$ESG$- with repeated coloring

"A". This is one of the (n-1)! previously mentioned valid colorings. This arrangement can be seen in 9 (c). We can then use coloring "A" to color the original partially colored clique from ESG since it preserved that partial coloring, fig. 9 (d). From this it follows that we can "glue" ESG with ESG' by an induced subgraph that includes the maximum clique colored "B". Let's call the resulting graph $<ESG+ESG'>$. Since both graphs are perfect with the same chromatic number, and we glue them by an induced subgraph that includes a maximum clique then $<ESG+ESG'>$ is also perfect and retains the same chromatic number. We can now repeat the procedure but now gluing $<ESG+ESG'>$ to ESG by an induced subgraph that includes the maximum clique colored "A", generation $<ESG+ESG'+ESG>$, which again retains perfectness and the chromatic number for the aforementioned reasons. We can continue doing this indefinitely. Since we only need one intermediate gluing graph ESG' before we can reuse the coloring of ESG, then it is obvious that the coloring has a maximum distance until it repeats. In the worst case, this distance is the width of the ESG in that particular direction.

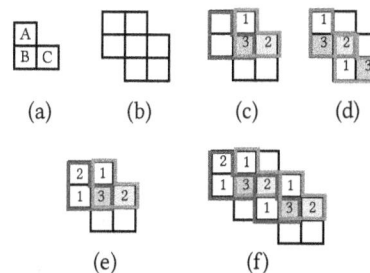

Figure 10: (a) An example stencil. (b) Extended stencil graph of the sample stencil. (c) ESG with valid coloring for one clique. (d) Glue extension graph ESG' with two cliques colored. (e) ESG with valid colorings for two cliques (f) Glued chain $ESG - ESG' - ESG$ for the sample stencil.

This idea can be seen in more detail with a real stencil in figure 10.Here (a) is a three point stencil with nodes A,B, and C. (b) Shows the *ESG* of the sample stencil. In (c) we see a partial coloring of the *ESG* with labels 1,2 and 3. Only the red clique is fully colored. The blue clique only has node C colored. The center node of the *ESG* is the node shaded in orange, is assigned label 3, and the "Link" node in green, is assigned label 2. Now, in (d) we see another instance of the *ESG*. The only clique where the coloring from Red will make the "Link" node to be the "pivot" node is the clique in brown. Since all cliques must have all coloring labels due to the chromatic number of the graph being equal to the number of nodes in the stencil, then it follows that there must exist a clique such that it has node C labeled 3 . Note that we have two options ((N-1)! with n=3), one with label 2 in position B, and another with the label 2 in position A, light blue. Only placing label 2 in position A allows for a valid coloring of the entire *ESG*, generating the coloring from the light blue clique. We can use this coloring to complete the partial coloring of the blue clique, since the *ESG* includes all interactions of a stencil with another (e). Finally in (f) we can see how we can indefinitely glue the graphs (by means of *ESG'*) while keeping the same chromatic number and with a repeating coloring. On top of that, since this graph is perfect, then there exists a polynomial time algorithm to color it.

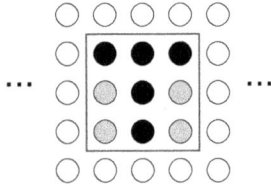

Figure 11: Stencil (black) and the circumscribing square (blue). Nodes in gray are potential candidates to be added

If, for a given stencil S, its extended stencil graph $ESG(S)$ is not perfect, i.e., $\chi(ESG(S)) > w(S)$, where $w(S)$ denotes the size of the stencil S. Unfortunately, the complete coloring of the entire memory access conflict graph can not be obtained by repeating the optimal coloring of the extended stencil graph. In this case, we have to iteratively add nodes to augment the original stencil until the resulting *ESG* of this modified stencil becomes perfect. To do this, we consider the smallest $m \times m$ circumscribing rectangle of the original stencil, perform an iterative search, and consider all C_n^k possible combinations of added nodes from inside the square, as seen in figure 11, where n is the number of nodes in the square but not in the stencil and for all k from 1 to n in incremental order to find a solution with the best chromatic number (and associated number of added nodes) that produces a perfect extended graph. Since we have a finite candidate solutions, this algorithm will terminate. However, why this search will result the optimal solution, i.e, the minimum number of memory banks to guarantee conflict-free coloring and periodic mapping, remains to be proven.

Fig. 1 presents the algorithm that performs the above iterative search. Note that if we add more nodes (and the corresponding edges) the original graph, with the original stencil, becomes a common induced subgraph. This means that if a valid periodic coloring for the new graph is found, then this solution will also solve the desired periodicity coloring scheme desired for the original one. We now prove that this algorithm results in the optimal partition factor. The following proof consists of two steps.

First we prove that this search algorithm terminates. Because the circumscribing square contains finite number of nodes, we only

---

Data: Stencil(P)
Result: Periodic coloring(PC)
CS ← smallest m×m square such that P ⊂ CS ;
TN ← CS - P;
for i ∈ 1...|*TN*| **do**
　forall the EN s.t. EN ⊆ TN and |EN|==i **do**
　　EG ← EG(P+EN);
　　if x(EG)==|P|+i **then**
　　　Terminate and return Optimal Coloring(EG);
　　end
　end
end

Algorithm 1: Node addition algorithm

have a finite number of possible candidate nodes sets to consider. Additionally, the final square augmented stencil is guaranteed to produce perfect extended stencil graph. This is because that any $m \times m$ square is always going to generate a perfect *ESG* since the Rook's graph has m^2 and can be directly mapped to an order m^2 Latin Square where every instance of the $m \times m$ stencil is surrounded by 3 or more same sized neighbors to form the aforementioned Latin square. One example of this condition is seen in the Sudoku game where 3×3 stencils form a larger 9×9 grid where each row and column has all the 9 symbols without repetition, but more importantly, each of the non-overlapping 3×3 squares has a permutation the 9 symbols, making it also a Gerechte square. Thus we know that since the geometry and maximum amount of nodes (and the largest number of colors) needed to obtain a periodic coloring for a given arbitrary stencil is the smallest circumscribing square that contains the stencil, then we can ensure that we will find at least one solution which is the all the nodes in the circumscribing square itself. In other words, we will always find a solution in the circumscribing square. This will also provide the upper limit to the number of colors needed to generate a periodic coloring.

Second, we argue optimality because of the incremental nature of the search in the solution space. We first try all sets of added nodes with cardinality 1 and increase it until we find an answer that generates a perfect Extended graph. We need to show that no better solution can be obtained by selecting nodes outside of it. We proceed to demonstrate by contradiction, using the properties of the Extended graph, that no such node exist that selecting it, will provide a better solution in terms of chromatic number. Assume the best solution found S_i has i added nodes from the circumscribing square with chromatic number k. Now assume that there exists a node(or set of nodes) outside the circumscribing square such that considering it would yield a periodic coloring with $i - 1$ added nodes and $k - 1$ colors. Given the vertex-transitive property of Rook's graphs, and the fact that this property is retained when the reduced graph is perfect, one can switch the relative position of the selected node(s) with nodes inside the circumscribing square and obtain an isomorphic graph using nodes entirely inside said region. Thus, since the search is done incrementally, considering all combinations of increasingly large sets of nodes inside the square, if such solution with $i - 1$ nodes and $k - 1$ colors exist, it must have been considered when exploring the previous sets considering only points inside the circumscribing square.

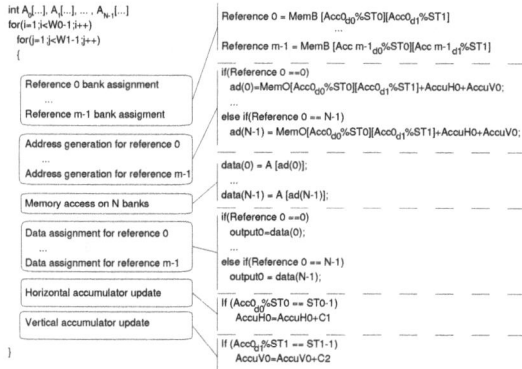

Figure 12: Template of transformed code

6 RESULTS AND ANALYSIS

To validate the performance benefits of our graph-based memory banking scheme, we start with inputting the memory access patterns of all test benchmarks into a Matlab script which computes the bank assignment and relative offset inside a super-tile for all memory locations. A Matlab script takes the information about the bank and offset super-tile and automatically generates new transformed code in C. This transformed C code is then used as an input to the Vivado HLS 2016.2 from Xilinx, which generates the HDL files in Verilog. The software also automatically generates a Vivado HLx 2016.2 project with the Verilog code already included. This project is synthesized and implemented. This software suite is also the same tool used to report post implementation resource usage and power estimation. To illustrate, we have listed a transformed code snippet in Fig. 12.

Six loop kernels with different access patterns are selected from a wide range of realistic applications, such as medical image processing and H.264 motion compensation. In our experiments, we mainly focus on the effects brought by different access patterns. The detailed experimental results are shown in Table 1 and Table 2. To compare, we also implemented the GMP method [9] for the same set of benchmarks and incorporated the results from [14] for the common ones (Bicubic, Deconv, Motion H, and Sobel). To do a fair comparison the original C code has the same structure for both sets of benchmarks, only calling different functions when testing GMP and our method. In all experimental runs, we turned on the loop pipelining setting in Vivado and set the target throughout with the iteration interval (II) to be 1, which requires all of the memory accesses in the same iteration to be in one clock cycle. For the hardware usage and energy consumption, we chose the target device to be the XC7K160tffg676-3 Kintex-7 FPGA for both Vivado HLS 2016.2 and Vivado Hlx 2016.2, and a bank size of 512 elements each in order to use one full RAMB18E1 block with a data width of 32 bits plus 4 bits of parity in single port mode. The results obtained can be seen in Table 1

Due to the regularity of the repeating pattern, the problem of computing intra bank offsets becomes an extension of the above memory bank mapping problem where we have a rectangle with a repeating pattern, this time intra bank offsets. First, for the upper $d-1$ dimensions, we want to calculate number of elements belonging to a particular bank that are in a $d-2$ dimensional space. This is, for 3-D matrix, we want to calculate how many elements are of each bank first in a cube with base vectors $[a_2, 0, 0], [0, w_1, 0], [0, 0, w_0]$, then in a rectangle with base vectors $[0, 0, 0], [0, a_1, 0], [0, 0, w_0]$, and finally in one of the repeating regions. The maximum of these

Table 1: Resource utilization and clock period comparison

		Bank #	CP(ns)	DSPs	FFs	LUTs	Pow.(mW)	Pipeline(#)
Denoise	GMP	4	2.1	0	254	438	754	8
	Ours	4	1.9	0	284	440	474	7
	Improv. (%)	0	9.52	0	-11.81	≈0	37.13	12.5
Bicubic	GMP	4	2.1	0	229	391	738	8
	Trace	4	3.66	0	212	184	N/R	N/R
	Ours	4	1.9	0	276	437	491	7
	Improv.(%)	0	9.52	0	-30.18	-137.5	33.45	12.5
Deconv	GMP	5	2.5	5	1320	1796	710	26
	Trace	5	3.37	10	383	541	N/R	N/R
	Ours	5	2	0	370	633	795	7
	Improv.(%)	0	20	100	3.39	-17	-11.97	73
MotionH	GMP	6	2.5	6	1783	2867	920	25
	Trace (Motion L)	6	3.31	6	392	425	N/R	N/R
	Ours	6	2	0	426	725	951	7
	Improv.(%)	0	20	100	-8.67	-70.59	-3.7	72
Sobel	GMP	9	2.5	9	3213	5792	1347	24
	Ours	9	2.2	0	606	1416	1340	7
	Improv.(%)	0	12	100	15.72	-33.71	≈0	70.8
12-Point	GMP	14	2.8	12	5108	9116	1687	34
	Ours	12	2.4	0	806	2159	1895	7
	Improv. (%)	14.3	14.3	100	84.22	76.3	-12.3	79
Average(%)		2.38	14.21	66.67	-8.77	-30.42	7.1	53.3

values for each dimension are then stored in memory. Once this is done, the intra bank offset becomes a function of the intra region offset and, 2 accumulators per access for the 2D case. One to store the number of elements before it in the same row of super-tiles, and another with the number of elements in the previous rows of super-tile. $\text{Offset}_{\text{Acc}_k} = \text{Mem}_O[X_0 \bmod a_0, \ldots, X_{d-1} \bmod a_{d-1}] + \text{Acc}_H + \text{Acc}_V$ Similarly as with the bank access, one can use accumulators and counters instead of costly modulo operation to access all the dimensions of the rectangle every iteration.

It is worth noting that the internal offset of the rectangle stored in Mem_O can be carefully arranged to reduce memory waste. By keeping the lower offsets in the area of the region that will always be within the bounds of the matrix under consideration, and assigning the higher ones to the areas that represent the smaller area for the other dimensions, we can effectively reduce the total memory waste. The highest offsets being located in the region that is less frequently accessed.

In figure 13 we see the size of the matrix in one dimension is an integer multiple of the size of the super-tile in dimension d_0, then we will only incur in wasted memory in the last iteration of the complementary loop. With this in mind, we can keep the lowest offsets in the area of the super-tile that are always going to be within the bounds, thus in the last iteration, such indexes will not be accessed and we have reduced memory waste to 0. The order of the offsets in each of the zones can be arbitrary and does not affect memory waste in any form.

The final amount of memory overhead can be calculated by:

$$\text{Overhead} = \sum_{i=0}^{d-1} ((\lceil \frac{w_i}{STi} \rceil - w_i) \times \prod_{k!=i} w_k) \qquad (3)$$

The main results, obtained from synthesizing both mapping functions and their respective address calculation logic ([9] and ours) and comparing it with the reported results from [14], can be seen in table 1. Here we see that our method can not only achieve better

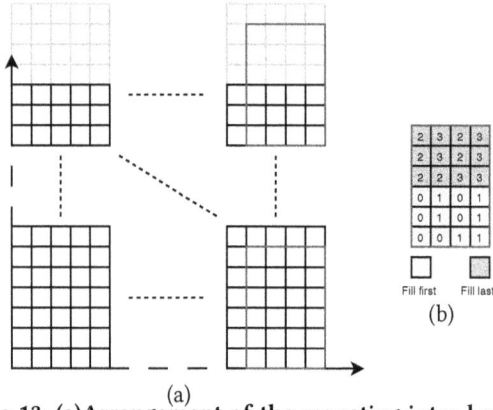

Figure 13: (a)Arrangement of the repeating intra bank off-set rectangle of for an m x n matrix using a 4 x 6 rectangle. (b)Mem_O offsets

partition factor for certain stencils, as seen in the 12-point stencil, and no worse in general but also achieve reduced resource utilization and clock period. The reduction of the clock period across the board comes from the capabilities of the FPGA fabric to synthesize a small distributed multidimensional array with fine grain access to all its elements with low hardware usage. The elimination of many of the division and multiplication operations from [9] and [14], using instead a quick access to the aforementioned memory, and only a few modulo operations, some multiplication, and additions (which are also needed in [9] and [14]) account for the 100% reduction in DSP usage and decrease hardware recourse utilization in general. For small stencils, such as Denoise, we see that the implementing the mapping and address calculation function from [9] is actually more efficient in terms of hardware utilization, but our method scales much better as the stencil size grows. But compared with [14] we have an increase in hardware utilization for both LUT's and FF.

Table 2: Memory waste comparison

		Memory overhead (elements)				
		SD	HD	FHD	WQXGA	4K
		640x480	1280x720	1920x1080	2560x1600	3840x2160
Denoise	GMP	0	0	0	0	0
	Ours	0	0	0	0	0
	Improv.	0%	0%	0%	0%	0%
Bicubic	GMP	0	0	0	0	0
	Ours	0	0	0	0	0
	Improv.	0%	0%	0%	0%	0%
Deconv	GMP	0	0	0	0	0
	Ours	0	0	0	0	0
	Improv.	0%	0%	0%	0%	0%
MotionH	GMP	960	2880	0	3200	0
	Ours	960	2880	0	3200	0
	Improv.	0%	0%	0%	0%	0%
Sobel	GMP	3840	5040	6480	8000	6480
	Ours	960	720	0	8324	0
	Improv.	75%	85.7%	100%	-4%	100%
12-Point	GMP	1920	5759	12960	3180	21591
	Ours	960	0	0	8324	0
	Improv.	50%	100%	100%	-2261.7%	100%
Average		20.8%	30.95%	33.33%	-34%	33.33%

Another important result is the comparison between the memory overhead resulting from the padding method in [9] and our address calculation method. In both cases, memory overhead is required to generate a regular and simple intra-bank address calculation function. The improved memory overhead in comparison

to [9] comes from the a ability to generate arbitrary offsets inside the repeating region. This in turn allows for a better control of how much space is wasted each row for different problem sizes while the method in [9] always needs to complete a sequence of N x B elements where N is the partition factor obtained by their method and B is the block size. There are some cases however that the k-dimensionality of our mapping function generates memory overhead in all dimensions while the method in [9] being one dimensional always generates overhead in just one. In this cases, the padding in [9] can be lower than ours, but this is not generally the case.

7 CONCLUSIONS

In this paper, we have presented a method based entirely on graph theory that allows for the automatic calculation of not only the optimal partition factor for any stencil, but also an usable mapping with said partition factor as a byproduct. This method not only ensures optimality, but also provides an actual upper bound to the partition factor needed to obtain an partition scheme that is finite but can be used to cover an arbitrarily larger memory space of any dimensionality.

ACKNOWLEDGEMENT

This material is based upon work supported by the National Science Foundation under Grant No. 1319884 and 1553056.

REFERENCES

[1] Alessandro Cilardo and Luca Gallo. 2015. Improving Multibank Memory Access Parallelism with Lattice-Based Partitioning. *ACM Trans. Archit. Code Optim.* 11 (2015), 45:1–45:25.
[2] Jason Cong, Wei Jiang, Bin Liu, and Yi Zou. 2009. Automatic Memory Partitioning and Scheduling for Throughput and Power Optimization. In *IEEE/ACM International Conference on Computer-Aided Design Digest of Technical Papers*.
[3] Alain Darte, IEEE Computer Society Member, Robert Schreiber, and Gilles Villard. 2005. Lattice-Based Memory Allocation. *IEEE Trans. Comput.* 10 (2005).
[4] Juan Escobedo and Mingjie Lin. 2017. Tessellating Memory Space for Parallel Access. In *ASP-DAC*.
[5] Chenyue Meng, Shouyi Yin, Peng Ouyang, Leibo Liu, and Shaojun Wei. 2015. Efficient Memory Partitioning for Parallel Data Access in Multidimensional Arrays. In *Proceedings of the 52Nd Annual Design Automation Conference*.
[6] Ed Scheinerman. 2008. Matgraph. Online. (March 2008). https://www.mathworks.com/matlabcentral/fileexchange/19218-matgraph.
[7] Henry D. Shapiro. 1978. Theoretical Limitations on the Efficent Use of Parallel Memories. *IEEE Trans. Comput.* c-27 (1978).
[8] Chariya Uiyyasathian and Supaporn Saduakdee. 2009. Perfect Glued Graphs at Complete Clones. *Journal of Mathematics Research* 1, 1 (2009), 25 – 30. https://doi.org/10.5539/jmr.v1n1p25
[9] Yuxin Wang, Peng Li, and Jason Cong. 2014. Theory and Algorithm for Generalized Memory Partitioning in High-level Synthesis. In *Proceedings of the 2014 ACM/SIGDA International Symposium on Field-programmable Gate Arrays (FPGA '14)*. 199–208. https://doi.org/10.1145/2554688.2554780
[10] Avi Wigderson. 1983. Improving the Performance Guarantee for Approximate Graph Coloring. *Journal of the Association for Computing Machinery* 30 (1983), 729–735.
[11] Harry A.G. Wijshoff. 1989. *Data Organization in Parallel Computers*. Springer US. XIV, 248 pages. https://doi.org/10.1007/978-1-4613-1711-1
[12] H. A. G. Wijshoff and J. Van Leeuwen. 1984. Arbitrary versus Periodic Storage Schemes and Tessellations of the Plane Using One Type of Polyomino. *Information and Control* 62 (1984), 1–25.
[13] H. A. G. Wijshoff and J. Van Leeuwen. 1987. On Linear Skewing Schemes and d-Ordered Vectors. *IEEE Trans. Comput.* C-36 (1987).
[14] Yuan Zhou, Khalid Musa Al-Hawaj, and Zhiru Zhang. 2017. A New Approach to Automatic Memory Banking Using Trace-Based Address Mining. In *Proceedings of the 2017 ACM/SIGDA International Symposium on Field-Programmable Gate Arrays (FPGA '17)*. ACM, New York, NY, USA, 179–188. https://doi.org/10.1145/3020078.3021734

Architecture Exploration for HLS-Oriented FPGA Debug Overlays

Al-Shahna Jamal
University of British Columbia
alshahnaj@ece.ubc.ca

Jeffrey Goeders
Brigham-Young University
jgoeders@byu.edu

Steven J.E. Wilton
University of British Columbia
stevew@ece.ubc.ca

ABSTRACT

High-Level Synthesis (HLS) promises improved designer productivity, but requires a debug ecosystem that allows designers to debug in the context of the original source code. Recent work has presented in-system debug frameworks where instrumentation added to the design collects trace data as the circuit runs, and a software tool that allows the user to replay the execution using the captured data. When searching for the root cause of a bug, the designer may need to modify the instrumentation to collect data from a new part of the design, requiring a lengthy recompile.

In this paper, we propose a flexible debug overlay family that provides software-like debug turn-around times for HLS generated circuits. At compile time, the overlay is added to the design and compiled. At debug time, the overlay can be configured many times to implement specific debug scenarios without a recompilation. This paper first outlines a number of "capabilities" that such an overlay should have, and then describes architectural support for each of these capabilities. The cheapest overlay variant allows selective variable tracing with only a 1.7% increase in area overhead from the baseline debug instrumentation, while the deluxe variant offers 2x-7x improvement in trace buffer memory utilization with conditional buffer freeze support.

CCS CONCEPTS

• **Hardware** → **VLSI**; **EDA**; **Design for debug**;

KEYWORDS

Field-Programmable Gate Array; Debugging; High-Level Synthesis

ACM Reference format:
Al-Shahna Jamal, Jeffrey Goeders, and Steven J.E. Wilton. 2018. Architecture Exploration for HLS-Oriented FPGA Debug Overlays. In *Proceedings of 2018 ACM/SIGDA International Symposium on Field-Programmable Gate Arrays, Monterey, CA, USA, February 25–27, 2018 (FPGA '18),* 10 pages.
https://doi.org/10.1145/3174243.3174254

1 INTRODUCTION

Recent years have seen the emergence of Field-Programmable Gate Arrays (FPGAs) as mainstream compute accelerators. Companies

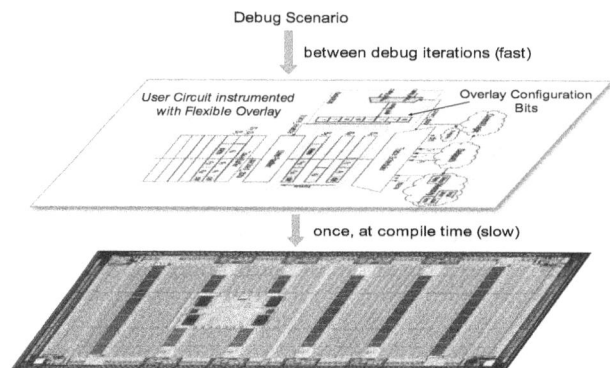

Figure 1: Debug Overlay

such as Amazon, IBM, Baidu, and Microsoft have invested significant resources understanding how FPGAs can be used to accelerate cloud-based computing. For FPGAs to thrive in this new role, new programming frameworks are essential. FPGA vendors such as Xilinx and Intel have responded by creating high-level synthesis (HLS) tools [3, 22] which allow designers to specify behaviour in a software language (C/OpenCL) and automatically compile this code to a hardware implementation. HLS technology promises significant productivity improvements and may someday open the door for software designers to enjoy the advantages of FPGAs.

An essential part of these frameworks is the ability to debug and optimize a design. Vendor tools allow for debug and optimization by compiling the design to RTL and using RTL simulation tools. When debugging and optimizing anything but a simple kernel, however, RTL simulation may not be sufficient. In larger systems, some bugs may only appear after long run-times, meaning they can not practically be observed using simulation. Other bugs may manifest only when running in conjunction with legacy IP that may not be designed using HLS technologies. When finding these kinds of bugs, the only option may be to run the design on an FPGA.

Debugging a design running on an FPGA is challenging. Limited I/O pins means that it is difficult to observe the internal behaviour of a design. FPGA vendors provide tools such as SignalTap II [1], and Vivado's ILA core [21] which store the behaviour of selected signals on-chip for later interrogation. However, these tools provide visibility in the context of the RTL design rather than the original source code. Understanding the waveforms produced by these tools and relating them to the original software-like code is difficult, especially if the HLS tool has heavily optimized the code. There has been a significant amount of work in recent years to address this problem. Prior work such as [5, 9, 12, 14, 17] provide the ability to debug an HLS design as it is running on an FPGA. Critically, these systems provide the ability to run the design at-speed, and record variables in on-chip memories for later replay using a familiar software-like debugging GUI.

Typically, many *debug turns* are required to find the root cause of unexpected behaviour. Each debug turn involves instrumenting and compiling the design, running the chip, observing the behaviour of selected variables, and using this information to either deduce the root cause or set up another debug run. In existing frameworks such as [9], the variables that are to be traced must be *determined at compile time*. As the user refines his or her understanding of the behaviour of the design, he or she may wish to change the set of signals observed, however, this requires a complete recompile of both the user design and the instrumentation. Recompiling the design for each debug turn is slow and can limit debug productivity.

For small circuits, it is possible to record all user-visible variables each time the circuit is run [9], however this is infeasible for large circuits (such as those with many parallel functional units), since it would require either extremely large trace buffers or recording activity for only very short periods of time.

In this paper, we present a configurable overlay architecture which provides *software-like turn-around times between debug turns for circuits created by an HLS tool* (i.e. on the order of milliseconds). As shown in Figure 1, an RTL description of the overlay architecture is added to the user circuit before it is compiled. The overlay is flexible enough to implement a variety of *debug scenarios*; debug scenarios may describe specific variables that should be captured or regions of code that should be traced. At debug time, between debug turns, the user can configure the overlay to implement a particular debug scenario *without recompiling the design or overlay*. In this way, the user can rapidly switch between debug scenarios as his or her understanding of the behaviour of the circuit evolves, while also ensuring that the user circuit does not change between debug turns. Unlike previous debug overlays [8] and commercial ILAs (eg. Chipscope/SignalTap), our architecture is optimized for HLS circuits and is intended to be tightly integrated into an HLS tool, allowing the instrumentation to take advantage of scheduling/allocation information within the HLS tool.

The flexibility of our overlay fabric comes at a cost. The debug scenario implemented by the fabric is encoded in a set of "overlay configuration bits" which represent area overhead in the fabric. Clearly, there is a trade-off between the amount of flexibility and the fabric's overhead. In addition to describing the basic overlay architecture, this paper presents an architecture study to better understand this trade-off. We identify a set of "capabilities" and determine how much overhead is incurred if each capability is supported by the fabric. Using this information, along with an estimate of how much chip area is left unused by a user circuit, an automatic tool could judiciously determine which capabilities to include when creating the overlay architecture for a given user circuit. The results of our architecture study would be essential information for FPGA vendors that wish to create such a tool.

This paper is organized as follows. Section 2 presents related work. Our overall debug flow is described in Section 3. Section 4 then describes the overlay debug capabilities that we consider. The architectural and CAD support for these capabilities will be described in Section 5. Section 6 will present results that quantify

the amount of overhead required for each capability. Section 7 will conclude the paper.

2 RELATED WORK

Early on-chip debugging work focused on scan-chains to read the values of internal signals, however, these solutions only offer a single snapshot of the state rather than a history of variable behaviour [20]. Later work considered instrumenting a user circuit with on-chip memories, called *trace buffers* and access networks to capture the behaviour of signals as the chip runs [13, 18]. Commercial offerings that revolve around trace buffers are available [1, 21]. To support rapid reconfiguration of the debug logic, [8] proposed a fine-grained overlay in which instrumentation can be added to the FPGA on-the-fly using resources not used by the user circuit. A similar solution was proposed in [14] in which the user circuit and instrumentation are compiled into a parameterized bitstream, allowing rapid specialization at debug time.

The above solutions all view the user design as hardware. Although this sort of instrumentation can be applied to designs written in C and compiled using an HLS tool, doing so has a number of challenges. Forcing HLS designers to understand their design at the hardware level defeats much of the purpose of using HLS. The situation is even worse if the HLS tool performs scheduling and allocation optimizations, meaning there is not a one-to-one correspondence between registers in the hardware and user variables in the original code. In addition, instrumenting an HLS design presents an opportunity not available while instrumenting an RTL hardware design: since the HLS tool understands the schedule of the generated circuit, it can use this information to optimize the instrumentation on a circuit-by-circuit basis, leading to much more effective trace buffer utilization [9].

Early work on developing an HLS-oriented debugger was presented in [12] which used an FPGA's readback feature to take a snapshot of the state and map it back to the original Java code. Later frameworks were described in [5, 9, 17], all of which revolve around trace buffers. The work in [9] is the framework in which we evaluate our ideas; details of their instrumentation architecture will be provided in Section 5.1.

The frameworks in [5, 9, 17] include instrumentation that is added to the design at compile time. If the user wants to change the instrumentation at debug time, the instrumentation and user circuit needs to be recompiled. This is addressed in [15] which shows that it is possible to use a commercial incremental design flow to recompile only the parts of the instrumentation that change. This leads to an improvement in debug turn-around time of about 40% which is still far short of the software-like debug turn-around times that HLS users might expect.

Our work has similarities to hardware performance monitoring circuitry that can be added to a CPU [16]. Like ours, these monitoring cores can be configured to watch for specific events within the processor. Unlike ours, they are not intended to be flexible enough to support an arbitrary HLS circuit.

There has been related work on automatically finding a bug (eg. [7]) often using formal methods. This is somewhat orthogonal to our approach. We believe that the most difficult and complex bugs that are the focus of run-time debugging are often multi-faceted in

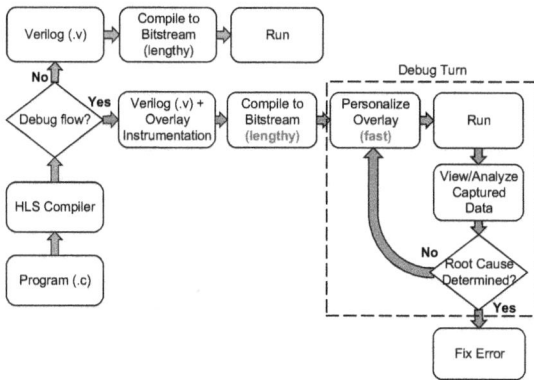

Figure 2: HLS Overlay Debug Flow

nature, and thus require a human engineer in the loop. Our goal is to give the user as much information as possible to help him or her find the root cause of a bug.

3 OVERALL DEBUG OVERLAY APPROACH

Figure 2 shows our overall framework. The user first compiles a C program to a Hardware Description Language (HDL) representation using an HLS tool (we use LegUp [6]). The HLS tool is modified to automatically add instrumentation to the user circuit, and creates a debug database, which contains a mapping between C-code variables and signals/memories in the RTL code, as well as scheduling information regarding when variables are updated. The circuit is then compiled using a vendor-specific tool-chain (we use Quartus II) and implemented on an FPGA.

Before running the circuit, the user sets up a *debug scenario*. A debug scenario is a collection of variables or region of code that is to be traced; Section 4 will describe the set of debug scenarios that we consider in this paper. The debug scenario is then mapped to the overlay. The flexibility of the overlay to implement a variety of debug scenarios comes from a set of *overlay configuration bits*, similar to FPGA configuration bits. Since our overlay is just flexible enough to implement common debug scenarios, we can keep the number of these overlay configuration bits low, limiting overhead. In our overlay, some configuration bits are stored in on-chip RAM blocks, meaning we can use vendor's in-system memory content editor to update these bits, and others are stored in registers that are accessible through the debug UART port. Unlike [8], the mapping from the debug overlay specification to the "bitstream" needed to configure the overlay is trivial, meaning the turn-around times between debug iterations is extremely small (milliseconds).

The circuit is then run, and the instrumentation records the behaviour of the selected signals in on-chip RAMs that have been configured as a circular buffer (the trace buffer); when the buffer fills up, old data is replaced with new data. The buffer continues to record data until either a breakpoint is reached or a predetermined condition indicates that recording should stop. At that point, the user can start a debug GUI (based on the one in [10]) and can single step through the design while observing the values of variables as they change. The data is taken from the recorded trace buffer, meaning the user is, in essence, *replaying* the execution that happened while the chip was running at-speed (the GUI in [10] also has

a "live mode" in which the design is single-stepped on the FPGA itself, however, this does not allow for running at-speed, which we believe is essential to capture many hard-to-find bugs).

Since the on-chip trace buffer is of a limited size, we can not store the entire run-time history of all variables and trace information. This means that, when debugging, the user can only view the behaviour of variables for a portion of the execution (called the *trace window*). After observing the behaviour of the code in the trace window, if the root cause of the bug can not be deduced, he or she can set up another debug scenario and repeat the process.

After debugging is complete, the user may choose to remove the overlay for production (possibly allowing the user to target a smaller FPGA) or leave the overlay in place, but disable it.

4 HLS DEBUG CAPABILITY INVENTORY

To quantify the flexibility of the overlay, we define three "capabilities" that an overlay can have: *Selective Variable Tracing*, *Selective Function Tracing*, and *Conditional Buffer Freeze*. An overlay can have any of these capabilities, or a combination of these capabilities. Each is described below.

Selective Variable Tracing: Selective Variable Tracing refers to the capability to configure the overlay, at debug time, to specify which variables should be traced. In [9], signals corresponding to *all* user-visible variables in the source code are traced. This provides the most software-like debug experience, since it allows the user to trace through a recorded execution and display the value of every variable at every step. However, for large designs, and in particular, designs with many parallel functional units, recording the behaviour of all variables may quickly consume the limited on-chip trace buffer. If fewer variables are recorded, then a longer *trace window* can be stored in the trace buffer, possibly making it easier for the user to understand the behaviour of the design and deduce the root cause of a bug.

In our implementation, the overlay is flexible enough that the user can specify any number of variables to trace (including all of them) within a debug turn. The user can therefore trade-off the number of variables for the trace window depth. Initially, the user may trace many variables to get a quick idea of the overall state of the system. In later debug iterations, the user may decide to focus on only a small subset of variables that he or she believes will reveal the problem.

Selective Function Tracing: Selective Function Tracing refers to the capability to specify, at debug time, specific function(s) of interest. Once the user identifies specific functions, the fabric records the activity only within those functions. This capability may be useful if the user has narrowed down the cause of a bug to a specific erroneous function output. By recording only data within the function, a longer trace of the function behaviour can be obtained.

There are two variants we will explore: (a) the user may wish to limit variable tracing to the specified function(s) but trace all control information (whether it is in the selected function or not), or (b) the user may wish to limit both the variable and control tracing to the specified function(s). The former mode would allow the user to single-step outside the function to understand the call path that led up to the invocation, and then focus on the variables within the function, while the latter would allow for a larger trace history within the function, but would not allow the user to single-step outside the selected function(s).

Conditional Buffer Freeze: Conditional Buffer Freeze refers to the capability to specify, at debug time, a condition that, when true, causes recording of data in the trace buffer to halt. After recording halts, the user can read out information in the trace buffer to understand what led up to that point. As an example, the user may set a freeze point to occur when a particular error flag goes high, or an argument to a function is not within an expected range. We distinguish between a freeze point and a breakpoint; in the former, the execution of the chip may continue, however, by freezing the contents of the trace buffer, the execution history up until the freeze point is preserved.

For efficiency reasons, our buffer freeze points are associated with *assignments* to variables rather than the variable itself. For example, the user may not specify that the buffer be frozen whenever a specified variable becomes a certain value. Instead the user can specify when a *specific assignment* to that variable results in the variable receiving a certain value (assignment is specified via source code line number). The reasons for this design decision will be described in Section 5.4.

Note that conditional buffer freeze is different than the conditional capture capability that may be familiar to hardware designers. Using conditional capture, designers can request that the trace buffer only record signals when a certain condition is true. If the condition changes over the execution of the circuit, this can create "gaps" in the recorded behaviour. In a hardware debug environment, these gaps can be clearly shown to the user using a waveform with X (unknown) regions to denote these gaps. In a software debug framework, however, it would be confusing if the user, while replaying the execution of the code by single-stepping, encountered unexpected short "dead zones" where the values of variables could not be displayed. In our system, the buffer freezes when a certain condition occurs, and does not start recording again until a new freeze point is configured or the design is re-run. This ensures that the area of code that can be replayed is contiguous, and provides the maximum visibility around a specified point of interest.

Although in our system, the designer specifies the conditional buffer freeze point in an interactive fashion, it would also be possible to create freeze points by automatically extracting assertions in the code, similar to [4]. In Section 5, we will consider several variants of an architecture that supports conditional buffer freeze; these variants differ in how complex a condition can be specified.

5 OVERLAY ARCHITECTURE

This section describes our overlay architecture family and algorithms to map a debug scenario to the overlay. Architectural support for each capability from Section 4 will be described separately.

5.1 Architectural Framework

The contributions presented in this paper build upon the HLS debug framework described in [9]. In this subsection, we describe this previously published framework.

Figure 3 shows the instrumentation from [9]. We assume that there is a single trace buffer, which is used to store the history of user-visible variables (both those stored within the user circuit

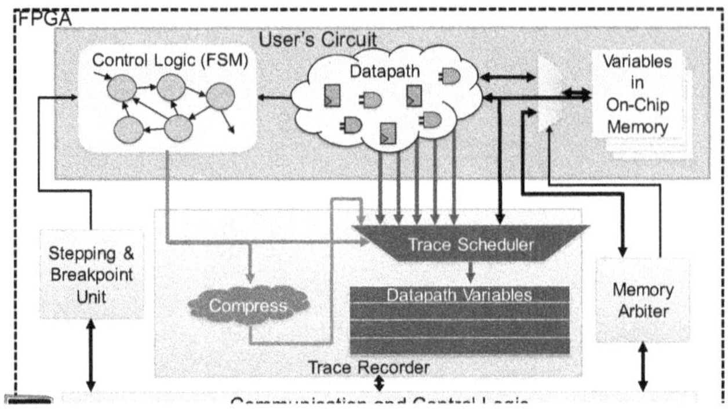

Figure 3: Baseline Instrumentation from [9] shows interaction with User Circuit and Debug Workstation

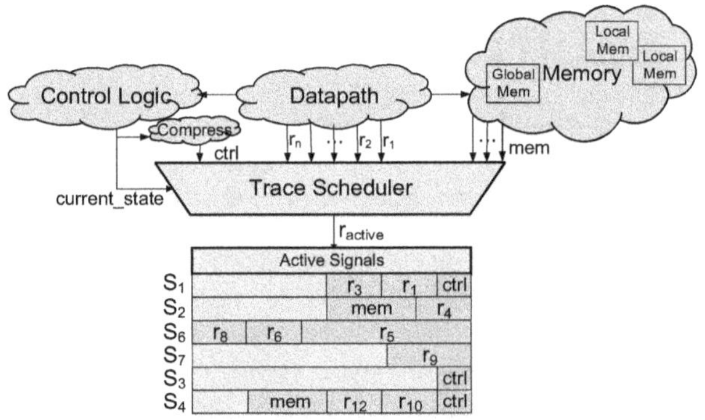

Figure 4: Baseline Trace Scheduler Instrumentation and trace buffer contents of hypothetical program

datapath and those that are mapped to memories), as well as sufficient control-flow information such that the control path can be reconstructed by the off-line debug GUI. The amount of memory allocated to the trace buffer can be chosen by the user.

In the simplest implementation, the trace buffer is updated every cycle in which any user variable is updated, or a new basic block in the source code is entered. In Figure 4, in the first cycle (State S_1), user variables r_3 and r_1 are updated, so their values are stored in the first line of the trace buffer. Control flow information is also stored in this cycle. In the second cycle (State S_2), user variable r_4 is updated, along with a variable that has been mapped to the global memory, so both updates are stored in the trace buffer. Notice that the width of the trace buffer must at least match the number of bits to be written in the worst-case state. Reference [9] describes optimization algorithms (named *delay-worst* and *delay-all*) which strategically delay writes to the trace buffer to balance the trace buffer width; these optimizations have been used in our framework.

Importantly, this trace scheduler is constructed on a circuit-by-circuit basis when the user circuit is instrumented and is optimized for both the user circuit and the set of variables to be recorded. Reference [9] shows that this leads to an improvement in the trace window size of between 50x and 100x.

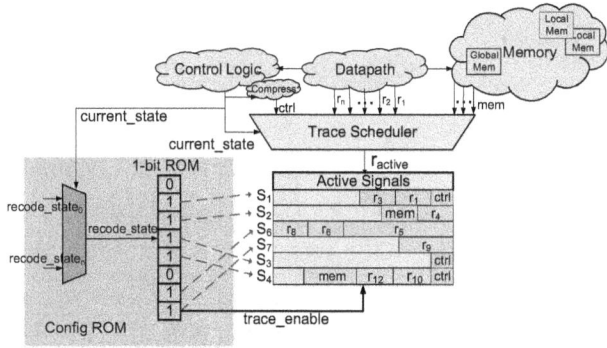

Figure 5: Selective Variable Selection - Variant A

5.2 Selective Variable Tracing

The remaining subsections of this section describes the architectural enhancements that are new in this paper. We first describe the architectural enhancements that will allow the user to select, at runtime, a subset of variables to trace. We present two variants of the architecture: *Variant A* which has the least overhead but may not make effective use of the trace buffer, and *Variant B* which will make more efficient use of the trace buffer, but at the expense of more area overhead.

Selective Variable Selection Architecture - Variant A: The first variant we consider is shown in Figure 5. The Signal Trace Scheduler and the Trace Buffer (both shown in green) are the same as in the baseline architecture (Figure 4). The 1-bit wide Config ROM and the multiplexer that feeds the address lines (shown on the bottom left) are new. The Config ROM contains the overlay configuration bits that encode which user variable(s) are to be recorded. Intuitively, it would make sense to include one configuration bit for each variable in the user circuit (to indicate if that variable should be recorded or not recorded), however, we found that this approach leads to large decoding logic which increases the overhead of our overlay unacceptably. Instead, we associate each configuration bit with one *state* in the user circuit. If a user variable is to be recorded, the configuration bits corresponding to all states in which that variable is updated are set to 1; this enables the write enable line of the trace buffer during those states. Since we wish to record all control flow information regardless of the user's variable selection, configuration bits corresponding to states in which control flow information is to be stored are also set to 1. As an example, Figure 6(a) shows the trace buffer contents after executing a hypothetical program in which all user variables are traced. If the user wishes to record only $r1$ and $r9$, then the trace buffer is *not* updated during states $S2$ and $S6$, leading to the more efficient packing in Figure 6(b) (note that the buffer still needs to be updated in states $S3$ and $S4$ because control-flow information is written during those states). This strategy causes the trace buffer to fill more slowly, meaning at the end of the run, a larger window of execution is available in the trace buffer, providing more information for the user as he or she seeks the root cause of a bug.

Note that, since several variables may be updated in the same state, unselected variables may also be inadvertently recorded. In Figure 6(b), even though the user has not selected $r3$, the value in $r3$ is still recorded in the first state, since $r1$ has been selected.

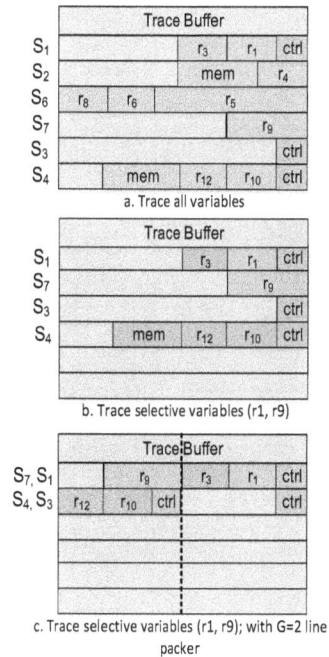

Figure 6: Selective Variable Tracing Examples

Similarly, $r12$ and $r10$ are recorded in the fourth line since the control flow information in that state must be recorded. This leads to a slightly less efficient use of trace buffer space than approaches such as [15] in which the compression circuitry is optimized to store *only* those variables that have been selected; in Section 6 we will quantify this impact.

In a naïve implementation, the depth of the 1-bit wide ROM would be equal to the number of states in the user circuit. However, in some states, no user variables are updated, and no control flow data needs to be captured, so no configuration bit is necessary. Thus, we use a multiplexer (the left-most multiplexer in Figure 5) to recode the state number (which is obtained from the user circuit) to a linear sequence of states in which at least one variable is updated (we call these *trace states*). The recoded state is then used to address the Config ROM to acquire the corresponding configuration bit for the trace buffer. In our benchmark circuits (listed in Section 6), we found that this approach reduces the depth of the ROM by about 50%. More importantly, it provides compatibility with HLS tools that do not encode their states sequentially.

The inputs to this recoding multiplexer are constants, inserted into the RTL by the modified HLS tool. It is important to emphasize that the circuitry in Figure 5 is constructed on a circuit-by-circuit basis. When the HLS tool compiles the user circuit, it knows the schedule and state encodings, and thus can create the instrumentation circuitry, including the values of these constants, optimized for that specific circuit. Since the multiplexer inputs are constant, significant area is reclaimed by the logic synthesis algorithm in the FPGA CAD suite as it optimizes the circuit.

In our implementation, the 1-bit ROM is implemented using one or more embedded FPGA memory blocks. This allows us to change the configuration bits at debug time, to implement a new debug scenario, without recompiling the circuit.

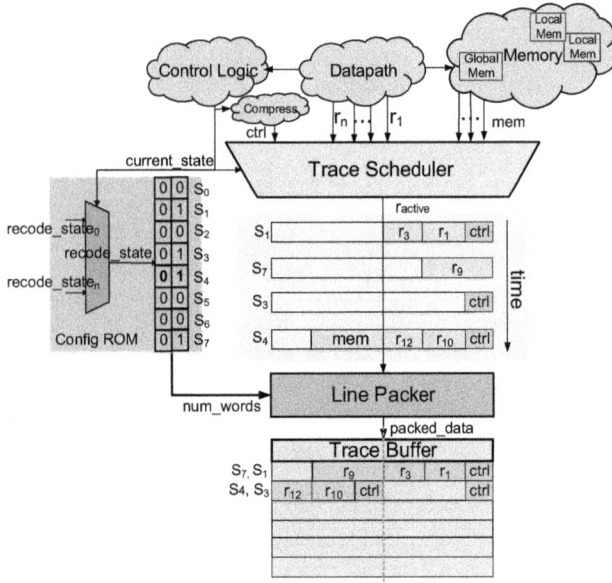

Figure 7: Selective Variable Selection - Variant B

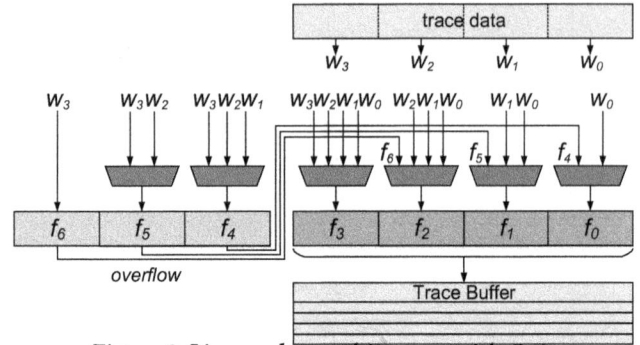

Figure 8: Line packer architecture with $G=4$

At debug time, an algorithm is needed to map a debug scenario (specified by the user using a GUI) to the values that will be stored in the overlay configuration cells. In the architecture of Figure 5, each overlay configuration bit corresponds to one state in the schedule of the user circuit. When the HLS tool creates the user circuit, it also creates a debug database which contains a list of all user variables that are updated in each state, as well as a list of when control flow information is generated. At debug time, when the user selects signals to observe, it is then straightforward to use this debug database to set the overlay configuration bits appropriately.

Selective Variable Selection Architecture - Variant B: When the overlay is constructed (at compile time), the trace buffer width is set to be equal to the largest number of bits that must be stored in a single state. In the example of Figure 6(a), the worst-case state is $S6$, so the width of the trace buffer is set to be the sum of the widths of all variables to be recorded in $S6$. At debug time, the trace buffer width can not be changed, meaning we may waste space in the trace buffer. In Figure 6(b), the trace buffer is not updated in $S6$, meaning the upper-order bits of every line in trace buffer remain unused. The severity of the problem increases as we reduce the number of variables selected. In this subsection, we show an alternative architecture, *Variant B*, which addresses this concern.

The major difference from the previous variant is the introduction of a *line packer* module, which is designed to pack partially used lines of trace data together into a single line in the trace buffer, thus making better use of memory. Figure 7 illustrates this module, and shows how data from two different states ($S1$ and $S7$) are combined into a single line in the trace buffer.

The line packer works by breaking up each incoming data line into G equally sized words (G is an architectural parameter representing the granularity of the line packer). As an example, Figure 7 shows a scenario where G=2. Increasing G splits the incoming data

into smaller words, allowing for a more fine grained packing, saving memory. However, as we will show shortly, increasing G also increases the area of the line packer.

In order for the line packer to operate, it must know which of the incoming G words contain important data to save to the buffer, and which contain data that can be discarded. To accomplish this, the 1-bit Config ROM from Variant A, is replaced with a multibit ROM. While in Variant A a single bit indicates whether or not the data line for a given state would be recorded, in Variant B, the ROM indicates how many words of the data line should be saved. Thus, if the data line is split into G words, the width of the Config ROM must be $\lceil log_2(G+1) \rceil$ bits.

It should be noted, that for a value n retrieved from the Config ROM, the line packer will save the *lower contiguous n* words of the data line. For example, in Figure 7, this means that if the user did not choose to observe the *mem* update in $S4$, then only the first word is saved. If *mem* was selected, then the entire line would be saved regardless of what the user chose to observe in the lower word. Although it would be possible to design a line packer that saved arbitrary (not necessarily contiguous) words from the data line, we found such a module would require a prohibitively large amount of area to build.

Like Variant A, Variant B is accompanied by a mapping algorithm that maps the user's variable selection to the ROM words. In this case, the algorithm can use the HLS schedule to determine how many selected variables are written each cycle, and the position of these variables in the trace buffer output, and set the ROM bits accordingly.

In the remainder of this subsection we describe how the line packer is constructed. Figure 8 illustrates the architecture of a $G=4$ line packer; we describe the operation in the context of this size line packer. The incoming data line is divided into G words ($w_3..w_0$). These incoming words are stored in a set of word-sized registers ($f_6..f_0$), which collect the incoming words and store them in the right-most unoccupied position. Once there are enough words stored to fill an entire line of the trace buffer (when $f_3..f_0$ are occupied), the four words are written out to the trace buffer.

While waiting for $f_3..f_0$ to populate, more words may arrive in a cycle than can be saved in the unpopulated $f_3..f_0$ registers. For this reason, the line packer includes overflow registers ($f_6..f_4$). In the $G=4$ line packer, the worst case occurs when three words are stored in registers ($f_2..f_0$) and four words arrive at the same time. This necessitates a total of seven registers to prevent data loss (or $2G - 1$ for the general case). After $f_3..f_0$ is full, and the data is written out to the trace buffer, the occupied overflow words $f_6..f_4$ are transferred over to $f_2..f_0$ and any incoming words are stored into the lowest empty positions, again using the overflow if necessary.

All of this data movement is controlled by the *num_words* signal, coming from the Config ROM, which indicates how many words of data are entering the line packer each cycle. This signal is used to generate steering logic to control all of the multiplexers shown in the example.

Although the example shown in Figure 8 is for $G=4$, the same design can be used for any value of G. However, as G increases, the number of inputs to the multiplexers increase by the same rate. In the example the multiplexers have up to four inputs, but for example, if G were increased to 16, the multiplexers would have up to 16 inputs.

5.3 Selective Function Tracing

This subsection describes enhancements needed to enable Selective Function Tracing, which allows the user to indicate specific functions in the source code that should be traced.

To implement this capability, no changes to the architecture described in Subsection 5.2 are required. Changes are required in the CAD algorithm that maps the debug scenario to the overlay configuration bits. When the user selects one or more functions to be traced, the algorithm uses the debug database to determine which user variable assignments are associated with each selected function, and which states correspond to these assignments. Using the techniques from Subsection 5.2, the algorithm can then turn on the configuration bits for these states. Control flow information can be handled in one of two ways, as described in Section 4. In the "full control flow" mode, the algorithm turns on all overlay configuration bits corresponding to all states in which control flow information is written. In the "partial control flow" mode, the algorithm does not turn on states outside the selected function(s) in which control flow information is written.

A complexity arises if the HLS tool makes extensive use of function inlining. In such cases, it is often difficult to crisply delineate which state(s) correspond to the inlined function, and which correspond to the parent function, since operations from each function can be mapped to the same state. To accommodate inlining, if an inlined function is selected for tracing, we conservatively trace all states in the parent function as well.

Because there are no changes required to the architecture, there are no area implications of supporting this capability. However, this capability does affect the achievable trace window; this will be investigated in Section 6.

5.4 Conditional Buffer Freeze

This subsection describes the architectural enhancements necessary to support the conditional buffer freeze capability.

Our conditional buffer freeze architecture is parameterized by C which is the number of conditions upon which a freeze point can depend. As shown in Figure 9, the architecture consists of C comparison subunits and a single Trace Buffer Write Controller.

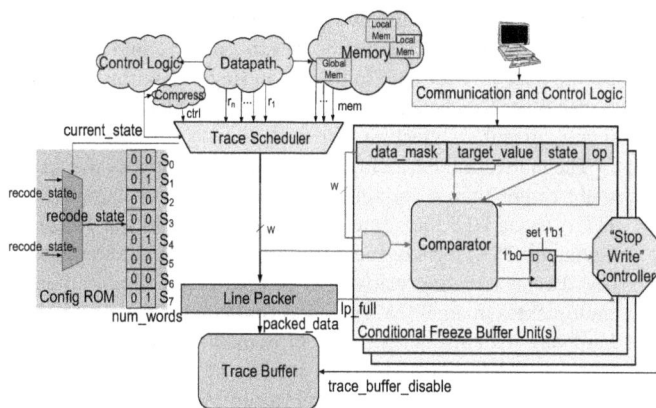

Figure 9: Conditional Buffer Freeze Architecture

Each comparison subunit monitors the running circuit for a single condition, and the supported operations of the comparator are $=$, $>$, $<$, $\geq$, $\leq$, and $\neq$. Each subunit contains a wide Configuration Register that can be configured at debug time via the debug UART port connected to the GUI; the values of this register are discussed next.

As described in Section 4, our freeze point architecture triggers when a specific *assignment* assigns a value that meets a specified condition. In the baseline architecture, the value of each assignment appears at the output of the trace scheduler multiplexer during a specific state. When the user wishes to set a conditional freeze point, the debug database is used to determine the state that the value from this assignment will appear at the output of the trace multiplexer, and this state is stored in the *state* field in the Configuration Register. Since several variable values may appear at the output of the trace multiplexer in the same cycle, it is necessary to select the proper subset of bits in the multi-bit trace multiplexer output. Rather than providing a barrel shifter (which would be large), a *data_mask* is generated (by the algorithm that maps the debug scenario to the overlay) to isolate the variable selected, along with a *target_value* which has been scaled appropriately so that the comparison can be performed without shifting. Both the mask and target values are fields within the Configuration Register, and each is as wide as the trace multiplexer output. During operation, the comparison subunit monitors the state of the user circuit, and when it matches the state specified in the Configuration Register, it masks the appropriate field and performs the comparison operation described in the *op* field of the Configuration Register. If the condition is true, a signal is sent to the Trace Buffer Write Controller.

The Trace Buffer Write Controller receives signals from all C comparison subunits, and when any of these signals becomes true, it stops writing to the trace buffer. In this way, the Trace Buffer Write Controller performs an "or" operation of the C comparison results. An "and" reduction is not supported; unlike a design specified at the RTL level, in an HLS design, the user can not be sure that any two assignments occur simultaneously in the hardware, due to optimizations that may be performed by the HLS tool. Because it may be useful to have some data in the trace buffer *after* the trigger, it is possible to continue to store data for several additional cycles, providing a sliding window of data around the point of interest selected by the user. The number of extra cycles could be specified by the user in another Configuration Register within the Trace Buffer Write Controller, however we do not implement this feature in our current architecture.

The motivation for basing each condition on a particular assignment rather than a variable value can now be explained. Many FPGA-based HLS tools (including LegUp) use a Static Single Assignment (SSA) form of the circuit's Intermediate Representation (IR). Because of the relatively high area required to implement multiplexers in an FPGA, HLS tools that target FPGAs often build hardware with distinct registers for each SSA IR assignment. If we were to monitor a variable, independent of a specific assignment, we would have to build a multiplexer to select the current value from all hardware registers corresponding to that variable. Even if there was only one register associated with each variable, since, at compile time, we do not know which variable the user would select, we would have to build a multiplexer to select from among all user variables in the circuit, which would be prohibitive in terms of area. By reusing the trace multiplexer, our overlay suffers much less overhead.

There is an extra complexity if the selected assignment is part of a function that the HLS tool inlines into multiple parents. In that case, it is impossible to uniquely identify which copy of the assignment should be used to perform the comparison. Our approach is to expose this complexity to the user if it occurs, asking him or her to identify the specific instantiation of the inlined function that is of interest. It is important to note that from a user's perspective, setting a condition can be very user-friendly in the debugger GUI interface (i.e. clicking on a line of source code and entering a condition on the variable of interest).

6 RESULTS

The architectural variants described in this paper all allow the user to trade-off the trace window size and area overhead, with essentially zero compile time between debug iterations. In this section, we describe this trade-off for the various variants and show the impact of several architectural parameters.

6.1 Selective Variable Trace: Variant A

We first evaluate basic selective variable tracing architecture (Variant A – without the line packer) shown in Figure 5, and compare it to previous work where the trace scheduler is recompiled between each debug iteration [9, 15]. Table 1 shows the impact on trace window size as we vary the proportion of user-visible variables that are traced. To gather these results, we used the CHStone benchmark suite and the FFT_Transpose benchmark from MachSuite [11, 19]. For each benchmark, we simulated the design using Modelsim and measured the number of cycles that are stored within the trace window, averaged over the run of the program (a higher number means that the trace buffer is being used more efficiently, and that there is more information available to the off-line debugging GUI). In all cases, a 100Kb trace buffer was assumed. In selecting a subset of variables to observe, we selected variables randomly; we average the results over five runs with different seeds to minimize the impact of especially bad or good variable selections.

Table 1: Trace Window Length Results

Benchmark	Baseline from [9]			Configurable Trace Variant A		
	Variable Selection			Variable Selection		
	100%	50%	25%	100%	50%	25%
adpcm	2247	2876	3562	2247	2412	2870
aes	3650	8972	17165	3650	5762	7321
blowfish	6113	8266	10525	6113	6873	9482
dfadd	1047	1366	1822	1047	1056	1095
dfdiv	3391	4363	5073	3391	3461	3490
dfmul	960	1169	1458	960	1043	1145
dfsin	2101	2410	2970	2101	2164	2230
gsm	386	1597	2391	386	386	386
jpeg	2201	3638	4652	2201	2233	2285
mips	739	1104	1949	739	739	739
motion	6212	6823	8771	6212	6222	6229
sha	3574	6702	9431	3574	3739	3790
FFT	636	1324	1627	636	662	675
Geomean	1860	2967	4035	1860	1991	2144
Improvement		1.60x	2.17x		1.07x	1.15x

In this table, Columns 2-4 show the results for the baseline architecture in which the trace scheduler is compiled between each debug iteration. Columns 5-7 show the results for our architecture. From this table, we can make two observations. First, by recording fewer user variables, we increase the achievable trace length using either architecture; we see an increase of 2.17x when recording 25% of the user variables using the baseline architecture and 1.15x using our architecture. This increase justifies the importance of being able to tailor the debug scenario as debug proceeds (rather than just recording everything). Second, we can observe that, our achievable trace length increases more slowly as the number of selected variables reduces, compared to the baseline. This is one of the prices we pay for software-like debug turn around times.

The other price we pay for software-like turn-around times is area. To measure area, we instrumented each benchmark circuit, and mapped the results to a Stratix IV FPGA. We report post place-and-route numbers to account for any physical design optimizations that Quartus II is able to perform. Over all benchmarks, the average area of the baseline architecture (based on the previous work [9]) was 2232 ALMs, not including the trace buffer itself. Our enhanced architecture, Variant A, required a total of 2271 ALMs plus one M9K memory block (this is an increase of 39 ALMs and one memory block). Of the 39 ALMs increase, 59% (on average) was due to logic required to make the memory block accessible using Intel's In-System Memory Content Editor [2].

We found little impact on the maximum clock speed of the circuit, ranging from -9% to +12% (average +1%), which we attribute to algorithmic noise in the CAD tool.

Even though our technique suffers in terms of area and trace window length, for our benchmarks, the time to personalize the overlay ranges from 0.887 seconds to 1.751 seconds (dominated by the time to update the ROM via the memory content editor). In contrast, the approach in [9] suffers a compile time of 454 seconds on average for the same benchmarks. In [15], this is improved to 231 seconds (assuming 50% traced signals) using Intel's incremental compilation flow in Quartus II v16.0.

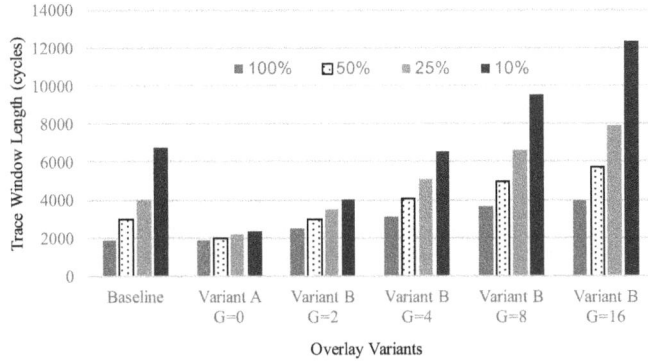

Figure 10: Impact of Line Packer Granularity (G) on Trace Window Size - Variant B

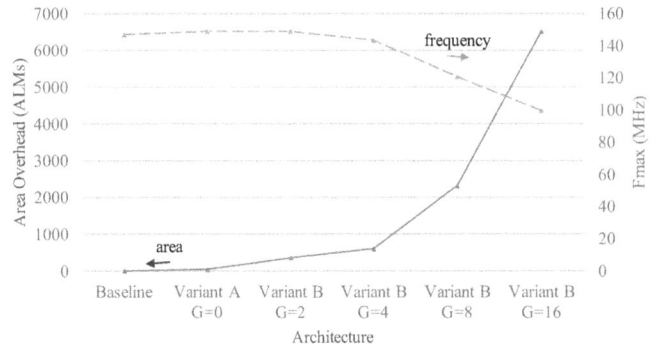

Figure 11: Impact of Line Packer Granularity (G) on Area - Variant B

6.2 Impact of Line Packer: Variant B

To improve the trace buffer capacity, Section 5 proposes Variant B, which contains a line packer. Figure 10 shows the impact of the trace length as a function of the line packer's granularity (G) for this variant. Compared to the trace lengths achieved by the baseline and Variant A architectures, G=2 reclaims the trace length lost with Variant A and G=16 performs 2x-7x better than the baseline. Figure 11 shows the impact of the overhead logic area versus the baseline as a function of G (all implementations also require one M9K memory block). As the graphs show, increasing G has a significant impact on the trace length. The area, on the other hand, grows more quickly as G increases, primarily due to the increased area of the steering logic.

Compared to Variant A, this variant requires more memory bits, however, for all benchmarks, only one M9K block was required to store all configuration bits, even for G=16.

Once again, we saw only a small impact on the clock frequency, except for the Variant B architecture where G=16 as shown in Figure 11. This is due to the increased chain of steering logic for a higher granularity line packer. At lower G, the frequency dropped slightly as compared to the baseline. The critical path of our instrumented circuits typically fall in the user circuit itself rather than the instrumentation. If we were instrumenting an extremely high-frequency circuit, we could pipeline our instrumentation to match the clock speed.

6.3 Selective Function Tracing

As described in Section 5.3, adding the selective function tracing capability may allow a user to use trace buffer space more efficiently by focusing on specific functions of interest. The benefit of this capability on trace buffer length is clearly very circuit-dependent and function-dependent, and thus overall averages may not be meaningful. However, as a data-point, we gathered the results in Table 2. This table shows the impact of tracing two functions on trace window size for a single benchmark circuit, *adpcm*, for two variants of the overlay mapping algorithm: *partial control flow* where control flow information that is outside the selected function is not recorded, and *full control flow* where all control flow information is recorded, regardless of whether it is outside the traced function. In

Table 2: Control Flow Tracing Results for adpcm

Function traced	Inlined?	Full Control Flow	Partial Control Flow
none		2613	2613
encode only	yes	4024	4278
upzero only	no	4932	6532

this experiment, the baseline trace window size (where everything is traced) was 2613 cycles. When we only trace the *encode* function, this rises to 4024 cycles for the full control flow method, and 4278 for the partial control flow method. For the *upzero* function, the trace window size is 4932 cycles for the full control flow method and 6532 cycles for the partial control flow method. Clearly, *upzero* benefits more from using partial control flow. One reason is that *encode* is inlined by the HLS tool; in this situation, we are conservative and trace the entire parent function. Thus, we would expect that the benefits of not tracing outside the selected function (in this case, the parent function) would be smaller than a function that is not inlined, such as *upzero*.

As described in Section 5, there is no area impact in supporting the selective function tracing capability.

6.4 Conditional Buffer Freeze

The area impact of the conditional buffer freeze capability is shown in Figure 12 as a function of C (the number of subunits, which affects the complexity of the conditional function that can be used). The left vertical axis is the increase in area when this capability is added to Variant B. As the graph shows, as C increases, the overall area increases significantly. As before, we saw negligible impact on clock speed as C increases.

The conditional buffer freeze capability has no impact on achievable trace length. The capability is meant to increase the likelihood that useful information is stored in the trace buffer. This is difficult to quantify and would be very specific to a particular circuit, designer, and bug.

6.5 Results Summary and Discussion

Overall, these results show the trade-off between trace window size and area overhead for the various capabilities we have discussed, along with the impact of various architectural parameters. These

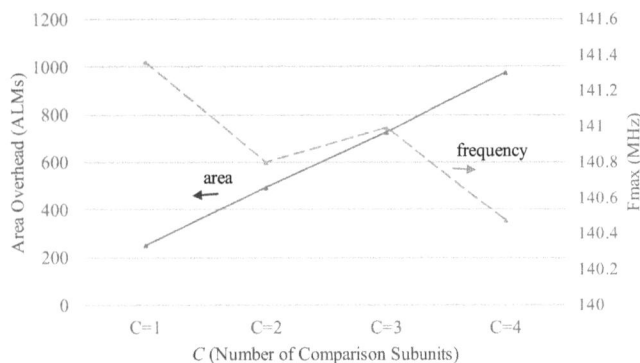

Figure 12: Impact of Number of Sub-units (C) on Area for Conditional Buffer Freeze Architecture

results are likely to be useful to an FPGA vendor who wishes to create an ecosystem containing an overlay such as ours. In such an ecosystem, the HLS tool could determine, based on an estimate of the amount of space left on the FPGA, how large an overlay to construct. If it is estimated that there is little space available, it might construct an "economy" version with only one or two capabilities. If more space is available, it may choose to construct a "deluxe" version that supports all capabilities we have discussed (and perhaps others). The results showed that the cost of our Selective Trace architecture is very small (Variant A required only 39 ALMs and one M9K block beyond the baseline), and that, when the user can be selective in which variables should be traced, the impact of including this capability on trace length is significant. This suggests that almost any overlay should likely have at least this capability. The conditional buffer freeze capability is more expensive (between 200 and 1000 ALMs depending on the complexity of the condition supported), so an automatic tool might only choose to include this capability in the overlay if there is sufficient space available.

We have purposefully not addressed the question of how useful each capability is in finding a bug (other than the extent to which some capabilities increase the trace window size). Understanding the trade-off between increased window size and improved buffer freeze capabilities, for example, would require user studies or interactions with a large user base that could provide experience and insight into what features help them find their most complex bugs.

7 CONCLUSIONS

This paper presents a flexible debug overlay that provides software-like debug turn around times for HLS circuits. At compile time, an overlay is constructed on a circuit-by-circuit basis, taking advantage of HLS scheduling information to maximize trace buffer utilization. At debug time, the user can configure the overlay without having to perform a lengthy recompilation. The range of debug scenarios that can be implemented by the overlay depend on the overlay itself; we presented architectural support for selective variable tracing, selective function tracing, and conditional buffer freeze. Compared to debug cores presented in previous work, our overlay adds only a small amount of extra overhead, but enables software-like debug turn around times, which we believe is essential if FPGAs are to reach their true potential as mainstream compute accelerators.

8 ACKNOWLEDGEMENTS

We would like to thank Intel for their FPGA Programming Optimizations ISRA (Intel Strategic Research Alliance) grant that funded this research.

REFERENCES

[1] Altera. 2015. *Quartus Prime Pro Edition Handbook*. Vol. 3. Chapter 9: Design Debugging Using the SignalTap II Logic Analyzer.
[2] Altera. 2016. Altera Virtual JTAG (altera_virtual_jtag) IP Core User Guide. https://www.altera.com/en_US/pdfs/literature/ug/ug_virtualjtag.pdf. (October 2016).
[3] Altera. 2016. SDK for OpenCL. https://www.altera.com/products/design-software/embedded-software-developers/opencl/overview.html. (2016).
[4] M. Boule and Z. Zilic. 2008. Automata-based Assertion-Checker Synthesis of PSL Properties. *ACM Trans. on Design Automation of Electronic Systems* 13, 1 (January 2008), 4.1–4.21.
[5] N. Calagar, S.D. Brown, and J.H. Anderson. 2014. Source-level Debugging for FPGA High-Level Synthesis. In *Int'l Conf. on Field Programmable Logic and Applications*.
[6] A. Canis, J. Choi, and others. 2013. LegUp: An Open-source High-level Synthesis Tool for FPGA-based Processor/Accelerator Systems. *ACM Trans. Embed. Comput. Syst.* 13, 2, Article 24 (Sept. 2013), 27 pages.
[7] Y. Chen, S. Safarpour, J. Marques-Silva, and A. Veneris. 2010. Automated Design Debugging With Maximum Satisfiability. *IEEE Trans. on Computer-Aided Design of Integrated Circuits and Systems* 29, 11 (Nov. 2010), 1804–1817.
[8] F. Eslami and S. J. E. Wilton. 2015. An adaptive virtual overlay for fast trigger insertion for FPGA debug. In *Int'l Conf. on Field Programmable Technology (FPT)*. 32–39.
[9] J. Goeders and S.J.E. Wilton. 2017. Signal-Tracing Techniques for In-System FPGA Debugging of High-Level Synthesis Circuits. *IEEE Trans. on Computer-Aided Design of Integrated Circuits and Systems* 36, 1 (Jan 2017), 83–96.
[10] J. Goeders and S.J. E. Wilton. 2015. Allowing Software Developers to Debug HLS Hardware. In *Workshop on FPGAs for Software Programmers*.
[11] Y. Hara, H. Tomiyama, S. Honda, and H. Takada. 2009. Proposal and Quantitative Analysis of the CHStone Benchmark Program Suite for Practical C-based High-level Synthesis. *Journal of Information Processing* 17 (2009), 242–254.
[12] K.S. Hemmert, J.L. Tripp, B.L. Hutchings, and P.A. Jackson. 2003. Source level debugger for the Sea Cucumber synthesizing compiler. In *Symposium on Field-Programmable Custom Computing Machines*. 228–237.
[13] F. Ko and N. Nicolici. 2009. Algorithms for state restoration and trace- signal selection for data acquisition in silicon debug. *IEEE Trans. on Computer-Aided Design of Integrated Circuits and Systems* 28, 2 (Feb. 2009), 285–297.
[14] A. Kourfali and D. Stroobandt. 2016. Efficient Hardware Debugging using Parameterized FPGA Reconfiguration. In *Int'l Parallel and Distributed Processing Symposium Workshop*. 277–282.
[15] P.B. Kumar, J. Goeders, and S.J.E. Wilton. 2017. Accelerating In-System FPGA Debug of High-Level Synthesis Circuits using Incremental Compilation Techniques. In *Int'l Conf. on Field-Programmable Logic and Applications*.
[16] E. Matthews, L. Shannon, and A. Fedorova. 2010. A Configurable Framework for Investigating Workload Execution. In *Int'l Conf. on Field-Programmable Technology*. 409–412.
[17] J. S. Monson and Brad L. Hutchings. 2015. Using Source-Level Transformations to Improve High-Level Synthesis Debug and Validation on FPGAs. In *Int'l Symp. on Field-Programmable Gate Arrays*. 5–8.
[18] B.R. Quinton and S.J.E. Wilton. 2005. Concentrator Access Networks for Programmable Logic Cores on SoCs. In *Int'l Symp. on Circuits and Systems*. 45–48.
[19] B. Reagen, R. Adolf, Y.S. Shao, Gu-Yeon Wai, and David Brooks. 2014. MachSuite: Benchmarks for accelerator design and customized architectures. In *Int'l Symp. on Workload Characterization*. 110–119.
[20] T. Wheeler, P. Graham, B. Nelson, and B. Hutchings. 2001. Using design-level scan to improve FPGA design observabilty and controllability for functional verification. In *Int'l Conf. on Field-Programmable Logic and Applications*. 483–492.
[21] Xilinx. 2016. Integrated Logic Analyzer v6.1: LogiCORE IP Product Guide. http://www.xilinx.com/support/documentation/ip_documentation/ila/v6_1/pg172-ila.pdf. (April 2016).
[22] Xilinx. 2016. Vivado Design Suite User Guide: High-Level Synthesis. http://www.xilinx.com/support/documentation/sw_manuals/xilinx2016_2/ug902-vivado-high-level-synthesis.pdf. (June 2016).

Memory-Efficient Fast Fourier Transform on Streaming Data by Fusing Permutations

François Serre
serref@inf.ethz.ch
Department of Computer Science
ETH Zurich

Markus Püschel
pueschel@inf.ethz.ch
Department of Computer Science
ETH Zurich

ABSTRACT

We propose a novel FFT datapath that reduces the memory requirement compared to state-of-the-art RAM-based implementations by up to a factor of two. The novelty is in a technique to fuse the datapaths for the required perfect shuffle and bit reversal and is applicable to an entire design space of FFT implementations with varying degrees of reuse and number of input ports. We implemented a tool to generate this FFT design space for a given input size and to benchmark against prior work. The results show a reduction of half the RAM banks and/or half the logic complexity used for the permutations. The technique for fusing permutations is more generally applicable beyond the FFT.

CCS CONCEPTS

• **Hardware** → **Digital signal processing**; *Application specific integrated circuits*; *High-level and register-transfer level synthesis*; • **Theory of computation** → *Circuit complexity*;

KEYWORDS

Streaming datapath; Fast Fourier Transform; Data reordering; Connection network; Linear permutation; Stride permutation; Bit-reversal

ACM Reference Format:
François Serre and Markus Püschel. 2018. Memory-Efficient Fast Fourier Transform on Streaming Data by Fusing Permutations. In *FPGA '18: 2018 ACM/SIGDA International Symposium on Field-Programmable Gate Arrays, February 25–27, 2018, Monterey, CA, USA*. ACM, New York, NY, USA, 10 pages. https://doi.org/10.1145/3174243.3174263

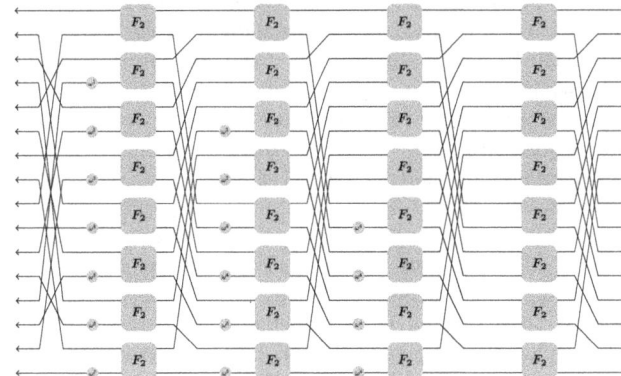

1 INTRODUCTION

The discrete Fourier transform (DFT) is a ubiquitous tool in signal processing and beyond, used in image and speech processing, radar, wireless communication (e.g., in the LTE standard), and many other domains. Thus, fast and efficient implementations of fast Fourier transforms (FFTs), in software and in hardware, and in particular for embedded systems are of high importance. Much work has been devoted to this topic and produced systematic methods to design efficient FFT circuits that cover the entire space of design tradeoffs from large and fast to small and slow [1–5]. In this paper

(a) Pease FFT dataflow

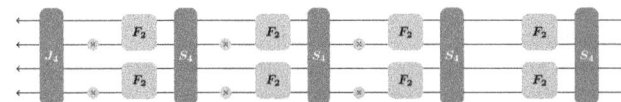

(b) Full streaming with $2^k = 4$ inputs

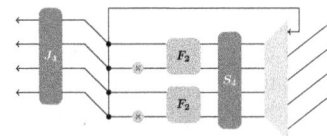

(c) Streaming plus iterative reuse

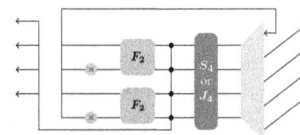

(d) Streaming plus iterative reuse with fused permutation

Figure 1: (a) Dataflow (right to left) of the radix-2 Pease FFT for size 2^4; (b) "vertically folded" design for $2^k = 2^2$ input ports; (c) in addition "horizontally folded" design in which the first four stages are iteratively reused; (d) our contribution: design with two permutations fused.

we extend prior work with a novel method that can reduce memory requirement by roughly one half. The method is more generally applicable beyond FFTs: it designs a circuit that can perform a small number of data permutations, which take the input streamed over several cycles. Our contribution is best explained with an example.

Example: FFT on 16 points. Fig. 1(a) shows the dataflow of a radix-2 Pease FFT [6, 7] on $2^n = 16$ points. Note that all dataflows in this paper are from right to left because of the corresponding matrix notation introduced later. The FFT comprises four identical stages (except for the twiddle scaling shown as little circles) of eight parallel butterflies F_2 preceded by a perfect shuffle, followed by the bit reversal permutation. This dataflow can be used for a fully-parallel implementation that has high throughput but also high cost.

The cost can be reduced by exploiting the repetitive structure of this FFT. A first method "folds the dataflow vertically" to obtain a design like Fig. 1(b) [8–10]. Now the circuit operates on streaming data, which means that the dataset arrives on 2^k ports during 2^t cycles, where $n = t + k$. In the figure $k = 2$. However, this design requires streamed permutation circuits (represented with blue boxes) between the butterfly stages. These require memory, as data may now be permuted across cycles, and routing components, as elements arriving on a given input port may need to be directed to different output ports. Efficient, and sometimes proven optimal methods, for implementing these have been developed in the literature. There are two classes of methods. One designs a circuit that can handle any permutation [11, 12], parameterized by the control logic at runtime. However, this flexibility comes at the price of a higher area cost. The second class consists of datapaths that are specialized for the desired permutation [13–17], which thus reduces cost.

Back to the FFT, Figure 1(a) has another symmetry: the first four stages are almost identical. Therefore, it is possible to "fold the dataflow horizontally" to reuse over time a single hardware stage [6]. The two types of folding can be combined [9, 10], resulting, for example, in the design shown in Fig. 1(c). If fully folded in both dimensions, the design is very compact. In the case shown it contains only two butterflies, two complex multipliers, and the hardware to perform the bit reversal (represented in Fig. 1(a) with the blue box labeled with J_4) and the perfect shuffle (labeled with S_4). The work in [9, 10] considers and generates the entire design space given by varying the degree of folding in both dimensions.

The architecture we propose is shown in Fig. 1(d) and fuses the hardware performing the two permutations to reduce cost, and in particular the memory required. Note that the entire discussion in this example can be extended to a Pease FFT of arbitrary radix. The method for fusing the streaming permutation is more generally applicable but the FFT was the motivation for this work.

Contributions. Our main contributions are as follows:

- We present a method to design a specialized datapath that can realize a given (small) set of permutations, taking the input streamed over several cycles. This datapath is cheaper than one capable of performing all permutations. The method is limited to the class of *linear* permutations, which contains bit reversal, perfect shuffle, matrix transpositions, and permutations needed in other FFTs beyond Pease, sorting networks, Viterbi decoders, filter banks, and other algorithms. The datapath we design consists of basic logic and RAMs, which is well-suited for implementation on FPGAs.

- As a major application, we propose a novel variant of a streamed FFT architecture (as shown in Fig. 1(d)) that reduces the RAMs required by prior work by up to one half.
- We implemented a generator [18] that can produce the entire design space sketched in Fig. 1. The input is the FFT size 2^n and the number of input ports for the design on Fig. 1(d). The output is RTL Verilog. The generator also supports different radices larger than 2.
- We show benchmarks to prior work confirming the benefits of the new FFT datapath.

2 STREAMED LINEAR PERMUTATIONS

As mentioned in the introduction, the bit reversal and the perfect shuffle used in the Pease FFT are *linear permutations*. In this section, we define this class, and review prior work on their implementation as streaming hardware.

Perfect shuffle. The perfect shuffle is the permutation that interleaves the first and second half of a list of 2^n elements. It appears in the first four stages of Fig. 1(a). For instance, if we consider 8 elements indexed from 0 to 7, these get rearranged such that the element i is mapped to the position $2i$ if $i < 4$, or $2i - 7$ otherwise. If we write the binary representation of i as a column vector i_b of 3 bits with the most significant bit on top, this means

$$\begin{pmatrix}0\\0\\0\end{pmatrix} \mapsto \begin{pmatrix}0\\0\\0\end{pmatrix}, \begin{pmatrix}0\\0\\1\end{pmatrix} \mapsto \begin{pmatrix}0\\1\\0\end{pmatrix}, \begin{pmatrix}0\\1\\0\end{pmatrix} \mapsto \begin{pmatrix}1\\0\\0\end{pmatrix}, \begin{pmatrix}0\\1\\1\end{pmatrix} \mapsto \begin{pmatrix}1\\1\\0\end{pmatrix},$$

$$\begin{pmatrix}1\\0\\0\end{pmatrix} \mapsto \begin{pmatrix}0\\0\\1\end{pmatrix}, \begin{pmatrix}1\\0\\1\end{pmatrix} \mapsto \begin{pmatrix}0\\1\\1\end{pmatrix}, \begin{pmatrix}1\\1\\0\end{pmatrix} \mapsto \begin{pmatrix}1\\0\\1\end{pmatrix}, \text{ and } \begin{pmatrix}1\\1\\1\end{pmatrix} \mapsto \begin{pmatrix}1\\1\\1\end{pmatrix}.$$

We observe that the perfect shuffle rotates up the binary representation i_b of its indexes.

More generally, for a set of 2^n elements, the perfect shuffle maps an index $0 \le i < 2^n$ to the index j such that

$$j_b = S_n \cdot i_b,$$

where S_n is the cyclic shift matrix:

$$S_n = \begin{pmatrix} & 1 & & \\ & & \ddots & \\ & & & 1 \\ 1 & & & \end{pmatrix}. \tag{1}$$

In summary, the invertible $n \times n$ bit matrix S_n defines the perfect shuffle permutation, which we denote with $\pi(S_n)$, on 2^n elements.

In the Pease FFT for a general radix 2^r, the shuffle between stages is given by $S_{n,r} = S_n^r$.

Linear permutations. In general, a linear permutation [19, 20] π on 2^n elements is a permutation such that there exists an $n \times n$ invertible bit matrix[1] P that satisfies, for $0 \le i < 2^n$,

$$\pi : i \mapsto j \Leftrightarrow j_b = P \cdot i_b. \tag{2}$$

Conversely, for any $n \times n$ invertible bit-matrix P, there is a unique linear permutation that satisfies (2), and we denote it with $\pi(P)$.

For a given n, there are a total of $\prod_{i=0}^{n-1}(2^n - 2^i)$ such P, and thus linear permutations. This means most permutations on 2^n points are not linear (e.g., linear requires that 0 is mapped to 0), but, interestingly, many permutations in signal processing algorithms are linear. Examples include permutations appearing in FFTs, fast

---

[1]mathematically, $P \in \mathrm{GL}(n, 2)$.

(a) RAM/SNW/RAM

(b) SNW/RAM/SNW

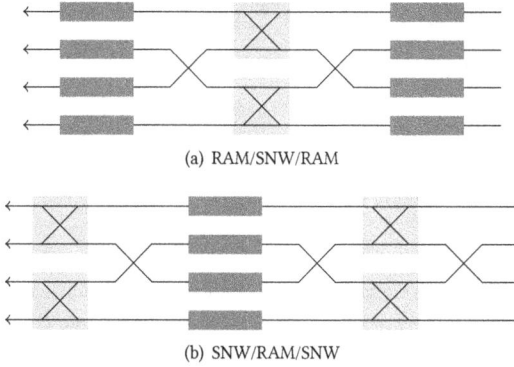

Figure 2: Perfect shuffle on $2^n = 16$ elements, streamed with $2^k = 4$ ports over $2^t = 4$ cycles. RAM banks permute *in time*, i.e., across cycles. Switching networks (SNWs) permute *in space*, i.e. across ports.

cosine transforms, Viterbi decoders, sorting networks, filter banks, and many others.

The linear permutations considered in this paper are even bit-index permutations, a subset of linear permutations for which P is itself a permutation matrix, such as the matrix in (1). However, the method we propose works with any linear permutation.

Bit reversal. Besides the perfect shuffle we consider the bit reversal, which is defined as the permutation that reverses the bits of the indices. Therefore, it is the linear permutation $\pi(J_n)$, where

$$J_n = \begin{pmatrix} & & 1 \\ & \cdot^{\cdot^{\cdot}} & \\ 1 & & \end{pmatrix}.$$

In the Pease FFT of a general radix 2^r, $r|n$ (r divides n), the bit reversal operates at coarser granularity and is given by $J_{n,r} = J_{n/r} \otimes I_r$. This means that every entry in $J_{n/r}$ is multiplied by the $r \times r$ identity matrix I_r.

Streamed linear permutations. In the streaming reuse structures (Figs. 1(b) and 1(c)), the linear permutations have to permute input data streamed in 2^t chunks of 2^k elements, where $2^n = 2^{t+k}$. Prior work provides optimal RAM-based implementations of such streaming linear permutation (SLP). The first one [17] uses an architecture composed of a *spatial SLP* block consisting of a network of 2×2-switches (SNW) framed by two *temporal SLPs*, each made of an array of 2^k RAM banks (See Fig. 2(a)). The second method [16, 17] uses a spatial SLP, a temporal SLP, and another spatial SLP (Fig. 2(b)). The corresponding generator is available at [18].

We explain these notions more formally next. If 2^n data are streamed through 2^k ports over 2^t cycles, $n = t + k$, then the cycle during which an element arrives corresponds to the t most significant bits of its index, while the port corresponds to the k least significant bits. For instance, for $t = k = 2$, the element indexed with

$$11_b = \begin{pmatrix} 1 \\ 0 \\ 1 \\ 1 \end{pmatrix} = \begin{pmatrix} 2_b \\ 3_b \end{pmatrix}$$

arrives during the second cycle on the third port. This suggests blocking the matrix P of a linear permutation $\pi(P)$ to be streamed as

$$P = \begin{pmatrix} P_4 & P_3 \\ P_2 & P_1 \end{pmatrix}, \text{ such that } P_4 \text{ is } t \times t.$$

Namely, an element arriving in cycle c on port p is output at port p' during the cycle c', where

$$p'_b = P_1 p_b + P_2 c_b \text{ and} \tag{3}$$

$$c'_b = P_4 c_b + P_3 p_b. \tag{4}$$

Spatial and temporal SLPs can now be identified using the structure of P [8]:

Spatial SLP. A permutation $\pi(P)$ such that

$$P = \begin{pmatrix} I_t & \\ P_2 & P_1 \end{pmatrix}$$

permutes only across ports, i.e., is spatial, and can be implemented with a switching network (SNW) consisting of rank P_2 stages of 2^{k-1} 2×2-switches [16, 17]. If in addition, $P_2 = 0$, the SNW thus requires no switches and corresponds to a simple rewiring. In this case we call $\pi(P)$ steady.

Temporal SLP. If

$$P = \begin{pmatrix} P_4 & P_3 \\ & I_k \end{pmatrix},$$

then $\pi(P)$ permutes only across cycles, i.e., is temporal, and can be implemented with an array of 2^k RAM banks of 2^t words with a simple control logic [17]. Alternatively, methods based on graph coloring can reduce the size of the RAM banks needed in certain cases [12].

General SLP. A general linear permutation $\pi(P)$ can now be decomposed into three linear permutations using the algorithms of [21]:

$$\pi(P) = \pi(L \cdot C \cdot R) = \pi(L) \cdot \pi(C) \cdot \pi(R), \tag{5}$$

where the factors alternate between spatial and temporal SLPs, yielding the two possibilities in Fig. 2.

Cost and optimality. The first structure in Fig. 2(a) requires 2^{k+1} RAM banks of 2^t elements, and rank$(P_2) \cdot 2^{k-1}$ 2×2-switches. This design always minimizes the number of 2×2-switches (Theorem 1 of [17]).

The second in Fig. 2(b) uses half the number of RAM banks, 2^k, and $\max(\text{rank}(P_2), n - \text{rank } P_1 - \text{rank } P_4) \cdot 2^{k-1}$ switches, which may be larger than in the first structure. It has the optimal logic complexity for such a structure, uses the minimal number of RAM banks, and has a minimal latency, if dual-ported memory banks are used (respectively Theorem 2 of [17], Corollary 1 and Lemma 2 of [12]). If in addition [12] is used to implement the temporal SLP, then the RAM size is also minimal.

Streaming the perfect shuffle. As an example, we consider the case of the perfect shuffle permutation in (1) for $n = 4$. For $t = k = 2$ and using the SNW/RAM/SNW structure, the corresponding bit-matrix S_4 would be decomposed as

$$S_4 = \left(\begin{array}{cc|cc} 1 & & & \\ & 1 & & \\ \hline & & 1 & \\ & 1 & & 1 \end{array} \right) \cdot \left(\begin{array}{cc|cc} & 1 & & \\ 1 & & & 1 \\ \hline & & & 1 \\ & & 1 & \end{array} \right) \cdot \left(\begin{array}{cc|cc} 1 & & & \\ & 1 & & \\ \hline & & & 1 \\ 1 & & 1 & \end{array} \right), \tag{6}$$

221

yielding the design shown in Fig. 2(b), consisting of 4 RAM banks of 2 word and 4 switches. More generally, implementing a streaming perfect shuffle requires 2^k banks of 2^{t-1} words, and 2^k switches [16].

3 STREAMING MULTIPLE LINEAR PERMUTATIONS

The prior techniques from Section 2 are sufficient to implement the streaming permutations, and thus the streaming FFTs shown in Fig. 1(b) and 1(c). However, they cannot be used for the structure in Fig. 1(d), where the same datapath has to handle two different SLPs[2]. An immediate solution would be to use general streaming permutation methods, like [11] or [12]. They propose, respectively, a structure as in Fig. 2(a) and 2(b), but replace the specialized SNWs by complete, and thus more expensive permutation networks. In this section, we propose a method to implement in hardware a datapath capable of rearranging streaming data according to a small number of given linear permutations, thus reducing the implementation cost compared to a general solution.

Problem statement. Formally, we are given a list

$$\pi(P^{(0)}), \pi(P^{(1)}), \ldots, \pi(P^{(s-1)})$$

of linear permutations, and a streaming width 2^k. Our goal is to implement an architecture that performs the permutation $\pi(P^{(i)})$ on the ith dataset, streamed over 2^k ports.

The main idea first decomposes each permutation as in (5), i.e., for all $0 \leq i < s$,

$$\pi(P^{(i)}) = \pi(L^{(i)}) \cdot \pi(C^{(i)}) \cdot \pi(R^{(i)}),$$

where each factor is either temporal or spatial. The global architecture can then be implemented by a sequence of blocks that each perform either a sequence of temporal or a sequence of spatial SLPs. We now consider these two cases and describe their implementation.

3.1 Sequence of Temporal SLPs

We assume a given list of bit matrices $P^{(0)}, P^{(1)}, \ldots, P^{(s-1)}$, such that all $\pi(P^{(i)})$ are temporal, i.e.,

$$P^{(i)} = \begin{pmatrix} P_4^{(i)} & P_3^{(i)} \\ & I_k \end{pmatrix}, \quad 0 \leq i < s.$$

RAM array. A structure that permutes a dataset i according to $\pi(P^{(i)})$ can be implemented using an array of 2^k dual-ported RAM banks of 2^t words. Each of these banks have a write port connected to one of the inputs of the block, and a read port connected to the corresponding output (see Fig. 3(a)). The write and read addresses ensure that data are correctly permuted (accordingly to (4)), and are respectively controlled using two t-bits timers: c, that starts when a new dataset arrives, and c', that starts when the output begins.

Latency. The output begins as early as possible, to minimize the latency, for each different permutation. Therefore, c' is triggered when c reaches the value corresponding to the maximal lifetime δ_i

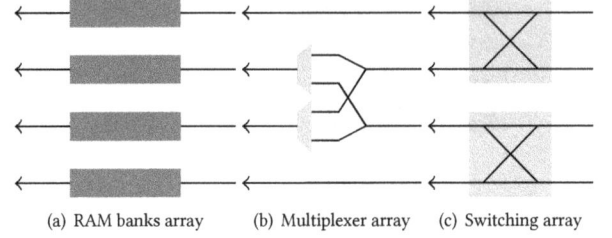

(a) RAM banks array   (b) Multiplexer array   (c) Switching array

Figure 3: The basic blocks we use, here for a streaming width of $2^k = 4$. (a) can pass any temporal permutation; (b) implements the two spatial steady SLPs $\pi(I_t \oplus J_2)$ and $\pi(I_n)$; (c) implements (9).

of an element in the permutation:

$$\delta_i = \max_{p,c}(c - d(i,p,c)), \quad \text{with } d(i,p,c)_b = P_4^{(i)}c_b + P_3^{(i)}p_b.$$

Conflict-free addressing. Besides permuting correctly the data, the read and write addresses need to ensure a conflict-free access. This means that an incoming element must not be written to a place where an element of a previous dataset has not been read yet. This issue occurs if $\delta_i < 2^t$. One solution is to use double buffering [11, 16], but this requires doubling the size of each RAM bank.

The solution we propose is to always write an element of a dataset where the same element of the previous dataset was read. Namely, for the pth port, the first dataset received is written consecutively in the bank, i.e., at address c_b. It is then read at the address $(P_4^{(0)})^{-1}c_b' + (P_4^{(0)})^{-1}P_3^{(0)}p_b$, to perform the first permutation $\pi(P^{(0)})$. Then, the second dataset is written where the first dataset was read to avoid conflicts, so at the address $(P^{(0)})_4^{-1}c_b + (P^{(0)})_4^{-1}P_3^{(0)}p_b$. It is then read at the address

$$(P_4^{(0)}P_4^{(1)})^{-1}c_b' + (P_4^{(0)}P_4^{(1)})^{-1}P_3^{(1)}p_b + (P_4^{(0)})^{-1}P_3^{(0)}p_b.$$

More generally, the ith dataset is written (resp. read) at the address $U_i c_b + u_{i,p}$, (resp. $U_{i+1}c_b' + u_{i+1,p}$), where U_i is such that

$$\begin{cases} U_{i+1} = U_i(P_4^{(i \bmod s)})^{-1}, \\ U_0 = I_t, \end{cases}$$

and u_i satisfies

$$\begin{cases} u_{i+1,p} = U_{i+1}P_3^{(i \bmod s)}p_b + u_{i,p}, \\ u_{0,p} = 0. \end{cases}$$

We store the values of (U_i) in a ROM, controlled by a counter. Using AND and XOR gates, the term $U_i c_b$ is computed once for all the banks. Then, this signal is XORed with $u_{i,p}$ for each bank p to obtain the write address. The number of terms of (U_i) stored in the ROM is the least that guarantees conflict-free access (this length is bounded by the period[3] of (U_i)) The read address is obtained similarly.

Alternative addressing. As remarked in [11], it is also possible to store all the addresses, for every cycle, and for every permutation in a bank. Using this technique with [12] allows to use banks of

---

[2]The direct sum, i.e. block diagonal composition of two linear permutations is in general not a linear permutation.

[3]The period of (U_i) is sq, where q is the smallest positive integer such that $(P_4^{(s-1)}P_4^{(s-2)}\cdots P_4^{(0)})^{-q} = I_t$.

size $\max_i \delta_i$ words. However, in our application, this value is close to 2^t due to the bit reversal.

3.2 Sequence of Spatial SLPs

We assume a given list of bit matrices $P^{(0)}, P^{(1)}, \ldots, P^{(s-1)}$, such that all $\pi(P^{(i)})$ are spatial, i.e.,

$$P^{(i)} = \begin{pmatrix} I_t & \\ P_2^{(i)} & P_1^{(i)} \end{pmatrix}, \quad 0 \le i < s. \tag{7}$$

This case is somewhat more complicated. We first design solutions for two special cases from which we then build the solution for the general case.

Multiplexer array. We first consider the case where all the SLPs $\pi(P^{(0)}), \ldots, \pi(P^{(s-1)})$ are steady spatial permutations, i.e., for every i,

$$P^{(i)} = I_t \oplus P_1^{(i)} = \begin{pmatrix} I_t & \\ & P_1^{(i)} \end{pmatrix}. \tag{8}$$

Since each such SLP is a different wiring, the list of those can be implemented with an array of 2^k d-input multiplexers, where d is the number of unique matrices in the list (see Fig. 3(b)).

For instance, if the list contains two different matrices $I_t \oplus A$ and $I_t \oplus B$, it is possible to implement both using a structure where each output port p is the output of a multiplexer connected to the inputs $A^{-1}p_b$ and $B^{-1}p_b$, and controlled by a counter. Of course, the multiplexers connected twice to the same input can be simplified to a simple wire, leaving an actual implementation consisting of

$$\left| \{p \mid A^{-1}p_b \ne B^{-1}p_b\} \right| = 2^k - 2^{k-\mathrm{rank}(A^{-1}+B^{-1})}$$

2-input multiplexers. If $A = B$, then $A^{-1} = B^{-1}$ and thus the sum is 0 (since addition is modulo 2), which means the implementation consists only of wires, as expected.

Switching array. We now consider another special case where, for every i, $P_1^{(i)} = I_k$ and all elements of $P_2^{(i)}$ are zero, except for its last row, which we denote with v_i^T. Formally, for every i,

$$P^{(i)} = \begin{pmatrix} I_t & & & \\ & 1 & & \\ & & \ddots & \\ v_i^T & & & 1 \end{pmatrix}. \tag{9}$$

In this case, (3) shows that $\pi(P^{(i)})$ is the permutation that exchanges each pair within a chunk of 2^k elements, every time the corresponding cycle c is such that $c_b \cdot v_{ib} = 1$.

Therefore, P can be implemented using an array of 2^{k-1} 2×2-switches. All these switches are controlled by the output of a single s-input multiplexer that chooses among the results of the scalar products $c_b \cdot v_{ib}$, for $0 \le i < s$. These scalar products are computed using XOR gates on a timer c_b.

Fig. 3(c) shows such a switching array that can implement any spatial $P^{(i)}$ in (9) for $k = 2$.

General Spatial SLP. We return now to the general case (7), which we will decompose into matrices of the form (8) and (9) to implement it with the previous structures. We first consider the matrix M of size $k \times st$ that concatenates the matrices $P_2^{(i)}$:

$$M = \begin{pmatrix} P_2^{(0)} & P_2^{(1)} & \cdots & P_2^{(s-1)} \end{pmatrix}.$$

Using Gaussian elimination, it is possible to find an invertible matrix K of size $k \times k$ such that KM has $m = \mathrm{rank}\, M$ non-zero rows at the top. This implies that for every i the matrix $KP_2^{(i)}$ has the form

$$KP_2^{(i)} = \begin{pmatrix} v_{1,i}^T \\ v_{2,i}^T \\ \vdots \\ v_{m,i}^T \\ 0 \\ \vdots \\ 0 \end{pmatrix},$$

where the m top rows are denoted with $v_{j,i}^T$. Note that some of these may be zero for a given i. Direct computation yields now the decomposition into the prior special cases:

$$P^{(i)} = \begin{pmatrix} I_t & \\ & K^{-1}S_k^{k-m} \end{pmatrix} \cdot \begin{pmatrix} I_t & & & \\ & 1 & & \\ & & \ddots & \\ v_{1,i}^T & & & 1 \end{pmatrix} \begin{pmatrix} I_t & \\ & S_k \end{pmatrix} \cdot$$

$$\vdots$$

$$\begin{pmatrix} I_t & & & \\ & 1 & & \\ & & \ddots & \\ v_{m,i}^T & & & 1 \end{pmatrix} \begin{pmatrix} I_t & \\ & S_k \end{pmatrix} \cdot$$

$$\begin{pmatrix} I_t & \\ & KP_1^{(i)} \end{pmatrix} \cdot$$

The corresponding architecture can now be read off from right to left:

(1) a multiplexer array that permutes the wires as $\pi(I_t \oplus KP_1^{(i)})$ for the ith dataset,
(2) a sequence of m switching arrays, parameterized, respectively, by $v_m, v_{m-1}, \ldots, v_1$, each preceded by a perfect shuffle of the wires, and
(3) a rewiring performing the permutation $\pi(I_t \oplus K^{-1}S_k^{k-m})$.

Cost. The structure that we derived consists of rank M arrays of 2^{k-1} switches each, and one array of at most 2^k multiplexers.

3.3 General sequence of SLPs

Now we consider the general case of arbitrary invertible bit matrices $P^{(0)}, P^{(1)}, \ldots, P^{(s-1)}$. Using [21], we get, for each i, the decomposition

$$P^{(i)} = \begin{pmatrix} I_t & \\ L^{(i)} & I_k \end{pmatrix} \begin{pmatrix} C_4^{(i)} & C_3^{(i)} \\ C_2^{(i)} & C_1^{(i)} \end{pmatrix} \begin{pmatrix} I_t & \\ R^{(i)} & I_k \end{pmatrix},$$

which can be rewritten as

$$P^{(i)} = \begin{pmatrix} I_t & \\ L^{(i)} & I_k \end{pmatrix} \begin{pmatrix} C_4^{(i)} & C_3^{(i)}(C_1^{(i)})^{-1} \\ & I_k \end{pmatrix} \begin{pmatrix} I_t & \\ C_1^{(i)}R^{(i)} & C_1^{(i)} \end{pmatrix}.$$

This decomposition yields two sequences of spatial permutations, and one of temporal permutations. These can be implemented in a straightforward way using the previous structures.

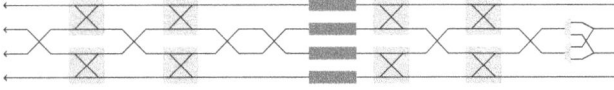

Figure 4: Datapath for the permutation block in Fig. 1(d).

Cost. The resulting architecture consists of one multiplexer array (as the leftmost sequence of spatial SLPs does not require one) containing a maximum of $2^k - 1$ multiplexers, an array of 2^k RAM banks (except in the special case where all the SLPs are spatial), and $(\text{rank } M_L + \text{rank } M_R) \cdot 2^{k-1}$ 2×2-switches, where

$$M_L = \begin{pmatrix} L_2^{(0)} & L_2^{(1)} & \cdots & L_2^{(s-1)} \end{pmatrix},$$
$$M_R = \begin{pmatrix} R_2^{(0)} & R_2^{(1)} & \cdots & R_2^{(s-1)} \end{pmatrix}.$$

Optimality. The number of RAM banks and the RAM latency match the bounds given in [12], and are therefore optimal. The number of switches, in the general case, depends on the different degrees of freedom appearing in the decompositions[4] [21], and no optimality can be claimed. Of course, if the sequence of SLPs only contains one unique SLP, the design we obtain only differs from [17] by rewirings, and it therefore inherits the optimality properties (Section 2).

Example: Fusing perfect shuffle and bit reversal. As an example, we design the permutation block in Fig. 1(d) capable of passing a perfect shuffle $\pi(S_4)$, and a bit reversal $\pi(J_4)$. Using the decomposition (6) for S_4, and the following (spatial/temporal/spatial) decomposition for J_4

$$J_4 = \left(\begin{array}{cc|cc} 1 & & & \\ & 1 & & \\ \hline & & 1 & 1 \\ 1 & & & 1 \end{array} \right) \cdot \left(\begin{array}{cc|cc} 1 & & & 1 \\ & 1 & 1 & \\ \hline & & 1 & \\ & & & 1 \end{array} \right) \cdot \left(\begin{array}{cc|cc} 1 & & & \\ & 1 & & \\ \hline & & 1 & 1 \\ 1 & & & 1 \end{array} \right),$$
(10)

we derive a datapath that consists of two blocks that performs a sequence of spatial SLPs around a block that performs a sequence of temporal SLPs. For example, this sequence of temporal SLPs contains the two middle permutations in (6) and (10):

$$\pi \left(\left(\begin{array}{cc|cc} & 1 & & \\ 1 & & & 1 \\ \hline & & 1 & \\ & & & 1 \end{array} \right) \right) \text{ and } \pi \left(\left(\begin{array}{cc|cc} 1 & & & 1 \\ & 1 & 1 & \\ \hline & & 1 & \\ & & & 1 \end{array} \right) \right).$$

The resulting implementation consists of an array of two 2-input multiplexers, two stages of two 2×2-switches each, an array of four RAM banks, and two additional stages of two 2×2-switches each (Fig. 4). Compared to an architecture performing only the bit reversal derived using [17] (Fig. 5), it requires only two additional 2-input multiplexers.

More generally, an architecture that can stream both the bit reversal and the perfect shuffle on 2^n points with a streaming width 2^k differs from a bit-reversal-only datapath with the same architecture by only $2^k - 2$ 2-input multiplexers. In other words,

---

[4]More precisely, the decomposition in [21] is optimal for each permutation taken individually, but as we compute independently these decompositions for each permutation, there is no guarantee in general that the global sequence yields an optimal rank for M_L and M_R.

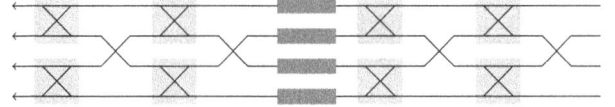

Figure 5: Datapath for a bit reversal on $2^n = 16$ elements streamed on $2^k = 4$ ports [17].

the additional support for the perfect shuffle is obtained almost for free.

4 APPLICATION: PEASE FFT

To evaluate our fused permutation in a concrete case, we have built a generator [18] capable of producing designs as in Fig. 1(d) for Pease FFTs of arbitrary radix (Fig 1 shows the special case of radix 2). This generator takes as input the size 2^n of the FFT, the number of ports 2^k, the bit-width of the input data, and the desired radix 2^r, with $r|n$ and $r \leq k \leq n$. It outputs the corresponding design in the form of Verilog code. In this section, we briefly explain how this generator works.

Derivation of the FFT architecture. The generator first considers a Pease FFT algorithm of the corresponding radix, and the sequence of permutations that have to be supported by the permutation block of Fig. 1(d). These are all linear, and the block is designed according to the techniques shown in Section 3. Butterflies and complex multipliers are then added to this permutation block within a loop, as in Fig. 1(d). Some optimizations occur at this time. For instance, with a radix 2, during the implementation of the leftmost spatial permutation, it is possible to choose K such that $v_{j,i} = 0$, for $i < n$ and $j < \min(t, k)$. Therefore, the $\min(t, k) - 1$ leftmost arrays of switches can safely be "unrolled," thus reducing the latency within the loop, and therefore improving the global throughput (see Fig. 6(b)). Only one stage of the leftmost spacial permutation remains in the loop.

Compared to the classic streaming reuse architecture (Fig. 6(a)), the design we obtain has an additional multiplexer stage and an additional switching array stage in the loop, but it does not have a dedicated structure to compute the bit reversal.

RTL graph. The design is then translated into an RTL graph, where additional optimizations are performed including the following:

- ROMs containing periodic values are simplified.
- ROMs containing a single value are replaced by a constant.
- Trivial arithmetic operations are simplified.
- A multiplexer with inputs coming from two multiplexers sharing the same inputs are fused into a single multiplexer.
- A 2-input multiplexer whose inputs come from two other multiplexers driven by the same control signal is fused to a 4-input multiplexer. This allows the efficient use of 6-input LUTs on current FPGAs.
- ROMs containing the same values are paired.

Additionally, in this step the design is pipelined and synchronized. In particular, if a control signal needs to be pipelined, the corresponding counters/timers are triggered in advance if possible. Otherwise, a reset value is computed for the registers that were added. As the design contains a loop, it must also be ensured that the

(a) Streaming iterative reuse with [17]

(b) Streaming iterative reuse with fused permutations

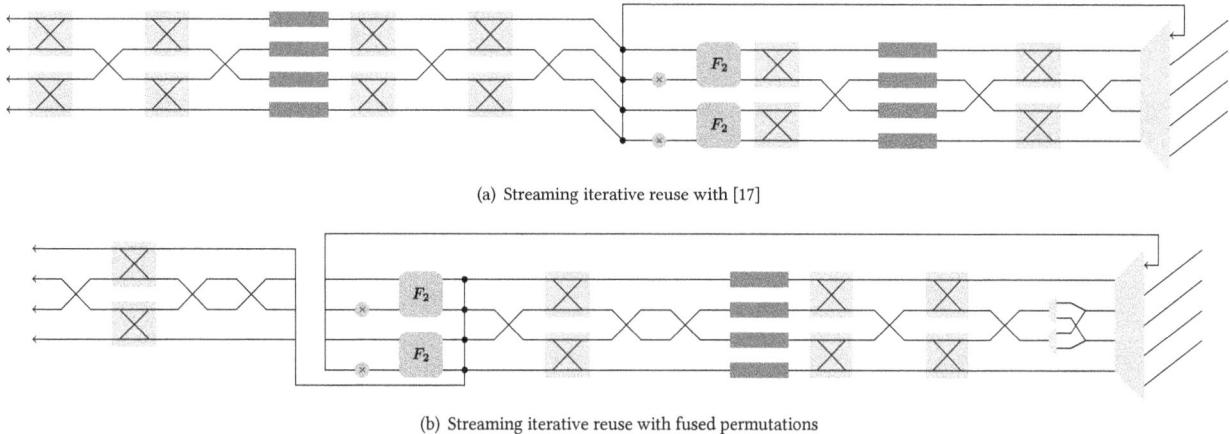

Figure 6: Radix-2 Pease FFT, iterative reuse with fused permutation $n = 4, k = 2$.

head of a dataset does not collide with its tail anywhere. Therefore, the design is first generated in a sandbox to measure the latency of its different parts. In a second pass, the latency of the inner temporal permutation is then increased if needed. Conversely, if the latency of the inner part of a loop is higher than the duration of the dataset, it means that the amount of time (the gap) between two datasets must be increased. This information is used in the second pass for the temporal permutation to reduce as much as possible the number of elements of (U_i) (see Section 3) stored in ROM, while ensuring conflict-free addressing in the RAM.

Once these simplifications have been performed, the design is output as Verilog code.

Limitations. Our generator was implemented with a main focus on the high level architecture and on the permutation part. It only supports fixed-point arithmetic, and the pipelining decisions are made with a basic heuristic. Using a more sophisticated approach like FloPoCo [22] for the low level implementation could reduce the area consumption of the produced designs, and add efficient support for floating point arithmetic.

Another limitation of our generator concerns the twiddle factors. In the designs we produce, each complex multiplier has a corresponding ROM that contains all the (real and imaginary) coefficients that it uses. A more distributed approach, along with a simple online computation of these coefficients could reduce further the number of BRAMs used.

5 RESULTS

In this section, we compare the cost and the performance of our generated FFT datapaths with other, state-of-the-art memory-efficient FFT architectures.

Table 1 lists the benchmarks we compare against. We consider two types of designs. The first type (A–D) is the prior iterative reuse structure from [10] exemplified in Fig. 1(c), with different solutions for the streaming permutations. The original [10] uses the permutations from [16], which is A in the table. B and C use different solutions that are not specific to linear permutations. Both,

A and B are available online at [23]. D improves the permutations in [16].

The second type (E–G) is the proposed architecture exemplified in Fig. 1(d), again with different solutions for the necessary fused permutation block. E and F is what can be built with prior work that provides a general streamed permutation network. G is our proposed solution specialized to the two permutations that need to be fused. Note that neither E or F has been used within an FFT architecture as proposed here.

Table 1 analyzes the cost and performance for a radix-2 Pease FFT. We discuss these next before we show results after place-and-route.

Cost. For the memory consumption, we list the RAM requirement for the permutation part, excluding the memory used to store the twiddle factors. C theoretically should allow the use of banks of 2^{t-1} words for the perfect shuffle, but when used with the structure in Fig. 1(c), the latency of the inner loop had to be increased to avoid dataset collisions, thus requiring 2^t words for all RAM banks. The gains compared to A–E are a factor of two or four; the only competitive method is F. However, the routing cost is at least a factor of two higher, and even more for t smaller than k.

For the routing requirements, we assume that the methods B, C, E, F using complete permutation networks implement them with [24], i.e., using $(k − 1/2) \cdot 2^k$ 2×2-switches. We counted 2 multiplexers per switch, and 2^k multiplexers for the loop. Figure 7 plots the formulas in Table 1 for three different numbers of ports and a range of FFT sizes. Our method is better compared to A–D and F. Only E use less multiplexers[5] for large values of t, but requires four times more RAM banks.

In summary, we improve routing cost compared to F (and B and C) and RAM cost compared to A–E, both by at least a factor of two.

Gap. Next we analyze the minimal number of cycles between two datasets, i.e., the gap, which is the inverse of the throughput. In our case, it is constrained by the duration of the input itself (2^t cycles), and by the time the dataset stays in the loop. In Table 1, we assumed that the designs were all targeting ≈ 400Mhz on a Virtex 7. This

---

[5]Using the RAM/SNW/RAM architecture instead would have yield better routing complexity, but for twice the amount of RAM.

Ref	Architecture	Permutation	Memory	Routing (2 : 1 Mux)	Gap (cycles per transform)
A	Fig. 1(c) [10]	Püschel [16]	2^{k+1} banks of 2^{t+1} words	$(\min(t,k)+3/2)\cdot 2^{k+1}$	$2^t+(n-1)\cdot\max(2^t,2^{t-1}+9)$
B	Fig. 1(c) [10]	Milder [11]	2^{k+2} banks of 2^{t+1} words	$(k-1/4)\cdot 2^{k+2}$	$\geq 2^t+(n-1)\cdot\max(2^t,2^{t-1}+\lceil k/2\rceil+8)$
C	Fig. 1(c) [10]	Koehn [12]	2^{k+1} banks of 2^t words	$(k-3/8)\cdot 2^{k+3}$	$2^t+(n-1)\cdot\max(2^t,2^{t-1}+2\lceil k/2\rceil+9)$
D	Fig. 1(c) [10]	Serre [17]	2^{k+1} banks of 2^t words	$(\min(t,k)+3/2)\cdot 2^{k+1}$	$2^t+(n-1)\cdot\max(2^t,2^{t-1}+9)$
E	Fig. 1(d) (novel)	Milder [11]	2^{k+1} banks of 2^{t+1} words	$k\cdot 2^{k+1}$	$\geq 2^t+n\cdot\max(2^t,2^{t-1}+\lceil k/2\rceil+8)$
F	Fig. 1(d) (novel)	Koehn [12]	2^k banks of 2^t words	$(k-1/4)\cdot 2^{k+2}$	$2^t+n\cdot\max(2^t,2^{t-1}+2\lceil k/2\rceil+9)$
G	Fig. 1(d) (novel)	Proposed	2^k banks of 2^t words	$(\min(t,k)+1)\cdot 2^{k+1}-2$	$2^t+n\cdot\max(2^t,2^{t-1}+\lceil\min(t,k)/2\rceil+8)$

Table 1: Comparison of different architectures using different permutation methods, for a radix-2 Pease FFT, for $k>1$.

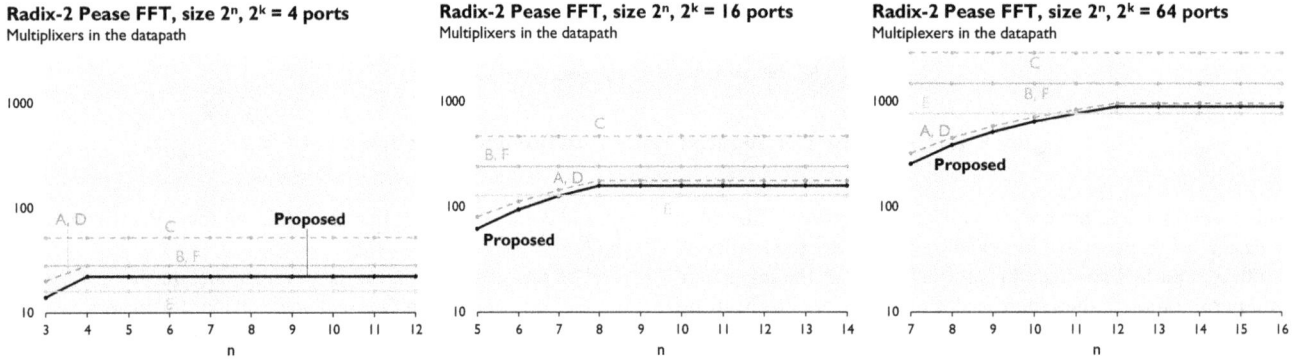

Figure 7: Number of 2-input multiplexers in the datapath of a radix-2 Pease FFT, for different streaming widths. Lower is better.

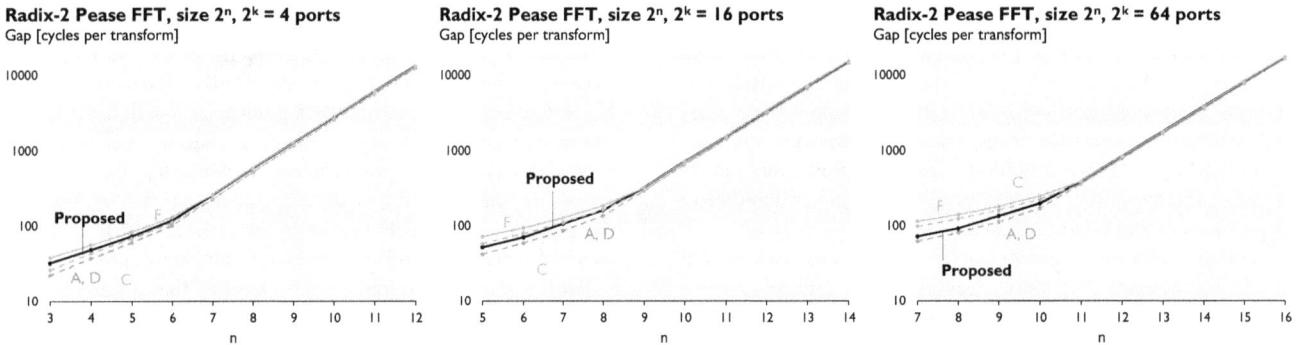

Figure 8: Gap of a radix-2 Pease FFT in number of cycles between two transforms, for different streaming widths. Lower is better.

requires a 4 cycles pipelining for the arithmetic part (butterfly and multiplications), and one register every 2 multiplexers (a complete permutation network has therefore a latency of $\lceil k/2\rceil+1$ cycles). Additionally, we assumed that all temporal permutations (even when fused) were done using the minimal possible latency; a feature that can easily be obtained using dual-ported RAM. However, with [11] (B and E), the total "temporal latency" depends on the chosen decomposition, and we can therefore only provide a lower bound. The corresponding formulas in Table 1 are plotted in Fig 8. It appears

that, for $n-k=t\geq 5$, the latency required to avoid two datasets overlapping in the loop dominates the intrinsic inner latency of the loop. Thus, the term 2^t becomes the dominant term in the max, and the gap becomes $n\cdot 2^t$ for all streaming iterative reuse architectures (A–D), and $(n+1)\cdot 2^t$ for the fused permutation structure (E–G). Thus, as n, and hence t, increases the gaps of the different solutions converge. The same is then also true for the throughputs.

Results after place and route. Among the prior FFT solutions only A ([10]) is available online at [23]. We compare these designs

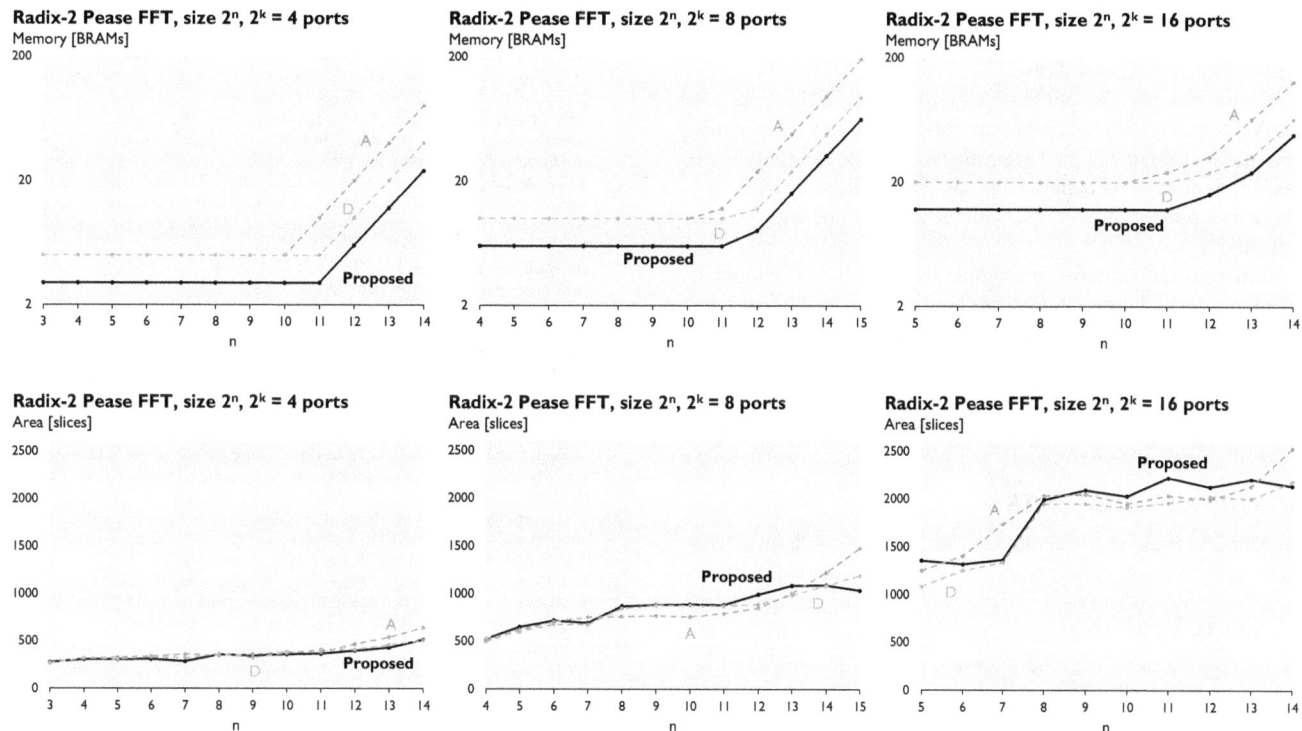

Figure 9: Resources used by a radix-2 Pease FFT. Lower is better.

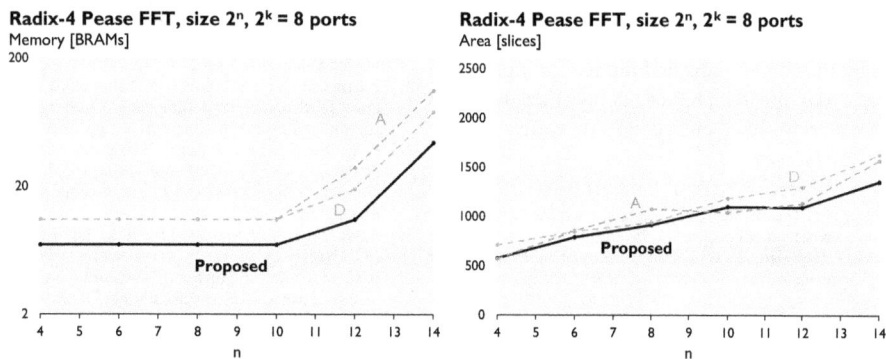

Figure 10: Resources used by a radix-4 Pease FFT. Lower is better.

with our solution G after place-and-route. For completeness we also implemented a variant of our generator [18] that produces the FFTs in D, which reduces the RAM cost of A.

The area and the RAM consumption of different designs for a radix-2 FFT are shown in Fig. 9, after place and route on a Xilinx Virtex 7 xc7vx1140 using Vivado 2014.4, using an element size of 16 bits. We observe that, as the number of RAM bank does not depend on n in the considered designs, the memory consumption stays constant until the capacity of the BRAM is reached. As expected from Table 1 our design requires fewer BRAMs; since the twiddle

factors are stored in BRAMs as well, the RAM usage is not exactly halved. The logic area is roughly comparable and includes the control, which was not included in Table 1. While our control logic is arguably more efficient than storing all the switch configuration and addresses for all cycles, it is more complex than the one used in A or D, which explains why we do not require fewer slices.

Fig. 10 shows some results for a radix-4 FFT, which slightly reduces the number of multiplications needed but can only be folded at the granularity of DFT$_4$ blocks, which themselves are implemented using four butterflies. The overall behavior and comparison is analogous to the radix-2 case.

Discussion. Because our main target is FPGA, which contains BRAM modules, we compared our work with other RAM-based permutation techniques. However, other approaches based on registers [13] or distributed buffers [15] could be beneficial on platforms where grouping several memory elements does not improve the cost (ASICs).

Hardware architectures to compute DFTs are a classic topic in the literature, and other approaches that also use a RAM capacity equal to the size of the dataset (2^n) exist. However, these works are based on in-place algorithms [25], or consist of parameterized architectures [26] that do not provide the same flexibility as a generated streamed architecture (for instance, the number of ports is constrained by the radix used in the algorithm).

ACKNOWLEDGMENTS

The authors would like to thank Peter A. Milder for helpful discussions, and the anonymous reviewers for their suggestions.

6 CONCLUSIONS

We proposed a novel method to design a datapath capable of realizing a number of fixed streamed linear permutations. As main application we proposed a new variant of a folded Pease FFT that requires only one permutation block for both, the internal shuffles and the final bit reversal. While in some FFT applications, the bit reversal can be omitted, in many others it cannot, e.g., if frequency components need to be processed in order from low to high. For those, our new architecture offers novel Pareto-optimal tradeoffs between performance and logic/memory cost across an entire design space of FFTs given by the chosen radix and number of input ports. These should directly translate to increased energy efficiency for a wide range of resource-constrained embedded applications.

REFERENCES

[1] D. Cohen, "Simplified control of FFT hardware," *IEEE Transactions on Acoustics, Speech, and Signal Processing*, vol. 24, no. 6, pp. 577–579, 1976.
[2] P. Kumhom, J. R. Johnson, and P. Nagvajara, "Design, optimization, and implementation of a universal FFT processor," in *Proc. International ASIC/SOC Conference (ASIC)*, pp. 182–186, 2000.
[3] A. Cortés, I. Vélez, and J. F. Sevillano, "Radix r^k FFTs: Matricial representation and SDC/SDF pipeline implementation," *IEEE Transactions on Signal Processing*, vol. 57, no. 7, pp. 2824–2839, 2009.
[4] S. He and M. Torkelson, "A new approach to pipeline FFT processor," in *Proc. Parallel Processing Symposium (IPPS)*, pp. 766–770, 1996.
[5] B. Akin, F. Franchetti, and J. C. Hoe, "FFTs with near-optimal memory access through block data layouts: Algorithm, architecture and design automation," *Journal of Signal Processing Systems*, vol. 85, no. 1, pp. 67–82, 2015.
[6] M. C. Pease, "An adaptation of the fast Fourier transform for parallel processing," *Journal of the ACM*, vol. 15, no. 2, pp. 252–264, 1968.
[7] J. H. Takala, T. S. Jarvinen, and H. T. Sorokin, "Conflict-free parallel memory access scheme for FFT processors," in *Proc. International Symposium on Circuits and Systems (ISCAS)*, vol. 4, pp. 524–527, 2003.
[8] K. J. Page, J. F. Arrigo, and P. M. Chau, "Reconfigurable-hardware-based digital signal processing for wireless communications," in *Advanced Signal Processing Algorithms, Architectures and Implementations* (P. SPIE, ed.), vol. 3162, pp. 529–540, 1997.
[9] G. Nordin, P. A. Milder, J. C. Hoe, and M. Püschel, "Automatic generation of customized discrete Fourier transform IPs," in *Proc. Design Automation Conference (DAC)*, pp. 471–474, 2005.
[10] P. A. Milder, F. Franchetti, J. C. Hoe, and M. Püschel, "Computer generation of hardware for linear digital signal processing transforms," *Transactions on Design Automation of Electronic Systems (TODAES)*, vol. 17, no. 2, pp. 15:1–15:33, 2012.
[11] P. A. Milder, J. C. Hoe, and M. Püschel, "Automatic generation of streaming datapaths for arbitrary fixed permutations," in *Proc. Design, Automation and Test in Europe (DATE)*, pp. 1118–1123, 2009.
[12] T. Koehn and P. Athanas, "Arbitrary streaming permutations with minimum memory and latency," in *Proc. International Conference on Computer-Aided Design (ICCAD)*, pp. 1–6, 2016.
[13] K. K. Parhi, "Systematic synthesis of DSP data format converters using life-time analysis and forward-backward register allocation," *IEEE Transactions on Circuits and Systems II (TCAS-II)*, vol. 39, no. 7, pp. 423–440, 1992.
[14] K. J. Page and P. M. Chau, "Folding large regular computational graphs onto smaller processor arrays," in *Advanced Signal Processing Algorithms, Architectures and Implementations* (P. SPIE, ed.), vol. 2846, pp. 383–394, 1996.
[15] T. Järvinen, P. Salmela, H. Sorokin, and J. Takala, "Stride permutation networks for array processors," in *Proc. International Conference on Application-Specific Systems, Architectures and Processors Proceedings (ASAP)*, pp. 376–386, 2004.
[16] M. Püschel, P. A. Milder, and J. C. Hoe, "Permuting streaming data using RAMs," *Journal of the ACM*, vol. 56, no. 2, pp. 10:1–10:34, 2009.
[17] F. Serre, T. Holenstein, and M. Püschel, "Optimal circuits for streamed linear permutations using RAM," in *Proc. International Symposium on Field-Programmable Gate Arrays (FPGA)*, pp. 215–223, 2016.
[18] F. Serre, "DFT and streamed linear permutation generator for hardware." https://acl.inf.ethz.ch/research/hardware/, 2018.
[19] M. C. Pease, "The indirect binary n-cube microprocessor array," *IEEE Transactions on Computers*, vol. 26, no. 5, pp. 458–473, 1977.
[20] J. Lenfant and S. Tahé, "Permuting data with the Omega network," *Acta Informatica*, vol. 21, no. 6, pp. 629–641, 1985.
[21] F. Serre and M. Püschel, "Generalizing block LU factorization: A lower-upper-lower block triangular decomposition with minimal off-diagonal ranks," *Linear Algebra and its Applications*, vol. 509, pp. 114–142, 2016.
[22] F. de Dinechin and B. Pasca, "Designing custom arithmetic data paths with FloPoCo," *IEEE Design & Test of Computers*, vol. 28, no. 4, pp. 18–27, 2011.
[23] P. A. Milder, "Spiral DFT/FFT IP core generator." http://www.spiral.net/hardware/dftgen.html, 2008.
[24] A. Waksman, "A permutation network," *Journal of the ACM*, vol. 15, no. 1, pp. 159–163, 1968.
[25] B. G. Jo and M. H. Sunwoo, "New continuous-flow mixed-radix (CFMR) FFT processor using novel in-place strategy," *IEEE Transactions on Circuits and Systems I (TCAS-I)*, vol. 52, no. 5, pp. 911–919, 2005.
[26] M. Garrido, M. Ángel Sánchez, M. L. López-Vallejo, and J. Grajal, "A 4096-point radix-4 memory-based FFT using DSP slices," *IEEE Transactions on Very Large Scale Integration (VLSI) Systems*, vol. 25, no. 1, pp. 375–379, 2017.

Degree-aware Hybrid Graph Traversal on FPGA-HMC Platform

Jialiang Zhang and Jing Li
Department of Electrical and Computer Engineering
University of Wisconsin-Madison
jialiang.zhang@ece.wisc.edu, jli@ece.wisc.edu

ABSTRACT

Graph traversal is a core primitive for graph analytics and a basis for many higher-level graph analysis methods. However, irregularities in the structure of scale-free graphs (e.g., social network) limit our ability to analyze these important and growing datasets. A key challenge is the redundant graph computations caused by the presence of high-degree vertices which not only increase the total amount of computations but also incur unnecessary random data access.

In this paper, we present a graph processing system on an FPGA-HMC platform, based on software/hardware co-design and co-optimization. For the first time, we leverage the inherent graph property i.e. vertex degree to co-optimize algorithm and hardware architecture. In particular, we first develop two algorithm optimization techniques: *degree-aware adjacency list reordering* and *degree-aware vertex index sorting*. The former can reduce the number of redundant graph computations, while the latter can create a strong correlation between vertex index and data access frequency, which can be effectively applied to guide the hardware design. We further implement the optimized hybrid graph traversal algorithm on an FPGA-HMC platform. By leveraging the strong correlation between vertex index and data access frequency made by degree-aware vertex index sorting, we develop two platform-dependent hardware optimization techniques, namely *degree-aware data placement* and *degree-aware adjacency list compression*. These two techniques together substantially reduce the amount of access to external memory. Finally, we conduct extensive experiments on an FPGA-HMC platform to verify the effectiveness of the proposed techniques. To the best of our knowledge, our implementation achieves the highest performance (45.8 billion traversed edges per second) among existing FPGA-based graph processing systems.

ACM Reference Format:
Jialiang Zhang and Jing Li. 2018. Degree-aware Hybrid Graph Traversal on FPGA-HMC Platform. In *Proceedings of 2018 ACM/SIGDA International Symposium on Field-Programmable Gate Arrays (FPGA '18)*. ACM, New York, NY, USA, 10 pages. https://doi.org/10.1145/3174243.3174245

1 INTRODUCTION

In response to the increasingly larger and more diverse graphs in social science[21], machine learning[8], search engine[11], and the

critical need of analyzing them, graph analytics, an essential class of big data analysis, has emerged as a new fundamental computing methodology to explore the comprehensive relationship among a vast collection of interconnected entities. Among all graph primitives in graph analytics, graph traversal has served as a basis for many higher-level graph analysis algorithms.

Unfortunately, graph traversal is notoriously inefficient due to the low computational intensity and irregular data access [2]. The problem is further aggravated in processing scale-free graphs — an essential class of real-world graphs where the distribution of vertex degrees (the number of edge connections per vertex) asymptotically follows a power law distribution. Scale-free graphs have been widely used in a number of important application domains including social science, computer network, finance, and biology. However, despite of their popularity, the unique topology of scale-free graphs creates additional challenges in processing. The reason is that the presence of high-degree vertices in scale-free graphs can cause a large number of redundant edge checks during the traversal, as reported by a number of prior work [2, 3, 14, 22]. The redundant edge checks not only increase the total number of graph computations but also incur unnecessary random data access, becoming the key performance bottleneck of existing graph processing systems.

To tackle such challenge, several existing work focus on algorithm optimization on conventional CPU- or GPU-based systems. For instance, Beamer *et al.* [3] proposes a *bottom-up* method, which takes an opposite direction of visiting the adjacency list of each vertex, compared to the traditional *top-down* approach. Experiment results confirm its effectiveness in reducing the number of redundant edge checks and achieving high throughput on large scale-free graphs on CPU-based systems. Gunrock *et al* [14, 22] further applies directional optimization to derive a *hybrid* graph traversal method by combining the best advantages of both *top-down* and *bottom-up* approaches. In their hybrid method, traversal direction (either top-down or bottom-up) can be optimally selected at each step during the traversal. The implementation on GPU-based systems with GPU specific optimizations has shown that the hybrid method is more effective than either of the prior methods (*bottom-up* or *top-down*) in reducing redundant graph computations and thus achieves better performance.

Although algorithm optimization has been demonstrated as an important approach to improve the efficiency of graph traversal, high-performance graph processing system could further benefit from careful optimization of the underlying hardware architectures, as often times the performance bottleneck of existing graph processing systems has shown to be bounded by the external memory [5]. Several recent works propose that customizing the hardware using FPGA can effectively alleviate the memory bottleneck [6, 10, 12, 26]. However, despite different system architectures, most of these works [6, 10, 12] are based on one common scheme: By placing hot data, which is used for synchronization between parallel kernels, on the on-chip block ram (BRAM) to alleviate the pressure on accessing external DRAM, the efficiency of processing scale-free graphs can be significantly improved. In addition to conventional DRAM-based FPGA graph processing systems, Zhang *et al* [25] propose to leverage the exceptional random access performance of the emerging hybrid memory cube (HMC) to further improve the external memory access. However, this body of research all implements the conventional *top-down* graph traversal algorithm and does not leverage the state-of-the-art direction optimization techniques, resulting in limited performance gain.

In this work, we leverage the inherent graph property i.e. *vertex degree* to co-optimize algorithm and hardware architecture to achieve a workload-optimized graph processing system. We will show that *vertex degree* contains rich information of graph topology in scale-free graphs and thus provides another key dimension in optimization space in both algorithm and hardware. To the best of our knowledge, we are the *first* to leverage the degree information to optimize graph traversal algorithm to reduce the redundant graph computation and thus improve memory access. Our work also differs from prior work on hardware customization, as we not only implement the state-of-the-art hybrid graph traversal but also optimize the system design by leveraging the essential graph property.

Specifically, we made the following contributions.

- We performed a comprehensive study on the properties of real-world scale-free graphs and found that the degree distribution of the graph is highly non-uniform. This non-uniform degree distribution forms the basis of the various optimization techniques in this paper.
- Based on these insights from graph analysis, we developed two algorithm optimization techniques: *degree-aware adjacency list reordering* and *degree-aware vertex index sorting*. The former can reduce the number of redundant edge checks in the *bottom-up* method, while the latter can create a strong correlation between vertex index and data access frequency, which can be effectively applied to guide the hardware design.
- We developed a new graph processing system to implement the optimized hybrid graph traversal algorithm on an FPGA-HMC platform. By leveraging the strong correlation between vertex index and data access frequency made by degree-aware vertex index sorting, we further developed two platform-dependent hardware optimization techniques, namely *degree-aware data placement* and *degree-aware adjacency list compression*. These two techniques together substantially reduce the amount of access to external memory.
- We conducted extensive experiments on an FPGA-HMC platform to verify the effectiveness of the proposed techniques. To the best of our knowledge, our implementation achieves the highest performance (45.8 billion traversed edges per second) among existing FPGA-based graph processing systems.

The rest of the paper is organized as follows. In section 2, we present the background of hybrid graph traversal algorithm and the FPGA-based graph processing system. In section 3, we present

the insights gained on analyzing the scale-free graphs followed by two algorithm optimization techniques, namely degree-aware adjacency list reordering and degree-aware vertex index sorting. In section 5, we present the software/hardware implementations including the key data structure, system architecture and two platform-dependent hardware optimization techniques, namely degree-aware data placement and degree-aware pointer compression. In section 6, we present the evaluation methodology and experimental results. In section 7, we conclude the paper.

2 BACKGROUND

In this section, we will first introduce the state-of-the-art hybrid graph traversal algorithm. Specifically, we will discuss the *top-down* method, the *bottom-up* method and the *inter-step* direction switching. Then, we will review existing work on the FPGA-based graph traversal system.

2.1 Hybrid graph traversal

Graph traversal is one of the most important kernels of many graph applications, and it is typically used to test the connectivity or to find the single-source shortest paths. As shown in figure 1, graph traversal starts from one source vertex, and the frontier expands to the neighbors of the source vertices during each step. All of the vertices at the same depth will be visited before visiting any vertices at a greater depth. The major portion of the computation in graph traversal is to find the unvisited neighbors of the frontier. The process ends when all vertices are visited, and yields a spanning tree, which contains all the connected source vertices. The number of edges in the spanning tree indicates the theoretical minimum number of edge check in a graph traversal. In the best case, if the spanning tree is known, we can achieve this minimum number. Here, we define the **redundant edge check**: the edge check which does not add an edge to the final spanning tree.

The conventional *top-down* method (figure 1) starts from the frontier, each vertex in the frontier checks all of its neighbors to see if any of them are unvisited. Each unvisited neighbor is marked as visited, added to the frontier of next step. The total number of edge checks with the *top-down* method is equal to the number of edges in the connected component containing the source vertex, as in each step every edge in the frontier is checked. When the number of edges to be checked from frontier is large, the *top-down* method becomes inefficient, as it checks all the edge connect to the same vertices from different vertices in the frontier, and only one check will update the final spanning tree. As a result, it performs a large number of redundant edge check.

To address this issue Beamer [3] proposes the *bottom-up* method for implementing the graph traversal algorithm. In this method, instead of iterating through the frontier, it iterate through the unvisited vertices array. For each, we test to see if any of its neighbors is in the frontier. When a neighbor is found in the frontier, *bottom-up* method terminates the edge check earilier, mark the vertex as visited and add it to the frontier of next step (figure 1(c)). Therefore, the *bottom-up* method can reduce the number of redundant edge check. This technique is advantageous when the frontier size is large, and disadvantageous when the frontier is small.

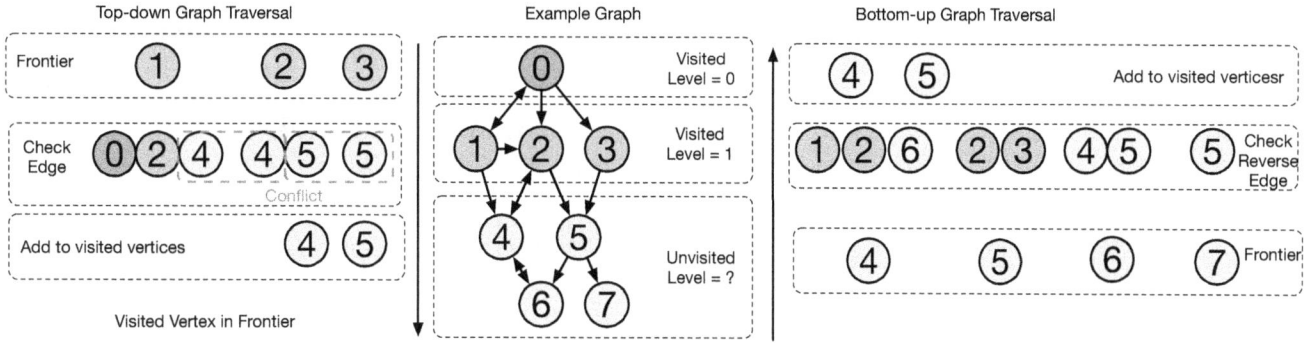

Figure 1: Example of *top-down* and *bottom-up* method in graph traversal

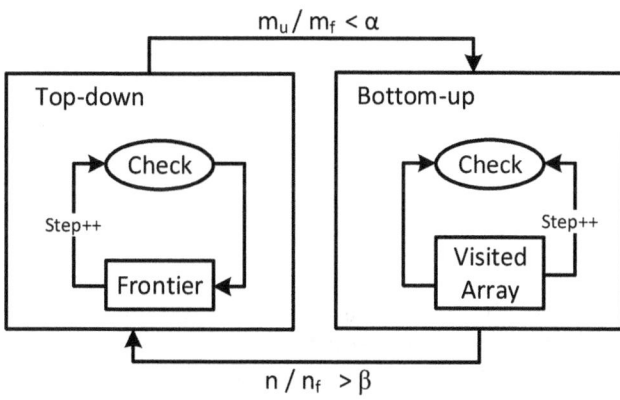

Figure 2: Hybrid (direction-optimizing) BFS

The *top-down* and *bottom-up* algorithms are complementary, since the *bottom-up* method performs well, when the frontier size is large, whereas the *top-down* method performs worse, and vice versa. To determine the graph traversal direction, Beamer et al. further introduce the Hybrid traversal algorithm. Figure 2 presents the flow of hybrid graph traversal. The hybrid graph traversal always starts from using *top-down* method as the frontier size is 1. As in figure 2, two thresholds(α and β) are used to control the direction switching, m_u represents the unexplored edge count, m_f is the number of edges to be checked from the frontier, and α determines when the number of edges to be checked fro the frontier is large enough to switch from *top-down* to *bottom-up*; n represents the number of vertices in the graph and n_f is the number of vertices in the frontier, and β determines when the frontier is small enough to use *top-down* method. Both of the two thresholds are heuristically determined. In this paper, we will show that there is still substantial to further improve the performance of hybrid graph traversal, and building an efficient hybrid graph traversal system on FPGA-HMC system will require a number of optimizations, including both platform-independent and platform-dependent techniques.

2.2 FPGA-based Graph Processing framework

There are several existing works on implementing graph accelerators using FPGAs. GRAPHGEN[18] proposed an FPGA-based graph

processing system using a vertex-centric model. However, it stores the whole graph in the on-board DDR DRAM, which severely limits the performance due to the bandwidth bottleneck of the memory. Also, the design does not provide any platform-aware software and hardware optimizations for implementing BFS. TorusBFS [13] proposed a 2-D message passing structure to reduce the latency between parallel BFS kernels, but its performance is also limited by the poor random access performance of DRAM and the available on-chip resources. FPGP [6] employed an interval-shared structure to maximize off-chip memory bandwidth and to exploit the parallelism of graph processing fully. However, its performance is still bounded by the capacity and bandwidth of FPGA's on-chip memory. ForeGraph[7] proposes to improve the scalability on multi-FPGA architectures. [25] implements the push method of graph traversal algorithms on an FPGA-HMC platform. All of these works are proposing new algorithms, data structures and hardware architectures to increase locality and utilization of memory bandwidth. However, none of these framework attempt to reduce the number of computations (number of edge checks). To the best of our knowledge, we are the first work to provide architectural support on FPGA for the hybrid graph traversal to reduce the number of computations.

3 ALGORITHM OPTIMIZATION

In this section, we will first present our observation on the non-uniform degree distribution of scale-free graphs. Then, we will propose two optimization techniques to reduce the redundancy in hybrid graph traversal based on the degree information. In particular, we effectively leverage the degree information of scale-free graphs to reduce the redundancy in the algorithm and provide insights to its data access frequency.

3.1 Non-uniform degree distribution in scale-free graphs

The performance of graph traversal is not only determined by the algorithm, but also by the topology of the graphs. In this work, we focus on the scale-free graph, which is one of the most important categories of the large-scale graph. A few examples of scale-free graphs include social networks, computer networks, financial networks, and protein-protein interaction networks. In a scale-free

Table 1: Comparisons of the number of edge checks with different method using *bottom-up* method. We also list the number of using *top-down* for reference

Step	Top-down	Bottom-up(Random)	Bottom-up(Desc)	Bottom-up(Asec)
2	346918235(25x)	52677691(3.9x)	**13455687**(1x)	91365756(6.79x)
3	1727195615(195x)	10568751(1.19x)	**8820854**(1x)	11065150(1.25x)
4	29557400(286x)	153245(1.48x)	**103184**(1x)	203844(1.97x)
5	82357(3.83x)	21467(1x)	**21467**(1x)	21467(1x)
Total	2103753607 (92.3x)	63421157 (2.79x)	**22701186**(1x)	102656217(4.52x)

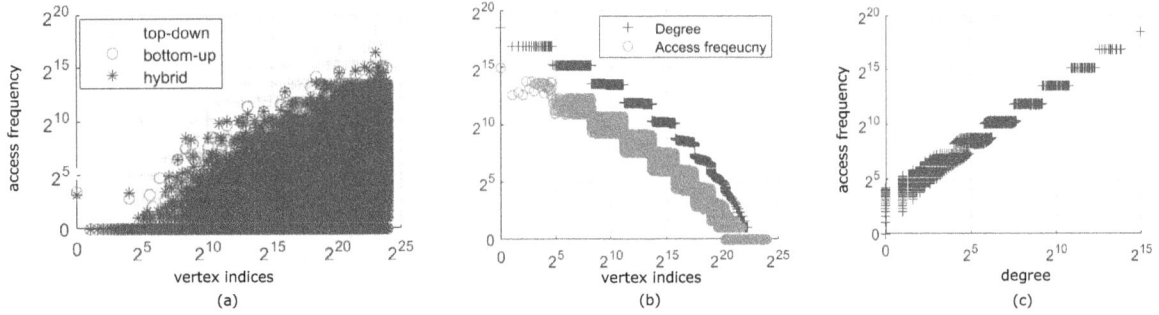

Figure 3: (a)Degree Access frequency distribution on unsorted graph; (b) Degree and access frequency of sorted vertex; (c) Strong correlation between access frequency and degrees

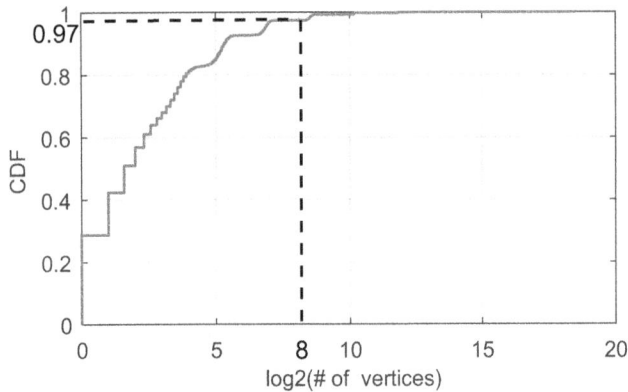

Figure 4: Cumulative distribution of vertex degree for rgg_s24_e16

graph, most vertices have only a small number of neighbors, and can reach others with a small number of hops. A scale-free graph typically has a degree distribution which follows a power-law, at least asymptotically [1, 24]. To show such power-law distribution, we plot the cumulative distribution of vertex degree of a Kronecker generated graph, which is a scale-free graph, as defined in GRAPH500 benchmark suite [16]. We can clearly see that 0.002% vertices with the largest degree contribute more than 97 % of the total edge connections.

Such a non-uniform degree distribution of scale-free graph is the basis of our optimizations. The degree distribution provides important information about the graph topology on which vertices have more connection to others. The more connection a vertex has,

it is more likely that its status will be checked during the graph traversal. Moreover, it is trivial to obtain the degree information. For that, we can subtract the two nearby elements of the vertex indices list, which is the data structure to store the edge information and will be shown in section 4. Leveraging the degree information, we can reduce the redundant calculation, as well as the memory access. In section 3.2, we show the degree-aware adjacency list reordering technique, which can reduce redundant edge checks by terminating the *bottom-up* edge checks at an earlier stage. In section 3.3, we show the strong correlation between access frequency and degree of vertices, which can be used to guide the data placement in the hardware design (section 5).

3.2 Degree-aware adjacency list reordering

In this section, we propose to sort the adjacency list based on the vertices degree in the *bottom-up* method to further reduce the number of the redundant edge checks. As discussed in section 2.1, the *bottom-up* method scans the neighbors of all unvisited vertices and terminates earlier when one neighbor is found in the frontier. The timing of the early termination, which indicates how many edge checks it can save, is determined by the order of checking the status of neighbors (order in the adjacency list). In the best case, for all unvisited vertices scanned in the *bottom-up* method, the first neighbor to check is in the frontier. In this case, there are no redundant edge checks, as it checks only one edge and skips all the others. However, it is non-trivial to obtain the optimal order for the adjacency list. The reason is that we need to run the graph traversal first to get the vertices in the frontier in each step. Moreover, the optimal order may not be the same for different source vertices, as the frontier in each step is different. Instead of finding the optimal

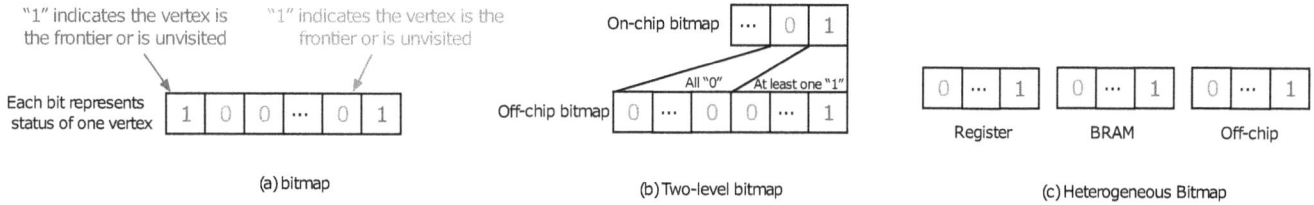

Figure 5: Illustration of bitmap

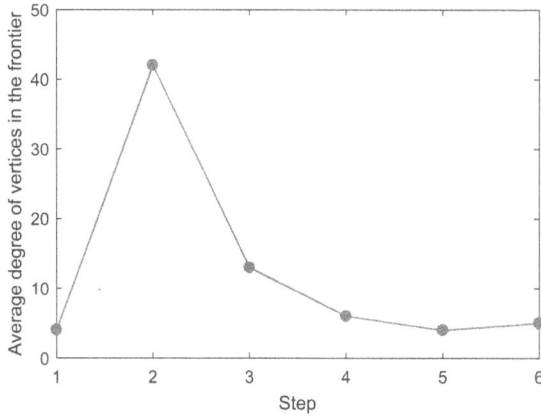

Figure 6: Average degree of vertices in the frontier of each step

order of the adjacency list , we propose a heuristic method, which sorts the adjacency list of each vertex based on the degree.

In table 1, we compare the number of checked edges for each step in both *top-down* and the *bottom-up* method using three different orders: **Descending order**, **Ascending order** and **Random order**. The table 1 shows that descending order can reduce the total number of edge checks and saves the most edge checks in step 2, which contributes most of edge checks. The reason is that veritices with higher degree tend to be visited in the first step in the *bottom-up* method. For example, as shown in figure 6, the average degree of the frontier of the step 2 is substantially larger than other steps. By sorting the adjacency list in the **descending order**, vertices in the frontier of the step 2, which have larger degree, are checked earlier than other vertices with lower degree. Though the number of reduced edge checks by using the **descending** compared to the **random** and the **ascending** order in other steps is not as large as the step 2, the adjacency list sorting still can reduce a substantial number of redundant edge checks, as the step 2 claims the most vertices.

3.3 Sorting Vertex Indices by degree

The locality in the scale-free graphs is considered weak due to its nature of sparsity and randomness[3]. In this section, we identify the relationship between degree and access frequency, which can be used to guide our hardware design.

More specifically, by sorting the vertex indices based on the degree in the descending order. We assign lower indices to vertices

with high-degree and vice versa. To check how the vertices sorting affects the locality, we plot the relationship between vertex indices and access frequency on the unsorted graph and sorted graph in figure 3 (a) and (b) separately. We can see figure 3(b) shows the correlation clearly. We further plot the correlation between vertex degree and the access frequency in (figure 3 (c)). By sorting the graph, it is possible to know the degree of vertices without counting its neighbor. Moreover, we can find a strong correlation between vertex degree (indices) and access frequency, which could be used to guide the data placement. Such strong correlation is very useful to us, as it connects a run-time determined statistic (access frequency) to an off-line known property (degree distribution). Therefore, we can predict the access frequency before running the program. We can place data with different access frequency to different types of memories to maximize the memory access efficiency. We will discuss such software-hardware co-optimization in section 5.2 and section 5.3.

4 SOFTWARE IMPLEMENTATION

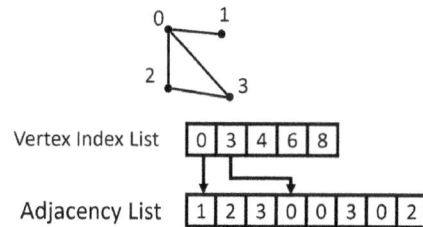

Figure 7: Illustration of adjacency list

As discussed in section 2.1, the *top-down* method needs to scan the frontier, read neighbor indices from the adjacency list ,and check the status of vertices. The *bottom-up* method follows the opposite order, which scans the status of vertices, reads the neighbor indices from the adjacency list and checks the frontier.

We first show the data structure for the frontier and the status of vertices. The key difference between scanning and checking is that the scanning reads the whole data structure *sequentially* and the checking reads the data structure *randomly* based on the indices reads from the adjacency list. The checking is considered costly, as random memory accesses have small granularities (sometimes 1 bit).

In this work, we use bitmaps, for bookkeeping both the frontier and the status of vertices, as [25] has already shown that the bitmap is a compact data structure for the frontier and can speed up the scanning. Figure5 (a) illustrates the idea of bitmap. Each bit in the bitmap indicates whether the corresponding vertices is in the frontier or has been already visited. Different from [25], which only accelerates the scanning, this work also leverage the bitmap to accelerate the checking for both the frontier and status of vertices. Between these two types of bitmap check, the frontier bitmap check is more critical to the performance. The reason is that the hybrid algorithm tends to have more edges checked in the *bottom-up* method compared to the *top-down* method, as listed in table 1. Hence, we choose to reduce the cost of the frontier bitmap reading in the *bottom-up* step by leveraging the correlation between vertex degree and access frequency (section 2.3). We will provide more details in section 5.2.

The other data structure used in the hybrid graph traversal is the adjacency list (figure 7), which stores all the edge information. Reading the adjacency list is also costly, as it has a large size and can only be stored off-chip. The reason is that each element in the adjacency list is an vertex index, as shown in figure5, and typically has 32 bits or 64 bits. In the hybrid graph traversal, both the *top-down* and *bottom-up* method needs to read each element of the adjacency list only once. Therefore, it is impossible to reuse the data to reduce the external memory traffic. Instead, we try to reduce the size of each element. In section 5.3, we present our technique of compressing the the vertex indices.

5 HARDWARE IMPLEMENTATION

In this section, we will first introduce the implementation of the hybrid graph traversal on the FPGA-HMC platform. Then, we will provide two degree-aware optimization techniques: degree-aware data placement and degree-aware pointer compression to further accelerate the graph traversal based on the degree information.

5.1 Hybrid graph traversal algorithm on FPGA-HMC platform

In this subsection, we will present details of our architecture for the optimized hybrid graph traversal. We show the architectural diagram of the proposed implementation of the hybrid graph traversal in figure 11. In contrast to the system architecture described in [25], which implements only *top-down* graph method, we add/modify several hardware components to adapt to the hybrid graph traversal algorithm. Particularly, we add a new pipeline to support the *bottom-up* method, as well as statistic counters and direction switching logic to support the optimized direction switching. To accelerate the scanning of vertex status bitmap in the *bottom-up* method, we adopt the two-level bitmap design to reduce the traffic to the external memory. Moreover, we introduce a new organization of the frontier bitmap, as the *bottom-up* method have massive random access to the frontier bitmap. Finally, we modify the *top-down* pipeline to adopt all the architectural changes above. The only component, which is from [25] is the interface design for reordering HMC requests. The details of each design component are described below:

- **Pipeline for *bottom-up* method:** We design a new pipeline for the *bottom-up* method, as it has a different data flow compared to the *top-down* method. As shown in figure 9(b), it first scans the vertices bitmap to find all the unvisited vertices.

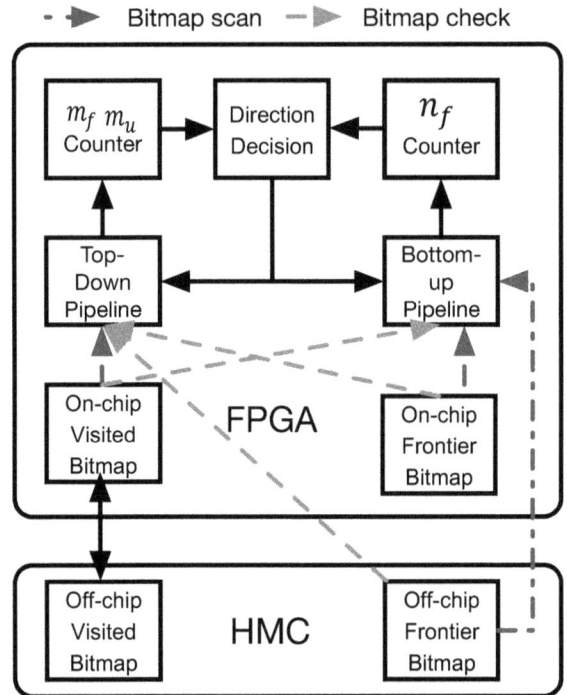

Figure 8: Architecture support for hybrid graph trveral

Then it reads the adjacency list from HMC to get the indices of neighbors to check. Finally, it checks all its neighbors to see if any of them is in the frontier. If so, the *bottom-up* pipeline marked the vertices as visited,and add it to the frontier of next step. As the *bottom-up* method only allows the child to update the visited flag by itself, the visited bitmap update doesn't need to be atomic.

- **Statistic counters:** We implement three counters to collect the statistics needed to support the direction switching: number of edges to check from the frontier(m_f), the size of the frontier(n_f) and the unexplored number of edges (m_u). These three statistics are calculated *sequentially* after each step in the CPU implementation[3] and the GPU implementation[22]. By taking advantage of the flexibility of FPGA, we implement three counters, which run in parallel to other components. These counters are updated when vertices are added to the frontier of next step. Therefore, we do not need an extra scan of the frontier after each step, which can take up to 20% of the total runtime in CPU implementation[2]. More specifically, the m_f and n_f are calculated by accumulating the degrees and the number of vertices when a vertex is added to the frontier of next step. The (m_u) is calculated by subtracting the sum of degrees of all visited vertices from the total number of edges.

- **Direction decision logic:** We implement a direction decision logic to support the optimized direction-switching. The direction decision logic compares the three statistics we collected from the last layer with the heuristic thresholds to

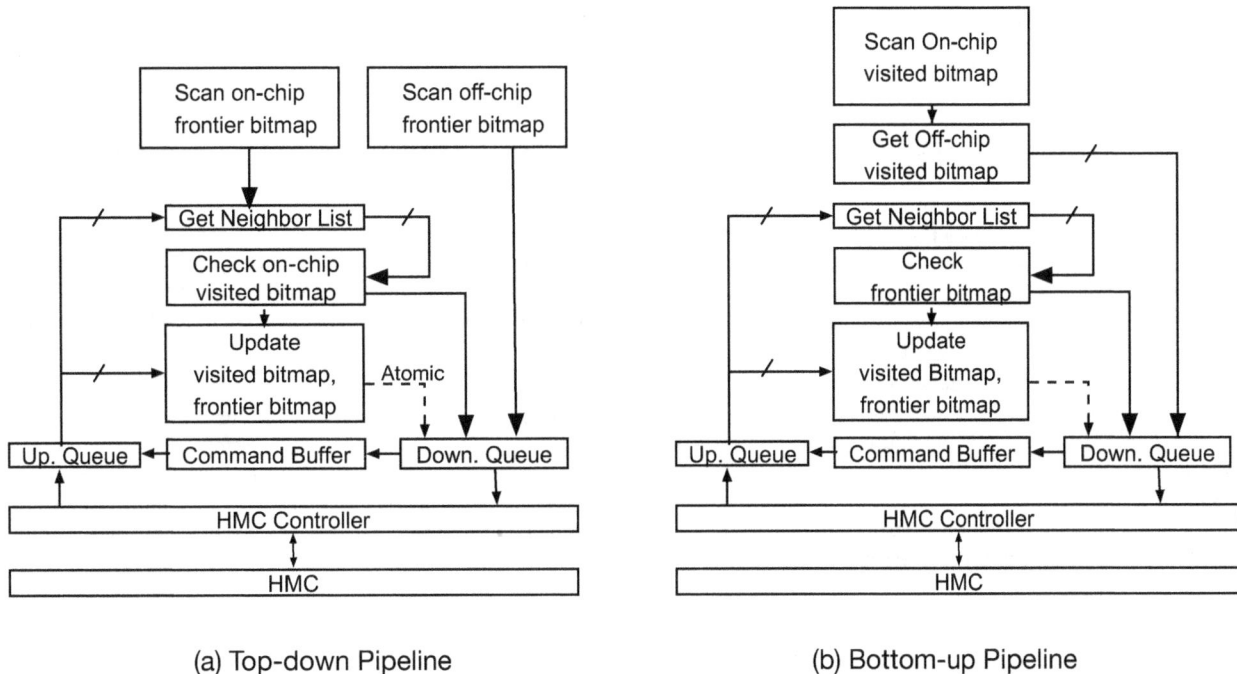

Figure 9: Data flow of the FPGA implementation of the (a) *top-down* (b) *bottom-up* graph traversal

determine whether *top-down* or *bottom-up* method should be invoked. We set these two thresholds to $\alpha = 15$ and $\beta = 20$, as in [3].

- **Bitmap of the status of vertices:** We use a two-level bitmap to store the unvisited vertices array instead of a single-level off-chip flag array (stores the parent of each vertices), as in Zhang *et al* [25]. As shown in Table 1, the number of unvisited vertices is relatively small, which makes the unvisited list very sparse. For every step using the *bottom-up* method, we need to scan the whole vertices status array to find all unvisited vertices. The sparsity of unvisited vertices leads a considerable amount of unnecessary external memory accesses. As discussed in Zhang *et al* [25], a two-level bitmap can accelerate the scanning of the frontier bitmap, which is also sparse in some steps. In this work, we adapt the two-level bitmap in [25] to the vertices status array. More particularly, as shown in figure 5 (b), the on-chip bitmap is initialized to all 0's at the beginning of the first *bottom-up* step. we first scan the on-chip bitmap to find the non-zero bits, which indicates there is at least 1 unvisited vertex in the corresponding vertices group. If the *bottom-up* method marks all of the vertices in this group visited, we set the on-chip bitmap to 1. During the *top-down* method, we do not check or update the on-chip bitmap. Checking whether all vertices in one group are visited in the *top-down* method has extra costs, as scanning the off-chip vertices status bitmap is not an essential step of *top-down* method. The vertices status bitmap is also used in the *top-down* method while checking whether a neighbor of the vertex in the frontier is visited or not.

- **Frontier bitmap:** In this work, we introduce a new heterogeneous bitmap organization, which can adapt to the access pattern of *bottom-up* method. Compared to the *top-down* method, which only needs to scan the frontier sequentially to find all the vertices to be checked, the *bottom-up* method access the frontier in a random parallel manner, as several unvisited vertices could have the same parent. As the two-level bitmap can only improve the efficiency of sequential bitmap scan during the *top-down* method, which only contributes a small portion of the total runtime, we choose to optimize the memory access in the *bottom-up* method. We use a heterogeneous bitmap to store the frontier, which can provide different random access performance. In the next subsection, we will further discuss the data-placement policy based on the relationship between degree and access frequency (section 3.3).

- ***Top-down* pipeline:** We also modify the *top-down* pipeline, as the memory organization of both visited veritices bitmap and the frontier bitmap has changed. Particularly, we first scan the heterogeneous bitmap to find the vertices that need to be checked. Then, we read the adjacency list from external memory and check whether neighbors are visited by reading the off-chip vertices status array. The unvisited vertices are marked through atomic updates to both the on-chip and HMC vertices status bitmaps as shown in figure 9a.

5.2 Degree-aware data placement

As discussed in section 4.1, the most performance critical operation is reading the frontier bitmap in the *bottom-up* method. In this section, we will show how to leverage the strong relationship between degree and access frequency (section 3.3) to guide the design of the frontier bitmap.

To take advantage of the correlation between vertex degree and access frequency, we introduce three types of bitmap to store the status of the vertices: register file, BRAMs and external HMC. The register file is bit addressable and is used to store the vertices with the highest degree. In our implementation, the size of the bitmap register is 4096 bits and has 64 read ports to support multiple simultaneous reads in one cycle. The second type of bitmap storage is stored in the on-chip BRAM, which stores the sorted vertices with indices from 2049 to 65536. From figure 3, we can see that the first 256 (0.002%) vertices contribute more than 97% of the edge checks in the rgg_s24_e16 graph. The rest of the visited vertices bitmap, which mainly consists of the vertices whose degrees are smaller than 4 (in the rmat graph dataset), can be stored off-chip.

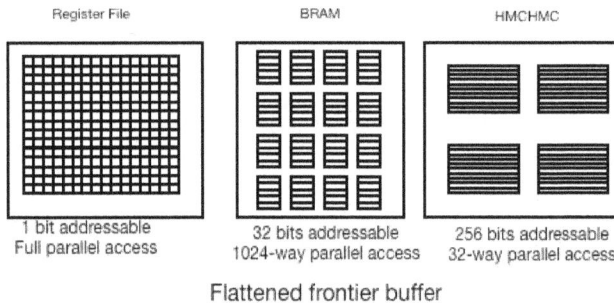

Figure 10: Flattened frontier buffer

5.3 Degree-aware adjacency list compression

To further leverage from non-uniform degree distribution, we propose to apply the coding technique to compress the adjacency list and reduce the runtime of neighbor accesses. The adjacency list stores the edge information on the external HMC, and will be accessed in both *top-down* and *bottom-up method*. Each element in the adjacency list is the index of a neighbor vertices. Vertices with higher degree will occurs more frequently in the adjacency list, and vice versa. For example , as shown in figure 7, vertex 0 occurs three time, and vertex 1 only occurs one time. However, prior works treat these vertices equally and use the same data format (e.g. uint32 or uint64), which is a waste of the storage and external memory bandwidth.

In this works, we apply a coding scheme to compress the adjacency list. By sorting vertices based on the degree in the descending order, as discussed in section 3.3, the vertices with lower indices have higher access frequency. In this case, Exp-Golomb coding [9], which is widely used in video compression [17] , can effectively compress the adjacency list to reduce the data access to the external memory. More specifically, It has been shown that Exp-Golomb coding has compression efficiency close to the more complex arithmetic

coding, and comparable to Huffman coding, if the input integer follows the assumption below: the larger the integer, the lower its probability of occurrence[9], which is exactly the the vertices list after sorting. Also, we choose the Exp-Golomb coding as its complexity is much lower than Huffman coding as it does not need to construct and store the Huffman tree.

In our design, we enable Exp-Golomb for a scale-free graph, such as indochina and rmat. As a uniformly generated graph, such as rgg, does not have enough variation of access frequency, the coding will essentially increase the length of the adjacency list. Our hardware implementation follows the parallel GR decoder design in [15].

6 PERFORMANCE EVALUATION

In this section, we will first present our evaluation methodology, which includes the experimental platform setup and the choice of dataset. Then, we will present the experimental results of the proposed design and compare it with the baseline design. Finally, we will project the performance with full HMC bandwidth and compare with the latest GPU implementation.

6.1 Hardware Platform

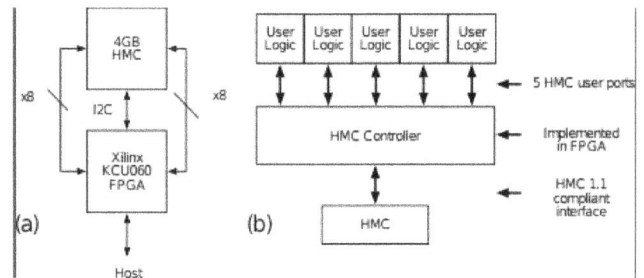

Figure 11: Diagram of experimental platform

We implement the proposed graph processor on an AC-510[20] and AC-520 FPGA-HMC platform from Micron. As shown in figure 11, the AC-510 platform has a Xilinx KCU060 FPGA and an 8GB HMC module. The HMC uses two half-width (8 lanes) 15G high-speed serial links, which provide a two-way bandwidth of 30GB/s, to communicate with the FPGA. The AC-520 platform has an Intel Arria 10 GX 1150 FPGA and a 4GB HMC module. The HMC interfaces with FPGA with four half-width links, which provide a two-way bandwidth of 60GB/s. The AC-520 also exposes the interface for power consumption measurement.

We implement our graph processing architecture using the PicoFramework, which provides an abstraction layer of the low level data transfer protocol. The kernel logic is driven by a 125 MHz clock, and on-chip memories are working at 250MHz in double-pump mode. The host machine is equipped with an Intel Xeon E5-1630V3 CPU and one DDR4 memory channel with a 16GB capacity. We use Ubuntu 14.04 as the host operating system and compile our CPU implementation using gcc with flags "-Ofast" and "-march=native." The GPU benchmark is running with a GTX Titan X graphics card with 12GB of GDDR5X VRAM. We summarize the resource utilization statistics in table 2. The high BRAM usage is

Table 2: FPGA resource utilization

	Available Resources	Proposed	Percentage
Logic	1506k	437k	64
BRAM	2713	2062	76
DSP	1518	64	4

because we hope to absorb as much off-chip memory access as possible by using a larger hierarchical frontier bitmap.

6.1.1 Datasets. We summarize the datasets used in our evaluations in table 3. Soc-orkut is a social graph; indochina-04 is a crawled hyperlink graph from indochina web domains; rmat_s22_e64, rmat_s23_e32, and rmat_s24_e16 are three generated R-MAT graphs with similar vertex counts. All five datasets are scale-free graphs with diameters less than 30 and unevenly distributed node degrees (80

Both rgg_n_24 and roadnet_usa datasets have large diameters with small and evenly distributed node degrees (most nodes have degree less than 12). soc-ork is from the Stanford Network Repository; Indochina-04 and roadnet are from the UF Sparse Matrix Collection; rmat_s22_e64 rmat_s23_e32, rmat_s24_e16, and rgg_n_24 are R-MAT and random geometric graphs we generated. For R-MAT, we use 16 as the edge factor, and the initiator parameters for the Kronecker graph generator are: a = 0.57, b = 0.19, c = 0.19, d = 0.05, which follows the Graph 500 Benchmark. For random geometric graphs, we set the threshold parameter to 0.000548.

Table 3: Test dataset (all directed graphs have been converted to un-directed graphs)

Dataset	Vertices	Edges	Max Degree	Diameter
soc-orkut	3M	212.7M	27,466	9
indochina-04	7.4M	302M	256425	26
rmat_s22_e64	4.2M	483M	451607	5
rmat_s23_e32	8.4M	505.6M	440396	6
rmat_s24_e16	16.8M	519.7M	432152	6
rgg_n_24	16.8M	265.1M	40	2622
roadnet_USA	23.9M	577.1M	9	6809

6.2 Experimental Results

We first compare the performance gain of the CPU-DRAM hybrid graph traversal algorithm and the FPGA+HMC based implementation in figure 12. The throughput gain of the proposed FPGA-HMC system is higher than the CPU-DRAM system[3] on the five scale-free graph datasets since the proposed FPGA-HMC system is optimized for the multiple random accesses of the frontier bitmap in the *bottom-up* graph traversal. Also, the five scale-free graphs with lower diameter have a large frontier size, which leads to more *bottom-up* method than *top-down* during the graph traversal and can benefit more from our optimization to the *bottom-up* method.

On the contrary, the performance gain difference on the scaled graph is relatively low, since nearly all steps use *top-down* method, which is hard for parallelization. We should note that most of the emerging graph analytics workloads, such as social networks, web, and communication networks are scale-free graphs[4].

In figure 13, we compare the performance gains of the three optimizations: degree-aware adjacency list reordering, degree aware

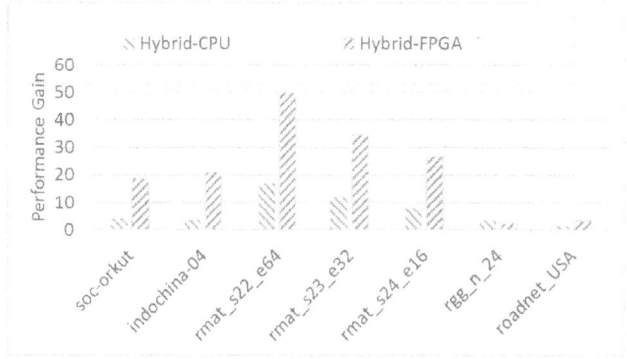

Figure 12: Performance gain comparison of CPU+DRAM and proposed FPGA+HMC implementation of hybrid graph traversal system

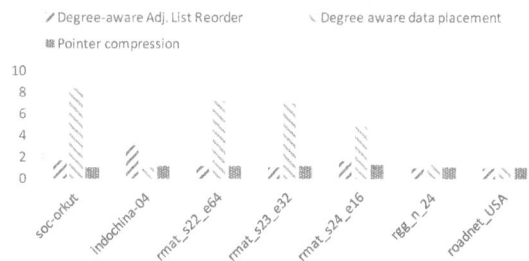

Figure 13: 8 Performance gain for degree-aware adjacency list reordering, degree-aware index sorting and degree-pointer compression

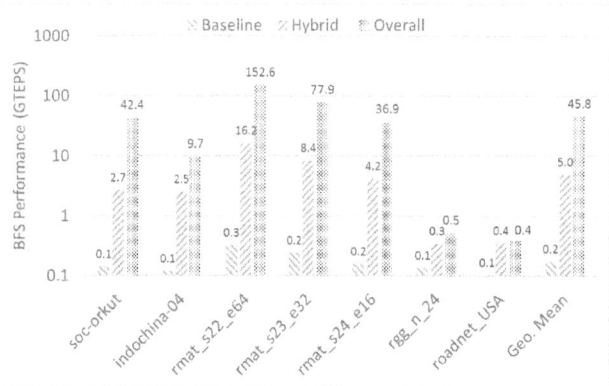

Figure 14: Graph traversal performance comparison

index sorting, and degree-aware pointer compression. We find that the degree-aware data-placement contributes to the major portion of the performance gain since the random access to the frontier bitmap is the most costly memory access in the *bottom-up* operation. Similar to the result in figure 10, the degree-aware data-placement also has fewer benefits in the rgg and roadnet graph due to its degree distribution being nearly uniform.

We summarize the overall graph traversal performance of the proposed system in figure 14 and compare it with the hybrid-only

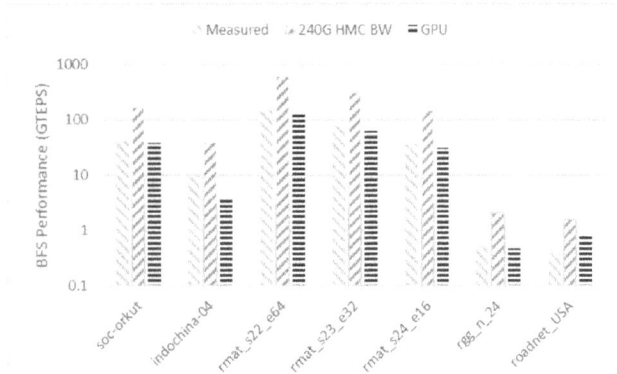

Figure 15: BFS performance projection and comparison with GPU

implementation and the baseline [3], which is the fastest existing FPGA-based graph traversal system. The geometric mean over the seven datasets is 45.8 GTEPS, which is significantly faster than the baseline design and the native implementation of hybrid graph traversal on an FPGA.

We further measure the graph traversal performance with 120GB/s HMC bandwidth on AC-520 system. We can achieve 79.8 GTEPS, which nearly doubles the performance compared to AC-510 platform. The power consumption of AC-520 board is 43.6 watts, which gives a power efficiency of 1.85 GTEPS per watt.

We further projects the performance on the system with the largest FPGA devices, XCKU115[23] and the HMC module, which can achieve the full two-way bandwidth of 240GB/s[19], and compare it with best single-GPU graph traversal performance[22]. As shown in figure 15, the proposed system achieves better performance than GPU for scale-free performance. By using the larger device with full HMC bandwidth, the proposed system can also outperform GPU on scaled graphs.

7 CONCLUSION

In this work, we present a high-performance graph traversal framework, which implements and optimizes the hybrid graph traversal on an FPGA-HMC platform. In particular, we first identify the improvement space of state-of-the-art hybrid graph traversal and provide two techniques to optimize the algorithm: degree-aware adjacency list reordering and degree-aware vertices sorting. Then, we introduce the implementation of the optimized hybrid traversal algorithm on an FPGA-HMC platform and provides two hardware optimization. Finally, we conduct experiments on eight different datasets to verify the effectiveness of the proposed techniques and provide a performance projection with higher HMC bandwidth. Our implementation on the AC-510 development board from Micron achieves 45 GTEPS, outperforming CPU and other FPGA-based large-scale graph processors, and can be compared with the latest GPU graph processing library.

ACKNOWLEDGEMENTS

We appreciate the insightful comments and feedback from the anonymous reviewers. We thank Micron for the donation of the development tool and hardware. We especially thank John Watson and Mark Hur for their support.

REFERENCES

[1] Albert-László Barabási and Réka Albert. 1999. Emergence of scaling in random networks. *science* 286, 5439 (1999), 509–512.
[2] Scott Beamer, Krste Asanovic, and David A Patterson. 2011. Searching for a parent instead of fighting over children: A fast breadth-first search implementation for graph500. (2011).
[3] Scott Beamer, Aydin Buluc, Krste Asanovic, and David Patterson. 2013. Distributed memory breadth-first search revisited: Enabling bottom-up search. In *Parallel and Distributed Processing Symposium Workshops & PhD Forum (IPDPSW), 2013 IEEE 27th International.* IEEE, 1618–1627.
[4] Béla Bollobás, Oliver Riordan, Joel Spencer, Gábor Tusnády, et al. 2001. The degree sequence of a scale-free random graph process. *Random Structures & Algorithms* 18, 3 (2001), 279–290.
[5] Aydin Buluç and Kamesh Madduri. 2011. Parallel breadth-first search on distributed memory systems. In *Proceedings of 2011 International Conference for High Performance Computing, Networking, Storage and Analysis.* ACM, 65.
[6] Guohao Dai, Yuze Chi, Yu Wang, and Huazhong Yang. 2016. FPGP: Graph Processing Framework on FPGA A Case Study of Breadth-First Search. In *ACM/SIGDA FPGA (FPGA '16).*
[7] Guohao Dai, Tianhao Huang, Yuze Chi, Ningyi Xu, Yu Wang, and Huazhong Yang. 2017. ForeGraph: Exploring Large-scale Graph Processing on Multi-FPGA Architecture. In *Proceedings of the 2017 ACM/SIGDA International Symposium on Field-Programmable Gate Arrays (FPGA '17).* ACM, New York, NY, USA, 217–226. https://doi.org/10.1145/3020078.3021739
[8] P. F. Felzenszwalb and R. Zabih. 2011. Dynamic Programming and Graph Algorithms in Computer Vision. *IEEE Transactions on Pattern Analysis and Machine Intelligence* 33, 4 (April 2011), 721–740. https://doi.org/10.1109/TPAMI.2010.135
[9] Solomon Golomb. 1966. Run-length encodings (Corresp.). *IEEE transactions on information theory* 12, 3 (1966), 399–401.
[10] Wook-Shin Han, Sangyeon Lee, Kyungyeol Park, Jeong-Hoon Lee, Min-Soo Kim, Jinha Kim, and Hwanjo Yu. 2013. TurboGraph: a fast parallel graph engine handling billion-scale graphs in a single PC. In *ACM SIGKDD.* ACM.
[11] T. H. Haveliwala. 2003. Topic-sensitive PageRank: a context-sensitive ranking algorithm for Web search. *IEEE Transactions on Knowledge and Data Engineering* 15, 4 (July 2003), 784–796. https://doi.org/10.1109/TKDE.2003.1208999
[12] Aapo Kyrola, Guy Blelloch, and Carlos Guestrin. 2012. GraphChi: large-scale graph computation on just a PC. In *USENIX OSDI.*
[13] Guoqing LEI, Rongchun LI, Song GUO, and Fei XIA. 2016. TorusBFS: A Novel Message-passing Parallel Breadth-First Search Architecture on FPGAs. (10 2016).
[14] Hang Liu and H Howie Huang. 2015. Enterprise: Breadth-first graph traversal on GPUs. In *Proceedings of the International Conference for High Performance Computing, Networking, Storage and Analysis.* ACM, 68.
[15] Roger Moussalli, Walid Najjar, Xi Luo, and Amna Khan. 2013. A high throughput no-stall golomb-rice hardware decoder. In *Field-Programmable Custom Computing Machines (FCCM), 2013 IEEE 21st Annual International Symposium on.* IEEE, 65–72.
[16] Richard C Murphy, Kyle B Wheeler, Brian W Barrett, and James A Ang. 2010. Introducing the graph 500. (2010).
[17] Savita Nargundmath and Archana Nandibewoor. 2013. Entropy coding of H. 264/AVC using Exp-Golomb coding and CAVLC coding. In *Advanced Nanomaterials and Emerging Engineering Technologies (ICANMEET), 2013 International Conference on.* IEEE, 607–612.
[18] Eriko Nurvitadhi, Gabriel Weisz, Yu Wang, Skand Hurkat, Marie Nguyen, James C. Hoe, José F. Martínez, and Carlos Guestrin. 2014. GraphGen: An FPGA Framework for Vertex-Centric Graph Computation. In *IEEE FCCM.*
[19] J Thomas Pawlowski. 2011. Hybrid memory cube (HMC). In *IEEE Hot Chips.*
[20] Picocomputing. 2016. UltraScale-based SuperProcessor with Hybrid Memory Cube. http://picocomputing.com/ac-510-superprocessor-module. (2016).
[21] John Scott. 2017. *Social network analysis.* Sage.
[22] Yangzihao Wang, Yuechao Pan, Andrew Davidson, Yuduo Wu, Carl Yang, Leyuan Wang, Muhammad Osama, Chenshan Yuan, Weitang Liu, Andy T Riffel, et al. 2017. Gunrock: GPU Graph Analytics. *arXiv preprint arXiv:1701.01170* (2017).
[23] Xilinx. 2011. Ultrascale Plus Fpga Product Selection Guide. https://www.xilinx.com/support/documentation/selection-guides/ultrascale-plus-fpga-product-selection-guide.pdf. (2011).
[24] Yuichiro Yasui, Katsuki Fujisawa, Eng Lim Goh, John Baron, Atsushi Sugiura, and Takashi Uchiyama. 2016. NUMA-aware scalable graph traversal on SGI UV systems. In *Proceedings of the ACM Workshop on High Performance Graph Processing.* ACM, 19–26.
[25] Jialiang Zhang, Soroosh Khoram, and Jing Li. 2017. Boosting the Performance of FPGA-based Graph Processor using Hybrid Memory Cube: A Case for Breadth First Search.. In *FPGA.* 207–216.
[26] Shijie Zhou, Charalampos Chelmis, and Viktor K Prasanna. 2016. High-throughput and energy-efficient graph processing on fpga. In *Field-Programmable Custom Computing Machines (FCCM), 2016 IEEE 24th Annual International Symposium on.* IEEE, 103–110.

Accelerating Graph Analytics by Co-Optimizing Storage and Access on an FPGA-HMC Platform

Soroosh Khoram
Department of Electrical and Computer Engineering
University of Wisconsin - Madison
khoram@wisc.edu

Jialiang Zhang
Department of Electrical and Computer Engineering
University of Wisconsin - Madison
jialiang.zhang@ece.wisc.edu

Maxwell Strange
Department of Electrical and Computer Engineering
University of Wisconsin - Madison
mbstrange@wisc.edu

Jing Li
Department of Electrical and Computer Engineering
University of Wisconsin - Madison
jli@ece.wisc.edu

ABSTRACT

Graph analytics, which explores the relationships among interconnected entities, is becoming increasingly important due to its broad applicability, from machine learning to social sciences. However, due to the irregular data access patterns in graph computations, one major challenge for graph processing systems is performance. The algorithms, softwares, and hardwares that have been tailored for mainstream parallel applications are generally not effective for massive, sparse graphs from the real-world problems, due to their complex and irregular structures.

To address the performance issues in large-scale graph analytics, we leverage the exceptional random access performance of the emerging Hybrid Memory Cube (HMC) combined with the flexibility and efficiency of modern FPGAs. In particular, we develop a collaborative software/hardware technique to perform a level-synchronized Breadth First Search (BFS) on a FPGA-HMC platform. From the software perspective, we develop an architecture-aware graph clustering algorithm that exploits the FPGA-HMC platform's capability to improve data locality and memory access efficiency. From the hardware perspective, we further improve the FPGA-HMC graph processor architecture by designing a memory request merging unit to take advantage of the increased data locality resulting from graph clustering. We evaluate the performance of our BFS implementation using the AC-510 development kit from Micron and achieve 2.8× average performance improvement compared to the latest FPGA-HMC based graph processing system over a set of benchmarks from a wide range of applications.

CCS CONCEPTS

• **Hardware** → **Hardware accelerators**; Reconfigurable logic applications; Emerging architectures; • **Theory of computation** → *Graph algorithms analysis*;

KEYWORDS

Graph Analytics; Graph Clustering; Hybrid Memory Cube; Reconfigurable Logic; Hardware Accelerators

ACM Reference Format:
Soroosh Khoram, Jialiang Zhang, Maxwell Strange, and Jing Li. 2018. Accelerating Graph Analytics by Co-Optimizing Storage and Access on an FPGA-HMC Platform. In *Proceedings of 2018 ACM/SIGDA International Symposium on Field-Programmable Gate Arrays (FPGA 2018)*. ACM, New York, NY, USA, Article 4, 10 pages. https://doi.org/10.1145/3174243.3174260

1 INTRODUCTION

Large-scale graph analytics, the class of big data analysis that essentially explores the relationship among a vast collection of interconnected entities, is becoming increasingly important for solving challenging problems in diverse fields including social networking [9], bioinformatics [12], text/graphics content analysis [8], and search engines [10]. In these applications, Breadth First Search (BFS) remains the most widely used algorithm and it often serves as a basis for complex graph algorithms.

Similar to many Big Data problems, one major challenge for graph processing systems is performance. Due to the highly irregular data access patterns, it is challenging to efficiently process a vast amount of linked data within a reasonable amount of time on traditional CPU-based systems. Such irregularity makes it difficult to exploit spatial or temporal locality using a standard on-chip cache. As a result, the system performance is often bounded by the random access bandwidth of the external memory. However, traditional DDR DRAM suffers from poor random access performance due to the lack of memory level parallelism [17]. To make matters worse, the high cost of frequent off-chip communication between the processor and memory makes it more challenging to parallelize large graph workloads efficiently on such systems as the synchronization and locking between parallel kernels have become key performance bottlenecks [13].

In response to the performance penalties inherently present within large graph workloads on the traditional CPU-based graph processing systems, in recent years, FPGAs have been explored as a promising alternative due to their flexibility, performance, and energy efficiency. Many existing works [6, 14, 21] have proposed various parallel architectures to implement BFS on FPGA. These works were all based on one common scheme. By placing some key data – those used for synchronization between parallel kernels – on the on-chip Block RAM (BRAM) to alleviate the pressure on accessing the external DRAM, the efficiency of processing large, sparse graphs on these architectures could be significantly improved. However, this scheme does not scale well with large graphs as the on-chip storage capacity of FPGA is very limited and external DRAM does not provide sufficient memory level parallelism. To address the memory capability and bandwidth issue, a recent work [24] proposed a graph processor design by effectively combining the high memory-level parallelism of the emerging Hybrid Memory Cube (HMC) with the superior parallel processing capability of FPGA. The experiments show such a FPGA-HMC based graph processing system significantly outperforms CPU and other FPGA-based large graph processors.

In this work, we develop a collaborative software/hardware technique that targets the FPGA-HMC platform and further improves the performance of the previous graph processing system [24]. We first perform an in-depth analysis on the data access patterns to HMC and observe that the flag read operations, in which the FPGA fetches a 1-bit flag from HMC using a 128-bit access granularity to check if a vertex has been visited, contributes the most to the HMC access frequency and, thus, severely affects performance. To address this issue, we then develop a software/hardware co-optimization technique. In particular, from the software point-of-view, we devise a novel architecture-aware graph clustering algorithm that can provide the most efficient graph data layout in the HMC. The goal is to minimize the number of requests to read the flag bit from the HMC by coalescing these requests into the largest possible HMC payload requests. As such, the saved random access bandwidth can be used to serve more parallel requests, resulting in improved performance and scalability. From the hardware point-of-view, we improve the previous architecture by adding a merging unit for the flag read operation to exploit the improved data locality resulting from graph clustering.

The key contributions of this paper are summarized as follows:

- We comprehensively analyze the data access patterns to the HMC and identify the performance bottleneck of existing FPGA-HMC based graph processing systems.
- We design an architecture-aware graph clustering algorithm that exploits the FPGA-HMC platform's capability by coalescing the bit-level irregular memory accesses into the largest possible HMC payload requests for high data locality and memory access efficiency.
- We further improve the FPGA-HMC graph processor architecture in [24] by adding a merging unit to take advantage of the increased data locality resulting from clustering.
- We conduct experiments to verify the effectiveness of the proposed techniques. Our implementation achieves **2.8×** average performance improvement compared to the latest FPGA-HMC based graph processing system [24] over a set of representative benchmarks from a variety of applications.

The rest of the paper is organized as follows. Section 2 presents the background of the graph clustering algorithm and BFS on the FPGA-HMC platform. In Section 3, we first show that the flag read operation is the performance bottleneck and present the architecture-aware graph clustering algorithm. In Section 4, we present the hardware design to implement the FPGA-HMC graph

processing system. Section 5 presents the experimental results and validates the proposed techniques. Section 6 concludes the paper.

2 BACKGROUND

2.1 Graph Clustering

Clustering algorithms are graph algorithms commonly used to gain insight into the high-level structure of a graph [4]. In addition to graph analysis, insights from these algorithms can be used to simplify and compress graphs or store them more efficiently. Many algorithms have been proposed in literature for this task such as Markov Clustering [22], Restricted Neighborhood Search Clustering (RNSC) [11], Super Paramagnetic Clustering [3], and Molecular Complex Detection [1]. Here, we first formally define a graph clustering algorithm. Then, we briefly discuss the first two clustering algorithms (MCL and RNSC) as they are more commonly used and can provide more robust clusterings [5].

A clustering of the graph $G = (V, E)$, where V is the set of vertices and E is a set of edges connecting members of V, is constructed by dividing members of V into several nonempty groups. Specifically, a clustering of G is a set like $C = \{C_1, ..., C_n\}$, where n is the number of clusters, $\forall 1 \leq i \leq n : C_i \subset V$, and $\forall 1 \leq i, j \leq n, i \neq j : C_i \cap C_j = \emptyset$. Each of the C_i is called a *cluster*. Furthermore, a subgraph of G corresponding to the cluster C_i is defined as $G_{C_i} = (C_i, E_{C_i})$ where $E_{C_i} \subset E$ only connects vertices of C_i. The goal of clustering a graph is usually to create clusters where the subgraphs are dense and with sparse inter-cluster edges.

Markov clustering (MCL) [22] is one of the most commonly used graph clustering algorithms that constructs clusters by simulating stochastic flows and detecting where they tend to gather. In other words, MCL calculates the probability of reaching from one vertex to another through randomly walking on the graph edges. If this probability is high, MCL puts the two vertices in the same cluster. This method can provide robust and accurate results for any form of weighted/unweighted directed/undirected graph. However, it is difficult to guarantee the number or the size of clusters (the number of vertices in each cluster) in MCL.

Restricted Neighborhood Search Clustering (RNSC) [11] takes another approach by defining cost functions for clusterings and trying to minimize these functions by trying different cluster arrangements. At the beginning, RNSC constructs a random clustering of the graph and calculates its cost. Then, it tries to optimize the clustering cost by moving vertices between clusters. RNSC continues this process until the cost converges to a minimum. This algorithm has the advantage that the number of the clusters can be predetermined; however, the original algorithm does not take weighted graphs into account.

2.2 Breadth-First Search

The BFS algorithm takes a graph and a source vertex as inputs, and finds the shortest path (disregarding edge weights) from the source to all other vertices of the graph. In the output, BFS produces an array which, for each vertex, specifies a parent, a vertex that is one step closer to the source than that vertex. To do so, BFS visits vertices in a breadth first manner meaning it visits vertices in the order of their distances from the source vertex. BFS does this by first visiting the neighbors of the source (vertices that are connected to it by an edge and thus have distance of 1). Then, in each iteration, it visits neighbors of the vertices that were visited in the previous iteration. We call each of these sets of vertices (vertices equidistant from the source) a *frontier*. We further refer to the frontier being visited in the current iteration the *current frontier* and the frontier that will be visited in the next iteration as *next frontier*. The process of visiting the frontiers continues until the next frontier is empty.

Algorithm 1 presents a detailed description of the BFS implementation that we use in this paper. Here, V and E are the vertex set and the edge set of the input graph G, the *flag* array is a bitmap that stores the visited status of vertices, *parent* is an array which stores the output parent information, and s is the source vertex. At the beginning, the source vertex s is added to the current frontier and its parent is set to be *NULL*. Then, the algorithm chooses a vertex from that frontier, reads its neighbors, and checks whether or not they have been visited by comparing their flag bits with 0 (a 0 flag bit means unvisited). Subsequently, the algorithm adds the unvisited neighbors to the next frontier. At the end of the loop, the current frontier is cleared, and the two frontiers are swapped to minimize the required storage. This process continues until the new current frontier (next frontier before swapping) is empty.

Algorithm 1 Level-synchronized BFS

1: **procedure** BFS(G, s)
2:     $flag[s] = 1$
3:     $parent[s] = NULL$
4:     $current\_frontier \leftarrow s$
5:     **while** $current\_frontier$ not empty **do**
6:         Clear $next\_frontier$
7:         **for** $v \in current\_frontier$ **do**
8:             $E_v = \{n \in V | (v, n) \in E\}$
9:             **for** $n \in E_v$ **do**
10:                 **if** $flag[n]$ is 0 **then**
11:                     $flag[n] = 1$
12:                     $parent[n] = v$
13:                     $next\_frontier.append(n)$
14:                 **end if**
15:             **end for**
16:         **end for**
17:         $current\_frontier = next\_frontier$
18:     **end while**
19: **end procedure**

2.3 Benchmark Graphs

We use a wide range of real-world graph benchmarks from the the University of Florida Sparse Matrix Collection [7] to evaluate our graph processing framework. Table 1 lists these benchmarks which cover a variety of scientific applications. For each graph $G = (V, E)$, this table includes its *scale* ($scale = log_2V$), its edge factor ($edge\ factor = \frac{|E|}{|V|}$), and its sparsity plot.

2.4 Hybrid Memory Cube

HMC is an emerging memory module that stacks multiple DRAM dies on top of a CMOS layer to form a cube using through-silicon-via (TSV) technology. The architecture of the HMC is optimized

Table 1: Benchmark graphs

Name	Sparsity plot	Description	Scale	Edge Factor
NACA0015		A 2-D Tri-Element mesh around an airfoil	19.99	3.00
nlpkkt80		Symmetric indefinite KKT matrix	20.02	14.01
Geo_1438		Geomechanical model of earth crust	20.46	22.46
belgium_osm		Real-world street network	20.46	2.16
kim2		2D complex mesh	18.80	24.79
mc2depi		2D Markov model of epidemic	19.00	3.99
coPapers DBLP		Citation and co-author network	19.04	28.21
dielFilter V2clx		High-order vector finite element method in EM	19.21	21.34
roadNet -CA		Road network of California	20.91	2.81
rggn224s0		Random geometric graphs	24.00	15.80

for parallel memory access. Each DRAM layer is divided into multiple partitions, and each partition is comprised of several memory banks. As shown in Figure 1, a vertically connected stack containing multiple partitions from different DRAM layers is called a *vault*. Moreover, each vault also contains a corresponding partition in the logic base layer, which serves as a vault controller. The vault controller manages the DRAM banks within the vault and thus eliminates the need for an off-chip memory controller compared to traditional DRAM modules.

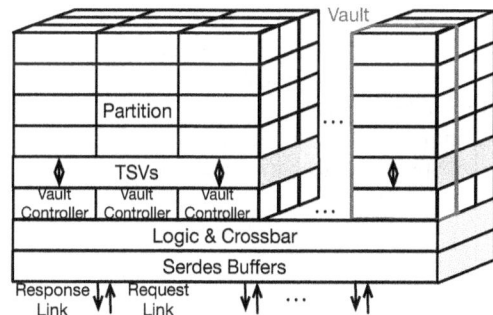

Figure 1: Architecture of Hybrid Memory Cube (HMC) [20]

As shown in Figure 1, vault memory controllers are connected to a high-speed interface to communicate with other HMCs or host devices (*e.g.* CPU, GPU, FPGA) via a crossbar switch. The high-speed interface consists of a serialized physical layer and a packetized transaction layer. The physical layer has several links, which can be used to connect to the different hosts. The base logic layer of HMC opens up opportunities for near-data computing. The HMC standard defines several locking and read-modify-write commands which are preferred to be executed by logic units near memory instead of by a host CPU. Although the idea of near data computing is not new, HMC is the first commercial device to practically implement the concept.

3 ARCHITECTURE-AWARE GRAPH CLUSTERING ALGORITHM

In this section, we first perform an in-depth analysis to identify the performance bottleneck in the previous implementation of the BFS algorithm on the FPGA-HMC platform. Then, we propose a new graph clustering algorithm to solve this bottleneck.

3.1 Performance Analysis

BFS is a memory-bound algorithm, as it performs relatively few simple computations and has a large number of irregular memory accesses. Thus, it can greatly benefit from the parallelism of FPGA and the high-speed random access of HMC. However, performance of this algorithm on the FPGA-HMC platform [24] is severely bounded by the accesses to the flag array (Algorithm 1). In this work, we first demonstrate this bottleneck by analyzing the breakdown of memory accesses of BFS. Then, we propose a new method to improve the storage of a graph to alleviate this problem.

We depict the breakdown of memory accesses for a sample graph in Figure 2. This figure shows the number of accesses to each of the arrays including: reading the graph (*vertex R*), reading the visited status flag (*flag R*), updating the visited status flag (*flag W*), reading the frontier bitmap (*bitmap R*), and updating the frontier bitmap (*bitmap W*). As shown in the figure, read accesses to the flag array comprise most of the accesses with an order of magnitude higher frequency. The reason for this high frequency is that BFS must access several bits in this array for each vertex (flag bits for its neighbors). However, these bits are randomly distributed throughout the flag array, which imposes generation of multiple read requests. In addition, even though BFS requires bit granularity of access to this array, the smallest read access of HMC is 16 bytes which further aggravates the problem. In the following section, we present a clustering technique that finds an optimized storage of the graph and improves memory access by reducing the randomness in the distributions of neighbors of vertices in the flag array.

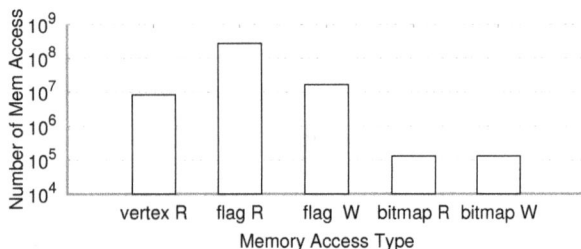

Figure 2: Distribution of HMC access for `rgg_n_2_24_s0`

3.2 Graph Clustering for Efficient Storage in HMC

Clustering algorithms provide useful tools for effective storage of a graph structure. These algorithms identify strongly connected vertices of a graph, which are often accessed successively and can be stored together for improve locality. In this case, however, our choice of clustering algorithm is limited since only a specific form of clustering would result in the higher access efficiency that we require, due to the unique characteristics of HMC. That is, we want the neighbors of a vertex, which themselves are *second-order neighbors* of each other connected through a *shared* vertex, to be placed in a cluster together. In the graph storage, we ideally want these neighbors to be accessible using one read. This is not easily realized through common clustering algorithms for two main reasons. First, the objective in these algorithms is to cluster vertices with strong connectivity. However, we need second-order neighbors to be clustered together, which might not have any connections themselves. Second, we desire small clusters with the exact size as the granularity of access in the HMC, so that each cluster can be read using one access. This is not possible using algorithms such as MCL or RNSC, since they often produce large clusters with arbitrary sizes. Therefore, we need to design a new algorithm that takes the granularity of access in the HMC into account and produces appropriately-sized clusters. By applying this algorithm to a graph as a preprocessing step, we can enhance the efficiency and performance of traversing the graph on the FPGA-HMC platform. In the rest of this section, we present our proposed clustering algorithm.

The proposed clustering algorithm performs the following steps:

(1) A large graph is divided into smaller subgraphs. These subgraphs will be clustered separately to keep computation load manageable.
(2) Each subgraph is converted into a *Second-Order Neighbors Subgraph* (SONS). We will argue that clustering this graph will result in our desired storage.
(3) Each SONS is clustered using our proposed clustering algorithm. The resulting clustering is then applied to the original subgraph.

Figure 3 depicts the three steps. Here we describe each of these steps in detail.

3.2.1 Dividing the original graph.
Our small choice for the cluster size results in a large number of clusters for large graphs. This makes the final clustering step computationally expensive. In order to avoid this problem, we divide the graph into smaller subgraph. For this purpose, we use the MCL algorithm due to its robustness [5]. This step does not affect the overall clustering of the graph. That is because we are not enforcing any strict constraints on sizes of the clusters, which results in most second-order neighbors to be grouped together in the same subgraph. This step has been illustrated in Figure 3 (a).

3.2.2 Generating the second-order neighbors graphs.
Achieving the desired storage by clustering the subgraphs produced in the previous step involves two difficulties. First, identifying second-order neighbors of a vertex (to put them in the same cluster) requires one level of indirection, and repetition of this process adds unnecessary computations. Second, it is often the case in

clustering algorithms that a vertex can be clustered with multiple groups of vertices. Naturally, we prefer to store this vertex together with the cluster that is more often read. However, access frequency to a cluster is not easily inferred based on the original subgraphs. Thus, we propose generating an equivalent subgraph called the *second-order neighbors subgraph* based on the original one. Next, we will explain how SONS is generated and how it addresses the problems.

A SONS is equivalent to its base subgraph (the subgraph it is generated from), in that, it comprises the same set of vertices. The difference is that the edges in the SONS connect all second-order neighbors in the base subgraph (Figure 3 (b)). This eliminates the unnecessary computations for finding second-order neighbors of a vertex. Furthermore, we assign weights to the edges of the SONS. These weights represent how likely it is for the two vertices connected by the edge to be accessed together. We note that two second-order neighbors are not always accessed together, since each can also be connected to *non-shared* vertices (in the base subgraph). By generating a weighted graph of second-order neighbors, the clustering problem turns into discovering strongly connected vertices in the SONS. When choosing a cluster for a vertex, we only need to find the one with which that vertex has stronger connections.

We assign weights to the edges of SONS based on two factors: 1) the total number of shared vertices between two second-order neighbors in the base subgraph, and 2) the total number of neighbors of those shared vertices, which determines the total number of common second-order neighbors each of the two has. To calculate the weight for each edge we just add these two values together. The idea behind this weight assignment is that a higher number of shared vertices means that the two second-order neighbors are more likely to be accessed together. Furthermore, clustering vertices with high number of common second-order neighbors together can result in high-efficiency accesses if all these vertices are accessed together.

The SONS generated using this procedure has a number of interesting features which we can utilize to further accelerate the computations in the next step.

First, a SONS is not necessarily a connected graph. Disconnected parts of the SONS can be processed separately reducing the computational load.

Second, a SONS can contain many cliques (fully connected subgraphs). We can identify cliques that are large and cluster them separately since they are already strongly interconnected. In our algorithm, we do this for cliques with the size equal or larger than the fixed cluster size.

3.2.3 Clustering algorithm.

The objective of this step, is to cluster each of the SONSs generated previously into strongly interconnected clusters. As discussed previously, we need the sizes of these clusters to be exactly the same as the HMC read granularity (128). We achieve this by devising a new clustering algorithm inspired by the RNSC algorithm [11]. Similar to the RNSC algorithm, the proposed technique uses cost functions to assign a cost to a specific clustering of the subgraph. Then, it tries to minimize the cost by moving the vertices between clusters, while making sure that the size constraint is maintained at all times. Below we describe the proposed algorithm.

The flow of the proposed algorithm is depicted in Figure 4 (a). In the first step, all clusters are randomly initialized. If a cluster is not filled completely (due to the number of vertices not being divisible by the memory access granularity) dummy isolated vertices are added to that cluster. Then, the cost of the clustering is calculated. We use two cost functions, which we call: 1) naïve and 2) scaled cost functions, similar to the RNSC algorithm. These functions are designed to inversely reflect our desired clustering, so that minimizing them would result in overall optimal read efficiency. The naïve function is easier to calculate while the scaled function more accurately represents the ideal clustering. Thus, we use the first one to quickly find a close to optimal clustering and then use the second one to tune that clustering. These two tasks are performed successively, following the cost initialization (Figure 4 (b)). Below, we present the two cost functions and describe the process of minimizing them in more detail.

In a specific clustering, the naïve cost function for a cluster c_i is defined below:

$$Cost_{c_i}^{na\"ive} = \sum_{v \in c_i} W_x(v, c_i) + W_A \sum_{v \in c_i} (S - N(v, c_i)) \qquad (1)$$

Here, $W_x(v, c_i)$ is the sum of the weights of the edges of vertex v incident to vertices outside of c_i, W_A is the average weight of the edges in the SONS, S is the size of each cluster, and $N(v, c_i)$ is the number of neighbors of v that are in c_i. In this function, the first term, $W_x(v, c_i)$, tries to minimize the weights of edges crossing the cluster borders while the second term, $S - N(v, c_i)$, tries to maximize the weights of the internal edges of the cluster. The second term effectively calculates the number of potential edges in the cluster that are absent. We multiply this term by W_A to balance the two terms. By summing this function over all clusters, we calculate the cost of the clustering.

The terms in the naïve cost function are all integer values and thus this function can be calculated using fixed-point operations (W_A is rounded to an integer as well). Conversely, the scaled cost function defined below requires floating-point division and is therefore more computationally expensive. The scaled cost function is defined similarly to the naïve function; however, this function has been scaled to balance the cost among all clusters. For this function, $W_i(v, c_i)$ is equal to the sum of the weights of the edges of vertex v that are incident to vertices inside the cluster c_i. Similar to the naïve cost function, we sum the scaled cost over all clusters to calculate the total cost of the clustering.

$$Cost_{c_i}^{scaled} = \frac{Cost_{c_i}^{na\"ive}}{Cost_{c_i}^{na\"ive} + W_i(v, c_i)} \qquad (2)$$

When minimizing each of the cost functions, we follow the procedure depicted in Figure 4 (b). At each step, two vertices from two different clusters are chosen to be swapped and the total cost before and after the swap are calculated. If the cost is improved due to the move, the move is taken. Otherwise, a counter (t_{last}) is incremented to hold the number of failed attempts since the last successful move. If this counter exceeds T, a constant, the algorithm assumes that the cost has converged and finishes this step.

To choose the two vertices to swap, the algorithm maintains a list of speculative cost changes for each vertex that specify the

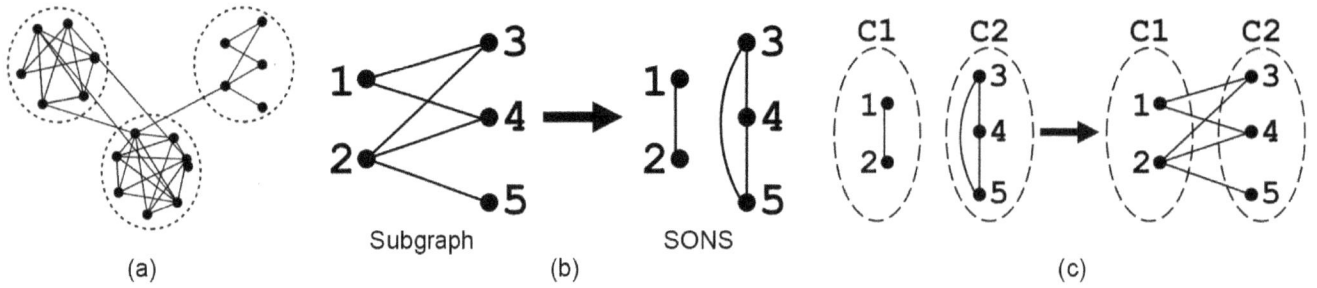

Figure 3: (a) Example of dividing a large graph into multiple subgraphs; (b) Generating the SONS for a subgraph; (c) Clustering the SONS of a subgraph

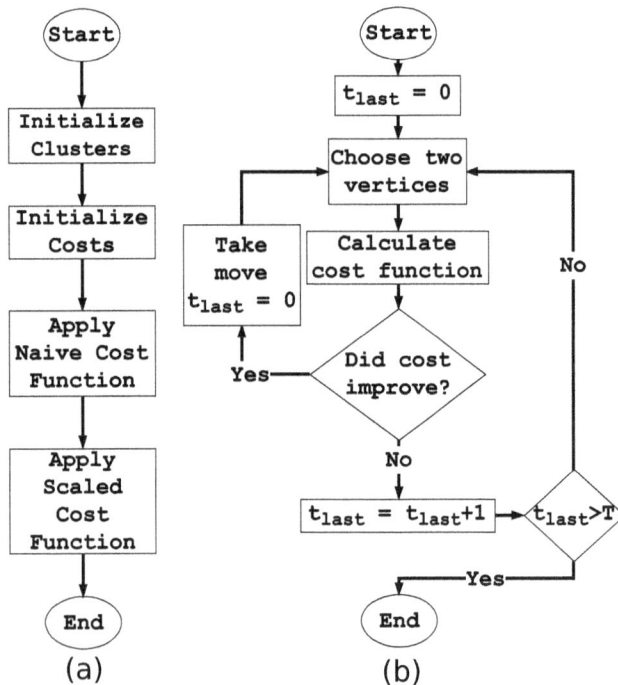

Figure 4: (a) Algorithm flow; (b) Optimizing cost functions

change in the total cost if the vertex is moved from its current cluster to other clusters in which it has neighbors. When choosing the vertices to move, the algorithm picks two clusters and chooses two vertices that are speculated to produce the maximum reduction in cost if swapped. As the actual change in cost might be different from the speculated change, the algorithm needs to reevaluate the change. If sufficient cost reduction is achieved, the move is taken. Subsequently, similar to the original RNSC algorithm, the vertices that were moved are put in a *taboo list*. Vertices in this list are not to be moved again until a specific number of successful moves have been taken. This is done to make sure the algorithm does not continuously cycle over the same subset of vertices. Following this procedure, the algorithm optimizes first the naïve cost function and then the scaled cost function until it finds the optimal clustering.

After clustering, read flags for vertices in the same cluster are stored in consecutive bit locations in memory. We can expect BFS to generate several requests to the same address in short periods of time. Our implementation (Section 4) utilizes this characteristic and merges these requests into one efficient read access. Thus, it effectively uses the limited available memory bandwidth.

4 HARDWARE SUPPORT FOR MERGING HMC ACCESS

In section III, we introduced the clustering algorithm, which stores vertices in each cluster consecutively. To leverage the improved locality from graph clustering, the hardware architecture should merge the memory accesses to the same HMC word address as much as possible. In this section, we introduce a new metric, namely *merging gain*, to quantify the effectiveness of merging flag read operations. Then, we briefly discuss the design of the FPGA-HMC graph processing framework from the previous work [24], which is used as a baseline here. Finally, we present a key design technique to improve the architecture [24] and to speed up BFS on a clustered graph using a Flag Read Merging Unit (FRMU).

4.1 Merging Gain for Graph Clustering

The clustering algorithm in section III improves spatial data locality by storing vertices in each cluster consecutively in the HMC. However, the existing hardware architecture [24] cannot take advantage of the improved locality as it issues a HMC request for each flag read request. Hence, we need to develop a hardware technique which can effectively support the merging of these requests and enable data reuse. To characterize the effectiveness of the merging support in hardware, we introduce merging gain: the speculative ratio of the average number of requests the BFS implementation must send to the HMC to read the flag array without merging, to that same number with merging. In theoretical terms:

$$Merging\ Gain = \frac{\sum_{u=1}^{V} |N_u|}{\sum_{u=1}^{V} NUnique(N_u/S)} \quad (3)$$

where N_u is the set of neighbors of vertex u, S is the cluster size in the clustering algorithm, which is equal to the memory access granularity, and $NUnique(N_u/S)$ is the number of unique elements in the set N_u when all the elements are divided by S. The lower and upper bounds of this factor are: 1 and the edge factor of the graph.

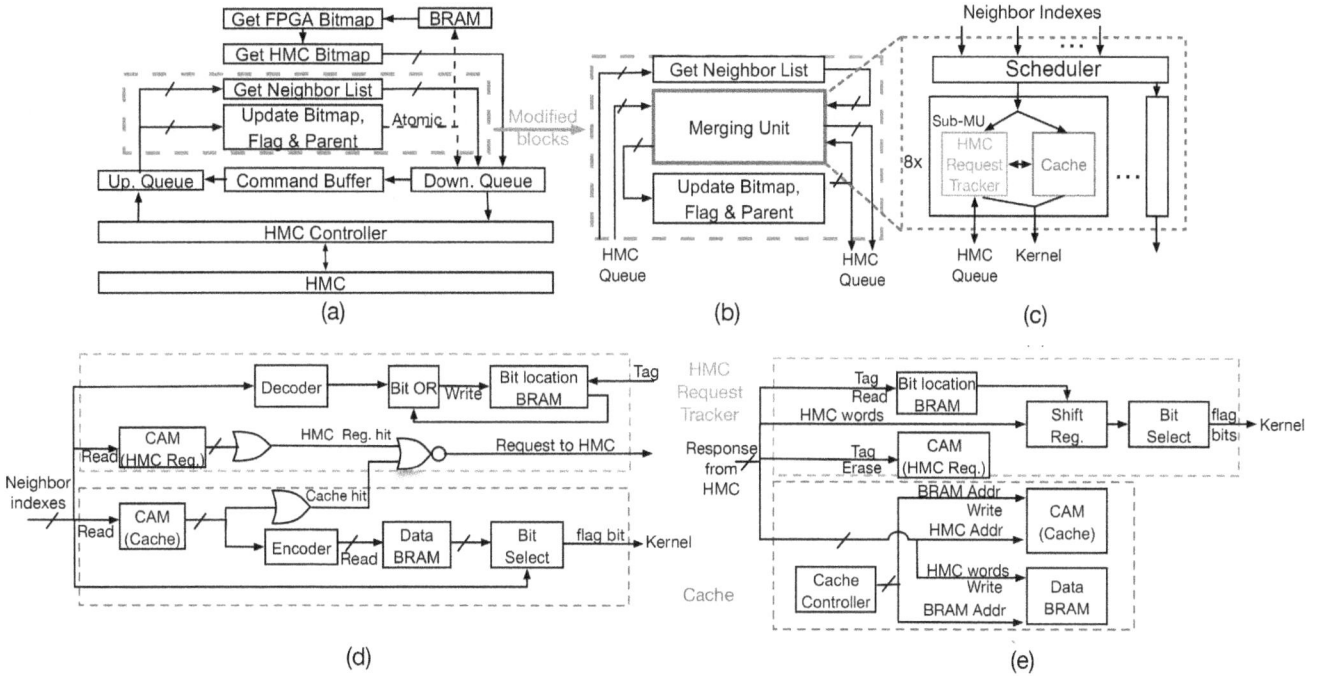

Figure 5: (a) Baseline design of FPGA-HMC graph processor [24]; (b) The modified blocks; (c) Overall architecture of merging unit; (d) Detailed design of merging unit related to incoming neighbor indexes (scheduler not shown) ; (e) Detailed design of merging unit related to incoming HMC responses (scheduler not shown)

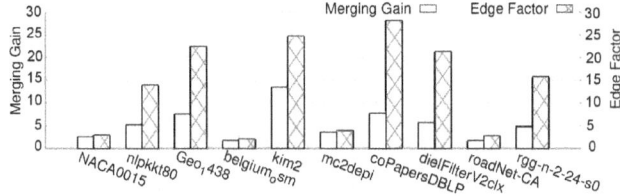

Figure 6: Merging gain of benchmark graphs when access granularity is $128b$

Table 2: Truth table of the Merging Unit (FRMU)

Cache hit	HMC Request hit	Merging unit operation
1	x	Get flag bit from cache
0	1	Log bit location
0	0	Send HMC request; Log bit location

Figure 6 shows the merging gain for the benchmark graphs when flag read operations use the $128b$ access granularity (128 vertices per cluster). As shown in this figure, the merging gain is generally much larger than 1, which verifies the effectiveness of merging. As the edge factors of the benchmark graphs increase, more opportunities to merge flag array read operations become available, increasing the merging gain. However, we also see a larger gap between the merging gain and the edge factor of graphs that have higher edge factors. This is due to the fact that in these graphs a vertex has more viable clusters in which it can be added. In the next subsection, we will introduce the design of our merging unit.

4.2   Design of the Merging Unit

The baseline design used in this implementation is taken from a previous work [24], which combined the parallelism of FPGA with the fast, random access capabilities of HMC to accelerate

BFS. It further introduced a 2-level coarse-grain/fine-grain bitmap system to further improve performance. The proposed design in this work benefits from the same optimizations in addition to its superior merging capability, by using this architecture as baseline and building on top of that.

The architecture of the baseline design has been depicted in Figure 5. At the beginning of the BFS execution, the bitmap will be reset except for the bit corresponding to the starting vertex. At each cycle, kernels send HMC requests to the downstream queue, which handles the communication between kernels and the HMC controller. Meanwhile, the upstream queue also checks if there are incoming HMC responses generated at the HMC controller. If so, it will fetch the response based on the tag field and forward the data to the next kernel stages.

To merge the flag read requests, we improve the architecture by adding a merging unit between the retrieval of the neighbor list and updating the bitmap, flag and parent, as shown in Figure 5 (b). More specifically, the merging unit consists of a scheduler and eight sub-merging units (sub-MUs), as shown in Figure 5. To achieve high parallelism in processing, we divide the whole address range of the flag array into 8 non-overlapping groups using the three lower address bits. The scheduler, which is a group of buffers and a crossbar, directs the flag read requests from different kernels to the corresponding sub-merging unit, which merges the HMC requests for the clustered graph.

The sub-merging unit has two components: a cache and a HMC request tracker. The cache is used to store recently checked flag words (128 bits) for future use. As the HMC access latency is typically several tens of cycles, a HMC request tracker is used to avoid issuing HMC requests to the same address multiple times before the first HMC response comes back. We show the detailed design of the sub-MU in Figure 5 (d), which is the data path design corresponding to incoming flag requests from a kernel, and Figure 5 (e) which is the data path design corresponding to incoming responses from the HMC. Both cache and HMC request trackers have a content addressable memory (CAM). The details of designing a CAM can be found in [15].

As shown in Figure 5(d), the sub-MU checks if the requested flag bit is in the cache or has already been requested when there is a flag read operation. The output of the two CAMs will pass through a pipelined OR gate to see whether the request is a hit, which determines the sources of the requested flag bit based on Table II. If the cache hits, the sub-MU will fetch the data from on-chip block RAM (BRAM) based on the CAM (cache) output and send the request bit to the next kernel stage. If the cache misses while the CAM of the HMC request tracker hits, the sub-MU will set the corresponding bit in BRAM. If both caches miss, the sub-MU needs to send a HMC request, write the tag from HMC controller to the CAM (HMC Request) using the HMC address as the CAM address, and set the corresponding bit in BRAM.

As shown in Figure 5 (e), when the sub-MU receives a response from HMC, it needs to: i) read the bit location in BRAM using the tag from the HMC; ii) burst out all the bits whose bit location is set; iii) select the cache line to be replaced based on the cache replacement policy; iv) write the BRAM address to CAM (cache), and write the data word to BRAM. We use the write-through policy for the cache. The sub-MU will set the bit in both cache and HMC when a flag write request is sent. Similar to the cache read in Figure 5(d), the sub-MU checks the CAM, and sets the BRAM bit.

5 EVALUATION

In this section, we will first present the experimental setup and then introduce the selected datasets. Finally, we will present and discuss the results.

5.1 Experimental Setup

We implement the proposed graph processor on an AC-510 FPGA module from Micron. As shown in Figure 7, an AC-510 consists of a Xilinx KCU060 FPGA and a 4GB HMC chip. The AC510 board uses two half-width (8 lanes) 15G HMC links to connect the HMC and the FPGA, and provides one-way bandwidth of 30GB/s. We implement our graph processing architecture under the PicoFramework, which provides communication between the host and the FPGA kernel. We use the HMC controller IP core from Micron as the interface between the FPGA kernels and the HMC. The clock frequency is 125 MHz for logic and 250MHz for all BRAMS, which work in double pump mode. We summarize the resource utilization in Table III. We can see the usage of BRAM is high as there is no native CAM in FPGA, and we need to implement CAM using BRAM. The host machine is equipped with an Intel Xeon E5-1630V3 CPU and one DDR4 memory channel with a 16GB capacity. We use Ubuntu 16.04.1 as the host operating system and compile our CPU implementation using gcc with flags "-Ofast" and "-march=native". The GPU benchmark is running with a GTX 1060 graphics card with 6GB of GDDR5 VRAM.

Table 3: Resource utilization

	FF	BRAM	DSP
Total	663360	2160	2760
Used	421424	1880	64
Utilization	63%	87%	2%

5.2 Results

We evaluate our proposed clustering algorithm and architecture on the benchmark graphs using three measures: 1) the performance in terms of Millions Traversed Edges Per Second (MTEPS), 2) the reduction of the number of accesses to the flags array in HMC using clustering and merging, and 3) the cache hit rate before and after the clustering. We then compare the performance of the clustered graph on the proposed architecture with two baseline implementations: the unclustered graph on the baseline architecture from the previous work [24] and the unclustered graph on the proposed cache-enabled architecture.

Figure 8 shows the performance comparison of the three BFS implementations based on their MTEPS values. Over the set of all benchmarks, our proposed implementation achieves an average of 2.8× performance improvement compared to the case without merging. On the other hand, the improvement achieved using merging but without clustering is almost insignificant which verifies the effectiveness of the proposed fine-grained clustering method. We also see that benchmarks with higher edge factors and merging gains achieve better performance improvements. This comes from the clustering of neighbors of high order vertices (vertices with a high number of neighbors) as these vertices cause generation of more read requests in the unclustered graphs.

The reduction in the number of flag read requests and the cache hit rate, as depicted in Figures 9 and 10, further explain the improvement in performance. There are, however, interesting cases such as NACA0015 and roadNet-CA where, despite a high cache hit rate, the performance improvement is not significant. This is because these graphs have small edge factors and, additionally, small frontiers (Section II.B) during the execution of BFS. As a result, reducing the number of flag accesses has a smaller impact on the overall performance. The effect of topological features of the benchmarks is also visible in belgium_osm which has small frontiers and as such experiences little performance improvement.

Finally, in Figure 11 we compare the performance of our implementation with the state-of-the-art GPU implementation of BFS

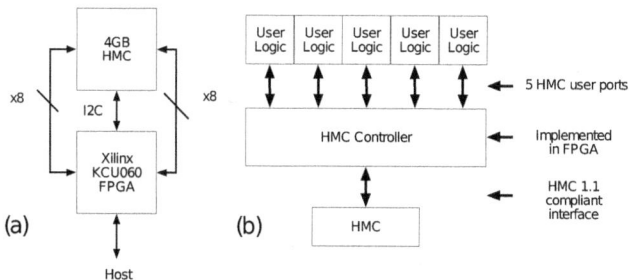

Figure 7: (a) Micron AC-510 board with two half-width HMC links[19] (b) HMC controller diagram [18]

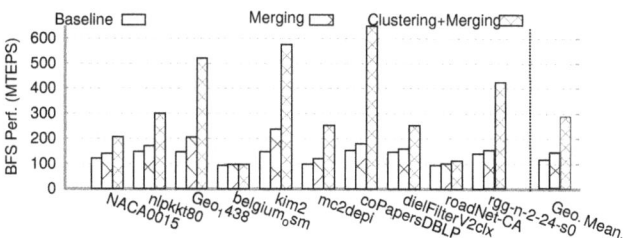

Figure 8: BFS Performance

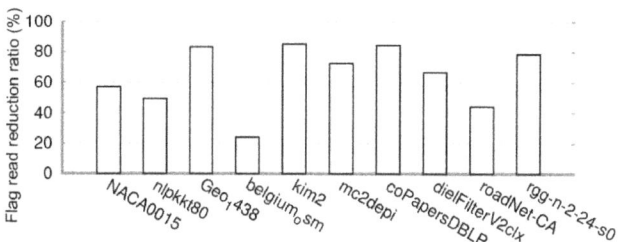

Figure 9: Percentage of flag read reduction

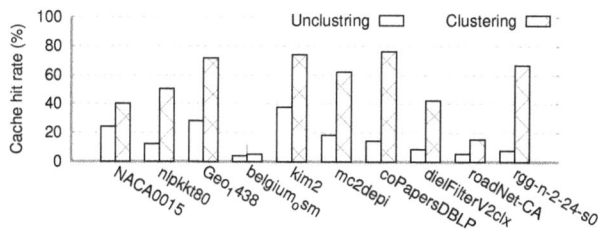

Figure 10: Cache hit rate

[16] which uses *culling* techniques to reduce the number of duplicate accesses to the main memory. We extract the numbers by running the available source code available on the Gunrock repository [23] on our GPU. For a fair comparison of the two implementations, we use a GeForce GTX 1060 GPU with $224GB/s$ memory bandwidth for the GPU implementation and project the FPGA results to a high-end FPGA-HMC board [17], which offers a similar $240GB/s$ memory bandwidth. In both cases we use the clustered graphs.

Figure 11 compares the performance results for the FPGA implementation combined with clustering with the GPU. We can see that in all cases FPGA offers at least comparable performance and in some cases outperforms GPU by a wide margin. We associate the high FPGA performance to the high-speed random access capability of HMC and effective clustering of the graph for the HMC hardware. Unlike HMC, which has been designed for optimal random access speed, GPU memory is less efficient when handling uncoalesced reads which, due to the irregular access pattern of BFS, are frequent. This can be observed in benchmarks such as NACA0015, roadNet-CA, and belgium_osm. In these cases, the performance improvement achieved through clustering was small (Figure 10) indicating a high irregular access rate. Thus, the FPGA improvement seen in Figure 11 over GPU comes from the parallelism of the HMC. In other cases where high performance improvement over baseline was achieved through clustering and merging, again we see a high performance on FPGA. In cases such as kim2 and rgg_n_2_24_s0 FPGA outperforms GPU by around 5× and 2× respectively, while it performs as well as GPU in nlpkkt80, Geo_1438, and coPapersDBLP. This shows that our clustering method performs similarly to the culling technique on GPU in the case where the culling works well, while performing better and identifying more merges when culling performs poorly.

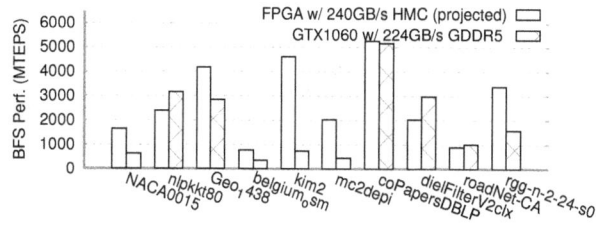

Figure 11: Projected Performance and comparison with GPU

6 CONCLUSION

In this paper, we present a new graph processing system to implement the level-synchronized BFS algorithm on an FPGA-HMC platform. We addressed the performance bottleneck of a previous implementation through software/hardware co-design. Specifically, we developed an efficient graph clustering algorithm tailored to the underlying FPGA-HMC hardware. We further developed a hardware technique, i.e. a merging unit that can exploit the benefits from our graph clustering algorithm.

We evaluated our graph processing system using a wide range of benchmark graphs. We showed that, through fine-grained clustering and merging of memory requests, the performance of the graph processing system is significantly improved. We further compared our implementation with a state-of-the-art GPU implementation, and showed that it not only provided a comparable performance, but also in many cases outperformed the GPU baseline.

Besides its direct performance benefits that were explored in this paper, the proposed design has the advantage of being flexible to the algorithm implementation. That is, this method can be integrated into any implementation on the FPGA-HMC platform with little need for modifications. Consequently, it can be easily combined with other runtime acceleration techniques, such as directional optimization method [2], to further improve their performances.

REFERENCES

[1] Gary D. Bader and Christopher W. Hogue. 2003. An automated method for finding molecular complexes in large protein interaction networks. *BMC Bioinformatics* 4, 1 (13 Jan 2003), 2. https://doi.org/10.1186/1471-2105-4-2

[2] Scott Beamer, Krste Asanovic, and David Patterson. 2012. Direction-optimizing Breadth-First Search. In *High Performance Computing, Networking, Storage and Analysis (SC), 2012 International Conference for.* 1–10. https://doi.org/10.1109/SC.2012.50

[3] Marcelo Blatt, Shai Wiseman, and Eytan Domany. 1996. Superparamagnetic Clustering of Data. *Phys. Rev. Lett.* 76 (Apr 1996), 3251–3254. Issue 18. https://doi.org/10.1103/PhysRevLett.76.3251

[4] Ulrik Brandes, Marco Gaertler, and Dorothea Wagner. 2003. *Experiments on Graph Clustering Algorithms.* Springer Berlin Heidelberg, Berlin, Heidelberg, 568–579. https://doi.org/10.1007/978-3-540-39658-1_52

[5] Sylvain Brohée and Jacques van Helden. 2006. Evaluation of clustering algorithms for protein-protein interaction networks. *BMC Bioinformatics* 7, 1 (06 Nov 2006), 488. https://doi.org/10.1186/1471-2105-7-488

[6] Guohao Dai, Yuze Chi, Yu Wang, and Huazhong Yang. 2016. FPGP: Graph Processing Framework on FPGA A Case Study of Breadth-First Search. In *Proceedings of the 2016 ACM/SIGDA International Symposium on Field-Programmable Gate Arrays (FPGA '16).* ACM, New York, NY, USA, 105–110. https://doi.org/10.1145/2847263.2847339

[7] Timothy A. Davis and Yifan Hu. 2011. The University of Florida Sparse Matrix Collection. *ACM Trans. Math. Softw.* 38, 1, Article 1 (Dec. 2011), 25 pages. https://doi.org/10.1145/2049662.2049663

[8] Pedro Felzenszwalb and Ramin Zabih. 2011. Dynamic Programming and Graph Algorithms in Computer Vision. *IEEE Transactions on Pattern Analysis and Machine Intelligence* 33, 4 (April 2011), 721–740. https://doi.org/10.1109/TPAMI.2010.135

[9] M. Gjoka, M. Kurant, C. T. Butts, and A. Markopoulou. 2010. Walking in Facebook: A Case Study of Unbiased Sampling of OSNs. In *2010 Proceedings IEEE INFOCOM.* 1–9. https://doi.org/10.1109/INFCOM.2010.5462078

[10] Taher Haveliwala. 2003. Topic-sensitive PageRank: a context-sensitive ranking algorithm for Web search. *IEEE Transactions on Knowledge and Data Engineering* 15, 4 (July 2003), 784–796. https://doi.org/10.1109/TKDE.2003.1208999

[11] Andrew D. King, Natasa Pržulj, and Igor Jurisica. 2004. Protein complex prediction via cost-based clustering. *Bioinformatics* 20, 17 (2004), 3013–3020. https://doi.org/10.1093/bioinformatics/bth351

[12] Mehmet Koyutürk, Ananth Grama, and Wojciech Szpankowski. 2004. An efficient algorithm for detecting frequent subgraphs in biological networks. *Bioinformatics* 20, suppl-1 (2004), i200–i207. https://doi.org/10.1093/bioinformatics/bth919

[13] Aapo Kyrola, Guy Blelloch, and Carlos Guestrin. 2012. GraphChi: Large-Scale Graph Computation on Just a PC. In *Presented as part of the 10th USENIX Symposium on Operating Systems Design and Implementation (OSDI 12).* USENIX, Hollywood, CA, 31–46. https://www.usenix.org/conference/osdi12/technical-sessions/presentation/kyrola

[14] Guoqing Lei, Rongchun Li, Song Guo, and Fei Xia. 2015. TorusBFS: A Novel Message-passing Parallel Breadth-First Search Architecture on FPGAs. *Engineering Science and Technology, an International Journal* 5, 5 (10 2015), 313–318.

[15] Kyle Locke. 2011. Parameterizable Content-Addressable Memory. https://www.xilinx.com/support/documentation/application_notes/xapp1151_Param_CAM.pdf. (2011).

[16] Duane Merrill, Michael Garland, and Andrew Grimshaw. 2012. Scalable GPU Graph Traversal. *SIGPLAN Not.* 47, 8 (Feb. 2012), 117–128. https://doi.org/10.1145/2370036.2145832

[17] J Thomas Pawlowski. 2011. Hybrid memory cube (HMC). In *2011 IEEE Hot Chips 23 Symposium (HCS).* 1–24. https://doi.org/10.1109/HOTCHIPS.2011.7477494

[18] Picocomputing. [n. d.]. Hybrid Memory Cube (HMC) and Controller IP. http://picocomputing.com/hybrid-memory-cube-hmc-controller-ip/. ([n. d.]).

[19] Picocomputing. [n. d.]. UltraScale-based SuperProcessor with Hybrid Memory Cube. http://picocomputing.com/ac-510-superprocessor-module. ([n. d.]).

[20] Paul Rosenfeld. 2014. *Performance exploration of the hybrid memory cube.* Ph.D. Dissertation. Department of Electrical Engineering at University of Maryland.

[21] Yaman Umuroglu, Donn Morrison, and Magnus Jahre. 2015. Hybrid breadth-first search on a single-chip FPGA-CPU heterogeneous platform. In *2015 25th International Conference on Field Programmable Logic and Applications (FPL).* 1–8. https://doi.org/10.1109/FPL.2015.7293939

[22] Stijn van Dongen. 2000. *Graph clustering by flow simulation.* Ph.D. Dissertation. University of Utrecht.

[23] Yangzihao Wang, Andrew A. Davidson, Yuechao Pan, Yuduo Wu, Andy Riffel, and John D. Owens. 2015. Gunrock: A High-Performance Graph Processing Library on the GPU. *CoRR* abs/1501.05387 (2015). arXiv:1501.05387 http://arxiv.org/abs/1501.05387

[24] Jialiang Zhang, Soroosh Khoram, and Jing Li. 2017. Boosting the Performance of FPGA-based Graph Processor Using Hybrid Memory Cube: A Case for Breadth First Search. In *Proceedings of the 2017 ACM/SIGDA International Symposium on Field-Programmable Gate Arrays (FPGA '17).* ACM, New York, NY, USA, 207–216. https://doi.org/10.1145/3020078.3021737

Configurable FPGA Packet Parser for Terabit Networks with Guaranteed Wire-Speed Throughput

Jakub Cabal
CESNET a.l.e.
Prague, Czech Republic
cabal@cesnet.cz

Pavel Benáček
CESNET a.l.e.
Prague, Czech Republic
benacek@cesnet.cz

Lukáš Kekely
CESNET a.l.e.
Prague, Czech Republic
kekely@cesnet.cz

Michal Kekely
Netcope Technologies
Brno, Czech Republic
kekely@netcope.com

Viktor Puš
Netcope Technologies
Brno, Czech Republic
pus@netcope.com

Jan Kořenek
IT4Innovations Centre of Excellence,
FIT BUT
Brno, Czech Republic
korenek@fit.vutbr.cz

ABSTRACT

As throughput of computer networks is on a constant rise, there is a need for ever-faster packet parsing modules at all points of the networking infrastructure. Parsing is a crucial operation which has an influence on the final throughput of a network device. Moreover, this operation must precede any kind of further traffic processing like filtering/classification, deep packet inspection, and so on.

This paper presents a parser architecture which is capable to currently scale up to a terabit throughput in a single FPGA, while the overall processing speed is sustained even on the shortest frame lengths and for an arbitrary number of supported protocols. The architecture of our parser can be also automatically generated from a high-level description of a protocol stack in the P4 language which makes the rapid deployment of new protocols considerably easier. The results presented in the paper confirm that our automatically generated parsers are capable of reaching an effective throughput of over 1 Tbps (or more than 2 000 Mpps) on the Xilinx UltraScale+ FPGAs and around 800 Gbps (or more than 1 200 Mpps) on their previous generation Virtex-7 FPGAs.

CCS CONCEPTS

• **Hardware** → *Networking hardware*; *Hardware accelerators*; *Hardware description languages and compilation*;

KEYWORDS

packet parser; HLS; P4; Ethernet; high-speed networks; VHDL

ACM Reference Format:
Jakub Cabal, Pavel Benáček, Lukáš Kekely, Michal Kekely, Viktor Puš, and Jan Kořenek. 2018. Configurable FPGA Packet Parser for Terabit Networks with Guaranteed Wire-Speed Throughput. In *FPGA '18: 2018 ACM/SIGDA*

FPGA '18, February 25–27, 2018, Monterey, CA, USA
© 2018 Association for Computing Machinery.
ACM ISBN 978-1-4503-5614-5/18/02...$15.00
https://doi.org/10.1145/3174243.3174250

International Symposium on Field-Programmable Gate Arrays, February 25–27, 2018, Monterey, CA, USA. ACM, New York, NY, USA, 10 pages. https://doi.org/10.1145/3174243.3174250

1 INTRODUCTION

The speeds of network links are growing very fast. This holds true not only in the core of carrier networks but also in a wide variety of application-specific cases. Parsing is a crucial operation that must precede any kind of further traffic processing like filtering/classification, deep packet inspection, and even basic routing/switching. With network lanes currently operating at hundreds of gigabits per second, and terabit requirements on the horizon, an effective design of packet parser capable of lossless wire-speed processing poses a major challenge.

Apart from high performance, current networks also require parsers to support an extensive set of various protocols. Furthermore, these requirements are changing rapidly as network protocols are constantly evolving. This trend is spearheaded by the success of Software Defined Networking and the end of network "ossification" that comes with it. The changing nature of networking ecosystem thus clearly favors flexible (programmable) technologies like FPGAs over fixed ASIC implementations. On top of that, utilization of some form of High-Level Synthesis in parser description is a must.

Fastest of current FPGA-based packet parsers are able to achieve a *raw (theoretical) throughput* of little over 400 Gbps by utilizing very wide (up to 2 048 b or 256 B) data buses. No approaches capable of 1 Tbps parsing has been presented so far. Nearly all of the existing parsers support some form of a higher-level protocol stack description followed by an automatic or semi-automatic HDL code generation. But the key issue, that still remains largely unaddressed in all of the previous works in this area, is the *effective throughput* achievable by the parsers at different traffic patterns. In the worst case, when bursts of the shortest possible packets are processed, the effective throughput of existing approaches drops to only a small fraction of advertised raw throughput as they can process only a single packet per clock cycle. This degradation of effective throughput is getting more severe as the raw throughput (bus width) increases and becomes unbearably large for wire-speed processing even at 100 Gbps or 400 Gbps.

The shortest allowed length of L2 Ethernet frame is 64 B (512 b). At the same time, a typical implementation of FPGA packet parser

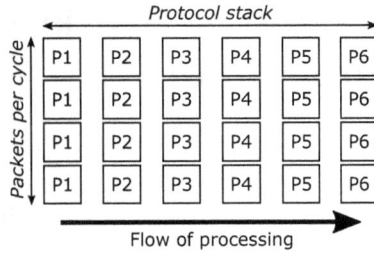

Figure 1: Proposed concept of main parser structure.

at 100 Gbps uses data bus that is 512 b wide and running at a clock frequency of at least 195 MHz. The shortest 64 B Ethernet frame fits nicely into a single data bus word. But what about 65 B, 66 B and similar frame lengths? When a few bytes spill into the second word, the rest of that word remains unused, yielding effective throughput of only around a half of the parser raw capacity. When data bus is wider than the length of the shortest frames, the effective throughput is even further reduced by insufficient packet rate. For example, a 400 Gbps parser operating with 2 048 b wide bus achieve effective throughput of only a fourth of its raw capacity when processing the shortest 64 B frames. Therefore, a processing of multiple packets or their fractions per clock cycle must be possible to achieve higher effective throughput of parsing.

This paper presents a novel packet parser design that not only advances achievable raw throughput of parsing in FPGAs above 1 Tbps mark but more importantly enables to retain sufficiently high effective throughput to guarantee the wire-speed processing of even the shortest packets at these speeds. In order to achieve such high degree of performance, the main feature of our proposed parser is to maximally exploit the means for massive processing parallelism that modern FPGAs offer.

The illustration of our key design concept is shown in Fig. 1. The complexity of fast packet parsing is divided into multiple simple parsers or analyzers (individual squares), where each of them can process at most one packet per clock cycle and parse only one protocol header from a supported protocol stack (P1, P2 . . .). The simple parsers are organized in a matrix-shaped structure that enables utilization of parallelism in two orthogonal dimensions. Firstly, each incoming packet traverses the structure from left to right going through a pipeline of simple parsers of different protocols, thus protocol stack complexity is divided into multiple steps (columns). Secondly, processing of multiple packets can start in every clock cycle as multiple simple parsers are working in parallel at each pipeline stage. In other words, the proposed matrix structure of our parser enables to use FPGA resources for scaling of both protocol stack complexity (width of the matrix) and achieved packet rate (height of the matrix).

The contribution of our work is a novel packet parser design for FPGAs that posses the following 3 key features:

(1) unprecedented raw throughput of over 1 Tbps;
(2) processing of multiple packets per clock cycle that leads to sufficient effective throughput for wire-speed processing;
(3) modular structure supporting automatic generation of HDL implementation from a high-level P4 description.

The rest of this paper is organized in the following manner. In section 2, we introduce several published approaches to parser design and compares them with our work. Section 3 describes our parser design concept and architecture in depth. In section 4, we provide a quick overview of the P4 language and description of the supported automated generation of the proposed parser from a P4 description. Section 5 contains results of achieved effective throughput, chip area and latency of our parser architecture in different configurations. Finally, the last section concludes the paper and discusses the obtained results.

2 RELATED WORK

Many fundamentally different approaches to FPGA packet parser design are present in published works with various benefits and disadvantages. However, many of them fail to scale well in a high-speed deployment that we aim for. Furthermore, none of them provide any robust and practical approach towards retainment of sufficient effective throughput ratio in the worst case.

Kobierský et al. [5] implement packet parsing using finite state machines generated from an XML description of protocol headers. This work shows achievable throughput of up to 20 Gbps. However, effective further scalability of the approach is poor. The size of generated FSMs (number of their states) rises rapidly with protocol stack complexity and data bus width, creating a performance bottleneck. Also, the crossbar used for extraction of fields values do not scale well with rising data bus width.

Unique Kangaroo parsing architecture of Kozanitis et al. [6] stores packets in memory and employs on-chip associative memory to perform a speculative lookahead into stored data. Based on lookahead results, the packet format is sequentially constructed, even moving through several headers in a single step (clock cycle). Authors showed achievable throughput of this architecture to be up to 40 Gbps line rate. However, this approach has the architectural limitation of storing the packets in the memory and fetching their data afterward. When scaling for higher throughput, the memory soon becomes a bottleneck. Also, higher complexity of parsed protocol stack can lead to considerably harder lookahead operation.

Wang et al. [10] introduce a rapid prototyping framework for mapping of a domain-specific HLS source code (P4 language) to the HDL description in BlueSpec language. The paper doesn't provide a detailed description of the generated parser's architecture but it provides results for its latency and throughput. The results show a raw throughput of up to 10 Gbps. But the effective throughput of the generated parser degrades with the growing complexity of supported protocol stack. With our parser design, we aim at throughput independent on the number of supported protocols to achieve wire-speed processing even in complex use cases. Also, the scalability of the parser from [10] on higher throughputs is questionable due to the generation of BlueSpec instead of HDL.

Another example of a domain-specific HLS generation of parsers is provided by Attig and Brebner in [1]. They propose their own Packet Parsing (PP) language to describe the structure of protocol headers and the methods which define parsing rules. From PP source code a pipelined implementation of a parser is generated. Thanks to the extreme pipelining and data bus width, generated parsers are able to achieve raw throughputs of up to 400 Gbps.

However, the results indicate a heavy price for such throughput in terms of the chip area and the latency. Also, authors themselves acknowledge the fact, that the effective throughput of their approach on the shortest frames is up to four times lower than presented raw throughput results (so only up to 100 Gbps). They propose to allocate the whole parser multiple times in parallel to workaround this issue, which would lead to even heavier resource price.

Similar pipeline architecture of parser is also proposed and elaborated by Kekely et al. in [3, 4]. Their approach achieves similar raw throughput of around 400 Gbps, but with considerably lower resource usage and latency compared to [1]. This is achieved thanks to hand-optimized implementation and not that heavy usage of pipelining. Authors also acknowledge the issue of degraded effective throughput of their parser on the shortest frames. They even propose a partial mitigation of the issue by unaligned frame starts and data bus words shared between parts of two consecutive frames. However, their approach is only sufficient for wire-speed processing of up to 100 Gbps (parsers with at most 512 b wide data bus). Further scaling of throughput (bus width) leads to similar throughput degradation as without this approach. Furthermore, in the original papers, the generation of the parser from the high-level description is not present at all. This is only supplemented later by Benáček et al. in [2], where they describe and generate these parsers using the P4 language.

The architecture of parser proposed in this paper is to some extent similar to pipelined approaches presented in the previous two paragraphs as protocol stack processing is divided into multiple parallel header parsers (columns in Fig. 1). However, the major contribution of this paper is the extension of parallelism utilization in the parser design towards another orthogonal dimension (packets per cycle or rows in Fig. 1). This extension in conceptual design is the key contribution that separates our parser from all previous works and enables us to achieve considerably higher effective throughput leading to lossless wire-speed processing.

3 PACKET PARSER DESIGN

The following section provides a bottom-up description of parser's architecture concept. We start with the proposition of our data convey bus protocol, more specifically the architecture of data word that would enable transfer of multiple packets per clock cycle. After that, the description of single protocol parser (analyzer) follows. Finally, the top-level parser architecture following the conceptual design from the Introduction is elaborated.

3.1 Data Convey Interface

The interface is used for transfer of packet's data into and through the whole parser. As already mentioned in the Introduction, it must be possible to transfer multiple packets (or their parts) in one bus word in order to retain the high ratio of effective to raw throughput even at higher speeds (bus widths).

To enable transfer of multiple packets per clock cycle, we define the data bus word structure illustrated in Fig. 2. The figure also shows an example of possible packet placements under the proposed bus structure. One should notice that without the support of multiple packets per clock cycle, each of the depicted data frames should occupy separate word on the bus (5 words would

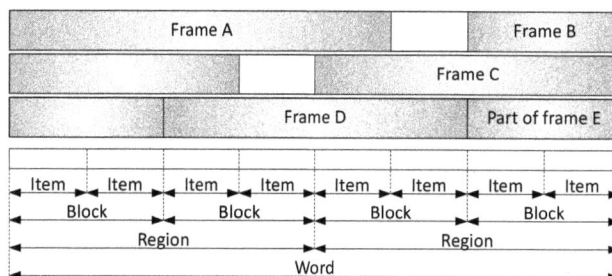

Figure 2: An example of possible packet placements under the proposed data bus structure (for $n = r = b = 2$).

be required), but word sharing enables more dense packing (only 3 words are needed). Now for the proposed structure (bottom of the Fig.), each data word of the bus consists of several *regions*. These restrain the maximal number of packets per cycle as at most one packet can start and one end (can be a different one) in each region. Each region is further separated into *blocks* of data *elements* (items) to constraint possible positioning of packet starts. All packets must start aligned with the start of a block, but can end in any element (e.g., frames A and B both end in the middle of a block).

General description of the proposed data word structure enables for definitions of multiple buses with different parameters. We formally describe them by the following four attributes:

- *Number of regions (n)* directly corresponds to the maximal number of packets transferred in each word.
- *Region size (r)* defines the number of blocks in each region, thus affects the size of overhead for very short packets. Usage of values that are powers of 2 is recommended here.
- *Block size (b)* states the number of elements in each start alignment block, thus controls the alignment overhead for frames. To simplify the processing complexity, usage of values that are powers of 2 is recommended.
- *Element width (e)* defines the size of the smallest distinguishable piece of data in bits. In networking, we always work with bytes (octets of bits), but in general, other values can be also utilized.

Using these main attributes, we derive bus word width in bits as: $dw = n \times r \times b \times e$. Now, we can also specify that illustration in Fig. 2 shows a bus with parameters $n = r = b = 2$.

When considering the processing of Ethernet frames, the aforementioned parameters of the bus should be configured to appropriate values. As already mentioned Ethernet operates with bytes (octets) as the smallest data elements – therefore we let $e = 8$. Lower layers of Ethernet (PCS/PMA layers) usually operate with frame starts aligned at 8 B blocks (lanes) – so $b = 8$ is convenient. Size of a region should correspond with the size of the smallest allowed packets (64 B) as smaller regions would needlessly allow transfer of more packets per word that is possible and on the other hand, larger regions would reduce effective bus saturation for the shortest packets – therefore we let $r = 64/b = 8$. Using these attribute values ($r = b = e = 8$) and considering the shortest packets to be 64 B long, the bus structure impose no more than $b - 1 = 7$ bytes of alignment

T [Gbps]	f [MHz]	n [-]	dw [b]
100	200	1	512
200	400	1	512
200	200	2	1024
400	400	2	1024
400	200	4	2048
800	400	4	2048
800	200	8	4096
1600	400	8	4096

Table 1: The throughput of selected combinations of bus attributes and frequency.

overhead per packet. Furthermore, as lower layers of Ethernet operate with larger overhead per packet (20 B of preamble and IFG), our bus enables us to achieve effective throughput sufficient for wire-speed processing of Ethernet packets even in the worst case.

In the previous paragraph, we left the value of attribute n unset, because we want to use it to control the number of transferred packets per clock cycle and also the total width of the bus. Thanks to different values of n and appropriately selected frequency, we can easily scale the supported throughput of the parser. Tab. 1 shows some considered configurations of the bus, where T stands for the achievable throughput, f stands for the FPGA frequency, n is the number of regions and dw is the total width of the data bus.

3.2 Simple Protocol Analyzers

The simple analyzers are the basic building blocks of our parser architecture. Fig. 3 shows how they are internally arranged. Each simple analyzer is able to start a processing of at most one packet per clock cycle and extract data from a single specific protocol header. From these, it computes control information for the next analyzer in the processing pipeline. The input information necessary to parse a single protocol header consists of: (1) packet data from the corresponding and the previous region of the data bus, (2) offset of the current word counted from the last start of packet, (3) type of the expected protocol header and (4) offset of the current header start. One should note that for $n > 2$, every simple analyzer does not have to operate with the full data bus width, only with two of its regions. The output information is similarly simple and includes: (1) type of the next expected protocol, (2) offset of the next header start and (3) extracted data of the current protocol header.

The Common logic block remains the same in all protocol analyzers. It is used to extract correct bytes from a data bus that corresponds to a protocol header based on given offsets. Only Protocol logic is specifically designed for each of the parsed protocols, it computes offset and type of the next header in a protocol-specific manner based on extracted data. As headers are not always aligned to region boundaries, the analyzer has to look into two regions, not just one. The data extraction is started when the end of a protocol header is detected in the current region of the data word. If the current region is occupied by two ends of the same protocol header, the second header is parsed by the protocol analyzer in the next region. This solution allows parsing of each frame on the bus without any stalling of the incoming data stream.

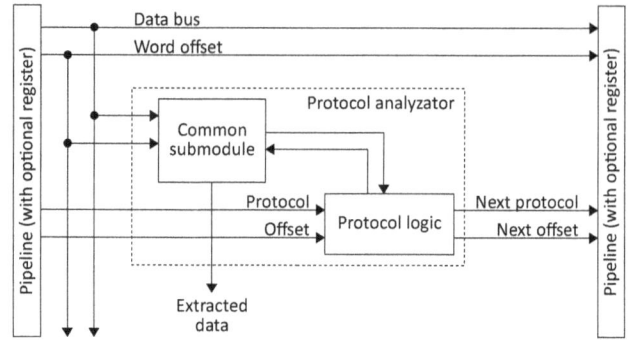

Figure 3: Internal structure of a single protocol analyzer.

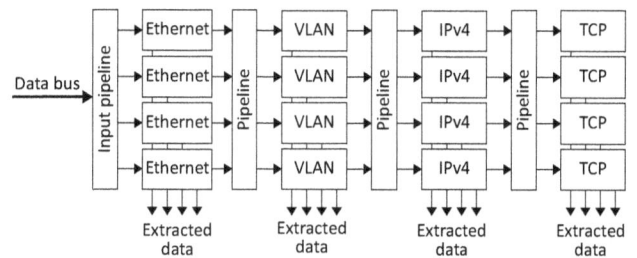

Figure 4: An illustration of complete parser arrangement.

3.3 Parser Top-Level Design

Our parser uses pipelining to achieve high working frequency and thus high throughput. However, pipeline steps are optional and we can control the trade-off between the frequency and used logic. For example, if many pipelines are enabled, the frequency (throughput) rises at the cost of longer latency and increased resources usage. Therefore, by careful selection of pipeline positions in the parser, we can find optimal configurations for any given use case.

Fig. 4 shows the example of parser pipeline with $n = 4$ and support of Ethernet, VLAN, IPv4 and TCP parsing. The shown pipeline arrangement corresponds to the conceptual matrix-like schema from Fig. 1. Each pipeline stage (column) contains one kind of protocol analyzers. The number of analyzers (in a pipeline stage) is equal to the number of regions n. Each protocol analyzer contains an inner bypass to solve the situations when the protocol is not found in processed data (i.e., the protocol analyzer is skipped if the currently processed packet does not contain the protocol which is being analyzed by the protocol analyzer). Thanks to this feature, the protocol analyzers can be arranged in a simple pipeline with a constant latency. This property also makes adding of new protocols into the pipeline very easy and it does not require any changes to the current protocol analyzer's architecture.

The shown arrangement contains two types of pipeline modules - *input pipeline* and *internal pipelines*. The input (first) pipeline stage also generates the initial control data for the first protocol analyzer stage (expecting Ethernet header at offset 0). There is also a word counter inside that counts the number of transferred words from the last packet start (i.e., word offset value). Both pipeline types

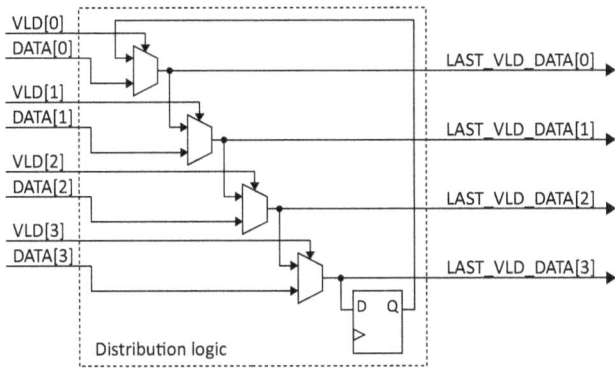

Figure 5: Internal structure of control data distribution login in pipelines.

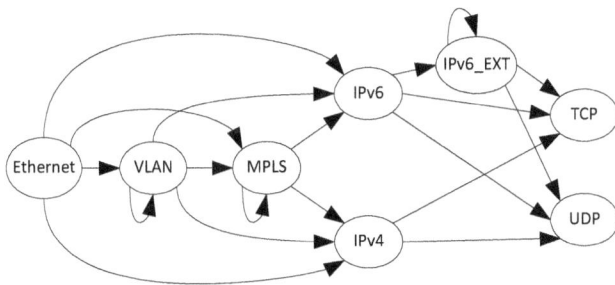

Figure 6: An example of protocol stack graph.

contain optional registers to achieve better timing and a logic for the distribution of control data across corresponding regions. The main task of the distribution block is to deliver control data to the correct protocol analyzer (region) in the next stage.

Fig. 5 shows the distribution logic for a control data. New valid control data are distributed to every following region until the start of a new packet is detected. Notice that each pipeline has registers to store data from the last region in the word because these data can be necessary for parsing in the next clock cycle (i.e., the remainder of header data is present in the following data word).

An example of the possible protocol stack that can be parsed by our parser is shown in Fig. 6. The order of protocol analyzer stages in the created pipeline directly depends on the selected protocol stack. The planning of parser stages order that accommodates any required stack is discussed in the next section of this paper, as we intend to use the P4$_{14}$[8] language for an automatic generation of packet parsers according to our proposed arrangement. This allows us to describe support for different protocol stacks very easily.

4　P4 HIGH-LEVEL SYNTHESIS

P4: Programming Protocol-independent Packet Processors is a high-level, platform-agnostic language. It represents a recent contribution to the broader idea of SDN and the SDN ecosystem. Its main purpose is to provide a way to define packet processing functionality of network devices, paying attention to reconfigurability, protocol independence and target (platform) independence. The idea

of programmable data plane in P4 language was introduced in [7]. There are two versions of P4 standard currently available: P4$_{14}$[8] and P4$_{16}$[9]. The P4$_{14}$ is earlier language specification which syntax was firstly introduced in 2014. The P4$_{14}$ standard is based on the abstract forwarding model which is capable to process the P4 program. The main advantage of this approach is easy portability to different platforms because the software tool is responsible for mapping of the P4 program to the target architecture. The disadvantage comes from the property of easy portability. That is, we cannot use the advanced functionality of a target because it is not used in the abstract forwarding model (the pattern matching for example). The P4$_{16}$ specification solves this problem directly in the language, as it allows us to describe the advanced functionality in the form of a library which is distributed with a network device. The library is then used by a user in a P4$_{16}$ program. The following text briefly introduces the P4$_{14}$ specification because we consider it to be more currently known by the P4 community.

Using relatively simple syntax, the P4$_{14}$ allows to define five basic aspects of packet processing:

- **Header Formats** describe recognized protocol headers.
- **Packet Parser** describes the (conceptual) state machine used to traverse packet headers from start to end, extracting field values as it goes.
- **Table Specification** defines how the extracted header fields are matched in possibly multiple lookup tables (e.g., exact match, prefix match, range search, and so on).
- **Action Specification** defines compound actions that may be executed for packets.
- **Control Program** puts all of the above together, defining the control flow mainly among the tables.

For our work, only the first two aspects of P4$_{14}$ are relevant. Header format description may look like this:

```
header_type ethernet {
    fields {
        dst_mac   : 48;
        src_mac   : 48;
        ethertype : 16;
    }
}
```

The description simply lists fields of the packet header and their width in bits. The example above shows the situation for a static header where the header length is the sum of lengths of all fields. This can't be done for protocols with a variable header length. The P4 solves this situation by the header length definition in form of an expression which uses fields from the protocol header declaration to compute the header length. Header format description with variable length may look like this:

```
header_type ipv6_ext {
    fields {
        next_hdr   : 8;
        total_len  : 8;
    }
    length : (total_len + 1) * 8;
    max_length : 1024;
}
```

Packet parser description constructs a parse graph using the header format description, for example:

```
header ethernet eth;
parser ethernet {
    extract(eth);
    switch(eth.ethertype) {
        case 0x8100: vlan;
        case 0x9100: vlan;
        case 0x800: ipv4;
    }
}
```

The example uses `switch` and `extract` statements. The `extract` instructs the parser to examine input packets and look for the data defined in the header. The parsed data is then used in the `switch` statement to determine the next state (protocol) to process.

4.1 Mapping from P4$_{14}$ to Parser Architecture

The transformation process from P4$_{14}$ to VHDL was introduced by Benáček et al. in [2]. The architecture of our parser is designed to be compatible with the parser generator from the mentioned paper: the parser consists of protocol analyzers and pipelines which form the processing chain of given protocol stack. Therefore, we can reuse the already presented algorithm for generation of our parser pipeline. In cooperation with authors of [2], we managed to integrate our parser into their generator, enabling it to create parsers with much higher effective throughput. The following text briefly introduces the transformation from P4$_{14}$ description to VHDL.

The main idea of the transformation is based on the topological ordering of Parse Graph Representation (PGR). The PGR is defined as an acyclic oriented graph (loop edges are allowed) from the P4's Packet Parser description. Each node of that graph represents one protocol header and each edge represents the next parsed protocol. A transition between nodes is based on a condition which is also inferred from the P4's Packet parser description. The PGR also contains loop edges which are used for the representation of more instances of the same protocol (e.g., two or more VLAN headers). Each non-finite node contains the edge to a special *Unknown* state. This state is not directly described in a P4 program but it is implicitly required by the transformation process because it represents the situation when none of the provided conditions match (in the currently processed protocol). The topological ordering of PGR nodes is based on a mark which is identified by the depth-first search (DFS) algorithm. The key for the ordering of nodes is to identify the latest possible usage of the protocol in a PGR. After that, we can connect all modules in any non-decreasing order, where: (1) each node will be translated to VHDL and (2) every two nodes will be divided by a pipeline module. The described planning algorithm fulfills the following requirements:

(1) The planned structure of modules forms a pipeline (i.e., it follows the processing flow of our parser in the protocol stack dimension).
(2) Protocol at the end of the transition has to be processed after the protocol at the beginning of the transition.
(3) Topologically ordered nodes (connected into the pipeline) are able to cover all paths through the PGR and we are able to parse any given combination of protocols because the PGR is acyclic and node skipping is allowed.

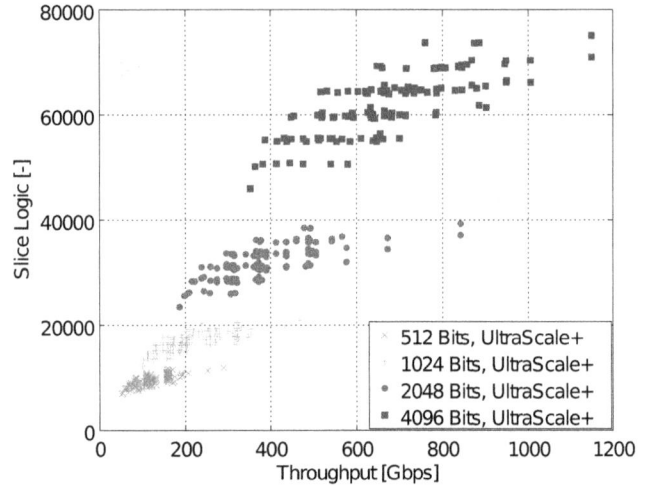

Figure 7: The relation between throughput and used resources of the simple L2 parsers on the UltraScale+ FPGA.

5 RESULTS

In this section, we provide a comparison of our generated parsers for two different protocol stacks:

- *full* – Ethernet, 4×VLAN, 4×MPLS, IPv4 or IPv6 (2×extension headers), TCP or UDP
- *simple L2* – Ethernet, IPv4 or IPv6 (2×extension headers), TCP or UDP

Thanks to the description in P4$_{14}$, we are able to easily generate parsers with the support of any protocols rather quickly. Of course, too big and complicated protocol stacks may require huge amounts of FPGA resources, but we will discuss it later in this section.

We described both mentioned protocol stacks in a P4$_{14}$ language. Then, translated the P4 source and synthesized it with different settings of data bus word width (512, 1024, 2048 and 4096 bits) and configuration of enabled pipeline registers. In all cases, we use data bus parameters that allow sufficient effective throughput for wire-speed processing of even the shortest packets ($r = b = e = 8$ with varying n as stated in subsection 3.1). The synthesis results of all the combinations form the state space of parsers with different throughput, working frequency, latency and resource usage. All values provided in the following text are after the synthesis for the Xilinx Virtex-7 XCVH870T FPGA or the Xilinx UltraScale+ XCVU7P FPGA using the Xilinx Vivado 2017.2 design tool. The achieved results were searched for sets of Pareto optimal parsers. From these, we can pick the best-fitting parser configurations for applications with different requirements. Notice that the FPGA resource usage is expressed as a sum of required LUTs and registers because it allows us to reflect the influence of enabled pipelines. Furthermore, selected Pareto optimal parsers were also integrated into our FPGA firmware and tested under real network conditions.

5.1 Simple L2 Protocol Stack

Figures 7 and Fig. 8 show the resource utilization and achieved throughput of generated simple L2 parsers, the first shows the UltraScale+ results and the second the Virtex7 results. Each point

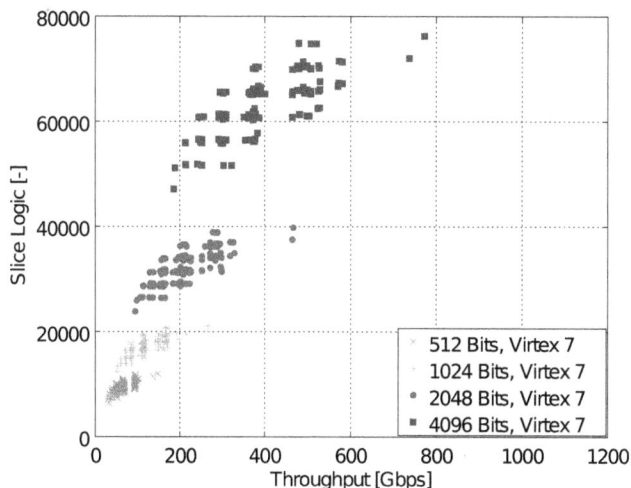

Figure 8: The relation between throughput and used resources of the simple L2 parsers on the Virtex-7 FPGA.

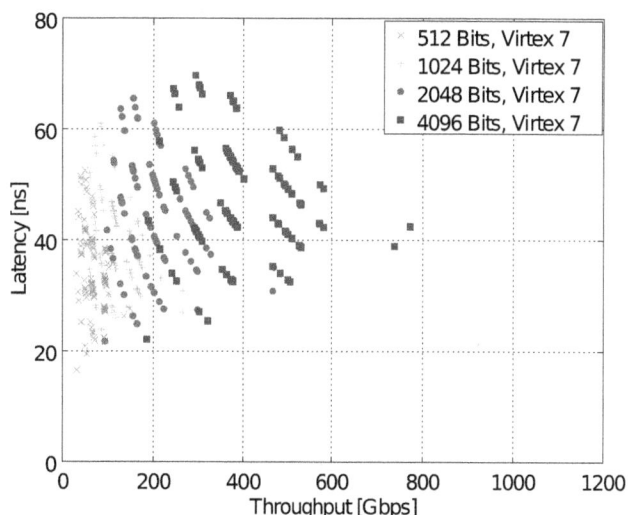

Figure 10: The relation between throughput and processing latency of the simple L2 parsers on the Virtex-7 FPGA.

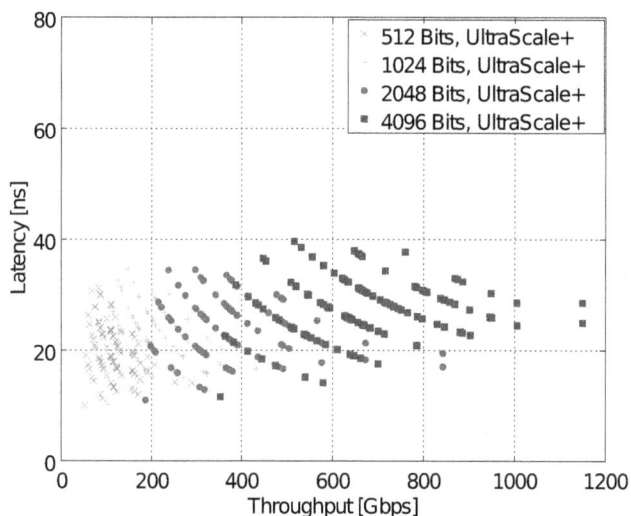

Figure 9: The relation between throughput and processing latency of the simple L2 parsers on the UltraScale+ FPGA.

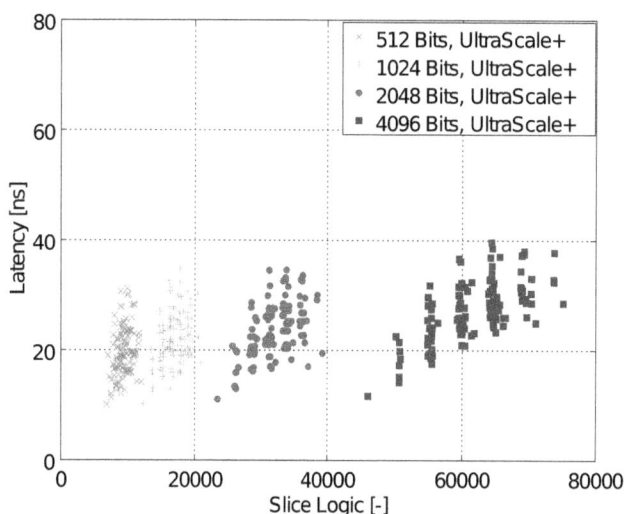

Figure 11: The relation between resources and latency of the simple L2 parsers on the UltraScale+ FPGA.

in the graphs represents one parser with a different combination of parameters. The FPGA resource utilization linearly increases with the achieved throughput in both graphs. In the case of the UltraScale+ FPGA, we are able to reach the effective throughput of well over 1 Tbps. Achieved throughputs for the Virtex7 FPGA are notably worse while the used resources remain very similar. This is because the same parsers reach lower frequencies when implemented on the Virtex-7 compared to the UltraScale+ FPGA – our results show the frequency to be 1.5 to 2 times lower.

Fig. 9 and Fig. 10 show the latency and throughput of different settings of the simple L2 parser on the UltraScale+ and the Virtex-7 FPGA. Generally, the latency depends on the configured number of enabled registers in pipeline stages and the working frequency.

From the graphs, we can see that the latencies of our parsers are increasing as the achieved throughput is rising. This is because higher throughput is achieved by more extensive registering (i.e., more clock cycles between start and end of parsing). The latency is again generally from 1.5 to 2 times better on the UltraScale+ because of the higher frequencies achieved.

Finally, Fig. 11 and 12 show the third point of view on the results – the relation between latency and resource utilization of the simple L2 parser on the UltraScale+ and the Virtex 7 FPGA. We can see that although resources utilization rises considerably with data bus width, the latency pretty much stays in the same boundaries.

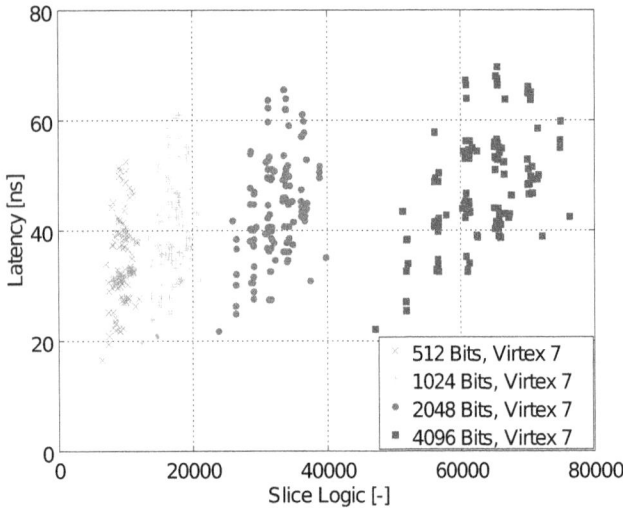

Figure 12: The relation between resources and latency of the simple L2 parsers on the Virtex-7 FPGA.

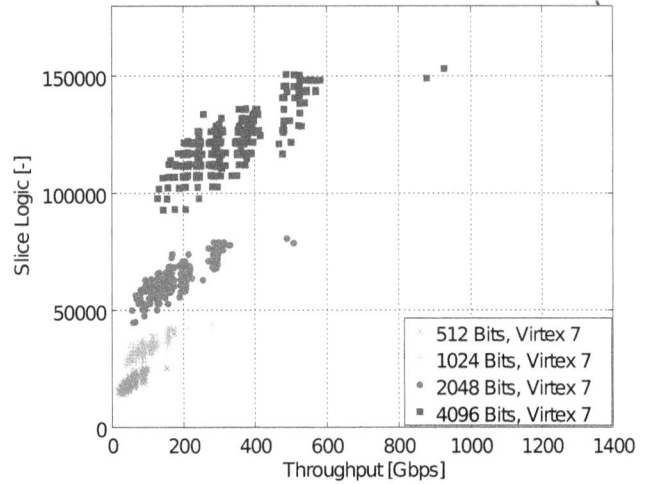

Figure 13: The relation between throughput and used resources of the full parsers on the UltraScale+ FPGA.

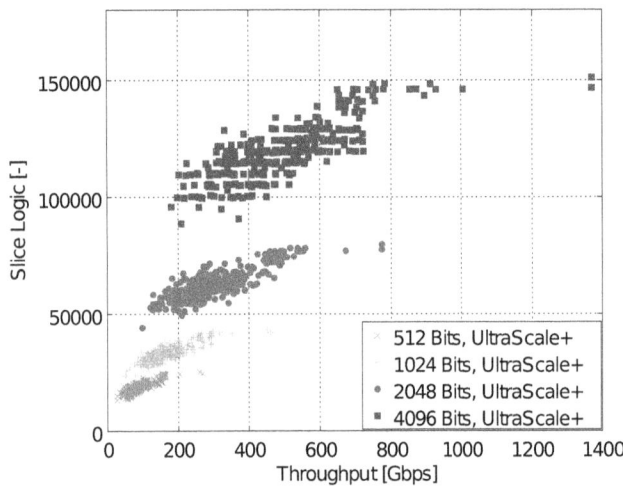

Figure 14: The relation between throughput and used resources of the full parsers on the Virtex-7 FPGA.

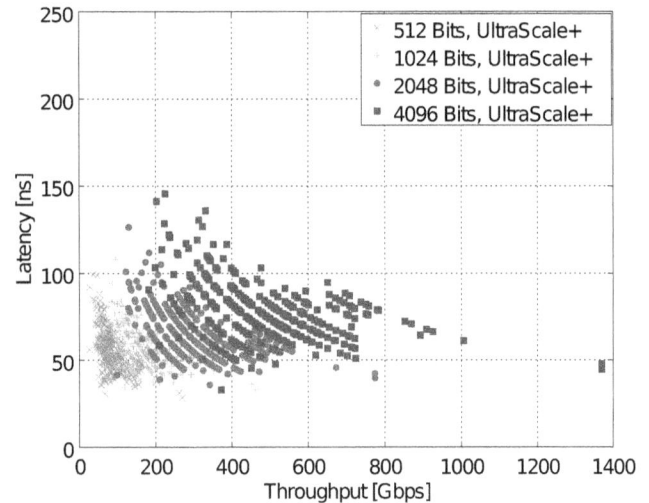

Figure 15: The relation between throughput and processing latency of the full parsers on the UltraScale+ FPGA.

5.2 Full Protocol Stack

The state space of the full protocol stack parser parameter combinations is huge – 2^{15} configurations for every bus width. Therefore we synthesized only some hand-picked and randomly selected configurations that account for about 1 % of all the possibilities.

Fig. 13 and Fig. 14 show the resource utilization and effective throughput of the synthesized full parsers on the UltraScale+ FPGA and the Virtex 7 FPGA. The full parsers are much larger because they support more protocols than the simple L2 parsers. Therefore, the resource utilization reaches nearly 2 times higher values here. However, we still managed to achieve effective throughput of well over 1 Tbps on the UltraScale+ FPGA. The results again show the 1.5 to 2 times lower achieved throughputs for the Virtex-7.

Fig. 15 and Fig. 16 show the the latency and throughput relation of different configurations of full parsers implemented on the UltraScale+ and the Virtex-7 FPGA. The full parsers have considerably more pipeline stages, and therefore their latency is much higher – nearly 4 times in some cases. Apart from that, we can see the same trends as for the simple L2 parser. This is also true for the relationship between latency and resource utilization of the full parser on the UltraScale+ (Fig. 17) and the Virtex-7 FPGA (Fig. 18).

5.3 Summary

Fig. 19 shows sets of tested parsers with Pareto optimal results of resource utilization to achieved throughput. From the graph, we can clearly see the difference between the simple L2 parsers (full line) and the full parsers (dashed line) in resource utilization – the

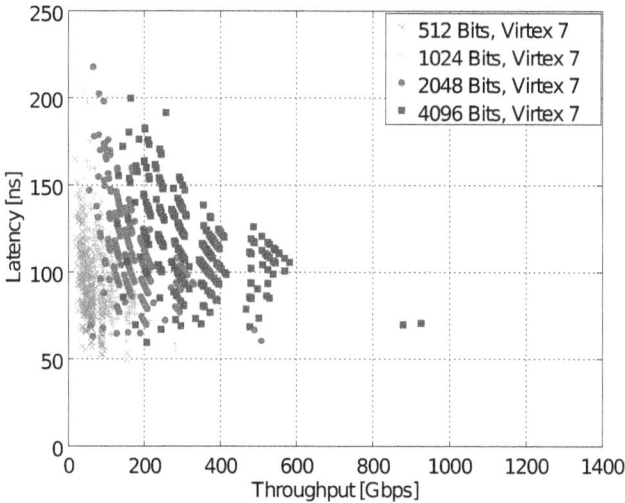

Figure 16: The relation between throughput and processing latency of the full parsers on the Virtex-7 FPGA.

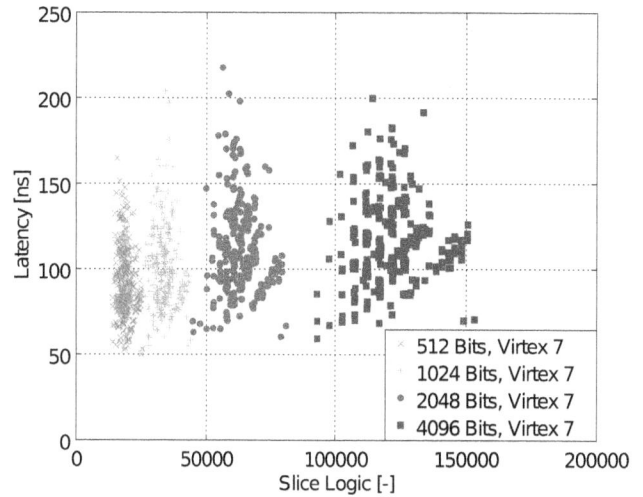

Figure 18: The relation between resources and latency of the full parsers on the Virtex-7 FPGA.

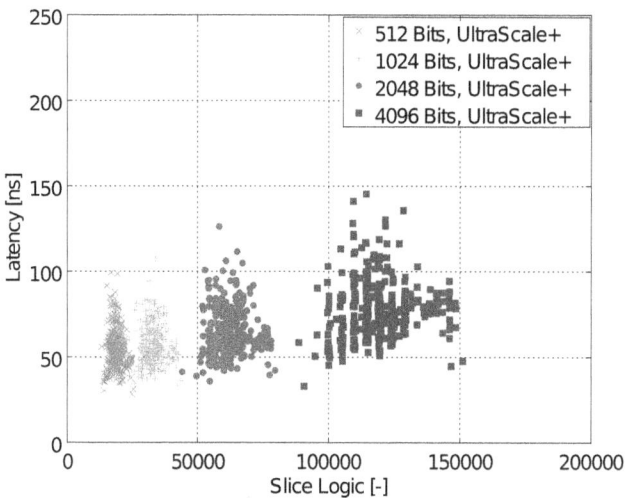

Figure 17: The relation between resources and latency of the full parsers on the UltraScale+ FPGA.

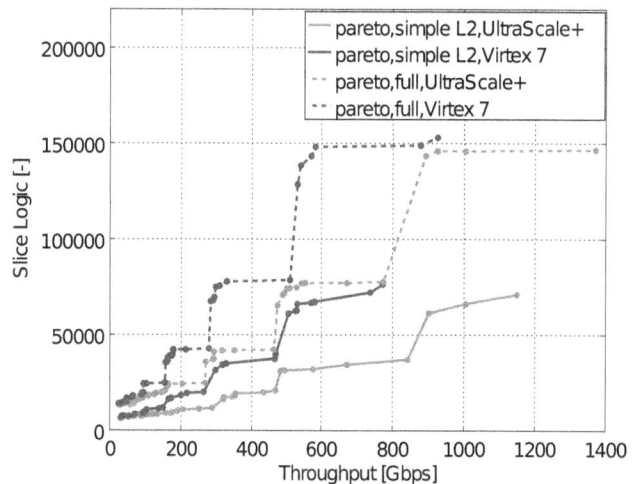

Figure 19: Pareto optimal sets of parsers in throughput × used resources space.

full parsers are up to 2 times larger. Also, the difference between target platforms (red for the UltraScale+ and blue for the Virtex-7 FPGA) is apparent. To compensate for the 1.5-2 times lower achieved frequencies on Virtex-7 and to achieve the same throughputs, nearly 2 times larger parsers must be used compared to UltraScale+. The stairs in the graphs are caused by the changing data bus width.

Fig. 20 shows Pareto optimal sets of parsers configurations in latency to throughput space. In all cases, the latency increases with the throughput. Again, we can see the positive effect of the higher frequencies on the UltraScale+, where the latency is only 10 to 30 ns for the simple L2 parsers and 30 to 50 ns for the full parsers.

To summarize, the measured results clearly show that the newer family of Xilinx FPGAs enable to achieve considerably better results of packet parsing implementation. Up to 2 times higher achieved

frequencies allow selection of parsers with a narrower data bus to conserve a significant portion of FPGA resources for a given throughput requirement. Or, on the other hand, allow our parser architecture to achieve effective throughput of over 1 Tbps using wider buses. As the throughput holds even in the worst case scenario, we are able to achieve an incredible processing rate of over 1 500 Mpps when parsing the shortest Ethernet frames. Furthermore, we can see that the number of supported protocols does not negatively affect the throughput (nor packet rate) of our parsers thanks to the proposed pipelined architecture.

The effective throughput of our parser architecture is better than any of the so far presented approaches to parsing in FPGAs. The highest raw throughputs have been presented by Attig and Brebner in [1] (AB parser) and by Kekely et al. in [3, 4] extended with automatic parser generation by Benáček et al. in [2] (KB parser). Their

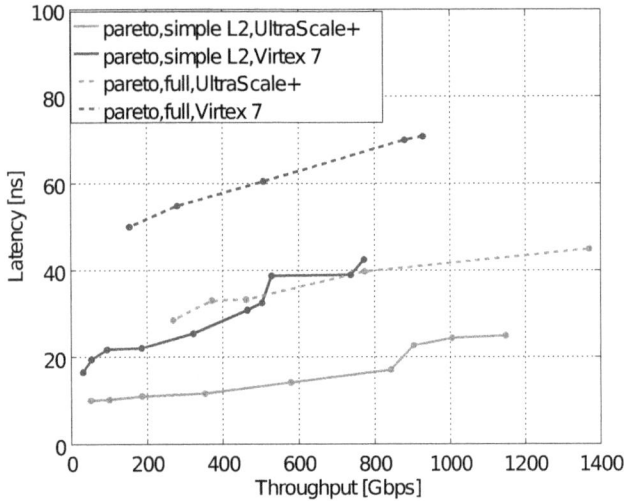

Figure 20: Pareto optimal sets of parsers in throughput × latency space.

Throughput	Parser	Utilization	Latency
over 100 Gbps	*our*	*2.05 %*	*69 ns*
	AB [1]	9.50 %	320 ns
	KB [2]	1.94 %	45 ns
over 400 Gbps	*our*	*6.38 %*	*67 ns*
	AB [1]	22.70 %	365 ns
	KB [2]	5.87 %	56 ns

Table 2: Comparison with other state of the art approaches.

approaches are discussed at the end of the section 2. Results of both of these parsers are presented for the Xilinx Virtex-7 XCVH870T FPGA – the same as we used for our Virtex-7 measurements. Also, both show results for similarly complex protocol stack as our full version of the parser (AllStack for AB and full stack for KB parser). Unfortunately, they use different metrics to describe the utilization of FPGA resources (percentage of the FPGA vs. LUT-FF pairs). Therefore, we transformed the utilization notation in the following paragraph to represent the percentage of used slices from the total available on the XCVH870T FPGA.

Under the specified common conditions, the AB parser is shown to achieve raw throughput of up to 578 Gbps and the KB parser of up to 478 Gbps. Our parser notably surpasses them both with the maximum of 926 Gbps. Furthermore, unlike the other approaches, the high throughput of our parser is retained even when processing the shortest packets. A comparison in terms of FPGA resources utilization and latency for specific throughput requirements (100 and 400 Gbps) is provided in the table 2. Compared to the AB parser, our approach (highlighted) requires several times fewer FPGA resources and operates with considerably smaller processing latency. The KB parser is only a little bit better in both metrics than our approach, but again, our approach guarantees sufficient throughput even in the worst case while the KB parser does not. To overcome this throughput limitation, the whole KB parser can be replicated (e.g., 4× for 400 Gbps) and traffic distributed between the copies.

But of course, this would considerably increase its utilization of FPGA logic and processing latency (well above our results).

6 CONCLUSIONS

This paper introduces and elaborates a novel parser architecture that enables processing of network traffic in current FPGAs at very high throughput. Unlike virtually all other approaches in this area, we do not focus solely on the raw achievable throughput but pay increased attention to sustainment of the performance even in the worst case – when parsing long bursts of very short packets. This way, the proposed parser architecture is able to guarantee wire-speed processing of network traffic at given link speed without any packet losses. Furthermore, HDL implementation of the parser can be automatically generated from a high-level description of a protocol stack in P4 language.

Our measurements show, that even for rather complex protocol stack the proposed parser concept enables to achieve high effective throughput at a cost of just a few percent of resources available in a single current FPGA. The achieved throughput is as high as 1.37 Tbps on the Xilinx UltraScale+ FPGAs and 926 Gbps on the Xilinx Virtex-7 FPGAs. Thanks to sustainment of the performance even for the shortest 64 B Ethernet frames, a huge packet rate is also reached – up to 2 038 Mpps on the UltraScale+ resp. 1 377 Mpps on the Virtex-7. The achieved throughput and, more notably, packet rate are considerably higher than in other published works. Moreover, they are well above the requirements for lossless wire-speed processing of 1 Tbps Ethernet traffic.

ACKNOWLEDGMENTS

This research has been partially supported by the project Reg. No. CZ.02.1.01/0.0/0.0/16_013/0001797 co-funded by the MEYS of the Czech Republic, IT4Innovations excellence in science project IT4I XS – LQ1602, and by the Technology Agency of the Czech Republic project TH02010214.

REFERENCES

[1] M. Attig and G. Brebner. 2011. 400 Gb/s Programmable Packet Parsing on a Single FPGA. In *Architectures for Networking and Communications Systems (ANCS), 2011 Seventh ACM/IEEE Symposium on.* 12–23. https://doi.org/10.1109/ANCS.2011.12
[2] P. Benáček, V. Puš, and H. Kubátová. 2016. P4-to-VHDL: Automatic Generation of 100 Gbps Packet Parsers. In *2016 IEEE 24th Annual International Symposium on Field-Programmable Custom Computing Machines (FCCM).* 148–155.
[3] L. Kekely, J. Kořenek, and V. Puš. 2012. Low-latency Modular Packet Header Parser for FPGA. In *Proceedings of the Eighth ACM/IEEE Symposium on Architectures for Networking and Communications Systems.* ACM, New York, NY, USA, 77–78.
[4] L. Kekely, V. Puš, and J. Kořenek. 2014. Design Methodology of Configurable High Performance Packet Parser for FPGA. In *17th IEEE Symposium on Design and Diagnostics of Electronic Circuits&Systems.* IEEE Computer Society, 189–194.
[5] P. Kobierský, J. Kořenek, and L. Polčák. 2009. Packet header analysis and field extraction for multigigabit networks. In *Proceedings of the 2009 12th International Symposium on Design and Diagnostics of Electronic Circuits&Systems (DDECS).* IEEE Computer Society, Washington, USA, 96–101.
[6] C. Kozanitis, J. Huber, S. Singh, and G. Varghese. 2010. Leaping Multiple Headers in a Single Bound: Wire-Speed Parsing Using the Kangaroo System. In *Proceedings of the 29th Conference on Information Communications.*
[7] P. Bosshart et al. 2014. P4: Programming Protocol-independent Packet Processors. *SIGCOMM Computer Communication Review* 44, 3 (July 2014), 87–95.
[8] The P4 Language Consortium. 2017. The P4 Language Specification. (24 May 2017). https://p4lang.github.io/p4-spec/p4-14/v1.0.4/tex/p4.pdf
[9] The P4 Language Consortium. 2017. P4$_{16}$ Language Specification. (22 May 2017). https://p4lang.github.io/p4-spec/docs/P4-16-v1.0.0-spec.pdf
[10] H. Wang, R. Soulé, H. T. Dang, K. S. Lee, V. Shrivastav, N. Foster, and H. Weatherspoon. 2017. P4FPGA: A Rapid Prototyping Framework for P4. In *Proceedings of the Symposium on SDN Research (SOSR '17).* ACM, New York, NY, USA, 122–135.

FASTCF: FPGA-based Accelerator for
STochastic-Gradient-Descent-based Collaborative Filtering

Shijie Zhou
University of Southern California
Los Angeles, CA 90089
shijiezh@usc.edu

Rajgopal Kannan
US Army Research Lab
Los Angeles, CA 90094
Rajgopal.kannan.civ@mail.mil

Yu Min
University of Southern California
Los Angeles, CA 90089
yumin@usc.edu

Viktor K. Prasanna
University of Southern California
Los Angeles, CA 90089
prasanna@usc.edu

ABSTRACT

Sparse matrix factorization using Stochastic Gradient Descent (SGD) is a popular technique for deriving latent features from observations. SGD is widely used for Collaborative Filtering (CF), itself a well-known machine learning technique for recommender systems. In this paper, we develop an FPGA-based accelerator, FASTCF, to accelerate the SGD-based CF algorithm. FASTCF consists of parallel, pipelined processing units which concurrently process distinct user ratings by accessing a shared on-chip buffer. We design FASTCF through a holistic analysis of the specific design challenges for the acceleration of SGD-based CF on FPGA. Based on our analysis of these design challenges, we develop a bipartite graph processing approach with a novel 3-level hierarchical partitioning scheme that enables conflict-minimizing scheduling and processing of on-chip feature vector data to significantly accelerate the processing of this bipartite graph. First, we develop a fast heuristic to partition the input graph into induced subgraphs; this enables FASTCF to efficiently buffer vertex data for reuse and completely hide communication overhead. Second, we partition all the edges of each subgraph into matchings to extract the maximum parallelism. Third, we schedule the execution of the edges inside each matching to reduce concurrent memory access conflicts to the shared on-chip buffer. Compared with non-optimized baseline designs, the hierarchical partitioning approach results in up to 60× data dependency reduction, 4.2× bank conflict reduction, and 15.4× speedup. We implement FASTCF based on state-of-the-art FPGA and evaluate its performance using three large real-life datasets. Experimental results show that FASTCF sustains a high throughput of up to 217 billion floating-point operations per second (GFLOPS). Compared with state-of-the-art multi-core and GPU implementations, FASTCF demonstrates 13.3× and 12.7× speedup, respectively.

KEYWORDS

Sparse matrix factorization; Training process; Bipartite graph representation

ACM Reference Format:
Shijie Zhou, Rajgopal Kannan, Yu Min, and Viktor K. Prasanna. 2018. FASTCF: FPGA-based Accelerator for STochastic-Gradient-Descent-based Collaborative Filtering. In *FPGA '18: 2018 ACM/SIGDA International Symposium on Field-Programmable Gate Arrays, February 25–27, 2018, Monterey, CA, USA.* ACM, New York, NY, USA, 10 pages. https://doi.org/10.1145/3174243.3174252

1 INTRODUCTION

Web-based services such as online shopping and social media have become extremely popular Internet services but also difficult to use effectively due to the surfeit of information available on the web. In order to provide accurate recommendations and enhance user satisfaction, many online companies such as Amazon, Netflix, and Facebook develop recommender systems [1, 2]. These systems analyze the patterns of user's interest in products and provide personalized recommendations that suit a user's taste. Collaborative Filtering (CF) is a widely used machine learning technique to design such recommender systems [1].

Sparse matrix factorization is an unsupervised machine learning technique to extract latent information from observations [1]. Stochastic Gradient Descent (SGD) is widely used to train the matrix factorization model for many applications, for which CF is a representative example. This approach has achieved the highest prediction accuracy in the Netflix challenge [2], which gives a partially observed rating matrix and asks to predict the missing ratings. In addition, SGD-based CF is adopted in many commercial recommender systems [1–4]. However, the training process of SGD-based CF algorithms is computation-intensive because the model needs to be iteratively updated for thousands of iterations [5]. When the volume of training data is huge, training time can become excessively long. Therefore, it becomes essential to develop hardware-based accelerators to reduce the training time.

Recently, there has been a growing interest in employing FPGA to accelerate machine learning techniques [6–10]. In this paper, we propose FASTCF, a high-throughput accelerator based on state-of-the-art FPGA to accelerate the training process of a popular SGD-based CF algorithm. FASTCF consists of parallel processing units concurrently working on distinct input data to sustain high throughput. On-chip buffers that store the feature data (vectors) of users and items feed the pipleines and are exploited for data reuse. The proposed design is also applicable to accelerating other applications that use matrix factorization to derive hidden features from observations (e.g., text mining [11]).

Our design of FASTCF is holistic and generalized: It is motivated by a careful analysis of the challenges involved in accelerating SGD-based CF on FPGA. We identify three principal design challenges 1) limited on-chip memory which can limit throughput if the long latencies of external memory accesses are not managed 2) data dependencies among feature vectors which can prevent concurrent processing within the FPGA pipeline and 3) pipeline stalls due to access conflicts between different pipelines when accessing single R/W ported on-chip memory banks. (Note that multi-ported memory banks [25, 26] can solve the access conflict problem but we must pay a significant memory capacity penalty to do so. Multi-port banks require significantly larger on-chip memory capacity for solving a similar sized problem due to quadratic factor duplication (Sec 5.3)). Based on our analysis of these design challenges, we develop a bipartite graph processing approach in which the input training data is first transformed into a bipartite graph representation. This is followed by a novel 3-level hierarchical partitioning scheme that enables conflict-minimizing scheduling and processing of on-chip feature vector data to significantly accelerate the processing of this bipartite graph. We handle the specific design challenges listed above through the following techniques:

- To overcome the first challenge, FASTCF first partitions the input graph into induced subgraphs. In lieu of more sophisticated partitioning algorithms with higher preprocessing costs, we develop a simple and fast partitioning heuristic that satisfies a necessary condition for storing feature vectors of vertices in the on-chip buffer. By overlapping the communication overhead with computation, FASTCF can absorb the long latencies of external memory accesses.

- To overcome the data dependency challenge, we maximize the available parallelism by partitioning the edges of each induced subgraph into matchings. This reduces the data dependencies among the edges by up to 60×, and thus enables FASTCF to efficiently process distinct edges in parallel.

- To overcome the bank-conflict challenge, we develop a greedy algorithm to partition each matching into batches and schedule the execution of the batches to reduce conflicts due to concurrent accesses to the shared on-chip buffer (i.e., bank conflicts). This optimization results in up to 4.2× bank conflict reduction.

Experimental results show that FASTCF sustains high throughput of up to 217 GFLOPS for training. Compared with a state-of-the-art multi-core implementation running on a 24-core Intel Xeon processor, FASTCF achieves 13.3× speedup. Compared with a state-of-the-art GPU implementation running on a 2880-core Tesla K40C, FASTCF attains 12.7× speedup.

The rest of the paper is organized as follows. Section 2 covers the background; Section 3 introduces the SGD-based CF algorithm and the challenges in accelerating it; Section 4 presents our 3-level hierarchical partitioning approach; Section 5 describes the architecture of FASTCF; Section 6 reports the experimental results; Section 7 discusses the related work; Section 8 concludes the paper.

2 BACKGROUND

CF relies on existing user ratings to predict the ratings that have not been given [5]. By collecting and analyzing past rating information from many users (collaborating), CF identifies new user-item associations and makes predictions (filtering). Most of the CF algorithms fall into two categories, namely memory-based and model-based algorithms [1, 5].

Memory-based CF algorithms use user ratings to compute the similarity between users or alternatively, between items. Several similarity metrics, such as Pearson correlation and Cosine similarity [6], can be used to compute the similarity. Once a matrix of similarities is formed, the prediction of a particular user's rating of an item is made based on similar users (i.e., users that have high similarity with this user) or similar items. Although memory-based CF algorithms are simple and fast, they cannot efficiently handle sparse datasets [5]. In addition, their prediction performance is not as accurate as model-based CF algorithms [5].

Model-based CF algorithms aim to develop a model of user ratings using machine learning techniques. After the model is obtained, model-based CF algorithms produce the prediction of a user's rating by computing the expected value of the rating in the model. Matrix factorization model, which is also called latent factor model [3], has shown great success to achieve high prediction accuracy for CF, and is widely adopted in recommender systems [1, 5, 14]. Stochastic Gradient Descent (SGD) and Alternate Least Square (ALS) are two primary methods to perform matrix factorization for CF [1, 13, 14]. ALS can converge in fewer iterations than SGD, but ALS is hardly scalable to large-scale datasets due to its cubic time complexity in each iteration [14]. In this paper, we focus on accelerating the SGD-based CF algorithm.

There are also hybrid approaches to combine CF technique with other recommendation techniques (e.g., content-based recommender [5]). Such hybrid CF algorithms can overcome the problems of native CF such as loss of information. However, the complexity and expense for the implementation are significantly increased as well [5].

3 ALGORITHM AND CHALLENGES

In this section, we briefly introduce the SGD-based CF algorithm and discuss the challenges in accelerating it.

3.1 SGD-based CF

Let U and V denote a set of users and items, $|U|$ and $|V|$ denote the number of users and items, respectively. The **input** training dataset is a partially filled rating matrix $R = \{r_{ij}\}_{|U| \times |V|}$, in which r_{ij} represents the rating of item v_j given by user u_i ($0 \leq i < |U|$, $0 \leq j < |V|$).

Assuming each user and item is associated with H latent features[1], the **output** model of the training process contains two matrices, P (a $|U| \times H$ matrix) and Q (a $|V| \times H$ matrix), such that their product approximates R (i.e., $R \approx P \times Q^T$). P and Q are called user feature matrix and item feature matrix, respectively. The i-th row of P (denoted as p_i) constitutes a **feature vector** of user u_i and the j-th row of Q (denoted as q_j) constitutes a feature vector of item v_j.

---

[1]A typical value of H is 32 [15–17].

The prediction of the rating of item v_j by user u_i is the dot product of p_i and q_j:

$$\hat{r}_{ij} = p_i \cdot q_j = \sum_{h=0}^{H-1} p_{ih} \cdot q_{jh} \tag{1}$$

Given a known rating r_{ij}, the prediction error is computed as $err_{ij} = r_{ij} - \hat{r}_{ij}$. The objective of the training process is to obtain such P and Q that minimize the overall regularized squared error based on all the known ratings:

$$\min_{P,Q} \sum_{u_i \in U, v_j \in V} err_{ij}^2 + \lambda \cdot (||p_i||^2 + ||q_j||^2) \tag{2}$$

In the objective function, λ is a constant used to introduce regularization to prevent overfitting. To minimize the objective function, SGD is used to update the feature vectors [1]. SGD randomly initializes all the feature vectors and then updates them by iteratively traversing all the known ratings until the overall squared error (i.e., $\sum err_{ij}^2$) converges. By taking a known rating r_{ij}, p_i and q_j are updated by a magnitude proportional to a constant α (learning rate) in the opposite direction of the gradient, yielding the following updating rules:

$$p_i^{new} = \beta \cdot p_i + err_{ij} \cdot \alpha \cdot q_j \tag{3}$$

$$q_j^{new} = \beta \cdot q_j + err_{ij} \cdot \alpha \cdot p_i \tag{4}$$

In Eq. (3) and (4), β is a constant whose value is equal to $(1 - \alpha\lambda)$. The algorithm requires to incrementally update the feature vectors **once per rating**; therefore, the ratings of the same item or given by the same user cannot be concurrently processed because they will result in the updates for the same q_j or p_i. Additional details of this algorithm can be found in [1, 4].

3.2 Challenges

There are three challenges in accelerating the SGD-based CF algorithm using FPGA.

First, since the feature vectors of users and items are repeatedly accessed and updated during the processing of ratings, it is desirable to store them in the on-chip memory of FPGA. However, for large training dataset that involves a large number of users and items, the feature vectors cannot fit in the on-chip memory. In this scenario, external memory such as DRAM is required to store them. However, accessing feature vectors from external memory can incur long access latency, which results in accelerator pipeline stalls and even no speedup [19].

Second, data dependencies exist among ratings, making it challenging to efficiently exploit the massive parallelism of FPGA for concurrent processing. More specifically, the ratings of the same item or given by the same user cannot be processed concurrently. This is because SGD requires to incrementally update feature vectors once per rating; concurrent processing of such ratings can lead to read-after-write data hazard. We define such data dependency among ratings as **feature vector dependency**.

Third, FPGA accelerators usually employ parallel processing units to increase processing throughput [8, 19, 20]. However, the on-chip RAMs (e.g., block RAM and UltraRAM) of FPGA support only dual-port accesses (one read port and/or one write port) [25–27]. When multiple processing units need concurrent accesses to the same RAM based on distinct memory addresses, these memory

accesses have to be serially served. This leads to additional latency to resolve the access conflicts and thus performance deterioration.

In order to overcome these challenges, we use a bipartite graph representation of CF (Section 4.1) and propose a 3-level hierarchical partitioning approach (Section 4.2).

4 GRAPH REPRESENTATION AND HIERARCHICAL PARTITIONING

4.1 Graph Representation

We transform SGD-based CF into a bipartite graph-processing problem so that graph theories can be leveraged to optimize the performance. The input rating matrix is converted into a bipartite graph G, whose vertices can be divided into two disjoint sets, U (user vertices) and V (item vertices). Each known rating in R is represented as an edge connecting a user vertex and an item vertex in G. We store G in the coordinate (COO) format [22], which is a commonly used graph representation [16–18, 22–24]. This format stores the graph as an edge list E; each edge is represented as a $< u_i, v_j, r_{ij} >$ tuple, in which u_i and v_j refer to the user and item vertices, and r_{ij} corresponds to the rating value of v_j given by u_i. Algorithm 1 illustrates the SGD-based CF using bipartite graph representation. Each vertex maintains a feature vector of length H. All the edges in E are iteratively processed to update the feature vectors of vertices until the overall squared error converges. When the training process terminates, the feature vectors of all the user vertices and item vertices constitute the output feature matrices P and Q, respectively.

Algorithm 1 SGD-based CF using graph representation

Let p_i denote the feature vector of user vertex u_i ($0 \le i < |U|$)
Let q_j denote the feature vector of item vertex v_j ($0 \le j < |V|$)
Let $edge_{ij}$ denote the edge connecting u_i and v_j
CF_Train $(G(U, V, E))$

1: **for** each user/item vertex **do**
2:     Randomly initialize its feature vector
3: **end for**
4: **while** Overall_squared_error_converages = false **do**
5:     Overall_squared_error= 0
6:     **for** each $edge_{ij} \in E$ **do**
7:         Read feature vectors p_i and q_j
8:         Compute $\hat{r}_{ij}$ based on Eq. (1)
9:         Compute err_{ij} based on r_{ij} and $\hat{r}_{ij}$
10:        Update p_i and q_j based on Eq. (3) and (4)
11:        Overall_squared_error+ = err_{ij}^2
12:     **end for**
13: **end while**
14: **Return** all the feature vectors of vertices

4.2 3-Level Hierarchical Partitioning

4.2.1 First-Level Partitioning: On-chip Buffering and Communication Hiding. In order to address the first challenge described in Section 3.2, we partition G into induced subgraphs to achieve two goals: (1) the feature vectors of the vertices in each induced subgraph can fit in the on-chip buffer; (2) the computation for processing each induced subgraph can completely hide the communication cost.

Let L (N) denote the on-chip buffer capacity in terms of the number of feature vectors for user (item) vertices. We partition U into l disjoint vertex subsets $\{U_0, \ldots, U_{l-1}\}$, each of size at most L, where $l = \lceil \frac{|U|}{L} \rceil$. Similarly, V is partitioned into $\{V_0, \ldots, V_{n-1}\}$, each of size at most N, where $n = \lceil \frac{|V|}{N} \rceil$. We will introduce the details to partition U and V in Algorithm 3. Let E_{xy} denote an subset of E that consists of all the edges connecting the vertices belonging to U_x and V_y in G ($0 \leq x < l, 0 \leq y < n$). Then U_x, V_y, and E_{xy} form an **Induced Subgraph** (*IS*) of G [28]. Since each user (item) vertex subset has no more than L (N) vertices, the feature vectors of all the vertices in each *IS* can fit in the on-chip buffer.

Because there are l user vertex subsets and n item vertex subsets, the total number of induced subgraphs after the partitioning is $l \times n$. Then, in each iteration of the training process, all the induced subgraphs are sequentially processed by FASTCF based on Algorithm 2. Note that during the processing of the edges in E_{xy}, all the feature vectors of the vertices in U_x and V_y have been prefetched into the on-chip buffer; therefore, the processing units of FASTCF can directly access the feature vectors from the on-chip buffer.

Algorithm 2 Scheduling of induced subgraph processing

1: **while** Overall_squared_error_converages = false **do**
2:   **for** x from 0 to $l - 1$ **do**
3:     Load feature vectors of U_x into on-chip buffer
4:     **for** y from 0 to $n - 1$ **do**
5:       Load feature vectors of V_y into on-chip buffer
6:       Process all the edges $\in E_{xy}$
7:       Write feature vectors of V_y into external memory
8:     **end for**
9:     Write feature vectors of U_x into external memory
10:   **end for**
11: **end while**

Using double buffering [8, 29], we can pipeline the processing of induced subgraphs while overlapping communication and computation of each *IS* with its predecessor/successor. Let $P(IS_z)$ denote the computation time to process all the edges of an induced subgraph IS_z; let T_z denote the *intra-subgraph* communication time (i.e., the total time for data transfers occurring during the processing of IS_z). As shown in Figure 1, we can pipeline the processing of induced subgraphs by overlapping the computation time $P(IS_z)$ of IS_z with the *writing* of feature vectors from IS_{z-1} and the *reading* of feature vectors from IS_{z+1}. Therefore, $T_z = T_{z-1}^{wr} + T_{z+1}^{rd}$. Here, T_z in general may include reads or writes of both user and item feature vectors. We can easily derive the **sufficient condition** for complete overlap of communication and computation: $P(IS_z) \geq T_z, \forall z \in [0, l \times n)$.

A vertex-index-based partitioning approach [30] has been widely used to perform graph partitioning for hardware accelerators [17, 20, 21]. This approach simply assigns a group of vertices with contiguous indices to each vertex subset. Although this approach is fast, it can lead to significant data imbalance such that some subgraphs may have very few edges; in this scenario, the communication cost cannot be completely hidden by the computation. Therefore, a desirable partitioning approach should balance the number of

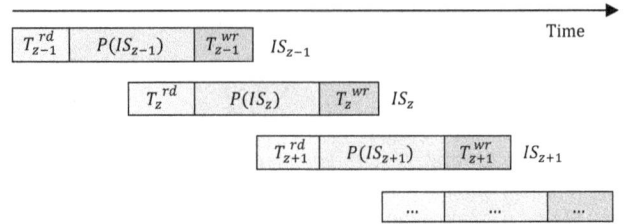

Figure 1: Pipelined induced subgraph processing

edges among the induced subgraphs. Many sophisticated graph partitioning approaches have been developed to achieve balanced partitioning and simultaneously minimize some other metrics [31]. For example, vertex-cut algorithm [31] balances the number of edges among subgraphs and meanwhile minimizes the number of vertex replicas in distributed computing environment. However, these sophisticated approaches usually introduce significant preprocessing overhead. Our intuition is that it is not necessary to invest significantly in developing complex partitioning algorithms (in terms of preprocessing time), rather any reasonably fast algorithm is acceptable as long as the derived sufficient condition is satisfied.

We propose a simple and fast heuristic partitioning approach. Our empirical results show that this approach leads to the balanced partitioning such that each *IS* has sufficient edges for the computation to completely hide the communication cost. We define the *subset degree* of a vertex subset as the total number of edges that connect to the vertices in the subset. When we partition U and V into vertex subsets, we attempt to pack vertices into each disjoint vertex subset such that the subset degrees are close to each other. However, the most important criteria is to ensure that subset sizes are bound by L and N as defined earlier. Algorithm 3 illustrates our approach to partition U into $U_0, \cdots, U_{l-1}$; V is partitioned based on the same methodology. We first identify the vertex degree of each vertex (i.e., the number of edges connected to the vertex) and sort all the vertices based on the vertex degree in non-increasing order. Then we greedily assign each vertex into the vertex subset which has not been full and has the minimum subset degree, until all the vertices are assigned, subject to the subset size condition.

When each vertex is assigned to a vertex subset, we assign a new vertex index to it (Algorithm 3, Line 18), which indicates the vertex subset that it belongs to and its index in the vertex subset. After U and V are partitioned, we reorder the vertices based on the new indices such that the feature vectors of the vertices belonging to the same vertex subset are stored contiguously in external memory. Since user and item vertices are reordered, we also re-index the user and item indices of each edge and partition the edges into induced subgraphs based on the new indices.

4.2.2 Second-Level Partitioning: Data Dependency Reduction. The second-level partitioning addresses the second challenge described in Section 3.2. Note that the edges having the same user vertex or item vertex cannot be concurrently processed due to the feature vector dependencies. We partition the edges in each *IS* into set of **matchings**, such that each matching consists of a set of

---

Algorithm 3 Partition U into l subsets $U_0, \cdots, U_{l-1}$

Let $u_{i \cdot degree}$ be the number of edges connected to u_i ($0 \le i < |U|$)
Let $U_{x \cdot size}$ be the number of vertices in U_x ($0 \le x < l$)
Let $U_{x \cdot degree}$ be the subset degree of U_x ($\sum u_{i \cdot degree}, \forall u_i \in U_x$)
Partition (U, L, l)

1: **for** x from 0 to $l - 1$ **do**
2:     $U_x = \varnothing$
3:     $U_{x \cdot degree} = 0$
4:     $U_{x \cdot size} = 0$
5: **end for**
6: Sort U based on vertex degree in descending order
7: **for** each $u_i \in U$ **do**
8:     $subset\_id = -1$
9:     $min\_degree = |E|$
10:     **for** x from 0 to $l - 1$ **do**
11:         **if** $min\_degree > U_{x \cdot degree}$ **and** $U_{x \cdot size} < L$ **then**
12:             $subset\_id = x$
13:             $min\_degree = U_{x \cdot degree}$
14:         **end if**
15:     **end for**
16:     $U_{subset\_id} = U_{subset\_id} \cup u_i$
17:     $U_{subset\_id \cdot degree} = U_{subset\_id \cdot degree} + u_{i \cdot degree}$
18:     $u_{i \cdot new\_user\_id} = subset\_id \times L + U_{subset\_id \cdot size}$
19:     $U_{subset\_id \cdot size} = U_{subset\_id \cdot size} + 1$
20: **end for**
21: **Return** $U_0, \cdots, U_{l-1}$

---

vertex-disjoint edges. As a result, the edges in the same matching do not have any feature vector dependencies and can be processed in parallel.

We perform the second-level partitioning by using edge-coloring [28], which colors all the edges of a bipartite graph such that any two adjacent edges do not have the same color. After all the edges are colored, the edges having the same color form a matching. However, the classic edge-coloring algorithm in [28] can result in small matchings, in which there are very few edges (e.g., only 1 edge). When processing such small matchings, the parallelism provided by the hardware accelerator (i.e., parallel processing units) is not fully utilized. We modify the edge-coloring algorithm by keeping track of the number of edges in each matching during the partitioning; when an edge can be partitioned into multiple matchings, we select the matching having the minimum number of edges.

4.2.3 Third-Level Partitioning: Bank Conflict Reduction. The architecture of the accelerator has M parallel processing units sharing an on-chip buffer, which is organized in $2M^*$ ($M^* \ge M$) banks with separate banks for users and items (see Section 5.3); therefore, a batch of M edges from a matching can be concurrently processed at a time. However, due to the dual-port nature of on-chip RAM [25–27], each bank can support only 1 read and 1 write request per clock cycle. If there is a bank conflict between two or more accesses within a batch, the memory requests to process the edges have to be serially served. Thus the latency for resolving the bank conflict(s) within a batch is equal to the *maximum* number of accesses to the same bank within the batch. We develop the following greedy

heuristic for reducing the bank conflicts. We sort all the edges in a matching in non-increasing order of their bank conflict index (BCI). The BCI of an edge is defined as the number of other edges in the matching that have bank conflict with this edge. We partition each matching into batches of size M by sequentially traversing the sorted edges. We greedily assign an edge to the first batch where its addition *does not increase* the current latency to resolve the bank conflicts of the batch. Note that this is different from assigning the edge to the batch where it has the minimum bank conflict.

5 ACCELERATOR DESIGN

5.1 Overall Architecture

The overall architecture of FASTCF is depicted in Figure 2. As shown, two DRAM chips, $DRAM_0$ and $DRAM_1$, are connected to FPGA as the external memory. $DRAM_0$ stores all the edges and $DRAM_1$ stores the feature vectors of all the vertices, respectively. When processing an *IS*, the feature vectors of all the vertices belonging to the *IS* are read from $DRAM_1$ and stored in the Feature Vector Buffer (FVB), which is organized as banks of UltraRAM. FPGA fetches edges from $DRAM_0$ and stores them into a first-in-first-out Edge Queue (EQ). Whenever the EQ is not full, FPGA pre-fetches edges from $DRAM_0$. A batch of edges are fed into the Bank Conflict Resolver (BCR) at a time and output in one or multiple clock cycles, such that the edges output in the same clock cycle do not have bank conflict accesses to the FVB. Then, each edge is checked by the Hazard Detection Unit (HDU) to determine whether it is data-hazard free to be processed. If an edge has no feature vector dependency with any edge being processed in the Processing Engine (PE), it is sent into the PE; otherwise, pipeline stalls occur until the dependency is resolved. The PE consists of multiple processing units that process distinct edges in parallel. These processing units access the feature vectors of vertices from the FVB.

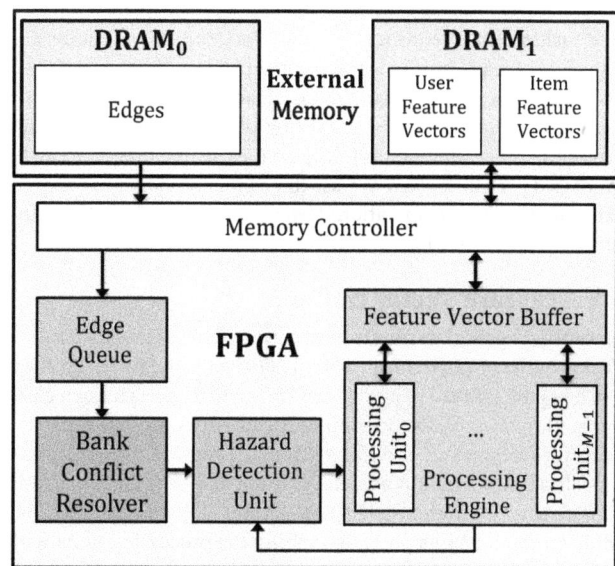

Figure 2: Overall architecture

5.2 Processing Engine

The processing engine (PE) consists of M parallel processing units that concurrently process distinct edges. We show the architecture of each processing unit in Figure 3. Each input edge is processed as follows: based on the user and item vertex indices, the processing unit reads the feature vectors, p_i and q_j, from the FVB; then, the prediction $\hat{r}_{ij}$ is computed based on p_i and q_j; meanwhile, p_i and q_j are multiplied with the constants (i.e., α and β) to obtain αp_i, αq_j, βp_i, and βq_j; once the prediction error err_{ij} is obtained, p_i^{new} and q_j^{new} are computed based on Eq. (3) and (4); finally, p_i^{new} and q_j^{new} are written into the FVB.

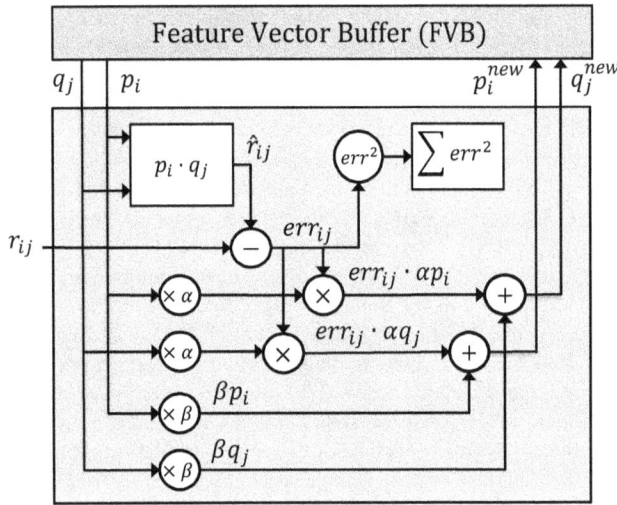

Figure 3: Architecture of processing unit

The dot product of p_i and q_j is computed in a binary-reduction-tree fashion [32], requiring H multipliers and $(H - 1)$ adders in total. Hence, each processing unit contains $7H$ multipliers, $(3H - 1)$ adders, 1 subtractor, 1 squarer, and 1 accumulator, sustaining a peak throughput of $(10H + 2)$ floating point operations per clock cycle. The processing unit is fully pipelined so that one edge can be processed per clock cycle. We use three pipeline stages to compute each floating point operation. Hence, the pipeline depth of the processing unit is $3(\log H + 4)$.

5.3 Feature Vector Buffer

Since the M processing units need concurrently access the Feature Vector Buffer (FVB) to read and write distinct feature vectors, there can be up to $2M$ read requests[2] and $2M$ write requests in each clock cycle. However, native on-chip RAMs of FPGA provide only two ports for reading and/or writing [25–27]. There are three major approaches to build multiport memory using dual-port on-chip RAMs, including multi-pumping [33], replication [25], and banking [34]. Multi-pumping gains ports by running the processing units with $M\times$ lower frequency than the multiport memory. However, this can significantly deteriorate the clock rate of the processing units for a large M (e.g., M=8) [25, 26]. Replication-based approaches,

[2] M for user feature vectors and M for item feature vectors

such as Live Value Table (LVT) and XOR [25], create replicas of all the stored data to provide additional ports and keep track of which replica has the most recently updated value for each data element [26]. However, the size of the RAM needed in implementing this grows quadratically with the number of ports, such that $M \times M$ replicas are required to support M read ports and M write ports. Additionally, the clock rate can degrade below 100 MHz when the width and depth of the memory are large (e.g., 1Kbit × 16K) [26].

In order to support large buffer capacity and sustain high clock rate, FASTCF adopts the banking approach [34] to build the FVB. This approach divides the memory into equal sized banks and interleaves these banks to provide higher access bandwidth (i.e., more read and write ports). As illustrated in Figure 4, the banked FVB contains two parts of equal size, one for storing user feature vectors and the other for storing item feature vectors. Each part is divided into M^* banks ($M^* \geq M$) and each bank is a dual-port UltraRAM [27]. Therefore, the FVB provides up to $2M^*$ read ports and $2M^*$ write ports. Feature vectors of vertices are stored into the FVB in a modular fashion based on the vertex indices, such that p_i is stored in the ($i\%M^*$)-th user bank and q_j is stored in the ($j\%M^*$)-th item bank. Hence, the feature vector of any user (item) can be accessed from the FVB based on the user (item) vertex index without complex index-to-address translation.

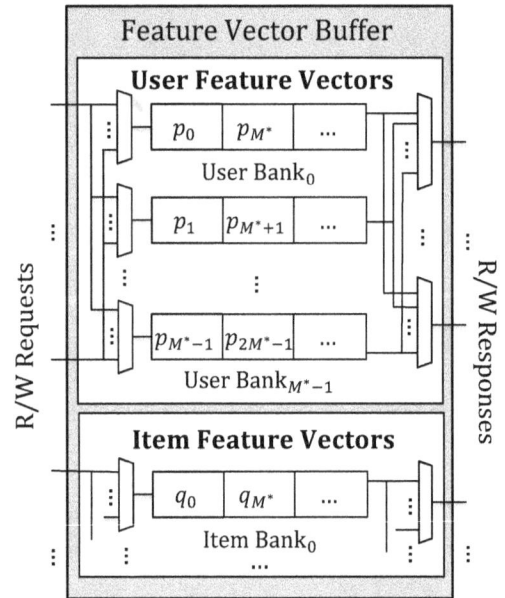

Figure 4: Banked FVB

However, the banked FVB cannot handle concurrent accesses to the same bank for distinct feature vectors. Such memory accesses are defined as bank conflict accesses. To address this issue, we develop a Bank Conflict Resolver (BCR) to avoid any bank conflict accesses. The BCR fetches a batch of M edges at a time and outputs them to the Hazard Detection Unit (HDU). The BCR ensures that all the edges output in the same clock cycle have the feature vectors of their vertices stored in distinct banks of the FVB. However, this can lead to additional clock cycles to resolve the bank conflicts within a batch; in the worst case, when all the edges in a batch have conflict with each other, the BCR takes M clock cycles to output all the edges in the batch.

5.4 Hazard Detection Unit

When the edges from the Bank Conflict Resolver and the edges being processed in the PE belong to different matchings, read-after-write data hazards due to feature vector dependencies may occur. The Hazard Detection Unit (HDU) is constructed by BRAMs and responsible for detecting feature vector dependencies and preventing read-after-write data hazards. We design the HDU using a fine-grained locking mechanism. For each vertex, we assign a 1-bit flag. A flag with value 1 means the feature vector of the corresponding vertex is being computed by the PE, and thus cannot be accessed. For each input edge, the HDU checks the flags of its user and item vertices; if both the flags are 0, the edge is fed into the PE and the flags are set to 1; otherwise, the pipeline stalls until both the flags become 0. When the PE writes any updated feature vector into the FVB, it also sends signals to the HDU to set the flag of the corresponding vertex back to 0. Therefore, deadlock will not occur.

6 EXPERIMENTAL RESULTS

6.1 Experimental Setup

Our FPGA designs are implemented on a state-of-the-art Virtex UltraScale+ xcvu9pflgb2104 FPGA [37]. The target FPGA device has 1,182,240 slice LUTs, 2,364,480 slice registers, 6,840 DSPs, and up to 43.3 MB of on-chip RAM. The FPGA uses two DDR4 chips as the external memory. Each DRAM has 16 GB capacity and a peak bandwidth of 19.2 GB/s. The host CPU is an 8-core Intel Xeon E5-2686 processor. Each core of the host CPU runs at 2.3 GHz and has a 32 KB L1 cache and a 256 KB L2 cache. All the cores share a 45 MB L3 cache. The host CPU and the FPGA are connected through PCIe 3.0×16 bus.

We use large real-life datasets (Table 1) to evaluate our designs. These datasets have been widely used in related works [12, 16, 22, 35]. In our experiments, the length of each feature vector is 32 (i.e., $H = 32$) with each element represented using IEEE 754 single precision format. We adopt a standard learning rate $\alpha = 0.0001$ and regularization parameter $\lambda = 0.02$ [4]. We use execution time and throughput (sustained floating point operations per second (GFLOPS)) as our performance metrics.

Table 1: Large real-life datasets used for experiments

Dataset	# users $|U|$	# items $|V|$	# ratings $|E|$	Description
Libimseti [23]	135 K	168 K	17,359 K	Dating ratings
Netflix [4]	480 K	17 K	100,480 K	Movie ratings
Yahoo [24]	1,200 K	136 K	460,380 K	Music ratings

6.2 Resource Utilization, Clock Rate, and Power Consumption

Table 2 shows the resource utilization, clock rate, and power consumption of FASTCF for $M = 8$ (i.e., the number of processing units

= 8). The reported results are post-place-and-route results evaluated by Xilinx Vivado Design Suite 2017.2. For $M = 8$, FASTCF uses up to 58.9% slice LUTs and 63.0% DSPs in the FPGA device. Therefore, we could not increase M further to 16 due to the resource limitations. The feature vector buffer (FVB) is organized in 32 banks and the capacity of the FVB is empirically set to 64K feature vectors (32K for user vertices and 32K for item vertices). We did not increase the capacity of the FVB to 128K because we observed that the clock rate degraded to 85 MHz when 75% UltraRAMs of the FPGA device were used.

Table 2: Resource utilization, clock rate, and power consumption of FASTCF

Slice LUT (%)	Register (%)	DSP (%)	On-chip RAM (%)	
			Block RAM	UltraRAM
58.9	27.1	63.0	1.2	37.5
Clock rate (MHz)			Power (Watt)	
150			13.8	

6.3 Pre-processing Time and Training Time

Table 3 and Table 4 report the pre-processing time and training time, respectively. The pre-processing is performed by the host CPU based on our proposed 3-level partitioning approach; the training is performed by FASTCF. Note that the pre-processing is performed only once, while the training is an iterative process; thus, the pre-processing time can be amortized and is negligible compared with the total training time. In Table 4, we also report the total training time and the average execution time for each iteration.

Table 3: Pre-processing time

Dataset	1st-level	2nd-level	3rd-level	Total
Libimseti	0.4 sec	4.4 sec	2.7 sec	7.5 sec
Netflix	1.0 sec	10.7 sec	7.0 sec	18.7 sec
Yahoo	5.5 sec	42.3 sec	23.0 sec	70.8 sec

Table 4: Training time

Dataset	Total training time	# iterations to converge	Avg. T_{exec} per iteration
Libimseti	360.8 sec	11,568	0.03 sec
Netflix	876.4 sec	5,766	0.15 sec
Yahoo	2536.5 sec	3,714	0.68 sec

6.4 Performance vs. Parallelism

To explore the impact of parallelism on the performance, we vary the number of processing units (M) from 1 to 8. Figure 5 shows the throughput performance for various M. We observe that the throughput performance significantly improves as M increases for all the three datasets. For $M = 8$, FASTCF sustains 165 GFLOPS

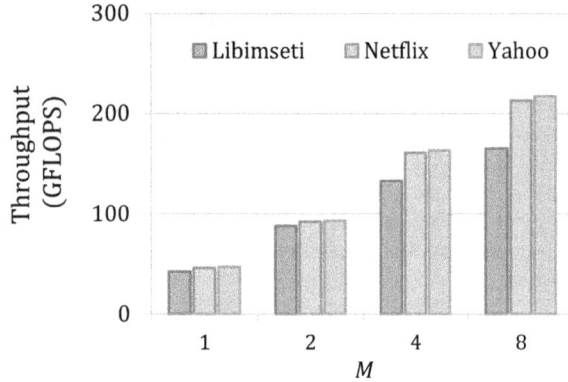

Figure 5: Throughput performance for various M

for Libimseti, 213 GFLOPS for Netflix, and 217 GFLOPS for Yahoo, respectively. However, we also observe that the number of pipeline stalls due to feature vector dependencies increases as M increases. This is because when a matching is to be processed, there can be up to $M \times D$ edges of other matching(s) remaining in the M processing units, where D is the pipeline depth of each processing unit. Thus, a larger M increases the chances of feature vector dependencies. It can also be observed that the throughput performance of Libimseti is worse than Netflix and Yahoo for $M = 4$ and 8. This is because the Libimseti dataset is much sparser than the other two datasets, thus resulting in more small matchings that cannot fill up the processing units. Since the edges belonging to different matchings can have common vertices, when multiple small matchings are consecutively processed, the pipeline stalls due to feature vector dependencies are more likely to occur.

6.5 Impact of the Optimizations

To show the effectiveness of our proposed 3-level hierarchical partitioning approach, we compare our optimized design with non-optimized FPGA-based baseline designs. All the comparisons are based on $M = 8$.

6.5.1 Bank Conflict Reduction. We first explore the effectiveness of the third-level partitioning in reducing the number of bank conflicts. Here, the baseline design used for the comparison only performs the first-level and second-level partitionings during the pre-processing. Table 5 summarizes the results of the comparison. We observe that our optimized design reduces the number of bank conflicts by 2.4× to 4.2× and thus results in 1.3× to 1.5× speedup.

Table 5: Bank conflict reduction

Dataset	# clocks to resolve bank conflicts per iteration		Reduc-tion	T_{exec} per iteration (sec)		Speedup
	Opt.	Base.		Opt.	Base.	
Libim.	1,165 K	2,798 K	2.4×	0.03	0.04	1.3×
Netflix	3,960 K	16,686 K	4.2×	0.15	0.23	1.5×
Yahoo	19,393 K	75,524 K	3.9×	0.68	1.03	1.5×

6.5.2 Data Dependency Reduction. We further explore the impact of the second-level partitioning to reduce the number of pipeline stalls due to feature vector dependencies. The baseline design used for the comparison performs the first-level and third-level partitionings only. Table 6 summarizes the effectiveness of this optimization. We observe that the optimization dramatically reduces the number of pipeline stalls due to feature vector dependencies by 28.7× to 60.1×; as a result, the execution time per iteration is reduced by 13.3× to 15.4×.

Table 6: Pipeline stall reduction

Dataset	# stalls due to dependencies per iteration		Reduc-tion	T_{exec} per iteration (sec)		Speedup
	Opt.	Base.		Opt.	Base.	
Libim.	2,005 K	57,524 K	28.7×	0.03	0.40	13.3×
Netflix	6,151 K	314,884 K	51.2×	0.15	2.19	14.6×
Yahoo	24,954 K	1,500,295 K	60.1×	0.68	10.45	15.4×

6.5.3 Communication Cost Reduction. Lastly, we study the impact of the first-level partitioning to reduce the communication cost. We define communication cost as the data transfer time between the FPGA and the external memory. Here, the baseline design also performs all the three levels of partitionings, but the first-level partitioning is based on the simple vertex-index-based partitioning approach [30] (described in Section 4.2.1) rather than our proposed approach (Algorithm 3). Table 7 summarizes the results of the comparison. For all the three datasets, the optimized design is able to completely hide the communication cost; while the baseline design cannot completely hide the communication cost for Libimseti and Yahoo datasets. This is because the vertex-index-based partitioning approach performs unbalanced graph partitioning and thus results in small induced subgraphs, which do not have sufficient edges to completely hide the communication cost.

Table 7: Communication cost reduction

Dataset	Unhidden communication cost per iteration (sec)		T_{exec} per iteration (sec)		Speedup
	Opt.	Base.	Opt.	Base.	
Libimseti	0	0.005	0.031	0.036	1.16×
Netflix	0	0	0.15	0.15	1.00×
Yahoo	0	0.04	0.68	0.72	1.06×

6.6 Comparison with State-of-the-art

We compare the performance of FASTCF with a state-of-the-art multi-core implementation [35] and a state-of-the-art GPU implementation [22]. Native [35] implements SGD-based CF on a 24-core Intel E5-2697 processor. It has shown the fastest training speed among the existing multi-core implementations [15, 36]. In [22], SGD-based CF algorithm is implemented on a 2880-core Tesla K40C GPU. The GPU design develops several scheduling schemes for parallel thread execution on the GPU. However, the lock-free static scheduling schemes are not able to efficiently exploit the thousands of cores on the GPU, and the dynamic scheduling schemes require memory locks to handle feature vector dependencies and thus have significant synchronization overhead. As a result, the achieved speedup by the GPU acceleration is quite limited.

Table 8 compares the performance of FASTCF with [22, 35] for training the same dataset (Netflix). Our design achieves 13.3× and 12.7× speedup compared with [35] and [22], respectively. Note that the feature vector length (H) used in FASTCF is larger than [22, 35]. Therefore, from throughput perspective, FASTCF achieves 21.3× and 25.4× improvement compared with [35] and [22], respectively. Moreover, the power consumption of FASTCF (13.8 W) is far less than the multi-core (130 W) and GPU (235 W) platforms.

Table 8: Comparison with state-of-the-art multicore and GPU implementations based on Netflix dataset

Approach	Platform	H	T_{exec} per iteration	Speedup
[35]	24-core Intel E5-2697	20	2.00 sec	1.0×
[22]	2880-core Tesla K40C	16	1.90 sec	1.1×
FASTCF	Virtex UltraScale+	32	0.15 sec	13.3×

7 RELATED WORK

7.1 Graph-processing Frameworks

There are several graph-processing frameworks that support CF. Representative examples include GraphMat [16], Graphicionado [17], and GraphLab [15]. However, most of these frameworks implement Gradient-Descend-based CF [15–17] because it can be easily expressed as a vertex-centric program. GD-based CF accumulates the intermediate updates for each feature vector and performs the update after all the ratings have been traversed in an iteration. Therefore, it updates each feature vector only once per iteration and thus requires more iterations to converge and more training time than SGD-based CF (e.g., 40× more iterations to train Netflix [35]). Native [35] implements SGD-based CF on multi-core platform. It pre-processes the input training matrix by partitioning it into submatrices, and concurrently processes the submatrices that do not have feature vector dependencies using distinct CPU cores. However, the design only exploits submatrix-level parallelism (i.e, each submatrix is serially processed by a CPU core) and the submatrices can vary significantly in size. This can result in load imbalance among the CPU cores and thus increase the synchronization overhead.

7.2 GPU-based CF Accelerators

GPUs are widely used to accelerate machine learning applications [38]. GPU-based accelerators for memory-based CF [39] and ALS-based CF [13] have been developed. However, it has been shown that GPUs are not suitable for accelerating SGD-based CF [22, 38, 40]. The main reasons include (1) the fine-grained synchronization of updated feature vectors is expensive on GPU platforms [38], and (2) the SIMD execution of GPU further inflates the cost of thread divergence when synchronization conflicts occur [22]. Siede et. al

[40] investigate the theoretical efficiency of SGD on GPUs, and conclude that fundamental changes in the algorithm are necessary to attain significant speedup. In [22], SGD-based CF is implemented on a Tesla K40C GPU. The design develops and compares several scheduling schemes for parallel execution of SGD on GPU, including dynamic scheduling schemes using locks and lock-free static scheduling schemes. However, none of the schemes is able to efficiently exploit the GPU acceleration and the achieved speedup compared with a CPU implementation is small (< 1.1×).

7.3 FPGA-based CF Accelerators

There have not yet been many efforts to exploit FPGA to accelerate CF. In [6], an FPGA-based accelerator for memory-based CF algorithms is proposed. The design accelerates three memory-based CF algorithms and achieves up to 16× speedup compared with multi-core implementations. However, the training dataset of the design is very small (4K users, 1K items, and 1M ratings), which can fit in the on-chip memory of state-of-the-art FPGAs. To the best of our knowledge, FASTCF is the first design to exploit FPGA to accelerate model-based CF algorithm for large training datasets.

8 CONCLUSION AND FUTURE WORK

In this paper, we presented FASTCF, an FPGA-based accelerator for SGD-based CF. FASTCF consisted of parallel processing units sharing an on-chip feature vector buffer. To optimize the performance of FASTCF, we proposed a novel 3-level hierarchical partitioning approach by using a bipartite graph representation of CF. Our focus was to obtain simple and fast heuristics based on identifying sufficient conditions for significant acceleration of the SGD-based CF algorithm on FPGA. By holistically considering the architectural characteristics of the FPGA platform, the proposed partitioning approach resulted in a complete overlap of communication and computation, up to 60× data dependency reduction, and 4.2× bank conflict reduction. As a result, our accelerator sustained a high throughput of up to 217 GFLOPS for training large real-life datasets. Compared with the state-of-the-art multi-core implementation and GPU implementation, FASTCF demonstrated 13.3× and 12.7× speedup, respectively.

In the future, we will explore multi-FPGA architectures, in which each FPGA device employs FASTCF, to further reduce the training time. We also plan to generalize our partitioning approach to support other SGD-based algorithms.

ACKNOWLEDGMENTS

This work is supported by the U.S. National Science Foundation grants ACI-1339756 and CNS-1643351. This work is also supported in part by Intel Strategic Research Alliance funding.

REFERENCES

[1] Y. Koren, R. Bell, and C. Volinsky, "Matrix Factorization Techniques for Recommender Systems," in IEEE Computer, vol. 42, iss. 8, 2009.

[2] C. A. Gomez-Uribe and N. Hunt, "The Netflix Recommender System: Algorithms, Business Value, and Innovation," ACM Transactions on Management Information Systems (TMIS), vol. 6, iss. 4, 2016.

[3] B. Chen, D. Agarwal, P. Elango, and R. Ramakrishnan, "Latent Factor Models for Web Recommender Systems," http://www.ideal.ece.utexas.edu/seminar/LatentFactorModels.pdf

[4] "Netflix Update: Try This at Home," http://sifter.org/~simon/journal/20061211.html

[5] X. Su and T. M. Khoshgoftaar, "A Survey of Collaborative Filtering Techniques," Advances in Artificial Intelligence, 2009.

[6] X. Ma, C. Wang, Q. Yu, X. Li, and X. Zhou, "An FPGA-based Accelerator for Neighborhood-based Collaborative Filtering Recommendation Algorithms," in Proc. of International Conference on Cluster Computing (CLUSTER), pp. 494-495, 2015.

[7] J. Zhang and J. Li, "Improving the Performance of OpenCL-based FPGA Accelerator for Convolutional Neural Network," in Proc. of International Symposium on Field-Programmable Gate Arrays February (FPGA), pp. 25-34, 2017.

[8] C. Zhang, P. Li, G. Sun, Y. Guan, B. Xiao, and J. Cong, "Optimizing FPGA-based Accelerator Design for Deep Convolutional Neural Networks," in Proc. of International Symposium on Field-Programmable Gate Arrays February (FPGA), pp. 161-170, 2015.

[9] G. Hegde, Siddhartha, N. Ramasamy, and N. Kapre, "CaffePresso: An Optimized Library for Deep Learning on Embedded Accelerator-based Platforms," in Proc. of International Conference on Compliers, Architectures, and Sythesis of Embedded Systems (CASES), 2016.

[10] R. Zhao, W. Song, W. Zhang, T. Xing, J. Lin, M. B. Srivastava, R. Gupta, and Z. Zhang, "Accelerating Binarized Convolutional Neural Networks with Software-Programmable FPGAs," in Proc. of International Symposium on Field-Programmable Gate Arrays February (FPGA), pp. 15-24, 2017.

[11] J. Pennington, R. Socher, and C. D. Manning, "Glove: Global Vectors for Word Representation," In Proc. of Conference on Empirical Methods in Natural Language Processing (EMNLP), pp. 1532-1543, 2014.

[12] M. Zhang, Y. Wu, K. Chen, X. Qian, X. Li, and W. Zheng, "Exploring the Hidden Dimension in Graph Processing," in Proc. of USENIX Symposium on Operating Systems Design and Implementation (OSDI), 2016.

[13] W. Tan, L. Cao, and L. Fong, "Faster and Cheaper: Parallelizing Large-Scale Matrix Factorization on GPUs," in Proc. of International Symposium on High-Performance Parallel and Distributed Computing (HPDC), pp. 219-230, 2016.

[14] H. Yu, C. Hsieh, S. Si, and I. Dhillon. "Parallel Matrix Factorization for Recommender Systems," in Journal of Knowledge and Information Systems (KAIS), pp. 793-819, 2014.

[15] "GraphLab Collaborative Filtering Library," http://select.cs.cmu.edu/code/graphlab/pmf.html

[16] N. Sundaram, N. Satish, M. A. Patwary, S. R. Dulloor, M. J. Anderson, S. G. Vadlamudi, D. Das, and P. Dubey, "GraphMat: High Performance Graph Analytics Made Productive," in Proc. of VLDB Endowment, vol. 8, no. 11, pp. 1214-1225, 2015.

[17] T. J. Ham, L. Wu, N. Sundaram, N. Satish, and M. Martonosi, "Graphicionado: A High-performance and Energy-efficient Accelerator for Graph Analytics," in Proc. of International Symposium on Microarchitecture (MICRO), 2016.

[18] S. Zhou, C. Chelmis, and V. K. Prasanna, "Accelerating Large-scale Single-source Shortest Path on FPGA," in Proc. of International Parallel and Distributed Processing Symposium Workshop (IPDPSW), 2015

[19] B. Betkaoui, Y. Wang, D. B. Thomas, and W. Luk, "A Reconfigurable Computing Approach for Efficient and Scalable Parallel Graph Exploration," in Proc. of International Conference on Application-specific Systems, Architectures and Processors (ASAP), pp. 8-15, 2012.

[20] S. Zhou, C. Chelmis, and V. K. Prasanna, "High-throughput and Energy-efficient Graph Processing on FPGA," in Proc of International Symposium on Field-Programmable Custom Computing Machines (FCCM), pp. 103-110, 2016.

[21] S. Zhou, C. Chelmis, and V. K. Prasanna, "Optimizing memory performance for FPGA implementation of pagerank," in Proc. of International

Conference on ReConFigurable Computing and FPGAs (ReConFig), 2015.

[22] R. Kaleem, S. Pai, and K. Pingali, "Stochastic Gradient Descent on GPUs," in Proc. of Workshop on General Purpose Processing using GPUs (GPGPU), pp. 81-89, 2015.

[23] L. Brozovsky and V. Petricek, "Recommender System for Online Dating Service," 2007, https://pdfs.semanticscholar.org/1a42/f06f368cf9b2ba8565e81d8e048caa5c2c9e.pdf.

[24] "Ratings and Classification Data," https://webscope.sandbox.yahoo.com/catalog.php?datatype=r

[25] C. E. Laforest, M. G. Liu, E. R. Rapati, and J. G. Steffan, "Multi-ported Memories for FPGAs via XOR," in Proc. of International Symposium on Field-Programmable Gate Arrays February (FPGA), pp. 209-218.

[26] S. N. Shahrouzi and D. G. Perera, "An Efficient Embedded Multiport Memory Architecture for Next-Generation FPGAs," in Proc. of International Conference on Application-specific Systems, Architectures and Processors (ASAP), pp. 83-90, 2017.

[27] "UltraRAM: Breakthrough Embedded Memory Integration on UltraScale+ Devices," https://www.xilinx.com/support/documentation/white_papers/wp477-ultraram.pdf

[28] R. J. Wilson, "Introduction to Graph Theory," ISBN 0-582-24993-7, 1996.

[29] E. Nurvitadhi, G. Weisz, Y. Wang, S. Hurkat, M. Nguyen, J. C. Hoe, J. F. Martnez, and C. Guestrin, "GraphGen: An FPGA Framework for Vertex-Centric Graph Computation," in Proc of International Symposium on Field-Programmable Custom Computing Machines (FCCM), pp. 25-28, 2014.

[30] R. Pearce, M. Gokhale, and N. M. Amato, "Faster Parallel Traversal of Scale Free Graphs at Extreme Scale with Vertex Delegates," in Proc. of International Conference for High Performance Computing, Networking, Storage and Analysis (SC), pp. 549-559, 2014.

[31] R. Chen, J. Shi, B. Zang, and H. Guan, "Bipartite-oriented Distributed Graph Partitioning for Big Learning," in Proc. of Asia-Pacific Workshop on Systems Article (APSys), 2014.

[32] G. R. Morris, V. K. Prasanna, and R. D. Anderson, "A Hybrid Approach for Mapping Conjugate Gradient onto an FPGA-Augmented Reconfigurable Supercomputer," in Proc. of International Symposium on Field-Programmable Custom Computing Machines (FCCM), pp. 3-12, 2006.

[33] H. E. Yantir, S. Bayar, A. Yurdakul, "Efficient Implementations of Multi-pumped Multi-port Register Files in FPGAs," in Proc. of Euromicro Conference on Digital System Design (DSD), pp. 185-192, 2013.

[34] J. Wawrzynek, K. Asanovic, J. Lazzaro, and Y. Lee, "Banked Multiport Memory," https://inst.eecs.berkeley.edu/~cs250/fa10/lectures/lec08.pdf.

[35] N. Satish, N. Sundaram, M. Patwary, J. Seo, J. Park, M. A. Hassaan, S. Sengupta, Z. Yin, and P. Dubey, "Navigating the Maze of Graph Analytics Frameworks using Massive Graph Datasets," in Proc. of ACM SIGMOD, pp. 979-990, 2014.

[36] A. Lenharth, "Parallel Programming with the Galois System," http://iss.ices.utexas.edu/projects/galois/downloads/europar2014-tutorial.pdf

[37] "Virtex UltraScale+ FPGA Data Sheet," https://www.xilinx.com/support/documentation/data_sheets/ds923-virtex-ultrascale-plus.pdf

[38] J. Dean, G. Corrado, R. Monga, K. Chen, M. Devin, Q. Le, M. Mao, M. Ranzato, A. Senior, P. Tucker, K. Yang, and A. Ng, "Large Scale Distributed Deep Networks," in Proc. of Neural Information Processing Systems Conference (NIPS), pp. 1232-1240, 2012.

[39] Z. Wang, Y. Liu, and S. Chiu, "An Efficient Parallel Collaborative Filtering Algorithm on Multi-GPU Platform," in Journal of Supercomputing, vol. 72, iss. 6, pp. 2080-2094, 2016.

[40] F. Seide, H. Fu, J. Droppo, G. Li, and D. Yu, "On Parallelizability of Stochastic Gradient Descent for Speech DNNs," In Proc. of International Conference on Acoustics, Speech and Signal Processing (ICASSP), pp. 235-239, 2014.

Rosetta: A Realistic High-Level Synthesis Benchmark Suite for Software Programmable FPGAs

Yuan Zhou[1]*, Udit Gupta[2]★, Steve Dai[1], Ritchie Zhao[1], Nitish Srivastava[1], Hanchen Jin[1], Joseph Featherston[1],
Yi-Hsiang Lai[1], Gai Liu[1], Gustavo Angarita Velasquez[3]★, Wenping Wang[4]★, Zhiru Zhang[1]*

[1] School of Electrical and Computer Engineering, Cornell University, USA
[2] Computer Science, Harvard University, USA
[3] Systems Engineering and Computer Science, National University of Colombia, Colombia
[4] Electronic and Information Engineering, Zhejiang University, China
*{yz882,zhiruz}@cornell.edu

ABSTRACT

Modern high-level synthesis (HLS) tools greatly reduce the turn-around time of designing and implementing complex FPGA-based accelerators. They also expose various optimization opportunities, which cannot be easily explored at the register-transfer level. With the increasing adoption of the HLS design methodology and continued advances of synthesis optimization, there is a growing need for realistic benchmarks to (1) facilitate comparisons between tools, (2) evaluate and stress-test new synthesis techniques, and (3) establish meaningful performance baselines to track progress of the HLS technology. While several HLS benchmark suites already exist, they are primarily comprised of small textbook-style function kernels, instead of complete and complex applications. To address this limitation, we introduce Rosetta, a realistic benchmark suite for software programmable FPGAs. Designs in Rosetta are fully-developed applications. They are associated with realistic performance constraints, and optimized with advanced features of modern HLS tools. We believe that Rosetta is not only useful for the HLS research community, but can also serve as a set of design tutorials for non-expert HLS users. In this paper we describe the characteristics of our benchmarks and the optimization techniques applied to them. We further report experimental results on an embedded FPGA device as well as a cloud FPGA platform.

ACM Reference Format:
Yuan Zhou, Udit Gupta, Steve Dai, Ritchie Zhao, Nitish Srivastava, Hanchen Jin, Joseph Featherston, Yi-Hsiang Lai, Gai Liu, Gustavo Angarita Velasquez, Wenping Wang, Zhiru Zhang. 2018. Rosetta: A Realistic High-Level Synthesis Benchmark Suite for Software Programmable FPGAs. In *FPGA '18: 2018 ACM/SIGDA International Symposium on Field-Programmable Gate Arrays, February 25–27, 2018, Monterey, CA, USA.* ACM, New York, NY, USA, 10 pages. https://doi.org/10.1145/3174243.3174255

★ Udit, Gustavo, and Wenping conducted this research when they were affiliated with or visiting Cornell.

1 INTRODUCTION

Field-programmable gate arrays (FPGAs) have become an attractive option for realizing specialized accelerators thanks to their reconfigurability, massive fine-grained parallelism, and performance per watt advantage. With the extreme-scale integration of modern system-on-chip (SoC) and escalating design complexity of emerging applications, designing at a higher level of abstraction has become crucial to achieving high productivity. To address this challenge, high-level synthesis (HLS) tools have emerged to allow application developers to describe the hardware accelerator using common software programming languages like C/C++ by automatically generating RTL from behavioral descriptions [7, 14]. With the recent advances on HLS techniques and algorithms, modern HLS tools enable designers to explore optimization opportunities that are infeasible at the register-transfer level.

Programming FPGAs with HLS tools is drastically different from writing traditional software code. HLS users typically need to apply many optimization pragmas/directives to meet design constraints. The success of such manual optimization often requires nontrivial hardware design knowledge. For example, in image/video processing, the right combination of SRAM-based line buffers and shift registers is needed to achieve the ideal throughput and resource usage for pipelining the stencil code in hardware. With a more complex dataflow structure, the user needs to further calculate and specify the right FIFO depth to obtain the best pipeline rate without causing too much area overhead. However, these advanced HLS optimizations are rarely used or even required in the existing HLS benchmark suites (e.g., [11], [23]), which primarily include relatively small kernels that are designed to test some of the basic capabilities of an HLS tool such as the synthesis support of high-level language constructs. In addition, for HLS tool developers and the HLS research community at large, there is also a growing demand for a common set of realistic and complex designs to evaluate the efficacy of new synthesis techniques.

To this end, we introduce Rosetta[1] — a suite of realistic HLS benchmarks for software programmable FPGAs. Rosetta includes popular machine learning workloads such as logistic regression and neural network inference, as well as real-time video processing applications including image rendering and face detection. Unlike previous efforts, Rosetta presents fully developed applications instead of small kernel programs, and specifies realistic design constraints for each

---

[1]Rosetta gets the name following the convention of a plethora of "stone" benchmark suites. It also symbolizes that our benchmarks are specified in multiple languages (i.e., C++, OpenCL) and useful for evaluating HLS across different tools and platforms.

application. These design constraints are satisfied by applying advanced optimizations of state-of-the-art HLS tools, which are not exercised by existing benchmark suites. With these features, Rosetta is not only a set of practical benchmarks for the HLS community, but also a design tutorial on how to build specialized FPGA accelerators with advanced HLS optimizations. More concretely, our main contributions are threefold:

- We design and present Rosetta, which couples a range of realistic applications with real-world design constraints under different programming models. Current Rosetta designs are written in C++ and OpenCL. The synthesized hardware accelerators are tested on both embedded and cloud FPGA platforms.

- Rosetta demonstrates how to effectively apply advanced optimizations provided by modern HLS tools to meet the design constraints and achieve high quality of results. Examples of these optimizations include fixed-point optimization, dataflow pipelining, and data reuse through customized memory.

- The proposed benchmark suite is freely available in open-source format[2]. We plan to continuously improve Rosetta by strengthening current cases and adding new applications from other domains.

The rest of this paper is organized as follows: in Section 2, we introduce related work on HLS benchmarking and optimizations; Section 3 outlines the Rosetta applications and key HLS optimization techniques leveraged by them; details of each benchmark are described in Section 4; we show our experimental results in Section 5, and conclude this work in Section 6.

2 RELATED WORK

FPGA programming currently differs significantly from the common practice of software programming, even with the use of HLS tools. Instead of simply focusing on functional correctness and execution time, FPGA programmers often have to explore various complex design trade-offs involving performance, power, area, and cost. Therefore, traditional software benchmark suites cannot directly be applied to HLS evaluation. In response, a number of HLS-specific benchmark suites have been developed by the research community for evaluating various aspects of hardware synthesis techniques and tool flows. CHStone [11] is a widely used C-based HLS benchmark suite, which contains function kernels selected from application domains such as arithmetic, signal processing, and security. Mach-Suite [23] is another popular HLS benchmark suite, which includes a more diverse set of kernels and provides different algorithms for the same kernel to facilitate comparisons at the algorithmic level. A more recent effort, Spector [10], offers OpenCL benchmarks that are ready to be executed on Intel (formerly Altera) FPGA platforms. Kernels in Spector are designed to have large design spaces, which is useful for experimentation of automatic design space exploration (DSE) techniques. Additionally, HLS researchers have also adopted benchmarks from other communities. For example, Rodinia [5], originally designed for GPU benchmarking, has been used to test OpenCL-based HLS flows [29, 31]. Polybench [21] from the software compiler community has been adopted for assessing HLS-targeted polyhedral transformations [22, 34, 42] and DSE techniques [24, 29, 38, 40].

While the popular kernel benchmarks are simple to run and analyze, they are insufficient for evaluating the increased capabilities of HLS optimizations and new technology advances in FPGA devices.

In particular, state-of-the-art HLS tools provide many advanced features for achieving high design quality. Examples include arbitrary-precision datatypes, parameterized hardware data structures (e.g., line buffers), and hierarchical dataflow pipelining. These features are often used in combination with other common HLS optimizations such as unrolling, loop pipelining [9, 15, 37], and array partitioning [30, 41]. Moreover, they are typically applied across multiple kernels exhibiting different characteristics to meet the stringent applicant-level design constraints.

We believe that a new set of full-application benchmarks is desirable to enable more realistic performance reporting of HLS tools and FPGA-based acceleration. Along this line, Liu et al. [16] conducted a comprehensive case study on an H.264 decoder, and they have open sourced their HLS implementation. Rosetta goes one step further by providing a suite of application benchmarks that can be used to (1) facilitate comparisons between HLS tools, (2) evaluate new synthesis techniques, and (3) establish meaningful baselines to track progress of the HLS and FPGA technologies. Each application in Rosetta includes a set of enforceable application-level design constraints based on real-world specifications. These constraints model the realistic use cases for FPGA-based hardware accelerators, which helps standardize the evaluation of future advancements in HLS tools. Furthermore, the applications in Rosetta leverage advanced features of HLS tools to achieve high quality of results (QoRs) across a distinct set of hardware designs. Hence these benchmarks can also serve as useful design tutorials for FPGA programmers to build high-performance hardware accelerators using HLS.

3 ROSETTA OVERVIEW

Rosetta currently contains six realistic benchmarks selected from machine learning and video processing fields, where FPGAs are competitive on energy efficiency compared to CPUs and GPUs.[3] For each Rosetta design, we provide the unoptimized software version, and the optimized HLS implementations written in either C++ or OpenCL. Table 1 lists the current Rosetta collection. Two of these benchmarks, binarized neural network and face detection, are adopted from our previously published work [25, 39], while the rest are new designs. Rosetta contains both compute-bound and memory-bound applications comprised of a rich set of kernels. These applications and kernels expose diverse sources of parallelism. Our current HLS implementations typically exploit instruction-level parallelism (ILP) through fine-grained pipelining, and in some cases also expose task-level parallelism (TLP) by overlapping the execution of different kernels. Additionally, each benchmark is associated with realistic design objectives — the machine learning applications require either low latency or high throughput depending on the use-case scenario, while video processing applications must meet a real-time throughput target of at least 30 frames per second. In order to achieve these application-level constraints, Rosetta designs are customized using a variety of HLS optimization techniques, which are concisely summarized as follows:

- **Datatype customization** – Customized data types such as fixed-point types allow an FPGA accelerator to compute at the desired numerical accuracy, and often lead to significant performance and area improvements over the design using full-precision floating-point types.

---

[2]Released on Github at https://github.com/cornell-zhang/rosetta

[3]For the time being, we are not targeting traditional benchmarks from cryptography (e.g., AES) and digital signal processing (e.g., DCT, FFT), since they are already included in several other benchmark suites [10, 23].

Table 1: The current set of the Rosetta applications — Rosetta contains both compute-bound and memory-bound applications with different workloads. Kernels in each application expose different sources of parallelism: SLP = subword-level parallelism; DLP = data-level parallelism; ILP = instruction-level parallelism. Different types of parallelism available in each compute kernel are listed in parentheses.

Application	Categorization	Major Compute Kernels	Major HLS Optimizations
3D Rendering	Video processing Compute bound Integer operation intensive	Integer arithmetics (ILP)	Dataflow pipelining Communication customization
Digit Recognition	Machine learning Compute bound Bitwise operation intensive	Hamming distance (SLP, DLP, ILP) KNN voting (ILP)	Loop unrolling Loop pipelining
Spam Filtering	Machine learning Memory bound Fixed-point arithmetic intensive	Dot product (DLP, ILP) Scalar multiplication (DLP, ILP) Vector addition (DLP, ILP) Sigmoid function (ILP)	Dataflow pipelining Datatype customization Communication customization
Optical Flow	Video processing Memory bound Floating-point arithmetic intensive	1D convolution (DLP, ILP) Outer product (DLP, ILP)	Dataflow pipelining Memory customization Communication customization
Binarized Neural Network (BNN) [39]	Machine learning Compute bound Bitwise operation intensive	Binarized 2D convolution (SLP, DLP, ILP) Binarized dot product (SLP, DLP, ILP)	Memory customization Datatype customization Communication customization
Face Detection [25]	Video processing Compute bound Integer arithmetic intensive	Image scaling (DLP, ILP) Cascaded classifiers (DLP, ILP)	Memory customization Datatype customization

- **Compute customization** – Compute customization improves the latency and/or throughput of the design through parallelization and pipelining. Loop unrolling, loop pipelining, and dataflow pipelining fall into this category.

- **Memory customization** – FPGA accelerators typically demand very high on-chip memory bandwidth to enable highly distributed control and computation. Therefore, it is critical to set up customized memory hierarchy to provide the required bandwidth through data reuse and memory banking.

- **Communication customization** – The limited data bandwidth between off-chip memories and the FPGA accelerators often becomes the performance bottleneck for memory-bound applications. Hence it is crucial to customize the communication channel and protocol used by the hardware accelerator to fully utilize off-chip memory bandwidth through proper data packing and careful design of the data layout.

4 BENCHMARK DESCRIPTION

This section discusses Rosetta applications in detail. For each benchmark, we first briefly introduce its functionality and design constraints; we then describe its major compute kernels, explain the rationale behind our categorizations in Table 1, and discuss the key HLS optimizations applied to this design.

4.1 3D Rendering

The 3D rendering benchmark renders 2D images from 3D triangle mesh models [20]. Taking in 3D coordinates of triangle vertices, the application projects the triangles onto a 2D image, and colors the image pixels according to the "altitude" of the projected triangle. Our implementation works on 256x256 images where pixels are represented with 8-bit integers. The provided dataset contains the

```
1  TRIANGLES: for (int i = 0; i < NUM_3D_TRI; i++) {
2      #pragma HLS dataflow
3      // five stages for processing each 3D triangle
4      projection(triangle_3ds, &triangle_2ds, angle);
5      flag = rasterization1(triangle_2ds, max_min,
6                            &triangle_2ds_same, max_index);
7      size = rasterization2(flag, max_min, max_index,
8                            triangle_2ds_same, fragment);
9      size_pixels = zculling(i, fragment, size, pixels);
10     coloringFB(i, size_pixels, pixels, frame_buffer);
11 }
```

Figure 1: Main loop for 3D Rendering. One triangle is processed by five image processing stages in each iteration.

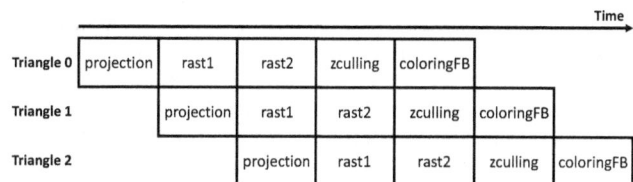

Figure 2: Dataflow optimization overlaps different pipeline stages in 3D rendering.

coordinates of 3192 triangles. Target throughput is 30 frames per second.

The HLS design contains a typical image processing pipeline as shown in Figure 1. The coordinates of each triangle go through four kernel functions before updating the output frame buffer in coloringFB. Integer operations form the primary workload inside the kernels: projection and rasterization2 are rich in integer

```
1  __local WholeDigitType training_set[NUM_TRAINING]
2  __attribute__((xcl_array_partition(block,PAR_FACTOR,1)));
3
4  __attribute__((xcl_pipeline_loop))
5  TRAINING_LOOP:
6  for (int i = 0; i < NUM_TRAINING / PAR_FACTOR; i ++) {
7    __attribute__((opencl_unroll_hint))
8    LANES:
9    for (int j = 0; j < PAR_FACTOR; j ++) {
10     // Read a new instance from the training set
11     int train_id = j * NUM_TRAINING / PAR_FACTOR + i;
12     WholeDigitType training_instance;
13     training_instance = training_set[train_id];
14     // Update the KNN set
15     update_knn(test_instance, training_instance,
16               &knn_set[j*K_CONST]);
17   }
18 }
```

Figure 3: Main compute loop nest for KNN calculation in OpenCL.

arithmetic, while rasterization1 and zculling are heavy on integer comparisons. Each triangle requires a large amount of computation relative to its memory size. Therefore, the application is categorized as compute-bound.

3D rendering is a prime example of dataflow optimization, which is applied in the HLS code on line 2 of Figure 1. Dataflow optimization exploits task-level parallelism by overlapping different stages of the image processing pipeline, as shown in Figure 2. Although the latency of processing each triangle is not reduced, dataflow optimization improves throughput and ensures no hardware module in the pipeline is idle in the steady state.

Design parameters. We provide a switch in the source code to enable/disable dataflow optimization.

4.2 Digit Recognition

Digit recognition classifies hand-written digits using the K-nearest-neighbor (KNN) algorithm. The application works on a downsampled subset of the MNIST database [13], with 18000 training samples and 2000 test samples evenly split amongst the ten digit classes. Each MNIST image is downsampled to 14x14 and each pixel is represented as a single bit; thus, each image can be stored as a 196-bit unsigned integer. The KNN algorithm computes the Hamming distance between a test input and each training sample, stores the labels of the training samples with the K shortest distances, and votes among the K labels to decide the label of the test sample. The design objective for digit recognition is to minimize the total latency of classifying the 2000 test samples.

Digit recognition includes two major compute kernels: Hamming distance calculation and KNN voting. The Hamming distance kernel computes the Manhattan distance between two samples; as each sample is comprised of 1-bit pixels, this is done via bitwise XOR on the inputs, followed by computing a population count of the result. The kernel is therefore rich in bitwise logic. The Hamming distance must be calculated between a test input and every training sample. As a result, Hamming distance calculation is the dominant workload of digit recognition. The KNN voting kernel examines the list of Hamming distances to find the K nearest training samples, and outputs the classification result as the most frequent label amongst them. The main workload in this kernel is integer comparison and sorting.

These two kernels have very different characteristics: while we can easily exploit the bit-level and data-level parallelism in the Hamming distance kernel, the KNN voting kernel is harder to parallelize.

Digit recognition has a high compute to communication ratio. For each test instance, Hamming distance calculation requires 100s-1000s of cycles depending on the parallelization factor, and KNN voting requires 10s-100s of cycles depending on K and the parallelization factor. The training samples and their labels are stored on-chip and reused for all test instances. As a result, digit recognition is a compute-bound application.

Figure 3 shows the main compute loop nest for KNN calculation, alongside key HLS optimizations. TRAINING_LOOP iterates over training samples, while the inner loop, LANES, instantiates different Hamming distance units. In addition to compute optimizations in the form of loop pipelining and unrolling (lines 4 and 7 of Figure 3), memory optimization is needed since the default implementation of on-chip array training_set only has two memory ports, it cannot supply PAR_FACTOR training instances per cycle. The training_set array is partitioned in line 2. With these optimizations, we can exploit the data-level parallelism between training instances.

Design parameters. The user can tune the following knobs:

- K: number of nearest neighbors.
- PAR_FACTOR: number of parallel Hamming distance units.

These two parameters present an interesting trade-off between classification accuracy, latency, and resource utilization. Increasing PAR_FACTOR reduces the latency of the Hamming distance kernel, but complicates the KNN voting kernel. Parallelization also causes frequency to drop. Furthermore, the complexity of both kernels increases with K. Additional results and analysis on the design space are presented in Section 5.

4.3 Spam Filtering

The spam filtering application uses stochastic gradient descent (SGD) to train a logistic regression (LR) model for spam email classification [19]. The input is a dataset containing 5000 emails, 4500 for training and 500 for testing [26]. Each email is represented as a 1024-dimensional vector whose elements are relative word frequencies stored as 16-bit fixed-point numbers. The SGD training process produces a vector of 32-bit fixed-point parameters for the LR model. We use five training epochs and a minibatch size of one; each epoch processes every training sample once and updates the parameters after each sample.

The performance target of spam filtering is to minimize training latency. Critical resource constraints are the number of hardened DSP blocks and the size of on-chip storage, which limits the level of compute parallelization and the amount of data stored on the FPGA. The SGD algorithm contains kernels commonly found in machine learning applications, including dot product, vector addition, and sigmoid.

Our spam filtering design exploits datatype customization and approximation of complex arithmetic operations on the FPGA. Figure 4 shows the optimized sigmoid function. Lines 1-3 show the customized datatypes used to avoid expensive floating-point arithmetic. We also eliminate most of the compute by taking advantage of the properties of the sigmoid function. Sigmoid asymptotically approaches one when the input is large and zero when the input is small (i.e. large negative). Sigmoid values when the input is between minus four and four are hardcoded in a look-up table.

```
1 typedef fixed<F_TWIDTH,F_IWIDTH> FeatureType;
2 typedef uint<LUT_TWIDTH> IdxFixed;
3 typedef fixed<LUT_TWIDTH, LUT_IWIDTH> LutInFixed;
4 // values of sigmoid function stored in a look-up table
5 FeatureType useLUT(LutInFixed in) {
6   IdxFixed index;
7   if (in < 0) {
8     in = -in;
9     index = LUT_SIZE - (in << (LUT_TWIDTH - LUT_IWIDTH));
10  }
11  else
12    index = (in << (LUT_TWIDTH - LUT_IWIDTH));
13  return lut[index];
14 }
15 // sigmoid function
16 FeatureType Sigmoid(FeatureType exponent) {
17   if (exponent > 4)
18     return 1.0;
19   else if (exponent < -4)
20     return 0.0;
21   else {
22     LutInFixed inLut = (LutInFixed)exponent;
23     return useLUT(inLut);
24   }
25 }
```

Figure 4: Datatype and compute optimization to the Sigmoid function — Specialized datatypes are used throughout the whole hardware function to avoid expensive floating-point arithmetic. We use a look-up table to store the values of the sigmoid function so that the complex arithmetic operations can be reduced. In our implementation F_TWIDTH = 32, F_IWIDTH = 13, LUT_TWIDTH = 12, LUT_IWIDTH = 4.

```
1 typedef uint<VDWIDTH> VectorDataType;
2 typedef fixed<D_TWIDTH, D_IWIDTH> DataType;
3 void read_data(VectorDataType* data,
4               DataType*      training,
5               int tid)
6 {
7   for (int i = 0; i < N_FEATURES/(VDWIDTH/D_TWIDTH); i++) {
8     #pragma HLS pipeline
9     // read in the data
10    int idx = tid * N_FEATURES / (VDWIDTH/D_TWIDTH) + i;
11    VectorDataType tmp = data[idx];
12    // distribute into local buffer
13    for (int j = 0; j < (VDWIDTH/D_TWIDTH); j++) {
14      int loc_idx = i * (VDWIDTH/D_TWIDTH) + j;
15      training[loc_idx] = tmp((j+1)*D_TWIDTH-1, j*D_TWIDTH);
16    }}
17 }
```

Figure 5: Communication optimization for spam filtering — In our implementation D_TWIDTH = 16, D_IWIDTH = 4, N_FEATURES = 1024. Users can tune the VDWIDTH parameter to control the off-chip communication bandwidth.

Our target FPGA devices do not have sufficient on-chip memory to store the complete training set, necessitating the streaming of training instances from off-chip memory. Dataflow optimization (introduced in Section 4.1) is applied to overlap communication and compute. To fully utilize off-chip memory bandwidth, we apply element packing as shown in Figure 5. Data is transferred from off-chip storage as VectorFeatureType, which is a wide, custom-bitwidth

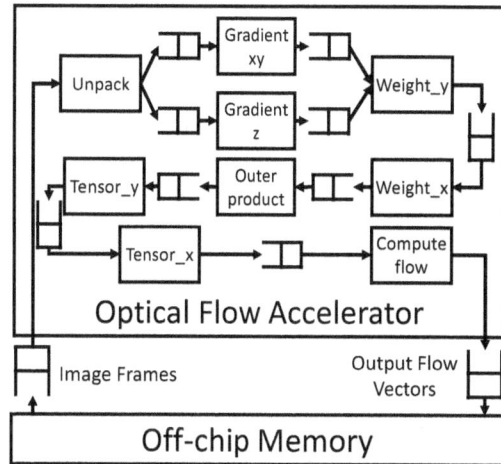

Figure 6: Hardware diagram for optical flow — The kernels are connected by FIFOs for streaming dataflow pipelining.

integer type. Inside the FPGA, the data is unpacked into 16-bit training vector elements, resulting in a communication throughput of multiple elements per cycle. Despite this optimization, the throughput of the dataflow pipeline is still determined by the communication latency because of the relatively simple and highly parallelized compute units for LR. Therefore, spam filtering is classified as a memory-bound application.

Design parameters. The design space of spam filtering consists of the following parameters:

- PAR_FACTOR: the parallelization factor of the vector compute kernels.
- VDWIDTH: the width of the packed vector data type, which controls the upper-bound of the off-chip communication bandwidth of the hardware function.

Our results and analysis on the design space are shown in Section 5.

4.4 Optical Flow

Optical flow captures the motion pattern of objects between consecutive image frames. It is an important step for object detection and is integrated into several image/video processing toolsets such as OpenCV and the Computer Vision toolbox of MATLAB. Our implementation is based on the Lucas-Kanade method which is friendly for FPGAs [32]. The output is a 2D vector field of the same size, where each vector shows the movement of the pixel in the input image frames. Currently, pixels of input images are represented with 8-bit integers, while the output and all intermediate results are represented with 32-bit floating-point numbers. We use the MPI Sintel dataset [4] for testing this benchmark. The resolution of the image frames in this dataset is 436x1024.

Optical flow must satisfy a real-time throughput constraint of 30 frames per second. In addition, the limited amount of on-chip storage prevents us from buffering the image frame on chip. Figure 6 shows the image processing pipeline with eight stages. The main compute kernel for stages Gradient, Weight, and Tensor is 1D convolution; the Outer product stage performs outer product of three-dimensional vectors. Output is generated in the Compute flow stage. Currently, we are using floating-point arithmetic in these kernels. Data packing optimization introduced in Section 4.3 is applied

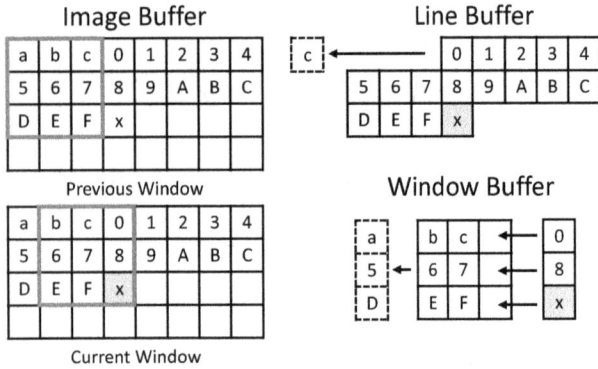

Figure 7: Example of a 2-row line buffer and a 3x3 window buffer — Pixels a, b, c and 0-F are already visited, while x is a new pixel. The line buffer stores pixels in the two most recently visited rows, and reads in one pixel from the image buffer every cycle. The 3x3 window buffer stores recently visited pixels in the 3x3 sliding window. When the sliding window shifts to the right, the left-most pixels in the window buffer are shifted out, while two pixels stored in the line buffer (0 and 8) and the new pixel x are shifted in. The new pixel x is also stored into the line buffer and pixel c is removed from the line buffer.

to avoid contention on the off-chip memory. Each packet contains one pixel from each image frame, and the Unpack stage distributes the pixels to on-chip FIFOs. Similar to 3D rendering, we use dataflow optimization to construct channels between stages of the image processing pipeline. The major difference between the two benchmarks is that all pipeline stages in optical flow produce and consume pixels in a strict sequential order. In addition, the pipeline stages have perfectly balanced rates. Therefore, the channels between pipeline stages can be implemented as fixed-depth FIFOs, as shown in Figure 6. The whole accelerator is a very deep, fine-grained pipeline with different stages perfectly overlapped.

Memory customization is also necessary for optical flow to achieve high throughput. Here we introduce the common specialized memory structures for image processing applications: line buffer and window buffer. Figure 7 gives a pictorial illustration of a 2-row line buffer and a 3x3 window buffer. The line buffer reads in one pixel per cycle and stores pixels in recently visited rows. The window buffer is completely partitioned into registers for parallel data access, and it consistently reads from the line buffer. These specialized memory structures exploit the data reuse in stencil applications with sliding processing windows, and minimize memory accesses to the next-level memory hierarchy. The convolution kernels in optical flow are good candidates for this memory customization. Figure 8 shows how we construct and maintain a line buffer and a window buffer in the gradient_xy kernel. Proper conditions need to be applied to avoid out-of-bound array accesses.

With the optimizations described above, we classify optical flow as a memory-bound application because the off-chip memory bandwidth directly determines the throughput of the streaming dataflow pipeline. However, this is because our current implementation does not exploit data reuse between input frames. We plan to further optimize this design to achieve a higher throughput.

```
1  void gradient_xy(pixel_t frame[MAX_HEIGHT][MAX_WIDTH],
2      pixel_t gradient_x[MAX_HEIGHT][MAX_WIDTH],
3      pixel_t gradient_y[MAX_HEIGHT][MAX_WIDTH])
4  {
5      // specialized line buffer and window buffer
6      hls::LineBuffer<5,MAX_WIDTH,pixel_t> buf;
7      hls::Window<5,5,pixel_t> window;
8      GRAD_XY_OUTER: for (int r = 0; r < MAX_HEIGHT + 2; r ++) {
9          GRAD_XY_INNER: for (int c = 0; c < MAX_WIDTH + 2; c ++) {
10             #pragma HLS pipeline II=1
11             // fill the line buffer
12             if (r < MAX_HEIGHT && c < MAX_WIDTH) {
13                 // shift up pixels in column c
14                 buf.shift_pixels_up(c);
15                 // insert new pixel into column c of the last row
16                 buf.insert_bottom_row(frame[r][c], c);
17             } else if (c < MAX_WIDTH) {
18                 buf.shift_pixels_up(c);
19                 // zero padding
20                 buf.insert_bottom_row(0,c);
21             }
22             // fill the window buffer
23             if (r < MAX_HEIGHT && c < MAX_WIDTH) {
24                 // shift pixels to the left
25                 window.shift_pixels_left();
26                 for (int i = 0; i < 4; i ++)
27                     // read from the line buffer
28                     // and insert to the right-most column
29                     window.insert_pixel(buf.getval(i, c), i, 4);
30             } else {
31                 window.shift_pixels_left();
32                 for (int i = 0; i < 4; i ++)
33                     // zero padding
34                     window.insert_pixel(0, i, 4);
35             }
36             // compute
37             // ......
38  }}}
```

Figure 8: Gradient kernel optimized with line buffer and window buffer — `hls::LineBuffer` and `hls::Window` classes provide parameterized implementations of line buffers and window buffers.

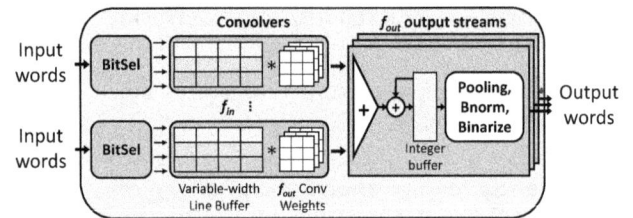

Figure 9: Hardware structure of the BNN accelerator (figure adapted from [39]).

4.5 Binarized Neural Network

Accelerating convolutional neural networks (CNNs) has become an important research topic for the FPGA community. Academic and industry researchers have implemented different CNN models on a variety of FPGA platforms [3, 18, 35, 36]. Recently, binarized neural networks (BNNs) were shown to be a natural fit for FPGA hardware [6, 27, 33, 39]. BNNs constrain weights and intermediate activations to +1 or -1; this converts most of its multiplies to binary XORs and takes full advantage of the FPGA logic fabric. We adopt an open-source implementation of BNN by Zhao et al. [39] as a representative neural network application in Rosetta.

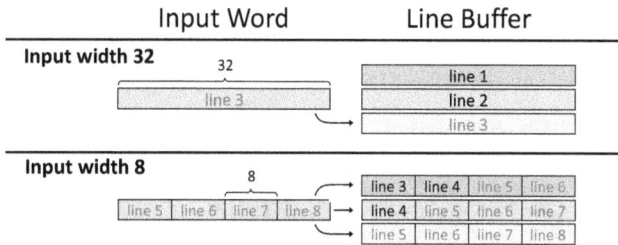

Figure 10: Example usage of variable-width line buffer for 8-wide and 32-wide feature maps (figure adapted from [39]).

Zhao et al. implement the BNN model described in [8], which operates on the CIFAR-10 dataset [12]. It contains six convolutional layers, three pooling layers, and three fully-connected layers. Figure 9 shows the hardware diagram of the BNN accelerator, which uses a configurable number of convolvers to exploit data-level parallelism in a scalable manner. The authors target a small FPGA device with limited on-chip storage. As a result, the BNN weights cannot fit on-chip and the accelerator must be invoked multiple times to classify an image; each time new weights are loaded from off-chip memory.

There are two major kernels in BNN: binarized convolution and binarized dot product. Both kernels are intensive of bitwise logic operations. Binarized convolution comprise the majority of operations in classifying an image, and is heavily parallelized as a result. In contrast, the binarized fully-connected layers, which use the dot product kernel, are limited by off-chip memory-bandwidth. We categorize BNN as compute-bound since latency improvement mostly comes from accelerating compute in the convolutional layers.

Since 2D convolutional layers have a sliding window access pattern, line buffers are used to exploit data locality. In particular, a variable-width line buffer (VWLB) is designed to keep the hardware convolvers fully utilized despite the varying sizes of the feature maps. Figure 10 shows how the VWLB works for different input widths. For input feature map with a width of 32, the VWLB operates identically to a conventional line buffer. For a smaller feature map with a width of 8, each row in the VWLB stores multiple rows of the input. The rows are carefully arranged in the VWLB so that the convolutional filter can slide through and produce correct results.

Design parameters. The BNN benchmark allows users to tune the number of convolvers in the accelerator. Other parameters such as the size of buffers are automatically scaled.

4.6 Face Detection

The face detection application is adopted from [25]. It uses the Viola-Jones algorithm [28] to detect human faces in a given image. More specifically, the accelerator takes an 320x240 greyscale image as input, which is scaled to construct an image pyramid; afterwards, an integral image is constructed from each image in the image pyramid, and a set of cascaded classifiers are applied to a fixed-size window which scans through the integral image; eventually, the positions and sizes of the human faces are returned.

As mentioned in [25], the throughput target for face detection is 30 frames per second. In addition, the application is subject to hardware constraints including limited on-chip storage and routing resources. The two major compute kernels in face detection are image scaling and cascaded classifiers. Image scaling is a common

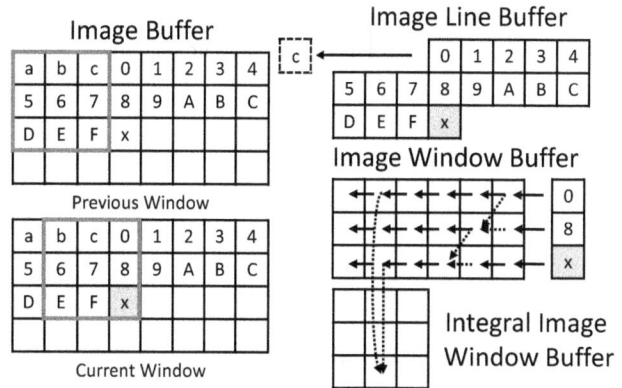

Figure 11: Specialized line buffer and window buffer for face detection [25] — Here we show a 3x3 example, but the actual implementation uses 25x25 windows. Solid arrows refer to normal register shifting, while dashed arrows refer to addition. The image window buffer accumulates the incoming pixels and construct the integral image on the fly. The integral image window buffer accesses the image window buffer for new data.

Table 2: Device capacity of the two FPGA platforms and the resource utilization of the platform logic (shell) on AWS F1 — The last row reports the average resource utilization of the shell, with the standard deviation in parentheses.

	# LUTs	# FFs	# BRAMs	# DSPs
AWS F1 Total	1181768	2363536	2160	6840
ZC706 Total	218600	437200	545	900
AWS F1 Shell	293209 (±3693)	381853 (±5138)	545 (±0)	12 (±0)

kernel in feature extraction applications such as SIFT [17], as well as the pooling layers of CNNs. The cascaded classifiers are the dominant workload for the face detection application. The authors of [25] parallelize the first three classifier stages and pipeline the rest of the stages to exploit data-level parallelism. This kernel also exposes an irregular memory access pattern — each classifier accesses either eight or twelve pixels, and the classifiers have different access patterns. This feature itself makes the kernel interesting for HLS memory optimization techniques. Customized memory partitioning is applied to improve kernel frequency and reduce routing effort [41].

The cascaded classifiers operate on a sliding window of the integral image. As a result, face detection can also benefit from the line buffer and window buffer optimization introduced in Section 4.4. However, constructing the whole integral image before applying the classifiers would require a significant amount of on-chip storage and incur performance loss. Therefore, the authors of [25] modified the window buffer to construct the integral image efficiently. The operation of this buffer is depicted in Figure 11, where the modified image window buffer accumulates pixels on the diagonal to compute the pixel values in the integral image.

5 EXPERIMENTAL RESULTS

We have synthesized the Rosetta benchmarks targeting an embedded FPGA as well as a cloud FPGA instance. We use Xilinx ZC706 for the embedded platform, which contains a Kintex-7 FPGA with a

Table 3: Rosetta results on Xilinx ZC706 Platform — The Runtime column shows overall execution time. Resource numbers show the *total* resource usage of the designs, including both kernel function and shell logic. Bitstreams are generated by Xilinx SDSoC 2017.1.

Benchmark	# LUTs	# FFs	# BRAMs	# DSPs	Runtime (ms)	Throughput
3D Rendering	8893	12471	48	11	4.7	213 frames/s
Digit Recognition[1]	41238	26468	338	1	10.6	189k digits/s
Spam Filtering[2]	12678	22134	49	160	78.9	285k samples/s
Optical Flow	42878	61078	54	454	24.3	41.2 frames/s
Binarized Neural Network[3]	46899	46760	102	4	4995.2	200 images/s
Face Detection	62688	83804	121	79	33.0	30.3 frames/s

1. K = 3, PAR_FACTOR = 40.   2. Five epochs, PAR_FACTOR = 32, VDWIDTH = 512.
3. Eight convolvers, 1000 test images.

Table 4: Rosetta results on AWS F1 Platform — Kernel: execution time on the FPGA; Comm.: time of data transfer between host and global memory; Runtime: overall execution time. Performance-Cost Ratio is calculated based on the hourly rate (in US Dollar/$) of the AWS f1.2xlarge instance [1]. Resource numbers are for kernel functions only. Bitstreams are generated by Xilinx SDAccel 2017.1.

Benchmark	# LUTs	# FFs	# BRAMs	# DSPs	Kernel (ms)	Comm. (ms)	Runtime (ms)	Throughput	Performance-Cost Ratio
3D Rendering	6763	7916	36	11	3.6	0.19	4.4	227 frames/s	496k frames/$
Digit Recognition[1]	39971	33853	207	0	9.9	0.55	11.1	180k digits/s	393M digits/$
Spam Filtering[2]	7207	17434	90	224	25.1	4.8	30.9	728k samples/s	1.6G samples/$
Optical Flow	38094	63438	55	484	2.6	4.8	8.4	119 frames/s	260k frames/$
Face Detection	48217	54206	92	72	20.2	0.47	21.5	46.5 frames/s	101k frames/$

1. K = 3, PAR_FACTOR = 40.   2. Five epochs, PAR_FACTOR = 32, VDWIDTH = 512.

target clock frequency of 140MHz. For the cloud FPGA platform, we choose the AWS f1.2xlarge instance (F1), which is equipped with a Xilinx VU9P FPGA. The target clock frequency for our experiments on F1 is 250MHz. These two platforms have different memory systems — on ZC706, the FPGA shares the same DRAM with the embedded CPU, while on F1 the FPGA has its own on-board DRAM and communicates with the CPU through PCIe. In the rest of this section, we use the term *global memory* to refer to the DRAM on the FPGA side, and use *host memory* for the DRAM on the CPU side. The BNN benchmark is originally designed for embedded FPGA platforms and requires nontrivial effort to be retargeted to AWS F1. We leave this for future work, and will only present BNN results on ZC706 in this paper. For other benchmarks, the HLS code for the two platforms share the same optimization techniques, with some platform-dependent variances such as datatype and interface. Xilinx SDSoC 2017.1 is used to generate bitstream for ZC706, and SDAccel 2017.1 is used for F1.

We run the F1 applications remotely through the FPGA developer AMI flow provided by AWS, whereas the experiments on ZC706 are performed locally. Table 2 shows the available resource counts of the two platforms. On the F1 platform, the AWS platform logic (or shell) consumes a considerable amount of resources to provide peripheral connections for PCIe data transfer, DRAM access, and interrupts [2]. In the third row of Table 2, we report the statistics of the resource usage by this shell across different applications. For ZC706, Xilinx SDSoC also automatically generates shell logic for communications among accelerators, processors, and DRAM. However, the size of these shells greatly vary across designs, and are typically small compared to that of the core logic. Hence we choose to simply report the total resource utilization for ZC706 results.

Table 5: 3D rendering without dataflow on AWS F1.

# LUTs	# FFs	# BRAMs	#DSPs	Kernel (ms)
6323	7737	36	11	5.3

Tables 3 and 4 show our experimental results on the two platforms. All resource usage numbers are extracted from Vivado reports after place and route. Resource numbers in Table 3 show the *total* resource utilization of the designs on ZC706, while Table 4 reports resource usage on F1 without the shell logic. The total runtime of the applications, including hardware kernel time, communication time, and the overhead of necessary software function calls, are measured on both platforms. On AWS F1, we further break down the kernel and communication time with the help of the SDAccel profiler. Rosetta benchmarks generally have better performance on AWS F1 because of its higher frequency and off-chip memory bandwidth, except for digit recognition. For some applications, however, this performance gap is narrow due to the communication latency and additional overhead incurred by OpenCL runtime.

Since cost efficiency is an important aspect of platform selection and accelerator design, we further provide the performance-cost ratio as a metric for F1 applications based on the hourly rate of the f1.2xlarge instance (currently at $1.65 per hour).

In the remainder of this section we summarize the results for the four new benchmarks. As for BNN and face detection, interested readers can refer to [39] and [25], respectively, for more results and detailed performance analysis.

3D Rendering. For our test dataset, the total execution time of 3D rendering is 4.7 ms and 4.4 ms on the two platforms, respectively. Converting to throughput, our design achieves 213 frames per second

Table 6: Digit recognition accuracy vs. K value.

K	2	3	4	5
Accuracy (%)	92.9	93.9	94.3	94.3

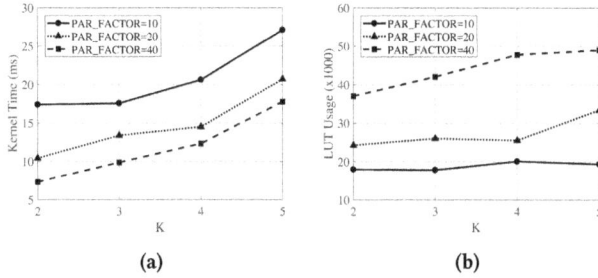

(a) (b)

Figure 12: Digit recognition design space, results are for AWS F1 platform — (a) Kernel time vs. K value. Difference in kernel time is caused by variance in latency and kernel frequency. (b) LUT usage vs. K value.

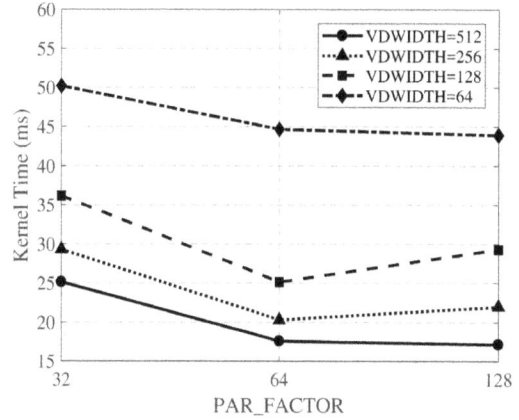

Figure 13: Spam filtering design space, results are for AWS F1 platform — Off-chip memory bandwidth is controlled by VDWIDTH. This parameter strictly limits the performance of the hardware kernel, showing that spam filtering is a memory-bound application.

on ZC706 and 227 frames per second on F1. While the throughput calculated with our test input is much higher than the target, both kernel time and communication time increase with more triangles in the input. Communication latency is not significant on F1, but the software API calls in OpenCL runtime incur a 0.6 ms overhead, which is not negligible for this specific application. These API calls initiate data transfer, enqueue the kernel function, and set proper kernel arguments.

Table 5 shows the resource utilization and kernel time of a baseline design where dataflow optimization is not applied. Comparing with the first row of Table 4, enabling dataflow optimization improves the kernel time by around 30% without significant resource overhead. This result demonstrates the efficacy of dataflow optimization in image processing pipelines.

Digit Recognition. In contrast to other benchmarks, the performance of digit recognition is currently slightly worse on F1 than ZC706. The overall throughput is 189k digits per second on ZC706 and 180k digits per second on F1. Although F1 has a shorter kernel time of 9.9ms, the latency of communication and other overhead in OpenCL runtime seem to have offset this advantage. According to our analysis, this is likely due to a missing feature in the specific version of the tool we are using, where async_group_copy is not pipelined to the full extent. Hence we expect to achieve a higher performance on F1 in the near future once this issue is resolved.

As mentioned in Section 4.2, digit recognition has a complex design space. Table 6 shows the classification accuracy of different K values. Figure 12 shows kernel time and resource utilization of different design points. We only show kernel time in Figure 12a because host-global memory communication time is not affected by kernel implementation. In Figure 12b, only the most critical resource LUT is shown. As we can see from Table 6 and Figure 12, the two design parameters expose interesting design trade-offs. Increasing the K value improves classification accuracy at a cost of significant increase in kernel time, which is caused by the frequency drop and the worsened latency of the KNN voting kernel. Additionally, the benefit of increasing PAR_FACTOR diminishes when PAR_FACTOR is

already large. When the Hamming distance kernel is highly parallelized, the KNN voting kernel, which is highly sequential, becomes the performance bottleneck. The performance can be further improved by optimizing the KNN voting kernel, and finding an optimal combination of the K value and PAR_FACTOR.

Spam Filtering. The performance of spam filtering significantly differs on two platforms. The kernel time on F1 is 3.1x shorter than ZC706, and the total execution time on F1 is 2.6x shorter, despite the additional 4.8 ms latency for host-global memory communication. In addition to the frequency improvement, this performance gap is mainly caused by the difference in off-chip memory bandwidth. Since we apply dataflow optimization to overlap communication and compute, the overall latency of the design is determined by the maximum of compute and communication latency. Because the compute kernels are highly parallel, the low communication bandwidth on ZC706 results in a much longer latency of the dataflow pipeline.

Figure 13 shows the kernel time on AWS F1 with different combinations of PAR_FACTOR and VDWIDTH. Here PAR_FACTOR specifies the degree of parallelism in vector kernels, and VDWIDTH controls the off-chip communication bandwidth. With the same off-chip bandwidth, increasing PAR_FACTOR beyond 64 does not result in much performance gain, since the communication latency already dominates the compute latency. When off-chip bandwidth is reduced, communication latency further increases, and kernel time degrades for all PAR_FACTOR values we tested. The best-achievable performance improves with a higher off-chip memory bandwidth. These results confirm that spam filtering is a memory-bound application.

Optical Flow. The total execution time of optical flow is 8.4 ms on F1 and 24.3 ms on ZC706. Both implementations satisfy the throughput constraint. On the AWS F1 platform, host-global memory communication time takes up approximately 60% of the total execution time due to the large input/output data size. If we only consider kernel time, it is 9.3x shorter on F1 than on ZC706. Similar with spam filtering, this behavior is also caused by the difference in off-chip memory bandwidth. The optical flow accelerator is reading from and writing to the off-chip memory at the same time due to the streaming dataflow optimization. The F1 platform has multiple off-chip

DDR banks to handle concurrent read and write requests. On ZC706, however, these concurrent requests would cause contention on the off-chip memory, and the accelerator is often stalled due to the lack of input data.

6 CONCLUSIONS AND FUTURE WORK

We have presented Rosetta, an open-source, realistic benchmark suite for high-level synthesis targeting modern FPGA platforms. Rosetta is designed to be a collection of real applications which are optimized for performance and resource constraints. All Rosetta applications are ready to be executed on the supported embedded and cloud platforms. We believe that Rosetta can serve as a useful benchmark suite for HLS algorithms and tools, as well as a set of design tutorials for application developers interested in FPGA-based accelerated computing.

Rosetta will be continuously improved in the future. We will extend Rosetta to include more realistic applications from emerging domains. For the existing benchmarks, we plan to provide both C++ and OpenCL implementations for every benchmark to embrace different programming models commonly supported by HLS tools. The benchmarks will also be further optimized for achieving higher performance and resource efficiency.

ACKNOWLEDGEMENTS

This research was supported in part by a DARPA Young Faculty Award, NSF Awards #1337240, #1453378, and a research gift from Xilinx, Inc. We thank Dr. Sumit Roy from Xilinx for providing helpful feedback on the Rosetta designs. We also thank Ackerley Tng, Edgar Munoz, Wendian Jiang, Lin Wang, Yun Qing, Nithya Subramanian, Nikita Patil, Surabhi Singh, Judy Stephen, and Ian Thompson for their contributions to the baseline designs of digit recognition, 3D rendering, spam filtering, and optical flow.

REFERENCES

[1] Amazon Web Services. AWS FPGA Developer AMI. *https://aws.amazon.com/marketplace/pp/B06VVYBLZZ*, Dec 2017.
[2] Amazon Web Services. AWS Shell Interface Specification. *https://github.com/aws/aws-fpga/blob/master/hdk/docs/AWS_Shell_Interface_Specification.md*, Dec 2017.
[3] U. Aydonat, S. O'Connell, D. Capalija, A. C. Ling, and G. R. Chiu. An OpenCL Deep Learning Accelerator on Arria 10. *Int'l Symp. on Field-Programmable Gate Arrays (FPGA)*, Feb 2017.
[4] D. J. Butler, J. Wulff, G. B. Stanley, and M. J. Black. A Naturalistic Open Source Movie for Optical Flow Evaluation. *European Conference on Computer Vision (ECCV)*, Oct 2012.
[5] S. Che, M. Boyer, J. Meng, D. Tarjan, J. W. Sheaffer, S.-H. Lee, and K. Skadron. Rodinia: A Benchmark Suite for Heterogeneous Computing. *Int'l Symp. on Workload Characterization (IISWC)*, Oct 2009.
[6] P. Colangelo, R. Huang, E. Luebbers, M. Margala, and K. Nealis. Fine-Grained Acceleration of Binary Neural Networks Using Intel Xeon Processor with Integrated FPGA. *Int'l Symp. on Field-Programmable Custom Computing Machines (FCCM)*, Apr/May 2017.
[7] J. Cong, B. Liu, S. Neuendorffer, J. Noguera, K. Vissers, and Z. Zhang. High-Level Synthesis for FPGAs: From Prototyping to Deployment. *IEEE Transactions on Computer-Aided Design of Integrated Circuits and Systems*, 30(4):473–491, 2011.
[8] M. Courbariaux, I. Hubara, D. Soudry, R. El-Yaniv, and Y. Bengio. Binarized Neural Networks: Training Deep Neural Networks with Weights and Activations Constrained to + 1 or -1. *arXiv preprint arXiv:1602.02830*, Mar 2016.
[9] S. Dai, R. Zhao, G. Liu, S. Srinath, U. Gupta, C. Batten, and Z. Zhang. Dynamic Hazard Resolution for Pipelining Irregular Loops in High-Level Synthesis. *Int'l Symp. on Field-Programmable Gate Arrays (FPGA)*, Feb 2017.
[10] Q. Gautier, A. Althoff, P. Meng, and R. Kastner. Spector: An OpenCL FPGA Benchmark Suite. *Int'l Conf. on Field Programmable Technology (FPT)*, Dec 2016.
[11] Y. Hara, H. Tomiyama, S. Honda, and H. Takada. Proposal and Quantitative Analysis of the CHStone Benchmark Program Suite for Practical C-Based High-Level Synthesis. *Journal of Information Processing, Vol. 17*, pages 242–254, Oct 2008.
[12] A. Krizhevsky and G. Hinton. Learning Multiple Layers of Features from Tiny Images. *Technical report, University of Toronto*, Apr 2009.
[13] Y. LeCun. The MNIST Database of Handwritten Digits. *http://yann.lecun.com/exdb/mnist/*, Dec 2017.
[14] Y. Liang, K. Rupnow, Y. Li, D. Min, M. N. Do, and D. Chen. High-Level Synthesis: Productivity, Performance, and Software Constraints. *Journal of Electrical and Computer Engineering*, 2012:1:1–1:1, Jan 2012.
[15] G. Liu, M. Tan, S. Dai, R. Zhao, and Z. Zhang. Architecture and Synthesis for Area-Efficient Pipelining of Irregular Loop Nests. *IEEE Trans. on Computer-Aided Design of Integrated Circuits and Systems (TCAD)*, 2017.
[16] X. Liu, Y. Chen, T. Nguyen, S. Gurumani, K. Rupnow, and D. Chen. High Level Synthesis of Complex Applications: An H. 264 Video Decoder. *Int'l Symp. on Field-Programmable Gate Arrays (FPGA)*, Feb 2016.
[17] D. G. Lowe. Object Recognition from Local Scale-Invariant Features. *Int'l Conf. on Computer Vision (ICCV)*, Oct 1999.
[18] Y. Ma, Y. Cao, S. Vrudhula, and J.-s. Seo. Optimizing Loop Operation and Dataflow in FPGA Acceleration of Deep Convolutional Neural Networks. *Int'l Symp. on Field-Programmable Gate Arrays (FPGA)*, Feb 2017.
[19] K. P. Murphy. *Machine Learning: A Probabilistic Perspective*. MIT Press, 2012.
[20] J. Pineda. A Parallel Algorithm for Polygon Rasterization. *ACM SIGGRAPH Computer Graphics*, 22(4):17–20, 1988.
[21] L.-N. Pouchet. Polybench: The Polyhedral Benchmark Suite. *http://www.cs.ucla.edu/pouchet/software/polybench*, Dec 2017.
[22] L.-N. Pouchet, P. Zhang, P. Sadayappan, and J. Cong. Polyhedral-Based Data Reuse Optimization for Configurable Computing. *Int'l Symp. on Field-Programmable Gate Arrays (FPGA)*, Feb 2013.
[23] B. Reagen, R. Adolf, Y. S. Shao, G.-Y. Wei, and D. Brooks. Machsuite: Benchmarks for Accelerator Design and Customized Architectures. *Int'l Symp. on Workload Characterization (IISWC)*, Oct 2014.
[24] Y. S. Shao, B. Reagen, G.-Y. Wei, and D. Brooks. Aladdin: A Pre-RTL, Power-Performance Accelerator Simulator Enabling Large Design Space Exploration of Customized Architectures. *Int'l Symp. on Computer Architecture (ISCA)*, Jun 2014.
[25] N. K. Srivastava, S. Dai, R. Manohar, and Z. Zhang. Accelerating Face Detection on Programmable SoC Using C-Based Synthesis. *Int'l Symp. on Field-Programmable Gate Arrays (FPGA)*, Feb 2017.
[26] The Apache Software Foundation. Public Corpus. *http://spamassassin.apache.org/old/publiccorpus/*, Apr 2017.
[27] Y. Umuroglu, N. J. Fraser, G. Gambardella, M. Blott, P. Leong, M. Jahre, and K. Vissers. FINN: A Framework for Fast, Scalable Binarized Neural Network Inference. *Int'l Symp. on Field-Programmable Gate Arrays (FPGA)*, Feb 2017.
[28] P. Viola, M. J. Jones, and D. Snow. Detecting Pedestrians using Patterns of Motion and Appearance. *International Journal of Computer Vision*, 63(2):153–161, Jul 2005.
[29] S. Wang, Y. Liang, and W. Zhang. FlexCL: An Analytical Performance Model for OpenCL Workloads on Flexible FPGAs. *Design Automation Conf. (DAC)*, Jun 2017.
[30] Y. Wang, P. Li, and J. Cong. Theory and Algorithm for Generalized Memory Partitioning in High-Level Synthesis. *Int'l Symp. on Field-Programmable Gate Arrays (FPGA)*, Feb 2014.
[31] Z. Wang, B. He, W. Zhang, and S. Jiang. A Performance Analysis Framework for Optimizing OpenCL Applications on FPGAs. *Int'l Symp. on High Performance Computer Architecture (HPCA)*, Mar 2016.
[32] Z. Wei, L. Dah-Jye, and B. E. Nelson. FPGA-Based Real-Time Optical Flow Algorithm Design and Implementation. *Journal of Multimedia*, 2:38–45, Sep 2007.
[33] H. Yonekawa and H. Nakahara. On-Chip Memory Based Binarized Convolutional Deep Neural Network Applying Batch Normalization Free Technique on an FPGA. *Int'l Parallel and Distributed Processing Symp. Workshops (IPDPSW)*, May 2017.
[34] C. Zhang, P. Li, G. Sun, Y. Guan, B. Xiao, and J. Cong. Optimizing FPGA-Based Accelerator Design for Deep Convolutional Neural Networks. *Int'l Symp. on Field-Programmable Gate Arrays (FPGA)*, Feb 2015.
[35] C. Zhang and V. K. Prasanna. Frequency Domain Acceleration of Convolutional Neural Networks on CPU-FPGA Shared Memory System. *Int'l Symp. on Field-Programmable Gate Arrays (FPGA)*, Feb 2017.
[36] J. Zhang and J. Li. Improving the Performance of OpenCL-Based FPGA Accelerator for Convolutional Neural Network. *Int'l Symp. on Field-Programmable Gate Arrays (FPGA)*, Feb 2017.
[37] Z. Zhang and B. Liu. SDC-Based Modulo Scheduling for Pipeline Synthesis. *Int'l Conf. on Computer-Aided Design (ICCAD)*, Nov 2013.
[38] J. Zhao, L. Feng, S. Sharad, W. Zhang, Y. Liang, and B. He. COMBA: A Comprehensive Model-Based Analysis Framework for High Level Synthesis of Real Applications. *Int'l Conf. on Computer-Aided Design (ICCAD)*, Nov 2017.
[39] R. Zhao, W. Song, W. Zhang, T. Xing, J.-H. Lin, M. B. Srivastava, R. Gupta, and Z. Zhang. Accelerating Binarized Convolutional Neural Networks with Software-Programmable FPGAs. *Int'l Symp. on Field-Programmable Gate Arrays (FPGA)*, Feb 2017.
[40] G. Zhong, A. Prakash, Y. Liang, T. Mitra, and S. Niar. Lin-Analyzer: A High-Level Performance Analysis Tool for FPGA-Based Accelerators. *Design Automation Conf. (DAC)*, Jun 2016.
[41] Y. Zhou, K. M. Al-Hawaj, and Z. Zhang. A New Approach to Automatic Memory Banking using Trace-Based Address Mining. *Int'l Symp. on Field-Programmable Gate Arrays (FPGA)*, Feb 2017.
[42] W. Zuo, P. Li, D. Chen, L.-N. Pouchet, S. Zhong, and J. Cong. Improving Polyhedral Code Generation for High-Level Synthesis. *Proc. of the 8th Int. Conf. on Hardware/Software Codesign and System Synthesis (CODES+ISSS)*, Sep/Oct 2013.

FPGA Fastfood - A High Speed Systolic Implementation of a Large Scale Online Kernel Method

Sean Fox
The University of Sydney
sean.fox@sydney.edu.au

David Boland
The University of Sydney
david.boland@sydney.edu.au

Philip Leong
The University of Sydney
philip.leong@sydney.edu.au

ABSTRACT

In this paper, we describe a systolic Field Programmable Gate Array (FPGA) implementation of the Fastfood algorithm that is optimised to run at a high frequency. The Fastfood algorithm supports online learning for large scale kernel methods. Empirical results show that 500 MHz clock rates can be sustained for an architecture that can solve problems with input dimensions that are 10^3 times larger than previously reported. Unlike many recent deep learning publications, this design implements both training and prediction. This enables the use of kernel methods in applications requiring a rare combination of capacity, adaption and speed.

ACM Reference Format:
Sean Fox, David Boland, and Philip Leong. 2018. FPGA Fastfood - A High Speed Systolic Implementation of a Large Scale Online Kernel Method. In *FPGA '18: 2018 ACM/SIGDA International Symposium on Field-Programmable Gate Arrays, February 25–27, 2018, Monterey, CA, USA*. ACM, New York, NY, USA, 6 pages. https://doi.org/10.1145/3174243.3174271

1 INTRODUCTION

Kernel methods are a popular class of machine learning algorithm capable of solving many problems, ranging from classification and regression to novelty detection and feature extraction. However, they are often limited to small datasets because their memory and computation requirements scale linearly with the number of input examples. To address this problem, Le et al. [7] proposed an efficient algorithm, called Fastfood, that builds an approximation to the kernel using combinations of random diagonal matrices and Hadamard transforms. This is advantageous because diagonal matrices require little storage and only involve elementwise multiplications, and the Hadamard transform can be computed in log linear time via the Fast Walsh Hadamard Transform (FWHT). Fastfood reduces $O(nd)$ storage and computation requirements to $O(n)$ and $O(n \log_2 d)$ respectively, where d is the length of the input vectors and n represents the number of basis functions used to preserve the statistical properties of the kernel function. To summarise, Fastfood only suffers minimal degradation in prediction accuracy and can solve problems which were previously intractable using exact kernel methods.

We describe the first known implementation of Fastfood using Field Programmable Gate Arrays (FPGAs). Our design, given in Section 3, is a systolic array architecture that creates local connections by grouping processing elements into designated blocks. This gives us the flexibility of compiling different configurations of Fastfood, and achieve a 500 MHz operating frequency. In fact, simply preserving module partitions during synthesis is enough to sustain high clock rates with our design.

In this article, we highlight that Fastfood is particularly suited for a hardware implementation because: 1) the computation requires simple arithmetic operations involving mainly addition and subtraction, 2) memory requirements are minimal allowing large parameter spaces to be stored in embedded memory, 3) the algorithm can be translated into a datapath that has a regular structure, is highly parallelisable, and benefits from high-speed local interconnections, and 4) the butterfly structure for computing the FWHT has an efficient hardware implementation.

Fastfood implements a form of model compression for kernel methods, however, unlike related deep learning algorithms that take advantage of reduced precision and sparsity [5], Fastfood also works during the learning phase. In addition, kernel methods are attractive in comparison to Neural Networks because they allow domain knowledge to be imparted in a statistical manner. Neural Networks have powerful generalisation properties because they are free to learn any data representation, but this can obfuscate the training process and yield results which are often less interpretable. The key contributions of this paper are:

- The first FPGA implementation of a large-scale online kernel method. Our design can solve problems with an input dimensionality up to 3 orders of magnitude larger than previous FPGA implementations of kernel methods, and achieves 245× speed up over a single-core Central Processing Unit (CPU).
- A novel hierarchical systolic architecture for sustaining high clock rates on FPGAs. Blocks of processing elements constrain the majority of computation to small physical spaces, and allow resource reuse. In particular, the design efficiently implements the computational bottleneck (FWHT) using the same processing elements that compute the rest of the Fastfood algorithm.

2 BACKGROUND

2.1 Machine Learning Regression Using Kernel Methods

Let x_i, $i = 1...m$ represent m input vectors of a given dimensionality d ($x_i \in \mathbb{R}^d$), and let y_i represent the corresponding desired output values for each input vector ($y_i \in \mathbb{R}$). In standard machine learning regression problems, the goal is to find a function $f(x)$ that results in the minimal prediction error (i.e. $\min \sum_{i=1}^{m}(y_i - f(x_i))^2$). For nonlinear problems, the input must first be transformed into a high dimensional space where patterns in x_i are linearly separable. The *kernel trick* does this implicitly, and thus, it is regularly employed to inexpensively evaluate $f(x)$, as described by (1).

$$f(x_i) = \sum_{j=1}^{N} \alpha_j \kappa(x_i, v_j) \tag{1}$$

Here, $\kappa(x_i, v_j)$ is the kernel function, and α_i are parameters to be optimised. The only caveat is that a length N subset of the input data must be stored in memory, also known as the *dictionary* or *support vectors* and denoted by v. The machine learning algorithm must update both the dictionary and parameters α to minimise the predictive error. On small datasets (less than 10^4 examples), (1) can be computed efficiently. However, this is not possible on large datasets because N tends to grow linearly with the number of input examples, m, [2]. To address this problem, Rahimi and Recht [10] proposed Random Kitchen Sinks (RKS) for shift-invariant kernels ($\kappa(x, x') = \kappa(x - x', 0)$). The main idea is to create a function, $z(x) = \frac{1}{\sqrt{n}} cos(Wx_i)$, such that the inner products $\langle z(x), z(x') \rangle$ are approximately equal to the high-dimensional features extracted from $k(x, x')$. Here, n is the number of basis functions used to approximate N dictionary elements, and W is a $n \times d$ matrix randomly sampled from the Fourier transform of $k(x, x')$. Importantly, n is fixed and means that Random Kitchen Sinks can be trained independent of the dataset size, making them much faster on problems with many inputs.

2.2 Fastfood

The Fastfood algorithm was introduced by Le et al. [7] to reduce the computational complexity of Random Kitchen Sinks. The main idea is that a random projection, given by Wx_i, can be approximated with a projection Vx_i, as described by (2), which requires much fewer operations to compute. [1]

$$Vx_i = [V_1 x_i, ..., V_h x_i], \text{ where } V_q x_i = SHGPHBx_i \tag{2}$$

We first break the computation down into $h = \lceil n/d \rceil$ separate stages, each working with d basis functions. By working from right to left, we can complete each intermediate computation of $V_q x_i$ by a sequence of matrix-vector operations, without storing the matrix V_q. Importantly, the matrix-vector operations are designed to involve minimal computation. Firstly, B, G and S are $d \times d$ diagonal matrices, where B_{ii} and G_{ii} are drawn i.i.d. from $\{-1, 1\}$ and $N(0, 1)$ distributions respectively, whilst S_{ii} depends on the choice of kernel function. In this work we assume a Gaussian RBF kernel, meaning S_{ii} is drawn from a chi-squared distribution [7]. Secondly, $P \in \{0, 1\}^{d \times d}$ is a permutation matrix which can be efficiently implemented in hardware. Finally, $H \in \{-1, 1\}^{d \times d}$ is a Hadamard matrix, as defined by (3). Matrix-vector multiplication with a Hadamard matrix can be done efficiently using the FWHT. For example, using the radix-2 FWHT algorithm, this reduces the number of operations from $O(d^2)$ to $O(d \log_2 d)$. The Hadamard matrix in (3) requires the input dimension, d, to be a power of 2

---

[1]For brevity, we limit the review to the key computation steps. Refer to [7] for a complete analysis, including derivations, proofs of convergence, and error bounds.

($d = 2^l$, where $l \in \mathbb{N}$). To meet this condition, the input vectors can be padded with zeros.

$$H = H_d = \begin{bmatrix} H_{d/2} & H_{d/2} \\ H_{d/2} & -H_{d/2} \end{bmatrix} \text{ where } H_2 = \begin{bmatrix} 1 & 1 \\ 1 & -1 \end{bmatrix} \tag{3}$$

The prediction is then formed by passing $Vx_i \in \mathbb{R}^n$ through a sinusoidal function, $\psi(x_i) = \frac{1}{\sqrt{n}} \cos(Vx_i)$, and taking a weighted sum as shown by (4).

$$f(x_i) = \sum_{j=1}^{n} \alpha_j \psi_j(x_i) \tag{4}$$

In this work, we train $f(x)$ for regression by solving the least squares problem $\min_\alpha \|y - \alpha^T \psi(x)\|_2^2$, where $y \in \mathbb{R}$ is the expected output. More specifically, we apply an online stochastic gradient descent algorithm, which incrementally updates α for each new (x_i, y_i), as given by (5). Alternatively, a batch-based training method could be used. However, this requires prior access to a large subset of the input data which is not available in real-time applications.

$$\alpha_{t+1} = \alpha_t + \eta[y_t - \alpha_t^T \psi(x_t)]\psi(x_t) \tag{5}$$

As with Random Kitchen Sinks, when $n = 16,384$, Fastfood achieves an accuracy on the CIFAR-10 dataset [6] which is among the top two for shift-invariant kernel representations [7].

2.3 Kernel Methods on FPGA

Efficient FPGA implementations of kernel methods have previously been studied and several architectures for performing simultaneous prediction and training have been reported. Fraser et al. [4] describe a floating point implementation of the KNLMS algorithm. They achieve very high efficiency using a fully-pipelined architecture and time-multiplexing independent parameter sets. This removes the data dependency in the update equation (similar to (5)) significantly improving overall throughput. Multiple parameter sets and deep pipelining increase the latency on a per input basis. Tridgell et al. [11] address this issue using a technique called "Braiding", which resolves data dependencies in pipelined architectures. Their design (in fixed point) operates at well over 10 Gb/s and achieves a latency around 10 cycles for $d = 8$ and a fixed $N = 200$, this coming at the cost of frequency and DSP resources. Neither explore re-utilisation of resources. Pang et al. [9] describe a micro-coded vector processor for the SW-KRLS algorithm which time-multiplexes resources to improve scalability. The works reviewed target a specific part of the design space, however, none can scale the input dimensionality, d, and dictionary size, N, to support the type of big-data applications dominating the machine learning community today. Our implementation of Fastfood fills this void.

3 ARCHITECTURE AND DESIGN

3.1 High-Level Description

From Equation (2), it is evident that $V_q x_i$ can be processed independently. Our architecture separates and localises their computation using blocks of Processing Elements (PEs), called Hadamard Blocks (HBs). A hierarchical diagram of the Fastfood processor is shown in Figure 1, and the following equation shows how the computation

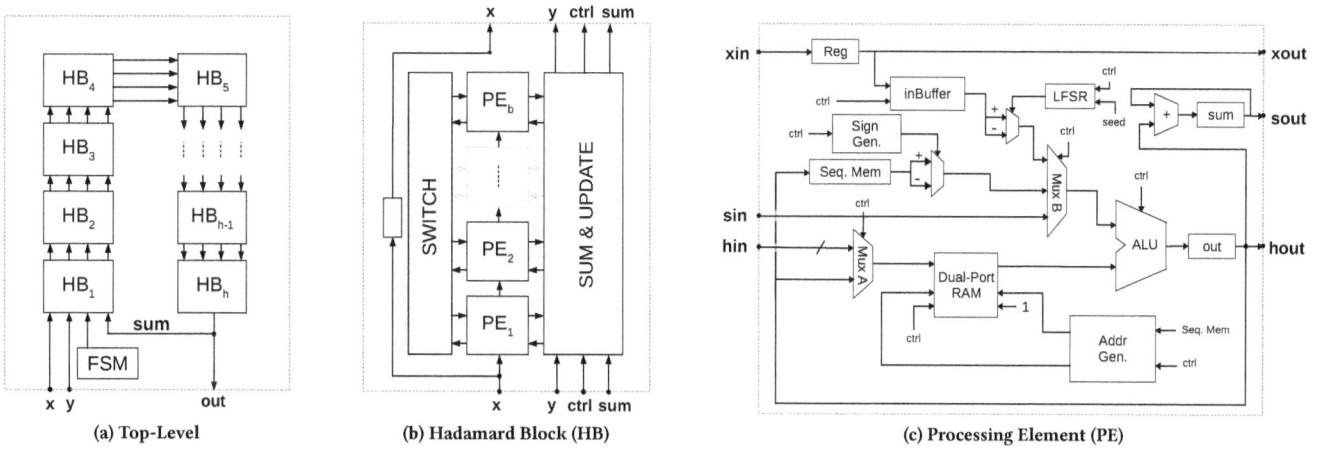

(a) Top-Level   (b) Hadamard Block (HB)   (c) Processing Element (PE)

Figure 1: A hierarchical block diagram of the Fastfood processor

of $f(x)$ (4) is unrolled into (6).

$$f(x) = \sum_{j=1}^{n} \alpha_j \psi_j(x) = \sum^{h} \sum^{b} \sum_{j=1}^{k} \alpha_j \psi_j(x) \qquad (6)$$

Here, n is the number of basis functions or expansion dimensions, k is the basis functions per PE, b is the PEs per HB, and h is the number of HBs. The other constraints are the input dimensionality, d, and total number of PEs, p. We adopted this architecture because 1) massive scalability can be achieved when PE compute resources are reused, 2) PEs with mostly local connections are more amenable to high-frequency implementations, and 3) blocks of PEs create the local connectivities needed to implement a fused and distributed FWHT. Parameters p, b and k should be chosen carefully, and depend on the FPGA device, task, and performance requirements: 1) p controls the parallelism and latency of the design; 2) $k = n/p$ is a portion of the algorithm distributed evenly across the PEs. k controls the computable size of n and scales the size of each PE; 3) $b = d/k$ is the number of PEs allocated to each HB. b controls the locality of connections between PEs; and in combination with k, also determines the computable size of d.

3.2 Top-Level Module

The top level diagram of our architecture is illustrated in Figure 1a (ignoring PCIe and memory bus interfaces). It mainly consists of an h-length array of HBs connected in a ring topology. Each HB accepts control logic from a finite state machine (FSM) and a stream of (x_i, y_i) pairs as input data. The Fastfood processor is an iterative architecture which does not have overlapping compute stages. This means that the inputs arrive with an initiation interval (II) equal to the number of cycles taken to compute a given sized input vector. Each HB computes a partial result for Fastfood, and an output is produced by summing each partial result as per the outer loop of (6). The HBs are connected in a ring array for two main reasons: 1) to minimise routing between HBs for computing the sum, and 2) to efficiently broadcast the input and FSM control logic across a large area of the chip.

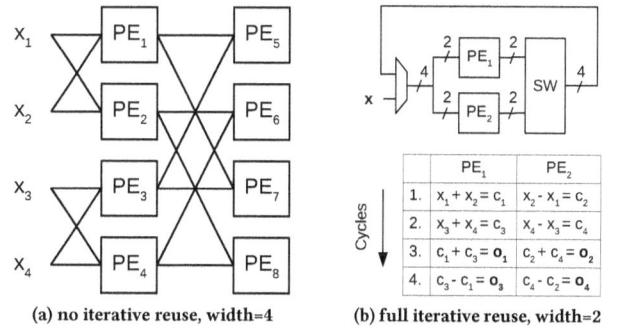

(a) no iterative reuse, width=4   (b) full iterative reuse, width=2

Figure 2: Two systolic array configurations for a 4-point FWHT, based on Milder et al. [8].

3.3 Hadamard Block

Each HB contains an array of b PEs, a switch, and a module for computing the HB sum and partial update. This is shown in Figure 1b. We created HBs with the aim of developing local structure between PEs for implementing the FWHT at high clock rates. A special emphasis is placed on the FWHT because its parallel implementation has data dependencies which require communication between multiple PEs.

The standard architecture for a radix-2 d-point FWHT is the fully pipelined version given in Figure 2a. It is constructed by cascading $\log_2 d$ stages of d PEs and connecting them in a butterfly structure to directly implement the required switching behaviour. This design executes the FWHT in a minimum number of cycles, but requires large amounts of additional hardware that are not reused. Given that the rest of Fastfood can be computed using a linear systolic array, we chose to implement the d-point FWHT by reusing one stage of b PEs over multiple cycles, like Figure 2b. This design has a compact and regular structure which makes it well suited to processing large amounts of data at a high frequency. The main overhead is the switching network between $\log_2 b$ PEs since the data buffering and reordering can be implemented locally in the PEs, using existing RAMs. We implemented the switch using a multiplexer in each PE,

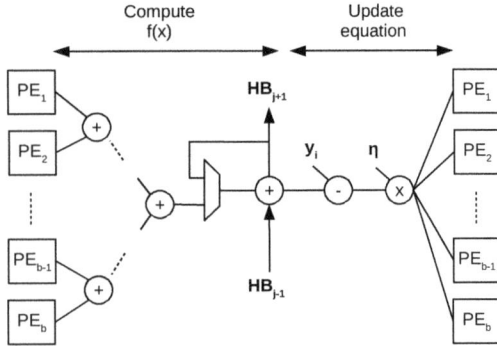

Figure 3: Dataflow diagram of the HB sum and update module (data moves from left to right)

Instr.	ALU	Active Cycles	Instr.	Active Cycles
Proc. Elem. (PE)			Had. Block (HB)	
Mul B	N	k	Adder-tree	$log_2 b$
Mul	Y	$3k$	Add	h
Perm.	N	k	Sub $(y-f(x))$	1
Add	Y	$2k \log_2 d + k$	Mul (η)	1
Cosine	N	k		
Mul-Add	Y	$k+1$		

Table 1: Fastfood instruction count for resources constrained in each PE and HB

and connected the PEs directly. For increasing b, the switch size increases. We experimented with $b = \{4, 8, 16, 32\}$, above which we observed a degradation in frequency due to routing congestion.

The *Sum & Update* unit routes the FSM control logic and also includes some logic to implement several instructions not allocated to the PEs. Figure 3 gives a dataflow diagram of the operations involved. We use $\log_2 b$ adders to compute the middle loop of (6). Each HB requires the results from every other HB to know the update (outer loop of (6)). These are passed around the ring array and accumulated here. The *Sum & Update* module then includes one subtract and multiply unit for computing part of update equation (5). The result is written back to each PE where the weights are ultimately updated. This creates a small resource inefficiency and means the PEs are idle for a short period of time. However, this only equates to an extra 1×DSP and between 2-5% in LUTs and FFs, while the PEs are idle for only 1% of total processing time.

3.4 Processing Element

The basic structure of each PE is given in Figure 1c. It mainly consists of one Arithmetic Logic Unit (ALU), two scalar operands, and a control mechanism for reading and writing to memory. Computation can only begin once a full input vector has been loaded into PE memory and the previous computation is finished. The *in-Buffer* shift register is used to buffer the input and allow the loading and computation stages to be overlapped. Table 1 summarises the compute requirements of each PE as a list of instructions. As per the table, not all the functionality is implemented with resources confined to the ALU. For instance, the first Fastfood operation is a

binary multiplication involving the input and a random variable $B \in \{-1, 1\}$ (in Eq. 2). We implemented this as a sign change using 1-bit from a 16-bit Linear Feedback Shift Register (LFSR). The Mul and Add instructions are implemented using 1×DSP slice and 1×adder in the ALU, and for Mul-Add we use an additional adder for the accumulator. The majority of Fastfood compute time is spent iteratively reusing the ALU adder. In fact, approximately 70% of total cycles are dedicated to Adds. The cosine function is implemented using a 256-point look-up table stored in a shared *Dual-Port RAM*. We read a result, i.e. $cos(x)$, using an address generated from x, where x is an intermediate result from the *Seq. Mem* shift register. The FWHT involves $2k \log_2 d$ add and subtract operations per PE. We reuse the ALU adder and perform sign switching on the top operand using the *Sign Generator* block. The *hin* and *hout* I/O ports connect multiple PEs together, and *MuxA* switches between them. For local permutations (or switching), the *Address Generator* develops the memory access patterns to buffer and reorder the data as required. The size of *MuxA* scales as $O(\log_2 b)$ which for $b = \{4, 8, 16, 32\}$ can be implemented efficiently with one layer of LUTs. The address and sign permutations are the same for each PE and can be generated using several counters and bit operations. This only contributes an additional 30 LUTs and 26 FFs for the *Address Generator* and *Sign Generator* modules combined. Given the small overhead, we have included these control units in every PE. This reduces the compute density of each PE, but removes a large fan-out problem which would likely require multiple stages of pipeline registers. Fastfood involves a data transformation from $\mathbb{R}^d \rightarrow \mathbb{R}^n$, where $n > d$. Our architecture distributes this computation across p PE's so that each PE works on $k = n/p$ dimensions, also known as basis functions. This requires k-length blocks of memory for intermediate results and Fastfood parameters G, S and α. We write intermediate results back to *Sequential Memory* every cycle, and load the Fastfood parameters to the *Dual-Port RAM* once at startup. For the FWHT switch, we read and write to a double buffer in *Dual-Port RAM* to avoid pipeline stalls. Therefore, including the *inBuffer* and 256-point cosine look-up table, each PE requires $(k + k + 3k + 2k + k + 256) \times bits$ of memory. The sequential memories are either implemented using two LUT-based shift registers (i.e. SRL) or the *Seq. Mem* shift register is also mapped to a BRAM. In Section 4, we present results for both configurations. The choice depends on whether we prefer a LUT-constrained or BRAM-constrained design. The PEs are fully pipelined. There are 4 register stages for reading and writing to memory, between 3 and 6 on the ALU, 1 on the ALU operands, 1 on the output, and 1 on the *MuxB* inputs. This minimises the number of logic levels between registered signals and keeps the frequency high.

3.5 Scalability: I/O and Latency

The top-level module takes 1× 18-bit feature as input per cycle. The data is loaded through the array via a d-length shift register, where d is the input dimensionality. Given that load and compute stages operate in parallel, one result can be retrieved every tc cycles, where tc is the total number of compute cycles given below:

$$tc = 8k + 2k \log_2 d + \log_2 b + 2h + 9 \qquad (7)$$

The above equation is taken from Table 1 for prediction and training, except a few extra cycles are added because the HB Control unit is

	LUT Total (203k)	LUT Mem. (112k)	FFs (406k)	BRAM (1080)	DSP (1700)	Max. PEs (p)
FF-L						
k=64	323	98	524	1	1	610
k=128	398	170	531	1	1	494
k=256	547	314	540	2	1	355
FF-B						
k=64	282	70	590	2	1	540
k=128	327	107	603	2	1	540
k=256	405	180	615	3	1	360

Table 2: PE resource utilisation for LUT and BRAM constrained 18-bit designs on a Kintex XCU035

not fully pipelined. The latency is thus $tc + d$ and the I/O required is $18d/8$ bytes every $max(d, tc)$ cycles. For large d and $d > tc$, the throughput is limited by loading of the input data. This equates to 18-bits per cycle, or 9Gb/s, assuming the memory bandwidth is not the bottleneck. This can be improved by broadcasting more of the input data in parallel. For fast designs, p should be large so a small k can be distributed to each PE.

4 RESULTS AND EVALUATION

Our designs were written in Chisel HDL [1] and are available at github.com/sfox14/chisel-fastfood.git. They were synthesised and implemented using Xilinx Vivado 2017.2, targeting a Kintex Ultrascale XCKU035-FBVA676-2-e FPGA. We present results for two designs: one which is LUT-constrained (FF-L) and the other BRAM-constrained (FF-B). In the FF-L design, the *Seq. Mem* and *inBuffer* shift registers are mapped to LUT SRL primitives, and in the FF-B design, *Seq. Mem* is implemented with a BRAM.

4.1 Resource Utilisation

Table 2 shows resource utilisation of FF-L and FF-B for an 18-bit design. Area scales with k because of two k-length shift-registers, *inBuffer* and *Seq. Mem*. The last column shows the maximum number of PEs that can be placed on the targeted device. These numbers are based on 97% of total LUTs, 99.8% of memory configurable LUTs, and all available BRAMs. The remaining resources are attributed to the FSM and HB modules, which contribute an additional 141 and $h \times 617$ LUTs respectively. In terms of parallelism, FF-L can support the most PEs for $k \leq 64$, FF-B is preferred for $k = 128$, and the designs are similar for $k = 256$.

4.2 Clock Frequency

Table 3 and 4 show the effect of design configurations on the clock frequency. Importantly, both tables show that a high operating frequency can be achieved for designs very close to the resource constraints given in Table 2. For $b = 32$, clock rates at or above 500 MHz can be sustained right up to $p = 544$, $p = 448$ and $p = 320$ for FF-L, and $p = 512$, $p = 480$ and $p = 320$ for FF-B. This corresponds to utilisation rates between 89-98% of available resources. Furthermore, the frequency is only slightly reduced to 483-495 MHz for

		Designs achieving Freq=500 MHz			For max. resources in Table 2	
		LUT %	BRAM %	PEs (p)	PEs (p)	Freq. (MHz)
k=64	b=32	91.6	50.4	544	576	483
	b=64	67.9	35.6	384	576	416
k=128	b=32	92.0	41.5	448	480	487
	b=64	54.8	23.7	256	448	465
k=256	b=32	89.2	59.3	320	320	508
	b=64	53.3	35.6	192	320	476

Table 3: Clock frequency for an 18-bit FF-L design - *Seq. Mem* implemented using a LUT SRL primitive

		Designs achieving Freq=500 MHz			For max. resources in Table 2	
		LUT %	BRAM %	PEs (p)	PEs (p)	Freq. (MHz)
k=64	b=32	82.1	94.8	512	512	501
	b=64	66.0	71.1	384	512	465
k=128	b=32	88.3	88.9	480	512	487
	b=64	59.7	59.3	320	512	455
k=256	b=32	76.6	97.8	352	352	501
	b=64	43.6	53.3	192	320	468

Table 4: Clock frequency for an 18-bit FF-B design - *Seq. Mem* implemented using a BRAM

PEs which are even closer to the resource limit. Both tables highlight the degradation in clock frequency observed for any $b > 32$. This occurs because 1) routing congestion increases between the PEs and *Sum & Update* unit, and 2) the size of each HB doubles in size which de-localises connections between them. Additional pipeline registers could manage both these issues, but on large designs, this creates even more congestion between CLBs. Instead we chose an architecture, where $b <= 32$, which guarantees an operating frequency close to 500 MHz for varying problem sizes. All of our designs were synthesised with cross module LUT optimisation turned off. This preserves the local structure in our architecture, and results are up to 20% faster.

4.3 Problem Size

The maximum problem size of the present design is compared with other online kernel methods in Table 5. For FF-B and FF-L, this translates to a 10^3 times increase in input dimensionality, and modelling capacity up to $90k$ basis functions. The massive modelling capacity allows our design to be used in problems with many input examples, m, because they approximate the kernel function for large dictionary sizes, N. Exact kernel methods such as KNLMS, KRLS and NORMA are intractable for datasets such as CIFAR-10 [2][6] because N is very large. In contrast, a floating point version of Fastfood with only $n = 16,384$ basis functions achieves an accuracy in the top two for RBF kernel representations [7].

---

[2]CIFAR-10 contains $m = 50,000$ images and $d = 3,072$ dimensions

	(d,n,B)	Lat (cyc)	Fmax (MHz)	Exec (ns)	Tput (Gb/s)
[4] (V7)	(8,16,32)	207	314	3.18	80.4
[11] (V7)	(8,200,18)	10	127	7.87	18.3
[9] (SV)	(-,128,32)	4396	157	28000	-
[7] (CPU)	(1024,16.4k,32)	-	-	580000	0.06
Ours (V7)	(1024,16.4k,18)	1893	432	2370	7.77
Ours (KU)	(8192,90.1k,18)	16930	508	17200	8.57

Table 5: Comparison of our implementation (FF-B only) with other online kernel methods (B=bit width, Lat=latency, Tput=throughput, Exec=execution time, V7=Virtex 7, SV=Stratix V, and KU=Kintex Ultrascale)

4.4 Speed-Up and Accuracy

Table 5 gives the speed-up of our FPGA implementation over a CPU. The execution time for the CPU version comes from the original Fastfood publication by Le et al. [7] and is only for prediction. The authors' code is written in C++ and uses the Spiral library for the FWHT. While details of the CPU are unclear from Le et al. [7], Spiral provides cache optimised C/C++ code which uses SSE vector instructions and up to four processor cores [3]. For a fairer comparison, we chose a previous generation Virtex 7 FPGA as the target for our design. The problem has $d = 1,024$ and $n = 16,384$, therefore, our implementation consists of 16 HBs, each of which compute a 1024-pt FWHT. For an FF-L design, the device operates at 432 MHz and has capacity for $p = 985$ PEs. However, only $p = 512$ could be used because p scales exponentially on fixed problem sizes. For $b = 32$ and $k = 32$, the number of compute cycles for prediction is $tc = 869$ (Eq. 7 minus $2h + k + 9$ cycles for the update). Therefore, our design is I/O constrained (i.e. $tc < d$), and one result can only be obtained every d cycles. The final result is a 245× speed-up although only 52% of available resources are used. We compared the mean square error (MSE) of floating point and fixed point versions, on the Mackey Glass regression benchmark [12] using a model consisting of $n = 16,384$ and $d = 1,024$. Competitive learning accuracies were achieved for floating point (MSE= 0.07), using 24-bit (MSE= 0.09) and 18-bit (MSE= 0.12) fixed point, although convergence of 18-bit is slower on average. This is only a minor problem since the additional latency gets hidden over time during online training.

4.5 Summary

Our implementation of Fastfood occupies a unique part in the design space of online kernel methods. This is observed in Table 5 [3]. The reported Fastfood configurations achieve an excellent combination of problem capacity and throughput for an 18-bit implementation. This yields 3 orders of magnitude increase in input dimensionality, 8.57 Gb/s of throughput, and a large number of basis functions. The last point gives us the ability to approximate much larger dictionary sizes than can otherwise be supported in [4][11][9]. Compared with Random Kitchen Sinks that have $O(nd)$ memory complexity, our Fastfood design only requires storage for $3n$ parameters. This

means that basis functions up to 1.66 GB (i.e. $n \times d \times 18/8$) can be approximated using only 0.61 MB, equating to a compression factor of 2730×. Future work will investigate how this result can be reinterpreted for DNNs, where state of the art compression factors are around 10× for full precision weights [5]. The main difference being that basis functions are learned in DNNs, whereas in Fastfood, they are randomly sampled from a distribution which closely approximates a kernel function.

5 CONCLUSION

This paper demonstrated the utility of employing the Fastfood algorithm for non-linear regression problems. Such an approach can be used to reduce the hardware requirements of kernel methods in applications demanding energy efficiency and real-time learning. A novel hierarchical systolic array architecture was described for minimising data transfers between processing elements in the computation of Fastfood. This utilised an efficient implementation of the FWHT, and our architecture is compatible with other fast transforms, such as the FFT. The reported design can sustain 500 MHz clock rates while supporting problems with an input dimensionality 10^3 times larger than other online kernel methods. Our work paves the way for real-time large-scale learning applications in control, communications and signal processing.

6 ACKNOWLEDGEMENTS

This research was supported under the Australian Research Councils Linkage Projects funding scheme (project number LP130101034) and Zomojo Pty Ltd.

REFERENCES

[1] Jonathan Bachrach, Huy Vo, Brian Richards, Yunsup Lee, Andrew Waterman, Rimas Avižienis, John Wawrzynek, and Krste Asanović. 2012. Chisel: constructing hardware in a scala embedded language. In Proc. DAC. ACM, 1216–1225.
[2] Ronan Collobert and Samy Bengio. 2001. SVMTorch: Support vector machines for large-scale regression problems. JMLR 1, Feb (2001), 143–160.
[3] Franz Franchetti, Markus Püschel, Yevgen Voronenko, Srinivas Chellappa, and José M. F. Moura. 2009. Discrete Fourier Transform on Multicores: Algorithms and Automatic Implementation. IEEE Signal Processing Magazine, special issue on "Signal Processing on Platforms with Multiple Cores" 26, 6 (2009), 90–102.
[4] Nicholas J Fraser, Duncan JM Moss, JunKyu Lee, Stephen Tridgell, Craig T Jin, and Philip HW Leong. 2015. A fully pipelined kernel normalised least mean squares processor for accelerated parameter optimisation. In Proc. FPL. IEEE, 1–6.
[5] Song Han, Huizi Mao, and William J Dally. 2015. Deep compression: Compressing deep neural networks with pruning, trained quantization and huffman coding. arXiv preprint arXiv:1510.00149 (2015).
[6] Alex Krizhevsky and Geoffrey Hinton. 2009. Learning multiple layers of features from tiny images. (2009).
[7] Quoc Le, Tamás Sarlós, and Alex Smola. 2013. Fastfood-approximating kernel expansions in loglinear time. In Proc. ICML, Vol. 85.
[8] Peter Milder, Franz Franchetti, James C Hoe, and Markus Püschel. 2012. Computer generation of hardware for linear digital signal processing transforms. ACM TODAES 17, 2 (2012), 15.
[9] Yeyong Pang, Shaojun Wang, Yu Peng, Nicholas J Fraser, and Philip HW Leong. 2013. A low latency kernel recursive least squares processor using FPGA technology. In Proc. FPT. IEEE, 144–151.
[10] Ali Rahimi and Benjamin Recht. 2007. Random features for large-scale kernel machines. In NIPS. 1177–1184.
[11] Stephen Tridgell, Duncan JM Moss, Nicholas J Fraser, and Philip HW Leong. 2015. Braiding: A scheme for resolving hazards in kernel adaptive filters. In Proc. FPT. IEEE, 136–143.
[12] Steven Van Vaerenbergh. 2012. Kernel methods toolbox KAFBOX: a Matlab benchmarking toolbox for kernel adaptive filtering. Grupo de Tratamiento Avanzado de Señal, Departamento de Ingeniería de Comunicaciones, Universidad de Cantabria, Spain (2012).

---

[3] 1) Input latency is included for Fastfood and KRLS [9] but not KNLMS [4] and NORMA [11], 2) n denotes both the number of basis functions and dictionary size, whereas in the text, N denotes the dictionary size and is applied only in the context of KNLMS, NORMA and KRLS, 3) (CPU) and Ours (V7) entries are for prediction only

Poster Session 1

Optimizations of Sequence Alignment on FPGA: A Case Study of Extended Sequence Alignment

Zheming Jin, *Argonne National Laboratory*
Kazutomo Yoshii, *Argonne National Laboratory*

Contact: zjin@anl.gov

Detecting similarities between sequences is an important part of Bioinformatics. In this poster, we explore the use of high-level synthesis tool and a field-programmable gate array (FPGA) for optimizing a sequence alignment algorithm. We demonstrate the optimization techniques to improve the performance of the extended sequence alignment algorithm in the BWA software package, a tool for mapping DNA sequences against a large reference sequence. Applying the optimizations to the algorithm using Xilinx SDAccel OpenCL-to-FPGA tool, we reduce the kernel execution time from 62.8 ms to 0.45 ms while the power consumption is approximately 11 Watts on the ADM-PCIE-8K5 FPGA platform.

Keywords: FPGA; OpenCL; Sequence alignment

DOI: https://doi.org/10.1145/3174243.3174958

Automatic Optimising CNN with Depthwise Separable Convolution on FPGA

Ruizhe Zhao, *Imperial College London*
Xinyu Niu, *Imperial College London*
Wayne Luk, *Imperial College London*
Contact: rz3515@ic.ac.uk

Convolution layers in Convolutional Neural Networks (CNNs) are effective in vision feature extraction but quite inefficient in computational resource usage. *Depthwise separable convolution* layer has been proposed in recent publications to enhance the efficiency without reducing the effectiveness by separately computing the *spatial* and *cross-channel* correlations from input images and has proven successful in state-of-the-art networks such as *MobileNets* [1] and *Xception* [2]. Based on the facts that depthwise separable convolution is highly structured and uses limited resources, we argue that it can well fit reconfigurable platforms like FPGA. To benefit FPGA platforms with this new layer, in this paper, we present a novel framework that can automatically generate and optimise hardware designs for depthwise separable CNNs. Besides, in our framework, existing conventional CNNs can be systematically converted to ones whose standard convolution layers are selectively replaced with functionally identical depthwise separable convolution layers, by carefully balancing the trade-off among speed, accuracy, and

resource usage through resource usage modelling and network fine-tuning. Results show that hardware designs generated by our framework can reach at most 231.7 frames per second regarding MobileNets, and for *VGG-16* [3], we gain 3.43 times speed-up and 3.54% accuracy decrease on the *ImageNet* [4] dataset comparing the original model and a layer replaced one.

Keywords: Design space exploration; Convolutional Neural Network; Depthwise separable convolution

DOI: https://doi.org/10.1145/3174243.3174959

Continuous Skyline Computation Accelerator with Parallelizing Dominance Relation Calculations

Kenichi Koizumi, *The University of Tokyo*
Kei Hiraki, *The University of Tokyo*
Mary Inaba, *The University of Tokyo*
Contact: koiken@is.s.u-tokyo.ac.jp

Skyline Computation is a method for extracting interesting entries from a large population with multiple attributes. These entries, called skyline or Pareto optimal entries, are known to have extreme characteristics that cannot be found by using outlier detection methods. Skyline computation is an important task for characterizing large amounts of data and selecting interesting entries with extreme features. When the population changes dynamically, the task of calculating a sequence of skyline sets is called a continuous skyline computation. This task is known to be difficult for the following reasons: (1) information must be kept for non-skyline entries, since they may join the skyline in the future; (2) the appearance or disappearance of even a single entry can change the skyline drastically; and (3) it is difficult to adopt a geometric acceleration algorithm for skyline computation tasks with high-dimensional datasets. A new algorithm, called jointed rooted-tree (JR-tree), has been developed that manages entries using a rooted-tree structure. JR-tree delays extend the tree to deeper levels to accelerate tree construction and traversal. In this study, we propose the JR-tree based continuous skyline computation acceleration algorithm. Our hardware algorithm parallelizes the calculations of dominance relation between a target entry and the skyline entries. We implemented our hardware algorithm on an FPGA and showed that high-speed tree construction and traversal can be realized. Comparing our FPGA-based implementation with an Intel CPU running state-of-the-art software algorithms, it was found to reduce the query processing time for synthetic and real-world datasets. Our hardware implementation is 1.7x to 35x faster than the software implementations.

Keywords: Continuous skyline Computation; Dominance Calculation; JR-tree

DOI: https://doi.org/10.1145/3174243.3174961

FastTrack: Exploiting Fast FPGA Wiring for Implementing NoC Shortcuts

Nachiket Kapre, *University of Waterloo*
Tushar Krishna, *Georgia Tech*
Contact: nachiket@uwaterloo.ca

The latency of packet-switched FPGA overlay Networks-on-Chip (NoCs) goes up linearly with the NoC dimensions, since packets typically spend a cycle in each dynamic router along the path. High-performance FPGA NoCs have to aggressively pipeline interconnects, thereby adding extra latency overhead to the NoC. The use of FPGA-friendly deflection routing schemes further exacerbates latency. Fortunately, FPGAs provide segmented interconnects with different lengths (speeds). Faster FPGA tracks can be used to reduce the number of switchbox hops along the packet path. We introduce FastTrack, an adaption to the NoC organization that inserts express bypass links in the NoC to skip multiple router stages in a single clock cycle. Our FastTrack design can be tuned to support different express link lengths for performance, and depopulation strategies for controlling cost. For the Xilinx Virtex-7 485T FPGA, an 8×8 FastTrack NoC is 2× larger than a base Hoplite NoC, but operates between 1.2–0.8× its clock frequency when using express links of length 2–4. FastTrack delivers throughput and latency improvements across a range of statistical workloads (2–2.5×), and traces extracted from FPGA accelerator case studies such as Sparse Matrix-Vector Multiplication (2.5×), Graph Analytics (2.8×), and Multi-processor overlay applications (2×). FastTrack also shows energy efficiency improvements by factors of up to 2× over baseline Hoplite due to higher sustained rates and high speed operation of express links made possible by fast FPGA interconnect.

Keywords: Network-on-chip; High-radix routers; FPGA Overlay NoC

DOI: http://dx.doi.org/10.1145/3174243.3174962

An Optimal Microarchitecture for Stencil Computation with Data Reuse and Fine-Grained Parallelism

Yuze Chi, *UCLA*
Peipei Zhou, *UCLA*
Jason Cong, *UCLA*
Contact: chiyuze@ucla.edu

Stencil computation is one of the most important kernels for many applications such as image processing, solving partial differential equations, and cellular automata. Nevertheless, implementing a high throughput stencil kernel is not trivial due to its nature of high memory access load and low operational intensity. In this work we adopt data reuse and fine-grained parallelism and present an optimal microarchitecture for stencil computation. The data reuse line buffers not only fully utilize the external memory bandwidth and fully reuse the input data, they also minimize the size of data reuse buffer given the number of fine-grained

parallelized and fully pipelined PEs. With the proposed microarchitecture, the number of PEs can be increased to saturate all available off-chip memory bandwidth. We implement this microarchitecture with a high-level synthesis (HLS) based template instead of register transfer level (RTL) specifications, which provides great programmability. To guide the system design, we propose a performance model in addition to detailed model evaluation and optimization analysis. Experimental results from on-board execution show that our design can provide an average of 6.5x speedup over line buffer-only design with only 2.4x resource overhead. Compared with loop transformation-only design, our design can implement a fully pipelined accelerator for applications that cannot be implemented with loop transformation-only due to its high memory conflict and low design flexibility. Furthermore, our FPGA implementation provides 83% throughput of a 14-core CPU with 4x energy-efficiency.

Keywords: Stencil Computation; High-Level Synthesis; Data Reuse; Fine-Grained Parallelism

DOI: http://dx.doi.org/10.1145/3174243.3174964

A FPGA Friendly Approximate Computing Framework with Hybrid Neural Networks

Haiyue Song, *Shanghai Jiao Tong University*
Xiang Song, *Shanghai Jiao Tong University*
Tianjian Li, *Shanghai Jiao Tong University*
Hao Dong, *Shanghai Jiao Tong University*
Naifeng Jing, *Shanghai Jiao Tong University*
Xiaoyao Liang, *Shanghai Jiao Tong University*
Li Jiang, *Shanghai Jiao Tong University*
Contact: jiangli@cs.sjtu.edu.cn

Neural approximate computing is promising to gain energy-efficiency at the cost of tolerable quality loss. The architecture contains two neural networks: the approximate accelerator generates approximate results while the classifier determines whether input data can be safely approximated. However, they are not compatible to a heterogeneous computing platform, due to the large communication overhead between the approximate accelerator and accurate cores, and the large speed gap between them. This paper proposes a software-hardware co-design strategy. With deep exploration of data distributions in the feature space, we first propose a novel approximate computing architecture containing a multi-class classifier and multiple approximate accelerator; this architecture, derived by the existing iterative co-training methods, can shift more data from accurate computation (in CPU) to approximate accelerator (in FPGA); the increased invocation of the approximate accelerator thus can yield higher utilization of the FPGA-based accelerator, resulting in the enhanced the performance. Moreover, much less input data is redistributed, by the classifier (also in FPGA), back to CPU, which can minimize the CPU-FPGA communication. Second, we design a pipelined data-path with batched input/output for the proposed hybrid architecture to efficiently hide the communication latency. A mask technique is proposed to decouple the synchronization between CPU and FPGA, in order to minimize the frequency of communication.

Keywords: Approximate computing; Neural network; FPGA

DOI: https://doi.org/10.1145/3174243.3174965

In-Package Domain-Specific ASICs for Intel® Stratix® 10 FPGAs: A Case Study of Accelerating Deep Learning Using TensorTile ASIC

Eriko Nurvitadhi, Jeff Cook, Asit Mishra, Debbie Marr, Kevin Nealis, Philip Colangelo, Andrew Ling, Davor Capalija, Utku Aydonat, Sergey Shumarayev, Aravind Dasu, *Intel Corporation*
Contact: eriko.nurvitadhi@intel.com

FPGAs or ASICs? There is a long-running debate on this. FPGAs are extremely *flexible* while ASICs offer top *efficiency* but inflexible. We believe that FPGAs *and* ASICs are better together, to offer both flexible and efficient solutions. We propose single-package heterogeneous 2.5D integration of FPGAs and ASICs, using Intel's Embedded Multi-Die Interconnect Bridge (EMIB). Since the ASICs are separate chips from the FPGA, this approach (1) does not change FPGA fabric, allowing re-use of existing ecosystems (FPGA chips/packaging/boards/software/etc), and (2) allows freedom in the ASIC design (area/freq/process/etc unconstrained by FPGA fabric). This approach is more effective than developing traditional stand-alone ASICs. Intel® Stratix® 10 FPGAs already have EMIBs, enabling single-package integration with other chips, or "tiles". We propose leveraging them to mix-and-match any domain-specific ASICs with Stratix10 FPGAs.

In particular, this work focuses on deep learning (DL) domain, which demands efficient tensor (matrix/vector) operations. We propose *TensorTile*, a family of ASICs to complement Stratix10 FPGAs to execute tensor operations with ASIC efficiency, while utilizing FPGA's flexibility for application-specific DL operations (e.g., Winograd). Our evaluation shows: (1) a small TensorTile (10s in mm^2, 14nm process) offer much better tensor throughput than a large Stratix10-2800 FPGA; (2) FPGAs and TensorTiles mix-and-match provide scalable solutions (e.g., ~69 peak INT8 TOPs with 1xTensorTile+small Stratix10-400 FPGA, to ~194 FP16 TOPs with 6xTensorTiles+large Stratix10-2800); (3) AlexNet performance and performance/Watt of Intel's DL OpenCL Stratix10 FPGA solution improved by 4x and 3.3x when enhanced with 2xTensorTiles. Overall, this approach is an effective, versatile, and scalable solution.

Keywords: multi-chip integration; accelerator; deep learning; ASIC; FPGA

DOI: https://doi.org/10.1145/3174243.3174966

Evaluation of OpenCL Performance-oriented Optimizations for Streaming Kernels on the FPGA

Zheming Jin, *Argonne National Laboratory*
Hal Finkel, *Argonne National Laboratory*
Contact: zjin@anl.gov

When Field-programmable gate arrays (FPGAs) can implement the streaming applications efficiently and High-level synthesis (HLS)

tools allow people without complex hardware design knowledge to evaluate an application on FPGAs, there is an opportunity and a need to understand where OpenCL and FPGA can play in the streaming domains. To this end, we evaluate the overhead of the OpenCL infrastructure on the Nallatech 385A FPGA board that features an Arria 10 GX1150 FPGA. Then we explore the implementation space and discuss the performance optimization techniques for the streaming kernels using the OpenCL-to-FPGA HLS tool. On the target platform, the infrastructure overhead requires 12% of the FPGA memory and logic resources. The latency of the single work-item kernel execution is 11 us and the maximum frequency of a kernel implementation is around 300 MHz. The experimental results of the streaming kernels show FPGA resources, such as block RAMs and DSPs, can limit the kernel performance before the constraint of memory bandwidth takes effect. Kernel vectorization and compute unit duplication are practical optimization techniques that can improve the kernel performance by a factor of 2 to 10. The combination of the two techniques can achieve the best performance. To improve the performance of compute unit duplication, the local work size needs to be tuned and the optimal value can increase the performance by a factor of 3 to 70 compared to the default value.

Keywords: FPGA; OpenCL; Streaming kernel

DOI: https://doi.org/10.1145/3174243.3174967

K-Flow: A Programming and Scheduling Framework to Optimize Dataflow Execution on CPU-FPGA Platforms

Jason Cong, *UCLA*
Zhenman Fang, *UCLA/Xilinx*
Yao Hu, *Falcon Computing Solutions, Inc.*
Di Wu, *Falcon Computing Solutions, Inc.*
Contact: allwu@falcon-computing.com

With the slowing down of Moore's law, major cloud service providers---such as Amazon Web Services, Microsoft Azure, and Alibaba Cloud---all started deploying FPGAs in their cloud platforms to improve the performance and energy-efficiency. From the perspective of performance per unit cost in the cloud, it is essential to efficiently utilize all available CPU and FPGA resources within a requested computing instance. However, most prior studies overlook the CPU-FPGA co-optimization or require a considerable amount of manual efforts to achieve it.

In this poster, we present a framework called K-Flow, which enables easy FPGA accelerator integration and efficient CPU-FPGA co-scheduling for big data applications. K-Flow abstracts an application as a widely used directed acyclic graph (DAG), and dynamically schedules a number of CPU threads and/or FPGA accelerator processing elements (PEs) to execute the dataflow tasks on each DAG node. Moreover, K-Flow provides user-friendly interfaces to program each DAG node and automates the tedious process of FPGA accelerator integration and CPU-FPGA co-optimization using the genomic read alignment application BWA-MEM as a case study. Experimental results show that K-Flow achieves a throughput that is on average 94.5% of the theoretical upper bound and 1.4x better than a straightforward FPGA integration.

Keywords: FPGA in the cloud; FPGA/CPU co-execution; dataflow programming; genomic sequences alignment

DOI: http://dx.doi.org/10.1145/3174243.3174968

FPGA-based LSTM Acceleration for Real-Time EEG Signal Processing

Zhe Chen, Andrew Howe, Hugh T. Blair, Jason Cong,
University of California, Los Angeles
Contact: zhechen@ucla.edu

Closed-loop neurofeedback is a growing area of research and development for novel therapies to treat brain disorders. A neurofeedback device can detect disease symptoms (such as motor tremors or seizures) in real time from electroencephalogram (EEG) signals, and respond by rapidly delivering neurofeedback stimulation that relieves these symptoms. Conventional EEG processing algorithms rely on acausal filters, which impose delays that can exceed the short feedback latency required for closed-loop stimulation. In this paper, we first introduce a method for causal filtering using long short-term memory (LSTM) networks, which radically reduces the filtering latency. We then propose a reconfigurable architecture that supports time-division multiplexing of LSTM inference engines on a prototype neurofeedback device. We implemented a 128-channel EEG signal processing design on a Zynq-7030 device, and demonstrated its feasibility. Then, we further scaled up the design onto Zynq-7045 and Virtex-690t devices to achieve high performance and energy efficient implementations for massively parallel brain signal processing. We evaluated the performance against optimized implementations on CPU and GPU at the same CMOS technology node. Experiment results show that the Virtex-690t can achieve 1.32x and 11x speed-up against the K40c GPU and the multi-thread Xeon E5-2860 CPU, respectively, while FPGA achieves 6.1x and 26.6x energy efficiency compared to the GPU and CPU.

Keywords: Electroencephalography; Multiplexing; Neurofeedback; Phase detection; Reconfigurable logic

DOI: https://doi.org/10.1145/3174243.3174969

Understanding Performance Differences of FPGAs and GPUs

Jason Cong, *UCLA*
Zhenman Fang, *UCLA and Xilinx*
Michael Lo, *UCLA*
Hanrui Wang, *UCLA and Fudan University*
Jingxian Xu, *UCLA*
Shaochong Zhang, *UCLA*
Contact: zhenman@cs.ucla.edu

The notorious power wall has significantly limited the scaling for general-purpose processors. To address this issue, various accelerators, such as GPUs and FPGAs, emerged to achieve better performance and energy-efficiency. Between these two programmable accelerators, a natural question arises: which applications are better suited for FPGAs, which for GPUs, and why?

In this paper, our goal is to better understand the performance differences between FPGAs and GPUs and provide more insights to the community. We intentionally start with a widely used GPU-friendly benchmark suite Rodinia, and port 11 of the benchmarks (15 kernels) onto FPGAs using the more portable and programmable high-level synthesis C. We provide a simple five-step strategy for FPGA accelerator designs that can be easily understood and mastered by software programmers, and present a quantitative performance breakdown of each step. Then we propose a set of performance metrics, including normalized operations per cycle (OPC_norm) for each pipeline, and effective parallel factor ($effective\_para\_factor$), to compare the performance of GPU and FPGA accelerator designs. We find that for 6 out of the 15 kernels, today's FPGAs can provide comparable performance or even achieve better performance, while only consume about 1/10 of GPUs' power (both on the same technology node). We observe that FPGAs usually have higher OPC_norm in most kernels in light of their customized deep pipeline but lower $effective\_para\_factor$ due to far lower memory bandwidth than GPUs. Future FPGAs should increase their off-chip bandwidth and clock frequency to catch up with GPUs.

Keywords: FPGA; GPU; Accelerator; Rodinia

DOI: https://doi.org/10.1145/3174243.3174970

Poster Session 2

Software/Hardware Co-design for Multichannel Scheduling in IEEE 802.11p MLME

Nan Ding, *Dalian University of Technology*
Wei Zhang, *Huawei Beijing Research Center*
Yanhua Ma, *Dalian University of Technology*
Zhenguo Gao, *Dalian University of Technology*
Contact: dingnan@dlut.edu.cn

The capacity of IEEE 802.11p communication in vehicular ad hoc networks (VANETs) is widely sensitive to the tradeoff between control channel (CCH) and service channels (SCHs), which is particularly obvious in the different traffic flow condition. This paper proposes a hybrid multichannel scheduling algorithm with FPGA and traffic flow forecasting based on Kalman Filter (HMS-FFK) according to the extended SCH access mechanism mentioned in IEEE 1609.4 protocol. In HMS-FFK, a Random CCH Transmission Request Probability is defined to describe the CCH message congestion probability according to the local traffic flow density. Then, a hardware prototype of MAC sublayer management entities (MLME) based on HMS-FFK scheduling (MLME-HMS) is designed with FPGA, which is flexible to be integrated in the 802.11p communication system by the PCI interface. Theoretical analysis and simulation results show that the proposed scheme and hardware prototype of MLME are able to help IEEE 1609.4 MAC to optimize the throughput of SCHs and reduce the transmission delay of CCH in the different traffic flow condition.

Keywords: IEEE 802.11p; MAC sublayer management entities; hardware/software co-design; traffic flow forecast

DOI: http://dx.doi.org/10.1145/3174243.3174971

Solving Satisfiability Problem on Quantum Annealer: A Lesson from FPGA CAD Tools

Juexiao Su, *University of California, Los Angeles*
Lei He, *University of California, Los Angeles*
Contact: sujuexiao@g.ucla.edu

Recently, a practical quantum annealing device has been commercialized by D-Wave Systems, sparking research interest in developing applications to solve problems that are intractable for classical computer. This paper provides a tutorial for using quantum annealer to solve Boolean satisfiability problem. We explain the computational model of quantum annealer and discuss the detailed mapping technique inspired by FPGA CAD flow, including stages such as logic optimization, placement and routing.

Keywords: Quantum Annealing; Boolean Satisfiability

DOI: https://doi.org/10.1145/3174243.3174972

Domino: An Asynchronous and Energy-efficient Accelerator for Graph Processing

Chongchong Xu, Chao Wang, Yiwei Zhang,
Lei Gong, Xi Li, Xuehai Zhou,
University of Science and Technology of China
Contact: xcc2448@mail.ustc.edu.cn

Large-scale graphs processing, which draws attentions of researchers, applies in a large range of domains, such as social networks, web graphs, and transport networks. However, processing large-scale graphs on general processors suffers from difficulties including computation and memory inefficiency. Therefore, the research of hardware accelerator for graph processing has become a hot issue recently. Meanwhile, as a power-efficiency and reconfigurable resource, FPGA is a potential solution to design and employ graph processing algorithms. In this paper, we propose Domino, an asynchronous and energy-efficient hardware accelerator for graph processing. Domino adopts the asynchronous model to process graphs, which is efficient for most of the graph algorithms, such as Breadth-First Search, Depth-First Search, and Single Source Shortest Path. Domino also proposes a specific data structure based on row vector, named Batch Row Vector, to present graphs. Our work adopts the naive update mechanism and bisect update mechanism to perform asynchronous control. Ultimately, we implement Domino on an advanced Xilinx Virtex-7 board, and experimental results demonstrate that Domino has significant performance and energy improvement, especially for graphs with a large diameter(e.g., roadNet-CA and USA-Road). Case studies in Domino achieve $1.47x$-$7.84x$ and $0.47x$-$2.52x$ average speedup for small-diameter graphs(e.g., com-youtube, WikiTalk, and soc-LiveJournal), over GraphChi on the Intel Core2 and Intel Core i7 processors, respectively. Besides, compared to Intel Core i7 processors, Domino also performs significant energy-efficiency that is $2.03x$-$10.08x$ for three small-diameter graphs and $27.98x$-$134.50x$ for roadNet-CA which is a graph with relatively large diameter.

Keywords: Graph Processing; Asynchronous; Energy-efficient; Accelerator

DOI: https://doi.org/10.1145/3174243.3174973

Towards Serial-Equivalent Parallel Routing for FPGAs

Minghua Shen, *Sun Yat-sen University*
Wentai Zhang, *Peking University*
Nong Xiao, *Sun Yat-sen University*
Guojie Luo, *Peking University*
Contact: shenmh6@mail.sysu.edu.cn

Serial equivalency can provide easier regression testing and customer support in production-grade CAD software. While existing parallel routing techniques have become sufficiently advanced to accelerate the execution time, support for serial equivalency has been very limited or ignored due to it was considered costly. In this paper, we propose serial-equivalent parallel routing for FPGAs. We use an optimal dependency-aware scheduling to facilitate serial equivalency of parallel routing algorithm. This capability enables the same answer as the serial version of the parallel algorithm, regardless of how many processing cores are used. We also validate this property across different hardware platforms. Further experimental results show that we achieve a 14.27x speedup on the MPI-based distributed parallel computer and a 19.65x speedup on the GPU-based massively parallel machine. To our knowledge, it is the first parallel routing with a serial equivalency guarantee.

Keywords: FPGAs; Physical Design; Routing; Parallelization;

DOI: https://doi.org/10.1145/3174243.3174974

Performance Comparison of Multiple Approaches of Status Register for Medium Density Memory Suitable for Implementation of a Lossless Compression Dictionary

Matěj Bartík, *CESNET a.l.e.*
Sven Ubik, *CESNET a.l.e.*
Pavel Kubalík, *CTU FIT*
Tomáš Beneš, *CTU FIT*
Contact: bartik@cesnet.cz

This paper presents a performance comparison of various approaches of realization of status register suitable for maintaining (in)valid bits in mid-density memory structures implemented in Xilinx FPGAs. An example of a such structure with status register could be a dictionary for Lempel-Ziv based lossless compression algorithms where the dictionary has to be initialized before each run of the algorithm with minimum time and logic resources consumption. The performance evaluation of designs has been made in Xilinx ISE and Vivado toolkits for the Virtex-7 FPGA. This research has been partially supported by the CTU project SGS17/017/OHK3/1T/18 "Dependable and attack-resistant architectures for programmable devices" and by the project "E-infrastructure CESNET – modernization" no. CZ.02.1.01/0.0/0.0/16 013/0001797.

Keywords: FPGA; performance; status; register; LZ77; memory; compression; algorithm; hash; table; dictionary

DOI: http://dx.doi.org/10.1145/3174243.3174976

BoxPlacer: Force Directed-Based Timing-Driven Placement for Large-Scale FPGAs

Minghua Shen, *Sun Yat-sen University*
Jiaxi Zhang, *Peking University*
Nong Xiao, *Sun Yat-sen University*
Guojie Luo, *Peking University*
Contact: shenmh6@mail.sysu.edu.cn

Placement is probably the most critical process in the FPGA design flow. The demand for high performance continues to increase, but existing placers are still faced with numerous

challenges including very long runtime, poor scalability, and restricted space exploration. In this paper we propose a novel timing-driven placement algorithm called BoxPlacer, which is supported by the force directed concept. BoxPlacer firstly uses a simple policy to create the initial box for placement. Then a force-directed iterative scheme is used to reduce the box size and determine the global placement. At last, the same concept is employed to eliminate the overlaps between reduced boxes to ensure the legalization in detailed placement. Notice that timing is always used to drive the placement in BoxPlacer. We demonstrate the effectiveness of our BoxPlacer by comparing the experimental results with that produced by the academic simulated annealing-based placer. Notably, our BoxPlacer achieves on average about 8x runtime advantage with 9% smaller critical path delay and 6% shorter wirelength.

Keywords: FPGAs; Physical Design; Placement;

DOI: https://doi.org/10.1145/3174243.3174977

DATuner: An Extensible Distributed Autotuning Framework for FPGA Design and Design Automation

Gai Liu, *Cornell University*
Ecenur Ustun, *Cornell University*
Shaojie Xiang, *Cornell University*
Chang Xu, *IBM Research, China*
Guojie Luo, *Peking University*
Zhiru Zhang, *Cornell University*
Contact: gl387@cornell.edu

Mainstream FPGA tools contain an extensive set of user-controlled compilation options and internal optimization strategies that significantly impact the design quality. These compilation and optimization parameters create a complex design space that human designers may not be able to effectively explore in a time-efficient manner. In this work we describe DATuner, an open-source extensible distributed autotuning framework for optimizing FPGA designs and design automation tools using an ensemble of search techniques managed by multi-armed bandit algorithms. DATuner is designed for a distributed environment that uses parallel searches to amortize the significant runtime overhead of the CAD tools. DATuner provides convenient interface for extension to user-supplied tools, which enables the end users to apply DATuner to design tools/flows of their interest. We demonstrate the effectiveness and extensibility of DATuner using three case studies, which include clock frequency optimization for FPGA compilation, fixed-point optimization, and autotuning logic synthesis transformations.

Keywords: Design automation; Distributed autotuning; Field-programmable gate array

DOI: https://doi.org/10.1145/3174243.3174978

Mapping Large-Scale DNNs on Asymmetric FPGAs

Wentai Zhang, Jiaxi Zhang, *Peking University*
Minghua Shen, Nong Xiao, *Sun Yat-sen University*
Guojie Luo, *Peking University*
Contact: shenmh6@mail.sysu.edu.cn

FPGAs are very attractive to accelerate the deep neural networks (DNNs). While single-FPGA can provide good performance for small-scale DNNs, support for large-scale DNNs is very limited due to they require higher resource demand. In this paper, we propose an efficient mapping approach for accelerating large-scale DNNs on an asymmetric multi-FPGA architecture. Relative to the state-of-the-art single-FPGA resource reuse for large-scale DNNs, we consider multi-FPGA fashion to strive for higher performance. In this fashion, the neural network mapping problem can be formulated as a resource allocation problem, and a dynamic programming-based partitioning is designed to solve this problem optimally. Notice that the network topology and communication bandwidth of multiple FPGAs are always used to guide the partitioning to boost the performance while satisfying the constraints of resource-performance trade-off in a single FPGA. Experimental results using the large-scale ResNet-152 demonstrate that our approach deploys sixteen FPGAs to provide an advantage of 16.4x GOPS over the state-of-the-art work.

Keywords: Multi-FPGAs; DNNs; Dynamic programming

DOI: http://dx.doi.org/10.1145/3174243.3174982

Software-Defined FPGA-Based Accelerator for Deep Convolutional Neural Networks

Yankang Du, Qinrang Liu, Shuai Wei, Chen Gao,
National Digital Switching System Engineering & Technology Research Center
Contact: duyankang@163.com

Convolutional Neural Network (CNN) has gained great popularity. Intensive computation and huge external data access amount are two challenged factors for the hardware acceleration. Besides these, the ability to deal with various CNN models is also challenged. At present, most of the proposed FPGA-based CNN accelerator either can only deal with specific CNN models or should be re-coded and re-download on the FPGA for the different CNN models. This would bring great trouble for the developers. In this paper, we designed a software-defined architecture to cope with different CNN models while keeping high throughput. The hardware can be programmed according to the demands. Several techniques are proposed to optimize the performance of our accelerators. For the convolutional layer, we proposed the software-defined data reuse technique to ensure that all the parameters can be only loaded once during the computing phase. This will reduce large off-chip data access amount and the need for the memory and the need for the memory bandwidth. By using the sparse property of the input feature map, almost 80% weight

parameters can be skipped to be loaded in the full-connected (FC) layer. Compared to the previous works, our software-defined accelerator has the highest flexibility while keeping relative high throughout.

Keywords: Software-defined, CNN, accelerator, FPGA

DOI: https://doi.org/10.1145/3174243.3174983

Design of an MTJ-Based Nonvolatile LUT Circuit with a Data-Update Minimized Shift Operation for an Ultra-Low-Power FPGA

Daisuke Suzuki, and Takahiro Hanyu, *Tohoku University*
Contact: daisuke.suzuki.e6@tohoku.ac.jp

Nonvolatile FPGAs (NV-FPGAs) have a potential advantage to eliminate wasted standby power which is increasingly serious in recent standard SRAM-based FPGAs. However, functionality of the conventional NV-FPGAs are not sufficient compared to that of standard SRAM-based FPGAs. For example, an effective circuit structure to perform shift-register (SR) function has not been proposed yet. In this paper, a magnetic tunnel junction (MTJ) based nonvolatile lookup table (NV-LUT) circuit that can perform SR function with low power consumption is proposed. The MTJ device is the best candidate in terms of virtually unlimited endurance, CMOS compatibility, and 3D stacking capability. On the other hand, large power consumption to perform SR function a serious design issue for the MTJ-based NV-LUT circuit. Since the write current for the MTJ device is large and all the data must be updated after the SR operation using CMOS-oriented method, large power consumption is indispensable. To overcome this issue, the address for read/write access is incremented at each cycle instead of direct data shifting in the proposed LUT circuit. In this way, the number of data update per 1-bit shift is minimized to one, which results in great power saving. Moreover, since the selector is shared both read (logic) and write operation, its hardware cost is small. In fact, 99% of power reduction and 52% of transistor counts reduction compared to those of SRAM-based LUT circuit are performed. The authors would like to acknowledge ImPACT of CSTI, CIES consortium program, JST-OPERA, and JSPS KAKENHI Grant No. 17H06093.

Keywords: Lookup table circuit; Nonvolatile logic; Magnetic tunnel junction device; Low power

DOI: https://doi.org/10.1145/3174243.3174984

High-Throughput Lossless Compression on Tightly Coupled CPU-FPGA Platforms

Weikang Qiao, Jieqiong Du, Zhenman Fang, Libo Wang,
Michael Lo, Mau-Chung Frank Chang, Jason Cong,
University of California, Los Angeles
Contact: wkqiao2015@ucla.edu

Data compression techniques have been widely used to reduce the data storage and movement overhead, especially in the big data era. Recent studies demonstrate the great promise of FPGAs to improve the throughput of lossless compression algorithms that are very computation-intensive. However, when such FPGA-based compression accelerators are integrated with the processors, the overall system throughput is typically limited by the communication between a CPU and an FPGA. This study proposes a novel scheme to achieve high-throughput lossless compression on modern Intel-Altera HARPv2 platforms, where a Xeon CPU and an Altera FPGA are tightly coupled to improve the CPU-FPGA communication. First, it implements a multi-way parallel and fully pipelined compression accelerator based on Deflate algorithm. The accelerator itself can achieve a maximum throughput of 12.8 GB/s and a compression ratio of 2.03 over standard benchmarks. In addition, various trade-offs among compression throughput, compression ratio, FPGA resource utilization and scalability are explored to optimize the accelerator design based on different application requirements. Moreover, this study exploits the high CPU-FPGA communication bandwidth of HARPv2 platforms to improve the compression throughput of the overall system, which can achieve an average practical end-to-end throughput of 10.0 GB/s (up to 12 GB/s for larger input files) on HARPv2.

Keywords: Lossless Compression; Deflate; End-to-End Communication Bandwidth

DOI: https://doi.org/10.1145/3174243.3174987

Poster Session 3

HexCell: a Hexagonal Cell for Evolvable Systolic Arrays on FPGAs

Fady Hussein, Luka Daoud, Nader Rafla,
Boise State University, Boise, Idaho
Contact: FadyHussein@u.BoiseState.edu

This paper presents a novel cell architecture for evolvable systolic arrays. HexCell is a tile-able processing element with a hexagonal shape that can be implemented and dynamically reconfigured on field-programmable gate arrays (FPGAs). The cell contains a functional unit, three input ports, and three output ports. It supports two concurrent configuration schemes: dynamic partial reconfiguration (DPR), where the functional unit is partially reconfigured at run time, and virtual reconfiguration circuit (VRC), where the cell output port bypasses one of the input data or selects the functional unit output. Hence, HexCell combines the merits of DPR and VRC including resource-awareness, reconfiguration speed and routing flexibility. In addition, the cell structure supports pipelining and data synchronization for achieving high throughput for data-intensive applications like image processing. A HexCell is represented by a binary string (chromosome) that encodes the cell's function and the output selections. Our developed evolvable HexCell array supports more inputs and outputs, a variety of possible datapaths, and has faster reconfiguration, compared to the state-of-the-art systolic array while maintaining the same resource utilization. Moreover, by using the same genetic algorithm on the two systolic arrays, results show that the HexCell array has higher throughput and can evolve faster than state-of-the-art array.

Keywords: HexCell; Systolic arrays; Dynamic partial reconfiguration (DPR); Virtual reconfiguration circuit (VRC); Evolvable hardware; FPGA

DOI: https://doi.org/10.1145/3174243.3174988

Label based Feature Analysis and Target Detection with Imager-driven Processing Mode for Ultrafast-Imager

Xiaoyu Yu, *Tencent*
Dong Ye, *Harbin Institute of Technology*
Contact: yxy_hit@163.com

Latest vision tasks trend to be the real-time processing with high throughput frame rate and low latency. High spatiotemporal resolution imagers continue to spring up but only a few of them can be used in real applications owing to the excessive computational burden and lacking of suitable architecture. This paper presents a solution for target detection task in imager-driven processing mode (IMP), which takes shorter time in processing than the time gap between frames, even if the ulreafast imager run at full frame rate. High throughput pixel stream outputted from imager is analyzed base on multi features in a fully pipelined and

bufferless architecture in FPGA. A pyramid shape model consisting of 2-D Processing Element (PE) array is proposed to search the connected regions of target candidates distributed at different time slices, and extract corresponding features when the stream pass through. A Label based 1-D PE Array collects the feature flow generated by the pyramid according to their labels, and output the feature vector of each target candidate in real time. The proposed model has been tested in simulation and experiments for target detection with 0.8Gpixel/sec (2320×1726 with 192FPS) data stream input, and the latency is less than 1 microsecond.

Keywords: feature extraction; high throughput data stream; connected components labeling; target detection; high speed camera; FPGA

DOI: http://dx.doi.org/10.1145/3174243.3174990

A Low-Power Deconvolutional Accelerator for Convolutional Neural Network Based Segmentation on FPGA

Shuanglong Liu, *Imperial College London*
Xinyu Niu, *Corerain Technologies Ltd.*
Wayne Luk, *Imperial College London*
Contact: s.liu13@imperial.ac.uk

Convolutional Neural Networks (CNNs) based algorithms have been successful in solving image recognition problems, showing very large accuracy improvement. In recent years, deconvolution layers are widely used as key components in the state-of-the-art CNNs for end-to-end training and models to support tasks such as image segmentation. However, the deconvolution algorithms are computationally intensive which limits their applicability to real time applications. Particularly, there has been little research on the efficient implementations of deconvolution algorithms on FPGA platforms. In this work, we propose and develop fully customized deconvolution architecture for CNN-based segmentation algorithms. Besides, memory sharing between the computation modules is proposed for the FPGA-based CNN accelerator as well as for other optimization techniques. Furthermore, a hardware mapping framework is developed to automatically generate the high-throughput hardware design for any given CNN model on the target device. Finally, we implement our designs on Xilinx Zynq-7030 and the deconvolution accelerator achieves a performance of 25.6 GOPS under 200MHz working frequency and a performance density of 0.064 GOPS/DSP using 32-bit quantization, which significantly outperforms previous designs on FPGAs. A real-time application of scene segmentation on Cityscapes Dataset is used to evaluate our CNN accelerator on Zynq-7030 board, and the system achieves a performance of 57.2 GOPS and 0.143 GOPS/DSP using 16-bit quantization, and supports up to 2 frames per second for 512x512 image inputs with a power consumption of only 3.2W.

Keywords: FPGA; Convolutional Neural Networks (CNNs); Deconvolution; Hardware Acceleration; Segmentation

DOI: https://doi.org/10.1145/3174243.3174991

FPGAs in the Datacenters: the Case of Parallel Hybrid Super Scalar String Sample Sort (pHS⁵)

Mikhail Asiatici, *EPFL*
Damian Maiorano, *Politecnico di Torino*
Paolo Ienne, *EPFL*
Contact: mikhail.asiatici@epfl.ch

String sorting is an important part of database and MapReduce applications; however, it has not been studied as extensively as sorting of fixed-length keys. Handling variable-length keys in hardware is challenging and it is no surprise that no string sorters on FPGA have been proposed yet. We present Parallel Hybrid Super Scalar String Sample Sort (pHS⁵) on Intel HARPv2, a heterogeneous CPU-FPGA system with a server-grade multi-core CPU. Our pHS⁵ is based on the state-of-the-art string sorting algorithm for multi-core shared memory CPUs, pS⁵, which we extended with multiple processing elements (PEs) on the FPGA. Each PE accelerates one instance of the most effectively parallelizable dominant kernel of pS⁵ by up to 33% compared to a single Intel Xeon Broadwell core running at 3.4 GHz. Furthermore, we extended the job scheduling mechanism of pS⁵ to enable our PEs to compete with the CPU cores for processing the accelerable kernel, while retaining the complex high-level control flow and the sorting of the smaller data sets on the CPU. We accelerate the whole algorithm by up to 10% compared to the 28 thread software baseline running on the 14-core Xeon processor and by up to 36% at lower thread counts.

Keywords: String Sorting; FPGA; Heterogeneous Computing

DOI: https://doi.org/10.1145/3174243.3174993

SIFT Keypoint Descriptor Matching Algorithm: A Fully Pipelined Accelerator on FPGA

Luka Daoud, M. Kamran Latif, and Nader Rafla
Department of Electrical and Computer Engineering, *Boise State University*
Boise, Idaho, USA
Contact: LukaDaoud@u.boisestate.edu

Scale Invariant Feature Transform (SIFT) algorithm is one of the classical feature extraction algorithms that is well known in Computer Vision. It consists of two stages: keypoint descriptor extraction and descriptor matching. SIFT descriptor matching algorithm is a computational intensive process. In this work, we present a design and implementation of a hardware core accelerator for the descriptor-matching algorithm on a field programmable gate array (FPGA). Our proposed hardware core architecture is able to cope with the memory bandwidth and hit the roofline performance model to achieve maximum throughput. The matching-core was implemented using Xilinx Vivado® EDA design suite on a Zynq®-based FPGA Development board. The proposed matching-core architecture is fully pipelined for 16-bit fixed-point operations and consists of

five main submodules designed in Verilog, High Level Synthesis, and System Generator. The area resources were significantly reduced compared to the most recent matching-core implemented on hardware. While our proposed hardware accelerator matching-core was able to detect 98% matching-points compared to the software approach, it is 15.7 × faster.

Keywords: Scale Invariant Feature Transform, SIFT; Matching algorithm; FPGA; Pipeline; Acceleration; High Level Synthesis; HLS

DOI: https://doi.org/10.1145/3174243.3174994

FGC: A Tool-flow for Generating and Configuring Custom FPGAs

Oluseyi A. Ayorinde, *US Army Research Lab – West (LA)*
He Qi, *University of Virginia*
Benton H. Calhoun, *University of Virginia*
Contact: oluseyi.a.ayorinde.civ@mail.mil

We introduce the FGC Toolflow, the only tool providing flexible custom-FPGA generation and configuration to-date. Currently, researchers building custom FPGAs must create for FPGA schematics and bitstreams by hand. Both tasks are prohibitively time intensive and error prone. Additionally, the simulation time for bitcell configuration is very long (often times longer than the functionality), making the verification of FPGA fabrics even more time consuming. Some existing toolflows and software packages designed to help with this process, but they only generate bitcell configurations, leaving schematics to be developed by hand. Others have limitations in circuit-level and architectural parameters, which prevent them from adequately exploring the FPGA design space. The FGC flow is the only flow available that generates a custom full-FPGA schematic from a single parameter text file, and generates the proper configuration bitstream for a target Verilog functionality. The parameter text file can accommodate 100s of different parameters, which include both circuit-level and architectural parameters to fully encompass the FPGA design space. The FGC flow generates both a schematic and a configuration bitstream for an FPGA with 100 CLBs (900,000 transistors) in only 8 minutes. The flow also generates simulation files, allowing the user to quickly set up and perform simulations to verify the FPGA and its configuration at the chip level with SPICE-level accuracy. This flow was used to create, verify, and test a taped-out ultra-low power FPGA.

Keywords: Custom FPGA Generation; Bitstream Generation; CAD for FPGAs; Automation; Simulation; Design Space Exploration

DOI: https://doi.org/10.1145/3174243.3174997

Exploration of Low Numeric Precision Deep Learning Inference Using Intel® FPGAs

Philip Colangelo, *Intel*
Nasibeh Nasiri, *Intel*
Eriko Nurvitadhi, *Intel*
Asit Mishra, *Intel*
Martin Margala, *Univ. of Massachusetts Lowell*
Kevin Nealis, *Intel*
Contact: philip.colangelo@intel.com

Convolutional neural networks have been shown to maintain reasonable classification accuracy when quantized down to 8-bits, however, quantizing to sub 8-bit activations and weights can result in classification accuracy falling below an acceptable threshold. Techniques exist for increasing accuracy of sub 8-bit networks typically by means of increasing computation resulting in a trade-off between throughput and accuracy and can be tailored for different networks through combinations of activation and weight precisions. Customizable hardware architectures like FPGAs provide opportunity for data width specific computation through unique logic configurations leading to highly optimized processing that is unattainable by full precision networks. Specifically, ternary and binary weighted networks offer an efficient method of inference for 2-bit and 1-bit data respectively. In this paper, we present a hardware design for FPGAs that takes advantage of the bandwidth, memory, and computation savings of limited numerical precision data. We provide insights into the trade-offs between throughput and accuracy for various networks and how they map to our framework. Further, we show how limited numeric precision computation can be efficiently mapped onto FPGAs for both ternary and binary cases. Starting with Arria 10, we show a 2-bit activation and ternary weighted AlexNet running in hardware that achieves 3,700 images per second on the ImageNet dataset with a top-1 accuracy of 0.49. Using a hardware modeler designed for our low numeric precision framework we project performance most notably for a 55.5 TOPS Stratix 10 device running a modified ResNet-34 with only 3.7% accuracy degradation compared with single precision.

Keywords: Arria 10; Stratix 10; Deep Learning; Low Precision Neural Network; CNN

DOI: https://doi.org/10.1145/3174243.3174999

LEOSoC: An Open-Source Cross-Platform Embedded Linux Library for Managing Hardware Accelerators in Heterogeneous System-on-Chips

Andrea Guerrieri, *EPFL*
Sahand Kashani-Akhavan, *EPFL*
Mikhail Asiatici, *EPFL*
Pasquale Lombardi, *Syderal SA*
Bilel Belhadj, *Syderal SA*
Paolo Ienne, *EPFL*
Contact: andrea.guerrieri@epfl.ch

Modern heterogeneous SoCs (System-on-Chip) contain a set of Hard IPs (HIPs) surrounded by an FPGA fabric for hosting custom Hardware Accelerators (HAs). However, efficiently managing such HAs in an embedded Linux environment involves creating and building custom device drivers specific to the target platform, which negatively impacts development cost, portability and time-to-market. To address this issue, we present LEOSoC, an open-source cross-platform embedded Linux library. LEOSoC reduces the development effort required to interface HAs with applications and makes SoCs easy to use for an embedded software developer who is familiar with the semantics of standard POSIX threads. Using LEOSoC does not require any specific version of the Linux kernel, nor to rebuild a custom driver for each new kernel release. LEOSoC consists of a base

hardware system and a software layer. Both hardware and software are portable across SoC from various vendors and the library recognizes and auto-adapts to the target SoC platform on which it is running. Furthermore, LEOSoC allows the application to partially or completely change the structure of the HAs at runtime without rebooting the system by leveraging the underlying platforms' support for dynamic full/partial FPGA reconfigurability. The system has been tested on multiple COTS (Commercial Off The Shelf) boards from different vendors, each one running different versions of Linux and, therefore, proving the real portability and usability of LEOSoC in a specific industrial design.

Keywords: FPGA; SoC; Reconfigurable Computing; Partial Reconfiguration; Heterogeneous Computing;

DOI: https://doi.org/10.1145/3174243.3175002

A Self-adaptation Method of Fitting Convolutional Neural Network into FPGA

Ning Mao, Institute of Electronics CAS & Univ. CAS
Zhihong Huang, Institute of Electronics CAS & Univ. CAS
Xing Wei, Institute of Electronics CAS & Univ. CAS
He Zhao, Institute of Electronics CAS & Univ. CAS
Xinkai Di, Institute of Electronics CAS & Univ. CAS
Le Yu, Beijing Technology and Business University
Haigang Yang, Institute of Electronics CAS & Univ. CAS
Contact: yanghg@mail.ie.ac.cn

In recent years, Convolutional Neural Networks (CNNs) have been used widely in many artificial intelligence (AI) related fields. Of many implementation platforms for CNNs, FPGA is regarded as an optimal platform because of its high power-efficiency and flexibility. Although various FPGA accelerators have been proposed to realize CNN, some of them are implemented by High-Level Synthesis such as in OpenCL. This may result in inefficiency in operation performance and resource utilization. Therefore, we propose to parameterize the RTL design at both algorithm and hardware implementation levels. Four types of parallelism are considered to model the parameterized design in terms of the input feature map, the output feature map, the layer and the convolution kernel. Meanwhile a library covering convolution layer, fully-connected layer, pooling layer, control module is established to cater for various CNN models. Further, an algorithm is proposed to find an optimal level of parallelism dedicated to limited resources. As a case study, four typical CNNs are implemented on Stratix III EP3SL110, taking up on-chip memory. Compared with some existing works using the automated design flow, the implementations obtained by the proposed approach have achieved up to 17.13× GOPS. To the best estimate, our design has also achieved 1.33× resource efficiency and 3.61× power efficiency.

Keywords: Convolutional Neural Network; Parallelism; Parameterize Design

DOI: http://dx.doi.org/10.1145/3174243.3175003

Author Index

www.ingramcontent.com/pod-product-compliance
Lightning Source LLC
Chambersburg PA
CBHW080935220326
41598CB00034B/5791